Canadian Family Law
THIRD EDITION

Canadian Family Law

THIRD EDITION

{*by*}

JULIEN D. PAYNE

MARILYN A. PAYNE

Canadian Family Law, Third Edition
© DANREB, 2008

Published in 2008 by

Irwin Law
14 Duncan Street
Suite 206
Toronto, Ontario
M5H 3G8

www.irwinlaw.com

ISBN: 978-1-55221-157-1

Library and Archives Canada Cataloguing in Publication

Payne, Julien D., 1934–
    Canadian family law / Julien Payne, Marilyn A. Payne. — 3rd ed.

Includes bibliographical references and index.
ISBN 978-1-55221-157-1

1. Domestic relations — Canada. I. Payne, Marilyn A II. Title.

KE539.P395 2008   346.7101'5   C2008-904951-9
KF505.ZA2P395 2008

The publisher acknowledges the financial support of the Government of Canada through the Book Publishing Industry Development Program (BPIDP) for its publishing activities.

We acknowledge the assistance of the OMDC Book Fund, an initiative of Ontario Media Development Corporation.

Printed and bound in Canada.

1 2 3 4 5   12 11 10 09 08

This book is dedicated to the unsung heroes of family law and family dispute resolution — namely judges, lawyers, and mediators — who conscientiously strive to protect the legitimate interests of all family members on the breakdown of their relationships.

SUMMARY
TABLE OF CONTENTS

PREFACE   *xxiii*

ACKNOWLEDGMENTS   *xxvii*

CHAPTER   1: **Family Structures and Canadian Family Law**   *1*

CHAPTER   2: **Marriage**   *21*

CHAPTER   3: **Cohabitational Relationships**   *45*

CHAPTER   4: **Domestic Contracts**   *65*

CHAPTER   5: **Family Violence**   *91*

CHAPTER   6: **The Crises of Marriage Breakdown and Processes for Dealing with Them**   *134*

CHAPTER   7: **Divorce: Jurisdiction; Judgments; Foreign Divorces; Ground for Divorce; Bars**   *179*

CHAPTER   8: **Spousal Support on or after Divorce**   *222*

CHAPTER   9: **Child Support on or after Divorce**   *353*

CHAPTER 10: **Parenting Arrangements after Divorce**   *474*

CHAPTER 11: **Remedies Available under Provincial and Territorial Legislation**   *519*

CHAPTER 12: **Matrimonial Property Rights**   *564*

APPENDIX 1: *DIVORCE ACT*   *633*

APPENDIX 2: *FEDERAL CHILD SUPPORT GUIDELINES*   *671*

APPENDIX 3: ONTARIO *FAMILY LAW ACT*   699

APPENDIX 4: ONTARIO *CHILDREN'S LAW REFORM ACT*   758

TABLE OF CASES   819

INDEX   851

ABOUT THE AUTHORS   858

DETAILED
TABLE OF CONTENTS

PREFACE *xxiii*

ACKNOWLEDGMENTS *xxvii*

CHAPTER 1:
FAMILY STRUCTURES AND CANADIAN FAMILY LAW *1*

A. Definitions of "Family" *1*

B. Functional Significance of Definitions *2*

C. Sources of Family Law *8*

D. Evolution of Family Law *8*

E. Fragmentation of Legislative Powers *16*

F. Fragmentation of Judicial Jurisdiction *17*

CHAPTER 2:
MARRIAGE *21*

A. Engagements *21*

B. Property Disputes on Termination of Engagement *21*

C. Change of Name *23*

D. Marriage: Status or Contract? *23*

E. Definition of Marriage; Monogamous and Polygamous Marriages *24*

   1)   Definition of "Marriage" *24*

   2)   Monogamous and Polygamous Marriages *27*

F.   Formal and Essential Validity   29

   1)   Validity of Marriage; Applicable Laws   29
   2)   Formal Validity   29
   3)   Essential Validity   30

G.   Jurisdiction   30

H.   Void and Voidable Marriages   31

I.   Absence of Consent   32

   1)   Unsoundness of Mind; Alcohol and Drug Intoxication   32
   2)   Duress   33
   3)   Fraud   34
   4)   Mistake   34
   5)   Intention and Motive; Marriages of Convenience   35

J.   Legal Capacity   37

   1)   Same-Sex Marriages   37
   2)   Age   37
   3)   Prior Marriage   38
   4)   Prohibited Degrees   39

K.   Non-consummation of Marriage   39

L.   Bars to Annulment   41

   1)   Collusion   42
   2)   Estoppel   42
   3)   Insincerity   42

M.   Religious Annulments and Divorce   44

CHAPTER 3:
COHABITATIONAL RELATIONSHIPS   45

A.   Introduction   45

B.   Legal Consequences of Unmarried Cohabitation As Compared to
   Marriage   48

C.   Cohabitation Agreements   50

D.   Support Rights and Obligations between Unmarried Cohabitants   53

E.   Property Rights   57

F.   Debts and Liabilities; Financial Planning   62

G.   Custody and Access   63

CHAPTER 4:
DOMESTIC CONTRACTS 65

A. **Types of Domestic Contracts** 65

B. **Domestic Contracts under the Ontario *Family Law Act*** 71

1) General Observations 71
2) Marriage Contracts 72
3) Cohabitation Agreements 74
4) Separation Agreements 75
5) Formal Requirements of Domestic Contracts 76
6) Capacity to Enter into Domestic Contracts 77
7) Contracts Subject to Best Interests of Child 78
8) *Dum Casta* Clauses 78
9) Setting Aside Domestic Contracts 79
10) Rights of Donors of Gifts 82
11) Contracts Made outside Ontario 83
12) Paternity Agreements 83
13) Application of Act to Pre-existing Contracts 84
14) Setting Aside Provision of Domestic Contract Respecting Spousal and Child Support 85
15) Incorporation of Provisions of Domestic Contract in Order under *Family Law Act* 86
16) Incorporation of Provisions of Domestic Contract in Divorce Judgment 87
17) Filing, Enforcement, and Variation of Support Provisions of Domestic Contract 87
18) Remedies for Breach of Domestic Contract 89
19) Termination of Domestic Contracts 90

CHAPTER 5:
FAMILY VIOLENCE 91

A. **Introduction** 91

B. **Abuse of the Elderly** 92

C. **Nature of Spousal Abuse** 94

D. **Social and Legal Responses to Spousal Abuse** 97

1) Shelters and Transition Houses 97
2) Counselling Services 98
3) Legal Responses to Spousal Abuse 99
4) Criminal Law 100
    a) *Criminal Code* Offences 100

b)   Specialized Criminal Courts   *105*

c)   Provincial Statutory Developments   *106*

5)   Matrimonial Proceedings   *107*

a)   *Divorce Act*   *107*

b)   Spousal and Child Support   *108*

c)   Custody and Access   *109*

d)   Orders for Exclusive Possession of Matrimonial Home   *110*

e)   Non-molestation or Restraining Orders   *111*

6)   Actions for Damages   *112*

E.   The Victim's Response to Spousal Abuse   *113*

F.   Proposals for Reform   *115*

G.   Nature of Child Abuse   *117*

H.   Social and Legal Responses to Child Abuse   *118*

1)   Criminal Sanctions   *119*

2)   Child Protection Proceedings   *122*

3)   Family Law Proceedings   *126*

4)   Damages for Child Abuse   *127*

5)   Institutional Child Abuse   *132*

CHAPTER 6:
THE CRISES OF MARRIAGE BREAKDOWN AND PROCESSES FOR DEALING WITH THEM   *134*

A.   The Crises of Marriage Breakdown   *134*

B.   The Emotional Divorce   *135*

C.   Recent Trends in Family Dispute Resolution   *138*

D.   Duty of Legal Profession to Promote Reconciliation, Negotiation, and Mediation   *139*

1)   Duty of Legal Adviser   *139*

2)   Duty of Court: Reconciliation   *141*

3)   Confidentiality   *142*

E.   Marriage and Family Counselling   *146*

F.   Negotiation   *148*

1)   The Importance of Negotiation   *148*

2)   Negotiation Techniques   *148*

3)   Aspects of Successful Negotiation on Family Breakdown   *150*

G.   Mediation   *152*

1)   Nature of Mediation   *152*

2) Approaches to Mediation *153*
3) Reasons for Mediation *154*
4) Goals of Mediation *154*
5) Arriving at a Fair Settlement *155*
6) Circumstances in Which Mediation Is Inappropriate *156*
7) Full Disclosure and Confidentiality *156*
8) Involvement of Third Parties *156*
9) Involvement of Children *157*
10) Involvement of Lawyers *157*
11) Issues to Be Mediated *158*
12) Neutrality of Mediators *158*
13) Common Impediments to Settlement *159*
   a) Emotional Barriers *159*
   b) "Stuck Spots" *159*
   c) Imbalances of Power *159*
   d) War Games *159*
14) Mediation Strategies to Circumvent or Remove Impediments to Settlement *160*
   a) Dealing with Anger and Hostility *160*
   b) Circumventing "Stuck Spots" *161*
   c) Private Caucusing *162*
   d) Restoring Trust and Respect *162*
   e) Redressing Power Imbalances *162*
15) Steps in Mediation Process *163*
   a) Setting the Stage *163*
   b) Defining the Issues *164*
   c) Processing the Issues *164*
   d) Resolving the Issues *164*
16) Court-Connected Mediation *165*
17) Pros and Cons of Mediation *166*
18) Professional and Community Responses to Mediation *166*
19) The Future of Family Mediation *167*

H. **Arbitration** *169*

1) Advantages of Arbitration *169*
   a) Selection of Arbitrator(s) *169*
   b) Type of Hearing *170*
   c) Flexibility and Speed *170*
   d) Definition of Issues *171*
   e) Privacy *171*
   f) Expense *171*
2) Disadvantages of Arbitration *172*
3) Court-Annexed Arbitration *172*

4)   Judicial and Legislative Responses to Arbitration   173

I.   Med-Arb   175

J.   Parenting Co-ordination   176

K.   Concluding Observations   178

CHAPTER 7:
DIVORCE: JURISDICTION; JUDGMENTS; FOREIGN DIVORCES;
GROUND FOR DIVORCE; BARS   179

A.   Judicial Separation; Separation Agreements;
       Divorce Settlements   179

B.   Jurisdiction over Divorce   181

      1)   Introduction   181
      2)   Definition of "Court"   181
      3)   Exercise of Jurisdiction by Judge Alone   181
      4)   Jurisdiction in Divorce Proceedings   181
            a)   Basic Statutory Criteria   181
            b)   Transfer of Divorce Proceeding to Another Province   182
            c)   Competing Foreign Proceeding   184
      5)   Jurisdiction in Corollary Relief Proceedings   184
            a)   Basic Statutory Criteria   184
            b)   Transfer of Corollary Relief Proceeding to Another Province   187
      6)   Jurisdiction in Variation Proceedings   187
            a)   Basic Statutory Criteria   187
            b)   Transfer of Variation Proceeding to Another Province   188
            c)   Variation of Foreign Orders   188
      7)   Ordinarily Resident   188

C.   Divorce Judgments   191

      1)   Effective Date of Divorce Judgment; Appeals; Rescission of Divorce
            Judgment   191
      2)   Expedition of Divorce Judgment   191
      3)   National Effect of Divorce and Corollary Orders   193
      4)   Right to Remarry   193

D.   Recognition of Foreign Divorces   193

      1)   General Criteria   193
      2)   Extra-Judicial Divorce   195
      3)   Substantive and Procedural Defects   195
      4)   Doctrine of Preclusion   195

E.   Marriage Breakdown As Sole Ground for Divorce   196

1) Spousal Separation As Proof of Marriage Breakdown *199*

2) Adultery and Cruelty As Proof of Marriage Breakdown: No Waiting Period *202*

3) Marriage Breakdown: Adultery *202*

4) Marriage Breakdown: Cruelty *205*

F. **Bars to Divorce** *211*

1) Collusion *213*

2) Connivance and Condonation *214*

3) Absence of Reasonable Arrangements for Child Support *217*

4) Barriers to Religious Remarriage *220*

CHAPTER 8:
SPOUSAL SUPPORT ON OR AFTER DIVORCE *222*

A. **Definition of "Spouse" and "Spousal Support"** *222*

B. **Formal Legal Equality between Spouses** *223*

C. **Types of Order** *223*

1) Diverse Types of Order *223*

2) Nominal Orders; Final Orders *224*

3) Interim Support Orders *224*

4) Lump Sum Support Orders *228*

5) Security *233*

6) Fixed-Term Spousal Support Orders; Review Orders *234*

D. **Terms, Conditions, and Restrictions** *242*

E. **Relevant Factors** *242*

1) Definition of "Condition" of the Spouses *243*

2) Definition of "Means" *244*

3) Needs and Capacity to Pay; Economic Self-Sufficiency; Relevance of Cohabitational Standard of Living *246*

4) Definition of "Other Circumstances" *247*

F. **Spousal Conduct** *248*

G. **Four Objectives of Spousal Support** *250*

H. **Broad Judicial Direction** *261*

I. **Overarching Principle of Equitable Sharing** *263*

J. **Needs and Capacity to Pay Not Excluded by Compensatory Model** *265*

K. **Implications of Child Care during Marriage and after Divorce** *267*

L. Alleviation of Feminization of Poverty *268*

M. No Pat Formula *268*

N. Effect of Separation Agreement or Consent Order on
    Subsequent Application for Spousal Support *269*

    1) The Impact of the Majority Judgment *274*
    2) Future Ramifications of *Miglin* *275*
        a) Finality of Spousal Agreement *275*
        b) Applicability of *Miglin* to Payors and Payees *277*
        c) Retrospective Implications of *Miglin* *277*
        d) Non-Cohabitation Covenants *277*
        e) Effect of Separation Agreement on Interim Orders *280*
        f) Effect of Marriage Contract or Cohabitation Agreement *282*
        g) Variation Orders *284*
        h) Effect of Spousal Agreement on Child Support *287*
        i) Applications under Provincial Statute *288*

O. Effect of Sponsorship Agreement *290*

P. Double Recovery or Double Dipping *290*

Q. Income Tax and Retroactive Orders *293*

R. Variation and Termination of Support Orders *295*

    1) General *295*
    2) Variation of Fixed-Term Orders *302*
    3) Effect of Remarriage or Common-Law Relationship *303*
        a) Effect of Remarriage *303*
        b) Effect of Common-Law Relationship *307*
    4) Finality of Orders *308*

S. Cost-of-Living Indexation *311*

T. Retroactive Spousal Support Orders *311*

U. *Spousal Support Advisory Guidelines* *312*
    1) Overview of the Guidelines *312*
        a) Introduction *312*
        b) The Nature of the Guidelines *314*
        c) Advantages and Disadvantages of the Guidelines *314*
        d) Basic Structure and Application of the Guidelines *315*
            i)   Income-Sharing Regime Deemed Consistent with Spousal
                Support Criteria under the *Divorce Act* *315*
            ii) The Proposed Applicability of the Guidelines *315*
            iii) Two Basic Formulas — Marriages without and with
                Dependent Children *316*
            iv) Floors and Ceilings *316*

v) Restructuring: Trade-Offs between Amount and
Duration *317*
vi) Exceptions *317*
e) The *Without Child Support Formula* *318*
f) The *With Child Support Formula* *320*
i) Reasons for Separate Model Where Dependent Children
Involved; Parenting Partnership Model *320*
ii) Primary Differences between the Two Basic Formulas *320*
iii) Sumarry of Basic *With Child Support Formula* *320*
iv) Narrowing the Range *322*
v) Duration under the Basic Formula *323*
vi) Shared and Split Custory *323*
vii) Hybrid Formula Where Spousal Support Paid by Custodial
Parent *324*
viii) Crossover between Formulas *324*
g) Quebec *324*
h) General Observations *325*
2) Judicial Responses to the *Spousal Support Advisory Guidelines* *326*
V. Appeals *351*

CHAPTER 9:
CHILD SUPPORT ON OR AFTER DIVORCE *355*

A. General Observations *353*

B. Income Tax — Child Support *353*

C. Presumptive Rule; Table Amount of Child Support;
Section 7 Expenses *354*

D. Exceptions to Presumptive Rule *355*

E. Obligation of *de facto* Parent *355*

1) Relevant Statutory Provisions *355*
2) Termination of Parent-Child Relationship: Impact on Child
Support *361*
3) Respective Obligations of Biological and Adoptive Parents and of
Persons Who Stand in the Place of Parents *362*

F. Children over Provincial Age of Majority *371*

1) Relevant Provisions of *Divorce Act* and *Federal Child Support
Guidelines* *371*
2) Status of Applicant; Payment to Parent or Child *373*
3) Statutory Definition of "Child of the Marriage"; Eligibility of Adult
Children for Child Support *373*
a) General *373*

b)   Sick or Disabled Children   *375*

c)   Unemployed Adult Children   *376*

4)   Post-Secondary Education or Training   *377*

a)   General   *377*

b)   Options Available to the Court under Section 3(2) of the *Federal Child Support Guidelines*   *381*

c)   Expenses for Post-Secondary Education under Section 7 of the *Federal Child Support Guidelines*   *388*

G.   Incomes over $150,000   *391*

H.   Split Custody; Section 8 of Guidelines   *393*

I.   Shared Custody: 40 Percent Rule   *395*

J.   Undue Hardship   *403*

K.   Effect of Order or Agreement   *407*

L.   Special and Extraordinary Expenses   *413*

1)   General   *413*

2)   Child-Care Expenses   *416*

3)   Medical and Dental Insurance; Medical, Dental, or Health-Related Expenses   *417*

4)   Extraordinary Educational Expenses; Private School   *420*

5)   Extraordinary Expenses for Extracurricular Activities   *421*

M.   Variation of Child Support Orders   *425*

1)   Variation of Amount of Child Support Made under Applicable Table   *425*

2)   Variation Where Amount of Child Support Not under Provincial or Territorial Table   *426*

3)   Variation of Orders Predating Implementation of Guidelines   *428*

4)   Remission of Arrears   *428*

N.   Determination and Disclosure of Income   *433*

O.   Disability Payments and Child Support   *454*

P.   Types of Orders   *455*

1)   Interim Orders   *455*

2)   Periodic and Lump Sum Orders   *456*

3)   Orders to Pay and Secure Child Support   *458*

Q.   Retroactive Child Support Orders under the *Divorce Act*   *458*

R.   Priority of Child Support over Spousal Support; Effect of Child Support Order on Assessment of Spousal Support   *468*

1)   Relevant Statutory Provisions   *468*

2)   Commentary   *468*

CHAPTER 10:
PARENTING ARRANGEMENTS AFTER DIVORCE *474*

A. Introduction *474*

B. Preservation of Family Bonds; Joint Custody; Maximum Contact Principle *475*

C. Terms and Conditions *483*

   1) General *483*
   2) Intended Change of Residence; Mobility Rights *485*

D. Best Interests of Child *492*

E. Conduct *497*

   1) General *497*
   2) Child Sexual Abuse Allegations *498*

F. Effect of Agreement *502*

G. Variation and Rescission of Custody and Access Orders *503*

H. Parental Conflict Resolution *510*

I. Voice of the Child *512*

J. Parenting Plans *513*

K. Third Parties *517*

L. Process *517*

CHAPTER 11:
REMEDIES AVAILABLE UNDER PROVINCIAL AND TERRITORIAL LEGISLATION *519*

A. Spousal Support *519*

   1) Diversity under Provincial and Territorial Statutes *519*
   2) Differences between Federal *Divorce Act* and Provincial and Territorial Legislation *521*

B. Child Support under Provincial and Territorial Legislation *522*

C. Need for Rationalization of Income Support Systems *525*

D. Enforcement of Support *526*

E. Custody of and Access to Children under Provincial and Territorial Legislation *526*

   1) Welfare or Best Interests of Child *526*
   2) Types of Order *530*
   3) Wishes of Child; Judicial Interviews; Legal Representation *532*

a) Hearsay Evidence 534

b) In-Court Testimony of Young Children 535

c) Interviewing Child in Chambers 536

d) Investigation by the Children's Lawyer 537

e) Court-Ordered Independent Assessment 539

4) Mediation and Reconciliation Attempts; Confidentiality of Process 543

5) Court-Ordered Investigations, Assessments, and Reports 544

6) Grandparents and Other Third Parties; Multiple Parents 554

7) Provincial Parenting Programs 563

CHAPTER 12:

MATRIMONIAL PROPERTY RIGHTS 564

A. Provincial and Territorial Legislative Diversity 564

1) Introduction 566

2) Objectives of *Family Law Act* 567

3) Definition of "Spouse" 567

4) Indian Lands; Foreign Immovable Property 568

5) Domestic Contracts 568

6) Applications Respecting Ownership and Possession of Property 568

a) General 568

b) Presumptions 569

7) Triggering Events for Equalization of Net Family Properties 571

a) Separation As a Triggering Event 571

b) Death As a Triggering Event 572

c) Improvident Depletion of Net Family Property 573

d) Alternative Triggering Events 573

8) Limitation Periods 573

9) Equalization of Net Family Properties 573

a) General Observations 573

b) Significance of Ownership to Equalization Scheme 578

c) Definition of "Property" 579

d) Pensions 581

e) University Degrees; Professional Licences; Goodwill 586

f) Value 587

g) Valuation of Business; Private Companies 587

h) Valuation Date 589

i) Income Tax and Other Prospective Liabilities 590

j) Expert Evidence: "Splitting the Difference" 592

k) Deduction of Debts and Liabilities 593

l) Valuation of Premarital Property 594

m) Excluded Property 597

n) Property Acquired by Gift or Inheritance   *598*

o) Income from Third-Party Postmarital Gift or Inheritance   *599*

p) Damages   *600*

q) Life Insurance Policies   *602*

r) Traceable Property   *603*

s) Property Excluded by Domestic Contract   *603*

t) Domestic Contracts: Canada Pension Plan   *604*

10) Unequal Division of Net Family Properties   *604*

a) Judicial Discretion Based on Unconscionability   *604*

b) Undisclosed Premarital Debts or Liabilities   *607*

c) Debts or Other Liabilities Incurred Recklessly or in Bad Faith   *607*

d) Interspousal Gifts   *608*

e) Depletion of Net Family Property   *608*

f) Duration of Cohabitation   *608*

g) Debts and Other Liabilities Incurred for Support of Family   *609*

h) Written Agreement   *610*

i) Any Other Circumstance Relating to the Acquisition, Disposition, or Management of Property   *610*

11) Entitlement on Death   *612*

a) Death As a Triggering Event   *612*

b) Election by Surviving Spouse   *612*

12) Property and Financial Statements   *616*

13) Powers of Court   *617*

a) General Observations   *617*

b) Order for Payment   *619*

c) Order for Security   *619*

d) Deferred or Instalment Payments   *620*

e) Transfers of Property; Partition and Sale   *620*

f) Financial Information and Inspections   *621*

g) Variation of Order for Instalment or Deferred Payments   *621*

h) Operating Business or Farm   *621*

i) Interest   *626*

14) Restraining Orders and Preservation Orders   *622*

15) Variation and Realization of Security   *622*

16) Retrospective Operation   *622*

17) Occupation Rent and Accountancy Claims   *624*

18) Disposition and Possession of the Matrimonial Home   *629*

a) General Observations   *625*

b) Definition and Designation of "Matrimonial Home"   *625*

c) Disposition of Matrimonial Home   *626*

d) Possessory Rights in Matrimonial Home   *626*

e) Penalties for Contravention of Exclusive Possession Order   *630*

    f)   Variation of Possessory Orders *630*

    g)   Severance of Third-Party Joint Tenancy in Matrimonial
         Home *631*

  19) Registration of Orders against Land *631*

  20) Situs of Matrimonial Home; Retrospective Operation of Part II of
       Family Law Act *631*

APPENDIX 1: *DIVORCE ACT* *633*

APPENDIX 2: *FEDERAL CHILD SUPPORT GUIDELINES* *671*

APPENDIX 3: ONTARIO *FAMILY LAW ACT* *699*

APPENDIX 4: ONTARIO *CHILDREN'S LAW REFORM ACT* *758*

TABLE OF CASES *819*

INDEX *851*

ABOUT THE AUTHORS *858*

PREFACE

Family law is a changing and dynamic field. In the twenty-first century, Canadian families will encounter new challenges. Marriage and the family are no longer synonymous. The traditional nuclear family of the 1950s, with its breadwinning husband, homemaking wife, and their two or more children, is a minority group. Two-income families, with or without children, high divorce and remarriage rates, and the increasing incidence of unmarried cohabitation, whether involving opposite or same-sex couples, have fostered new family structures and radical legal reforms. At the same time, there has been increased recognition of the inherent limitations of the law in regulating marriage and the family.

The public and the legal profession are aware of the devastating impact that family breakdown can have on women and children. The feminization of poverty that results from single parenthood, family breakdown, and divorce continues to be of pressing concern to provincial and federal governments as they seek to enforce spousal and child support payments that have fallen into default, and endeavour to provide a socio-economic safety net for sole parents and children.

Canadian family law is a fascinating blend of old and new. It is continually in transition as it responds to evolving family structures. Chapter 1 of *Canadian Family Law* identifies the changing character of Canadian families and poses fundamental questions concerning possible future directions of law and social policy in Canada. In addition, it provides a review of the legal consequences of marriage breakdown and divorce since the enactment of the first dominion-wide *Divorce Act* in 1968. The fragmentation of legislative powers between the Parliament of Canada and the provincial and territorial legislatures is also addressed, together with the inefficient fragmentation of jurisdiction between diverse courts that has led to the emergence of specialized Family Courts.

Chapter 2 focuses on the nature of marriage and the legal prerequisites to a valid marriage. Much of the legal analysis in this chapter has a long history that can be traced back to ecclesiastical origins in England. However, Chapter 2 does not ignore contemporary issues that have confronted Canadian courts, such as the validity of same-sex relationships and marriages of convenience that are entered into for the sole purpose of gaining preferred immigration status.

Chapter 3 examines cohabitational relationships between persons of the same or opposite sex in light of the guarantee of equality under section 15 of the *Canadian Charter of Rights and Freedoms*, which has resulted in increasing legal recognition being given to unmarried heterosexual cohabitation and to same-sex relationships for a variety of purposes, including contracts, support rights and, under some provincial statutes, succession and property rights.

Chapter 4 reviews the statutory regulation of "domestic contracts" as a means of determining the rights and obligations of married persons and of unmarried cohabitants during their relationship and upon its termination. One of the most significant trends in Canadian family law is the degree of contractual autonomy that is now afforded to spouses and unmarried cohabitants to regulate their own affairs, provided that their agreements do not undermine the best interests of any children of the family. Chapter 4 analyzes in-depth the provisions of the Ontario *Family Law Act* that provide a comprehensive legislative framework for marriage contracts, cohabitation agreements, and separation agreements.

Chapter 5 addresses one of society's best kept secrets: family violence. Some people believe that abuse of the elderly, spousal abuse, and child abuse have reached epidemic proportions. Social and legal responses to these urgent problems are comprehensively reviewed in Chapter 5.

Chapter 6 deals with the emotional dynamics of marriage breakdown for spouses and their children. This chapter points out the inability of the law to respond to the emotional trauma of family breakdown. Although the *Divorce Act* imposes a duty on lawyers to promote reconciliation, negotiation, and mediation between divorcing partners, the use of innovative processes, such as mediation, arbitration, med-arb, and parenting coordination, is still evolving in Canadian family dispute resolution.

Chapter 7 reviews the ground rules for determining whether Canadian courts can assume jurisdiction over a divorce petition, the criteria for recognizing foreign divorces, the ground for divorce in Canada, and bars or impediments to a divorce judgment.

Chapter 8 analyzes the basic principles for determining spousal support rights and obligations under the *Divorce Act,* having special regard to the judgments of the Supreme Court of Canada in *Moge v. Moge, Bracklow v. Bracklow, Miglin v. Miglin, Boston v. Boston,* and *Leskun v. Leskun,* and the impact of the *Spousal Support Advisory Guidelines.* This chapter has undergone radical changes since the last edition of *Canadian Family Law* to accommodate the judgment of the Supreme Court of Canada in *Leskun v. Leskun* and the various responses of Canadian courts to the *Spousal Support Advisory Guidelines.*

Chapter 9 provides an overview of the judicial determination of child support under the *Divorce Act* and the *Federal Child Support Guidelines.* A much more detailed analysis may be found in Julien D. Payne and Marilyn A. Payne, *Child Support Guidelines in Canada, 2006,* published by Irwin Law. On 1 May 2006, changes to the *Federal Child Support Guidelines* were implemented. They involved (i) overall changes in the table amounts of child support; (ii) a redefinition of "extraordinary expenses" under section 7 of the Guidelines; (iii) changes to the comparison of household incomes under the undue hardship provisions of section 10 of the Guidelines; and (iv) judicial determination of the income of foreign residents. Equally important, there have been a number of important judicial decisions that affect child support in shared-parenting situations, the support of adult children, and retroactive child support. These changes are incorporated in Chapter 9 and in Appendix 2.

Chapter 10 examines issues relating to parenting disputes and their resolution in proceedings instituted pursuant to the *Divorce Act.*

Chapter 11 briefly reviews spousal support, child support, and custody and access under provincial and territorial statutes in Canada. It complements the analysis of these issues in Chapter 3 (Cohabitational Relationships), Chapter 4 (Domestic Contracts), Chapter 5 (Family Violence), and Chapter 6 (The Crises of Marriage Breakdown and Processes for Dealing with Them).

Chapter 12 analyzes matrimonial property rights on marriage breakdown or death. Because of wide differences among current provincial and territorial statutes, Chapter 12 concentrates on the Ontario *Family Law Act.*

Four appendices are provided, namely, Appendix 1 (*Divorce Act*), Appendix 2 (*Federal Child Support Guidelines*), Appendix 3 (Ontario *Family Law Act*), and Appendix 4 (Ontario *Children's Law Reform Act*).

Although *Canadian Family Law* cannot provide an encyclopedic digest of all aspects of Canadian family law, it does provide insights into most of the fundamental legal issues that confront Canadian families today.

This book is current to 1 May 2008.

Julien D. Payne

Marilyn A. Payne

ACKNOWLEDGMENTS

The authors thank Jeff Miller for his co-operation in facilitating this publication and arranging for the in-house preparation of a comprehensive case list. The authors much appreciate the efforts of Alisa Posesorski, who discharged editorial responsibilities in her usual efficient manner.

Special thanks are also due to Rebecca Payne and Andrew Payne for word processing and proofreading that went far beyond the call of filial duty.

Julien D. Payne
Marilyn A. Payne

NOTICE

CITATIONS

For the most part, the authors cite cases in Reports of Family Law, for example, *Rosario v. Rosario* (1991), 37 R.F.L. (3d) 24 (Alta. C.A.) or on Quicklaw (LexisNexis). The latter source identifies cases by their year and province or territory of origin and a J number, for example, *Lagace v. Lagace*, [1999] N.B.J. No. 556 (C.A.).

CHAPTER 1

FAMILY STRUCTURES AND CANADIAN FAMILY LAW

A. DEFINITIONS OF "FAMILY"

The term "family" does not have a precise legal definition. Law tends to regulate the rights and obligations of individuals, as distinct from groups, such as families, however they may be constituted. Canadian family law might more properly be called the Law of Persons insofar as it concentrates on the rights of individuals whose family relationships have become dysfunctional. In short, Canadian family law deals primarily with the pathology of family breakdown and its legal consequences.

People often perceive "marriage" and "family" as synonymous but these words are not interchangeable in law. The term "family" is elusive and defies exact definition. Many, but not all, Canadian families are the product of a marriage. More often than not, the presence of children signifies a family relationship. Children may be born within or outside of marriage. Their parents may or may not live together. The parents may have lived together before or after the birth of the child but may no longer do so by reason of separation or divorce. Some children are adopted. In relatively rare situations, a child's birth may have resulted from surrogate parenting arrangements or the use of new reproductive technologies. Children are usually family members of the household in which they reside but this is not invariably true. Some children do not live with either of their parents or with aunts, uncles, or grandparents. They may live in foster homes or even with friends or neighbours. A new *de facto* family may co-exist with the family of origin.

Family relationships can exist when there is neither marriage nor a parent-child or ancestral relationship. Unmarried couples of the opposite sex or same-sex may be regarded as members of the same family for social or legal purposes.

Whether the indicia of a family relationship involve marriage, parenthood, a common household, or the sharing of responsibilities, there are many unresolved legal questions concerning the characterization of "families" and the rights and obligations of diverse family members.

Although some will look back with nostalgia to the traditional nuclear family, with its breadwinning husband, its homemaking wife, and their children, that is a minority group in terms of contemporary family structures in Canada. Today, Canadian families take a wide variety of forms. They include childless marriages, two-parent families, single parent families in which the mother is the primary caregiver, single parent families where the father is the primary caregiver, unmarried cohabitants with or without children, and blended or reconstituted families that are the product of sequential cohabitational relationships inside or outside marriage. Family structures may also vary according to ethnic and cultural factors. Customary Inuit adoptions, for example, bear little resemblance to the statute-based systems of adoption that exist in Canadian provinces and territories.

Traditional notions of the family must clearly be re-examined in the search for rational and equitable social and legal policies. In the final analysis, it may be impractical for the law to endorse a monolithic definition of "family" that applies for all legal purposes. As in the past, the extent to which the law will recognize a family relationship may turn on the nature of the relationship and the purpose for which such recognition is sought.

B. FUNCTIONAL SIGNIFICANCE OF DEFINITIONS

Family law in Canada has focused on the traditional nuclear family. Our federal divorce laws are based on monogamous marriage. Scant attention is directed towards the rights and responsibilities of members of the extended family, such as grandparents, aunts, and uncles. Even provincial legislation tends to focus on regulating the economic and parenting consequences of marriage breakdown, although issues of spousal and child support and custody and access can arise independently of the status of marriage. Recent years have witnessed changes in the identification of issues relating to changing family structures in Canada.

The two-income family, the high divorce rate, the increasing incidence of unmarried cohabitation, the changing needs of the labour force, cultural diversity resulting from immigration, the ageing of the Canadian population, and many other factors have generated new challenges for Canada. Contemporary policy issues include the following:

(i)   Is a national child-care program desirable?

(ii)   To what extent should Canadian law recognize rights and responsibilities between unmarried cohabitants of the opposite sex or of the same-sex?[1]

(iii)   How should law and society respond to the growing awareness of family violence?

(iv)   To what extent should Canadians be entitled to regulate the legal consequences of family breakdown by marriage contracts, cohabitation agreements, or separation agreements?

(v)   How should new human reproductive technologies be regulated?[2]

(vi)   How can the economic interests of women and children be protected in the event of marriage breakdown or divorce?

(vii)   How can parental ties be preserved notwithstanding separation and divorce?

(viii) How will Canada address the problem of an ageing population? What will be its impact on health care, residential care, or family care for the elderly?

(ix)   How should Canada respond to declining birth rates? Are financial incentives for parenthood, such as those adopted in Quebec, a solution? Does the answer lie in increased immigration?

(x)   How should Canadian family law be administered? By traditional courts? By Unified Family Courts? By administrative tribunals? By governmental or community agencies? What do innovative processes, such as mediation and arbitration, offer as alternative means of resolving family disputes? Should they be subsidized by the state?

---

1   See William N. Eskridge, Jr., "Comparative Law and the Same-Sex Marriage Debate" (2000) 31 McGeorge L. Rev. 641.

2   See Weldon E. Havins & James J. Dalessio, "Reproductive Surrogacy at the Millennium: Proposed Model Legislation Regulating 'Non-Traditional' Gestational Surrogacy Contracts" (2000) 31 McGeorge L. Rev. 673.

(xi)   How should Canadian law respond to aboriginal families with their own cultural identity and heritage? Does the answer lie in new substantive laws or in delegating decision-making authority to their communities? Do immigrant families require special recognition?[3]

In order to address issues such as these, it is important to discover the reality of Canadian families today and to destroy popular myths.[4] The following information may offer some insight for future policy directions:

(i)   In 2006, 51.5 percent of the Canadian population over fifteen years of age were unmarried.

(ii)   One-third of all marriages are terminated by divorce but the majority of divorcees marry again or form cohabitational relationships. Marriages that end in divorce have an average duration of fourteen years. By the end of the 1990s, one-third of all marriages involved a spouse who had married before — most of whom had been divorced, not widowed.

(iii) In 1968, 171,766 marriages were performed, and 11,000 divorces were granted by Canadian courts. In 1994, 160,000 couples were married, and 78,800 marriages were judicially dissolved. During this quarter of a century, therefore, marriages were somewhat less frequent, notwithstanding an increase in the Canadian population. Divorces, on the other hand, shot up dramatically. Over the last four decades, the Canadian divorce rate has increased by more than 500 percent. In 2002, a total of 70,155 divorces were granted.

(iv)   The divorce rate in Canada is lower than that in the United States and in England, but higher than that in most European countries.

(v)   The older you are when you get married, the more likely you are to stay married. In 1987, about 57 percent of Canadian women who

---

3   As to the impact of cultural and religious factors on dispute resolution processes, see the report of Marion Boyd, *Dispute Resolution in Family Law: Protecting Choice, Promoting Inclusion*, December 2004, Ontario Ministry of Attorney General, online: www.attorneygeneral.jus.gov.on.ca/english/about/pubs/boyd/.

4   See generally, Canada, *National Longitudinal Survey of Children and Youth*, 1994–; Canada, Department of Justice, *Evaluation of the Divorce Act; Phase II: Monitoring and Evaluation* (May 1990); M. Baker, Ph.D., ed., *Canada's Changing Families: Challenges to Public Policy* (Ottawa: Vanier Institute of the Family, 1994) at 14–15; Vanier Institute of the Family, *Transition*, December 1997, "Till Death Do Us Part: Divorce in Canada"; Vanier Institute of the Family, *Transition*, Spring 1999, "Lone-parents and Their Children"; Canadian Council on Social Development, *Income and Child Well-Being: A New Perspective on the Poverty Debate*, 1999; and 1996, 2001, and 2006 census data provided by Statistics Canada.

got married when they were fifteen to nineteen years old had divorced. The rate drops to about 40 percent for those who married between twenty and twenty-four years of age, and to about 33 percent for those who married after they turned twenty-five.

(vi)   Seven out of ten Canadians who left marriages or common-law unions in 1993 were in their twenties or thirties. In 2002, the average age of males and females at the time of divorce was forty-three and forty respectively.

(vii)   Over three decades, children have experienced their parents' separation at an increasingly younger age. Between 1961 and 1963, 20 percent of Canadian children experienced parental separation before they were sixteen years old. Between 1987 and 1988, the same percentage of children had experienced parental separation by the time they were five years old.

(viii)   Seventy-five percent of all Canadian children under the age of twelve live with both of their biological parents. Sixteen percent of children under twelve live with a lone-parent, 55 percent of whom are separated or divorced. Ten percent of children under twelve live in a step-family.

(ix)   Unmarried cohabitation of the parents provides a far less stable family environment for children than marriages. By the time they are ten years old, 63 percent of children with parents living in a common-law union have seen their parents separate, compared with only 14 percent of children whose parents were married and had not previously lived common law.

(x)   The 2006 census showed that an increasing proportion of couples are living in common-law relationships. Married couples accounted for 68.6 percent of all families in 2006, down from 83 percent in 1981. At the same time, the proportion of common-law couples rose from 6 percent to 15.5 percent. In 2006, the census counted 6,105,910 married couples, 1,376,865 common-law couples, and 1,414,060 lone-parent families. The trend towards common-law relationships was strongest in Quebec where 611,855 common-law relationships accounted for 44.4 percent of the national total. Almost 29 percent of children were living with common-law parents in Quebec, more than double the national average. The number of common-law couples in Canada with children under the age of twenty-five is also increasing. In 2001, they accounted for 7 percent of all couples in Canada, compared with only 2 percent two decades earlier. About 732,900 children, or 13 percent of the total, lived with common-law parents in 2001, more than four times the proportion of 3 percent two decades ago. Younger children were more likely to live with common-law parents.

(xi) The 2001 census is the first to provide data on same-sex partnerships. A total of 34,200 couples identified themselves as same-sex couples, accounting for 0.5 percent of all couples in the country. There were more male same-sex couples than female. The census counted about 19,000 male same-sex couples, 55 percent of the total. Female same-sex couples were five times as likely to have children living with them as their male counterparts. About 15 percent of the 15,200 female same-sex couples were living with children, compared with only 3 percent of male same-sex couples. The number of same-sex couples increased by 32.6 percent between 2001 and 2006. Given the legalization of same-sex marriage in 2005, the 2006 census identifies 45,345 same-sex couples, of whom 7,465 or 16.5 percent were married couples.

(xii) People are getting married later in life and are deferring the birth of children while they get an education and establish themselves in the labour force. Men who divorced in 2002 had an average age of twenty-nine years when they married; women who divorced in 2002 were twenty-six years old, on average, when they married.

(xiii) Two-income families are the norm in Canada. The number of married women in the Canadian labour force has increased over the last twenty years from 35 percent to over 60 percent. If married women suddenly stopped working outside the home, the number of Canadian families living in poverty would double overnight.

(xiv) There are more than 14 million lone-parent families in Canada. These households represent 15.9 percent of all Canadian families with children. More than 80 percent of lone-parent households are headed by women. Separation and divorce result in lone-parenthood more frequently than death.

(xv) Separated and divorced women who are incapable of achieving economic self-sufficiency in the labour force are likely to live in poverty, unless they remarry or form a new permanent marriage-like relationship.

(xvi) Families are smaller than they were a generation ago. Canada has a declining birth rate because parents usually have only one or two children.

(xvii) Three generational families living under the same roof represent approximately 6 percent of all families. With an ever-increasing ageing population, this statistic may increase dramatically over the next twenty years.

(xviii) Estimates of the cost of raising a child from birth until the age of eighteen range between $80,000 and $180,000. One out of every six children in Canada lives in poverty. There is an extremely high rate of poverty among single-parent families. Children from aboriginal, immigrant, and visible minority families are twice as likely to experience poverty than other Canadian children. Associated with poverty are poorer health, lower educational achievements, and emotional and behavioural problems.

(xix) Two million families have no children living at home. Of the 4.5 million families who have children, 80 percent of them are two-parent families. Approximately a quarter of a million single-parent families have children under six years of age in the home.

(xx) When children are living with their mother in a single-parent household, they are five times more likely to live in poverty than children who are living with two parents. It is not true, however, that children in poverty are more frequently living in a single-parent household. Two-parent families with children represent the largest group of families living in poverty.

(xxi) Custody dispositions were granted by the courts in 2001 and 2002 in three out of ten divorces. In 2002, sole custody was granted to the wife with respect to 49.5 percent of the children and sole custody was granted to the husband with respect to 8.5 percent of the children. Joint custody of 41.8 percent of the children was granted to the husband and wife in 2002. These figures present a sharp contrast with 1988 when sole custody was granted to the wife with respect to 75.8 percent of the children. Because joint custody typically refers to equal decision-making authority in both parents, it should not be assumed that joint custody orders involve the parents in equal or substantial time sharing. More often than not, the children reside primarily with their mother.

(xxii) When financial support agreements have been made by court order or privately, support payments are received regularly or with occasional delays for six of ten children. Regular financial payments are received for 76 percent of children whose parents reached their own financial arrangements, but only 53 percent of children for whom financial support has been ordered by the court receive it regularly. In addition, 31 percent of court-ordered support payments were in arrears for at least six months.

(xxiii) At first glance, the likelihood of children maintaining regular contact with a non-custodial parent appeared to be linked to the type of financial arrangements made between the parents. Seventy-five percent of children whose parents have a private agreement for financial support see their non-custodial parent regularly (at least once a month), compared with just 51 percent of children whose parents had a court-ordered financial arrangement.

(xxiv) Today, two out of three immigrants are from Asia, the Caribbean, Africa, or Central America. One in five Canadians have a cultural heritage that is neither English nor French.

C. SOURCES OF FAMILY LAW

The primary sources of family law in Canada are found in provincial, territorial, and federal statutes. In some areas, such as nullity proceedings, judge-made principles of law prevail. In Quebec, the *Civil Code* regulates family law other than divorce.

D. EVOLUTION OF FAMILY LAW

Federal, provincial, and territorial legislation regulating the rights and obligations of family members has been largely piecemeal in its evolution and no coherent family policy has been articulated, particularly in the context of the relationship between the so-called private system of family law, which regulates the personal rights and obligations of spouses, parents, and children as between themselves, and the public system that provides social assistance, tax concessions, pension and medical health schemes, and the like.

The predominant legislative trend has been towards the assertion of individual rights and obligations, rather than the assertion of any family right. Family law statutes are largely premised on the notion that any form of government intervention is an intrusion upon privacy that can only be justified in the event of a breakdown in the family relationship, a reasonable apprehension of domestic violence, or child abuse and neglect.

Revolutionary changes to family law occurred in Canada with the passage of the first dominion-wide *Divorce Act* in 1968. With this federal legislation serving as a catalyst, Canadians have witnessed radical changes in all aspects of family law. The dimensions of change have been immense. Before 1968, adultery constituted the sole ground for divorce, except in Nova Scotia where matrimonial cruelty constituted an alternative ground for relief. In Quebec and Newfoundland, divorce was only available by private Act of Parliament. With the enactment of the *Divorce Act* in 1968, "no-fault" divorce grounds were introduced in addition to an extended list of "offence" grounds. In addition, formal legal equality of support rights and obligations was established for the first time in Canada between divorcing and divorced men and women. Although the *Divorce Act* of 1986 amended the law relating to the criteria for divorce, spousal and child support, and custody and access in such a way as to shift the focus of the courts from the grounds of divorce to an almost exclusive emphasis on the economic and parenting consequences of divorce, the truly radical breakthroughs occurred with the *Divorce Act* of 1968, which paved the way for future federal, provincial, and territorial statutory changes.

Before 1968, the support of divorcing or divorced spouses was regulated by provincial and territorial statutes that imposed a unilateral obligation on a guilty husband to maintain his innocent wife in the event of a breakdown of their marriage ensuing from his commission of adultery, cruelty, or desertion. The same principles applied to spousal support claims brought independently of divorce proceedings. During the 1970s and 1980s, many provinces and territories enacted legislation that eliminated the offence concept as the foundation of spousal support rights and obligations. In addition, following the precedent established by the federal *Divorce Act* of 1968, the right to spousal support on marriage breakdown in the absence of divorce became no longer confined to wives under provincial and territorial legislation; a financially dependent spouse of either sex might look to his or her marital partner for financial support. The governing consideration was no longer sex-based but turned upon the financial needs of the claimant and the ability of his or her spouse to pay. Each spouse was expected, however, to strive for financial self-sufficiency. Thus, marriage was no longer legally perceived as creating a presumed right to lifelong financial support for a dependent spouse in the event of marriage breakdown.

These changes in the right to divorce and the right to spousal support on divorce or marriage breakdown were accompanied by equally fundamental changes in provincial and territorial statutes governing the division of property on marriage breakdown or divorce. Separated and divorced wives no longer found themselves in the prejudicial position in which Irene Murdoch found herself in 1973 when the Supreme Court of

Canada denied her any interest in a ranch registered in her husband's name because her contributions in the home and in the fields were perceived as non-financial contributions ordinarily expected of a rancher's wife.[5] Although three years later the Supreme Court of Canada abandoned *Murdoch* in favour of a more enlightened approach in *Rathwell*,[6] the inequities of the *Murdoch* case triggered provincial and territorial legislation that provided for property sharing on marriage breakdown that was no longer based on ownership or who purchased the property.

Another fundamental change in family law has been the evolution of legal rights and obligations between unmarried cohabitants. Following the pattern established in cases like *Rathwell* from Saskatchewan, which involved married couples before the implementation of statutory property rights in the 1970s and 1980s, unmarried cohabitants have been accorded property rights on the dissolution of their relationships on the basis of the constructive trust and the doctrine of unjust enrichment. Rosie Becker, who did not live to enjoy the fruits of her legal victory in the Supreme Court of Canada in 1980, paved the way for the application of the doctrine of unjust enrichment to unmarried cohabiting couples of the opposite sex,[7] although there is nothing in the Supreme Court of Canada's analysis that precludes the application of similar principles to same-sex couples. Contemporaneously with these judicial developments dealing with property rights, many Canadian provincial statutes provided an extended definition of "spouse" so as to establish spousal support rights and obligations between cohabiting couples of the opposite sex who lived together for a designated period of time or had a child together. A more recent development in this context has been the extension of similar support rights and obligations as between cohabiting couples of the same-sex. This was achieved in 1999 by the Supreme Court of Canada's *M. v. H.*[8] judgment applying the equality provisions of section 15 of the *Canadian Charter of Rights and Freedoms*.

Major statutory reforms in children's rights have also occurred in the last thirty years. One of the most significant changes might be characterized as an aspect of criminal law, rather than family law. In the early 1980s, the *Juvenile Delinquents Act* was superseded by the *Young Offend-*

---

5   *Murdoch v. Murdoch*, [1975] 1 S.C.R. 423.

6   *Rathwell v. Rathwell*, [1978] 2 S.C.R. 436.

7   *Pettkus v. Becker*, [1980] 2 S.C.R. 834. And see *Sorochan v. Sorochan*, [1986] 2 S.C.R. 38; *Peter v. Beblow*, [1993] 1 S.C.R. 980; *Nova Scotia (Attorney General) v. Walsh*, [2002] 4 S.C.R. 325, (*sub nom. Walsh v. Bona*) (2002), 32 R.F.L. (5th) 81.

8   [1999] 2 S.C.R. 3.

ers Act. The paternalistic, or perhaps maternalistic, approach under the former statute perceived children before the court as misguided youth who needed help without the protection of due process. Not only did the *Young Offenders Act* implement the principle that juveniles should be held responsible for criminal conduct; it also acknowledged the responsibility of the state to accord legal rights to juveniles in the conduct of legal proceedings. The *Young Offenders Act* thereby endorsed the realization that we do it to the children, and not simply for the children. Due process changes respecting children were also promulgated in the late 1970s and early 1980s in the context of child protection legislation. In the 1960s, no one questioned the practices of residential schools or inter-provincial and international transracial adoptions of children from aboriginal communities. Contrast this with the 1990s when child abuse by institutional personnel led to criminal convictions in several Canadian provinces as well as to multiparty civil litigation and multifaceted mediated settlements for victims of abuse. The door has been opened to address the mistreatment of aboriginal children in residential schools and other institutions but closure has yet to be achieved. Fifteen years ago, it was extremely rare for children to sue their parents for damages for emotional, physical, and sexual abuse and recover very substantial compensation. In cases of spousal abuse, few people envisaged domestic violence statutes and specialized domestic violence courts. In the realm of what is somewhat artificially referred to as "private family law," the former legal distinctions between marital and extramarital children have long been abolished, either in consequence of express provincial legislation or because of the judicial application of the equality provisions in section 15 of the *Canadian Charter of Rights and Freedoms*, which were implemented in 1985.

The above substantive changes in the rights and obligations of family members have been accompanied by the evolution of new procedures for resolving family disputes. It is now mandatory for litigating spouses to file financial and property statements to provide data that will expedite the adjudication of support and property disputes. In contested custody disputes, independent expert assessments may be ordered by the court to determine the needs of the children and the respective abilities of the parents to accommodate those needs. It is only a matter of time before parenting plans become mandatory in contested custody proceedings. Diverse pre-trial processes are now in place to help reduce or eliminate contentious issues. The discretionary jurisdiction of the court over costs is being exercised aggressively by some courts to promote the consensual resolution of issues, including parenting disputes.[9] The consolidation of disputed issues in a single court proceeding has been facilitated by statutory changes and by amendments to provincial rules of court. These and other procedural changes have proved their worth but the legal system has remained adversarial. Separating and divorcing parents are still legally perceived as being in conflict with each other. "Fighting it out" is the legal norm. Significant progress has, nevertheless, been made. In several provinces and territories, parenting education for separating and divorce couples is readily available and voluntary recourse to mediation is encouraged. In some urban centres across Canada, specialized Family Courts have been established with a comprehensive jurisdiction over family law matters and access to support services that may deflect the need for lengthy and costly litigation. There still remains, however, considerable room for improvement in the development of alternative processes to litigation that can facilitate in the constructive resolution of family conflict.

Before addressing potential future developments in family law, a few words are appropriate concerning the legal profession. Although the public opinion of lawyers engaged in the practice of family law may not have changed as much as it should over the span of forty years in Canada, the divorce lawyer of the 1960s is a different breed from the family law practitioner of today. In the 1960s, divorce practitioners were often scorned by other lawyers, many of whom were proud to assert that "they didn't take divorce cases." Today, the responsible family law practitioner is no longer perceived as running a divorce mill where the sole grounds for relief are adultery or perjury. Family law practice has come of age. This is not to say that the family law specialist is held in high regard by the legal profession. Corporate and commercial practitioners and civil litigation lawyers still enjoy prestigious reputations that are not shared by dedicated family law practitioners. With the development of specialized Family Courts and very extensive family law dockets in courts of general jurisdiction, far more family law specialists have found their way to the Bench over the last twenty years. A new type of family law practitioner is slowly emerging in Canada. Following developments that have occurred in California, Minnesota, and elsewhere in the United States, some Canadian family law practitioners have opted into Collaborative

---

9   As to a "successful" parent's right to costs in contested custody proceedings, see the compelling analysis of the Alberta Court of Appeal in *Metz v. Weisgerber*, [2004] A.J. No. 510 (C.A.). See also *J.G.W. v. A.C.S.*, [2004] B.C.J. No. 889 (S.C.).

Family Law. This approach differs from the traditional practice of family law in that its practitioners focus on settlement to the exclusion of litigation. Written agreements are executed to provide full disclosure and to waive discovery and recourse to litigation for a stipulated period of time. During this period, negotiations are undertaken by the clients and their lawyers in an effort to achieve a settlement. If no settlement is reached, the lawyers withdraw from the case and cannot participate in any subsequent litigation. Opportunities exist for made-to-measure individualized Collaborative Family Law Participation Agreements that can reflect the specific interests of the disputants.

For many years, provincial and federal governments have provided booklets and pamphlets on family law for the general public. More recently, they have created relatively sophisticated websites to provide information. In particular, the federal Department of Justice currently provides a veritable mine of information on diverse aspects of Canadian family law. Its materials on the *Federal Child Support Guidelines* are remarkably informative for both lawyer and lay person alike. The provinces of Alberta, British Columbia, and Saskatchewan currently reproduce full trial and appellate family law judgments on their websites and the same is true in Ontario with respect to appellate judgments. Prince Edward Island identifies relevant provincial family law judgments on its website but does not provide the contents of those judgments. This website preserves a high degree of privacy by referring to cases by the initial letters of the names of the parties. This is one step removed from Quebec's system of referring to family law cases under the generic heading: "*Droit de la famille, No. ...*" but it is a step in the right direction. Books, pamphlets, audio and video cassettes are now commonplace in various court-connected information centres. Steps have also been taken to provide relevant information on the web. Some farsighted Canadian family law practitioners are providing wide-ranging information on the web. Information is the primary source of the lawyer's stock in trade but legal practitioners will have to work harder to communicate information to potential clients, if they are to compete with increasing numbers of paralegals, mediators, and facilitators. It is insufficient to have a web page geared to self-promotion. Potential clients need to be informed of their basic substantive rights and of the diverse processes available for the resolution of disputes both within and outside the judicial system. The strategic use of the web, hard copy, disks, and videos will become an integral part of the practice of family dispute resolution. With an increasing number of self-represented litigants, the unbundling of legal services will become widespread within the next few years. "Unbundling" signifies that the lawyer will provide information and input into a client's case, without assuming the responsibility to appear for that client in the courtroom or elsewhere. For the more traditional practitioner, hourly billing may be largely replaced in family law practice by block billings, whereby the lawyer will undertake the carriage of a case through its diverse possible stages, with a maximum global amount being payable at each stage.

The uncontested divorce under the auspices of the judiciary is on its last legs. If the stumbling block of section 96 of the *Constitution Act, 1867* can be overcome, administrative divorce will replace the desk order divorces that are currently processed on affidavit evidence without any court appearance. In the meantime, paralegals will assume this task with input from court-based information facilities. Adultery and cruelty will disappear as criteria of marriage breakdown under the *Divorce Act*, leaving no-fault separation as the sole criterion. Collusion, connivance, and condonation will disappear from the statute book as bars to divorce, thereby formalizing their present *de facto* status. Divorces, like marriages, will become subject to an administrative registration system. Current spousal and child support laws will need to be re-addressed with the expanded legal recognition of non-marital domestic partnerships and in light of the ageing Canadian population. Spousal Support Guidelines of an advisory nature are on the horizon.[10]

The obligation of children to support their elderly parents who are not economically self-sufficient has long existed under provincial legislation in Canada but has been relatively rarely invoked. The present legislation is a sleeping giant awaiting arousal. The clock is ticking but the wake up alarm is not yet ringing. But it will. In all likelihood, governmental agencies will more actively pursue liable relatives as the state becomes less capable of absorbing the costs in an ageing population with a substantially reduced work force.

With respect to parenting disputes, cultural diversity will attract greater attention than it has in the past. The processing of disputes relating to the treatment of aboriginal children in residential schools underlines the need to more aggressively recognize cultural heritage in resolving parenting disputes on family breakdown. Children will become more actively involved in the dispute resolution process in cases where their parenting is at stake. The voice of the child will be heard more ef-

---

10   See Department of Justice, Canada, *Spousal Support Advisory Guidelines: A Draft Proposal*, January 2005.

fectively in the formulation of parenting plans. The proprietary legal terminology of "custody" and "access" will disappear; parenting plans involving extended family members will become common; and mediation may become a preferred alternative to the traditional legal process for the majority of parents. Private arbitration may also become an integral part of family dispute resolution across Canada and arbitration may ultimately become court-connected with recourse to a panel of screened arbitrators. Courts will, nevertheless continue to play a major role in the resolution of family disputes. New processes for family dispute resolution are complementary to the legal system. They cannot exist without it. Their efficacy lies in the fact that the legal system is there to fall back on when there are no options available or they have proved wanting. But courts themselves face major changes in an age when 30 to 40 percent of all family litigants, depending on the issue and the province of residence, seek access to the courts without legal representation. As a first step, several provinces are following Ontario's example by seeking to simplify the Family Law Rules so as to make them comprehensible to non-lawyers. The next step will be to develop improved informational resources to assist self-represented litigants to present relevant information before the court. Videos and computer disks that inform litigants how to fill in the requisite forms and what financial or other material to provide for the court are absolutely vital, if courts are to cope with the increasing number of self-represented litigants. Court lists may need to be divided into cases where one or both of the parties are self-represented and those where both sides are independently legally represented. The assignment of judges may be structured according to their willingness and ability to cope with self-represented litigants. Judges will diversify their roles. They will no longer be confined to an adjudicator's role. They will become case managers in the fullest sense from the time when litigation commences. Court-connected mediation will become the norm.

The private certificate system of legal aid in Ontario is destined to disappear. It will initially be replaced by a family law clinic system, such as already exists in other jurisdictions. Within the next twenty years, family legal aid clinics may themselves yield pride of place to community-based family dispute resolution centres, with ready access to a network of lawyers, psychologists, social workers, mediators, business valuators, actuaries, and a host of other paid professionals as well as para-professionals and volunteers.

Multidisciplinary private law practices will emerge in the field of family conflict management and family dispute resolution. One can only look back in wonder at the foresight of James (Jim) C. MacDonald and Lee Ferrier (now an Honourable Justice of the Superior Court of Ontario), the first lawyers in Canada to establish a specialized family law practice. That was in the 1960s. Now family law boutiques are the rage in Ontario, after brief liaisons with the corporate/commercial law elite proved largely unsuccessful. As long ago as the 1970s, Jim MacDonald and Lee Ferrier introduced a social worker into their practice on an as-needed consultancy basis. They were true pioneers in the practice of family law in Canada. They were also largely responsible for the evolution of family law Continuing Legal Education programs in Ontario in the 1970s and 1980s.

Whether past, present, and future changes should be perceived as good or bad for family stability in Canada is a matter of opinion. Some will view changes in family law and family life in Canada over the last thirty years as undermining the institution of marriage. Others will conclude that the changes already encountered and those yet to be experienced merely reflect the family in transition, rather than the family in crisis. In the absence of sophisticated empirical research, strongly held opinions or convictions on the past, present, or future state of the Canadian family will remain unsubstantiated and unabated.

E. FRAGMENTATION OF LEGISLATIVE POWERS

Exclusive legislative jurisdiction over "marriage and divorce" is conferred on the Parliament of Canada by section 91(26) of the *Constitution Act, 1867*, which was formerly known as the *British North America Act, 1867*. By way of qualification of the above jurisdiction, section 92(12) grants exclusive power to the provincial legislatures to enact laws relating to the "solemnization of marriage." Section 92(13) also confers exclusive authority on the provincial legislatures to make laws in relation to "property and civil rights in the province." Subject to the overriding provisions of section 96, which controls the power of appointment and the jurisdictional competence of federally and provincially appointed judges, section 92(14) gives the provinces authority over the "administration of justice in the province, including the constitution, maintenance and organization of provincial courts, both of civil and criminal jurisdiction, and including procedure in civil matters in those courts." This distribution of legislative powers is ratified by the *Canada Act, 1982*.

It is significant that the Parliament of Canada has never seen fit to exercise its potentially broad legislative authority over "marriage." Since the enactment of the first comprehensive federal *Divorce Act* in 1968, a dual system of support and custody has existed in Canada. Where a claim for support or custody arises in divorce proceedings, the dispute is governed by federal divorce legislation, which is currently found in the *Divorce Act, 1986* as amended. Where, however, such claims arise independently of divorce, they are governed by provincial and territorial legislation.

In federal-provincial consultations on constitutional reform in the late 1970s and early 1980s, the federal government initially proposed that the legislative jurisdiction over "marriage and divorce" be transferred to the provinces. This proposal reflected the opinions expressed in *The Report of the Special Joint Committee of the Senate and House of Commons on the Constitution of Canada* (The Molgat/McGuigan Report, Canada, 1972). This Committee concluded that such a transfer of legislative jurisdiction would permit "the laws [to] conform more closely to the social and ethical values of the Canadians living in that Province" and "would allow for a more integrated approach to Family Law within provincial jurisdiction." Although a transfer of legislative jurisdiction over "marriage and divorce" from the Parliament of Canada to the provincial and territorial legislatures would facilitate the development of a unified family law regime within a single province or territory, any advantage thereby resulting must be weighed against the disadvantages that would flow from a proliferation of diverse regimes. Having regard to the mobility of Canadians, a transfer of legislative jurisdiction over "marriage and divorce" to the provinces and territories would undoubtedly exacerbate the problems currently encountered with respect to the recognition and enforcement of extraprovincial support and custody orders.

It remains to be seen whether the federal government will ultimately transfer legislative jurisdiction over "marriage and divorce" to the provinces and territories. Any decision on this matter must await the outcome of future constitutional negotiations.

F. FRAGMENTATION OF JUDICIAL JURISDICTION

The aforementioned distribution of legislative powers contributes to, but is not the sole reason for, fragmentation in the jurisdiction of Canadian courts that adjudicate family disputes.

In most Canadian provinces, two levels of court share the responsibility for resolving family disputes, namely, courts presided over by federally appointed judges and courts presided over by provincially appointed judges. Overlapping and competing jurisdictions are rife, especially with respect to spousal and child support and the custody, care, and upbringing of children. Thus, lawyers can play the game of "forum shopping" and this can materially affect the cost and outcome of legal proceedings. Despair, confusion, and frustration may ensue as family members are shunted from court to court in their search for elusive legal remedies. The problems are aggravated by the differing approaches to family conflict resolution adopted in this two-tiered system of courts.

Matrimonial proceedings before federally appointed judges for the most part follow the traditional adversarial approach adopted in civil proceedings. Technical and formal procedures are adhered to and involve substantial costs to the litigants at a time when there may be insufficient money to accommodate the basic needs of two separate households. These courts are often presided over by judges who have never specialized in the field of family law and whose contact with the adjudication of family disputes is sporadic. They rarely look to agencies or facilities in the community that might promote family counselling and the mediation of disputes between family members. The responsibility for any out-of-court settlement of disputes is left to the lawyers and their clients. Although the vast majority of disputes are in fact settled by the lawyers, one of the most significant factors contributing to settlement is the prohibitive cost of litigation, both in terms of dollars and cents and the psychological wear and tear of protracted legal proceedings. Courts presided over by provincially appointed judges are more accessible, simpler, cheaper, and less formal than those presided over by federally appointed judges, but the case loads are extremely high and offer little opportunity to make use of community-based agencies to assist family members cope with stress and the economic or parenting realities of family breakdown.

Although public expectations with respect to the constructive resolution of family disputes may far exceed the realistic potential of any court of law, the present fragmentation of jurisdiction, coupled with the absence of any coherent legal philosophy towards the resolution of family conflicts, cannot be justified.

In an effort to redress some of the problems arising out of the present fragmentation of judicial jurisdiction, Unified Family Courts or specialized Family Courts have been established in several Canadian provinces. There are two essential features of a Unified Family Court:

(i) The court must exercise an exclusive and comprehensive jurisdiction over legal issues directly arising from the formation or dissolution of the family.

(ii) Auxiliary services must be available to the court in the exercise of its judicial functions and also to litigants having recourse to the judicial process. These auxiliary services include (a) information and intake services; (b) counselling and conciliation or mediation services; (c) investigative or assessment services; (d) legal services; and (e) enforcement services.

Pursuant to the recommendations of the Law Reform Commission of Canada and provincial law reform agencies, Unified Family Court projects were first established in the 1970s on a pilot or experimental basis in various urban centres across Canada, including the Richmond, Surrey, Delta districts in British Columbia; Fredericton, New Brunswick; St. John's, Newfoundland; Hamilton, Ontario; and Saskatoon, Saskatchewan. Internal and external evaluations of several of the aforementioned pilot projects attested to their success in promoting the resolution of spousal and family disputes.[11] The British Columbia pilot project, though successful, was discontinued. The Saskatoon and Hamilton projects have long existed on a permanent basis. In both Saskatoon and Regina, the Court of Queen's Bench now has a Family Division, with a core of specialized judges. In the late 1990s, Ontario established specialized Family Courts in a dozen or more other judicial districts. In 1983, Manitoba established a Family Division of the Court of Queen's Bench but its jurisdiction was initially confined to Winnipeg.[12] It has since been expanded to Brandon and, with judges going on circuit, virtually all of the province is now covered. In New Brunswick, Newfoundland, and Prince Edward Island, specialized Family Courts have been established on a permanent and province-wide basis. The establishment of such specialized courts, coupled with a shift of judicial emphasis towards case management that

---

11   See, for example, Bergen Amren & Flora MacLeod, *The British Columbia Unified Family Court Pilot Project, 1974–1977, A Description and Evaluation* (British Columbia: Ministry of Attorney General, Spring 1979); Andrea Maurice & John A. Byles, *A Report on the Conciliation Services of the Unified Family Court, Judicial District of Hamilton-Wentworth* (Ontario: Ministry of Attorney General and Canada: Department of Justice, 1980); *Attempting to Restructure Family Law: Unified Family Court Experiments in Canada, Discussion Draft* (Canada: Department of Justice, August 1983).

12   Freda M. Steel, "Recent Family Law Developments in Manitoba" (1983) 13 Man. L.J. 323 at 324–29.

can facilitate the resolution of family disputes, promise a more conciliatory climate for families on their breakdown than has been afforded in the past under traditional adversarial legal and judicial processes.

CHAPTER 2

MARRIAGE

A. ENGAGEMENTS

Engagements are a common prelude to marriage. At the time when the parties agree to marry at some future date, they often exchange gifts as a token of their commitment. The most common gift, of course, is the engagement ring that is traditionally given by the prospective bridegroom to his prospective bride. Not every engagement, however, results in marriage. The parties may mutually agree to abandon their plans to marry. Or either of them may unilaterally break off the engagement. At one time, it was possible for the jilted lover to sue the other party for breach of promise of marriage. These actions have now been abolished in England, Scotland, Australia, New Zealand, and in several American states and Canadian provinces, including British Columbia, Manitoba, and Ontario. Most people would agree that it is better for an engagement to be broken than for a marriage to be entered into after the parties have second thoughts.

B. PROPERTY DISPUTES ON TERMINATION OF ENGAGEMENT

Statutory abolition of actions for breach of promise of marriage does not interfere with the remedies legally available to resolve property or other disputes that arise on the termination of an engagement. For example, an engaged couple may have acquired property for their future married life together, either from their individual or joint efforts. In these circumstances, if the engagement is subsequently broken off, either party may invoke established legal doctrines to determine their interest in the property. If it was a product of their joint financial contributions, whether direct or indirect, the value of the property will be shared between them. If it was acquired solely through the efforts of one of the parties, that person will be exclusively entitled to the property. The reason for terminating the engagement would be irrelevant to any such claims. Different principles apply to gifts made in contemplation of marriage, including the engagement ring. In the absence of express statutory provision to the contrary, the general common-law rule is that the engagement ring is forfeited by the party who refused to honour the engagement.[1] If the woman breaks off the engagement, she must return the ring. On the other hand, if the man breaks off the engagement, he cannot demand the return of the engagement ring. In Ontario, the action for breach of promise of marriage was abolished in 1977 but section 33 of the Ontario *Marriage Act*[2] expressly provides for the recovery of gifts made in contemplation of marriage. Pursuant to this statutory provision, where one person makes a gift to another "in contemplation of or conditional upon" their marriage to each other and the marriage fails to take place or is abandoned, the question of whether the failure or abandonment was caused by the fault of the donor is irrelevant to a determination of the right of the donor to recover the gift. Whether a gift has been made in contemplation of or conditional upon marriage is a question of fact to be determined in light of the attendant circumstances. Birthday presents, for example, would not be regarded as conditional gifts. On the other hand, an engagement ring could properly be regarded as a pledge made in contemplation of marriage and should, therefore, be returned under the Ontario statutory provision if the intended marriage did not take place.[3]

---

1   *Seiler v. Funk* (1914), 32 O.L.R. 99 (S.C.); *Jacobs v. Davies*, [1916–17] All E.R. Rep. 374; *McArthur v. Zaduk* (2001), 21 R.F.L. (5th) 142 (Ont. Sup. Ct.); *Cohen v. Sellar*, [1926] All E.R. Rep. 312; *Robinson v. Cumming* (1742), 26 E.R. 646. See also *Marcon v. Cicchelli* (1993), 47 R.F.L. (3d) 403 (Ont. Gen. Div.); for criticism of this conclusion, see J.G. McLeod, "Case Comment: *Marcon v. Cicchelli*" (1993), 47 R.F.L. (3d) 411 at 412. Compare *Zimmerman v. Lazare*, [2007] B.C.J. No. 932 (S.C.).

2   R.S.O. 1990, c. M.3.

3   But see *contra*: *Marcon v. Cicchelli* (1993), 47 R.F.L. (3d) 403 (Ont. Gen. Div.).

Gifts received from third parties in contemplation of marriage, such as wedding presents, are returnable to the donors if the marriage fails to take place for any reason.[4]

C. CHANGE OF NAME

It has been traditional for the bride to take the surname of the bridegroom after their marriage. This tradition is based on convention and is not a legal requirement. In the absence of any statutory provision to the contrary, any person may assume the surname of his or her choice, provided that its use is not calculated to deceive or inflict pecuniary loss. A bride is, therefore, free to retain her birth name in preference to adopting her husband's surname or they may agree on some hybrid form of their joint names. When persons marry and give birth to children, however, statutory restrictions are often imposed that restrict their ability to change their surnames at will. In Canada, such legislation is found in provincial and territorial *Change of Name Acts*. These statutes sometimes require applications for a change of family surname to be made through the courts. The current trend of legislation, as exemplified by the Ontario *Change of Name Act*, R.S.O. 1990, c. C.7, provides for official changes of name to be made through administrative processes at a modest cost.

D. MARRIAGE: STATUS OR CONTRACT?

Marriage is more than a simple contract between two people who live together as husband and wife. Marriage is a status that is conferred on individuals by the state. Marriage has a public character and, as such, is subject to general laws that dictate and control the rights, obligations, and incidents of marriage, independently of the wishes of those who marry. Although based on a contract between the parties, marriage is a status to which the state attaches its own conditions as to its creation, duration, and consequences.[5] The principle of the contractual autonomy of the parties has, nevertheless, been endorsed in judicial decisions and statutory provisions that expressly confer certain powers on married persons to regulate their own affairs during marriage and on its termination

---

4   *Jeffreys v. Luck* (1922), 153 L.T.J. 139.
5   *Newson v. Newson and Davidson*, [1936] O.R. 117 at 126 (H.C.J.).

by death or divorce. Marriage contracts and separation agreements are of particular importance in this context; they will be examined later.[6]

E. DEFINITION OF MARRIAGE; MONOGAMOUS AND POLYGAMOUS MARRIAGES

1) Definition of "Marriage"

Between 2003 and 2005, the courts of eight provinces and two territories held that the traditional common-law definition of "marriage" as "the voluntary union for life of one man and one woman to the exclusion of all others"[7] contravenes section 15 of the *Canadian Charter of Rights and Freedoms* by precluding same-sex marriage and cannot be saved under section 1 of the *Charter*. Consequently, marriage was judicially redefined to mean the voluntary or lawful union of two persons to the exclusion of all others.[8] Instead of appealing any of these rulings to the Supreme Court of Canada, the Canadian government decided to introduce legislation to reflect the judicial redefinition of marriage to include same-sex marriage.[9] Before doing so, however, it invoked section 53 of the *Supreme Court Act*,[10] pursuant to which the Governor in Council referred the following questions to the Supreme Court of Canada:[11]

> 1. Is the annexed Proposal for an Act respecting certain aspects of legal capacity for marriage for civil purposes within the exclusive legislative authority of the Parliament of Canada? If not, in what particular or particulars, and to what extent?

---

6   See *Miglin v. Miglin*, [2003] 1 S.C.R. 303; *Hartshorne v. Hartshorne*, [2004] 1 S.C.R. 550.

7   *Hyde v. Hyde and Woodmansee* (1866), L.R. 1 P. & D. 130.

8   *Egale Canada Inc. v. Canada (Attorney General)*, [2003] B.C.J. No. 994 (C.A.) and [2003] B.C.J. No. 1582 (C.A.); *Vogel v. Attorney General of Canada, Attorney General of Manitoba and Director of Vital Statistics Agency, Yard J. Winnipeg Centre*, FD04-01-74476 (Man. Q.B.); *Harrison v. Canada (Attorney General)*, [2005] N.B.J. No. 257 (Q.B.); *Pottle v. Canada (Attorney General)* (21 December 2004) (Nfld. & Lab. S.C.) [unreported], Green C.J.; *Boutilier v. Nova Scotia (Attorney General)*, [2004] N.S.J. No. 357 (S.C.); *Halpern v. Canada*, [2003] O.J. No. 2268 (C.A.); *Hendricks c. Québec (Procureur général)*, [2002] J.Q. no 3816 (S.C.), aff'd [2004] J.Q. no 2573 (C.A.); *N.W. v. Canada (Attorney General)*, [2004] S.J. No. 669 (Q.B.); *Dunbar v. Yukon*, [2004] Y.J. No. 61 (S.C.).

9   See *Civil Marriage Act*, S.C. 2005, c. 33.

10 R.S.C. 1985, c. S-26.

11 *Reference Re Same-Sex Marriage*, [2004] 3 S.C.R. 698.

2. If the answer to question 1 is yes, is section 1 of the proposal, which extends capacity to marry to persons of the same sex, consistent with the *Canadian Charter of Rights and Freedoms*? If not, in what particular or particulars, and to what extent?

3. Does the freedom of religion guaranteed by paragraph 2(a) of the *Canadian Charter of Rights and Freedoms* protect religious officials from being compelled to perform a marriage between two persons of the same sex that is contrary to their religious beliefs?

4. Is the opposite-sex requirement for marriage for civil purposes, as established by the common law and set out for Quebec in section 5 of the *Federal Law-Civil Law Harmonization Act, No. 1*, consistent with the *Canadian Charter of Rights and Freedoms*? If not, in what particular or particulars and to what extent?

The operative sections of the proposed legislation read as follows:

1. Marriage, for civil purposes, is the lawful union of two persons to the exclusion of all others.

2. Nothing in this Act affects the freedom of officials of religious groups to refuse to perform marriages that are not in accordance with their religious beliefs.

The responses of the Supreme Court of Canada were as follows:

General responses
Question 1 was answered in the affirmative with respect to section 1 of the proposed legislation but in the negative with respect to section 2. Questions 2 and 3 were both answered in the affirmative. The Supreme Court of Canada declined to answer question 4.

Question 1
In ruling that section 1 of the proposed legislation is *intra vires* Parliament, the Supreme Court of Canada held that section 91(26) of the *Constitution Act, 1867* does not entrench the common-law definition of marriage as it stood in 1867, when marriage was perceived as "the voluntary union for life of one man and one woman to the exclusion of all others.[12] Accepting an expansive definition of "marriage" to include same-sex marriage, the Supreme Court of Canada concluded that, while the proposed federal legislative recognition of same-sex marriage would have an impact in the provincial legislative sphere, these effects

---

12   *Hyde v. Hyde and Woodmansee* (1866), L.R. 1 P. & D. 130 at 133.

are incidental and do not relate to the core of the provincial powers relating to the "solemnization of marriage" and "property and civil rights" under sections 92(12) and 92(13) of the *Constitution Act, 1867*. Section 2 of the proposed legislation was found to be *ultra vires* Parliament, however, because it pertains to the solemnization of marriage which falls within the provincial legislative domain under section 92(12) of the *Constitution Act, 1867*.

Question 2
Section 1 of the proposed legislation, which reflects the government's policy stance towards equality rights under section 15(1) of the *Canadian Charter of Rights and Freedoms*, was perceived by the Supreme Court of Canada as flowing from the *Charter* and was, therefore, consistent with the values protected by section 15(1), notwithstanding any potential conflicts that might arise between the right to same-sex marriage and the right to freedom of religion, which conflicts should be resolved within the ambit of the *Charter* itself by way of internal balancing and delineation.

Question 3
The Supreme Court of Canada held that, absent unique circumstances about which the Court would not speculate, the guarantee of religious freedom in section 2(a) of the *Charter* is broad enough to protect religious officials from being compelled by the state to perform civil or religious same-sex marriages that are contrary to their religious beliefs.

Question 4
The Supreme Court of Canada declined to answer question 4 for the following reasons:
(i)   The federal government had announced its intention to address the issue of same-sex marriage, regardless of the Court's opinion on this question.
(ii) Same-sex couples have relied upon the finality of previous appellate and trial court rulings that have recognized same-sex marriage and these acquired rights are entitled to protection.
(iii) While a negative answer to question 4 would promote uniformity with respect to civil marriage across Canada, an affirmative answer would throw the law into confusion because previous judicial decisions that have upheld the validity of same-sex marriages would be cast in doubt, though they would not be technically overruled by an advisory opinion of the Supreme Court of Canada on question 4.

Having received these responses, section 2 of the *Civil Marriage Act*[13] currently provides that "marriage, for civil purposes, is the lawful union of two persons to the exclusion of all others." Notwithstanding the response of the Supreme Court of Canada to question 1, section 3 of the *Civil Marriage Act* invades the provincial domain of legislative authority by providing that officials of religious groups are free to refuse to perform services that are not in accordance with their religious beliefs.

Because the right of same-sex couples to marry is an issue relating to capacity to marry, the validity of same-sex marriage is to be determined by the domiciliary law of the parties, not by the law of the place of solemnization of the marriage that governs only the formalities of marriage. This legal distinction may be of no significance to same-sex couples who are domiciled in Canada but is of critical importance to same-sex couples who are domiciled elsewhere and who come to Canada to solemnize their marriage.

In response to the recognition of the legal validity of same-sex marriage by the Ontario Court of Appeal in *Halpern v. Canada*,[14] the Ontario legislature enacted the *Spousal Relationships Statute Law Amendment Act*[15] in 2005, which revised more than seventy provincial statutes to assimilate the legal rights and obligations of opposite-sex and same-sex married couples. This statute also amended the Ontario *Marriage Act* to affirm the freedom of religious officials to decline to solemnize same-sex marriages or to provide a venue for such marriages against their religious beliefs.[16]

The criterion to determine whether the parties contracted a lifelong union is the intention that they had at the time when the marriage took place. It is immaterial that the spouses may subsequently divorce.[17]

2) Monogamous and Polygamous Marriages

It is generally, but not universally, accepted that the characterization of a marriage as monogamous or polygamous is to be determined by reference to the law of the country where the marriage was celebrated.[18] It

---

13   S.C. 2005, c. 33.

14   [2003] O.J. No. 2268 (C.A.).

15   S.O. 2005, c. 5.

16   *Marriage Act*, R.S.O. 1990, c. M-3, s. 20(b) as amended by S.O. 2005, c. 5, s. 39.

17   *Nachimson v. Nachimson*, [1930] P. 217.

18   *Chetti v. Chetti*, [1909] P. 67; *Srini Vassan v. Srini Vassan*, [1946] P. 67; *Cheni (otherwise Rodriguez) v. Cheni*, [1965] P. 85.

has, nevertheless, been held that a husband's acquisition of a domicile of choice in a monogamous jurisdiction is sufficient to convert his potentially polygamous marriage into a monogamous marriage.[19]

Marriages in Canada are monogamous. Polygamous marriages that were validly solemnized in a foreign country may be recognized for some, but not for all purposes, of Canadian federal, provincial, or territorial laws. For example, parties to a polygamous marriage may be denied access to Canadian courts for the purpose of obtaining a divorce.[20] They may, nevertheless, be entitled to pursue claims for spousal and child support or for custody or access under provincial or territorial legislation in Canada.[21] Parties to a polygamous marriage that was validly solemnized abroad are prohibited from entering into a subsequent monogamous marriage in Canada.[22] A polygamous marriage may be recognized as valid in Canada for the purpose of determining the succession rights of surviving spouses.[23] Under subsection 1(2) of the Ontario *Family Law Act*,[24] "spouse" is defined to include a party to "a marriage that is actually or potentially polygamous, if it was celebrated in a jurisdiction whose system of law recognizes it as valid." Accordingly, polygamous spouses in Ontario are entitled to pursue claims for an equalization of net family property between the spouses on separation or death. They may also pursue claims under the Ontario *Family Law Act* for spousal and child support and may enter into marriage contracts and separation agreements. In addition, they can sue a third party for damages where that third party kills or injures their polygamous spouse. For almost all practical purposes under the law of Ontario, a spouse who contracted a valid polygamous marriage abroad has the same legal rights and obligations as a spouse who is party to a traditional monogamous marriage. Legislative changes such as these broadly reflect the changing nature of family relationships in a multicultural society such as currently exists in Canada. Ironically, although foreign polygamous marriages have been recognized for many purposes of Canadian law, the practice of polygamy is an indictable criminal offence

---

19   *Ali v. Ali*, [1968] P. 564, [1966] 1 All E.R. 665; *Re Hassan and Hassan* (1976), 12 O.R. (2d) 432, 28 R.F.L. 121, 69 D.L.R. (3d) 224.

20   See *Hyde v. Hyde and Woodmansee*, (1866), L.R. 1 P. & D. 130. *Quaere* whether this prohibition violates s. 15 (equality rights) of the *Canadian Charter of Rights and Freedoms*.

21   *Lim v. Lim*, [1948] 1 W.W.R. 298 (B.C.S.C.).

22   *Kaur v. Ginder* (1958), 25 W.W.R. 532 (B.C.S.C.).

23   *Yew v. British Columbia (Attorney General)* (1924), 33 B.C.R. 109 (C.A.).

24   R.S.O. 1990, c. F.3.

under section 293 of the *Criminal Code* of Canada.[25] No successful prosecution has been pursued under this provision since the late-nineteenth century. It remains on the statute books, however, and is quite distinct from the criminal offence of bigamy, which is regulated by sections 290 and 291 of the *Criminal Code*.

F. FORMAL AND ESSENTIAL VALIDITY

1) Validity of Marriage; Applicable Laws

The formal validity of marriage is determined by the application of the *lex loci celebrationis*, that is, the law of the place where the marriage was contracted.[26] A party who asserts that a marriage is void because of lack of compliance with the requirements of the law of the country in which it was celebrated has the burden of proving the foreign law by means of an expert witness. Absent such proof, the foreign law will be presumed to be the same as the law of the forum wherein the marriage is impugned.[27]

Matters pertaining to the essential validity of a marriage, which include the capacity to marry and consent to marriage, are governed by the law of the domicile of the parties, or possibly the law of their intended matrimonial domicile.[28]

2) Formal Validity

In Canada, the formal requirements of marriage are governed by provincial and territorial legislation. For example, the Ontario *Marriage Act*[29] regulates the solemnization of marriage in that province. It stipulates that no marriage may be solemnized in Ontario except under the authority of

---

25 See *R. v. Bear's Shin Bone* (1899), 4 Terr. L.R. 173 (N.W.T. S.C.); *R. v. Nan-E-Quis-A-Ka* (1899), 1 Terr. L.R. 211 (N.W.T. C.A.); *Ali v. Canada (Minister of Citizenship and Immigration)*, [1998] F.C.J. No. 1640 (T.D.) (application for permanent residence in Canada denied because the applicant was likely to practise polygamy, an indictable offence under section 293 of the *Criminal Code*).

26 *Hassan v. Hassan*, [2006] A.J. No. 955 (Q.B.); *Davison v. Sweeney*, [2005] B.C.J. No. 1196 (S.C.); *Berthiaume v. Dastou*, [1930] 1 D.L.R. 849 (J.C.P.C.).

27 *Davison v. Sweeney*, [2005] B.C.J. No. 1196 (S.C.); *Ali v. Ahmed*, [2002] O.J. No. 397 (Sup. Ct.).

28 *Sangha v. Mander*, [1985] B.C.J. No. 2688 (S.C.); *Davison v. Sweeney*, [2005] B.C.J. No. 1196 (S.C.); *Brook v. Brook* (1861), 9 H.L. Cas. 193; *De Reneville v. De Reneville*, [1948] P. 100 at 114 (Eng. C.A.).

29 R.S.O. 1990, c. M.3.

a licence or the publication of banns. It also defines specific requirements concerning waiting periods, parental consents, the attendance of the parties and witnesses, and penalties for false declarations. Non-compliance with statutorily presented formalities, though subject to penalties, does not render the marriage void unless the statute expressly or by necessary implication invalidates the marriage.[30] Section 31 of the Ontario *Marriage Act* expressly provides that "[if] the parties to a marriage solemnized in good faith and intended to be in compliance with this Act are not under a legal disqualification to contract such marriage and after such solemnization have lived together and cohabited as man and wife, such marriage shall be deemed a valid marriage, notwithstanding that the person who solemnized the marriage was not authorized to solemnize marriage, and notwithstanding the absence of or any irregularity or insufficiency in the publication of banns or the issue of a licence."[31] The good faith of one of the parties will be sufficient to satisfy this statutory validation clause.[32] Failure to comply with a curative provision, such as section 31 of the Ontario *Marriage Act*, may imply invalidity.[33]

3) Essential Validity

A valid marriage requires the voluntary consent of both parties and the absence of any legal incapacity to marry.[34] These prerequisites to a valid marriage can be traced back to the jurisprudence of the ecclesiastical courts in England prior to 1857.

G. JURISDICTION

Canadian courts may assume jurisdiction in nullity proceedings, whether the marriage is void or voidable, if either party is domiciled within the territorial jurisdiction of the court at the commencement of the proceedings, or if the respondent is *bona fide* resident within the jurisdiction of

---

30   *Clause v. Clause*, [1956] O.W.N. 449 (S.C.).

31   *Upadyhaha v. Sehgal* (2000), 11 R.F.L. (5th) 210 (Ont. Sup. Ct.).

32   *Alspector v. Alspector*, [1957] O.R. 454 (C.A.).

33   See *Gilham v. Steele*, [1953] 2 D.L.R. 89 (B.C.C.A.); see also H.R. Hahlo, *Nullity of Marriage in Canada* (Toronto: Butterworths, 1979) at 19.

34   *Moss v. Moss*, [1897] P. 263 at 268.

the court, or when the marriage has been solemnized within the territorial jurisdiction of the court.[35]

H. VOID AND VOIDABLE MARRIAGES[36]

Marriages may be valid, void, or voidable according to law. A void marriage is one that is null and void from its inception. It is regarded as though it had never taken place. A voidable marriage, on the other hand, is treated in law as a valid and subsisting marriage unless and until it is annulled by a court of competent jurisdiction.[37] A voidable marriage can only be annulled on the petition of one of the spouses and the annulment must occur during the lifetime of both spouses.[38] Third parties cannot seek to annul a voidable marriage entered into by other people. The parties to a voidable marriage may elect to treat it as valid. A voidable marriage can only be terminated by the judgment of a court of competent jurisdiction at the request of one of the parties to that marriage. A void marriage, however, is impeachable by third parties who "have an interest of some kind; for the object of the suit must be to procure the marriage to be voided on the ground that its validity may affect some right, or interest of the party promoting the suit."[39] A "slight interest" will suffice.[40] A void marriage may also be impugned collaterally after the death of one or both spouses.[41] Where the marriage is void, either party is entitled to institute

---

35   See J.D. Payne, "Jurisdiction in Nullity Proceedings" (1961) 26 Sask. Bar Rev. 20; *Stevenson v. Stevenson*, [1997] B.C.J. No. 1154 (S.C.) (domicile); *Meunier v. Meunier*, [1997] B.C.J. No. 1156 (S.C.); *Sangha v. Aujla*, [2002] B.C.J. No. 2388 (S.C.) (residence); *Grewal v. Sohal*, [2004] B.C.J. No. 4802 (S.C.) (domicile); *Davison v. Sweeney*, [2005] B.C.J. No. 1196 (S.C.); *Ward v. Ward* (1985), 66 N.B.R. (2d) 44 (Q.B.).

36   For a detailed analysis of the differing consequences of void and voidable marriages, including their effect on marriage settlements, separation agreements, gifts, intestate succession rights, the revocation of wills, dependants' maintenance claims against the estate of a deceased person, changes of name, the legitimacy of children, support and property rights, tax consequences, and the like, see H.R. Hahlo, *Nullity of Marriage in Canada* (Toronto: Butterworths, 1979) at 41–57.

37   *Meunier v. Meunier*, [1997] B.C.J. No. 1156 (S.C.) (void marriage); *Davison v. Sweeney*, [2005] B.C.J. No. 1196 (S.C.); *De Reneville v. De Reneville*, [1948] P. 100 at 110 (Eng. C.A) (voidable marriage).

38   *A. v. B.* (1868), 1 P. & D. 559; *Cowell v. Prince* (1866), L.R. 1 Ex. 246; *Brown v. Brown* (1907), 13 B.C.R. 73 (Co. Ct.); *Fleming v. Fleming*, [1934] O.R. 588 (C.A.).

39   *Sherwood v. Ray* (1837), 12 E.R. 848, Parke B.

40   *Faremouth v. Watson* (1811), 161 E.R. 1009.

41   *Fenton v. Livingstone* (1859), 3 Macq. 497; *Spier v. Bergen*, [1947] W.N. 46.

nullity proceedings and a decree may be granted to the party under the disability.[42] If the marriage is voidable, only the party under the disability may be barred from securing an annulment of the marriage.[43] The doctrine of insincerity may bar the annulment of a voidable marriage but is, in principle, inapplicable to a void marriage.[44]

I. ABSENCE OF CONSENT

As stated previously, marriage is "a voluntary union for life." It is not a status that can be imposed on a person without his or her consent. In principle, the absence of consent should render a marriage null and void, regardless of the factor that precluded consent. Judicial decisions have differed, however, on whether factors such as insanity, duress, or mistake render a marriage void or only voidable at the option of the non-disabled or innocent party.[45]

1) Unsoundness of Mind; Alcohol and Drug Intoxication

Freedom of consent to marry may be negated by unsoundness of mind or the effects of excessive alcohol or drug consumption.[46] The degree of impairment must be such that the afflicted person was incapable of understanding the ceremony of marriage and the duties and responsibilities that flow from marriage.[47] The affliction must have existed at the time

---

42   *Miles v. Chilton (falsely called Miles)* (1849), 163 E.R. 1178; *Andrews v. Ross* (1884), 14 P.D. 15; *Pugh v. Pugh*, [1951] P. 482.

43   *Harthan v. Harthan*, [1948] 2 All E.R. 639 (Eng. C.A.).

44   See Section L(3), below in this chapter.

45   See generally, H.R. Hahlo, *Nullity of Marriage in Canada* (Toronto: Butterworths, 1979) especially at 43–44.

46   *Sullivan v. Sullivan* (1818), 2 Hag. Con. 238, aff'd *(sub nom. Sullivan v. Oldacre)* 3 Phillim. 45; *Meilen v. Anderson* (1977), 6 A.R. 427 (T.D.) (drugs); *Barrett Estate v. Dexter*, [2000] A.J. No. 955 (Q.B.) (senility); *Davison v. Sweeney*, [2005] B.C.J. No. 1196 (S.C.) (drunkenness); *Ward v. Ward* (1985), 66 N.B.R. (2d) 44 (Q.B.) (intoxication); *Feng v. Sung Estate*, [2004] O.J. No. 4496 (C.A.) (mental and physical incapacity).

47   *Brosseau v. Belland*, [1932] 2 W.W.R. 632 (Alta. T.D.); *Barrett Estate v. Dexter*, [2000] A.J. No. 955 (Q.B.); *Davison v. Sweeney*, [2005] B.C.J. No. 1196 (S.C.); *Feng v. Sung*, [2004] O.J. No. 4496 (C.A.); *Reynolds v. Reynolds* (1966), 58 W.W.R. 87 (B.C.S.C.); compare *Milson v. Hough*, [1951] 3 D.L.R. 725 (Ont. C.A.).

when the marriage was solemnized.[48] The burden of proof falls on the person who seeks to impugn the marriage.[49]

2) Duress

Where improper pressure undermines a person's ability to consent, the marriage is voidable at the option of the coerced party. Duress implies the exertion of pressure that induces fear but it does not require the use of physical force. Although fear is a necessary ingredient, it is unnecessary for the person coerced to feel a threat to his or her personal life, limb, or liberty. It is sufficient if fear for some other person is induced.[50] Coercion sufficient to undermine the consent to marry may arise from external sources, as, for example, where a person marries for the purpose of escaping political oppression in his or her homeland.[51] The threat of false criminal charges being laid against a person may constitute duress negating that person's consent to marry.[52] It may be different if the person is in fact guilty of the charges advanced,[53] although one would have thought that the greater the truth, the greater the coercion. Judicial opinion is divided on the question whether duress renders the marriage null and void or voidable only at the option of the party under duress.[54]

---

48   *Durham v. Durham* (1885), 10 P.D. 80.

49   *Chertkow v. Feinstein*, [1930] S.C.R. 335; *Davison v. Sweeney*, [2005] B.C.J. No. 1196 (S.C.); *Deal v. Deal* (1966), 60 D.L.R. (2d) 411 (N.S.S.C.).

50   *Pascuzzi v. Pascuzzi*, [1955] O.W.N. 853 (H.C.J.).

51   *H. v. H.*, [1953] 2 All E.R. 1229.

52   *Buckland v. Buckland*, [1967] 2 All E.R. 330.

53   See *Griffith v. Griffith*, [1944] I.R. 35; see also C. Davies, "Duress and Nullity of Marriage" (1972) 88 Law Q. Rev. 549.

54   See, for example, *H. v. H.*, [1953] 2 All E.R. 1229 (void); *Parojcic v. Parojcic*, [1959] 1 All E.R. 1 at 3 (void); compare *Mahadervan v. Mahadervan*, [1962] 3 All E.R. 1108 (voidable); *A.S. v. A.S.* (1988), 65 O.R. (2d) 720 (U.F.C.); *Kawaluk v. Kawaluk*, [1927] 3 D.L.R. 493 (Sask. K.B.) (voidable); *Thompson v. Thompson* (1971), 19 D.L.R. (3d) 608 (Sask. Q.B.) (voidable). In *Shepherd v. Shepherd* (1917), 192 S.W. 658, Hurt J. observed:

> A marriage procured by fraud or duress is not absolutely void for all purposes, but it can only be declared so at the option of the injured party, since all the authorities are to the effect that it may be ratified or affirmed by the injured party by the exercise of marital rights after constraint has been removed. Furthermore to have such a marriage dissolved or declared null is a privilege personal to the injured party, and cannot be effected by the heirs of such party, or by the party in fault.

3) Fraud

Fraudulent misrepresentations that induce a person to marry will not undermine consent except where the misrepresentations lead to an operative mistake. As a Saskatchewan judge has observed,

> No degree of deception can avail to set aside a contract of marriage duly celebrated by consenting parties with the capacity to enter into the marriage.[55]

4) Mistake

There are only two kinds of mistake that can render a marriage void for lack of consent. They are (i) mistake as to the identity of the person with whom the marriage is entered into; and (ii) mistake as to the nature of the ceremony.[56]

A mistake of identity presupposes that A intended to marry B but in fact married C.[57] Mistakes as to the attributes of a person with whom marriage is contracted, for example, his or her age, health, virginity, or wealth, do not amount to mistaken identity and do not negate the consent to marry. Thus, a woman's wilful concealment of her pregnancy by another man at the time of the marriage has been found insufficient to undermine her husband's consent to the marriage.[58]

Consent will be negated, however, where a person was unaware that the ceremony to which he or she was a party was one of marriage. For example, belief that the ceremony is one of betrothal rather than marriage will negate consent.[59] In determining whether a person was acting under a misapprehension with respect to the nature of the ceremony, credibility

---

55   *Kokkalas v. Kokkalas* (1965), 50 D.L.R. (2d) 193 at 194 (Sask. Q.B.). See also *Swift v. Kelly* (1835), 12 E.R. 648 (H.L.), wherein it was stated:

> No marriage shall be held void merely upon proof that it had been contracted upon false representations, and that but for such contrivances, consent never would have been obtained. Unless the party imposed upon has been deceived as to the person, and thus has given no consent at all, there is no degree of deception which can avail to set aside a contract of marriage knowingly made.

56   See *Iantsis (Papatheodorou) v. Papatheodorou* (1971), 3 R.F.L. 158 (Ont. C.A.).

57   *C. v. C.*, [1942] N.Z.L.R. 356 at 359.

58   *Moss v. Moss*, [1897] P. 263.

59   *Ford v. Stier*, [1896] P. 1; *Valier v. Valier* (1925), 133 L.R. 830; *Kelly v. Kelly* (1932), 49 T.L.R. 99; *Mehta v. Mehta*, [1945] 2 All E.R. 690; *Vamvakidis v. Kirkoff*, [1930] 2 D.L.R. 877 (Ont. C.A.); *Nane (Sykiotis) v. Sykiotis* (1966), 57 D.L.R. (2d) 118 (Ont. S.C.); *Sobush v. Sobush*, [1931] 2 W.W.R. 900 (Sask. Q.B.).

becomes a critical factor. In an Ontario case,[60] the trial judge took account of the following circumstances: the parties had recently arrived from Greece where marriage ceremonies take a different form; the parties never cohabited or consummated the marriage; and the petitioner only spoke Greek whereas the language of the marriage ceremony was English. Custom, language, cohabitation, and consummation are, therefore, important considerations in determining credibility. Where the nature of the ceremony is understood, however, a mistake as to the consequences of the marriage is not sufficient to negate the consent to marry. A mistaken belief that the marriage is polygamous,[61] or that the other spouse would be free to leave her Russian homeland,[62] or that a religious ceremony is required in addition to the civil ceremony,[63] have all been deemed insufficient to render the marriage void.

5) Intention and Motive; Marriages of Convenience

From the legal standpoint, the intention of the parties to contract marriage is all-important; their motive for doing so is irrelevant.[64] In the words of a Manitoba judge,

> In English law, while the purely sham marriage is of no effect, e.g., a masquerade, theatre performance, party entertainment, things of that kind, generally the mental reservations or motive of the parties, or one of them, will not serve to destroy the validity of the ceremony. So, the parties were held to their mutual promises in *Brooks-Bischoffberger v. Brooks-Bischoffberger* (1930), 149 A. 606 at 607, 129 Me. 52, where a marriage performed through the dare of a third party was held to be valid, Dunn J. observing that marriage is "a status wherein public policy rises superior to mere sympathy"; or to win a bet, *Parker v. Parker* (1757), 2 Lee, 382, 161 E.R. 377; to obtain employment open only to married persons, *Crouch v. Wartenberg* (1920), 104 S.E. 117, 11 A.L.R. 212, 91 W. Va. 91 (West Virginia C.A.); to comply with the terms of a settlement conferring gifts subject to the beneficiary's marriage, *Coppo v. Coppo* (1937), 297 N.Y.S. 744, 163 Misc. 249; to avoid a court martial, *Dumoulin v. Druitt* (1860), 13 Ir. C.L. 212 (Q.B.).

---

60   *Nane (Sykiotis) v. Sykiotis*, (1966), 57 D.L.R. (2d) 118 (Ont. S.C.).

61   *Kassim v. Kassim*, [1962] P. 224.

62   *Kenward v. Kenward*, [1951] P. 124 (Eng. C.A.).

63   *Caro v. Cebryk* (1965), 54 W.W.R. 447 (Alta. Q.B.).

64   *K.J.W. v. M.D.W.W.*, [2003] B.C.J. No. 1125 (C.A.).

In all those cases the protests of the petitioner that the marriage was no more than a sham, an event which one or both of the parties regarded as fictitious or simulated, went unheard, English law considering it irrelevant to consider the motives which prompt a party to enter into the union; and see *Nash v. Nash*, [1940] P. 60, [1940] 1 All E.R. 206.[65]

The relevance of motive has most frequently arisen when marriages have been contracted solely for the purpose of immigration. In a leading case in the United States, the judge stated:

> Mutual consent is necessary to every contract; and no matter what forms or ceremonies the party may go through indicating the contrary, they do not contract if they do not in fact assent, which must always be proved .... Marriage is no exception to this rule: a marriage in jest is not a marriage at all .... It is quite true that a marriage without subsequent consummation will be valid; but if the spouses agree to a marriage only for the sake of representing it as such to the outside world and with the understanding that they will put an end to it as soon as it has served its purpose to deceive, they have never really agreed to be married at all. They must assent to enter into the relation as it is ordinarily understood, and it is not ordinarily understood as merely a pretence, or cover, to deceive others.[66]

The preponderance of authority in England and Canada, however, has rejected this opinion and concluded that a marriage is not invalidated by reason only that it was entered into solely as a device to evade immigration regulations.[67] It may be otherwise where the marriage was induced by coercion,[68] or the petitioner was deluded by the respondent into believing that he meant to take her as his wife, whereas he went through the marriage ceremony solely as a means of establishing permanent residence in

---

65   *Fernandez (Alarcio) v. Fernandez* (1983), 34 R.F.L. (2d) 249 at 253–54 (Man. Q.B.), Wilson J.

66   *U.S. v. Rubenstein*, 151 F.2d 915 at 918 (1945), Learned Hand J.

67   *Silver v. Silver*, [1955] 2 All E.R. 614; *Iantsis (Papatheodorou) v. Papatheodorou* (1971), 3 R.F.L. 158 (Ont. C.A.), overruling *Johnson v. Smith* (1968), 70 D.L.R. (2d) 374 (Ont. H.C.J.); *Leonotion v. Leonotion* (1977), 4 R.F.L. (2d) 94 (Ont. C.A.); *Kaur v. Brar*, [2003] O.J. No. 745 (Sup. Ct.). See also *Merchant v. Dossani*, [2007] A.J. No. 815 (Q.B.); *Peters v. Murray*, [2006] O.J. No. 4871 (C.A.); *Said v. Said* (1986), 33 D.L.R. (4th) 382 (B.C.C.A.); compare *Grewal v. Sohal*, [2004] B.C.J. No. 2487 (S.C.).

68   *H. v. H.*, [1953] 2 All E.R. 1229.

Canada,[69] or where the marriage does not comply with the formal require-ments of the place of celebration.[70] Where both parties voluntarily enter into an "immigration" marriage of convenience, the marriage is valid and cannot be annulled by reason of non-consummation but a divorce may be available under paragraph 8(2)(a) of the *Divorce Act*, which empowers a court to grant a divorce on the basis of a breakdown of the marriage when the spouses have lived separate and apart for at least one year.[71] A finding of collusion, however, would bar the granting of a divorce.[72]

J. LEGAL CAPACITY

A valid marriage presupposes that both parties have the capacity to marry and intermarry. Legal incapacity may arise because the parties are of the same sex or by reason of age, prior marriage, or under prohibited degrees of consanguinity or adoption.

1) Same-Sex Marriages

As stated previously, marriage for civil purposes has been legislatively redefined as the lawful union of two persons. Consequently, members of the same sex can now intermarry.[73]

2) Age

Pursuant to principles upheld by the ecclesiastical courts in England more than 150 years ago, any marriage involving a person under the age of seven years is null and void. Marriages of males between the ages of seven and fourteen years and of females between the ages of seven and twelve years are voidable at the option of the underage party but may be ratified

---

69　*Kalyan v. Lal* (1976), 28 R.F.L. 229 (B.C.S.C.); *Torfehnejad v. Salimi*, [2006] O.J. No. 4633 (Sup. Ct.) (fraudulent deception by wife); compare *Ali v. Ahmed*, [2002] O.J. No. 397 (Sup. Ct.).

70　*McKenzie v. Singh* (1972), 29 D.L.R. (3d) 380 (B.C.S.C.).

71　*Ciresi (Ahmad) v. Ahmad* (1983), 31 R.F.L. (2d) 326 (Alta. Q.B.); *Tefera v. Yergu*, [2002] A.J. No. 258 (Q.B.); *Fernandez (Alarcio) v. Fernandez* (1983), 34 R.F.L. (2d) 249 (Man. Q.B.).

72　See *Johnson v. Ahmad* (1981), 22 R.F.L. (2d) 141 (Alta. Q.B.); *Kaur v. Brar*, [2003] O.J. No. 745 (Sup. Ct.); compare *Ciresi (Ahmad) v. Ahmad* (1983), 31 R.F.L. (2d) 326 (Alta. Q.B.).

73　See Section E(1), above in this chapter.

by continued cohabitation after the upper age limit has been reached.[74] Provincial and territorial Marriage Acts in Canada also regulate the age of marriage by licensing and other requirements, including parental consent for children under the age of majority, which is eighteen or nineteen years of age depending on which province or territory the child lives in.

3) Prior Marriage

Marriage presupposes exclusivity between the spouses.[75] Accordingly, a valid and subsisting marriage bars any subsequent marriage by either spouse. Any purported second marriage is null and void, regardless of whether it will ground a charge of bigamy or polygamy under the Canadian *Criminal Code*.[76] An order may be made pursuant to section 9 of the Ontario *Marriage Act*,[77] which presumes the death of a missing spouse and permits the applicant to remarry under the authority of a licence or the publication of banns. An order of presumed death has limited effect; it does not validate the remarriage in the event that the missing spouse reappears.[78] The more appropriate course of action, therefore, for a spouse whose consort has disappeared without trace is the institution of divorce proceedings to terminate his or her marital status. Any subsequent remarriage with a third party will then be valid. But divorcees must not jump the gun. Pursuant to section 12 of the *Divorce Act*,[79] a divorce judgment in Canada does not usually become effective until the thirty-first day after the day on which the judgment granting the divorce was rendered. The Ontario Superior Court of Justice has jurisdiction to declare a foreign marriage a nullity where the defendant was already party to a subsisting marriage that had not been terminated at the time of his second marriage.[80]

---

74 *R. v. Bell* (1857), 15 U.C.Q.B. 287.

75 *Hyde v. Hyde and Woodmansee* (1866), L.R. 1 P. & D. 130.

76 *Stevenson v. Stevenson*, [1997] B.C.J. No. 1154 (S.C.); *Meunier v. Meunier*, [1997] B.C.J. No. 1156 (S.C.); *Bolentiru v. Radulescu*, [2004] O.J. No. 3325 (Sup. Ct.); *Peters v. Murray*, [2006] O.J. No. 4871 (C.A.).

77 R.S.O. 1990, c. M.3.

78 *McCullough v. Ralph*, [1942] 2 D.L.R. 389 (Ont. S.C.); *Tomberg v. Tomberg (Gilbert)*, [1942] 2 W.W.R. 319 (Alta. C.A.); see also *Tomberg (Gilbert), Re*, [1942] 3 W.W.R. 542 (Alta. C.A.).

79 R.S.C. 1985 (2d Supp.), c. 3.

80 *Bolentiru v. Radulescu*, [2004] O.J. No. 3325 (Sup. Ct.).

4) Prohibited Degrees

Marriages between certain persons who are closely related are prohibited by federal legislation. The *Marriage (Prohibited Degrees) Act,*[81] as amended, currently provides a codification and amendment of the former law governing the prohibited degrees of consanguinity, affinity, and adoption. Consanguinity involves blood relationships whereas affinity involves relationships arising from marriage. Subsection 3(1) of the *Marriage (Prohibited Degrees) Act* stipulates that "a marriage between persons related by consanguinity, affinity or adoption is not invalid by reason only of their relationship" except where it contravenes the express prohibitions set out under subsection 2(2) of the Act.[82] Subsection 3(2) provides that "a marriage between persons who are related in the manner described in subsection 2(2) is void." Subsection 2(2) of the *Marriage (Prohibited Degrees) Act* provides as follows:

> *Prohibition*
> 2(2) No person shall marry another person if they are related lineally, or as brother or sister or half-brother or half-sister, including by adoption.[83]

Former prohibited degrees based on affinity have been abolished. It is now possible, for example, for a man to marry his divorced wife's sister or niece or for a woman to marry her divorced husband's brother or nephew. Prior to the *Marriage (Prohibited Degrees) Act*, there was some doubt on this issue.

K. NON-CONSUMMATION OF MARRIAGE

Impotence, which is the inability to consummate the marriage, renders a marriage voidable. Canadian law draws a distinction between the inability to consummate a marriage and wilful refusal to do so. It is impotence, not wilful refusal, that constitutes a ground for annulment of marriage in

---

81   S.C. 1990, c. 46, as amended by S.C. 2005, c. 33.
82   See *P.A. v. C.G.*, [2002] J.Q. no 4585 (C.A.) (foreign marriage between husband and divorced wife's sister subsequently validated by enactment of the *Marriage (Prohibited Degrees) Act*, S.C. 1990, c. 46).
83   For the amendments accommodating same-sex marriages, see *Civil Marriage Act*, S.C. 2005, c. 33, ss. 13 & 14.

Canada.[84] A continuing and persistent refusal to consummate the marriage may, nevertheless, be indicative of impotence.[85]

Either or both parties to a marriage that has not been consummated may petition the courts for annulment of the marriage. Even the impotent spouse can seek the annulment provided that he or she did not knowingly deceive the other spouse.[86]

Impotence is not to be confused with the inability to have children. Impotence signifies an incapacity in one or both spouses to engage in normal sexual intercourse with each other.[87] As was stated in an old English case,

> The only question is whether the [spouse] is or is not capable of sexual intercourse, or, if at present incapable, whether that incapacity can be removed. ... If there be a reasonable probability that the lady can be made capable of a *vera copula* — of the natural sort of *coitus*, though without power of conception — I cannot pronounce this marriage void. If, on the contrary, she is not and cannot be made capable of more than incipient, imperfect, and unnatural *coitus*, I would pronounce the marriage void.[88]

With respect to same-sex married couples, section 4 of the *Civil Marriage Act*[89] provides that "for greater certainty, a marriage is not void or voidable by reason only that the spouses are of the same sex."

The use of contraceptives or the practice of *coitus interruptus* does not preclude consummation of the marriage.[90] Conversely, the impregnation of the wife by artificial insemination does not constitute consummation of the marriage even if the husband's semen is used.[91]

---

84 *Heil v. Heil*, [1942] S.C.R. 160; *K.H.L. v. G.Q.L.*, [2003] B.C.J. No. 1249 (C.A.); *Davison v. Sweeney*, [2005] B.C.J. No. 1196 (S.C.).

85 *K.H.L. v. G.Q.L.*, [2003] B.C.J. No. 1249 (C.A.); *H.L.C. v. M.A.L.*, [2003] B.C.J. No. 2224 (S.C.); *LeBlanc v. LeBlanc*, [1955] 1 D.L.R. 676 (N.S.S.C.).

86 *Harthan v. Harthan*, [1948] 2 All E.R. 639 (Eng. C.A.); *Sallam v. Sallam*, [1988] N.J. No. 386 (S.C.).

87 *Baxter v. Baxter*, [1948] A.C. 274 (H.L.); *K.H.L. v. G.Q.L.*, [2003] B.C.J. No. 1249 (C.A.).

88 *D. v. A.* (1845), 1 Robb Ecc. 279 at 296 and 299 (Dr. Lushington). See *Civil Marriage Act*, Canada (Bill C-38), 2005, c. 33, s. 4, which provides that "For greater certainty, a marriage is not void or voidable by reason only that the spouses are of the same sex."

89 S.C. 2005, c. 33.

90 *Baxter v. Baxter*, [1948] A.C. 274 (H.L.); *Wilkinson v. Wilkinson*, [1950] 3 D.L.R. 236 (B.C.C.A.) (but see dissenting judgment of O'Halloran J.A.).

91 *R.E.L. v. E.L.*, [1949] P. 211 (Eng. H. Ct.).

The inability to consummate the marriage may arise from a physical incapacity or from an invincible repugnance or aversion to sexual intercourse.[92] The sexual incapacity may be general in character or it may exist only as between the spouses themselves.[93]

A marriage is consummated on the first occasion when the spouses engage in postmarital sexual intercourse. Once consummated, always consummated, is the criterion.[94] Premarital intercourse cannot constitute consummation of a subsequent marriage between the parties, although it may be presumptive evidence of the capacity of the spouses to engage in sexual intercourse.[95]

The sexual incapacity must exist at the time of the marriage and throughout the marriage,[96] although courts have frequently recognized psychological impotence manifested after the marriage has been solemnized.[97] It must also be incurable but will be regarded as incurable when the condition can only be remedied by an operation attended by danger or when the spouse under the disability persistently refuses to undergo treatment that carries no significant risk.[98]

L. BARS TO ANNULMENT

There are three potential bars to a person obtaining a decree of nullity or other relief from a court of competent jurisdiction. They are (i) collusion; (ii) estoppel; and (iii) insincerity.

---

92 *G. v. G.*, [1924] A.C. 349 (H.L.); *Heil v. Heil*, [1942] S.C.R. 160; *Juretic v. Ruiz* (1999), 49 R.F.L. (4th) 299 (B.C.C.A.); *Sangha v. Aujla*, [2002] B.C.J. No. 2388 (S.C.); *K.H.L. v. G.Q.L.*, [2003] B.C.J. No. 1249 (C.A.); *H.L.C. v. M.A.L.*, [2003] B.C.J. No. 2224 (S.C.); *Grewal v. Sohal*, [2004] B.C.J. No. 4802 (S.C.).

93 *C. v. C.*, [1921] P. 399; *Sallam v. Sallam*, [1988] N.J. No. 386 (S.C.); *H.L.C. v. M.A.L.*, [2003] B.C.J. No. 2224 (S.C.); *Greenlees v. Greenlees*, [1959] O.R. 419 (H.C.); *Hardick v. Fox* (1970), 3 R.F.L. 153 (Ont. H.C.J.).

94 *Goodman v. Goodman* (1973), 9 R.F.L. 261 (Ont. Prov. Ct.).

95 *Ibid.*

96 *Greenstreet v. Cumyns* (1812), 2 Hag. Con. 332 (postmarital defect); *S. v. S.*, [1956] P. 1 (cure effected after institution of nullity proceedings); *K.H.L. v. G.Q.L.*, [2003] B.C.J. No. 1249 (C.A.); *C. v. C.*, [1949] 1 W.W.R. 911 (Man. Q.B.).

97 *H.L.C. v. M.A.L.*, [2003] B.C.J. No. 2224 (S.C.); see also cases cited in note 90 above.

98 *S. v. S.*, [1956] P. 1; *C. v. C.*, [1949] 1 W.W.R. 911 (Man. Q.B.); *Deo v. Kumar*, [1993] B.C.J. No. 2051 (S.C.); *H.L.C. v. M.A.L.*, [2003] B.C.J. No. 2224 (S.C.); *Ryan v. Ryan* (1985), 74 N.S.R. (2d) 49 (S.C.).

1) Collusion

Collusion constitutes a bar to relief in any matrimonial proceeding, including nullity proceedings.[99] Collusion signifies an agreement or conspiracy between the spouses to subvert the administration of justice, as, for example, by fabricating or suppressing evidence.

2) Estoppel

A spouse who has obtained a decree of nullity from a foreign court that was incompetent to assume jurisdiction, is precluded from attacking the validity of the foreign decree for the purpose of securing a pecuniary advantage against his or her spouse or the estate of that spouse.[100] Assume, for example, that a wife obtained a decree of nullity of marriage from a foreign court that was not entitled to deal with the issue. The foreign decree would not be recognized as valid by Canadian courts; the marriage would still be valid in Canada. But, if the husband were to die, his wife would be estopped from asserting succession rights in his estate under a provincial or territorial statute in Canada.

3) Insincerity

The doctrine of "insincerity" may constitute a bar to the judicial annulment of a voidable marriage. A spouse may be precluded from impugning a voidable marriage if it has been previously approbated by the conduct of the parties. In an old English case, the doctrine of insincerity was explained in the following terms:

> I think I can perceive that the real basis of reasoning which underlines that phraseology is this, and nothing more than this, that there may be conduct on the part of the person seeking this remedy, which ought to estop that person from having it; as, for instance, any act from which the inference ought to be drawn that during the antecedent time the party has, with a knowledge of the facts and of the law, approbated the marriage which he or she seeks to get rid of, or has taken advantages and derived benefits from the matrimonial relation which it would be unfair and inequitable to permit him or her, after having received them, to treat as if no such relation had ever existed. Well now, that explanation can be referred to known principles of equitable, and, I may say,

---

99 *Synge v. Synge*, [1900] P. 180; *Menzies v. Farnon* (1909), 18 O.L.R. 174 (C.A.).
100 *Downton v. Royal Trust Co.* (1973), 15 R.F.L. 43 (S.C.C.).

general jurisprudence. The circumstances which may justify it are various, and in cases of this kind many sorts of conduct might exist, taking pecuniary benefits, for example, living for a long time together in the same house, or family with the status and character of husband and wife, after knowledge of everything which it is material to know. I do not at all mean to say that there may not be other circumstances which would produce the same effect.[101]

An indirect or improper motive is not an adequate test of insincerity. Approbation of the marriage presupposes a knowledge of the facts that render the marriage defective and an awareness of the availability of a legal remedy.[102] There may be cases in which approbation may be found even in the absence of actual knowledge, if there has been the means of procuring knowledge.[103] Delay in the institution of nullity proceedings is not, of itself, a bar to relief,[104] but a culpable delay, with knowledge of the facts and law, is a significant factor in considering the insincerity of the petitioner.[105] The fact that each party continues to share, while under the same matrimonial roof, the normal domestic services derivable from a joint establishment, does not inevitably constitute the bar of insincerity,[106] but if such conduct is accompanied by a premarital agreement whereby the parties undertake not to engage in sexual intercourse after their marriage, the court may properly refuse to annul the marriage on the ground of non-consummation by reason of the petitioner's insincerity.[107] The annulment of a voidable marriage on the ground of non-consummation may also be barred by the petitioner's knowledge of his own or his spouse's impotence at the time of the marriage.[108]

Judicial opinion is divided on the question whether insincerity constitutes an absolute or only a discretionary bar to relief.[109] In an English

---

101 *G. v. M.* (1985), 10 App. Cas. 171 (H.L.), Earl of Selbourne (L.C.), quoted in *J. v. J.*, [1940] O.R. 284 (H.C.), aff'd [1940] 4 D.L.R. 807 (Ont. C.A.); see also *Aisaican v. Khanapace* (1996), 24 R.F.L. (4th) 143 (Sask. Q.B.).

102 *Hill v. Hill*, [1959] 3 All E.R. 754; *B. v. B.*, [1935] S.C.R. 231.

103 *Pettit v. Pettit*, [1962] 3 All E.R. 37 (Eng. C.A.).

104 *J. v. J.*, [1940] O.R. 284 (H.C.), aff'd [1940] 4 D.L.R. 807 (Ont. C.A.).

105 *W. v. W.*, [1952] 1 All E.R. 858 (Eng. C.A.); *B. v. B.*, [1935] S.C.R. 231.

106 *Scott v. Scott*, [1959] 1 All E.R. 531, Sachs J.

107 *Norman v. Norman* (1979), 9 R.F.L. (2d) 345 (Ont. U.F.C.); *Aisaican v. Khanapace* (1996), 24 R.F.L. (4th) 143 (Sask. Q.B.); see also *Scott v. Scott*, [1959] 1 All E.R. 531; compare *Morgan v. Morgan*, [1959] 1 All E.R. 539.

108 *Harthan v. Harthan*, [1948] 2 All E.R. 639 (Eng. C.A.).

109 See *Clifford v. Clifford*, [1948] 1 All E.R. 394 (Eng. C.A.); *R.E.L. v. E.L.*, [1949] P. 211 (Eng. H. Ct.); *Scott v. Scott*, [1959] 1 All E.R. 531; *G. v. G.*, [1960] 3 All E.R. 56.

case wherein the wife was granted an annulment of the marriage by reason of her husband's impotence, notwithstanding that she had given birth to a child after her artificial insemination with the husband's semen, the trial judge stated:

> If I am right the question of discretion does not arise, and it is irrelevant to weigh the public and private advantages of granting or refusing a decree. If I am wrong, I should, in the exercise of my discretion, grant a decree [because] I see no hope of happiness by keeping these two people married .... If I grant a decree it seems quite possible that the wife, who seems affectionate and likely to be a good wife, may marry again, and even the husband might marry again and conquer his inhibitions and enjoy normal married happiness. The future holds better augury for the child, I think, if I grant the decree than if he is brought up by an embittered mother who may be tied for life to a marriage that has never been a real marriage and which, only through the unnatural aid of science, has produced the fruit of a real marriage.[110]

The proper approach would seem to be for the court to initially determine whether the conduct of the parties constitutes approbation of the marriage and, if so, to then determine whether it is in the public interest and that of the parties and their children, if any, to grant or refuse a decree of nullity. In considering the public interest, the court should weigh the sanctity of marriage against the legal futility of preserving a marriage that has irretrievably broken down.

The doctrine of insincerity is confined to voidable marriages and has no application to void marriages at least where the invalidity arises because of lack of capacity to marry.[111]

M. RELIGIOUS ANNULMENTS AND DIVORCE

Some religious faiths, such as the Roman Catholic, Jewish, and Muslim faiths, provide for religious annulment or divorce. A religious annulment or divorce is valid only for the purpose of religious practices. It does not terminate a marriage according to Canadian law. If spouses wish to terminate their marriage in law, they must petition the state courts for annulment or divorce. It is insufficient to obtain a religious annulment or divorce.

---

110   *R.E.L. v. E.L.*, [1949] P. 211 (Eng. H. Ct.).
111   *Hayward v. Hayward*, [1961] 1 All E.R. 236; *Saari v. Nykanen*, [1944] O.R. 582; *Dejardin v. Dejardin*, [1932] 2 W.W.R. 237 (Man. Q.B.).

CHAPTER 3

COHABITATIONAL RELATIONSHIPS[1]

A. INTRODUCTION

Cohabitational relationships involve two people who share their lives together but are not married to each other. Cohabitational relation-

---

1   For excellent sources dealing with the legal implications of unmarried cohabitation in Canada, see Alberta Law Reform Institute, *Towards Reform of the Law Relating to Cohabitation Outside Marriage*, Report No. 53 (Edmonton: The Institute, 1989); Ontario Law Reform Commission, *Report on The Rights and Responsibilities of Cohabitants under the* Family Law Act, (Toronto: The Commission, 1993); Winifred H. Holland & Barbro E. Stalbecker-Pountney, *Cohabitation: The Law in Canada* (Toronto: Carswell, 1990); Winifred H. Holland, "Marriage and Cohabitation: Has the Time Come to Bridge the Gap" in The Law Society of Upper Canada, *Special Lectures of the Law Society of Upper Canada, Family Law: Roles, Fairness and Equality* (Scarborough, ON: Carswell, 1994) at 369; Nicholas Bala, "Controversy Over Couples in Canada: The Evolution of Marriages and Other Adult Interdependent Relationships," online: http://qsilver.queensu.ca/law/papers/evolutionapril. html; Nicholas Bala, "Alternatives For Extending Spousal Status in Canada," online: www.familylawcentre.com/ccbalaspousal.html; Winnifred H. Holland, "Intimate Relationships in the New Millennium," online: www.familylawcentre. com/ccholland.html. For a useful summary of other legal systems, see William N. Eskridge, Jr., "Comparative Law and the Same-Sex Marriage Debate: A Step-by-Step Approach to State Recognition" (2000) 31 McGeorge L. Rev. 641. As to the possibility of extending legal rights and obligations to a broader range of personal relationships, see Law Commission of Canada, Discussion Paper, "Recognizing and Supporting Close Personal Relationships Between Adults," online: www.lcc.gc.ca.

ships may involve members of the opposite sex or members of the same sex. Unmarried heterosexual cohabitation is sometimes referred to as a common-law relationship. Unmarried cohabitants go under a variety of names, including common-law spouse, co-vivant, significant other, mate, life partner, cohabitee, and cohabitant.

Although the Canadian census includes no data on same-sex relationships, approximately 14 percent of Canadian families involve unmarried cohabitants of the opposite sex. On 14 October 1997, Statistics Canada released its data from the 1996 Census on the subject of marital status, common-law unions, and families. Included in that report is the following:

Families: growth strongest among common-law couple families

Of all family structures, growth was strongest among common-law couple families. In 1996, 920,635 such families were counted, up 28% from 1991. (The Census defines common-law partners as two persons of opposite sex who are not legally married to each other, but live together as husband and wife in the same dwelling).

In 1996, one couple in seven in Canada was living common law, compared to about one in nine in 1991. The marital status of individuals in common-law unions remained almost the same between 1991 and 1996: nearly two-thirds of them were single, while over a quarter were divorced.

Almost half of the common-law couple families included children, whether born to the current union or brought to the family from previous unions.

Common-law families were by far most frequent in Quebec, which had 400,265, or 43% of all such families in Canada. One couple in four (24%) in Quebec lived common law.

Between 1991 and 1996, the number of common-law families grew fastest in New Brunswick and the Northwest Territories. Increases were also above the national average of 28% in Newfoundland, Prince Edward Island and Quebec, and in the Yukon.

And further:

Substantially more children in common-law couple families

In 1996, 735,565 children were living in common-law couple families, a substantial 52% increase from 1991.

Nationally, 14% of all children under the age of six were living in common-law couple families.

In Quebec, by comparison, 31% of all children in this age group were in common-law couple families.

Every province and territory recorded substantial increases among children living with common-law couples. In Quebec, 343,050 children lived in families of common-law couples in 1996, up 69% from 1991, the biggest increase among the provinces.

In Ontario, there were 164,550 children living in common-law couple families, up 45% from five years earlier.

What the above data fail to reveal is that "common-law" relationships are less enduring than marital relationships and the risk of children under the age of ten encountering family breakdown is much greater when they are children of unmarried cohabitants than when they are children of married couples. For example, based on a longitudinal study of approximately 23,000 children in Canada, a report entitled *Growing Up With Mom and Dad: The Intricate Family Life of Canadian Children*[2] concludes that only 13.6 percent of the children under ten experienced family breakdown when they were born after their parents' marriage whereas more than 63 percent of the children whose parents cohabited but never married encountered family breakdown before the age of ten.

There are various reasons why some members of the opposite sex enter into unmarried cohabitational relationships instead of marriage. They include the following:

(i)   There may be a legal impediment to marriage — as, for example, where one of the parties has been previously married but is not divorced.

(ii)   There may be some religious obstacle to marriage.

(iii)   Marriage may be perceived by one or both of the parties as a patriarchal straitjacket that involves traditional homemaking and breadwinning roles that fail to recognize equality between the sexes.

(iv)   Marriage imposes certain legal rights and obligations that one or both parties might wish to avoid. They may have been involved in a previous marriage breakdown that carries emotional and economic scars and may assume that history cannot repeat itself if they avoid the marriage "trap." Any such assumption is misplaced, however, because

---

2   Statistics Canada, by Nicole Marcil-Gratton (Ottawa: Ministry of Industry, 1998) Catalogue No. 89-566-XIE.

the emotional trauma of the breakdown of a relationship is not conditioned on whether the parties are married. Furthermore, unmarried cohabitation may carry significant economic consequences that are legally enforceable on the breakdown of the relationship.

(v)   Changing social mores and the weakening of religious influences have largely removed the stigma that formerly attached to unmarried cohabitants of the opposite sex.

(vi)   Many young couples enter into unmarried cohabitation as a "trial marriage" that can be informally terminated or legally formalized at some time in the future. Conversion to marital status is often triggered by the anticipated birth of a child.

(vii) Unmarried cohabitation may enable one or both of the parties to preserve their entitlement to certain benefits, such as support payments or pension payments, which would be lost in the event of remarriage.

(viii) Many couples who begin sleeping over at each other's house slip into a cohabitational relationship as a matter of convenience rather than in consequence of carefully weighing the pros and cons of marital and unmarried cohabitation.

B. LEGAL CONSEQUENCES OF UNMARRIED COHABITATION AS COMPARED TO MARRIAGE

In previous generations, unmarried cohabitants were disentitled to the protection of the law. By the 1980s, social attitudes and the law had undergone radical changes, at least with respect to unmarried cohabitants of the opposite sex. The social stigma that formerly attached to unmarried heterosexual cohabitation has now largely disappeared. The law has, nevertheless, been cautious in its response to unmarried cohabitation. The law does not assimilate the consequences of marriage and unmarried cohabitation, although legal recognition has been extended to unmarried cohabitation in various contexts in light of the judgments of the Supreme Court of Canada in *Miron v. Trudel*[3] and *M. v. H.*[4] In consequence of *M.*

---

3   [1995] 2 S.C.R. 18 (spouse judicially redefined pursuant to s. 15 of the *Canadian Charter of Rights and Freedoms* to include unmarried heterosexual cohabitants of three years' standing under automobile insurance policy).

4   [1999] 2 S.C.R. 3 (assimilation of statutory support rights of cohabitants of the same sex with those of cohabitants of opposite sex); and see Section D, below in this chapter.

v. H., federal, provincial, and territorial statutes have established diverse rights and obligations as between unmarried cohabitants of the opposite sex and unmarried cohabitants of the same sex. In July 2000, the federal government passed omnibus legislation, entitled the *Modernization of Obligations and Benefits Act,* which amended sixty statutes for the purpose of assimilating the rights and obligations of same-sex couples and opposite sex couples. In 1999, Ontario enacted the *Amendments Because of the Supreme Court of Canada Decision in* M. v. H. *Act,*[5] which amended the *Family Law Act* so that its support provisions apply to same-sex couples as well as opposite-sex couples. The provisions of the *Family Law Act* with respect to cohabitation agreements, separation agreements, and claims for damages by family dependents were also amended to include same-sex cohabitants. Various other Ontario statutes were also extended to same-sex couples, namely the *Change of Name Act,*[6] the *Child and Family Services Act,*[7] the *Children's Law Reform Act,*[8] the *Courts of Justice Act,*[9] the *Family Responsibility and Support Orders Arrears Enforcement Act, 1996,*[10] the *Pension Benefits Act,*[11] and the *Succession Law Reform Act.*[12] It is noteworthy, however, that spousal property rights and intestate succession rights in Ontario have not been extended to either same-sex or opposite-sex unmarried cohabitants.[13] Other provinces and territories have introduced amendments to their legislation so as to bring it in line with the ruling of the Supreme Court of Canada in *M. v. H.*[14]

Provincial and territorial legislation confers the same legal status on children whether they are born to married or unmarried parents. Discrimination against children born out of wedlock contravenes the equal-

---

5   S.O. 1999, c. 6.

6   R.S.O. 1990, c. C.7.

7   R.S.O. 1990, c. C.11.

8   R.S.O. 1990, c. C.12.

9   S.O. 1994, c. 12.

10 S.O. 1996, c. 31.

11 R.S.O. 1990, c. P.8.

12 R.S.O. 1990, c. S.26.

13 See Lorne H. Wolfson & Carol A. Dalgado, "Some Thoughts on Family and Estates Matters After *M. v. H.* (Part I)" (February 2000) 15:2 Money & Family Law at 9–12; Lorne H. Wolfson & Carol A. Dalgado, "Some Thoughts on Family and Estates Matters After *M. v. H.* (Part II)"; "Testate and Intestate Succession and Dependants Relief Post *M. v. H.*" (March 2000) 15:3 Money & Family Law at 17–19.

14 See, for example, *Adult Interdependent Relationships Act,* S.A. 2002, c. A-4.5; *Common Law Partners' Property and Related Amendments Act,* S.M. 2002, c. 48; *Law Reform (2000) Act,* S.N.S. 2000, c. 9; *An Act instituting civil unions and establishing new rules of filiation,* Quebec, Bill 84, passed June 2002.

ity guarantee established by section 15 of the *Canadian Charter of Rights and Freedoms*. Some provincial adoption statutes expressly allow individuals, including gay men and lesbians, to adopt children.

The *Canadian Charter of Rights and Freedoms* and federal and provincial Human Rights Codes have generated claims by unmarried cohabitants of the same sex to benefits that were hitherto confined to married couples and to unmarried couples of the opposite sex. These include pension benefits; welfare assistance; workers' compensation; life, health, and disability insurance; and tax advantages. These benefits may be regulated by either federal, provincial, or territorial legislation but the restrictive application of such legislation to married persons or unmarried heterosexual cohabitants is being successfully challenged for the most part. Former "common-law spouses," like divorced spouses, are not eligible to receive a survivor's pension under the Canada Pension Plan on the death of their former partner who contributed to the plan. No distinction is drawn on the basis of marital status between these two comparator groups. Accordingly, the definition of "spouse" under section 2(1) of the Canada Pension Plan does not contravene equality rights under section 15(1) of the *Canadian Charter of Rights and Freedoms*.

C. COHABITATION AGREEMENTS

In the distant past, courts refused to recognize or enforce agreements entered into by unmarried cohabitants. Such agreements were regarded as illegal and contrary to public policy on the basis of immorality. In view of fundamental changes in social attitudes in the latter part of the twentieth century, courts have abandoned their original stance by upholding the validity and enforceability of contracts entered into by unmarried cohabitants. In *Chrispen v. Topham*,[15] for example, where unmarried heterosexual cohabitants entered into a written agreement respecting the sharing of household expenses and a collateral oral agreement respecting the performance of domestic chores, both agreements were found to be in default and were held enforceable by way of damages or monetary compensation. Recognition has also been granted to contractual arrangements entered into by unmarried cohabitants of the same sex. In *Anderson v. Luoma*,[16] a British Columbia court acknowledged the right

---

15   (1986), 3 R.F.L. (3d) 149 (Sask. Q.B.), aff'd (1987), 9 R.F.L. (3d) 131 (Sask. C.A.).
16   (1986), 50 R.F.L. (2d) 127 (B.C.S.C.).

of a lesbian to pursue contractual and property claims against her mate. The contractual claim was dismissed, however, on the ground that the evidence did not support a finding that a contract had been entered into. The alternative claim to share in property on the basis of the doctrine of unjust enrichment was upheld. Accordingly, the claimant was entitled to a 20 percent interest in certain property that had been acquired by her mate during their relationship. These judicial developments occurred in the absence of any express statutory authority.

Although provincial and territorial legislation in Canada throughout the twentieth century remained silent on the question of whether same-sex cohabitants could enter into legally binding contracts, several provinces and one territory enacted legislation that expressly permitted unmarried cohabitants of the opposite sex to enter into "cohabitation agreements." The relevant statutory provisions in New Brunswick, Newfoundland, Ontario, Prince Edward Island, and the Yukon are broad in scope. In general, they empower unmarried cohabitants of the opposite sex to enter into "cohabitation agreements" for the purpose of regulating ownership in or the division of property, spousal and child support rights and obligations, and other matters in the settlement of their affairs. Except in British Columbia and the Yukon, matters relating to custody of and access to children fall outside the scope of cohabitation agreements, although such agreements may regulate the religious or secular education of children. In Ontario, a cohabitation agreement may be entered into before the commencement of cohabitation or during cohabitation. In New Brunswick, Newfoundland, Prince Edward Island, and the Yukon, the parties must be cohabiting at the time when they enter into a cohabitation agreement. However, these jurisdictions, together with Ontario, also entitle former unmarried cohabitants to enter into "separation agreements" after cohabitation has ceased. Separation agreements may regulate custody of and access to children in addition to the same matters that can be regulated by cohabitation agreements. The provisions of a cohabitation agreement may anticipate a future separation. Indeed, a cohabitation agreement may regulate the rights and obligations of the parties during cohabitation, on separation, or on the death of either party. It may be wise, however, for cohabitants to substitute a new separation agreement for the old cohabitation agreement in the event of a termination of their relationship. This is especially important if children are involved and arrangements for their support and for custody and access must be determined.

All domestic contracts that are governed by provincial or territorial statutes must be in writing, signed by the parties, and witnessed.[17] Independent legal representation or advice is not legally required, although a court is more likely to set aside a domestic contract on the ground of duress, undue influence, or unconscionability if a party was not legally represented. Relevant provincial or territorial legislation empowers a court to set aside any provisions of a domestic contract that are contrary to the best interests of children. In addition, the courts are statutorily empowered to override the support provisions of a cohabitation agreement or any other domestic contract in specified circumstances.[18]

Although the aforementioned provincial and territorial legislation specifically extended a qualified contractual autonomy only to unmarried cohabitants of the opposite sex, the decision of the Supreme Court of Canada in *M. v. H.*, which assimilates the rights of unmarried cohabitants of the same sex with those of unmarried cohabitants of the opposite sex pursuant to section 15 of the *Canadian Charter of Rights and Freedoms*, has caused provincial and territorial legislatures to revisit and amend current provincial and territorial statutes so as to assimilate the legal rights and obligations of unmarried cohabitants of either sex.

In *Doe v. Alberta*,[19] the Alberta Court of Appeal held that cohabiting partners cannot contractually oust the jurisdiction of the court to grant future orders determining their parental rights and obligations under the *Family Law Act*[20] with respect to a child born to the mother as a result of her artificial insemination by an unknown sperm donor. In upholding the trial judgment, the Alberta Court of Appeal observed that an express declaration in a written agreement that the mother's male cohabitant does not intend to assume a parental role or the legal obligations of a parent will not preclude a finding that the cohabitant's subsequent conduct has demonstrated a settled intention to treat the child as his own within the meaning of section 48(2) of the *Family Law Act*, thus triggering a child support obligation. The Alberta Court of Appeal further concluded that sections 53, 85, and 86 of the *Family Law Act*, which provide qualified recognition of parental agreements subject to the court's supervisory

---

17   Compare *Chrispen v. Topham*, (1986), 3 R.F.L. (3d) 149 (Sask. Q.B.), aff'd (1987), 3 R.F.L. (3d) 131 (Sask. C.A.).

18   *Family Services Act*, S.N.B. 1980, c. F-2.2, s. 115(5); *Family Law Act*, R.S.N. 1990, c. F-2, s. 39(5); *Family Law Act*, R.S.O. 1990, c. F.3, s. 33(4); *Family Law Act*, S.P.E.I. 1995, c. 12, s. 18(4); *Family Property and Support Act*, R.S.Y. 1986, c. 63, s. 34(4).

19   2007 ABCA 50, [2007] A.J. No. 138.

20   S.A. 2003, c. F-4.5.

jurisdiction, do not contravene section 7 of the *Charter of Rights and Freedoms*.

D. SUPPORT RIGHTS AND OBLIGATIONS BETWEEN UNMARRIED COHABITANTS

Provincial and territorial statutes currently confer mutual support rights and obligations on unmarried cohabitants, whether of the opposite sex or the same sex, provided that the prescribed statutory conditions are satisfied.

Some statutes require that the parties cohabit or live together in a conjugal relationship for a minimum period, which usually ranges from one year to three years according to the particular province where the parties reside. Several provinces also impose support obligations upon unmarried cohabitants who have lived in a relationship of some permanence and are the natural or adoptive parents of a child. In the context of provincial and territorial statutory support rights and obligations, cohabitation signifies a marriage-like relationship. Not all arrangements whereby a man and a woman live together and engage in sexual activity will suffice to trigger statutory support rights and obligations.[21] As was observed by Morrison J.A. of the Nova Scotia Court of Appeal,

> I think it would be fair to say that to establish a common-law relationship there must be some sort of stable relationship which involves not only sexual activity but a commitment between the parties. It would normally necessitate living under the same roof with shared household duties and responsibilities as well as financial support.[22]

More specific judicial guidance as to what constitutes cohabitation or a conjugal or marriage-like relationship is found in a judgment of the Ontario District Court,[23] wherein Kurisko D.C.J. identified the following issues as relevant:

---

21 See *Jansen v. Montgomery* (1982), 30 R.F.L. (2d) 332 (N.S. Co. Ct.).
22 *Soper v. Soper* (1985), 67 N.S.R. (2d) 49 at 53 (C.A.).
23 *Molodowich v. Penttinen* (1980), 17 R.F.L. (2d) 376 at 381–82 (Ont. Dist. Ct.). See also *Gostlin v. Kergin* (1986), 3 B.C.L.R. (2d) 264 at 267–68 (C.A.); *Austin v. Goerz*, 2007 BCCA 586, [2007] B.C.J. No. 2546; *MacMillan-Dekker v. Dekker*, [2000] O.J. No. 2957 (Sup. Ct.). For endorsement of *Molodowich v. Penttinen* by the Supreme Court of Canada, see *M. v. H.*, [1999] 2 S.C.R. 3 at paras. 56–60. And see *Milot v. Canada*, [1995] T.C.J. No. 412; *Lavoie v. Canada*, [1999] T.C.J. No. 688; *Hendricken v. Canada*,

1. Shelter:
    (a) Did the parties live under the same roof?
    (b) What were the sleeping arrangements?
    (c) Did anyone else occupy or share the available accommodation?

2. Sexual and Personal Behaviour:
    (a) Did the parties have sexual relations? If not, why not?
    (b) Did they maintain an attitude of fidelity to each other?
    (c) What were their feelings toward each other?
    (d) Did they communicate on a personal level?
    (e) Did they eat their meals together?
    (f) What, if anything, did they do to assist each other with problems or during illness?
    (g) Did they buy gifts for each other on special occasions?

3. Services:
    What was the conduct and habit of the parties in relation to:
    (a) preparation of meals;
    (b) washing and mending clothes;
    (c) shopping;
    (d) household maintenance; and
    (e) any other domestic services?

4. Social:
    (a) Did they participate together or separately in neighbourhood and community activities?
    (b) What was the relationship and conduct of each of them toward members of their respective families and how did such families behave towards the parties?

5. Societal:
    What was the attitude and conduct of the community toward each of them and as a couple?

[2008] T.C.J. No. 30; *Sprackin v.* Kichton, [2000] A.J. No. 1329 (Q.B.); *Medora v. Kohn,* [2003] A.J. No. 1027 (Q.B.); *Paff v. Postnikoff,* [2007] B.C.J. No. 139 (S.C.); *McGee v. Ranson,* [2003] M.J. No. 304 (Q.B.); *Huberdeau v. Reid,* [2007] M.J. No. 90 (Q.B.); *Maresich v. Penner,* [2007] M.J. No. 113 (Q.B.); *Wolinski v. Olynyk,* [2008] M.J. No. 2 (Q.B.); *Cooper v. Cooper* (1998), 42 R.F.L. (4th) 317 (Nfld. U.F.C.); *Evely v. Evely,* [2003] N.J. No. 85 (S.C.); *Bakes v. Bakes,* [2002] N.S.J. No. 202 (S.C.); *Ross v. Reaney,* [2003] O.J. No. 2366 (Sup. Ct.); *Yakiwchuk v. Oaks,* [2003] S.J. No. 216 (Q.B.); *Bzowy v. Grover,* [2005] S.J. No. 130 (Q.B.).

6. Support (economic):
    (a) What were the financial arrangements between the parties regarding the provision of or contribution toward the necessaries of life (food, clothing, shelter, recreation, etc.)?
    (b) What were the arrangements concerning the acquisition and ownership of property?
    (c) Was there any special financial arrangement between them which both agreed would be determinant of their overall relationship?

7. Children:
    What was the attitude and conduct of the parties concerning children?

These seven elements may be present in varying degrees and not all of them need exist in order for the relationship to be regarded as "spousal" or conjugal.[24] Similar factors were identified by Hunter J. of the Saskatchewan Court of Queen's Bench in *Tanouye v. Tanouye*[25] who observed:

> The authorities seem to indicate that a common-law relationship or marriage requires perhaps not all but at least a majority of the following characteristics: economic interdependence including an intention to support; a commitment to the relationship, express or implied, for at least an extended period of time; sharing of a common principal residence; a common desire to make a home together and to share responsibilities in and towards that home; where applicable, shared responsibilities of child rearing; and a sexual relationship. As well, it appears that, superimposed on the relationship, there should be the general recognition of family, friends, and perhaps to some extent the larger community, that the particular man and woman appear as a "couple", i.e. a family unit.

Additional factors that may be relevant include the following:

1. Provisions made in the event of illness or death. For example, were they named as beneficiaries in each other's wills, RRSPs, pensions, life insurance or health plans? Did they give each other powers of attorney or decision-making authority on health care?

---

24 *Molodowich v. Penttinen* (1980), 17 R.F.L. (2d) 376 (Ont. Dist. Ct.).
25 (1973), 117 Sask. R. 196 at para. 36 (Q.B.), var'd on other grounds (1995), 134 Sask. R. 159 (C.A.).

2. Are documents available that identify their relationship as spousal, such as income tax returns and elections under pension or health plans?
3. Did their future plans include each other? For example, were there plans to marry, have children, or for a joint retirement?
4. What is the motivation for the relationship, i.e. why are they together?[26]

Because of the wide variety of interpersonal relationships, no single factor is determinative of whether a spousal relationship exists. All relevant factors must be weighed to reach a judicial determination, although some may be given more weight than others. After considering sixteen factors relating to the interpersonal relationship between the parties in *Yakichuk v. Oaks*,[27] Ryan-Froslie J., of the Saskatchewan Court of Queen's Bench, had no hesitation in concluding that a spousal relationship had existed for more than two years within the meaning of section 2(1) of the *Family Property Act* (Saskatchewan).

A flexible objective approach to the relevant factors, rather than a focus on the subjective intentions of either party, is preferable if society and its laws are to respond to the diversity of interpersonal relationships that generate dependence such as justifies the existence of support rights and obligations on the breakdown of intimate relationships.[28]

When support rights and obligations arise pursuant to provincial or territorial legislation, the needs of the applicant and the ability of the other party to pay are critical factors, but the court should also consider legislatively stipulated objectives of support orders that encompass both compensatory and non-compensatory support principles.[29]

In *Bracklow v. Bracklow*,[30] McLachlin J., as she then was, refers to three conceptual bases for spousal support orders, namely, (i) compensatory; (ii) contractual; and (iii) non-compensatory. In addressing the common-law wife's claims to lump sum and ongoing periodic spousal support in *Johnstone v. Wright*,[31] the British Columbia Court of Appeal had no hesitation

---

26 *Yakichuk v. Oaks*, [2003] S.J. No. 216 (Q.B.).

27 *Ibid.*

28 *Spracklin v. Kichton*, [2000] A.J. No. 1329 (Q.B.); *MacMillan-Dekker v. Dekker*, [2000] O.J. No. 2957 (Sup. Ct.).

29 Diebert v. *Calder* (2001), 289 A.R. 228 (Q.B.); *Medora v.* Kohn, [2003] A.J. No. 1027 (Q.B.); *McGee v.* Ranson, [2003] M.J. No. 304 (Q.B.); *Halliday v. Halliday* (1997), 37 R.F.L. (4th) 192 (Ont. C.A.).

30 [1999] 1 S.C.R. 420.

31 [2005] B.C.J. No. 928 (C.A.).

in declaring that these claims could not be advanced on either a contractual or a compensatory basis. With respect to non-compensatory support, the British Columbia Court of Appeal stated that the common-law wife's enjoyment of an affluent lifestyle during cohabitation did not imply that the law should turn her emotional need to continue that lifestyle into a legal obligation on the part of her former common-law husband. While accepting that some transitional spousal support was appropriate to cushion the common-law wife's difficulty in adjusting to her pre-cohabitation lifestyle, the British Columbia Court of Appeal concluded that her receipt of interim support for three and a half years after the breakdown of the relationship had already provided a generous period of adjustment, and to allow any additional support would defeat the statutory goal of encouraging spouses to strive for economic self-sufficiency to the extent that this is reasonable and practicable on the breakdown of their relationship: see section 65(1)(e) of the *Family Relations Act*[32] and section 15.2(6)(d) of the *Divorce Act*.[33] An equalization of incomes does not reflect the law either for former unmarried cohabitants or for married couples who separate or divorce. Generosity during the spousal relationship does not require equal generosity on its breakdown.[34]

E. PROPERTY RIGHTS

Every Canadian province and territory has enacted legislation to provide for the sharing of property between spouses on marriage breakdown or divorce. Unmarried cohabitants are not always covered by this legislation and cannot invoke section 15 of the *Canadian Charter of Rights and Freedoms* to claim statutory property rights. In *Nova Scotia (Attorney General) v. Walsh and Bona*,[35] by a majority of eight to one, the Supreme Court of Canada determined that the exclusion of unmarried heterosexual cohabitants from the definition of "spouse" in section 2(g) of the *Matrimonial Property Act*[36] is not discriminatory within the meaning of section 15(1) of the *Canadian Charter of Rights and Freedoms*. The three-part test for determining whether an impugned statute violates the equality guarantee under section 15(1) of the *Charter* is set out in *Law v. Canada*

---

32 R.S.B.C. 1996, c. 128.
33 R.S.C. 1985 (2d Supp.), c. 3.
34 *Roberts v. Clough*, [2005] P.E.I.J. No. 38 (S.C.A.D.).
35 [2002] S.C.J. No. 84.
36 R.S.N.S. 1989, c. 275.

(Minister of Employment and Immigration).[37] It was conceded by counsel that the first two requirements under *Law* were satisfied in that (i) the *Matrimonial Property Act* promotes substantively differential treatment between married and unmarried cohabitants; and (ii) this differential treatment is based on martial status, which is an analogous ground of discrimination under section 15(1) of the *Charter.* Where the majority and minority judgments disagreed is on the third part of the *Law* test which, in the present case, involved a determination whether a reasonable unmarried heterosexual cohabitant would find the failure of the *Matrimonial Property Act* to include him or her within its ambit has the effect of demeaning his or her dignity. In undertaking the necessary comparison of unmarried heterosexual cohabitants and married cohabitants, the majority judgment acknowledged that there are certain functional similarities between these two groups, but these similarities were not perceived as adequately addressing the full range of circumstances that characterize unmarried heterosexual cohabitants. In particular, the majority judgment observed that the decision whether or not to marry is intensely personal. Many opposite-sex individuals in conjugal relationships of some permanence have opted to avoid marriage and its legal consequences. To equate the legal status of married and unmarried cohabitants pursuant to section 15(1) of the *Charter* would, according to the majority judgment, effectively nullify the individual's freedom to choose alternative family forms and have that choice respected by the state. The decision to marry, which requires the consent of both parties, encapsulates within it a consent to be bound by the property-sharing regime established by the *Matrimonial Property Act.* Unmarried cohabitants are not deprived of property rights by the *Matrimonial Property Act.* Indeed if they choose to do so, they may avail themselves of all the benefits applicable to married couples under the *Matrimonial Property Act.* This can be achieved by a decision to marry, or by their joint ownership of property, or more recently, by registering as domestic partners in accordance with the *Law Reform (2000) Act.*[38] The majority judgment, therefore, concluded that there is no discriminatory denial of a benefit to unmarried heterosexual cohabitants under the *Matrimonial Property Act,* given the diverse steps already available to them to deal with their property in such a way as to create a marriage-like equal partnership. The fact that the freedom to marry might in some cases be illusory and the fact that in-

---

37   [1999] 1 S.C.R. 497.
38   S.N.S, 2000, c. 29.

equities might result on the breakdown of some unmarried cohabitational relationships were deemed an insufficient basis, in the opinion of the majority, for imposing a constitutional requirement that the state extend the provisions of the *Matrimonial Property Act* to unmarried heterosexual cohabitants. Alternative choices and remedies were regarded as available even to persons unwilling or unable to marry. In conclusion, the majority judgment states that the applicability of the *Matrimonial Property Act* only to married couples reflects the difference between married and unmarried heterosexual cohabitants and acknowledges the fundamental personal autonomy and dignity of the individual without any affront to the dignity of unmarried heterosexual cohabitants. There is no deprivation of a benefit based on stereotype or presumed characteristics perpetuating the idea that unmarried couples are less worthy of respect or are not valued as members of Canadian society. All cohabitants have the liberty to make fundamental choices in their lives, and the object of section 15(1) of the *Charter* is thereby respected. Moreover, the alleged discriminatory aspect of a legislative distinction must be determined in light of *Charter* values. One of the essential *Charter* values is liberty, which can be defined as the absence of coercion and the existence of the ability to make fundamental choices with respect to one's life. Limitations imposed by the Supreme Court of Canada that restrict such freedom of choice among persons in conjugal relationships would be contrary to the liberty interest. In a separate concurring judgment, Gonthier J. concluded that it is fitting that certain attributes, rights, and obligations, which serve to give marriage its unique character as a chosen life commitment, are not conferred on unmarried couples. When couples choose to marry, they commit themselves to respect the rights and obligations flowing from their choice. It is this choice that legitimates the system of benefits and obligations flowing from their marriage, including those relating to the sharing of matrimonial assets. To extend the presumption of an equal division of matrimonial assets to unmarried heterosexual cohabitants would intrude into the most personal and intimate of life choices by imposing a system of obligations on persons who never consented to that system. To presume that unmarried heterosexual cohabitants want to be bound by the same obligations as married couples is contrary to their choice to live in a non-marital relationship. Although there is recognition that unmarried cohabitants, whether of the opposite sex or of the same sex, are entitled to the same spousal support rights and obligations as married couples (see *M. v. H.*[39]), such recognition does not extend to

---

39   [1999] 2 S.C.R. 3.

matrimonial property division. The reason for this distinction lies in the different objectives that underlie matrimonial property regimes and spousal support regimes. The former seeks to divide assets according to a property regime chosen by the spouses, either directly by contract or indirectly by the fact of marriage. It reflects the individual choice of the parties. A spousal support regime, on the other hand, is designed not to reflect an individual choice but to fulfill a social objective, namely, to ensure the provision of financial support to family dependants in need and to alleviate the burden that might otherwise fall on the public purse. In a dissenting judgment, L'Heureux-Dubé J. concluded that the *Matrimonial Property Act* violates section 15(1) of the *Canadian Charter of Rights and Freedoms* by failing to extend the same benefits to unmarried heterosexual cohabitants as are provided to married cohabitants on the breakdown of their relationship. Viewed from a functional perspective, unmarried heterosexual cohabitants make similar contributions to the family as their married counterparts and they experience similar needs on the breakdown of the relationship. To deny these realities implies that unmarried heterosexual cohabitants are not worthy of the same recognition, solely because they have not married. The *Matrimonial Property Act* is not premised on choice or consensus; it is a legislative regime that is designed to ensure an equitable apportionment of the economic consequences of the relationship on its breakdown. Although some of the legal disadvantages historically suffered by unmarried heterosexual cohabitants have already been erased from the law, others remain, one of which is the unwarranted denial of property sharing on the breakdown of the relationship. Judicial and legislative recognition of past injustices has resulted in various benefits being conferred on unmarried heterosexual cohabitants. These developments demonstrate the historical demeaning of the dignity of unmarried heterosexual cohabitants, which is perpetuated by the *Matrimonial Property Act*. It is no answer to suggest that alternative remedies are available to achieve property sharing between unmarried heterosexual cohabitants on the breakdown of their relationship because these remedies are inadequate when compared to those accorded to married couples by the *Matrimonial Property Act*. Given these conclusions, L'Heureux-Dubé J. found that the *Matrimonial Property Act* violates the equality guarantee under section 15(1) of the *Canadian Charter of Rights and Freedoms* and this violation cannot be saved by section 1 of the *Charter*.

Although Manitoba, Nova Scotia, Nunavut, the Northwest Territories, Quebec, Saskatchewan, and the Yukon currently confer statutory rights on unmarried cohabitants under defined circumstances, Alberta, New Brunswick, and Newfoundland and Labrador continue to exclude unmarried cohabitants from their matrimonial property regimes. In British Columbia, unmarried cohabitants can opt into the statutory matrimonial property regime by agreement. Consequently, there is a patchwork quilt of diverse provincial and territorial regimes in Canada, which will continue to generate litigation that may become relatively complex in light of the inter-provincial mobility of Canadians and the implications of private international law rules.

Unmarried cohabitants receive some measure of protection across Canada under the judge-made doctrine of unjust enrichment, but this doctrine, unlike statutory matrimonial support regimes, does not trigger any presumption of equal sharing on the breakdown of the relationship.[40] In order for the doctrine of unjust enrichment to apply, three conditions must be satisfied; there must be

(i)   a benefit or enrichment of one party;
(ii) a corresponding deprivation of the other party; and
(iii) the absence of any legal justification for the enrichment, such as a contract or gift.

In the leading case of *Pettkus v. Becker*,[41] wherein these prerequisites were spelled out, it was further observed that there must exist a substantial connection between the contribution made by the one cohabitant and the property acquired or preserved by the other cohabitant. An indirect contribution of money will suffice, as for example, where one cohabitant pays the mortgage instalments and the other buys the food or pays other household expenses. Unmarried cohabitants who work together for many years on a farm or in a family business are usually entitled to share equally in the fruits of their joint enterprise.[42] The issues become more cloudy when the relationship is more limited in its duration and the cohabitant claims an interest in property owned or acquired by the other cohabitant solely by reason of household services or child-care services rendered. In these situations, courts may be more reluctant to find a causal connection between the alleged contribution made and the asset

---

40   *Gould v. Sandau*, [2005] B.C.J. No. 694 (C.A.); *Wylie v. Leclair*, [2003] O.J. No. 1938 (C.A.); *Roberts v. Clough*, [2005] P.E.I.J. No. 38 (S.C.A.D.).

41   (1980), 19 R.F.L. (2d) 165 (S.C.C.). See also *Sorochan v. Sorochan* (1986), 2 R.F.L. (3d) 225 (S.C.C.); *Peter v. Beblow*, [1993] 1 S.C.R. 980; *Thomas v. Fenton*, [2006] B.C.J. No. 1345 (C.A.); *Goddard v. Hambleton*, [2005] N.S.J. No. 381 (C.A.).

42   *Peter v. Beblow*, [1993] 1 S.C.R. 980.

acquired or maintained. In long-term cohabitational relationships, however, the causal connection will usually be found and an equal sharing of specified property may be found appropriate. An unmarried cohabitant who has rendered household or child-care services may alternatively be entitled to reasonable compensation for the services, either pursuant to a contract[43] or in an action for *quantum meruit*. Although the doctrine of unjust enrichment has most frequently been applied to unmarried cohabitants who have claimed a share of the value of the family home on the breakdown of the cohabitational relationship, it has also been applied to enable a "common-law wife" to share her "husband's" pension.[44]

F. DEBTS AND LIABILITIES; FINANCIAL PLANNING

Unmarried cohabitants, whether of the same or opposite sex, often share household expenses. They may purchase a home, cottage, furniture, household appliances, or a car, and finance these transactions through a bank, credit union, or finance company. They may also share the use of the same credit card. Questions may subsequently arise as to who is responsible for any outstanding loan or debt after the cohabitants separate.

When loans are obtained from financial institutions, they are reduced to writing and signed by the party or parties legally responsible for the loan. For example, if unmarried cohabitants co-sign a promissory note to finance the purchase of a car, either or both of them can be called upon to discharge the obligation to the creditor. Not surprisingly, financial institutions are likely to look to the person who is better able to pay, even though they can sue either or both of the parties who signed the note. Liability on a mortgage will also be determined by the signature or signatures on the mortgage document.

When property or services are paid for by credit card, the owner of the card is liable to pay for the goods or services rendered. If an unmarried cohabitant applies for an additional card for his or her partner, the applicant is liable to pay all charges against that card. The important factor

---

43   See *Chrispen v. Topham* (1986), 3 R.F.L. (3d) 149 (Sask. Q.B.), aff'd (1987), 3 R.F.L. (3d) 131 (Sask. C.A.).

44   *Maloney v. Maloney* (1993), 109 D.L.R. (4th) 161 (Ont. Gen. Div.); see also *Bigelow v. Bigelow* (1995), 15 R.F.L. (4th) 12 (Ont. Div. Ct.); compare *MacPhee v. Russel* (2000), 6 R.F.L. (5th) 340 (N.B.C.A.); *Brownie v. Hoganson*, [2005] N.S.J. No. 470 (S.C.).

is not who uses the credit card but whose name is on the account. The same principle applies to unmarried cohabitants and to married couples. If they separate, the person whose name is on the credit card should cancel the privileges formerly provided to his or her partner by notifying the bank or financial institution that issued the card. Otherwise, the card owner may be responsible for debts incurred by the other party even after their separation.

Unmarried cohabitants of the same or opposite sex should also review other documents, such as wills, insurance policies, pension plans, and bank accounts in order to determine changes that might be appropriate. They are well-advised to enter into agreements to regulate their debts and liabilities as well as their rights. Although such an agreement cannot be relied upon as a defence to any third-party claim against either cohabitant, the agreement can provide for remedies between the cohabitants themselves. For example, it might provide for either cohabitant to be indemnified for any third-party debt or liability incurred on behalf of the other cohabitant.

G. CUSTODY AND ACCESS

Custody and access disputes on family breakdown are legally resolved by reference to the elusive criterion of the "best interests of the child." If the parents lived together in a stable relationship after the birth of the child, it is immaterial whether or not they were married to each other.

In theory, the formation of a same-sex relationship after a heterosexual family breakdown does not affect a parent's right to custody of or access to a child. Although the sexual orientation or conduct of a parent may be irrelevant to parenting capacity or the best interests of the child, some judges are inclined to place children with the heterosexual parent. Judicial preference for the heterosexual parent has been displaced from time to time by expert evidence that the child's growth and development will be unaffected by the sexual orientation of the gay or lesbian parent but the need for such evidence underlines the existence of a discriminatory perspective.[45] Judicial attitudes towards gay and lesbian parents are undergoing a change, however, as a result of the *Canadian Charter of*

---

45   See Susan B. Boyd, "Lesbian (and Gay) Custody Claims: What Difference Does Difference Make?" (1997) 15 Can. J. Fam. L. 131.

Rights and Freedoms. In *Re K.*,[46] Nevins Prov. J. concluded that the *Child and Family Services Act*[47] contravened section 15 of the *Charter* by its requirement that spouses be of the opposite sex before they can apply for the adoption of a child. Having found that the infringement was not justified under section 1 of the *Charter*, Nevins Prov. J. held that the appropriate remedy was to modify the definition of "spouse" to include same-sex couples. Pursuant to section 6 of the *Amendments Because of the Supreme Court of Canada Decision in* M. v. H. *Act, 1999*,[48] section 146(4) of the *Child and Family Services Act* has been amended to permit adoption applications by "any other individuals that the court may allow, having regard to the best interests of the child."

---

46   (1995), 23 O.R. (3d) 679 (Prov. Div.); see also *Re C.G.E.* (No. 1), [1995] O.J. No. 4072 (Gen. Div.); and see *Re Nova Scotia Birth Registration No 1999-02-004200*, [2001] N.S.J. No. 261 (S.C.).

47   R.S.O. 1990, c. C.11.

48   S.O. 1999, c. 6, s. 6.

CHAPTER 4

DOMESTIC CONTRACTS

A. TYPES OF DOMESTIC CONTRACTS

The following analysis will focus on "domestic contracts" insofar as they have been statutorily defined in Ontario. Even in the absence of statutory provisions, however, married and unmarried cohabitants[1] are legally entitled to enter into binding and enforceable contracts. In some circumstances, the law restricts the extent to which spouses or unmarried cohabitants can contractually waive rights that would otherwise vest in them pursuant to statute. For example, the splitting of credits under the Canada Pension Plan between divorced spouses cannot be circumvented by a spousal contract or separation agreement, except where provincial legislation specifically permits such contracting out.[2] In addition, courts are entitled to override the terms of spousal contracts that purport to waive child support rights and obligations.[3]

Domestic contracts, as defined under provincial and territorial statutes in Canada, are formal written contracts signed by the parties and

---

1   See *Chrispen v. Topham* (1986), 3 R.F.L. (3d) 149 (Sask. Q.B.), aff'd (1987), 9
     R.F.L. (3d) 131 (Sask. C.A.). See also *Anderson v. Luoma* (1986), 50 R.F.L. (2d) 127
     (B.C.S.C.).
2   *An Act to Amend the Canada Pension Plan and the Federal Court Act*, R.S.C. 1985
     (2d Supp.), c. 30, s. 23; see also *An Act to Amend the Canada Pension Plan (Spousal
     Agreement)*, S.C. 1991, c. 14.
3   *Richardson v. Richardson* (1987), 7 R.F.L. (3d) 304 (S.C.C.).

witnessed, whereby married couples and unmarried cohabitants may regulate their rights and obligations during their relationship or on its termination. There are three different kinds of domestic contracts: (i) marriage contracts; (ii) cohabitation agreements; and (iii) separation agreements.[4]

The right of men and women to enter into agreements or domestic contracts to regulate their affairs is expressly recognized by statute in several provinces and territories[5] but the legislation is not uniform throughout Canada. Because space does not permit a detailed description of the different provincial and territorial statutes, the following analysis will examine the Ontario legislation, which has provided the precedent for similar legislation in several other provinces. Before doing so, however, it is pertinent to review *Hartshorne v. Hartshorne*,[6] a judgment of the Supreme Court of Canada, which dealt with the impact of a marriage contract on an application for spousal property division under the *Family Relations Act (British Columbia)*. While this judgment specifically addresses that particular topic, it also provides insight into how such contracts might be interpreted and applied under statutory property regimes in the provinces and territories.

In *Hartshorne v. Hartshorne*, the parties cohabited for twelve and one-half years and were married for nine of those years. It was a second marriage for both of them. They had two children. After the birth of their first child, the wife, a lawyer, withdrew from the practice of law to assume a full-time homemaking and child caregiving role. The husband, also a lawyer, made it clear to her prior to their marriage that he would never again allow his property to be divided by reason of a marriage breakdown.

---

4   See, for example, *Family Law Act*, R.S.O. 1990, c. F.3, s. 51. And see text to and contents of note 5, below in this chapter.

5   See *Matrimonial Property Act*, R.S.A. 2000, c. M-8, ss. 37–38; *Family Relations Act*, R.S.B.C. 1996, c. 128, s. 120.1; *Marital Property Act*, S.N.B. 1980, c. M-1.1, ss. 33–41 (marriage contracts, cohabitation agreements, separation agreements); *Family Law Act*, R.S.N. 1990, c. F-2, ss. 61–71 (marriage contracts, cohabitation agreements separation agreements); *Matrimonial Property Act*, R.S.N.S. 1989, c. 275, ss. 23–29 (marriage contracts, separation agreements); *Family Law Act*, S.N.W.T. 1997, c. 18, ss. 2–13 (marriage contracts, cohabitation agreements; separation agreements); *Family Law Act*, R.S.O. 1990, c. F.3, ss. 51–60 (marriage contracts, cohabitation agreements, separation agreements); *Family Law Act*, S.P.E.I. 1995, c. 12, ss. 50–58 (marriage contracts, cohabitation agreements, separation agreements); *Matrimonial Property Act*, 1997, S.S. 1997, c. M-6.11, ss. 38–42 (interspousal contracts); *Family Property and Support Act*, R.S.Y. 1986, c. 63, ss. 58–64 (marriage contracts, cohabitation agreements, separation agreements).

6   [2004] 1 S.C.R. 550.

The husband brought assets of $1.6 million into the marriage, which included his law practice, whereas the wife had no assets and was heavily in debt at the time of the marriage. At the husband's insistence, the spouses executed a marriage agreement declaring the parties separate as to property, subject to the wife being entitled to a 3 percent interest in the matrimonial home for each year of marriage up to a maximum of 49 percent. The wife received independent legal advice that the agreement was grossly unfair but signed it with a few amendments, including her right to spousal support. Pursuant to the agreement, the wife was entitled to property valued at $280,000 on the spousal separation and the husband's entitlement was to property worth $1.2 million. In subsequent divorce proceedings, the husband sought to rely on the agreement to avoid the operation of the statutory property regime in British Columbia while the wife contended that the agreement should be set aside on common-law principles or that the distribution of assets should be reapportioned under section 65(1) of the *Family Relations Act* (B.C.) because the agreement was unfair. The trial judge concluded that the agreement was unfair and ordered a 60:40 reapportionment of most of the assets, including the husband's law practice, in favour of the husband. Each spouse was held entitled to a one-half interest in the matrimonial home and contents. This judgment was upheld by a majority judgment (2–1) of the British Columbia Court of Appeal. On further appeal to the Supreme Court of Canada, the husband's appeal was allowed by a majority of 6–3. In the majority judgment, Bastarache J., with whom McLachlin C.J. and Iaccobucci, Major, Arbour, and Fish JJ. concurred, formulated the following principles:

(i)   The primary policy objective underlying the statutory property regime in British Columbia is to achieve fairness.

(ii)   Marriage agreements are expressly recognized by the *Family Relations Act* (B.C.) as providing an appropriate means of regulating the division of property upon the breakdown or dissolution of marriage. As a prerequisite to enforceability, however, any such agreement must operate fairly at the time of the property division. Otherwise, judicial reapportionment of the property pursuant to section 65(1) of the *Family Relations Act* will be available to achieve fairness.

(iii)   To implement the legislative intention, courts must encourage parties to enter into marriage agreements that are fair and to respond to changing circumstances by revisiting and revising their agreements from time to time to ensure continued fairness. Parties should also be encouraged to take personal control over their own financial well-being upon the dissolution of marriage and courts should be reluctant to second-guess the arrangement upon which both spouses reasonably expected to rely. Spouses may choose to structure their financial affairs in a number of ways and it is their prerogative to do so, provided that the legal boundaries of fairness are observed.

(iv) The outcome of matrimonial proceedings should reconcile respect for the intentions of the spouses and the assurance of an equitable result.

(v) There is no hard and fast rule regarding the judicial deference to be accorded to marriage agreements as compared to separation agreements. In some cases, for example, where a marriage agreement is intended to protect premarital assets or an anticipated inheritance for the children of a prior marriage, marriage agreements may be accorded a higher degree of deference than separation agreements. In other cases, marriage agreements may be accorded less deference than separation agreements because the former type of agreement may be anticipatory and fail to take account of the financial means, needs, or other circumstances of the parties as they exist at the time of the marriage breakdown.

(vi) In addressing the issue of judicial deference to spousal agreements in the context of property division on marriage breakdown, the court may apply *Miglin v. Miglin*,[7] to support the general legal proposition that some weight should be given to marriage agreements. *Miglin v. Miglin* is also helpful for its general propositions that "a court should be loathe to interfere with a pre-existing agreement unless it is convinced that the agreement does not comply substantially with the overall objectives" of the governing legislation and that the court "must look at the agreement or arrangement in its totality, bearing in mind that all aspects of the agreement are inextricably linked and that the parties have a large discretion in establishing priorities and goals for themselves." Beyond these parameters, however, the *Miglin* judgment, which deals with the effect of a separation agreement on an application for a support order under the *Divorce Act*, cannot be directly applied to regulate property distribution on the dissolution of marriage because this would distort the analytical structure provided by the *Family Relations Act* (B.C.).

---

7   [2003] 1 S.C.R. 300.

(vii) In determining whether a marriage agreement is unfair so as to entitle the court to reapportion property pursuant to section 65(1) of the
Family Relations Act, the court must determine whether the agreement is substantively fair when the application for reapportionment
is made. The essence of this inquiry is whether the circumstances
of the parties on their separation were within their reasonable contemplation when the agreement was entered into and, if so, whether
at that time the parties made adequate arrangements in response to
their anticipated circumstances. In determining whether a marriage
agreement operates unfairly, the court must first apply the agreement. In particular, the court must assess and award the financial
entitlements of each spouse under the agreement and their entitlements from all other sources, including spousal and child support.
The court must then review the list of factors set out in section 65(1)
of the *Family Relations Act* for the purpose of determining whether
the agreement operates unfairly. At the second stage of the inquiry,
consideration must be given to the personal and financial circumstances of both parties and in particular to the manner in which
these circumstances evolved.

Because the financial and domestic arrangements of the parties unfolded
as expected, and they remained completely independent with respect to
their real and personal property during their relationship, the economic
impact of the wife's assumption of homemaking and child caregiving responsibilities during the twelve and one-half year spousal relationship,
though relevant under sections 65(1)(a) and (e) of the *Family Relations Act*
(B.C.), was found to be offset by her right to spousal support and the fact
that the bulk of the property existing at the time of the spousal separation was property that the husband had acquired prior to their spousal
relationship, the latter being a relevant factor to consider under section
65(1)(c) of the *Family Relations Act* (B.C.). Given the availability of spousal
support to accommodate any economic disadvantage resulting to the wife
from her assumption of homemaking and child caregiving responsibilities
during the spousal relationship, coupled with the express preservation of
her right to spousal support by the terms of the marriage agreement and
the wife's postseparation return to employment as a lawyer, the majority
judgment of the Supreme Court of Canada in *Hartshorne v. Hartshorne*
concluded that the judicial reapportionment of property ordered by the
trial judge and affirmed on appeal to the British Columbia Court of Appeal was unjustified and the marriage contract should be upheld.

On an incidental question relating to the characterization of the husband's law corporation, the majority judgment cited section 59(1) of the *Family Relations Act* (B.C.) whereby property is not a family asset if it "is owned by one spouse to the exclusion of the other and is used primarily for business purposes and if the spouse who does not own the property made no direct or indirect contribution to the acquisition of the property by the other spouse or to the operation of the business." Having regard to the husband's ownership of the law corporation prior to the spousal relationship and the fact that its value did not increase after the marriage, the majority judgment concluded that the trial judge had erred in finding that the corporation constituted a family asset.

The statutory threshold for judicial intervention where the provisions of a spousal agreement purport to govern the division of property on marriage breakdown is lower in British Columbia than in other provinces.[8] In the words of Bastarache J. in *Hartshorne v. Hartshorne*, at paragraphs 13–14,

> 13. Specifically, s. 65(1) provides that if the provisions for division of property between spouses either under their marriage agreement or under the statutory regime would be unfair having regard to: (a) the duration of the marriage; (b) the duration of the period during which the spouses have lived separate and apart; (c) the date when property was acquired or disposed of; (d) the extent to which property was acquired by one spouse through inheritance or gift; (e) the needs of each spouse to become or remain economically independent and self-sufficient; or (f) any other circumstances relating to the acquisition, preservation, maintenance, improvement or use of property or the capacity or liabilities of a spouse, the Supreme Court, on application, may order that the property covered by such agreement or statutory regime be divided into shares fixed by the court.

> 14. Most of the provinces provide for judicial oversight of marriage agreements. For example, s. 56(4) of the Ontario's *Family Law Act*, R.S.O. 1990, c. F.3, permits a court to set aside a domestic contract or a provision thereof if a party failed to disclose significant assets or liabilities, if a party did not understand the nature or consequences of the contract, or otherwise, in accordance with the law of contract. See also *Family Law Act*, R.S.N.L. 1990, c. F-2, s. 66(4); *Family Law Act*, S.P.E.I. 1995, c. 12, s. 55(4), for this language. The threshold in Nova Scotia is a

---

8   *Jasinski v. Jasinski*, [2006] B.C.J. No. 1325 (S.C.).

finding that any term is "unconscionable, unduly harsh on one party or fraudulent": see *Matrimonial Property Act*, R.S.N.S. 1989, c. 275, s. 29.[9] Saskatchewan allows a court to redistribute property where an inter-spousal contract was unconscionable or grossly unfair at the time it was entered into: see *Family Property Act*, S.S. 1997, c. F.-6.3, s. 24(2). New Brunswick permits a court to disregard a provision of a domestic con-tract where a spouse did not receive independent legal advice and appli-cation of the provision would be inequitable: see *Marital Property Act*, S.N.B. 1980, c. M-1.1, s. 41. By contrast, in British Columbia, as earlier noted, a court may reapportion assets upon finding that to divide the property as provided for in the agreement or the FRA would be "unfair." Clearly, the statutory scheme in British Columbia sets a lower threshold for judicial intervention than do the schemes in other provinces.

B. DOMESTIC CONTRACTS UNDER THE ONTARIO *FAMILY LAW ACT*

1) General Observations

Ontario was the first province to introduce comprehensive statutory pro-visions regulating domestic contracts. This was first achieved by the *Fam-ily Law Reform Act, 1978*,[10] which was superseded in 1986 by the *Family Law Act*,[11] Part IV of which is specifically entitled "Domestic Contracts."

Part IV of the *Family Law Act* endorses contractual autonomy by en-abling persons to contract out of rights and obligations that would other-wise arise pursuant to the *Family Law Act*. Subsection 2(10) of the *Family Law Act* specifically provides that "[a] domestic contract dealing with a matter that is also dealt with in this Act prevails unless this Act provides otherwise." A significant qualification to the paramountcy of a domestic contract is found in subsection 33(4) of the *Family Law Act*. This subsec-tion empowers a court to set aside a provision for support or a waiver of the right to support in a domestic contract or paternity agreement, if the terms of the agreement (i) result in unconscionable circumstances,

---

9   *Rogerson v. Rogerson*, [2004] N.S.J. No. 152 (S.C.).

10 S.O. 1978, c. 2.

11 S.O. 1986, c. 4, now R.S.O. 1990, c. F.3. For proposed changes, see Ontario Law Re-form Commission, *Report on Family Property Law* (including Executive Summary) (Toronto: The Commission, 1993); Ontario Law Reform Commission, *Report on the Rights and Responsibilities of Cohabitants under the* Family Law Act (including Executive Summary) (Toronto: The Commission, 1993).

(ii) shift the prospective burden of supporting family dependants to the public purse, or (iii) the domestic contract or paternity agreement is in default at the time of an application for support under Part III of the *Family Law Act*.[12] Somewhat limited powers are also conferred on the court to vary all or part of a domestic contract under section 56 of the *Family Law Act*, although it is always open to the court to set aside any provision of a domestic contract that undermines the best interests of a child.[13]

Section 51 of the *Family Law Act* defines a domestic contract to mean "a marriage contract, separation agreement or cohabitation agreement." This definition applies for all purposes of the *Family Law Act* pursuant to the supplementary definition of "domestic contract" in subsection 1(1) of the Act.

Except insofar as the *Family Law Act* expressly provides to the contrary, the general principles of the law of contract apply to "domestic contracts" within the meaning of the *Family Law Act*, 1986. Non-compliance with the explicit requirements of the *Family Law Act* does not necessarily preclude an action on the agreement at common law.

2) Marriage Contracts

Section 51 of the *Family Law Act* empowers persons to enter into marriage contracts before or during their marriage, provided that in the latter circumstance they are still cohabiting at the time of the execution of the agreement.[14] Marriage contracts cannot be entered into by cohabitants of the same sex nor by persons living in a permanent common-law relationship.[15] In light of the extended definition of "spouse" in subsections 1(1) and (2) of the *Family Law Act*, marriage contracts may be entered into by parties to a void or voidable marriage celebrated in good faith or by parties to a valid foreign polygamous marriage.

Pursuant to subsection 52(1) of the *Family Law Act*, the parties to a marriage contract may regulate their respective legal rights and obligations during the marriage, on separation, annulment or dissolution of the marriage, or on death. A valid marriage contract that regulates "the ownership" and "division of property" takes precedence over the statutory equalization entitlements conferred by Part I of the *Family Law Act*.[16] Specific property may also be excluded from the equalization pro-

---

12   See Section B(14), below in this chapter.
13   See Sections B(7) and B(9), below in this chapter.
14   See Section B(4), below in this chapter.
15   See Section B(3), below in this chapter.
16   *Family Law Act*, R.S.O. 1990, c. F.3, s. 2(10).

cess pursuant to paragraph 4(2)6 of the Act.[17] A marriage contract may also preclude an order for support being granted under Part III of the Act, subject to the court's discretionary jurisdiction to override the contract under the conditions specified in subsection 33(4) of the *Family Law Act* or under section 56 of the Act.

If spouses wish to predetermine their property rights on marriage breakdown or death, declarations of ownership may be insufficient to exclude an equalization claim under section 5 of the *Family Law Act* because such claims are not dependent on ownership.[18]

A marriage contract, unlike a separation agreement, cannot limit the rights conferred on a spouse by Part II of the *Family Law Act*.[19] Pursuant to section 19 of the Act, both spouses have an equal right to possession of the matrimonial home in the absence of a separation agreement or court order to the contrary. Furthermore, neither spouse can unilaterally dispose of or encumber an interest in the matrimonial home in the absence of authority conferred by a separation agreement or court order. However, subsection 52(2) of the *Family Law Act* does not preclude a marriage contract from determining rights of ownership in the home or excluding the home or its value from any spousal equalization claim based on section 5 of the Act. The language of the marriage contract should be carefully drawn so as to make it clear that possessory interests remain unaffected by its terms. In *Ramboer v. Ramboer*,[20] for example, a marriage contract was declared void pursuant to subsection 51(2) of the *Family Law Reform Act, 1978*,[21] where the husband paid a lump sum "in full satisfaction and payment of the wife's interest in the home." The wife was consequently entitled to an equal share in the value of the matrimonial home pursuant to subsection 4(1) of the *Family Law Reform Act, 1978*. A different conclusion would presumably have been reached if the terms of the marriage contract had not inextricably intertwined possessory, proprietary, and division rights in the general release. The language of subsection 51(2) of the *Family Law Reform Act, 1978* and of its successor, subsection 52(2) of the *Family Law Act*,[22] with the express reference to "[a] *provision* in a marriage contract," clearly envisages the possibility of severing the offending

17   *Nurmi v. Nurmi* (1988), 16 R.F.L. (3d) 201 (Ont. U.F.C.).
18   *Bosch v. Bosch* (1991), 36 R.F.L. (3d) 302 (Ont. C.A.); *Webster v. Webster Estate*, [2006] O.J. No. 2749 (Sup. Ct.).
19   *Family Law Act*, R.S.O. 1990, c. F.3, s. 52(2).
20   (1979), 11 R.F.L. (2d) 320 (Ont. S.C.).
21   S.O. 1978, c. 2.
22   R.S.O. 1990, c. F.3.

provision from the contract as a whole, if this is practicable under the terms of the marriage contract. It is also important to observe that an offending provision was rendered void by subsection 51(2) of the *Family Law Reform Act, 1978*, which was applied in *Ramboer v. Ramboer*, above, but is now merely unenforceable pursuant to subsection 52(2) of the *Family Law Act*.[23]

Paragraph 52(1)(c) of the *Family Law Act* precludes the parties to a marriage contract from determining prospective rights to the custody of or access to their children. A marriage contract may, nevertheless, define the right to direct the education and moral upbringing of the children. Any such provision is subject to the court's discretionary jurisdiction under section 56 of the *Family Law Act* to disregard the provision where the best interests of the child are not thereby served.

3) Cohabitation Agreements

Section 53 of the *Family Law Act* provides that cohabitation agreements may be entered into by persons of the opposite sex or of the same sex who are cohabiting or intend to cohabit but who are not married and have no present intention to marry. The fact that two people are sharing accommodation does not necessarily constitute cohabitation. Subsection 1(1) of the *Family Law Act* defines "cohabit" as meaning "to live together in a conjugal relationship, whether within or outside marriage." Same-sex cohabitants fall within the scope of section 53 of the *Family Law Act* pursuant to statutory amendments[24] that were implemented in Ontario in consequence of the judgment of the Supreme Court of Canada in *M. v. H.*[25]

Cohabitation agreements, as defined by section 51 of the *Family Law Act*, may regulate the rights and obligations of the respective parties during cohabitation, on the cessation of cohabitation, or on death. Such agreements, like marriage contracts, may predetermine the ownership or division of property, support rights and obligations, the right to direct the education or moral upbringing of children, and any other matter in the settlement of the cohabitants' affairs.[26]

---

23 See *Nurmi v. Nurmi* (1988), 16 R.F.L. (3d) 201 (Ont. U.F.C.).
24 *Amendments Because of the Supreme Court of Canada Decision in* M. v. H. *Act, 1999*, S.O. 1999, c. 6.
25 [1999] 2 S.C.R. 3.
26 See Section B(2), above in this chapter.

If the parties to a cohabitation agreement subsequently marry each other, the agreement is deemed to be a marriage contract pursuant to subsection 53(2) of the *Family Law Act*.

4) Separation Agreements

Section 54 of the *Family Law Act* provides that a separation agreement may be entered into by persons of the opposite sex or of the same sex who have cohabited and are living separate and apart. The term "cohabit" is defined in subsection 1(1) of the *Family Law Act* as meaning "to live together in a conjugal relationship, whether within or outside marriage." The words "living separate and apart" in section 54 of the Act bear the same meaning as paragraph 4(1)(e) of the *Divorce Act*.[27] Accordingly, the fact of separation and an intention to separate must co-exist before spouses or other persons can be found to be living separate and apart.[28] Continued residence under the same roof does not preclude a finding that the parties are living separate and apart, provided that they are living independent lives while sharing common accommodation.[29] Furthermore, isolated or casual acts of postseparation sexual intercourse do not preclude a finding that the parties are living separate and apart.[30]

At common law, married couples could enter into valid separation agreements before withdrawing from cohabitation, provided that a cessation of cohabitation was imminent. The language of sections 52 and 54 of the *Family Law Act* imply that preseparation agreements are now characterized as marriage contracts. The difference between marriage contracts and separation agreements is not merely a matter of form. Paragraph 52(1)(c) and subsection 52(2) of the *Family Law Act* preclude a marriage contract from regulating custody and access rights and render unenforceable any provision thereof relating to the limitation of possessory or disposition rights in the matrimonial home arising under Part II of the *Family Law Act*. No corresponding qualifications apply to separation agreements.[31] Where separation is imminent, therefore, the execution, as distinct from the drafting of an agreement, should be deferred until the

---

27   R.S.C. 1985 (2d Supp.), c. 3.

28   Compare *Herman v. Herman* (1969), 3 D.L.R. (3d) 551 (N.S.S.C.).

29   Compare *Cooper v. Cooper* (1972), 10 R.F.L. 184 (Ont. H.C.J.); *Dupere v. Dupere* (1975), 19 R.F.L. 270 (N.B.S.C.), aff'd (1975), 10 N.B.R. (2d) 148 (C.A.).

30   Compare *Deslippe v. Deslippe* (1974), 16 R.F.L. 38 (Ont. C.A.); *Leaderhouse v. Leaderhouse* (1971), 4 R.F.L. 174 (Sask. Q.B.).

31   See ss. 54(d), 19(2)(b), and 21(1)(b) of the *Family Law Act*, R.S.O. 1990, c. F.3.

parties have ceased cohabitation. Otherwise, there may be serious impediments to a complete and final settlement of all outstanding issues.

The fact that one spouse failed to obtain independent legal advice, when advised to do so, does not invalidate a separation agreement.[32]

Where a valid and enforceable separation agreement has been executed, its terms prevail over family property and matrimonial home rights that might otherwise have arisen under Parts I *and* II of the *Family Law Act*.[33] Spousal support claims under Part III of the *Family Law Act* may also be barred by the provisions of a separation agreement, subject to the possible application of subsection 33(4) of the *Family Law Act*.[34]

Although a separation agreement, unlike a marriage contract or cohabitation agreement, may regulate the right to custody of and access to children,[35] it is subject to the overriding provisions of subsection 56(1) of the *Family Law Act*, whereby the court may disregard any custody or access provision in a domestic contract where such a course of action is in the best interests of a child. Pursuant to paragraph 54(e) of the *Family Law Act*, parties to a separation agreement may agree on their respective rights and obligations including any other matter in the settlement of their affairs. This allows spouses to determine responsibility for outstanding debts.

5) Formal Requirements of Domestic Contracts

Subsection 55(1) of the *Family Law Act* provides that a domestic contract and an agreement to amend or rescind a domestic contract are unenforceable unless made in writing, signed by the parties, and witnessed.

Subsection 55(1) of the *Family Law Act* is the successor to subsection 54(1) of the *Family Law Reform Act, 1978*.[36] There is, however, one marked difference between these two provisions. Non-compliance with the formal requirements of subsection 54(1) of the *Family Law Reform Act, 1978* rendered the domestic contract void. Pursuant to subsection 55(1) of the *Family Law Act*, non-compliance with the formal requirements of domestic contracts does not invalidate the contract but merely renders it unenforceable.

---

32 *Kristoff v. Kristoff* (1987), 7 R.F.L. (3d) 284 (Ont. Dist. Ct.).
33 See *Puopolo v. Puopolo* (1986), 2 R.F.L. (3d) 73 (Ont. S.C.); *Cipens v. Cipens* (1987), 8 R.F.L. (3d) 325 (Ont. U.F.C.), Steinberg U.F.C.J.; compare Section B(2), above in this chapter.
34 See Section B(14), below in this chapter.
35 *Family Law Act*, R.S.O. 1990, c. F.3, s. 54(d).
36 S.O. 1978, c. 2.

An agreement to amend a separation agreement, negotiated by letters between the parties' lawyers, will not be enforceable unless it has met the formal requirements of subsection 55(1).[37] The provisions of subsection 55(1) of the *Family Law Act* are inapplicable, however, to authorized settlements entered into by the lawyers for the respective parties after the institution of legal proceedings.[38]

One judge has stated that the relevant statutory provisions "do not require that the signature of each party be expressly witnessed but only that the agreement be witnessed."[39] Another judge has concluded that, despite the fact that the witness was not present when the wife signed the agreement, the formalities of subsection 55(1) were satisfied because the wife did not dispute the authenticity of her signature in the presence of the witness.[40]

6) Capacity to Enter into Domestic Contracts

In Ontario, a person attains the age of majority and ceases to be a minor on reaching the age of eighteen years.[41] Subsection 55(2) of the *Family Law Act* confers a qualified capacity on minors to enter into a marriage contract, cohabitation agreement, or separation agreement, in that any such contract or agreement is subject to the approval of the court, either before or after the minor enters into the contract.

The guardian of property of a mentally incapable person other than his or her spouse is empowered to enter into a domestic contract on behalf of the person under such incapacity and may also give any waiver or consent required by the *Family Law Act*. In all cases, however, the domestic contract, waiver, or consent is subject to the prior approval of the court.[42] The aforementioned powers cannot be exercised by the spouse of the mentally incapable person even if that spouse is the guardian of the property of the mentally incapable person. In such a case or where no guardian has been appointed, the Public Guardian and Trustee may act on behalf of the mentally incapable person.

---

37 *Miller v. Bozzi* (1991), 34 R.F.L. (3d) 371 (Ont. Div. Ct.).
38 *Geropoulos v. Geropoulos* (1982), 26 R.F.L. (2d) 225 (Ont. C.A.); *Campbell v. Campbell* (1986), 47 R.F.L. (2d) 392 at 396–98 (Ont. S.C.); *Pastoor v. Pastoor*, [2007] O.J. No. 2851 (Sup. Ct.).
39 *Campbell v. Campbell* (1991), 33 R.F.L. (3d) 99 (Ont. Gen. Div.), Steele J.
40 *Hyldtoft v. Hyldtoft* (1991), 33 R.F.L. (3d) 99 (Ont. Gen. Div.), Haines J.
41 *Age of Majority and Accountability Act*, R.S.O. 1990, c. A.7, s. 1.
42 *Family Law Act*, R.S.O. 1990, c. F.3, s. 55(3).

7) Contracts Subject to Best Interests of Child

Subsection 56(1) of the *Family Law Act* confers a broad discretionary jurisdiction on the court to disregard the provisions of a domestic contract relating to the support, education, moral training, or custody of or access to a child, where the best interests of the child are not thereby served. It is generally acknowledged that parents cannot contract out of their obligations to provide child support.[43] Furthermore, a parent cannot avoid obligations to pay child support under a separation agreement simply because of an inability to exercise a right of reasonable access.[44]

The power of a court to override the provisions of a spousal agreement respecting custody or access has long been established. No spousal agreement can deprive the court of its traditional responsibility for the custody and guardianship of children.[45] In matters of custody and access, the courts are clearly entitled to override the terms of a spousal agreement, if the terms of the agreement do not harmonize with the welfare or best interests of the child.[46] Opinions may differ, however, as to how a child's welfare or best interests will be served in controversial situations and the wishes of the parents may be entitled to considerable weight.[47]

8) *Dum Casta* Clauses

The rights and obligations of the parties to a domestic contract cannot be made contingent upon the chastity of either party following separation. Any provision to such effect is unenforceable pursuant to subsection 56(2) of the *Family Law Act*. It is permissible, however, for the terms of a domestic contract to take account of any subsequent marriage or cohabitational relationship. A domestic contract does not offend subsection 56(2) of the *Family Law Act* if, for example, periodic "spousal" support is payable only until the payee's marriage or remarriage or non-marital cohabitation with another person.

It is no longer the practice of the courts to incorporate a *dum casta* clause in an order for periodic support.[48] It is not unusual, however, for

---

43   See Section B(14), below in this chapter.
44   *Wright v. Wright* (1974), 12 R.F.L. 200 (Ont. C.A.).
45   *Voegelin v. Voegelin* (1980), 15 R.F.L. (2d) 1 (Ont. Co. Ct.); *Statia v. Statia* (1981), 29 Nfld. & P.E.I.R. 464 (P.E.I.S.C.).
46   *Liang v. Liang* (1979), 5 R.F.L. (2d) 103 (Ont. S.C.).
47   *Ibid.*
48   *Seeman v. Seeman* (1976), 28 R.F.L. 275 (Ont. S.C.); *Sleigh v. Sleigh* (1979), 23 O.R. (2d) 336 (S.C.).

a court to order periodic spousal support to be payable until the payee's marriage, remarriage, or non-marital cohabitation in circumstances similar to marriage.

9) Setting Aside Domestic Contracts

Judicial opinion has been divided in the past concerning the effect of non-disclosure on a domestic contract.[49] The uncertainty has now been resolved by paragraph 56(4)(a) of the *Family Law Act*, which empowers the court to set aside the domestic contract or a provision thereof, if a party failed to disclose significant assets, debts, or other liabilities in existence when the domestic contract was made. The court should first determine whether a failure to disclose within the meaning of paragraph 56(4)(a) is proven. Only where such non-disclosure is established can the court be called upon to exercise its statutory discretion. The fact of non-disclosure does not compel the court to set aside all or part of the domestic contract. In *Demchuk v. Demchuk*,[50] an application to rescind or amend a separation agreement executed prior to the commencement of the *Family Law Act* on 1 March 1986 was coupled with a claim for lump sum and periodic spousal support under subsection 11(1) of the *Divorce Act, 1968*.[51] In denying relief to the claimant, Clarke J. reached the following conclusions. Non-disclosure, whether consensual or innocent, falls within the ambit of paragraph 56(4)(a) and waiver of full disclosure is not permissible by virtue of subsection 56(7). Full disclosure presupposes the identification of all significant assets and their value. The trial judge, nevertheless, refused to exercise the statutory discretion to re-open the agreement having regard to the attendant circumstances of the case, including the absence of concealment of the husband's pension and deferred profit-sharing plan; the absence of material misrepresentation, duress, or unconscionable circumstances in the making of the agreement; the neglect of the wife to pursue full legal disclosure and her subsequent failure to expeditiously seek a variation; the absence of any catastrophic change in the wife's situation that would compel judicial intervention; the substantial benefits received by the wife pursuant to the agreement; the social desirability

---

49　See *Farquar v. Farquar* (1984), 35 R.F.L. (2d) 287 at 299 (Ont. C.A.), Zuber J.A., and compare dissenting judgment of Matas J.A. in *Tutiah v. Tutiah* (1986), 48 R.F.L. (2d) 337 at 356–59 (Man. C.A.).

50　(1986), 1 R.F.L. (3d) 176 (Ont. S.C.). For a detailed review of relevant case law on s. 56 of the Ontario *Family Law Act*, see *Loy v. Loy*, [2007] O.J. No. 4274 (Sup. Ct.).

51　S.C. 1967–68, c. 24.

of a clean break following the discharge of the obligations imposed by the agreement; the wife's attainment of financial self-sufficiency; and the husband's willingness to assume continuing responsibility for the cost of the children's post-secondary education. The trial judge further concluded that interference with the terms of the separation agreement was also unwarranted because the pension and deferred profit-sharing plan was not a "significant asset" within the meaning of paragraph 56(4)(a) of the *Family Law Act* at the time when the agreement was entered into. Accordingly, the court upheld the separation agreement and refused to order spousal support pursuant to subsection 11(1) of the *Divorce Act*, 1968, notwithstanding the judicial discretion to order such support even when the validity of a separation agreement has not been successfully impugned. The trial judge also concluded that paragraph 56(4)(a) of the *Family Law Act* does not impose a reverse onus. Although each party is now under a positive and absolute duty to disclose, the party who seeks to rescind the separation agreement in whole or in part must demonstrate that the other party has failed to discharge that duty.

The duty to disclose the value, and not merely the extent, of significant assets must be realistically applied by the courts. In the absence of any definition of "value" in the *Family Law Act*, opinions may differ as to its meaning, and even if this is agreed upon, there may be legitimate differences of opinion respecting the manner of determining the value of particular assets. Accordingly, it is submitted that paragraph 56(4)(a) of the *Family Law Act* will be satisfied if the court concludes that the valuation of an asset was not inherently misleading and constituted a realistic estimate in light of established valuation practices.[52]

While paragraph 56(4)(a) restricts the court's jurisdiction to set aside domestic contracts to instances of lack of financial disclosure, a court may set aside a separation agreement, at least in part, where there has been a failure to disclose personal information material to the contract, as, for example, where the wife withholds information concerning the paternity of one of the children from her husband.[53] If the offending covenant does not constitute the only consideration for the contract, a separation agreement may be enforced without the offending covenant.[54]

---

52   See *Greenwood v. Greenwood* (1988), 18 R.F.L. (3d) 273 (Ont. H.C.J.); *Dearing v. Dearing* (1991), 37 R.F.L. (3d) 102 (Ont. Gen. Div.).

53   *Kristoff v. Kristoff* (1987), 7 R.F.L. (3d) 284 (Ont. Dist. Ct.).

54   *Tuxford v. Tuxford* (1913), 6 Sask. L.R. 96 (S.C.); and see *Lotton v. Lotton* (1979), 11 R.F.L. (2d) 112 (Ont. C.A.).

Paragraph 56(4)(b) of the *Family Law Act* indicates that a court may set aside a domestic contract or a provision in it if a party did not understand the nature or consequences of the domestic contract. Paragraph 56(4)(b) underlines the importance of independent legal advice. A separation agreement signed by a spouse without independent legal advice may be ignored by the court,[55] although the absence of independent legal advice does not inevitably undermine an agreement.[56] Conversely, a court is not prevented from overriding a separation agreement merely because the partners to it have received independent legal advice.[57]

The jurisdiction of a court to set aside a domestic contract or any provision thereof pursuant to the application of established principles of the law of contract is expressly recognized by paragraph 56(4)(c) of the *Family Law Act*. A separation agreement secured through the exertion of undue influence may be set aside pursuant to paragraph 56(4)(c) of the *Family Law Act* at the instance of the spouse influenced even though the agreement appears to be fair and reasonable on its face. Cases are divided on the issue of whether the defence of undue influence will succeed if the spouses have had the benefit of independent legal advice. In *Hyldtoft v. Hyldtoft*,[58] Haines J. observed that there is no presumption of undue influence between spouses. In refusing, however, to give effect to an amendment to a marriage contract that gave the husband significantly more than originally provided, Haines J. found specific evidence of undue influence because the husband's repeated threats to leave the wife and force her to manage the business alone amounted to the improper use of unequal bargaining power, notwithstanding that the wife's lawyer had drafted the amendment. Undue influence may be defined as "the unconscientious use by one person of power possessed by [that person] over another in order to induce the other to do something."[59]

Where one party takes advantage of inequality in spousal bargaining power and this brings about an improvident bargain, the spousal agreement will be set aside by the court at the instance of the injured party but

---

55   *Grossmann v. Grossmann* (1982), 29 R.F.L. (2d) 300 (Ont. S.C.).
56   *Kristoff v. Kristoff,* (1987), 7 R.F.L. (3d) 284 (Ont. Dist. Ct.); see also *Smith v. Smith* (1977), 25 R.F.L. 133 (Ont. Co. Ct.); *Loy v. Loy,* [2007] O.J. No. 4274 (Sup. Ct.).
57   *Woods v. Woods* (1976), 22 R.F.L. 370 (Ont. H.C.J.).
58   (1991), 33 R.F.L. (3d) 99 (Ont. Gen. Div.).
59   *Berdette v. Berdette* (1991), 33 R.F.L. (3d) 113 at 125 (Ont. C.A.), citing *Brooks v. Alker* (1975), 22 R.F.L. 260 at 266 (Ont. S.C.), Henry J..

a spouse's failure to make a good bargain will not itself satisfy the legal requirements of unconscionability.[60]

Rescission of a separation agreement for duress requires proof of coercion by the use of or threat of the use of physical force or mental pressure. There is no need to establish a pre-existing relationship of dependence as in undue influence.[61]

Subsection 56(5) of the *Family Law Act* empowers the court to set aside all or part of a separation agreement in circumstances where one party has brought pressure to bear on the other by means of the former party's control over the latter's freedom to remarry within his or her religious faith. It is open to question how far, if at all, this subsection qualifies the doctrine of unconscionability previously established by judicial decisions.[62] An issue could arise as to the constitutional validity of subsection 56(5) in light of section 15 of the *Canadian Charter of Rights and Freedoms*. It has been suggested that any constitutional challenge of subsection 56(5) is likely to prove unsuccessful[63] but this opinion has been questioned.[64]

10) Rights of Donors of Gifts

Section 57 of the *Family Law Act* qualifies the common-law doctrine of privity of contract by providing a means of protecting the rights of a donor who has imposed conditions on specific gifts made to one or both parties, whereby any subsequent disposition or encumbrance of the property requires the donor's consent. Where a domestic contract prohibits the alienation of third-party gifts without the donor's consent, the parties to the domestic contract cannot subsequently circumvent the donor's interest. Should they attempt to do so, the donor has *locus standi* to enforce the terms of the gift or amend the provisions of the domestic contract.

---

60 *Rosen v. Rosen* (1994), 18 O.R. (3d) 641 (Ont. C.A.); *Loy v. Loy*, [2007] O.J. No. 4274 (Sup. Ct.).

61 *Mundinger v. Mundinger*, [1969] 1 O.R. 606 (C.A.), aff'd (1970), 14 D.L.R. (3d) 256n (S.C.C.).

62 See, generally, Michel G. Picher, "The Separation Agreement As an Unconscionable Transaction: A Study in Equitable Fraud" (1972) 7 R.F.L. 257.

63 See John T. Syrtash, "Removing Barriers to Religious Remarriage in Ontario: Rights and Remedies" with "Memorandum of Law" by J. Whyte (1987) 1 Can. Fam. L.Q. 309.

64 Edwin A. Flak, "'Get' Law May Promote Invalid Marriages" *The Lawyers Weekly* (7 May 1993) 5.

11) Contracts Made outside Ontario

When parties negotiate a contract, they may expressly choose the "proper law of the contract," which is the system of law that will determine their rights and liabilities under the contract. In the absence of a *bona fide* choice of law clause in the domestic contract, "the proper law of the contract" will be the system of law that has the most real and substantial connection with the contract.[65]

The "proper law of a contract" ordinarily governs its essential validity and effect. Pursuant to the provisions of paragraph 58(a) of the *Family Law Act*, however, the validity and enforceability of a domestic contract will be upheld, notwithstanding non-compliance with a foreign proper law, if the contract is valid and enforceable according to the laws applicable in Ontario. Pursuant to paragraph 58(b) of the Act, domestic contracts that are governed by a foreign proper law cannot circumvent the application of subsection 33(4) or of section 56 of the *Family Law Act*, which empower a court to set aside all or part of a domestic contract in designated circumstances.[66] Such contracts are also subject to limitation under paragraph 56(c) of the Act, whereby a provision in a marriage contract or cohabitation agreement that purports to regulate custody and access rights is unenforceable in Ontario.

12) Paternity Agreements

Section 59 of the *Family Law Act* regulates paternity agreements. It provides as follows:

> *Paternity Agreements*
>
> 59. (1) If a man and a woman who are not spouses enter into an agreement for,
> (a) the payment of the expenses of a child's prenatal care and birth;
> (b) support of a child; or
> (c) funeral expenses of the child or mother,
>
> on the application of a party, or a children's aid society, to the Provincial Court (Family Division) or the Unified Family Court, the court may incorporate the agreement in an order, and Part III (Support Obliga-

---

65   See *Vien v. Vien Estate* (1988), 12 R.F.L. (3d) 94 (Ont. C.A.).
66   See Sections B(1), B(7), and B(9), above in this chapter; and Section B(14), below in this chapter.

tions) applies to the order in the same manner as if it were an order made under that Part.

Absconding respondent

(2)   If an application is made under subsection (1) and a judge of the court is satisfied that the respondent is about to leave Ontario and that there are reasonable grounds to believe that the respondent intends to evade his or her responsibilities under the agreement, the judge may issue a warrant in the form prescribed by the rules of the court for the respondent's arrest.

Bail

(3)   Section 134 (interim release by justice of the peace) of the *Provincial Offences Act* [R.S.O. 1980, c. 400], applies, with necessary modifications, to an arrest under the warrant.

Capacity of minor

(4)   A minor has capacity to enter into an agreement under subsection (1) that is approved by the court, whether the approval is given before or after the minor enters into the agreement.

Application to existing agreements

(5)   This section applies to paternity agreements that were made before the day this Act comes into force.

13)   Application of Act to Pre-existing Contracts

Pursuant to subsection 60(1) of the *Family Law Act*, a marriage contract, cohabitation agreement, or separation agreement that was validly made before the *Family Law Act* came into force on 1 March 1986 is deemed to be a domestic contract for the purposes of the Act. Such a contract or agreement accordingly prevails over the rights conferred by the *Family Law Act*, except insofar as the Act provides otherwise.[67] Having regard to the fundamental differences between the *Family Law Act*[68] and its predecessor, the *Family Law Reform Act, 1978*,[69] subsection 70(3) of the *Family Law Act* expressly provides as follows:

---

67   S.O. 1986, c. 4, now R.S.O. 1990, c. F.3, s. 2(10).
68   *Ibid.*
69   S.O. 1978, c. 2.

Interpretation of Existing Contracts

70.(3) A separation agreement or marriage contract that is validly made before the 1st day of March, 1986 and that excludes a spouse's property from the application of sections 4 and 8 of the *Family Law Reform Act*,

(a) shall be deemed to exclude that property from the application of section 5 of this Act; and

(b) shall be read with necessary modifications.

Subsection 60(2) of the *Family Law Act* upholds the validity of prior domestic contracts entered into in contemplation of the Act, provided that such contracts would have been valid if entered into after the commencement of the *Family Law Act* on 1 March 1986.

Subsection 60(3) of the *Family Law Act* validates transfers of property that occurred before the commencement of the *Family Law Reform Act, 1978*.[70]

14) Setting Aside Provision of Domestic Contract Respecting Spousal and Child Support

Subsection 33(4) of the *Family Law Act* confers a limited discretionary jurisdiction on the court to set aside a provision for spousal or child support in a domestic contract or paternity agreement *and* to determine the right to and amount of support, if any, in an application under Part III of the Act, notwithstanding that the contract or agreement purports to exclude any such right. The discretionary jurisdiction of the court is exercisable pursuant to the subsection: (a) if the provision for support of the waiver of support results in unconscionable circumstances; (b) where the provision for support, if any, is in favour of a dependent spouse or child who qualifies for public assistance; or (c) if there is default in the payment of support under the contract or agreement at the time when an application is made pursuant to section 33 of the *Family Law Act*. It is submitted that paragraph 33(4)(a) of the Act may be invoked by either spouse, where the contract or agreement is unconscionable.[71] A distinction is to be drawn between the doctrine of unconscionability applicable under the general law of contract and section 56(4) of the *Family Law Act* and the notion of "unconscionable results" of a domestic contract under section

---

70   See *Cushman v. Cushman* (1979), 10 R.F.L. (2d) 305 (Ont. S.C.).

71   Compare *Porter v. Porter* (1979), 8 R.F.L. (2d) 349 (Ont. S.C.) and *Gergely v. Gergely* (1979), 11 R.F.L. (2d) 221 at 230 (Ont. S.C.).

33(4) of the *Family Law Act*. The former doctrine addresses whether the separation agreement was unconscionable at the time of its execution. Section 33(4) is directed at whether the agreement is unconscionable at the time when an order for spousal support is sought under section 33 of the *Family Law Act*.[72] A wife who seeks to set aside a marriage contract on the ground that her waiver of support rights results in unconscionability within the meaning of subsection 33(4) of the *Family Law Act* is not prevented from examining the husband's financial status by a covenant in the marriage contract whereby she undertook not to compel disclosure for the purpose of pursuing any legal proceeding against the husband.[73]

Subsection 33(4) of the *Family Law Act* is supplemented by subsection 56(1) of the Act, which empowers the court to disregard any provision respecting child support in a domestic contract, where such a course of action is justified in light of the best interests of the child. The provisions of the *Family Law Act* have no direct application to corollary claims for spousal or child support in divorce proceedings.[74]

15) Incorporation of Provisions of Domestic Contract in Order under *Family Law Act*

Subsection 2(9) of the *Family Law Act* expressly provides that a provision of a domestic contract respecting a matter that is dealt with by the Act may be incorporated in an order made pursuant to the Act.[75] Insofar as the domestic contract regulates matters pertaining to property rights or entitlements under Part I or possessory or dispositional rights in the matrimonial home under Part II of the *Family Law Act*, such incorporation may only be ordered by the Unified Family Court or the Ontario Court (General Division).[76] The provisions of a domestic contract respecting spousal or child support may, however, be incorporated in a judgment of the Ontario Court (Provincial Division).[77]

---

72   *Scheel v. Henkelman* (2001), 11 R.F.L. (5th) 376 (Ont. C.A.); *Desramaux v. Desramaux*, [2002] O.J. No. 3251 (C.A.); *Mongillo v. Mongillo*, [2007] O.J. No. 1705 (Sup. Ct.); *Loy v. Loy*, [2007] O.J. No. 4274 (Sup. Ct.).

73   *Lipson v. Lipson* (30 June 1986), Doc. 11969/86 (Ont. S.C. Master).

74   *McMeekin v. McMeekin* (1978), 21 O.R. (2d) 72 (S.C.).

75   *Cipens v. Cipens* (1987), 8 R.F.L. (3d) 325 (Ont. U.F.C.).

76   See definitions of "court" in ss. 4(1) and 17 of *Family Law Act*, R.S.O. 1990, c. F.3; compare s. 34(2); see also *Reference Re S. 6 of Family Relations Act*, [1982] 1 S.C.R. 62; *Lamb v. Lamb* (1985), 46 R.F.L. (2d) 1 (S.C.C.).

77   See definition of "court" in s. 1(1) of *Family Law Act*, R.S.O. 1990, c. F.3.

A litigant may not, however, bring an action to incorporate the terms of a domestic contract into a court order pursuant to subsection 2(a) of the *Family Law Act* in the absence of judicial jurisdiction to deal with the subject matter sought to be incorporated.[78]

16) Incorporation of Provisions of Domestic Contract in Divorce Judgment

The current *Divorce Act*, like its predecessor, the *Divorce Act, 1968*,[79] is silent on matters relating to property rights or entitlements and perhaps necessarily so by virtue of section 92(13) of the *Constitution Act, 1867*, which confers exclusive legislative jurisdiction over "Property and Civil Rights" on the provinces. The jurisdiction of a court to incorporate the provisions of a domestic contract in a divorce judgment is accordingly fettered. The court has a discretionary jurisdiction to incorporate the terms of a separation agreement, with or without amendment, in the divorce judgment, but this jurisdiction is limited to those corollary relief matters that fall within the ambit of the *Divorce Act*. The court may, therefore, incorporate in the divorce judgment the provisions of a separation agreement insofar as they relate to spousal and child support or custody and access, but there is no jurisdiction to include covenants respecting the ownership or distribution of real or personal property.[80] Where the provisions of a separation agreement are properly incorporated in a divorce judgment, the spouses must look to the judgment, which supersedes the separation agreement. The agreement continues to be operative and enforceable, however, insofar as its provisions cannot be legitimately incorporated in the divorce judgment, being matters falling outside the jurisdiction of the court under the *Divorce Act*.[81]

17) Filing, Enforcement, and Variation of Support Provisions of Domestic Contract

Subsection 35(1) of the *Family Law Act* empowers a party to a domestic contract or paternity agreement to file the contract or agreement with the

---

78   *Cipens v. Cipens* (1987), 8 R.F.L. (3d) 325 (Ont. U.F.C.).

79   S.C. 1967–68, c. 24.

80   *Spooner v. Spooner* (1979), 89 D.L.R. (3d) 685 (Sask. C.A.).

81   See *Oeming v. Oeming* (1985), 43 R.F.L. (2d) 175 (Alta. Q.B.); *Finnie v. Rae* (1977), 16 O.R. (2d) 54 (S.C.); *Campbell v. Campbell* (1976), 27 R.F.L. 40 (Sask. Q.B.); compare *Horne v. Roberts* (1971), 5 R.F.L. 15 (B.C.S.C.); see also *McLeod v. McLeod*, [2006] A.J. No. 1663 (Q.B.).

clerk of the Ontario Court (Provincial Division) or of the Unified Family Court with an accompanying affidavit stating that the contract or agreement is still in effect and has not been set aside or varied by court order or agreement. Upon such filing, any provision for spousal or child support in the domestic contract may be enforced in the same manner as a support order. The enforcement power conferred by paragraph 35(2)(a) is expressly confined to support rights and obligations and has no application to any provision of the domestic contract relating to such matters as property entitlements or possessory or dispositional rights in the matrimonial home. Subsection 35(1) and paragraph 35(2)(a), being discretionary, do not preclude a party to a domestic contract from pursuing a contractual remedy in the event of non-compliance with support provisions of a domestic contract. Any action arising from default under the domestic contract may fall subject, however, to the two-year limitation period imposed by subsection 50(2), as qualified by subsection 2(8), of the *Family Law Act*.

Pursuant to paragraph 35(2)(b) of the Act, the support provisions of a duly filed domestic contract may be varied under section 37 of the Act. But where a court order as to support has been disregarded and followed by a subsequent agreement, signed by the parties, the court's jurisdiction to vary the original order is exhausted. If under the agreement itself no right to support exists, the agreement cannot then be filed, enforced, or varied under section 35 of the Act.[82] The onus is on the party seeking to amend the agreement to show clear and compelling reasons to justify change.[83] An application under this section may be made by either party and the court may discharge, vary, or suspend the support provisions of the domestic contract, either prospectively or retroactively, with consequential remission of all or part of any arrears or interest thereon.

Paragraph 35(2)(b) also provides for an annual increase in the amount of support provided under a duly filed domestic contract or paternity agreement by means of a court-ordered indexation of the amount based on the Consumer Price Index. The jurisdiction of the court to index support payments and the definition of the indexing factor to be used are specifically defined in subsections 34(5) and 34(6) and in section 38 of the *Family Law Act*.[84]

---

82   See *Cipens v. Cipens* (1987), 8 R.F.L. (3d) 325 (Ont. U.F.C.).

83   *Ditullio v. Ditullio* (1974), 16 R.F.L. 148 (Ont. S.C.); *Woods v. Woods* (1976), 22 R.F.L. 370 (Ont. H.C.J.); *Nador v. Nador* (1977), 19 O.R. (2d) 728 (S.C.), aff'd (1978), 22 O.R. (2d) 685 (C.A.).

84   See *Davidson v. Davidson* (1987), 62 O.R. (2d) 145 (S.C.).

The provisions of subsection 33(4) of the Act, which fetter the jurisdiction of a court to interfere with the support provisions of a domestic contract or paternity agreement, continue to apply, however, where the contract or agreement is filed with the Ontario Court (Provincial Division) or the Unified Family Court.[85]

The statutory rights respecting the filing, enforcement, and variation of domestic contracts and paternity agreements under section 35 of the *Family Law Act* cannot be ousted by the terms of any domestic contract or paternity agreement.[86] The overall provisions of the domestic contract or paternity agreement will, nevertheless, remain significant in the exercise of the court's discretionary jurisdiction. The onus is on the party seeking to avoid a domestic contract to show why the court ought not to attach to it the weight ordinarily given any binding contract.

Domestic contracts or paternity agreements entered into before 1 March 1986 fall subject to the aforementioned statutory provisions, as do arrears that accrued before that date.[87]

18) Remedies for Breach of Domestic Contract

Traditional contractual remedies such as damages, rectification, rescission, specific performance, and injunctions provide means of enforcing the terms of a domestic contract. Declaratory relief is also available and the appropriate remedy may be specified in the domestic contract.[88]

In the absence of express provision to the contrary, the paragraphs of a separation agreement are deemed to be independent of each other. Therefore, a breach of one or more does not automatically entitle the aggrieved party to refuse to perform his or her own covenants and he or she may be limited to damages for the breach.[89] Only a major breach of the agreement will permit the innocent party to treat the separation agreement as repudiated and so refuse his or her own performance.[90] There is

---

85   *Family Law Act*, R.S.O. 1990, c. F.3, s. 35(3).

86   *Ibid.*, s. 35(4).

87   *Ibid.*, ss. 35(5) & 35(6).

88   *Griffith v. Griffith*, [2001] S.J. No. 411 (Q.B.); see also *Carwick v. Carwick* (1972), 6 R.F.L. 286 (Ont. C.A.).

89   *Graves v. Legg* (1854), 156 E.R. 304; *Quinn v. Quinn*, [1949] O.W.N. 614 (H.C.J.); *Marshall v. Marshall*, [1923] 4 D.L.R. 175 (Sask. C.A.); *Griffith v. Griffith*, [2001] S.J. No. 411 (Q.B.).

90   *T. v. T.* (1966), 55 D.L.R. (2d) 183 (Man. Q.B.); *Balcombe v. Balcombe*, [1908] P. 176; *Shoot v. Shoot*, [1957] O.W.N. 22 (C.A.).

no reason, however, why certain covenants cannot be made the essence of the separation agreement.[91]

19) Termination of Domestic Contracts

A domestic contract does not automatically terminate any more than any ordinary contract does. As it is always a matter of intent and construction, obligations that are to terminate on the happening of one or more events should be clearly indicated.

The effect that any reconciliation or resumption of cohabitation is to have on a separation agreement should be agreed on between the parties. In the absence of such a paragraph, the separation agreement will ordinarily terminate as of the date of reconciliation but the reconciliation does not affect rights that have already accrued or parts of the agreement that have already been executed.[92]

In the absence of a provision to the contrary, a separation agreement is not automatically terminated by divorce. Courts are usually more willing to imply a termination of the separation agreement upon remarriage of the dependent spouse than upon divorce.[93] However, this is not the case where there is a specific term in the separation agreement that defines its duration.[94]

Unless the domestic contract provides to the contrary, the death of either spouse will normally terminate the obligation to pay spousal support. An unconditional promise to pay, however, raises the implication that a deceased spouse's estate is bound by the agreement even though not expressly mentioned.[95]

---

91   *Marshall v. Marshall*, [1923] 4 D.L.R. 175 (Sask. C.A.).
92   *Negus v. Forster* (1882), 46 L.T. 675; *Christofferson v. Christofferson* (1924), 21 Alta. L.R. 13 (C.A.); *Bosley v. Bosley*, [1958] 2 All E.R. (C.A.); *Fraser v. Capital Trust Corp.*, [1938] O.W.N. 210 (H.C.J.); see also *Berman v. Berman* (1980), 12 R.F.L. (2d) 165 (Man. Q.B.); *McConnell v. McConnell* (1980), 12 R.F.L. (2d) 108 (Ont. H.C.J.); *Livermore v. Livermore* (1992), 43 R.F.L. (3d) 163 (Ont. Gen. Div.).
93   *Murdoch v. Ransom*, [1963] 2 O.R. 484 (S.C.); compare *Rust v. Rust*, [1972] 1 W.W.R. 491 (Alta. C.A.).
94   *Richards v. Richards* (1972), 6 R.F.L. 99 (Ont. H.C.J.), aff'd (1972), 7 R.F.L. 101 (Ont. C.A.).
95   *Baker, Re* (1923), 24 O.W.N. 44 (H.C.).

CHAPTER 5

FAMILY VIOLENCE[1]

A. INTRODUCTION

One of the best kept secrets of the twentieth century was the incidence of domestic violence in supposedly intact families. It is only in the last twenty years that family violence has been recognized as a serious social problem that encompasses the abuse of elderly parents or grandparents as well as spousal and child abuse. Until the early 1960s, when Dr. Kempe coined the phrase "battered child syndrome," physical injuries to children were almost invariably assumed to be caused by accidents inside or outside the home, such as falling off a bike, tumbling down the stairs, or getting into a scalding bath. Sexual abuse, ritual abuse, and incest were not widely publicized until the 1980s. Spousal violence was formerly regarded as a private affair and police were reluctant to interfere. The only form of spousal abuse that would guarantee police intervention and criminal prosecution was murder. But the exposure of spousal and child abuse in the courts, in the press, and on television has triggered public concern and the interest of provincial and federal governments in seeking solutions to these social and family crises.

---

1   See, generally, Department of Justice, Canada, Family Violence Initiative, online: www.phac-aspc.gc.ca/ncfv-cnivf/familyviolence/initiative_e.html.

B. ABUSE OF THE ELDERLY

A sadly neglected aspect of abuse that has come to the forefront in the 1990s is abuse of the elderly.[2] Although such abuse has been found in situations involving institutional care, it frequently involves younger family members, often children or grandchildren.

The most common abuse of the elderly is financial abuse, which is often accompanied by emotional abuse. The retirement savings of an elderly parent or grandparent may be squandered by children or grandchildren. Monthly pension or disability cheques may be withheld. Children and grandchildren may "jump the gun" on prospective inheritances without any thought for the impact of such conduct on the elderly parent or grandparent. Theft of money or possessions represents more than 60 percent of all cases of abuse of the elderly. In some instances, resistance by the elderly person may result in physical abuse.

It has been estimated that at least 4 percent and perhaps as many as 15 percent of the elderly in Canada are abused financially, emotionally, or physically by their children, grandchildren, spouses, or caregivers. Health and Welfare Canada has estimated that more than 315,000 Canadians over sixty-five years of age are victims of abuse. However, the incidence of abuse is likely to be much higher because of the ease with which it can be concealed by family members.

The characteristics of the abused victim are similar to those identified with respect to the "battered wife syndrome." Victims of elder abuse feel helpless and sense that they have no place to go in order to avoid the abuse. They often have low self-esteem, are dependent on the abuser, and lack the physical, emotional, and often financial ability to withdraw from the abusive environment. They are fearful of being abandoned or sent to an institution; they are ignorant of their legal rights; and they are often isolated or unable to communicate.

Abuse of the elderly is not a new social problem but its incidence is increasing with the ageing of the Canadian population. In 1991, 11.6 percent of the population of Canada was over sixty-five years of age. By 2031, it will be more than 22 percent. Although federal and provincial governments, universities, and social agencies are beginning to show some in-

---

2   See, generally, P. Lynn McDonald, Joseph P. Hornick *et al.*, *Elder Abuse and Neglect in Canada* (Toronto: Butterworths, 1991). See also Manitoba Law Reform Commission, Report No. 103, *Adult Protection and Elder Abuse* (Winnipeg: The Commission, December 1999).

terest in defining the boundaries and potential solutions to the societal problem of abuse of the elderly, no concerted effort has yet been undertaken to come to grips with it. There is evidence, however, of increased awareness of the need for change. A parliamentary study on abuse of the elderly in 1993[3] recommended that federal funding should be available to provide shelters for elderly victims of abuse.[4] It also recommended that the federal government should work with organizations responsible for professional standards and for the education of physicians, nurses, social workers, bankers, and lawyers so that abuse of the elderly could be identified and dealt with. It further recommended that a large-scale federal study should be undertaken to ascertain the scope of the problem and the means of dealing with it.

One project in the mid-1990s that was funded by the federal government sought to develop an education program and a police response protocol to deal with abuse of the elderly. This project was a joint venture of the Nepean Police and the Queensway Carleton Hospital. Its objectives were as follows:

(i)   to sensitize police officers to the problem of elder abuse;

(ii) to develop a protocol for police intervention;

(iii) to devise policies and procedures that will provide more constructive responses from the criminal justice system;

(iv) to develop and monitor a multidisciplinary and collaborative consultation and case review service between the police and social agencies;

(v)   to develop educational programs for police officers to deal with the three Rs of intervention — namely, Recognition, Responsibility, and Response;

(vi) to recognize the special needs of racial minorities, the aboriginal communities, different linguistic groups, and persons with disabilities; and

(vii) to standardize terminology.

Much more is needed! Social attitudes towards the elderly must undergo a radical shift. We must cease to question their competence sim-

---

3   Canada, House of Commons Standing Committee on Health and Welfare, Social Affairs, Seniors and the Status of Women, *Breaking the Silence on the Abuse of Older Canadians: Everyone's Concern* (Ottawa: The Committee, June 1993).

4   The first seniors' shelter in Canada was opened in east-end Montreal in 1992: *Ottawa Citizen* (12 August 1994) B7.

ply because they are old. Institutionalized prejudice against the elderly is amply demonstrated in three judgments of the Supreme Court of Canada wherein mandatory retirement at the age of sixty-five was held to be perfectly acceptable, regardless of the wishes or ability of the affected parties.[5] And this notwithstanding the *Canadian Charter of Rights and Freedoms*!

C. NATURE OF SPOUSAL ABUSE[6]

Although the expression "spousal abuse" has been traditionally confined to persons who are married, it is also frequently used to refer to conduct between divorced spouses or persons living in a cohabitational relationship. "Spousal abuse" takes various forms but all involve domination or the improper exercise of power or control over a spouse, divorced spouse, or quasi-marital partner. Spousal abuse may involve physical, sexual, psychological, or economic oppression. It is not usually an isolated event; it is a systematic course of conduct over a sustained period of time.

Physical abuse involves the application of force. It includes beating, slapping, punching, kicking, choking, stabbing, shooting, and throwing objects at the victim. Even when physical assaults are intermittent or isolated, they have a long-term impact because the threat of repetition is never far from the victim's mind. Domination established through a single act of violence often produces long-term emotional abuse that is reinforced by subsequent threats, isolation, degradation, or economic control.

Spousal homicide accounts for 15 percent of all homicide deaths in Canada. Four times as many women as men are killed by their spouses or partners.

Sexual abuse is usually an aspect of physical abuse that involves the perpetration of sexual acts against the will of a spouse and may include "marital rape." The fact that a couple is married or living together does not entitle either of them to insist that their partner engage in any form of sexual activity. Marital rape or any other forced sexual activity is an

---

5   *McKinney v. University of Guelph*, [1990] 3 S.C.R. 229; see also *Stoffman v. Vancouver General Hospital*, [1990] 3 S.C.R. 483; *Douglas/Kwantlen Faculty Association v. Douglas College*, [1990] 3 S.C.R. 570.

6   For an excellent overview of spousal abuse, see "A Special Report — Spousal Abuse: The Shocking Truth" *Toronto Star* (9–16 March 1996); "A Special Report — Spousal Abuse: The Vicious Cycle" *Toronto Star* (3 November 1996).

offence under the *Criminal Code* of Canada. In 1983, the criminal offence of "rape" was replaced by the offence of sexual assault, which can be committed by a spouse or partner as well as by a stranger.

Emotional or psychological abuse most frequently arises from verbal assaults, such as threats or disparaging comments directed towards a spouse. Emotional abuse often accompanies physical or sexual abuse, but can exist in the absence of physical or sexual abuse. Emotional abuse signifies that one party demeans, belittles, degrades, or threatens the other party to such a degree that the victim's psychological well-being is in jeopardy. Economic abuse arises from an improper exercise of control over personal or household finances by one spouse to the exclusion and deprivation of the other.

Spousal abuse is not confined to any age group or socio-economic class. Many victims of spousal abuse suffer in silence. Consequently, statistics on spousal abuse are notoriously speculative. A frequently cited statistic is that one in ten Canadian women are victims of abuse by their spouse or male partner. In a national survey of 12,300 women, released by Statistics Canada in November 1993, it was found that 51 percent of women had been victims of at least one incident of physical or sexual assault since the age of sixteen. The survey further indicated that 25 percent of these women had been victimized by their marital partner. A more subsequent national survey suggests that men are just as likely as women to be the victims of spousal abuse. In a random telephone survey of 26,000 Canadians conducted by Statistics Canada in 1999, 8 percent of women and 7 percent of men claimed to have been victims of violence from their spouses or partners at least once in the preceding five years. Sixty percent of those reporting violence had been victimized more than once. The survey revealed that women living in violent relationships were five times more likely than men to have feared for their life and the same ratio was found with respect to the need for subsequent medical attention. However, the survey also found that men are more likely than women to be slapped, kicked, or have something thrown at them. Rates of domestic violence against women ranged from 12 percent in Prince Edward Island to 4 percent in Newfoundland; rates for men ranged from 9 percent in Alberta to 5 percent in Newfoundland and Ontario.[7] More recent data

7   *Ottawa Citizen* (26 July 2000) A8. And see *Family Violence in Canada: A Statistical Profile*, 2000, at Statistics Canada, online: www.statcan.ca/english/freepub/85-224-XIE/0000085-224-XIE.pdf. And see Statistics Canada, "Violence against Women: Statistical Trends" *The Daily* (2 October 2006).

published by Statistics Canada assert that 7 percent of women and 6 percent of men encountered spousal violence during the five years up to and including 2004.[8] In a ground-breaking decision, the Alberta Human Rights Commission in June, 2000 ruled that family violence brochures published by an Edmonton counselling centre discriminated against men by perpetuating the myth that only men are abusive in relationships.[9]

Opinions differ on whether spousal abuse is increasing or whether there is simply an increase in the number of reported incidents. Opinions also differ on the causes and appropriate steps to be taken to deter such behaviour.

Dr. Lenore Walker, a clinical psychologist, has observed that physical abuse may involve a cycle or pattern of behaviour that is divided into three phases, namely, (i) a tension-building phase; (ii) the acute battering incident; and (iii) a loving contrition phase.[10] During the first phase, there is a gradual escalation of tension manifested by verbal abuse and less extreme acts of physical abuse. The victim tries to placate the abuser and avoid confrontation. The tension continues to mount until the atmosphere becomes explosive and an acute battering incident occurs. This is characterized by the batterer unleashing a torrent of verbal and physical abuse that leaves the victim severely shaken and injured. The acute battering incident is followed by a reduction in tension and the batterer's expression of remorse, promises to change, and the showering of gifts or affection on the victim. This third phase provides positive reinforcement for the victim to remain in the relationship. In due course, the cycle repeats itself, again and again. With the passage of time, things progress from bad to worse, with the most significant differences being that the tension-building phase and the loving contrition phase become shorter in duration and the frequency and degree of violence in the explosion or acute battering phase increase.

---

8   Statistics Canada, "Family Violence in Canada: A Statistical Profile" *The Daily* (14 July 2005). See also Donald G. Dutton, *Rethinking Domestic Violence* (Vancouver: U.B.C. Press, 2006).

9   *National Post*, online (Monday, 19 June 2000).

10   Lenore E. Walker, *The Battered Woman Syndrome* (New York: Springer, 1984) at 95–96, cited in *R. v. Lavallee*, [1990] 1 S.C.R. 852. For insight into five basic types of interparental violence and corresponding patterns in parent-child relationships, see Janet R. Johnston & Linda E.G. Campbell, "Parent-Child Relationships in Domestic Violence Families Disputing Custody" (July 1993) 31:3 Family and Conciliation Courts Review 282–98.

D. SOCIAL AND LEGAL RESPONSES TO SPOUSAL ABUSE

Domestic violence, and especially spousal abuse, has triggered various social and legal responses during the past twenty years. Although community agencies and resources are limited, they provide services and facilities that were virtually non-existent twenty years ago. Spousal assault "hotlines" and shelters for battered wives are now found in most Canadian urban centres. The medical and legal professions, as well as the police, are more responsive to problems engendered by spousal abuse than they were hitherto.

1) Shelters and Transition Houses

There are approximately 550 women's emergency shelters and transition houses in Canada that provide temporary shelter and counselling to battered women. They are run by a combination of full-time and part-time staff together with volunteers. Their location is closely guarded for the purpose of ensuring the safety of the residents, but relevant telephone numbers are listed in the front of the telephone directory.

According to a recent report from Statistics Canada,[11] there were 3,274 women and 2,835 children in emergency shelters or transition houses on 14 April 2004. Eighty-two percent of the women were escaping abuse; the remainder were there for other reasons such as housing, addiction, or mental health problems. Forty percent of them had been to the facility once in the previous year; 38 percent had been there two to four times; and about 10 percent had been there five or more times during the preceding year. The total number of admissions over the one-year period from 2003 to 2004 was 95,326, of whom 58,486 were women and 36,840 were children. Two-thirds of the women went to shelters to escape the abuse of a current spouse or common-law partner and ten to escape an abusive ex-spouse or ex-partner.

> Women's shelters provide several services for abused women. First and foremost, they provide temporary free shelter and counselling that empowers victims of abuse to regain self-esteem and reassert control over their own lives. They do not provide permanent accommodation

---

11 Statistics Canada, "Shelters for Abused Women" *The Daily* (15 June 2005), a report based on Juristat, "Canada's Shelters for Abused Women, 2003/04" (using data from a biennial Transition Home Survey).

for their residents. Most shelters will not allow their occupants to stay more than six months. During their stay, residents are expected to plan longer term solutions to their problems. In addition to shelter, they provide (i) hotline telephone services and crisis counselling; (ii) individual counselling and support groups for battered women; (iii) information and referral assistance with respect to medical, legal, housing, welfare assistance, job training and educational programs; (iv) food, clothing, and transportation; and (v) counselling to help children deal with the violence.

For the minority of men who are victims of spousal abuse, there are few comparable resources.

2) Counselling Services

Victims of spousal abuse use a variety of counselling services in urban communities. Family Service Agencies provide counselling services for all dysfunctional families but specialized counselling services are also available to abused women. Governmental funding of specialized services, such as sexual assault centres, distress centres, alcohol and drug abuse treatment facilities, transition houses, and information services for abused women, is often short-term and subject to budgetary cutbacks. Furthermore, few facilities exist in rural communities or to serve special ethnic or cultural groups or recent immigrants.

Counselling for abused women is not confined to dealing with their emotional needs. Housing and financial needs as well as medical and legal needs must also be met. Above all, the future safety of victims of abuse must be assured to the fullest extent possible.

Counselling services are not always limited to the victims of abuse. Where domestic violence is linked to alcohol or drug abuse, many communities offer counselling for the abuser. In addition, there are a few men's self-help groups for the perpetrators of domestic violence. These groups engage in counselling or therapy under the guidance of a professionally qualified group leader. Their objective is to enable abusers to take responsibility for their misconduct and develop alternatives to violence in dealing with interpersonal relationships. Although there has been some success with individual and group therapy for abusers, there are probably no more than thirty-five self-help groups for abusers in all of Canada.

3) Legal Responses to Spousal Abuse

The law provides a veritable arsenal of weapons to deal with problems generated by spousal abuse. How effective they are is open to question. The following are some reasons the Ontario Women's Directorate gives as explanations for the reluctance of abused women to use the legal system:

(i)   fear of retaliation or revenge instilled in the victim by threats made over an extended period of time;

(ii) fear that the police and the courts will not believe that the abuse has occurred, will blame the victim for the abuse, or will take no action to protect the victim and her children;

(iii) desire to keep the family together;

(iv) fear of living in poverty on social assistance after a family breakdown;

(v)   lack of information regarding community services such as counselling, shelters, the Children's Aid Society, victim crisis units, and legal rights after marriage breakdown; and

(vi) for immigrant women, a fear that they or their partners will be deported, and mistrust of the police.

Battered women have traditionally encountered two primary obstacles to invoking legal remedies. First, they often have no money to hire a lawyer and must obtain a legal aid certificate in order to pursue civil proceedings, including matrimonial relief. Legal aid pays notoriously low hourly rates for civil proceedings, regardless of the province involved, and therefore attracts junior lawyers in an area where experience and excellent judgment are vital. Second, criminal prosecutions necessitate the intervention of the police, some of whom still perceive domestic violence as a private affair that should be resolved by the spouses rather than as a crime in which the public has an overriding interest. Sustained police intervention in domestic violence may also be deterred by their realization that a criminal conviction may be difficult to secure, especially if the victim refuses to testify against the perpetrator. Although police have traditionally been disinclined to use the criminal process as a means of controlling or deterring spousal assaults except in cases of severe bodily injury or death, the Solicitor General of Ontario has chartered a new course of action for police in that province by issuing policy directives to provincial police forces stipulating that, in the absence of exceptional circumstances, charges should be laid and prosecutions pursued regardless of the wishes of the victim. At the same time, the training of police has been improved by their introduction to new techniques of intervention in domestic disputes. Improving the response of the criminal justice system for abused women requires changes that include the following:

(i)   continuing training for everyone involved;
(ii)   women's advocacy services;
(iii) a legal clinic for women;
(iv)   beefed-up victim crisis units in the police service, and victim/witness assistance programs in the courts;
(v)   emphasis on front-end police investigation to reduce court costs by providing more guilty pleas and by shifting resources from police court activity to police investigations;
(vi)   specialized prosecutors and courts;
(vii) making the court process more accessible and supportive of complainants;
(viii) preventing defence lawyers from intimidating victim/witnesses;
(ix)   maintaining a zero-tolerance policy for breach of restraining orders, conditions of bail, or probation;
(x)   insisting on mandatory counselling services for men who batter; and
(xi)   all sectors of the criminal justice system working together to send a clear message to abusers that violence against women is a crime and will not be tolerated.

4) Criminal Law

a) *Criminal Code* Offences

A person who commits a spousal assault may be charged with one or more of several offences under the *Criminal Code* of Canada. The specific offences vary according to the type of conduct and the gravity of the injuries sustained.

Any person who intentionally applies force to another person, or attempts or threatens to do so, commits an "assault" under section 265 of the *Criminal Code* of Canada. This section applies to all forms of assault, including sexual assault. It carries a maximum penalty of five years' imprisonment. If the person committing an assault uses a weapon or causes bodily injury to the victim that is not transient in nature, this constitutes the separate offence of "assault with a weapon or assault causing bodily harm" under section 267 of the *Criminal Code*, which carries a maximum penalty of ten years' imprisonment. An even heavier penalty is imposed by section 268 of the *Criminal Code* for "aggravated assault."

This offence is committed by any person who "wounds, maims, disfigures or endangers the life of the complainant." It carries a maximum penalty of fourteen years' imprisonment. Sexual assaults are regulated by additional provisions of the *Criminal Code*. Section 271 imposes a maximum penalty of ten years' imprisonment for sexual assault. Section 272 regulates sexual assaults with a weapon, sexual assaults induced by threats to a third party, and sexual assaults causing bodily harm. These offences carry a maximum penalty of fourteen years' imprisonment. Section 273 defines the offence of "aggravated sexual assault," which involves wounding, maiming, disfiguring, or endangering the life of the victim. This offence is punishable by a maximum term of imprisonment for life. With respect to the evidence required to sustain a conviction for physical or sexual assault, corroboration is not required. Section 278 of the *Criminal Code* specifically provides that a husband or wife may be charged with an offence under sections 271, 272, or 273 of the *Criminal Code*, whether or not the spouses were living together at the time of the conduct complained of. The former notion that marriage necessarily implied consent to sexual intercourse between the spouses has been abandoned. Spouses may, of course, be charged with other offences under the *Criminal Code*, including murder.

In 1993, the *Criminal Code* was amended to include the new offence of criminal harassment, also known as "stalking," which offers some measure of protection to separated and divorced spouses. Section 264 of the *Criminal Code* imposes a maximum penalty of five years' imprisonment on any person who knowingly or recklessly harasses another person by engaging in conduct causing that person to reasonably fear for his or her own safety or the safety of anyone known to that person. The section identifies four kinds of conduct that will sustain a conviction, namely,

- repeatedly following, from place to place, the other person or anyone known to him or her;
- repeatedly communicating with, either directly or indirectly, the other person or anyone known to him or her;
- besetting or watching the dwelling-house or place where the other person, or anyone known to him or her, resides, works, carries on business, or happens to be; or
- engaging in threatening conduct directed at the other person or any member of his or her family.

There are three elements to the crime of criminal harassment:

(i) The accused must be found to have engaged in one or more of the types of conduct prescribed.

(ii) It must be established that, while engaging in one of the types of prohibited conduct, the accused either intended to harass the complainant, or was reckless as to whether or not his conduct would harass the complainant. The court may infer intent to recklessness if it finds that the accused had no legitimate purpose for engaging in the conduct complained of.

(iii) It must be established that the complainant had reasonable fears for her safety or the safety of anyone known to her. This includes both physical and psychological safety.

The court must apply an objective standard when determining whether or not the complainant reasonably feared for his or her safety or the safety of another person. In making this objective determination, the court must look at all of the circumstances, including the gender of the complainant and the history of the circumstances surrounding the relationship with the accused.

The aforementioned provisions of the *Criminal Code* are triggered by the commission of an offence. Preventative justice is also available, however, under section 810 of the *Criminal Code.* This section empowers a Provincial Court judge or a justice of the peace to require a person to enter into a recognizance or financial bond to keep the peace where there is a reasonable apprehension that he or she will cause personal injury to a spouse or child or damage their property. The recognizance can be required for any period not exceeding twelve months. It may contain such conditions as the court considers desirable for securing good behaviour. Typical conditions preclude access to the complainant's residence, place of employment, or to any school attended by the children, and restrictions or prohibitions concerning telephone or written communications. A person who refuses to enter in a recognizance or who breaches a recognizance is guilty of an offence under sections 810 and 811 of the *Criminal Code.*

The threat of criminal prosecution has not been an unqualified success in deterring spousal assaults. Convictions are difficult to secure when wives refuse to testify against their husbands, against whom charges have been laid. Some wives fear further violence or feel financially threatened by the prospect that criminal prosecution may result in a conviction. Other victims wish to put the past behind them rather than relive it in the witness box. Still others have reconciled with the abuser, notwithstanding that the cycle of abuse may be indicative of future risk. Ironically, wives who refuse to testify against their husbands may themselves be charged with the offence of obstructing justice under section 139 of the *Criminal Code*. In addition to the difficulties encountered in securing convictions for spousal assaults, whether physical or sexual, the sentencing practices of some courts evoke strong criticism. Some judges are inclined to extol the virtues of preserving the marriage by imposing a lenient sentence. Absolute and conditional discharges are too frequently the outcome of criminal prosecutions for spousal assault. Although opinions may differ on whether imprisonment is an appropriate sanction, one alternative that has been effective in less heinous offences is treatment as a condition of probation. This joint application of a carrot-and-stick approach to spousal abusers may offer a constructive response to the complex dynamics of spousal assault. There is, however, a public interest that must also be considered in criminal prosecutions for spousal abuse. The Alberta Court of Appeal has emphasized the significance of criminal sanctions as a general and individual deterrent to spousal abuse. Pleas by the abused victim that a lengthy sentence of imprisonment will produce further victimization, whether economically or otherwise, may have to yield to the pressing need for an effective deterrent.[12] In a sentencing study released in 2004, it was found that family members convicted of violent crimes against spouses, children, and seniors are less likely to receive a prison sentence than other violent offenders. According to police and court records from 1997 to 2002, judges handed down prison sentences in 19 percent of convictions for spousal violence. The comparable figure for non-spousal violence convictions was 29 percent. The only exception occurred with respect to the offence of criminal harassment where one-third of the spouses received a prison term compared with one-quarter of non-spousal offenders.[13] Family members convicted of physical violence against their children also received less harsh sentences than non-family members, except with respect to convictions for sexual abuse when the converse was true.

Many people find it incomprehensible that victims of spousal abuse do not withdraw from the threatening environment. Why do they stay? This issue attracted the attention of the Supreme Court of Canada in a

---

12   *R. v. Brown* (1992), 13 C.R. (4th) 346 (Alta. C.A.); *R. v. Bell*, [1992] A.J. No. 495 (C.A.), discussed in *The Lawyers Weekly* (3 July 1992) 17.

13   Statistics Canada, "Family Violence in Canada: A Statistical Profile" *The Daily* (6 July 2004), online: www.statcan.ca/english/freepub/85-224-XIE/85-224-XIE2004000.pdf.

celebrated case where a victim of abuse had been charged with murdering her abusive common-law husband. In acquitting the accused on the ground of self-defence, the Supreme Court of Canada acknowledged the need for expert evidence to negate popular myths surrounding spousal abuse. Madam Justice Wilson summarized the principles upon which expert evidence is properly admitted in the following observations:

1. Expert testimony is admissible to assist the fact-finder in drawing inferences in areas where the expert has relevant knowledge or experience beyond that of the lay person.

2. It is difficult for the lay person to comprehend the battered wife syndrome. It is commonly thought that battered women are not really beaten as badly as they claim, otherwise they would have left the relationship. Alternatively, some believe that women enjoy being beaten, that they have a masochistic strain in them. Each of these stereotypes may adversely affect consideration of a battered woman's claim to have acted in self-defence in killing her mate.

3. Expert evidence can assist the jury in dispelling these myths.

4. Expert testimony relating to the ability of an accused to perceive danger from her mate may go to the issue of whether she "reasonably apprehended" death or grievous bodily harm on a particular occasion.

5. Expert testimony pertaining to why an accused remained in the battering relationship may be relevant in assessing the nature and extent of the alleged abuse.

6. By providing an explanation as to why an accused did not flee when she perceived her life to be in danger, expert testimony may also assist the jury in assessing the reasonableness of her belief that killing her batterer was the only way to save her own life.

Quite apart from Dr. Shane's testimony there was ample evidence on which the trial judge could conclude that the appellant was battered repeatedly and brutally by Kevin Rust over the course of their relationship. The fact that she may have exhibited aggressive behaviour on occasion or tried (unsuccessfully) to leave does not detract from a finding of systematic and relentless abuse. In my view, the trial judge did not err in admitting Dr. Shane's expert testimony in order to assist the jury in determining whether the appellant had a reasonable apprehension of death or grievous bodily harm and believed on reasonable grounds that she had no alternative but to shoot Kevin Rust on the night in question.

Obviously the fact that the appellant was a battered woman does not entitle her to an acquittal. Battered women may well kill their partners other than in self-defence. The focus is not on who the woman is, but on what she did. ...

Ultimately, it is up to the jury to decide whether, in fact, the accused's perceptions and actions were reasonable. Expert evidence does not and cannot usurp that function of the jury. The jury is not compelled to accept the opinions proffered by the expert about the effects of battering on the mental state of victims generally or on the mental state of the accused in particular. But fairness and the integrity of the trial process demand that the jury have the opportunity to hear them.[14]

The expert evidence adduced before the Supreme Court of Canada on the "battered wife syndrome" demonstrated that a woman who lives in a battering relationship is paralyzed by the tyranny of the abuser. She is psychologically incapable of withdrawing from the abusive relationship regardless of her economic ability to do so. She loses her sense of self-worth and becomes helpless. Some wives find the strength to leave. Others may strike back in self-defence, but few can hope to resist the more powerful aggressor.

b) Specialized Criminal Courts[15]

In Winnipeg, Manitoba, a provincial criminal court has been established since 1990 to deal exclusively with family violence, which encompasses elder, spousal, and child abuse. Specialized Crown Attorneys prosecute these cases. There is a victim assistance service called the Women's Advocacy Program. There is also a Family Violence Unit within the probation services that provides individual assessments, counselling, and long-term treatment for offenders.

Independent evaluation of this project suggests that it provides a more efficient legal process and a more sensitive legal service for victims of family violence. It has resulted in an increase in the number of criminal charges laid and an increase in the conviction rates.

Since 1997, Ontario has established new domestic violence courts in Ottawa, London, Hamilton, North Bay, Oshawa, and North York.

---

14 *R. v. Lavallee*, [1990] 1 S.C.R. 852 at 889–91.
15 See E. Jane Ursel, "The Family Violence Court of Winnipeg" (1992) 21 Man. L.J. 100.

c) Provincial Statutory Developments

Several provinces have enacted legislation to protect victims of family violence. For example, in 1994 the *Victims of Domestic Violence Act* was enacted in Saskatchewan. It confers broad powers on justices of the peace, police officers, and social workers to intervene in cases of domestic violence. Justices of the peace are empowered to grant emergency orders at any time during the day or night and such orders may be granted over the telephone. These intervention orders can grant exclusive possession of the family home to alleged victims, can direct the police to remove the alleged abuser from the home, and can restrain the alleged abuser from contacting the victim. Police officers can also obtain entry warrants to allow them to enter a home and assist a suspected victim even when no complaint has been laid. The Act also empowers judges of the Court of Queen's Bench to issue assistance orders to compel abusers to pay compensation to their victims and to give victims temporary possession of personal property.

Provincial legislation regulating domestic violence has withstood constitutional challenge. Thus, in *Baril v. Obelnicki*,[16] it was held that the pith and substance of the *Domestic Violence and Stalking Prevention, Protection and Compensation Act*[17] is in the nature of crime prevention and thus falls within the provincial legislative domain. Protection orders granted pursuant to the Act are in the nature of preventive justice, similar to orders historically granted by magistrates and justices of the peace, and therefore do not violate section 96 of the *Constitution Act, 1867*. Although the provincial statute infringes the respondent's freedom of expression in contravention of section 2(b) of the *Canadian Charter of Rights and Freedoms*, such infringement is justified under section 1 of the *Charter*. An order limiting the respondent's freedom of movement in relation to the applicant so as to prevent contact and end stalking behaviour constitutes an infringement of the respondent's liberty under section 7 of the *Charter*. However, such infringement accords with the principles of fundamental justice so long as the respondent is provided a fair trial with fair procedures, the nature of those procedures being determined within the context of the Act's purpose and objectives. The statutory provisions allowing for a protection order to be granted without notice, and for the transcribed evidence from the without notice hearing to be used at the review hearing, are in accord with the principles of fundamental

---

16   2007 MBCA 40, [2007] M.J. No. 110 (C.A.).

17   C.C.S.M. c. D93.

justice. However, section 12(2) of the Act is problematic in that it places the burden of proof on the respondent rather than the applicant by requiring the respondent "to demonstrate, on the balance of probabilities, that the protection order should be set aside." Rather than strike it down as the motion court judge had done, the Manitoba Court of Appeal read the provision down to constitute an evidentiary burden. Instead of being required to show that the without notice order was granted in error, the respondent need only show, on a balance of probabilities, that there is an issue arising from the without notice hearing that warrants the order being set aside on the basis of an absence of full disclosure or based on the weight of all the evidence adduced at both the without notice and review hearings. This would accord with the principles of fundamental justice.

5) Matrimonial Proceedings

With the exception of divorce proceedings, which may include corollary issues relating to support and custody, matrimonial relief available to abused spouses is regulated by provincial laws. Issues of spousal and child support and of custody and access are governed by the federal *Divorce Act* if they arise on divorce. If they arise independently of divorce, they are governed by provincial statute.

a) *Divorce Act*

Spousal abuse, whether physical, sexual, psychological, or economic, may constitute mental or physical cruelty of such a kind as to render matrimonial cohabitation intolerable. In that event, the victim of abuse may petition the courts for divorce on the basis that such conduct manifests a permanent breakdown of the marriage. A husband's violent attack on his wife on a single occasion may justify a finding of physical cruelty that will warrant the granting of a divorce.[18] In the ordinary course of events, however, cruelty involves a course of conduct over a period of time. The cumulative effect of such conduct on the petitioner is the critical test of cruelty.[19] Verbal abuse may constitute "mental cruelty" for the purpose of divorce,[20] as may also a husband's domineering, unloving, and inconsiderate attitude to his wife in the home and his belittling her in public.[21]

---

18   *Aucoin v. Aucoin* (1976), 28 R.F.L. 43 (N.S.C.A.).
19   *Pongor v. Pongor* (1976), 27 R.F.L. 109 (Ont. C.A).
20   *Greggain v. Hunter* (1984), 31 Sask. R. 311 (U.F.C.).
21   *Ratcliffe v. Ratcliffe* (1977), 27 R.F.L. 227 (B.C.S.C.); *Nichols v. Nichols* (1968), 1 N.S.R. (1965–69) 503 (T.D.).

Excessive or improper sexual demands on a spouse,[22] or the withholding of necessary financial support,[23] may also constitute "mental cruelty" within the meaning of federal divorce legislation. The following quotation aptly summarizes the law:

> When the acts of cruelty relied upon take the form of abuse, quarrels, nagging, selfishness, etc. there is a greater danger of their being categorized as examples of incompatibility rather than of cruelty. However, where one spouse insists on totally dominating the other or deprives the other of his company or ridicules and belittles his spouse or is selfish and ignores his obligations of support he or she may be found guilty of cruelty. Similarly, threats of physical violence towards the petitioner, her children or towards the respondent himself, false accusations of theft, of non-support or of infidelity, vulgar abuse, constant nagging, and unseemly "scenes" before others, can amount to cruelty.[24]

In the final analysis, each case of alleged cruelty must be decided on its own facts.

b) Spousal and Child Support

An abused spouse who has separated from the abuser may institute legal proceedings for spousal and child support. These claims can be brought as part of a divorce petition, or independently under provincial or territorial legislation. If an abused wife is unable to meet her own financial needs, and those of any children, she may seek a court order for spousal and child support. Entitlement to spousal support under provincial or territorial legislation will depend on whether she satisfies the statutory definition of "spouse." Married people do. Some "common-law spouses" may do so; other "common-law spouses" may not. It depends on the express provisions of the statute in the particular province or territory wherein the legal proceedings are instituted. If the statutory definition of "spouse" is met, spousal support orders will usually be granted or denied on the basis of the applicant's needs and the ability of the other spouse to pay. In divorce proceedings, only married persons or already divorced spouses are eligible to bring claims for "spousal" support.

---

22   *Rankin v. Rankin* (1970), 13 D.L.R. (3d) 630 (B.C.S.C.); *M. v. M.* (1971), 3 R.F.L. 350 (Ont. C.A.); *M. v. M.* (1975), 16 R.F.L. 291 (N.B.C.A.).

23   *Brewer v. Brewer* (1978), 21 N.B.R. (2d) 154 (Q.B.); *Gollins v. Gollins*, [1963] 2 All E.R. 966 (H.L.).

24   *Brewer v. Brewer* (1978), 21 N.B.R. (2d) 154 at 157 (Q.B.), Stevenson J., citing *Power on Divorce*, 3d ed. (Toronto: Carswell, 1976–) at 64–65.

Although claims for spousal and child support may be triggered by spousal abuse that brings matrimonial cohabitation to an end, courts cannot punish the abusing spouse by increasing the amount of support payable to a dependent spouse or child. Subsection 15.2(5) of the *Divorce Act* expressly stipulates that "the court shall not take into consideration any misconduct of a spouse in relation to the marriage" in making an order for spousal or child support. Similar, though not identical provisions, can be found in many provincial and territorial statutes that regulate spousal and child support proceedings arising independently of divorce. Spousal and child support are usually based on need and are not intended to punish spousal misconduct. If, however, spousal abuse impairs the ability of a dependent spouse to achieve financial self-sufficiency, the need thereby arising can be met by an order for a reasonable level of spousal support.[25]

c) Custody and Access
Federal divorce legislation and many provincial and territorial statutes stipulate that spousal misconduct is irrelevant to issues of custody of and access to the children unless such conduct reflects on that person's ability to parent. Subsection 24(4) of the Ontario *Children's Law Reform Act*[26] specifically identifies domestic violence as of special significance to custody and access disputes. Some judges fail to appreciate that spousal abuse to which children are witnesses may be just as detrimental to a child's development as abuse where the child is the primary victim. Other judges show enlightenment by recognizing that, even in the absence of physical or sexual abuse, psychological spousal abuse may constitute a compelling reason for denying custody of the children to the abusive parent.

If an abused wife leaves home to secure her own safety, she may take the children with her. If the children do not accompany her but she wishes to obtain sole legal custody, she should institute legal proceedings as soon as possible. Substantial delay can be fatal to a claim for custody. Courts do not normally grant custody to an abusive spouse. They may, however, grant access privileges that enable an abusive spouse to preserve meaningful contact with the children. The abusive parent is not free to see or contact the child whenever he wants to. The terms of access will

---

25   *Anderson v. Anderson* (1990), 27 R.F.L. (3d) 358 (Man. Q.B.); see also *Jones v. Jones*, [1975] 2 All E.R. 12 (C.A.), wherein the right to and amount of spousal support were affected by the husband's physical assault of his wife that prevented her from pursuing her nursing career and rendered her prospects of alternative employment somewhat doubtful.

26   R.S.O. 1990, c. C.12, s. 24, as amended by S.O. 2006, c. 1, s. 3(1).

be spelled out in the court order. If the children would be at risk, sexually, physically, or emotionally, access may be denied. Alternatively, the court may order that an abusive parent exercise access privileges under the supervision of a neutral third party. The Attorney General of Ontario has provided funding for supervised access from time to time but there has been no permanently guaranteed funding.

d) Orders for Exclusive Possession of Matrimonial Home

Matters relating to property rights, including rights to exclusive possession of the matrimonial home, are regulated by provincial legislation in Canada. Federal divorce legislation is silent on these issues. In Ontario, section 24 of the *Family Law Act*[27] expressly empowers a court to grant exclusive possession of the matrimonial home and its contents to either spouse regardless of ownership rights. Similar legislation exists in other provinces and territories. Subsection 24(3) of the Ontario *Family Law Act* identifies the following six factors that must be considered on an application to the court for exclusive possession of the matrimonial home: (a) the best interests of the children affected; (b) any existing court orders; (c) the financial position of both spouses; (d) any written agreement between the parties; (e) the availability of other suitable and affordable accommodation; and (f) any violence committed by a spouse against the other spouse or children. "Violence" within the meaning of paragraph 24(3)(f) of the Ontario *Family Law Act* includes psychological violence.[28] Orders for exclusive possession of the matrimonial home may also be granted pursuant to section 34 of the Ontario *Family Law Act* in proceedings for spousal support. In this latter context, section 29 of the Ontario *Family Law Act* defines "spouse" to include unmarried persons who have cohabited continuously for not less than three years or who have cohabited "in a relationship of some permanence" and are the natural or adoptive parents of a child. Judicial opinion is, nevertheless, divided on the question whether unmarried cohabitants are entitled to claim exclusive possession rights in a "matrimonial" home under the Ontario *Family Law Act*.[29] However, protection may be available to an unmarried cohabitant pursuant to the Ontario *Domestic Violence Protection Act*, 2000[30] which empowers a court to make a temporary or final intervention order, if it is

---

27   R.S.O. 1990, c. F.3. See, generally, Chapter 12, Section A(18)(d).
28   *Hill v. Hill* (1987), 10 R.F.L. (3d) 225 (Ont. Dist. Ct.).
29   See *Czora v. Lonergan* (1987), 7 R.F.L. (3d) 458 (Ont. Dist. Ct.).
30   S.O. 2000, c. 33.

satisfied on a balance of probabilities that domestic violence has occurred — such an order may include provision whereby the applicant is granted exclusive possession of the residence shared by the applicant and the respondent, regardless of ownership.

e) Non-molestation or Restraining Orders

In addition to or instead of granting an exclusive possession order of the matrimonial home, a court may grant a non-molestation order. This type of order prohibits a person from molesting, annoying, or harassing his or her spouse, divorced spouse, or common-law spouse or any children in his or her custody. In Ontario, non-molestation orders, or restraining orders as they are called, are regulated by statutory provisions. Subsection 46(1) of the Ontario *Family Law Act* provides as follows:

> *Order restraining harassment*
>
> 46(1) On application, a court may make an interim or final order restraining the applicant's spouse or former spouse from molesting, annoying or harassing the applicant or children in the applicant's lawful custody, or from communicating with the applicant or children, except as the order provides, and may require the applicant's spouse or former spouse to enter into the recognizance that the court considers appropriate.

Specific penalties for contravention of a restraining order are set out in subsection 46(2) of the Ontario *Family Law* Act. This subsection stipulates that the first offence carries a maximum fine of $5,000 and/or a maximum term of imprisonment of three months. Any subsequent offence carries increased penalties of a maximum fine of $10,000 and/or a maximum term of imprisonment of two years. Subsection 46(3) of the Ontario *Family Law Act* empowers a police officer to arrest, without warrant, a person whom the police officer believes, on reasonable and probable grounds, to have contravened a restraining order. Similar sanctions and powers of arrest exist under section 24 of the Ontario *Family Law Act* for contravention of a court order granting a spouse or former spouse exclusive possession of the matrimonial home.

Additional powers to grant restraining orders are also granted by the Ontario *Domestic Violence Protection Act*.

6) Actions for Damages

If a person causes bodily injury to any other person, including a spouse or common-law spouse, monetary compensation is available in a civil action for damages. Assault and battery constitute actionable torts in every Canadian province and territory. Unlawful restraints on the freedom of movement of another person may constitute the tort of false imprisonment and the intentional infliction of mental suffering may also ground an action for damages in tort. Most successful claims for damages in Canadian courts have been confined, however, to damages for physical assaults that caused bodily injury. This is, nevertheless, an evolving field of liability, particularly with respect to such matters as the transmission of diseases, such as genital herpes and AIDS.

In an Ontario case, a wife sued her husband for substantial damages on the basis of breach of fiduciary duty, negligent or intentional infliction of emotional distress, negligent or fraudulent misrepresentations, and battery. She alleged that her husband was a practising bisexual who had failed to disclose his premarital and extramarital affairs with the consequence that she was fearful of contracting AIDS. The husband brought a preliminary application to strike out the wife's action because it disclosed no foundation for the imposition of legal liability and constituted an abuse of the judicial process. This application was dismissed, thus allowing the merits of the wife's alternative claims to go to trial.[31]

In an Alberta case, harassing telephone calls were characterized as an actionable tort that entitled the wife to damages in addition to an injunction prohibiting future calls. Remedies in tort law do not stand in the place of criminal prosecution. They provide a financial remedy for the victim as distinct from the *Criminal Code*, which imposes financial or other penalties on the perpetrator.

As an alternative to suing an abuser, who may be incapable of paying damages, a victim of a crime of violence may seek compensation from the appropriate provincial or territorial Criminal Injuries Compensation Board. The criteria for such compensation are prescribed by provincial legislation. Recovery of compensation is not dependent upon the prior criminal conviction of the abuser.

In 1994, three women were granted $15,000 each by the Ontario Criminal Injuries Compensation Board because they contracted the AIDS virus after engaging in sexual intercourse with a man who died

---

31   *Bell-Ginsburg v. Ginsburg* (1993), 48 R.F.L. (3d) 208 (Ont. Gen. Div.).

from AIDS some months before the Board's ruling. The criminality of the man's conduct arose not simply from his transmission of the virus but from his wanton and reckless disregard for the women's lives that he placed at risk by lying about his health and engaging in unprotected sex when he was aware that he had tested positive to the AIDS virus.[32]

E. THE VICTIM'S RESPONSE TO SPOUSAL ABUSE

Abused spouses must develop a plan of action to accommodate their basic needs for the following:

- safety;
- medical assistance;
- housing;
- financial assistance;
- legal assistance; and
- emotional support.

The minimum amount of information needed by an abused spouse involves awareness of the wide variety of support services available in the community. As a starting point, an abused spouse should have the local and emergency telephone numbers for the following:

- the police;
- the hospital;
- women's shelters;
- general welfare assistance;
- legal aid services;
- family service agencies; and
- community hotlines.

Police are on call twenty-four hours every day to provide emergency intervention for any person whose personal safety is threatened, but police cannot be at a home all day and every day in order to guarantee protection. As stated previously, there are legal means whereby an abuser may be ordered by a court to leave the victim alone. A recognizance or peace bond can be obtained under the *Criminal Code* of Canada. An order can also be obtained in civil proceedings whereby the abuser is ordered to refrain from molesting or harassing the victim or her children.

---

32   *Ottawa Citizen* (8 February 1994) A3.

An order for exclusive possession of the matrimonial home may also be obtainable in civil proceedings. These orders provide some measure of protection to an abused spouse. If they are unlikely to be respected by the abuser, however, the victim must have a fall-back position. Safety must be the paramount concern. Where can an abused spouse go to ensure her safety? Relatives or friends may be available to provide or find a safe place for her. She should also contact a women's shelter. The advantage of this last course of action is that she will then be provided with information concerning other agencies and services that may accommodate her longer-term needs.

An abused spouse should be ready to leave home at any time when she foresees that violence will erupt. She should keep clothes handy for herself and the children so as to be prepared for a quick departure. She should remember to take any necessary documents with her, such as her marriage certificate, birth certificates for herself and the children, passports, medical insurance cards, social insurance cards, and court orders. Keys, a telephone list, and a favourite toy for each child should not be forgotten. If she leaves home and needs to return for something she has forgotten, she should be accompanied by the police or some third person. If there is time to plan, she should put away an emergency fund.

Abused spouses have great difficulty in disclosing what has happened to them. If a lawyer is to give sound advice, full disclosure is essential. Details of specific incidents, rather than bald assertions of violence, must be provided to the lawyer and, ultimately, the court. Visits to a doctor or hospital should be noted so that medical and hospital records may be obtained as evidence of the violence.

Many spouses fear that as soon as any legal documents are served on the abuser, this will itself trigger further violence. If this is a real danger, a lawyer can institute *ex parte* civil proceedings to obtain an order against the abusing spouse before any legal documents are served. The order is then served on the abusing spouse who is given the opportunity to challenge it on the basis that the allegations were improper.

Court orders do not provide any guarantee that violence will not occur. A court order may be contravened. The benefits of an order are, nevertheless, worthwhile. Court orders underline for the community at large the gravity of the behaviour complained of. They are also helpful if the police are called. The police will know that they are dealing with an abusing spouse and they are less likely to regard the matter as one to be resolved by the spouses themselves. Contravention of court orders also carries certain penalties, such as fines or imprisonment.

F. PROPOSALS FOR REFORM

In 1991, the federal government established the Canadian Panel on Violence against Women to examine the incidence of spousal violence and the measures necessary to combat it. The panel presented its report on 29 July 1993. It contains 494 recommendations. Many of the panel members were familiar with spousal abuse by virtue of their involvement with women's shelters, the courts, or public health. They were, nevertheless, shocked by the evidence presented to them at public hearings in 139 Canadian communities. Among the statistics compiled, the following figures paint an alarming picture:

(i)   Interviews with a random sample of 420 women between the ages of 18 and 64 revealed that 51 percent of them had been the victims of rape or attempted rape and 43 percent reported at least one experience of incest and/or extrafamilial sexual abuse before the age of 16.

(ii) More than 78,000 people were admitted to protective shelters in 1992.

(iii) In 1991, 270 women were murdered. Of the 225 cases that were solved, all but 15 women were killed by men — more than half by husbands or lovers.

Using what is termed a "feminist lens," the report characterizes violence against women as inextricably linked to women's social and economic inequality. In consequence, the recommendations in the report are extremely ambitious and far-reaching, so much so that some early critics regarded them as utopian, while others contend that the $10 million cost of the report would have been far better spent on funding women's shelters, sexual assault centres, and advocacy groups, all of which are chronically underfunded.

The following summary highlights the wide range and multiplicity of the recommendations:

(1)   *Equality Rights*: Make sexual orientation a prohibited ground for discrimination; strengthen human rights laws to address systemic discrimination; recognize persecution on the basis of gender as an explicit ground for granting refugee status; reinstate and expand the Court Challenges Program to enable women to fight for equality rights in the courts.

(2)   *Services*: Provide core funding for women's shelters, sexual assault and rape crisis centres; establish national standards for the provi-

sion of adequate services, such as a crisis toll-free telephone number in each community in remote communities and an emergency shelter or services within one hour commuting distance from each community; set up a committee in every community to co-ordinate services to survivors of violence against women.

(3) *Legal System*: Develop mandatory training programs on violence against women for judges and parole board members; support the development of specialized courts to deal with crimes of violence; identify ways to reduce acquittals based on "legal" technicalities; train legal aid lawyers to deal with spousal abuse; initiate programs to remove the abuser rather than the victim from the home whenever possible and use technology such as electronic monitoring devices to safeguard potential victims.

(4) *Criminal Code*: Repeal soliciting law, change obscenity provisions to prohibit sexually violent and degrading material; collect DNA evidence from all those accused of sex offences and create a DNA data bank to identify serial offenders.

(5) *Family*: Implement a national child care program and encourage workplace child care services through funding or tax relief, implement educational programs for men, women, and young boys and girls to create greater awareness of shared obligations within the family.

(6) *Taxes*: Analyze all proposed tax system changes for bias or adverse effects based on gender; address the taxation and collection problems associated with child support obligations; acknowledge through the tax system the costs of raising children and the reduced capacity of families with children to pay taxes.

(7) *Police*: Create and enforce the implementation of policies to ensure that initial police response, decisions on arrest, detention and terms of any release, support the safety of the victim and prevent revictimization; establish a women's safety advisory board locally and nationally in the R.C.M.P. which includes representation from Aboriginal and Inuit Women.

(8) *Workplace*: Develop a written code of conduct based on zero tolerance for violence which promotes equality and guarantees safety for all workers and clients.

(9) *Military*: Counterbalance combat readiness training which can make men very aggressive and domineering with human relations training that emphasizes the inappropriateness and danger of aggression in interpersonal relationships.

(10) *Education*: Make violence prevention a part of all school curricula; implement effective policies against sexual and racial violence; train staff to recognize the linkages between inequality and violence and to incorporate this knowledge in their work; make awareness of such linkages a formal rating factor in staff performance appraisals; hold all staff and students accountable for sexist and racist behaviour.

(11) *Media*: Broadcasters should develop significantly more women's programming; print media should dedicate space as frequently as possible to issues of violence, women's safety, and equality; advertisers should commit support to non-violent productions and should create anti-violence advertising.

(12) *Churches*: Religious institutions must work to revise teachings that promote inequality of women and support violence against women and adopt democratic structures to balance power between religious leaders and followers.

(13) *Government*: Adopt and implement zero-tolerance policy against violence and an equality action plan; require organizations that receive contracts for more than $100,000 to do the same; enact a Status of Women Act to identify the specific obligations and responsibilities of the federal government to ensure that the rights to equality and safety of all Canadian women are supported and advanced.

Many of the above recommendations signify that violence against women will not be checked until we live in an egalitarian society.

G. NATURE OF CHILD ABUSE

Child abuse may involve physical, sexual, or emotional oppression of children. Some definitions include economic deprivation, such as failure to provide adequate food, clothing, housing, or medical care for a child. Other definitions identify these situations as "child neglect" as distinct from "child abuse."

Physical abuse typically signifies an improper application of force that results in bruises, cuts, burns, broken bones, internal injuries and, in its most extreme form, death.

Sexual abuse is conduct that involves the sexual molestation or exploitation of children. Examples include incest, rape, sodomy, carnal knowledge, sexual touching, or procuring a child's involvement in prostitution or pornography.

Emotional abuse refers to conduct that produces psychological harm to the child. Emotional abuse undermines a child's sense of well-being and impairs the child's development and ability to reach his or her full potential. It often produces lifelong difficulties for the emotionally abused victim.

Canadians have been shocked by media reports of multiple incidents of child abuse in New Brunswick, Newfoundland, and Ontario. In several instances, the victims have been children who were taken from their families and placed in supposedly safe institutions. These children were physically and sexually abused by their so-called protectors or caregivers. Bizarre allegations of satanic ritual abuse are raised from time to time, but have never been substantiated by proof. Between 1985 and 1987, for example, a judge of the Ontario Unified Family Court in Hamilton spent 150 days sifting through evidence and legal submissions relating to allegations of physical, sexual, and ritual abuse against the mother of two young girls, her boyfriend, and the estranged father of the children. While the evidence was insufficient to warrant any finding of ritual abuse, the three accused were all found guilty of sexual abuse.[33] Rumours of ritual abuse also arose in the mid-1990s in Prescott-Russell, Ontario, where sexual abuse allegations led to a significant number of criminal convictions. Highly publicized cases involving such matters as alleged satanic ritual abuse, sexual abuse involving three generations of the same family, or physical and sexual abuse by supposed pillars of the community, such as the clergy or police, are exceptional. It is for that reason that they have attracted so much publicity in the media. Typical cases of child abuse do not involve the occult or multiparty conspiracy. They involve physical assaults and sexual molestation behind closed doors in family homes.

H. SOCIAL AND LEGAL RESPONSES TO CHILD ABUSE

Child abuse is found in all societies. It has often been hidden or ignored. "Spare the rod and spoil the child" has only recently been displaced by the realization that "violence breeds violence." Research studies demonstrate that child abuse must be prevented not only to save this generation

---

33   See Kevin Marron, *Ritual Abuse* (Toronto: Seal Books, 1989).

of children but also to save the next generation. Far too often, an abused child in turn becomes the abusing parent of his or her own child.

Statistics indicate that sexual abuse of children is predominantly a male offence, although there are a significant number of cases where mothers have been involved. Mothers are just as likely to physically or emotionally abuse their children as fathers.[34] Many instances of child abuse involve preschool children and single-parent households.[35] These factors may partially explain the statistics concerning female perpetrators in that many mothers are left to carry the responsibility of parenthood with little or no help from the fathers.

Canada, like many other countries, historically offered greater protection to animals than to children. Canadian legislation prohibiting cruelty to animals can be traced back to 1824. The first statute to prohibit cruelty to children was enacted in 1893 when the Ontario legislature passed an *Act for the Prevention of Cruelty to and Better Protection of Children.*[36] Manitoba enacted similar legislation in 1898 and the other provinces followed these precedents in the early-twentieth century.

Today, every province and territory in Canada has relatively sophisticated legislation that is aimed at providing protection to abused and neglected children. These statutes call for the mandatory reporting of child abuse to provincial child welfare authorities by any professional or other person who reasonably suspects that child abuse has occurred. In addition to provincial child welfare legislation, the *Criminal Code* of Canada may be invoked to punish conduct that constitutes child abuse. It is also possible for the victim of child abuse to claim damages for assault and battery from the perpetrator of the abuse.

1) Criminal Sanctions

The criminal offences relating to physical and sexual assaults, which were previously identified as potentially applicable to spousal abuse, may also be invoked in cases of child abuse. Sexual abuse of a child that involves carnal knowledge may also constitute incest, which is punishable by a maximum term of fourteen years' imprisonment under section 154 of the *Criminal Code.* In the event that child abuse results in the death of the

---

34 See Honourable Senator Anne C. Cools, *Senate Debates* (21 March 1996) at 113, citing a study of the Toronto Institute for the Prevention of Child Abuse entitled *The Ontario Incidence of Reported Child Abuse and Neglect 1994.*

35 *Ibid.*

36 S.O. 1893, c. 45.

victim, murder or manslaughter charges may ensue. The *Criminal Code* of Canada includes many additional offences that are specifically directed at the protection of children. Sections 151, 152, and 153 of the *Criminal Code* prohibit sexual interference with children, invitations for sexual touching, and sexual exploitation of children. "Sexual touching" includes touching a child for a sexual purpose or having the child touch himself or herself or touch other persons for a sexual purpose. Section 170 prohibits a parent or guardian from procuring his or her child to engage in sexual activities with third parties. Section 215 imposes a duty on parents and guardians to provide necessaries of life to children under the age of sixteen years. Section 223 prohibits the killing of a child once it has proceeded in a living state from the mother. Section 237 prohibits infanticide and section 238 prohibits killing an unborn child during the act of birth.

A parent's infliction of corporal punishment on a child for disciplinary reasons does not constitute a criminal assault unless the force used was excessive. Section 43 of the *Criminal Code* of Canada provides as follows:

Correction of Child by Force

43. Every schoolteacher, parent or person standing in the place of a parent is justified in using force by way of correction toward a pupil or child, as the case may be, who is under his care, if the force does not exceed what is reasonable under the circumstances.

In *Canadian Foundation for Children Youth and the Law v. Canada (Attorney General)*,[37] the majority judgment of the Supreme Court of Canada rejected the appellant's contention that section 43 of the *Criminal Code* contravenes sections 7, 12, and 15 of the *Canadian Charter of Rights and Freedoms*. The dividing line between corporal punishment and physical abuse is not always clear. There are many people, including experts, who regard any degree of corporal punishment as bordering on child abuse. Criminal assault charges are, however, rarely brought against parents. If the police consider that state intervention is appropriate, they will usually refer the matter to the local child protection agency.

The multiplicity of criminal offences that can be committed against children does not guarantee adequate protection for victims of parental child abuse. Indeed, a child may be re-victimized as a witness against an accused parent in a criminal prosecution. The child faces the terror of

---

37   [2004] 1 S.C.R. 76. See also *R. v. B.S.*, [2008] O.J. No. 975 (Sup. Ct.) (parent not precluded from using force as corrective restraint of his teenage child).

revisiting the abuse and is subject to cross-examination by the lawyer representing the alleged offender.

In 1988, federal legislation was enacted to reduce the tension and anxiety faced by children who are called as witnesses in sexual molestation and sexual abuse prosecutions against parents or any other persons.[38] The court, on application of the Crown prosecutor, will prohibit the publication or broadcasting of any information that could disclose the identity of the child. In addition, any interviewing of the child by the police or a child protection agency may be videotaped. The videotape can then be admitted as evidence at the trial, although its contents must be confirmed by the child at the trial. A child's testimony may also be presented by closed-circuit television to avoid the need to have the child present in court. Alternatively, a screen may be used in the courtroom so that the child does not have to face the accused while giving evidence. Irrespective of how the child gives his or her evidence, the lawyer for the accused has the right to cross-examine the child. Corroboration of a child's evidence is not required in order to obtain conviction of the accused. The judge must decide what weight should be given to the evidence and will direct a jury accordingly. In two recent decisions of the Supreme Court of Canada, it was held that the use of videotaped evidence[39] and the practice of allowing witnesses below the age of eighteen to testify behind screens[40] in sexual abuse prosecutions does not violate the accused's right to a fair trial under the *Canadian Charter of Rights and Freedoms*. No similar statutory concessions apply to child protection proceedings instituted pursuant to provincial legislation, although a judge of the Ontario Court (Provincial Division) has allowed a fifteen-year-old child to give videotaped evidence of sexual abuse allegations against her stepfather in child protection proceedings,[41] and the Ontario Law Reform Commission has advocated changes that go even further than the federal legislation.[42]

Criminal prosecution of a parent, without the availability of support services for the family, may generate additional problems. For example,

---

38 R.S.C. 1985 (3d Supp.), c. 19. See Canada, House of Commons, *Four-Year Review of the Child Sexual Abuse Provisions of the* Criminal Code *and the* Canada Evidence Act by Chair, Dr. Bob Horner, M.P. (June 1993).

39 *R. v. L.(D.O.)* (1993), 161 N.R. 1 (S.C.C.).

40 *R. v. Levogiannis*, [1993] 4 S.C.R. 475.

41 *Children's Aid Society of Brant v. R.(E.)*, [1993] O.J. No. 2382, digested in *The Lawyers Weekly* (3 December 1993) 8 (Prov. Div.).

42 Ontario Law Reform Commission, *Report on Child Witnesses* (including Executive Summary) (Toronto: The Commission, 1991).

the child accuser may face hostility from other members of the family, or economic deprivation may be suffered by all family members, including the abused child, as a result of the conviction of an abusing parent. A fine or imprisonment may impair or undermine the abusing parent's ability to provide financial support for his or her family dependants. Punishment of an abusive parent does not always coincide, therefore, with the best interests of the family or those of the abused child. Of course, abuse cannot go unchecked. It must be terminated. But whether this is better accomplished by invoking the *Criminal Code* or by resort to provincial child protection legislation is a matter that necessitates careful evaluation by the police and child protection agencies.

2) Child Protection Proceedings[43]

Child protection legislation exists in every Canadian province and territory.[44] Although the statutes vary in content, their fundamental character is consistent. Child protection statutes in Canada usually include declarations of the basic philosophy underlying the detailed statutory provisions. These declarations vary in length but provide some direction for child protection agencies and the courts in their interpretation and application of the statute. In Prince Edward Island, for example, the *Family and Child Services Act*[45] simply states that "[in] the administration and interpretation of this Act the best interests of the child shall be the paramount consideration." Other provinces, such as Alberta, Manitoba, New Brunswick, Ontario, and Quebec, have relatively detailed declarations that stress such matters as (i) family autonomy and the vital importance of parents assuming the responsibility for child rearing; (ii) the adoption of the least restrictive and disruptive alternative when state intervention is necessary; (iii) the importance of continuity and stability for children;

---

43   See, generally, Nicholas Bala, Joseph P. Hornick, & Robin Vogl, *Canadian Child Welfare Law: Children, Families and the State* (Toronto: Thompson Educational, 1990); see also Nicholas Bala, "Reforming the *Children and Family Services Act*: Is the Pendulum Swinging Back Too Far?" (Quicklaw, SFLN).

44   *Child Welfare Act*, R.S.A. 2000, c. C-12; *Child, Family and Community Services Act*, R.S.B.C. 1996, c. 46; *Child and Family Services Act*, R.S.M. 1987, c. C80; *Family Services Act*, S.N.B. 1980, c. F-2.2; *Child, Youth and Family Services Act*, S.N.L. 1998, c. C-12.1; *Children and Family Services Act*, S.N.S. 1990, c. 5; *Child and Family Services Act*, R.S.O. 1990, c. C.11; *Family and Child Services Act*, R.S.P.E.I. 1988, c. F-2; *Youth Protection Act*, R.S.Q. 1977, c. P-34.1; *Child and Family Services Act*, S.S. 1989, c. C-7.2; *Child and Family Services Act*, S.N.W.T. 1997, c. 13; *Children's Act*, R.S.Y. 1986, c. 22, Part 4.

45   R.S.P.E.I. 1988, c. F-2, s. 2.

and (iv) cultural and religious differences. In Ontario, the statutory "declaration of principles" in section 1 of the *Child and Family Services Act*[46] also includes a specific reference to Indian and native families by providing as follows:

> *Declaration of principles*
>
> 1. The purposes of this Act are:
>
> ...
>
> 5. To recognize that Indian and native people should be entitled to provide, wherever possible, their own child and family services, and that all services to Indian and native children and families should be provided in a manner that recognizes their culture, heritage and traditions and the concept of the extended family.

The dominant theme of declarations of purpose in child protection legislation reflects a distinct preference for children to be raised by their parents in their own home, except in those circumstances where there is no practical alternative to removing the children and placing them elsewhere.

Child protection agencies, which are often called Children's Aid Societies or Child and Family Services, are responsible for investigating allegations of child abuse or neglect and bringing any necessary application before the courts. They may remove a child from his or her home with or without a warrant but must bring the child before a judge within a stipulated time.

In child protection proceedings, there are two key issues. First, is the child an "endangered child," "child in need of guidance," or a "child in need of protection," as defined in the applicable provincial or territorial statute? Second, if so, what judicial disposition will satisfy the best interests of the child?

The child protection agency has the legal burden of proving that state intervention is justified because the parents do not meet even minimal standards in discharging their obligations to their children. In the words of one Ontario judge,

> Society's interference in the natural family is only justified when the level of care of the children falls below that which no child in this country should be subjected to.[47]

---

46   R.S.O. 1990, c. C.11.
47   *Re Brown* (1975), 9 O.R. (2d) 185 at 189 (Co. Ct.).

Central to every provincial and territorial child protection statute is the definition of "child in need of protection" or the analogous terms "endangered child" or "child in need of guidance." Circumstances that justify a finding that a child is in need of protection include the actuality or substantial risk of the following:

(i)   physical harm;
(ii)   sexual molestation or exploitation;
(iii) emotional harm;
(iv)   abandonment; and
(v)   parental inability to care for the child.

These factors are spelled out in detail in Alberta[48] and Ontario[49] where the legislation is more precise than that found in other provinces or territories. In most statutes, the definition of a child in need of protection includes such vague terms as "a child without adequate care, supervision or control," "a child living in unfit or improper circumstances," or a child beyond the control of the parent or guardian.[50]

If a child is found to be in need of protection, the judge must determine the most appropriate placement for the child. In this context, the judge is required to have regard to the best interests of the child. Many provincial and territorial statutes identify specific factors that are relevant to a determination of a child's best interests. In Ontario, twelve factors have been singled out for consideration. Subsection 37(3) of the Ontario *Child and Family Services Act*[51] provides as follows:

Best interests of child

37(3) Where a person is directed in this Part to make an order or determination in the best interests of a child, the person shall take into consideration those of the following circumstances of the case that he or she considers relevant:

1. The child's physical, mental and emotional needs, and the appropriate care or treatment to meet those needs.
2. The child's physical, mental and emotional level of development.
3. The child's cultural background.
4. The religious faith, if any, in which the child is being raised.

---

48   *Child, Youth and Family Enhancement Act*, R.S.A. 2000, c. C-12, s. 2.
49   *Child and Family Services Act*, R.S.O. 1990, c. C.11, s. 37(2).
50   See, for example, *Family Services Act*, S.N.B. 1980, c. F-2.2, s. 31(1).
51   R.S.O. 1990, c. C.11.

5. The importance for the child's development of a positive relationship with a parent and a secure place as a member of a family.
6. The child's relationship by blood or through an adoption order.
7. The importance of continuity in the child's care and the possible effect on the child of disruption of that continuity.
8. The merits of a plan for the child's care proposed by a society, including a proposal that the child be placed for adoption or adopted, compared with the merits of the child remaining with or returning to the parent.
9. The child's views and wishes, if they can be reasonably ascertained.
10. The effects on the child of delay in the disposition of the case.
11. The risk that the child may suffer harm through being removed from, kept away from, returned to or allowed to remain in the care of a parent.
12. The degree of risk, if any, that justified the finding that the child is in need of protection.

Section 53 of the Ontario *Child and Family Services Act* further provides that a court shall not make an order removing a child from the care of a parent unless the court is satisfied that less restrictive alternatives would be unsuccessful or inadequate to protect the child.

A judge may make any one of three different types of order in respect of a child who is found to be in need of protection: (i) a supervision order; (ii) a temporary wardship order; or (iii) a permanent wardship order.

Under a supervision order, the child is placed in the care of his or her parents and resides at home. However, the child protection agency assumes supervisory responsibilities and periodicially visits the child's home.

A temporary wardship order places the child in the custody of the child protection agency for a specified period of time. Temporary wards are placed in foster homes or group homes. Temporary wardship orders envisage that a positive parent-child relationship can be established in due course. To promote this goal, parents are granted reasonable access to the child.

A permanent wardship order, sometimes called Crown wardship, is the most intrusive type of order. It terminates all parental rights of guardianship over the child. Children, who have been made permanent wards may be placed for adoption without parental consent. The parent-child relationship is severed in the hope of finding a new permanent home for the child. Several statutes, including those in British Columbia, Ontario, and the Yukon, expressly prohibit or severely circumscribe rights of access by natural parents whose child has been made a permanent ward. In Ontario, for example, subsection 59(2) of the *Child and Family Services Act* provides as follows:

> *Access: Crown ward*
>
> 59(2) The court shall not make or vary an access order with respect to a Crown ward under section 58 (access) or section 65 (status review) unless the court is satisfied that,
>
> (a) the relationship between the person and the child is beneficial and meaningful to the child; and
>
> (b) the ordered access will not impair the child's future opportunities for a permanent or stable placement.[52]

Dispositive orders that have been made in child protection proceedings are subject to review. Review hearings are conducted for the purpose of extending, terminating, or varying the prior order. In some provinces, such as Alberta and British Columbia, parents may only seek a review of orders for supervision or temporary wardship. In Ontario, parents may seek a review of a permanent wardship order but a status review hearing cannot be commenced after a Crown ward has been placed for adoption.

3) Family Law Proceedings

When child abuse is accompanied by spousal separation or divorce, the non-abusing parent may seek matrimonial relief by way of spousal support, child support, custody of the child, or exclusive possession of the family home. These remedies have been previously analyzed in the context of spousal abuse. Suffice it to say, therefore, that it is the parent, rather than the child, who seeks such relief. Although there have been isolated cases where children have personally instituted proceedings for child support against one or both parents, such actions are extremely rare. Almost invariably, claims on behalf of a child are brought by the parent. Indeed, in divorce proceedings, the child has no legal standing to pursue remedies on his or her own behalf.

Allegations of child abuse are of crucial significance in contested custody and access disputes. Where allegations of child abuse are substantiated, the abusive parent has virtually no chance of obtaining an or-

---

52   *Ibid.*, as amended by S.O. 1999, c. 2, s. 16.

der for custody of the child. Access privileges are not necessarily denied, however, to an abusing parent, although a court is likely to impose conditions whereby the access arrangements will be under the supervision of a neutral third party.

Concern has been expressed from time to time that spouses may seek to affect the outcome of disputed custody and access proceedings by making false allegations of child abuse. Allegations of sexual abuse, in particular, are often difficult to either substantiate or refute. Where a spouse or parent is faced by what he or she claims to be false allegations of child abuse, the appropriate course of action is to seek the assistance of a lawyer and of the local child protection agency that has a statutory responsibility to investigate all allegations of child abuse.

Research studies indicate that children are usually telling the truth when they relate incidents of abuse without prompting or coaching by a parent or any other person. Different considerations may apply when allegations of child abuse are made by a hostile spouse or parent who is caught up in the emotional trauma of marriage breakdown or divorce. Even in these circumstances, however, there is a reasonable probability that there was some foundation for the allegations made, although they were ultimately shown to lack substance. False allegations of abuse are rarely vindictive. They are far more likely to result from a misunderstanding of the circumstances or a misrepresentation of a particular event.

4) Damages for Child Abuse

There are no legal impediments to an action for damages being brought by a child against his or her parent for harm inflicted on the child. A physically or sexually abused child may sue an abusing parent, step-parent, foster parent, or sibling for damages in the torts of assault, battery, and intentional infliction of mental harm. Alternatively, the child victim may sue a parent for breach of his or her fiduciary obligation to protect the child.[53]

Children rarely sue for damages while living in the same home as the abuser. There have been several cases, however, where women have obtained substantial damages for incest committed against them during their childhood. In Manitoba, a twenty-three-year-old woman, who during childhood had been persistently sexually abused by her father,

---

53   See Bruce Feldthusen, "The Civil Action for Sexual Battery: Therapeutic Jurisprudence" (1993) 25 Ottawa L. Rev. 203; James W.W. Neeb & Shelly J. Harper, *Civil Action for Childhood Sexual Abuse* (Toronto:, Butterworths, 1994).

was held entitled to damages of $170,000, which comprised $100,000 for psychological trauma, $50,000 for aggravated general damages, and $20,000 for future therapy.[54] In Ontario, a father has been ordered to pay to his adult daughter, who had been sexually abused by him for more than twelve years of her childhood, the following amounts: $100,000 as general damages, $75,000 as aggravated damages, $50,000 as punitive damages, $50,000 for future therapy, and $9,037.50 as special damages for unpaid expenses for psychotherapy. The father was also ordered to pay interest on all the damages except the $50,000 for future therapy, the interest being declared retroactive to a point midway through the period during which the sexual assaults occurred.[55]

Although actions for damages arising from childhood sexual abuse are most frequently instituted by female victims against male perpetrators, a few instances involve claims by male victims against either male or female perpetrators. In British Columbia, a man has been granted damages of $350,000 for childhood sexual assaults perpetrated upon him by his uncle, these damages representing $80,000 in aggravated general damages, $70,000 for pre-trial loss of wages, and $200,000 for loss of future career opportunities attributable to the traumatization resulting from the frequent sexual assaults.[56] In a subsequent British Columbia case, a man received $260,000 in a successful action against both of his parents who had subjected him to frequent verbal and physical abuse during his childhood.[57]

Courts have overcome procedural hurdles that ordinarily require the commencement of judicial proceedings within a limited period of time after the commission of any tort. The Supreme Court of Canada has decided that a victim of incest can sue an abusing parent for the torts of assault and battery and also for breach of the fiduciary obligation owed by the parent to the child.[58] With respect to the applicability of statutory limitation periods on the right of a victim of childhood incest to sue the abuser, the Supreme Court of Canada concluded that time begins to run only when the victim appreciates the harmful effect that the childhood

---

54   *B.(K.L.) v. B.(K.E.)* (1991), 71 Man. R. (2d) 265 (Q.B.). See also *L.(B.) v. B.(A.R.)* (1994), 91 Man. R. (2d) 1 (Q.B.).

55   *B.(P.) v. B.(W.)* (1992), 11 O.R. (3d) 161 (Gen. Div.).

56   *D.S. v. D.A.M.*, [1993] B.C.J. No. 315, digested in *The Lawyers Weekly* (19 March 1993) 7 (S.C.).

57   *Y.(A.D.) v. Y.(M.Y.)*, [1994] B.C.J. No. 375, digested in *The Lawyers Weekly* (25 March 1994) 1 (S.C.).

58   *M.(K.) v. M.(H.)* (1992), 142 N.R. 321 (S.C.C.).

incest has had on his or her psychological and emotional well-being as an adult. Several of the judges observed that the victim's appreciation of the harmful effects of the incestuous abuse will not usually occur until the child victim seeks therapy as an adult. Some provincial legislatures have amended their legislation so as to provide a statutory extension of time for the institution of civil proceedings by victims of child abuse. Substantial delay in the institution of proceedings for abuse perpetrated during childhood may, nevertheless, present difficulties of proof.

In two British Columbia cases wherein damages were sought against the provincial government by former foster children who had been abused by foster parents, the following principles were endorsed by the Supreme Court of Canada.[59] The provincial government has a duty under the *Protection of Children Act* (British Columbia) to place children in adequate foster care and to monitor such placements. Liability in damages for the tort of negligence may arise where the provincial government has breached its duty by failing to follow proper placement and supervision procedures to prevent the abuse of children in their foster home. Although the provincial government may be liable on the basis of its own direct negligence, no vicarious liability can be imposed on the provincial government for the activities of foster parents. There are two prerequisites to a successful claim for vicarious liability. The relationship between the tortfeasor and the person against whom liability is sought must be sufficiently close to make a claim of vicarious liability appropriate. In addition, the tort must be sufficiently connected to the tortfeasor's assigned tasks that the tort can be regarded as a materialization of the risks created by the enterprise. In determining whether the tortfeasor was acting "on his or her own account" or acting on behalf of the employer, the level of control the employer has over the tortfeasor's activities will always be a factor. Other relevant factors include whether the worker provides his or her own equipment, whether the worker hires his or her own helpers and whether the worker has managerial responsibilities. These factors suggest that the government is not vicariously liable for wrongs committed by foster parents against children entrusted to them. It is inherent in the nature of family-based care for children that foster parents are independent in important respects and the government cannot exercise sufficient control over their activities for them to be seen as acting "on account" of the government. Foster parents do not hold themselves out as govern-

---

59   *K.L.B. v. British Columbia*, [2003] 2 S.C.R. 403; *M.B. v. British Columbia*, [2003] 2 S.C.R. 477.

ment agents in their daily activities with their children, nor are they reasonably perceived as such. Foster families serve a public goal — the goal of giving children the experience of a family, so that they may develop into confident and responsible members of society. However, they discharge this public goal in a highly independent manner, free from close government control. The *Protection of Children Act* (British Columbia) offers no basis for imposing on the Superintendent of Child Welfare a non-delegable duty to ensure that no harm comes to children through the abuse or negligence of foster parents. Nor can liability be grounded in an alleged breach of the provincial government's fiduciary obligation to children where there is no evidence that the government put its own interests ahead of those of the children or committed acts that harmed the children in a way that amounted to a betrayal of trust or loyalty. In *K.L.B. v. British Columbia*, the Supreme Court of Canada concluded that the provincial government's liability to four siblings who had suffered abuse in two foster homes could only arise in consequence of the provincial government's direct negligence. Vicarious liability was deemed untenable and the provincial government did not breach any non-delegable duty or any fiduciary duty owed to the children. In the context of negligence liability, the Supreme Court of Canada addressed the issue of whether the action was statute barred. The *Limitation Act* (British Columbia) imposes a two-year limitation period for actions based on personal injuries resulting from torts (section 3(2)), with the two-year period commencing when a child attains the age of majority (section 7(1)(a)(i)). Having regard to the fact that the youngest of the children reached the age of majority in 1980 and the actions by the four siblings were not commenced until the mid-1990s, the Supreme Court of Canada concluded that the negligence action was statute barred because the children, as adults, had acquired sufficient awareness of the relevant facts to start the limitation period running and they had established no disability that would override the two-year limitation period. In *M.B. v. British Columbia*, the trial judge and the British Columbia Court of Appeal had imposed vicarious liability on the provincial government for the sexual assault of a foster child by her foster father. Alternative liability was also found on the basis of the provincial government's breach of a non-delegable duty. In the absence of any finding that the sexual abuse of the foster child was attributable to negligence on the part of the provincial government and in light of the aforementioned legal analysis, the Supreme Court of Canada concluded that no liability could be imposed on the provincial government and the appeal to the Supreme Court of Canada was allowed.

In an Ontario case, a child, who had been sexually assaulted by her mother's "common-law spouse," pursued concurrent claims for damages in tort and for breach of fiduciary duty. She was held entitled to recover general damages and future-care expenses in the amount of $90,700 against the sexually abusing *de facto* parent and the mother. In addition, she recovered punitive damages of $45,000 against the mother who had negligently failed to prevent the abuse and was in breach of the fiduciary obligation to protect her daughter against known sexual abuse.[60]

In a tort action for assault, damages have been awarded to a child who suffered emotional abuse at the hands of his father, which included witnessing the serious consequences of a violent physical assault perpetrated against the child's mother.[61] Claims for damages may not be feasible, however, if the abuser has no ability to pay the damages to which the victim is entitled. In that event, it should first be determined whether there is any household insurance policy that might cover the claim for damages. Although such policies do not insure against intentional wrongdoing, they may leave the door open to claims for damages arising from negligence or breach of fiduciary duty. If there is no insurance coverage and the abuser is "judgment-proof," the victim of abuse may look for monetary compensation from the appropriate provincial or territorial Criminal Injuries Compensation Board, although the amount of compensation available will not match that available through the courts.

A victim of sexual assault may be entitled to a publication ban and to the use of initials in court documents to prevent the disclosure of his or her identity in an action for damages against the alleged perpetrator.[62]

Actions for damages that focus on allegations of sexual abuse are not exclusively brought by the victims of abuse. In an Ontario case, a Children's Aid Society was ordered to pay $120,000 damages to a father who sued the agency for its mishandling of unsubstantiated sexual abuse allegations made against the father during a custody battle between the parents.[63]

Canadian courts have grappled with the so-called "false memory syndrome"[64] The underlying thesis of advocates of the "false memory syn-

---

60   *J.(L.A.) v. J.(H.)* (1993), 13 O.R. (3d) 306 (Gen. Div.).

61   *Valenti v. Valenti*, [1996] O.J. No. 522 (Gen. Div.), aff'd [1998] O.J. No. 2242 (C.A.).

62   *C.W. v. L.G.M.*, [2004] B.C.J. No. 2435 (S.C.).

63   *D.B. (Litigation guardian of) v. Children's Aid Society of Durham Region*, [1994] O.J. No. 643, digested in *The Lawyers Weekly* (29 April 1994) 1 (Gen. Div.).

64   See Lynda Shorten, "False Memory Syndrome" *Canadian Lawyer* (May 1994) at 16. In a Manitoba case, the trial judge acquitted a man of incest charges on the basis

drome" is that an alleged victim of assault honestly believes that she or he was assaulted when, in fact, no assault occurred. The "false memory syndrome" has attracted vigorous debate among psychiatrists and clinical psychologists as to its validity.

In a majority decision of the Supreme Court of Canada dealing with the unsworn evidence of a four and one-half year old child, whose grandparent was charged with aggravated assault under the *Criminal Code*, it was held that the ultimate conclusion as to the credibility or truthfulness of a witness is for the trier of fact and is not the proper subject of expert opinion. A judge or jury that simply accepts an expert's opinion on the credibility of a witness would be abandoning its own duty to determine the credibility of the witness. Experts may, nevertheless, testify about human conduct and the psychological or physical factors that could lead to certain behaviour relevant to credibility, such as delay in reporting abuse or the recantation of testimony. With respect to the child's own evidence, the court concluded that it would be admissible if the witness is capable of perceiving, remembering, and communicating events to the court.

5) Institutional Child Abuse

There have been a series of instances where childhood victims of physical and sexual abuse have successfully pursued claims for compensation and other relief against institutions, such as churches, hospitals, school boards, children's aid societies, and provincial and federal governments. These cases involved multiple claimants and several have led to innovative consensual resolution. In several instances, a "healing package" was negotiated that went beyond monetary compensation by including psychological counselling, remedial education, the right to remain on social assistance despite the monetary compensation, a healing centre, and a twenty-four-hour crisis hotline. The most notable settlement is the Indian Residential Schools Settlement reached in May 2006, in which the federal government set aside 1.9 billion dollars for the direct benefit of former students. This settlement also provided for a Truth and Reconciliation Commission to promote public education about residential schools. Former students, their families, and their communities will be given the opportunity to share their experiences in a safe and culturally appropriate environment.

---

that they were attributable to the false memory syndrome: *Ottawa Citizen* (23 June 1994) A3.

The use of non-adversarial dispute resolution processes in preference to litigation has attracted both supporters and critics. Non-adversarial processes, such as facilitation and mediation, can provide more flexibility than litigation, even when class actions in the courts are permissible. Non-adversarial processes can also shield abuse victims from the glare of publicity, whereas adversarial legal processes and attendant media publicity aggravate the risk of abuse victims being re-victimized. Non-adversarial processes may, however, result in abuse victims receiving less financial compensation than would be likely if they had recourse to the courts.[65]

---

65 For a settlement wherein New Brunswick approved a multimillion-dollar compensation package for victims of molestation and rape at provincial reform schools, see *Globe and Mail* (9 June 1995) A5. For a similar settlement in Nova Scotia, see *Ottawa Citizen* (4 May 1996) A9. For a multimillion-dollar settlement in Ontario, see *Ottawa Citizen* (16 March 1996) C7. On 10 May 2006, the Canadian government announced a $2.2 billion compensation package for the cultural, emotional, physical, and sexual abuse of aboriginal children who had attended church-run native residential schools: online, www.residentialschoolsettlement.ca/English.html.

CHAPTER 6

THE CRISES OF MARRIAGE BREAKDOWN AND PROCESSES FOR DEALING WITH THEM

A. THE CRISES OF MARRIAGE BREAKDOWN

For most families, marriage breakdown provokes three crises: an emotional crisis; an economic crisis; and a parenting crisis. Both of the spouses and their children suffer severe emotional upheaval when the unity of the family disintegrates. Failure in the most basic of life's commitments is not lightly shrugged off by its victims. Marriage breakdown, whether or not accompanied by divorce, is a painful experience. Furthermore, relatively few families encounter separation or divorce without encountering financial setbacks. The emotional and economic crises resulting from marriage breakdown are compounded by the co-parental divorce when there are dependent children. Bonding between children and their absent parent is inevitably threatened by spousal separation and divorce.

Paul Bohannan identified six "stations" in the highly complex human process of marriage breakdown:

- the emotional divorce;
- the legal divorce;
- the economic divorce;
- the co-parental divorce;
- the community divorce; and
- the psychic divorce.[1]

---

1   Paul Bohannan, "The Six Stations of Divorce" in *Divorce and After* (New York: Doubleday & Co., 1971) c. II.

Each of these stations of divorce involves an evolutionary process and there is substantial interaction among them. The dynamics of marriage breakdown, which are multifaceted, cannot be addressed in isolation.

History demonstrates a predisposition to seek the solution to the crises of marriage breakdown in external systems. During the past 150 years, the Church, law, and medicine have each been called upon to deal with the crises of marriage breakdown. Understandably, each system has been found wanting in its search for solutions. People are averse to losing control over their own lives. Decrees and "expert" rulings that exclude affected parties from the decision-making process do not pass unchallenged. Omniscience is not the prerogative of any profession. Nor should the family's right to self-determination be lightly ignored.

B. THE EMOTIONAL DIVORCE

For many people, there are two criteria of self-fulfilment. One is satisfaction on the job. The second, and more important one, is satisfaction with one's marriage or family. When marriage breakdown occurs, the spouses and their children experience a grieving process. Separated spouses find themselves living alone in a couples-oriented society. The concept of the swinging single was belied by reality long before the AIDS crisis. The devastating effect of marriage breakdown is particularly evident with the displaced long-term homemaking spouse whose united family has crumbled and who is ill-equipped, psychologically and otherwise, to convert homemaking skills into gainful employment.

Most legal divorces in Canada are uncontested. Issues relating to the economic and parenting consequences of marriage breakdown are usually resolved by negotiation between the spouses, who are often represented by independent lawyers. Because the overwhelming majority of all divorces are uncontested, it might be assumed that the legal system works well in resolving the economic and parenting consequences of marriage breakdown. That assumption cannot pass unchallenged.

In the typical legal divorce scenario, spouses negotiate a settlement at a time when one or both are undergoing the emotional trauma of marriage breakdown. Psychiatrists and psychologists agree that this "emotional divorce" passes through a variety of states, including denial, hostility, and depression, to the ultimate acceptance of the death of the marriage. Working through the spousal emotional divorce rarely takes less than two years. In the interim, permanent and legally binding decisions are often made to regulate the economic and parenting consequences of the marriage breakdown. From a legal perspective, the economic and parenting consequences of the marriage breakdown are interdependent. Decisions respecting any continued occupation of the matrimonial home, the amount of child support, and the amount of spousal support, if any, are conditioned on the arrangements made for the future upbringing of the children. The perceived legal interdependence of property rights, support rights, and parental rights after divorce naturally affords opportunities for abuse by lawyers and their clients. The lawyer who has been imbued with the "will to win" from the outset of his or her career, coupled with the client who negotiates a settlement when his or her emotional divorce is unresolved, can wreak future havoc on the spouses and on their children. All too often, when settlements are negotiated, children become pawns or weapons in the hands of game-playing or warring adults and the battles do not cease with the judicial divorce.

The interplay between the emotional dynamics of marriage breakdown and regulation of the economic consequences of marriage breakdown may be demonstrated by the following examples. A needy spouse who insists that no claim for spousal support should be pursued may be manifesting a hope for reconciliation or a state of depression. A spouse who makes excessive demands is often manifesting hostility. A spouse who proffers an unduly generous financial settlement may be expiating guilt. Denial, depression, hostility, and guilt are all typical manifestations of the emotional divorce that elicit inappropriate responses to dealing with the practical economic and parenting consequences of marriage breakdown. Furthermore, like most emotional states they change with the passage of time. Separated spouses, lawyers, and mediators should be aware of the dangers of premature settlements when one or both of the spouses are still going through emotional turmoil. Indeed, the notion of a "cooling-off" period, though unsuccessful as a means of divorce avoidance, might have significant advantages with respect to negotiated spousal settlements on marriage breakdown. Certainly, spouses and their lawyers should more frequently assess the strategic potential of interim agreements as a stage in a longer-term divorce adjustment and negotiation process.

The legal divorce and the emotional divorce usually involve different time frames. Furthermore, the emotional divorce is rarely contemporaneous for both spouses. Lawyers frequently encounter situations where one spouse regards the marriage as over but the other spouse is unable or unwilling to accept that reality. In circumstances where one of the spouses is adamantly opposed to cutting the marital umbilical cord, embittered negotiations or contested litigation over support, property division, or custody or access often reflect an unresolved emotional divorce. Spouses who have not worked their way through the emotional divorce displace what is essentially a non-litigable issue relating to the preservation or dissolution of the marriage by fighting over the litigable issues of support, property-sharing, custody, and access. In such cases, the judicial disposition often fails to terminate spousal hostilities. Even when the legal battles over support and property have been finally adjudicated by the courts, spousal conflict can continue to rage over the children.

The multifaceted aspects of marriage breakdown require more than the typical adversarial legal response. In the words of Paul Bohannan,

> A "successful" divorce begins with the realization by two people that they do not have any constructive future together. That decision itself is a recognition of the emotional divorce. It proceeds through the legal channels of undoing the wedding, through the economic division of property and arrangements for alimony and support. The successful divorce involves determining ways in which children can be informed, educated in their new roles, loved and provided for. It involves finding a new community. Finally, it involves finding your own autonomy as a person and as a personality.[2]

The emotional trauma experienced by the spouses on the breakdown of their marriage is mirrored in the experience of the children of divorcing parents. The manifestation of these trauma takes a variety of forms that are largely conditioned upon the child's stage of development.[3]

Although divorce is rarely painless, especially when children are involved, the trauma of divorce can be eased with the help of therapy or counselling and even by access to informational and educational programs. In some jurisdictions, divorcing parents are required to attend courses that examine the impact of their conduct on the children and offer advice to parents that may reduce potentially harmful conduct such as

---

2   *Ibid.* at 62.
3   For an excellent overview of the impact of separation and divorce on children, see Canada, Ministry of Health and Welfare, *Because Life Goes On: Helping Children and Youth Live with Separation and Divorce*, 1994. For a guide to constructive parenting after divorce, see Julien D. Payne & Kenneth L. Kallish, "A Behavioural Science and Legal Analysis of Access to the Child in the Post-Separation/Divorce Family," Appendix, Proposed Visiting Code in *Payne's Digest on Divorce in Canada, 1968–1980*, looseleaf (Don Mills, ON: R. De Boo, 1982) at 775–77.

using children as weapons or pawns in the spousal conflict, fighting over the children, criticizing the other spouse in the presence of the children, or competing for the children's affection. Time may also be spent in dealing with practical matters such as household budgets, reaching fair child support arrangements, and providing guidelines or structures for parenting arrangements. Several jurisdictions also provide separate courses for the children of divorcing parents that are designed to help the children deal with the feelings of loss, guilt, fear, and grief.

C. RECENT TRENDS IN FAMILY DISPUTE RESOLUTION

Many lawyers and judges have now joined their critics from other disciplines by acknowledging the inefficacy of the law in resolving parenting disputes between separated and divorced spouses. The limitations of the law in resolving the economic consequences of marriage breakdown have been more cautiously acknowledged by the legal profession. However, the emergence of statutory provisions, regulations, and rules of court governing such matters as mandatory financial disclosure, case management, mediation, independent expert assessments, pre-trials, and formal offers to settle manifest a growing realization that litigation should be regarded as a last resort in the resolution of all family disputes. These and other developments signal a need for family law to focus much more on processes for dispute resolution. Sections 9 and 10 of the *Divorce Act*[4] pay lip-service to the potential benefits of counselling, negotiation, and mediation as processes for resolving disputes arising on divorce but do little to foster the use of these processes. More far-reaching statutory provisions are found in provincial legislation, such as section 3 of the Ontario *Family Law Act*,[5] which endorses voluntary mediation as a process for resolving any matter falling within the ambit of that Act, including spousal support, child support, and property entitlements on marriage breakdown. These are all indicia for the future.

To assert the truism that law and lawyers, like all other systems and professions, can lay no claim to omniscience in the resolution of family conflict is not the same as saying that law and lawyers have no contribution to make. We should not overlook the fact that the viability of dispute

---

4   See Section D(1), below in this chapter.
5   S.O. 1986, c. 4, now R.S.O. 1990, c. F.3.

resolution processes, including negotiation, mediation, and arbitration, cannot be divorced from the legal process as the ultimate means of resolving intractable disputes. Nor should we forget that lawyers, in practice, on the Bench, in federal and provincial legislatures, and in academe, have been at the forefront of welcome reforms in promoting dispute resolution processes. To take only one example, the Alberta Court of Queen's Bench has engaged in various judicial dispute resolution processes, as an alternative to the conventional trial, for more than ten years. These judicial dispute resolution processes include judicial mediation, mini-trials, summary trials, case management, and pre-trial conferences.[6]

D. DUTY OF LEGAL PROFESSION TO PROMOTE RECONCILIATION, NEGOTIATION, AND MEDIATION

1) Duty of Legal Adviser

Section 7 of the *Divorce Act*, 1968[7] imposed a duty on lawyers representing a divorce petitioner or respondent to discuss the possibility of spousal reconciliation and to inform the client of marriage counselling or guidance facilities that might assist the spouses in achieving reconciliation. This duty is restated in subsection 9(1) of the current *Divorce Act* and is now complemented by additional duties under subsection 9(2) that are designed to promote negotiated settlements and the mediation of support and custody disputes arising on divorce.[8]

The experience under section 7 of the *Divorce Act*, 1968 suggests that the duty to promote reconciliation tends to be regarded as a *pro forma* requirement by the legal profession. Once divorce proceedings are instituted, thereby triggering the statutory duty, few lawyers view spousal reconciliation as a viable option. The institution of the divorce proceeding is perceived as an extremely strong, if not conclusive, indication that at least one of the spouses is adamantly of the opinion that the marriage

---

6   *Botros v. Botros*, [2002] A.J. No. 1500 (Q.B.); *Yeoman v. Luhtala*, [2002] A.J. No. 1504 (Q.B.).

7   S.C. 1967–68, c. 24.

8   As to certification by the lawyer that the aforementioned duties have been discharged, see *Divorce Act*, R.S.C. 1985 (2d Supp.), c. 3, s. 9(3). As to the impact of s. 9 on the finality of separation agreements dealing with spousal support, see *Miglin v. Miglin*, [2003] 1 S.C.R. 303.

has irretrievably broken down and that any attempts to reconcile will prove futile. Most lawyers will, therefore, discharge their statutory duty by a brief discussion to ensure that their client is "a serious client" and by handing out a list of available marriage counselling services in the community.

Lawyers are effective, however, in promoting the negotiation of settlements. This is amply demonstrated by the fact that 86 percent of all divorce cases are uncontested from the outset and less than 4 percent involve a trial. Subsection 9(2) of the current *Divorce Act* may, therefore, be directed primarily towards providing mediation as an alternative process to litigation in those cases where no agreement can be reached by the lawyers on behalf of their clients.

The long-term impact of subsection 9(2) of the *Divorce Act* and the value of mediation will largely depend on the attitude of the legal profession. Whether mediation is viewed by lawyers as practical and beneficial or as an unwarranted invasion of the legal domain will be answered in the years ahead. Just as successful mediation requires the co-operation of the parties, so too, an interdisciplinary professional approach to the resolution of family conflict requires the co-operation of the involved professions. In all probability, lawyers will themselves increasingly engage in the mediation of spousal support and property disputes on marriage breakdown or divorce. Several provincial governing bodies of the legal profession in Canada have reviewed the canons of ethics in order to accommodate this practice. The Law Society of British Columbia addressed this issue in 1984 and permits lawyers to engage in family mediation under certain conditions.[9] Other provincial Law Societies have also endorsed the practice of lawyers engaging in mediation.[10]

Lawyers acting within the scope of their actual or apparent authority may bind their clients to a settlement negotiated on their behalf. If a lawyer negotiates a settlement without actual authority to do so, the client is still bound by the settlement so long as the other party was not aware of any limitation placed on the lawyer's authority.[11]

---

9   See Julien D. Payne, "The Mediation of Family Disputes" in *Payne's Divorce and Family Law Digest*, looseleaf (Don Mills, ON: R. De Boo, 1982), 1984 tab at 84-1861; see also Julien D. Payne & Eileen Overend, *ibid.*

10 See, for example, *Ontario Rules of Professional Conduct*, Rule 4.07 "Lawyers As Mediators" (22 June 2000).

11 *Correia v. Danyluk*, [2001] A.J. No. 799 (C.A.); *Cosper v. Cosper* (1995), 14 R.F.L. (4th) 152 (N.S.C.A.); *Landry v. Landry* (1981), 48 N.S.R. (2d) 136 (S.C.A.D.); *Rother v. Rother*, [2005] N.S.J. No. 138 (C.A.).

Findings of credibility and reliability are for the trial judge, as are findings of fact. Where there is nothing in the record indicating that the trial judge erred in law or made a palpable and overriding error of material facts or inferences drawn therefrom, an appellate court will not disturb the trial judge's finding that the appellant's former solicitor had actual authority to negotiate the settlement or, alternatively, any limitation placed on her authority was unknown to the other party, thus entitling that party to a declaration that a binding settlement had been reached.[12]

2) Duty of Court: Reconciliation

Subsections 10(1), (2), and (3) of the current *Divorce Act* substantially correspond to section 8 of the *Divorce Act, 1968*.[13] Subsection 10(1) of the *Divorce Act* imposes a duty on the court, before considering the evidence in a divorce proceeding, to satisfy itself that there is no possibility of the reconciliation of the spouses, unless the circumstances are of such a nature that it would clearly not be appropriate to do so. Subsection 10(2) further provides that, where at any stage of a divorce proceeding, the court sees a possibility of reconciliation, the court shall adjourn the proceeding to afford the spouses an opportunity to achieve a reconciliation. With the consent of the spouses or in its own discretion, the court may nominate a duly qualified person or agency to assist the spouses to achieve a reconciliation. Pursuant to subsection 10(3) of the *Divorce Act*, when fourteen days have elapsed from the date of any adjournment, the court must resume the proceeding on the application of either or both spouses.

The duty of the court under section 10 is confined to examining the prospects of reconciliation. By its nature, reconciliation implies a bilateral intention to re-establish the marital relationship. Where the court is faced with a complete denial of any prospect of reconciliation by the petitioner, the court should find against the possibility of reconciliation, notwithstanding a fervent desire for reconciliation on the part of the respondent.[14]

---

12 *Rother v. Rother*, [2005] N.S.J. No. 138 (C.A.).

13 S.C. 1967–68, c. 24.

14 *Pires v. Pires*, [2006] B.C.J. No. 698 (C.A.); *Challoner v. Challoner* (1973), 12 R.F.L. 311 (N.S.C.A.); *Gordon v. Keyes* (1985), 45 R.F.L. (2d) 177 at 185 (N.S.C.A.), citing *Payne's Digest on Divorce in Canada, 1968–1980*, above note 3 at 130, leave to appeal to S.C.C. refused (1985), 69 N.S.R. (2d) 358n, 163 A.P.R. 358n (S.C.C.); *McDermid v. McDermid* (1989), 21 R.F.L. (3d) 47 (Sask. C.A.); compare *Sheriff v. Sheriff* (1983), 31 R.F.L. (2d) 434 at 436 (Ont. S.C.); see also *Acchione v. Acchione* (1987), 9 R.F.L. (3d) 215 (Ont. S.C.). And see *Perchaluk v. Perchaluk* (1988), 56 Man. R. (2d) 46 (Q.B.).

3) Confidentiality

Subsections 10(4) and 10(5) of the current *Divorce Act* correspond to section 21 of the *Divorce Act*, 1968.[15] They provide as follows:

> *Nominee not competent or compellable*
> 10.(4) No person nominated by a court under this section to assist spouses to achieve a reconciliation is competent or compellable in any legal proceedings to disclose any admission or communication made to that person in his or her capacity as a nominee of the court for that purpose.

> *Evidence not admissible*
> (5) Evidence of anything said or of any admission or communication made in the course of assisting spouses to achieve a reconciliation is not admissible in any legal proceedings.

Pursuant to these provisions, the confidentiality of the reconciliation process is guaranteed by a statutory prohibition against the admissibility of evidence which, unlike a common-law privilege, cannot be waived.[16] Statements made during marriage counselling aimed at promoting a spousal reconciliation are inadmissible in subsequent divorce proceedings, even though the statements might themselves have been tantamount to cruelty. But a draft domestic contract presented to the wife by the husband is admissible as indicative of the husband's cruelty where no prior settlement negotiations had been entered into by the spouses.[17]

Judicial opinions have divided on the question whether the statutory prohibition is confined to reconciliation attempts undertaken by a court-appointed conciliator. In *Robson v. Robson*[18] and in *Cronkwright v. Cronkwright*,[19] Wright J. of the Ontario Supreme Court endorsed a restrictive interpretation of subsection 21(2) of the *Divorce Act*, 1968[20] so as to confine its application to admissions or communications made to a court-nominated counsellor. In *Shakotko v. Shakotko*,[21] however, Grant J. of the Ontario Supreme Court concluded that the statutory evidential

---

15   S.C. 1967–68, c. 24.
16   *Piercy v. Piercy* (1990), 29 R.F.L. (3d) 18 (B.C.S.C.).
17   *de Araujo v. de Araujo* (1986), 11 C.P.C. (2d) 272 (Ont. S.C.); see also *Osmond v. Osmond* (1989), 89 N.S.R. (2d) 333 (S.C.).
18   [1969] 2 O.R. 857 (S.C.).
19   (1970), 2 R.F.L. 214 (Ont. S.C.).
20   S.C. 1967–68, c. 24.
21   (1976), 27 R.F.L. 1 (Ont. S.C.).

prohibition applied to all reconciliation attempts and not merely to those conducted by a court-appointed person. It is submitted that the latter broad interpretation is to be preferred as implementing the social policy underlying the applicable statutory provisions, which is to promote reconciliation between the spouses wherever possible.

Although subsection 10(5) of the current *Divorce Act* prohibits the admission "in any legal proceedings" of any evidence as to what occurred during an endeavour to assist spouses to reconcile, the legislative authority of the federal government does not extend to prohibit the admission of evidence in a proceeding concerning property rights under provincial statute. Furthermore, if a party to such a proceeding seeks to obtain the protection of the common-law privilege that attaches to settlement negotiations, there must be some evidence to support the inference that the parties considered the occasions to be confidential and without prejudice, that matrimonial proceedings were being contemplated, and that the focus was on the settlement of a litigious issue.[22]

In *L.M.B. v. I.J.B.*,[23] the appellant sought to refute allegations of spousal and child abuse by seeking the production of third-party records relating to marriage counselling and the personal counselling of his oldest child, who had behavioural problems. The Alberta Court of Appeal unanimously refused to order production of either of the records on the ground that they were protected by common-law privilege, having regard to the four principles set out in the "Wigmore test," which was endorsed by the Supreme Court of Canada in *M.(A.) v. Ryan*.[24] The Alberta Court of Appeal was divided, however, on the question of whether admissibility of the marriage-counselling records was prohibited by subsection 10(5) of the *Divorce Act*, which provides that "[e]vidence of anything said or of any admission or communication made in the course of assisting spouses to achieve a reconciliation is not admissible in any legal proceeding." While conceding that this prohibition might well apply only to divorce proceedings, the majority judgment of Berger J.A., which was concurred in by Wittman J.A., concluded that the legislative jurisdictional authority of Parliament over divorce "extends to the enactment of a provision that renders all communications made in the course of assisting spouses to reconcile inadmissible whenever they occurred." In their opinion, the object and purpose of subsection 10(5) of the *Divorce Act* is to promote rec-

---

22 *Piercy v. Piercy* (1990), 29 R.F.L. (3d) 18 (B.C.S.C.).

23 [2005] A.J. No. 214 (C.A.).

24 [1997] 1 S.C.R. 157.

onciliation attempts, regardless of whether they occur before or after the institution of divorce proceedings. In a dissenting opinion on this aspect of the appeal, McFadyen J.A. concluded that, when viewed in the context of section 10 as a whole, subsection 10(5) refers only to court-sanctioned reconciliation attempts after divorce proceedings have been instituted.

In *Duits v. Duits*,[25] the mother alleged emotional and verbal abuse in contested custody proceedings, and she brought a motion to call a marriage counsellor as a witness. The motion was judicially dismissed on the bases of the inherent unreliability of the evidence and common-law privilege. As Turnbull J. observed, the common law views communications made during marriage counselling as privileged, provided that the following four criteria in *Wigmore on Evidence* are satisfied:

(i)   The communications must originate in a confidence that they will not be disclosed.

(ii) The element of confidentiality must be essential to the full and satisfactory maintenance of the relation between the parties.

(iii) The relation must be one which in the opinion of the community ought to be sedulously fostered.

(iv) The injury that would inure to the relation by the disclosure of the communications must be greater than the benefit thereby gained for the correct disposal of litigation.

As Turnbull J. further observed, however, in *M.(A.) v. Ryan*, in which the mother alleged emotional and verbal abuse, the Supreme Court of Canada has effectively ruled that privilege should not be a bar to justice. Thus, the court must determine if the evidence must be produced to get at the truth and prevent an unjust verdict. After conducting a *voir dire* with respect to the evidence of the marriage counsellor, Turnbull J. concluded that there was arguably some relevant evidence that might be considered if it met the tests of reliability and necessity. In this case, the test of reliability was not satisfied because both parties had, *inter alia*, violated the trust essential to marriage counselling by tape recording sessions for an ulterior motive and the marriage counsellor's observations and opinions might be attributable to planning and manipulation to "push the button" of one of the parties to create an adverse inference against that party. In addition to finding that the evidence of the marriage counsellor was inadmissible because it was inherently unreliable, Turnbull J. concluded that the public interest in maintaining the confidentiality of marriage

25   [2006] O.J. No. 1762 (Sup. Ct.).

counselling would have taken precedence over the immediate relevance of any evidence proffered in the custody litigation (the fourth step in *Wigmore's* test). Having regard to the evolution of diverse processes aimed at promoting the consensual resolution of family disputes, Turnbull J. expressed the opinion that the sanctity of these community-based and court-connected processes should be recognized in most cases. While there may be exceptional cases where the common-law recognition of the paramountcy of confidentiality must be abrogated, such cases should be relatively rare.

Subsections 10(4) and 10(5) of the *Divorce Act* are expressly confined to attempts at reconciliation. They have no application to a mediation process where the focus of the negotiations is not on reconciliation but on the resolution of the economic and parenting consequences of divorce.[26] The confidentiality of the mediation process is, nevertheless, protected by common-law principles governing privileged communications, subject to waiver of the privilege by both spouses.[27] When the safety of children is at risk, however, the confidentiality of the mediation process must yield to the overriding welfare of the children.[28]

Provincial laws of evidence apply in divorce proceedings.[29] In several provinces, specific legislation regulates the confidentiality of the mediation process, but there is some doubt respecting the applicability of these provisions to disputes arising in divorce proceedings.[30] Their questionable applicability to spousal and child support or to custody and access disputes arising in divorce proceedings is of limited significance because of the aforementioned applicability of common-law principles respecting privileged communications.

Whether the confidentiality of reconciliation or mediation processes is compatible with the *Canadian Charter of Rights and Freedoms* is a question that will, no doubt, engage the attention of the courts. In *M.*

---

26   See *McDonald v. McDonald* (1987), 6 R.F.L. (3d) 17 (B.C.S.C.).

27   *Porter v. Porter* (1983), 32 R.F.L. (2d) 413 (Ont. U.F.C.); *Keizars v. Keizars* (1982), 29 R.F.L. (2d) 223 (Ont. U.F.C.); see also *Sinclair v. Roy* (1985), 47 R.F.L. (2d) 15 (B.C.S.C.) and compare *McDonald v. McDonald* (1987), 6 R.F.L. (3d) 17 (B.C.S.C.). See also *A.H. v. J.T.H.*, [2004] B.C.J. No. 321 (S.C.) and compare *Rudd v. Trossacs Investments Inc.* (2004), 244 D.L.R. (4th) 758 (Ont. Sup. Ct.).

28   *Pearson v. Pearson*, digested in *The Lawyers Weekly* (3 July 1992) (Yukon S.C.).

29   *Divorce Act*, s. 23(1).

30   See Julien D. Payne, "New Approaches to the Resolution of Custody Disputes on Marriage Breakdown or Divorce" in *Payne's Divorce and Family Law Digest*, above note 9, 1983 tab at 83-1255 *et seq.*; and see *Sinclair v. Roy* (1985), 47 R.F.L. (2d) 15 (B.C.S.C.).

v. K.,[31] it was held that, in proceedings where the custody of a child is in issue, a statutory privilege respecting spousal communications to a marriage counsellor constitutes a violation of the child's right to due process under the United States and New Jersey Constitutions.

In *P.E.C. v. C.E.G.*,[32] it was held that, in very exceptional circumstances, the common-law privilege that attaches to a "without prejudice" report in a contested custody proceeding may be judicially overridden in the exercise of the court's *parens patriae* jurisdiction in order to ensure the protection and best interests of the children. In this case, the parents attended a settlement conference to address issues of custody and access. At the conference, the father raised concerns about the mother's alleged erratic and bizarre behaviour. To address these concerns, counsel for both parents agreed that the mother's mental state would be assessed by a psychiatrist whose report would be "without prejudice." In the report, the mother was diagnosed as having a borderline personality disorder that placed the children at risk. In consequence of this report, *ex parte* orders were granted that transferred the primary residential care of the children from the mother to the father and severely limited the mother's contact with the children. The psychiatrist's report was trenchantly criticized and was inconsistent with expert opinions presented on behalf of the mother, one of which involved a psychological assessment with psychometric testing. Being of the opinion that the mother could not properly reply to the damaging opinion expressed in the psychiatrist's report unless she were permitted access to the psychiatrist's background notes, Guerette J., of the New Brunswick Court of Queen's Bench, issued an order for the production of these notes and for the attendance of the psychiatrist on discovery, if requested. A similar direction was issued with respect to the experts who had presented reports on behalf of the mother.

E. MARRIAGE AND FAMILY COUNSELLING

In decades past, families would take their problems to the doctor, priest, or rabbi. These days, family crises are more likely to attract the attention of the police, lawyers, and the courts. Counselling is, nevertheless, available to families in crisis. In urban centres, professionals in private practice who have expertise in social work, psychology, or psychiatry offer

---

31   186 N.J. Super. 363, 452 A.2d 704 (N.J. Super. Ct. Ch. Div. 1982).
32   [2003] N.B.J. No. 193 (Q.B.).

marriage, family, and individual counselling on a fee-paying basis. They can be found in the Yellow Pages of any telephone directory together with listings for community services such as Family Service Agencies and Children's Aid Societies. Community agencies may provide counselling services free of charge or assess a fee based on a sliding scale to reflect the ability to pay.

Counselling may deal with an ongoing problem within an intact family or it may involve a family threatened by separation or divorce. In previous generations, marriage counselling existed to promote reconciliation. A couple heading for divorce was urged to reconcile. Today, reconciliation is regarded as only one of the options. Much of the effort of family counsellors is now directed towards helping families understand how they will be affected by separation or divorce and how they can deal with the emotional, economic, and parenting consequences of marriage breakdown.

Of course, not everybody who lives together goes through a ceremony of marriage. People who live in common-law relationships encounter similar types of problems to married couples whose relationship is threatened or terminated. They may need family counselling. Family Service Agencies and private practitioners also provide counselling services for people after separation or divorce. Of particular significance in this regard are blended or reconstituted families arising when divorced people remarry. Although step-parents are not inevitably related to the "wicked witch of the west," notwithstanding fairy tales to the contrary, the blending of children into new family structures is not always a smooth transition and may require insightful family counselling.

Marriage and family counselling has traditionally placed emphasis on the emotional dynamics of dysfunctional families and is regarded as therapeutic in nature, even if it falls short of being a sustained program of family therapy. The day-to-day consequences of marriage breakdown are also important aspects of family counselling. For example, families may be offered advice and assistance on such matters as child care and budgetary planning in light of separation or divorce.

Family Service Agencies are familiar with other support services available in the community, such as safe havens for battered women, alcohol and drug addiction treatment centres, vocational retraining programs, social assistance benefits, and housing services to which needy family members can be referred. In recent years, community agencies have moved into the field of mediation or conciliation, which is aimed at promoting a settlement of disputed issues between separated or divorcing adults. For the most part, however, Family Service Agencies confine their attention to dealing with the parenting consequences of separation or divorce. They do not get involved in issues of property sharing or spousal support.

F. NEGOTIATION

Less than 4 percent of divorces involve a trial of contested issues in open court. People normally settle their differences by negotiation. If each spouse is represented by an independent lawyer, the husband instructs his lawyer, the wife instructs her lawyer, and the lawyers engage in negotiation on behalf of their respective clients. Although information may become distorted in its transmission through the lawyers, the emotional divorce usually presents obstacles to divorcing spouses negotiating directly with each other without the benefit of legal representation. Couples caught up in the emotional dynamics of marriage breakdown often have great difficulty in communicating with each other because their emotions cloud their judgment. Fair and reasonable settlements in the emotionally charged atmosphere of marriage breakdown or divorce may, therefore, necessitate the intervention of lawyers or other third parties, such as mediators, who can bring objectivity to the bargaining table.

1) The Importance of Negotiation

Negotiation is the most effective way of resolving disputes. It leaves the decision-making authority with the disputants and is cost-efficient and timesaving when compared to other means of dispute resolution. Some people have the erroneous impression that lawyers spend most of their time in court. In reality, most lawyers spend the bulk of their time consulting with their clients and engaging in negotiations that will lead to settlements. Good negotiation skills are a prerequisite to the constructive resolution of family disputes.

2) Negotiation Techniques

There are three basic approaches to negotiation:

(i)   hard bargaining;
(ii) soft bargaining; and
(iii) principled negotiation.

These approaches are reviewed in detail by Roger Fisher and William Ury in their bestselling book, *Getting to Yes*. At the risk of oversimplification, the following summary may shed some light on their differences.

Hard bargaining reflects a competitive or adversarial approach to negotiation. The hard bargainer takes a position and is difficult to shift from that position. He or she makes concessions reluctantly but demands liberal concessions from the other side. Hard bargaining does not necessarily involve unethical or improper conduct but does imply that the dispute involves a contest of wills that the hard bargainer is seeking to win.

Soft bargaining implies an excessive degree of co-operation and the avoidance of confrontation. Soft bargainers are inclined to make too many concessions without demanding a fair return. Soft bargainers are particularly vulnerable when negotiating with hard bargainers, although soft bargainers may reach a point when they say "enough is enough."

So-called principled negotiators, unlike hard and soft bargainers, strive to avoid positional bargaining. They perceive themselves as joint problem solvers. Fisher and Ury have identified the following four characteristics of principled negotiation:

(i)   Separate the people from the problem.
(ii) Focus on interests, not positions.
(iii) Generate options that will be advantageous to both parties.
(iv) Insist that the result be based on objective standards.

In separating the people from the issues in family disputes, it is imperative that settlement negotiations avoid blaming one spouse over the other. Issues of "who is to blame" lead to guilt and hostility, neither of which is helpful in the search for equitable solutions to the financial and parenting consequences of marriage breakdown. The focus of discussions should not be on why things have happened but on how they are to be dealt with. Successful negotiations normally require the parties to re-establish some measure of trust and mutual respect, at least when there will be ongoing parental responsibilities.

Fisher and Ury's insistence that negotiations focus on interests, not positions, signifies that behind any position there is a need, desire, or concern that should be identified. Interests may be material, such as money or property, or they may be psychological, such as the need for recognition or security.

Generating options for mutual gain is acknowledged to be a vital feature of effective negotiations. For example, it may be better for both of the parents to share the responsibility for raising the children rather than leaving the responsibility to one parent and relegating the other parent to the status of a passive bystander. Sharing the responsibility will encourage both parents to contribute to the growth and development of their children and also enables them to have time for themselves when they can enjoy the freedom of not being tied to the children. Options that are advantageous to both sides increase the prospect of reaching a mutually acceptable solution.

The use of objective standards to evaluate possible solutions promotes reasonable and fair settlements that can survive the test of time. Objective criteria that are relied on by family law practitioners include relevant statutory provisions and judgments from cases involving comparable facts.

The notion that principled negotiation will substitute win-win solutions for the win-lose philosophy of adversarial bargaining is not without its critics. It may, nevertheless, prove attractive to separated, divorcing, and divorced spouses who can ill-afford to engage in hostile legal negotiations or protracted litigation.

3) Aspects of Successful Negotiation on Family Breakdown

Successful negotiations are dependent on timing, preparation, and effective use of leverage.

Timing is especially crucial in family disputes. Both parties must be ready and willing to abandon their personal hostilities. They must be capable of controlling emotions that can slow down or prevent reasonable settlements. They must have confidence in their lawyers but should not place the ultimate responsibility for a settlement in the hands of their lawyers. They are the persons who must live with the outcome. They should not lightly ignore legal advice but must make their own decisions.

Many people see no need to prepare for negotiation. After all, they can always "play it by ear." They are mistaken. Successful negotiations require careful planning. Just as good musicians do not "play it by ear," neither do good negotiators. Preparation for negotiation requires a knowledge of the relevant facts, an awareness of your own strengths and weaknesses and those of the other side, and a sense of those factors that can be used as leverage or bargaining chips. It can be useful for the disputants and their lawyers to prepare a written negotiation plan itemizing such matters as the following:

(i)   issues to be resolved;

(ii)   your needs and interests, both financial and psychological;

(iii) the needs and interests of the other side;

(iv)   the needs and interests of any third parties, such as children or grandparents;

(v)   those matters that are of paramount importance to you and those where you would be willing to make concessions;

(vi)   the strengths and weaknesses of your case;

(vii) the strengths and weaknesses of the other side's case;

(viii) your best alternative to a negotiated agreement ("BATNA"); and

(ix)   options for resolution of the issues.

An agenda should be established for the negotiations in order to keep issues on track and to accommodate the anticipated time frame for completion of the negotiations. Be aware that deadlines can be used to force concessions. Family dependants who are in financial need cannot withstand a long negotiation process. It is, nevertheless, possible to negotiate issues in stages. For example, issues of spousal and child support and temporary occupation of the matrimonial home may take on a much greater urgency than the sharing of property acquired by the spouses during their marriage. Lawyers frequently draft "interim settlements" that are intended to apply until they are replaced by a permanent and comprehensive settlement.

Knowledge is power. Experienced lawyers can predict the legal outcome of some of the issues arising between spouses on the breakdown of their relationship. In the ordinary course of events, for example, the value of property acquired by either or both of the spouses during their marriage will be equally shared. The amount and duration of child support is reasonably predictable by family law specialists. But spousal support is not nearly so predictable even though it may be vital to the economic security of a custodial parent and the children. There are, of course, no guarantees that an experienced lawyer's predictions on any of the issues will be borne out if the matter goes to trial. Judges are not always predictable — the human factor can get in the way. In any event, litigation is expensive. It costs money to litigate, even for the so-called winner. And in family law, there are rarely any clear winners. Even clients with a relatively weak legal case have something to bargain with, namely, the financial cost and uncertainty of litigation and the emotional wear and tear of protracted negotiations or litigation.

Knowledge of the relevant facts is an obvious necessity for successful negotiation. Negotiators must know what they are talking about. In family disputes, there is often a significant difference between relevant facts from a legal point of view and relevant facts in the minds of the disputants. Here again, emotions tend to get in the way. For example, many provincial statutes, as well as the federal *Divorce Act*, stipulate that matrimonial misconduct must be disregarded in any legal determination of the right to, amount, and duration of spousal support. Spousal misconduct is also irrelevant to claims for property division on marriage breakdown. Yet, for many separated and divorcing spouses, the misconduct of their partner is foremost in their minds. The dichotomy between *legal and personal* perceptions of relevant facts tends to become blurred in negotiations as compared to litigation, because psychological factors come into play.

Insofar as relevant legal facts are regulated by provincial legislation, as distinct from federal divorce legislation, they will not be uniform throughout Canada. For example, different provinces have different statutory criteria that regulate property sharing on marriage breakdown. Consequently, property rights for separated and divorcing spouses may vary according to whether the spouses live in British Columbia, Ontario, Quebec, or Saskatchewan.

Negotiators must always keep in mind their "BATNA" — their best alternative to a negotiated agreement. It operates as a tripwire against making too many unreciprocated concessions. It also empowers a person to walk away from a bad deal. Unconscionable settlements in family disputes are to be avoided like the plague. They undermine ongoing relationships involving the children. In addition, they are an open invitation to re-open issues by way of litigation or for a party to abandon his or her commitment by taking the law into his or her own hands.

G. MEDIATION

1) Nature of Mediation

The essence of mediation is that the family members are themselves responsible for determining the consequences of their divorce. Self-determination with the aid of an impartial third party is the cornerstone of mediation. Divorce mediation is a process aimed at facilitating the consensual resolution of the economic and parenting consequences of marriage breakdown.

The mediator must defuse family conflict to a level where the parties can communicate with each other. They can then look at their options and apply objective standards with a view to negotiating a fair settlement. Mediation is neither medication nor meditation. Mediation is not to be confused with family therapy. Mediation aims to resolve the practical economic and parenting consequences of marriage breakdown. It is a time-limited process that is intended to produce a formal written settlement. Mediation looks to the future rather than the past. Mediators are usually unconcerned with the reasons for family dysfunction or the search for possible cures. They are not marriage counsellors or therapists. They deal with the practical consequences, not the causes, of marriage breakdown.

Mediation must also be distinguished from arbitration. In mediation, disputants seek a mutually acceptable solution. In arbitration, they agree to be bound by the decision of a third party.

2) Approaches to Mediation

Mediators come in diverse shapes and sizes. They may be engaged in private practice. They may be connected with courts. They may work in community-based services, such as Family Service Agencies.

Many mediators are professional social workers. Some are psychologists; a few are psychiatrists or lawyers. Some mediators have no direct link with the established professions and are self-made, and in some cases self-proclaimed. For many professionals, mediation is still a sideline generated by clientele demands. Some mediation models favour a team approach where a social worker or psychologist and a lawyer jointly or sequentially engage in the mediation process, but there is no one single or preferred model.

Many mediators confine their practice to parenting disputes. Those mediators whose expertise lies in psychiatry may adhere to a therapeutic model in which marital history and the family of origin are regarded as significant in the search for solutions to parenting problems. Marriage counsellors of a traditional persuasion, who perceive their function as promoting both reconciliation and mediation, may also look to the past in order to plan for the future. Social workers or family therapists whose practice has centred on short-term crisis counselling are inclined to focus on the present and future rather than on the distant past. Lawyer mediators adopt a pragmatic approach to the resolution of economic and parenting consequences of marriage breakdown by emphasizing legal rights and obligations.

Mediation is not a monolithic process. Systems and processes vary even though the goal of consensual resolution is constant.

3) Reasons for Mediation

The most common responses to conflict are "fight or flight." Often neither is the right response. Mediation provides an alternative to conflict when spouses or former spouses are unable to negotiate directly with each other but wish to avoid the adversarial postures of the legal process.

- Negotiated settlements achieved through mediation may be more likely to be respected by the disputants than court-imposed orders.
- The privacy of mediation is less threatening than open conflict in a public courtroom.

Mediation can provide more personal or "tailor-made" solutions than traditional legal procedures.

Successful mediation is much cheaper than protracted litigation. However, comparing the costs of successful mediation and litigation is misleading. The vast majority of divorces involve the negotiation of settlements by lawyers. Very few divorces involve a trial. Negotiation through a mediation process is not necessarily cheaper than negotiation through the traditional legal process. Indeed, many mediators insist that any mediated settlement must be reviewed by independent lawyers hired by each spouse.

Although mediation is not always cheaper, it appears to have several advantages not enjoyed by the legal process. Family members are often intimidated by the formal complexity and adversarial nature of the legal process. When the trial date looms, they would rather surrender than engage in warfare through the courts. For many divorcing couples, mediation offers opportunities for them to retain control over their own lives. In parenting disputes, in particular, mediation can establish a framework for future communication and an ongoing exchange of information and ideas respecting the upbringing of the children.

4) Goals of Mediation

As already noted, mediation is goal-oriented. It aims at an end product — namely, a negotiated settlement. First and foremost, mediation is a process by which people attempt to resolve their disputes by agreement. Important secondary goals may include improving communication and reducing tension between the disputants.

A mediated agreement should be reduced to writing and executed in accordance with established legal requirements. Mediators without legal expertise tread on dangerous ground if they assume the responsibility for drafting a formal settlement. They may even be accused of engaging in the unauthorized practice of law. The law of contract that regulates the validity and enforceability of agreements, and the statutes and family law doctrine that have an impact on contractual autonomy, are relatively complex. Although spousal agreements do not normally oust the jurisdiction of the courts over custody and access disputes, different considerations may apply to spousal support and property agreements. Consequently, many non-legally trained mediators prepare only a memorandum of understanding for submission to the lawyers for each party. This memorandum identifies the areas of consensus reached by the disputants and may be expressly declared as not legally binding on the parties until a formal contract has been executed.

5) Arriving at a Fair Settlement

When parties talk about "a fair settlement," they usually mean a workable agreement that meets their subjective needs. Of course, the parties' own sense of what is fair may not be consistent with standards applied by third parties called in to assist them. When mediators talk about the fairness of the final settlement they may mean any one or more of the following:

- "not unconscionable" (i.e., no undue influence or duress);
- "not disproportionate";
- "workable," "legally fair" (i.e., in line with decided cases and applicable statute law);
- "objectively fair" (i.e., meets actual as opposed to perceived needs); or
- "meets each party's sense of what is fair."

An American commentator has concluded that the mediator's duty is to facilitate an agreement "that (1) meets the participants' own senses of fairness; (2) does not violate minimal societal notions of fairness between persons who make agreements; and (3) does not violate minimal standards of fairness towards unrepresented third parties."[33]

---

33   L. Riskin, "Towards New Standards in the Neutral Lawyer in Mediation" (1984) 26 Ariz. L. Rev. 329 at 354.

6) Circumstances in Which Mediation Is Inappropriate

Various techniques exist to enable mediators to effectively redress imbalances of power. If the imbalance of power cannot be redressed and an uninformed or intimidated party may be induced to agree to an unrealistic or unfair settlement, the mediator should consider terminating the negotiations. Where an imbalance of power will lead to an abuse of power, mediation is inappropriate. In some disputes, inequalities of bargaining power between spouses may be more satisfactorily handled by the legal process.

Clearly, mediation is not suitable for all persons. Many mediators contend that mediation is inappropriate when either of the parties is physically violent, addicted to alcohol or drugs, or cannot face the reality of the death of the marriage. People with a "winner-take-all" mentality are not likely to benefit from mediation, which requires an attitude of "give and take" and compromise.

7) Full Disclosure and Confidentiality

Full disclosure is a prerequisite to effective mediation. A frank exchange of information concerning income and assets is essential to the mediation of support and property disputes on marriage breakdown.

Mediators stress the advisability of predetermining what can or cannot be disclosed to third parties, including lawyers and the courts, during or following an ongoing mediation process. The parties are free to select "open" or "closed" mediation. Open mediation signifies that the parties waive their rights to confidentiality. Closed mediation implies that confidentiality is critical and that neither the parties nor the mediator will be permitted to give evidence in any subsequent litigation as to what transpired during mediation.

8) Involvement of Third Parties

There is a difference between using third parties, such as lawyers and accountants, for information purposes and involving third parties, such as live-ins or in-laws, as active participants in the mediation process. At an early stage, it is important for the mediator and the disputants to define the direct or indirect involvement of other parties. These decisions will partly depend on the preferences of the negotiating parties and partly on the approach taken by the mediator. For example, a "family systems" mediator may adopt an holistic approach that directly involves third parties, such as grandparents or common-law spouses. A lawyer/mediator would be more inclined to see only the disputants themselves.

9) Involvement of Children

There are differences of opinion respecting the role of the children and, indeed, of the mediator, when the mediation process concerns the resolution of parenting disputes. Ignoring the children's perceptions, wishes, and preferences raises a significant risk of the children undermining the settlement. When children are involved in the process, however, the parents must not delegate the decision making to the children.

A distinction needs to be drawn between involving the children in the mediation process on a continuing basis and consulting them on an *ad hoc* basis in order to ascertain their views or preferences. Whether or not the children are consulted, it is important that their anxieties be allayed, that loyalty conflicts be avoided, that they be kept informed of progress, and that they understand the consequences of any mediated settlement.

10) Involvement of Lawyers

Access to independent legal advice must be assured once the dispute has been resolved. The injection of legal expertise into the mediation process itself, whether directly or indirectly, may also be of vital importance before specific decisions are taken. For example, lawyers for the respective parties might be called upon to provide information about the legal and tax implications of particular types of property division or to advise about the probable disposition that would be reached in the event of contested litigation. In the latter case, the legal input provides criteria against which the fairness of a prospective settlement can be measured.

A mediated settlement of financial and property issues on marriage breakdown should always be reviewed by independent lawyers for each of the disputants. Because review of any proposed settlement opens the door to one or both of the independent lawyers sabotaging the agreement, family disputants are wise to select and consult their respective lawyers at an early stage in the mediation process. Early involvement of the lawyers in the mediation process enables the disputants to evaluate the opportunities for, and the potential obstacles to, a mediated settlement.

11) Issues to Be Mediated

At an early stage, the mediator and the parties must define the issues to be examined. They should also agree that new issues are not to be unilaterally sprung on a party at a later stage. The parties should be discouraged from predetermining what is not negotiable when the parameters of the dispute are being set. Rather, the presumption should be that everything to be discussed is negotiable; otherwise, parties become entrenched and immovable.

The mediator's attitudes and expertise may have as much bearing on the subject matter to be mediated as the views of the parties themselves. For example, many mediators shy away from comprehensive divorce mediation, which includes parenting, support, and property disputes; they prefer to confine their practice to parenting disputes. The inclination of non-legally trained mediators to restrict their roles to parenting disputes may be explicable in part by the readiness of lawyers to opt out of such disputes and confine their attention to the economic consequences of marriage breakdown, such as support arrangements and property division. It is questionable, however, how far parenting disputes can be viewed as separate from the economic reorganization of the fractured family. The potential relationship between parenting arrangements and continued occupation of the family residence and child support is self-evident. Parenting arrangements may also be relevant to spousal support for a custodial parent. Mothers worried about economic security may be prepared to make reasonable concessions in parenting areas in order to obtain appropriate financial benefits. Conversely, fathers who place a high value on maintaining a close relationship with their children are usually more open to discussion of issues such as the amount of support payable or continued occupation of the family residence by the custodial parent and children. The mediator must ensure that neither parent takes undue advantage of his or her position as the primary parent or the primary breadwinner.

12) Neutrality of Mediators

Mediators must not only preserve a neutral stance; they must also be perceived as neutral by the disputants. The term "neutral" does not mean a mediator will be passive. Mediators can take active roles to facilitate settlement and their training and personal value systems will clearly affect their overall approach to the mediation process. Intervention, though quite legitimate for the purpose of restructuring the lines of communication or identifying new options, has to stop short of taking the decision-making authority away from the parties. If a mediator is perceived as taking sides, his or her credibility is destroyed and the parties will lose confidence in the process.

13) Common Impediments to Settlement

a) Emotional Barriers

Marriage breakdown spawns emotional crises that may totally frustrate any attempt at mediation. Realization by both parties that the marriage is over is usually a necessary prerequisite to a satisfactory and lasting settlement. If one spouse is committed to terminating the marital relationship but the other spouse is unwilling to cut the marital tie, then disputes over property, support, and parenting arrangements may be projections of the unresolved emotional divorce, which, if unaddressed, can present a serious stumbling block to any mediated settlement. Spouses who arrive at the divorce mediator's door are often emotionally distraught. They may be angry and resentful; they usually lack respect for and are deeply mistrustful of each other; they may feel rejected and desolate; and they may lack self-confidence or be full of grief or guilt. Such manifestations of an unresolved emotional divorce may demonstrate a need for counselling or therapy either before or during the mediation process.

b) "Stuck Spots"

At times, the parties may reach impasses on specific issues that are not symptomatic of irreconcilable conflict but are simply temporary failures to find a workable compromise. D.T. Saposnek aptly calls these "stuck spots." They must be overcome but rarely undermine the success of the mediation process in reaching a final comprehensive settlement.

c) Imbalances of Power

Imbalances of power between the parties may hinder a fair settlement. They may be so severe that the mediator will find it impossible to redress them without being perceived as favouring one spouse over the other.

d) War Games

Mediators are in agreement that war games must be suppressed if mediation is to succeed. There should be no clearing out the bank account, no removal of the children without consent, no poisoning the minds of the children, and no acrimonious litigation. The first step of any mediator or lawyer should be to establish a truce between the parties and the cessation of hostile activities.

14) Mediation Strategies to Circumvent or Remove Impediments to Settlement

Mediators have developed techniques for avoiding or removing impediments to settlement. Not all mediators use the same techniques; the strategies are numerous and have many variations.

a) Dealing with Anger and Hostility

The mediator's main task is to divert the emotional energy generated by anger and hostility into a constructive mediation process. One technique widely used by mediators is to neutralize highly emotional outbursts such as accusations by reframing what was said in such a way as to focus on the issues — not the personalities. Another way to defuse tension and also to clarify feelings is to allow what mediators commonly refer to as "controlled venting." There is general agreement that this should be attempted only if the venting will reduce the emotional charge. Mediators may have to adopt an assertive interventionist role when emotional outbreaks threaten the lines of communication. If a session becomes hostile and unproductive, the mediator may temporarily withdraw and resume discussion after tempers have cooled. Alternatively, the mediator may adjourn the whole session to allow the intensity of feeling to abate.

Hostilities that are manifested in parenting disputes can often be controlled or diverted if the mediator reframes issues so as to place emphasis on the child's need to preserve positive relationships with both parents and the psychological damage that the children may suffer as a consequence of continued friction. Many separated and divorced parents can be brought to reason by asking them to address their child's welfare rather than their personal gratification. Spouses, who may be disinclined to be financially generous to their marriage partners, may loosen their purse strings when the emphasis is placed on the economic and emotional well-being of their children, even though the custodial parent will indirectly benefit from any generosity extended to the children. In the childless marriage, where spouses project their hostility in support and property disputes, the mediator will often encounter much more difficulty appealing to the "better judgment" of the spouses. Much greater emphasis may be placed on the legal rights and obligations of the parties, the degree of uncertainty inherent in the substantive law and the legal process, and the relative ability of each spouse to absorb the risk of uncertain litigation and the financial and emotional consequences of contested legal proceedings.

b) Circumventing "Stuck Spots"

Spacing the sessions and strategic use of an adjournment can be particularly effective to resolve deadlock when an impasse has been caused by lack of information. Disputants may, for example, be given assigned tasks of gathering or supplying additional information or seeking input from third parties. The late O.J. Coogler, a pioneer of family mediation in the United States, endorsed arbitration as a means of resolving an impasse, but this should only be used as a last resort to avoid litigation. The better route may be to seek an expert opinion on the matter. If legal norms are applicable, a written opinion may be sought from an independent senior counsel when the facts are not in dispute. This obviates the expense, inconvenience, or apprehension of a personal appearance by the disputants at an arbitration hearing. Information or an independent expert opinion may also be sought from accountants, appraisers, and estate planners. The use of expert custody assessments prepared by psychologists or psychiatrists is, however, more problematic. Proper testing and evaluation necessitates the direct participation of all affected family members and tends to shift decision-making authority from the disputants to the assessor. The use of counselling or therapy to complement the mediation process may, on the other hand, be advantageous and can sometimes eliminate emotional roadblocks to a mediated settlement.

Adjournment is only one of many strategies available to the mediator when discussions reach an impasse. Deadlocks may also be broken by broadening the terms of reference beyond those of the spouses, by reformulating or reframing the issue, or by asking the disputants to generate options to resolve the "stuck spot." The objective is to change adversarial perspectives into co-operative perspectives. With some disputants, it is useful to emphasize the emotional and financial cost of not resolving the impasse. A number of mediators stress the value of temporary agreements as a way of preserving the status quo during mediation or of consolidating progress made. Short-term experimental agreements may provide an effective means of testing the viability of options that have been identified. Temporary or limited-issue agreements have the advantage of emphasizing the positive and relegating an impasse to the status of a negotiable obstacle en route to comprehensive resolution of the dispute.

c) Private Caucusing

Opinions differ on whether private caucusing is an appropriate means of breaking an impasse between disputants. Private caucusing involves the mediator meeting with each of the disputants separately. Some mediators consider that private caucusing can reduce or eliminate logjams when either party is extremely sensitive or hostile. Other mediators are uncomfortable with private caucusing. At the very outset of the mediation process, the parties and the mediator should resolve whether private caucusing will be used.

d) Restoring Trust and Respect

Setting the right tone for settlement is critically important. The mediator must foster co-operative solutions by re-establishing trust and respect between the disputants. In order to establish a positive ambience, mediators adopt a number of useful strategies, such as setting joint budgetary assignments, or encouraging trial parenting arrangements. The rationale is clear; joint tasks promote the search for mutually acceptable solutions and shift attention away from recriminations and fault finding. Mediators and disputants cannot expect to resolve chronic emotional problems, but more limited success may be within their grasp if they focus their attention on workable solutions to practical pressing problems.

Co-operation is harder to achieve in some circumstances than in others. In "zero-sum negotiation," for example, where the interests of the two parties are diametrically opposed and any gain to one spouse represents a loss to the other, co-operation may not be possible. In contrast, in "mixed motive negotiation," where the interests of the parties are partially opposed and partially coincidental, parties may be convinced of the value of co-operating in order to maximize their respective interests.

e) Redressing Power Imbalances

Mediation can be an empowering process insofar as it fosters respect and co-operation but its success depends on active participation by both parties and requires a relatively balanced capacity to negotiate. True equality in the balance of power may be impossible to achieve, but mediators must prevent an abuse of power by either party. Mediators can use a variety of techniques to redress an imbalance of power between the parties. For example, if inequality of bargaining power stems from lack of knowledge, information can be provided. Unequal negotiating skills can sometimes be balanced by insightful intervention and restructuring by the mediator or by the allocation of joint assignments to the parties. Intimidating negotiation patterns can be interrupted and reframed in order to provide support to the disadvantaged party. However, where the imbalance of power is considered to be so great that the mediator cannot intervene without endangering his or her neutrality, the mediator should refuse to sanction the process and suggest other means of dispute resolution.

15) Steps in Mediation Process

Sheila Kessler, in workshop materials entitled *Creative Conflict Resolution*,[34] identified four basic steps in the mediation process, namely,

(i)   setting the stage;
(ii) defining the issues;
(iii) processing the issues; and
(iv) resolving the issues.

a) Setting the Stage

Even when people consider the possibility of mediation as a means of resolving their family disputes, they usually have very little awareness of the mediation process. After the couple meets with the mediator and exchanges preliminary information concerning the couple's needs and the qualifications and experience of the mediator, the stage is set for the mediator to explain the process and the ground rules that will be applied. The mediator explains his or her approach to mediation, how the meetings will be conducted, and how issues will be dealt with. The mediator emphasizes that mediation is voluntary and may compare mediation to alternative methods of conflict resolution. Most mediators insist that the process be confidential so that the mediator cannot be called as a witness in any subsequent litigation between the parties. The mediator will explain his or her role as that of an impartial facilitator who will assist the parties in their endeavours to find a solution to the problems with which they are faced. The mediator will impress on the parties that, while the mediator controls the process, the parties themselves control the substantive outcome of their dispute.

---

34   Atlanta National Institute for Professional Training, 1978.

b) Defining the Issues

In divorce mediation, the fundamental issues relate to one or more of the following matters:

(i)   property sharing;
(ii) spousal support;
(iii) child support; and
(iv) parenting arrangements ("custody" and "access").

The parties may have dramatically opposite views on all or any of these matters. At the outset, the areas of agreement and disagreement must be identified. The mediator will then assist the parties in segregating their feelings from the substantive issues. Relationship issues may warrant counselling but mediation must focus on dealing with the practical consequences of the breakdown of the relationship.

In assisting the parties to define the specific issues, the mediator tends to move them from positional bargaining to an identification of their needs and interests.

c) Processing the Issues

Processing the issues involves an examination of the options. The mediator will encourage the parties to "brainstorm," which signifies generating a wide variety of options without evaluating them. After the listing of options has been exhausted, the parties can then evaluate their respective strengths and weaknesses. This presupposes effective communication between the parties. Mutual trust, self-confidence, and the ability to exchange opinions without rancour may need to be re-established between the spouses by the mediator's use of diverse techniques that can promote a climate for meaningful dialogue between the parties. A co-operative search for options that will maximize the advantages to both parties goes a long way towards providing the basis for a fair and reasonable settlement. Mutually advantageous options may be easier to discover when issues relating to the children are the focal point or an integral part of the mediation process. Even in property and support disputes, however, it is usually advantageous to both parties to avoid expensive and emotionally wearing litigation.

d) Resolving the Issues

Resolving the issues involves sifting through all the options until a comprehensive settlement is reached. Although the parties may have temporarily resolved specific issues at different times in the mediation process, it is generally understood that these arrangements are tentative until such time as all issues have been resolved. At that point, the mediator will prepare a draft memorandum of understanding that can be subsequently converted into a formal legal contract.

16) Court-Connected Mediation

In North America, court-connected mediation of family disputes can be traced back to 1939 and the pioneering efforts of the Los Angeles Conciliation Court. For twenty years, counsellors working in this court concentrated their attention on attempts to reconcile the spouses. It was not until the 1960s that the counselling orientation changed to one of facilitating the reasonable settlement of the consequences of divorce.

Following the example of the Los Angeles Conciliation Court, other counties in California developed Conciliation Courts, as did other states. Procedures and systems established in these courts do not adhere to a single model but have a common philosophy of approach.

Some features of the Los Angeles Conciliation Court were imported into Canada in 1972, largely through the efforts of Marjorie M. Bowker, a former judge of the Edmonton Family Court. She secured funding from the federal government to establish what became known as the Edmonton Conciliation Project on a pilot or experimental basis for a fixed term of three years. She sought the assistance of Franklin Bailey, a former senior marriage counsellor with the Los Angeles Conciliation Court. Franklin Bailey was appointed as Project Consultant and was actively involved in the development of policies, techniques, and administrative structures necessary for effective implementation of the court-connected conciliation service. On the expiry of the pilot project in 1975, the subsequently re-named Family Conciliation Service became funded exclusively by the province of Alberta. It is now a permanent agency under the authority of the provincial Department of Social Services and Community Health. Although its procedures and focus have been adjusted over the years, the Family Conciliation Service still concentrates on the conciliation or mediation of family disputes arising on divorce. Counselling staff are accessible to families through referral by lawyers, judges, Family Court counsellors, or paralegal workers. The stated objective of the Family Conciliation Service is "to help parties make decisions about the marriage and/or related issues of custody, access, and sometimes maintenance."

Since the mid-1970s, court-connected conciliation services have been developed in other cities, including Vancouver, Montreal, Kingston, Toronto, and Windsor. Some have encountered funding difficulties and have died. Others have survived. Conciliation or mediation services continue to be an integral part of Unified Family Courts, which have been established in some Canadian provinces.

17) Pros and Cons of Mediation

Mediation can facilitate tailor-made solutions to individual problems. It is usually less threatening than the legal process and its self-determined agreements may prove more durable and adaptable than court-ordered settlements. However, mediation is not appropriate for everybody, nor is it appropriate in all circumstances. Not all self-styled mediators are qualified. Successful mediation presupposes high professional standards because of the control a mediator exercises over the process, and because the clients are frequently psychologically disadvantaged by the trauma of family breakdown. Mediation may "belong" to the parties, but a successful outcome is crucially dependent on the expertise of the mediator. Practising mediators are still grappling with problems relating to techniques and procedures as well as professional qualifications, standards, and ethics. Family members who look to private mediation as a means of conflict resolution must, therefore, undertake careful inquiries to ensure that they have recourse to a qualified and experienced mediator.

Some feminist commentators have suggested that mediation is disadvantageous to women because of an inherent imbalance of power between the sexes. It is doubtful, however, whether legal processes assure any greater protection to women.

18) Professional and Community Responses to Mediation

The future of mediation will largely depend on its receptivity by existing professional groups, and by the lay community — its potential consumers. There is a dire need for broadly-based ongoing sources of information, whether provided through the mass media, the schools, community agencies, or under professional auspices, such as the Church, medicine, and the law. The professions must themselves become educated.

Information is required to dispel the myths of mediation. Members of the legal community who view their vested interests as being threatened by the emerging process of mediation have to be reassured. Mediation must be better understood by lawyers, among whom are to be found both its strongest supporters and its strongest opponents. The legal system is not undermined by mediation. Indeed, the legal system and mediation are complementary, rather than competing or contradictory, processes. Both seek to provide a solution to disputes. Each has its place. Neither is self-sufficient: no profession has a monopoly or omniscience in the resolution of human conflict.

Although court-connected conciliation or mediation services are not new to Canada in family dispute resolution, they are likely to play a more substantial role in the future as governments seek to reduce the costs of access to justice. Budgetary restraints will, of course, continue to limit the resources available to promote the consensual resolution of family disputes with the aid of court-connected or community-based conciliation and counselling services. Consequently, there will be a growing demand for community and private services.

19) The Future of Family Mediation

Predictions as to the future of family and divorce mediation may be reflected in its past. Mediation, whether court-connected or private, has found a growing place in the resolution of family disputes during the last seventeen years. The statutory endorsement of mediation in provincial legislation,[35] and the acknowledgment of a role for mediation in the federal *Divorce Act*, constitute signposts for the future, as do the availability of legal aid certificates for mediation processes in some provinces and the authority for lawyers to engage in the practice of mediation under provincial rules of professional conduct. These changes, together with the influence of Family Mediation Canada and provincial Associations for Family Mediation augur well for the future.

In the short term, divorce mediation in Canada will be more common in parenting disputes. This is done primarily by mediators with training in social work, psychology, or psychiatry. When support and property disputes on marriage breakdown are mediated, the mediator is much more likely to be a lawyer. This division of function, whereby non-lawyers mediate parenting disputes while lawyers mediate the economics of divorce, is a division of convenience that is currently acceptable to most, but not all, mediators. In the long term, comprehensive or "total package" mediation will become commonplace.

---

35   Such as the New Brunswick *Family Services Act*, S.N.B. 1980, c. F-2.2, the Ontario *Children's Law Reform Act*, R.S.O. 1990, c. C.12, the Ontario *Family Law Act*, R.S.O. 1990, c. F.3, and the Quebec *Civil Code*.

As family mediation continues to develop, there will be increasing recognition that mediation is, first and foremost, a process. Far too many people confuse substance with process. It is this confusion that causes lawyers to assert that, even though parenting disputes arising on marriage breakdown lend themselves to mediation by non-legally trained persons, the economic consequences of marriage breakdown, such as property division or spousal and child support, belong in the hands of lawyers or, at least, legally trained mediators. This thinking shows a lack of understanding of what mediation is. Mediation is the process of bringing about consensus between persons involved in a dispute. The substantive issues must not be confused with the process for resolving the dispute. Though incidental to the process, the dispute in itself does not determine the process. Expertise on substantive issues, such as the legal or tax implications of a proposed support or property settlement, can and should be incorporated in the mediation process. Such expertise need not reside in the mediator provided that all relevant information is brought to the bargaining table before a final settlement is reached. The mediator's role is to promote consensus in light of all relevant data, rather than to personally furnish the necessary expertise on the substantive issues.

The role of the "neutral lawyer" or lawyer-mediator, who will advise the family as a whole in an attempt to reach a negotiated settlement, will emerge to complement the traditional role of lawyers who advise and represent individual family members. Some family law practitioners will discharge both mediation and lawyering functions but not in relation to the same family. A closer association must be established between lawyers and other professionals engaged in advising and assisting families in crisis. Sequential team mediation involving lawyers and other professionals, such as social workers or psychologists, will likely develop as an effective means of promoting the consensual resolution of family conflict.

Although the day may come when community centres, staffed by lawyers, doctors, psychologists, social workers, and other professionals, as well as volunteers, will provide a multidisciplinary approach to the resolution of the multifaceted crises of marriage breakdown, that development lies in the future. In the meantime, the various professions and, indeed, federal and provincial governmental agencies (including Departments as diverse as Employment, Finance, Revenue Canada, Health and Welfare, and Justice), which are directly or indirectly involved in the systemic management of the human process of marriage breakdown, must recognize their own limitations and foster effective lines of communication in the search for constructive and comprehensive solutions to the human and socio-economic problems associated with marriage breakdown.

H. ARBITRATION[36]

The conciliation or mediation of family disputes leaves decision making in the hands of the parties. If they cannot resolve the issues, an independent arbiter must determine their respective rights and obligations. Traditionally, this function has been discharged by courts.

The use of binding arbitration has recently emerged in Canada as a viable alternative to contested litigation as a means of resolving spousal disputes respecting property division, support, and child custody and access on marriage breakdown or divorce. During the last thirteen years, Canadian lawyers have made increasing use of arbitration clauses in drafting separation agreements and minutes of settlement.

1) Advantages of Arbitration

Private arbitration has the following potential advantages over litigation as a dispute resolution process.

a) Selection of Arbitrator(s)

The parties are directly involved in the appointment of the arbitrator(s). An arbitrator can be selected having regard to the nature of the dispute and the arbitrator's qualifications and expertise. A lawyer or accountant might be appointed to resolve a complex financial dispute whereas a psychiatrist or psychologist might be preferred when the dispute focuses on the custody, care, and upbringing of children. More than one arbitrator can be appointed if the parties wish to take advantage of several fields of expertise.

In litigation, the parties have little or no choice. Once proceedings have been instituted in a particular court, the issues will be adjudicated by one of the judges assigned to that court. The parties are not free to

---

36　See, generally, Julien D. Payne, "Family Conflict Resolution: Conciliation and Arbitration As Alternatives to the Adversarial Legal Process" in *Payne's Divorce and Family Law Digest*, above note 9, 1983 tab at 83-1601, especially 1611/1615. See also The Law Society of Upper Canada, *Alternatives*: The Report of the Dispute Resolution Subcommittee, February 1993. And see *Practice Direction Concerning Alternative Dispute Resolution Pilot Project in the Ontario Court (General Division)* (22 February 1994) 16 O.R. (3d) Pt. 7 at 481–503.

select a particular judge. Furthermore, if proceedings are instituted in a court of superior jurisdiction, the judge is not usually a specialist in family law and may have no interest in, or even an aversion to, adjudicating spousal or parental disputes.

b) Type of Hearing

Litigants are often intimidated by the formality and adversarial atmosphere of the court. An arbitration hearing can be as formal or informal as the parties desire. The arbitration process can be tailored to the needs of the parties and the circumstances of the particular case. The parties may favour an adversarial type of proceeding in which pleadings and affidavits are filed, witnesses are examined and cross-examined, and the rules of evidence are strictly observed. Alternatively, they may prefer an informal approach by way of a round-table conference. The role of the arbitrator can be specifically defined by the parties. In custody and access disputes, if the arbitrator is a psychiatrist or psychologist, he or she may be given authority to act as a fact-finder as well as the decision maker. The fact-finding may include authorized access to school records and personnel and to doctors and medical records. It may also involve interviewing members of the immediate or extended family and other persons who may be involved in future arrangements for the care and upbringing of the children. Psychological tests might also be appropriate.

c) Flexibility and Speed

Litigation, at least in courts of superior jurisdiction, necessitates formal pleadings, production of documents, and discoveries. Interlocutory motions are often brought pending a trial of the issues. The parties, their counsel, and any witnesses must accommodate the demands or convenience of the court. There is no guarantee when the case will be heard and time is often wasted in waiting to be reached on the court list. Procedural requirements imposed by provincial Rules of Court must be observed and the judge must have regard to previous decisions in matters of substantive law. It is not difficult for experienced counsel to invoke established procedures to delay a resolution of the issues.

In contrast, arbitration does not normally require formal pleadings, productions, and discoveries. Interlocutory motions are usually unnecessary and the issues can be resolved without delay. An arbitrator can resolve the issues on the facts of the particular case and is not fettered by the doctrine of precedent. The extent to which formal procedural rules shall govern is determined by the parties themselves. The parties and the arbitrator can negotiate a suitable time and location for any hearing: long summer vacations, weekends, and evenings are not precluded, as they would be in the judicial process. The arbitrator has only one case to resolve and can give it undivided attention. Hearings and adjournments can be scheduled to accommodate the parties. Even complex issues can usually be resolved by arbitration within a few weeks. Contested litigation rarely takes less than eighteen months and may take several years, particularly if appeals are taken.

d) Definition of Issues

Parties specifically define the limits of the arbitrator's decision-making power. It can be as broad or as narrow as the parties determine. The jurisdiction and powers of the arbitrator are fixed by the agreement of the parties and cannot be exceeded. An arbitrator may be required to make decisions not only about the present but also the future. For example, an arbitrator may be asked to determine what spousal or child support shall be payable before and after retirement. In contrast, litigants cannot fetter the statute-based discretionary jurisdiction of a court respecting spousal or child support, custody, and access. In addition, courts look to the present and not the future; they cannot, or will not, decide issues that depend on future contingencies.

e) Privacy

Even when the arbitration process selected by the parties has a formal and adversarial character, the hearing is conducted in private. Only the parties, their counsel, and witnesses attend the hearing before the arbitrator. Courts of law are generally open to the public and the press with the consequential risk of embarrassing publicity.

f) Expense

Whereas judges and courts are provided at the taxpayer's expense, arbitrators in family disputes are paid for their services by the disputants. These additional costs are usually more than offset by the time and expense saved as a result of the arbitration process.

The costs of arbitration are more predictable than those arising from contested litigation. Parties to the arbitration process may predetermine who shall pay the costs. It is not uncommon for each spouse to pay his or her own lawyer and for the costs of the arbitrator to be shared equally between the spouses. In contested litigation, it is often difficult to predict the costs that will be involved in a trial. The time likely to be expended and the results of the dispute are often unpredictable. In addition, after contested litigation, it is the responsibility of the court to determine who shall pay the legal costs. The jurisdiction to order costs falls within the unfettered discretion of the court and judicial practices vary widely. In some cases, the court will make no order for costs; in others, costs will be ordered on a party-party basis, whereby the recipient will usually recover between one-third and one-half of his or her lawyer's fees; in exceptional circumstances, a court may order costs on a solicitor-client basis, which indemnifies the recipient for all costs reasonably incurred.

2) Disadvantages of Arbitration

Opponents of arbitration argue that the arbitration process denies the protection guaranteed by "due process of law." Any failure to adhere to substantive and procedural laws, including the rules of evidence, creates a vacuum within which the arbitrator's discretion is unfettered and may produce unpredictable results or an unfair process.[37] Arbitrators are sometimes accused of being too inclined to "split the difference." Some years ago, after contending that "a refined adversarial process of judicial decision making is necessary to avoid the erosion and dilution of the integrity of the law of the family" and that this can be achieved by refinements of the existing process, including the use of expert evidence, pre-trials, mediation, and the legal representation of children, Justice Rosalie Silberman Abella, now of the Supreme Court of Canada, concluded that arbitration is essentially "the adversary process without the judicial atmosphere, and therefore not generally considered a real alternative to it."

3) Court-Annexed Arbitration

Some form of court-annexed arbitration might ultimately be endorsed in Canada as an alternative process for the resolution of family disputes. Court-annexed arbitration has been introduced in several jurisdictions in the United States to cope with the flood of civil litigation. Court-annexed arbitration differs from private arbitration in several ways. Court-annexed arbitration is often mandatory rather than voluntary and the arbitrator is assigned and not chosen by the disputants. Most importantly, court-annexed arbitration is usually advisory rather than binding. If the disputants accept the arbitration award, it is entered as a court judgment and is enforceable as such. If the arbitration award is rejected by either

---

37   See *Kainz v. Potter*, [2006] O.J. No. 2441 (Sup. Ct.).

party, the issues go to trial and are adjudicated without reference being made to the arbitration award. Most court-annexed programs impose penalties on a disputant, however, if the trial judgment affords no greater relief than that given under the arbitration award.

4) Judicial and Legislative Responses to Arbitration

There are relatively few Canadian judicial decisions dealing with the enforceability of agreements to arbitrate family disputes, although it is generally conceded that spousal and parental disputes can be referred to binding arbitration.[38] As long ago as 1917, in *Harrison v. Harrison*,[39] it was held that spouses may agree to submit the right to and amount of spousal support to binding arbitration. In *Crawford v. Crawford*,[40] however, Berger J. of the British Columbia Supreme Court observed that it is still open to either spouse to invoke the jurisdiction of the court conferred by the *Divorce Act*. The impact of the dispute resolution movement over the last twenty years may have tempered this opinion,[41] although courts have tended to jealously guard their *parens patriae* jurisdiction over custody and access disputes. Different considerations may apply to spousal property disputes[42] or to spousal and child support claims arising under provincial statutes that include express provisions dealing with spousal agreements or the arbitration of spousal disputes.[43] For example,

---

38   *Marchese v. Marchese*, [2007] O.J. No. 191 (C.A.); see also *Dormer v. McJannet*, [2006] O.J. No. 5106 (Sup. Ct.) (custody and access); *Kay v. Korakianitis*, [2007] O.J. No. 2905 (Sup. Ct.); *Costa v. Costa*, [2008] O.J. No. 930 (Sup. Ct.).

39   (1917), 41 O.L.R. 195 (S.C.), aff'd (1918), 42 O.L.R. 43 (C.A.).

40   (1973), 10 R.F.L. 1 at 3 (B.C.S.C.). See also *Merrell v. Merrell* (1987), 11 R.F.L. (3d) 18 (B.C.S.C.) (arbitration clause in separation agreement no bar to judicial exercise of jurisdiction to vary support order that incorporated financial terms of separation agreement).

41   See, for example, *Harsant v. Portnoi* (1990), 27 R.F.L. (3d) 216 (Ont. H.C.J.) (shared parenting arrangement); *Wentzell v. Schumacher*, [2004] O.J. No. 1892 (Sup. Ct.) (high-conflict parenting dispute; judicial endorsement of recourse to arbitration).

42   See *Walker v. Tymofichuk* (1984), 38 R.F.L. (2d) 330 (Alta. Q.B.); compare *Keyes v. Gordon* (1985), 45 R.F.L. 177 at 187 (N.S.C.A.); see also *Childs v. Childs Estate*, [1988] 1 W.W.R. 746 (Sask. C.A.).

43   For decisions where arbitration awards were upheld or varied in family disputes, see *Willick v. Willick* (1994), 118 D.L.R. (4th) 51 (Alta. Q.B.) (judicial review of arbitrator's award respecting property and fixed-term spousal support); *Lalonde v. Lalonde* (1994), 9 R.F.L. (4th) 27 (Ont. Gen. Div.) (custody, access, costs); *Olmstead v. Olmstead*, [1991] O.J. No. 609 (Gen. Div.) (registration and variation of arbitral award concerning custody, support, and property); *Nagoda v. Nagoda*, [1992] O.J. No. 136 (C.A.) (voidability of separation agreements); *Newham v. Newham* (10

many provincial statutes regulating matrimonial property include express provisions that recognize some degree of contractual autonomy that may facilitate a submission to binding arbitration in accordance with the applicable provincial *Arbitration Act*. In Nova Scotia, section 30 of the *Matrimonial Property Act*[44] specifically endorses arbitration as an appropriate means of dispute resolution. Section 30 reads as follows:

Arbitration

30(1) Parties to a marriage contract or separation agreement may, where both persons consent, refer any question as to their rights under this Act or the contract or agreement for determination by arbitration and the *Arbitration Act* then applies.

Order of court

(2)   A copy of an arbitration award made pursuant to this Section, certified by the arbitrator to be a true copy, may be made an order of the court by filing it with the prothonotary of the court who shall enter the same as a record and it thereupon becomes and is an order of the court and is enforceable as such.

Arbitrations in Ontario fall subject to amendments to the *Arbitration Act, 1991*, and the *Family Law Act*, which came into force on 1 February 2006.[45] These amendments were directed towards controlling the arbitration of family disputes based on religious laws that are fundamentally different from Ontario or Canadian family law. The primary changes thereby effectuated are as follows:

• Family arbitration agreements and family arbitration awards are governed by the *Family Law Act* and by the *Arbitration Act, 1991*. In

---

December 1993) (Ont. Gen. Div.) [unreported] (variation of support provisions of separation agreement); *Ross v. Ross*, [1999] O.J. No. 3971 (Sup. Ct.) (confirmation of arbitral award respecting property); *Robinson v. Robinson*, [2000] O.J. No. 3299 (Sup. Ct.) (confirmation of arbitral award respecting property and costs). Compare *Deane v. Pawluk*, [2006] S.J. No. 731 at para. 29 (Q.B.).

44   R.S.N.S. 1989, c. 275.

45   See *Family Statute Law Amendment Act*, S.O. 2006, c. 1 and *Family Arbitration*, O. Reg. 134/07 (effective 30 April 2008). See also Anne Marie Predko & John D. Gregory, "Overview of the *Family Statute Law Amendment Act, 2006*"; and Phillip M. Epstein & Sheila R. Gibb, "Family Law Arbitrations: Choice and Finality under the *Amended Arbitration Act, 1991* and *Family Law Act*" in The Law Society of Upper Canada, *Special Lectures 2006: Family Law* (Toronto: Irwin Law, 2007) at 1–20 and 21–46 respectively.

the event of any conflict of statutory provisions, the *Family Law Act* prevails.

• Family arbitration agreements constitute domestic contracts under Part IV of the *Family Law Act*. They must be in writing and each party must receive independent legal advice before entering into such an agreement. Their enforceability is regulated by the provisions of the *Family Law Act*.

• A family arbitration agreement and any arbitration award made thereunder is unenforceable, unless the family arbitration agreement was entered into after the dispute to be arbitrated arose.

• Family arbitrations in Ontario must be resolved exclusively in accordance with the law of Ontario or some other Canadian jurisdiction. Arbitration awards that are not in accordance with the law of Ontario or another Canadian jurisdiction have no legal force in Ontario.

• Regulations passed pursuant to the statutory amendments require all family arbitrators who are not members of the Ontario or another Canadian Bar to complete thirty hours of training in Ontario family law provided by a recognized source of such training. All family arbitrators must have received a training program of fourteen hours in screening parties for power imbalances and domestic violence. They must also keep proper records and submit reports to the Ministry of the Attorney General.

• The current statutory provisions and regulations confining the nature, effect, and enforceability of family arbitration agreements and arbitration awards cannot be waived by the parties.

The wisdom of these statutory amendments and regulations has been seriously questioned by some lawyers who have assumed the role of arbitrators in the past.

I. MED-ARB

Mediation and arbitration need not be exclusive of one another. "Med-Arb" is a process that utilizes both approaches. Typically, a fixed time will be set aside for mediation, with the understanding that, if no consensus is reached, the mediator will then act as an arbitrator who will give a final and binding decision.[46] Knowing that the negotiations will proceed to arbitration may help parties to reach a consensus in the final stages of the mediation process.[47]

On an application to confirm or set aside a parenting arbitral award ensuing from a med-arb agreement, a court must ensure that the process reflects the expectations of the parties as set out in their written agreement and that it is conducted not only in accordance with the terms and conditions of the agreement but also the governing legislation.[48] An anomaly is created by agreements that incorporate a med-arb process in that either party is free to withdraw from the mediation process at any time, but any such withdrawal triggers the mandatory arbitration process.[49]

A court is not bound by a parental agreement to accept med-arb to resolve an access dispute, and a consequential arbitral award may be set aside in the exercise of the court's *parens patriae* jurisdiction.[50]

J. PARENTING CO-ORDINATION

Pursuant to the initiative of an interdisciplinary group of legal and mental health professionals in Denver, Colorado in the early 1990s, a process known as "parenting co-ordination" has evolved in several American states and is beginning to spread into Canada.[51] Parenting co-ordination usually involves mental health professionals assisting parents who

---

46   *Marchese v. Marchese*, [2007] O.J. No. 191 (C.A.).
47   For a brief analysis of the advantages and disadvantages of med-arb, see Stephen B. Goldberg, Frank E.A. Sander, & Nancy H. Rogers, *Dispute Resolution* (Boston: Little, Brown and Company, 1992) at 226–28.
48   *Marchese v. Marchese*, [2007] O.J. No. 191 (C.A.).
49   *Hercus v. Hercus*, [2001] O.J. No. 534 (Sup. Ct.) (arbitral award set aside). Compare *Marchese v. Marchese*, [2007] O.J. No. 191 (C.A.).
50   *Duguay v. Thompson-Duguay*, [2000] O.J. No. 1541 (Sup. Ct.).
51   See Linda Chodos, "Parenting Coordination: The Cutting Edge of Conflict Management with Separated and Divorced Families" in The Law Society of Upper Canada, *Special Lectures 2006: Family Law* (Toronto: Irwin Law, 2007) 389–412. See also C.B. Garrity & M.A. Baris, *Caught in the Middle: Protecting the Children of High-Conflict Divorce* (New York: Lexington Books, 1994); M.A. Baris *et al.*, *Working with High Conflict Families of Divorce: A Guide for Professionals* (Northvale, NJ: Jason Aronson, 2001). For examples of relevant legislation in the U.S.A., see *The Parenting Coordinator Act*, enacted June 2001, *Oklahoma Statutes*, Title 43, § 120.1 *et seq*; see also *Oregon Laws*, ORS 107.425, enacted 1 January 2002, which implements a general statutory scheme authorizing a court to appoint an individual to assist

encounter ongoing conflict after custody and access issues have already been the subject of a parenting agreement or court order. Parenting co-ordinators usually counsel and advise parents on how to develop a more positive co-parenting relationship. They may be authorized to mediate disputes arising between the parents and, if the parents cannot settle a dispute, to assume the role of an arbitrator and issue a final decision on the dispute. It is customary for parents to agree to med-arb being used to resolve relatively minor disputes that will not fundamentally change the character of an existing parenting agreement or court order. For example, med-arb may be agreed upon by the parents to resolve issues relating to the children's extracurricular activities, vacation plans, preschool and after-school child care, existing communication problems, pick-up and drop-off arrangements, or minor changes to the parenting schedule. Fundamental issues, such as a change of custody, extraprovincial relocation of the children, or substantial changes in the parenting schedule usually fall outside the authority of parenting co-ordinators.[52] Although parents may delegate such functions as they see fit to parenting co-ordinators and some Canadian courts may refer consenting parents to a court-appointed parenting co-ordinator, a court has no jurisdiction to delegate its decision-making authority to a parenting co-ordinator.[53]

---

the court and parents in creating parenting plans or resolving disputes regarding parenting time, including the following:

    (i)   gathering information;

    (ii)   monitoring compliance with court orders;

    (iii) providing the parents, their attorneys, if any, and the court with recommendations for new or modified parenting time provisions; and

    (iv) providing parents with problem solving, conflict management, and parenting time co-ordination services or other services approved by the court.

See also *J.M.M. v. K.A.M.*, [2005] N.J. No. 27 (S.C.). Compare *Kaplanis v. Kaplanis*, [2005] O.J. No. 275 (C.A.). And see Association of Family and Conciliation Courts, "Guidelines for Parenting Coordination" in (2006) 44 Fam. Ct. Rev. 164.

52   For examples of the functions of a court-appointed parenting co-ordinator, see *J.M.M. v. K.A.M.*, [2005] N.J. No. 27 at paras. 92–98 (S.C.).

53   See *contra: J.M.M. v. K.A.M.*, [2005] N.J. No. 27 at para. 92(h) (S.C.), where the responsibilities of a court-appointed parenting co-ordinator included making changes to access arrangements. As to the incapacity of a court to delegate its decision-making authority, see *Stewart v. Stewart* (1990), 30 R.F.L. (3d) 67 (Alta. C.A.); *S.L.T. v. A.K.T.*, [2007] A.J. No. 797 (Q.B.), subsequent proceedings [2007] A.J. No. 1468 (Q.B.); *Lake v. Lake* (1988), 11 R.F.L. (3d) 234 (N.S.C.A.); *Strobridge v. Strobridge* (1994), 4 R.F.L. (4th) 169 (Ont. C.A.); *C.A.M. v. D.M.*, [2003] O.J. No. 3707 (C.A.); *Reid v. Catalano*, [2008] O.J. No. 912 (Sup. Ct.). Compare *Hunter v. Hunter*, 2008 BCSC 403.

K. CONCLUDING OBSERVATIONS

This chapter has focused on counselling, negotiation, mediation, arbitration, and med-arb as processes that can be used as alternatives to, or in conjunction with, litigation as means of resolving the emotional, economic, and parenting consequences of marriage breakdown. It does not canvass or even catalogue all of the processes that can be applied or adapted to family conflict management and dispute resolution. Nor does it recommend the outright rejection of traditional legal processes in favour of other processes. Indeed, separated and divorced spouses will usually find it advantageous to avoid locking themselves into a single process in their attempts to resolve the multifaceted problems generated by their marriage breakdown. A few examples may serve to demonstrate that it is appropriate to utilize more than one process. Negotiations do, and must, continue after legal proceedings have been instituted. Indeed, the very institution of legal proceedings may trigger an early negotiated settlement and, even when matters proceed further, eve of trial settlements are common. Divorcing or divorced couples may also use different processes to deal with different aspects of their marriage breakdown. Individual or family counselling and therapy may be appropriate as a prelude to mediation. Arbitration may be used to resolve an impasse that has been reached in mediation. Parenting mediation may co-exist with a motion to a court, perhaps on consent, to determine urgent matters relating to interim possession of the family home or the amount of spousal or child support.

Separated and divorced couples must be made aware of the diversity of processes available to foster family conflict management and dispute resolution. Only then can they examine their options in such a way as to reflect their respective interests and those of any children.

CHAPTER 7

DIVORCE: JURISDICTION; JUDGMENTS; FOREIGN DIVORCES; GROUND FOR DIVORCE; BARS

A. JUDICIAL SEPARATION; SEPARATION AGREEMENTS; DIVORCE SETTLEMENTS

In most provinces and territories, it is possible for spouses to obtain a decree of judicial separation from the courts. Judicial separation is not available as a remedy from the courts in Ontario or Prince Edward Island. Spouses may separate without seeking any order from the courts. If they do so, they usually regulate the consequences of their separation by entering into a separation agreement dealing with such matters as division of property, support rights, and custody of or access to the children.

Rights and obligations under a separation agreement are not automatically terminated by a subsequent spousal reconciliation. For example, if property has already been transferred by one spouse to the other under the terms of a separation agreement, a subsequent reconciliation does not revest the property in the original owner. When lawyers draft a separation agreement, they usually include a provision that specifically deals with the effect of a subsequent reconciliation.

Separation agreements or minutes of settlement can also be entered into by divorcing spouses, but a divorce judgment must be obtained from the court in order to terminate the marriage and render the parties free to remarry a third party. Separated spouses who do not reconcile may subsequently petition for divorce, but may choose not to do so. Some postpone divorce for a few years; others never get a divorce. Separated spouses who never divorce are wise to put their affairs in order by way of a separation agreement and by reviewing their wills, insurance policies, pension plans, and other important documents.

Spousal separation is the conventional prelude to a divorce. Separated spouses who wish to obtain spousal or child support, or custody of or access to their children, may apply to the courts pursuant to provincial or territorial legislation. In the alternative, they may immediately institute divorce proceedings and claim spousal and child support or custody of or access to the children as corollary relief in the divorce proceedings. In this event, the relevant legislative provisions will be found in the *Divorce Act*. In most cases, it is immaterial whether a separated spouse or parent seeks support, custody, or access under the federal *Divorce Act* or under provincial or territorial legislation. The outcome of the dispute will not normally be affected. Spousal claims for property division are regulated by provincial or territorial legislation and fall outside the scope of the *Divorce Act*. Spousal property disputes can, nevertheless, be joined with a divorce petition so as to enable all economic and parenting issues between the spouses to be determined by the same court at the time of the divorce. The vast majority of divorces are uncontested, with the spouses settling their differences by a negotiated agreement or settlement. Less than 4 percent of all divorces involve a trial of contested issues where the spouses give evidence in open court.

Before examining provincial and territorial legislation regulating such matters as support, custody, access, and property division, it is appropriate to summarize the basic provisions of the *Divorce Act*. They relate to

- jurisdiction,
- the ground for divorce,
- bars to divorce,
- spousal and child support,
- parenting arrangements, and
- process.

The first three of these will be dealt with in this chapter; spousal support will be dealt with in Chapter 8, child support in Chapter 9, parenting arrangements in Chapter 10, and process in Chapter 6.

B. JURISDICTION OVER DIVORCE

1) Introduction

Sections 3 to 7 of the current *Divorce Act* include detailed provisions respecting the exercise of judicial jurisdiction over a "divorce proceeding," "corollary relief proceeding," or "variation proceeding." Each of these terms bears a technical meaning that is defined in section 2(1) of the Act.

2) Definition of "Court"

The definition of "court" in section 2(1) of the *Divorce Act* designates a particular court in each province or territory that has jurisdiction to entertain proceedings under the Act. A designated court must be presided over by federally appointed judges. This reflects the constitutional limitations imposed on both the Parliament of Canada and the provincial legislatures by section 96 of the *Constitution Act, 1867*.[1]

3) Exercise of Jurisdiction by Judge Alone

Section 7 of the *Divorce Act* expressly provides that the jurisdiction to grant a divorce is exercisable only by a judge without a jury.

4) Jurisdiction in Divorce Proceedings

a) Basic Statutory Criteria

Pursuant to section 3(1) of the *Divorce Act*, a court of a province, as defined in section 2(1), has jurisdiction to hear and determine an application for divorce and any accompanying application for corollary relief by way of spousal or child support or custody or access, if either spouse has been ordinarily resident within the province for at least one year immediately preceding the commencement of the proceeding.[2] There is a potential conflict of jurisdiction if the one spouse's ordinary residence has been in one province or territory and the other spouse's ordinary residence has been in another. If, for example, the husband had always lived in Ontario but his wife, after separation, returned to her home province of Saskatchewan, where she has been living for the past year, the Ontario Superior

---

1   (U.K.), 30 & 31 Vict., c. 3. See *McEvoy v. New Brunswick (A.G.)*, [1983] 1 S.C.R. 704, (*sub nom. Re Court of Unified Criminal Jurisdiction*) 46 N.B.R. (2d) 219.

2   See Section B(7), below in this chapter.

Court of Justice as well as the Saskatchewan Court of Queen's Bench could deal with a divorce petition filed by either spouse. To avoid any such judicial conflict, section 3(2) of the *Divorce Act* provides that, if petitions have been filed in two courts that otherwise would have jurisdiction under section 3(1), the first in time prevails if it is not discontinued within thirty days of its commencement; thus the second proceeding shall be deemed to be discontinued, and the court of the province or territory in which the first petition was filed will assume exclusive jurisdiction over the divorce.[3] If both petitions have been filed on the same day, the conflict of judicial jurisdiction is resolved by exclusive jurisdiction being vested in the Trial Division of the Federal Court.[4] Section 3(2) of the *Divorce Act* does not apply when divorce petitions have been filed in two different registries in the same province. In that event, the appropriate course of action may be to consolidate the two proceedings.[5]

There is no constitutional right to a divorce that allows a court to reduce or eliminate the one-year ordinary residence requirement imposed by section 3(1) of the *Divorce Act*.[6] The imposition of a one-year ordinary residence requirement under section 3(1) of the *Divorce Act* does not contravene the mobility right guaranteed to every citizen of Canada by section 6(2) of the *Canadian Charter of Rights and Freedoms*, nor the right to life, liberty, and security of the person that is guaranteed under section 7 of the *Charter*.[7]

Where jurisdiction over a divorce petition arises pursuant to section 3(1) of the *Divorce Act*, a Canadian court may grant orders for spousal support and child support even though the applicant and children live abroad. In determining whether Ontario is the appropriate forum for resolving the issues of spousal and child support after concurrent proceedings have been brought by the wife in both Ontario and a foreign country, the court will consider which jurisdiction has the closer connection to the parties and the issues.[8]

b) Transfer of Divorce Proceeding to Another Province

A court that is seized of jurisdiction under section 3 of the *Divorce Act* has the discretionary power to transfer the "divorce proceeding" to a

---

3   See *Astle v. Walton* (1987), 10 R.F.L. (3d) 199 (Alta. Q.B.).
4   *Divorce Act*, R.S.C. 1985 (2d Supp.), c. 3, s. 3(3).
5   *Hiebert v. Hiebert*, [2005] B.C.J. No. 1409 (S.C.).
6   *Garchinski v. Garchinski*, [2002] S.J. No. 465 (Q.B.).
7   *Thurber v. Thurber*, [2002] A.J. No. 992 (Q.B.).
8   *Follwell v. Holmes*, [2006] O.J. No. 4387 (Sup. Ct.).

competent court in another province, if the divorce proceeding includes a contested application for an interim or permanent custody and access order and the child of the marriage is most substantially connected with the province to which the transfer is contemplated.[9] The application for transfer must be made to the court in which the divorce proceedings were commenced and not the court to which the transfer is requested.[10] The primary factor in analyzing the facts of the case is the best interests of the child; a secondary factor is the proper administration of justice.[11] Section 6 empowers but does not compel a transfer to be ordered.[12] The word "may" rather than "shall" in matters affecting custody signifies a judicial discretion that is exercisable having regard to the best interests of the child. A transfer should be denied where the best interests of the child would not be served by a transfer.[13] The transfer jurisdiction conferred by section 6(1) of the *Divorce Act* may be exercised on the application of a spouse or by the court acting on its own motion. Pursuant to section 6(4), where a transfer of the divorce proceeding has been made under the authority of section 6(1), the court to which the divorce proceeding has been transferred has exclusive jurisdiction to hear and determine the proceeding. Although section 6 of the *Divorce Act* enables a court to transfer a petition for divorce instituted in its jurisdiction to another provincial jurisdiction, it does not permit a court to transfer to its jurisdiction a petition commenced in another province.[14]

---

9   See *Astle v. Walton* (1987), 10 R.F.L. (3d) 199 (Alta. Q.B.). See also *Chenkie v. Chenkie* (1987), 6 R.F.L. (3d) 371 (Alta. Q.B.); *Shields v. Shields* (2001), 18 R.F.L. (5th) 357 (Alta. C.A.); *Kern v. Kern* (1989), 19 R.F.L. (3d) 350 (B.C.S.C.); *Tibbs v. Tibbs* (1988), 12 R.F.L. (3d) 169 (Man. Q.B.); *D.(T.W.) v. D.(Y.M.)* (1989), 20 R.F.L. (3d) 183 (N.S.T.D.); *Riehl v. Key*, [2007] N.W.T.J. No. 66 (S.C.); *Ruyter v. Samson* (1992), 44 R.F.L. (3d) 35 (Ont. Gen. Div.); *Mohrbutter v. Mohrbutter* (1991), 34 R.F.L. (3d) 357 (Sask. Q.B.); *Garchinski v. Garchinski*, [2002] S.J. No. 465 (Q.B.); *Rude v. Rude*, [2007] S.J. No. 398 (Q.B.). For a review of the words "most substantially connected," see *Cormier v. Cormier* (1990), 26 R.F.L. (3d) 169 at 171–72 (N.B.Q.B.). See, generally, Vaughan Black, "Section 6 of the *Divorce Act*: What May Be Transferred?" (1992), 37 R.F.L. (3d) 307.

10   *Ruyter v. Samson* (1992), 44 R.F.L. (3d) 35 (Ont. Gen. Div.).

11   *Mohrbutter v. Mohrbutter* (1991), 34 R.F.L. (3d) 357 at 358 (Sask. Q.B.), citing *D.(T. W.) v. D.(Y.M.)* (1989), 20 R.F.L. (3d) 183 (N.S.T.D.).

12   *Palahnuk v. Palahnuk* (1991), 33 R.F.L. (3d) 194 (Man. C.A.).

13   *Newman v. Newman* (1993), 89 Man. R. (2d) 254 (Q.B.); *Ketler v. Peacey* (1990), 28 R.F.L. (3d) 266 (N.W.T.S.C.).

14   *Springer v. Springer*, [1994] O.J. No. 450 (Gen. Div.).

c) Competing Foreign Proceeding

While conflicts in Canadian provincial divorce jurisdiction are resolved by section 3(2) of the *Divorce Act*, whereby the first to be initiated prevails, this is not the dominant factor when there are contemporaneous proceedings in a Canadian province and in a foreign jurisdiction. The principles applicable to an injunction to restrain foreign proceedings and those applicable to a stay of the Canadian proceedings in favour of a foreign court are not the same. A party should not be enjoined from pursuing foreign proceedings that are not vexatious or oppressive. Since the court is concerned with the ends of justice, account must not only be taken of injustice to the defendant if the plaintiff is allowed to pursue the foreign proceedings but also of injustice to the plaintiff if he or she is not allowed to do so. Whether the Canadian proceedings should be stayed depends on whether the foreign court provides an alternative forum that is clearly or distinctly more appropriate. In deciding which of two jurisdictions offer the more convenient forum, the court should ordinarily consider which jurisdiction can deal more comprehensively with the issues in dispute. It is not *prima facie* unjust or vexatious to commence two actions about the same issues in different jurisdictions. Furthermore, a court will lean against interference where the plaintiff in one jurisdiction is the defendant in the other.[15]

5) Jurisdiction in Corollary Relief Proceedings

a) Basic Statutory Criteria

Section 2(1) of the *Divorce Act* defines "a corollary relief proceeding" as "a proceeding in a court in which either or both former spouses seek a support order or a custody order or both such orders." Sections 3(1) and 4 of the *Divorce Act* respectively provide that an original application for support or custody may be brought at the time of the divorce or thereafter.[16]

---

15   *Kornberg v. Kornberg* (1990), 30 R.F.L. (3d) 238 (Man. C.A.), leave to appeal to S.C.C. refused (1991), 32 R.F.L. (3d) 157*n* (S.C.C.). See also *Follwell v. Holmes*, [2006] O.J. No. 4387 (Sup. Ct.). And see *Harris v. Murray* (1995), 11 R.F.L. (4th) 450 (Alta. Q.B.), where the court reached a questionable conclusion that recognition of the foreign divorce would not preclude subsequent corollary relief being granted pursuant to the Canadian *Divorce Act*. Compare *Rothgiesser v. Rothgiesser* (2000), 46 O.R. (3d) 577, 2 R.F.L. (5th) 266 (C.A.).

16   See *Evans v. Evans* (1987), 6 R.F.L. (3d) 166 (B.C.S.C.); *Currie v. Currie* (1987), 6 R.F.L. (3d) 40 (Man. Q.B.), aff'd (1987), 10 R.F.L. (3d) 207 (Man. C.A.); *Arsenault v. Arsenault*, [2006] N.S.J. No. 114 (C.A.); *Standing v. Standing* (1991), 37 R.F.L. (3d) 90 at 92–93 (Sask. Q.B.); and see Section B(4), above in this chapter.

A court has jurisdiction to hear and determine a corollary relief proceeding if either former spouse is ordinarily resident in the province or both former spouses accept the jurisdiction of the court.[17] Where corollary relief proceedings are pending in two courts of competing jurisdiction, the first to be instituted prevails unless that proceeding is discontinued within thirty days of its commencement;[18] and if the two proceedings are commenced on the same day, the Federal Court – Trial Division has exclusive jurisdiction to hear and determine the corollary relief proceedings.[19]

The following statement appears in *Payne on Divorce*:

> The amended section 4 of the *Divorce Act*, which became effective 25 March 1993, appears sufficiently broad to enable a foreign divorcee to institute proceedings for support and custody under sections 15 and 16 of the Act, if he or she has established ordinary residence in a Canadian province.[20]

In the opinion of the British Columbia Court of Appeal in *L.R.V. v. A.A.V.*,[21] and of the Ontario Court of Appeal in *Rothgiesser v. Rothgiesser*,[22] the above statement is untenable. In *L.R.V. v. A.A.V.*, the British Columbia Court of Appeal traced the evolution of relevant jurisdictional rules in the *Divorce Act*, 1968 and the *Divorce Act*, 1986, as subsequently amended in 1993, before concluding that there is nothing to lead to the conclusion that Parliament, by section 4, intended to confer jurisdiction on Canadian courts to grant "corollary" relief with respect to foreign divorces.

---

17 *Divorce Act*, R.S.C. 1985 (2d Supp.), c. 3, s. 4, as amended by S.C. 1993, c. 8, s. 4(1). See *Arsenault v. Arsenault*, [2006] N.S.J. No. 114 (C.A.).

18 *Divorce Act, ibid.*, as amended by s. 4(2).

19 *Ibid.*, as amended by s. 4(3).

20 Julien D. Payne, *Payne on Divorce*, 4th ed. (Scarborough, ON: Carswell, 1996).

21 [2006] B.C.J. No. 264 (C.A.), supplementary reasons, (*sub nom. Virani v. Virani*) [2006] B.C.J. No. 1610 (C.A.); compare *Shokohyfard v. Sotoodeh*, [2006] B.C.J. No. 1348 (S.C.) (application for division of immovable property in British Columbia is not precluded by foreign divorce).

22 [2000] O.J. No. 33 (C.A.); see also *Leonard v. Booker*, 2007 NBCA 71, [2007] N.B.J. No. 381; *Okmyansky v. Okmyansky*, 2007 ONCA 427, [2007] O.J. No. 2298; *Jahangiri-Mavaneh v. Taheri-Zengekan*, [2003] O.J. No. 3018 (Sup. Ct.); *Ziemann v. Ziemann*, [2001] B.C.J. No. 733 (S.C.); *Wlodarczyk v. Spriggs*, [2000] S.J. No. 703 (Q.B.). For relevant judgments relating to the jurisdiction of the Quebec Superior Court to provide relief to persons who are ordinarily resident in Quebec after the dissolution of their marriage in a foreign jurisdiction, see *Droit de la famille — 3148*, [2000] R.J.Q. 2339, (*sub nom. O.M. v. A.K.*) [2000] Q.J. No. 3224 (Sup. Ct.), and *G.M. c. M.A.F.*, [2003] J.Q. no 11325 (C.A.).

The British Columbia Court of Appeal found it unnecessary to determine whether Parliament has the constitutional authority to enact legislation that would empower Canadian courts to grant orders for support, custody, or access to a foreign divorcee who is ordinarily or habitually resident in a Canadian province or territory, but whose former spouse is ordinarily or habitually resident in a foreign country. However, the British Columbia Court of Appeal did volunteer the statement that "much can be said for the proposition that such an enactment would be invading provincial jurisdiction over 'property and civil rights in the Province': see *Ontario (Attorney-General) v. Scott*, [1956] S.C.R. 137."[23] In *Rothgiesser v. Rothgiesser*, the Ontario Court of Appeal had previously concluded that the aforementioned suggestion in *Payne on Divorce* is untenable, being of the firm opinion that Parliament did not intend to give Canadian courts jurisdiction over foreign divorcees. In the opinion of the Ontario Court of Appeal, "[a]ny attempt to deal with [spousal] support obligations in the absence of a Canadian divorce would encroach on provincial jurisdiction [*Constitution Act, 1867*] (s. 92, 'Property and Civil Rights')."[24] It does not follow that relief is unavailable to a foreign divorcee who has established his or her home in Canada. However, in the opinion of the British Columbia and Ontario Courts of Appeal, such relief must be found under provincial or territorial legislative authority. In *L.R.V. v. A.A.V.*, the British Columbia Court of Appeal held that the *Family Relations Act* (B.C.) does not empower British Columbia courts to make an original order for child support against a non-resident parent for the simple reason that, by enacting the *Interprovincial Support Orders Act* (B.C.), the legislature intended to provide a code that is complementary to legislation existing in jurisdictions with which British Columbia has reciprocal arrangements.[25] Absent reciprocity, however, a foreign divorcee may have no alternative but to seek a remedy against his or her former spouse in the appropriate foreign jurisdiction. The unfairness that can result from this situation has been specifically addressed in England by the *forum conveniens* provisions of the *Matrimonial and Family Proceedings Act, 1984*, which

---

23   [2006] B.C.J. No. 264 at para. 60 (C.A.).
24   [2000] O.J. No. 33 at para. 59 (C.A.).
25   See *D.P.C. v. T.N.C.*, [2005] A.J. No. 1634 (Q.B.) (Florida divorce; child support order registered in Alberta and varied pursuant to *Reciprocal Enforcement of Maintenance Orders Act*).

were enacted in response to the recommendations of the Law Commission (England).[26]

b) Transfer of Corollary Relief Proceeding to Another Province

Pursuant to section 6(2) of the *Divorce Act*, a court with jurisdiction under section 4 to entertain "a corollary relief proceeding," as defined in section 2(1), may transfer that proceeding to a court in a province with which a child of the marriage is most substantially connected, if the corollary relief proceeding includes an application for interim custody or access under section 16 and that application is opposed.[27] Pursuant to section 6(4), a court to which a corollary relief proceeding has been transferred under the authority of section 6(2) has exclusive jurisdiction to hear and determine the proceeding.

6) Jurisdiction in Variation Proceedings

a) Basic Statutory Criteria

Pursuant to section 5(1) of the current *Divorce Act*, the jurisdiction to vary, rescind, or suspend a permanent order for spousal or child support, custody, or access vests in the court of the province in which either former spouse is ordinarily resident, or in a court whose jurisdiction is accepted by the former spouses, provided that any such court falls within the definition of "court" under section 2(1).[28]

Pursuant to sections 5(2) and 5(3), where variation proceedings are pending in two courts that would have jurisdiction under section 5(1), the first to be instituted prevails unless it is discontinued within thirty days of its commencement,[29] and if the two proceedings are commenced on

---

26 See Solicitors Family Law Association, *International Aspects of Family Law*, 2d ed. (Orpington: SFLA, Spring 2004) c. 6; and see David Truex, "Matrimonial Financial Applications in England and Wales after Foreign Divorce" (Paper presented to CLT Seminar, London, 1 December 2004), online: www.internationalfamilylaw. com/pub/clt1004.html.

27 See Vaughan Black, "Section 6 of the *Divorce Act*: What May Be Transferred?" (1992), 37 R.F.L. (3d) 307.

28 See *Lavoie v. Yawrenko* (1992), 44 R.F.L. (3d) 89 (B.C.C.A.); *Hiscocks v. Marshman* (1991), 34 R.F.L. 12 (Ont. Gen. Div.); *Dixon v. Dixon* (1995), 13 R.F.L. (4th) 160 (Alta. Q.B.).

29 See *Winram v. Cassidy* (1991), 37 R.F.L. (3d) 230 (Man. C.A.); *Droit de la famille — 541*, [1988] R.D.F. 484 (Que. C.A.).

the same day, the Federal Court — Trial Division has exclusive jurisdiction to hear the variation proceedings.

b) Transfer of Variation Proceeding to Another Province

Where a variation application in respect of a custody order is opposed in a "variation proceeding" as defined in section 2(1) of the *Divorce Act*, and the child is most substantially connected with another province, a court with jurisdiction over the variation proceeding under section 5 may transfer the variation proceeding to a court in that other province.[30] In that event, the court to which the variation proceeding has been transferred has exclusive jurisdiction to hear and determine the proceeding by virtue of section 6(4).

c) Variation of Foreign Orders

Section 5 of the *Divorce Act* confers no jurisdiction on any Canadian court to vary a foreign support order, although such jurisdiction may be exercisable under provincial legislation respecting the reciprocal enforcement of support orders.[31]

7) Ordinarily Resident

A person is "ordinarily resident" in a Canadian province when that person has his or her customary residence in that province. Ordinary residence signifies that a spouse has taken up residence in the province with the intention of remaining there indefinitely. It is not dependent on citizenship, domicile, or immigration status.[32] Residence in a place on a temporary basis for a specific purpose does not constitute ordinary residence within the meaning of sections 3(1), 4(1), and 5(1) of the *Divorce Act*, which regulate the jurisdiction of Canadian courts over divorce proceedings, corollary relief proceedings, and variation proceedings instituted pursuant to the *Divorce Act*. The test to be applied is "Where is [the spouse's]

---

30   See *Ellet v. Ellet* (1994), 4 R.F.L. (4th) 358 (Alta. Q.B.); *Staranowicz v. Staranowicz* (1990), 30 R.F.L. (3d) 185 (Ont. Gen. Div.); *Turnbull v. Turnbull* (1989), 80 Sask. R. 277 (Q.B.); *Rempel v. Reynolds* (1991), 34 R.F.L. (3d) 82 (Sask. Q.B.); *Erhardt v. Erhardt* (1992), 43 R.F.L. (3d) 159 (Sask. Q.B.). See also *Kermeen v. Kermeen* (1989), 93 N.S.R. (2d) 28 (Fam. Ct.). Compare *Naylen v. Naylen* (1987), 6 R.F.L. (3d) 350 (B.C.S.C.); but see Vaughan Black, "Section 6 of the *Divorce Act*: What May Be Transferred?" (1992), 37 R.F.L. (3d) 307.

31   *Leonard v. Booker*, 2007 NBCA 71, [2007] N.B.J. No. 381; see also *Rothgiesser v. Rothgiesser* (2000), 46 O.R. (3d) 577, 2 R.F.L. (5th) 266 (C.A.).

32   *Murphy v. Wulkowicz*, [2003] N.S.J. No. 324 (S.C.).

real home?" Accordingly, a spouse may retain an ordinary residence in a Canadian province, even though that spouse spends a number of years in another jurisdiction to which he or she has been posted by an employer.[33] A voluntary change of a spouse's home and private business may, however, terminate the period of ordinary residence previously established in another province.[34] The arrival of a person in a new province with intention of making a home there for an indefinite period makes that person ordinarily resident in that province. Future intentions unaccompanied by any change of residence will not, however, terminate an existing ordinary residence.[35] A person does not lose his or her place of ordinary residence until he or she has determined to give up that residence and arrives in another province with the intention of remaining there.[36]

A spouse may be ordinarily resident in a province within the meaning of the *Divorce Act*, notwithstanding that the initial entry and continued residence in Canada is illegal. Some degree of volition may be required, however, to establish an ordinary residence in a particular province.[37]

The jurisdictional requirements of section 3(1) of the *Divorce Act* cannot be waived or changed by consent of the spouses.[38]

Where neither spouse has been ordinarily resident in any single province for at least one year, no Canadian court can entertain an application for divorce.[39] It has been held that the term "ordinary residence" should not be construed too restrictively when it could create a jurisdictional

---

33 *Marsellus v. Marsellus* (1970), 2 R.F.L. 53 (B.C.S.C.).

34 See *Anema v. Anema* (1976), 27 R.F.L. 156 (Man. Q.B.); *Quigley v. Willmore*, [2007] N.S.J. No. 426 (S.C.); *Masse v. Sykora* (1979), 13 R.F.L. (2d) 68 (Que. C.S.); *Nunan v. Nunan* (1982), 18 Sask. R. 191 (Q.B.); *Cable v. Cable* (1981), 130 D.L.R. (3d) 381 (Sask. Q.B.).

35 *MacPherson v. MacPherson* (1976), 28 R.F.L. 106 (Ont. C.A.); see also *Nowlan v. Nowlan* (1970), 2 R.F.L. 67 (N.S.S.C.T.D.); *Quigley v. Willmore*, [2008] N.S.J. No. 144 (C.A.).

36 *Re Beaton* (1980), 42 N.S.R. (2d) 536 (T.D.); *Cadot v. Cadot* (1982), 49 N.S.R. (2d) 202 (T.D.); compare *Wrixon v. Wrixon* (1982), 30 R.F.L. (2d) 107 (Alta. Q.B.).

37 See *Blair v. Chung*, [2006] A.J. No. 882 (Q.B.); *Murphy v. Wulkowicz*, [2003] N.S.J. No. 324 (S.C.); *Jablonowski v. Jablonowski* (1972), 8 R.F.L. 36 (Ont. S.C.); *Wood v. Wood* (1987), 4 R.F.L. (2d) 182 (P.E.I.S.C.T.D.); compare *Spek v. Lawson* (1983), 43 O.R. (2d) 705 (C.A.).

38 *Byrn v. Mackin* (1983), 32 R.F.L. (2d) 207 (Que. S.C.); *Quigley v. Willmore*, [2007] N.S.J. No. 426 (S.C.); *N.K. c. R.V.*, [2004] Q.J. No. 8238 (C.S.); compare s. 5(1) of the *Divorce Act*, R.S.C. 1985 (2d Supp.), c. 3.

39 See *Winmill v. Winmill* (1975), 47 D.L.R. (3d) 597 (Fed. C.A.); *Lietz v. Lietz* (1990), 30 R.F.L. (3d) 293 (N.B.Q.B.).

vacuum.[40] No corresponding time limitation of one year applies with respect to variation proceedings under section 5(1).

The residence requirement is a fundamental condition and is unqualified by the effect of a delay in raising the issue under the Quebec *Code of Civil Procedure.*[41]

Section 3(1) of the *Divorce Act*, which imposes a minimum one-year period of ordinary residence, does not contravene section 6(2)(a) (mobility rights) or section 15 (equality rights) of the *Canadian Charter of Rights and Freedoms.* The imposition of the one-year ordinary residence requirement should also be upheld as a reasonable limit on guaranteed rights and freedoms under section 1 of the *Charter*, having regard to the ramifications of divorce, which go beyond the personal interests of the spouses.[42]

The period of ordinary residence required by section 3(1) of the *Divorce Act* is not limited to one year and may exceed it, but the required period of ordinary residence must continue without interruption for at least one year immediately preceding the commencement of the divorce proceedings.[43] An application for divorce that is presented before expiry of the minimum one-year period of ordinary residence must be dismissed, even though either or both spouses have been ordinarily resident in the province for more than one year at the time of a divorce hearing. Under these circumstances, however, a new application could be successfully launched without delay.[44]

In calculating the minimum one year of ordinary residence for the purposes of section 3(1) of the *Divorce Act*, the court may take account of premarital residence in the province. Section 3(1) is not confined to ordinary residence *qua* spouse.[45]

---

40 *Droit de la famille — 1006*, [1986] R.D.F. 81 (Que. C.S.). See also *Mills v. Butt* (1990), 82 Nfld. & P.E.I.R. 42 (Nfld. U.F.C.).

41 See *Droit de la famille — 360*, [1987] R.D.F. 171 (Que. C.S.).

42 *Canadian Charter of Rights and Freedoms*, Part I of the *Constitution Act, 1982*, being Schedule B to the *Canada Act 1982* (U.K.), 1982, c. 11. See *Koch v. Koch* (1985), 23 D.L.R. (4th) 609 (Sask. Q.B.); see also *Tit v. Manitoba (Director of Vital Statistics)* (1986), 28 D.L.R. (4th) 150 (Man. Q.B.) (application under the *Change of Name Act*, S.M. 1982–83–84, c. 56).

43 See *Anema v. Anema* (1976), 27 R.F.L. 156 (Man. Q.B.); *Robichaud v. Robichaud* (1974), 20 R.F.L. 14 (N.B.Q.B.); *Cullen v. Cullen* (1969), 9 D.L.R. (3d) 610 (N.S.T.D.).

44 *Anema v. Anema* (1976), 27 R.F.L. 156 (Man. Q.B.); *Stapleton v. Stapleton* (1977), 1 R.F.L. (2d) 190 (Man. C.A.).

45 See *Navas v. Navas*, [1969] 3 All E.R. 677; *Zoldester v. Zoldester* (1974), 13 R.F.L. 398 (B.C.S.C.).

The requirements of section 3(1) may be satisfied if either spouse was ordinarily resident in the province for at least one year immediately preceding the commencement of the divorce proceeding, notwithstanding that such ordinary residence was abandoned before the application is adjudicated.[46]

C. DIVORCE JUDGMENTS

1) Effective Date of Divorce Judgment; Appeals; Rescission of Divorce Judgment

Pursuant to section 12 of the *Divorce Act*, a divorce judgment normally takes effect on the thirty-first day after the day on which the judgment granting the divorce was rendered, or at such later date as all rights of appeal have been exhausted. A divorce is not effective until an appeal has been determined and the time for any further appeal from the appellate judgment has expired.[47] Pursuant to sections 12(3), 12(4), 12(5), and 21(2) of the *Divorce Act*, no appeal lies from a judgment granting a divorce on the expiry of the time fixed by law for instituting an appeal, unless an extension of the time for appeal has been granted prior to expiry of the normal period. Less restrictive conditions apply to appeals respecting corollary relief in divorce proceedings, as distinguished from the judgment on marital status. Pursuant to section 21(4), an appellate court or a judge thereof may, on special grounds, grant an extension of the time for appealing corollary relief even after expiry of the normal period. Although no appeal lies from a divorce judgment that has taken effect under section 12 of the *Divorce Act*, the judgment may be set aside where it was obtained by irregular or illegal means,[48] as, for example, where fraud is involved, where statutory provisions or rules of court are contravened, or where principles of natural justice are infringed. Infringement of principles of natural justice should not, however, render the divorce judgment void but only voidable, so that the court can do justice to all affected parties.[49] Any application for rescission is properly made to the

---

46   See *Martin v. Martin* (1970), 9 R.F.L. 1 at 5 (N.S.W.S.C.); *Battagin v. Battagin* (1980), 28 A.R. 586 (Q.B.); *Weston v. Weston* (1972), 5 R.F.L. 244 (B.C.S.C.); compare *Baia v. Baia* (1970), 1 R.F.L. 348 (Ont. H.C.J.).

47   *Bast v. Bast* (1990), 30 R.F.L. (3d) 181 (Sask. C.A.).

48   *Geci v. Gravel*, [1970] R.P. 402 (Que. B.R.).

49   *Rivas v. Rivas* (1977), 28 R.F.L. 342 (Alta. T.D.); *Harding v. Harding* (1985), 47 R.F.L. (2d) 52 at 57 (Man. Q.B.); *Chadderton v. Chadderton* (1973), 8 R.F.L. 374 (Ont. C.A.);

trial court and not to the court of appeal. A court has the inherent jurisdiction to amend a divorce judgment so as to correct an error respecting the date of the marriage dissolved, notwithstanding that there is no ability to appeal the judgment and notwithstanding that the error goes beyond what can be corrected under the slip rule.[50]

2) Expedition of Divorce Judgment

Section 12(2) of the *Divorce Act* empowers the court to reduce or eliminate the thirty-one day waiting period that must ordinarily elapse before the divorce judgment takes effect. The exercise of this jurisdiction is conditioned on (i) the existence of special circumstances;[51] and (ii) the agreement of the spouses and their undertakings that no appeal will be taken from the judgment or that any pending appeal has been abandoned.[52] Such agreement and undertakings may be oral[53] or they may be submitted to the court in writing without any requirement that the respondent appear personally before the court.[54] A divorce judgment cannot be expedited unless the parties positively agree to the abridgement and undertake not to appeal. Where a party cannot be found or refuses to agree, there can be no expedition of the divorce judgment.[55] Unlike the position under section 13(2) of the *Divorce Act*, 1968, section 12(2) of the current *Divorce Act* no longer requires the applicant to show that the public interest would be served by expediting the operative date of the divorce. Consequently, cases under the former *Divorce Act* that refused to expedite the divorce judgment must be viewed with circumspection.

Where the special circumstances were that reconciliation was impossible, the petition for divorce was not contested, no children were born of the marriage, the parties had reorganized their lives separately, and they agreed not to appeal, there were found to be sufficient reasons to expedite

---

Polsinelli v. Polsinelli (1992), 11 O.R. (3d) 541 (Gen. Div.); *Brown v. Brown* (1980), 19 R.F.L. (2d) 225 (P.E.I.T.D.).

50   *Tschudi v. Tschudi*, [2007] B.C.J. No. 2428 (S.C.), citing *Thynne v. Thynne*, [1955] 3 All E.R. 129 (Eng. C.A.).

51   *Baia v. Baia* (1970), 1 R.F.L. 348 (Ont. H.C.J.).

52   Compare *Bast v. Bast* (1990), 30 R.F.L. (3d) 181 (Sask. C.A.).

53   *Dippel v. Dippel* (17 February 1970) (Alta. T.D.) [unreported].

54   *Cooper v. Cooper* (1969), 1 R.F.L. 338 (N.S.S.C.). Compare *Baia v. Baia* (1970), 1 R.F.L. 348 (Ont. H.C.J.) wherein Wright J. stated that although *viva voce* evidence can be given by the parties, the records of the court should in every case include a written agreement and undertaking properly attested.

55   *Baia v. Baia* (1970), 1 R.F.L. 348 (Ont. H.C.J.).

the granting of the divorce judgment.[56] Special circumstances may be found if the failure to waive the thirty-one day waiting period would cause a great deal of inconvenience, heartache, and possibly expense.[57]

If it is not waived by court order and either spouse attempts to remarry a third party before the thirty-one days have elapsed, the second marriage will be null and void. In law, the second marriage would be bigamous, although a criminal prosecution for bigamy would not result in a conviction if the remarriage occurred in ignorance of the thirty-one days requirement.

3) National Effect of Divorce and Corollary Orders

Section 13 of the *Divorce Act* provides that a divorce granted pursuant to the Act shall have legal effect throughout Canada. The recognition of foreign divorce judgments is independently regulated by section 22 of the *Divorce Act*. Pursuant to section 20(2) of the *Divorce Act*, 1968, any corollary order granted under the *Divorce Act*, other than a provisional order under section 18(2), also has legal effect throughout Canada.

4) Right to Remarry

Section 14 of the *Divorce Act* provides that "[o]n taking effect, a divorce granted under this Act dissolves the marriage of the spouses." A respondent's fundamental freedom to practise his or her own religion, which is guaranteed by section 2(a) of the *Canadian Charter of Rights and Freedoms*,[58] is not violated by a divorce judgment granted to the petitioning spouse.[59]

D. RECOGNITION OF FOREIGN DIVORCES[60]

1) General Criteria

Consistent with the jurisdiction conferred on Canadian courts by section 3(1) of the *Divorce Act*, section 22(1) provides that recognition shall be afforded to a foreign divorce granted on or after the commencement of the

---

56   *Bitard v. Ritztallah*, [1981] R.P. 408 (Que. C.S.).

57   *Mundle v. Jurgaitis* (1994), 127 N.S.R. (2d) 88 (T.D.).

58   Part I of the *Constitution Act, 1982*, being Schedule B to the *Canada Act 1982* (U.K.), 1982, c. 11.

59   *Gordon v. Keyes* (1986), 72 N.S.R. (2d) 172 (T.D.).

60   See James G. McLeod, *The Conflict of Laws* (Calgary: Carswell, 1983) c. 4.1.

Act, if either spouse was ordinarily resident[61] in the foreign jurisdiction for at least one year immediately preceding the commencement of the proceedings for divorce. In the common law provinces, at least, section 22(1) of the *Divorce Act* may be superfluous in light of the law as defined in *Robinson-Scott v. Robinson-Scott.*[62]

Sections 22(2) and 22(3) of the current *Divorce Act* substantially preserve the contents of section 6(2) of the *Divorce Act*, 1968. The continued recognition thereby afforded to foreign divorce decrees granted after 1 July 1968 on the jurisdictional basis of the wife's independent domicile reflects the provisions of section 6(1) of the *Divorce Act*, 1968, coupled with the doctrine of comity and reciprocity endorsed in *Travers v. Holley.*[63] Section 22(3) of the *Divorce Act* expressly preserves pre-existing judge-made rules of law pertaining to the recognition of foreign divorces. It may be appropriate to summarize these rules.[64] Canadian courts will recognize a foreign divorce:

- where jurisdiction was assumed on the basis of the domicile of the spouses;[65]
- where the foreign divorce, though granted on a non-domiciliary jurisdictional basis, is recognized by the law of the domicile of the parties;[66]
- where the foreign jurisdictional rule corresponds to the Canadian jurisdictional rule in divorce proceedings;[67]
- where the circumstances in the foreign jurisdiction would have conferred jurisdiction on a Canadian court if they had occurred in Canada;[68]
- where either the petitioner or respondent had a real and substantial connection with the foreign jurisdiction wherein the divorce was granted;[69] and

---

61   As to the significance of the term "ordinarily resident," see Section B(7), above in this chapter.

62   [1958] P. 71; see text below and see Julien D. Payne, "Recognition of Foreign Divorce Decrees in Canadian Courts" (1961) 10 I.C.L.Q. 846. Compare *Droit de la famille — 1221*, [1989] R.D.F. 161 (Que. C.S.).

63   [1953] P. 246 (Eng. C.A.); see text below.

64   The following summary was endorsed in *Janes v. Pardo*, [2002] N.J. No. 17 (S.C.), citing *Payne on Divorce*, 4th ed. (Scarborough, ON: Carswell, 1996) at 110–11. See also *Orabi v. El Qaoud*, [2005] N.S.J. No. 76 (C.A.).

65   *Le Mesurier v. Le Mesurier*, [1895] A.C. 517.

66   *Armitage v. Attorney General*, [1906] P. 135.

67   *Travers v. Holley*, [1953] P. 246 (Eng. C.A.).

68   *Robinson-Scott v. Robinson-Scott*, [1958] P. 71.

69   *Indyka v. Indyka*, [1969] 1 A.C. 33 (H.L.); *Mayfield v. Mayfield*, [1969] P. 119.

- where the foreign divorce is recognized in another foreign jurisdiction with which the petitioner or respondent has a real and substantial connection.[70]

If jurisdiction vests in the foreign court in accordance with the above criteria, the substantive ground for the foreign divorce is of no concern.[71]

Although the aforementioned rules were established by decisions of the English courts, they have generally been followed by Canadian courts, at least in those provinces that adhere to common-law tradition.

Judicial recognition of a foreign divorce pursuant to section 22 of the *Divorce Act* does not imply that recognition automatically extends to any corollary order for financial relief granted in the foreign divorce judgment.[72]

2) Extra-Judicial Divorce

Canadian courts may recognize an extra-judicial foreign divorce.[73]

3) Substantive and Procedural Defects

The perpetration of fraud upon a foreign tribunal that goes to the question of jurisdiction will preclude recognition of the foreign divorce in Canada.[74] A foreign divorce may also be denied recognition where principles of natural justice have been contravened.[75]

4) Doctrine of Preclusion

A person who has invoked the jurisdiction of a foreign tribunal cannot be heard to question the validity of the foreign divorce so as to obtain a material or pecuniary advantage based on its invalidity in Canada. The

---

70 *Mather v. Mahoney*, [1968] 3 All E.R. 223. This criterion has been deemed applicable even though the foreign divorce was granted prior to that ruling: *Edward v. Edward Estate* (1987), 8 R.F.L. (3d) 370 (Sask. C.A.).

71 *Powell v. Cockburn*, [1977] 2 S.C.R. 218; *Pitre v. Nguyen*, [2007] B.C.J. No. 1708 (S.C.).

72 *Vargo v. Saskatchewan (Family Justice Services Branch)*, [2006] S.J. No. 350 (Q.B.).

73 *Schwebel v. Ungar* (1963), 42 D.L.R. (2d) 622 (Ont. C.A.), aff'd [1965] S.C.R. 148; *Goldenberg v. Triffon*, [1955] C.S. 341 (Que.).

74 *Redl v. Redl* (1983), 35 R.F.L. (2d) 117 (Ont. H.C.J.); see also *Powell v. Cockburn*, [1977] 2 S.C.R. 218; *Pitre v. Nguyen*, [2007] B.C.J. No. 1708 (S.C.).

75 *Holub v. Holub*, [1976] 5 W.W.R. 527 (Man. C.A.); *Orabi v. El Qaoud*, [2005] N.S.J. No. 76 (C.A.).

foreign divorce is not validated for all purposes in such a case; it is merely recognized for the purpose of applying an estoppel.[76]

E. MARRIAGE BREAKDOWN AS SOLE GROUND FOR DIVORCE

Section 8 of the *Divorce Act*[77] defines the ground for divorce. In light of its importance, it is appropriate to reproduce it in its entirety:

Divorce

8.(1) A court of competent jurisdiction may, on application by either or both spouses, grant a divorce to the spouse or spouses on the ground that there has been a breakdown of their marriage.

Breakdown of marriage

(2) Breakdown of a marriage is established only if
   (a) the spouses have lived separate and apart for at least one year immediately preceding the determination of the divorce proceeding and were living separate and apart at the commencement of the proceeding; or
   (b) the spouse against whom the divorce proceeding is brought has, since celebration of the marriage,
      (i) committed adultery, or
      (ii) treated the other spouse with physical or mental cruelty of such a kind as to render intolerable the continued cohabitation of the spouses.

Calculation of period of separation

(3) For the purposes of paragraph (2)(a),
   (a) spouses shall be deemed to have lived separate and apart for any period during which they lived apart and either of them had the intention to live separate and apart from the other; and
   (b) a period during which spouses have lived separate and apart shall not be considered to have been interrupted or terminated

---

76   See *Downton v. Royal Trust Co.*, [1973] S.C.R. 437; see also *Stephens v. Falchi*, [1938] S.C.R. 354; *Re Plummer*, [1941] 3 W.W.R. 788 (Alta. C.A.).
77   *Divorce Act*, R.S.C. 1985 (2d Supp.), c. 3.

   (i)   by reason only that either spouse has become incapable of forming or having an intention to continue to live separate and apart or of continuing to live separate and apart of the spouse's own volition, if it appears to the court that the separation would probably have continued if the spouse had not become so incapable, or

  (ii)   by reason only that the spouses have resumed cohabitation during a period of, or periods totalling, not more than ninety days with reconciliation as its primary purpose.

Pursuant to section 8 of the *Divorce* Act, there is only one ground for divorce in Canada, namely, a "breakdown of [the] marriage."[78] It is not sufficient for one or both spouses to simply assert that their marriage has irretrievably broken down. In order to obtain a divorce under the *Divorce Act*, breakdown of a marriage is established "only if" the spouses have lived separate and apart for at least one year immediately preceding the divorce judgment, or the spouse against whom the divorce is sought has since the celebration of the marriage committed adultery or treated the other spouse with physical or mental cruelty of such a kind as to render continued marital cohabitation intolerable.[79]

In light of the recognition accorded to same-sex marriage in *Halpern v. Canada (Attorney General)*[80] Mesbur J., of the Ontario Superior Court of Justice, held in *M.M. v. J.H.*[81] that same-sex couples who are legally married may invoke the primary and corollary relief provisions of the *Divorce Act*. She found that section 2(1) of the *Divorce Act*, whereby "'spouse' means either of a man or woman who are married to each other," discriminates against same-sex married couples and contravenes equality rights guaranteed by section 15(1) of the *Canadian Charter of Rights and Freedoms*. Such contravention is not saved by section 1 of the *Charter* and the appropriate remedy is for the court to sever the words "a man and a woman" and read in the words "two persons" instead, so that section 2(1) will now provide that "'spouse' means either of two persons who are married to one another."

---

78   *Ibid.*, s. 8(1).

79   *Ibid.*, s. 8(2).

80   (2003), 65 O.R. (3d) 161 (C.A.). See Chapter 2, Section E(1).

81   [2004] O.J. No. 5314 (Sup. Ct.). See also *S.E.P. v. D.D.P.*, 2005 CarswellBC 2137 (S.C.) and *Thebeau v. Thebeau*, [2006] N.B.J. No. 178 (Q.B.) wherein "adultery" was judicially redefined pursuant to the *Canadian Charter of Rights and Freedoms* to include extramarital sexually intimate acts between a same-sex couple.

In *M.M. v. J.H.*, the parties entered into a same-sex marriage on 18 June 2003 but separated five days later. The petition for divorce was filed on 15 June 2004 and a divorce judgment was granted on 13 September 2004 pursuant to section 8(2)(a) of the *Divorce Act* on the basis that the spouses had "lived separate and apart for at least one year immediately preceding the determination of the divorce proceeding and were living separate and apart at the commencement of the proceeding." The judgment in *M.M. v. J.H.* substantially reflects the reasoning of the Ontario Court of Appeal in *Halpern v. Canada (Attorney General)*,[82] where the common-law definition of "marriage" was reformulated pursuant to the *Charter* to mean "the voluntary union for life of two persons to the exclusion of all others."

It is important to bear in mind that not all same-sex couples choose to marry. Only those who marry can avail themselves of the corollary relief provisions of the *Divorce Act* that relate to spousal support, child support, custody, and access. If same-sex couples, who cohabited but did not marry, wish to obtain any of the aforementioned types of relief, they must, like unmarried cohabitants of the opposite sex, have recourse to applicable provincial legislation. While this may be of little practical importance because applications for spousal support, child support, custody, and access usually generate the same result whether such relief is sought pursuant to provincial legislation or the *Divorce Act*, fundamental differences between same-sex married couples and same-sex unmarried couples may arise in the context of provincial statutory property rights on the breakdown of their relationships. For example, in Ontario, a same-sex married partner may obtain an equalization of the net spousal properties pursuant to Part I of the *Family Law Act*[83] as amended by the *Spousal Relationships Statute Law Amendment Act*.[84] However, in light of the judgment of the Supreme Court of Canada in *Nova Scotia (Attorney General) v. Walsh and Bona*,[85] a same-sex former unmarried cohabitant cannot avail himself or herself of similar relief and must rest content with such relief as might be available at common law or by way of resulting or constructive trusts.

Section 8(1) of the *Divorce Act* provides that "either or both spouses" may apply for divorce. A joint petition for divorce may be based on mar-

---

82   (2003), 65 O.R. (3d) 161 (C.A.).

83   R.S.O. 1990, c. F.3.

84   S.O. 2005, c. 5.

85   [2002] 4 S.C.R. 325.

riage breakdown as manifested by the separation of the spouses within the meaning of section 8(2)(a) but a joint petition cannot be brought where the facts relied upon, in whole or in part, involve the adultery or cruelty of the respondent as defined in section 8(2)(b).[86]

1) Spousal Separation As Proof of Marriage Breakdown

Spouses who rely on the one-year separation period in order to obtain their divorce are not required to wait until that period has expired before filing for divorce. A divorce petition can be filed on the day following the spousal separation but a divorce judgment cannot be obtained until the one-year period has elapsed. Once a divorce petition has been filed, either spouse may obtain interim corollary relief, such as support, custody, or access, to tide him or her over until the issues can be permanently resolved by a trial in open court or settled by the parties, with or without the aid of lawyers or mediators.

Subject to the provisions of section 8(3)(b) of the *Divorce Act*, the designated period of separation under 8(2)(a) must be continuous and uninterrupted up to the time when the divorce judgment is granted.

The words "living separate and apart" in section 8(2)(a) of the *Divorce Act* require proof of an intention to bring the marriage to an end in addition to the fact of separation. Subject to section 8(3)(b)(i) of the *Divorce Act*, the physical separation and the intention to end the marriage must co-exist for the requisite one-year period. Neither factor standing alone can satisfy the statutory requirements of section 8(2)(a).[87] No account will be taken of any period of physical separation that occurred prior to the formation of an intention to terminate the marriage.[88]

Section 8(2)(a) of the *Divorce Act* draws no distinction between deserted and deserting spouses. It is immaterial whether the separation occurred by consent of the spouses or by reason of an unjustifiable withdrawal from cohabitation by one of the spouses. In either event, it is open to one or both spouses to commence proceedings for divorce. Unilateral

---

86   *Droit de la famille — 304*, [1986] R.D.F. 589 (Que. C.S.); *Droit de la famille — 471*, [1988] R.D.F. 236 (Que. C.S.).

87   *Raven v. Raven* (1984), 30 Man. R. (2d) 71 (Q.B.); *Shorten v. Shorten* (1986), 65 N.B.R. (2d) 429 (Q.B.).

88   *Devani v. Devani* (1976), 8 Nfld. & P.E.I.R. 273 (Nfld. T.D.); *Singh v. Singh* (1976), 23 R.F.L. 379 (Ont. H.C.J.).

abandonment of the matrimonial relationship is sufficient to satisfy the requirements of section 8 of the *Divorce Act*.[89]

Section 8(3)(b)(i) of the *Divorce Act* provides that the designated period of separation will not be interrupted or terminated by reason that either spouse has become incapable of forming or having an intention to live separate and apart, if it appears to the court that the separation would probably have continued in any event. Thus, supervening physical or mental illness that precludes a spouse from retaining a prior intention to treat the marriage as ended will not bar relief under section 8(2)(a). An enforced physical separation will satisfy the requirements of section 8(2)(a) of the *Divorce Act* but only if it is accompanied by a co-existing intention to end the marriage.[90]

Spouses may have been living "separate and apart" within the meaning of section 8(2)(a) of the *Divorce Act*, notwithstanding their continued residence under the same roof, provided that they have been living independent lives while sharing common accommodation.[91] In *Cooper v. Cooper*,[92] Holland J. of the Ontario Supreme Court pointed out that a finding that the spouses have been living separate and apart, albeit under the same roof, may be made where the following circumstances are present:

- occupation of separate bedrooms;
- absence of sexual relations;
- little, if any, communication between the spouses;
- the wife is providing no domestic services for her husband;
- eating meals eaten separately; and
- no social activities together.

---

89   *Lachman v. Lachman* (1970), 2 R.F.L. 207 (Ont. C.A.).
90   *Dorchester v. Dorchester* (1971), 3 R.F.L. 396 (B.C.S.C.); *Norman v. Norman* (1973), 12 R.F.L. 252 (N.S.C.A.); *Burgoyne v. Burgoyne* (1974), 14 R.F.L. 92 (N.S.C.A.); *Lachman v. Lachman* (1970), 2 R.F.L. 207 (Ont. C.A.).
91   *Rushton v. Rushton* (1969), 1 R.F.L. 215 (B.C.S.C.); *Galbraith v. Galbraith* (1969), 1 R.F.L. 77 (Man. C.A.); *Dupere v. Dupere* (1974), 19 R.F.L. 270 (N.B.S.C.), aff'd (1975), 10 N.B.R. (2d) 148 (C.A.); *Bance v. Bance* (1977), 18 N.B.R. (2d) 262 at 264–65 (Q.B.); *Boulos v. Boulos* (1980), 14 R.F.L. (2d) 206 (Nfld. S.C.); *McDonald v. McDonald* (1988), 15 R.F.L. (3d) 268 (N.S.T.D.); *Williams v. Williams*, [1991] N.W.T.R. 53 (S.C.); *Mayberry v. Mayberry* (1971), 3 R.F.L. 395 (Ont. C.A.); *Cooper v. Cooper* (1972), 10 R.F.L. 184 (Ont. H.C.J.); *Thorogood v. Thorogood* (1987), 11 R.F.L. (3d) 82 (Ont. U.F.C.); *Oswell v. Oswell* (1992), 43 R.F.L. (3d) 180 (Ont. C.A.); *Hébert v. Dame Houle*, [1973] C.S. 868 (Que.); *Ginter v. Ginter* (1988), 15 R.F.L. (3d) 203 (Sask. Q.B.).
92   (1972), 10 R.F.L. 184 (Ont. S.C.). See also *Ashworth v. Ashworth* (1995), 15 R.F.L. (4th) 379 (Ont. Gen. Div.).

It is not necessary, however, to establish all six elements and each case must stand or fall on its own merits.[93] In determining whether the spouses are living separate and apart within the meaning of section 8(2)(a) of the *Divorce Act*, the court must give greater weight to those matters that should be peculiar to a husband and wife relationship, such as sexual relations, joint social ventures, communication, and discussion of family problems, rather than to the performance or non-performance of domestic chores.[94] Similarly, the payment of household expenses does not negate a finding that the spouses have been living separate and apart under the same roof where there were no activities of any kind as a family.[95]

The cessation of sexual intercourse is relevant but not conclusive on the issue whether the spouses have been living separate and apart within the meaning of section 8(2)(a) of the *Divorce Act*.[96] Where the spouses remain under the same roof and continue to discharge their marital responsibilities, the cessation of sexual intercourse will not suffice to justify a finding that the spouses are living separate and apart within the meaning of section 8(2)(a) of the *Divorce Act*.[97]

Isolated or casual acts of postseparation sexual intercourse between the spouses do not preclude a finding that they have continued to live separate and apart within the meaning of section 8(2)(a) of the *Divorce Act*, nor justify a finding that they have resumed cohabitation within the meaning of section 8(3)(b)(ii). In the absence of a mutual intention to become reconciled, the continuance or resumption of sexual intercourse between separated spouses is not to be equated with matrimonial cohabitation.[98] Just as sexual activity between separated spouses does not

---

93 *Ibid.* See also *Bance v. Bance* (1977), 18 N.B.R. (2d) 262 (Q.B.).

94 *McKenna v. McKenna* (1975), 19 R.F.L. 357 at 358 (N.S.C.A.). See also *Kobayashi v. Kobayashi* (1972), 6 R.F.L. 358 (Man. Q.B.); *Woolgar v. Woolgar* (1995), 10 R.F.L. (4th) 309 (Nfld. U.F.C.); *Smith v. Smith* (1980), 28 Nfld. & P.E.I.R. 99 (P.E.I.T.D.).

95 *Byzruki v. Byzruki* (1982), 26 R.F.L. (2d) 243 (Ont. S.C.).

96 *Smith v. Smith* (1970), 2 R.F.L. 214 (B.C.S.C.); *Dick v. Dick* (1971), 2 R.F.L. 225 (B.C.S.C.); *Newman v. Newman* (1971), 2 R.F.L. 219 (Ont. C.A.); *Seminuk v. Seminuk* (1970), 72 W.W.R. 304 (Sask. C.A.).

97 *Cridge v. Cridge* (1974), 12 R.F.L. 348 (B.C.S.C.); *Davies v. Davies* (1980), 29 N.B.R. (2d) 207 (Q.B.); *Burt v. Burt* (1974), 7 R.F.L. 155 (N.S.T.D.).

98 *Roadburg v. Braut* (1994), 4 R.F.L. (4th) 96 (B.C.C.A.); *Singh v. Singh* (1982), 130 D.L.R. (3d) 130 (Man. Q.B.); *Sampson v. Sampson* (1994), 3 R.F.L. (4th) 415 (N.B.Q.B.); *Morrow v. Morrow* (1982), 36 N.B.R. (2d) 117 (Q.B.); *Deslippe v. Deslippe* (1974), 16 R.F.L. 38 (Ont. C.A.); *McGeachy v. McGeachy* (1980), 15 R.F.L. (2d) 274 (Ont. H.C.J.); *Spinney v. Spinney* (1982), 33 Nfld. & P.E.I.R. 61 (P.E.I.C.A.); *Leaderhouse v. Leaderhouse* (1971), 4 R.F.L. 174 (Sask. Q.B.); *Geransky v. Geransky* (1980), 16 R.F.L. (2d) 193 (Sask. Q.B.).

necessarily signify a resumption of the matrimonial relationship, so too, a resumption of cohabitation can occur even though sexual intercourse is restricted.[99]

Section 8(3)(b)(ii) of the *Divorce Act* confers a limited right on the spouses to resume cohabitation in an attempt to achieve a reconciliation without interrupting or terminating the period of separation that preceded the attempted reconciliation. The spouse are free to resume cohabitation on any number of occasions and are not confined to a single reconciliation attempt. However, they have a maximum of ninety days during which they can resume cohabitation in any attempt(s) at reconciliation.[100]

2) Adultery and Cruelty As Proof of Marriage Breakdown: No Waiting Period

If either spouse has committed adultery or treated the other spouse with cruelty, a speedy divorce is obtainable without waiting for spousal separation to run for one year. Marriage breakdown as a ground for divorce where a spouse has committed adultery or cruelty is only available to the innocent spouse. The spouse who commits adultery or treats the other spouse with cruelty cannot petition for divorce on the basis of his or her own misconduct having caused a breakdown of the marriage. The guilty spouse can, nevertheless, invoke the no-fault separation criterion of marriage breakdown and obtain a divorce after the spouses have been separated for one year. In short, when separation is relied upon in proof of marriage breakdown, a mandatory one-year period must elapse before a divorce can be obtained by either spouse. With adultery or cruelty, the innocent spouse can proceed to obtain a divorce right away.

3) Marriage Breakdown: Adultery

Section 8(2)(b)(i) of the *Divorce Act* provides that marriage breakdown as a ground for divorce may be established if the spouse against whom the divorce proceeding is brought has committed adultery since the celebration of the marriage.

In the absence of any statutory definition, adultery has been traditionally defined by the courts as voluntary sexual intercourse between

---

99 *Sampson v. Sampson* (1994), 3 R.F.L. (4th) 415 at 421 (N.B.Q.B.).
100 *Williams v. Williams*, [1991] N.W.T.R. 53 (S.C.); *Thorogood v. Thorogood* (1987), 11 R.F.L. (3d) 82 (Ont. U.F.C.).

a married person and another person of the opposite sex other than his or her spouse.[101] Full and complete sexual intercourse is not required to prove adultery; partial penetration will suffice.[102] Masturbation or other activities that fall short of penetration of the male sexual organ into the female have been held not to constitute adultery, although such activities may lead to an inference that adultery has been committed.[103] Judicial opinion has been divided on the question of whether artificial insemination by a third party constitutes adultery.[104]

In *S.E.P. v. D.D.P.*,[105] Garson J., of the British Columbia Supreme Court, observed that the *Civil Marriage Act*,[106] which has redefined "marriage, for civil purposes, as the lawful union of two persons to the exclusion of all others," reflects current values of our society consistent with the *Canadian Charter of Rights and Freedoms*. It therefore provides a guide to the current definition to be accorded to "adultery" in section 8(2)(b)(i) of the *Divorce Act*. Because same-sex couples can now marry and divorce, the common-law definition of adultery would be anomalous if same-sex couples were not bound by the same legal and social restraints against extramarital sexual relationships that apply to heterosexual spouses. As Iacobucci J. observed in *R. v. Salituro*,[107] "[j]udges can and should adapt the common law to reflect the changing social, moral and economic fabric of the country" but "the judiciary should confine itself to those incremental changes which are necessary to keep the common law in step with the dynamic and evolving fabric of our society." And as McLachlin C.J. observed in *Retail, Wholesale and Department Store Union, Local 558 v. Pepsi-Cola Canada Beverages*,[108] "the common law does not exist in a vacuum. The common law reflects the experience of the past, the reality of modern concerns and a sensitivity to the future. As such, it does not grow in isolation from the *Charter*." Garson J., in *S.E.P. v. D.D.P.*, agreed with counsel for the wife and counsel for the Attorney General of Canada (who had intervened in the case) that it was unnecessary to undertake

---

101 *Orford v. Orford* (1921), 49 O.L.R. 15 (S.C.); *Kahl v. Kahl*, [1943] O.W.N. 558 (S.C.).

102 *Thompson v. Thompson*, [1939] P. 1; *Sapsford v. Sapsford*, [1954] P. 394; *Dennis v. Dennis*, [1955] P. 153.

103 *Sapsford v. Sapsford*, [1954] P. 394; *Dennis v. Dennis*, [1955] P. 153.

104 See *Orford v. Orford* (1921), 49 O.L.R. 15 (S.C.); compare *MacLennan v. MacLennan*, [1958] S.C. 105 (Scot.).

105 [2005] B.C.J. No. 1971 (S.C.).

106 S.C. 2005, c. 33.

107 [1991] 3 S.C.R. 654 at 670.

108 [2002] 1 S.C.R. 156 at para. 19.

a section 15 *Charter* analysis to determine whether section 8(2)(b)(i) of the *Divorce Act* was discriminatory and therefore unconstitutional. Instead she accepted the submissions of both counsel that an incremental change in the definition of adultery, to include sexual acts between same-sex couples, was consistent with the *Civil Marriage Act*, the *Charter*, and the principles enunciated in *Salituro* and *Pepsi-Cola*, above. Having regard to the husband's admission of adultery with another man, Garson J. did not consider it necessary or desirable to define what type of intimate sexual activity between persons of the same sex would constitute adultery, leaving this to be resolved over time on a case-by-case basis. It is submitted that the wiser course of action in *S.E.P. v. D.D.P.* would have been for the court to strike down section 8(2)(b)(i) of the *Divorce Act* as a violation of section 15 of the *Canadian Charter of Rights and Freedoms*, leaving it to Parliament to address the issue of whether (or what type of) sexual infidelity should continue to provide a basis for the dissolution of marriage on the ground of marriage breakdown. If this course of action had been pursued, it would have been open to Garson J. to allow the wife petitioner to amend her pleadings to seek a divorce pursuant to section 8(2)(b)(ii) of the *Divorce Act* on the basis of her husband's cruelty. In its *Report on Family Law*,[109] the original Law Reform Commission of Canada proposed the abolition of matrimonial offences as grounds for divorce and the substitution of "marriage breakdown" as the sole criterion for divorce. The Commission envisaged that the dissolution process would be commenced by either spouse filing with the court a simple and non-accusatory notice of intention to seek dissolution of marriage and that marriage breakdown would be non-justiciable, being conclusively established by the evidence of either spouse. Perhaps the time is ripe for Parliament to implement the Commission's proposal.

It is impossible to generalize about the circumstances that will warrant an inference of adultery being drawn by the court save to say that the circumstances of the particular case must be such as to lead to a fair and reasonable inference of adultery.[110] Where the evidence of adultery is circumstantial, the circumstances must be such as would lead the guarded discretion of a reasonable and just person to the conclusion that adultery

---

109   Ottawa: Information Canada, March 1976.
110   *Stacey v. Stacey*, [1977] 1 W.W.R. 821 (Alta. S.C.); *Furlong v. Furlong* (1963), 49 M.P.R. 377 (N.B.C.A.); *Harrison v. Harrison* (1975), 12 N.S.R. (2d) 149 (T.D.).

has been committed.[111] Evidence that creates only suspicion, surmise, or conjecture is insufficient.[112]

Adultery may be proved by the respondent's admission under oath.[113] The court may find that both spouses have committed adultery on the basis of their respective admissions.[114] The wife's evidence of the husband's out-of-court admissions of adultery may be sufficient to warrant a finding of adultery in divorce proceedings.

4) Marriage Breakdown: Cruelty

Section 8(2)(b)(ii) of the *Divorce Act* provides that marriage breakdown as a ground for divorce may be established if the spouse against whom the divorce proceeding is brought has, since the celebration of the marriage, treated the other spouse with physical or mental cruelty of such a kind as to render intolerable the continued cohabitation of the spouses.

Cruelty does not lend itself to any precise definition. Generally speaking, cruelty signifies a disposition to inflict suffering, to delight in or exhibit indifference to the pain and misery of others, mercilessness, or hard-heartedness as manifested by conduct.[115] It is impossible to categorize particular types of conduct as constituting mental or physical cruelty.[116] Cruelty is a question of fact and degree to be determined in light of the particular circumstances of each case.[117] Danger to life, limb, or health is not a prerequisite to a finding of cruelty under the *Divorce Act*.[118] The conduct complained of in the divorce petition must be grave and weighty; it must go beyond incompatibility of temperament between the spouses.[119]

---

111 *Coates v. Coates* (1974), 16 R.F.L. 117 (N.B.Q.B.), citing *MacCurdy v. MacCurdy* (1971), 8 R.F.L. 125 (N.B.C.A.).

112 *Carson v. Carson* (1985), 46 R.F.L. (2d) 102 at 105 (N.B.Q.B.); *George v. George*, [1950] O.R. 787 (C.A.); *Zawatsky v. Zawatsky* (1976), 21 R.F.L. 370 (Sask. Q.B.).

113 *d'Entremont v. d'Entremont* (1992), 44 R.F.L. (3d) 224 (N.S.C.A.); *Ewasiuk v. Ewasiuk* (1969), 66 W.W.R. 509 (N.W.T.T.C.); *Mark v. Mark* (1974), 15 R.F.L. 73 (Ont. H.C.J.); *Morice v. Morice* (1972), 8 R.F.L. 283 (Sask. C.A.).

114 *Elligott v. Elligott* (1977), 3 R.F.L. (2d) 61 (Alta. S.C.).

115 See *Knoll v. Knoll* (1970), 1 R.F.L. 141 (Ont. C.A.).

116 *Re Tremaine* (1968), 2 N.S.R. 787 (S.C.).

117 *Stevens v. Stevens* (1977), 17 N.B.R. (2d) 656 at 659–60 (Q.B.); *Ebenal v. Ebenal* (1971), 3 R.F.L. 303 (Sask. C.A.).

118 *Zalesky v. Zalesky* (1968), 67 W.W.R. 104 (Man. Q.B.); *Knoll v. Knoll* (1970), 1 R.F.L. 141 (Ont. C.A.); *Stevens v. Stevens* (1977), 17 N.B.R. (2d) 656 (Q.B.).

119 *Ibid.*

Mere estrangement of the spouses or a breakdown of their marriage arising from incompatibility of temperament will not constitute cruelty within the meaning of the *Divorce Act*.[120] In the words of Schroeder J.A., of the Ontario Court of Appeal:

> Care must be exercised in applying the standard set forth in ... [the *Divorce Act*] that conduct relied upon to establish cruelty is not a trivial act, but one of a "grave and weighty" nature, and not merely conduct which can be characterized as little more than a manifestation of incompatibility of temperament between the spouses. The whole matrimonial relations must be considered, especially if the cruelty consists of reproaches, complaints, accusations, or constant carping criticism. A question most relevant for consideration is the effect of the conduct complained of upon the mind of the affected spouse. The determination of what constitutes cruelty in a given case must, in the final analysis, depend upon the circumstances of the particular case having due regard to the physical and mental condition of the parties, their character and their attitude towards the marriage relationship.[121]

It is not necessary that the allegedly cruel spouse acted with a culpable intention.[122] The impact of the alleged conduct on the victim is far more important.[123] Where the two spouses are of normal physical and mental health and the conduct of the respondent is so bad that the petitioner should not be called on to endure it, cruelty is established irrespective of

---

120 *Takenaka v. Takenaka* (1981), 24 B.C.L.R. 273 (S.C.); *Galbraith v. Galbraith* (1969), 1 R.F.L. 96 (Man. Q.B.); *Chouinard v. Chouinard* (1969), 1 R.F.L. 101 (N.B.C.A.), 1 (1971), 3 N.B.R. (2d) 357 (C.A.); *Goudie v. Goudie* (1970), 2 R.F.L. 128 (Nfld. S.C.); *Hiltz v. Hiltz* (1971), 2 R.F.L. 178 (N.S.T.D.), aff'd (1973) 11 R.F.L. 35 (N.S.C.A.); *Knoll v. Knoll* (1970), 1 R.F.L. 141 (Ont. C.A.); *Storey v. Storey* (1973), 10 R.F.L. 170 (P.E.I.T.D.); *Pawelko v. Pawelko* (1970), 1 R.F.L. 174 (Sask. Q.B.).

121 *Knoll v. Knoll* (1970), 1 R.F.L. 141 at 150 (Ont. C.A.), cited with approval in *Krause v. Krause* (1975), 19 R.F.L. 230, var'd (1976), 23 R.F.L. 219 (Alta. C.A.); *Edwards v. Edwards* (1973), 12 R.F.L. 35 (B.C.C.A.); *Zunti v. Zunti* (1971), 15 D.L.R. (3d) 369 (B.C.C.A.); *Shumila v. Shumila* (1975), 21 R.F.L. 110 (Man. C.A.); *Aucoin v. Aucoin* (1976), 28 R.F.L. 43 (N.S.C.A.); *Horner v. Horner* (1973), 13 R.F.L. 117 at 126 (N.S.C.A.); *Pongor v. Pongor* (1976), 27 R.F.L. 109 (Ont. C.A.); *Wittstock v. Wittstock* (1971), 3 R.F.L. 326 (Ont. C.A.); *Storey v. Storey* (1973), 10 R.F.L. 170 (P.E.I.T.D.); *Powell v. Powell* (1972), 5 R.F.L. 194 (Sask. C.A.); *Ebenal v. Ebenal* (1971), 3 R.F.L. 303 (Sask. C.A.). See also *Anderson v. Anderson* (1972), 8 R.F.L. 299 at 304 (Alta. C.A.), aff'd (1973), 10 R.F.L. 200 (S.C.C.); *Stevens v. Stevens* (1977), 17 N.B.R. (2d) 656 (Q.B.).

122 *Gollins v. Gollins*, [1964] A.C. 644 (H.L.); *Williams v. Williams*, [1964] A.C. 698 (H.L.).

123 *Ibid.*

the respondent's state of mind. It is immaterial whether the respondent's conduct was deliberately aimed at the petitioner or due to unwarranted indifference.[124] Malevolent intention, though not essential to cruelty, is a most important element where it exists.[125]

Where the conduct complained of would amount to cruelty in the absence of any culpable intention,[126] the insanity of the respondent is no answer to the charge of cruelty.[127]

The test of cruelty is largely subjective because the paramount question is whether "*this* conduct by *this* man towards *this* woman, or *vice versa*, is cruelty" such as renders matrimonial cohabitation intolerable.[128] The law has been aptly summarized by Disbery J., of the Saskatchewan Court of Queen's Bench, in the following observations:

> In dealing with the ingredient of cruelty it has been widely held that the conduct and actions of the respondent spouse upon which the petitioner relies must be conduct or acts of a serious, grave and weighty nature. Lesser marital misconduct such as rudeness, personal slovenliness, slovenly housekeeping, inability to hold steady employment, wasteful spending and the tit for tat irritations bestowed by each spouse upon the other are all part of the stresses and strains of marriage and, save for rare and exceptional cases, such conduct and actions do not constitute the kind of cruelty defined in [section 8(2)(b)(ii) of the *Divorce Act*]. Again incompatibilities, which of course include sexual incompatibility, resulting in an unhappy marriage do not constitute, *per se*, cruelty so defined in the said section .... Pearce J., in *Lauder v. Lauder*, [1949] P. 277 at p. 308; [1949] 1 All E.R. 76, said: "For in a cruelty case the ques-

---

124 *Goldstein v. Goldstein* (1970), 15 D.L.R. (3d) 95 (Alta. S.C.). See also *Gollins v. Gollins*, [1964] A.C. 644 (H.L.); *Gollins v. Gollins (No. 2)* (1964), 108 S.J. 941; *Rankin v. Rankin* (1970), 13 D.L.R. (3d) 630 (B.C.S.C.); *Martin v. Martin* (1971), 1 R.F.L. 154 (B.C.S.C.); *Schnerch v. Schnerch* (1982), 13 Man. R. (2d) 277 (Q.B.); *White v. White* (1968), 69 D.L.R. (2d) 60 (N.S. Div. Ct.); *Knoll v. Knoll* (1970), 1 R.F.L. 141 (Ont. C.A.); *Wakefield v. Schrogl*, [1976] C.S. 222 (Que.).

125 *King v. King*, [1953] A.C. 124 (H.L.); *Feldman v. Feldman* (1970), 2 R.F.L. 173 (Alta. C.A.); *Krause v. Krause* (1976), 23 R.F.L. 219 at 222 (Alta. C.A.); *Knoll v. Knoll* (1970), 1 R.F.L. 141 (Ont. C.A.); *Wittstock v. Wittstock* (1971), 3 R.F.L. 326 (Ont. C.A.).

126 Above note 119.

127 *Williams v. Williams*, [1964] A.C. 698 (H.L.); *Novak v. Novak* (1969), 1 R.F.L. 58 (B.C.S.C.). See also *Baker v. Baker* (1970), 1 R.F.L. 106 (B.C.S.C.); *McGrath v. McGrath* (1977), 16 N.B.R. (2d) 462 (Q.B.); *Herman v. Herman* (1969), 1 R.F.L. 41 (N.S.T.D.); *MacKay v. MacKay* (1978), 1 R.F.L. (2d) 80 (P.E.I.C.A.); *Ifield v. Ifield* (1976), 24 R.F.L. 237 (Sask. C.A.).

128 *Lauder v. Lauder*, [1949] P. 277 at 308 (Eng.).

tion is whether this conduct by this man to this woman, or vice versa is cruelty." This subjective test has been approved and applied in this Province by the Court of Appeal in *Austin v. Austin* (1970), 13 D.L.R. (3d) 498 at p. 500; 2 R.F.L. 136; 73 W.W.R. 289 at p. 291. ... Having regard to the endless variations in the conduct, habits, dispositions, sensitivities, intelligence, temperaments and character of married persons, it immediately becomes apparent that when a divorce is sought on the ground of cruelty, each case must be determined on its own facts including, of course, the personalities of the spouses. Identical conduct and acts of a respondent spouse would [in one case] constitute cruelty within the ambit of [the section] having regard to the personality of the recipient spouse; while in another case identical acts and conduct would not suffice because of the different personality of the recipient spouse.[129]

The court has regard to the cumulative effect of the respondent's conduct on the petitioner.[130] The cumulative effect of the respondent's conduct may constitute cruelty although each of the individual incidents complained of would not, standing alone, be sufficiently grave and weighty to satisfy the requirements of section 8(2)(b)(ii) of the *Divorce Act*.[131]

It is for the court and not the petitioner to determine whether the conduct of the respondent is sufficiently grave to warrant dissolution of the marriage pursuant to section 8(2)(b)(ii) of the *Divorce Act*.[132]

Diverse types of conduct may constitute cruelty, although whether cruelty actually exists will always depend on the facts of the particular case, having regard to the history of the marriage and the sensibilities of the spouses. Physique, temperament, culture, habits of verbal expression and of action, and the interaction of the spouses in their daily lives are vital considerations.[133] The court must have regard to the society in which the parties live, socially, morally, and materially.[134]

---

129 *Ifield v. Ifield* (1976), 24 R.F.L. 237 at 242–44 (Sask. Q.B.).
130 *Knoll v. Knoll* (1970), 1 R.F.L. 141 (Ont. C.A.); *Pongor v. Pongor* (1976), 27 R.F.L. 109 (Ont. C.A.).
131 *Cochrane v. Cochrane* (1976), 10 Nfld. & P.E.I.R. 86 (Nfld. T.D.); *Zwicker v. Zwicker* (1973), 3 R.F.L. 333 (N.S.T.D.); compare *Wyman v. Wyman* (1971), 2 R.F.L. 190 at 195 (Sask. Q.B.).
132 *Lake v. Lake* (1983), 30 R.F.L. (3d) 5 (B.C.S.C.); *B. v. B.*, [1970] C.S. 212 (Que.); *Jordahl v. Jordahl* (1972), 5 R.F.L. 189 (Sask. Q.B.); *Summerfelt v. Summerfelt* (1983), 31 R.F.L. (2d) 240 (Sask. Q.B.).
133 *Watt v. Thomas*, [1947] A.C. 484 at 488 (H.L.).
134 *Goudie v. Goudie* (1970), 2 R.F.L. 128 (Nfld. T.D.).

Cruelty may be established on the basis of commission or omission. The conduct of the respondent may be active or passive; it may consist of deliberate ill treatment, by word or deed, or it may arise from thoughtless neglect.[135]

A husband's violent assault committed on his wife on a single occasion may justify a finding of physical cruelty of such a kind as to render cohabitation intolerable within the meaning of the *Divorce Act*. Older cases that required repeated acts of physical violence for a finding of cruelty to be made[136] must be viewed with extreme caution in light of the current state of awareness concerning the battered wife syndrome. Courts have shown no hesitation in finding cruelty such as renders cohabitation intolerable within the meaning of the *Divorce Act* where there have been long-term or repeated incidents of violence[137] or where physical violence has been accompanied by other intolerable conduct.[138]

Verbal abuse,[139] false accusations of infidelity,[140] and domineering and demeaning conduct,[141] if of sufficient gravity, may constitute cruelty within the meaning of the *Divorce Act*. However, differences of opinion or verbal squabbles, even though accompanied by gross or vulgar language on isolated occasions, may fall short of satisfying the statutory requirements,[142] as may also the respondent's continual complaints about the petitioner's absence from home in the discharge of professional responsibilities.[143]

---

135 *Ibid.*
136 See *Peskett v. Peskett* (1980), 14 R.F.L. (2d) 134 (B.C.S.C.); *McEvoy v. McEvoy* (1984), 55 N.B.R. (2d) 269 (Q.B.).
137 *Curran v. Curran* (1973), 3 Nfld. & P.E.I.R. 395 (Nfld. S.C.); *Betts v. Betts* (1979), 25 N.B.R. (2d) 478 (Q.B.); *Othberg v. Othberg* (1979), 2 N.B.R. (2d) 339 (Q.B.); *MacLeod v. MacLeod* (1979), 32 N.S.R. (2d) 137 (T.D.).
138 *Curran v. Curran* (1973), 3 Nfld. & P.E.I.R. 395 (Nfld. S.C.); *MacLeod v. MacLeod* (1979), 32 N.S.R. (2d) 137 (T.D.).
139 *Chorney v. Chorney* (1971), 4 R.F.L. 347 (Alta. C.A.); *Fisher v. Fisher* (1978), 11 A.R. 359 (T.D.); *Humeniuk v. Humeniuk* (1970), 4 R.F.L. 163 (Ont. H.C.J.); *Giesbrecht v. Giesbrecht* (1975), 16 R.F.L. 399 (Sask. Q.B.).
140 *Chorney v. Chorney* (1971), 4 R.F.L. 347 (Alta. C.A.); *Ivany v. Ivany* (1971), 2 R.F.L. 172 (B.C.S.C.); *Wakefield v. Schrogl*, [1976] C.S. 222 (Que.).
141 *Ratcliffe v. Ratcliffe* (1977), 27 R.F.L. 227 (B.C.S.C.); *Dowell v. Dowell* (1978), 30 R.F.L. 278 (Man. Q.B.); *Nichols v. Nichols* (1968), 1 N.S.R. (1965–69) 503 (T.D.); *Ells v. Ells* (1971), 2 R.F.L. 186 (N.S.T.D.); *Rowe v. Rowe* (1977), 26 R.F.L. 91 (Ont. H.C.J.); *Pavlinek v. Pavlinek* (1976), 22 R.F.L. 236 (Ont. H.C.J.); *L. v. L.*, [1970] C.S. 222 (Que.).
142 *B. v. R.*, [1970] C.S. 21 (Que.).
143 *Turnbull v. Turnbull* (1977), 28 R.F.L. 92 (Man. Q.B.).

Stevenson J., of the New Brunswick Court of Queen's Bench, has observed:

> When acts of cruelty relied upon take the form of abuse, quarrels, nagging, selfishness, etc. there is a greater danger of their being categorized as examples of incompatibility rather than of cruelty. However, where one spouse insists on totally dominating the other or deprives the other of his company or ridicules and belittles his spouse or is selfish and ignores his obligations of support he or she may be found guilty of cruelty. Similarly, threats of physical violence towards the petitioner, her children or towards the respondent himself, false accusations of theft, of non-support or of infidelity, vulgar abuse, constant nagging, and unseemly "scenes" before others, can amount to cruelty.[144]

Habitual drinking, drug-taking, or gambling does not necessarily constitute cruelty[145] but will be found to do so when it has a detrimental impact on the petitioner who finds continued cohabitation intolerable under those circumstances.[146]

Inattentiveness or insensitivity that is simply a manifestation of a spouse's personality ordinarily falls short of cruelty.[147]

A husband's addiction to work with consequential neglect of his wife and children may constitute cruelty within the meaning of the *Divorce Act*,[148] although the court may decline to make such a finding when the wife did not complain of his conduct until the last stage of their marriage and the conduct had continued from the very early stages of the marriage.[149]

A court may find cruelty by reason of the respondent's refusal to work and support the family.[150]

Notwithstanding the wide diversity of standards between one married couple and another as to what is normal,[151] excessive demands for

---

144   *Brewer v. Brewer* (1978), 21 N.B.R. (2d) 154 at 157 (Q.B.).

145   *Kulyk v. Kulyk* (1980), 5 Sask. R. 235 (Q.B.).

146   *Le Blanc v. Le Blanc* (1984), 54 N.B.R. (2d) 388 (Q.B.) (excessive drinking); *Bramley v. Bramley* (1974), 15 R.F.L. 152 (Ont. Sup. Ct.) (heroin addiction); *Rauch v. Rauch* (1976), 22 R.F.L. 143 (Ont. H.C.J.) (addiction to gambling).

147   *Cavalier v. Cavalier* (1977), 25 R.F.L. 118 (B.C.S.C.).

148   *Mark v. Mark* (1974), 15 R.F.L. 73 (Ont. H.C.J.).

149   *Koch v. Koch* (1978), 30 R.F.L. 269 (Man. Co. Ct.); see also *Kastrau v. Kastrau* (1979), 7 R.F.L. (2d) 318 (Ont. U.F.C.).

150   *Durant v. Durant* (1971), 2 Nfld. & P.E.I.R. 138 (P.E.I.T.D.).

151   *M. v. M.* (1974), 14 R.F.L. 1 (Ont. H.C.J.).

sexual intercourse[152] or the persistent denial of sexual intercourse[153] may constitute cruelty within the meaning of the *Divorce Act*. Several courts have declined to find cruelty where the refusal of sexual intercourse was attributable to physical or psychological difficulties,[154] although it is doubtful whether any binding precedents have been thereby established.

The court may grant a divorce judgment to each spouse on the ground of mutual cruelty.[155]

The clear trend of the law is to remove fault from most spousal disputes. As it usually takes a year to bring a contested matter to trial, a divorce will usually be available on the basis of one year of separation. Where this is the case, a court should avoid dealing with any cruelty allegation that has been made and the divorce should be granted on the no-fault separation basis. While a no-fault divorce is preferable where fault and no-fault bases for relief co-exist, there is no objection to a trial judge granting a divorce on the basis of cruelty, if the statutory one-year period of separation has not been fully satisfied at the time when the judgment was granted.[156]

F. BARS TO DIVORCE

Section 11 of the *Divorce Act* establishes the following four bars or impediments to divorce:

- collusion;
- connivance;
- condonation; and
- the absence of reasonable arrangements for child support.[157]

---

152   *Hock v. Hock* (1971), 3 R.F.L. 353 (B.C.C.A.).

153   *Lewis v. Lewis* (1983), 44 N.B.R. (2d) 268 (Q.B.); *Delaney v. Delaney* (1971), 5 R.F.L. 44 (Ont. C.A.); *Perry v. Perry* (1971), 1 Nfld. & P.E.I.R. 325 (P.E.I.S.C.T.D.).

154   *Sheldon v. Sheldon*, [1966] P. 62 (Eng. C.A.); *Anderson v. Anderson* (1972), 8 R.F.L. 299 (Alta. C.A.), aff'd (1973), 10 R.F.L. 200 (S.C.C.); *Piette v. Therrien*, [1976] C.S. 1634 (Que.); *Rouleau v. Wells*, [1980] C.S. 915 (Que.). Compare *Katapodis v. Katapodis* (1980), 27 O.R. (2d) 711 (C.A.).

155   *Lehman v. Lehman* (1989), 95 A.R. 383 (Q.B.); *Krause v. Krause* (1976), 23 R.F.L. 219 (Alta. C.A.); *Hock v. Hock* (1970), 2 R.F.L. 333 (B.C.S.C.), aff'd (1971), 3 R.F.L. 353 (B.C.C.A.); *Farkasch v. Farkasch* (1972), 4 R.F.L. 339 (Man. Q.B.); *McGrath v. McGrath* (1977), 16 N.B.R. (2d) 462 (Q.B.); *MacNeil v. MacNeil* (1976), 25 R.F.L. 82 (N.S.C.A.).

156   *B.K.K. v. H.D.*, [2002] B.C.J. No. 2683 (C.A.).

157   And see s. 21.1 of *Divorce Act*, R.S.C. 1985 (2d Supp.), c. 3, as amended by S.C. 1990, c. 18, and Section F(4), below in this chapter.

It expressly provides as follows:

Duty of court – bars

11.(1) In a divorce proceeding, it is the duty of the court
  (a) to satisfy itself that there has been no collusion in relation to the application for a divorce and to dismiss the application if it finds that there was collusion in presenting it;
  (b) to satisfy itself that reasonable arrangements have been made for the support of any children of the marriage, and, if such arrangements have not been made, to stay the granting of the divorce until such arrangements are made; and
  (c) where a divorce is sought in circumstances described in paragraph 8(2)(b), to satisfy itself that there has been no condonation or connivance on the part of the spouse bringing the proceeding, and to dismiss the application for a divorce if that spouse has condoned or connived at the act or conduct complained of unless, in the opinion of the court, the public interest would be better served by granting the divorce.

Revival

(2) Any act or conduct that has been condoned is not capable of being revived so as to constitute a circumstance described in paragraph 8(2)(b).

Condonation

(3) For the purpose of this section, a continuation or resumption of cohabitation during a period of, or periods totalling, not more than ninety days with reconciliation as its primary purpose shall not be considered to constitute condonation.

Definition of "collusion"

(4) In this section, "collusion" means an agreement or conspiracy to which an applicant for a divorce is either directly or indirectly a party for the purpose of subverting the administration of justice, and includes any agreement, understanding or arrangement to fabricate or suppress evidence or to deceive the court, but does not include an agreement to the extent that it provides for separation between the parties, financial support, division of property or the custody of any child of the marriage.

1) Collusion

A finding of collusion constitutes an absolute bar to divorce that compels a court to dismiss the divorce petition regardless whether the divorce is sought on the basis of no-fault separation, adultery, or cruelty.[158] Collusion will not be found unless there is an agreement or conspiracy to subvert the administration of justice, as for example, where there is an agreement to fabricate or suppress evidence or to deceive the court.[159] Spousal agreements to separate and to regulate the economic and parenting consequences of their separation are not collusive.[160] It is also not collusive for one spouse to co-operate with the other spouse by providing evidence that will substantiate the facts relied upon to establish marriage breakdown in the divorce proceeding.[161]

Judicial opinion is divided on the question whether collusion may be found where a marriage was entered into solely for the purpose of obtaining immigration or citizenship benefits and the spouses never intended to cohabit and went their separate ways after the marriage ceremony.[162] Although section 11(1)(a) of the *Divorce Act* imposes a duty on the court to satisfy itself that there has been no collusion, the role of the court is not inquisitorial. If the pleadings or evidence justify an inference of collusion, however, it falls upon the applicant to negate collusion and a mere denial of collusion does not discharge the burden of negating collusion.[163] Where the evidence is clear that the petitioner has been duped and was not a party to an agreement or conspiracy to circumvent the immigration laws of the country, or to any agreement that was collusive, he or she has satisfied any onus placed upon him or her by virtue of section 11(1)(a) of the *Divorce Act*.[164]

---

158 *Divorce Act*, R.S.C. 1985 (2d Supp.), c. 3, s. 11(1)(a).

159 *Ibid.*, s. 11(4); *Gillett v. Gillett* (1979), 9 R.F.L. (2d) 97 (Alta. S.C.T.D.); *Merchant v. Dossani*, [2007] A.J. No. 815 (Q.B.); *Sattar v. Sattar* (1975), 26 R.F.L. 127 (Ont. H.C.J.).

160 *Ibid.*; see *Tannis v. Tannis*, [1970] 1 O.R. 323 (H.C.J.).

161 *Milne v. Milne*, [1970] 1 O.R. 381 (C.A.).

162 See *Johnson v. Ahmad* (1981), 22 R.F.L. (2d) 141 (Alta. Q.B.); *Ciresi v. Ahmad* (1983), 31 R.F.L. (2) 326 at 329 and 333–34 (Alta. Q.B.); *Singh v. Singh* (1977), 25 R.F.L. 20 (B.C.S.C.); *Fernandez v. Fernandez* (1983), 34 R.F.L. (2d) 249 (Man. Q.B.); *McKenzie v. McKenzie* (1982), 26 R.F.L. (2d) 310 at 312 (Ont. C.A.); *Chaudhry v. Chaudhry* (21 March 1983) (Ont. C.A.) [unreported]; *Sattar v. Sattar* (1975), 26 R.F.L. 127 (Ont. H.C.J.); compare *Merchant v. Dossani*, [2007] A.J. No. 815 (Q.B.).

163 *Singh v. Singh* (1977), 25 R.F.L. 20 (B.C.S.C.).

164 *Gentles v. Gentles* (1980), 12 R.F.L. (2d) 287 (Ont. C.A.).

2) Connivance and Condonation

Connivance[165] and condonation[166] constitute provisional, rather than absolute, bars to divorce where marriage breakdown is sought to be proven by way of a spouse's adultery or cruelty. These bars have no application where the divorce petition is based on spousal separation for one year or more. Being provisional, and not peremptory or absolute bars to divorce, a court will grant a divorce, notwithstanding the petitioner's connivance or condonation of the other spouse's adultery or cruelty, if the court is of the opinion that the public interest would be better served by granting the divorce.[167]

Connivance signifies that the petitioner has actively promoted or encouraged the commission of the offence complained of. A corrupt intention is an essential ingredient of connivance. If, for example, the petitioner has actively induced his or her spouse to commit adultery or has passively stood by and made no attempt to prevent the commission of the offence, connivance will be found.[168]

The basic principles of law respecting connivance are succinctly defined in *Maddock v. Maddock*, wherein Laidlaw J.A. of the Ontario Court of Appeal observed:

> It will be convenient and helpful to state certain propositions or principles of law respecting connivance, and which I extract from the following and other cases: *Rogers v. Rogers* (1830), 3 Hagg. Ecc. 57, at p. 59, *Gipps v. Gipps* (1864), 11 H.L. Cas. 1, *Lloyd v. Lloyd*, [1938] P. 174, *Churchman v. Churchman*, [1945] P. 44, *Woodbury v. Woodbury*, [1948] 2 All E.R. 684, *Mudge v. Mudge*, [1950] 1 All E.R. 607.
>
> 1. Connivance may consist of any act done with corrupt intention of a husband or wife to promote or encourage either the initiation or the continuance of adultery of his or her spouse, or it may consist of passive acquiescence in such adultery.
>
> 2. Corrupt intention of the husband or wife seeking a divorce is an essential ingredient of connivance, and the conduct of the husband or wife seeking the divorce must show that he or she, as the case may be, willingly consented to the adultery of the other spouse.

---

165 *Divorce Act*, R.S.C. 1985 (2d Supp.), c. 3, s. 11(1)(c).
166 *Ibid.*
167 *Ibid.*
168 *Maddock v. Maddock*, [1958] O.R. 810 at 818 (C.A.).

3. The issue is whether on the facts of the particular case, the husband or wife seeking the divorce was or was not guilty of the corrupt intention of promoting or encouraging either the initiation or the continuance of the adultery of the other spouse.

4. Acts done by a husband or wife seeking a divorce or by any person employed by him or her, as the case may be, to keep watch on the other spouse to see whether or not his or her suspicions of adultery are well-founded or unfounded, do not necessarily constitute connivance and, likewise, if one spouse does nothing without lulling into a sense of security, the other spouse about whom he or she, as the case may be, is suspicious, but merely watches her, he is not necessarily guilty of passive acquiescence amounting to connivance.

5. "The Court should not allow its judgment to be affected by importing, as principles of universal application, pronouncements made with regard to wholly different circumstances and be led to a conclusion contrary to the justice of the case": *Churchman v. Churchman*, [1945] P. 44, at p. 52.

6. There is a presumption of law against the existence of connivance and the court should not find a spouse guilty of connivance unless the evidence shows clearly that all the essential ingredients thereof exist in the particular facts under consideration.[169]

In determining whether the public interest would be better served by granting a divorce, notwithstanding the petitioner's connivance at the offence complained of, a court is more likely to excuse passive acquiescence than active procurement of the offence.[170]

Condonation arises where a divorce petitioner, with knowledge of his or her spouse's adultery or cruelty, forgives the offence and continues or resumes matrimonial cohabitation with the offending spouse. The essence of condonation is spousal reconciliation. Condonation requires a mutual intention to be reconciled coupled with a reinstatement of the guilty spouse to his or her former position.[171] It is not necessary for spouses to achieve the same degree of mutual devotion that they enjoyed when they were first married. The matrimonial relationship must, nevertheless, be restored to a settled rhythm in which the past offences, if not forgotten,

---

169 *Ibid.*; cited with approval in *Fleet v. Fleet* (1972), 7 R.F.L. 355 (Ont. C.A.).
170 See *Berger v. Berger* (1974), 17 R.F.L. 88 (B.C.S.C.).
171 *Mackrell v. Mackrell*, [1948] 2 All E.R. 858 (Eng. C.A.); *Leaderhouse v. Leaderhouse* (1971), 4 R.F.L. 174 (Sask. Q.B.).

no longer undermine the continued commitment of the spouses to each other.[172]

There can be no condonation of a matrimonial offence unless the innocent spouse has knowledge of all the material facts. It is the duty of the guilty spouse to make full disclosure of any factor that might reasonably weigh with the innocent spouse in deciding whether to remit the offence and reinstate the guilty spouse to his or her former position.[173] The innocent spouse may, however, expressly or impliedly waive the requirement of further knowledge of any material fact.[174]

Condonation requires a bilateral intention to be reconciled or to resume cohabitation. Although sexual intercourse is a significant factor to be considered in determining whether condonation exists, a continuation or resumption of sexual intercourse is not a prerequisite to a finding of condonation. When the spouses engage in sexual intercourse without the slightest thought of reinstatement, no question of condonation can arise.[175]

Condonation is ordinarily manifested by a resumption of cohabitation that reflects a reconciliation of the spouses. Spousal residence under the same roof is not conclusive evidence of condonation and reconciliation will not be inferred from the mere continuation of an increasingly cold and sexless co-existence.[176] Spouses who are living independent lives, albeit under the same roof, will not be deemed to have continued or resumed cohabitation or to have achieved a spousal reconciliation.[177]

If spouses separate after one of them has committed adultery or matrimonial cruelty, subsequent attempts to reconcile do not necessarily constitute condonation so as to bar a divorce, if the reconciliation ul-

---

172 *Mackrell v. Mackrell*, [1948] 2 All E.R. 858 (Eng. C.A.).

173 *Inglis v. Inglis*, [1968] P. 639; *Watkins v. Watkins* (1980), 14 R.F.L. (2d) 97 (Nfld. T.D.).

174 *Ibid.*

175 *Henderson v. Henderson*, [1944] A.C. 49 (H.L.). See also Julien D. Payne, "The Concept of Condonation in Matrimonial Causes: A Restatement of *Henderson v. Henderson and Crellin*" (1961) 26 Sask. Bar Rev. 53. And see *Roschuk v. Roschuk* (1979), 12 R.F.L. (2d) 34 (Man. Q.B.); *Watkins v. Watkins* (1980), 14 R.F.L. (2d) 97 (Nfld. T.D.); *Grandy v. Grandy* (1972), 7 R.F.L. 69 at 74 (N.S.C.A.); *Wood v. Wood*, [1944] 1 D.L.R. 493 at 494 (Ont. H.C.J.), Robertson C.J.O.: "To constitute condonation there must be an actual intention to forgive and be reconciled"; *H. v. H.* (1978), 30 R.F.L. 122 (Ont. H.C.J.); *Pellegrini v. Pellegrini* (1978), 30 R.F.L. 293 (Ont. H.C.J.); *MacDougall v. MacDougall* (1970), 3 R.F.L. 174 (Ont. C.A.); *Leaderhouse v. Leaderhouse* (1971), 4 R.F.L. 174 at 182 (Sask. Q.B.).

176 *Aucoin v. Aucoin* (1976), 28 R.F.L. 43 (N.S.C.A.).

177 *McAllister v. McAllister* (1976), 14 N.B.R. (2d) 552 (T.D.); *Aucoin v. Aucoin* (1976), 28 R.F.L. 43 (N.S.C.A.); *Woerz v. Woerz* (1977), 17 N.S.R. (2d) 697 (T.D.).

timately fails.[178] The *Divorce Act* encourages spousal reconciliation. Section 11(3) of the *Divorce Act* specifically provides that "a continuation or resumption of cohabitation during a period of, or periods totalling not more than ninety days with reconciliation as it primary purpose shall not be considered to constitute condonation." Consequently, spouses may attempt to reconcile on any number of occasions following the commission of adultery or cruelty provided that the aggregate period of cohabitation does not exceed ninety days.

Prior to the *Divorce Act*, 1968, the ecclesiastical doctrine of revival enabled a spouse to petition for divorce on the basis of a previously condoned offence. Condonation was conditional on future behaviour; if the guilty spouse misbehaved subsequent to the condonation, the condoned offence would be revived so as to constitute a ground for divorce. By virtue of section 11(2) of the current *Divorce Act*, the doctrine of revival no longer applies but section 11(2) does not circumscribe the power of the court to grant a divorce pursuant to section 11(1)(c) of the *Divorce Act*, notwithstanding condonation, where the public interest so requires.[179]

In recent years, courts have rarely denied a divorce by reason of the petitioner's condonation of the offence complained of. To do so would tend to discourage attempts to reconcile. Furthermore, the public interest is best served by granting a divorce where the marriage has irretrievably broken down, rather than insisting that the parties preserve the mere legal shell of a marriage.[180]

3) Absence of Reasonable Arrangements for Child Support

Regardless whether the divorce petition relies on adultery, cruelty, or no-fault separation, it is a statutory duty of the court to satisfy itself that reasonable arrangements have been made for the support of any children of the marriage. In determining whether reasonable arrangements have been made for the support of children of the marriage, the court has re-

---

178 *Goldstein v. Goldstein* (1970), 15 D.L.R. (3d) 95 (Alta. S.C.); *Nielsen v. Nielsen* (1971), 2 R.F.L. 109 (Ont. H.C.J.).

179 See J.D. Payne, "The *Divorce Act* (Canada), *1968*" (1969) 7 Alta. L. Rev. 1. See also *Raney v. Raney* (1974), 13 R.F.L. 156 at 158 (Ont. H.C.J.). Compare *Grant v. Grant* (1979), 9 B.C.L.R. 306 (S.C.), applying *Lyons v. Lyons* (1971), 1 R.F.L. 328 (N.S.T.D.).

180 See, generally, Kenneth L. Kallish & Julien D. Payne, "Current Controversies Concerning Condonation" in Julien D. Payne, Freda M. Steel, & Marilyn A. Bégin, *Payne's Digest on Divorce in Canada, 1968–1980* (Don Mills, ON: R. De Boo, 1982) at 134, and especially at 141–43.

gard to the *Federal Child Support Guidelines.* If reasonable arrangements for child support could be but have not been made, the court cannot grant the divorce until such arrangements are made[181] but a court cannot discriminate between rich and poor by denying a divorce to spouses who have insufficient means to provide reasonable support for their children.[182] Furthermore, a court should not speculate about future contingencies, such as the impact of a non-custodial parent's remarriage, which could result in some reduction of the financial security provided for children of his or her dissolved marriage.[183] The reasonableness of arrangements for the support of children must be determined by the court in the particular circumstances of each case, which may include assistance from other members of the family or friends, social assistance, and any other relevant circumstances.[184] Where, however, the divorcing spouses can afford to support their own children, this financial burden cannot be transferred by the parents to the welfare system.[185]

A parent cannot escape the obligation to make reasonable arrangements for child support by voluntarily relinquishing well-paid employment. In such a case, reasonable arrangements for child support will be based on the respondent's earning capacity, not on a self-induced unemployed status. Consequently, if an agreed amount of child support is clearly insufficient in light of the respondent's earning capacity, the court must stay the granting of the divorce until reasonable arrangements are made.[186] The existence of a separation agreement or subsisting court order does not abrogate the duty of the court under section 11(1)(b) of the *Divorce Act* to satisfy itself that reasonable arrangements are thereby provided for the support of the children of the marriage.[187]

In uncontested divorce proceedings where spouses rely on affidavits, instead of appearing in person before a judge, the petitioner's affidavit must contain sufficient information to enable the court to discharge its statutory duty. It must include information concerning the spousal income and the number, age, and circumstances of the children so that the

---

181   *Divorce Act*, R.S.C. 1985 (2d Supp.), c. 3, s. 11(1)(b).
182   *F. (R.D.) v. F. (S.L.)* (1987), 6 R.F.L. (3d) 413 (B.C.S.C.); *Williams v. Williams* (1971), 5 R.F.L. 72 (N.S.S.C.); see also *Shore-Kalo v. Kalo*, [2007] M.J. No. 297 (Q.B.).
183   *Williams v. Williams* (1971), 5 R.F.L. 72 (N.S.S.C.).
184   *F.(R.D.) v. F.(S.L.)* (1987), 6 R.F.L. (3d) 413 (B.C.S.C.).
185   *Simpson v. Simpson* (1987), 8 R.F.L. (3d) 216 at 219–20 (B.C.S.C.).
186   *Eddy v. Eddy* (1992), 39 R.F.L. (3d) 339 (Alta. Q.B.).
187   *K.(L.A.) v. K.(G.N.)* (1987), 12 B.C.L.R. (2d) 9 (S.C.); *M.(B.J.) v. M.(J.H.)* (1987), 12 B.C.L.R. (2d) 16 (S.C.).

court can determine whether proposed arrangements for the support of the children are reasonable having regard to the applicable guidelines.[188] Bare assertions that the spouses have made reasonable arrangements for child support are not enough. If the court has insufficient information to determine whether the arrangements are suitable, it must withhold the divorce until this omission has been corrected.

The court can raise the bar created by section 11(1)(b) of the *Divorce Act* on its own motion.[189] In that event, either or both spouses must satisfy the court that reasonable arrangements have been made for the support of the children of the marriage or that any such arrangements are impracticable under the circumstances. Although the role of the court may be inquisitorial, there is no independent duty imposed on the court itself to make an order for child support that will guarantee the financial security of dependent children. If the court is not satisfied that reasonable efforts have been made to protect the financial security of the children of the marriage, the court must stay the granting of a divorce until reasonable arrangements are made for the support of any children of the marriage or the court is satisfied that the spouses cannot, by reason of the attendant circumstances, make any such arrangements.[190] Where an application for child support has been included in the divorce petition but the amount is insufficient, rather than imposing a stay under section 11(1)(b) of the *Divorce Act*, the court may allow amendment of the petition to reflect a proper amount of child support, provided that the obligor has notice of this and is given an opportunity to make submissions thereupon at trial.[191]

Failure to comply with section 11(1)(a) of the *Divorce Act* renders the divorce judgment voidable, not void. Where innocent third parties have acquired rights and interests in consequence of the ostensible validity of the divorce judgment and no party has any superior equity, it is thereafter too late to set the judgment aside.[192]

---

188 *F.(R.D.) v. F.(S.L.)* (1987), 6 R.F.L. (3d) 413 (B.C.S.C.); *Money v. Money* (1987), 5 R.F.L. (3d) 375 (Man. C.A.); *MacKinnon v. MacKinnon* (1986), 78 N.S.R. (2d) 361 (S.C.).

189 *Wallace v. Wallace* (1973), 9 R.F.L. 393 (Alta. S.C.T.D.); *Money v. Money* (1987), 5 R.F.L. (3d) 375 (Man. C.A.).

190 *Money v. Money* (1987), 5 R.F.L. (3d) 375 (Man. C.A.); see also *Dumas v. Dumas* (1992), 43 R.F.L. (3d) 260 (Alta. Q.B.); *Acchione v. Acchione* (1987), 9 R.F.L. (3d) 215 (Ont. Sup. Ct.).

191 *Almeida v. Almeida* (1995), 11 R.F.L. (4th) 131 (Alta. Q.B.). See also *Fowler v. Szabo-Fowler*, [2006] S.J. No. 101 (C.A.).

192 *P. v. P.*, [1971] 2 W.L.R. 510 (Eng. C.A.). See *Practice Direction*, [1970] 3 All E.R. 1023. And see *Wallin v. Wallin* (1973), 13 R.F.L. 305 at 311 (Ont. H.C.J.), var'd (1975), 18

4) Barriers to Religious Remarriage

In some religions, one spouse may control the availability of religious divorce. The other spouse is powerless. State law does not interfere with religious doctrine. However, section 21.1 of the *Divorce Act* imposes legal sanctions on a spouse who unjustifiably refuses to remove a barrier to the religious remarriage of the other spouse. For example, a Jewish husband who refuses to deliver a *get* (a Jewish bill of divorcement) stands in the way of his wife's remarriage in the Jewish faith. If that husband were to seek a divorce or any corollary relief such as support or custody of the children from a Canadian court in proceedings instituted under the *Divorce Act*, his claim may be stayed unless and until he removes the barrier to his wife's religious remarriage. This sanction only applies where the removal of the barrier lies exclusively with a spouse, as distinct from a religious body or official. Its purpose is to prevent a spouse from withholding the right to a religious divorce or remarriage for the purpose of negotiating an unconscionable settlement of legal rights respecting spousal support, child support, child custody or access, or property division. Section 21.1 of the *Divorce Act* constitutes a temporary bar to the offending spouse's right to seek a divorce or corollary relief under the *Divorce Act*. If the offending spouse rectifies the situation by removing the obstacles to religious remarriage of the other spouse, the substantive claims of the previously offending spouse may proceed on their merits, although costs consequences may ensue for the spouse who acted improperly.[193]

In *Bruker v. Marcovitz*,[194] the spouses negotiated a "Consent to Corollary Relief," which included an undertaking to obtain a Jewish divorce or *get* from the rabbinical court (*Beth Din*) once their Quebec divorce became final. Under Jewish law, a wife cannot obtain a *get* unless her husband agrees to give it. So long as the husband refuses to give the *get*, his wife is unable to remarry under Jewish law and any children born after a civil marriage are illegitimate. In this case, the husband refused his wife's repeated requests to provide a *get* for fifteen years. The wife sought damages for breach of contract. The husband argued that his agreement to give a *get* was unenforceable under Quebec law and that he was protected from any liability for damages by his right to freedom of religion. The

---

R.F.L. 122 (Ont. C.A.). See also *Rivas v. Rivas*, [1977] 2 W.W.R. 345 (Alta. S.C.).

193   *Tanny v. Tanny*, [2000] O.J. No. 2472 (Sup. Ct.) (wife not precluded from pursuing substantive relief under federal and provincial legislation where she withdrew her earlier refusal of consent to receive *get*).

194   2007 SCC 54, [2007] S.C.J. No. 54.

trial judge held the agreement to be a valid and binding contract that was enforceable by an award of damages in a Quebec court. The Court of Appeal allowed the husband's appeal, holding that the substance of his commitment was religious in character and was not enforceable by secular courts. On appeal to the Supreme Court of Canada, the majority judgment of seven to two held that the fact that a civil dispute involves a religious aspect does not, by itself, render it non-justiciable. The undertaking by the husband to provide a *get* was part of a voluntary exchange of promises that was intended to have legally enforceable consequences. The Court was not being asked to determine doctrinal religious issues and there is nothing in the *Civil Code* to prevent someone from transforming his or her moral obligations into legal and binding obligations. Nor was the husband entitled to immunity from his contractual breach by invoking his freedom of religion under section 3 of the Quebec *Charter of Human Rights and Freedoms*. Section 9.1 of the *Charter* confirms the principle that a claim to religious freedom must be reconciled with countervailing rights, values, and harm. Determining when such a claim must yield to a more pressing public interest is a complex, nuanced, fact-specific exercise. In this case, the husband's claim did not survive the balancing mandated by the Quebec *Charter* and by previous judgments of the Supreme Court of Canada. Any impairment of the husband's religious freedom was outweighed by the harm both to the wife personally and to the public's interest in protecting fundamental values such as equality rights and autonomous choice in marriage and divorce. These, as well as the public benefit in enforcing valid and binding contractual obligations, were among the interests that outweighed the husband's claim. The wife's appeal to the Supreme Court of Canada was accordingly allowed and the trial judge's award of damages was reinstated.

CHAPTER 8

SPOUSAL SUPPORT ON OR AFTER DIVORCE

A. DEFINITION OF "SPOUSE" AND "SPOUSAL SUPPORT"

Pursuant to section 3 of the *Civil Marriage Act*, S.C. 2005, c. 33, "marriage, for civil purposes, is the lawful union of two persons to the exclusion of all others." Consequential on this parliamentary recognition of the validity of same-sex marriages, section 8(1) of the *Civil Marriage Act* has amended section 2(1) of the *Divorce Act* to provide that "'spouse' means either of two persons who are married to each other." A same-sex couple, who are married according to the law, may, therefore, invoke the primary and corollary relief provisions of the *Divorce Act*.[1]

The expression "spousal support" is somewhat misleading because it includes the payment of support to an ex-spouse. Furthermore, some provincial and territorial statutes impose "spousal" support obligations on unmarried cohabitants who have lived together for a designated period of time or who are the parents of a child.

---

1   *M.M. v. J.H.*, [2004] O.J. No. 5314 (S.C.J.).

B. FORMAL LEGAL EQUALITY BETWEEN SPOUSES

Formal legal equality exists between divorcing spouses insofar as support rights and obligations are concerned. A husband in need has just as much right to seek spousal support from his financially independent wife as she has if their financial situation is reversed. In reality, divorcing or divorced husbands rarely need or obtain spousal support. Even wives, who are in need, rarely apply for or receive spousal support. Separated and divorced women who stay at home for sustained periods of time to raise their children are the new poor in Canada. They are often untrained for the labour force and cannot regain lost years when they were unemployed and consequently had no opportunity to build a career or contribute to a pension plan. A federal study has concluded that "[for] women whose labour force interruptions have lasted for ten years or longer, the cumulative present value of post re-entry earnings losses will typically exceed $80,000."[2] Or in everyday language, women who are out of the labour force for more than ten years sacrifice more than $80,000 in lost future income potential that will never be recaptured when they enter or return to the labour force.

C. TYPES OF ORDERS

1) Diverse Types of Order

The diverse types of spousal support orders that may be granted pursuant to subsection 15.2 of the *Divorce Act* are as follows:

(i)   An order to secure a lump sum;
(ii) An order to pay a lump sum;
(iii) An order to secure and pay a lump sum;
(iv) An order to secure periodic sums;
(v)   An order to pay periodic sums;
(vi) An order to secure and pay periodic sums.

The court is not restricted to making only one type of order. A combination of the various types of order may be accommodated. Any of the aforementioned orders may be granted by way of interim or permanent

---

2   Department of Justice and Status of Women Canada, *An Economic Model to Assist in the Determination of Spousal Support* by Richard Kerr (Ottawa: Department of Justice, 1992).

relief, although they are always subject to variation or rescission in the event of a material change of circumstances.

2) Nominal Orders; Final Orders

An order for nominal spousal support is not necessary for the purpose of preserving a future right to claim spousal support following a divorce.[3] Nominal orders have, nevertheless, been granted where the applicant establishes a present need but the respondent has no ability to pay or where there is no current need but there is a predictable future need. A nominal order for spousal support may be vacated on appeal where no current need has been demonstrated and any future need would be unrelated to the marriage.[4] According to the judgment of the British Columbia Court of Appeal in *Gill-Sager v. Sager*,[5] the law is unsettled on the question whether the dismissal of an application for spousal support under section 15.2 of the *Divorce Act* precludes the applicant from ever succeeding on a subsequent application, regardless of a change in his or her circumstances. Only the Supreme Court of Canada can provide a definitive answer to this question. If the applicant is disentitled to spousal support at the time of the original application but might reasonably be subsequently entitled to relief in the event of a change of circumstances, for example, by reason of deteriorating health, an appropriate order should be couched in terms that do not preclude a subsequent application for spousal support.

3) Interim Support Orders

Section 15.2(2) of the *Divorce Act* empowers a court to grant an interim order requiring a spouse to secure and/or pay such lump sum and/or periodic sums as the court deems reasonable for the support of the other spouse. An interim spousal support order is intended to provide a reasonably acceptable short-term solution until the trial when an in-depth examination can be undertaken, if the spouses have not previously

---

3   *Traversy v. Glover*, [2006] O.J. No. 2908 (Sup. Ct.).

4   *Vickers v. Vickers*, [2001] N.S.J. No. 218 (C.A.). For the suggestion that nominal orders are not "support orders" within the meaning of the *Divorce Act*, see *Gill-Sager v. Sager*, [2003] B.C.J. No. 121 (C.A.).

5   *Gill-Sager v. Sager*, *ibid.*; see also *B.G.D. v. R.W.D.*, [2003] B.C.J. No. 1098 (C.A.). Compare *Tierney-Hynes v. Hynes*, [2005] O.J. No. 2661 (C.A.).

reached a consensual resolution of their support rights and obligations.[6] The nature of interim spousal support dictates that the court does not have to embark upon a detailed examination of the merits of the claim for permanent spousal support. Nevertheless, entitlement to interim support must be established in accordance with the provisions of section 15.2 of the *Divorce Act*.[7] Section 15.2(2) of the *Divorce Act* includes no explicit reference to the variation of an interim spousal support order, but the court has an inherent jurisdiction to vary such an order in response to a material change of circumstances.[8] However, Canadian courts have consistently asserted that interim support orders should only be varied when they are patently inappropriate. Otherwise, any fine tuning or necessary adjustment can be accommodated at trial.[9]

Absent some reasonably sound prospect of success at trial, interim spousal support should be denied.[10] Interim spousal support should not be ordered in the face of conflicting affidavits on crucial issues relating to spousal support entitlement.[11] Where interim spousal support is in dispute, a court will ordinarily focus on the needs of the applicant and the respondent's ability to pay because of the difficulty of applying the objectives set out in section 15.2(6) of the *Divorce Act*, relating to compensatory spousal support.[12] This relatively narrow perspective is inevitable in the ordinary course of events for the following reasons:

---

6   *Lapp v. Lapp*, [2008] A.J. No. 208 (C.A.); *Kowalski v. Grant*, [2007] M.J. No. 386 (Q.B.); *Gabel v. Gabel*, [2000] N.W.T.J. No. 54 (S.C.); *Turk v. Turk*, [2008] O.J. No. 397 (Sup. Ct.).

7   *Noonan v. Noonan*, 2007 PEICAD 5, [2007] P.E.I.J. No. 17. Compare *Muchekeni v. Muchekeni*, [2008] N.W.T.J. No. 19 (S.C.).

8   *Carvell v. Carvell*, [1969] 2 O.R. 513 (C.A.); *Lipson v. Lipson* (1972), 7 R.F.L. 186 (Ont. C.A.); *Dumont v. Dumont*, [1987] N.B.J. No. 1054 (Q.B.); *Torres v. Marin*, [2007] Y.J. No. 94 (S.C.).

9   *Owokalu v. Owokalu*, [2000] A.J. No. 1519 (Q.B.); *Hama v. Werbes*, [2000] B.C.J. No. 1556 (S.C.); *Aschenbrenner v. Aschenbrenner*, [2000] B.C.J. No. 1950 (S.C.) (spousal support) and *Hope v. Hope*, [2000] O.J. No. 4532 (Sup. Ct.) (child support). As to retroactive adjustment of an interim spousal support order, see also *Lapp v. Lapp*, [2008] A.J. No. 208 (C.A.); *Fisher v. Fisher*, 2008 ONCA 11, [2008] O.J. No. 38.

10 *Kowalski v. Grant*, [2007] M.J. No. 386 (Q.B.); *Belcourt v. Chartrand*, [2006] O.J. No. 1500 (Sup. Ct.).

11 *Duder v. Rowe*, [2006] A.J. No. 868 (Q.B.).

12 *Vauclair v. Vauclair* (1998), 126 Man. R. (2d) 136 (C.A.); *Gale v. Gale*, 2007 MBCA 162, [2007] M.J. No. 459; *Muchekeni v. Muchekeni*, [2008] N.W.T.J. No. 19 (S.C.); *Byerley v. Byerley* (1998), 41 R.F.L. (4th) 50 (Ont. Gen. Div.); *Borger v. Jan*, [2006] O.J. No. 2075 (Sup. Ct.); *Turk v. Turk*, [2008] O.J. No. 397 (Sup. Ct.); *D'Vaz v. D'Vaz*, [2008] O.J. No. 1063 (Sup. Ct.); *Hein v. Hein*, [2004] S.J. No. 458 (Q.B.); *Kovitch v. Kovitch*, [2006] S.J. No. 256 (Q.B.).

(i)   The marriage breakdown is usually recent. Consequently, the applicant, if unemployed prior thereto, will have been afforded insufficient opportunity to find suitable employment or obtain the requisite skills to become economically self-sufficient.

(ii) The property of the spouses still remains to be divided.

(iii) The nature of the hearing is such that insufficient evidence exists to determine issues of credibility and make the requisite findings of fact in light of statutorily designated factors and objectives that regulate spousal support entitlement.

Interim spousal support proceedings are, therefore, summary in nature and provide "rough justice" at best. If a substantial period of time has elapsed between the spousal separation and the time of the application, a court may find it possible to determine whether the allegedly dependent spouse has made reasonable efforts to achieve economic self-sufficiency. Such a finding is easier to make if the court has the benefit of oral evidence instead of affidavit evidence. Where an interim order for spousal support is expressly declared subject to review after the filing and delivery of the Property and Financial Statement, a payor who seeks remission or reduction of the amount payable is not required to prove any material change of circumstances since the granting of the order. A reduction may be judicially perceived as appropriate where the recipient spouse is found capable of supplementing pension income through part-time employment.[13]

An appellate court should not interfere with an interim order for support, unless it is demonstrated that the interim order is clearly wrong and exceeds the wide ambit of reasonable solutions that are available on a summary interim proceeding.[14] This standard of appellate review reflects the following characteristics of interim and permanent support orders:

(i)   Interim orders are intended to provide short-term reasonable relief pending trial.

(ii) Interim orders are usually granted on the basis of affidavit evidence that is often conflicting or contradictory. This limited evidence renders interim orders more susceptible to error than permanent orders made after a trial.

(iii) Appeals from interim orders can provide an inappropriate means of deferring a trial. Appeals from interim orders have been generally

---

13   *Threlfall v. Threlfall*, [2001] B.C.J. No. 2474 (S.C.).

14   *Sypher v. Sypher*, [1986] O.J. No. 536, 2 R.F.L. (3d) 413 (C.A.).

discouraged and will usually be dismissed, unless the trial date is so far in advance as to require immediate appellate review of an interim disposition.

(iv) Interim orders do not fetter the discretion of trial judges to determine the appropriate disposition after a full investigation of the facts. Where it is deemed appropriate, a trial judge may make a retroactive order to address any inequity or inadequacy arising under an interim order.

(v) The use of case conferences and pre-trials may also address matters of interim relief without furthering a war of affidavits.[15]

Where an interim order provides for periodic spousal support to be paid from the date of the filing of the application, but payment of the instant arrears thereby created is to be deferred pending the resolution of outstanding monetary issues, the arrears may be subsequently expunged by a trial judge without proof of a change of circumstances since the granting of the interim order. In addressing the wife's contention that section 17(4.1) of the *Divorce Act* required the trial judge to find a change of circumstances before varying the interim spousal support order, the Newfoundland and Labrador Court of Appeal in *Whelan v. Whelan*[16] observed that section 17(4.1) applies only when the court is considering an application to vary a "spousal support order," which is explicitly defined in section 2(1) of the *Divorce Act*. Since that definition stipulates that a "spousal support order" means an order made under section 15.2(1) of the *Divorce Act*, whereas interim spousal support orders are granted pursuant to section 15.2(2) of the *Divorce Act*, section 17(4.1) of the *Divorce Act* can have no application to the variation of interim orders. The Newfoundland and Labrador Court of Appeal further observed that the argument that finding a change of circumstance is required before a judge can grant a final order that is different from an interim order lacks any logical foundation. There would then be no difference between interim and final orders under the *Divorce Act* and both spouses would feel obliged to fully argue the whole case at the interim stage because of their concern that any subsequent adjustment would require a demonstrated change of circumstances. This would defeat Parliament's objective of enabling temporary orders to be made expeditiously pending a final determination of the issue of spousal support. The Newfoundland and Labrador Court of Appeal also rejected the wife's alternative contention that the trial judge

15   *Wellman v. Gilcash*, [2003] N.B.J. No. 214 (C.A.).
16   [2005] N.J. No. 134 (C.A.).

had erred in failing to consider the five factors listed by Noonan J. in *Tremblett v. Tremblett*[17] as relevant to the remission of support arrears. In the opinion of the Newfoundland and Labrador Court of Appeal, these criteria relate to applications under section 17(4.1) of the *Divorce Act* to retroactively vary final orders for spousal support and have no application to original applications of the *Divorce Act*. In this latter context, the relevant factors to be applied are those specified in section 15.2(4) of the *Divorce Act*, namely, the condition, means, needs, and other circumstances of the spouses, which the Newfoundland and Labrador Court of Appeal found to have been properly applied by the trial judge in exercising his discretion to expunge the arrears under the interim order after a full and thorough review of the evidence.

4) Lump Sum Support Orders

Section 15.2(1) of the *Divorce Act* empowers a court to order a lump sum in addition to or in lieu of periodic sums for the support of a spouse.[18] The same statutory criteria apply to lump sum and periodic support orders.[19] When spousal support is granted, it is usually ordered to be paid on a periodic basis — weekly, fortnightly, or monthly. A spouse may receive a lump sum instead of or in addition to periodic support payments.[20] Although the court has a wide discretion to order a lump sum under section 15.2 of the *Divorce Act*, this discretion can only be exercised for the purpose of providing support in accordance with the provisions of the *Divorce Act*. Lump sum support payments cannot be made to redress inequities in the division of matrimonial property under provincial legislation. Section 15.2 of the *Divorce Act* does not empower a court to redistribute property in the guise of lump sum support,[21] although an equitable distribution of the economic consequences of the marriage and its breakdown may be achieved by a combination of property and support entitlements.[22] Sup-

---

17   (1998), 75 Nfld. & P.E.I.R. 175 (Nfld. U.F.C.).
18   *Mollot v. Mollot*, 2007 ABCA 183, [2007] A.J. No. 583.
19   *Waterman v. Waterman* (1995), 16 R.F.L. (4th) 10 (Nfld. C.A.).
20   *Vynnk v. Baisa*, [2007] O.J. No. 274 (Sup. Ct.).
21   *Young v. Young*, [1993] 4 S.C.R. 3, 49 R.F.L. (3d) 117; *Newstone v. Newstone* (1994), 2 R.F.L. (4th) 129 (B.C.C.A.); *Mosher v. Mosher* (1995), 13 R.F.L. (4th) 385 (N.S.C.A.); *Gossen v. Gossen*, [2003] N.S.J. No. 113 (S.C.); *Mannarino v. Mannarino* (1992), 43 R.F.L. (3d) 309 (Ont. C.A.); *Tweel v. Tweel* (1994), 7 R.F.L. (4th) 204 (P.E.I.S.C.T.D.); *Droit de la famille — 221* (1985), 49 R.F.L. (2d) 194 (Que. C.A.); *Osborne v. Osborne* (1973), 14 R.F.L. 61 (Sask. Q.B.), var'd (1974), 23 R.F.L. 358 (Sask. C.A.).
22   *Moge v. Moge*, [1992] 3 S.C.R. 813, 43 R.F.L. (3d) 345 at 374.

port payments may be secured by way of a trust imposed on the obligor's property entitlement.[23] A lump sum support order may be granted notwithstanding a prior or contemporaneous property division,[24] but any substantial property entitlement affects the "means" and "needs" of the respective spouses for the purpose of subsection 15.2(4) of the *Divorce Act* and may render support unnecessary or inequitable.[25]

Some courts have expressed the view that lump sum orders should be the exception and not the rule.[26] This opinion is by no means universally held and each case must be decided on its merits.[27] Lump sum orders in divorce proceedings have not been confined to persons with very substantial capital assets and a wide variety of circumstances may justify such a disposition.[28]

Because lump sum orders may not fairly anticipate future changes of circumstances, lump sum support is a solution that must be carefully weighed before implementation.[29] Lump sum support may be impractical by reason of the insufficient means of the obligor to pay.[30]

Diverse circumstances have justified orders for lump sum support.[31] For example, a lump sum payment may be appropriate where

---

23   *Glazier v. Glazier* (1991), 36 R.F.L. (3d) 84 (Ont. Gen. Div.); *Balogh v. Balogh*, [1993] O.J. No. 2897 (U.F.C.). See also *MacNeil v. MacNeil* (1994), 2 R.F.L. (4th) 432 (N.S.C.A.); *Pettigrew v. Pettigrew*, [2006] N.S.J. No. 321 (C.A.). Compare *Cohen v. Cohen* (1995), 16 R.F.L. (4th) 408 (B.C.C.A.).

24   *Cunningham v. Cunningham* (1990), 30 R.F.L. (3d) 159 (B.C.C.A.); *Smith v. Smith* (1985), 55 Nfld. & P.E.I.R. 85, 162 A.P.R. 85 (Nfld. S.C.); *Wilson v. Wilson* (1985), 66 N.S.R. (2d) 361, 152 A.P.R. 361 (S.C.); *Crawford v. Crawford* (1987), 6 R.F.L. (3d) 308 (Ont. H.C.J.).

25   *Rafuse v. Rafuse* (1984), 43 R.F.L. (2d) 282 (N.S.S.C.A.D.); *Mannarino v. Mannarino* (1992), 43 R.F.L. (3d) 309 (Ont. C.A.); see also *Newson v. Newson* (1993), 45 R.F.L. (3d) 115 (B.C.C.A.).

26   See, for example, *Krause v. Krause*, [1976] 2 W.W.R. 622, 64 D.L.R. 351 (Alta. C.A.); *Hauff v. Hauff* (1994), 95 Man. R. (2d) 83 (C.A.); *Ramantanis v. Ramantanis*, [2004] M.J. No. 332 (C.A.); *Powers v. Powers* (1990), 92 N.S.R. (2d) 337, 237 A.P.R. 337 (S.C.); *Mannarino v. Mannarino* (1992), 43 R.F.L. (3d) 309 (Ont. C.A.); *T.A.E. v. M.E.E.*, [2003] O.J. No. 3300 (C.A.).

27   *Main v. Main* (1978), 5 R.F.L. (2d) 1 (Man. C.A.); *Jensen v. Jensen* (1986), 43 Man. R. (2d) 241, 5 R.F.L. (3d) 346 (C.A.).

28   *Raffin v. Raffin*, [1972] 1 O.R. 173, 5 R.F.L. 274 (C.A.).

29   *Stricker v. Stricker* (1991), 33 R.F.L. (3d) 367 (Alta. Q.B.); *Patten v. Patten*, [2005] N.B.J. No. 70 (Q.B.); *R.B. v. I.B.*, [2005] N.B.J. No. 134 (C.A.).

30   *Ramantanis v. Ramantanis*, [2004] M.J. No. 332 (C.A.); *Fraser v. Fraser* (1994), 143 N.B.R. (2d) 189 (C.A.); *Elliot v. Elliot* (1993), 48 R.F.L. (3d) 237 (Ont. C.A.).

31   For listing of relevant factors, see *Carter v. Carter* (1978), 19 Nfld. & P.E.I.R. 411 (Nfld. S.C.) and *Boland v. Boland*, [2006] N.J. No. 206 (U.F.C.).

- the obligor has substantial assets but a limited income,[32]
- periodic payments are plainly inadequate by themselves,[33]
- it is necessary to provide security,[34]
- there is a history of default with respect to periodic payments,[35]
- a lump sum would recoup unpaid periodic support,[36]
- the obligor has an unstable employment record,[37]
- the obligor's income is unpredictable,[38]
- the obligor's future employment prospects are uncertain,[39]
- there is evidence that the obligor will fritter away the capital,[40]
- the obligor is unlikely or unable to pay periodic support at all or for the appropriate length of time,[41] or
- the conduct of the obligor has been to unnecessarily protract litigation and force the dependent spouse to live on social assistance.[42]

Lump sum support may provide transitional financial relief to enhance a spouse's economic self-reliance[43] or to allow a spouse to become self-supporting where periodic support would serve as a disincentive to the recipient to make a genuine effort to obtain employment.[44] Persistent conflict between the spouses may justify a "clean break" by way of an order for lump sum support instead of periodic payments.[45] Similarly,

---

32   *Baker v.* Baker, [2003] A.J. No. 778 (Q.B.); *Maillet v. Maillet* (1975), 25 R.F.L. 126 (N.B.Q.B.); *Battaglini v. Battaglini* (1994), 4 R.F.L. (4th) 235 (Ont. Gen. Div.).

33   *Stricker v. Stricker* (1994), 4 R.F.L. (4th) 29 (Alta. C.A.).

34   *Rossiter-Forrest v. Forrest* (1994), 129 N.S.R. (2d) 130 (S.C.).

35   *Brodytsch v. Brodytsch* (1977), 7 A.R. 541 (C.A.); *Baker v. Baker*, [2003] A.J. No. 778 (Q.B.); *Verdun v. Verdun* (1994), 9 R.F.L. (4th) 54 at 67 (Ont. Gen. Div.).

36   *Magne v. Magne* (1990), 26 R.F.L. (3d) 364 (Man. Q.B.); *Boland v. Boland*, [2006] N.J. No. 206 (U.F.C.).

37   *Clarke v. Clarke* (1974), 14 R.F.L. 190 (Alta. S.C.T.D.), aff'd (1974), 15 R.F.L. 115 (Alta. C.A.).

38   *Murphy v. Murphy* (1989), 77 Nfld. & P.E.I.R. 51 (Nfld. U.F.C.).

39   *Barker v. Barker* (1993), 144 A.R. 314 (Q.B.); *Bhatti v. Bhatti* (1994), 45 B.C.A.C. 87.

40   *Krause v. Krause* (1976), 23 R.F.L. 219 (Alta. C.A.).

41   *Babowech v. Von Como* (1989), 18 R.F.L. (3d) 365 (B.C.C.A.); *Boland v. Boland*, [2006] N.J. No. 206 (U.F.C.); *Poisson v. Poisson* (1993), 46 R.F.L. (3d) 105 (Ont. Gen. Div.).

42   *Droit de la famille — 1184*, [1988] R.D.F. 272 (Que. C.S.).

43   *Boland v. Boland*, [2006] N.J. No. 206 (U.F.C.); *Tauber v. Tauber*, [2003] O.J. No. 1083 (C.A.); *Vynnk v. Baisa*, [2007] O.J. No. 274 (Sup. Ct.).

44   *Andrews v. Andrews* (1995), 11 R.F.L. (4th) 117 (B.C.S.C.).

45   See *Baker v. Baker*, [2003] A.J. No. 778 (Q.B.); *Carmichael v. Carmichael* (1976), 27 R.F.L. 325 (B.C.C.A.); *Foster v. Foster*, 2007 BCCA 83, [2007] B.C.J. No. 244; *Parish v. Parish* (1993), 46 R.F.L. (3d) 117 (Ont. Gen. Div.).

where continued contact between the spouses would hamper a spouse's recovery from illness, a lump sum order promoting a clean break may be appropriate.[46]

Judicial opinion has been divided on whether the applicant must show that a lump sum is required for a specific or immediate purpose or project.[47]

Lump sum orders have been granted to achieve a variety of objectives, many of which contain a compensatory element.[48] Lump sum orders may

- facilitate the purchase or repair of a residence,[49]
- provide reasonable accommodation for a custodial parent and child,[50]
- enable a spouse to acquire furnishings for a new residence,[51]
- promote a spouse's economic self-sufficiency,[52]
- compensate a spouse for loss of career development or future earnings potential,[53]
- compensate a spouse for assuming the primary responsibility for child care,[54]
- compensate a spouse for assisting the other to further his or her education to the detriment of the contributing spouse's own education,[55]

---

46 *Poisson v. Poisson* (1993), 46 R.F.L. (3d) 105 (Ont. Gen. Div.).

47 See *Jensen v. Jensen* (1986), 5 R.F.L. (3d) 346 (Man. C.A.). Compare *Mosher v. Mosher* (1995), 13 R.F.L. (4th) 385 (N.S.C.A.); *Tweel v. Tweel* (1994), 7 R.F.L. (4th) 204 (P.E.I.S.C.T.D.).

48 *Sword v. Sword* (1994), 118 Nfld. & P.E.I.R. 69 at 74 (Nfld. U.F.C.).

49 *Krause v. Krause* (1976), 23 R.F.L. 219 (Alta. C.A.); *Evans v. Evans* (1988), 16 R.F.L. (3d) 437 (Ont. H.C.J.); compare *Gossen v. Gossen*, [2003] N.S.J. No. 113 (S.C.).

50 *Meltzer v. Meltzer* (1989), 22 R.F.L. (3d) 38 (Man. Q.B.).

51 *Krause v. Krause* (1976), 23 R.F.L. 219 (Alta. C.A.); *Baker v. Baker*, [2003] A.J. No. 778 (Q.B.); *MacNaughton v. MacNaughton* (1991), 32 R.F.L. (3d) 312 (N.S.C.A.).

52 *Lacroix c. Valois*, [1990] 2 S.C.R. 1259, 29 R.F.L. (3d) 337; *Krause v. Krause* (1976), 23 R.F.L. 219 (Alta. C.A.); *Amaral v. Amaral* (1993), 50 R.F.L. (3d) 364 (Ont. Gen. Div.).

53 *Monks v. Monks* (1993), 84 Man. R. (2d) 268 (Q.B.), aff'd (1993), 88 Man. R. (2d) 149 (C.A.); *MacNeil v. MacNeil* (1994), 2 R.F.L. (4th) 432 (N.S.C.A.); *Henderson v. Sharma-Henderson* (1993), 47 R.F.L. (3d) 388 (Ont. Gen. Div.).

54 *Wegert v. Wegert* (1994), 6 R.F.L. (4th) 430 (Man. Q.B.); *Pearson v. Pearson* (1995), 16 R.F.L. (4th) 75 (Man. Q.B.).

55 *Doiron v. Doiron* (1994), 153 N.B.R. (2d) 113 (Q.B.).

- assist a spouse with education expenses or retraining for the labour market,[56]
- facilitate the purchase or repair of an automobile,[57]
- accommodate a spouse's temporary dislocation after separation and assist that spouse in reorganizing his or her life,[58]
- provide for transportation and relocation expenses in order for the spouse to return to her native country,[59]
- reimburse a spouse for household and other expenses incurred for the sake of the other spouse,[60] and
- reimburse a spouse for post-separation debts,[61] and facilitate the discharge of debts.[62]

Lump sum spousal support should not be ordered in lieu of periodic payments when the timing and extent of the recipient's economic self-sufficiency is not reasonably ascertainable. However, lump sum payments to supplement periodic payments may be appropriate to facilitate a particular legitimate need for a larger immediate sum, for such purposes as education tuition, home repairs, etc.[63]

When quantifying a lump sum spousal support order by reference to the capitalized value of periodic payments over a fixed period of time, a discounting for present value may be required and due account should also be taken of the different income tax consequences of lump sum and periodic spousal support payments. Faced with inadequate reasons to justify a trial judge's lump sum order, an appellate court may substitute an order for fixed-term periodic spousal support with the amount to be secured against the obligor's assets.[64]

---

56 *Baker v. Baker*, [2003] A.J. No. 778 (Q.B.); *K.K.C. v. A.P.C.*, [2003] B.C.J. No. 1312 (C.A.); *Mosher v. Mosher* (1995), 13 R.F.L. (4th) 385 (N.S.C.A.); *Ross v. Ross* (1993), 12 O.R. (3d) 705 (C.A.); compare *Gossen v. Gossen*, [2003] N.S.J. No. 113 (S.C.); *Rust v. Rust*, [2003] S.J. No. 394 (C.A.).

57 *MacNaughton v. MacNaughton* (1991), 32 R.F.L. (3d) 312 (N.S.C.A.); *Gossen v. Gossen, ibid.*

58 *Mroz v. Mroz* (1987), 7 R.F.L. (3d) 66 (Alta. C.A.); *Nurmi v. Nurmi* (1988), 16 R.F.L. (3d) 201 (Ont. U.F.C.).

59 *Memisoglu v. Memiche* (1994), 154 N.B.R. (3d) 30 (Q.B.).

60 *Desrochers v. Desrochers* (1987), 47 Man. R. (2d) 135 (Q.B.); *Van Stavern v. Van Stavern* (1987), 10 R.F.L. (3d) 354 (Sask. Q.B.).

61 *MacNeil v. MacNeil* (1994), 2 R.F.L. (4th) 432 (N.S.C.A.).

62 *Droit de la famille — 1115*, [1987] R.D.F. 356 (Que. C.S.); *Vieira v. Vieira* (1987), 46 Man. R. (2d) 74 (Q.B.); *Greenall v. Greenall* (1984), 39 R.F.L. (2d) 225 (Ont. H.C.J.).

63 *Maber v. Maber*, [2007] N.B.J. No. 128 at para. 253 (Q.B.).

64 *Dudla v. Lemay*, [2005] A.J. No. 117 (C.A.).

5) Security

Section 15.2(1) of the *Divorce Act* empowers a court to order a spouse to pay and/or secure such lump sum and/or periodic sums for the support of the other spouse. The power to order security does not extend to confer jurisdiction on the court to deprive a spouse of his or her property by ordering its transfer to the other spouse.[65] In determining whether court-ordered periodic spousal support payments should be secured pursuant to section 15.2 of the *Divorce Act*, section 8 of the *Family Maintenance Act* (Saskatchewan), or section 65 of the *Queen's Bench Act* (Saskatchewan), case law has established that the court should consider

(i)   whether the obligor has a history of dissipating assets;

(ii) whether the obligor is likely to leave the jurisdiction and become an absconding debtor;

(iii) whether the obligor has previously refused to discharge a support obligation;

(iv) whether the obligor has a poor employment history or has indicated that he or she will leave his or her employment;

(v)   the extent to which an order to secure interferes with the obligor's ability to manage his or her business affairs; and

(vi) the availability of other substantial resources to enforce the support order.[66]

Section 15.2 of the *Divorce Act* empowers a court to order a spouse to secure a support payment against his interest in the former matrimonial home or the proceeds of sale thereof[67] but the court order does not, in and of itself, constitute a security interest. This stands to reason because the rationale behind the registration systems applicable to land and personal property under the *Land Titles Act* (Alberta) and the *Personal Property Security Act* (Alberta) is that persons claiming a security interest in particular property must give notice of that interest to other potential creditors in order to claim priority over them. A support order, without more, does not provide notice of its contents to persons other than those involved in the particular proceedings. Although there is provision in some provincial statutes, including the *Land Titles Act* (Alberta) and the *Maintenance Enforcement Act* (Alberta), for support orders to be

---

65   *Switzer v. Switzer* (1969), 1 R.F.L. 262 (Alta. C.A.); *Metz v. Metz*, [2004] A.J. No. 925 (Q.B.); *McConnell v. McConnell* (1975), 11 N.B.R. (2d) 19 (C.A.).

66   *Saleh v. Saleh*, [2002] S.J. No. 426 (Q.B.).

67   *R.B. v. I.B.*, [2005] N.B.J. No. 134 (C.A.).

registered so as to give notice to other potential creditors, in the absence of registration, a support order does not give rise to a secured interest that takes priority over other secured interests. Furthermore, even when registered, the support debtor will not have priority over previously registered secured creditors of the obligor.[68]

6) Fixed-Term Spousal Support Orders; Review Orders

Subsection 15.2(3) of the *Divorce Act* specifically empowers the court to make a support order for a definite or indefinite period or until the happening of a specified event, such as the retirement of the payor.

Orders for periodic spousal support for a fixed-term or on a sliding scale have been used in the past as a means of promoting a dependent spouse's return to economic self-sufficiency where that spouse lacked occupational skills at the time of the divorce but could reasonably be expected to acquire or upgrade such skills in the foreseeable future. Given the uncertainties of the labour market and the impact of the judgment of the Supreme Court of Canada in *Moge v. Moge*,[69] however, many courts are now disinclined to grant fixed-term orders for spousal support except in marriages of short duration. Such orders are improper where there is no evidence that the dependent spouse can secure employment within a stipulated period.[70] In these circumstances, a court may order the recipient spouse to furnish the payor with periodic sworn statements respecting employment efforts.[71] Time-limited orders have no place where a displaced homemaking spouse lacks marketable skills or has suffered a permanent economic disadvantage from the role assumed during a lengthy marriage.[72] Ongoing parental responsibilities may also render

---

68   *Minaei v. Brae Centre Ltd.*, [2004] A.J. No. 943 (Q.B.).

69   [1992] 3 S.C.R. 813, 43 R.F.L. (3d) 345.

70   *Hudson v. Hudson* (1989), 19 R.F.L. (3d) 409 (B.C.C.A.); *Rayvals v. Rayvals*, [2004] B.C.J. No. 2538 (C.A.); *Nataros v. Nataros* (2000), 4 R.F.L. (5th) 290 (B.C.C.A.); *Patten v. Patten*, [2005] N.B.J. No. 70 (Q.B.); *S.C. v. J.C.*, [2006] N.B.J. No. 186 (C.A.); *MacLennan v. MacLennan*, [2003] N.S.J. No. 15 (C.A.); *Chadder v. Chadder* (1986), 2 R.F.L. (3d) 433 (Ont. C.A.); *Droit de la famille — 683*, [1989] R.D.F. 390 (Que. C.A.).

71   *Epstein v. Epstein* (1988), 86 N.B.R. (2d) 326, 219 A.P.R. 326 (Q.B.), supp. reasons (1988), 91 N.B.R. (2d) 98 (Q.B.).

72   *Moge v. Moge*, [1992] 3 S.C.R. 813, 43 R.F.L. (3d) 345; *Jean v. Jean*, [2006] A.J. No. 1687 (Q.B.); *Tedham v. Tedham*, [2005] B.C.J. No. 2186 (C.A.); *Doherty v. Doherty*, [2001] O.J. No. 2400 (Sup. Ct.).

fixed-term support inappropriate.[73] It is an error in principle for a trial judge to grant an order for fixed-term spousal support where there is no reasonably identifiable time within which the recipient can be expected to become economically self-sufficient. Furthermore, the ability to become self-sufficient is only one of the four objectives of spousal support orders that the court must consider pursuant to section 15.2(6) of the *Divorce Act*. In *Lacroix v. Lacroix*,[74] the Ontario Divisional Court upheld the amount of periodic spousal support ordered by the trial judge which, combined with the wife's earned income, her entitlement to child support, and her receipt of the Child Tax Credit, provided her with 58.1 percent of the total family net disposable income. With respect to the duration of the spousal support order, which had a fixed-term of three years, the Ontario Divisional Court referred to the trial judge's declaration that the wife "has the potential for self-sufficiency" but concluded that there was no evidence before the trial judge to indicate that the wife had any prospect of increasing her modest annual income in the foreseeable future. Given the substantial disparity between the spousal annual incomes, with the husband's being $56,500 and the wife's being $18,000, and the wife's on-going parenting responsibilities, which placed limitations on her employment opportunities, the Ontario Divisional Court held that the trial judge erred in limiting the duration of the spousal support order to three years. Accordingly, that provision in the order was set aside by the Ontario Divisional Court, which substituted a provision whereby the spousal support order would be of unlimited duration but subject to review after three years. Having regard to this change, the wife was held entitled to security that had been denied by the trial judge, such security being provided by a direction that the husband designate his wife as an irrevocable beneficiary of death benefits under his employment pension plan and group life insurance plan for so long as spousal support remained payable.

It is unusual for a court to order time-limited spousal support on the breakdown of a marriage of significant duration.[75] On the other hand, fixed-term spousal support may be appropriate where both spouses have experienced relatively few or similar advantages or disadvantages from

---

73　*Moge v. Moge*, [1992] 3 S.C.R. 813, 43 R.F.L. (3d) 345; *Ripley v. Ripley* (1991), 30 R.F.L. (3d) 41 (B.C.C.A.); *Ross v. Ross* (1993), 12 O.R. (3d) 705 (C.A.).

74　[2005] O.J. No. 5240 (Div. Ct.); see also *Ingram v. Ingram*, [2005] S.J. No. 342 (C.A.).

75　*Riad v. Riad* (2002), 317 A.R. 201 (C.A.); *Thomas v. Thomas and Abel v. Abel*, [2005] A.J. No. 61 (C.A.); *Ickovich v. Tonken*, [2005] A.J. No. 98 (C.A.); *Walsh v. Walsh*, [2006] N.B.J. No. 441 (Q.B.); *Foran v. Foran*, [2007] O.J. No. 1340 (Div. Ct.).

the marriage or its breakdown.[76] The dissolution of a lengthy marriage does not inevitably signify that spousal support should be granted for an indefinite term as distinct from a fixed period of time.[77] In the final analysis, each marriage in each case is different and different judges might well reach different conclusions as to how to best achieve justice in the particular case. Provided that the trial judge paid proper regard to the factors relevant to spousal support orders under section 15.2(4) of the *Divorce Act* and to the objectives of spousal support orders set out in section 15.2(b) of the Act, an appellate court should not disturb the trial judge's order for fixed-term support that is premised on findings that the recipient is capable of achieving economic self-sufficiency and has not been disadvantaged by the marriage, which changed from its original "traditional" character well before its breakdown.[78]

As the British Columbia Court of Appeal observed in *Foster v. Foster*,[79] shorter-term marriages usually result in shorter-term spousal support orders, although exceptions are admitted based on the facts of the particular case as, for example, where the dependent spouse assumes primary responsibility for the children or the marriage has dislocated a spouse from his or her country of origin and support networks there.

If a fixed-term spousal support order is granted on the assumption that the recipient spouse will become economically self-sufficient within the prescribed time period, the failure of the recipient to achieve that goal for reasons beyond his or her control can justify variation of the order by means of its renewal or extension.[80]

The special significance of a fixed-term order becomes apparent under subsection 17(10) of the *Divorce Act*, which imposes strict limitations on the discretionary jurisdiction of the court to vary a periodic order after expiry of the term therein defined.[81]

Fixed-term orders must not be confused with support orders that are declared subject to review on the application of either spouse after a specified period of time. The latter order is a mandate to revisit the issue

---

76   *Dobson v. Dobson*, [2005] S.J. No. 722 (C.A.).

77   *Fisher v. Fisher*, 2008 ONCA 11, [2008] O.J. No. 38.

78   *Spencer v. Spencer*, [2002] B.C.J. No. 984 (C.A.); compare *MacLean v. MacLean*, [2004] N.B.J. No. 363 (C.A.).

79   2007 BCCA 83, [2007] B.C.J. No. 244.

80   *Morgan v. Morgan*, [2001] B.C.J. No. 1244 (S.C.); *Fisher v. Fisher*, 2008 ONCA 11, [2008] O.J. No. 38.

81   See *Bergeron v. Bergeron*, [1999] O.J. No. 3167 (Sup. Ct.); and see Section R(2), below in this chapter.

of support after expiry of the designated period to determine again the right to, amount, and duration of a spousal support order. An order that is declared to be reviewable after a fixed period of time may be reconsidered without proof of any material change of circumstances.[82] The advantage of such orders is that, unlike variation applications, they enable a court to modify its order to take account of significant changes of circumstances that were anticipated at the time of the original order but about which there was no certainty. They are usually granted when there is a reasonable expectation that there will soon be changes or the payee will or should become partially or fully self-sufficient within the time set for review.[83] They may also be granted to take account of an anticipated reduction in the payor's ability to pay ongoing spousal support in the amount originally ordered. The disadvantage of review orders is that they generate an air of unfinished business and have the potential for unduly increasing litigation costs and suspending the ability of divorced spouses to get on with their lives. In *Tedham v. Tedham*,[84] the British Columbia Court of Appeal upheld the paragraph in the chambers judge's order that provided for further review of the issue of spousal support because the husband's eyesight was deteriorating and that could significantly reduce his future earning capacity. In *Leskun v. Leskun*,[85] the trial judge at the time of the divorce granted the wife periodic support of $2,250 per month until she "returns to full employment, when both entitlement and quantum will be reviewed." The Supreme Court of Canada accepted the divorced husband's submission that his application to terminate the spousal support order should be characterized as a review application rather than a variation application under section 17 of the *Divorce Act*, which would have re-

---

82 *Leskun v. Leskun*, [2006] 1 S.C.R. 920; *Abbott v. Taylor* (1988), 14 R.F.L. (3d) 9 (Man. C.A.), var'g (1987), 11 R.F.L. (3d) 407 (Man. Q.B.); *Schmidt v. Schmidt*, [1999] B.C.J. No. 2757 (C.A.); *Xu v. Leung*, [2002] B.C.J. No. 131 (C.A.); *S.E.J. v. G.P.J.*, [2004] B.C.J. No. 137 (C.A.); *Tedham v. Tedham*, [2005] B.C.J. No. 2186 (C.A.); *Skelly v. Skelly*, [2007] B.C.J. No. 1243 (S.C.); *Maber v. Maber*, [2007] N.B.J. No. 128 (Q.B.); *MacPherson v. MacPherson*, [2007] N.B.J. No. 392 (Q.B.); *Hill v. Hill*, 2003 NSCA 33 at para. 26; *Gossen v. Gossen*, [2003] N.S.J. No. 113 (S.C.); *Bergeron v. Bergeron*, [1999] O.J. No. 3167 (Sup. Ct.); *Brown v. Brown*, [2007] O.J. No. 1558 (Sup. Ct.); *Rea v. Rea*, [2007] O.J. No.4990 (Sup. Ct.); *Fisher v. Fisher*, 2008 ONCA 11, [2008] O.J. No. 38.

83 *Stein v. Stein*, [2006] B.C.J. No. 2020 (C.A.); *T.H. v. W.H.*, [2007] N.S.J. No. 27 (S.C.); *Brown v. Brown*, [2007] O.J. No. 1558 (Sup. Ct.); *Rea v. Rea*, [2007] O.J. No. 4990 (Sup. Ct.); *Hinz v. Hinz*, [2007] S.J. No. 216 (Q.B.); *Peterson v. Peterson*, [2007] S.J. No. 474 (Q.B.).

84 [2005] B.C.J. No. 2186 (C.A.).

85 [2006] S.C.J. No. 25 at para. 7.

quired him to prove a material change of circumstances since the granting of spousal support at the time of the divorce. However, this proved of no assistance to the divorced husband, given his continued capacity to pay the previously ordered amount and his divorced wife's continuing need for such support in light of her inability to achieve economic self-sufficiency. In the opinion of the Supreme Court of Canada, the review order was justified by serious doubt at the time of the trial as to the financial prospects of the wife and the level of support that might be needed in the future. While affirming the judicial jurisdiction to grant a review order pursuant to section 15.2(3) of the *Divorce Act* that enables the court to revisit the order after the occurrence of a specified event or the passage of a fixed period of time without any need for proof of a material change in circumstances, the Supreme Court of Canada observed that review orders are not to be routinely granted. Although they have a useful role, it is a very limited one. They are appropriate where either of the spouses lacks the ability to cope with the economic disadvantages arising from the marriage or its breakdown at the time of the divorce but his or her economic circumstances are reasonably expected to improve in the future. Common examples of circumstances wherein review orders may be appropriate were identified by the Supreme Court of Canada in *Leskun*, namely, "the need to establish a new residence, start a program of education, train or upgrade skills, or obtain employment."[86] The Supreme Court of Canada asserted that "[i]nsofar as possible, courts should resolve the controversies before them and make an order which is permanent subject only to change under section 17 [of the *Divorce Act*] on proof of a change in circumstances."[87] Having regard to the fact that review orders impose no onus on either party to prove changed circumstances, and the risk that such orders may be perceived as an invitation to the parties to simply re-argue their case, the Supreme Court of Canada further stated that any review order should identify the issue for future review and it should be "tightly delineated."[88] Given the examples provided by the Supreme Court of Canada as to the circumstances wherein review orders are appropriate, the role of review orders may not be unduly limited. Indeed, the listed circumstances reflect those that have been previously identified in appellate and trial judgments across Canada. However, the routine use of re-

---

86   *Ibid.* at para. 36.

87   *Ibid.* at para. 39. See also *Litton v. Litton*, [2006] B.C.J. No. 2916 (C.A.); *Walsh v. Walsh*, [2006] N.B.J. No. 441 (Q.B.); *Fisher v. Fisher*, 2008 ONCA 11, [2008] O.J. No. 38.

88   See *Fisher v. Fisher, ibid.*; *Hinz v. Hinz*, [2007] S.J. No. 216 (Q.B.).

view orders is clearly impermissible since *Leskun*.[89] In the words of Tuck J., of the New Brunswick Court of Queen's Bench, in *Maber v. Maber*,[90] "[t]he Supreme Court of Canada did not by any stretch signal the demise of review orders. Review orders are still with us; they still have a role. The court just emphasized the importance of using them on a principled basis when needed and not just as a matter of course." Review orders are only justified where there is a genuine and material uncertainty with regard to a particular matter at the time when a spousal support order is granted.[91] Furthermore, as Perkins J., of the Ontario Superior Court of Justice, observed in *Bemrose v. Fetter*,[92] "Spousal support reviews are best conducted against stated goals and expectations." Given the wife's lack of any significant earning capacity in her previously chosen field, Perkins J. coupled his spousal support order, which was declared subject to review after 1 May 2007, with a directive that the wife devise a realistic career plan and provide it to her husband within two months.

The fact that the order is reviewable after a fixed period of time does not preclude an earlier application to vary the order pursuant to subsections 17(1)(a) and 17(4.1) of the *Divorce Act*, if a material change does occur in the condition, means, or needs of other circumstances of either former spouse after the granting of the reviewable order.[93]

The Ontario Court of Appeal has asserted that review orders should not be granted routinely and has acknowledged that a failure to make reasonable efforts to obtain full-time employment when able to do so can constitute a material change of circumstances that will justify an application to vary an existing order.[94] Since the decision of the Supreme Court of Canada in *Moge v. Moge*,[95] courts in Ontario have been disinclined to grant orders for fixed-term spousal support, because they fail to address the uncertainties of future gainful employment and often fail to satisfactorily address the long-term economic consequences that ensue from the

---

89 *Long-Beck v. Beck*, [2006] N.B.J. No. 398 (Q.B.).

90 [2007] N.B.J. No. 128 at para. 246 (Q.B.).

91 *Parker v. Vik*, [2006] B.C.J. No. 1794 (S.C.); *Tsurugida v. Romero*, [2006] B.C.J. No. 3067 (S.C.); *Austin v. Austin*, [2008] O.J. No. 421 (Sup. Ct.).

92 [2005] O.J. No. 3362 at para. 44 (Sup. Ct.).

93 *Lidstone v. Lidstone* (1993), 46 R.F.L. (3d) 203 (N.S.C.A.); *Bemrose v. Fetter*, [2007] O.J. No. 3488 (C.A.); see also *Gossen v. Gossen*, [2003] N.S.J. No. 113 (S.C.); *Bergeron v. Bergeron*, [1999] O.J. No. 3167 (Sup. Ct.).

94 *Andrews v. Andrews* (1999), 45 O.R. (3d) 577 (C.A.); *Choquette v. Choquette* (1998), 39 R.F.L. (4th) 384 (Ont. C.A.); see also *Bergeron v. Bergeron*, [1999] O.J. No. 3167 (Sup. Ct.); *Doherty v. Doherty*, [2001] O.J. No. 2400 (Sup. Ct.).

95 [1992] 3 S.C.R. 813, 43 R.F.L. (3d) 345.

division of spousal homemaking and breadwinning functions during the marriage.[96] However, an appellate court may refuse to disturb a fixed-term order where the trial judge concluded that the recipient was pursuing unrealistic career goals, rather than seeking to maximize an existing earning potential.[97]

A useful and succinct summary of relevant Ontario cases dealing with situations in which time-limited spousal support orders have been granted and those in which such orders have been refused may be found in the judgment of G. Campbell J., of the Ontario Superior Court of Justice, in *Ramdatt v. Ramdatt*[98] who expressed the following opinions:

> Recent cases appear to decide that spousal support is more likely to be time-limited when the marriage is of short duration.
>
> …
>
> Cases also appear to suggest that spousal support is more likely to be time-limited where the party receiving the support is able to be self-sufficient.
>
> …
>
> Recent case law also seems to suggest that a court is not precluded from awarding indefinite spousal support for marriages of medium duration.
>
> …
>
> The unique circumstances of each of the parties in each case must be considered in determining whether spousal support should be time-limited, but courts at all appeal levels have indicated that spousal support should be time-limited only in unusual circumstances.

---

96 *Schmuck v. Reynolds-Schmuck*, [1999] O.J. No. 3104 (Sup. Ct.); *Foran v. Foran*, [2007] O.J. No. 1340 (Div. Ct.).

97 *Mero v. Mero*, [2001] O.J. No. 2042 (Div. Ct.).

98 [2004] O.J. No. 578 (Sup. Ct.). See also *Schmuck v. Reynolds-Schmuck*, [1999] O.J. No. 3104 (Sup. Ct.), wherein Himel J. also provides a succinct review of Ontario cases dealing with the issue of fixed-term spousal support orders. And see *Maber v. Maber*, [2007] N.B.J. No. 128 (Q.B.). For a corresponding review of Nova Scotia case law by Goodfellow J., see *Bray-Long v. Long*, [2000] N.S.J. No. 10 (S.C.). And see *Rondeau v. Kirby*, [2004] N.S.J. No. 143 (C.A.), wherein Oland J.A., delivering the opinion of the appellate panel, stated at para. 7 that "[t]he time limitation in a spousal support order is to be decided on the facts of each case and not in accordance with facts which may or may not occur." See also *R.B. c. N.A.*, [2004] Q.J. No. 2778 (C.A.).

Section 17 of the *Divorce Act* empowers either former spouse to apply for a variation of spousal support in the event of a subsequent material change of circumstances and there is no requirement that an order for an indefinite term include provision for an automatic review.[99]

While a judicial direction that a periodic spousal support order should be reviewed after a designated period of time may be inappropriate on the dissolution of a long traditional marriage, it may be appropriate for the court to direct the recipient of spousal support to keep the payor informed of the recipient's efforts to improve employment skills and find suitable employment.[100]

The Quebec Court of Appeal has frequently acknowledged that fixed-term orders for spousal support are inappropriate to deal with uncertain and unpredictable future contingencies. In some circumstances a review order may be granted. Two types of spousal support review orders have been used. The first type involves the passage of a specified period of time, after which spousal support will be re-evaluated without any constraints being imposed, such as proof of a change in circumstances. The second type involves an order that terminates after a specified period of time, unless the payee justifies its continuance or establishes a need for further spousal support payments. The underlying rationale for this second type of review order is the assumption that the term indicated will likely suffice to allow the payee to achieve the required financial autonomy. Fixed-term orders or review order conditions are rarely imposed when a court is dealing with the dissolution of a long, traditional marriage. They are more likely to be imposed when the obligor has already been paying spousal support for a significant number of years. If a spouse's current lack of economic self-sufficiency is attributable more to the breakdown of her long traditional marriage than to her postseparation refusal to take steps to achieve financial autonomy, the court may find it inappropriate to grant a spousal support review order, but may find it appropriate to order the payee to inform the payor every six months of her efforts to find employment or improve her workforce skills and to advise him of any future income earned.[101]

---

99 *Thomas v. Thomas and Abel v. Abel*, [2005] A.J. No. 61 (C.A.).
100 *Rose v. Ferguson*, [2001] B.C.J. No. 2477 (S.C.).
101 *A.C. c. O.F.*, [2005] Q.J. No. 5259 (S.C.).

D. TERMS, CONDITIONS, AND RESTRICTIONS

Pursuant to section 15.2(3) of the *Divorce Act*, a court may order spousal support for a definite or indefinite period or until a specified event occurs, and the court may impose terms, conditions, and restrictions on its order.[102]

E. RELEVANT FACTORS

Subsection 15.2(4) of the *Divorce Act* defines the "factors" that a court must consider in determining the right to, amount, and duration of spousal support. It provides that the court shall take into consideration the condition, needs, means, and other circumstances of each spouse, including (a) the length of time the spouses cohabited; (b) the functions performed by each spouse during cohabitation; and (c) any order, agreement, or arrangement relating to support of either spouse.

These statutory criteria confer a virtually unfettered discretion on the court to have regard to any facts that the trial judge considers relevant, with the exception of matrimonial misconduct.

Spousal support cases are fact-driven because terms such as "means" and "needs" in subsection 15.2(4) of the *Divorce Act* and "economic self-sufficiency" in subsection 15.2(6) of the *Divorce Act* have no absolute meaning. They must be interpreted and applied having regard to the circumstances of the particular spouses. In high-end cases, a critical assessment of the means made available from a matrimonial property settlement must be undertaken in the context of the factors and objectives set out in subsections 15.2(4) and (6) of the *Divorce Act* to determine whether spousal support should be ordered and, if so, in what amount. A very substantial matrimonial property entitlement on the breakdown of marriage does not imply that a spousal support order is inappropriate. In determining the impact of a matrimonial property entitlement on an application for spousal support, a distinction is to be drawn between

---

102   See, generally, *Re Muslake and Muslake* (1987), 58 O.R. (2d) 615, 6 R.F.L. (3d) 280 (U.F.C.). See also *Torres v. Marin*, [2007] Y.J. No. 94 (S.C.) (obligor to pay periodic spousal support while earning employment income); *Lockyer v. Lockyer*, [2000] O.J. No. 2939 (Sup. Ct.) (order for periodic spousal support declared subject to conditions whereby amount payable would be unaffected by either spouse earning an annual income below a specified amount). As to child support orders, see *Divorce Act*, R.S.C. 1985 (2d Supp.), c. 3, s. 15.1(4), as amended by S.C. 1997, c. 1.

income-producing assets derived from the settlement, and assets, such as a home and an automobile, which are not income-producing. The income-earning capacity of a matrimonial property settlement should be taken into account in determining the "means" factor under subsection 15.2(4) of the *Divorce Act*, and the preseparation lifestyle of the spouses is pertinent to the "needs" factor under that subsection. As was observed in *Moge v. Moge*,[103] the longer a marriage endures, the greater the presumptive claim to equal standards of living on its dissolution. An onus, nevertheless, remains on the applicant to prove need by establishing a shortfall between the amount required to cover a reasonable budget based on the preseparation standard of living and the means available to the applicant from employment income and investment income from the matrimonial property settlement.[104]

1) Definition of "Condition" of the Spouses

The "condition" of the spouses has been defined to include their age, health, needs, obligations, dependants, and the station in life of the parties.[105]

Courts must look to the economic consequences of the marriage and its breakdown on a sick or disabled spouse and not simply to whether the illness or disability is causally connected to the marriage.[106] Consequently, previous judicial decisions that denied spousal support on the basis that the applicant's illness or disability had no causal connection to the marriage must be re-examined in light of the judgments of the Supreme Court of Canada in *Moge v. Moge*[107] and *Bracklow v. Bracklow*.[108] As McLachlin J., as she then was, observed in the latter case,

---

103 [1992] 3 S.C.R. 813.

104 *Spiers v. Spiers*, [2003] A.J. No. 1223 (Q.B.).

105 *Moge v. Moge*, [1992] 3 S.C.R. 813, 43 R.F.L. (3d) 345; *Robichaud v. Robichaud* (1988), 17 R.F.L. (3d) 285 (B.C.C.A.); *Thomas v. Thomas and Abel v. Abel*, [2004] A.J. No. 30 (Q.B.); *Bennett v. Bennett*, [2005] A.J. No. 1824 (Q.B.); *Chalifoux v. Chalifoux*, [2006] A.J. No. 883 (Q.B.); *Robichaud v. Robichaud* (1992), 124 N.B.R. (2d) 332, 312 A.P.R. 332 (Q.B.).

106 *Moge v. Moge*, [1992] 3 S.C.R. 813, 43 R.F.L. (3d) 345; *Hillhouse v. Hillhouse* (1992), 43 R.F.L. (3d) 266 (B.C.C.A.); *McKean v. McKean* (1992), 38 R.F.L. (3d) 172 (Man. C.A.); *Currie v. Currie* (1991), 32 R.F.L. (3d) 67 (P.E.I.S.C.A.D.).

107 *Ibid.*

108 [1999] 1 S.C.R. 420, 44 R.F.L. (4th) 1. See also *Bracklow v. Bracklow*, [1999] B.C.J. No. 3028 (S.C.) (order for fixed-term support after matter remitted to trial court by Supreme Court of Canada).

Divorce ends the marriage. Yet in some circumstances the law may require that the healthy party continue to support a disabled party, absent contractual or compensatory entitlement. Justice and considerations of fairness may demand no less.[109]

It does not follow that divorcing or divorced sick or disabled persons can always look to their healthy spouses or former spouses for support, without limitation as to the amount or duration of such support. As McLachlin J., as she then was, further observes in *Bracklow v. Bracklow*,

Need is but one factor to be considered. This is consistent with the modern recognition, captured by the statutes, of the variety of marital relationships in modern society. A spouse who becomes disabled towards the end of a very short marriage may well be entitled to support by virtue of her need, but it may be unfair, under the circumstances, to order the full payment of that need by the supporting spouse for the indefinite future.[110]

2) Definition of "Means"

In considering a divorced husband's contention that the chambers judge and the British Columbia Court of Appeal had both erred by having regard to his capital assets for the purpose of determining his obligation to pay ongoing periodic spousal support, the Supreme Court of Canada in *Leskun v. Leskun*[111] observed that section 15.2(4) of the *Divorce Act* empowers the court to have regard to the "means" of each spouse. On the authority of *Strang v. Strang*,[112] which defines the term "means" to include all pecuniary resources, capital assets, income from employment or earning capacity, and any other source from which a person received gains or benefits are received, together with, in certain circumstances, money that a person does not have in possession but that is available to such person, no error was found in the chambers judge's decision to have regard to the capital assets of the divorced husband in determining his capacity to pay ongoing periodic spousal support. Given that the doctrine of "double dipping" was inapplicable to the divorced husband's capital acquired after

---

109   *Ibid.* at para. 48 (S.C.C.).
110   *Ibid.* at para. 54.
111   [2006] S.C.J. No. 25.
112   [1992] 2 S.C.R. 112 at 119. See also *Droit de la Famille — 08316*, [2008] J.Q. no 872 (C.A.).

the dissolution of the marriage,[113] the Supreme Court of Canada observed that the failure of a court to take into account after-acquired capital assets in determining the right to and amount of spousal support can create the potential for injustice where a spouse attempts to shield his true worth to avoid paying spousal support, even though his or her financial position is far superior to that of the other spouse. In *Leskun*, wherein the ex-husband invested earned income in a bagel business, he was found by the chambers judge to have demonstrated a significant earning capacity[114] and to own assets worth approximately $1 million, and enjoyed a lifestyle with his new wife that was far superior to that of his divorced wife. The Supreme Court of Canada agreed with the British Columbia Court of Appeal that the chambers judge was entitled to have regard to the husband's capital assets in determining his capacity to pay continued spousal support. As for the divorced husband's submission that the chambers judge had overestimated the value of his capital assets, the Supreme Court of Canada affirmed the right of the chambers judge to draw an adverse inference against the divorced husband as a result of his failure to make full and complete financial disclosure. In the words of Binnie J. of the Supreme Court of Canada, "[i]f problems of calculation exist the appellant is largely the author of his own difficulties" and the court "would not interfere on that basis."[115]

Although the term "means" in sections 15.2(4) and 17(4.1) of the *Divorce Act* clearly encompasses capital assets, periodic spousal support is ordinarily payable out of the income of the obligor. This includes investment income from capital assets. Where a spouse chooses to live off his or her capital rather than pursue available employment, income may be imputed to that spouse based on his or her unrealized earning capacity as well as on the basis of the actual or potential income yield of the capital assets.[116] If capital assets have already been divided pursuant to the provincial matrimonial property regime, the principle of "double dipping" or "double recovery" may preclude an order for spousal support or

---

113 See text at Section P, below in this chapter.

114 For insight into the differing statutory and regulatory foundations for judicially imputing income for the purposes of spousal support and child support respectively, see *Jean v. Jean*, 2006 ABQB 938, [2006] A.J. No. 1687, Greckol J.

115 *Leskun v. Leskun*, [2006] 1 S.C.R. 920 at para. 34.

116 *Bartole v. Parker*, [2006] S.J. No. 349 (Q.B.) (application to vary child support order having regard to father's cessation of employment after winning a lottery). See also *Scott v. Scott*, [2007] B.C.J. No. 1863 (S.C.); *Gainer v. Gainer*, [2006] O.J. No. 1631 (Sup. Ct.).

reduce the amount that would otherwise have been ordered.[117] "Means" under section 17(4.1) of the *Divorce Act* takes account of capital assets but the same standards apply to each former spouse in the overall evaluation of their financial circumstances.[118] A financially dependent wife who is incapable of achieving economic self-sufficiency will not be expected to erode her capital assets to support herself while her former spouse continues to build a retirement nest egg and preserve his asset base.[119] Conversely, a husband with insufficient income to pay spousal support is not obliged to erode his capital assets for the purpose of paying spousal support where the overall means of both spouses are relatively comparable.[120] In the final analysis, whether one or both spouses are required to use their capital for the purposes of supporting themselves or their (former) spouse will depend on the facts of the particular case. As is pointed out in *Moge v. Moge*,[121] the overarching principle of the *Divorce Act* is to provide an equitable distribution of the economic consequences of the marriage and its breakdown. If this requires either spouse to draw on their capital to support themselves or their former partner, then so be it.

3) Needs and Capacity to Pay; Economic Self-Sufficiency; Relevance of Cohabitational Standard of Living

Subsection 15.2(4) of the *Divorce Act* requires the court to have regard to the "needs" of each spouse. The "needs" of a spouse are relative and may be determined, at least in part, by reference to the lifestyle enjoyed by both spouses during long-term matrimonial cohabitation.[122] The needs of a spouse may also be relative to the standard of living of the other spouse after their separation. Having regard to financial practicalities, it may not be possible for a spousal support order to provide the standard

---

117   See Section P, below in this chapter.
118   *Campese v. Campese*, [2006] B.C.J. No. 1412 (S.C.).
119   *Kranenburg v. Kranenburg*, [1999] B.C.J. No. 574 (C.A.); *Campese v. Campese*, [2006] B.C.J. No. 1412 (S.C.); *Petz v. McNulty-Petz*, [2001] O.J. No. 1735 (Sup. Ct.).
120   *Wagstaff v. Wagstaff*, [2002] N.S.J. No. 527 (S.C.).
121   [1992] 3 S.C.R. 813, 43 R.F.L. (3d) 345.
122   *Moge v. Moge, ibid.*; *Corbeil v. Corbeil*, [2001] A.J. No. 1144 (C.A.); *Riad v. Riad*, 2002 ABCA 254; *Thomas v. Thomas and Abel v. Abel*, [2004] A.J. No. 30 (Q.B.); *Bennett v. Bennett*, [2005] A.J. No. 1824 (Q.B.); *Chalifoux v. Chalifoux*, [2006] A.J. No. 883 (Q.B.); *Boudreau v. Brun*, [2005] N.B.J. No. 501 (C.A.); *O. v. C.*, [2004] N.J. No. 19 (S.C.); *Pettigrew v. Pettigrew*, [2006] N.S.J. No. 321 (C.A.); *Martin v. Martin*, [2006] O.J. No. 3238 (C.A.); *Fisher v. Fisher*, 2008 ONCA 11, [2008] O.J. No. 38.

of living experienced during matrimonial cohabitation but courts are unwilling to allow one party to a long marriage to maintain a substantially higher standard of living than the other party on the dissolution of their marriage. On the breakdown of a long marriage, there should not be a large discrepancy in the standard of living enjoyed by each spouse. An indefinite long-term order for spousal support may, therefore, be required to ensure that the benefits and detriments that were shared during the marriage continue to be shared on its dissolution. However, such an order does not negate the obligation of the recipient spouse to strive for some degree of self-support, where this is reasonable and practicable under the circumstances of the particular case. In order to promote justice for both spouses and to avoid future litigation, the court may devise a formula whereby the amount of spousal support originally ordered shall be reduced by a designated amount when the recipient spouse's annual income exceeds a specified total. In order to retain an incentive for the support recipient spouse, the reduction may not be a dollar-for-dollar reduction.[123]

The "needs" and entitlement of the obligor to a reasonable standard of living are also to be considered.[124] If the obligor is insolvent, in a precarious financial position, or in a worse financial position than the claimant, support may be modest or may be denied.[125]

4) Definition of "Other Circumstances"

It is impossible to catalogue all the "other circumstances" of the parties that might be deemed relevant under subsection 15.2(4) of the *Divorce Act*, although it has been stated that the circumstances must be "so nearly touching the matter in issue as to be such that a judicial mind ought to regard it as a proper thing to be taken into consideration."[126] "Other circumstances" have been said to include "a deficiency in language skills, the state of the employment market, a lack of professional qualifications, an innate shortage of skills, a shortfall of ambition and motivation, ... mismanagement of funds," and the "likelihood of remarriage, cessation

---

123 *Thomas v. Thomas and Abel v. Abel*, [2004] A.J. No. 30 (Q.B.).

124 *Boyd v. Boyd* (1992), 41 R.F.L. (3d) 182 (B.C.C.A.); *Giorno v. Giorno* (1992), 39 R.F.L. (3d) 345 (N.S.S.C.A.D.); *Hawkins v. Hawkins* (1992), 40 R.F.L. (3d) 456 (Ont. C.A.); *Elliot v. Elliot* (1993), 48 R.F.L. (3d) 237 (Ont. C.A.).

125 *Graham v. Graham* (1988), 17 R.F.L. (3d) 380 (B.C.S.C.); *Powers v. Powers* (1990), 92 N.S.R. (2d) 337, 237 A.P.R. 337 (S.C.); *Botchett v. Botchett* (1990), 94 N.S.R. (2d) 339, 247 A.P.R. 339 (S.C.).

126 *Rogers v. Rogers* (1962), 3 F.L.R. 398 at 402 (N.S.W.S.C.).

of employment, possibility of inheritance and many other unforeseen events."[127]

The short duration of the marriage is a "circumstance" that the courts have considered in denying spousal support, unless a significant sacrifice was made for the sake of the marriage.[128]

F. SPOUSAL CONDUCT

Section 15.2(5) of the *Divorce Act* provides that "the court shall not take into consideration any misconduct of a spouse in relation to the marriage" when considering an application for spousal support. Pursuant to section 17(6) of the *Divorce Act*, the same criterion applies to an application to vary an existing order. In addressing the impact of the husband's conduct on the wife's state of mind and her inability to strive for economic self-sufficiency, the Supreme Court of Canada in *Leskun v. Leskun*[129] draws a distinction between misconduct, as such, which is irrelevant to the determination of spousal support, and the impact of such misconduct on a spouse's economic status, which is a relevant consideration under sections 15.2(4), 15.2(6), 17(4), and 17(7) of the *Divorce Act*. While courts have long since abandoned the notion that spousal support orders are intended to punish the guilty and reward the innocent,[130] sections 15.2(5) and 17(6) of the *Divorce Act* do not preclude the court from taking account of the economic implications of spousal misconduct. Thus, the commission of a matrimonial offence, such as adultery or cruelty or other misconduct that may have caused or contributed to the breakdown of the marriage, is *per se* irrelevant to the determination of spousal support under the *Divorce Act*. However, the economic implications of such conduct may be relevant in determining spousal support. For example, the financial aspects of a spouse's "common-law relationship" may be taken into account in determining spousal support rights and obligations. Or, to use the example presented by the Supreme Court of Canada in *Leskun*[131] "[i]f ... spousal

---

127 *Brockie v. Brockie* (1987), 5 R.F.L. (3d) 440 (Man. Q.B.), aff'd (1987), 8 R.F.L. (3d) 302 (Man. C.A.).

128 *South v. South* (1992), 40 R.F.L. (3d) 179 (Man. C.A.); *Fleming v. Fleming*, [2001] O.J. No. 1117 (Div. Ct.).

129 [2006] 1 S.C.R. 920.

130 See *Connelly v. Connelly* (1974), 16 R.F.L. 171 at 176–78 (N.S.C.A.); *Hockey-Sweeney v. Sweeney*, [2004] O.J. No. 4412 (C.A.).

131 [2006] 1 S.C.R. 920 at para. 21.

abuse triggered a depression so serious as to make a claimant spouse unemployable, the consequences of the misconduct would be highly relevant (as here) to the factors which must be considered in determining the right to support, its duration and its amount. The policy of the 1985 *[Divorce] Act* however, is to focus on the consequences of spousal misconduct not the attribution of fault." Similarly, if spousal misconduct has caused a financial loss or assets have been depleted, these consequences of the misconduct may be relevant to the determination of spousal support.[132] Spouses may enhance, diminish, or negate their mutual support rights and obligations by their conduct. However, economic misconduct is only one consideration and the nature and extent of any harm done will dictate its significance to the mandatory judicial review of all the factors and objectives to be considered on an application for spousal support pursuant to sections 15.2(4) and 15.2(6) of the *Divorce Act*. In applying these criteria in *Sibbet v. Sibbet*,[133] Little J., of the Manitoba Court of Queen's Bench, held that a wife who was suffering from ill-health should be denied a spousal support order where her deliberate misconduct in bringing the family business to an end placed ongoing burdens on her husband whom she had forced out of the business when it was a going concern. In addition, a spouse cannot sit idly by and expect to collect support. Each spouse must strive to attain financial self-sufficiency, if it is practicable to do so.[134]

A husband's cruel or abusive conduct, which impairs his divorced wife's ability to secure economic self-sufficiency through employment, may trigger a spousal support order, although the diminishing effect of the husband's misconduct on her earning capacity over a period of time may subsequently justify variation or termination of the order.[135]

Retroactive orders for spousal support and child support are not precluded by the husband/father's past imprisonment for assaulting his son and sexually assaulting his stepdaughter and such conduct is not excluded from consideration in the context of spousal support by section 15.2(5) of the *Divorce Act*.[136]

---

132   See *Sibbet v. Sibbet*, [2001] M.J. No. 181 (Q.B.).
133   *Ibid.*
134   *Fisher v. Fisher*, [2001] N.S.J. No. 32 (C.A.).
135   *Kurcz v. Kurcz* (1989), 20 R.F.L. (3d) 206 (B.C.C.A.); *Martin v. Martin* (1993), 50 R.F.L. (3d) 77 (Sask. C.A.). See also *Gainer v. Gainer*, [2006] O.J. No. 1631 (Sup. Ct.).
136   *R.B. v. I.B.*, [2005] N.B.J. No. 134 (C.A.).

In *Harris v. Harris*,[137] a motion to strike the husband's pleadings because of his refusal to answer questions, on an examination for discovery relating to his alleged alcoholism, was dismissed because the allegation of alcoholism was found irrelevant to the issues in the wife's claim for spousal support and for equalization of the spousal net family properties. Having determined that the wife's application for spousal support was governed by section 15.2 of the *Divorce Act* and the wife's alternative claim for spousal support under the Ontario *Family Law Act* should be stayed, Olah J., of the Ontario Superior Court of Justice, found that the wife's pleadings did not support any correlation between the husband's alleged alcoholism and his ability to pay spousal support or the wife's entitlement thereto. After observing that section 15.2(5) of the *Divorce Act* precludes the court from taking into consideration "any misconduct of a spouse in relation to the marriage," Olah J. concluded that the wife's argument, that the husband's alcoholism constituted a relevant "condition" to be considered pursuant to section 15.2(4) of the *Divorce Act*, was a thinly disguised attempt to circumvent section 15.2(5) of the *Divorce Act*. Rule 20 of the Ontario *Family Law Rules* allows wide latitude during questioning, so long as the questions have a semblance of relevance. Olah J. concluded that this low threshold of relevance was not satisfied in the present case because the applicant had failed to establish that any economic consequences flowed from the husband's alleged alcoholism that would affect her entitlement to or the quantum of spousal support.

G. FOUR OBJECTIVES OF SPOUSAL SUPPORT

Subsection 15.2(6) of the *Divorce Act* defines four objectives of spousal support orders. They are as follows:

(i) to recognize any economic advantages or disadvantages arising from the marriage or its breakdown;

(ii) to apportion between the spouses any financial consequences arising from child care;

(iii) to relieve any economic hardship arising from the marriage breakdown; and

(iv) insofar as practicable, to promote the economic self-sufficiency of each spouse within a reasonable period of time.

---

137 [2005] O.J. No. 1310 (Sup. Ct.).

Legislative endorsement of these four policy objectives manifests the realization that economic variables of marriage breakdown and divorce do not lend themselves to the application of any single objective. Long-term marriages that ultimately break down may leave in their wake a condition of permanent financial dependence because wives have assumed the role of full-time homemakers. The legitimate objectives of spousal support in such a case rarely coincide with the objectives that should be pursued with respect to short-term childless marriages. Substantial periodic spousal support for an indefinite term will customarily be granted to an older spouse whose primary role during a long marriage was that of a homemaker or caregiver, whereas a young able-bodied spouse with no children whose marriage was of short duration is unlikely to be granted substantial or long-term spousal support. Childless marriages cannot be treated in the same way as marriages with dependent children. The two-income family cannot be equated with the one-income family. A "clean break," with or without an order for lump sum support in lieu of periodic spousal support, may provide a workable and desirable solution for a wealthy couple or for a two-income family where there is no substantial difference between the spousal incomes, but is unlikely to be feasible for most families on the dissolution of marriage. Quite apart from the question whether a spouse can afford to pay a lump sum, such an order will not normally accommodate long-term needs, where they exist.

Periodic spousal support orders that are reviewable after a designated period of time may be appropriate where rehabilitative support is required until a dependent spouse returns to economic self-sufficiency by means of gainful employment, although continued support may be appropriate to top up the earned income of a recipient spouse who continues to suffer economic disadvantages in consequence of the marriage and its breakdown. There can be no fixed rules, however, whereby particular types of orders are tied to the specific objectives sought to be achieved. In the final analysis, the court must determine the most appropriate kind of order, having regard to the attendant circumstances of the case, including the present and prospective financial well-being of both the spouses and their dependent children. Much of the above analysis was cited with approval in *Moge v. Moge*.[138]

Judicial implementation of the statutorily defined objectives has, to some degree, resulted in a shift from the former narrow perspective of a "needs" and "capacity to pay" approach, particularly in cases where one of

---

138 [1992] 3 S.C.R. 813, 43 R.F.L. (3d) 345 at 375–76, L'Heureux-Dubé J.

the spouses has substantial means.[139] In the words of L'Heureux-Dubé J., of the Supreme Court of Canada,

> The most significant change in the new Act when compared to the 1970 *Divorce Act* may be the shift away from the "means and needs" test as the exclusive criterion for support to a more encompassing set of factors and objectives which requires courts to accommodate a much wider spectrum of considerations. This change, of course, does not signify that "means and needs" are to be ignored. Section 15(5) [now 15.2(4)] of the Act specifically states that "the court shall take into consideration the condition, means, needs and other circumstances of each spouse."[140]

The dual operation of compensatory and needs-based considerations under the *Divorce Act* was specifically acknowledged by McLachlin J., as she then was, in *Bracklow v. Bracklow,*[141] who observed:

> In summary, nothing in the *Family Relations Act* or the *Divorce Act* suggests that the only foundations for spousal support are compensatory. Indeed, I find it difficult to confine the words of the statutes to this model. It is true that in 1986 the *Divorce Act* was amended to place greater emphasis on compensation. This represented a shift away "to some degree" from the "means and needs" approach of the 1968 Act: *Payne on Divorce*, supra, at p. 267. But while the focus of the Act may have shifted or broadened, it retains the older idea that spouses may have an obligation to meet or contribute to the needs of their former partners where they have the capacity to pay, even in the absence of a contractual or compensatory foundation for the obligation. Need alone may be enough. More broadly, the legislation can be seen as a sensitive compromise of the two competing philosophies of marriage, marriage breakdown, and spousal support.

The four objectives defined in the *Divorce Act* are not necessarily independent of each other. They may overlap or they may operate independently, according to the circumstances of the particular case.

All four of the objectives defined in the *Divorce Act* should be examined in every case wherein spousal support is claimed or an order for

---

139 *Moge v. Moge,* [1992] 3 S.C.R. 813, 43 R.F.L. (3d) 345; *Bracklow v. Bracklow,* [1999] 1 S.C.R. 420, 44 R.F.L. (4th) 1.

140 *Moge v. Moge, ibid.* at 374–75 (R.F.L.).

141 [1999] 1 S.C.R. 420, 44 R.F.L. (4th) 1 at 29.

spousal support is sought to be varied. There is nothing in the *Divorce Act* to suggest that any one of the objectives has greater weight or importance than any other objective.[142] The fact that one of the objectives, such as economic self-sufficiency, has been attained, does not obviate the need to ascertain whether the remaining objectives have also been satisfied.[143]

The aforementioned objectives, which operate in the context of a wide judicial discretion under subsections 15.2(4) and 17(4.1) of the *Divorce Act*, provide opportunities for a more equitable distribution of the economic consequence of divorce between the spouses. As has been stated by L'Heureux-Dubé J., of the Supreme Court of Canada in *Moge v. Moge*,

> Equitable distribution can be achieved in many ways: by spousal and child support, by the division of property and assets or by a combination of property and support entitlements. But in many if not most cases, the absence of accumulated assets may require that one spouse pay support to the other in order to effect an equitable distribution of resources.[144]

Paragraphs 15.2(6)(a) and 17(7)(a) of the *Divorce Act* respectively provide that an original order for spousal support or a variation order should recognize any economic advantages or disadvantages to the spouses arising from the marriage or its breakdown. In the words of L'Heureux-Dubé J. of the Supreme Court of Canada in *Moge v. Moge*,

> [T]he focus of the inquiry when assessing spousal support after the marriage is ended must be the effect of the marriage in either impairing or improving each party's economic prospects.[145]

Thus, a wife who has contributed to her husband's career development, or a wife whose earning potential has been eroded, restricted, or

---

142 *Moge v. Moge*, [1992] 3 S.C.R. 813, 43 R.F.L. (3d) 345; *Bracklow v. Bracklow, ibid.*; *Chalifoux v. Chalifoux*, [2006] A.J. No. 883 (Q.B.); *Fisher v. Fisher*, 2008 ONCA 11, [2008] O.J. No. 38; *Phinney v. Phinney*, [2002] N.S.J. No. 540 (C.A.); *Mason v. Mason*, [2006] N.S.J. No. 227 (S.C.).

143 *Moge v. Moge, ibid.*; *Renouf v. Bertol-Renouf*, [2004] A.J. No. 1402 (Q.B.); *Travers v. Travers*, [2003] A.J. No. 786 (C.A.); *Linton v. Linton* (1990), 1 O.R. (3d) 1, 30 R.F.L. (3d) 1 (C.A.); *Allaire v. Allaire*, [2003] O.J. No. 1069 (C.A.); *Mullin v. Mullin* (1991), 37 R.F.L. (3d) 139 at 148 (P.E.I.S.C.A.D.).

144 *Moge v. Moge*, [1992] 3 S.C.R. 813, 43 R.F.L. (3d) 345 at 374; see also *Newson v. Newson* (1993), 45 R.F.L. (3d) 115 (B.C.C.A.); *Robinson v. Robinson* (1993), 48 R.F.L. (3d) 265 (Ont. C.A.) (order for fixed-term support on sliding scale pursuant to *Family Law Act*, R.S.O. 1990, c. F.3).

145 *Moge v. Moge, ibid.* at 373 (R.F.L.).

deferred by reason of the assumption of homemaking responsibilities, is entitled to have these circumstances taken into consideration in any determination of the right to, amount, and duration of spousal support.[146] It does not follow that a court must compensate for every economic disadvantage, no matter how minimal,[147] or that one spouse should shoulder the entire responsibility for redressing economic advantages or disadvantages arising from the marriage or its breakdown.[148] Lack of resources may, of course, stand in the way of adequate compensation.[149]

Compensatory spousal support may be granted to a wife who has sacrificed her own earning potential by assuming primary responsibility for homemaking and child care during the marriage[150] or who has contributed to the career development of her husband.[151] Cultural dislocation on marriage that does not generate an economic loss will not justify a compensatory spousal support order.[152]

In quantifying a spousal support order on the dissolution of a long marriage with respect to a wife who has discharged the primary responsibility for household management and child care while maintaining full-time employment, the court may have regard to a substantial increase in the husband's postseparation income that is found to be attributable to the considerable time and effort that the husband put into his business activities while the spouses were living together. Equalization of the spousal incomes by means of a spousal support order may be inappropriate, however, because the court should take account of the ongoing substantial efforts of the husband to earn his increased income.[153]

---

146 *Moge v. Moge, ibid.; Elliot v. Elliot* (1993), 48 R.F.L. (3d) 237 (Ont. C.A.).

147 *Grohmann v. Grohmann* (1991), 37 R.F.L. (3d) 71 at 83 (B.C.C.A.), Southin J.A.

148 *Moge v. Moge*, [1992] 3 S.C.R. 813, 43 R.F.L. (3d) 345 at 387; *Elliot v. Elliot* (1993), 48 R.F.L. (3d) 237 (Ont. C.A.).

149 *Ibid.*

150 *Moge v. Moge*, [1992] 3 S.C.R. 813, 43 R.F.L. (3d) 345; *Bracklow v. Bracklow*, [1999] 1 S.C.R. 420, 44 R.F.L. (4th) 1; *Chalifoux v. Chalifoux*, [2006] A.J. No. 883 (Q.B.); *MacLean v. MacLean*, [2004] N.B.J. No. 363 (C.A.); *Caratun v. Caratun*, (1992), 10 O.R. (3d) 385, 42 R.F.L. (3d) 113 (C.A.); see also *Ross v. Ross* (1993), 12 O.R. (3d) 705 (C.A.); *Elliot v. Elliot* (1993), 48 R.F.L. (3d) 237 (Ont. C.A.).

151 See *MacLean v. MacLean, ibid.; Caratun v. Caratun, ibid.; Keast v. Keast* (1986), 1 R.F.L. (3d) 401 (Ont. Dist. Ct.) (application under *Family Law Act*, S.O. 1986, c. 4); *Magee v. Magee* (1987), 6 R.F.L. (3d) 453 (Ont. U.F.C.).

152 *Dyal v. Dyal*, [2000] B.C.J. No. 1937 (C.A.).

153 *Giguere v. Giguere*, [2003] O.J. No. 5102 (Sup. Ct.); see also *Chalifoux v. Chalifoux*, [2006] A.J. No. 883 at paras. 105–6 (Q.B.); *Pettigrew v. Pettigrew*, [2006] N.S.J. No. 321 (C.A.).

Financial consequences arising from the care of a child of the marriage that are personal to the custodial parent, in that they arise from the limitations and demands of parenting, are additional to the direct costs of raising the children that are addressed by means of the *Federal Child Support Guidelines*. Such personal financial consequences, therefore, fall properly within the ambit of paragraphs 15.2(6)(b) and 17(7)(b) of the *Divorce Act*, as well as subsections 15.2(4) and 17(4.1) of the Act.[154]

Paragraph 15.2(6)(c) of the *Divorce Act* provides that an order for spousal support should "relieve any economic hardship of the spouses arising from the breakdown of the marriage." The same criterion applies to variation proceedings pursuant to paragraph 17(7)(c) of the Act. As L'Heureux-Dubé J. stated in *Moge v. Moge*,

> Sections 15(7)(a) [now 15.2(6)(a)] and 17(7)(a) of the Act are expressly compensatory in character while ss. 15(7)(c) [now 15.2(6)(c)] and 17(7)(c) may not be characterized as exclusively compensatory. These latter paragraphs may embrace the notion that the primary burden of spousal support should fall on family members *not* the state.[155]

A similar opinion is voiced by McLachlin J., as she then was, in *Bracklow v. Bracklow*. She asserts:

> Section 15.2(6) of the *Divorce Act*, which sets out the objectives of support orders, also speaks to these non-compensatory factors. The first two objectives — to recognize the economic consequences of the marriage or its breakdown and to apportion between the spouses financial consequences of child care over and above child support payments — are primarily related to compensation. But the third and fourth objectives are difficult to confine to that goal. "[E]conomic hardship ... arising from the breakdown of the marriage" is capable of encompassing not only health or career disadvantages arising from the marriage breakdown properly the subject of compensation (perhaps more directly covered in s. 15.2(6)(a): see *Payne on Divorce*, supra at pp. 251–53), but the mere fact that a person who formerly enjoyed intra-spousal entitlement to support now finds herself or himself without it. Looking only at compensation, one merely asks what loss the marriage or marriage breakup

---

154 *Moge v. Moge*, [1992] 3 S.C.R. 813, 43 R.F.L. (3d) 345; *Brockie v. Brockie* (1987), 46 Man. R. (2d) 33, 5 R.F.L. (3d) 440 (Q.B.), aff'd (1987), 8 R.F.L. (3d) 302 (Man. C.A.); *J.H.A. v. C.G.A.*, [2008] M.J. No. 94 (Q.B.); *Ray v. Ray* (1993), 121 N.S.R. (2d) 340, 335 A.P.R. 340 (S.C.); *D.P.O. v. P.E.O.*, [2006] N.S.J. No. 205 (S.C.).

155 [1992] 3 S.C.R. 813, 43 R.F.L. (3d) 345 at 386.

caused that would not have been suffered but for the marriage. But even where loss in this sense cannot be established, the breakup may cause economic hardship in a larger, non-compensatory sense. Such an interpretation supports the independent inclusion of s. 15.2(6)(c) as a separate consideration from s. 15.2(6)(a). Thus, Rogerson sees s. 15.2(6)(c), "the principle of compensation for the economic disadvantages of the marriage breakdown as distinct from the disadvantages of the marriage" as an explicit recognition of "non-compensatory" support ("Spousal Support After *Moge*", supra, at pp. 371-72).

Similarly, the fourth objective of s. 15.2(6) of the *Divorce Act* — to promote economic self-sufficiency — may or may not be tied to compensation for disadvantages caused by the marriage or its breakup. A spouse's lack of self-sufficiency may be related to forgoing career and educational opportunities because of the marriage. But it may also arise from completely different sources, like the disappearance of the kind of work the spouse was trained to do (a career shift having nothing to do with the marriage or its breakdown) or, as in this case, ill-heath.[156]

In addressing the economic advantages and disadvantages arising from the marriage and its breakdown and the economic implications of childcare responsibilities both before and after the marriage breakdown, as required by sections 15.2(6)(a) and (b) of the *Divorce Act*, judges are not excused from hearing relevant evidence and fully applying the law. However, as L'Heureux-Dubé J. observed in *Moge v. Moge*,[157] adducing evidence to identify and quantify the economic consequences of marriage or marriage breakdown is an impossible task in most family law cases or one that is beyond the financial capability of litigating spouses. Consequently, trial judges should temper their expectations for detailed evidence and are encouraged to resort, where necessary, to judicial notice of certain realities. In the words of Richard J.A. in *MacLean v. MacLean*,

> It is certainly amenable to judicial notice that one who has not been in the workforce for over 14 years will generally be less competitive on the job market than one who has acquired working experience over that same period. It is also evident that one who has foregone vocational pursuits for a significant period because of family priorities will not be able to re-enter the workforce as the level that he or she would likely

---

156   (1999), 44 R.F.L. (4th) 1 at 28–29 (S.C.C.). See also *Thomas v. Thomas and Abel v. Abel*, [2004] A.J. No. 30 (Q.B.).

157   [1992] 3 S.C.R. 813, 43 R.F.L. (3d) 345.

have reached otherwise. It seems to me that these propositions are self-evident and that they ought to be properly considered in the complex and difficult analysis expected of trial judges when assessing a claim for spousal support.[158]

In situations, such as that which arose in *MacLean v. MacLean*, where the evidence demonstrates an entitlement to spousal support without enabling the trial judge to determine its duration, the appropriate order is one that is declared subject to review after a specified period of time without the need for proof of any change in circumstances. If a change does occur prior to expiry of the prescribed period, an application for variation of the order can always be brought.

A homemaking wife, who is entitled to only a modest property entitlement on the breakdown of her long traditional marriage, may be presumed to have suffered economic disadvantages under sections 15.2(6)(a) and (b) of the *Divorce Act* but this does not obviate the need for evidence as to the preseparation standard of living of the spouses and their present health and earning capacities. In the absence of sufficient evidence respecting the wife's needs and the husband's ability to pay, a court should refuse to grant an order for spousal support, whether interim or permanent, but such refusal may be declared to be without prejudice to the wife's right to renew her application once the material evidence has been assembled.[159]

Although the objectives of spousal support, as defined in the *Divorce Act*, provide a legal foundation for fair and reasonable spousal support orders on or after divorce, they must be applied in light of the economic realities facing Canadians who divorce and thereafter enter into new family obligations. It is for that reason that many judges still tend to focus on needs and ability to pay as the fundamental basis of spousal support laws

---

158 [2004] N.B.J. No. 363 (C.A.). Compare *Sylvestre v. Sylvestre*, [2004] B.C.J. No. 1813 (S.C.). See also *Tweel v. Tweel* (1994), 7 R.F.L. (4th) 204 at 207 (P.E.I.S.C.T.D.), wherein DesRoches J. remained "unconvinced that *Moge* stands for the proposition that a party can resort to judicial notice alone to quantify the economic advantages and disadvantages of marriage and its breakdown." And see Justice James Williams, "Grasping a Thorny Baton ... A Trial Judge Looks at Judicial Notice and Courts' Acquisition of Social Science" (1996) 14 Can. Fam. L.Q. 179; L.H. Wolfson, "The Use of Judicial Notice after *Moge*" in The Law Society of Upper Canada, *Family Law à la* Moge (Toronto: The Law Society of Upper Canada, 1993) at section D. Compare Madam Justice Claire L'Heureux-Dubé, "Re-examining the Doctrine of Judicial Notice in the Family Law Context" (1994) 26 Ottawa L. Rev. 551.

159 *Walker v. Walker*, [2004] B.C.J. No. 1876 (S.C.).

in Canada. Compensating a homemaking wife for her years of service in the home is not only appropriate, but may also be feasible when the courts are dealing with spouses, one of whom is a well-established professional or business man. It is more problematic when the husband is an unskilled labourer in receipt of a modest income or unemployment insurance. It does not follow that a divorced spouse can jettison support obligations owed to a former spouse by assuming new family obligations. Thus, in *Bracklow v. Bracklow*, McLachlin J., as she then was, observed:

> Mr. Bracklow makes a final policy argument. In an age of multiple marriages, he asserts, the law should permit closure on relationships so parties can move on. Why, he asks, should a young person whose marriage lasts less than a year be fixed with a lifelong obligation of support? When can a former spouse finally move on, knowing that he or she cannot be drawn back into the past by an unexpected application for support?

> Again the answer is that under the statutes, the desirability of freedom to move on to new relationships is merely one of several objectives that might guide the judge. Since all the objectives must be balanced, it often will not be possible to satisfy one absolutely. The respondent in effect seeks a judicially created "statute of limitations" on marriage. The Court has no power to impose such a limitation, nor should it. It would inject a rigidity into the system that Parliament and the legislatures have rejected. Marriage, while it may not prove to be "till death do us part", is a serious commitment not to be undertaken lightly. It involves the *potential* for lifelong obligation. There are no magical cut-off dates.[160]

If the economic plight of separated and divorced women is to be resolved, however, laws regulating spousal and child support rights and obligations are not sufficient. Federal and provincial governments must search for a more rational and cohesive system of income security for all needy families that reconstitutes the inter-relationship between spousal and child support payments, public assistance, and earned income.

Paragraphs 15.2(6)(d) and 17(7)(d) of the *Divorce Act* underline the responsibility of each spouse to become economically self-sufficient within a reasonable time to the extent that this is practicable. Although the court should not focus unduly on the recipient spouse's obligation to strive for

---

160   *Bracklow v. Bracklow*, [1999] 1 S.C.R. 420, 44 R.F.L. (4th) 1 at para. 57.

economic self-sufficiency, given that this is only one of the four object-ives of spousal support orders under section 15.2(6) of the *Divorce Act*, it remains a legitimate concern insofar as it is practicable and may justify the court granting an order for periodic spousal support that is subject to review after a specified time.[161] A dependent spouse, who can reasonably be expected to acquire economic self-sufficiency, cannot assert a lifetime support entitlement, unless there is some ongoing economic disadvan-tage resulting from the marriage or its breakdown that compels financial redress in order to promote an equitable sharing of the economic conse-quences of the marriage and its dissolution. A dependent spouse must be diligent in pursuing full-time employment and is not entitled to pursue a less economically advantageous career and look to the other spouse to make up the shortfall.[162] Where a spouse enters marriage with an edu-cation, a profession, and good health and leaves it with these attributes intact, an order for spousal support may be inappropriate.[163]

Where both spouses have pursued their respective careers prior to the dissolution of their long-term "modern marriage" and there is no evi-dence of any significant economic advantage or disadvantage to either spouse arising from the marriage or its breakdown, an ongoing disparity between their professional incomes does not justify an order for spousal support in favour of the lower-income spouse.[164]

A court may order one spouse to furnish the other spouse with in-formation concerning efforts to achieve economic self-sufficiency.[165] Eco-nomic self-sufficiency does not necessarily connote equality, although it should include fairness.[166] A dependent spouse's capacity to become self-sufficient must be examined in light of the particular case and having regard to the realities of the marketplace.[167] In *Moge v. Moge*,[168] L'Heureux-Dubé J., of the Supreme Court of Canada, stressed the impracticability of applying a principle of economic self-sufficiency to many long-term

---

161   *Gossen v. Gossen*, [2003] N.S.J. No. 113 (S.C.).

162   *Hedley v. Hedley* (1989), 22 R.F.L. (3d) 309 (B.C.C.A.).

163   *Zimmer v. Zimmer* (1989), 90 N.S.R. (2d) 243, 230 A.P.R. 243 (S.C.).

164   *Grams v. Grams*, [2004] B.C.J. No. 28 (S.C.); see also *Sylvestre v. Sylvestre*, [2004] B.C.J. No. 1813 (S.C.).

165   *Romanoff v. Romanoff* (1992), 41 R.F.L. (3d) 433 (Man. Q.B.); *Melanson v. Melanson* (1990), 98 N.B.R. (2d) 357, 248 A.P.R. 357 (S.C.); see also *Walsh v. Walsh* (1988), 16 R.F.L. (3d) 8 (N.B.C.A.).

166   *Faulkner v. Faulkner* (1986), 4 R.F.L. (3d) 182 (B.C.S.C.); see also *Veres v. Veres* (1987), 9 R.F.L. (3d) 447 (Ont. S.C.).

167   See *Messier v. Delage*, [1983] 2 S.C.R. 401, R.F.L. (2d) 337.

168   [1992] 3 S.C.R. 813, 43 R.F.L. (3d) 345.

homemaking spouses and the "unmitigated parsimony" of many courts in fixing the level of support that would reflect economic self-sufficiency for a dependent spouse.

Economic self-sufficiency does not signify a bare subsistence level of survival. Economic self-sufficiency is a relative term and its significance depends on the financial circumstances of the spouses during the marriage and at the time of the marriage breakdown. Subject to financial practicalities following divorce, a long-term spouse may be entitled to support sufficient to meet the cost of preserving a lifestyle not unlike that enjoyed during matrimonial cohabitation.[169] Where that is not feasible, as is frequently the case, a dependent long-term homemaking spouse should not be relegated to a significantly inferior standard of living than that enjoyed by the breadwinning spouse.[170]

Periodic spousal support will usually be denied to a young spouse who has no children and whose economic status was not materially affected by a marriage of short duration, although a modest lump sum may be ordered to compensate for any economic loss sustained.[171] The short duration of a marriage is no bar to periodic spousal and child support where a dependent spouse is unable to take full-time employment by reason of her responsibilities as the mother of a young child.

Economic self-sufficiency does not preclude an order for periodic spousal support where one of the spouses has suffered economic disadvantage in consequence of the marital role and the breakdown of the marriage. Gauging spousal support based on need is rather straightforward and arithmetically predictable. Fixing support on the basis of the amorphous notion of economic disadvantage where the disadvantage is not capable of calculation is extremely difficult but the court must do the best it can.[172]

On the dissolution of a long traditional marriage that has had a detrimental impact on the lower-income spouse's earning capacity, the quan-

---

169 *Moge v. Moge*, [1992] 3 S.C.R. 813, 43 R.F.L. (3d) 345; *Boudreau v. Brun*, [2005] N.B.J. No. 501 (C.A.); *Heinemann v. Heinemann* (1989), 91 N.S.R. (2d) 136, 20 R.F.L. (3d) 236 (S.C.A.D.); *Pettigrew v. Pettigrew*, [2006] N.S.J. No. 321 (C.A.); *Elliot v. Elliot* (1993), 48 R.F.L. (3d) 237 (Ont. C.A.); *Fisher v. Fisher*, 2008 ONCA 11, [2008] O.J. No. 38.

170 *Attwood v. Attwood*, [1968] P. 591 (Eng.); *Marcus v. Marcus*, [1977] 4 W.W.R. 458 (B.C.C.A.); *Elias v. Elias*, [2006] B.C.J. No. 146 (S.C.).

171 See *Fisher v. Giles* (1987), 75 N.S.R. (2d) 395, 186 A.P.R. 395 at 398 (Fam. Ct.), Niedermayer F.C.J., citing *Newman v. Newman* (1979), 24 N.S.R. (2d) 12, 35 A.P.R. 12 at 15 (S.C.A.D.).

172 *Higgins v. Higgins*, [2001] O.J. No. 3011 (Sup. Ct.).

tification of a spousal support order should promote similar lifestyles for both spouses until the economic disadvantages of the marriage and its breakdown can be overcome.[173]

An order for periodic spousal support, which provides for the future reduction of the designated monthly amount by one dollar for every dollar that the recipient earns in excess of $1,200 per month, provides no incentive for the recipient to return to economic self-sufficiency. To provide such an incentive, an appellate court may substitute its own order whereby the reduction in the monthly amount of spousal support shall be by one dollar for every three dollars earned in excess of $1,200 per month.[174]

H. BROAD JUDICIAL DISCRETION

As McLachlin J., as she then was, observed in *Bracklow v. Bracklow,*

> [T]he law recognizes three conceptual grounds for entitlement to spousal support: (1) compensatory; (2) contractual; and (3) non-compensatory. These three bases of support flow from the controlling statutory provisions and the relevant case law, and are more broadly animated by differing philosophies and theories of marriage and marital breakdown.[175]

As *Bracklow* further points out, the judicial role is not to select one particular model but to apply the relevant factors to the statutory objectives and strike a balance that best achieves justice in the particular case before the court.[176] Although *Moge v. Moge* placed great emphasis on the concept that spousal support should seek to redress the advantages and disadvantages arising from the marriage or its breakdown, it does not seek to reduce the issue of spousal support to a simple equation conditioned on the notion of compensation. *Moge v. Moge* confirms that there is a broad judicial discretion to determine the right to, amount, and duration of spousal support under the *Divorce Act.* This judicial discretion is exercisable having regard to the factors signified under sections 15.2(4) and 17(4.1) of the

---

173   *Moge v. Moge,* [1992] 3 S.C.R. 813 at 870; *Ross v. Ross* (1995), 168 N.B.R. (2d) 147 at 158–59 (C.A.); *Adams v. Adams,* [2003] N.B.J. No. 51 (C.A.).

174   *Carmichael v. Carmichael,* 2007 ABCA 3, [2007] A.J. No. 1.

175   [1999] 1 S.C.R. 420, 44 R.F.L. (4th) 1 at 21. See also Bruce B. Clark, "Spousal Support after *Bracklow*" (2001), 16 R.F.L. (5th) 225.

176   *MacLean v. MacLean,* [2004] N.B.J. No. 363 (Q.B.).

Divorce Act and having regard to all four of the policy objectives defined in sections 15.2(6) and 17(7). A court cannot bypass the statutory provisions nor formulate criteria that fly in the face of them. The authority to order both spousal[177] and child[178] support is statute-based. The combined application of *Moge v. Moge* and *Bracklow v. Bracklow* requires courts to be flexible and to avoid formulaic approaches to spousal support applications. There is no single model or objective that underlies spousal support orders. The governing statute, be it the *Divorce Act* or provincial legislation, is central to the right to, duration, and amount of spousal support, if any, to be ordered. It is a discretion-driven analysis that is geared towards overall fairness.[179]

On the dissolution of a long marriage, a spouse is not automatically entitled to a spousal support order solely because that spouse stayed home with the children. The right to, duration, and amount of spousal support, if any, is dependent on all the circumstances of the particular case. Spousal support in Canada is frequently referred to as (i) compensatory; (ii) contractual, or (iii) non-compensatory. These categories reflect the combined operation of sections 15.2(4) and (6) of the *Divorce Act*. The law of spousal support continues to evolve, particularly with respect to the balancing of the factors and objectives contained in these subsections to determine whether, and how much, support should be ordered. There is no magic formula for the resolution of spousal support disputes. It is a matter for the exercise of judicial discretion and is fact-driven. The following principles may nevertheless be extrapolated from the judgments of the Supreme Court of Canada in *Moge v. Moge*,[180] and *Bracklow v. Bracklow*:[181] (i) The focus of the inquiry is on the economic consequences of the marriage for each spouse. (ii) There is no single model of support and no stipulated objective is paramount. The right to support and its quantum involve a balancing of all the factors and objectives specified in section 15.2 of the *Divorce Act*. This involves analysis of a wide range of issues, such as the length of the marriage, spousal contributions, means, needs and self-sufficiency. (iii) A fair distribution of the economic consequences

---

177 *Moge v. Moge*, [1992] 3 S.C.R. 813, 43 R.F.L. (3d) 345.

178 *Willick v. Willick*, [1994] 3 S.C.R. 670.

179 *Dreichel v. Dreichel*, [2000] A.J. No. 664 (Q.B.); *Fritz v. Day*, [2001] A.J. No. 281 (Q.B.); *Connor v. Rakievich*, [2002] A.J. No. 206 (Q.B.); *Mason v. Mason*, [2006] N.S.J. No. 227 (S.C.). For an excellent overview of relevant criteria, see *Cymbalisty v. Cymbalisty*, [2002] M.J. No. 526 (Q.B.), Beard J.

180 [1992] 3 S.C.R. 813, 43 R.F.L. (3d) 345.

181 [1999] 1 S.C.R. 420.

of the marriage through the medium of spousal support does not require a detailed accounting of the spousal day-to-day financial and other contributions to their married life nor does it require expert evidence as to the economic consequences of the marriage. Courts are entitled to take judicial notice of the economic effects of the division of labour during the marriage when the spouses divorce. A spouse's homemaking contributions and child-care responsibilities are highly relevant in terms of their ongoing economic impact on the spouses after the divorce but they must be addressed in the context of all of the attendant circumstances that fall within the ambit of sections 15.2(4) and (6) of the *Divorce Act*. Applications for retroactive and prospective spousal support should take account of the assets, income, and earning capacity of the spouses following the breakdown of the marriage. Lump sum retroactive spousal support orders made after or contemporaneously with an order dividing matrimonial property can be especially problematic in that the payment of lump sum spousal support has an impact on the property that would or should have been available for division. The global means and current net worth of the spouses must be considered when determining the right to and quantum of spousal support, if any, in light of the factors and objectives specified in sections 15.2(4) and (6) of the *Divorce Act*.[182]

I. OVERARCHING PRINCIPLE OF EQUITABLE SHARING

Moge v. Moge provides a comprehensive rationale for all four of the statutory objectives of spousal support orders by endorsing the overarching principle of an equitable sharing of the economic consequences of marriage and divorce.[183] Such a sharing can be achieved by spousal property division, or by spousal support, or child support, or any combination thereof. In order to achieve an equitable distribution of economic resources on or after divorce, it is necessary to consider the circumstances of the parties as they existed during the marriage and at the time of the application for support or variation, and as they may reasonably be expected to emerge in the future.[184]

---

182 *Corbeil v. Corbeil*, [2001] A.J. No. 1144 (C.A.).

183 *MacLean v. MacLean*, [2004] N.B.J. No. 363 (C.A.).

184 *Smyth v. Smyth* (1993), 48 R.F.L. (3d) 280 (Alta. Q.B.); *Beaulac v. Beaulac*, [2005] S.J. No. 15 (Q.B.).

The overarching principle in *Moge v. Moge* that spousal support orders should seek to achieve an equitable distribution of the economic consequences of the marriage and its breakdown applies not only to the amount of a spousal support order but also to its duration.[185]

When spouses divorce after a long marriage during which they jointly developed a successful business in addition to sharing the responsibilities of child rearing, a substantial property settlement may fall short of an equitable distribution of the economic consequences of the marriage and its breakdown, if one spouse is left in control of the business and continues to earn a substantial income, whereas the other spouse is unable to find alternative employment and receives a significantly lower income from investing the property settlement. On the dissolution of such a marriage, the lower-income spouse may be granted a spousal support order in an amount that reflects the lifestyle enjoyed during matrimonial cohabitation and provides a standard of living that is not substantially inferior to that enjoyed by the higher income spouse.[186]

On an application for a spousal support order brought pursuant to section 15.2 of the *Divorce Act*, it may be unproductive to characterize the marriage as traditional or non-traditional. Instead, a functional analysis should be undertaken by examining the choices that the spouses made and their economic consequences. A wife who postponed her career aspirations to advance those of her husband may be entitled to substantial periodic spousal support for an indefinite term, where their marital roles resulted in ongoing economic disparity between the spouses in terms of their future earning capacity on the dissolution of their long marriage. The fact that the wife will continue to earn a reasonable annual income after the divorce does not preclude an order for permanent periodic spousal support because of her alleged self-sufficiency, where the economic consequences of the marriage and its breakdown continue to operate to the husband's advantage and to the wife's disadvantage after their divorce.[187]

---

185 *MacDonald v. MacDonald*, [2004] N.S.J. No. 488 (C.A.).
186 *Brown v. Rae*, [2001] A.J. No. 1516 (Q.B.).
187 *Allaire v. Allaire*, [2003] O.J. No. 1069 (C.A.).

J. NEEDS AND CAPACITY TO PAY NOT EXCLUDED BY COMPENSATORY MODEL

The judgment of L'Heureux-Dubé J. in *Moge v. Moge* endorses the concept of an equitable redistribution of resources, rather than a fixed compensation model. If the notion of compensation were regarded as paramount, this would fly in the face of the four objectives identified in the *Divorce Act* and could prove prejudicial rather than beneficial to spouses in certain cases, especially those where sickness or disability exists. It would also open the door to spousal misconduct, which is explicitly rejected as a relevant consideration by sections 15(6) and 17(6) of the *Divorce Act*.

As is amply demonstrated by *Bracklow v. Bracklow*, needs and capacity to pay as the basis of spousal support have not been superseded by the notion of compensatory support. They have been complemented by it.[188] As *Moge v. Moge* categorically points out, there are four objectives of spousal support set out in the *Divorce Act* — not one, not two, not three, but four. Every case must be reviewed in light of the potential applicability of each and all of these objectives. *Moge v. Moge* pays special attention to the disservice to women that has resulted from undue emphasis being placed on the self-sufficiency objective defined in paragraphs 15.2(6)(d) and 17(7)(d) of the *Divorce Act*. Lawyers and judges must avoid moving from one extreme to another. A compensatory model of spousal support, like that of deemed self-sufficiency, if applied as the sole criterion of spousal support, would provoke more problems than solutions. The concept of compensatory support espoused in *Moge v. Moge* was intended to foster a more equitable distribution of economic rights on divorce. It was not intended to provide a straitjacket where litigants, lawyers, and courts would debate the legitimacy of so-called expert valuations of the losses and gains flowing from marriage or its breakdown nor was it intended to exclude the possibility of spousal support orders on bases other than compensation. Needs and means (or the ability to pay) have not been relegated to an inferior status by the notion of compensatory support.[189]

---

188 [1999] 1 S.C.R. 420, 44 R.F.L. (4th) 1. See also *Ross v. Ross* (1995), 16 R.F.L. (4th) 1 (N.B.C.A.); *Robinson v. Robinson* (1993), 48 R.F.L. (3d) 265 (Ont. C.A.); *Tweel v. Tweel* (1994), 7 R.F.L. (4th) 204 (P.E.I.S.C.T.D.).

189 *Bracklow v. Bracklow*, [1999] 1 S.C.R. 420, 44 R.F.L. (4th) 1. See also *Colp (Silmarie) v. Colp* (1994), 1 R.F.L. (4th) 161 (N.S.C.A.) where, on an application to vary, Hallet J.A. found that, while the disadvantages and advantages arising from the marriage and its breakdown had been addressed, support was nevertheless appropriate based on the recipient spouse's dire need and the other spouse's ability to pay.

Even if compensatory-based spousal support is no longer appropriate, ongoing needs-based spousal support may be required where a divorced wife would be left with no viable means of support and the divorced husband has the continuing ability to pay.[190] As McLachlin J., as she then was, observed in *Bracklow v. Bracklow*,

> Judges must exercise their discretion in light of the objectives of spousal orders as set out in section 15.2(6), and after having considered all the factors set out in section 15.2(4) of the *Divorce Act*. By directing that the judge consider factors like need and ability to pay ..., the *Divorce Act* left in place the possibility of non-compensatory support.[191]

Professor Christine Davies has stated that "[c]ompensatory and needs-based support have different philosophical bases and should be kept apart."[192] This statement may be consistent with some, but not all, of the observations of McLachlin J. in *Bracklow v. Bracklow*.[193] It is open to question, however, whether such pigeon-holing is realistic, or even conceptually sound, under the express provisions of the *Divorce Act*, bearing in mind that, as Professor Davies correctly points out, "[s]pousal support is from first to last a matter of statutory interpretation."[194] That being the case, it is unfortunate that commentators and the courts have frequently failed to discriminate between the "factors" designated by section 15.2(4) of the *Divorce Act* that must be taken into consideration by the court and the "objectives" or goals that should be achieved by spousal support orders. Compensatory considerations do not so readily lend themselves to monetary assessment as needs-based support. Whether needs are measured by reference to a subsistence level, or by reference to the standard of living enjoyed during cohabitation, or by seeking to equalize the income of the spouses on the dissolution of marriage, there is a specific financial pool that can be readily divided in accordance with the governing criterion. The attribution of monetary values to perceived advantages and disadvantages arising from the marriage or its breakdown is much more elusive, if not illusory, in most cases. Furthermore, the justification for needs-based support is usually premised on the notion that it is a right

---

190   *Stier v. Stier*, [2004] B.C.J. No. 2343 (S.C.).
191   [1999] 1 S.C.R. 420, 44 R.F.L. (4th) 1 at 22.
192   "Spousal Support under the *Divorce Act*: From *Moge* to *Bracklow*" (1999), 44 R.F.L. (4th) 61 at 62.
193   [1999] 1 S.C.R. 420, 44 R.F.L. (4th) 1.
194   *Ibid.* at 61 (R.F.L.).

that has been earned in consequence of the division of functions between the spouses during the marriage and the ongoing child-rearing functions that survive divorce. In other words, though needs-based, it is also compensatory in character. For these reasons, this author would qualify the suggestion of McLachlin J., as she then was, in *Bracklow v. Bracklow* that the starting point of the inquiry is to address "the objectives which the *Divorce Act* stipulates the support order should serve."[195] Instead the court should first address the factors under section 15.2(4) of the *Divorce Act* that "the court shall take into consideration." As Bastarache J.A., as he then was, pointed out in *Ross v. Ross,* "It is in cases where it is not possible to determine the extent of the economic loss of the disadvantaged spouse that the court will consider need and standard of living as the primary criteria, together with the ability to pay of the other party."[196] And those cases are the norm.

K. IMPLICATIONS OF CHILD CARE DURING MARRIAGE AND AFTER DIVORCE

Sections 15.2(6)(b) and 17(7)(b) of the *Divorce Act* seek to equitably apportion the financial consequences of child rearing between divorcing or divorced spouses by means of spousal support insofar as those consequences are not dealt with by child support orders. As L'Heureux-Dubé J. observed in *Moge v. Moge,*[197] a woman's ability to support herself after divorce is often significantly affected by her role as primary caregiver to the children both during the marriage and after the divorce. Her sacrifices include loss of training, workplace security and seniority, absence of pension and insurance plans and decreased salary levels. These losses may arise from the woman's role as primary caregiver, regardless of whether or not she was employed outside the home.

---

195   *Ibid.* at 26 (R.F.L.).
196   [1995] N.B.J. No. 463 at para. 15 (C.A.).
197   [1992] 3 S.C.R. 813 at 867–69 citing *Brockie v. Brockie* (1987), 5 R.F.L. (3d) 440 (Man. Q.B.), Bowman J., aff'd (1987), 8 R.F.L. (3d) 302 (Man. C.A.). See also *Gale v. Gale,* [2002] M.J. No. 177 (C.A.); *Anderson v. Anderson,* [2002] M.J. No. 176 (C.A.); *J.H.A. v. C.G.A.,* [2008] M.J. No. 94 (Q.B.); *Snodgrass v. Snodgrass,* [2004] N.B.J. No. 27 (Q.B.); *Ierullo v. Ierullo,* [2006] O.J. No. 3912 (C.A.).

L. ALLEVIATION OF FEMINIZATION OF POVERTY

On marriage breakdown and divorce, poverty is usually associated with parenting responsibilities, whether past or present. Divorced women often shoulder both economic and parenting burdens. This must be borne in mind with respect to spousal support under sections 15.2(6)(a), (b), and (c) and 17(7)(a), (b), and (c) of the *Divorce Act*. As L'Heureux-Dubé J. has stated extra-judicially, "Through judicial discretion, these objectives must be interpreted and applied in a way that does not perpetuate the feminization of poverty and further diminish the economic condition of women after divorce."[198]

M. NO PAT FORMULA

For the purpose of determining the amount of spousal support to be ordered pursuant to section 15.2 of the *Divorce Act*, the court may impute income to one or both of the spouses. The court may find it appropriate to impute investment income to the applicant in light of the attendant circumstances, including rental income and tax write-offs relating thereto and a prospective equalization payment. However, the court may refuse to impute employment income where the applicant's historical and current child-care responsibilities render it impractical for her to pursue employment opportunities for some time, even though future part-time employment is judicially envisaged once the demands of the children have diminished.[199]

Section 18 of the *Federal Child Support Guidelines* empowers a court to include corporate profits in the income of a parent who has control over whether dividends are paid and what corporate earnings will be retained. There is no reason why the principles enunciated in section 18 of the Guidelines and in case law interpreting that section should not apply to spousal support as well. If a court decides to exercise its discretion to include corporate profits in the obligor's income for spousal support purposes, the extent to which such profits should be imputed to the obligor will be determined by the individual facts of the case.[200]

---

198   Justice Claire L'Heureux-Dubé, "Economic Consequences of Divorce: A View from Canada" (1994) 31 Hous. L. Rev. 451 at 489.

199   *Brophy v. Brophy*, [2002] O.J. No. 3658 (Sup. Ct.); compare *Marshall v. Marshall*, [2002] O.J. No. 3653 (Sup. Ct.).

200   *Brophy v. Brophy, ibid.*

There is no general philosophy that spousal support should be assessed in an amount that will equalize the incomes of the spouses or their respective households, after due account is taken of existing child support obligations. Any such general approach would impose a superficial response to a complex problem, whereas the law must seek to balance competing interests in light of the diverse factors and objectives specified in the applicable legislation.[201] Of course, an equalization of incomes may sometimes be appropriate after due regard is paid to the income, assets, means, and needs of the spouses. Such a result tends to occur more frequently on the dissolution of long traditional marriages involving spouses of low income who have little or no future earning potential.[202] It may also be appropriate in circumstances involving middle-income spouses where the differential between their respective incomes is perceived as attributable to the career sacrifices made by one spouse by virtue of homemaking and child-rearing responsibilities assumed during the marriage or on its dissolution.

N. EFFECT OF SEPARATION AGREEMENT OR CONSENT ORDER ON SUBSEQUENT APPLICATION FOR SPOUSAL SUPPORT

By a majority of seven to two, the Supreme Court of Canada in *Miglin v. Miglin*[203] endorsed the following principles to be judicially applied pursuant to section 15.2 of the *Divorce Act* when a spousal support order is sought that would override the provisions of a pre-existing spousal agreement.

(i) The courts retain a supervisory jurisdiction to determine whether an order for spousal support should be granted pursuant to sections 15.2 or 17 of the *Divorce Act* in the face of a purportedly final spousal agreement or consent order.[204]

---

201 *Lockyer v. Lockyer*, [2000] O.J. No. 2939 (Sup. Ct.); see also *Creelman v. Creelman*, [2000] P.E.I.J. No. 86 (S.C.).

202 *Lockyer v. Lockyer, ibid.*

203 [2003] 1 S.C.R. 303. See Carol Rogerson, "The Legacy of *Miglin*: Are Spousal Support Agreements Final?" and H. Hunter Phillips, "The Legacy of *Miglin*: A Practitioner's Response" in The Law Society of Upper Canada, *Special Lectures 2006: Family Law* (Toronto: Irwin Law, 2007) at 119–34 and 135–52 respectively.

204 *B.G.D. v. R.W.D.*, [2003] B.C.J. No. 1098 (C.A.).

(ii) The narrow test imposed by the *Pelech* trilogy under the 1968 *Divorce Act* is inappropriate under the 1986 *Divorce Act*. The provisions of a spousal agreement that limits the amount or duration of spousal support or waives any right to spousal support may be overridden by an order for spousal support granted pursuant to section 15.2 of the *Divorce Act* on grounds that are somewhat broader than those defined in the *Pelech* trilogy. It is no longer necessary for the applicant who seeks a support order under that section to prove that there has been a radical and unforeseen change of circumstances that generates a need for spousal support that is causally connected to the roles assumed by the spouses during their marriage. The emphasis of the *Pelech* trilogy on economic self-sufficiency and a clean break is inconsistent with the current model of compensatory support espoused in *Moge v. Moge*[205] and the conceptual analysis of compensatory and non-compensatory support in *Bracklow v. Bracklow*.[206] Economic self-sufficiency, nevertheless, remains as one of the objectives of spousal support orders and the policy of encouraging spouses to resolve their disputes by agreement remains of vital importance.

(iii) Although a material change in the condition, means, needs, or other circumstances of either of the former spouses is a threshold requirement on an application to vary a pre-existing spousal support order pursuant to section 17 of the *Divorce Act*, no similar prerequisite applies where an original order for spousal support is sought pursuant to section 15.2 of the *Divorce Act*. In the latter context, a change of circumstances since the execution of a pre-existing spousal agreement has no relevance except with respect to its impact when the court has regard to "any order, agreement or arrangement relating to support of either spouse" as required by section 15.2(4)(b) of the *Divorce Act*.

(iv) Where an application for spousal support under section 15.2 of the *Divorce Act* is inconsistent with a pre-existing spousal agreement, the court should examine the agreement in two stages. First, the agreement should be reviewed in light of the circumstances that existed at the time of its negotiation and execution. As of this date, the court should ascertain whether one spouse was vulnerable and whether the other spouse took advantage of that vulnerability. In assessing the issue of vulnerability, the court need not adhere to the stringent

---

205 [1992] 3 S.C.R. 813, 43 R.F.L. (3d) 345.
206 [1999] 1 S.C.R. 420, 44 R.F.L. (4th) 1.

requirements of the doctrine of unconscionability that are applied to commercial transactions. Vulnerability and an imbalance of power should not be assumed, however, in the absence of evidence of a fundamental flaw in the negotiation process. The existence of emotional stress on separation or divorce should not be judicially perceived as negating the ability of the spouses to freely negotiate a mutually acceptable agreement. Any systemic imbalance of power between spouses will usually, but not always,[207] be overcome if each spouse has independent legal representation. After addressing the circumstances attendant on the execution of the agreement, the contents of the spousal agreement should be examined as of the date of its execution to see whether they substantially comply with the overall objectives of the *Divorce Act*, which include an equitable sharing of the economic consequences of the marriage and its breakdown in accordance with section 15.2(6) of the *Divorce Act* and the promotion of certainty, autonomy, and finality that is implicitly acknowledged by section 9(2) of the *Divorce Act*. Where the spousal agreement is unimpeachable as of the date of its execution, the court will pursue the second stage of its inquiry by examining the spousal agreement in light of the facts existing at the time of the application for a support order under section 15.2 of the *Divorce Act*. As of that date, the court should determine whether the applicant has established that the agreement no longer reflects the original intention of the spouses and whether it is still in compliance with the overall objectives of the *Divorce Act*.[208] In this context, the applicant must show that new circumstances have arisen that were not reasonably anticipated by the spouses when their agreement was executed and that these changes have led to a situation that cannot be condoned. Changes that occur in the ordinary course of people's lives, such as health problems, changes in the job market, business upswings or downturns, remarriage, or increased parenting responsibilities will not justify judicial interference with a final spousal settlement. It is only where the current circumstances represent a significant departure from the range of reasonable outcomes anticipated by the spouses, in a manner that puts them at odds with the overall objectives of the *Divorce Act*, that

---

207 *Gauthier v. Gauthier*, [2004] O.J. No. 4698 (C.A.); *Gammon v. Gammon*, [2008] O.J. No. 603 (Sup. Ct.). See also *Rogerson v. Rogerson*, [2004] N.S.J. No. 152 (S.C.) (waiver of spousal support vitiated where wife not legally represented).

208 *D.K.N. v. M.J.O.*, [2003] B.C.J. No. 2164 (C.A.); *R.S.M. v. M.S.M.*, [2006] B.C.J. No. 1756 (C.A.).

the court may be persuaded to give little weight to the agreement on the application for a spousal support order under section 15.2 of the *Divorce Act*.[209] The co-existence of diverse competing and conflicting objectives under the *Divorce Act* manifests Parliament's intention to vest a significant discretion in trial judges to assess the weight to be given to each objective against the particular backdrop of the spouses' circumstances. However, the objectives of spousal support orders that are set out in section 15.2(6) of the *Divorce Act* do not confer an unfettered discretion on trial judges to substitute their own view of what is required for that which the spouses found mutually acceptable. A court should be loath to interfere with a pre-existing spousal agreement, unless the court is convinced that the agreement does not comply substantially with the overall objectives of the *Divorce Act*. Courts should not condone spousal agreements that are manifestly prejudicial to one spouse but, equally important, they should not stand in the way of spouses bringing their personal concerns, desires, and objectives to the bargaining table in their negotiation of a mutually acceptable agreement that they regard as balancing economic fairness with the need for certainty and finality on the dissolution of their marriage. This is especially important when spousal support provisions constitute only one aspect of a comprehensive settlement that encompasses such interrelated matters as family property division and child support. In reviewing a comprehensive settlement, the court must look beyond the parameters of section 15.2(6) of the *Divorce Act*, which is written in permissive language and is expressly confined to defining the objectives of spousal support orders. *Moge v. Moge* clearly affirms that an equitable sharing of the economic consequences of the marriage and its breakdown can be achieved by means of property division, spousal support, child support, or any combination thereof. A policy of promoting negotiated settlements is clearly endorsed by section 9(2) of the *Divorce Act*, which imposes a duty on every lawyer to discuss with his or her client the advisability of negotiating matters that may be the subject of a support or custody order. Certainty and finality that is achieved by means of freely negotiated settlements are fundamental objectives of the *Divorce Act* when it is viewed as a whole. If that were not the case and agreements could be

---

209 *Borrett v. Borrett*, [2006] B.C.J. No. 1012 (S.C.); *Kerr v. Kerr*, [2005] N.S.J. No. 593 (S.C.).

lightly set aside, spouses would have little incentive to negotiate the economic consequences of their divorce.

Applying the aforementioned principles, the judgment of the Ontario Court of Appeal granting the wife periodic support for an indefinite term was reversed by the majority judgment of the Supreme Court of Canada, which vacated the order on the basis that the wife was bound by her waiver of spousal support, which constituted one aspect of a final spousal settlement.

Where a spousal support agreement includes no expiry or review date, public policy may compel a court to intercede where the contract leaves one party in penury, but there are no public policy grounds for disturbing a contract that pays too much support or tolerates the recipient's failure to secure full-time gainful employment.[210]

Whether the spousal support provisions of a spousal agreement are contractually valid, and whether they are impeachable under the criteria defined by the Supreme Court of Canada in *Miglin v. Miglin*, are questions to be determined in a single proceeding. In determining whether the spousal support provisions of a purportedly final settlement comply with the objectives of the *Divorce Act* as defined in *Miglin*, the court must guard against analyzing particular clauses in isolation; rather, the settlement must be viewed as a whole to determine whether the spousal support provisions comply with the statutory objectives.[211]

In the post-*Miglin* era, courts have experienced no difficulty in stating the principles to be applied when a spousal support order is sought under section 15.2 of the *Divorce Act* in the face of a purportedly final settlement previously negotiated by the spouses. Where difficulty may be encountered is in the application of those principles to the facts of the particular case. This is clearly demonstrated in *Lang v. Lang*[212] wherein the majority judgment of Hamilton J.A., with whom Scott C.J.M. concurred, upheld the trial judge's order for ongoing spousal support for an indefinite term, whereas the minority judgment of Monnin J.A. would have allowed the husband's appeal and set aside the order that he continue to pay spousal support beyond the five-year period specified by a pre-existing separation agreement. It would be comforting if the conflicting opinions espoused in the majority and minority judgments in *Lang v. Lang* could be explained by the fact that the trial judgment preceded *Miglin* whereas the

---

210 *Schultz v. Schultz*, [2002] A.J. No. 1493 (C.A.).
211 *S.M. c. S.K.*, [2006] J.Q. no 778 (C.A.).
212 [2003] M.J. No. 463 (C.A.).

Manitoba Court of Appeal had to review the trial judge's reasons in light of the *Miglin* criteria. Such comfort may be misplaced. Although post-*Miglin* decisions have manifested a strong reluctance to interfere with final settlements, the weighing of contractual autonomy, certainty, and finality as an objective of the *Divorce Act* against the objective of promoting an equitable distribution of the economic consequences of the marriage and its breakdown is not an easy task, even when both spouses are represented by competent lawyers throughout the entire negotiation process. If spouses have not previously sought independent legal advice, the finality of an unfair "kitchen table" agreement may be readily disturbed by an order for spousal support on the basis that the agreement fails to reflect the financial objectives of spousal support orders under section 15.2(6) of the *Divorce Act*.

1) The Impact of the Majority Judgment

In the post-*Pelech* and pre-*Miglin* era, Canadian courts followed diverse and inconsistent paths in their treatment of applications for support orders under section 15.2 of the *Divorce Act* where the spouses had previously negotiated a purportedly final settlement. In an article by Martha Shaffer and Daniel S. Melamed,[213] which is cited in the dissenting judgment of LeBel and Deschamps JJ. in *Miglin*,[214] four basic types of approach were identified, namely,

> Cases in which courts strictly apply the *Pelech* standard, requiring a radical change causally connected to the marriage before intervening in settlement agreements;

> Cases in which courts purport to apply the *Pelech* standard, but in fact apply a standard that is less stringent;

> Cases in which courts explicitly reject the trilogy standard in favour of some other variation standard, for instance applying a lower threshold such as material or substantial change or endorsing the minority opinion in *G.(L.) v. B.(G.)*, and determining whether to intervene in an agreement by having regard to the extent to which it meets the objectives in s. 15.2 of the *Divorce Act*; and

---

213   M. Shaffer & D.S. Melamed, "Separation Agreements Post-*Moge, Willick* and *L.G. v. G.B.*: A New Trilogy?" (1999) 16 Can. J. Fam. L. 51.

214   [2003] 1 S.C.R. 303 at para. 169.

Cases in which courts have shown an increased willingness to adopt a broad definition of change, defining for instance as a "change" the parties' failed expectations where the dependent spouse does not achieve the predicted economic self-sufficiency.

None of these alternative approaches will be tenable in future. The majority judgment in *Miglin* defines the parameters governing judicial intervention today. Up to this point in time, courts have exhibited a strong disinclination to disturb the support provisions of a purportedly final and comprehensive spousal settlement in light of the principles of contractual autonomy endorsed in the majority judgment in *Miglin*.[215]

2) Future Ramifications of *Miglin*

a) Finality of Spousal Agreement

The fundamental significance of the majority judgment in *Miglin* relates to purportedly final spousal agreements that either limit the amount or duration of spousal support or waive it absolutely. Because final settlements envisage no future adjustments, spouses are expected to consider and guard against foreseeable changes such as increases or decreases in income that may occur in the future and changes of this nature cannot ordinarily be relied upon as a basis for the court to override the agreement or settlement by an order for spousal support that is inconsistent with its terms. However, if minutes of settlement expressly provide that spousal support payments may be varied by reason of a material change of circumstances, the stringent criteria that attach to purportedly final settlements under *Miglin v. Miglin* will be inapplicable.[216] Furthermore, where the minutes of settlement expressly provide for the variation of child support and spousal support if a material change of circumstances occurs, a spouse whose financial circumstances thereafter change as a result of the exercise of stock options and a substantial increase in salary may owe an implied obligation to notify the other spouse of the changes and a failure to do so may justify orders for retroactive child support and retroactive spousal support to a date preceding that on which an applica-

---

215 See, for example, *Borrett v. Borrett*, [2006] B.C.J. No. 1012 (S.C.); *Kerr v. Kerr*, [2005] N.S.J. No. 593 (S.C.); *Stening-Riding v. Riding*, [2006] N.S.J. No. 295 (S.C.); compare *Routley v. Paget*, [2006] B.C.J. No. 554 (S.C.) (prenuptial agreement).

216 *Stones v. Stones*, [2004] B.C.J. No. 378 (C.A.); *Marinangeli v. Marinangeli*, [2003] O.J. No. 2819 (C.A.); *Poitras v. Poitras*, [2006] S.J. No. 113 (Q.B.). See also *Katz v. Katz*, [2004] M.J. No. 206 (C.A.); *Henteleff v. Henteleff*, 2005 MBCA 50; compare *Gobeil v. Gobeil*, [2007] M.J. No. 19 (C.A.).

tion is made to the court.[217] If periodic spousal support payments under a separation agreement and subsequent consent order are based on the obligor's overly optimistic appraisal of his future annual income and the separation agreement and consent order envisage variation in the event of a material change of circumstances, an order for the termination of spousal support may be upheld on appeal if the obligor's business reversals result in an incapacity to pay ongoing spousal support.[218]

When a separation agreement provides for a review of spousal support, the agreement is only one of the factors to be considered under section 15.2(4) of the *Divorce Act*. In reviewing the diverse factors identified in that section, the court must also have regard to the four objectives of spousal support orders under section 15.2(6) of the *Divorce Act*.[219]

A spouse who seeks to rely upon a negotiated settlement must establish, as a preliminary matter, that its provisions were intended to constitute a final and binding determination of the matters with which they deal. In ascertaining the intention of the spouses, the court will have regard to all the attendant circumstances. The intention may be manifested by express terms of the settlement, for example, by the use of a "no variation clause" or by the inclusion of an automatic escalator clause coupled with an exchange of mutual releases. A court may also conclude that the parties have inextricably intertwined the settlement of property matters and the issue of spousal support in such a way as to demonstrate intended finality. Where the terms of the agreement or minutes of settlement are not perceived as constituting a binding and final determination (as, for example, where the agreement either includes the words "or until further order," contains a variation clause, provides for review after a period of time, has undergone several variations, or provides for nominal support with the intention of preserving the right to re-apply for support), the court is free to exercise its statutory jurisdiction to order spousal support in light of a material change in the circumstances of the parties since the execution of the agreement or minutes of settlement.[220]

A final agreement is one that is intended by the parties to govern all aspects of their future economic relationship; contemplation of variation in the amount of support does not necessarily deprive the agreement of

---

217 *Marinangeli v. Marinangeli, ibid.*

218 *Kehler v. Kehler,* [2003] M.J. No. 217 (C.A.).

219 *McEachern v. McEachern,* [2006] B.C.J. No. 2917 (C.A.).

220 *Drewery v. Drewery* (1986), 50 R.F.L. (2d) 373 (Ont. U.F.C.).

its finality if the changes or the mechanism to effect changes are defined in the document.[221]

Where an agreement contains contradictory paragraphs as to its finality, the court should presume that its jurisdiction remains unfettered.[222]

b) Applicability of *Miglin* to Payors and Payees

The principles formulated by the majority in *Miglin* are conceptually gender neutral and apply equally to payors and payees. In practice, men will fare better than women under *Miglin* because men are typically payors and women are typically payees and finality usually favours the former group. In addition, the principles set out in *Miglin* are inevitably subject to the practicability of the payor's retention of an ability to pay.

c) Retrospective Implications of *Miglin*

Soon after the *Pelech* trilogy came down, the Manitoba Court of Appeal asserted that a separation agreement executed before the trilogy was no bar to a spousal support order because the applicable law concerning the mutability of spousal agreements is to be determined by reference to the date of the agreement.[223] Given the subsequent emergence of a wide diversity of judicial opinions on the impact of spousal settlements on subsequent applications for spousal support orders under the *Divorce Act*,[224] the reasoning of the Manitoba Court of Appeal would be virtually impossible to apply today. Consequently, the majority judgment in *Miglin* will be applied retroactively to final agreements that were negotiated before the Supreme Court of Canada's judgment came down.[225]

d) Non-Cohabitation Covenants

In a bygone era, separation agreements frequently included a "*dum casta et sola*" clause, whereby periodic spousal support payments following separation or divorce would cease if the recipient spouse or former spouse committed adultery or remarried. No difficulty was encountered in the interpretation and application of these clauses. By the late 1970s, however,

---

221   *Tully v. Tully* (1993), 49 R.F.L. (3d) 31 (Ont. Gen. Div.).

222   *Debacker v. Debacker* (1993), 49 R.F.L. (3d) 106 at 113 (Alta. Q.B.).

223   *Horn v. Horn* (1987), 11 R.F.L. (3d) 23 (Man. C.A.); *Weir v. Weir* (1987), 12 R.F.L. (3d) 160 (Man. C.A.).

224   M. Shaffer & D.S. Melamed, "Separation Agreements Post-*Moge, Willick* and *L.G. v. G.B.*: A New Trilogy?" (1999) 16 Can. J. Fam. L. 51.

225   See *Lang v. Lang*, [2003] M.J. No. 463 (C.A.); *Marks v. Tokarewicz*, [2004] O.J. No. 92 (C.A.).

they had fallen into disfavour, at least so far as the *dum casta* (chastity) component was concerned. In 1978, *dum casta* clauses were declared void under the Ontario *Family Law Reform Act*. Section 56(2) of the Ontario *Family Law Act*, R.S.O. 1990, c. F.3, which can be traced back to the 1978 Act, currently provides that "[a] provision in a domestic contract to take effect on separation whereby any right of a party is dependent upon remaining chaste is unenforceable, but this subsection shall not be construed to affect a contingency upon marriage or cohabitation with another." The *dum casta* clause thus became displaced by a "non-cohabitation" clause, which would typically refer to a "marriage-like relationship," or to "living with another man as husband and wife," or to "an unmarried cohabitational relationship," or to a "common-law relationship."

Unlike the term "*dum casta*," which is self-explanatory, problems of interpretation and application have arisen with the new phraseology. The question whether a spouse is "cohabiting" or living in a "common-law relationship" to use the modern, if somewhat inaccurate, idiom is far more complex than whether they have remained chaste. In order to determine whether parties are "cohabiting" or living in a "common-law relationship," the court must analyze the nature, quality, and duration of the relationship. Sexual intercourse between two persons, even while living under the same roof, may fall short of "cohabitation" or a "common-law relationship." In *Molodowich v. Penttinen*,[226] Kurisko D.C.J., of the Ontario District Court, formulated a seven-stage test for determining whether cohabitation exists. This test was recently applied by Noonan J., of the Newfoundland and Labrador Unified Family Court, in *Evely v. Evely*.[227] In this case, the wife's sexual relationship with a man who had been living with her for several months in the former matrimonial home was found not to constitute a "common-law relationship" that would terminate her right to periodic spousal support under a pre-existing separation agreement, because there was no evidence of any long-term commitment between the parties and the attendant circumstances were indicative of the absence of any close socio-economic partnership. Even if a "common-law relationship" had been found to exist, it is by no means obvious that the wife would have lost all rights to statutory spousal support, as distinct from contractual spousal support. In the post-*Miglin* era, a wife who has lost a right to spousal support under the terms of a pre-existing separation agreement is not automatically disentitled to seek an order for spousal support under

---

226 (1980), 17 R.F.L. (2d) 376 (Ont. Dist. Ct.); see Chapter 3, Section D.
227 [2003] N.J. No. 85 (U.F.C.).

section 15.2 of the *Divorce Act*. In *Bakes v. Bakes*,[228] the spouses executed a separation agreement whereby the husband's obligation to pay periodic spousal support would terminate upon the wife's "cohabiting in a common-law relationship." After citing *Molodowich v. Penttinen*,[229] Scanlan J., of the Nova Scotia Supreme Court, observed that the legal test for determining whether a couple is living in a "common-law relationship" must be determined on an objective standard, having regard to the degree of commitment between the parties combined with the length of the relationship and their socio-economic interaction. On the facts, Scanlan J. concluded that a "common-law relationship" did exist so as to terminate the wife's right to contractual support. It became necessary, therefore, to consider her statutory entitlement, if any, to a spousal support order under section 15.2 of the *Divorce Act*, having regard to the two-step process defined by the Supreme Court of Canada in *Miglin v. Miglin*. Applying the first step in *Miglin*, Scanlan J. reviewed the separation agreement as a whole at the time of its negotiation and execution. After reviewing its terms, including those relating to the division of matrimonial assets, the assumption of debts, spousal support, and child support, Scanlan J. concluded that the separation agreement was initially far more advantageous to the wife than to the husband who had assumed extremely onerous obligations to the subsequent prejudice of his physical and mental health. Consequently, the wife who, unlike the husband, had been legally represented during the negotiations, could not complain of oppression, pressure, or vulnerability at the time of the execution of the separation agreement. Scanlan J. then proceeded to the second step articulated in *Miglin*, which requires the court to review the separation agreement at the time of the divorce in light of any changed circumstances and the objectives of the *Divorce Act*, which encompass the promotion of autonomy, certainty, and finality with respect to spousal agreements as well as an equitable sharing of the economic consequences of the marriage and its breakdown as envisaged by the four objectives of spousal support orders that are specifically identified in section 15.2(6) of the *Divorce Act*. In this case, there was one substantial change in circumstance that existed at the time of divorce. The wife's health had deteriorated to the point where it might have a long-term impact on her earning capacity. In this context, Scanlan J. cited paragraph 89 in *Miglin* wherein the Supreme Court of Canada observed that negotiating spouses should know that

---

228 [2003] N.S.J. No. 202 (S.C.).
229 (1980), 17 R.F.L. (2d) 376 (Ont. Dist. Ct.).

their health may deteriorate and such a change is unlikely to be sufficient for a court to override the terms of a purportedly final separation agreement by granting an order for spousal support pursuant to section 15.2 of the *Divorce Act*. After adverting to the fact that the wife's "common-law spouse" could be reasonably expected to make a greater contribution to their common household expenses, Scanlan J. observed that there was nothing inherent in the twenty-year marriage or the roles assumed by the spouses during their marriage that warranted spousal support being paid to the wife indefinitely. Scanlan J. then found that the terms of the separation agreement, which provided generous financial provision for the wife initially, while providing for the termination of spousal support when she formed a "common-law relationship," did not represent a significant departure from the range of reasonable spousal expectations so as to put them at odds with the objectives of the *Divorce Act*. Accordingly, the provisions of the separation agreement were judicially upheld and the husband's spousal support obligation was terminated in accordance with its terms.

e) Effect of Separation Agreement on Interim Orders

Although similar considerations apply to both interim and permanent orders for corollary financial relief granted pursuant to section 15.2 of the *Divorce Act*, courts are especially reluctant to order interim support where a separation agreement has been freely entered into by the spouses and it provides a reasonable standard of living pending trial.[230]

Where the validity of the separation agreement is impugned and only a trial can resolve the matter, an order for interim spousal support is not precluded,[231] but a court must be careful not to pre-judge the issue where, as is often the case in interim proceedings, there is insufficient evidence to determine the issues necessary for a proper *Miglin* analysis.[232] The objective of interim orders is to adjust the situations of the parties so that their immediate requirements are met with as little prejudice to the ultimate outcome as possible. An interim spousal support order may be

---

230 *Hubbell v. Hubbell* (1984), 43 R.F.L. (2d) 94 (B.C.C.A.) citing *Macy v. Macy* (1984), 40 R.F.L. (2d) 11 (Ont. C.A.); *Trinchan v. Trinchan* (1983), 34 R.F.L. (2d) 331 (Ont. C.A.); compare *Ziniuk v. Ziniuk* (1986), 2 R.F.L. (3d) 398 at 401 (B.C.C.A.).

231 *Desimone v. Desimone* (1993), 48 R.F.L. (3d) 161 (B.C.S.C.); *Kerr v. Kerr*, [2003] B.C.J. No. 1890 (S.C.); *Carlsen v. Carlsen* (1990), 25 R.F.L. (3d) 461 (Ont. H.C.J.); *Salzmann v. Salzmann*, [2004] O.J. No. 166 (Sup. Ct.).

232 *Palmer v. Palmer*, 2003 SKQB 438, [2003] S.J. No. 671; *Hill v. Hill*, [2008] S.J. No. 3 (Q.B.).

refused because of a mutual waiver of spousal support in a comprehensive separation agreement, where there is no suggestion of fraud, duress, undue influence, or unconscionable conduct, and the applicant signed the agreement with the benefit of independent legal advice. Such preservation of the *status quo* under the separation agreement operates without prejudice to the applicant's right to have the agreement reviewed at trial for the purpose of determining whether a permanent order for spousal support is appropriate having regard to the criteria defined in *Miglin v. Miglin*. If the applicant is successful at trial, the court may then adjust the equities between the spouses, including any hardship leading up to the trial.[233]

An interspousal agreement that purports to limit the period of time during which spousal support shall be payable does not oust the discretionary jurisdiction of the court to grant an interim spousal support order pursuant to section 15.2(2) of the *Divorce Act* after the time limit has expired. However, the discretionary jurisdiction to order interim spousal support in the face of such a covenant should only be exercised in exceptional circumstances. Although an interspousal agreement is a relevant factor for the court to consider on an application for interim spousal support by virtue of section 15.2(4) of the *Divorce Act*, a review of the agreement in light of the principles defined in *Miglin v. Miglin* is usually impractical because the court is often presented with limited and contradictory affidavit evidence at the interim stage of a proceeding. Pending trial when the circumstances surrounding the agreement can be more fully addressed, a purportedly final and comprehensive agreement that structures the spouses' affairs should ordinarily be respected and upheld. If a trial judge finds that the agreement should be set aside, a retroactive spousal support order may be appropriate.[234]

In *Chaitos v. Christopoulos*,[235] the parties executed a marriage contract two days before their wedding under which they mutually released spousal property rights under the Ontario *Family Law Act* and any rights to spousal support. Applying the first stage of a *Miglin* analysis, Sachs J. found that the circumstances attendant on the negotiation and execu-

---

233 *Rodrigues v. Rodrigues*, [2004] B.C.J. No. 1353 (S.C.).

234 *Palmer v. Palmer*, [2003] S.J. No. 671 (Q.B.). See also *Kelly v. Kelly*, [2004] O.J. No. 3108 (C.A.), wherein it was held that a motion for summary judgment under Rule 20 of the Ontario *Rules of Civil Procedure* is often poorly suited to dispose of spousal support claims that must be resolved by applying the detailed two-stage analysis required by *Miglin v. Miglin*, [2003] 1 S.C.R. 303.

235 [2004] O.J. No. 907 (Sup. Ct.).

tion of the marriage contract raised a serious issue as to its validity and enforceability. Applying the second stage of a *Miglin* analysis, Sachs J. found that the marriage contract gave the husband the lion's share of the wealth accumulated by the spouses during their marriage and, in addition, the wife's earning capacity had been detrimentally affected by the marriage breakdown. Given these findings, Sachs J. held that the marriage contract did not reflect any of the objectives set out in section 15.2(6) of the *Divorce Act*, which are applicable to interim spousal support orders. Indeed, the only objective under the *Divorce Act* that was achieved was that of certainty, finality, and autonomy and this objective, while an important one, does not negate the significance of the other objectives. For these reasons, Sachs J. determined that the waiver of spousal support in the marriage contract did not constitute a bar to the wife's application for interim spousal support. In addressing the amount of such support, having regard to the wife's needs and the husband's ability to pay, Sachs J. observed that the wife should not be expected to deplete her capital in order to reduce the husband's liability to pay interim spousal support. The husband, whose annual income was determined to be $143,000, was ordered to pay $5,000 per month as interim spousal support. On the separate issue of financial disclosure, Sachs J. stated that the requirement of full financial disclosure is not satisfied by simply filing a financial statement with figures in it. The party who files the statement has to provide a basis for the figures provided. Accordingly, the husband was directed to provide specific documentation to support the value attributed to condominiums that he owned.

f)   Effect of Marriage Contract or Cohabitation Agreement

In *Charles v. Charles*,[236] Bouck J. observed that the statutory jurisdiction of the court to order spousal support under section 15.2 of the *Divorce Act* cannot be ousted by the provisions of a premarital contract. Consequently, a court may order spousal support, notwithstanding a clause in the marriage contract whereby both parties agreed to be self-supporting in the event of a marriage breakdown. However, Bouck J. further observed that "like a separation agreement, a court should not ignore the maintenance provisions of a pre-marital agreement unless for good reason."[237] In *Miglin* the majority judgment states that "the appeal raises the question

---

236   (1991), 32 R.F.L. (3d) 316 at 328–29 (B.C.S.C.).
237   *Ibid.* at 329; see also *Culen v. Culen*, [2003] A.J. No. 680 (Q.B.); *Andrews v. Andrews* (1992), 42 R.F.L. (3d) 454 (N.S.T.D.).

of the proper weight to be given to any type of agreement"[238] that one of the spouses wishes to have modified by a spousal support order under section 15.2 of the *Divorce Act*. There are undoubtedly distinctions that can be drawn between marriage contracts, separation agreements, and minutes of settlement drawn up at the time of divorce. When spouses seek to regulate the economic consequences of an already existing marriage breakdown by negotiating a comprehensive separation agreement or minutes of settlement to determine their property rights and their support rights and obligations, courts legitimately exhibit a strong reluctance to isolate and interfere with the support provisions of that agreement.[239] Such an agreement will ordinarily have been negotiated at arm's length with independent legal advice and with knowledge of the capital assets and income-earning potential of both spouses. In contrast, where a marriage contract is negotiated prior to the marriage, an election by the spouses in favour of economic independence on the breakdown of marriage is anticipatory and may not accommodate their condition, means, needs, or other circumstances at the time of divorce.[240] A marriage contract might, therefore, carry less weight with the court than a separation agreement, if a spousal support order were subsequently sought pursuant to section 15.2 of the *Divorce Act*. This result would ensue, however, not because of any judicial refusal to extend *Miglin* to marriage contracts but because the application of *Miglin* to marriage contracts would require the court to have regard to the different circumstances attendant upon the execution of a marriage contract and those attendant upon the execution of a separation agreement or minutes of settlement.

In *Culen v. Culen*,[241] the wife's application for a spousal support order under section 15.2 of the *Divorce Act* was dismissed on the ground that such an order was inappropriate in the face of the waiver provisions of a prenuptial agreement executed with independent legal advice on the wife's initiative. In reaching this conclusion, Verville J., of the Alberta Court of Queen's Bench, applied the principles defined in *Miglin v. Miglin*, being of the opinion that "the same principles should apply when considering prenuptial agreements as apply to separation agreements." The wife's current reliance on the public purse was found to provide no basis for an order in light of her waiver of spousal support and the absence of evidence before

---

238 [2003] 1 S.C.R. 303 at para. 2.
239 See *Hartshorne v. Hartshorne*, [2004] 1 S.C.R. 550; see also Chapter 4, Section A.
240 *Roberts v. Salvador*, [2006] A.J. No. 715 at para. 72 (Q.B.).
241 [2003] A.J. No. 680 (Q.B.).

the court that the spouses had established an interdependent financial relationship during their nine years of matrimonial cohabitation. And in *Frazer v. van Rootselaar*,[242] the British Columbia Court of Appeal found no error in the trial judge's refusal to order spousal support where a waiver of such support was included in a marriage contract executed to protect the wife's capital assets.

Pursuant to section 53 of the Ontario *Family Law Act*, a cohabitation agreement shall be deemed to be a marriage contract if the cohabitants marry. Although a waiver of spousal support in the cohabitation agreement does not preclude a court order for spousal support under section 15.2 of the *Divorce Act*, the applicant's entitlement may be tempered by the provisions of the cohabitation agreement.[243]

g) Variation Orders

The spousal support provisions of a separation agreement or minutes of settlement may be incorporated in an order of the court on the pronouncement of the divorce judgment. In that event, the spouses must look to the order because it supersedes the spousal support provisions of their agreement.[244] The agreement continues to be operative and enforceable with respect to its provisions on such matters as property sharing that fall outside the jurisdiction of the court under the corollary provisions of the *Divorce Act* and cannot, therefore, be incorporated in the divorce judgment.[245]

The financial provisions of a separation agreement, including a clause that provides for full and final satisfaction and discharge of all future support obligations, may be incorporated in a divorce judgment although it is questionable whether a court has jurisdiction to grant a final order under the *Divorce Act* that precludes any future application respecting spousal support.[246] Even if a court lacks jurisdiction to bind its successors if a

---

242 [2006] B.C.J. No. 875 (C.A.).

243 *Johnston v. Burns*, [2002] O.J. No. 1805 (Sup. Ct.). Compare *L.M. v. I.M.*, [2007] N.J. No. 379 (U.F.C.).

244 *King Estate v. King* (1994), 8 R.F.L. (4th) 380 at 388 (N.B.Q.B.); *Re Finnie and Rae* (1977), 16 O.R. (2d) 54 (H.C.J.); compare *Horne v. Roberts* (1971), 5 R.F.L. 15 (B.C.S.C.); see also *McLeod v. McLeod*, [2006] A.J. No. 1663 (Q.B.).

245 *Walker v. Tymofichuk* (1984), 38 R.F.L. (2d) 330 (Alta. Q.B.); *Campbell v. Campbell* (1976), 27 R.F.L. 40 (Sask. Q.B.).

246 *Gill-Sager v. Sager*, [2003] B.C.J. No. 121 (C.A.); *B.G.D. v. R.W.D.*, [2003] B.C.J. No. 1098 (C.A.); see also *Tierney-Hynes v. Hynes*, [2005] O.J. No. 2661 (C.A.), leave to appeal to the S.C.C. refused, [2005] S.C.C.A. No. 424; see also Section R(4), below in this chapter.

subsequent application respecting spousal support were to be brought, a purportedly final consent order, such as an order for lump sum spousal support in lieu of periodic spousal support, would trigger the *Miglin* criteria on any future application for variation. Furthermore, any order, whether on consent or otherwise, which fixes the duration of spousal support for a definite period or until the occurrence of a specified event, falls subject to the additional stringent requirements imposed by section 17(10) of the *Divorce Act*, if an application to vary is brought after expiry of the order.[247] In that event, the court must be satisfied that a variation order is necessary to relieve economic hardship arising from a change that is related to the marriage and that the changed circumstances would have resulted in a different order had they occurred at the time of the making of the order that is sought to be varied.[248] Economic hardship that arises from extrinsic circumstances unconnected with the marriage, such as an involuntary loss of employment due to illness or disability or an inability to find employment before expiry of the fixed-term that is unrelated to the duration of and functions performed during the marriage and arises solely by reason of the economic climate, falls outside the protection of section 17(10) of the *Divorce Act*.[249] The more stringent criteria imposed by section 17(10) of the *Divorce Act* apply even when the purpose of the variation application is simply to extend the term of support. Where the termination date arises from spousal agreement, the original order will be assumed to have correctly and equitably redistributed the economic consequences of the marriage and its breakdown and the order will be varied only when the changed circumstances distort the equity of the original redistribution of those economic consequences when measured by the objectives defined in sections 15(7) and 17(7) of the *Divorce Act*.[250]

Pursuant to section 17(4.1) of the *Divorce Act*, it falls on the applicant to satisfy the court that there has been a change in the condition, means, needs, or other circumstances of either former spouse since the existing order was made. The court has no discretionary jurisdiction to revisit the existing order *de novo* and cannot second-guess the merits of the order that is sought to be varied.[251] Consequently, the first stage of a *Miglin* in-

---

247 *H.L. v. M.H.L.*, [2003] B.C.J. No. 2098 (C.A.).

248 *Ambler v. Ambler*, [2004] B.C.J. No. 2076 (C.A.); *Hiscock v. Dickie* (1994), 6 R.F.L. (4th) 149 (N.B.Q.B.).

249 *Paredes v. Paredes* (1992), 38 R.F.L. (3d) 267 (B.C.S.C.); *Hiscock v. Dickie, ibid.*; *Kirby v. Kirby* (1991), 31 R.F.L. (3d) 162 (N.S.T.D.).

250 *Ginn v. Ginn* (1995), 11 R.F.L. (4th) 377 (Alta. Q.B.).

251 *Oakley v. Oakley* (1985), 48 R.F.L. (2d) 307 at 313 (B.C.C.A.); *Willick v. Willick*, [1994] 3 S.C.R. 670 (child support); *B.(G.) v. G.(L.)*, [1995] 3 S.C.R. 370.

quiry, insofar as it involves a review of the spousal settlement at the time of its negotiation and execution, would seem more readily applicable to an original application for a spousal support order under section 15.2 of the *Divorce Act* than to a variation application brought pursuant to section 17 of the *Divorce Act*, unless new evidence comes to light that would vitiate the settlement as of the date of its execution. As the Ontario Court of Appeal concluded in *McCowan v. McCowan*,[252] a consent order for spousal support can only be set aside on the same grounds as the agreement giving rise to the order. These grounds go to the formation of the agreement and not to any subsequent non-performance of the consent order. While the court may find no basis on which to set aside a consent order for support, such an order may be varied under section 17 of the *Divorce Act*, subject to the strictures imposed by *Miglin* and the possible application of section 17(10) of the *Divorce Act*.[253]

Where a consent order envisages that spousal support will not be paid indefinitely but provides for a review of the order after three years, a motion judge, in reviewing the consent order may find that an extension is warranted but should not grant an order for an indefinite term. Such an order would contravene the principles articulated by the Supreme Court of Canada in *Miglin v. Miglin*,[254] which require courts to uphold spousal agreements that are fair and in substantial compliance with the overall objectives of the *Divorce Act*. In *Bourque v. Bourque*,[255] the New Brunswick Court of Appeal concluded that a new review date would be objectively fair and would relieve the applicant from having to overcome the difficult hurdle of establishing a change of circumstances under section 17 of the *Divorce Act*.

The fact that the divorced husband has been forced into early retirement by ill health does not justify variation of the agreed amount of spousal support where that amount is relatively modest, having regard to the divorced wife's role during a long, traditional marriage, and the divorced husband has benefited from a substantially increased income over several years since the divorce, and he currently owns an RRSP that can be converted to an annuity to increase his household income. Based on

---

252   (1995), 14 R.F.L. (4th) 325 (Ont. C.A.).

253   *Kehler v. Kehler*, [2003] M.J. No. 217 (C.A.); see also *Gobeil v. Gobeil*, [2007] M.J. No. 19 (C.A.); *Kemp v. Kemp*, [2007] O.J. No. 1131 (Sup. Ct.); *Roy v. Roy*, [2007] N.B.J. No. 247 (Q.B.).

254   [2003] 1 S.C.R. 303.

255   [2004] N.B.J. No. 343 (C.A.).

these factors, the Alberta Court of Appeal in *Templeton v. Templeton*[256] concluded that the minutes of settlement, which had been incorporated in the divorce judgment, should be accorded determinative weight. On the assumption that the minutes of settlement might not constitute a final agreement so as to trigger the *Miglin* criteria, the Alberta Court of Appeal further concluded that, even if a material and unforeseen change of circumstances had occurred by reason of the divorced husband's forced early retirement due to ill health, the circumstances of the case did not justify the reduction or termination of the agreed spousal support payments because, in addition to the aforementioned factors, the divorced wife, who had respected the finality of the agreement by not seeking increased spousal support after her divorced husband's income increased, should not suffer the consequences of poor choices made by the divorced husband, who chose to spend his income without saving anything, while knowing of his ongoing obligation to support his divorced wife.

It is uncertain whether a court has jurisdiction to retroactively incorporate the support provisions of a separation agreement in the divorce judgment for the purpose of allowing a variation proceeding under section 17 of the *Divorce Act*.[257]

h) Effect of Spousal Agreement on Child Support

Courts will not hesitate to order child support where a spousal agreement or settlement prejudicially affects the financial welfare of children. Child support, like access, is the right of the child and neither parent has the authority to waive or restrict the statutory support obligations that each parent owes to his or her dependent children.[258] That is not to say that parents cannot negotiate settlements or other arrangements to stand in the place of child support payments that would otherwise be ordered pursuant to the *Federal Child Support Guidelines*. However, it is not open

---

256 [2005] A.J. No. 349 (C.A.).

257 See *Posener v. Posener* (1981), 123 D.L.R. (3d) 493 (B.C.S.C.), aff'd (1984), 4 D.L.R. (4th) 385 (B.C.C.A.), leave to appeal to S.C.C. refused (1984), 55 N.R. 159n (S.C.C.); *Kramer v. Kramer* (1983), 36 R.F.L. (2d) 297 (B.C.S.C.); *Pousette v. Pousette* (1993), 46 R.F.L. (3d) 152 (B.C.S.C.); *Cawker v. Cawker* (1994), 7 R.F.L. (4th) 282 (B.C.S.C.); *Zimmerman v. Shannon*, [2006] B.C.J. No. 2887 (C.A.). See also *Champion v. Champion* (1994), 2 R.F.L. (4th) 455 (P.E.I.T.D.). For various options available in British Columbia to enforce or vary the support provisions of a separation agreement, see Georgialee Lang, "An Agreement Today, an Order Tomorrow: Incorporating Agreement Terms into a Divorce Order" (1995) 53 Advocate 385.

258 *Richardson v. Richardson*, [1987] 1 S.C.R. 857; *Willick v. Willick*, [1994] 3 S.C.R. 670; *C.N.G. v. S.M.R.*, [2007] B.C.J. No. 1251 (S.C.); *Jay v. Jay*, [2003] P.E.I.J. No. 68 (C.A.).

to parents to trade off child support against non-access to the children by the non-custodial parent.[259] The test of whether parents have made adequate provision for their child must be measured against the *Federal Child Support Guidelines* and the provisions of sections 15.1(5) to (8) (original applications) and sections 17(6.2) to (6.5) of the *Divorce Act*.[260]

i)   Applications under Provincial Statute

In *Zimmerman v. Shannon*,[261] the British Columbia Court of Appeal observed that the power of the court under section 15.2 of the *Divorce Act* is to order or refuse to order spousal support. It was not the intention of Parliament to supersede provincial legislative jurisdiction over contracts regulating spousal support, and the judgment of the Supreme Court of Canada in *Miglin v. Miglin*[262] affirmed the jurisdiction to order spousal support inconsistent with a private contract without commenting on the effect of such an order on the enforceability of the private contract. Several provinces have enacted legislation whereby the support provisions of a separation agreement may be filed with a designated court and thereafter varied in the same way as a court order.

As McLachlin J., as she then was, observed in *Moge v. Moge*,[263] "it seems to me important to emphasize that this is, first and last, a case of statutory interpretation ...." It may be important to bear this observation in mind when the impact of a purportedly final spousal agreement on a subsequent application for a spousal order arises, not in the context of the *Divorce Act* but under provincial statute. Given the diversity of provincial legislation, this writer will focus on section 33(4) of the Ontario *Family Law Act*, which provides as follows:

Setting Aside Domestic Contract

33.(4) The court may set aside a provision for support or a waiver of the right to support in a domestic contract or paternity agreement and may determine and order support in an application under subsection (1) although the contract or agreement contains an express provision excluding the application of this section,

---

259   *Black v. Black* (1995), 19 R.F.L. (4th) 442 (B.C.C.A.); *D.A.W. v. W.M.Z.*, [2000] O.J. No. 2391 (Sup. Ct.).

260   *Gobeil v. Gobeil*, [2007] M.J. No. 19 (C.A.); *Kudoba v. Kudoba*, [2007] O.J. No. 3765 (Sup. Ct.); see, generally, Chapter 9, Section K.

261   [2006] B.C.J. No. 2887 (C.A.).

262   [2003] 1 S.C.R. 303.

263   [1992] 3 S.C.R. 813 at para. 102.

(a) if the provision for support or the waiver of the right to support results in unconscionable circumstances;

(b) if the provision for support is in favour of or the waiver is by or on behalf of a dependant who qualifies for an allowance for support out of public money; or

(c) if there is default in the payment of support under the contract or agreement at the time the application is made.[264]

It is noteworthy that counsel for the appellant in *Miglin v. Miglin*[265] invited the Supreme Court of Canada to adopt the criterion set out in section 33(4)(a) of the Ontario *Family Law Act* as the basis for judicial intervention where a spousal support order is sought pursuant to section 15.2 of the *Divorce Act* in contravention of the express terms of a spousal settlement. In declining this invitation, the majority judgment in *Miglin v. Miglin* stated that "our approach … takes greater account of the parties' subjective sense of equitable sharing than the objective 'unconscionable circumstances' standard proposed by counsel for the appellant." If that is true, it is difficult to see how Ontario courts can incorporate the *Miglin* criteria in cases that fall subject to the express provisions of section 33 of the Ontario *Family Law Act*, unless they judicially redefine "the objective … standard" referred to in *Miglin*. Such redefinition is not unlikely, given the reality that a married couple on the breakdown of their relationship has the option of seeking a spousal support order under either the federal *Divorce Act* or pursuant to provincial statute and, if these statutes are perceived to be in conflict from an operational standpoint, the doctrine of paramountcy would be triggered to give precedence to the *Divorce Act* and the interpretation given to section 15.2 of that Act in *Miglin*.

In *Patan v. Patan*,[266] a waiver of spousal support in a prenuptial agreement was held to constitute no bar to a needs-based interim order for spousal support when section 33(4)(b) of the Ontario *Family Law Act* was triggered by the wife being on welfare. In reaching this conclusion, Coates J., of the Ontario Superior Court, stated that the court was not required to apply a *Miglin* analysis.

---

264 *Armstrong v. Armstrong*, [2006] O.J. No. 3823 (C.A.).
265 [2003] 1 S.C.R. 303 at paras. 68–73.
266 [2004] O.J. No. 5365 (Sup. Ct.).

O. EFFECT OF SPONSORSHIP AGREEMENT

A sponsorship agreement entered into by one spouse to facilitate the other spouse's immigration defines obligations owed to the Canadian government rather than spousal support obligations arising pursuant to the *Divorce Act* or provincial statute. Though it may be deemed relevant on the issue of spousal support, it is not determinative of the appropriate amount or duration of spousal support to be ordered.[267]

P. DOUBLE RECOVERY OR DOUBLE DIPPING

Court-ordered spousal support rights and obligations may survive the payor's retirement. In some instances, the payee will have received an equal share of the value of the payor's pension upon their separation or divorce, either by way of a lump sum or a trade-off of assets such as the pension against the matrimonial home. If that is the case, when addressing the issue of spousal support after the payor's retirement, the court should seek to avoid "double dipping" or "double recovery." Consequently, the court should not take account of an already divided pension, except insofar as its value to the pension-holding spouse may have increased since the separation or divorce. A spouse who receives money or assets in satisfaction of his or her pension-sharing entitlement on separation or divorce must use those resources in a reasonable attempt to generate income, at least by the time pension benefits begin to be paid to the pensioned spouse. Failure to do so may result in the judicial imputation of income to the support payee, based on actuarial evidence. It is unfair to allow a support payee to reap the benefit of the pension both as a divisible asset and thereafter as a source of income to the payor, particularly when the payee previously received capital assets that have appreciated in value. To avoid double recovery, the court should, where practicable, focus on the portion of the payor's income and assets that have not been a part of the property division when the payee spouse's continuing need for support

---

267   *Szczur v. Szczur*, [1999] A.J. No. 1523 (Q.B.); *Poelen v. Poelen*, [2000] A.J. No. 900 (Q.B.); *Nathoo v. Nathoo*, [2005] A.J. No. 255 (Q.B.); *Sarai v. Sarai*, [1999] B.C.J. No. 2786 (S.C.); *Achari v. Sami*, [2000] B.C.J. No. 1651 (S.C.); *Aujla v. Aujla*, [2004] B.C.J. No. 2496 (S.C.); *Paulina v. Dudas*, [2005] B.C.J. No. 172 (S.C.); *Gossen v. Gossen*, [2003] N.S.J. No. 113 (S.C.); *Camilleri v. Camilleri*, [2000] O.J. No. 4136 (Sup. Ct.); *Segal v. Ou*, [2001] O.J. No. 2646 (Sup. Ct.); *Gidey v. Abay*, [2007] O.J. No. 3693 (Sup. Ct.).

is shown. This would include the portion of the payor's pension earned after separation and not subject to equalization. Double recovery cannot always be avoided, and a pension previously divided can also be viewed as a maintenance asset where the payor has the ability to pay and the payee has made a reasonable effort to use equalized assets in an income-producing way and, despite this, economic hardship from the marriage or its breakdown persists. Double recovery may also be permitted in spousal support orders based upon need as opposed to compensation.[268]

While the principle of "double dipping" articulated in *Boston v. Boston* may be trumped by the needs of an elderly recipient divorced spouse who suffers from ill health, her failure to conserve and invest her share of the family assets that were received at the time of the divorce may justify a reduction in the amount of spousal support to a level that reflects the minimum needs required to provide for her welfare.[269]

A wife, whose financial needs arise to a significant degree from her retaining the matrimonial home in lieu of sharing the husband's pension that would have generated a monthly income for her, cannot expect the husband to support her lifestyle indefinitely, although a transitional adjustment period may be deemed appropriate to enable the wife to generate income from her capital assets.[270]

Early retirement due to ill health, which results in a significant reduction in the retiree's income, constitutes a material change of circumstances that warrants a court-ordered reduction in the amount of spousal support previously ordered. The principles of "double dipping" do not preclude the court from taking account of the husband's pension income, if the wife is in need, and the pension was undervalued at the time of the previously negotiated spousal property settlement, and was enriched by the contributions of the husband and his employer after the spousal separation. Where the husband's pension income is fully indexed, the variation order for reduced periodic spousal support may be declared subject to annual cost-of-living indexation.[271]

---

268 *Boston v. Boston*, [2001] 2 S.C.R. 413 (variation proceeding); *Bennett v. Bennett*, [2003] O.J. No. 5295 (Sup. Ct.); *Perry v. Perry*, [2008] O.J. No. 1118 (Sup. Ct.); *Rimmer v. Adshead*, [2004] S.J. No. 834 (Q.B.) (contemporaneous applications for property sharing and spousal support); *Napper v. Napper*, [2007] S.J. No. 350 (Q.B.).

269 *Prendergast v. Prendergast*, [2004] B.C.J. No. 1934 (S.C.).

270 *Beaton v. Beaton*, [2001] N.S.J. No. 478 (S.C.).

271 *Meiklejohn v. Meiklejohn*, [2001] O.J. No. 3911 (C.A.); see also *Napper v. Napper*, [2007] S.J. No. 350 (Q.B.).

After reviewing the response to *Boston v. Boston* in subsequent judicial decisions, Philp J.A., who delivered the judgment of the Manitoba Court of Appeal in *Cymbalisty v. Cymbalisty*,[272] expressed the following opinion:

> The general principles that the court enunciated in *Boston* were founded on unique factual circumstances that are not the fodder that usually feeds family law litigation. The goal of self-sufficiency is one that is not often attained following the break-up of a long-term marriage. Economic disadvantage or hardship will often persist. For this reason, it is not surprising that trial and appellate courts have found in the facts before them the circumstances that permit double recovery in spousal support orders/agreements. Balancing the needs of the wife who remains disadvantaged by the marriage and its breakdown against the right of the husband to enjoy his pension entitlement that had been equalized, the courts have come down, properly in my view, in favour of the wife.

If spouses have executed minutes of settlement at the time of their divorce that were intended to be final and to exclude all future claims for spousal support, a court will dismiss a subsequent application for spousal support that is continued against the divorced husband's estate after his death where the applicant seeks to attach assets that were previously dealt with under the minutes of settlement and consequently fall subject to the "double dipping" or "double recovery" principles set out in *Boston v. Boston*.[273] The rationale underlying the judgment of Major J. in *Boston v. Boston* applies to a claim for spousal support under the Ontario *Succession Law Reform Act* as well as to a claim under the Ontario *Family Law Act*. Although double recovery may be permitted when the applicant establishes need, an application for spousal support must be dismissed where the divorced wife's needs are already being met by the assets received from the settlement and her entitlement to an employment pension, CPP disability payments, and investment income. Section 57 of the Ontario *Succession Law Reform Act* defines a "dependant" as someone "to whom the deceased was providing support or was under a legal obligation to provide support immediately before his or her death." Where it is clear that the minutes of settlement would have precluded a successful claim for spousal support being brought during the divorced husband's

---

272   [2003] M.J. No. 398 at para. 37 (C.A.).
273   [2000] 2 S.C.R. 413.

lifetime, his former wife is not a "dependant" within the meaning of the Ontario *Succession Law Reform Act*.[274]

In *Litton v. Litton*,[275] the principle of double dipping was held inapplicable to the husband's income earned from his business after a court-ordered division of property involved a trade-off of the matrimonial home and the business.

Q. INCOME TAX AND RETROACTIVE ORDERS[276]

Periodic spousal support payments made pursuant to an order of a competent tribunal or a written agreement after marriage breakdown are tax deductible by the payor and are taxable in the hands of the payee, whereas lump sum payments involve no such consequences.[277] In *R. v. McKimmon*,[278] Hugessen J.A., of the Federal Court of Appeal, sets out a nonexhaustive list of eight factors to be taken into account for the purpose of differentiating between periodic spousal support payments and lump sum spousal support payable by instalments:

1. the length of the periods at which the payments are made;
2. the amount of payments in relation to the income and living standards of both payor and recipient;
3. whether the payments are to bear interest prior to their due date;
4. whether the amounts envisaged can be paid by anticipation at the option of the payor or can be accelerated as a penalty at the option of the recipient in the event of default;
5. whether the payments allow a significant degree of capital accumulation by the recipient;

---

274 *Friedt v. Friedt Estate*, [2004] O.J. No. 2227 (Div. Ct.).

275 [2006] B.C.J. No. 2916 (C.A.).

276 For detailed information on income tax (including Interpretation Bulletins), GST, Child and Family Benefits, and Tax Credits, see Canada Revenue Agency (formerly Revenue Canada) online: www.ccra-adrc.gc.ca.

277 *Income Tax Act*, R.S.C. 1985 (5th Supp.), c. 1, ss. 56 and 60. See *Krause v. Krause* (1976), 23 R.F.L. 219 (Alta. C.A.); *Caston v. Caston* (1990), 28 R.F.L. (3d) 222 (Alta. Q.B.); *James v. James* (1992), 41 R.F.L. (3d) 70 (B.C.C.A.); *Meltzer v. Meltzer* (1992), 41 R.F.L. (3d) 257 (Man. C.A.); *Boland v. Boland*, [2006] N.J. No. 206 (U.F.C.); *Osborne v. Osborne* (1973), 14 R.F.L. 61 at 72 (Sask. Q.B.), var'd (1974), 23 R.F.L. 358 (Sask. C.A.); see also *Coward v. Coward* (1991), 30 R.F.L. (3d) 227 (B.C. Master) (retroactivity of income tax deductions), applying *Meltzer v. Meltzer* (1989), 22 R.F.L. (3d) 38 (Man. Q.B.) (retroactive effect of order unacceptable to Revenue Canada; application to vary dismissed).

278 [1990] 1 C.T.C. 109 (Fed. C.A.); see also *Asselin v. Canada*, [2007] T.C.J. No. 366.

6. whether the payments are stipulated to continue for an indefinite period or whether they are for a fixed-term;

7. whether the agreed payments can be assigned and whether the obligation to pay survives the lifetime of either the payor or recipient;

8. whether the payments purport to release the payor from any future obligations to pay maintenance.

The income tax implications of periodic spousal support can be taken into consideration after the court has determined the net amount of support that a spouse needs to live on.[279]

Where, by prior agreement, the payor spouse agrees to pay directly to the recipient an amount equal to the recipient's tax liability on the support payments, that amount may be deducted from the payor's taxable income and must be included by the recipient spouse as income.[280]

In *Watt v. Watt*,[281] Wright J. formulated the following guidelines to determine whether a support order should be declared retroactive in order to facilitate the payor obtaining tax relief with respect to prior consensual periodic support payments:

> It is desirable to encourage the prompt commencement of payments for support. There must be a recognition that the paperwork necessary for tax purposes may take some time to effect. The court should encourage support to be paid notwithstanding that the documentation for tax relief has not yet been prepared. This can be done by indicating its willingness, in a proper case, to grant the necessary order retroactively.

> There is a difference between support which is being paid unilaterally and support which is being paid pursuant to a parol agreement.

> Where support is being paid pursuant to a parol agreement, the surrounding circumstances must be looked at to determine whether it was within the contemplation of the parties that the payments would be tax deductible by the husband. The fact that the agreement was to be embodied in a written document or court order is *prima facie* proof that the parties contemplated the tax deductibility of the payments.

> If it was contemplated that payments would be tax deductible, then generally a retroactive order will follow.

---

279 *Au v. Au* (1993), 47 R.F.L. (3d) 342 (Alta. Q.B.).
280 *Guerin v. R.* (1994), 1 R.F.L. (4th) 396 (T.C.C.).
281 [1995] O.J. No. 1758 at para. 14 (Gen. Div.).

If it was not contemplated that the payments would be deductible, then the court must consider whether the issue was considered and rejected by the wife to the knowledge of the husband.

If that aspect had been considered and rejected by the wife to the knowledge of the husband, then generally a retroactive order will not follow.

Where support is being paid unilaterally or where deductibility has not been considered, the amount is suspect and the presumption is that the wife should receive the money tax-paid.

Whether the amount is being paid unilaterally or in accordance with a parol agreement, where the parties did not contemplate the issue, the sum must be reasonable considering that the husband will receive a tax benefit and the wife will receive the money with a tax liability.

The fact that some support is being paid unilaterally may lull the wife into inaction. Should the husband later seek tax relief and the amounts paid, while adequate on a tax deductible basis, reasonably give rise to the argument that if the wife had known that she would have to pay tax she would have asked for more, then the court might consider making a retroactive order on terms. In such circumstances the court may direct the payment of a lump sum for support in addition to the periodic payments. This lump sum can be paid from the tax refund realized by the husband in consequence of the retroactive order. The funds can be used by the wife to pay her additional tax. Generally speaking her additional tax will be less than his tax saving.

R. VARIATION AND TERMINATION OF SUPPORT ORDERS

1) General

Section 17(4.1) of the *Divorce* Act empowers a court to vary an existing order for spousal support upon proof of a substantial, unforeseen, and continuing change in the condition, means, needs, or other circumstances of either former spouse since the granting of the order that is sought to be varied.[282] An order for spousal support is subject to variation, rescission,

---

282 *B.(G.) v. G.(L.)*, [1995] 3 S.C.R. 370; *Oakley v. Oakley* (1985), 48 R.F.L. (2d) 307 (B.C.C.A.); *Poulter v. Poulter*, [2005] B.C.J. No. 895 (C.A.); *Hamilton v. Hamilton*, [2006] B.C.J. No. 1616 (S.C.) (application to cancel support arrears); *Fehr v. Fehr*,

or suspension on the application of either former spouse brought pursuant to section 17 of the *Divorce Act*. Similar factors and objectives govern variation proceedings under section 17 as those applicable to original applications under section 15.2 of the *Divorce Act*.

Although interim orders are specifically authorized by subsections 15.1(2), 15.2(2), and 16(2) of the *Divorce Act*, no jurisdiction to grant interim orders is explicitly conferred by section 17 of the *Divorce Act*, which empowers a court to make an order varying, rescinding, or suspending, prospectively or retroactively, a permanent spousal support order, child support order, or custody order. In British Columbia and Saskatchewan, appellate courts have addressed the issue of whether interim variation orders could be granted under section 11 of the *Divorce Act*, S.C. 1967–68, c. 24 (R.S.C. 1970, c. D-4), the predecessor to section 17 of the *Divorce Act*, R.S.C. 1985, c. 3 (2d Supp.). While acknowledging that there was no jurisdiction to grant interim orders on an application under section 11(2) of the *Divorce Act*, 1968 where variation was sought in respect of an existing permanent order for corollary financial relief, the judgments of *Burton v. Burton*[283] and *Frey v. Frey*[284] stated that an order could be varied pursuant to section 11(2) of the *Divorce Act*, 1968, and then varied again, if injustices might otherwise arise from delay prior to a full review of the attendant circumstances. On the other hand, in *Yeo v. Yeo*,[285] the Prince Edward Island Court of Appeal concluded that injustices and hardships that can arise from delay in the full hearing of an application to vary an order under section 17(1) of the current *Divorce Act* cannot be addressed by successive orders, the first of which is merely transitional pending a full review of the attendant circumstances. Instead, injustices and hardships must be addressed by expedited hearings and/or by orders for retroactive variation, the latter jurisdiction being explicitly recognized by section 17(1) of the current *Divorce Act* but not by section 11(2) of the *Divorce Act*, 1968. Notwithstanding their different perspectives, the three aforementioned judgments have two features in common. First, they openly acknowledge that the relevant statutory provisions confer no jurisdiction on a court to grant an interim order varying an existing permanent or-

---

[2006] B.C.J. No. 2611 (S.C.); *R.M. v. M.M.*, [2006] N.B.J. No. 157 (C.A.); *House v. House*, [2007] N.J. No. 383 (T.D.); *Purdy v. Hazelden*, [2006] N.S.J. No. 229 (C.A.); *Levinson v. Levinson*, [2006] O.J. No. 2566 (Div. Ct.). And see discussion, below in this chapter.

283   (1982), 27 R.F.L. (2d) 170 (B.C.C.A.).

284   (1987), 8 R.F.L. (3d) 154 (Sask. C.A.).

285   (1998), 42 R.F.L. (4th) 418 (P.E.I.S.C.A.D.).

der. Second, they acknowledge the need for the avoidance of injustices or hardships that might arise from delay. Where they differ is in the means whereby such avoidance is secured. Where the interests of children are concerned, some courts have purported to exercise their *parens patriae* jurisdiction as a means of securing the interim variation of a final order for child support.[286] There is, nevertheless, room for doubt whether such jurisdiction can properly be invoked in a proceeding relating to child support, as distinct from a guardianship, custody, or adoption proceeding.[287] Even if such jurisdiction can be invoked to protect the economic interests of a child, there is no reason to assume that it can be invoked to reduce pre-existing child support obligations for the benefit of a parent. Furthermore, the *parens patriae* jurisdiction has no application in situations involving the variation of spousal support orders. As McQuaid J. observed in *Yeo v. Yeo*, "[t]he *parens patriae* jurisdiction of the court, as broad as it may be, may only be invoked when the person for whose benefit it is being invoked is incompetent. [See *Re Eve* (1986), 61 Nfld. & P.E.I.R. 273 (S.C.C.), at para 36]."[288] After a detailed review of relevant case law in *Keogan v. Weekes*,[289] R.S. Smith J., of the Family Law Division of the Saskatchewan Court of Queen's Bench, found himself "in harmony with the analytical chord struck by the Saskatchewan Court of Appeal in *Frey* ... [which] permits the court to address a manifest injustice but at the same time respects the strictures of the *Divorce Act*."[290] Applying that approach, Smith J. concluded that changes in the children's parenting arrangements were insufficient in themselves to justify an interim or temporary reduction in the amount of child support payable under a pre-existing permanent order in circumstances where the father's current income as a farmer could not be resolved on affidavit evidence and required a *viva voce* hearing in which income issues and assertions could be tested by cross-examination.

On an application to vary a spousal support order pursuant to section 17(4.1) of the *Divorce Act*, the onus falls on the applicant to prove a material change in the condition, means, needs, or other circumstances

---

286 See *Dixon v. Dixon* (1995), 13 R.F.L. (4th) 160 (Alta. Q.B.); *Parlee v. Lavallée* (1992), 42 R.F.L. (3d) 58 (Ont. Gen. Div.); *Bradley v. Bradley* (1995), 15 R.F.L. (4th) 33 (Ont. Gen. Div.); *Daher v. Daher*, [2002] O.J. No. 3671 (Sup. Ct.).

287 See *Harris v. Harris* (1978), 90 D.L.R. (3d) 699 (B.C.S.C.).

288 *Yeo v. Yeo*, [1998] P.E.I.J. No. 97 at para. 12 (S.C.A.D.).

289 [2005] S.J. No. 170 (Q.B.).

290 *Ibid.* at para. 33.

of either former spouse. As Sopinka J. observed in *Willick v. Willick*,[291] a material change is a change that was not contemplated by the court and that would have led to different terms, if the change had been known when the order was granted. Court-ordered variation of a spousal support presupposes that the change is not trivial or insignificant. In a variation proceeding, the existing support order must be assumed to have been correct when it was granted. Absent proof of a material change since then, the judge hearing a variation application has no jurisdiction to vary the order because he or she regards it as inappropriate or unrealistic. If a material change is established sufficient to warrant judicial intervention, the variation order should reflect the objectives set out in section 17(7) of the *Divorce Act*.[292] Whether retirement constitutes a material change depends upon the attendant circumstances of the case.[293] Having regard to the factors and objectives set out in sections 17(4.1) and 17(7) of the Act, a reduction in the amount of spousal support previously ordered may be appropriate because of the recipient's increased income and the payor's reduced income but termination of the order may not be warranted where the recipient continues to suffer economic disadvantages in consequence of the long traditional marriage and its breakdown. For the purpose of providing security for arrears and future payments of spousal support, the court may exercise its discretionary statutory jurisdiction to order the obligor to designate the obligee as the beneficiary under the obligor's life insurance policy. Orders of this nature have begun to be granted on a routine basis, even though no specific mention of life insurance policies is found in the provisions of sections 15.2(1), (2), and (3) and 17(3) of the *Divorce Act*, which relate to the court's jurisdiction to order security for spousal support payments.[294]

The requirement of a material change within the meaning of section 17(4.1) of the *Divorce Act* is not met where the applicant, who seeks a reduction in the amount of spousal support, fails to explain a change in his employment status and provides no evidence that he has made

---

291 [1994] 3 S.C.R. 670; see also *B.(G.) v. G.(L.)*, [1995] 3 S.C.R. 370; *Smith v. Smith*, [2007] M.J. No. 284 (Q.B.); *R.M. v. M.M.*, [2006] N.B.J. No. 157 (C.A.); *Bemrose v. Fetter*, [2007] O.J. No. 3488 (C.A.); *McGoey v. McGoey*, [2008] O.J. No. 7 (Sup. Ct.).

292 *McMurchy v. McMurchy*, [2002] B.C.J. No. 2681 (C.A.); *Petrowski v. Waskul*, [2003] M.J. No. 151 (C.A.); *Hayward v. Hayward*, [2006] N.B.J. No. 283 (Q.B.); *Winsor v. Winsor*, [2002] N.J. No. 195 (C.A.); *R.K. c. H.S.*, [2006] Q.J. No. 4996 (Sup. Ct.).

293 *Fehr v. Fehr*, [2006] B.C.J. No. 2611 (S.C.); see also *Benson v. Benson*, [2008] O.J. No. 578 (Sup. Ct.).

294 *Murphy v. Murphy*, [2002] N.S.J. No. 180 (S.C.).

reasonable efforts to find comparable employment commensurate with his earning capacity based on his education, skill, experience, age, and health. A self-induced reduction in income does not satisfy the statutory requirement.[295] Similarly, self-induced increased needs cannot be relied upon to justify increased spousal support. A recipient spouse is not entitled to spend her way into a "change of circumstances" for the purposes of section 17 of the *Divorce Act*. Applying the above principles, the British Columbia Court of Appeal in *W.C.P. v. C.P.*[296] found no error on the part of the chambers judge who had dismissed the wife's application for increased spousal support because her increased expenses and reduced investment income were attributable to her lifestyle choice in purchasing a luxury condominium rather than more modest accommodation such as was envisaged by the trial judge when the original spousal support order was granted.

Where spousal support has been ordered after the breakdown of a long traditional marriage, the subsequent explicable failure of the recipient to achieve anticipated economic self-sufficiency within a specified period of time constitutes a material change of circumstances that justifies extending the duration of the order.[297]

Where a divorced wife has been adequately compensated for the economic disadvantages sustained in consequence of her previous marriage and its breakdown, and her new career and remarriage negate any continuing need for spousal support, an order for termination of the divorced husband's reviewable consensual spousal support obligation should be affirmed on appeal. A divorced wife has no proprietary interest in her divorced husband's increased earning capacity and she cannot sustain a claim for ongoing support based simply on a substantial disparity between their current incomes. Economic self-sufficiency, which is one of the objectives of the *Divorce Act*, is to be determined by the divorced spouses' standard of living during their marriage, not by reference to the divorced husband's current income. An appellate court should not overturn a support judgment unless the reasons disclose an error in principle, a significant misapprehension of the evidence, or unless the order is clearly wrong.[298] In *Roberts v. Beresford*,[299] the British Columbia Court of Appeal found that the trial judge had considered all the relevant factors

---

295 *Poitras v. Poitras*, [2006] S.J. No. 113 (Q.B.).
296 [2005] B.C.J. No. 179 (C.A.).
297 *Cottreau v. Pothier*, [2002] N.S.J. No. 556 (C.A.).
298 *Hickey v. Hickey*, [1999] 2 S.C.R. 518 at para. 11.
299 [2006] B.C.J. No. 291 (C.A.).

and objectives under the *Divorce Act* and had placed no undue emphasis on the objective of promoting economic self-sufficiency, due regard
having been paid to the review clause in the prior spousal agreement
that addressed the issues of economic self-sufficiency and the divorced
husband's income. The British Columbia Court of Appeal declined to
interfere with the trial judge's fixing of the date of the review as the appropriate termination date.

On an application to vary a spousal support order, section 17 of the
Divorce Act requires the "means" of each divorced spouse to be addressed
and this includes their unrealized earning capacity[300] or capital assets.[301]
Section 15.2(5) of the *Divorce Act* provides that "the court shall not take
into consideration any misconduct of a spouse in relation to the marriage"
when considering an application for spousal support. Pursuant to section
17(6) of the *Divorce Act*, the same criterion applies to an application to
vary an existing order. These provisions do not disentitle a fifty-seven-
year-old divorced wife to ongoing spousal support when she is incapable
of achieving economic self-sufficiency due to her age, medical problems,
and the emotional devastation that she suffered in consequence of her
former husband's unilateral withdrawal from their twenty-year marriage
and the death of close family members.[302]

In determining whether to vary a spousal support order pursuant to
section 17 of the *Divorce Act*, the court must have regard to whether the
alleged changes are of sufficient magnitude to warrant variation in light
of the conceptual basis of the original order. In *Bracklow v. Bracklow*,[303]
McLachlin J., as she then was, acknowledged three conceptual grounds
for entitlement to spousal support: (i) compensatory; (ii) contractual; and
(iii) non-compensatory. Where all three of these grounds are likely to
have co-existed as bases for the original spousal support order on the
dissolution of a twenty-two-year traditional marriage, the court may conclude that the changes largely resulting from the recipient's relatively new
cohabitational relationship, namely, the sharing of household expenses
and the sale of her former home, coupled with her modest earning cap-

---

300 *Hayward v. Hayward*, [2006] N.B.J. No. 283 (Q.B.) (income imputed to spousal
support recipient who failed to take reasonable steps to find employment; order for
reduced amount); *House v. House*, [2007] N.J. No. 383 (T.D.); *Walsh v. Walsh*, [2006]
O.J. No. 2480 (Sup. Ct.).

301 *Leskun v. Leskun*, [2006] 1 S.C.R. 920; *Prendergast v. Prendergast*, [2004] B.C.J. No.
1934 (S.C.).

302 *Leskun v. Leskun, ibid.*

303 [1999] 1 S.C.R. 420.

acity, are not material changes sufficient to warrant the elimination or reduction of her former husband's court-ordered spousal support obligation.[304]

Moge v. Moge,[305] though decided under section 17 of the *Divorce Act* in the context of a variation proceeding, has produced its major impact on original applications for spousal support under section 15.2 of the *Divorce Act*. Although empirical evidence is lacking, legal practitioners throughout Canada acknowledge that *Moge v. Moge* has strengthened the pre-existing trend towards higher amounts of spousal support and for longer periods of time. Fixed-term orders are no longer regarded as appropriate to address the economic consequences of long traditional marriages where the woman as wife and mother assumed the primary responsibility for homemaking and child care.

The impact of *Moge v. Moge* on variation applications is explained in the following observations of Baker J., of the British Columbia Supreme Court, in *Patrick v. Patrick*,[306] who sets out the evidential requirements faced by obligors in seeking to reduce or terminate spousal support orders:

> The *Divorce Act* does not rule out the possibility that an economically disadvantaged spouse may be only temporarily disadvantaged. As a result of post-divorce career developments, education or training, or other fortuitous circumstances, economic disadvantage may be reduced or even eliminated. Where the economic disadvantage sought to be remedied by the payment of spousal support has been eliminated or significantly reduced, termination or a reduction in support is envisioned by the Act. In my view, however, where an order for spousal support has been made with the primary objective of compensating the receiving spouse for economic disadvantage accruing during several years of marriage and expected to continue after divorce, a court should not readily reduce or terminate spousal support. The evidence on an application to vary a so-called "compensatory support" order must establish not only that there has been a significant change in the means and needs of the parties since trial but also that the factors which resulted in economic disadvantage during the marriage and after its breakdown no longer exist and that the lost advantage has been recovered.[307]

---

304 *Goudy v. Malbeuf*, [2002] S.J. No. 466 (Q.B.).
305 [1992] 3 S.C.R. 813, 43 R.F.L. (3d) 345.
306 (1994), 92 B.C.L.R. (2d) 50 (S.C.).
307 *Ibid.* at 53–54.

Many lawyers and judges assume that spousal support like child support should be reduced or eliminated once there are no longer any dependent children. Although it is appropriate to terminate child support when the child is economically self-sufficient, it does not follow that spousal support should be terminated, or even reduced, because the custodial parent's responsibilities for the child have ceased to exist. The economic consequences of child rearing for the custodial parent are often permanent and irreversible in terms of loss of employment potential, including loss of the fringe benefits usually associated with employment. As Palmeter A.C.J.S.C., of the Nova Scotia Supreme Court, observed in *Gillis v. Gillis,*

> In my opinion, the fact that the two youngest children have left the respondent's home does not necessarily mean that maintenance has to be reduced on any pro rata basis, or even be reduced at all.[308]

On the same basis, it is submitted that, on an original application for spousal support or on a variation application, lawyers and judges should reject any assumption that short-term marriages warrant only short-term spousal support when these marriages have produced children. The notion that spousal support should terminate or be reduced when the youngest child is old enough to attend school is one that must be rejected if the observations of Bowman J. in *Brockie v. Brockie,*[309] which were quoted with approval in *Moge v. Moge,*[310] are to have a real impact. Child-care responsibilities do not end when a child enters school, although the direct and hidden costs of child rearing may change.

2) Variation of Fixed-Term Orders

Subsection 17(10) of the *Divorce Act* provides that, where a spousal support order provides for support for a definite period or until a specified event occurs, a court may not vary that order after expiry of the period or the occurrence of the stipulated event for the purpose of resuming support, unless the court is satisfied that (i) a variation order is necessary to relieve economic hardship arising from a change in the condition, means, needs, or other circumstances of the spouse that is related to the

---

308 (1994), 3 R.F.L. (4th) 128 at 131 (N.S.S.C.A.D.). And see judgment of L'Heureux-Dubé J. in *Willick v. Willick,* [1994] 3 S.C.R. 670, 6 R.F.L. (4th) 161 at 216.

309 (1987), 5 R.F.L. (3d) 440 at 447–48 (Man. Q.B.), aff'd (1987), 8 R.F.L. (3d) 302 (Man. C.A.).

310 [1992] 3 S.C.R. 813, 43 R.F.L. (3d) 345 at 388–89, L'Heureux-Dubé J.

marriage; and (ii) the change, had it existed at the time when the current order was made, would likely have resulted in a different order.[311] The explicit requirement that the effect of the change must be causally connected to the marriage imposes a significant limitation on the jurisdiction of the court once an order has terminated by the effluxion of time or by the occurrence of the stipulated event. Given a material change, therefore, an application to vary should be brought before expiry of the order so as to avoid the explicit stringent requirements of subsection 17(10) of the *Divorce Act*.

The change relied upon must be of a substantial, unforeseen, and continuing nature.[312] In an annotation of *Therrien-Cliché v. Cliché*[313] Professor James G. McLeod identified two kinds of changed circumstances: "1) something happens that was not taken into account when the prior order was made; and 2) something that was expected to happen does not occur." This latter circumstance is exemplified in *O'Neill v. Wolfe*,[314] wherein the wife was granted a spousal support order in the amount of $1,000 monthly for a fixed-term of two years in January, 2001. The term was fixed in the expectation that she would recover from her depression, which had its origins in the marriage, and establish her economic self-sufficiency with the two-year period. This expectation was not realized but there was still hope that she would overcome her depression and that her acquisition of a bed and breakfast in a tourist centre would enable her to become economically self-sufficient at some future date. Having regard to this future potential and the fact that the business had enjoyed a significant capital gain, even though it had yet to earn a profit, Brooke J., of the British Columbia Supreme Court, granted a variation order to the wife but in the reduced amount of $750 monthly from the date of her application (1 April 2003) to 1 March 2004, with the amount to be further reduced to $500 monthly thereafter, and the amount to be reviewed in May 2005.

3) Effect of Remarriage or Common-Law Relationship

a) Effect of Remarriage

There is no express requirement in section 17 of the *Divorce Act* that the court shall vary or rescind a spousal or child support order in the event

---

311 *Higgins v. Higgins*, [2006] A.J. No. 1550 (Q.B.); *Hancock v. Hancock*, [2006] B.C.J. No. 550 (S.C.).

312 *Carter v. Carter* (1991), 34 R.F.L. (3d) 1 (B.C.C.A.).

313 (1997), 30 R.F.L. (4th) 97 (Ont. C.A.).

314 *O'Neill v. Wolfe*, [2004] B.C.J. No. 807 (S.C.).

of the subsequent remarriage of either party. The remarriage of either divorced spouse is a relevant but not a decisive factor on any subsequent application to vary or discharge a subsisting order.[315]

Remarriage of the obligor may either increase or reduce the ability to pay support under a pre-existing support order. Where the obligor has remarried and the new spouse contributes to their common household expenses, the obligor's ability to pay support for a former spouse or a child of a prior marriage is thereby increased and the amount of support may be varied in light of that factor.[316]

There have been conflicts of judicial opinion on the question of whether a divorced spouse should be relieved of court-ordered obligations to the first family by reason of newly acquired obligations owed to a second family.[317] Some courts have concluded that the primary responsibility is owed to the first family.[318] Other courts have held that the new family should take precedence where the obligor cannot support both families because it is in the public interest for the new family to survive.[319] Still other courts have adopted a middle ground whereby no preference is given to either family.[320] In the final analysis, each case will be determined on its

315   *Ewing v. Ewing* (1990), 26 R.F.L. (3d) 115 (B.C.S.C.); *Richards v. Richards* (1972), 7 R.F.L. 101 (Ont. C.A.); *May v. May* (1993), 48 R.F.L. (3d) 432 (Ont. Gen. Div.); *Kinghorn v. Kinghorn* (1960), 29 D.L.R. (2d) 168 (Sask. Q.B.); *Ceulemans v. Ceulemans* (1986), 50 Sask. R. 120 (C.A.); *Grainger v. Grainger* (1992), 39 R.F.L. (3d) 101 (Sask. C.A.).

316   *Watson v. Watson* (1991), 35 R.F.L. (3d) 169 (B.C.S.C.); *Hersey v. Hersey* (1993), 47 R.F.L. (3d) 117 (N.B.C.A.); *Garwood v. Garwood* (1995), 15 R.F.L. (4th) 53 (N.B.C.A.); *Bartlett v. Bartlett* (1994), 2 R.F.L. (4th) 202 (Nfld. U.F.C.); *Edwards v. Edwards* (1994), 5 R.F.L. (4th) 321 (N.S.C.A.).

317   As to the effect of support obligations arising on a second divorce, see *Harvey v. Harvey* (1995), 14 R.F.L. (4th) 128 (B.C.C.A.).

318   *Doole v. Doole* (1991), 32 R.F.L. (3d) 283 (Alta. Q.B.); *Firth v. Firth* (1991), 35 R.F.L. (3d) 445 (B.C.S.C.); *Jenkins v. Jenkins* (1993), 47 R.F.L. (3d) 219 (B.C.S.C.); *Wallis v. Wallis* (1989), 61 Man. R. (2d) 199 (Q.B.); *Fournier v. Fournier* (1990), 97 N.B.R. (2d) 309 (Q.B.); *Zinck v. Zinck* (1989), 93 N.S.R. (2d) 374 (Fam. Ct.); *Somers v. Somers* (1990), 79 Nfld. & P.E.I.R. 1 (P.E.I.T.D.); *Fredrickson v. Fredrickson* (1993), 48 R.F.L. (3d) 48 (Sask. Q.B.); see also *Greco v. Levin* (1991), 33 R.F.L. (3d) 405 (Ont. Gen. Div.); *Burton v. Burton* (1994), 9 R.F.L. (4th) 108 (Ont. Gen. Div.).

319   *Wolfe v. Wolfe* (1995), 15 R.F.L. (4th) 86 (B.C.S.C.); *Burt v. Burt* (1990), 25 R.F.L. (3d) 92 (Nfld. T.D.); *Upshall v. Janvier* (1994), 120 Nfld. & P.E.I.R. 49 (Nfld. T.D.); *L.(G.M.) v. L.(V.A.)* (1993), 127 N.S.R. (2d) 66 at 69–70 (Fam. Ct.); *Kelly v. Kelly* (1992), 44 R.F.L. (3d) 214 (P.E.I.T.D.).

320   *Koop v. Polson* (1991), 31 R.F.L. (3d) 1 (Man. C.A.); *Pilon v. Pilon* (1993), 48 R.F.L. (3d) 99 (Man. Q.B.); *Ralph v. Ralph* (1994), 7 R.F.L. (4th) 238 (Nfld. S.C.); *Smith v. Smith*

own facts.[321] The intractable problem of reconciling the respective interests of sequential families often produces a collision between questions of principle and economic realities. While it is proper for courts to recognize that a person should respect his or her obligations to the first family, children in the second family also have needs that should not be forgotten.[322] Human nature and the economic demands of children may wreak havoc with analytical doctrines or any cohesive philosophy that seeks to balance the legal rights of competing families. Courts are inescapably reduced, therefore, to making the best of a bad situation by seeking to promote a situation that is tolerable for the children of both families.[323]

Different considerations apply where it is the divorced recipient spouse who remarries. In the absence of any direction to the contrary in the support order, the remarriage of a divorced spouse entitled to court-ordered support from a former spouse does not automatically justify the variation or discharge of a subsisting order for spousal or child support, but such remarriage is a relevant circumstance to be considered on any application for variation or discharge.[324] Where the parties to the second marriage are financially self-sufficient, courts have traditionally relieved the former spouse of any continuing obligation to support his or her divorced and remarried spouse.[325] In the final analysis, however, the effect of the obligee's remar-

---

(1992), 40 R.F.L. (3d) 316 (N.S. Fam. Ct.); *Grant-Hose v. Grant-Hose* (1991), 32 R.F.L. (3d) 26 (Ont. U.F.C.); *Greco v. Levin* (1991), 33 R.F.L. (3d) 405 (Ont. Gen. Div.); *Wills v. Wills* (1994), 9 R.F.L. (4th) 78 (Ont. Ct. Prov. Div.) (balancing of family income in each household); *Cass v. Cass* (1995), 15 R.F.L. (4th) 436 (P.E.I.S.C.T.D.); see also *Willick v. Willick*, [1994] 3 S.C.R. 670, 6 R.F.L. (4th) 161 at 217, L'Heureux-Dubé J.

321   *Jackson v. Jackson*, [1993] O.J. No. 1713 (Gen. Div.); *Droit de la famille — 1404*, [1991] R.J.Q. 1561 at 1566 (Que. C.A.). See, generally, Judge Norris Weisman, "The Second Family in the Law of Support" (1984), 37 R.F.L. (2d) 245.

322   *Young v. Konkle* (1993), 1 R.F.L. (4th) 211 (Alta. Q.B.).

323   *Smith v. Smith* (1992), 40 R.F.L. (3d) 316 at 318–19 (N.S. Fam. Ct.), Levy Fam. Ct. J.; see also *Magder v. Magder*, [1994] O.J. No. 1334 (C.A.).

324   See *Caron v. Caron*, [1987] 1 S.C.R. 892, 7 R.F.L. (3d) 274; *Range v. Range* (1995), 14 R.F.L. (4th) 11 (B.C.S.C.); *MacDougall v. MacRae* (1989), 19 R.F.L. (3d) 329 (N.B.Q.B.); *Smith v. Smith*, ibid.; *May v. May* (1993), 48 R.F.L. (3d) 432 (Ont. Gen. Div.); *Wilson v. Wilson*, [2005] O.J. No. 3478 (Sup. Ct.); *Campbell v. Rooney* (1995), 10 R.F.L. (4th) 351 (P.E.I.S.C.T.D.); and see Judge Norris Weisman, "The Second Family in the Law of Support" (1984), 37 R.F.L. (2d) 245.

325   *Wrobel v. Wrobel* (1994), 8 R.F.L. (4th) 403 (Alta. Q.B.); *Beaumont v. Beaumont* (1988), 19 R.F.L. (3d) 33 (N.B.Q.B.); *Oxenham v. Oxenham* (1982), 26 R.F.L. (2d) 161 (Ont. C.A.); *Bush v. Bush* (1989), 21 R.F.L. (3d) 298 (Ont. U.F.C.); *Droit de la famille — 1404*, [1991] R.J.Q. 1561 (Que. C.A.); *Impey v. Impey* (1973), 13 R.F.L. 240 (Sask. Q.B.).

riage on a subsisting spousal support order should be determined in light of the rationale upon which the order was based. A needs-based order for spousal support may be terminated by a court if the recipient remarries or enters into a non-marital cohabitational relationship, but if the spousal support order was compensatory in nature, remarriage or unmarried co-habitation may not justify its termination.[326] Repartnering has an impact on needs-based spousal support simply because the recipient's needs are usually reduced in that current household expenses are shared by his or her new partner.[327]

A helpful list of issues to consider is found in Marie Gordon's paper entitled "Glass Ceilings in Spousal Support".[328] The listed issues include:

1. Does the recipient spouse still need support in view of her new relationship and the income of her new partner?

2. Is there a way to terminate the periodic support obligation while acknowledging an ongoing entitlement (i.e. by a final lump sum payment)?

3. Did the parties specify the reasons why support was being paid when they signed their agreement?

4. Was it foreseeable at the time of the agreement that the spouse would remarry or cohabit?

5. Can it be said with any degree of certainty that the new relationship will last?

6. What effort is the recipient spouse making to achieve economic self-sufficiency?

7. Will the new relationship compensate the recipient for the economic consequences of the first marriage?

---

326 *Rosario v. Rosario* (1991), 37 R.F.L. (3d) 24 (Alta. C.A.); *Bracewell v. Bracewell* (1994), 4 R.F.L. (4th) 183 (Alta. Q.B.) (periodic support for husband not precluded by his cohabitation with another woman); *Heimbecker v. Heimbecker*, [2007] A.J. No. 1172 (Q.B.); *Rideout v. Rideout* (1995), 13 R.F.L. (4th) 191 (B.C.S.C.) (fixed-term spousal support for further two years to compensate for economic hardship resulting from marriage breakdown); *R.S.R. v. S.M.R.*, [2006] B.C.J. No. 2109 (S.C.); *Murphy v. Murphy*, 2007 BCCA 500, [2007] B.C.J. No. 2258; *K.A.M. v. P.K.M.*, [2008] B.C.J. No. 121 (S.C.); *Lagacé v. Lagacé*, [1999] N.B.J. No. 556 (C.A.) (unmarried cohabitation); see also *May v. May* (1993), 48 R.F.L. (3d) 432 (Ont. Gen. Div.). Compare *Lockyer v. Lockyer*, [2000] O.J. No. 2939 (Sup. Ct.).

327 *Locke v. Ledrew*, [2006] A.J. No. 759 (Q.B.); *Smith v. Smith*, [2007] M.J. No. 284 (Q.B.).

328 Paper presented to the National Family Law Symposium 1998.

A spouse who wants to be able to argue that remarriage or cohabitation was foreseeable at the time of entering into minutes of settlement should assume the obligation to "lay that relationship on the table" at the time of signing the minutes of settlement. After reviewing the aforementioned issues in *Wilson v. Wilson*,[329] the motions judge concluded that the wife's medical condition rendered part-time employment reasonable but that she continued to suffer an ongoing economic disadvantage from her homemaking role during her first marriage that was not eliminated by her remarriage. Having regard to the divorced husband's increased income and the divorced wife's reduced needs after her remarriage, the motions judge concluded that she should continue to receive indexed periodic spousal support, but in a reduced amount from that provided by the minutes of settlement.

b) Effect of Common-Law Relationship

In the absence of any express term or condition whereby court-ordered spousal support shall cease in the event that the recipient enters into a common-law relationship,[330] the formation of such a relationship does not automatically justify termination of an order for spousal support.[331]

In *Juvatopolos v. Juvatopolos*,[332] an order for compensatory spousal support granted to a homemaking wife on the dissolution of her traditional twenty-four-year marriage was found subject to reduction under section 17 of the *Divorce Act*, where the recipient failed to take reasonable steps to increase her earning capacity because of ongoing monthly payments that she received from her current common-law partner.

A divorced spouse who is under a court-ordered obligation to support his or her former spouse is not automatically released from that obligation

---

329 [2005] O.J. No. 3478 (Sup. Ct.).

330 See *Caron v. Caron*, [1987] 1 S.C.R. 892, 7 R.F.L. (3d) 274; *Neufeld v. Neufeld* (1986), 3 R.F.L. (3d) 435 (Ont. H.C.J.); *Rogers v. Rogers* (1992), 42 R.F.L. (3d) 410 (N.B.Q.B.) (unsuccessful attempt to arrange affairs so as to stop short of "cohabitation"); see also *Gillham v. Gillham* (1993), 48 R.F.L. (3d) 156 (Alta. C.A.) (separation agreement; onus of proof).

331 See *McMullen v. McMullen* (1993), 141 N.B.R. (2d) 297 at 304 (Q.B.); *Horlock v. Horlock* (1984), 42 R.F.L. (2d) 164 (Ont. C.A.), aff'g (1983), 37 R.F.L. (2d) 198 (Ont. H.C.J.); *Ewart v. Ewart* (1979), 10 R.F.L. (2d) 73 (Ont. C.A.); *Droit de la famille — 333*, [1987] R.D.F. 45 (Que. C.A.); compare *Barnard v. Barnard* (1982), 30 R.F.L. (2d) 337 (Ont. C.A.). See also *Janz v. Harris* (1993), 86 Man. R. (2d) 300 (Q.B.) (same-sex relationship; wife granted $50,000 lump sum for homemaking contributions to marriage).

332 [2005] O.J. No. 4181 (C.A.). See also *K.A.M. v. P.K.M.*, [2008] B.C.J. No. 121 (S.C.).

because of voluntarily assumed new financial obligations arising from a common-law relationship. Where the divorced spouse's obligation to support the "common-law spouse" is legally recognized, the court may feel compelled to strike a balance between the competing obligations owed to the respective families.[333] As with remarriage, each case will be determined on its own facts.[334]

The *Miglin* criteria apply where the terms of a comprehensive separation agreement, which includes a third-party non-cohabitation clause, are incorporated in a divorce judgment.[335]

4) Finality of Orders

It is doubtful whether courts have a discretionary jurisdiction to direct that a support order shall be final and irrevocable.[336] Incidental to the above question is the jurisdiction, if any, of the court to vary a support order that has been completely discharged and has spent its force. Judicial opinions have been divided on this issue.[337] The objective of economic self-sufficiency defined in sections 15(7)(d) and 17(7)(d) of the *Divorce Act* implies that the courts may now direct that a spousal support order shall be final and irrevocable.[338] On the other hand, the jurisdiction of the court under section 4 to entertain an original application for support after the divorce and the jurisdiction to vary a subsisting support order under section 17(1), regardless of its type and subject only to the express limitations of section 17(10), imply that the court has no jurisdiction to order a final settlement

---

333   *Cooper v. Cooper* (1983), 33 R.F.L. (2d) 359 (Ont. Prov. Ct.); compare *McKinney v. Polston* (1992), 42 R.F.L. (3d) 141 (B.C.S.C.).

334   See Section R(3)(a), above in this chapter. As to the contributions of a "common-law spouse" to household expenses, see *Underwood v. Underwood* (1994), 3 R.F.L. (4th) 457 (Ont. Gen. Div.).

335   See Section N, above in this chapter.

336   See *Gill-Sager v. Sager*, [2003] B.C.J. No. 121 (C.A.); *B.G.D. v. R.W.D.*, [2003] B.C.J. No. 1098 (C.A.); see also *Dipper v. Dipper*, [1981] Fam. 31, [1980] 3 W.L.R. 626, [1980] 2 All E.R. 722 (Eng. C.A.), wherein such jurisdiction was denied, but which has since been abrogated by statutory provisions expressly conferring such jurisdiction on the English courts.

337   See *Collins v. Collins* (1978), 2 R.F.L. (2d) 385 (Alta. S.C.T.D.); *Wyatt v. Wyatt* (1986), 1 R.F.L. (3d) 252 (Nfld. U.F.C.); *Droit de la famille — 382* (1988), 16 R.F.L. (3d) 379 (Que. C.A.); *A.(C.) v. F.(W.)*, [1988] R.D.F. 358 at 360 (Que. C.A.). But see s. 17(10) of the *Divorce Act*.

338   See *Smith v. Smith* (1987), 5 R.F.L. (3d) 398 (Man. Q.B.).

or preclude a future application for spousal support.[339] In *Tierney-Hynes v. Hynes*,[340] in response to the appellant's request for a review of the principles hitherto endorsed by the Ontario Court of Appeal with respect to the finality of orders dismissing applications for spousal support, the Chief Justice appointed a five-judge panel to hear the appeal. In granting the divorced wife's appeal against a summary judgment that had dismissed her variation application, on the ground that the court had no jurisdiction to reinstate spousal support in the face of a prior variation order that had terminated an original order for spousal support granted at the time of divorce, the five-judge panel set out the following reasons. The question whether a court has jurisdiction to vary a prior denial, or a court-ordered termination, of spousal support is solely one of statutory interpretation. The judgments of the Ontario Court of Appeal in *Cotter v. Cotter*[341] and *McCowan v. McCowan*[342] have long supported the proposition that a court lacks jurisdiction under the *Divorce Act* to vary the prior dismissal of an application for spousal support. The economic self-sufficiency and finality objectives emphasized in *Cotter* were endorsed by the Supreme Court of Canada in *Pelech v. Pelech*,[343] *Caron v. Caron*,[344] and *Richardson v. Richardson*.[345] However, the language of section 17 of the current *Divorce Act* differs from its predecessor and there has been a significant jurisprudential shift away from the former prioritization of the goals of finality, certainty, and self-sufficiency as a result of the judgments of the Supreme Court of Canada in *Moge v. Moge*,[346] *Bracklow v. Bracklow*,[347] and *Miglin v. Miglin*.[348] Given significant changes in the legislative language and significant jurisprudential changes in the formulation of principles guiding spousal support, the judgments of the Ontario Court of Appeal in *Cotter* and *McCowan* are no longer authoritative. Under the current provisions of the *Divorce Act*, a court has jurisdiction to vary its previous denial of spousal support, whether such denial arose by dismissal of

---

339 See *Droit de la famille — 382* (1988), 16 R.F.L. (3d) 379 (Que. C.A.).

340 [2005] O.J. No. 2661 (C.A.), leave to appeal to the S.C.C. refused, [2005] S.C.C.A. No. 424. See also *Gill-Sager v. Sager*, [2003] B.C.J. No. 121 (C.A.) and *B.G.D. v. R.W.D.*, [2003] B.C.J. No. 1098 (C.A.).

341 (1986), 53 O.R. (2d) 449 (C.A.).

342 (1995), 24 O.R. (3d) 707 (C.A.).

343 [1987] 1 S.C.R. 801.

344 [1987] 1 S.C.R. 892.

345 [1987] 1 S.C.R. 857.

346 [1992] 3 S.C.R. 813.

347 [1999] 1 S.C.R. 420.

348 [2003] 1 S.C.R. 303.

an original application brought pursuant to section 15.2 of the *Divorce Act*, or by way of a variation order terminating a previous order providing spousal support. Such jurisdiction is inferentially supported by section 15.3 of the *Divorce Act*, which specifically contemplates an application for spousal support after an earlier dismissal of such a claim because of the priority accorded to child support orders. Section 15.3 provides powerful and persuasive support for the existence of a similar jurisdiction in analogous situations where the obligor previously lacked, but no longer lacks, the ability to pay or where there was no previous need for spousal support, but a need currently exists that is related to the marriage or its breakdown. Another reason for allowing a court to revisit the issue of spousal support lies in the fact that the language of section 17(1)(a) of the *Divorce Act* does not distinguish between child support and spousal support in addressing variation applications, and courts have readily acknowledged their jurisdiction to vary a prior denial of child support. The right of a court to revisit the issue of spousal support is also consistent with the structure and terms of the current *Divorce Act*, which was last amended in 1997 to accommodate the implementation of the *Federal Child Support Guidelines*. The current legislative provisions, particularly sections 15 and 17, differ substantially from the provisions in section 11 of the *Divorce Act* of 1968 and also introduce significant amendments to the *Divorce Act* of 1986.[349] In particular, the language of section 17(7) of the *Divorce Act* was amended in 1997 so that a court, in looking to the objectives of variation orders, is not confined to reviewing positive orders that previously provided for the support of a spouse. The current *Divorce Act* does not require a spouse to seek support at the time of divorce. Instead, it implements a structure that contemplates subsequent applications for spousal support. In addition, Parliament has provided the courts with broad jurisdiction to structure a wide range of support relief that includes the authority to order spousal support for a definite or indefinite term, to order support until a specified event occurs, and to impose any terms, conditions, or restrictions that are deemed appropriate. The broad range of options available on both original applications for spousal support and variation applications reflects parliamentary recognition that the courts require significant flexibility to tailor a just result for individual cases, given the multitude of circumstances in which spouses find themselves. The legislative changes and the expansive language used throughout the current legislation thus lead to the conclusion that a court now has the

---

349 See R.S.C. 1985 (2d Supp.), c. 3.

jurisdiction to vary the prior dismissal of an application for spousal support. This does not signify that the proverbial floodgates will open; applications to vary previous denials of spousal support will still be required to meet the threshold tests necessary to establish a meritorious claim. Furthermore, the spectre of adverse cost consequences will continue to discourage applications for relief that are without merit.

S. COST-OF-LIVING INDEXATION

In granting orders for periodic spousal support on separation or divorce, courts may order the payments to be annually adjusted in accordance with a designated cost-of-living index.[350] This eliminates the need for repeated applications to the court to increase the amount of support because of the impact of inflation on the purchasing power of the original order. It does not prevent either spouse from applying to vary an order by reason of changes of circumstances that are unconnected with the cost of living.

T. RETROACTIVE SPOUSAL SUPPORT ORDERS

The following non-exhaustive list of relevant considerations have been endorsed by the Ontario Court of Appeal as relevant to applications for retroactive spousal support orders:

(i)   the extent to which the claimant established past need (including any requirement to encroach on capital) and the payor's ability to pay;
(ii) the underlying basis for the ongoing support obligation;
(iii) the requirement that there be a reason for awarding retroactive support;
(iv) the impact of a retroactive award on the payor and, in particular, whether a retroactive order will create an undue burden on the payor or effect a redistribution of capital;
(v)   the presence of blameworthy conduct on the part of the payor such as incomplete or misleading financial disclosure;
(vi) notice of an intention to seek support and negotiations to that end;
(vii) delay in proceeding and any explanation for the delay; and

---

350   *Meiklejohn v. Meiklejohn*, [2001] O.J. No. 3911 (C.A.); *Martin v. Martin*, [2004] O.J. No. 5170 (Sup. Ct.).

(viii) the appropriateness of a retroactive order predating the date on which the application for divorce was issued.[351]

Post-application spousal support is not retroactive support that requires an analysis of the aforementioned factors. In the absence of any unusual reason arising from the factors and objectives governing spousal support orders under sections 15.2(4) and (6) and 17(4.1) and (7) of the *Divorce Act*, "an applicant, who requests financial disclosure in preparation for the negotiation or litigation of a spousal support claim and thereafter proceeds reasonably to a disposition of that claim, is presumptively entitled to prospective support from the date of notice that a support claim is being pursued."[352]

A court may grant an order for lump sum retroactive spousal support, notwithstanding a prior interim order for spousal support, but such an order is the exception rather than the rule.[353] In determining whether an order for lump sum retroactive spousal support is appropriate, the court should carefully consider the impact it can have on the matrimonial property distribution.[354]

U. *SPOUSAL SUPPORT ADVISORY GUIDELINES*[355]

1) Overview of the Guidelines

a) Introduction

In January 2005, the Department of Justice, Canada released a report entitled *Spousal Support Advisory Guidelines: A Draft Proposal*.[356] The re-

---

351 *Bremer v. Bremer*, [2005] O.J. No. 608 (C.A.), citing *Horner v. Horner*, [2004] O.J. No. 4268 (C.A.); *Marinangeli v. Marinangeli* (2003), 66 O.R. (3d) 40 (C.A.); *Price v. Price*, [2002] O.J. No. 2386 (C.A.); *Soper v. Soper*, [2006] O.J. No. 4728 (Sup. Ct.); *Galeano v. Dubail*, [2006] O.J. No. 5159 (C.A.); *Albert v. Albert*, [2007] O.J. No. 2964 (Sup. Ct.); *Emery v. Emery*, [2008] O.J. No. 844 (Sup. Ct.); compare also *J.W. v. M.H.W.*, [2007] B.C.J. No. 1597 (S.C.) and *Gehla v. Gehla*, [2008] B.C.J. No. 218 (S.C.), applying *L.S. v. E.P.*, [1999] B.C.J. No. 1451, 50 R.F.L. (4th) 302 (C.A.).

352 *MacKinnon v. MacKinnon*, [2005] O.J. No. 1552 at paras. 22–23 (C.A.); compare *Martin v. Blanchard*, [2007] O.J. No. 2713 (Sup. Ct.).

353 *Pettigrew v. Pettigrew*, [2006] N.S.J. No. 321 (C.A.), citing *Hauff v. Hauff* (1994), 95 Man. R. (2d) 83, 5 R.F.L. (4th) 419 (C.A.) and *Elliot v. Elliot* (1994), 15 O.R. (3d) 265 (C.A.).

354 *Corbeil v. Corbeil*, [2001] A.J. No. 1144 (C.A.); *E.S. v. J.S.S.*, [2007] A.J. No. 832 (Q.B.).

355 For a short critical practitioner's review of the *Spousal Support Advisory Guidelines*, see Lorne Wolfson, "The Emperor's New Guidelines" (May 2005) 20:5 Money and Family Law 33.

356 (Ottawa: Department of Justice, 2005), online: www.justice.gc.ca/eng/dept-min/pub/ss-pae/proj/ssag-idpa.pdf.

port was written by Professor Carol Rogerson of the Faculty of Law at the University of Toronto and by Professor D. Rollie Thompson of the Faculty of Law at Dalhousie University, who were retained by the Department of Justice in 2001 to prepare practical spousal support guidelines that could assist mediators, lawyers, and the courts in resolving spousal support disputes arising on divorce. In preparing the report, Professors Rogerson and Thompson engaged in a consultative process with an advisory working group of thirteen members composed of judges, lawyers, and mediators. As directors of the project, Professors Rogerson and Thompson engaged in consensus building but exercised the final decision-making authority when opinions were divided. A final report was published by the Department of Justice in 2008. This final report incorporates revisions made to their original report by Professors Rogerson and Thompson. The basic structure of the Guidelines as originally envisaged remains unchanged but the language and organization of the final report seek to clarify meaning, to incorporate the three years of experience with the Guidelines, and to focus attention on issues such as entitlement, application, using the ranges, restructuring, and exceptions. The following significant revisions to the 2005 report have been endorsed in the 2008 report:

(i) All social assistance is excluded from income for spousal support purposes, although the Universal Child Care Benefit is included.

(ii) An additional formula has been recommended to address cases where child support is determined under section 3(2)(b) of the *Federal Child Support Guidelines* and there are no children for whom a table amount of child support is being paid. Under this additional formula, once each spouse's contribution to the adult child's budget has been allocated under section 3(2)(b), those child support payments are grossed-up and deducted from each spouse's gross income. Then the *Without Child Support Formula* is applied, using the gross income disparity and the length of the marriage factor to determine the amount and duration of spousal support.

(iii) The *Without Child Support Formula* has been modified so that the recipient of spousal support will never receive more than 50 percent of the couple's net disposable income.[357]

(iv) The *Shared Custody Formula* has been adjusted to always include an equal split of the couple's net disposable income.

The following summary highlights the major proposals of Professors Rogerson and Thompson.

---

357   See *Bentley v. Bentley*, [2007] B.C.J. No. 1780 (S.C.).

b) The Nature of the Guidelines

The Guidelines are informal, voluntary, and advisory. They have not been legislatively endorsed and are not legally binding. The report envisages that lawyers and mediators will use the Guidelines as a principled basis for negotiation or as a test for determining the reasonableness of offers to settle derived from a budgetary analysis. The report also envisages that judges will use the ranges established by the prescribed formulas in the Guidelines as a check or litmus test to assess the positions of the parties at pre-trial conferences or in argument at hearings and trials and that the formulas will assist judges in adjudication by providing a structural approach to the exercise of the judicial discretion conferred by the *Divorce Act*.

c) Advantages and Disadvantages of the Guidelines

The following six potential advantages of the *Spousal Support Advisory Guidelines* are identified:

1. To provide a starting point for negotiations and decisions.
2. To reduce conflict and to encourage settlement.
3. To reduce the costs and improve the efficiency of the system.
4. To avoid budgets and to simplify the process.
5. To provide a basic structure for further judicial elaboration.
6. To create consistency and legitimacy.

The following five potential disadvantages of the Guidelines are identified:

1. They are too rigid.
2. Spousal support is too complicated.
3. Discretion allows intuitive reasoning.
4. Regional variations are too great.
5. Litigation will be foreclosed.

Given the inherent uncertainty of the present law of spousal support, Professors Rogerson and Thompson conclude that the advantages of the Guidelines far outweigh their disadvantages, especially in light of the inclusion of more than one formula in the Guidelines, the provision of ranges for the amount and duration of spousal support rights and obligations, and specified exceptions and other features of the Guidelines that balance consistency and certainty against the necessary flexibility that is permitted under the Guidelines.

d) Basic Structure and Application of the Guidelines

i) *Income-Sharing Regime Deemed Consistent with Spousal Support Criteria under the* Divorce Act

The most fundamental aspect of the Guidelines is that they are based on income sharing, as distinct from a budgetary analysis. Income sharing does not imply equal sharing of the combined income of the spouses. Mathematical formulas have been devised to determine the proportion of the spousal incomes to be shared. The report states that the income-sharing regime is consistent with existing legal principles and does not purport to change them. It stipulates that the Guidelines do not deal with entitlement but, nevertheless, asserts that the post-*Bracklow* era has introduced a "very expansive basis for entitlement to spousal support" and "effectively any significant income disparity generates an entitlement to some support."[358] While this may be true of long, traditional marriages in which one spouse, usually the wife, forgoes employment for a significant period of time to assume a parenting role, it is by no means a self-evident universal truth. The report further states that the Guidelines do not deal with the effect of a prior agreement on spousal support, which will continue to be governed by *Miglin v. Miglin*.[359] The Guidelines are, nevertheless, expected to play an important role in the negotiation of spousal agreements by providing a more structured framework for negotiation and some benchmarks of fairness.

ii) *The Proposed Applicability of the Guidelines*

The Guidelines are intended to apply to interim as well as final orders.[360] Although they may also be applied in variation proceedings based on an increase in the recipient's income or a decrease in the payor's income,[361] the Guidelines are not intended to be of general application in variation proceedings. Postseparation increases in the payor's income,[362] repartner-

---

358   Compare *Duder v. Rowe*, [2006] A.J. No. 868 (Q.B.); *Dubey v. Dubey*, [2008] B.C.J. No. 605 (S.C.); *Eastwood v. Eastwood*, 2006 NBQB 413, [2006] N.B.J. No. 513.

359   [2003] 1 S.C.R. 303. See *Duder v. Rowe*, *ibid*; *K.A.M. v. P.K.M.*, [2008] B.C.J. No. 121 (S.C.); *Campbell v. Campbell*, [2008] B.C.J. No. 202 (S.C.); *Vanderlinden v. Vanderlinden*, 2007 NSSC 80, [2007] N.S.J. No. 107.

360   See *D.R.M. v. R.B.M*, 2006 BCSC 1921, [2006] B.C.J. No. 3299; *Williams v. Williams*, [2007] N.J. No. 257 (U.F.C.); *Fisher v. Fisher*, 2008 ONCA 11, [2008] O.J. No. 38.

361   *Beninger v. Beninger*, 2007 BCCA 619, [2007] B.C.J. No. 2657.

362   *Logan v. Logan*, [2007] B.C.J. No. 1371 (S.C.); *Bryant v. Gordon*, [2007] B.C.J. No. 1460 (S.C.); *Emery v. Emery*, [2007] B.C.J. No. 2579 (S.C.) (review order); *Beninger v. Beninger*, *ibid*.

ing,[363] remarriage, and second families are left to be resolved under the evolving framework of existing law.

Having regard to the legislative redefinition of "marriage" in the *Divorce Act* to include same-sex couples, the Guidelines apply to them in the same way as to opposite-sex divorcing or divorced couples.

The Guidelines have been specifically developed for use under the *Divorce Act*. Their applicability to claims for spousal support under provincial or territorial legislation will depend on the extent to which such legislation endorses principles and a conceptual approach consistent with the *Divorce Act*.[364]

iii) *Two Basic Formulas — Marriages without and with Dependent Children*

The Guidelines establish two basic mathematical formulas to determine both the amount and duration of spousal support. The first formula, which applies to marriages without dependent children, is relatively simple, being based on the duration of marital and premarital cohabitation. As the duration of the cohabitational relationship increases, so too does the amount and duration of spousal support. A more complex formula is devised to deal with marriages with dependent children. Both formulas provide ranges for both the amount and duration of spousal support, rather than fixed amounts or periods. The particularly wide ranges used in the *Without Child Support Formula* reflect regional variations and uncertainty in current practice, and could be refined after some period of experience under the Guidelines. For the purpose of applying both formulas, spousal income is defined in accordance with the criteria defined in the *Federal Child Support Guidelines*. However, the report opts to use different methods of calculating income under the two formulas. Under the *Without Child Support Formula*, gross income is used, whereas the *With Child Support Formula* relies upon net income calculations. Both formulas generate a gross amount of spousal support that remains subject to the current inclusion/deduction rules under the *Income Tax Act*.

iv) *Floors and Ceilings*

The Guidelines establish both a floor and a ceiling for their application. Subject to exceptional circumstances, such as where the payor is living

---

363 *K.A.M. v. P.K.M.*, [2008] B.C.J. No. 121 (S.C.).

364 See *McCulloch v. Bawtenheimer*, [2006] A.J. No. 361 (Q.B.); *Brown v. Brown*, [2007] N.B.J. No. 330 (Q.B.); *Snyder v. Pictou*, [2008] N.S.J. No. 77 (C.A.).

with parents or otherwise has significantly reduced expenses, the report does not envisage that the formulas would apply to payors earning a gross annual income of $20,000.[365] The formulas are also inapplicable to the apportionment of income between the spouses insofar as the payor's gross annual income exceeds $350,000.[366]

v) *Restructuring: Trade-Offs between Amount and Duration*

The report provides for the possible restructuring of spousal support by trade-offs between the amount and duration of support. For example, the formula amount could be increased or reduced to reflect corresponding reductions or increases in the duration of spousal support or a lump sum payment of spousal support could influence the amount and duration of periodic support.[367]

vi) *Exceptions*

While acknowledging that the Guidelines are not binding and departures are always possible on a case-by-case basis, the report provides a non-exhaustive list of "recognized categories of departures" or "exceptions" where it might be inappropriate to apply the prescribed formulas. By way of example, compensatory spousal support awards might exceed the prescribed formula in cases of shorter marriages that have generated disproportionate economic losses or gains to either spouse.[368] An inability to achieve economic self-sufficiency due to illness or disability might also justify deviation from the formulas, as might a disproportionate responsibility for family debts, support obligations to children and spouses from previous relationships, or compelling financial circumstances at the interim stage.[369]

Additional specific exceptions have been introduced since the publication of the 2005 report. These relate to the following:

---

365 *Torres v. Marin*, [2007] Y.J. No. 94 (S.C.).

366 See *D.R.M. v. R.B.M.*, 2006 BCSC 1921, [2006] B.C.J. No. 3299.

367 See *McCulloch v. Bawtinheimer*, [2006] A.J. No. 361 (Q.B.) (restructuring of spousal support payments under the *Family Law Act* (Alberta) by front-end loading to reflect the applicant's current unemployment and to promote her economic self-sufficiency within two years); *Pickford v. Pickford*, [2008] B.C.J. No. 548 (S.C.); *Fisher v. Fisher*, 2008 ONCA 11, [2008] O.J. No. 38 (amount higher; duration shorter).

368 See *Ahn v. Ahn*, [2007] B.C.J. No. 1702 (S.C.).

369 Compare *Vanderlinden v. Vanderlinden*, 2007 NSSC 80, [2007] N.S.J. No. 107.

- reapportionment of property under the *Family Relations Act* (B.C.)
- the inability of low-income recipients to meet basic needs in shorter marriages under the *Without Child Support Formula*
- special needs of a child under the *With Child Support Formula*
- inadequate spousal support under the *With Child Support Formula* due to the priority given to child support under s. 15.3 of the *Divorce Act*
- non-taxable payor income
- the addition of a minimum duration to the *With Child Support Formula*

e) The *Without Child Support Formula*

The underlying premise of the *Without Child Support Formula*, which applies when there are no longer dependent children for whom child support is payable, is the concept of "merger over time." This signifies that as the duration of a marriage increases, the spouses merge their economic and non-economic lives to complement each other.

The two essential elements of this formula relate to the gross income differential between the spouses and the duration of their cohabitational relationship. The report recommends as follows:

The *Without Child Support Formula*

Amount ranges from 1.5 to 2 percent of the difference between the spouses' gross incomes (the *gross income difference)* for each year of marriage, (or more precisely, years of cohabitation), up to a maximum of 50 percent. The range remains fixed for marriages twenty-five years or longer, at 37.5 to 50 percent of income difference.

Duration ranges from .5 to one year for each year of marriage. However support will be *indefinite* if the marriage is *twenty years or longer* in duration *or*, if the marriage has lasted five years or longer, when years of marriage and age of the support recipient (at separation) added together total sixty-five or more (the *rule of 65*).

Gross income (i.e., pretax) income under this formula is based on the same definition of income as that in the *Federal Child Support Guidelines* and courts are free to impute income to either spouse who unreasonably fails to achieve his or her earning potential. It is important to observe that the percentages in the formula are not percentages of the payor's annual income; they are percentages of the gross income difference between the spouses. Chapter 5 of the report sets out fact-specific examples to demonstrate the application of the formula and the ranges that it produces for marriages of different lengths and incomes.

Although the ranges for the duration of spousal support are very broad, a tighter range was found to be unattainable because of uncertainties under the current law. The interrelationship between the amount and duration of spousal support is, nevertheless, regarded as of critical importance. In the words of the report, "using one part of the formula without the other would undermine its integrity and importance."[370] The proposed formula provides for spousal support awards of indefinite duration if cohabitation has lasted for twenty years or more or if the years of marriage plus the age of the support recipient at the time of separation equals or exceeds sixty-five (the so-called "rule of 65"). Under the proposed formula, short childless marriages will generate very modest spousal support awards in terms of both amount and duration. Medium-term childless marriages will generate transitional orders of varying amounts and duration that increase with the length of the relationship. Long childless marriages will generate generous spousal support for an indefinite term that provides comparable standards of living for each of the spouses. As under the current law, orders made under the Guidelines will be subject to variation in the event of a subsequent material change of circumstances and may also include provisions for review.[371]

The report identifies a non-exhaustive list of several situations that could be taken into account in narrowing the prescribed range of spousal support generated by the formula. Five examples are provided. First, a strong compensatory claim for spousal support might generate an award at the higher end of the range whereas a non-compensatory claim based simply upon loss of the marital standard of living might result in an award at the lower end of the range. Second, a recipient's needs arising because of age or disability might push an award to the higher end of the range. Conversely, the absence of any compelling need might push the award to the lower end of the range. Third, the absence of any property to be divided might trigger a spousal support order at the higher end of the range whereas an unequal division of property in favour of the recipient could trigger a spousal support order at the lower end of the range. Fourth, the needs and limited means of the payor spouse might also push an award

---

370　Above note 356 at 30.
371　See *Snyder v. Pictou*, [2008] N.S.J. No. 77 at para. 25 (C.A.).

to the lower end of the range. Fifth, the need to promote the economic self-sufficiency of a recipient spouse could push in different directions. A spousal support award at the lower end of the range could be used to encourage a spouse to make greater efforts to achieve self-sufficiency. Alternatively, an award at the higher end of the scale might facilitate the recipient spouse's pursuit of retraining or education for the purpose of achieving economic self-sufficiency.

f)   The *With Child Support Formula*

i)   *Reasons for Separate Model Where Dependent Children Involved; Parenting Partnership Model*
Having regard to the impact of child support obligations on the ability to pay spousal support, the priority accorded to child support under section 15.3 of the *Divorce Act*, the income tax implications of child support, which differ radically from those governing periodic spousal support, and child-related federal and provincial benefits and credits, a separate formula has been devised for calculating spousal support in circumstances where child support is concurrently being paid by one spouse to the other. The underlying rationale of this formula is a "parental partnership model" premised on the compensatory notions espoused in both *Moge* and *Bracklow*. The parental partnership rationale looks not only at past loss but also at the continuing economic disadvantages that result from ongoing parenting responsibilities.

ii)   *Primary Differences between the Two Basic Formulas*
There are three important differences between the *Without Child Support Formula* and the *With Child Support Formula*. First, the *With Child Support Formula* uses the net incomes of the spouses, not their gross incomes. Second, it divides the pool of combined net incomes between the two spouses, instead of using the gross income difference. Third, the upper and lower percentage limits of net income division do not change with the length of the marriage.

iii) *Summary of Basic* With Child Support Formula
The following basic *With Child Support Formula* applies where the higher-income spouse is paying both child support and spousal support to the lower-income spouse, who is the parent with primary care of the child:

The *With Child Support Formula*

(1) Determine the *individual net disposable income (INDI)* of each spouse:

Guidelines Income *minus* Child Support *minus* Taxes and Deductions = Payor's *INDI*

Guidelines Income *minus* Notional Child Support *minus* Taxes and Deductions *plus* Government Benefits and Credits = Recipient's *INDI*

(2) Add together the individual net disposable incomes. Determine the range of spousal support amounts that would be required to leave the lower income recipient spouse with between 40 and 46 percent of the combined INDI.

Calculation of a spouse's individual net disposable income under this formula will require access to computer software. Existing computer programs will need modification to accommodate the formula.

The *With Child Support Formula* seeks to isolate a pool of net disposable income available to the spouses after adjustment for child support obligations. In the interests of uniformity and efficiency, the same definition of income is used as that found in the *Federal Child Support Guidelines*. There is, however, one important variation under the formula. In calculating the recipient's individual net disposable income, the formula requires the inclusion of government benefits and refundable credits, such as the Child Tax Benefit, the National Child Benefit, the GST credit, the refundable medical credit, and various provincial benefit and credit schemes.

After undertaking the necessary steps to assign a Guidelines income to each spouse under the formula, the respective child support contributions of each spouse must be deducted. For the payor spouse, these contributions will typically comprise the applicable table amount of child support plus the payor's share of special and extraordinary expenses under section 7 of the *Federal Child Support Guidelines*. For the payee spouse, the deduction will be the notional table amount of child support payable by that spouse plus his or her contributions to section 7 expenses. The next stage in the calculations is to subtract income taxes and additional deductions from the income of each spouse to obtain his or her net incomes. These additional deductions include CPP contributions, E.I. contributions, medical and dental insurance premiums, group life insurance premiums, and other family benefit plans. Mandatory pension plan

contributions are not an allowable deduction, although they might sometimes be used as a factor to justify fixing spousal support at the lower end
of the formulaic range. Finally, with respect to the payee spouse, government benefits or credits such as those mentioned above must be included
in the recipient's net disposable income.

After the individual net disposable income of each spouse has been
ascertained, they must be added together and hypothetical calculations
will then be undertaken to determine the amount of spousal support that
will provide the lower-income recipient spouse with between 40 and 46
percent of the combined pool of their individual net disposable incomes.

iv) *Narrowing the Range*
To assist in determining where spousal support should be fixed within the
aforementioned range, the report lists the following six circumstances for
consideration:

1. Compensatory principles would suggest that the more the recipient
   spouse gave up in the paid labour market, the higher one should go
   in the range.
2. The age, number, and needs of the children will affect placement
   within the range. For example, the demands of very young children or special needs children may have a significant impact on
   the caregiving parent's earning potential which would point to a
   higher range award of spousal support.
3. The needs and ability of the payor spouse will have special importance at the lower end of the income spectrum, as, for example,
   where the payor is making mandatory pension deductions or incurring significant but reasonable costs in exercising access to the
   children.
4. At lower income levels, the needs and standard of living of the recipient spouse and children may point towards spousal support at
   the higher end of the range, subject to a balancing of the needs of
   the payor spouse who falls under the third category.
5. Other things being equal, which they rarely are, the longer the
   marriage, the more likely one might move towards the higher end
   of the range.
6. Economic self-sufficiency incentives, as, for example, where a
   spouse might be reasonably expected to train for re-entry into the
   paid labour force, might favour an award at the higher end of the
   range. Conversely, spousal support might be fixed at the lower end

of the range to induce an unwilling spouse to make greater efforts towards economic self-sufficiency.

v) Duration under the Basic Formula

Initial orders under the basic *With Child Support Formula* would be indefinite in form (i.e., duration not specified), but would be subject to outside time limits that would inform the processes of subsequent review or variation.

While endorsing the criterion that the maximum duration of a spousal support order would be the longer of either one year of support for each year of the marriage or until the youngest or last child completed high school, Professors Rogerson and Thompson saw no reason to impose any kind of minimum duration in their 2005 report. However, lawyers and judges treated the maximum duration test as the norm and this was never intended by Professors Rogerson and Thompson. Consequently, they introduced a minimum time limit for spousal support orders in their final report, namely, the longer of either one-half year of support for each year of marriage or until the date one year after the youngest child starts attending school full-time.

vi) Shared and Split Custody

Split custody and shared custody arrangements, which fall subject to sections 8 and 9 of the *Federal Child Support Guidelines* respectively, trigger adjustments to the computation of the individual net disposable income of each spouse under the basic *With Child Support Formula.*

In split custody arrangements, where one or more children are primarily resident with each parent, the report acknowledges the costs faced by each parent in supporting the child in his or her primary care by deducting a notional table amount of child support from the income of each parent, not just the recipient parent.

In cases of shared custody, Professors Rogerson and Thompson propose that, in computing the individual net disposable income of each spouse, the full table amount of child support, plus section 7 contributions, be deducted from the payor's income; and the notional table amount, plus any section 7 contributions, be deducted from the recipient's income, even though the child support actually paid and received is a straight set-off amount under section 9(a) of the *Federal Child Support Guidelines.*[372]

---

372 See *Swallow v. De Lara*, [2006] B.C.J. No. 2060 (S.C.); *Fell v. Fell*, [2007] O.J. No. 1011 (Sup. Ct.).

vii) *Hybrid Formula Where Spousal Support Paid by Custodial Parent*

The basic *With Child Support Formula* is premised on the higher income spouse's paying both child and spousal support to the lower-income parent. Cases do arise, however, where child support and spousal support flow in opposite directions. To address these cases, the report provides the following distinct formula:

Formula for Spousal Support Paid by Custodial Parent

(1) Reduce the payor spouse's Guidelines income by the *grossed-up notional table amount* for child support (plus a gross-up of any contributions to s. 7 expenses).

(2) If the recipient spouse is paying child support, reduce the recipient's Guidelines income by the *grossed-up amount of child support paid* (table amount plus any s. 7 contributions).

(3) Determine the *adjusted gross income difference* between the spouses and then quantum ranges from 1.5 percent to 2 percent for each year of marriage, up to a maximum of 50.

(4) *Duration* ranges from .5 to one year of support for each year of marriage, with the same rules for indefinite support as under the *Without Child Support Formula*.[373]

viii) *Crossover between Formulas*

The report provides for a crossover between the *With Child Support Formula* and the *Without Child Support Formula* after the children cease to be eligible for support.

g) **Quebec**

As stated previously, the *Without Child Support Formula* is based on both marital and premarital cohabitation. Whether this will prove to be acceptable in Quebec is open to question because there is no entitlement to spousal support for unmarried cohabitants under the *Civil Code of Québec*. Subject to that caveat, Professors Rogerson and Thompson perceive the basic *Without Child Support Formula* as readily applicable in Quebec. Although Quebec has its own *Child Support Guidelines*, which differ in

---

373   See *Puddifant v. Puddifant*, [2005] N.S.J. No. 558 (S.C.); *Martin v. Martin*, [2007] O.J. No. 467 (Sup. Ct.).

some important ways from the *Federal Child Support Guidelines*, they foresee no obstacles to the application of the basic *With Child Support Formula* in Quebec after due account is taken of the differences between the provincial and federal *Child Support Guidelines*. Where one of the divorcing parents is ordinarily resident outside Quebec, the *Federal Child Support Guidelines* govern child support and no adjustments to the basic *With Child Support Formula* are necessary.

h) General Observations

It is evident from the above overview that the Guidelines are complex. Some of the terminology is new and the detailed commentary of the authors is vital to a proper understanding of the formulas. Professors Carol Rogerson and Rollie Thompson fully explain their rationale and the underlying bases of the formulas as well as identifying specific limitations and exceptions to their application. Twenty-seven years ago, Justice Abella, now of the Supreme Court of Canada, observed that spousal support is a "Rubik's cube for which no one yet has written the Solution Book."[374] The highly sophisticated report prepared by Professors Rogerson and Thompson with input from their consultative group constitutes an important step towards providing a much needed Solution Book. However, progress towards achieving that objective is impeded by the fact that the Guidelines currently have no formal legal status. At this point in time, no steps have been taken to implement them by regulation pursuant to section 26(1) of the *Divorce Act*. Pending any such implementation or a judgment of the Supreme Court of Canada, the Guidelines must be viewed with some degree of caution by the judiciary. Notwithstanding this *caveat*, there are no legal obstacles to prevent judges from calling on counsel to address the Guidelines at pre-trial conferences or at hearings or trials. If lawyers are far apart on the amount and/or duration of a spousal support order, the presiding judge can legitimately draw their attention to the Guidelines and seek an explanation as to whether or not their application is appropriate and, if appropriate, how they should be applied. However, while some judges clearly perceive the Guidelines as facilitating the exercise of their discretion in fixing the amount and duration of spousal support orders, other judges perceive them as imposing an unwarranted fetter on the broad discretion conferred by the *Divorce Act*.

---

374 Rosalie S. Abella, "Economic Adjustment on Marriage Breakdown: Support" (1981) 4 Fam. L. Rev. 1.

2) Judicial Responses to the *Spousal Support Advisory Guidelines*

Between January 2005 and February 2008, the Rogerson/Thompson report on the *Spousal Support Advisory Guidelines: A Draft Proposal* was considered in 420 judicial decisions across Canada.[375] A broad spectrum of differing judicial attitudes towards the *Spousal Support Advisory Guidelines* is manifested by the following cases from across Canada.

In *Modry v. Modry*,[376] wherein the Guidelines were deemed inapplicable because of pre-existing minutes of settlement and because the annual income differential between the spouses exceeded $350,000, Germain J., of the Alberta Court of Queen's Bench, provided the following cautious judicial perspective:

> [para. 67] These Guidelines are not mandatory and are only a suggestion. There has been very little judicial analysis of the Guidelines as they are new.
>
> ...
>
> [para. 68] The Guidelines offer no guidance for handling income differences over $350,000.
>
> ...
>
> [para. 70] I suggest that courts will likely use these Guidelines as a bench mark to see what the support amount would be if the Guidelines were applied. Thus it will serve as another method of calculation, which when coincidentally echoing judicial discretion, will become referenced with approval. In other cases where the courts are either astounded by the payment proposition, that is that the math creates a number that is perceived to be too high or inadequate, the courts will shy away from its application.
>
> [para. 71] Of significant importance is that the Guidelines were never intended to be applied in the face of an existing contractual payment regime.
>
> ...
>
> [para. 73] Lastly, being income stream based, they do not directly take into account property division aspects of each case, although on an in-

375 See Professors Carol Rogerson & Rollie Thompson, "The *Spousal Support Advisory Guidelines* Three Years Later" (8 February 2008), online: www.law.utoronto. ca/documents/rogerson/spousal_3Years_en.pdf.

376 [2005] A.J. No. 442 (Q.B.).

come deeming approach their supporters point out that assets could be indirectly measured and taken into account.

[para. 74] In this case I will not apply the Guidelines but I recognize their worth and I suspect most judges will find use for them. Their limitations must be recognized, and they should not have an inflationary impact on spousal support that overshadows the statutory objectives for spousal support set out in the *Divorce Act*.

In *V.S. v. A.K.*,[377] Trussler J., of the Alberta Court of Queen's Bench, presented a vigorous challenge of the *Spousal Support Advisory Guidelines* and expressed the following concerns. The provisions of the *Divorce Act*, as interpreted by the Supreme Court of Canada in *Moge v. Moge*,[378] and *Bracklow v. Bracklow*,[379] constitute the law of Canada with respect to spousal support. In contrast, the *Spousal Support Advisory Guidelines: A Draft Proposal*[380] has no binding legal authority. The Guidelines have not been enacted by the Parliament of Canada nor by any provincial legislature, nor have they been implemented by any governmental regulation. The Guidelines report represents the opinions of two university law professors, Carol Rogerson and Rollie Thompson, assisted by a small committee of judges and lawyers. Persons with strong contrary views were not party to the deliberations and there was no widespread discussion of the report prior to its publication. While the formulas prescribed might be useful for judges who want quick answers without undertaking a thorough and careful analysis of each case, it is not the role of judges to opt for easy "cookie cutter" answers. They are bound by the *Divorce Act* and by judgments of the Supreme Court of Canada to do justice according to the circumstances of the individual case. Trussler J. rejects the contention of Professors Rogerson and Thompson that their Guidelines do not change the law.[381] In Trussler J.'s opinion, they attempt to do so by advo-

---

377   [2005] A.J. No. 1357 (Q.B.). See also *S.M.A. v. S.F.H.*, [2007] A.J. No. 610 at para. 124 (Q.B.), Romaine J.

378   [1992] 3 S.C.R. 813, 43 R.F.L. (3d) 345.

379   [1999] 1 S.C.R. 420, 44 R.F.L. (4th) 1.

380   Above note 356.

381   See also *Megyesi v. Megyesi*, [2005] A.J. No. 1261 (Q.B.), wherein Watson J. observed that the *Spousal Support Advisory Guidelines* apply a concept of income sharing that may produce results that do not necessarily accord with the compensatory and non-compensatory (i.e., needs-based) approach to spousal support orders formulated in *Bracklow v. Bracklow*, [1999] 1 S.C.R. 420, 44 R.F.L. (4th) 1. After a detailed review of the evidence in light of ss. 15.2(4) and (6) of the *Divorce Act*, Watson J. concluded that the range of income sharing proposed by the Guidelines was exces-

cating income sharing, a concept that has rarely been accepted by Canadian courts save in exceptionally long marriages. Trussler J. fears that it will not be long before someone will argue that income disparity signifies spousal support entitlement, notwithstanding Chouinard J.'s observation in *Messier v. Delage*,[382] that marriage is not an insurance policy that guarantees a lifetime pension on its dissolution. Trussler J.'s fear is somewhat reinforced by the report of Professors Rogerson and Thompson,[383] wherein, after asserting that "[t]he proposed advisory guidelines do not deal with entitlement," they go on to state that in the post-*Bracklow* era "[e]ffectively any significant income disparity generates an entitlement to some support, leaving amount and duration as the main issues to be determined in spousal support cases." On the issue of entitlement, Trussler J. adds the further comment that there are many possible degrees of entitlement under the *Divorce Act* that are based on a multitude of factors and the formulaic ranges under the *Spousal Support Advisory Guidelines* are not sufficient to cover them. She further observes that the Guidelines are experimental, being a work in progress, and it is not the function of Canadian courts to experiment on litigants. Trussler J. also states that the Guidelines ignore the interrelationship between matrimonial property division and spousal support and the potential problem of "double dipping" or double recovery that is explained in *Boston v. Boston*.[384] In Trussler J.'s opinion, the Guidelines also ignore the goal of economic self-sufficiency, insofar as it is practicable, as set out in section 15.2(6)(d) of the *Divorce Act*. In addition, they fail to take account of the growing trend, in Alberta at least, towards shared parenting. Trussler J. perceives the Guidelines formulas as setting an arbitrary and presumptive range for both the amount and duration of spousal support orders that imposes an onus on the obligor to justify judicial deviation therefrom and relieves the applicant from substantiating his or her claim by supporting evidence. While acknowledging that the Guidelines were intended to bring greater certainty and predictability to the determination of spousal support, Trussler J. concludes that every case is factually different and flexibility and discretion are required to address the many variables. By way of summation, Trussler J. states:

---

sive on the facts of this case. Watson J., nevertheless, found the Guidelines influential in ordering spousal support for a fixed-term of eight years on the dissolution of the thirteen-year marriage.

382   [1983] 2 S.C.R. 401.

383   Above note 356 at 4.2.2 "Entitlement."

384   [2001] 2 S.C.R. 413. See also *Smith v. Smith*, [2006] B.C.J. No. 2920 (S.C.).

Judges should exercise extreme caution in using the Guidelines. The
Divorce Act and the decisions of the Supreme Court of Canada call on
a judge to undertake a thorough analysis of each case. Not to do so is to
disregard the views of the highest court in this country and to make a
mockery of *stare decisis*.[385]

Given a paucity of verified information on relevant issues, the motion for
interim spousal support in *V.S. v. A.K.* was adjourned for two weeks to
permit evidence to be submitted that would enable the court to weigh all
of the factors and objectives set out in the *Divorce Act* for the purpose of
determining the appropriate disposition.

In *Law v. Law*,[386] Clackson J., of the Alberta Court of Queen's Bench,
concluded that the Rogerson/Thompson report provides a reasonable
synopsis of the law of spousal support, at least for long-term marriages
without children remaining in care. Consistent with previous judicial responses to the Guidelines, Clackson J. stated that they are useful as a
check upon the reasoning process that leads to an order and the amount
and duration of the order. Ultimately, however, the court must apply
binding judicial precedents and consider the reasons for decision made
by other courts. While acknowledging that the Guidelines formulas are
somewhat arbitrary, notwithstanding that they establish a bracket or
range of potential awards as opposed to a fixed amount, Clackson J. observed that the range serves to protect the payor from supporting the
payee at a higher standard of living than that enjoyed by the payor. After
finding that the relative standards of living of the spouses were not as
uneven as their annual income differential, the husband was ordered to
pay spousal support of $3,000 per month, which compared to a range of
$2,500 to $3,333 under the Guidelines. On the issue of the duration of the
order, Clackson J. departed from the Guidelines, which suggested that it
should be of indefinite duration. Having regard to the husband's planned
retirement and the court-ordered matrimonial property division that had
already addressed the husband's pension, the wife's spousal support order
was to terminate once the husband fully retired because any claim for
ongoing compensatory spousal support after that date would no longer
be sustainable. Given the wife's annual income of $51,000, she laid no
claim to needs-based (non-compensatory) support, being content to rest
her case on the basis of compensatory support that would be payable out
of the husband's pre-retirement annual income of $131,000. A retroactive

---

385 *V.S. v. A.K.*, [2005] A.J. No. 1357 at para. 25 (Q.B.).
386 [2005] A.J. No. 1315 (Q.B.).

spousal support order totalling just under $50,000 was deemed appropriate but only from the date when the wife's application was launched.

The *Family Law Act* (Alberta)[387] permits both spouses and adult interdependent partners to apply for support. An adult interdependent relationship is used to describe unmarried cohabiting couples of the opposite sex or of the same sex. Similar criteria apply to support rights and obligations under the *Family Law Act* (Alberta) as apply to divorcing or divorced couples under the *Divorce Act*. In *McCulloch v. Bawtinheimer*,[388] the parties had cohabited for almost six years. Applying sections 58 (factors) and 60 (objectives) of the *Family Law Act* (Alberta) to the facts of the case, including the duration of the relationship, the applicant's age, her position as a secondary earner in the relationship in consequence of the respondent's multiple employment transfers, and the significant disparity between the parties' incomes, Sullivan J. found the applicant entitled to spousal support. Using the *Spousal Support Advisory Guidelines: A Draft Proposal* as a starting point to determine an appropriate level of support, Sullivan J. observed that, while provincial-territorial legislation may differ from the *Divorce Act*, and the Guidelines were developed for use under the *Divorce Act*, the similarities between the criteria applicable to spousal support applications under the *Family Law Act* (Alberta) and the *Divorce Act* justified the Guidelines being used under the provincial statute. After referring to the Guidelines' application to initial orders, which are subject to variation in the event of a material change of circumstances within the meaning of section 77 of the *Family Law Act*, Sullivan J. observed that judicial responses to the Guidelines have varied in Alberta. After pointing out the aversion to the Guidelines articulated by Trussler J. in *V.S. v. A.K.*,[389] Sullivan J. referred to *Modry v. Modry*,[390] wherein it was concluded that the courts can consider the amount payable under the applicable Guidelines formula but the individual facts of the case must ultimately determine the amount to be ordered. Sullivan J. also cited the judgment of the British Columbia Court of Appeal in *Yemchuk v. Yemchuk*,[391] which regarded the Guidelines as a useful tool to assist judges in assessing the amount and duration of spousal support. In

---

387   S.A. 2003, c. F-4.5.

388   [2006] A.J. No. 361 (Q.B.). See also *Girouard v. Girouard*, [2006] O.J. No. 762 (S.C.), Sedgwick J. (*Spousal Support Advisory Guidelines* applied to proceeding under the *Family Law Act*).

389   [2005] A.J. No. 1357 (Q.B.).

390   [2005] A.J. No. 442 (Q.B.).

391   [2005] B.C.J. No. 1748 (C.A.).

considering the *Without Child Support Formula* under the Guidelines, Sullivan J. observed that, as stated in the Guidelines report, courts may impute income to a spouse who is not achieving his or her earning potential.[392] Furthermore, a pre-existing obligation to pay support to a previous spouse or prior children is to be taken into account. Although the amount of support and the duration of support under the Guidelines are premised on the number of years of cohabitation, the range of support generated by the applicable formula may negate any need for the court to round up or down to the nearest number of years. After examining the Guidelines to determine the duration of the spousal support order, the court may adopt the option in the Guidelines report of restructuring the monthly amount and the duration of spousal support by front-loading the amount of spousal support to reflect the applicant's current unemployment and to promote financial self-sufficiency within a designated time (in this case, two years). More specifically, in the present case, Sullivan J. ordered retroactive spousal support of $2,000 monthly for nine months, followed by $1,000 monthly for eight months, and then $500 per month for a further seven months, for a total of $29,500.

In *Lust v. Lust*,[393] the mother appealed the trial judge's order for spousal support of $700 per month for four years, pointing to the *Spousal Support Advisory Guidelines* as suggesting an order of $1,229 per month for ten years. In response to this contention, the Alberta Court of Appeal stated that, whereas the *Federal Child Support Guidelines* have the force of law and are mandatory, the *Spousal Support Advisory Guidelines* are not. While observing that the *Spousal Support Advisory Guidelines* "are instructive as to one route to proper exercise of discretion in arriving at an award," the Alberta Court Appeal stated that "[t]hey do not fully fetter a trial judge's discretion."[394] Because the trial judge considered that his order would enable the appellant to acquire experience and training to secure rewarding employment and concluded that his order recognized the length of the marriage and its negative impact on the mother, and account was also taken of her receipt of $170,000 from matrimonial property, all of which were deemed to constitute proper factors in the setting of a spousal support order, the Alberta Court of Appeal concluded that,

---

392 See *Wilm v. Wilm*, 2007 ABQB 65, [2007] A.J. No. 109; *P.G.A. v. B.M.A.*, 2006 BCSC 1964, [2006] B.C.J. No. 3386; *S.C. v. J.C.*, [2006] N.B.J. No. 186 (C.A.); see text below in this chapter.

393 2007 ABCA 202, [2007] A.J. No. 654.

394 *Ibid.* at para. 10.

on the deferential standard of appellate review, there was no basis for interfering with the trial judge's award.

In *Lapp v. Lapp*,[395] the Alberta Court of Appeal noted that, "although the Guidelines are not binding, they are a suggested measure of support that can be considered." However, "a guideline is just that — a guideline. It is always incumbent on a trial judge to look at all of the circumstances of the parties — their means, needs, and ability to pay. It is also necessary for the trial judge to consider the objectives of spousal support."

Strong judicial endorsement of the Rogerson/Thompson report, *Spousal Support Advisory Guidelines: A Draft Proposal* is found in judgments of the British Columbia Court of Appeal.[396] In *Yemchuk v. Yemchuk*,[397] the first appeal on the issue, the British Columbia Court of Appeal expressed the following conclusions. The Rogerson/Thompson report is a useful tool to assist judges in assessing the amount and duration of spousal support. While decisions undoubtedly exist in which the result differs from the Guidelines, the report and its formulas seek to build upon current law rather than devise an entirely new approach to the determination of spousal support. The Guidelines do not operate to displace judicial reliance on decided cases to the extent that they are forthcoming, but to supplement relevant case law. In that regard, they do not constitute evidence but are properly considered as part of counsel's submissions. The ranges of spousal support set out under the applicable formula in the Guidelines are appropriate for consideration when the court attempts to give effect to the principles espoused in *Moge v. Moge*[398] and *Bracklow v. Bracklow*[399] in light of the overall financial circumstances of the particular spouses.

---

395   2008 ABCA 15, [2008] A.J. No. 208 at paras. 23 and 33.

396   See *Yemchuk v. Yemchuk*, [2005] B.C.J. No. 1748 (C.A.), citing *W. v. W.*, [2005] B.C.J. No. 1481 (S.C.), Martinson J.; see also *Tedham v. Tedham*, [2005] B.C.J. No. 2186 (C.A.); *Kopelow v. Warkentin*, [2005] B.C.J. No. 2412 (C.A.); *Toth v. Kun*, [2006] B.C.J. No. 739 (C.A.); *Redpath v. Redpath*, [2006] B.C.J. No. 1550 (C.A.); *Stein v. Stein*, [2006] B.C.J. No. 2020 (C.A.); *McEachern v. McEachern*, [2006] B.C.J. No. 2917 (C.A.); *Foster v. Foster*, [2007] B.C.J. No. 244 (C.A.); *Beninger v. Beninger*, 2007 BCCA 619, [2007] B.C.J. No. 2657; *Shellito v. Bensimhon*, [2008] B.C.J. No. 425 (C.A.). See also Carol Rogerson & Rollie Thompson, "The Spousal Support Guidelines in B.C.: The Next Generation" (July 2007), online: www.law.utoronto. ca/documents/rogerson/spousal_bc07.pdf.

397   [2005] B.C.J. No. 1748 (C.A.).

398   [1992] 3 S.C.R. 813, 43 R.F.L. (3d) 345.

399   [1999] 1 S.C.R. 420, 44 R.F.L. (4th) 1.

In the subsequent judgment of the British Columbia Court of Appeal in *Redpath v. Redpath*,[400] an order for spousal support was increased on appeal from $3,500 to $5,000 per month due to the fact that the former amount fell substantially short of the range of $4,542 to $5,510 per month established by the *Spousal Support Advisory Guidelines*. Addressing the amount of spousal support, Newbury J.A. stated that she did "not read *Yemchuk*, [*Tedham* or *Kopelow*] as indicating that the Guidelines must as a matter of law be used by a judge in determining support .... However, as a 'useful tool,' the Guidelines may indicate whether a proposed award is 'in the range' of what should be a pattern of predictable maintenance across the province and across Canada." While acknowledging that the judgment of the Supreme Court of Canada in *Hickey v. Hickey*[401] instructs appellate courts that they are not entitled to overturn spousal support orders simply because they would have balanced the factors differently than the trial judge, Newbury J.A. observed that *Hickey* was decided before the introduction of the *Spousal Support Advisory Guidelines*. Consequently, Newbury J.A. opined that "[n]ow that they are available to provide what is effectively a 'range' within which awards in most cases of this kind should fall, it may be that if a particular award is substantially lower or higher than the range and there are no exceptional circumstances to explain the anomaly, the standard of review should be reformulated to permit appellate intervention."[402] While finding that the trial judge had considered the appropriate factors and did not misapprehend the evidence, Newbury J.A. concluded that his award of $3,500 per month was "simply too low in light of the Guideline range of $4,542 and $5,510 per month."[403]

In *Dunnigan v. Park*, Prowse J.A., of the British Columbia Court of Appeal states: "In determining the quantum of support the trial judge referred to the *Spousal Support Advisory Guidelines* as he is obliged to do. ... In so doing, he properly used the Spousal Support Guidelines as just that, a guide to a range of awards, rather than as a set figure which must be applied or awarded."[404]

---

400 [2006] B.C.J. No. 1550 at para. 38 (C.A.). See also *McEachern v. McEachern*, [2006] B.C.J. No. 2917 (C.A.); *Stein v. Stein*, [2006] B.C.J. No. 2020 (C.A.); *R.S.R. v. S.M.R.*, [2006] B.C.J. No. 2109 (S.C.); *Williston v. Williston*, [2006] B.C.J. No. 3248 (S.C.). Compare *J.H.A. v. C.G.A.*, [2008] M.J. No. 94 (Q.B.).

401 [1999] 2 S.C.R. 518 at paras. 10–11.

402 *Redpath v. Redpath*, [2006] B.C.J. No. 1550 at para. 42 (C.A.).

403 *Ibid.*

404 2007 BCCA 329, [2007] B.C.J. No. 1364.

In British Columbia, property division and spousal support orders are closely intertwined. Pursuant to section 65 of the *Family Relations Act* (B.C.), property may be judicially reapportioned between the spouses to reflect their relative abilities to become or remain economically independent and self-sufficient and their respective capacities and liabilities. These concepts are also relevant to the judicial determination of spousal support applications under section 15.2 of the *Divorce Act*. A judicial reapportionment of property may render an order for spousal support inappropriate[405] but this does not inevitably ensue. Whether spousal support should be ordered will turn on the extent to which the judicial reapportionment of property has adequately compensated for the economic dislocation caused to the recipient spouse as a result of the marriage and its breakdown and any continuing need that spouse may have for support arising from other factors and objectives set out in section 15.2 of the *Divorce Act*. Where the judicial reapportionment of property only partially compensates the recipient spouse for the economic disadvantages flowing from the marriage or its breakdown, a spousal support order is appropriate. However, in order to avoid double recovery, account should be taken of the judicial reapportionment of property in fixing the amount of spousal support to be paid.[406] Such an accounting may lead the court to conclude that spousal support should be ordered in an amount that is somewhat less than the low end of the range recommended by the *Without Child Support Formula* under the *Spousal Support Advisory Guidelines (SSAG)*.[407]

In *Shellito v. Bensimhon*,[408] the parties cohabited for seventeen months prior to their marriage, which lasted just under four years. This appeal by the husband was from a judgment ordering the equal division of family assets and spousal support for the wife of $1,800 monthly for four months, $1,500 monthly for the next eighteen months, and $1,200 monthly for a further eighteen months ending in October 2010, by which time the disabled wife should have moved from part-time to full-time employment. The British Columbia Court of Appeal found no reviewable error in the trial judge's equal apportionment of family assets, not-

---

405 *Narayan v. Narayan*, [2006] B.C.J. No. 3178 (C.A.).

406 *Smith v. Smith*, 2006 BCSC 1655, [2006] B.C.J. No. 2920.

407 *Tedham v. Tedham*, [2005] B.C.J. No. 2186 (C.A.). See also *W. v. W.*, [2005] B.C.J. No. 1481 (S.C.); *Vazzaz v. Vazzaz*, [2006] B.C.J. No. 625 (S.C.), Myers J.; *McEachern v. McEachern*, [2006] B.C.J. No. 2917 (C.A.). Compare *Smith v. Smith*, 2006 BCSC 1655, [2006] B.C.J. No. 2920 (application of Guidelines deemed inappropriate).

408 [2008] B.C.J. No. 425 (C.A.).

withstanding the relatively short duration of the marriage, because the equity value in the four properties largely resulted from market appreciation. With respect to spousal support, the husband argued that the amounts ordered substantially exceeded the range in the *Without Child Support Formula* under the *Spousal Support Advisory Guidelines* and they also double-counted the consequences of the wife's disability, which had already been considered in the court-ordered apportionment of family assets. The British Columbia Court of Appeal observed that the trial judge had expressly recognized that his award would exceed the *SSAG* level by approximately $700 per month. Addressing the trial judge's statement that the *SSAG* amounts were too low "in all the circumstances of this case," the British Columbia Court of Appeal pointed out that the wife's disability was obviously the largest factor in the award, which was structured to reflect a gradual recovery from an occupational disability and a return to full employment in about three years. Having regard to its previous judgment in *Yemchuk v. Yemchuk*,[409] wherein it was decided that the *SSAG* amounts are not determinative but are "a useful tool to assist judges in assessing the quantum and duration of spousal support," the British Columbia Court of Appeal found no error in principle in the trial judge's departure from the *SSAG* amounts to reflect the wife's disability. Furthermore, the trial judge had explicitly stated that he was taking account of the asset apportionment in fixing spousal support and there was no evidence of inadvertent double counting. The husband's appeal was accordingly dismissed.

In *Toth v. Kun*,[410] the amount of spousal support was reduced on the basis that the application judge had failed to give effect to her finding that the divorced wife's health would improve with the passage of time and thus enable her to earn income from employment. In light of the divorced husband's reduction in income from the $70,000 range to approximately $42,000 per annum, the application judge had reduced the monthly spousal support obligation from $2,400 per month to $1,500 per month. On the divorced husband's appeal, he contended that he could not afford this reduced amount, which was substantially more than the range of between $500 and $700 per month generated by the *Without Child Support Formula* in the *Spousal Support Advisory Guidelines*. In response, the divorced wife submitted that the authors of the Guidelines

---

409 [2005] B.C.J. No. 1748 (C.A.).
410 [2006] B.C.J. No. 739 (C.A.).

and the judgment in *Yemchuk v. Yemchuk*[411] both acknowledge that the Guidelines are advisory only; they do not cover all situations and, in some cases, an appropriate result will not be achieved by applying the Guidelines uncritically. The British Columbia Court of Appeal found force in the respondent's submission, having regard to her past health problems and her present English language skills, which affected her short-term earning capacity. At the same time, the British Columbia Court of Appeal found that the financial burden imposed by the spousal support order of $1,500 per month for an indefinite term was too onerous an obligation to impose on the divorced husband. For the purpose of achieving a period of transition from the current regime to a fairer and more realistic balance based on the respective positions of the parties that reflected their ages, their prospective annual incomes, and the ten-year duration of the marriage, the British Columbia Court of Appeal ordered that from 1 May through 1 September 2006, the wife should receive spousal support of $1,200 per month. The wife would then receive $1,000 per month from 1 October 2006 for three years, and by November 2009, when the retired husband would be in his late sixties and the wife about forty-seven years of age, the divorced wife would be expected to support herself.

The authors of the *Spousal Support Advisory Guidelines*, Professors Carol Rogerson and Rollie Thompson, have identified certain situations where the Guidelines apply on review and variation applications, including increases in the recipient's income and decreases in the payor's income. Other situations, such as postseparation increases in the payor's income, repartnering, remarriage, and second families, were left to be resolved by the exercise of judicial discretion because of the uncertain state of current substantive law in these contexts and the threshold issue of entitlement that may arise in these situations. In *Beninger v. Beninger*,[412] the British Columbia Court of Appeal found that the complications, referred to by Professors Rogerson and Thompson as arising on a variation application, were not a barrier to using the Guidelines as a tool in determining the amount and duration of spousal support. At the time of the original order, the Guidelines were not available and, therefore, played no part in the spousal support determination. It was apparent, however, that the criteria applied under section 15.2 of the *Divorce Act*, which are mirrored on variation applications under section 17 of the *Divorce Act*, led the trial judge to conclude that the wife was entitled to substantial

---

411 [2005] B.C.J. No. 1748 (C.A.).
412 2007 BCCA 619, [2007] B.C.J. No. 2657.

spousal support for an indefinite term on both compensatory and non-compensatory principles. While there was some prospect of the wife's obtaining employment thereafter, this expectation was not realized due to the wife's marital role and her persistent and increasing health problems. On the other hand, the divorced husband's increased income was directly related to the career that he embarked on during the marriage while his wife assumed the role of a full-time homemaker and relinquished her own career prospects. Given these circumstances, and the fact that the divorced wife continued to struggle with the adverse economic consequences of the marriage breakdown, the British Columbia Court of Appeal concluded that almost all of the same factors that were relevant on the wife's original application for spousal support continued to apply with equal force to the current variation application. In these circumstances, the British Columbia Court of Appeal held that it would be appropriate to apply the Guidelines as a guide to the appropriate level and duration of support. At the same time, the British Columbia Court of Appeal made it clear that the decision whether to use the Guidelines as a guide on variation applications will have to be made cautiously and on a fact-specific basis.

In *J.H.A. v. C.G.A.*,[413] Little J. articulates the following response to the *Spousal Support Advisory Guidelines* as appropriate in Manitoba pending an appellate ruling:

[160] The *SSAG* have been referred to or used in at least four trial level decisions in the Manitoba Courts (see *Shore-Kalo v. Kalo*, 2007 MBQB 197; [2007] M.J. No. 297; *Hykle v. Hykle*, 2007 MBQB 243; [2007] M.J. No. 360; *Graham v. Graham*, 2008 MBQB 25; and *Huntly v. Huntly*, 2008 MBQB 42).

[161] The *SSAG* have received increased judicial endorsement over time. This includes a number of appellate decisions in other jurisdictions, most notably and early on, the British Columbia Court of Appeal's decision in *Yemchuk v. Yemchuk*, 2005 BCCA 406, [2005] B.C.J. No. 1748 (C.A.). Others have followed including *Redpath v. Redpath*, 2006 BCCA 338; [2006] B.C.J. No. 1550 (BCCA). Most recently, the Ontario Court of Appeal indicated (in *Fisher v. Fisher*, 2008 ONCA 11 at para. 103) that appellate review of decisions would be assisted by the trial judge's inclusion of reasons explaining why the *SSAG* in a particular case do not provide an appropriate result, the court likening the use of the *SSAG*

---

as being "no different than a trial court distinguishing a significant authority relied upon by a party". (Also see *Redpath, supra*, at para. 42).

[162] Given the broad and growing use of and reference to the *SSAG* by appellate courts in other jurisdictions, and as a matter of comity within this court, I think it would take an appellate decision in this Province to direct me not to use or consider the *SSAG*, should I regard them as applicable or helpful in this or another case. Whether reasons are necessary to explain why the *SSAG* in a particular case do not provide an appropriate result I leave for another day.

[163] That said, I do not think the *SSAG* create a regime where evidence, its reliability or completeness, no longer matters. I do not think that the *SSAG* have created a regime (at least not yet) where one can stand up, file three tax returns, a financial statement dealing with assets, debts and expenses and a computer generated calculation offered by the *SSAG*, close the evidence and proceed to argument. (See *Morash v. Morash*, 2005 SKQB 411, [2005] S.J. No. 618.)

...

[237] In my view the *SSAG* may offer useful guidance in some cases when it comes to issues of duration.

...

[240] While the aggregate period over which needs based support is paid is two years less than the low end of the range provided for in the *SSAG*, the *SSAG* offer a formulaic approach that leads to "average" justice rather than individualized justice. It is important to remember that the *SSAG*'s philosophical underpinnings are not reflected *per se* in the legislation although they do emerge from the case law (some of it at the highest level). These include "income sharing", "merger over time" and "parental partnership".

In *S.C. v. J.C.*,[414] a decision of the New Brunswick Court of Appeal, on the dissolution of a twenty-five-year marriage, the trial judge, having attributed an annual income of $100,000 to the husband and $46,764 to the wife, had ordered the husband to pay spousal support of $1,625 per month for a fixed-term of five years. The wife appealed both the amount and duration of the spousal support order. There was no dispute concerning the wife's entitlement to spousal support and the amount of the order was

---

414 2006 NBCA 46, [2006] N.B.J. No. 186, leave to appeal to S.C.C. refused, [2006] S.C.C.A. No. 246.

upheld by the New Brunswick Court of Appeal, being an amount that fell at the lower end of the range of support indicated by the *Without Child Support Formula* under the *Spousal Support Advisory Guidelines*. In endorsing the trial judge's use of the Guidelines, the New Brunswick Court of Appeal accepted the opinion of the British Columbia Court of Appeal in *Yemchuk v. Yemchuk*[415] that the Guidelines "reflect the current law" and "[provide] a useful tool to assist judges in assessing the quantum and duration of spousal support." The New Brunswick Court of Appeal further observed that the Guidelines have been characterized in various ways, namely, "a check, a cross-check, a litmus test, a useful tool and a starting point" but, whatever term is preferred, "their use, through the available software, will help in the long run to bring consistency and predictability to spousal support awards. Not only will they foster settlement; they will also allow spouses to anticipate their support responsibilities at the time of separation."[416] In rejecting the wife's contentions that a higher amount of spousal support should have been ordered and the trial judge had erred in imputing an annual income to her that was twice the amount payable to her under her then current six months' contract with the Ontario government, the New Brunswick Court of Appeal observed that there was no evidence to suggest that the wife's contract would not be renewed and she had in fact been working continuously for more than eighteen months prior to the date of the trial. While testing the amount of spousal support in light of the range suggested by the *Without Child Support Formula* under the Guidelines, the New Brunswick Court of Appeal ignored the Guidelines' formula relating to the duration of the spousal support order under appeal. In the *Spousal Support Advisory Guidelines: A Draft Proposal*,[417] Professors Rogerson and Thompson set out the following criteria:

The *Without Child Support Formula*

Amount ranges from 1.5 to 2 percent of the difference between the spouses' gross incomes (the *gross income difference*) for each year of marriage, (or more precisely, years of cohabitation), up to a maximum of 50 percent. The range remains fixed for marriages twenty-five years or longer, at 37.5 to 50 percent of income difference.

---

415   [2005] B.C.J. No. 1748 (C.A.).
416   2006 NBCA 46 at para. 5, [2006] N.B.J. No. 186, leave to appeal to S.C.C. refused, [2006] S.C.C.A. No. 246.
417   Above note 356 at 5.1.

Duration ranges from .5 to one year for each year of marriage. However support will be *indefinite* if the marriage is *twenty years or longer* in duration *or*, if the marriage has lasted five years or longer, when years of marriage and age of the support recipient (at separation) added together total sixty-five or more (the *rule of 65*).

The authors observe that "amount and duration are interrelated parts of the formula — they are a package deal. Using one part of the formula without the other would undermine its integrity and coherence," although the report envisages restructuring, which allows duration to be extended by lowering the monthly amount of support. In *S.C. v. J.C.*, the New Brunswick Court of Appeal upheld the trial judge's direction that the spousal support order terminate after five years, namely, in August 2008. The most troubling aspect of this time-limited order arises from the fact that the spouses had been married for twenty-five years. In the opinion of the New Brunswick Court of Appeal, "[i]t would almost seem that there would be a presumption that support would be paid for an indefinite period after what is regarded as a long-term marriage."[418] However, the court observed that previous case law in New Brunswick and elsewhere indicated that long-term marriages do not automatically negate time-limited orders. After charting fifteen appellate rulings in New Brunswick indicating that more time-limited orders have been overturned than upheld in cases involving long-term marriages, the New Brunswick Court of Appeal in *S.C. v. J.C.* stated that the recent trend in that province was to set a date for a review of the payee's self-sufficiency three years after the original order. Given the findings of the trial judge that the wife, in her mid-forties, had the ability and drive to become self-sufficient and her temporary loss of earning capacity and career development during the marriage was counterbalanced by her marital property entitlement, which included $300,000 in pension benefits as her share of the husband's military pension, the New Brunswick Court of Appeal found no fault with the trial judge's comment that "[i]t is important to use a flexible approach when the parties are left with significant assets from the marriage"[419] and saw no reason to interfere with the trial judge's determination that the spousal support order terminate after five years. The stated trend in New Brunswick to review the economic self-sufficiency of the payee after three years from the date of the original spousal support

---

418   2006 NBCA 46 at para. 14, [2006] N.B.J. No. 186, leave to appeal to S.C.C. refused, [2006] S.C.C.A. No. 246.

419   *Ibid.* at para. 18 (C.A.).

order needs to be re-examined in light of the restraints placed on review orders by the more recent judgment of the Supreme Court of Canada in *Leskun v. Leskun.*[420]

In *Carrier v. Carrier,*[421] in dismissing the husband's appeal of an order requiring him to pay $700 per month spousal support, the New Brunswick Court of Appeal held that a separation agreement negotiated by the spouses some thirteen years prior to their divorce constituted no bar to an order for spousal support under section 15.2 of the *Divorce Act* because the terms of the separation agreement were appallingly unfair to the wife and failed to comply with the overall objectives of the *Divorce Act* under each of the two stages of the required *Miglin* analysis. In ordering spousal support of $700 per month, the trial judge had stated that this amount represented "about 25–26 per cent of [the husband's] pay and that for a 21 year marriage it was a fair amount."[422] In the opinion of the New Brunswick Court of Appeal, it might have been preferable for the trial judge to apply the *Spousal Support Advisory Guidelines.*[423] However, because the amount of the order was not raised on the appeal and the respondent wife viewed it as "fair and reasonable," the New Brunswick Court of Appeal declined to interfere with the amount ordered by the trial judge.

In a more recent ruling, *D.L.M. v. J.A.M.,*[424] Larlee J.A., delivering the judgment of the New Brunswick Court of Appeal, went so far as to say: "I would remit the matter of spousal support to the trial judge to assess entitlement and, if there is entitlement, to apply the federal *Spousal Support Advisory Guidelines.*"[425]

In *Morgan v. Morgan,*[426] LeBlanc J., of the Newfoundland and Labrador Supreme Court, examined several aspects of the *Spousal Support Advisory Guidelines* with a critical eye. Reviewing the "parental partnership rationale" as the basis of spousal support obligations under the Guidelines, LeBlanc J. stated that the rationale is not applicable in every case.

---

420 [2006] S.C.J. No. 25. See *Walsh v. Walsh*, [2006] N.B.J. No. 441 (Q.B.).

421 2007 NBCA 23, [2007] N.B.J. No. 115.

422 *Ibid.* at para. 28.

423 Citing *S.C. v. J.C.*, 2006 NBCA 46, [2006] N.B.J. No. 186, leave to appeal to S.C.C. refused, [2006] S.C.C.A. No. 246.

424 2008 NBCA 2, [2008] N.B.J. No. 9.

425 *Ibid.* at para. 46.

426 [2006] N.J. No. 9 (S.C.). For two Newfoundland and Labrador judgments wherein the *Spousal Support Advisory Guidelines* were considered on applications to vary an existing order for spousal support, see *Upshall v. Upshall*, [2006] N.J. No. 23 (U.F.C.), Dunn J. and *Walsh v. Walsh*, [2006] N.J. No. 33 (U.F.C.), Cook J. See also *Puddifant v. Puddifant*, [2005] N.S.J. No. 558 (S.C.), Gass J.

There will be cases where the preseparation and postseparation arrangements involving the children will not create any ongoing economic disadvantage or negative financial consequences, as for example, where both parents have established careers during the marriage, which are not materially affected by child-care responsibilities. Cases will also arise where the duration of the spousal relationship will be so short that the presence of children will make no difference to spousal support. In LeBlanc J.'s opinion, the parenting partnership rationale will most likely constitute the basis of spousal support entitlement where, due to the needs of the children, their age, or other special circumstances, one parent ends up having restricted employment or educational opportunities. A parent who has flexibility in his or her employment and educational opportunities may not face the same limitations or restrictions. Consequently, the fact that the spouses have cohabited for a period of time and have children will not, of itself, be determinative as to the applicability of the parenting partnership rationale. Each case must be determined on its own facts. In *Morgan v. Morgan*, LeBlanc J. found that the wife's parenting responsibilities, including those relating to a special-needs child, established a clear entitlement to spousal support. If the *With Child Support Formula* under the *Spousal Support Advisory Guidelines* had been applied, the husband would have been required to pay monthly spousal support in the range of $329 to $546. However, after reviewing the husband's net income after the payment of child support and having regard to his monthly expenses, including housing and automobile expenses, which were not excessive and were affected by his exercise of access to the children, LeBlanc J. concluded that the husband lacked the capacity to pay any spousal support. In this context, it is noteworthy that the *Spousal Support Advisory Guidelines* suggest that no spousal support should be payable until the obligor's gross annual income exceeds $20,000 and in cases where his or her gross annual income falls between $20,000 and $30,000, "consideration should be given to the percentages sought under the applicable formula, the net disposable income left to the payor spouse, and the impact of a spousal support payment upon the work incentives and marginal gains of the payor." While conceding that the Rogerson/Thompson proposal might constitute an appropriate floor in most cases, LeBlanc J. concluded that it was too low in the present case and it would be preferable to have the father continue in his present lifestyle, which was not excessive or extravagant, with him meeting his child support and access obligations rather than risk placing him in such poor financial shape as to jeopardize his child support obligations and his relationship with the children.

LeBlanc J. also expressed reservations about the Rogerson/Thompson proposals respecting the duration of child support when there are young children residing with the applicant spouse and the spousal relationship is of short duration. In the present case, LeBlanc J. would have been inclined to favour a short period of time-limited spousal support whereas the maximum duration under the *Spousal Support Advisory Guidelines* would have been up to the date when the youngest child finished high school. In LeBlanc J.'s opinion, such an order would require exceptional circumstances under the current law in Newfoundland and Labrador.

In *Phinney v. Phinney*,[427] Warner J., of the Nova Scotia Supreme Court, observes:

> The prerequisite to the determination of the quantum of spousal support is entitlement. While the draft proposal for the *Spousal Support Advisory Guidelines* states that the Guideline amounts are premised on a finding by a court that entitlement exists, the application of the ranges, and the basis for the calculation of quantum, does not appear to fully take into account circumstances where entitlement, based on the objectives in s. 15.2(6), is weak.

In *Phinney*, Warner J. reviewed the four objectives of spousal support orders under section 15.2(6) of the *Divorce Act* in concluding that the wife was disentitled to spousal support after September 2004. Warner J. held that no foundation had been established for compensatory spousal support and any right to non-compensatory support based on the wife's needs was negated by her earning capacity and her entry into a stable common-law relationship with a man whose income significantly exceeded that of the husband. In addressing section 15(2)(6)(d) of the *Divorce Act*, whereby the fourth objective of spousal support orders is to promote the economic self-sufficiency of each of the spouses, insofar as is practicable, Warner J. observed that economic self-sufficiency does not have to be achieved through employment income. Alternative means of achieving economic self-sufficiency include good fortune, investments, inheritance, or entering into a new partnership with a person with a significant and secure financial status.

In *Vanderlinden v. Vanderlinden*,[428] Campbell J., of the Nova Scotia Supreme Court, set aside a separation agreement negotiated by the spouses with minimal legal advice on the ground that the spouses had

---

427   [2005] N.S.J. No. 224 at para. 26 (S.C.).
428   2007 NSSC 80, [2007] N.S.J. No. 107.

mistakenly applied the *Spousal Support Advisory Guidelines* in effectuating a trade-off between spousal support and the future discharge of family and personal debts and thereby produced an agreement that was not even remotely affordable by the husband.

In *Pettigrew v. Pettigrew*,[429] the appellant husband argued that the trial judge erred in setting the amount of spousal support by applying the *Spousal Support Advisory Guidelines* instead of assessing the evidence and applying the law. The Nova Scotia Court of Appeal held that the trial judge had only referred to the Guidelines as a cross-check and, applying the customary standard of appellate review, was not satisfied that the trial judge erred in law, misapprehended the evidence, or was clearly wrong in determining the amount of spousal support to be paid.

In *Fisher v. Fisher*,[430] the Ontario Court of Appeal sought to provide the wife with a reasonable financial transition after the breakdown of her nineteen-year marriage. Lang J.A., with whom Doherty and Goudge JJ.A. concurred, concluded that the wife should receive support for seven years running from the date of spousal separation to facilitate her attainment of economic self-sufficiency, either by earning a higher income or by adapting her lifestyle to her earned income. With respect to the trial judge's refusal to revisit the amount of interim spousal support, Lang J.A. stated that "retroactive support should be available when the recipient establishes at trial that he or she was entitled to a greater amount of interim support, the respondent had the ability to pay, and the imposition of retroactive support would not create undue hardship for the payor."[431] Lang J.A. further stated that this approach accords with the structure of the *Spousal Support Advisory Guidelines*, which apply to both interim and permanent orders, and it avoids distortions that would otherwise arise under the Guidelines in determining the interdependent issues of the amount and duration of spousal support orders. To achieve an equitable outcome in determining the amount of spousal support, Lang J.A. averaged the annual income of each spouse during the last three years of matrimonial cohabitation and during the year in which they separ-

---

429 [2006] N.S.J. No. 321 (C.A.).

430 2008 ONCA 11, [2008] O.J. No. 38. See also *Pagnotta v. Malozewski*, [2008] O.J. No. 1318 (Div. Ct.); *Grinyer v. Grinyer*, [2008] O.J. No. 290 (Sup. Ct.); *Langdon v. Langdon*, [2008] O.J. No. 418 (Sup. Ct.); *Benson v. Benson*, [2008] O.J. No. 578 (Sup. Ct.); *Havrot v. Moore*, [2008] O.J. No. 1315 (Sup. Ct.). And see *J.H.A. v. C.G.A.*, [2008] M.J. No. 94 (Q.B.).

431 2008 ONCA 11, [2008] O.J. No. 38 at para. 76.

ated. This produced an average annual income of $89,825 for the husband and $35,500 for the wife. Based on these averages, Lang J.A. concluded that the wife should receive spousal support in the amount of $3,000 per month for three and one-half years from the date of the interim order, followed by monthly spousal support of $1,500 for a further three and one-half years, whereafter spousal support would terminate. Although she assessed the amount and duration of spousal support on the basis of the circumstances of the case, Lang J.A. stated that "it is helpful to consider the reasonableness of this award by reference to the Guidelines."[432] After referring to "the seminal case" of *Yemchuk v. Yemchuk*,[433] wherein the *Spousal Support Advisory Guidelines* were characterized as a "useful tool," and after identifying specified circumstances wherein their application is limited or excluded, Lang J.A. expressed the following general conclusion:

> [96] Importantly, in all cases, the reasonableness of an award produced by the Guidelines must be balanced in light of the circumstances of the individual case, including the particular financial history of the parties during the marriage and their likely future circumstances.
>
> [97] Accordingly, the Guidelines cannot be used as a software tool or a formula that calculates a specific amount of support for a set period of time. They must be considered in context and applied in their entirety, including the specific consideration of any applicable variables and, where necessary, restructuring.[434]

Lang J.A. further observed:

> [98] Because they purport to represent a distillation of current case law, they are comparable to counsel's submissions about an appropriate range of support based on applicable jurisprudence. However, if the Guidelines suggest a range that conflicts with applicable authorities, the authorities will prevail.[435]

She noted that counsel had advised her that the Guidelines are widely used by lawyers "as a starting point for the purpose of assessing an appro-

---

432 *Ibid.* at para. 92.
433 [2005] B.C.J. No. 1748 (C.A.).
434 *Fisher v. Fisher*, 2008 ONCA 11, [2008] O.J. No. 38 at paras. 96–97.
435 *Ibid.* at para. 98.

priate level of spousal support, or for checking the validity of a proposed settlement."[436] And she stated:

> [103] In my view, when counsel fully address the Guidelines in argument, and a trial judge decides to award a quantum of support outside the suggested range, appellate review will be assisted by the inclusion of reasons explaining why the Guidelines do not provide an appropriate result. This is no different than a trial court distinguishing a significant authority relied upon by a party.[437]

Applying the Guidelines to the *Fisher* marriage, Lang J.A. found that the amount proposed under the *Without Child Support Formula* ranged from $1,290 to $1,720 monthly and the duration formula would provide support for a period ranging from nine and one-half years to nineteen years. Since the award deemed appropriate by the Ontario Court of Appeal exceeded the range for the amount of spousal support and fell well below the range for the duration of spousal support, Lang J.A. applied the restructuring concept endorsed in the *SSAG* report, which allows amount and duration to be traded off against each other, as long as the overall value of the re-structured award remains within the global amount generated by the formulas when the amount is multiplied by the duration of the award. After undertaking the necessary arithmetical calculations, Lang J.A. observed that the global amount under the spousal support order was $189,000, an amount that fell within the Guidelines global range of a low of $147,000 to a high of $392,236.[438]

Ontario courts are fortunate to have a provincial precedent-based formulaic resource available to assist them in their determination of spousal support. A review of the quantification of spousal support orders in judgments of the Ontario Superior Court of Justice, between 1 January 2002 to and including 31 December 2003, has been prepared by Justice V. Jennifer MacKinnon and E. Jane Murray, a legal practitioner.[439] In a follow-up study of later Ontario judgments,[440] the same authors express the following conclusions:

---

436   *Ibid.* at para. 99. Compare *J.H.A. v. C.G.A.*, [2008] M.J. No. 94 at paras. 159–63 (Q.B.).
437   *Fisher v. Fisher, ibid.* at para. 103.
438   See also *Grinyer v. Grinyer*, [2008] O.J. No. 290 (Sup. Ct.).
439   See "'Magical Mystery Tour': Seeking Consistency in Spousal Support Awards" (2004) 22 Can. Fam. L.Q. 215.
440   Justice Jennifer Mackinnon & E. Jane Murray, "Let It Be?: Spousal Support Update" (Paper presented to 15th Annual Institute of Family Law, 2006, County of Carleton

We have commented on the impact of the introduction of the *SSAG*. It has had the effect of increasing awards in longer marriages without child support. The formula for cases where the children are in the care of the payor produces ranges that are low and are less than the amounts observed in the 2002/2003 study and in the 2005 study. This may be a function of the fact that the formula starts with the *Without Child Support Formula* which is influenced by the length of the marriage. And, if our prediction is correct, the *SSAG* will result in lower awards in shorter marriages than has been customary in Ontario.[441] There is a lower percentage of time limited/review awards in the 2005 study, which may suggest that the durational aspects of the *SSAG* are not being embraced by the court. However a large percentage of the cases in the current study were long-term marriages that would lead to indefinite awards under the *SSAG* in any event. In *Zalman v. Zalman*, [2002] O.J. No. 1818, Quinn J. said:

> It is unfortunate that something cannot be done to bring some measure of consistency to determining spousal support. Throughout the land, hundreds of thousands of dollars, as well as incalculable hours of court time would be saved if only the assessment of spousal support was more predictable.

Today one can state with confidence that "something" has been done. The introduction of the *SSAG* provides a tool to assist in predicting spousal support awards. The cases in this study show a degree of consistency that is comparable but not greater than the degree of consistency observed in the 2002/2003 study. It cannot yet be concluded that the introduction of the *SSAG* has increased the level of consistency in spousal support awards. Having said that, awards of spousal support, with and without child support, are predictable more often than not, within reasonably well-defined ranges. The ranges are evolving. A final point of repose has not yet been reached.

In *Johnston v. Johnston*,[442] Lalonde J., of the Ontario Superior Court of Justice, relied on the following finding in the 2002–2003 review: "Where no child support is in pay, most awards of spousal support are in an amount to bring the recipient's share of gross family income into

---

Law Association, 2 June 2006).

441   See *Simpson v. Grignon*, [2007] O.J. No. 1915 (Sup. Ct.).

442   [2004] O.J. No. 4793 at para. 39 (Sup. Ct.). See also *Havrot v. Moore*, [2008] O.J. No. 146 (Sup. Ct.); *Havrot v. Moore*, [2008] O.J. No. 1315 (Sup. Ct.).

the 34–43 percent range. The comparative percentage of the net disposable income range is 36.6–44.5 percent." Having regard to the husband's high debt load, from which his wife escaped liability under the terms of their marriage contract, Lalonde J. fixed the amount of the wife's interim spousal support at the lower end of the spectrum, namely at 35.3 percent of the husband's income. Compare *Bourget v. Bourget*,443 wherein interim spousal support was fixed at $600 per month, which reflected 40 percent of the husband's net disposable income, an amount that falls within the mid-range of pre-existing case law in Ontario as compared to the *Spousal Support Advisory Guidelines*, which produced a significantly higher range of support between $755 and $1,000 based on the gross income differential between the spouses.

The strongest opposition of an appellate court to the *Spousal Support Advisory Guidelines* is to be found in the judgment of the Quebec Court of Appeal in *G.V. c. C.G.*444 On the dissolution of a thirty-two-year marriage that produced three children, one of whom was living with the husband, where the wife earned $50,000 and the husband earned $227,000 per annum, the husband was ordered to pay annual child support of $15,948 which, being paid in after-tax dollars, was grossed up to $33,000 for the purpose of determining his capacity to pay spousal support. The trial judge endorsed the approval extended to the *Spousal Support Advisory Guidelines* by the British Columbia Court of Appeal in *Yemchuk v. Yemchuk*, citing *W. v. W.*, and ordered spousal support of $4,500 per month for an indefinite term, which amount reflected the low end of the range suggested by the Guidelines. On the husband's appeal, the Quebec Court of Appeal reduced the amount of spousal support to $2,750 per month after undertaking a budgetary analysis. After reviewing the approval extended to the Guidelines by the British Columbia Court of Appeal in *Yemchuk v. Yemchuk*,445 *Tedham v. Tedham*,446 and *Kopelow v. Warkentin*,447 the Quebec Court of Appeal referred to the trenchant criticism of the Guidelines by Julien J. in *D.S. v. M.S.*,448 who observed that spousal support must be determined after a global appraisal of the factors and objectives defined

---

443 [2006] O.J. No. 419 (Sup. Ct.), Smith J., citing MacKinnon & Murray, "'Magical Mystery Tour': Seeking Consistency in Spousal Support Awards" (2004) 22 Can. Fam. L.Q. 215.

444 [2006] J.Q. no 5231 (C.A.).

445 [2005] B.C.J. No. 1748 (C.A.).

446 [2005] B.C.J. No. 2186 (C.A.).

447 [2005] B.C.J. No. 2412 (C.A.).

448 [2006] J.Q. no 506 (C.S.).

in sections 15(2), 15(4), and 15(6) of the *Divorce Act* as exemplified in *Moge v. Moge* and *Bracklow v. Bracklow,* whereas the Guidelines focus only on the duration of the marriage and provide a cookie-cutter approach that fails to take account of the individual circumstances of the particular case. The Quebec Court of Appeal also referred to the observations of Gendreau J. in *B.D. v. S.D.,*[449] who concluded that the Guidelines have no official status and involve ongoing research and consultation that have no place in the judicial disposition of current applications for spousal support. While declining to rule on the utility of the Guidelines as a facilitative supplementary tool in the determination of spousal support, the Quebec Court of Appeal in *G.V. c. C.G.* clearly disapproves of their direct application in the absence of a review of the governing legal criteria defined by statute and relevant case law coupled with a budgetary analysis to determine needs and ability to pay.

By way of an overview of the case law, the following opinions are tendered:

(i)   Absent statutory or regulatory adoption, the Guidelines are informal and advisory. Blind adherence to the ranges established by the formulas under the Guidelines is not endorsed by the authors of the report, nor by the courts. In the opinion of the majority of courts that have considered the Guidelines, the prescribed formulas provide a useful supplementary tool to assist the court in determining the amount and duration of spousal support orders after the evidence has been reviewed in light of the statutory and judicial criteria governing such orders which are elucidated in *Moge v. Moge* [450] and *Bracklow v. Bracklow.*[451]

(ii) Even if the formulas in the Guidelines can be used as a starting point, as proposed by Professors Rogerson and Thompson[452] and endorsed by Sullivan J. in *McCulloch v. Bawtinheimer,*[453] and by Heeney J. in *Hesketh v. Hesketh,*[454] but opposed by Trussler J. in *V.S. v. A.K.,*[455] they are no substitute for a factual analysis of evidence and a legal analy-

---

449   [2006] J.Q. no 1670 (C.S.).

450   [1992] 3 S.C.R. 813, 43 R.F.L. (3d) 345.

451   [1999] 1 S.C.R. 420, 44 R.F.L. (4th) 1.

452   See *Fisher v. Fisher,* 2008 ONCA 11, [2008] O.J. No. 38 at para. 99.

453   [2006] A.J. No. 361 (Q.B.).

454   [2005] O.J. No. 4053 (Sup. Ct.).

455   [2005] A.J. No. 1357 (Q.B.).

sis of the factors and objectives that are prescribed as relevant by the governing statute and relevant case law.[456]

(iii) On the breakdown or dissolution of long-term marriages in which the wife has assumed the primary homemaking and child caregiving roles, income splitting under the *Spousal Support Advisory Guidelines* substantially accords with *Moge v. Moge*, wherein L'Heureux-Dubé J. observed that "[a]s marriage should be regarded as a joint endeavour, the longer the relationship endures, the closer the economic union, the greater will be the presumptive claim to equal standards of living upon its dissolution."[457]

(iv) Although Professors Rogerson and Thompson perceive an interdependence between the amount and duration of spousal support orders, especially under the *Without Child Support Formula*,[458] courts use the Guidelines more frequently when addressing the amount of support to be ordered than in addressing the duration of the order.

(v) The Guidelines are inapplicable until an entitlement to spousal support is established.[459] In exceptional circumstances, the Guidelines may operate to negate any entitlement to spousal support.[460]

(vi) Given the informal, voluntary, and advisory status of the Guidelines, courts are disinclined to apply the proposed formulas as the sole or primary determinant of the amount and duration of spousal support orders. Courts have, nevertheless, accepted the Guidelines as providing an appropriate benchmark for the judicial determination of spousal support orders, whether made pursuant to the *Divorce Act* or provincial legislation.[461]

---

456 *V.S. v. A.K., ibid.; J.H.A. v. C.G.A.,* [2008] M.J. No. 94 (Q.B.); *Fisher v. Fisher,* 2008 ONCA 11, [2008] O.J. No. 38; *Morash v. Morash,* [2005] S.J. No. 618 (Q.B.); *Nasby v. Nasby,* [2005] S.J. No. 619 (Q.B.); *McCorriston v. McCorriston;* [2006] S.J. No. 277 (Q.B.).

457 [1992] 3 S.C.R. 813 at 870.

458 See *Fisher v. Fisher,* 2008 ONCA 11, [2008] O.J. No. 38.

459 *Duder v. Rowe,* [2006] A.J. No. 868 (Q.B.); *Dubey v. Dubey,* [2008] B.C.J. No. 605 (S.C.); *Eastwood v. Eastwood,* [2006] N.B.J. No. 513 (Q.B.).

460 *Rossi v. Rossi,* [2005] O.J. No. 4136 (Sup. Ct.).

461 See, for example, *Modry v. Modry,* [2005] A.J. No. 442 (Q.B.), Germain J.; *J.H.A. v. C.G.A.,* [2008] M.J. No. 94 (Q.B.), Little J.; *Simmonds v. Simmonds,* [2005] N.J. No. 144 (U.F.C.), Handrigan J.; *Garland v. Garland,* [2005] N.J. No. 139 (U.F.C.), Cook J.; *Barter v. Barter,* [2006] N.J. No. 52, B.G. Welsh J.A. (C.A.); *Harding v. Harding,* [2006] N.J. No. 64 (S.C.), Fowler J.; *Denton v. Denton,* [2005] N.S.J. No. 245 (S.C.), Moir J.; *Kerr v. Kerr,* [2005] O.J. No. 1966 (Sup. Ct.), Blishen J.; and *Fleming v. Flem-*

(vii)　Since computer software on the *Spousal Support Advisory Guidelines* has become available, their application as benchmarks or cross-checks has been more frequent. Lawyers and judges are cautioned against attempting to apply the prescribed *With Child Support Formula* under the *Spousal Support Advisory Guidelines* without recourse to available computer software.

(viii)　Although they have not gained universal acceptance as a "cross-check," "benchmark," "litmus test," or starting point in the judicial assessment of the amount and duration of spousal support orders, many judges now appear to have established a comfort level with the formulas and principles presented by Professors Rogerson and Thompson. It is becoming increasingly frequent for courts to look beyond the prescribed formula by examining the underlying principles set out in the Rogerson/Thompson report.

(ix)　Some previous judicial reservations about applying the *Spousal Support Advisory Guidelines* because they are a "work in progress" have been laid to rest since the Department of Justice, Canada released a final version of the Rogerson/Thompson report in 2008. However, that version introduces no major substantive changes. The differing responses of Canadian appellate courts to the *Spousal Support Advisory Guidelines* will, therefore, continue until such time as the Supreme Court of Canada addresses the issue.

V. APPEALS

The role of appellate courts in reviewing spousal support orders is clearly defined by L'Heureux-Dubé J. in *Hickey v. Hickey*.[462] Because the application of the relevant factors and objectives governing spousal support orders under sections 15.2(4) and (6) (original orders) and sections 17(4.1) and (7) of the *Divorce Act* (variation orders) necessarily involves the exercise of a broad judicial discretion, appellate courts afford considerable deference to the decisions of trial judges. In the words of L'Heureux-Dubé J., appellate courts "should not overturn support orders unless the reasons disclose an error in principle, a significant misapprehension of the

---

ing, [2005] S.J. No. 251 (Q.B.), Sandomirsky J. Compare *Large v. Large*, [2005] P.E.I.J. No. 43 (S.C.), Mitchell C.J.P.E.I. And see text below in this chapter.

462　[1999] 2 S.C.R. 518 at paras. 11–12.

evidence, or unless the award is clearly wrong."[463] The fact that the appellate court finds the amount of spousal support to be relatively low is insufficient, in itself, to warrant appellate intervention. It is only when the decision of the application judge falls outside the general ambit within which reasonable disagreement is possible and the order is, in fact, plainly wrong, that an appellate court is entitled to interfere.[464]

---

463 See, for example, *F.C.W. v. B.E.W.*, [2005] A.J. No. 143 (C.A.); *Greither v. Greither*, [2005] B.C.J. No. 2502 (C.A.); *Boudreau v. Brun*, [2005] N.B.J. No. 501 (C.A.); *Lu v. Sun*, [2005] N.S.J. No. 314 (C.A.); *Pettigrew v. Pettigrew*, [2006] N.S.J. No. 321 (C.A.); *Morton v. Morton*, [2005] S.J. No. 719 (C.A.).

464 *Silver v. Silver* (1985), 54 O.R. (2d) 591 (C.A.); *Juvatopolos v. Juvatopolos*, [2005] O.J. No. 4181 (C.A.).

CHAPTER 9

CHILD SUPPORT ON OR AFTER DIVORCE

A. GENERAL OBSERVATIONS

Fundamental changes to child support laws in Canada occurred on 1 May 1997, when the *Federal Child Support Guidelines* were implemented. These Guidelines, as amended, regulate the jurisdiction of the courts to order child support in divorce proceedings or in subsequent variation proceedings.

Since 1 May 1997, most provinces and territories have implemented similar guidelines for application in child support proceedings instituted pursuant to provincial or territorial statute.[1]

B. INCOME TAX — CHILD SUPPORT

Periodic child support payments under agreements or orders made after 1 May 1997 are free of tax. They are not deductible from the taxable income of the payor, nor are they taxable in the hands of the recipient. This represents a radical change from the former income tax regime, which applied similar criteria to both periodic spousal support and periodic child sup-

---

1   For detailed analysis of the *Federal Child Support Guidelines*, see Julien D. Payne & Marilyn A. Payne, *Child Support Guidelines in Canada, 2006* (Toronto: Irwin Law, 2006).

port in that periodic payments were deductible from the payor's taxable income and were taxable as income in the hands of the payee.

C. PRESUMPTIVE RULE; TABLE AMOUNT OF CHILD SUPPORT; SECTION 7 EXPENSES

In the absence of specified exceptions, section 3(1) of the *Federal Child Support Guidelines* requires the court to order the designated monthly amount of child support set out in the applicable provincial table. The table amount of child support is fixed according to the obligor's annual income and the number of children in the family to whom the order relates. Where the obligor resides in Canada, the applicable provincial or territorial table is that of the province or territory in which the obligor resides.[2] If the obligor's residence is outside of Canada, the applicable table is that of the province or territory wherein the recipient parent resides. Section 3(1) of the Guidelines also empowers a court to order a contribution to be made towards necessary and reasonable special or extraordinary expenses that are specifically listed under section 7 of the Guidelines. Although the court has a discretion in ordering section 7 expenses, it has no corresponding discretion with respect to ordering the table amount. It must order the table amount except where the Guidelines or the *Divorce Act* expressly provide otherwise.

In determining a father's concurrent obligations to pay court-ordered support for his two children born of different mothers, where neither child is living with the father, section 3(1) of the *Federal Child Support Guidelines* requires the court to separately determine the table amount of support payable for each child. It is not open to the court to treat the children as members of the same family unit by using the column in the applicable provincial table for the total number of children and then dividing the specified amount so that each child receives an equal share. In *M.L. v. R.S.E.*,[3] Sullivan J. granted two orders that required the father, whose annual income was $22,900, to pay the full table amount of $203 to each of his two children, in addition to specified section 7 expenses. Because the table amounts of child support reflect economies of scale as the number of children residing in the same household increases, but no such economies apply when two children reside in different households,

---

2   *Federal Child Support Guidelines*, s. 3(3).
3   [2006] A.J. No. 642 (C.A.).

Sullivan J. held that, in fixing the table amount of child support, the two children must be treated as members of distinct family units and the two families could not be treated as a single unit by determining the table amount payable for two children and then dividing this equally between the two children. The Alberta Court of Appeal found no error in Sullivan J.'s order respecting the full table amount of child support being payable for each child in addition to the specified section 7 expenses. Given the obligor's limited means, however, the Alberta Court of Appeal stayed the monthly payment of child support arrears ordered by Sullivan J., but directed that the parties were at liberty to apply to the Court of Queen's Bench to lift the stay in the event of a change of circumstances.

D. EXCEPTIONS TO PRESUMPTIVE RULE

The presumptive rule endorsing orders for the applicable table amount of child support may be deemed inapplicable in the following circumstances:

(i) where child support is sought from a person who is not a biological parent but who stands in the place of a parent;

(ii) where a child is over the provincial age of majority;

(iii) where the obligor earns an income of more than $150,000;

(iv) in split custody arrangements whereby each parent has custody of one or more of the children;

(v) in shared custody or access arrangements where a child spends not less than 40 percent of the year with each parent;

(vi) where undue hardship arises and the household income of the party asserting undue hardship does not exceed that of the other household;

(vii) where there are consensual arrangements in place that attract the operation of sections 15.1(5), (7), and (8) or sections 17(6.2), (6.4), and (6.5) of the *Divorce Act*.

E. OBLIGATION OF *DE FACTO* PARENT

1) Relevant Statutory Provisions

The definition of "child of the marriage" in section 2(2) of the *Divorce Act* reads as follows:

2(2) For the purposes of the definition of "child of the marriage" in sub-section (1), a child of two spouses or former spouses includes:

(a) any child for whom they both stand in the place of parents; and

(b) any child of whom one is the parent and for whom the other stands in the place of a parent.

A divorcing spouse can, therefore, be ordered to pay child support even though he or she is not the biological parent of the child. For example, a divorcing step-parent, who stands "in the place of a parent" to his or her spouse's children from a previous marriage, may be ordered to support those children.[4]

A spouse stands in the place of a parent within the meaning of section 2(2) of the *Divorce Act* when that spouse by his or her conduct manifests an intention of placing himself or herself in the situation ordinarily occupied by the biological parent by assuming the responsibility for providing the child's economic and parenting needs. Judicial opinion is divided on the question whether the requisite intention can exist when a husband who is alleged to be standing in the place of the parent erroneously believes that he is the father of the child.[5] In *Peters v. Graham*,[6] Boudreau J., of the Nova Scotia Supreme Court, concluded that a husband, who unknowingly stands in the place of a parent to his wife's children because he erroneously believes that he is their biological father, may be ordered to support the children but the amount of support to be paid may be reduced pursuant to section 5 of the *Federal Child Support Guidelines* in light of the concurrent obligations owed by the children's biological father and the wife's "common-law spouse" who currently stands in the place of a parent to the children.

While financial contribution towards the support of the child is a material consideration, it is not decisive in determining whether the con-

---

4   *Chartier v. Chartier*, [1999] S.C.J. No. 79. See, generally, Nicholas Bala, "Who Is a 'Parent'? 'Standing in the Place of a Parent' and Section 5 of the *Child Support Guidelines*" in The Law Society of Upper Canada, *Special Lectures 2006: Family Law* (Toronto: Irwin Law, 2007) 71–118.

5   See *T.A. v. R.C.A.*, [1999] B.C.J. No. 1382 (S.C.); *Aksugyuk v. Aksugyuk* (1975), 17 R.F.L. 224 (N.W.T.S.C.); compare *W. v. W.* (1973), 10 R.F.L. 351 (Eng.). See also *Bumbacco v. Bumbacco*, [1999] O.J. No. 3690 (S.C.J.); *D.R.D. v. S.E.G.*, [2001] O.J. No. 320 (Sup. Ct.); *S.E. v. D.E.*, [1998] S.J. No. 223 (Q.B.). And see *H.R. v. R.P.*, [2001] O.J. No. 4374 (Sup. Ct.) (portions of statement of claim for damages against wife and alleged father of child struck out).

6   [2001] N.S.J. No. 452 (S.C.); see also *J.S. v. D.W.*, [2005] A.J. No. 8 (Q.B.).

tributor stands in the place of a parent. Accordingly, a step-parent is not liable to pay support where his or her relationship with the stepchildren "never jelled into a family unit," even though he or she made indirect contributions to an educational trust for the children by way of contributions being paid out of joint family accounts.[7] Evidence of financial support may simply be indicative of kindness and compassion and is insufficient in itself to justify a finding that a spouse stands in the place of a parent where there is no evidence of any relationship akin to that of parent and child.[8] Such a status implies an intention on the part of the person alleged to stand in the place of a parent to fulfill the office and duty of a parent in both a practical and legal sense.[9] Courts look to a variety of objective factors for the purpose of determining intention. For example, they may consider the duration of the relationship, the age of the children, whether psychological parenting has taken place, day-to-day care of the children, involvement in vital activities such as the child's education or discipline, how the child and the person in question acknowledge each other in their daily roles, as well as any financial contribution to the children.[10] In *Chartier v. Chartier*, Bastarache J., speaking for the Supreme Court of Canada as a whole, observed:

> [para. 39] Whether a person stands in the place of a parent must take into account all factors relevant to that determination, viewed objectively. What must be determined is the nature of the relationship. The *Divorce Act* makes no mention of formal expressions of intent. The focus on voluntariness and intention in *Carignan, supra,* was dependent on the common-law approach discussed earlier. It was wrong. The Court must determine the nature of the relationship by looking at a number of factors, among which is intention. Intention will not only be ex-

---

7   *Fair v. Jones*, [1999] N.W.T.J. No. 17, 44 R.F.L. (4th) 399 (S.C.); see also *Henderson v. Henderson*, [1999] B.C.J. No. 2938 (S.C.).

8   *Fournier v. Fournier*, [1997] B.C.J. No. 2299 (S.C.).

9   *Wuzinski v. Wuzinski* (1987), 10 R.F.L. (3d) 420 (Man. Q.B.); *Andrews v. Andrews* (1992), 38 R.F.L. (3d) 200 (Sask. C.A.); *Anderson v. Lambert*, [1997] S.J. No. 725 (Q.B.).

10   *Motuzas v. Yarnell*, [1997] M.J. No. 520 (Q.B.); *See v. See*, [1999] O.J. No. 698 (Gen. Div.); *Halliday v. Halliday*, [1998] S.J. No. 53 (Q.B.); *Campbell v. Campbell*, [1998] S.J. No. 180 (Q.B.). See also *McDonald v. McDonald*, [1998] B.C.J. No. 3150 (S.C.); *A.(D. R.) v. M.(R.M.)* (1997), 30 R.F.L. (4th) 269 (Ont. Gen. Div.) (application under *Family Law Act*); *Do Carmo v. Etzkorn* (1995), 16 R.F.L. (4th) 341 (Ont. Gen. Div.) (application under *Family Law Act*); *Cassar-Fleming v. Fleming* (1996), 20 R.F.L. (4th) 201 (Ont. Gen. Div.) (application under *Family Law Act*); *Prieur v. Prieur*, [1998] O.J. No. 5378 (Gen. Div.); *Marud v. Marud*, [1999] S.J. No. 478 (Q.B.).

pressed formally. The court must also infer intention from actions, and take into consideration that even expressed intentions may sometimes change. The actual fact of forming a new family is a key factor in drawing an inference that the step-parent treats the child as a member of his or her family, i.e., a child of the marriage. The relevant factors in defining the parental relationship include, but are not limited to, whether the child participates in the extended family in the same way as would a biological child; whether the person provides financially for the child (depending on ability to pay); whether the person disciplines the child as a parent; whether the person represents to the child, the family, the world, either explicitly or implicitly, that he or she is responsible as a parent to the child; the nature or existence of the child's relationship with the absent biological parent. The manifestation of the intention of the step-parent cannot be qualified as to duration, or be otherwise made conditional or qualified, even if this intention is manifested expressly. Once it is shown that the child is to be considered, in fact, a "child of the marriage", the obligations of the step-parent towards him or her are the same as those relative to a child born of the marriage with regard to the application of the *Divorce Act*. The step-parent, at this point, does not only incur obligations. He or she also acquires certain rights, such as the right to apply eventually for custody or access under s. 161(1) of the *Divorce Act*.

[para. 40] Nevertheless, not every adult-child relationship will be determined to be one where the adult stands in the place of a parent. Every case must be determined on its own facts and it must be established from the evidence that the adult acted so as to stand in the place of a parent to the child.

[para. 41] Huband J.A., in *Carignan*, [above,] expressed the concern that individuals may be reluctant to be generous towards children for fear that their generosity will give rise to parental obligations. I do not share those concerns. The nature of a parent relationship is complex and includes more than financial support. People do not enter into parental relationships with the view that they will be terminated.[11]

---

11   [1999] 1 S.C.R. 242.

A spouse's subjective feelings[12] and motivation[13] are not relevant when his or her objective behaviour has manifested an intention to treat the child as a member of his or her family.[14] Contractual covenants do not suffice to negate child support obligations that would otherwise ensue from the parent-child relationship.[15]

The judgment in *Chartier v. Chartier* leaves open the question whether a person can or should be deemed to stand in the place of a parent in circumstances where both biological parents continue to play a significant role in their child's life. This question was examined by Campbell J. of the Supreme Court of Nova Scotia in *Cook v. Cook.*[16] He concluded that Parliament endorsed the use of the words "in the place of" to indicate that parental status, with its concomitant child support obligations and the right to apply for custody of or access to the child, would arise only when a person has "substantially replaced the biological parent with respect to the various needs of the [child]." Campbell J. acknowledged that the judgment of the Supreme Court of Canada "clearly implies that both the biological parent and the step-parent can be required to pay support in appropriate circumstances" and that there are circumstances where concurrent payments would be appropriate as, for example, where the biological parent is paying inadequate support and the step-parent has provided "financial, emotional and physical support and guidance over a sufficient period of time in substitution for the natural parent."

Both before and after the implementation of the *Federal Child Support Guidelines* on 1 May 1997, several courts have shared the opinion expressed by Campbell J. in *Cook v. Cook*, above, and have been disinclined to impose long-term child support obligations on cohabitants who assume parental responsibilities during a relatively brief relationship with

---

12 *Cassar-Fleming v. Fleming* (1996), 20 R.F.L. (4th) 201 (Ont. Gen. Div.); *Seeley v. McKay*, [1998] O.J. No. 2857 (Gen. Div.).

13 *F.(R.L.) v. F.(S.)* (1996), 26 R.F.L. (4th) 393 (Ont. Gen. Div.) (application under *Family Law Act*).

14 *A.(D.R.) v. M.(R.M.)* (1997), 30 R.F.L. (4th) 269 (Ont. Gen. Div.) (application under *Family Law Act*), citing *Spring v. Spring* (1987), 61 O.R. (2d) 743 (Gen. Div.).

15 See *Chartier v. Chartier*, [1999] S.C.J. No. 79; *Richardson v. Richardson*, [1987] S.C.R. 857, 7 R.F.L. (3d) 304; *Doe v. Alberta*, 2007 ABCA 50, [2007] A.J. No. 138; *Seeley v. McKay*, [1998] O.J. No. 2857 (Gen. Div.) (application under *Family Law Act*); *See v. See*, [1999] O.J. No. 698 (Gen. Div.).

16 [2000] N.S.J. No. 19 (S.C.); see also *Lewcock v. Natili-Lewcock*, [2001] O.J. No. 2051 (Sup. Ct.); *Anderson v. Lambert*, [1997] S.J. No. 725 (Q.B.); compare *Hearn v. Bacque*, [2006] O.J. No. 2385 (Sup. Ct.); *Widdis v. Widdis*, [2001] S.J. No. 614 (Q.B.).

the child's custodial parent.[17] However, it should not be overlooked that the parties in *Chartier v. Chartier*[18] lived together in premarital cohabitation and marital cohabitation for an aggregate period of less than three years and the marriage itself lasted only fifteen months.

On the stepfather's application to vary an existing order in *Swindler v. Belanger*,[19] the mother's renewal of her relationship with the biological father did not release the stepfather from his obligation to support his stepchild in addition to his biological child born of the same mother. In fixing the amount of support payable for the two children, the Saskatchewan Court of Appeal took account of the fact that the biological father earned no income but, in the exercise of the discretion conferred with respect to the stepchild by section 5 of the *Federal Child Support Guidelines*, the stepfather was ordered to pay the full table amount of support for his biological child and an additional one-half of the differential between that amount and the full table amount normally payable for two children. The stepfather's application to remit the support arrears that had accrued under the original order was dismissed where there was no evidence that he was unable to pay the arrears and the mother had taken reasonable steps to enforce the arrears, but with little success. The Saskatchewan Court of Appeal acceded to the stepfather's request that he be granted reasonable access to his stepchild in addition to his biological child.

The uncertainties that continue to exist after *Chartier v. Chartier* have been explained by a Saskatchewan legal practitioner in the following words:

> In summary, although the *Chartier* case has outlined the principles which should be applied in determining whether or not a person stands in the place of a parent, it is still not clear how those principles will be applied to future cases. The result will depend very much on the amount of evidence and how this evidence is presented to the court. It may also depend on the judge's own beliefs whether a high or low threshold test should be applied. The finding will be in the judge's discretion and will likely not be subject to an appeal providing the principles as set out in the *Chartier* case have been applied.[20]

---

17   See, for example, *Weicholz v. Weicholz* (1987), 81 A.R. 236 (Q.B.); *Gavigan v. Gavigan* (1990), 30 R.F.L. (3d) 314 (Alta. Q.B.); *M.(C.F.) v. M.(M.F.)* (1996), 23 R.F.L. (4th) 55 (N.B.Q.B.); *Sloat v. Sloat* (1990), 102 N.B.R. (2d) 390 (Q.B.).

18   [1999] S.C.J. No. 79 at para. 2.

19   [2005] S.J. No. 709 (C.A.).

20   Marcia E. Jackson, "Multiple Parents" (Paper presented to Saskatchewan Legal Education Society Inc., University of Saskatchewan College of Law, and Law

2) Termination of Parent-Child Relationship: Impact on Child Support

The time for determining whether a person stands in the place of a parent for the purpose of ascertaining child support rights and obligations under the *Divorce Act* or under provincial-territorial statute is the time when the parties were cohabiting as a family unit.[21] A person who has established an enduring parent-child relationship during matrimonial cohabitation cannot be permitted to escape the statutory child support obligations that flow from that relationship simply by a unilateral abandonment of the relationship after the separation of the spouses.[22]

Although a person who has stood in the place of a parent cannot unilaterally sever the relationship and thereby avoid child support obligations, the question arises whether a parent can or should be required to support a child who is instrumental in severing the parent-child relationship. In *Cox v. Cox*,[23] Adams J. of the Newfoundland Unified Family Court concluded on the basis of *Chartier v. Chartier* that the obligation to support a child is not discharged, even if the child is responsible for severing the parent-child relationship. However, in *Ollinger v. Ollinger*,[24] Sandominski J., of the Saskatchewan Court of Queen's Bench, held that standing in the place of a parent is not static and such a relationship, with its attendant rights and obligations, can cease when a stepchild of sufficient maturity unilaterally withdraws from the step-parent or where there is a bilateral or mutual withdrawal from each other. There are several judicial decisions, the earliest ones of which predated the judgment of the Supreme Court of Canada in *Chartier v. Chartier*, in which judges have concluded that, where support is claimed for an adult child pursuing post-secondary education, it may be relevant for the court to consider whether or not the child has unilaterally terminated his or her relation-

---

Foundation of Saskatchewan, Family Law Conference: Economic and Parenting Consequences of Separation and Divorce, Saskatoon, 31 March and 1 April 2000) at 5–6.

21 *Chartier v. Chartier*, [1999] S.C.J. No. 79; *Dutrisac v. Ulm*, [1999] B.C.J. No. 591 (S.C.) (application under *Family Relations Act*); *H.(U.V.) v. H.(M.W.)*, 2008 BCCA 177, [2008] B.C.J. No. 717; *M.(C.F.) v. M.(M.F.)* (1996), 23 R.F.L. (4th) 55 (N.B.Q.B.) (application under *Family Services Act*); *Swindler v. Belanger*, [2005] S.J. No. 709 (C.A.).

22 *Ibid.*

23 [1999] N.J. No. 242 (U.F.C.); see also *Necemer v. Necemer*, [1999] B.C.J. No. 3023 (S.C.).

24 2006 SKQB 433.

ship with the parent from whom child support is sought.[25] It has also been asserted that, while an estranged relationship between an adult child and the paying parent may not justify the immediate denial or reduction of child support, the child may ultimately be called upon to bear the consequence of persisting in the estrangement and that consequence may be cessation of child support.[26] This approach has been judicially questioned in circumstances of long-term estrangement on the basis that it is unfair to place such a burden on the child, when the responsibility for cementing a meaningful relationship with the child lay with both parents.[27] It is apparent from the case law that the quality of the parent-child relationship is rarely determinative in the absence of other factors negating the child support obligation,[28] unless the circumstances are extremely grave and exceptional as, for example, where the parent was the victim of abuse and the child had other resources to fall back on.[29]

3) Respective Obligations of Biological and Adoptive Parents and of Persons Who Stand in the Place of Parents

Section 26.1(2) of the *Divorce Act* provides that the *Federal Child Support Guidelines* "shall be based on the principle that spouses have a joint financial obligation to maintain the children of the marriage in accordance with their relative abilities to contribute to the performance of that obligation."

Section 5 of the *Federal Child Support Guidelines* provides as follows:

---

25   *Wahl v. Wahl*, [2000] A.J. No. 29 (Q.B.); *Farden v. Farden* (1993), 48 R.F.L. (3d) 60 (B.C.S.C.); *Darlington v. Darlington*, [1997] B.C.J. No. 2534 (C.A.); *M.T.R. v. I.S.R.*, [2003] B.C.J. No. 545 (S.C.); *Hrecka v. Andries*, [2003] M.J. No. 114 (Q.B.); *Swaine v. Swaine*, [1996] N.S.J. No. 553 (T.D.); *Khoee-Solomonescu v. Solomonescu*, [1997] O.J. No. 4876 (Gen. Div.); *Rudulier v. Rudulier*, [1999] S.J. No. 366 (Q.B.); *Fernquist v. Garland*, [2005] S.J. No. 747, 22 R.F.L. (6th) 371 (Q.B.); *Ollinger v. Ollinger*, 2006 SKQB 433; compare *Necemer v. Necemer*, [1999] B.C.J. No. 3023 (S.C.).

26   *Wahl v. Wahl*, [2000] A.J. No. 29 (Q.B.); *Khoee-Solomonescu v. Solomonescu*, [1997] O.J. No. 4876 (Gen. Div.); *Fraser v. Jones* (1995), 17 R.F.L. (4th) 218 (Sask. Q.B.).

27   *J.K. v. S.D.*, [1999] Q.J. No. 4155 (S.C.); but see *Marsland v. Gibb*, [2000] B.C.J. No. 558 (S.C.).

28   *Wahl v. Wahl*, [2000] A.J. No. 29 (Q.B.); *Rebenchuk v. Rebenchuk*, 2007 MBCA 22; *Nitkin v. Nitkin*, [2006] O.J. No. 2769 (Sup. Ct.).

29   *Dalep v. Dalep* (1987), 11 R.F.L. (3d) 359 (B.C.S.C.).

> Where a spouse against whom a child support order is sought stands in the place of a parent for a child, the amount of the child support order is, in respect of that spouse, such amount as the court considers appropriate, having regard to these Guidelines and any other parent's legal duty to support the child.

It is noteworthy that *Chartier v. Chartier* does not address the implications of section 5 of the *Federal Child Support Guidelines*.[30] The *Divorce Act* and section 5 of the *Federal Child Support Guidelines* do not establish any ranking so far as support obligations are concerned between biological parents and persons who stand in the place of parents to children. There is no fixed formula or criterion whereby biological parents have the primary obligation to support their children or whereby a step-parent is only responsible for child support for the number of years or months that the step-parent has lived with the child. Parliament requires the courts to determine what is "appropriate" in light of all the circumstances of the particular case. It has been suggested that the overriding principle to be applied is to do what is in the best interests of the child,[31] although this principle is neither articulated in the child support provisions of the *Divorce Act* nor in the *Federal Child Support Guidelines* and the observations of Bastarache J. in *Chartier v. Chartier* that advert to this principle were expressed in the context of determining whether a person who stands in the place of a parent can unilaterally terminate the parent-child relationship and thereby evade child support obligations. If the best interests of the child were the determinative criterion, it might be argued that a child with sequential or multiple parents would have an automatic right to receive at least the applicable provincial-territorial table amount of child support from each parent, but this appears to fly in the face of the wide judicial discretion accorded by the express language of section 5 of the *Federal Child Support Guidelines*.

Where a support order is sought against a person who stands in the place of a parent to the child, section 5 of the *Federal Child Support Guidelines* confers a broad discretion on the court to apportion the child support obligation between the biological and non-biological parents. There is no consistency in the judicial approach to section 5 of the Guide-

---

30 *Dutrisac v. Ulm*, [2000] B.C.J. No. 1078 (C.A.); *H.(U.V.) v. H.(M.W.)*, 2008 BCCA 177, [2008] B.C.J. No. 717 (C.A.); *Marud v. Marud*, [1999] S.J. No. 478 (Q.B.).

31 *Janes v. Janes*, [1999] A.J. No. 610 (Q.B.); *Squires v. Severs*, [1999] B.C.J. No. 1653 (Prov. Ct.); *S.M. v. R.P.*, [1998] Q.J. No. 4119 (S.C.).

lines. In *Adler v. Jonas*,[32] Hardinge J., of the Supreme Court of British Columbia, identified the following six different methods of apportioning child support between multiple obligors but did not suggest that the list was exhaustive:

(a) Apportion mathematically, taking as the amount due the total expenses of the child and distributing this among payors according to the ability of each to pay (*Garad v. Garad*, [1996] B.C.J. No. 1165 (S.C.), a pre-Guidelines case under the *Divorce Act*);

(b) Add the incomes to get the total incomes of all the parents, find the Guideline amount for that figure and then divide that amount pro rata among the payors based on the percentage of the total income earned by each. (This approach was rejected in *Beatty v. Beatty*, [1997] B.C.J. No. 2269 (S.C.), and *Gordon v. Paquette*, [1998] B.C.J. No. 225 (S.C.));

(c) Apportion the amount of support due according to the role each contributor plays in the life of the child (*Dusseault v. Dolfo* (28 March 1998), Kamloops Reg. 6157, 6158 and 6159 (Prov. Ct.));

(d) Treat each payor individually and apply the Guidelines, with the possibility of an excess of support (*Gordon v. Paquette*, above);

(e) Determine the amount due from the last payor under the Guidelines, then subtract from it any [amount] being paid by a previous payor (*Ruth v. Young*, [1997] B.C.J. No. 1848 (S.C.) and *Nay v. Nay* (1998), New West. (S.C.), Bennett J.); and

(f) Consider Guidelines amount for each payor, but also consider the means, needs and circumstances of the parties, the relationship between each potential payor and the child, its length, whether it continues and the extent to which the child relies on the support of the payor (*Singh v. Singh*, [1997] B.C.J. No. 2195 (S.C.) and *White v. Rushton*, [1998] B.C.J. No. 422 (S.C.)).

When additional evidence was subsequently adduced in *Adler v. Jonas*[33] so as to require a choice to be made between the aforementioned alternatives, Hardinge J. expressed the following conclusions. The provision in section 5 of the *Federal Child Support Guidelines* that refers to "such amount as the court considers appropriate having regard to the Guidelines and any other parent's legal ability to support the child" mandates

---

32   [1998] B.C.J. No. 2062 (S.C.).
33   [1999] B.C.J. No. 358 (S.C.); compare *MacArthur v. Demers*, [1998] O.J. No. 5868 (Gen. Div.); see also *H.(U.V.) v. H.(M.W.)*, 2008 BCCA 177, [2008] B.C.J. No. 717.

a consideration not only of the legal duty of another non-custodial parent but also that of the custodial parent. Although the provisions of the *Family Relations Act* (B.C.) acknowledge the child support obligation of a step-parent, section 5 of the Guidelines empowers the court to reduce the amount of support payable, depending on the circumstances of the case. This may ensue because, if another non-custodial parent, such as a biological or adoptive parent, has an income equal to or exceeding that of a step-parent, the legal duty of the step-parent might become purely nominal. That approach might be unsatisfactory in some cases, particularly where a step-parent's income, though less than that of another non-custodial parent, is still substantial. The problem would then arise as to how to determine the contribution of the step-parent. Section 5 of the Guidelines may provide an answer to what could be a perplexing situation. It mandates consideration not only of the Guidelines but also "any other parent's legal duty to support the child." Consequently, when seeking to determine the fair contribution to child support of a step-parent, the court must first determine the appropriate amount specified by the Guidelines for that step-parent's liability. The next step would be to determine the legal duty of "any other parent," including that of the non-custodial and custodial parent. If the total amount of "any other parent's" basic financial contribution would be sufficient to provide "a fair standard of support" for the child, the determination of the extent of the step-parent's legal duty could end there and his or her required contribution could be nominal. If the sum of the other parent's basic financial contribution were insufficient to provide a fair standard of support for the child, the step-parent could be called on to top up the available funds to a point where they are sufficient for that purpose. One way, but not the only way, of determining a fair standard of support for the child is to look at what funds would have been available for the child's support, if the marriage of the biological parents had not broken down.

In *Mancuso v. Weinrath*,[34] Groves J., of the Supreme Court of British Columbia, provides an updated in-depth analysis of the principles underlying section 5 of the Guidelines and of the diverse methods that British Columbia courts have used to calculate the amount of child support payable by a non-custodial step-parent where the non-custodial biological parent is also paying support for the child. Groves J. formulates the following five principles governing the exercise of judicial discretion under section 5 of the Guidelines:

---

34   [2005] B.C.J. No. 2509 (S.C.).

1.   The court should have regard to the specific objectives set out in section 1 of the Guidelines.
2.   The biological parents generally bear the responsibility for the support of their children, but their obligation does not necessarily displace that of the non-custodial step-parent.
3.   The upper limit of the step-parent's obligation is generally the amount set out in the applicable income-based Guidelines table.
4.   Each case must be determined on the basis of its own particular facts.
5.   British Columbia courts have adopted a broad approach to the factors that may be considered in exercising the judicial discretion under section 5 of the Guidelines. There is no exhaustive list of the factors to be considered.

Having reviewed relevant case law from British Columbia and elsewhere, Groves J. identifies the following four primary approaches to section 5 of the Guidelines without foreclosing the possibility that new approaches might be devised to meet particular situations:

1.   Non-Mathematical Approach
This approach, unlike the remaining approaches, does not rely upon any particular equation to determine the step-parent's liability. Instead, it weighs the factors in the particular case to determine the extent to which the step-parent's liability should fall below the normal Guidelines amount, if at all. This approach, which is endorsed in *Singh v. Singh*,[35] appears to be the method most frequently applied by British Columbia courts.

2.   Subtraction Approach
This method subtracts the child support payments of the non-custodial biological parent from the full amount that the step-parent would otherwise be ordered to pay under the Guidelines.

3.   Cumulative Approach
The cumulative approach signifies that the court requires the step-parent to pay the full amount under the Guidelines without any right to a deduction in consequence of the non-custodial biological parent's payment of child support. This method is rarely applied in British Columbia.

---

35   [1997] B.C.J. No. 2195 at para. 17 (S.C.).

4. *Apportionment Based on Fair Standard of Support*

Under this approach, the court determines a step-parent's liability for child support based on a "fair standard of support" for the child and then apportions the responsibility for meeting that standard between the parents. Four methods of quantifying a fair standard of support are suggested by Groves J. First, it might be either the table amount for the combined incomes of the separated spouses prior to their separation or the combined table amounts for those incomes. Second, it might be the step-parent's table amount multiplied by two on the basis that table amounts represent half of the expense of raising the child. Third, the fair standard of support might be determined by reference to the specific expenses incurred by the custodial parent in raising the child. Fourth, it might be appropriate in certain cases to combine the preseparation or postseparation incomes of the biological parents and the step-parent and determine the table amount for the aggregated income. Having determined the fair standard of support by one of these methods, the court then apportions the child support obligation between the parents by using one of the following three alternatives. First, the court may opt for a top-up approach whereby it determines the shortfall between the fair standard of support for the child and the ability of the biological parents to meet it. It then assigns liability for the shortfall to the step-parent to the extent that it is lesser than or equal to his or her table amount. A second method differs from the top-up method in that it apportions the child support obligation between the parents and step-parent in proportion to their ability to pay. A third method, which was firmly rejected by Aston J. in *MacArthur v. Demers*,[36] would determine the fair amount of support and then require the non-custodial parents to share the responsibility in proportion to their involvement with the child.

Having canvassed the aforementioned principles and diverse methods of approach to section 5 of the *Federal Child Support Guidelines*, and having regard to the unique facts of *Mancuso v. Weinrath*, in which prior negotiations had led to a creative mediated settlement, Groves J. concluded that it would be appropriate to apply a "slightly modified method," whereby the stepfather would be required to pay the full amount of table support minus one-half of the amount payable by the biological non-custodial parent. In devising this formula, Groves J. responded to the request of the parties that the method of approach be spelled out to enable them to make appropriate adjustments in the future.

---

36 (1998), 166 D.L.R. (4th) 172 at 184 (Ont. Gen. Div.).

In determining the respective child support obligations of the natural father and the stepfather in *H.(U.V.) v. H.(M.W.)*[37] the judgment of the British Columbia Court of Appeal endorses the following principles:

(i) A non-custodial natural parent cannot invoke section 5 of the Guidelines even though a non-custodial step-parent is concurrently liable to pay child support.[38] There can be no "balancing" or "apportionment" of the table amount of child support payable by the non-custodial natural parent by reason of the non-custodial step-parent's concurrent liability. The obligation of the non-custodial natural parent to pay the applicable table amount of child support, pursuant to section 3(1) of the Guidelines, can only be modified or affected by the obligation of the step-parent in those discretionary situations specified by the Guidelines, namely, in circumstances involving children over the provincial age of majority (section 3(2)(b)), incomes over $150,000 (section 4), special or extraordinary expenses (section 7), shared custody (section 9), or undue hardship (section 10).[39]

(ii) A non-custodial natural parent is not released from his or her obligation to pay the applicable table amount of child support by a prior consensual undertaking on the part of the step-parent to shoulder primary responsibility for supporting the natural parent's children.

(iii) The non-custodial natural parent's legal obligation to pay the applicable table amount of child support is not discharged by voluntary payments of his own choosing made for the benefit of the children.

(iv) As was stated by the British Columbia Court of Appeal in *Dutrisac v. Ulm*,[40] in the context of the provincial *Child Support Guidelines*, the judgment of the Supreme Court of Canada in *Chartier v. Chartier*[41] does not preclude a court from concluding that a step-parent should pay a reduced amount or no amount of child support, if that is deemed appropriate in the exercise of the judicial discretion conferred by section 5 of the Guidelines.

(v) Where it is practicable to do so, the amount of child support payable by the non-custodial natural parent must be determined in order to determine the appropriate amount of child support to be paid by the non-custodial step-parent. Once the former amount has been ascer-

---

37   2008 BCCA 177, [2008] B.C.J. No. 717.
38   See also *Wright v. Zaver*, [2002] O.J. No. 1098 (C.A.).
39   See also *Pevach v. Spalding*, [2001] S.J. No. 469 (Q.B.).
40   [2000] B.C.J. No. 178 (C.A.).
41   [1999] 1 S.C.R. 242.

tained, the step-parent's obligation should be determined in light of that amount and the notional amount of child support payable by the custodial parent, having regard to the objectives specified in section 1 of the Guidelines. In the words of Newbury J.A., in *H.(U.V.) v. H.(M.W.)*,

Thus a "fair standard of support", objectivity of calculation, and reduction of conflict between parents are relevant to the determination of "appropriate" support by the stepparent. On the other hand, s. 5 does not, in my view, confer a discretion that is so broad as to encompass "*all*" the circumstances of a case ... or "fairness" to the father arising from a kind of promissory estoppel against the stepparent (as was suggested by the chambers judge in this case).

Given the "children-first" perspective of the Guidelines ..., primacy should be given to the children's standard of living. Where for example the stepparent provided a standard to the children during the period of cohabitation that was materially higher than that which the natural parents can provide by means of their Guidelines amounts, a court might find it appropriate to make an order against the stepparent that is designed to provide the higher standard, or something approximating it, "on top of" the other parents' support. However, where the "piling" of Guidelines amounts would result in a standard beyond one that is reasonable in the context of the standard the children have previously enjoyed, such a "windfall" or "wealth transfer" ... is unlikely to be "appropriate". At the other end of the spectrum, where the three (or more) parents' Guidelines "contributions" together are needed to provide the children with a reasonable standard of living, then both the stepparent and the non-custodial parent(s) may well be required to pay full Guidelines amounts. Or, where one of the natural or adoptive parents is not present or is unable to pay any support, the stepparent may well have to pay his or her full table amount.[42] The Legislature has left it to the judgment of trial and chambers judges in the first instance to fashion orders that are "appropriate" under s. 5. At the same time, the Guidelines system is not thereby jettisoned in favour of a "wide open" discretion. The inquiry must, like the Guidelines themselves, focus on the children and their needs.[43]

---

42   See *Janes v. Janes*, [1999] A.J. No. 610 (Q.B.); *Clarke v. Clarke*, [1998] B.C.J. No. 2370 (S.C.); compare *Cook v. Kilduff*, [2000] S.J. No. 482 (Q.B.).

43   2008 BCCA 177, [2008] B.C.J. No. 717 at paras. 40–41 [emphasis in original].

Applying the above criteria to the facts of the case, the British Columbia Court of Appeal held that, notwithstanding the stepfather's prior consensual undertaking to support the children, the chambers judge erred in his approach to determining the stepfather's child support obligation under section 5 of the *British Columbia Child Support Guidelines* without due regard for the natural father's obligation under section 3 of the Guidelines. Where he erred was in approaching the father's obligation as a secondary obligation, and losing sight of the father's non-discretionary obligation to pay the table amount of child support pursuant to section 3 of the Guidelines. In the result, the British Columbia Court of Appeal set aside the chambers judge's order that the stepfather pay the full table amount of child support based on his income while requiring the natural father to pay substantially less than his table amount. In its place, the British Columbia Court of Appeal substituted an order whereby the natural father was required to pay the full table amount of child support and the stepfather was ordered to pay a designated "top up" amount as his contribution towards the custodial mother's child-related expenses.

In *McBride v. McBride*,[44] Vertes J., of the Northwest Territories Supreme Court, concluded that a non-custodial step-parent, against whom a child support order is sought, may initiate a concurrent application for child support under provincial statute against the non-custodial biological parent. If this is done, the court may order the non-custodial biological parent to pay the applicable table amount of child support and may then proceed to determine whether the step-parent's child support obligation should be reduced because of the non-custodial biological parent's court-ordered child support payments. Vertes J. further observed that a court should not order the full table amount of child support to be paid by the non-custodial step-parent as a matter of course. Evidence should be adduced as to the needs and circumstances of the child so that the appropriate amount of child support to be paid by the non-custodial step-parent can be determined.

---

44   [2001] N.W.T.J. No. 69 (S.C.).

F. CHILDREN OVER PROVINCIAL AGE OF MAJORITY

1) Relevant Provisions of *Divorce Act* and *Federal Child Support Guidelines*

For the purpose of determining the right of adult children to child support, section 2(1) of the *Divorce Act* defines "age of majority" and "child of the marriage" as follows:

Definitions

2.(1) In this Act,

"age of majority"

"age of majority", in respect of a child, means the age of majority as determined by the laws of the province where the child ordinarily resides, or, if the child ordinarily resides outside of Canada, eighteen years of age;

…

"child of the marriage"

"child of the marriage" means a child of two spouses or former spouses who, at the material time,

    (a) is under the age of majority and who has not withdrawn from their charge, or

    (b) is the age of majority or over and under their charge but unable, by reason of illness, disability or other cause, to withdraw from their charge or to obtain the necessaries of life;

In determining an adult child's right, if any, to child support, sections 3 and 7 of the *Federal Child Support Guidelines* are the key provisions. The relevant provisions read as follows:

Amount of Child Support

Presumptive rule

3.(1) Unless otherwise provided under these Guidelines, the amount of a child support order for children under the age of majority is

    (a) the amount set out in the applicable table, according to the number of children under the age of majority to whom the order relates and the income of the spouse against whom the order is sought; and

(b)   the amount, if any, determined under section 7.

Child the age of majority or over

(2)   Unless otherwise provided under these Guidelines, where a child to whom a child support order relates is the age of majority or over, the amount of the child support order is

(a)   the amount determined by applying these Guidelines as if the child were under the age of majority; or

(b)   if the court considers that approach to be inappropriate, the amount that it considers appropriate, having regard to the condition, means, needs and other circumstances of the child and the financial ability of each spouse to contribute to the support of the child.

Special or extraordinary expenses

7.(1) In a child support order the court may, on either spouse's request, provide for an amount to cover the following expenses, or any portion of those expenses, taking into account the necessity of the expense in relation to the child's best interests and the reasonableness of the expense, having regard to the means of the spouses and those of the child and to the family's spending pattern prior to the separation:

...

(e)   expenses for post-secondary education; and

...

Sharing of expense

(2)   The guiding principle in determining the amount of an expense referred to in subsection (1) is that the expense is shared by the spouses in proportion to their respective incomes after deducting from the expense, the contribution, if any, from the child.

Subsidies, tax deductions, etc.

(3)   In determining the amount of an expense referred to in subsection (1), the court must take into account any subsidies, benefits or income tax deductions or credits relating to the expense, and any eligibility to claim a subsidy, benefit or income tax deduction or credit relating to the expense.

2) Status of Applicant; Payment to Parent or Child

An application for a child support order or for variation thereof can only be brought under the *Divorce Act* by either or both spouses or former spouses.[45] An adult child has no standing to bring an application for support under the *Divorce Act* on his or her own behalf.[46]

On the application of either or both of the spouses, a court may order support to be paid directly to the child. Such orders are relatively unusual, even for adult children. Where a child resides with a parent who provides his or her basic needs, a court should not order support payments to be made directly to the child, unless that parent consents or there are exceptional circumstances.[47] An order for direct payment to a child should be denied where the payor's past conduct manifested control and manipulation by means of money,[48] where undue friction would be thereby caused,[49] or where the applicable table amount is ordered for two or more children, only one of whom is an adult child who qualifies for child support.[50] On the other hand, direct payments to an adult child may be deemed appropriate where the child attends an out-of-town college or university.[51]

Where child support is ordered to be paid to the custodial parent, the obligor is not entitled to make payments to the child instead or to purchase things for the child in partial discharge of the support obligation.[52]

3) Statutory Definition of "Child of the Marriage"; Eligibility of Adult Children for Child Support

a) General

A divorcing spouse may be ordered to pay support for a child under the age of provincial majority (which is either eighteen or nineteen years of

45   *Divorce Act*, s. 15.2(1) (original application), s. 17(1)(a) (variation application).

46   *Tapson v. Tapson* (1970), 2 R.F.L. 305 (Ont. C.A.); *M.V. v. D.V.,* [2005] N.B.J. No. 505 (Q.B.); *Skolney v. Herman,* [2008] S.J. No. 73 (Q.B.).

47   *Morgan v. Morgan,* [2006] B.C.J. No. 1795 (S.C.); *Marshall v. Marshall,* [1998] N.S.J. No. 311 (S.C.); *Lu v. Sun,* [2005] N.S.J. No. 314 (C.A.); compare *M.V. v. D.V.,* [2005] N.B.J. No. 505 (Q.B.).

48   *Baker v. Baker,* [1997] O.J. No. 2196 (Gen. Div.).

49   *Sherlock v. Sherlock,* [1998] B.C.J. No. 116 (S.C.).

50   *Walls v. Walls,* [1998] N.B.J. No. 246 (Q.B.).

51   *Wesemann v. Wesemann,* [1999] B.C.J. No. 1387 (S.C.); *Morgan v. Morgan,* [2006] B.C.J. No. 1795 (S.C.); *Chapple v. Campbell,* [2005] M.J. No. 323 (Q.B.); *Merritt v. Merritt,* [1999] O.J. No. 1732 (Sup. Ct.).

52   *Haisman v. Haisman,* [1994] A.J. No. 553, 7 R.F.L. (4th) 1 (C.A.).

age according to the province or territory in which the child ordinarily resides) or for an adult child who is unable to achieve self-sufficiency by reason of "illness, disability or other cause."

Children under the provincial age of majority who are financially dependent while they continue with their schooling satisfy the definition of "children of the marriage" under section 2(1) of the *Divorce Act*, even though they are alienated from the non-custodial parent who is called upon to pay child support.[53] The definition of "child of the marriage" in section 2(1) of the *Divorce Act* is not simply one of age; it is one of dependence.[54] In *A.A.C. v. M.A.B.*,[55] an adult child, who was pursuing post-secondary education that was largely financed by summer-employment income, scholarships, and student loans, was held disentitled to ongoing child support from her parent once she married. MacDonald J. observed that the marriage, which would take place in July 2006, constituted a declaration of independence and a "withdrawal from [parental] charge" under the definition of "child of the marriage" in section 2(1) of the *Divorce Act*. It is noteworthy that an adult child who lives with his girlfriend or boyfriend while pursuing university studies does not automatically cease to be a "child of the marriage" where the adult child remains economically dependent on his or her parents.[56] In *Karol v. Karol*,[57] an adult child, who withdrew from her mother's home because of overcrowding, was not disentitled to child support while pursuing post-secondary education, merely because she was sharing household expenses with a common-law partner. Wilkinson J. undertakes a review of the case law and identifies the following factors as relevant in determining the impact of an adult child's common-law relationship upon his or her eligibility for child support to meet the costs of post-secondary education:

> [para. 19] Similarly, the fact that Sharla resides in a common-law relationship does not automatically disqualify her for support. A review of the case law shows mixed results, depending on a number of factors, including the child's age, whether the parents approved the relationship, how long the common-law relationship has lasted, and whether

53   *Marsh v. Marsh*, [2006] B.C.J. No. 615 (C.A.).

54   *Ivany v. Ivany* (1996), 24 R.F.L. (4th) 289 (Nfld. S.C.); *Martell v. Height* (1994), 3 R.F.L. (4th) 104 (N.S.C.A.).

55   [2006] N.S.J. No. 169 (S.C.).

56   See *Robertson v. Hibbs*, [1997] B.C.J. No. 1305 (S.C.); *Taylor v. Taylor*, [2002] N.J. No. 52 (S.C.); *Crowdis v. Crowdis*, [2003] S.J. No. 371 (Q.B.); compare *Hrechka v. Andries*, [2003] M.J. No. 114 (Q.B.); *Ritchie v. Ritchie*, [2003] S.J. No. 326 (C.A.).

57   [2005] S.J. No. 349 (Q.B.).

the common-law partner is working full-time or part-time or attending school and without income. Other considerations are how long the child has been in school, how much the child has been able to contribute from other sources, and whether the parents would provide assistance in any event, whether ordered to or not. Another relevant consideration is whether the parents had provided any financial assistance at all towards the child's post-secondary training and, if so, for how long.

Child support is transitional; it is not an income security plan for the indolent child or the perennial student. A court must be careful not to be carried away with claims on behalf of the would-be "hanger on" in perpetuity.[58]

b) Sick or Disabled Children

Adult children who are incapable of economic self-sufficiency because of illness or disability fall within the definition of "child of the marriage" under section 2(1) of the *Divorce Act*.[59] State subsidized financial assistance for special-needs adult children does not necessarily absolve parents of their child support obligation.[60] In *Krangle (Guardian ad litem of) v. Brisco*,[61] McLachlin C.J., of the Supreme Court of Canada, addressed the issue of a disabled adult child's withdrawal from the charge of his parents in the context of an action for damages for medical malpractice. She observed that the relevant statutory amendments "were not aimed at shifting the burden of caring for adult children from the state to parents, but rather with ensuring that in situations where one parent is charged with the care of an adult disabled child, the other parent is obliged to assist." A similar approach is tenable when interpreting federal or provincial legislation dealing with the support of adult disabled children.[62] State-subsidized financial assistance for disabled adult children does not necessarily absolve the parents from their child support obligations.[63]

---

58 *Yashuk v. Logan* (1992), 39 R.F.L. (3d) 417 at 438 (N.S.C.A.), Chipman J.A.

59 *Harris v. Harris*, [2006] N.S.J. No. 257 (C.A.). Compare s. 46(b) of the *Family Law Act*, S.A. 2003, c. F-4.5 (effective 1 October 2005); *L.L.M. v. W.L.K.*, [2007] A.J. No. 1424 (Q.B.)

60 *Hellinckx v. Large*, [1998] B.C.J. No. 1462 (S.C.); compare *Harrington v. Harrington* (1981), 22 R.F.L. (2d) 40 (Ont. C.A.); *Hill v. Davis*, [2006] N.S.J. No. 331 (S.C.).

61 [2002] 1 S.C.R. 205 at para. 35.

62 *Hill v. Davis*, [2006] N.S.J. No. 331 (S.C.); *Hanson v. Hanson*, [2003] S.J. No. 514 (Q.B.).

63 *Lougheed v. Lougheed*, [2007] B.C.J. No. 1648 (C.A.).

An adult child, with serious addictions that are treatable, must make reasonable efforts to achieve economic independence. Although addiction is a disease, courts have not condoned chronic financial dependence in cases where individuals refuse to help themselves. An addicted child, who has squandered opportunities to overcome the disease and become economically self-sufficient, may cease to be a "child of the marriage" within the meaning of section 2(1) of the *Divorce Act*. Even if that status were deemed to continue, the adult child cannot look to a parent to continue to underwrite the costs of the post-secondary education or training, where the adult child has already wasted several opportunities in the past and has demonstrated no aptitude for a proposed new field of study. Section 4 of the *Federal Child Support Guidelines* empowers a court to deviate from the applicable table amount of child support insofar as a parent's annual income exceeds $150,000, where the reasonable needs of the adult child are already being met and anything other than a modest lifestyle would be an obstacle to recovery.[64]

c) Unemployed Adult Children

Some courts have held that a child's inability to obtain employment, which does not result from illness or disability but from restrictions on job availability, falls outside the meaning of "other cause" in section 2(2) of the *Divorce Act*. Given this interpretation, parents cannot be ordered to support a child who cannot withdraw from the charge of his or her parents or provide himself or herself with the necessities of life because of the state of the labour market.[65] Other courts have opted for a broader interpretation of "other cause" and have ordered child support in cases where the economic climate makes it impossible for a diligent child to find employment and become self-supporting.[66] Such orders are typically transitional, rather than long-term.[67]

---

64 *R.W.G. v. S.I.G.*, [2002] S.J. No. 231 (Q.B.), var'd [2003] S.J. No. 250 (C.A.).

65 See, for example, *Gartner v. Gartner* (1978), 5 R.F.L. (2d) 270 at 274 (N.S.S.C.); *Sproule v. Sproule* (1986), 2 R.F.L. (3d) 54 (N.S.C.A.); *Murray v. Murray* (1982), 30 R.F.L. (2d) 222 (Sask. Q.B.).

66 See, for example, *Baker v. Baker* (1994), 2 R.F.L. (4th) 147 at 155–56 (Alta. Q.B.); *Bruehler v. Bruehler* (1985), 49 R.F.L. (2d) 44 (B.C.C.A.); *McAdam v. McAdam* (1994), 8 R.F.L. (4th) 252 at 255–56 (Man. Q.B.).

67 *C.L.B. v. B.T.C.*, [2006] B.C.J. No. 3112 (S.C.).

4) Post-Secondary Education or Training

a) General

Pursuit of post-secondary education or training constitutes "other cause" within the meaning of the definition of "child of marriage" in section 2(1) of the *Divorce Act,* thus rendering an adult child eligible for support in appropriate circumstances.[68]

Post-secondary education or training is not confined to pursuit of a university degree. It includes vocational training[69] and may extend to an adult child's pursuit of a career in professional sport, where the child has the requisite aptitude and realistic career aspirations.[70]

Where support is sought for an adult child pursuing post-secondary education or vocational training, the onus of demonstrating that the child cannot provide for himself or herself and is, therefore, unable to withdraw from the parents' charge, rests with the applicant seeking child support.[71]

Relevant considerations in determining the right to child support include the following:

- the age of the child,
- his or her academic achievements,
- the ability to profit from further education,
- the possibility of securing employment having regard to the standard of education already achieved and the state of the labour market, and
- the capacity of the parents to bear the costs of a college education for a child who evinces an aptitude therefor.[72]

Additional considerations include the following:

- whether the child is a full-time or part-time student,
- whether the child is eligible for student loans or other financial assistance,

---

68   *Sherlow v. Zubko,* [1999] A.J. No. 644 (Q.B.).

69   *Blake v. Blake* (1994), 121 Nfld. & P.E.I.R. 263 (Nfld. S.C.) (technical college); *Van Wynsberghe v. Van Wynsberghe,* [1997] O.J. No. 2566 (Gen. Div.) (film school).

70   *Olson v. Olson,* [2003] A.J. No. 230 (C.A.); *Thompson v. Thompson,* [1999] S.J. No. 317 (Q.B.). See also *Maxwell v. Maxwell,* [2007] B.C.J. No. 43 (S.C.).

71   *Albo v. Albo,* [2006] A.J. No. 1330 (Q.B.); *Jean v. Jean,* [2006] A.J. No. 1687 (Q.B.); *MacDonald v. Rasmussen,* [2000] S.J. No. 660 (Q.B.); *Loos v. Schneider,* [2007] S.J. No. 33 (Q.B.); *Hiebert v. Hiebert,* [2007] S.J. No. 569 (Q.B.).

72   *Douglas v. Campbell,* [2006] N.S.J. No. 350 (S.C.); *Hiebert v. Hiebert, ibid.* See also *Albert v. Albert,* [2007] O.J. No. 2964 (Sup. Ct.).

- whether the child has reasonable career plans,
- the ability of the child to contribute to his or her own support through part-time employment,
- parental plans for the child's education, particularly those made during cohabitation, and
- (at least in the case of a mature child who has reached the age of majority,) whether or not the child has unilaterally terminated his or her relationship with the parent from whom child support is sought.[73]

Evidence need not be adduced on all the aforementioned considerations in order for an application for child support to be successful.[74] Although relevant authorities have developed lengthy lists of factors relevant to determining whether an adult child remains a "child of the marriage" for support purposes,[75] such lists, helpful though they are, must not be used in place of the language of the statute nor should they be invoked to impose a burden on parents to call evidence about the obvious, or on judges to address non-issues in their reasons for judgment. Judges are entitled to draw reasonable, common-sense inferences from the proven facts and may take into account notorious facts such as, that post-secondary education is expensive, well-paid part-time employment for full-time students is scarce, and the demands of a full-time course load limit the time available for part-time work.[76]

The governing principle in determining whether child support should be ordered is reasonableness.[77] There is no arbitrary cut-off point based

---

73   *Farden v. Farden* (1993), 48 R.F.L. (3d) 60 (B.C.S.C.); see also *Albo v. Albo*, [2006] A.J. No. 1330 (Q.B.); *Jean v. Jean*, [2006] A.J. No. 1687 (Q.B.); *Miller v. Joynt*, 2007 ABCA 214, [2007] A.J. No. 959; *Mighton v. Mighton*, [2007] A.J. No. 976 (Q.B.); *Darlington v. Darlington*, [1997] B.C.J. No. 2534 (C.A.); *Morgan v. Morgan*, [2006] B.C.J. No. 1795 (S.C.); *Maxwell v. Maxwell*, [2007] B.C.J. No. 43 (S.C.); *Winsemann v. Donaldson*, [2007] B.C.J. No. 1936 (S.C.); *Matwichuk v. Stephenson*, [2007] B.C.J. No. 2347 (S.C.); *Green v. Green*, [2005] N.J. No. 165 (C.A.); *Nitkin v. Nitkin*, [2006] O.J. No. 2769 (Sup. Ct.); *Kemp v. Kemp*, [2007] O.J. No. 1131 (Sup. Ct.); *Albert v. Albert*, [2007] O.J. No. 2964 (Sup. Ct.); *Bradley v. Zaba* (1996), 137 Sask. R. 682 (C.A.); *Loos v. Schneider*, [2007] S.J. No. 33 (Q.B.); *Hiebert v. Hiebert*, [2007] S.J. No. 569 (Q.B.).

74   *Albo v. Albo*, [2006] A.J. No. 1330 (Q.B.); *Darlington v. Darlington*, [1997] B.C.J. No. 2534, 32 R.F.L. (4th) 406 (C.A.); *Brandner v. Brandner*, [2002] B.C.J. No. 1398 (C.A.); *Morgan v. Morgan*, [2006] B.C.J. No. 1795 (S.C.); *MacDonald v. Rasmussen*, [2000] S.J. No. 660 (Q.B.).

75   See, for example, *Farden v. Farden* (1993), 48 R.F.L. (3d) 60 (B.C.S.C.); *Rebenchuk v. Rebenchuk*, 2007 MBCA 22; *Cole v. Cole*, [1995] N.S.J. No. 362 (Fam. Ct.).

76   *MacLennan v. MacLennan*, [2003] N.S.J. No. 15 (C.A.).

77   *Ivany v. Ivany* (1996), 24 R.F.L. (4th) 289 (Nfld. S.C.); *Hiebert v. Hiebert*, [2007] S.J. No. 569 (Q.B.).

on age or academic achievement,[78] although the onus of proving a child's continued financial dependence on his or her parents grows heavier as these increase.[79] There must be some degree of congruency between the financial circumstances of the parents and the child's educational plans.[80] Parents of modest means may not be able to afford to underwrite their children's post-secondary education. Middle-class parents may be called on to make some sacrifice to put their children through college, but they are not required to assume more debt than they can repay or sell capital assets if their estates are modest. They may, nevertheless, be expected to make reasonable adjustments to their lifestyle by reducing their consumption of luxuries.[81]

Academically qualified children with reasonable expectations of undertaking post-secondary education will normally receive support to permit their completion of an undergraduate university degree or college diploma, provided that their parents have the means to pay.[82] The parental support obligation does not necessarily extend to postgraduate or professional education or training,[83] although it may do so in appropriate circumstances.[84] As a general rule, parents of a *bona fide* adult student remain financially responsible until the child has reached a level of education commensurate with his or her demonstrated abilities that fits the child for entry-level employment in an appropriate field within a reasonable period of time.[85] In making this determination, the court must be aware of prevailing socio-economic conditions whereby an undergraduate degree no longer assures economic self-sufficiency,[86] although this awareness must be tempered by the realization that the majority of children

---

78   *Ivany v. Ivany* (1996), 24 R.F.L. (4th) 289 (Nfld. S.C.); *Martell v. Height* (1994), 3 R.F.L. (4th) 104 (N.S.C.A.); *Erickson v. Erickson*, [2007] N.S.J. No. 483 (S.C.).

79   *McArthur v. McArthur*, [1998] A.J. No. 1522 (Q.B.).

80   *Jarzebinski v. Jarzebinski*, [2004] O.J. No. 4595 (Sup. Ct.).

81   *J.C.R. v. J.J.R.*, [2006] B.C.J. No. 2150 (S.C.).

82   *Rebenchuk v. Rebenchuk*, 2007 MBCA 22; *Matwichuk v. Stephenson*, [2007] B.C.J. No. 2347 (S.C.); *Holizki v. Reeves*, [1997] S.J. No. 746 (Q.B.).

83   *Rebenchuk v. Rebenchuk*, 2007 MBCA 22; *Smith v. Smith* (1990), 27 R.F.L. (3d) 32 (Man. C.A.).

84   *Jamieson v. Jamieson* (1995), 14 R.F.L. (4th) 354 (N.B.C.A.); *Martell v. Height* (1994), 3 R.F.L. (4th) 104 (N.S.C.A.); *J.C. v. A.M.M.*, [2007] O.J. No. 3887 (Sup. Ct.); *English v. English* (1995), 16 R.F.L. (4th) 250 (Sask. Q.B.); *D.J.F. v. E.K.*, 2005 SKQB 131, 264 Sask. R. 119.

85   *W.P.N. v. B.J.N.*, [2005] B.C.J. No. 12, 10 R.F.L. (6th) 440 (C.A.); *Martell v. Height* (1994), 3 R.F.L. (4th) 104 (N.S.C.A.); *Erickson v. Erickson*, [2007] N.S.J. No. 483 (S.C.).

86   *Martell v. Height* (1994), 3 R.F.L. (4th) 104 (N.S.C.A.).

find their place in the world without the benefit of any post-secondary education.[87] Additional considerations include the means and standard of living of the parent and the legitimate expectations of the children.[88]

Full-time post-secondary education by means of correspondence courses may render an adult child eligible for support.[89] Post-secondary education that is pursued on a part-time basis by an adult child with a clear career plan may entitle the child to support where his or her income from employment is insufficient to enable the child to fully withdraw from the charge of his or her parents.[90] The failure of an adult child to obtain exemplary grades in his or her university studies is not a sufficient basis in itself to justify a finding that the child is no longer a "child of the marriage" within the meaning of the *Divorce Act*, where the evidence does not support allegations that the child is taking advantage of the situation and is not serious in his or her studies.[91] A court may conclude that a financially contributing parent should be kept informed of the child's marks and academic progress, [92] and a condition to this effect may be imposed on the child support order pursuant to section 15.1(4) of the *Divorce Act*.[93]

It has been judicially asserted that an estranged relationship between an adult child and the paying parent may not justify the immediate denial or reduction of child support, but that the child may ultimately be called upon to bear the consequence of persisting in the estrangement and that consequence may be cessation of child support.[94] As the Manitoba Court of Appeal observed in *Rebenchuk v. Rebenchuk*,[95] parent-child estrangement is a particularly difficult issue. "[S]elfish or ungrateful children who reject the non-custodial parent without justification should not expect to be supported through their years of higher education. But this fac-

---

87   *Jonasson v. Jonasson*, [1998] B.C.J. No. 726 (S.C.).

88   *Douglas v. Campbell*, [2006] N.S.J. No. 350 (S.C.).

89   *Kirkpatrick v. Kirkpatrick*, [1997] S.J. No. 212 (Q.B.).

90   *Kovich v. Kreut*, [1998] B.C.J. No. 2586 (S.C.).

91   *Budyk v. Sol*, [1998] M.J. No. 252 (C.A.).

92   *Ciardullo v. Ciardullo* (1995), 15 R.F.L. (4th) 121 (B.C.S.C.).

93   *Brown v. Brown* (1993), 45 R.F.L. (3d) 444 (B.C.S.C.).

94   *Fraser v. Jones* (1995), 17 R.F.L. (4th) 218 (Sask. Q.B.); see, generally, *Farden v. Farden* (1993), 48 R.F.L. (3d) 60 (B.C.S.C.); *Bradley v. Zaba* (1996), 137 Sask. R. 682 (C.A.); *Hamel v. Hamel*, [2001] S.J. No. 692 (C.A.). See also Phillip M. Epstein & Ilana I. Zylberman, "Support for Adult Children in Cases of Estrangement: The Parent As Wallet" in The Law Society of Upper Canada, *Special Lectures 2006: Family Law* (Toronto: Irwin Law, 2007) 233–71.

95   2007 MBCA 22 at para. 56.

tor rarely stands alone as the sole ground for denying support unless the situation is 'extremely grave' (*Pepin v. Jung*, [2003] O.J. No. 1779 (S.C.J.))."

A parent is not relieved of the obligation to support an adult child pursuing post-secondary education or training at an accredited institution merely because the parent disapproves of the child's career choice.[96]

There is nothing in the *Divorce Act* to suggest that a child may not move from being a child of the marriage to being outside the category and thereafter within it again.[97] An adult child who has ceased to be a "child of the marriage" under the *Divorce Act* and the *Federal Child Support Guidelines* may regain that lost status by reason of the pursuit of further education.[98] Whether the status has been regained is a question of fact that may be determined by whether the educational program and the resources of the parent render such a course realistic. When the child in respect of whom support is brought has already been provided with the means to be independent and the parent against whom support is sought has assumed new obligations to a second family, a court may conclude that the parent should not be called upon to support an adult child's pursuit of postgraduate professional training.[99]

b) Options Available to the Court under Section 3(2) of the *Federal Child Support Guidelines*

Section 3(2) of the *Federal Child Support Guidelines* stipulates that, unless otherwise provided under the Guidelines, where a child who is entitled to support is the age of majority or over, the amount of the child support order is

(a) the amount determined by applying the Guidelines as if the child were under the age of majority; or

(b) if the court considers that approach to be inappropriate, the amount that it considers appropriate, having regard to the condition, means, needs and other circumstances of the child and the financial ability of each spouse to contribute to the support of the child.

---

96 *Evans v. Evans*, [1998] S.J. No. 91 (Q.B.).

97 *Stocchero v. Stocchero* (1997), 29 R.F.L. (4th) 223 (Alta. C.A.); *Jean v. Jean*, [2006] A.J. No. 1687 (Q.B.); *M.V. v. D.V.*, [2005] N.B.J. No. 505 (Q.B.); *Olsen v. Olsen*, [1997] S.J. No. 476 (Q.B.).

98 *Horvath v. Horvath*, [2000] M.J. No. 428 (C.A.); *Leonard v. Leonard* (1996), 29 R.F.L. (4th) 237 (N.W.T.S.C.).

99 *Jonasson v. Jonasson*, [1998] B.C.J. No. 726 (S.C.).

Pursuant to the presumptive rule established by section 3(1) of the *Federal Child Support Guidelines*, a child under the age of majority is entitled to the applicable provincial table amount of basic child support and to such special or extraordinary expenses as may fall within section 7 of the Guidelines. If section 3(1)(a) of the Guidelines is deemed applicable, the basic amount of child support fixed by the applicable provincial table cannot be reduced to reflect the child's ability to contribute to his or her own support, but any supplementary amount ordered pursuant to section 7 of the Guidelines will be determined having regard to the guiding principle set out in subsection 7(2), whereby the expense is shared by the spouses in proportion to their respective incomes after deducting from the expense the contribution, if any, from the child.[100]

If a child under the age of majority is pursuing post-secondary education away from home, a court has no authority to deviate from the presumptive rule, unless the attendant circumstances trigger the discretionary jurisdiction of the court by reason of a parent's annual income exceeding $150,000 (Guidelines, section 4), split or shared custody arrangements (Guidelines, sections 8 and 9), or undue hardship (Guidelines, section 10). A court cannot refuse to apply the presumptive rule by invoking section 3(2)(b) of the Guidelines simply because the parents are agreeable to this course of action, even though the child is under the provincial age of majority. In quantifying the living expenses associated with the child's post-secondary education, clothing expenses, spending money, and personal expenses will be excluded from the allowable expenses under section 7 of the Guidelines. This consequence ensues from the fact that these expenses are incorporated in the applicable table amount of child support and they are moveable and not dependent on "economy of scale" when the applicable table amount relates to two or more children. Some, but not all, of the child's food costs are also covered by the applicable table amount of child support, so an adjustment of these expenses is warranted under section 7 of the Guidelines. However, the same is not true of the child's out-of-town accommodation costs, which are allowable under section 7 of the Guidelines to the extent that they are reasonable. In fixing the respective parental contributions to the child's post-secondary education expenses, including tuition, books, and incidental fees, as well as the aforementioned expenses, the court may have regard to money previously set aside or otherwise available to defray the costs of the child's post-secondary education, including scholarship funds

---

100 *Glen v. Glen*, [1997] B.C.J. No. 2806 (S.C.).

and any income tax refund received by a parent as a tuition and educa-tion tax credit.[101] In *Lu v. Sun*,[102] the Nova Scotia Court of Appeal held that the trial judge had erred in apportioning the child's overall university expenses, including accommodation and food costs, between the parents in accordance with their respective incomes, given that the mother also received the full table amount of child support (which includes provision for accommodation and food) during the months that the child was liv-ing away from home while attending university. The father's contribution to the child's section 7 expenses was accordingly reduced on appeal. No error was found in the trial judge's order that the father pay one-half of the table amount of child support in addition to a parental income-based proportionate contribution to section 7 expenses for the second and sub-sequent years of the child's attendance at university, such attendance oc-curring after the child had attained the provincial age of majority, thus triggering a permissible discretionary deviation from the aforementioned presumptive rule pursuant to section 3(2)(b) of the *Federal Child Support Guidelines*. The Nova Scotia Court of Appeal accepted the trial judge's finding that the attendant circumstances justified the child's attendance at an out-of-town university, even though her estranged father had not been consulted on this matter.

The problem of applying section 3(1) of the *Federal Child Support Guidelines* to children under the age of majority who are attending col-lege or university away from home is particularly acute in provinces where the age of majority is nineteen years. This problem is not addressed in *Children Come First: A Report to Parliament Reviewing the Provisions and Operation of the Federal Child Support Guidelines*.[103] Provincial rep-resentations to the federal Minister of Justice might elicit a response. In the meantime, some courts may opt to depart from the "guiding prin-ciple" of a *pro rata* sharing of allowable expenses based on the respective parental incomes under section 7 of the *Federal Child Support Guide-lines*, if a forced payment of the applicable table amount of child support under section 3(1) of the Guidelines generates financial inequity between the parents.

---

101 *Callaghan v. Callaghan*, [2002] N.J. No. 117 (S.C.). Had a step-parent been involved in *Callaghan v. Callaghan*, the discretionary provisions of s. 5 of the Guidelines might have been invoked. As to additional circumstances where a court may devi-ate from the *Federal Child Support Guidelines*, see *Divorce Act*, ss. 15.1(5)–(8) and 17(6.2)–(6.5).

102 [2005] N.S.J. No. 314 (C.A.).

103 Department of Justice, Canada (Ottawa: Department of Justice, 2002).

Section 3(2) of the Guidelines involves a two-stage analysis where a child has attained the provincial age of majority. The initial approach involves a determination of the applicable table amount, together with such amounts for special or extraordinary expenses as may be justified under section 7 of the Guidelines. Only when the court considers that approach inappropriate can the court invoke the broader discretionary jurisdiction that is exercisable under section 3(2) of the Guidelines, having regard to the condition, means, needs, and other circumstances of the child and the financial ability of each spouse to contribute to the support of the child.[104] The words "inappropriate approach" in section 3(2)(b) of the Guidelines may be interpreted as signifying an unreasonable amount of child support. If section 3(2)(b) of the Guidelines is triggered, the court must undertake the budget-driven approach that was in vogue before implementation of the Guidelines.[105]

The party who invokes section 3(2)(b) of the *Federal Child Support Guidelines* has the onus of establishing that the application of section 3(2)(a) of the Guidelines would be inappropriate.[106]

It is a reasonable expectation of a parent that an adult child will pursue post-secondary education at their home-town university, if the desired source of study is available there. If the child wishes to pursue studies elsewhere, reasonable evidence should be offered to justify that decision; for example, evidence that the chosen university offers a program that better accommodates the child's anticipated career path.[107]

Double counting must be avoided. If the applicable provincial table amount is deemed appropriate for a child attending college, it will be necessary to exclude the residence, meals, and other costs that are subsumed in the table amount from any supplementary order for post-secondary expenses under section 7 of the *Federal Child Support Guidelines*.[108]

The judicial flexibility conferred by section 3(2) of the Guidelines is justified by the generally different situations of adult children and of children under the age of majority. Although section 3(2) of the Guidelines

---

104   *S.D.P. v. P.W.*, [1998] N.S.J. No. 565 (Fam. Ct.); *MacDonald v. Rasmussen*, [2000] S.J. No. 660 (Q.B.); *Hiebert v. Hiebert*, [2007] S.J. No. 569 (Q.B.).

105   *Welsh v. Welsh*, [1998] O.J. No. 4550 (Gen. Div.).

106   *Glen v. Glen*, [1997] B.C.J. No. 2806 (S.C.); *Rebenchuk v. Rebenchuk*, 2007 MBCA 22; *M.V. v. D.V.*, [2005] N.B.J. No. 505 (Q.B.); *J.C. v. A.M.M.*, [2007] O.J. No. 3887 (Sup. Ct.); *MacDonald v. Rasmussen*, [2000] S.J. No. 660 (Q.B.).

107   *Woods v. Woods* (1998), 42 R.F.L. (4th) 123 (Sask. Q.B.); *Krueger v. Tunison*, [1999] S.J. No. 482 (Q.B.).

108   *Degagne v. Sargeant*, [1999] A.J. No. 506 (C.A.); see also *Lu v. Sun*, [2005] N.S.J. No. 314 (C.A.).

contemplates that the applicable provincial table amount of basic child support may be inappropriate in relation to children who have attained the age of majority, it offers no guidance how the determination of propriety is to be made. The amount of child support ordered pursuant to that section may be higher or lower than the table amount, depending upon the circumstances, such as the additional costs attributable to an adult child's reasonable pursuit of post-secondary education at an out-of-town university, or the ability of the child to contribute to his or her own living and university expenses.[109]

There is insufficient judicial consistency of approach to lay down any hard and fast rules with respect to adult children who are pursuing university studies while living at home or away from home. Helpful guidance has been furnished, however, by the following analysis of Martinson J., of the Supreme Court of British Columbia, in *Wesemann v. Wesemann*.[110] The law relating to adult children involves a four-step process. The court must first determine whether an adult child falls within the definition of a "child of the marriage" under section 2(1) of the *Divorce Act*. Second, the court must determine whether the approach of applying the Guidelines as if the child were under the age of majority is challenged. If not, the court shall apply the same criteria as those applicable to children under the age of majority.[111] Third, if this approach is challenged, the court must determine whether the challenger has satisfied the burden of proving that it is inappropriate. If not, the usual Guidelines apply. Fourth, if the usual Guidelines approach is proven to be inappropriate, the court must decide what amount is appropriate, having regard to the condition, means, needs, and other circumstances of the child and the financial ability of each parent to contribute to the support of the child.

Where it is appropriate to apply the same approach under the Guidelines to adult children as that applied to children under the age of provincial majority, this can result in an order for the applicable table amount or an order for the applicable table amount and an additional amount under section 7 of the Guidelines for the expenses of post-secondary education. Martinson J. suggests a third alternative, whereby an order could be made under section 7 of the Guidelines without any table amount, but this sug-

---

109   *Whitley v. Whitley*, [1999] B.C.J. No. 3116 (S.C.); *St. Arnaud v. St. Arnaud*, [1998] B.C.J. No. 3155 (S.C.); *Rudulier v. Rudulier*, [1999] S.J. No. 366 (Q.B.).

110   [1999] B.C.J. No. 1387 (S.C.); see also *Winsemann v. Donaldson*, [2007] B.C.J. No. 1936 (S.C.); *Bainbridge v. Bainbridge*, [2007] B.C.J. No. 2614 (S.C.).

111   *Pollock v. Rioux*, [2004] N.B.J. No. 467 (C.A.). Compare *W.P.N. v. B.J.N.*, [2005] B.C.J. No. 12 (C.A.).

gestion negates the significance of the word "and" that links paragraphs (a) and (b) in section 3(1) of the Guidelines. This third alternative would be available, however, by recourse to section 3(2)(b) of the Guidelines in circumstances where the concurrent allocation of the applicable table amount is inappropriate.

Section 3(2) of the Guidelines does not inform a court how to determine whether or not the usual Guidelines approach is appropriate. The usual Guidelines approach is based on certain factors that normally apply to children under the age of majority; namely, they reside with one or both parents, are not earning an income, and are financially dependent on their parents. The closer the circumstances of an adult child are to those upon which the usual Guidelines approach is based, the less likely it is that the usual Guidelines will be found inappropriate. The opposite is also true. Children over the age of majority may reside away from home and/or earn a significant income. In these circumstances, the adult child's expenses will be quite different from those of a typical child under the age of majority. In exercising the discretion to move away from the usual approach under the Guidelines, a court will find it helpful to consider

(i)   the reasonable needs of the child;
(ii) the ability and opportunity of the child to contribute to those needs; and
(iii) the ability of the parents to contribute to those needs.

The reasonable needs of the child has two aspects, namely,

(i)   the child's needs for accommodation, food, clothing, and miscellaneous expenses, and
(ii) the child's actual post-secondary expenses.

Children have an obligation to make a reasonable contribution to their own post-secondary education or training. This does not signify that all of a child's income should be applied to the costs of the child's further education. A child should be entitled to some personal benefit from the fruits of his or her labours. It is not appropriate to require a child to pursue part-time employment during the academic year where that would interfere with the child's academic progress, nor should the availability of student loans automatically require the child to obtain such loans. Student loans are not to be equated with bursaries, grants, or scholarships. A student loan delays the payment of expenses, rather than defraying them. After considering the ability of both parents to contribute to an adult child's reasonable needs, the court may choose to apportion the parental contributions in accordance with their respective incomes.

After reviewing relevant case law, including *Wesemann v. Wesemann*,[112] the British Columbia Court of Appeal in *W.P.N. v. B.J.N.*[113] concluded that, even when a party has not challenged the appropriateness of applying the presumptive rule pursuant to section 3(2)(a) of the Guidelines, it is open to the court to find the application of the presumptive rule to be inappropriate on the facts of the particular case, in which event the court should apply section 3(2)(b) of the Guidelines and order an appropriate amount of child support having regard to the condition, means, needs, and other circumstances of the child and the financial ability of each parent to contribute to the support of the child. Given a reasonable expectation that an adult child will contribute to his or her own expenses and the fact that the table amount is based solely on the obligor's income and can take no account of the child's contribution, the British Columbia Court of Appeal stated that, in principle, support for an adult child who is in attendance at a post-secondary institution should generally be determined under section 3(2)(b) of the Guidelines. The British Columbia Court of Appeal further concluded that concurrent orders may be made under section 3(2)(b) and section 7 of the Guidelines and suggested that a separation agreement providing for specific expenses might lead to such an approach.

A court is more likely to order the applicable table amount of support with respect to an adult child attending university where that child is pursuing his or her studies while living at home with a parent and any other siblings.[114] In addition to ordering the table amount of basic child support in these circumstances, the court may order a contribution towards tuition, books, and incidental expenses pursuant to section 7 of the Guidelines, unless the child can reasonably be expected to meet these

---

112 [1999] B.C.J. No. 1387 (S.C.).

113 [2005] B.C.J. No. 12 (C.A.); see also *Roberts v. Beresford*, [2006] B.C.J. No. 291 (C.A.); *Park v. Thompson*, [2005] O.J. No. 1695 (C.A.); *Rebenchuk v. Rebenchuk*, 2007 MBCA 22; *Lewi v. Lewi*, [2006] O.J. No. 1847 (C.A.); *Shillington v. Shillington*, [2007] S.J. No. 241 (Q.B.); *Royko v. Royko*, [2008] S.J. No. 155 (Q.B.). Compare *Pollock v. Rioux*, [2004] N.B.J. No. 467 (C.A.); *Ferguson v. Thorne*, [2007] N.B.J. No. 45 (Q.B.).

114 *Sherlow v. Zubko*, [1999] A.J. No. 644 (Q.B.) (support to be reviewed, if children pursued post-secondary education away from home); *Glen v. Glen*, [1997] B.C.J. No. 2806 (S.C.); *Morgan v. Morgan*, [2006] B.C.J. No. 1795 (S.C.); *Lewi v. Lewi*, [2006] O.J. No. 1847 (C.A.); *Coghill v. Coghill*, [2006] O.J. No. 2602 (Sup. Ct.); *Holizki v. Reeves* (1998), 34 R.F.L. (4th) 414 (Sask. Q.B.); *Carnall v. Carnall* (1998), 37 R.F.L. (4th) 392 (Sask. Q.B.); *Hiebert v. Hiebert*, [2007] S.J. No. 569 (Q.B.).

expenses.[115] The table amount of support under the Guidelines may be deemed inappropriate for an adult child attending a home-town university, where the child is capable of contributing to his or her own support from earned income, in which event the court should invoke its discretionary jurisdiction under section 3(2)(b) of the Guidelines.[116]

Where children attend university away from home, courts do not normally resort to the provincial table amount, but to the means and needs approach set out in section 3(2)(b) of the *Federal Child Support Guidelines.*[117] Economies of scale, which are reflected in the provincial and territorial tables under the *Federal Child Support Guidelines* where several children are residing in the same household, are inapplicable where one or more of the children are residing elsewhere while pursuing post-secondary education. It is, therefore, more appropriate to calculate the actual costs of providing for the needs of any child in another residence, factoring in a contribution towards the cost of maintaining the family home to return to on weekends or college breaks where appropriate, and apportioning that between the spouses on a means and needs basis after considering the child's own ability to contribute.[118]

c) Expenses for Post-Secondary Education under Section 7 of the *Federal Child Support Guidelines*

Section 7(1)(e) of the *Federal Child Support Guidelines* empowers a court to provide for the payment of some or all of post-secondary education expenses. Post-secondary education expenses do not have to be "extraordinary" in order to satisfy section 7 of the Guidelines.[119]

Expenses for post-secondary education may include tuition, books and other supplies, and transportation costs.[120] Where the table amount of basic child support is deemed inappropriate because the adult child is living away from home while attending university, the post-secondary

---

115 *Mills v. Mills*, [1999] S.J. No. 177 (Q.B.).

116 *Phillipchuk v. Phillipchuk*, [1999] A.J. No. 438 (Q.B.); *Hagen v. Rankin*, [2002] S.J. No. 15 (C.A.).

117 *W.P.N. v. B.J.N.*, [2005] B.C.J. No. 12 (C.A.); *Rebenchuk v. Rebenchuk*, 2007 MBCA 22; *Merritt v. Merritt*, [1999] O.J. No. 1732 (Sup. Ct.); *Lewi v. Lewi*, [2006] O.J. No. 1847 (C.A.); *Coghill v. Coghill*, [2006] O.J. No. 2602 (Sup. Ct.); *Krueger v. Tunison*, [1999] S.J. No. 482 (Q.B.); see also *Power v. Hunt*, [2000] N.J. No. 315 (U.F.C.). Compare *Pollock v. Rioux*, [2004] N.B.J. No. 467 (C.A.); *S. v. S.*, [2007] N.B.J. No. 422 (Q.B.).

118 *Merritt v. Merritt*, [1999] O.J. No. 1732 (Sup. Ct.).

119 *Odermatt v. Odermatt*, [1998] B.C.J. No. 55 (S.C.).

120 *St. Amour v. St. Amour*, [1997] N.S.J. No. 363 (S.C.).

education expenses under section 7 of the Guidelines will include tuition and institutional expenses, room and board or equivalent expenses, and books, travel, and miscellaneous expenses reasonably attributable to the pursuit of that education.[121]

There are a number of things that the court is required to consider in relation to post-secondary education expenses. The court must determine whether the expenses are reasonable having regard to the means of the spouses and child and the family's spending pattern before separation. It is also necessary to determine whether an expense has arisen solely as a result of post-secondary education or whether some portion is already factored into the basic amount provided by the applicable provincial or territorial table. Contributions of the child made possible from his or her earnings or available student loans may be deducted from the expenses. The court must also take into account subsidies, benefits, and income tax deductions or credits relating to the expenses.[122]

Adult children have an obligation to make a reasonable contribution towards the costs of their post-secondary education or training, whether by scholarships, bursaries, loans, or summer employment, but availability for part-time employment while at college is to be determined in light of the academic demands for successful completion of the program.[123] The extent to which an adult child can reasonably be expected to contribute to his or her living or post-secondary education expenses should be determined by seeking to achieve a fair balance between the child's means and capabilities and those of the parents.[124] Support may be denied where a child who attends university can totally finance his or her own studies through savings, and student loans, or employment income.[125] Gifts received by the child may also be taken into account, although it does not follow that the child should exhaust his or her savings before seeking support from a parent.[126] Although a court lacks jurisdiction to compel adult children to expend trust funds to underwrite the costs of their post-secondary education, the amount of support payable by a parent may be

---

121   *Johnson v. Johnson*, [1998] B.C.J. No. 1080 (S.C.).

122   *Magnes v. Magnes*, [1997] S.J. No. 407 (Q.B.).

123   *Matwichuk v. Stephenson*, [2007] B.C.J. No. 2347 (S.C.); *Rebenchuk v.* Rebenchuk, 2007 MBCA 22; *Coghill v. Coghill*, [2006] O.J. No. 2602 (Sup. Ct.); *Zaba v. Bradley* (1996), 140 Sask. R. 297 at 300 (Q.B.), Archambault J.

124   *Whitley v. Whitley*, [1997] B.C.J. No. 3116 (S.C.); *Barbeau v. Barbeau*, [1998] O.J. No. 3580 (Gen. Div.); *MacDonald v. Rasmussen*, [2000] S.J. No. 660 (Q.B.).

125   *Clark v. Clark*, [1998] B.C.J. No. 1934 (S.C.); *Evans v. Evans*, [1998] S.J. No. 91 (Q.B.).

126   *Griffiths v. Griffiths*, [1998] B.C.J. No. 2000 (S.C.); *Lewi v. Lewi*, [2006] O.J. No. 1847 (C.A.).

reduced to reflect the children's ability to use their trust funds or a reasonable portion thereof as a contribution towards the costs of their post-secondary education. The term "means, " which appears in both sections 3(2)(b) and 7 of the Guidelines, includes both capital assets and income, and requires the means of the children as well as those of the parents to be considered in determining the parental contributions towards the costs of the post-secondary education of adult children. In *Lewi v. Lewi*,[127] the motions judge was found to have erred in confining the adult children's contribution to their post-secondary education expenses to their summer employment income, while disregarding trust funds of approximately $41,820 for each child that had been provided by their grandfather. In determining the respective contributions to be made by each of the children, Juriansz J.A., delivering the majority judgment of the Ontario Court of Appeal, observed that there is no provision in the Guidelines that implies that children over the age of majority should contribute all their capital assets towards their post-secondary education before their parents will be required to provide support, or that such children should not have to make any contribution out of their capital. As a general rule, however, the amount of child support that a parent is ordered to pay should be determined in the expectation that a child with means, such as independent assets, will contribute something from those means towards his or her post-secondary education. The extent of the contribution expected depends on the circumstances of the case. Neither section 3(2)(b) nor section 7 of the Guidelines contains any indication whatsoever of the level of contribution an adult child with capital should be expected to make to his or her post-secondary education expenses. There is no standard formula. Under both provisions, the question is largely a matter of discretion for the trial judge.

The applicant and child may be judicially required to keep the payor parent fully informed about the child's educational progress and expenses and about the child's employment income and student loans.[128]

Section 7 of the *Federal Child Support Guidelines* confers a discretion on the court to order a parent to make a contribution to a child's post-secondary education expenses. The court is under no compulsion

---

127   [2006] O.J. No. 1847 (C.A.). For an excellent detailed summary of the principles espoused in *Lewi v. Lewi*, see *Razavi-Brahimi v. Ershadi*, [2007] O.J. No. 3736 (Ct. Just.), Murray J.

128   *Adams v. Adams*, [1997] M.J. No. 621 (Q.B.); *Evans v. Evans*, [1998] S.J. No. 91 (Q.B.); *Rosenberg v. Rosenberg*, [2003] O.J. No. 2962 (Sup. Ct.).

to make such an order and may conclude that any contribution would be inappropriate, having regard to the parent's inability to pay.[129]

G. INCOMES OVER $150,000

Obligors with annual incomes exceeding $150,000 must pay the basic table amount of child support on the first $150,000. With respect to the income over $150,000, the court has one of two alternatives. It can order the additional amount prescribed by a percentage formula in the applicable provincial or territorial table. Or, if it finds that additional amount "inappropriate," the court can exercise its discretion to order a different amount, having regard to the child's condition, means, needs, and other circumstances and the financial ability of each parent to contribute to the support of the child. Deviation from the table formula presupposes a finding that the amount thereby prescribed is "inappropriate." In *Francis v. Baker*,[130] the Supreme Court of Canada concluded that the word "inappropriate" in section 4(b) of the *Federal Child Support Guidelines* does not mean "inadequate"; it bears its ordinary dictionary meaning of "unsuitable" or "inadvisable." Consequently, insofar as the obligor's annual income exceeds $150,000, a court has the discretion to increase, decrease, or confirm the amount of child support prescribed by a strict application of the table formula. A point may be reached where the overall table amount is so far in excess of the child's reasonable needs as to justify the court ordering a lower supplementary amount than that prescribed by the table formula relating to the obligor's income in excess of $150,000. Some obligors, such as sports stars, may have astronomic incomes but short professional careers. In *Bachorick v. Verdejo*,[131] the Saskatchewan Court of Appeal concluded that a court has no jurisdiction to build a fund to cover future contingencies, such as a child's education, out of monthly table amounts of child support. Any judicial direction to such effect would negate the underlying premise of the *Federal Child Support Guidelines* that the amount of child support ordered reflects the current needs of the children. It would also constitute an unwarranted intrusion on the spending priorities of the custodial parent.

---

129   *Giebelhaus v. Bell*, [1998] B.C.J. No. 627 (S.C.); *Jarzebinski v. Jarzebinski*, [2004] O.J. No. 4595 (Sup. Ct.).

130   [1999] 3 S.C.R. 250.

131   [1999] S.J. No. 450 (C.A.); see also *Simon v. Simon*, [1999] O.J. No. 4492 (C.A.).

The relevant principles that were laid down in *Francis v. Baker* are aptly summarized as follows by Finch J.A. (now Finch C.J.) in *Metzner v. Metzner*:

1) It was Parliament's intention that there be a presumption in favour of the table amount in all cases.

2) The Guidelines figures can only be increased or reduced under s. 4 if the party seeking such a deviation has rebutted the presumption that the applicable table amount is appropriate.

3) There must be clear and compelling evidence for departing from the Guidelines figures.

4) Parliament expressly listed in s. 4(b)(ii) the factors relevant to determining both appropriateness and inappropriateness of the table amount or any deviation therefrom.

5) Courts should determine table amounts to be inappropriate and so create more suitable awards only after examining all circumstances including the factors expressly set out in s. 4(b)(ii).

6) Section 4(b)(ii) emphasizes the "centrality" of the actual situation of the children. The actual circumstances of the children are at least as important as any single element of the legislative purpose underlying the section. A proper construction of s. 4 requires that the objectives of predictability, consistency and efficiency, on the one hand, be balanced with those of fairness, flexibility and recognition of the actual "condition, means, needs and other circumstances of the children" on the other.

7) While child support payments unquestionably result in some kind of wealth transfer to the children which results in an indirect benefit to the non-paying parent, the objectives of child support payments must be kept in mind. The Guidelines have not displaced the *Divorce Act* which has as its objective the maintenance of children rather than household equalization of spousal support.

8) The court must have all necessary information before it in order to determine inappropriateness under s. 4. If the evidence provided is a child expense budget then "the unique economic situation of high income earners" must be considered.

9) The test for reasonableness of expenses will be a demonstration by the paying parent that the budgeted expense is so high as to exceed the generous ambit within which reasonable disagreement is possible.[132]

---

132 [2000] B.C.J. No. 1693 (C.A.). See also *Hollenbach v. Hollenbach*, [2000] B.C.J. No. 2316 (C.A.); *MacDonald v. MacDonald*, [2002] B.C.J. No. 121 (C.A.); *Debora v. Debora*, [2006] O.J. No. 4826 (C.A.). For a review of Ontario appellate judgments

In *Hogkinson v. Hodgkinson*,[133] wherein the father's annual income exceeded $150,000, the trial judge awarded the table amount of child support ($2,415 per month) pursuant to section 4 of the *Federal Child Support Guidelines*. In addressing the presumptive rule in favour of the full table amount of child support under section 4, the Supreme Court of Canada in *Francis v. Baker*[134] observed that, where the table amount is "inappropriate" with respect to the portion of the parent's annual income that exceeds $150,000, the court has "the discretion to both increase and reduce the [full table] amount." In *Hodgkinson v. Hodgkinson*, the British Columbia Court of Appeal accepted the wife's submission that the trial judge had erred by viewing the discretion conferred by section 4 as being triggered only when the overall table amount is excessive. Having regard to the trial judge's finding that the expenses in relation to the child totaled $2,716, all of which were reasonable, and having regard also to the vast discrepancy between the parental incomes, the British Columbia Court of Appeal held that the trial judge's order, in failing to cover all the reasonable expenses of the child, was "inappropriate," which, according to *Francis v. Baker*, means "unsuitable." Consequently, the British Columbia Court of Appeal in *Hodgkinson v. Hodgkinson* increased the amount of the trial judge's child support order by $300 per month, retroactive to the date of the order.

H. SPLIT CUSTODY; SECTION 8 OF GUIDELINES[135]

Section 8 of the *Federal Child Support Guidelines* provides that, where each spouse or former spouse has custody of one or more children, the amount of a child support order is the difference between the amount that each would otherwise pay if a child support order were sought against each of them.[136] Given possible future changes in the parental incomes,

---

dealing with the child support of parents with annual incomes exceeding $150,000, see *R. v. R.*, [2002] O.J. No. 1095 (C.A.).

133 [2006] B.C.J. No. 678 (C.A.).

134 [1999] 3 S.C.R. 250 at para. 40.

135 See, generally, Carol Rogerson, "Child Support under the Guidelines in Cases of Split and Shared Custody" (1998) 15 Can. J. Fam. L. 11 (Quicklaw, db SFLN).

136 *S.E.H. v. S.R.M.*, [1999] B.C.J. No. 1458 (S.C.) (split custody involving biological child and stepchild; set off under s. 8 of *Federal Child Support Guidelines*); *Fitzpatrick v. Fitzpatrick*, [2000] N.J. No. 62 (U.F.C.); *Watson v. Watson*, [1999] N.S.J. No. 272 (S.C.); *Bergman-Illnik v. Illnik*, [1997] N.W.T.J. No. 93 (S.C.); *J.P. v. B.G.*, [2000] O.J. No. 1753 (Sup. Ct.); *MacLean v. MacLean*, [2003] P.E.I.J. No. 16 (S.C.T.D.); *Rudulier*

the parents may be judicially directed to exchange complete copies of their income tax returns by May 15th of each year.[137] Where the parents earn the same income and each is responsible for the support of a child of the marriage, the court may decline to make any order for child support.[138] Bilateral orders may be granted for child support where each parent had custody of one or more children of the marriage.[139] Section 8 of the *Federal Child Support Guidelines*, unlike section 9, provides no judicial discretion in the assessment of child support.[140]

Section 8 of the *Federal Child Support Guidelines* may be applied where each of the parents provides a home for one or more of their dependent children, even though one of the children is an adult attending university in respect of whom "neither parent has custody."[141] Section 8 of the Guidelines will not be satisfied, however, where the evidence is insufficient to establish that the adult child is a "child of the marriage" within the meaning of the *Divorce Act*.[142]

Where parents have a split custody arrangement but the income of one of the parents falls short of the minimum threshold under the applicable provincial table, the other parent will be required to pay the full table amount of support for the child in the custody of the low- or no-income parent.[143]

In addition to ordering payment of the differential between the two table amounts pursuant to section 8 of the *Federal Child Support Guidelines*, a court may order a sharing of special or extraordinary expenses

---

v. *Rudulier*, [1999] S.J. No. 366 (Q.B.); *Hladun v. Hladun*, [2002] S.J. No. 476 (Q.B.). Compare *Dudka v. Dudka*, [1997] N.S.J. No. 526 (T.D.).

137   *Hladun v. Hladun*, [2002] S.J. No. 476 (Q.B.).

138   *Cram v. Cram*, [1999] B.C.J. No. 2518 (S.C.).

139   *Mayer v. Mayer*, [1999] O.J. No. 5286 (Sup. Ct.) (cost-of-living indexation of orders); *Holman v. Bignell*, [2000] O.J. No. 3405 (Sup. Ct.).

140   *Wright v. Wright*, [2002] B.C.J. No. 458 (S.C.); *Kavanagh v. Kavanagh*, [1999] N.J. No. 358 (S.C.).

141   *Khoee-Solomonescu v. Solomonescu*, [1997] O.J. No. 4876 (Gen. Div.); see also *Sutcliffe v. Sutcliffe*, [2001] A.J. No. 629 (Q.B.); *Davis v. Davis*, [1999] B.C.J. No. 1832 (application of s. 8 of *Federal Child Support Guidelines* in circumstances involving split custody over summer months when adult child not away at university); *Kavanagh v. Kavanagh*, [1999] N.J. No. 358 (S.C.).

142   *Tanner v. Simpson*, [1999] N.W.T.J. No. 71 (S.C.).

143   *Estey v. Estey*, [1999] N.S.J. No. 226 (S.C.); *Fraser v. Gallant*, [2004] P.E.I.J. No. 5 (S.C.T.D.); *Hamonic v. Gronvold*, [1999] S.J. No. 32 (Q.B.). Compare *K.O. v. C.O.*, [1999] S.J. No. 29 (Q.B.) (shared custody).

under section 7 of the Guidelines in proportion to the respective parental incomes,[144] or in such other proportion as the court deems reasonable.[145]

I. SHARED CUSTODY: 40 PERCENT RULE

Section 9 of the *Federal Child Support Guidelines* permits a court to deviate from the normal guidelines amount of child support, where a parent exercises access to or has physical custody of a child for not less than 40 percent of the time over the course of a year. Shared custody or access for 40 percent of the time over the course of a year is the equivalent of 146 days[146] or 3504 hours[147] of the year. The 40 percent criterion must be satisfied before section 9 of the Guidelines is triggered.[148] Time spent by a child sleeping, in day care, or at school is credited to the parent who has care and control over the child at that time. Parents who exercise access for part of a day, such as midweek evening access, cannot be credited with a full day, when the custodial parent would be called upon, if anything happened while the child was at school.[149] A custodial parent will ordinarily be credited with time that a child spends sleeping, or at day care, or at school,[150] except for those hours when the non-custodial parent is actually exercising rights of access or the child is sleeping in that parent's home.[151]

The amount of child support to be paid pursuant to section 9 of the *Federal Child Support Guidelines* when the minimum 40 percent criterion has been satisfied must be determined by taking into account (a)

---

144 *Sutcliffe v. Sutcliffe*, [2001] A.J. No. 629 (Q.B.); *Patrick v. Patrick*, [1999] B.C.J. No. 1245 (S.C.); *Sayong v. Aindow*, [1999] N.W.T.J. No. 63 (S.C.); *Fraser v. Fraser*, [2001] O.J. No. 3765 (Sup. Ct.); *Fransoo v. Fransoo*, [2001] S.J. No. 121 (Q.B.).

145 Compare *Tooth v. Knott*, [1998] A.J. No. 1395 (Q.B.), and see Section I, below in this chapter.

146 *Handy v. Handy*, [1999] B.C.J. No. 6 (S.C.); *Gardiner v. Gardiner*, [2007] N.S.J. No. 367 (S.C.).

147 *Claxton v. Jones*, [1999] B.C.J. No. 3086 (Prov. Ct.); *D'Urzo v. D'Urzo*, [2002] O.J. No. 2415 (Sup. Ct.).

148 *L.C. v. R.O.C.*, 2007 ABCA 158, [2007] A.J. No. 513; *Campolin v. Campolin*, [2007] B.C.J. No. 2090 (S.C.).

149 *McGrath v. McGrath*, [2006] N.J. No. 201 (U.F.C.); *Lepage v. Lepage*, [1999] S.J. No. 174 (Q.B.).

150 *Walker v. Rutledge*, [2002] O.J. No. 4521 (Sup. Ct.); *Gardiner v. Gardiner*, [2007] N.S.J. No. 367 (S.C.); *Cross v. Cross*, [2004] O.J. No. 2341 (Sup. Ct.); *Jarocki v. Rice*, [2003] S.J. No. 178 (Q.B.).

151 *Cusick v. Squire*, [1999] N.J. No. 206 (S.C.); *Jarocki v. Rice*, [2003] S.J. No. 178 (Q.B.).

the amounts set out in the applicable tables for each spouse; (b) the increased costs of shared custody; and (c) the conditions, means, needs, and other circumstances of each spouse and of any child for whom support is sought. A court is not compelled to make a formal finding of the precise percentage of time that each parent is responsible for the child. There is nothing in section 9 of the Guidelines to suggest that the amount of child support must invariably reflect the percentages of shared parenting. A contextual approach that does not place undue reliance upon percentages or formulas is required. Shared parenting is usually expensive for both parents and it cannot be assumed that, once the 40 percent threshold is met, the parent who spends more time with the child will have higher costs than the parent who spends less time with the child. Even if a finding is made with respect to the percentage of the year that each parent is responsible for the child, this neither avoids nor assists in the financial analysis that must be undertaken pursuant to sections 9(b) and (c) of the Guidelines, which respectively require the court to have regard to any proven increased costs of the shared-parenting regime and to the relative standards of living available in the two households and the ability of each parent to absorb the costs required to maintain an appropriate standard of living.[152]

In *Contino v. Leonelli-Contino*,[153] the Supreme Court of Canada, by a majority of eight to one, held that section 9 of the Guidelines promotes flexibility and fairness by ensuring that the economic reality and particular circumstances of each family are accounted for. The three listed factors all structure the exercise of judicial discretion and no single factor prevails. The weight given to each of the three factors will vary according to the particular circumstances of each case. There is no presumption in favour of awarding at least the amount prescribed by section 3 of the Guidelines. Nor is there any presumption in favour of reducing a parent's child support obligation below that amount, because after an analysis of all three factors in section 9, a court may conclude that the normal Guidelines amount should be paid in full under the circumstances of the particular case. A simple set-off between the table amounts payable by each parent is an appropriate starting point under section 9(a), but it must be

---

152 *Stewart v. Stewart*, 2007 MBCA 66, [2007] M.J. No. 178.

153 [2005] 3 S.C.R. 217, [2005] S.C.J. No. 65. For insightful commentary, see D.A. Rollie Thompson, Annotation, *Contino v. Leonelli-Contino* (2006), 19 R.F.L. (6th) 239, and Justice Jennifer Blishen & Michèle Labrosse, "Shared Custody and Child Support after *Contino*" (Paper presented to the County of Carleton Law Association, 15th Annual Institute of Family Law, 2 June 2006, Ottawa) at tab 1Cii.

followed by an examination of the continuing ability of the recipient parent to meet the financial needs of the child, especially in light of the fact that many costs are fixed. Where both parents are making effective contributions, it is necessary to verify how each parent's actual contribution compares to the table amount that is provided for each of them. This will provide the judge with better insight when deciding whether the adjustments to be made to the set-off amount are based on the actual sharing of child-related expenses. The court retains the discretion to modify the set-off amount where, considering the financial situation of the parents, it would lead to a significant variation in the standard of living experienced by the children as they move between the respective households. Section 9(b) of the *Federal Child Support Guidelines* recognizes that the total cost of raising children may be greater in shared-custody situations than in sole-custody situations. The court will examine the budgets and actual expenditures of both parents in addressing the needs of the children and determine whether shared custody has resulted in increased costs globally. These expenses will be apportioned between the parents in accordance with their respective incomes. Lastly, section 9(c) vests the court with a broad discretion to analyze the resources and needs of both the parents and the children. It is important to keep in mind the objectives of the Guidelines that require a fair standard of support for the child and fair contributions from both parents. The court will look at the standard of living of the child in each household and the ability of each parent to absorb the costs required to maintain the appropriate standard of living in the circumstances. Financial statements and/or child-expense budgets are necessary for a proper evaluation of section 9(c). There is no need to resort to section 10 and section 7[154] of the Guidelines either to increase or to reduce support, since the court has full discretion under section 9(c) to consider "other circumstances" and order the payment of any amount above or below the table amounts. It may be that section 10 would find application in an extraordinary situation. It is important that the parties lead evidence relating to sections 9(b) and 9(c), and courts should demand information from the parties when the evidence is deficient. A court should neither make "common-sense" assumptions about costs incurred by the payor parent, nor apply a multiplier to account for the fixed costs of the recipient parent, such as has been done by some courts in the past. Although the Comparison of Household Standards of Living Test in Schedule II of the Guidelines, which is included in Child View Calculations, is

---

154 *Stewart v. Stewart*, 2007 MBCA 66, [2007] M.J. No. 178.

normally used in the context of the undue hardship provisions of section 10 of the Guidelines, its use in the broad discretionary context of section 9(c) of the Guidelines is neither required nor precluded. In some situations it will provide assistance. Provided that it is not overemphasized at the expense of the required consideration of the relevant personal factors applicable to the parties under section 9(c) of the Guidelines, its use by the trial judge does not constitute a reviewable error.[155]

The majority judgment in *Contino* denounces a strict formulaic approach to the determination of child support in shared-parenting situations, and emphasizes the need for relevant financial evidence to be adduced so that the court can address the factors specified in paragraphs 9(b) and (c) of the Guidelines, in addition to taking account of the table amount payable by each parent, as required by paragraph 9(a). After reviewing diverse formulas that had previously been applied, especially in British Columbia, the Supreme Court of Canada in *Contino* rejects the use of prorated set-offs between the applicable table amounts of child support payable by each parent, which have been frequently used in the past in situations involving unequal time-sharing arrangements falling within section 9 of the Guidelines. The Supreme Court of Canada also discredits the judicial application of a multiplier (usually 1.5 times the determined set-off amount), which some courts previously applied on the assumption that part of the recipient parent's costs are fixed and unaffected by increased time that the child spends with the payor parent. The majority judgment in *Contino*, nevertheless, accepts that a simple set-off between the full table amount of child support payable by each parent is a useful starting point in shared-parenting situations, but emphasizes the need for a facts-based and child-related budgetary analysis that reflects the factors specified in paragraphs 9(b) and (c) of the Guidelines. Given the Supreme Court of Canada's assertion that a child should not suffer a noticeable decline in his or her standard of living from any change in the parenting regime, a distinction may need to be drawn between original applications for child support and variation applications, which can trigger the so-called cliff effect, in that a modest increase in the time spent with the child could result in an unjustifiable reduction in the amount of child support payable if a strict formulaic approach were applied.[156] The cliff effect can only be resolved by the court paying due regard to the

---

155 *Ibid.*
156 *Martin v. Martin*, [2007] M.J. No. 449 (Q.B.); *Costa v. Petipas*, [2006] P.E.I.J. No. 39 (S.C.T.D.).

criteria specified in paragraphs 9(b) and (c) of the Guidelines. If evidence relating to these criteria is not initially adduced, the court may grant an adjournment to permit the necessary evidence to be provided. It is not open to the court to make unsubstantiated assumptions as to the increased costs of a shared-custody arrangement or to apply any arbitrary multiplier to the set-off amount instead of requiring relevant evidence to be adduced. While mandatory financial statements and child-related budgets may be fraught with difficulties, as parents confuse necessary expenditures with their preferred wish lists, trial judges are well-placed to resolve any such conflict. The majority judgment in *Contino* states that the broad discretion conferred by paragraph 9(c) of the Guidelines empowers the court to order an overall amount of child support that includes special or exceptional expenses that would otherwise fall within section 7 of the Guidelines.[157] As was observed in *Slade v. Slade*,[158] special or extraordinary expenses may be ordered in shared-parenting situations pursuant to section 7 of the Guidelines, or they may be considered under the broad provisions of paragraph 9(c) of the Guidelines. Neither option is foreclosed by the majority judgment in *Contino*, and a severance of the basic amount of child support from allowable section 7 expenses may be advantageous in facilitating future variations. The majority judgment of the Supreme Court of Canada in *Contino* represents a balanced approach to reconciling the inherent flexibility of the judicial discretion conferred by section 9 of the *Federal Child Support Guidelines* with the objective of providing some measure of consistency and predictability. If there is limited information available to the court and the incomes of the parents are not widely divergent, a simple set-off between the table amounts of child support may be deemed appropriate. Where there is a substantial disparity between the parental incomes and the child's standard of living would be significantly reduced by a simple set-off approach, it behooves the court to adjourn the proceeding so that requisite evidence can be provided that will enable the court to apply the criteria defined in paragraphs 9(b) and (c) of the Guidelines. In addressing the application of section 9 to the shared-parenting arrangement that existed in *Dillon v. Dillon*,[159] the Nova Scotia Court of Appeal found no error on the part of the trial judge who fixed child support at the set-off amount created by the differential between the table amount of child support payable by each parent. In up-

---

157 *Stewart v. Stewart*, 2007 MBCA 66, [2007] M.J. No. 178.
158 [2000] N.J. No. 5 (C.A.); see also *Costa v. Petipas*, [2006] P.E.I.J. No. 39 (S.C.T.D.).
159 [2005] N.S.J. No. 548 (C.A.).

holding the set-off amount, the Nova Scotia Court of Appeal held that the judgment of the Supreme Court of Canada in *Contino v. Leonelli-Contino* does not rule out the fixing of child support on the basis of a simple set-off of the respective table amounts, provided that, in so doing, the additional factors in sections 9(b) and (c) of the *Federal Child Support Guidelines* are considered.

In a summary of their review of post-*Contino* cases published in June 2006, Justice Jennifer Blishen and Michèle Labrosse, a family law practitioner, express the following conclusion:

> Given the Supreme Court of Canada's emphasis on a discretionary rather than a "formulaic" or "mathematical" approach to calculating child support under s. 9 of the *Child Support Guidelines*, it is not surprising that recent cases have widely differing results depending on their circumstances. The results range from a determination that no child support was payable (see *Lowe v. Lowe*, [2006] O.J. No. 128 (S.C.J.)), to the use of a straight set-off (see *Dillon v. Dillon*, [2005] N.S.J. No. 548 (C.A.)), to orders for the full Table amount or close to it in situations where there is a significant disparity in the incomes, assets and/or expenses of the parties (see *Kennedy v. Kennedy*, [2006] B.C.J. No. 509 (S.C.), *Elliot v. MacAskill*, [2005] N.S.J. No. 479 (Fam. Ct.), *Mendler v. Mendler*, [2006] O.J. No. 878 (S.C.J.) and *Easton v. McAvoy*, [2005] O.J. No. 5479 (O.C.J.)).[160]

Canadian case law has manifested divergent approaches to the application of section 9 of the *Federal Child Support Guidelines* when there is a hybrid of parenting arrangements in that different time-sharing regimes apply to different children in the family.[161] In *Wouters v. Wouters*,[162] the oldest of three children lived with the mother and the two younger children spent equal time with each parent. M.-E. Wright J., of the Saskatchewan Court of Queen's Bench, concluded that a two-stage analysis should be undertaken to determine the amount of child support to be ordered. First, child support should be fixed for the oldest child whose custody was not shared. After determining the table amount payable

---

160   Above note 153.

161   See, for example, *Ferster v. Ferster*, [2002] B.C.J. No. 172 (S.C.); *Earles v. Earles*, [2006] B.C.J. No. 346 (S.C.); *Doyle v. Doyle*, [2006] B.C.J. No. 3015 (S.C.); *Burns v. Burns* (1998), 40 R.F.L. (4th) 32 (Ont. Gen. Div.); *Seguin v. Masterson*, [2004] O.J. No. 2176 (Sup. Ct.); *Tweel v. Tweel* (2000), 186 Nfld. & P.E.I.R. 99 (P.E.I.S.C.T.D.); *Costa v. Petipas*, [2006] P.E.I.J. No. 39 (S.C.T.D.).

162   (2001), 205 Sask. R. 215 (Q.B.).

with respect to this child in accordance with the presumptive rule under section 3(1) of the Guidelines, Wright J. turned to support for the two children whose custody was shared. Their entitlement was determined by ordering a set-off between the table amount of support payable by each parent when there are two children. In *Hofsteede v. Hofsteede*,[163] Marshman J., of the Ontario Superior Court of Justice, conceded that the wording of the Guidelines might, at first blush, dictate that the approach in *Wouters v. Wouters* is the proper one. However, Marshman J. accepted the reasoning of Vogelsang J. in *Burns v. Burns*,[164] who observed that the table amounts prescribed by the Guidelines recognize the principle of economies of scale when children are residing under the same roof. Thus, the table amount for three children is less than the table amount for one child plus the table amount for two children before any *Contino* adjustment is made by virtue of a set-off or the application of paragraphs 9(b) and (c) of the Guidelines. Applying the reasoning in *Burns* to the facts in *Hofsteede v. Hofsteede*, wherein the older of two children resided primarily with the mother and the younger child spent equal time with both parents, Marshman J. found it more appropriate to apply sections 8 (split custody) and section 9 (shared custody) to the situation rather than sections 3 and 9. Consequently, in calculating the child support to be paid, Marshman J. first determined the father's table amount of support for the two children and the wife's table amount of support for one child and effectuated a set-off between these two amounts. Marshman J. then reviewed the children's budgets prepared by both parents and increased the set-off amount to reflect the increased costs of the shared-parenting arrangement with respect to the younger child and the mother's assumption of a disproportionate share of the overall child-related expenses. In *Doyle v. Doyle*,[165] the British Columbia Court of Appeal found that the chambers judge had erred by failing to apply the *Federal Child Support Guidelines* on a variation application after finding that a change of circumstances had occurred in consequence of the older of two children taking up residence with the father and thereby changing the equal time-sharing regime that had previously been implemented with respect to both of the children. After reviewing the submissions of both parties with respect to the potential application of sections 8 and 9 of the Guidelines, the British Columbia Court of Appeal concluded that additional evidence was

---

163 [2006] O.J. No. 304 (Sup. Ct.).
164 (1998), 40 R.F.L. (4th) 32 (Ont. Gen. Div.).
165 [2006] B.C.J. No. 523 (C.A.).

required and the application to vary should be remitted to the British Columbia Supreme Court for a new hearing to enable both parents to provide the necessary evidence and to permit a proper determination to be made as to whether the parenting arrangements fell within section 8 or 9 of the Guidelines, or some combination thereof and, if within section 9, to consider and weigh each of the factors listed in paragraphs (a), (b), and (c). It is noteworthy that *Wouters v. Wouters* predates the judgment of the Supreme Court of Canada in *Contino v. Leonelli-Contino*. Given the broad discretion conferred by section 9, and especially 9(c) of the Guidelines, as manifested by *Contino*, equitable and reasonably consistent results can be reached regardless of whether courts prefer the *Wouters* or the *Hofsteede* approach. A similar approach to *Wouters v. Wouters* was endorsed by Vertes J. in *McBride v. McBride*,[166] wherein the following conclusions were expressed. If there is a hybrid of custody arrangements whereby one child is living in a shared-parenting arrangement but a second child is not, the court must segregate the determination of support for each child. A hybrid of custody arrangements calls for the application of different formulas under the *Federal Child Support Guidelines*. The court cannot simply mix different arrangements into a mélange and then apply one formula. Where section 9 of the Guidelines is triggered with respect to one child and section 5 of the Guidelines applies to the other child, the court cannot simply pull a number out of the air that appears to be fair. Although both sections 9 and 5 of the Guidelines confer a discretion on the court, different factors must be taken into account under each section. In the more recent case of *T.L.R. v. R.W.R.*,[167] wherein a shared-parenting arrangement involved the defendant's biological child and his stepchild, Taylor J. first examined section 5 of the *Federal Child Support Guidelines*. Having observed that the full table amount payable by the defendant for the two children would be $678 per month and for the one child would be $415 per month, Taylor J. stated that the primary consideration in exercising the discretion conferred by section 5 to reduce a step-parent's obligation to support a child because of the biological parent's concurrent support obligation is fairness and societal expectations. Having regard to the defendant's close relationship with his stepchild, which would continue under a joint-custody and joint-guardianship order, and the absence of the biological father's involvement in the life of the child and his failure to pay court-ordered support, Taylor J. concluded that the

---

166 [2001] N.W.T.J. No. 69 (S.C.).
167 [2006] B.C.J. No. 409 (S.C.).

defendant's obligation to pay support for his stepchild should be reduced by only 10 percent of $263 per month, which total amount represents the difference between the table amount that he would be required to pay for his biological child and the additional amount that would be payable for a second child, his stepchild. The full table amount of child support was, therefore, reduced by $26 per month, leaving his Guidelines obligation for the two children at $652 per month. Taylor J. then proceeded to apply section 9 of the Guidelines in light of *Contino v. Leonelli-Contino* by effectuating a set-off of the table amount payable by the mother for her two biological children and thereafter increasing the balance pursuant to paragraphs (b) and (c) of section 9 of the Guidelines to take account of the fact that the children spent more time with their mother, who had the primary financial responsibility for them notwithstanding that she had fewer resources than the defendant, and to accommodate a comparable standard of living for the children in each of the two households.

J. UNDUE HARDSHIP

Section 10 of the *Federal Child Support Guidelines* confers a discretion of the court to deviate from the normal Guidelines amount of child support in cases of undue hardship. Undue hardship is a tough threshold to meet. Hardship is not sufficient. It must be hardship that is excessive, extreme, improper, unreasonable, or unjustified.[168] Absent a finding of undue hardship within the meaning of section 10 of the *Federal Child Support Guidelines*, bankruptcy does not relieve the obligor of child support obligations.[169] The undue hardship provisions of section 10 of the Guidelines may be invoked to increase or reduce the amount of child support that would otherwise be payable.[170] However, courts must be cautious where undue hardship is pleaded by a recipient spouse because of the potential for its abuse as an indirect vehicle for the payment of spousal support or for imposing the child support obligation on other members of the obligor's household.[171] The undue hardship provisions of section 10 of the Guidelines are inapplicable to claims for special or extraordinary

---

168 *Hanmore v. Hanmore*, [2000] A.J. No. 171 (C.A.); *Van Gool v. Van Gool*, [1998] B.C.J. No. 2513 (C.A.); *Schenkeveld v. Schenkeveld*, [2002] M.J. No. 69 (C.A.); *Green v. Green*, [2005] N.J. No. 165 (C.A.).

169 *Court v. McQuaid*, [2005] P.E.I.J. No 24 (S.C.T.D.).

170 *Gandy v. Gandy*, [2000] B.C.J. No. 2294 (S.C.).

171 *Middleton v. MacPherson*, [1997] A.J. No. 614 (Q.B.).

expenses under section 7 of the Guidelines, being unnecessary to such claims by virtue of the broad discretion conferred on the court by that section.[172]

Section 10(2) of the Guidelines sets out the following non-exhaustive list of five circumstances that may constitute undue hardship:

a)   the spouse has responsibility for an unusually high level of debts reasonably incurred to support the spouses and their children prior to the separation or to earn a living;

b)   the spouse has unusually high expenses in relation to exercising access to the child;

c)   the spouse has a legal duty under a judgment, order or written separation agreement to support any person;

d)   the spouse has a legal duty to support any child, other than a child of the marriage, who is (i) under the age of majority, or (ii) the age of majority or over but is unable, by reason of illness, disability, or other cause to obtain the necessaries of life; and

e)   the spouse has a legal duty to support any person who is unable to obtain the necessaries of life due to an illness or disability.

Undue hardship may arise from a combination of the circumstances listed under paragraphs (a) to (e) of subsection 10(2) of the *Federal Child Support Guidelines*,[173] or from a combination of circumstances some of which fall within the categories listed while others fall outside.[174] All five circumstances listed under section 10(2) of the Guidelines relate in one way or another to the financial costs associated with past or present obligations to children or other family members. The circumstances listed in section 10(2) of the Guidelines are not exhaustive, nor does their existence mandate a conclusion that undue hardship exists. Before adding to the list, however, a court must be satisfied that the circumstances pleaded as constituting undue hardship are as serious, exceptional, or excessive as those listed in section 10(2) of the Guidelines.[175] Obligors have frequently asserted undue hardship as a consequence of their assumption of new

---

172   *Dean v. Friesen*, [1999] S.J. No. 424 (Q.B.).

173   *MacFarlane v. MacFarlane*, [1999] B.C.J. No. 3008 (S.C.); *Deveau v. Groskopf*, [2000] S.J. No. 281 (Q.B.); *Kaatz v. Kaatz*, [2001] S.J. No. 661 (Q.B.).

174   *Goudie v. Buchanan*, [2001] N.J. No. 187 (U.F.C.) (application under *Newfoundland Child Support Guidelines*); *Hollett-Collins v. Hollett*, [2002] N.J. No. 292 (S.C.); *Wainman v. Clairmont*, [2004] N.S.J. No. 69 (S.C.).

175   *Adams v. Loov*, [1998] A.J. No. 660 (Q.B.); *Goudie v. Buchanan*, [2001] N.J. No. 187 (U.F.C.).

family support obligations. Subjective perceptions of undue hardship do not satisfy the requirements of section 10 of the Guidelines. Sequential families may inevitably introduce some degree of hardship, but undue hardship is not to be equated with financial difficulty, budgetary cutbacks, or financial restraints or re-evaluations. As stated previously, the hardship must be excessive or extreme. The fact that the standard of living in the obligor's household is lower than that in the recipient household does not, of itself, constitute evidence of undue hardship.[176]

Even assuming a finding of undue hardship, a court cannot deviate from the amount ordinarily payable under the Guidelines, if the household of the party pleading undue hardship would, after payment of the Guidelines amount, have a higher standard of living than that of the other party. This is expressly provided by section 10(3) of the Guidelines.

Section 10 of the Guidelines thus involves a two-step process. First, the court must make a finding of undue hardship. Second, if, and only if, such a finding is made, the court must undertake a comparison of the standard of living in each household in order to ensure that the obligor is not better off even after payment of the Guidelines amount.[177] In comparing the standard of living in the respective households, section 10(4) of the Guidelines empowers, but does not compel, a court to apply the steps set out in Schedule II of the Guidelines.[178] Given a finding of undue hardship and a lower standard of living in the household of the parent who invokes section 10 of the Guidelines, the court retains a residual discretion as to whether it should reduce the child support normally payable and, if so, by what amount.[179]

Where undue hardship is found, a court should seek to ensure as much as possible that the children of both families are treated equitably.[180] In the absence of undue hardship as defined above, the "first in time prevails" as between the children of sequential families.[181]

---

176 *Van Gool v. Van Gool*, [1998] B.C.J. No. 2513 (C.A.); *Schenkeveld v. Schenkeveld*, [2002] M.J. No. 69 (C.A.); *Steele v. Koppanyi*, [2002] M.J. No. 201 (C.A.); *Gaetz v. Gaetz*, [2001] N.S.J. No. 131 (C.A.); *Ross v. Ross*, [2001] N.S.J. No. 171 (C.A.); *Birss v. Birss*, [2000] O.J. No. 3692 (Div. Ct.); *Messier v. Baines*, [1997] S.J. No. 627 (Q.B.).

177 *Van Gool v. Van Gool*, [1998] B.C.J. No. 2513 (C.A.); *Green v. Green*, [2005] N.J. No. 165 (C.A.); *Douglas v. Ward*, [2006] S.J. No. 57 (Q.B.).

178 *Williams v. Smith*, [2001] A.J. No. 248 (Q.B.).

179 *Pelletier v. Kakakaway*, [2002] S.J. No. 448 (C.A.) (herein referred to as a third condition).

180 *Messier v. Baines*, [1997] S.J. No. 627 (Q.B.); *Douglas v. Ward*, [2006] S.J. No. 57 (Q.B.).

181 *Schenkeveld v. Schenkeveld*, [2002] M.J. No. 69 (C.A.); *Steele v. Koppanyi*, [2002] M.J. No. 201 (C.A.).

Pursuant to section 10(5) of the *Federal Child Support Guidelines*, where the court orders a different amount of child support after making a finding of undue hardship under section 10(1) of the Guidelines, it may specify, in the child support order, a reasonable time for the satisfaction of any obligation arising from the circumstances that cause undue hardship and the amount payable at the end of that time. This provision is likely to be most frequently invoked in situations where unusually high family debts are the cause of the hardship[182] but it is by no means expressly confined to those situations. In *Bourque v. Phillips*,[183] undue hardship was found under section 10(2)(c) of the *Nova Scotia Child Support Guidelines*, where the father was obliged to pay fixed-term spousal support under a separation agreement, but the court concluded that the undue hardship would cease to exist once the time-limited spousal support obligation terminated.

A reduction of the applicable table amount of child support on the basis of unusually high access expenses is permissible under the undue hardship provisions of section 10 of the *Federal Child Support Guidelines*. Nothing in the Guidelines, however, authorizes a court to order a custodial parent to make a financial contribution towards access costs.[184] Prior to the implementation of the *Federal Child Support Guidelines* on 1 May 1997, a court could make an order for the payment of access costs pursuant to either section 15(4) or section 16(6) of the *Divorce Act*.[185] It is questionable whether section 10 of the *Federal Child Support Guidelines* impliedly limits this jurisdiction, given that the provisions of section 15(4) are currently mirrored in section 15.1(4) of the *Divorce Act*, as amended by the S.C. 1997, c. 1, and section 16(6) of the *Divorce Act* is unaffected by the 1997 amendments.[186] This issue was not specifically addressed in *Curniski v. Aubert*,[187] wherein the custodial parent was ordered to pay the transportation expenses of the children to enable them to visit the non-custodial parent, but the court refused to set off these expenses against the court-ordered child support payments. In *Holtskog v. Holtskog*,[188] the Saskatchewan Court of Appeal concluded that the trial judge erred in or-

---

182 *Aker v. Howard*, [1998] O.J. No. 5562 (Gen. Div.).
183 [2000] N.S.J. No. 13 (S.C.).
184 *South v. South*, [1998] B.C.J. No. 962 (S.C.).
185 R.S.C. 1985 (2d Supp.), c. 3.
186 See *Ruel v. Ruel*, [2006] A.J. No. 621 (C.A.); *Cofell v. Moyer*, [2003] O.J. No. 2050 (Sup. Ct.); *MacPhail v. MacPhail*, [2000] P.E.I.J. No. 41 (S.C.T.D.).
187 [1998] S.J. No. 825 (Q.B.).
188 [1999] S.J. No. 304 (C.A.).

dering the custodial parent to contribute one-half of the monthly airfare arising from extraprovincial access in light of the non-custodial parent's failure to substantiate the plea of unusually high access expenses generating undue hardship within the meaning of section 10 of the Guidelines. In *R.B.N. v. M.J.N.*,[189] Campbell J., of the Nova Scotia Supreme Court, questioned whether *Holtskog v. Holtskog* precluded an order for the payment or sharing of access costs in the absence of a finding of undue hardship. In ordering the custodial parent to pay all of the extraprovincial access transportation costs resulting from her relocation of the children, Campbell J. stated that the authority to order a contribution to access costs comes from the *Divorce Act* itself both under section 15.1(4), which permits the court to impose terms, conditions, or restrictions in connection with a support order, and under section 16(6) of the *Divorce Act*, which provides a similar jurisdiction with respect to a custody order. As Campbell J. observes, "there is no logical reason to deny a claim for a contribution or full payment of access costs by the custodial parent merely because the undue hardship claim failed."

K. EFFECT OF ORDER OR AGREEMENT

Sections 15.1(5) to (8) and sections 17(6.2) to (6.5) of the *Divorce Act* confer limited powers on parents to deviate from their child support obligations as set out in the *Federal Child Support Guidelines*.[190]

Given that these provisions are substantially similar, except insofar as section 15.1 relates to applications for an original child support order whereas section 17 relates to applications for the variation of an existing order, it will suffice for the purposes of this analysis if section 15.1 is reproduced. Section 15.1 reads as follows:

Child support order

15.1(1) A court of competent jurisdiction may, on application by either or both spouses, make an order requiring a spouse to pay for the support of any or all children of the marriage.

---

189 [2002] N.S.J. No. 530 (S.C.); see also *Morrone v. Morrone*, [2007] O.J. No. 5341 (Sup. Ct.).

190 *Gobeil v. Gobeil*, [2007] M.J. No. 19 (C.A.); *Kudoba v. Kudoba*, [2007] O.J. No. 3765 (Sup. Ct.).

Interim order

(2) Where an application is made under subsection (1), the court may, on application by either or both spouses, make an interim order requiring a spouse to pay for the support of any or all children of the marriage, pending the determination of the application under subsection (1).

Guidelines apply

(3) A court making an order under subsection (1) or an interim order under subsection (2) shall do so in accordance with the applicable guidelines.

Terms and conditions

(4) The court may make an order under subsection (1) or an interim order under subsection (2) for a definite or indefinite period or until a specified event occurs, and may impose terms, conditions or restrictions in connection with the order or interim order as it thinks fit and just.

Court may take agreement, etc., into account

(5) Notwithstanding subsection (3), a court may award an amount that is different from the amount that would be determined in accordance with the applicable guidelines if the court is satisfied

    (a)   that special provisions in an order, a judgment or a written agreement respecting the financial obligations of the spouses, or the division or transfer of their property, directly or indirectly benefit a child, or that special provisions have otherwise been made for the benefit of a child; and

    (b)   that the application of the applicable guidelines would result in an amount of child support that is inequitable given those special provisions.

Reasons

(6) Where the court awards, pursuant to subsection (5), an amount that is different from the amount that would be determined in accordance with the applicable guidelines, the court shall record its reasons for having done so.

Consent orders

(7) Notwithstanding subsection (3), a court may award an amount that is different from the amount that would be determined in accordance

with the applicable guidelines on the consent of both spouses if it is satisfied that reasonable arrangements have been made for the support of the child to whom the order relates.

Reasonable arrangements

(8) For the purposes of subsection (7), in determining whether reasonable arrangements have been made for the support of a child, the court shall have regard to the applicable guidelines. However, the court shall not consider the arrangements to be unreasonable solely because the amount of support agreed to is not the same as the amount that would otherwise have been determined in accordance with the applicable guidelines.

It is not clear whether the term "special provisions" in sections 15(1)(5)(a) and 17(6.2)(a) of the *Divorce Act* means "particular" or "out of the ordinary or unusual."[191] It has been generally acknowledged, however, that "special provisions" must be of a nature that, in whole or in part, replace the need for ongoing child support.[192]

Courts will be called upon to examine a wide variety of agreements to determine whether they contain "special provisions" within the meaning of sections 15.1(5) and 17(6.2) of the *Divorce Act*. Some agreements will have been prepared by legal counsel; others will not. Some will have been entered before, and others after, the Guidelines were implemented. Some will expressly purport to set out "special provisions"; others will not. Some agreements will provide more, others will provide less, than the amounts payable under the Guidelines. The particular circumstances facing each family and their children will obviously differ from case to case. Consequently, the determination whether an agreement contains "special provisions" will depend on the unique circumstances of the individual case.[193]

An agreement made with knowledge of the Guidelines that provides for child support in an amount greater than the amount payable under the Guidelines may, in itself, be a "special provision."[194]

---

191 *Wang v. Wang*, [1997] B.C.J. No. 1678 (S.C.), Saunders J., aff'd [1998] B.C.J. No. 1966 (C.A.); compare *Wright v. Zaver*, [2002] O.J. No. 1098 (C.A.). See also *Danchuk v. Danchuk*, [2001] B.C.J. No. 755 (C.A.).

192 *Wright v. Zaver*, [2002] O.J. No. 1098 (C.A.).

193 *Finney v. Finney*, [1998] B.C.J. No. 1848 (S.C.).

194 *Ibid*; compare *Biggar v. Biggar*, [1998] S.J. No. 570 (Q.B.).

The term "inequitable" in sections 15(1)(5)(b) and 17(6.2)(b) of the *Divorce Act* is capable of several meanings depending on the subject of comparison. It could refer to inequity as between the parties, or as between a child and parent, or as between these parties and others in the community to whom the Guidelines apply. The last construction is raised by section 1(d) of the Guidelines, which defines one of their objectives as being "to ensure consistent treatment of spouses and children who are in similar circumstances." Notwithstanding this declared objective, the term "inequitable" relates to the parties and requires consideration of both the circumstances giving rise to the written agreement or order and their circumstances at the time of the application. This interpretation recognizes the give and take of settlement negotiations and the interrelationship of the terms reflected in an agreement or order.[195]

In the absence of evidence of undue hardship within the meaning of section 10 of the *Federal Child Support Guidelines*, a pre-existing spousal agreement with special provisions that benefit the children constitutes no bar to the application of the Guidelines where the needs and circumstances of the children have changed since the agreement and where no inequitable consequences would ensue from the application of the Guidelines in these circumstances.[196]

A lump sum payment, which purports to constitute a final and binding resolution of child support rights and obligations, does not preclude a subsequent application for periodic support under the Guidelines, although it may constitute a "special provision" for the benefit of the child that renders inequitable an order for the future payment of the full monthly table amount of child support under the Guidelines.[197]

In addressing sections 15.1(5) and 17(6.2) of the *Divorce Act*, whereby special provisions in a written agreement or order that directly benefit a child may justify deviation from the *Federal Child Support Guidelines* but only if the application of the Guidelines would be inequitable having regard to the special provisions, the court must first decide whether it should exercise its discretion not to apply the *Federal Child Support Guidelines*. If it concludes that the Guidelines should be applied, the court must then decide whether an amount less than that required by the Guidelines should be ordered on the basis that the written agreement

---

195   *Wang v. Wang*, [1997] B.C.J. No. 1678 (S.C.); *Eilers v. Eilers*, [1998] B.C.J. No. 1021 (S.C.); *Epp v. Robertson*, [1998] S.J. No. 684 (Q.B.).

196   *Fisher v. Heron*, [1997] P.E.I.J. No. 77 (S.C.T.D.).

197   *MacKay v. Bucher*, [2001] N.S.J. No. 326 (C.A.); *Wright v. Zaver*, [2002] O.J. No. 1098 (C.A.).

contains special provisions that directly or indirectly benefit the child so as to render application of the Guidelines inequitable within the meaning of section 15.1(5) of the *Divorce Act*. A six-step procedure has been formulated by Martinson J., of the British Columbia Supreme Court, to address these two issues:

(i) identify the child support provisions in the agreement;

(ii) identify any special provisions in the agreement as defined in section 15.1(5) of the *Divorce Act*;

(iii) determine the Guidelines amount as though there were no separation agreement;

(iv) compare the Guidelines amount to the provisions of the separation agreement to see whether reasonable arrangements have been made in light of the Guidelines standard;

(v) if reasonable arrangements have been made, the court will decline to make an order under the Guidelines and the terms of the separation agreement will prevail; if reasonable arrangements have not been made, the Guidelines should be addressed;

(vi) in addressing the Guidelines, compare the Guidelines amount to the special provisions and child support provisions to see if an order different from the Guidelines amount should be ordered; if it should be, decide what amount is appropriate; if it should not be, apply the Guidelines amount determined in the third step.[198]

Spousal reapportionment of property, transfers of property, or the payment of a substantial lump sum may constitute examples of "special provisions" that benefit the children and justify deviation from the Guidelines under sections 15.1(5) and 17(6.2) of the *Divorce Act*.[199] Such deviation will only be justified, however, where the special provisions replace or reduce the need for ongoing child support.[200]

A custodial parent's willingness to accept less child support than the amount provided by the Guidelines cannot justify a court deviating from the Guidelines where no compensatory benefits are conferred on the children.[201]

---

198 *Baum v. Baum*, [1999] B.C.J. No. 3025 (S.C.).

199 *Fonseca v. Fonseca*, [1998] B.C.J. No. 2772 (S.C.); *Handy v. Handy*, [1999] B.C.J. No. 6 (S.C.).

200 *Hall v. Hall*, [1997] B.C.J. No. 1191 (S.C.); *Garard v. Garard*, [1998] B.C.J. No. 2076 (C.A.); *Wright v. Zaver*, [2002] O.J. No. 1098 (C.A.).

201 *Howe v. Kendall*, [1997] N.S.J. No. 310 (S.C.).

The phrase "or that special provisions have otherwise been made for the benefit of the child" in sections 15.1(5)(a) and 17(6.2)(a) of the *Divorce Act* does not specifically require that special provisions be made by the divorcing or divorced spouses. A family trust established by a parent[202] or by a grandparent[203] may satisfy either section.

Where a court deviates from the Guidelines pursuant to section 15.1 (5) or section 17(6.2) of the *Divorce Act*, the court must record its reasons for doing so.[204]

Sections 15.1(7) and (8) and 17(6.4) and (6.5) of the *Divorce Act* empower a court to grant a consent order for child support that deviates from the *Federal Child Support Guidelines*, if the court is satisfied that reasonable arrangements have been made for the support of the child to whom the order relates. It has been suggested that a court should be loath to change negotiated child support arrangements to which the parents wish to adhere, even though they provide an amount of support modestly lower than the applicable table amount under the Guidelines.[205] It is submitted, however, that courts should be cautious about allowing parents the freedom to pay or receive lower periodic child support payments than those required by the applicable provincial or territorial table, unless there are circumstances other than the agreement itself that warrant deviation from the table amount. On the other hand, the Guidelines should not blind the courts to the realities of comprehensive negotiations, which lead the parties to a complex settlement of their financial affairs, in which the components are finely balanced, and alteration of one term may upset the balance and thereby render the remaining terms unfair.[206]

With respect to consent orders, a finding under section 15.1(7) of the *Divorce Act* that reasonable arrangements have been made for the support of a child to whom the order relates presupposes that adequate information has been provided to the court about the economic and other circumstances of the spouses and the children, including any special or extraordinary expenses likely to be incurred on behalf of the children. Sufficient evidence must be presented to the court to enable it to make an informed judgment. A bald assertion that reasonable arrangements have been made for the support of a child does not warrant a consent order that deviates from the Guidelines. Such a bald assertion is not evidence

---

202 *Davidson v. Davidson*, [1998] A.J. No. 1040 (Q.B.).
203 See *Tauber v. Tauber*, [1999] O.J. No. 359 (Gen. Div.).
204 *Divorce Act*, R.S.C. 1985 (2d Supp.), c. 3, ss. 15.1(6) and 17(6.3).
205 *McIllwraith v. McIllwraith*, [1999] N.B.J. No. 129 (Q.B.).
206 *Eilers v. Eilers*, [1998] B.C.J. No. 1021 (S.C.).

but a conclusion to be determined by the court after an evaluation of any supporting evidence.[207]

L. SPECIAL AND EXTRAORDINARY EXPENSES

1) General

Section 7 of the *Federal Child Support Guidelines* empowers a court to grant an order for designated special or extraordinary expenses relating to a child of the marriage. The list of expenses under section 7 of the Guidelines is exhaustive. Expenses that fall outside the categories specified cannot be the subject of any order. The expenses must be necessary in light of the child's best interests.[208] The expenses must also be reasonable, having regard to the means of the spouses and child and the family's previous spending pattern.[209] The family's preseparation spending pattern may need to be re-assessed in light of the increased costs generated by the split into two households. Relevant factors to be considered in determining whether special or extraordinary expenses are reasonable include (i) the combined income of the parents; (ii) the fact that two households must be maintained; (iii) the extent of the expenses in relation to the combined income level of the parents; (iv) the debts of the parents; (v) any prospect for a decline or increase in the parents' means in the near future; and (vi) whether the other parent was consulted prior to the expenses being incurred.[210]

Child-care expenses, dental and medical insurance premiums, health care expenses, and post-secondary education expenses, if necessary and reasonable, will be ordinarily shared in proportion to the respective parental incomes. These expenses need not be "extraordinary" in order to satisfy the requirements of section 7 of the Guidelines.[211] Expenses relating to primary or secondary school or special educational needs and expenses for extracurricular activities must be "extraordinary" in order

---

207 Compare *Dumas v. Dumas* (1992), 43 R.F.L. (3d) 260 (Alta. Q.B.), applying *Divorce Act*, s. 11(1)(b); see, generally, Chapter 7, Section F(3).

208 *Holeman v. Holeman*, [2006] M.J. No. 456 (Q.B.) (private school); see also *Fritz v. Tate*, [2006] N.J. No. 336 (U.F.C.).

209 *Park v. Thompson*, [2005] O.J. No. 1695 (C.A.); *T.H. v. W.H.*, [2007] N.S.J. No. 27 (S.C.).

210 *Holeman v. Holeman*, [2006] M.J. No. 456 (Q.B.), citing *Bland v. Bland*, [1999] A.J. No. 344 (Q.B.) and *Correia v. Correia*, [2002] M.J. No. 248 (Q.B.).

211 *MacKinnon v. MacKinnon*, [2005] O.J. No. 1552 (C.A.).

to trigger an order under section 7 of the Guidelines.[212] A contribution to affordable "special" (as distinct from "extraordinary") expenses listed under section 7(1) of the *Federal Child Support Guidelines* is generally ordered more or less as a routine matter where these expenses are sought in a child support proceeding.[213]

In the past, there has been a lack of judicial consistency in the interpretation accorded to the term "extraordinary expenses" under paragraph 7(1)(d) (extraordinary education expenses) and paragraph 7(1)(f) (extraordinary expenses for extracurricular activities) of the *Federal Child Support Guidelines*.[214] To promote clarity and consistency, section 7 of the *Federal Child Support Guidelines* has been amended as of 1 May 2006 by SOR/2005-400, to include subsection 7(1.1), which sets out a specific two-part definition of "extraordinary expenses."[215] Pursuant to paragraph 7(1.1)(a), expenses are extraordinary if they exceed an amount that the requesting spouse can reasonably cover, taking into account that spouse's income and the basic amount of child support received (usually the applicable table amount). Where paragraph 7(1.1)(a) is inapplicable because the expenses do not exceed the amount that the requesting spouse can reasonably cover, paragraph 7(1.1)(b) directs the court to determine whether the expenses are extraordinary having regard to the following five factors:

- the amount of the expense in relation to the income of the spouse requesting the amount (including the child support amount);
- the nature and number of the educational programs and extracurricular activities;
- any special needs and talents of the child or children;
- the overall costs of the programs and activities; and
- any other similar factor that the court considers relevant.

The definition of "extraordinary expenses" under section 7(1.1) of the amended *Federal Child Support Guidelines* mirrors the definition adopted in 2001 under paragraph 7(1.1) of the *Manitoba Child Support Guidelines*. Insight into its application may accordingly be sought in Manitoba

---

212   See Section L(5), below in this chapter.

213   *Slade v. Slade*, [2001] N.J. No. 5 (C.A.); *Sharf v. Sharf*, [2000] O.J. No. 4052 (Sup. Ct.).

214   See Julien D. Payne & Marilyn A. Payne, *Child Support Guidelines in Canada* (Toronto: Irwin Law, 2004) at 242–43.

215   As to ongoing judicial uncertainty and lack of consistency, see *Simpson v. Trowsdale*, [2007] P.E.I.J. No. 7 (S.C.T.D.), MacDonald J.

judgments.[216] The additional requirements of necessity and reasonableness within the meaning of subsection 7(1) of the *Federal Child Support Guidelines* are unaffected by the explicit definition of "extraordinary expenses" under paragraph 7(1.1) of the Guidelines.

In determining the amount of an expense, section 7(3) of the Guidelines requires the court to take into account any subsidies, benefits, and income tax deductions or credits that are available with respect to the expense. Contributions to expenses made by family relatives or community groups are taken into account.[217] Eligibility for income tax relief must be taken into account, even if such relief is not sought by the recipient spouse.[218] Although a court must take the income tax implications into account, it may be impossible to quantify this until the end of the tax year. One way of addressing this problem is for the court to direct each parent to pay his or her proportionate share of the expenses when they fall due and to later share in the tax benefit on the same proportionate basis, when it is ascertained.[219] In order to accommodate this result, the court may direct the parties to exchange their income tax returns within a specified time after filing.[220]

Pursuant to section 13(e) of the *Federal Child Support Guidelines*, where a court orders the payment of special or extraordinary expenses, the particulars of the expense must be specified in the order, including the child to whom the expense relates, the amount of the expense, or where the amount cannot be determined, the proportion to be paid in relation to the expenses.

An order for the payment of special or extraordinary expenses need not specify periodic payments on a regular basis. The expenses may be isolated, sporadic, or recurring at irregular intervals. Pursuant to section 11 of the *Federal Child Support Guidelines*, a court may require expenses to be discharged on a periodic basis or by a lump sum or by a combination of both. Where the expenses cannot be predetermined, a court may

---

216 See *Correia v. Correia*, [2002] M.J. No. 248 (Q.B.); *Laurie v. Laurie*, [2004] M.J. No. 87 (Q.B.); *Chambers v. Chambers*, [2004] M.J. No. 397 (Q.B.); *Fong v. Charbonneau*, [2005] M.J. No. 124 (Q.B.); *Holeman v. Holeman*, [2006] M.J. No. 456 (Q.B.).

217 *Giles v. Villeneuve*, [1998] O.J. No. 4492 (Gen. Div.).

218 *Laskosky v. Laskosky*, [1999] A.J. No. 131 (Q.B.); *Skiba v. Skiba*, [2000] O.J. No. 76 (Sup. Ct.); *Leibel v. Davis*, [2001] S.J. No. 208 (Q.B.); compare *Mundle v. Mundle*, [2001] N.S.J. No. 111 (S.C.).

219 *Murphy v. Murphy*, [1998] N.J. No. 304 (S.C.); compare *Jackson v. Punga*, [1998] S.J. No. 633 (Q.B.) (order for adjustment of payments either by additional disbursement or rebate after requisite tax calculations).

220 *Murphy v. Murphy*, [1998] N.J. No. 304 (S.C.).

simply order that all or a fixed percentage of the expenses shall be paid after a proper account is presented, although such an order may trigger difficulty if automatic enforcement processes are invoked to secure due compliance with the order.

2) Child-Care Expenses

Section 7 of the *Federal Child Support Guidelines* confers a discretion on the court to order the payment of all or part of child-care expenses incurred as a result of the custodial parent's employment, illness, disability, or education or training for employment. No corresponding discretion is conferred on the court where child-care expenses are incurred for the above reasons by a non-custodial parent.[221] Child-care expenses may be denied under section 7 of the Guidelines where the non-custodial parent's family is able to provide child care,[222] although a court may refuse to disturb existing day-care arrangements that have worked well for a substantial period of time.[223] Section 7 of the Guidelines does not cover babysitting expenses that are incidental to a custodial parent's recreational activities.[224] A contribution to child-care expenses may be reduced to take account of child-connected expenses incurred by the contributing spouse.[225] In situations where resources are available, the court will allow child-care costs for an employed parent as a legitimate expense.[226] Even though child care may be a necessity, the amount of the non-custodial parent's contribution may be limited by the ability to contribute.[227] A court should refuse to order a contribution towards child-care expenses where the non-custodial parent lacks the financial ability to meet this additional obligation.[228] An application for a contribution to child-care costs may also be denied because of the non-custodial parent's access costs.[229] Where child-care costs are found excessive, the court may reduce

221 *S.M. v. R.P.*, [1998] Q.J. No. 4119 (S.C.).
222 *Shipka v. Shipka*, [2001] A.J. No. 213 (Q.B.); compare *E.C.H. v. W.E.H.*, [2003] B.C.J. No. 715 (S.C.).
223 *Erickson v. Erickson*, [2001] B.C.J. No. 71 (S.C.).
224 *Forrester v. Forrester*, [1997] O.J. No. 3437 (Gen. Div.).
225 *Enman v. Enman*, [2000] P.E.I.J. No. 48 (S.C.T.D.).
226 *Murray v. Murray* (1991), 35 R.F.L. (3d) 449 (Alta. Q.B.).
227 *Zsiak v. Bell*, [1998] B.C.J. No. 2233 (S.C.); *Wedsworth v. Wedsworth*, [2000] N.S.J. No. 209 (S.C.).
228 *Kennedy v. Kennedy*, [1997] N.S.J. No. 450 (Fam. Ct.); *Wedsworth v. Wedsworth*, [2000] N.S.J. No. 209 (C.A.).
229 *Chaput v. Chaput*, [1997] O.J. No. 4924 (Gen. Div.); *Keller v. Black*, [2000] O.J. No. 79 (Sup. Ct.).

the amount before calculating the respective contributions of each spouse or former spouses to these costs.[230] A claim for child-care expenses may be denied where the child is twelve years of age and, therefore, old enough to care for herself,[231] but a twelve-year-old child should not be expected to regularly babysit a younger sibling in order to reduce child-care expenses.[232] Child-care expenses, like health-related expenses and expenses for post-secondary education, do not need to be extraordinary in order to satisfy the requirements of section 7(1)(a) of the *Federal Child Support Guidelines*.[233] Child-care costs can vary substantially according to the age of the child, the type of care, whether the care is full-time or part-time, and the ability to pay, but they must be reasonable and necessary. Section 7(1) of the *Federal Child Support Guidelines* specifically limits the judicial discretion to provide for the payment of all or any expenses by requiring the court to take into account the necessity of the expense in relation to the child's best interests and the reasonableness of the expense, having regard to the means of the spouses and those of the child and to the family's spending pattern before the separation.[234] Notwithstanding the last mentioned consideration, courts will, no doubt, take account of reasonable and necessary child-care expenses triggered by the fact of separation.

3) Medical and Dental Insurance; Medical, Dental, or Health-Related Expenses

Section 6 of the *Federal Child Support Guidelines* provides that, in making a child support order, where medical or dental insurance coverage is available to either or both[235] of the spouses or former spouses through his or her employer or otherwise at a reasonable rate, the court may order

---

230 *Tallman v. Tomke*, [1997] A.J. No. 682 (Q.B.); *Kramer v. Kramer*, [1999] M.J. No. 338 (Q.B.).

231 *Acorn v. DeRoche*, [1997] P.E.I.J. No. 82 (S.C.T.D.); compare *Gormley v. Gormley*, [1999] P.E.I.J. No. 83 (S.C.T.D.) (contribution to child-care expenses for eleven-year-old child deemed appropriate).

232 *Levesque v. Levesque*, [1999] O.J. No. 3056 (Sup. Ct.).

233 *Tang v. Tang*, [1998] B.C.J. No. 2890 (S.C.); *Crawley v. Tobin*, [1998] N.J. No. 293 (S.C.); *Smith v. Smith*, [2001] N.S.J. No. 505 (S.C.).

234 *Wait v. Wait*, [2000] B.C.J. No. 1282 (C.A.) (custodial parent entitled to contribution from non-custodial parent towards child's daycare expense but not entitled to incur higher expenses by enrolling child in Montessori school); *Kramer v. Kramer*, [1999] M.J. No. 338 (Q.B.).

235 *Young v. Vincent*, [1997] N.S.J. No. 163 (T.D.).

that coverage be acquired or continued.[236] Child support orders normally include a provision whereby health insurance coverage will be maintained for eligible dependants. Where this is placed at risk by an obligor's threat to quit employment the court may order an additional amount of support to replace the health insurance coverage.[237]

Where there is existing medical and dental insurance coverage through employment, its continuance should be virtually automatic.[238] The court may grant an order under section 6 of the *Federal Child Support Guidelines* for the reinstatement of cancelled medical and dental insurance available to a spouse through employment.[239]

Section 6 is complemented by sections 7(1)(b) and (c) of the *Federal Child Support Guidelines*, which provide that in a child support order the court may, on either spouse's or former spouse's request, provide for the payment of all or a portion of the following expenses, taking into account the necessity of the expenses in relation to the child's best interests and the reasonableness of the expenses, having regard to the means of the spouses and the family's preseparation spending pattern: "(b) that portion of the medical and dental insurance premiums attributable to the child;[240] and (c) health-related expenses that exceed insurance reimbursement by at least $100 annually,[241] including orthodontic treatment;[242] professional counselling provided by a psychologist, social worker, psychiatrist, or any other person;[243] physiotherapy, occupational therapy, speech therapy;[244] and prescription drugs, hearing aids, glasses, and contact lenses." Section

---

236 *Faulkner v. Faulkner*, [1997] A.J. No. 730 (Q.B.); *Dempsey v. Dempsey*, [1997] N.S.J. No. 327 (T.D.); *Kingston v. Kelly*, [1999] P.E.I.J. No. 52 (S.C.T.D.) (order under *P.E.I. Child Support Guidelines*); *Martel v. Martel*, [2000] S.J. No. 322 (Q.B.); compare *M.D.L. v. C.R.*, [2004] S.J. No. 326 (Q.B.).

237 *Dickinson v. Dickinson*, [1998] O.J. No. 4815 (Gen. Div.).

238 *Robski v. Robski*, [1997] N.S.J. No. 444 (T.D.).

239 *Jackson v. Holloway*, [1997] S.J. No. 691 (Q.B.).

240 *Rudulier v. Rudulier*, [1999] S.J. No. 366 (Q.B.).

241 *Federal Child Support Guidelines*, s. 7(1)(c), as amended by SOR/2000-337, s. 1; *Corkum v. Clarke*, [2000] N.S.J. No. 285 (Fam. Ct.); *Baram v. Bakshy*, [2000] O.J. No. 2349 (Sup. Ct.); *Woode v. Woode*, [2002] S.J. No. 55 (Q.B.).

242 *Moss v. Moss*, [1997] N.J. No. 299 (S.C.); *Kennedy-Dalton v. Dalton*, [2000] N.J. No. 41 (U.F.C.); *O'Brien v. O'Brien*, [1999] N.W.T.J. No. 56 (S.C.); *Bell v. Griffin*, [1997] P.E.I.J. No. 86 (S.C.T.D.).

243 *Massler v. Massler*, [1999] A.J. No. 206 (Q.B.); *Moss v. Moss*, [1997] N.J. No. 299 (S.C.) (need for counselling not established); *Sharf v. Sharf*, [2000] O.J. No. 4052 (Sup. Ct.) (counselling expenses deemed excessive).

244 *Tubbs v. Phillips*, [2000] S.J. No. 282 (Q.B.).

6 of the *Federal Child Support Guidelines* should be utilized whenever possible before resorting to section 7 of the Guidelines, because section 6 provides a significant benefit to children at little or no expense to the parents in that the insurance premiums, if any, will normally be significantly less than the amount of the expenses that would otherwise be incurred if no insurance coverage were available.[245] Any expenses in excess of those reimbursed through a medical or dental insurance plan may be ordered to be shared proportionately in accordance with the respective spousal incomes.[246] Reciprocal obligations may be imposed on the parents to maintain coverage for the children under their employment health and dental plans, with any expenses not covered being shared proportionately in accordance with the respective parental incomes.[247]

Medical expenses may be viewed as a whole, rather than individually, in determining whether they are reasonable and necessary within the meaning of section 7(1) of the *Federal Child Support Guidelines*.[248]

With respect to necessary health-related expenses, ability to pay is the deciding factor.[249] Expenses for private nursing care will be denied where there is no money available to meet such expenses.[250]

As was observed by Johnstone J., of the Alberta Court of Queen's Bench, in *A.L.Y. v. L.M.Y.*,[251] Canadian judgments are divided on the question whether respite care provided for the benefit of the parent of a special needs child can constitute a child care-related expense or health-related expense under sections 7(1)(a) and (c) respectively of the *Federal Child Support Guidelines*. While disallowing the expense under either of these two headings, Johnstone J. concluded that it would be appropriate for the court to address the issue of respite care through a spousal support order premised on section 15(2)(6)(b) of the *Divorce Act*.

---

245 *Hansvall v. Hansvall*, [1997] S.J. No. 782 (Q.B.); see also *Budden v. Combden*, [1999] N.J. No. 199 (S.C.).

246 *MacLellan v. MacLellan*, [1998] N.S.J. No. 349 (T.D.); *Hansvall v. Hansvall*, [1997] S.J. No. 782 (Q.B.).

247 *Bellman v. Bellman*, [1999] B.C.J. No. 1196 (S.C.).

248 *Giles v. Villeneuve*, [1998] O.J. No. 4492 (Gen. Div.).

249 *Bell v. Griffin*, [1997] P.E.I.J. No. 86 (S.C.T.D.); *Sharf v. Sharf*, [2000] O.J. No. 4052 (Sup. Ct.).

250 *Van Harten v. Van Harten*, [1998] O.J. No. 1299 (Gen. Div.).

251 [2001] A.J. No. 506 (Q.B.).

4) Extraordinary Educational Expenses; Private School[252]

Section 7(1)(d) of the *Federal Child Support Guidelines* confers a discretion on the court to provide for the payment of all or part of extraordinary expenses for primary or secondary school education or for any educational programs that meet the child's particular needs.[253] The expenses must satisfy the tests of reasonableness and necessity under section 7(1) of the Guidelines.[254]

Extraordinary education expenses are those that extend beyond the basic school program.[255] Routine school fees, general school supplies, and normal transportation are regarded as "usual expenses" rather than "extraordinary expenses" within the meaning of section 7 of the *Federal Child Support Guidelines*.[256]

Laura W. Morgan, an American commentator,[257] has identified the following factors as relevant to the provision of expenses for private schooling: "whether one or both parents attended private school; whether the child has been enrolled in a private school prior to the divorce;[258] whether there has been an expectation that the child would have a private education, by express agreement or otherwise;[259] whether the parents can afford

---

252 For a revised definition of "extraordinary expenses," see Section L(1), above in this chapter, citing SOR/2005-400.

253 *Crofton v. Sturko*, [1997] B.C.J. No. 38 (S.C.); *Hogan v. Johnston*, [1998] B.C.J. No. 2055 (S.C.); *Hoover v. Hoover*, [1997] N.W.T.J. No. 43 (S.C.); *McCoy v. Hucker*, [1998] O.J. No. 4982 (Gen. Div.); *Andrews v. Andrews*, [1999] O.J. No. 3578 (C.A.) (application under Ontario *Family Law Act* and Ontario *Child Support Guidelines*); *Jonas v. Jonas*, [2002] O.J. No. 2117 (Sup. Ct.) (partial contribution); *Tubbs v. Phillips*, [2000] S.J. No. 282 (Q.B.) (tutoring expenses); *Wurmlinger v. Cyca*, [2003] S.J. No. 247 (Q.B.).

254 *Fisher v. Pade*, [2001] B.C.J. No. 1469 (S.C.); *N.M.M. v. N.S.M.*, [2004] B.C.J. No. 642 (S.C.) (fees to be paid until end of current school year); *Casals v. Casals*, [2006] O.J. No. 5602 (Sup. Ct.).

255 *Middleton v. MacPherson*, [1997] A.J. No. 614 (Q.B.); *Lavoie v. Wills*, [2000] A.J. No. 1359 (Q.B.); *Ebrahim v. Ebrahim*, [1997] B.C.J. No. 2039 (S.C.).

256 *Cowan v. Cowan*, [2001] A.J. No. 669 (Q.B.); *Smith v. Smith*, [2001] A.J. No. 1420 (C.A.); *Callaghan v. Brett*, [2000] N.J. No. 354 (S.C.); *McEachern v. McEachern*, [1998] S.J. No. 507 (Q.B.).

257 Laura W. Morgan, *Child Support Guidelines: Interpretation and Application*, loose-leaf (New York: Aspen Law and Business, 1996–2004) at §4.05[b]; see also *Andrews v. Andrews*, [1999] O.J. No. 3578 (C.A.).

258 *Van Deventer v. Van Deventer*, [2000] B.C.J. No. 37 (C.A.); *Rivett v. Bylund*, [1998] O.J. No. 325 (Gen. Div.); compare *B.A.C. v. D.L.C.*, [2003] B.C.J. No. 1303 (S.C.).

259 *Barker v. Barker*, [2000] B.C.J. No. 388 (S.C.).

a private education;[260] and whether the child has a special need for private school that public schools cannot provide,[261] making private education in the best interests of the child." She further asserts that "[these] considerations would also justify... [expenses] for music lessons or other cultural activities" and that "[when] private education costs are awarded, the court should award such expenses only to the extent that they are actually incurred and not paid from other sources."[262]

In determining the extent, if any, to which a parent should contribute to private school expenses of children of the marriage, the court may assess each child independently and thereby reach differing outcomes.[263] However, a court should not lightly deny one child the same benefits of private school as those enjoyed by another sibling, where there are no financial obstacles to the payment of the requisite costs.[264] Private school expenses, though reasonable for a short period of transition, may become unreasonable in the long term, especially where a change in circumstances reduces the parental income.[265]

5) Extraordinary Expenses for Extracurricular Activities

Section 7(1)(f) of the *Federal Child Support Guidelines* confers a discretion on the court to provide for the payment of all or part of any extraordinary expenses for extracurricular activities. In consequence of the prior lack of judicial consistency in defining "extraordinary expenses" under both section 7(1)(d) (extraordinary education expenses) and section 7(1)(f) (extraordinary expenses for extracurricular activities) of the *Federal Child Support Guidelines*, section 7 has been amended as of 1 May 2006 to include section 7(1.1), which sets out a specific definition of "extraordinary expenses."[266] The amendment, which mirrors the defin-

---

260 *Stelter v. Klingspohn*, [1999] B.C.J. No. 2926 (S.C.); *Steele v. Koppanyi*, [2002] M.J. No. 201 (C.A.); *Grierson v. Brunton*, [2004] O.J. No. 3043 (Sup. Ct.); *Maloney v. Maloney*, [2004] O.J. No. 5828 (Div. Ct.).

261 *Greenwood v. Greenwood*, [1998] B.C.J. No. 729 (S.C.); *Shankman v. Shankman*, [2001] O.J. No. 3798 (Sup. Ct.).

262 Morgan, *Child Support Guidelines*, above note 257.

263 *Burton v. Burton*, [1997] N.S.J. No. 560 (T.D.); see also *Ostlund v. Ostlund*, [2000] B.C.J. No. 1158 (S.C.).

264 *Bell-Angus v. Angus*, [2000] O.J. No. 2074 (Sup. Ct.).

265 *McDonald v. McDonald*, [2001] B.C.J. No. 2570 (B.C.C.A.).

266 SOR/2005-400, s. 1 (28 November 2005), published in Canada Gazette, Vol. 139, No. 25 (14 December 2005).

ition adopted in 2001 under the *Manitoba Child Support Guidelines*,[267] provides a two-part definition. First, pursuant to paragraph 7(1.1)(a), expenses are extraordinary if they "exceed those that the spouse requesting an amount for the extraordinary expenses can reasonably cover." This is determined having regard to the income of the requesting spouse as well as any child support received. This element of the definition relates to the requesting spouse's ability to pay for the expenses. If the expenses exceed those that the requesting spouse can reasonably cover, they are extraordinary. The tests of necessity and reasonableness set out in section 7(1) of the Guidelines continue to apply to extraordinary expenses under sections 7(1)(d) and 7(1)(f). Where paragraph 7(1.1)(a) does not apply (because the expense does not exceed the amount that the requesting spouse can reasonably cover), the second part of the definition, set out in paragraph 7(1.1)(b), applies. Paragraph 7(1.1)(b) directs the court to determine whether the expenses are extraordinary having regard to the following five factors:

- the amount of the expense in relation to the income of the spouse requesting the amount (including the child support amount);
- the nature and number of the educational programs and extracurricular activities;
- any special needs and talents of the child or children;
- the overall costs of the programs and activities; and
- any other similar factor that the court considers relevant.

It is impossible to list specific categories of expenses as falling within the ambit of section 7(1)(f) of the Guidelines. Although the table amounts of child support under the *Federal Child Support Guidelines* apparently include some allowance for expenditures incurred for the extracurricular activities of children, there is no readily available information to indicate what portion of the applicable table amount is allocated to meet these expenses. Accordingly, courts lack any clear guidance as to when expenses for extracurricular activities are ordinary and when they are extraordinary. As Veit J., of the Alberta Court of Queen's Bench, observed in *MacIntosh v. MacIntosh*, "it would be helpful if some guideline, based perhaps on a percentage of the total income of the parents, could help identify

---

267   See *Correia v. Correia*, [2002] M.J. No. 248 (Q.B.); *Laurie v. Laurie*, [2004] M.J. No. 87 (Q.B.); *Chambers v. Chambers*, [2004] M.J. No. 397 (Q.B.); *Fong v. Charbonneau*, [2005] M.J. No. 124 (Q.B.).

which extracurricular activities belong in the 'extraordinary' category."[268] Given the absence of any such guidance, there is a substantial lack of consistency in the judicial disposition of applications for extraordinary expenses for extracurricular activities under section 7(1)(f) of the *Federal Child Support Guidelines.*

Not all expenses for extracurricular activities will qualify for sharing between the spouses or former spouses. The expenses must be "extraordinary" in order to qualify under section 7 of the *Federal Child Support Guidelines.*[269] Basic expenses, such as the costs of registration in a community sports league, or normal costs commonly associated with sport, such as the purchase of ordinary equipment and minimal travel costs, are not extraordinary expenses and should be discounted from any exceptional expenses.[270] In determining whether a child support order should provide for an amount to cover all or some extraordinary expenses for extracurricular activities, the court takes into account the necessity of the expense in relation to the child's best interests and the reasonableness of the expense, having regard to the current means of the spouses and those of the child and to the family's spending pattern prior to the separation.[271] The test of necessity relates to the best interests of the child and is not one of strict necessity;[272] money spent on a child will usually benefit that child and thereby satisfy the necessity criterion imposed by section 7(1) of the Guidelines.[273] A child does not require any special talent for an activity's expenses to qualify as necessary.[274] Expenses may be deemed necessary when they relate to activities, such as sports, that aid in the development of the child's character and health to their full potential.[275] The issue of

---

268 [2003] A.J. No. 728 at para. 42 (Q.B.).

269 *Lavoie v. Wills*, [2000] A.J. No. 1359 (Q.B.); *Pomroy v. Greene*, [2000] N.J. No. 38 (U.F.C.); *Pitcher v. Pitcher*, [2002] N.J. No. 358 (U.F.C.); *Cane v. Newman*, [1998] O.J. No. 1776 (Gen. Div.); *Kofoed v. Fichter*, [1998] S.J. No. 338 (C.A.); *Fransoo v. Fransoo*, [2001] S.J. No. 121 (Q.B.).

270 *Bruno v. Bruno*, [2000] O.J. No. 3057 (Sup. Ct.).

271 *Trueman v. Trueman*, [2000] A.J. No. 1301 (Q.B.); *Kinasewich v. Kinasewich*, [2001] A.J. No. 1185 (Q.B.); *Ackland v. Brooks*, [2001] B.C.J. No. 1733 (S.C.); *Myers v. Myers*, [2000] N.S.J. No. 367 (S.C.); *Doherty v. Doherty*, [2001] O.J. No. 2400 (Sup. Ct.); *Fransoo v. Fransoo*, [2001] S.J. No. 121 (Q.B.).

272 *Omah-Maharajh v. Howard*, [1998] A.J. No. 173 (Q.B.); *Stewart v. Stewart*, [2004] A.J. No. 362 (Q.B.).

273 *Trueman v. Trueman*, [2000] A.J. No. 1301 (Q.B.).

274 *Omah-Maharajh v. Howard*, [1998] A.J. No. 173 (Q.B.); *Raftus v. Raftus*, [1998] N.S.J. No. 119 (C.A.).

275 *DiPasquale v. DiPasquale*, [1998] N.W.T.J. No. 58 (S.C.); *Yeo v. Yeo*, [1998] P.E.I.J. No. 100 (S.C.T.D.).

whether expenses are reasonable, given the means of the spouses and those of the child and the family's established spending pattern before separation, will depend on the circumstances of the particular case.[276] Although each case should be determined on its own facts, orders for such expenses should be the exception, not the rule;[277] they should not be routinely included in an order for child support.[278] Even if a child is extremely talented, an order for a contribution to the extraordinary expenses of that activity will be denied where the cost is not reasonable in light of the modest means of the parents.[279]

Having regard to the fact that the table amount of child support builds in a certain amount for extracurricular expenses,[280] the norm for what are ordinary expenses increases as the family income increases;[281] ordinary expenses for a family income of $30,000 are less than what is normal for a family income of $60,000.[282] It may be difficult to determine where ordinary expenses for extracurricular activities end and extraordinary expenses begin but the court must make that determination based on the facts of each particular case.[283] To the extent that extracurricular expenses are found to be extraordinary, the court still retains a discretion whether to order any contribution to be paid, having regard to the necessity of the expenses and their reasonableness as defined in section 7 of the *Federal Child Support Guidelines*.[284] In most middle-income families, the expenses of extracurricular activities are ordinary and largely covered by the applicable table amount. The same expenses for a low-income family

---

276 *Omah-Maharajh v. Howard*, [1998] A.J. No. 173 (Q.B.); *Morrissette v. Ball*, [2000] B.C.J. No. 73 (S.C.); *DiPasquale v. DiPasquale*, [1998] N.W.T.J. No. 58 (S.C.).

277 *Johnston v. Johnston*, [2004] A.J. No. 333 (Q.B.); *McEachern v. McEachern*, [1998] S.J. No. 507 (Q.B.); *Fransoo v. Fransoo*, [2001] S.J. No. 212 (Q.B.).

278 *Yeo v. Yeo*, [1998] P.E.I.J. No. 100 (S.C.T.D.).

279 *Bland v. Bland*, [1999] A.J. No. 344 (Q.B.). Compare *Strickland v. Strickland*, [1998] O.J. No. 5869 (Gen. Div.) (interim order for contribution to extremely high costs of teenage Olympic hopeful; fixed-term order; payment conditioned upon other parent's undertaking to reimburse payor for one-half of mortgage payments and municipal taxes on matrimonial home).

280 *Nataros v. Nataros*, [1998] B.C.J. No. 1417 (S.C.); *Shambrook v. Shambrook*, [2004] B.C.J. No. 1410 (S.C.).

281 *Nataros v. Nataros*, [1998] B.C.J. No. 1417 (S.C.); *Yeo v. Yeo*, [1998] P.E.I.J. No. 100 (S.C.T.D.).

282 *Campbell v. Martijn*, [1998] P.E.I.J. No. 33 (S.C.T.D.).

283 *Nataros v. Nataros*, [1998] B.C.J. No. 1417 (S.C.).

284 *Ibid.*

would be extraordinary because the applicable table amount of child support would be required to meet basic needs.[285]

M. VARIATION OF CHILD SUPPORT ORDERS

Pursuant to section 17(4) of the *Divorce Act* and section 14 of the *Federal Child Support Guidelines*, a court may vary an order for child support in any one of the following circumstances:

(a) an order providing the applicable table amount of child support is variable on proof of any change of circumstances that would result in a different disposition;

(b) an order that does not include any table amount of child support is variable on proof of any change in the condition, means, needs or other circumstances of either spouse or of any child who is entitled to support;

(c) any order granted before the implementation of the *Federal Child Support Guidelines* on 1 May 1997 may be varied in light of their implementation.

1) Variation of Amount of Child Support Made under Applicable Table

Pursuant to section 17(4) of the *Divorce Act* and section 14(a) of the *Federal Child Support Guidelines*, a court may vary a child support order whenever the amount of child support was determined in accordance with the applicable provincial or territorial table and any change has occurred that would result in a different child support order. Any change that triggers a different order, whether it is a change in form, in substance, or in dollar amounts, is sufficient justification for a variation application.[286] Such a change will occur when the obligor's annual income and consequential capacity to pay child support has increased[287] or has deteriorated for reasons beyond his or her control.[288] An obligor who seeks to retroactively

---

285 *Trueman v. Trueman,* [2000] A.J. No. 1301 (Q.B.); *DiPasquale v. DiPasquale,* [1998] N.W.T.J. No. 58 (S.C.).

286 *Blais v. Blais,* [2001] S.J. No. 468 (S.C.).

287 *A.D.B. v. S.A.M.,* [2006] N.S.J. No. 252 (S.C.); *Khoee-Solomonescu v. Solomonescu,* [2000] O.J. No. 743 (Div. Ct.).

288 *A.D.B. v. S.A.M.,* [2006] N.S.J. No. 252 (S.C.); *Guillet v. Guillet,* [1999] S.J. No. 266 (Q.B.).

and prospectively reduce the amount of child support payable must provide reliable and credible evidence that his annual income is less than the amount previously attributed to him.[289] The basic amount of child support payable under the applicable provincial or territorial table is unaffected by a reduction in the payee's income, unless such reduction triggers a successful claim of undue hardship under section 10 of the *Federal Child Support Guidelines.*[290] The judicial jurisdiction to vary an order for child support based on a provincial or territorial table is not confined to circumstances where the obligor's income has increased or decreased. For example,

- a complementary provision could be included with respect to newly encountered special or extraordinary expenses, or
- a reconstitution of either household might justify a claim of undue hardship under subsections 10(1) and 10(3) of the *Federal Child Support Guidelines,* or
- the residence of the obligor might change so as to trigger the application of a different provincial or territorial table under section 3(3)(a) of the Guidelines, or
- the accumulation of arrears might warrant the variation of an order for periodic support into an order for lump sum support in accordance with section 11 of the Guidelines.

Section 14(a) of the *Federal Child Support Guidelines* deems that there is a change in circumstances for the purposes of section 17(4) of the *Divorce Act* if section 9 of the Guidelines is triggered.[291]

2) Variation Where Amount of Child Support Not under Provincial or Territorial Table

Variation of an order for child support under section 14(b) of the *Federal Child Support Guidelines,* where the amount of child support was not determined under a provincial or territorial table, may be granted when there has been a change in the condition, means, needs, or other circumstances of either spouse or former spouse or a change in the condition, means, needs, or other circumstances of any child who is entitled to support.[292] The terms "condition," "means," "needs," and "other cir-

---

289 *Murphy v. Murphy,* 2007 BCCA 500, [2007] B.C.J. No. 2258.
290 *Saby v. MacIntosh,* [2002] B.C.J. No. 1813 (S.C.); *Williams v. Williams,* [1997] N.W.T.J. No. 49 (S.C.).
291 *Kolada v. Kolada,* [2000] A.J. No. 342 (Q.B.).
292 *Birks v. Birks,* [2003] B.C.J. No. 949 (S.C.); *Sikler v. Snow,* [2000] S.J. No. 271 (Q.B.).

cumstances" of either former spouse provide an extremely wide range of relevant considerations that leave the court with an extremely broad discretionary jurisdiction to vary, rescind, or suspend a support order.[293] In determining the obligor's available means, the nature and source of those means (whether salary, pension, other income, or capital) are not material.[294] Misconduct is ordinarily an irrelevant consideration.[295] Income may be imputed to a spouse in the context of an application to vary child support for the purpose of determining whether a material change of circumstances has occurred within the meaning of section 14(b) of the Guidelines.[296]

A material change has been defined by the Supreme Court of Canada in *Willick v. Willick*,[297] as being a change of such magnitude that, if the court had known of the changed circumstances at the time of the original order, it is likely that the order would have been made on different terms.[298] The change must be significant and long lasting.[299] A parent has a continuing obligation to support his or her children in spite of temporary unemployment,[300] or a fluctuating income; some degree of budgeting may be required.[301] If the change was known at the relevant time, it cannot be relied on as the basis for variation.[302] Subject to the express provisions of section 14 of the *Federal Child Support Guidelines*, the principles of *Willick v. Willick* continue to apply to the variation of child support orders under the *Federal Child Support Guidelines*.[303]

---

293 *Willick v. Willick*, [1994] 3 S.C.R. 670, 6 R.F.L. (4th) 161.

294 *Bartlett v. Bartlett* (1994), 2 R.F.L. (4th) 202 (Nfld. U.F.C.).

295 See ss. 17(6) and 15.2(5) of the *Divorce Act*; see also *Single v. Single* (1986), 5 R.F.L. (3d) 287 at 291 (N.S. Fam. Ct.); and see Chapter 8, Section F.

296 *Daku v. Daku*, [1999] S.J. No. 330 (Q.B.).

297 [1994] 3 S.C.R. 670, 6 R.F.L. (4th) 161.

298 *Bushell v. Bushell*, [2000] A.J. No. 1499 (Q.B.); *Meuser v. Meuser*, [1998] B.C.J. No. 2808 (C.A.); *Birks v. Birks*, [2003] B.C.J. No. 949 (S.C.); *Basi v. Basi*, [2007] B.C.J. No. 2680 (S.C.); *A.C. v. R.R.*, [2006] N.B.J. No. 204 (C.A.); *Collins v. Collins*, [2003] N.J. No. 278 (S.C.); *A.D.B. v. S.A.M.*, [2006] N.S.J. No. 252 (S.C.); *Osmar v. Osmar*, [2000] O.J. No. 2060 (Sup. Ct.); *Demeria v. Demeria*, [1998] S.J. No. 898 (Q.B.); *Vezina v. Vezina*, [2006] S.J. No. 105 (C.A.).

299 *Bushell v. Bushell*, [2000] A.J. No. 1499 (Q.B.); *Pagani v. Pagani*, [1999] B.C.J. No. 3051 (S.C.); *Martin v. Martin*, [2000] B.C.J. No. 303 (S.C.); *Birks v. Birks*, [2003] B.C.J. No. 949 (S.C.); *Cook v. McManus*, [2006] N.B.J. No. 334 (Q.B.).

300 *N.B. v. K.J.B.*, [1999] B.C.J. No. 1584 (S.C.).

301 *Pagani v. Pagani*, [1999] B.C.J. No. 3051 (S.C.).

302 *Meuser v. Meuser*, [1998] B.C.J. No. 2808 (C.A.).

303 *Bushell v. Bushell*, [2000] A.J. No. 1499 (Q.B.); *Khoee-Solomonescu v. Solomonescu*, [2000] O.J. No. 743 (Div. Ct.).

An obligor cannot reduce an existing child support obligation by a self-imposed reduction of income.[304] It may be otherwise if an obligor's change of employment that resulted in a reduced income was not made for selfish or illogical reasons and could prove sensible in the longer term.[305] Parents who are subject to support obligations are entitled to make decisions in relation to their careers so long as the decisions are reasonable at the time having regard to all the circumstances. Those circumstances include the age, education, experience, skills, historical earning capacity and health of the payor, the standard of living experienced during marriage, the availability of work, the payor's freedom to relocate, the reasonableness of the career aspirations and of the motives behind any change, as well as any other obligations of the payor.[306]

3) Variation of Orders Predating Implementation of Guidelines[307]

Appellate rulings in Canada are divided on the question whether the implementation of the *Federal Child Support Guidelines* on 1 May 1997 compels a court to vary a pre-Guidelines agreement or order for child support or whether a residual discretion vests in the court to leave the order unchanged so as to retain the income tax inclusion and deductibility rules that continue to apply to pre-Guidelines agreements and orders.[308]

4) Remission of Arrears

In *Earle v. Earle*,[309] Martinson J., of the Supreme Court of British Columbia, set out the following propositions with respect to applications to reduce or cancel child support arrears:

---

304 *Aziz v. Aziz*, [2000] B.C.J. No. 1134 (C.A.); *Donovan v. Donovan*, [2000] M.J. No. 407 (C.A.) (application under *Manitoba Child Support Guidelines*); *Hart v. Neufeld*, [2004] S.J. No. 232 (C.A.).

305 *Darvill v. Chorney*, [1999] S.J. No. 551 (Q.B.).

306 *Kozub v. Kozub*, [2002] S.J. No. 407 (Q.B.).

307 See Carol Rogerson, "Of Variation, 'Special Provisions' and 'Reasonable Arrangements' — The Effect of Prior Orders and Agreements on Child Support Determinations under the Guidelines" (Quicklaw, db SFLN).

308 For a detailed review of this subject, see Julien D. Payne & Marilyn A. Payne, *Child Support Guidelines in Canada*, 2006 (Toronto: Irwin Law, 2006) at 466–72.

309 [1999] B.C.J. No. 383 (S.C.); see also *Morgan v. Morgan*, [2006] B.C.J. No. 1795 (S.C.); *McIntosh v. McIntosh*, [2007] B.C.J. No. 1956 (S.C.). And see *Ghisleri v. Ghisleri*, 2007 BCCA 512, [2007] B.C.J. No. 2356; *Luney v. Luney*, 2007 BCCA 567, [2007] B.C.J. No. 2483; *Nielsen v. Nielsen*, 2007 BCCA 604, [2007] B.C.J. No. 2599.

Basic Principles

a.   There is a heavy duty on the person asking for a reduction or a cancellation of arrears to show that there has been a significant and long lasting change in circumstances. Arrears will not be reduced or cancelled unless it is grossly unfair not to do so.

b.   If arrears are not reduced or cancelled, the court can order a payment plan over time if convinced the arrears cannot be paid right away.

Examples

a.   Arrears will only be cancelled if the person is unable to pay now and will be unable to pay in the future.

b.   A reduction or a cancellation requires detailed and full financial disclosure, under oath (usually in the form of an affidavit) that at the time the payments were to be made:

   i.   the change was significant and long lasting and

   ii.   the change was real and not one of choice and

   iii.   every effort was made to earn money (or more money) during the time in question, and those efforts were not successful.

c.   Responsibility for a second family cannot relieve the parent of his or her legal obligation to support the first family.

d.   Delay in enforcement is generally not a legal basis to cancel or reduce child support arrears.

e.   Judges will not cancel arrears because the other party gets a lot of money at once. Otherwise, people would be encouraged to not pay maintenance and rewarded for not paying maintenance.

f.   Judges will not cancel arrears because the children were looked after in spite of the non-payment.

g.   Nor will judges cancel arrears because the children no longer need the money. The children should be compensated for what they missed.

h.   An agreement between parents that the maintenance for the children does not have to be paid will not be considered.

i.   Lack of access between a parent and child is not a legal reason to reduce or cancel arrears.

j.   Judges will not reduce or cancel arrears because other money has been spent to buy things for the children.

k.   The fact that a person did not have legal advice when the order was made or during the time when the arrears added up, is not, by itself, a reason to reduce or cancel arrears.

In *Sewell v. Grant*,[310] Gower J., of the Yukon Territory Supreme Court, questioned the validity of several of the principles set out in *Earle v. Earle*, above, in concluding that the court has no discretion to refuse to reduce arrears of child support where the payor's income is less than that previously judicially imputed to him.

Both parents have a joint legal obligation to support their children according to their respective abilities. Courts must avoid giving the appearance of favouring non-custodial parents who fail to discharge their support obligations diligently, thus casting additional financial burdens on the more diligent custodial parents.[311]

In *Haisman v. Haisman*,[312] the Alberta Court of Appeal drew an important distinction between child support and spousal support arrears. It concluded that a child should not be penalized by a custodial parent's delay in enforcing a child support order and the obligor should not be allowed to shift the burden of child support to the custodial parent or to the public purse unless there was an inability to pay over a substantial period of time during which the child support payments fell due and this inability would have necessitated a suspension of the child support order or a reduction in the amount of the order, had a timely application for variation or rescission been instituted. A present inability to pay child support arrears does not itself warrant judicial remission of the arrears, although it may justify a suspension of their enforcement for a limited term or an order for instalment payments against the arrears.[313]

In determining whether to remit arrears of child support, the court should consider

---

310   [2005] Y.J. No. 37 (S.C.).

311   *Labell v. Labell*, [2006] B.C.J. No. 185 (C.A.), citing *Longstaff v. Longstaff* (1993), 49 R.F.L. (3d) 1 (B.C.C.A.) at para. 54.

312   (1994), 7 R.F.L. (4th) 1 (Alta. C.A.), leave to appeal to S.C.C. refused (1995), 15 R.F.L. (4th) 51 (S.C.C.); see also *Blyth v. Brooks*, [2008] A.J. No. 100 (C.A.); *E.M.V. v. T.D.H.V.*, [2008] A.J. No. 328 (C.A.); *Bernard v. Bernard*, [2008] A.J. No. 302 (Q.B.) (obligor in prison); *Johnston v. Johnston*, [1997] B.C.J. No. 418, 26 R.F.L. (4th) 131 (C.A.); *Heiden v. British Columbia (Director of Maintenance Enforcement)* (1995), 19 R.F.L. (4th) 320 (B.C.C.A.); *A.E. v. M.G.*, [2004] N.W.T.J. No. 8 (S.C.); *Filipich v. Filipich*, [1996] O.J. No. 3081 (C.A.); *White v. Gallant*, [2001] P.E.I.J. No. 115 (S.C.T.D.); *Diebel v. Diebel*, [1997] S.J. No. 165 (Q.B.); *Johnston v. Johnston*, [2006] S.J. No. 653 (Q.B.); *M.L.C. v. G.C.C.*, [2000] Y.J. No. 114 (S.C.).

313   *Haisman v. Haisman*, (1994), 7 R.F.L. (4th) 1 (Alta. C.A.), leave to appeal to S.C.C. refused (1995), 15 R.F.L. (4th) 51 (S.C.C.); *DiFrancesco v. Couto*, [2001] O.J. No. 4307 (C.A.); *Wiome v. Wiome*, [2002] S.J. No. 613 (Q.B.); *Johnston v. Johnston*, [2006] S.J. No. 653 (Q.B.); *Ross v. Vermette*, [2007] S.J. No. 483 (Q.B.).

- the nature of the support obligation sought to be varied,
- the obligor's ability to pay the arrears when they fell due,
- the ongoing financial capacity of the obligor,
- the ongoing needs of the payee and child,
- unreasonable and unexplained delay by the payee in enforcing the arrears,
- unreasonable and unexplained delay by the payor in seeking relief from the support obligation, and
- whether enforcement of payment will cause hardship to the payor.

The court is at liberty to consider whether hoarding has occurred or whether the payee has rested on his or her rights in such a manner as to mislead the payor but the court is not bound to discharge any arrears solely because they have been outstanding for more than one year.[314] Other factors that have been singled out include whether there is a reasonable explanation for the delay, the obligor's efforts to comply with the order, the ability of the obligor to pay, the creditor's means and needs, whether denial of retroactive variation would result in a windfall hoarding, whether the obligor was lulled by the creditor into believing that the order would not be enforced, and the futility of making an order that would be impossible to perform.[315] A failure to enforce a child support order without more is not evidence of waiver.[316] In *Turecki v. Turecki*,[317] judicial remission of child support arrears was deemed appropriate because the custodial parent deliberately refrained from enforcing court-ordered child support payments so as to avoid disclosing her whereabouts, thereby

---

314 *Moriarty v. Hood* (1993), 142 N.B.R. (2d) 334 (Q.B.); *Owen v. Sears*, [1997] N.B.J. No. 65 (Q.B.); *Gray v. Gray* (1983), 32 R.F.L. (2d) 438 at 440 (Ont. H.C.J.); *Filipich v. Filipich*, [1996] O.J. No. 3081 (C.A.); *DiFrancesco v. Couto*, [2001] O.J. No. 4307 (C.A.); *Adamson v. Steed*, [2007] O.J. No. 219 (Sup. Ct.); *Loshney v. Hankins* (1993), 48 R.F.L. (3d) 67 (Sask. Q.B.) (wherein the court also identifies the evidence that must be adduced when remission of arrears is sought); *Wiome v. Wiome*, [2002] S.J. No. 613 (Q.B.); *Wurmlinger v. Cyca*, [2003] S.J. No. 247 (Q.B.); *Creighton v. Klyne*, [2006] S.J. No. 679 (Q.B.); *McLaughlin v. Braun*, [2006] S.J. No. 796 (Q.B.); *Zawada v. Zawada*, [2007] S.J. No. 44 (Q.B.); *Ross v. Vermette*, [2007] S.J. No. 483 (Q.B.); *Criddle v. Mohl*, [2008] S.J. No. 86 (Q.B.); *Allaire v. Greyeyes*, [2008] S.J. No. 107 (Q.B.); *Gilchrist v. Keith*, [2008] S.J. No. 128 (Q.B.).

315 *Hawko v. Knapp*, [2001] N.J. No. 300 (U.F.C.); *Hickey v. Hickey*, [2002] N.J. No. 157 (S.C.); *Lynch v. Lundrigan*, [2002] N.J. No. 185 (S.C.).

316 *Boehmer v. Boehmer*, [1997] A.J. No. 69 (Q.B.); *Belcourt v. Belcourt* (1987), 6 R.F.L. (3d) 396 (Alta. Q.B.); *Poyntz Estate v. Poyntz*, [1998] O.J. No. 1024 (Gen. Div.).

317 (1989), 19 R.F.L. (3d) 127 (B.C.C.A.). See also *Misener v. Muir*, [2007] B.C.J. No. 2029 (S.C.).

denying the non-custodial parent court-ordered access to which both he and the child were entitled. The British Columbia Court of Appeal reasoned that a custodial parent, who has been required to draw on his or her own resources to properly maintain the children of the marriage, is entitled to recover child support arrears from the non-custodial parent, but this reasoning does not apply where the encroachments are self-induced.

Full or partial remission of arrears may be granted for a variety of reasons, the most compelling of which is the obligor's inability to pay by reason of unemployment, reduction of income, or illness.[318]

The court has jurisdiction to order the payment of arrears in an orderly manner. A schedule for payment must be realistic, having regard to the potential for compliance and its sufficiency in addressing the needs of the children for whose benefit the payments are being made. Enforcement of some or all of the arrears may be postponed with a direction for them to be discharged by future instalments.[319]

Although a mother may be deemed to have waived court-ordered child support during ten months of a trial reconciliation with the father with the result that no arrears of child support will accrue during that period, the order remains in existence and arrears accrue thereunder after a subsequent cessation of cohabitation. Forcing a recipient parent to return to court for a new order after a failed reconciliation attempt would not only discourage reconciliation; it would also disrupt the continuity of support and potentially the standard of living of the child.[320]

---

318 *Doole v. Doole* (1991), 32 R.F.L. (3d) 283 (Alta. Q.B.); *Smith v. Smith* (1990), 27 R.F.L. (3d) 32 (Man. C.A.); *Domanski v. Domanski* (1992), 83 Man. R. (2d) 161 (C.A.); *Klassen v. Klassen* (1993), 44 R.F.L. (3d) 443 (Man. C.A.); *Stacey v. Hacking* (1993), 142 N.B.R. (2d) 99 (Q.B.); *Pidgeon v. Hickman*, [2000] N.J. No. 44 (S.C.); *Rector v. Hamilton* (1989), 94 N.S.R. (2d) 284 (Fam. Ct.); *Propper v. Vanleeuwen*, [1999] O.J. No. 2297 (S.C.J.); *Stewart v. Stewart*, [2000] S.J. No. 149 (Q.B.); *Turnbull v. Turnbull*, [1998] Y.J. No. 145 (S.C.); See also *Bernard v. Bernard*, [2008] A.J. No. 302 (Q.B.) (partial remission of arrears accrued during obligor's imprisonment).

319 *Young v. Konkle* (1993), 1 R.F.L. (4th) 211 (Alta. Q.B.); *Sampson v. Sampson*, [1998] A.J. No. 1214 (Q.B.); *B.L. v. S.S.*, [2003] A.J. No. 696 (Q.B.); *Beaudoin v. Beaudoin* (1993), 45 R.F.L. (3d) 412 (B.C.S.C.); *P.H. v. P.H.*, [2008] N.B.J. No. 52 (C.A.); *Delorme v. Woodham* (1993), 89 Man. R. (2d) 16 (Q.B.); *Adamson v. Steed*, [2006] O.J. No. 5306 (Sup. Ct.); *Stewart v. Stewart*, [2000] S.J. No. 149 (Q.B.).

320 *Fitzell v. Weisbrood*, [2005] O.J. No. 791 (Sup. Ct.).

N. DETERMINATION AND DISCLOSURE OF INCOME

The obligor's income is the foundation on which the provincial and territorial tables in the *Federal Child Support Guidelines* fix the monthly amount of basic child support. The recipient parent's income or that of the child only becomes relevant in those cases where the court is empowered to deviate from the table amount.[321]

Martinson J., of the Supreme Court of British Columbia, has formulated the following step-by-step guide to the determination of a parent's income under the *Federal Child Support Guidelines*.[322] The steps are divided in two parts, each of which has four steps. The following summary is extracted from her judgment:

Part I — Actual Earnings

Step One: Gather mandatory information pursuant to financial disclosure requirements.

Step Two: Examine separately each source of income identified in the C.R.A. T1 General form and use the most current information available to predict the parent's prospective annual earnings from each source.

Step Three: Review historical patterns of income over the last three taxation years to determine whether the predicted income under Step Two is the fairest determination of annual income from each source. If it is not, the historical pattern of earnings can be used to predict the parent's prospective annual income from each source.

Step Four: Total the predicted income from each source.

Part II — Imputing Income

Step Five: Assess the parent's earning capacity in light of whether a parent is under-employed, unreasonably deducts expenses from income, is not using property to generate income, or is hiding income behind a corporate veil.

Step Six: Determine whether the parent receives any income tax benefits or concessions or benefits under a trust.

---

321 See Section D, above in this chapter.
322 *Murphy v. Murphy*, [2000] B.C.J. No. 1253, 8 R.F.L. (5th) 338 (S.C.); *Hamilton v. Pearce*, [2000] B.C.J. No. 1953 (S.C.).

Step Seven: Decide whether a parent is seeking to avoid the payment of child support by diverting income or not making full financial disclosure.

Step Eight: Decide whether any other supplemental income should reasonably be attributed to the parent.

Sections 16 to 20 of the *Federal Child Support Guidelines* define how income is to be determined for the purpose of applying the Guidelines.[323] Section 16 of the *Federal Child Support Guidelines* provides that, subject to sections 17 to 20 of the Guidelines, a spouse's annual income is determined by reference to the sources of income set out under the heading "Total income" in the Canada Revenue Agency's T1 General form, with adjustments being made in accordance with sections 1 to 10 of Schedule III of the Guidelines.[324] Specified adjustments to the spouse's income provided under Schedule III of the Guidelines include the following:

a) the spouse's employment expenses that would be deductible under paragraphs 8(1)(c) to (j) and (n) to (q) of the *Income Tax Act* are deducted;[325]

b) CPP contributions and Employment Insurance premiums under section 8(1)(1.1) of the *Income Tax Act* are deducted if paid in respect of another employee who has acted as an assistant or substitute for the spouse;[326]

c) child support that is included to determine total income in the T1 General form issued by the Canada Revenue Agency is to be deducted;

d) spousal support received from the other spouse is deducted in calculating income for the purpose of determining the amount of child support under the applicable provincial or territorial table;[327]

---

323 For an excellent detailed analysis of this topic, see V. Jennifer MacKinnon, "Determining Income under the *Child Support Guidelines*" in The Law Society of Upper Canada, *Child Support Guidelines: Recent and Important Caselaw* (16 December 1998). See also Aaron Franks, "Deferred Compensation versus Current Support Obligations" in The Law Society of Upper Canada, *Special Lectures 2006: Family Law* (Toronto: Irwin Law, 2007) 273–89.

324 *Lavergne v. Lavergne*, 2007 ABCA 169, [2007] A.J. No. 580.

325 *Jarbeau v. Pelletier*, [1998] O.J. No. 3029 (Prov. Div.) (meals and lodgings of railway employee held deductible under *Income Tax Act*, paragraph 8(1)(e); union dues deductible under paragraph 8(1)(i); motor vehicle expenses deductible under paragraph 8(1)(j)); *Haimanot v. Haimanot*, [2002] S.J. No. 12 (C.A.) (union dues).

326 *Guidelines to Amend the Federal Child Support Guidelines*, SOR/97-563, s. 12 amending SOR/97-175, para. 1(i) of Schedule III.

327 *Westcott v. Westcott*, [1997] O.J. No. 3060 (Gen. Div.); *Moro v. Miletich*, [1998] O.J. No. 1799, 40 R.F.L. (4th) 115 (Gen. Div.); *Schick v. Schick*, [1997] S.J. No. 447 (Q.B.).

e) spousal support paid to the other spouse is deducted in calculating income for the purpose of determining an amount respecting special or extraordinary expenses under section 7 of the Guidelines;[328]

f) social assistance income is adjusted to only include the amount determined to be attributable to the spouse;[329]

g) the taxable amount of dividends from Canadian corporations received by the spouse is replaced by the actual amount of those dividends received by the spouse;[330]

h) the taxable capital gains realized in a year by the spouse are replaced by the actual amount of capital gains realized by the spouse in excess of actual capital loss suffered by the spouse in that year;[331]

i) the actual amount of business investment losses suffered by a spouse during the year is deducted;[332]

j) the spouse's carrying charges and interest expenses that are paid by the spouse and that would be deductible under the *Income Tax Act* are deducted;[333]

k) where the net self-employment income of the spouse is determined by deducting an amount in respect of salaries, wages or management fees, or other payments, paid to or on behalf of persons with whom the spouse does not deal at arm's length, that amount shall be added, unless the spouse establishes that the payments were necessary to earn the self-employment income and were reasonable in the circumstances;[334]

l) where the spouse reports income from self-employment that includes income for the reporting year plus a further amount earned

---

328 *Russell v. Russell*, [2002] B.C.J. No. 1983 (S.C.); *Galloway v. Galloway*, [2008] B.C.J. No. 94 (C.A.); *Margee v. Magee*, [1997] S.J. No. 468 (Q.B.).

329 *Martell v. Martell*, [2001] O.J. No. 759 (Ct. Just.).

330 *Shaw v. Shaw*, [1997] M.J. No. 400 (Q.B.); *Johnson v. Checkowy*, [1997] S.J. No. 451 (Q.B.); *Wilson v. Wilson*, [1998] S.J. No. 236 (Q.B.); *Stephen v. Stephen*, [1999] S.J. No. 479 (Q.B.). See also *Boniface v. Boniface*, [2007] B.C.J. No. 2303 (S.C.).

331 *Kendry v. Cathcart*, [2001] O.J. No. 277 (Sup. Ct.); *Andersen v. Andersen*, [1997] B.C.J. No. 2496 (S.C.); *Coghill v. Coghill*, [2006] O.J. No. 2602 (Sup. Ct.).

332 *Omah-Maharajh v. Howard*, [1998] A.J. No. 173 (Q.B.).

333 *Tynan v. Moses*, [2002] B.C.J. No. 197 (S.C.); *Andres v. Andres*, [1999] M.J. No. 103 (C.A.) (mortgage payments respecting rental property; principal not deductible under s. 18(1)(b) of *Income Tax Act*; interest deductible under s. 20(1)(c) of *Income Tax Act*); *Haimanot v. Haimanot*, [2002] S.J. No. 12 (C.A.).

334 *Holtby v. Holtby*, [1997] O.J. No. 2237 (Gen. Div.); *Finn v. Levine*, [1997] O.J. No. 2201 (Gen. Div.); *Stewart v. Stewart*, [2000] S.J. No. 149 (Q.B.).

in the prior year, the spouse may deduct the amount earned in the prior period, net of reserves;

m)   spousal income includes any deduction for an allowable capital cost allowance with respect to real property;

n)   where the spouse earns income from a partnership or sole proprietorship, any amount included in income that is properly required by the partnership or sole proprietorship for purposes of capitalization shall be deducted from the spouse's income;[335] and

o)   where the spouse has received, as an employee benefit, stock options to purchase shares of a Canadian controlled private corporation, or a publicly traded corporation that is subject to the same tax treatment as a Canadian controlled private corporation, and has exercised the options during the year, the difference between the value of the shares at the time the options are exercised and the amount paid for the shares and any amount paid to acquire the options is added to the spouse's income for the year in which the options are exercised.[336]

Pursuant to SOR/2007-59, which became effective on 1 April 2007, the *Federal Child Support Guidelines* have been amended to address the impact of the Universal Child Care Benefit (UCCB). Although the UCCB does not constitute spousal income for the purpose of determining the table amount of child support, it must be taken into account in determining the reasonableness of section 7 expenses and in apportioning those expenses between the spouses insofar as the UCCB is paid for the child in respect of whom section 7 expenses are ordered.[337]

The calculation of income under sections 16 to 20 of the *Federal Child Support Guidelines* can be exceedingly complex and the problems are compounded by the fact that accounting procedures applicable under the *Income Tax Act* are not necessarily the same as those applicable under the Guidelines.

Judicial determination of the income of wage earners is relatively simple, because they usually have only one source of income and their income tax returns are likely to provide a true reflection of their annual

---

335   *Austin v. Austin*, [2007] O.J. No. 4283 (Sup. Ct.).

336   See Franks, "Deferred Compensation versus Current Support Obligations," above note 323.

337   For the specific language of the amendments and an excellent "Regulatory Impact Analysis Statement," see *Canada Gazette*, Vol. 141, No. 7 (4 April 2007), online: http://canadagazette.gc.ca/partII/2007/20070404/html/sor59-e.html.

income. Where spouses are self-employed, the net income reported on their income tax return is not necessarily a true reflection of their income for the purpose of determining their child support obligations. Business expenses that may be legitimately deducted under the *Income Tax Act* are not necessarily allowed under the *Federal Child Support Guidelines*.[338] For example, capital cost allowances permitted for the depreciation of business equipment may be permissible for income tax purposes, but disallowed in whole or in part for the purpose of determining a spouse's income under the *Federal Child Support Guidelines*.[339]

Section 2(3) of the *Federal Child Support Guidelines* requires a court to use "the most current information" to determine a spouse's annual income.[340] Historical information, based on personal or corporate tax returns or other available data, is often predictive of a spouse's current annual income and may be relied upon in the absence of any contrary indication.[341] Reliable current information should be used where it conflicts with historical information because child support is payable out of current and future income, not out of past earnings.[342] In determining a spouse's (parent's) income for the purpose of determining child support, section 2(3) of the *Federal Child Support Guidelines* mandates the use of the most current information, but this is only appropriate when the most recent information is likely to accurately reflect the spouse's prospective annual income. In *L.A.K. v. A.A.W.*,[343] Johnstone J. found that the father's pay stubs from January through May 2005 were not necessarily reflective of his anticipated annual income. Accordingly, the father's income for 2005 was determined by reference to his income tax return for 2004. In *Green v. Green*,[344] the father contended that ill-health would continue to reduce his prospective annual income, as it had over the preceding three years. The applications judge, nevertheless, calculated the father's prospective annual income by extrapolation from his year-to-date earnings. The Newfoundland and Labrador Court of Appeal concluded that the applications judge had made no palpable and overriding error in determin-

338 *Cook v. McManus*, [2006] N.B.J. No. 334 (Q.B.).
339 *Andries v. Andries*, [1999] M.J. No. 103 (C.A.); see also *Huber v. Yaroshko*, [2000] S.J. No. 201 (Q.B.).
340 *Lavergne v. Lavergne*, 2007 ABCA 169, [2007] A.J. No. 580.
341 *Rasmussen v. MacDonald*, [1997] S.J. No. 667 (Q.B.).
342 *Halley v. Halley*, [1998] N.J. No. 104 (S.C.); *Lee v. Lee*, [1998] N.J. No. 247 (C.A.); *Coghill v. Coghill*, [2006] O.J. No. 2602 (Sup. Ct.); *Luckett v. Luckett*, [2002] S.J. No. 232 (Q.B.).
343 [2005] A.J. No. 1140 (Q.B.).
344 [2005] N.J. No. 165 (C.A.).

ing the father's annual income for 2004 in this manner because, if his income continued to decrease due to ill-health, the father could apply to vary the amount of child support payable.

Historical patterns of income from overtime employment and the continued availability of overtime are relevant factors to consider but they are not necessarily determinative of what is a fair and reasonable level of income to be imputed to a parent. In seeking to provide guidance as to the circumstances that a court should take into account in determining what, if any, income from overtime employment should be imputed to a parent who is already engaged in regular full-time employment, Tuck J. in *R.S. v. T.S.*[345] offers the following opinion and non-exhaustive list of relevant factors for consideration:

> [para. 44] Each overtime case is of course unique and fact driven. In the result there can not be developed a list of factors or guideposts to be considered in relation to the overtime issue that are exhaustive or weighted. Some obvious factors that may be considered in a principled approach to the issue of assessing reasonableness in this regard I think would have to include some of the following considerations as appropriate.
>
> 1. The necessity of overtime in relation to appropriate support needs. The determination of said necessity to include as appropriate a consideration of the condition, means and needs of the affected parents, and the extent of the effect of removal of the disputed overtime amount from income on the pre-existing standard of living enjoyed by affected parties.
> 2. The issue of any potential reasonable detrimental reliance created by the past working of the disputed overtime.
> 3. Are the best interests of any children adversely impacted by working the questioned overtime hours, i.e. does same adversely affect the appropriate care of or the appropriate exercise of access to the children in question.
> 4. The extent to which the elimination of the questioned overtime is a deliberate attempt to avoid otherwise necessary support obligations.
> 5. A consideration, in context of the overtime in question, of the age and health of the payor.
> 6. The training, experience and education of the payor.

---

345 [2005] N.B.J. No. 448 (Q.B.).

7. The nature of the actual overtime work, i.e. quantity, type of work (sedentary or labour intensive), how much notice of the availability or obligation with respect to particular overtime is provided and the effect of same.

8. The amount of overtime with respect to which there is reason to believe there will be some consistency of availability and appropriate ability to work.

9. The purpose of past overtime worked. Was it worked of necessity or for a specific purpose i.e. debt reduction, purchase of luxury item etc. and to what extent said need still exists.

10. Whether the working of the overtime is mandatory or discretionary from the employer's perspective. Is the working of the questioned overtime to some measure expected or advisable in relation to a person's employment, i.e. employer expectation, historical practice, trade practice or otherwise?

11. The potential affect of overtime on lifestyle and life quality issues, recognizing the need for all persons not to be unnecessarily thwarted in their pursuit of [a] rewarding balanced and fulfilled life.

12. Recognition of legitimately arising obligations of others with respect to the support in question.

13. Such other factors and considerations as [are] appropriate in particular circumstances.

[para. 45] The considerations noted of course are not necessarily mutually exclusive.

Section 17 of the *Federal Child Support Guidelines* provides various means whereby a court can address erratic or fluctuating annual incomes. The most widely used means of dealing with this problem under section 17 of the Guidelines is by way of averaging the annual income over the three most recent taxation years. It is inappropriate to rely on the averaging provisions of section 17 of the Guidelines to reduce an obligor's income where his or her current income is known and will not decrease in future years.[346] Section 17 of the Guidelines confers discretionary, not mandatory, powers on the court that are exercisable in the search for the fairest determination of a spouse's income.[347] When averaging a parent's

---

346 *Johnson v. Checkowy*, [1997] S.J. No. 451 (Q.B.).

347 *Wilson v. Wilson*, [1998] S.J. No. 236 (Q.B.); *Schnell v. Schnell*, [2001] S.J. No. 704 (C.A.); *Luckett v. Luckett*, [2002] S.J. No. 232 (Q.B.).

income over the three preceding taxation years pursuant to section 17 of the *Federal Child Support Guidelines,* section 16 of the Guidelines does not require the court to rely on the pattern of income revealed in the parent's income tax returns. Additional income may be imputed to the parent pursuant to section 19 of the Guidelines before the averaging of the last three years of income is undertaken. While section 16 of the Guidelines permits recourse to sections 17 and 19 of the Guidelines to enable a court to make the fairest determination of the parent's prospective annual income, section 16 does not treat sections 17 and 19 as mutually exclusive.[348]

Pursuant to section 18 of the *Federal Child Support Guidelines,* income may be attributed to a spouse whose income is artificially low because of low draws from a personal corporation.[349] Section 18 of the Guidelines can be invoked whenever a spouse's income, as determined under section 16 of the Guidelines, does not fairly reflect all the money that ought reasonably to be available for child support, after the legitimate needs of the corporation are taken into account. Given such a finding, the court has the discretionary jurisdiction under section 18(1) of the Guidelines to consider the spouse's income as including (a) all or part of the pretax income of the corporation; or (b) an amount commensurate with the services rendered to the corporation provided that the amount does not exceed the corporation's pretax income.[350] Only the pretax income of a corporation for the most recent taxation year may be included in a spouse's annual income under section 18(1)(a) of the Guidelines. Section 18 is not directed at retained corporate earnings over several years, although such retained earnings could result in an imputation of income to a spouse under section 19 of the Guidelines.[351] In determining the pretax income of a corporation, money paid to persons with whom the corporation does not deal at arm's length must be added to the pretax income, unless the payment is shown to be reasonable in the circumstances.[352]

Two appellate judgments from British Columbia and Manitoba offer significant guidance as to the interpretation to be accorded to section 18

---

348   *Schnell v. Schnell,* [2001] S.J. No. 704 (C.A.).

349   *Bhopal v. Bhopal,* [1997] B.C.J. No. 1746 (S.C.).

350   *Stephen v. Stephen,* [1999] S.J. No. 479 (Q.B.); see also *Goldberg v. Goldberg,* [1998] M.J. No. 536 (Q.B.).

351   *Morley v. Morley,* [1999] S.J. No. 31 (Q.B.).

352   *Federal Child Support Guidelines,* s. 18(2); *Needham v. Needham,* [1998] B.C.J. No. 202 (S.C.).

of the Guidelines. The first is *Kowalewich v. Kowalewich*,[353] wherein the British Columbia Court of Appeal formulated the following principles:

- A court need not look for signs of bad faith or undeclared personal benefits before imputing income to a parent pursuant to sections 17 or 18 of the Guidelines. Nor should a court look only to section 18(1)(b) of the Guidelines to determine the value of the parent's services to a company that the parent owns or controls.

- The attribution of pretax corporate income to a parent pursuant to section 18(1)(a) of the Guidelines does not strip that parent or his or her corporation of the income attributed. It is simply used as a measuring rod for the purpose of fixing the parent's annual income on the basis of which the amount of child support will be determined.

- The purpose of section 18 of the Guidelines is to allow the court to lift the corporate veil to ensure that money received as income by the paying parent fairly reflects all of the income reasonably available for the purpose of assessing child support. A court's effort to ensure fairness does not require a court to second-guess business decisions. What it does require is that a parent's allocation of pretax corporate income between business and family purposes be assessed for fairness by an impartial tribunal when parents cannot reach agreement on priorities as they would in an intact family. To determine whether "Total income" in the T1 General form issued by the Canada Revenue Agency fairly reflects a parent's income in the context of child support, a court might ask what a reasonable and well-informed parent would make available for child support in the circumstances of the particular business over which the parent exercises control, having regard to the objectives under section 1 of the Guidelines, the underlying parental obligation to support children in accordance with parental means under section 26(2) of the *Divorce Act*, and any applicable situation arising from income fluctuations or non-recurring gains or losses under section 17 of the Guidelines.

- No explicit guidance is provided as to how a parent or a court might go about choosing whether to use the corporate income method of attribution under section 18(1)(a) of the Guidelines or the personal

---

353 [2001] B.C.J. No. 1406 (C.A.); see also *Miller v. Joynt*, 2007 ABCA 214, [2007] A.J. No. 959; *Cook v. McManus*, [2006] N.B.J. No. 334 (Q.B.); *Beeching v. Beeching*, [2006] S.J. No. 792 (Q.B.); *Hannah v. Warner*, [2008] S.J. No. 46 (Q.B.).

services attribution method under section 18(1)(b) of the Guidelines. Section 18 suggests, however, two considerations in the preconditions for its application: (1) which method produces an annual income that more fairly reflects all the income available for the assessment of child support? and (2) which method does the nature of the parent's relationship with the corporation support? Section 18 also permits reference to the "situations described in section 17" and thus to the parent's income pattern over the preceding three years. The nature of the parent's relationship with the corporation may sometimes be decisive. Section 18 of the Guidelines applies not only to a parent who wholly controls a corporation; it also applies to a parent who shares corporate ownership and control with others. Where a parent wholly owns a corporation, the attribution of corporate income under section 18(1)(a) of the Guidelines is likely to be the fairer method of determining parental income, because it allows a court to include not only reasonable payment for personal services rendered to the corporation but also a reasonable return on the parent's entrepreneurial capacity and investment. These are sources of income that an intact family would utilize. Moreover, it not only permits but requires the inclusion of the income of companies related within the meaning of the *Income Tax Act* and of non-arms length payments made without value to the company.

- There may be factors in particular cases that will recommend to the court the personal services method of attributing income under section 18(1)(b) of the Guidelines, as for example, where the corporation's only business is the provision of the personal services of its owner. There may also be cases where stability of income will persuade a trial judge to use the personal services method, having regard to situations under section 17 of the Guidelines.

- Section 18(1)(a) of the Guidelines allows a court to include all the pretax income of a corporation for the most recent taxation year in a parent's annual income for Guidelines purposes, but this is not required and courts should not make the inclusion of pretax corporate income the default position.

- The only explicit guidance provided as to how much of a corporation's pretax income should be included in the parent's annual income is found in the words "the court may consider the situations described in section 17." That section refers to the historical income pattern of a spouse and to non-recurring gains and losses. Regard should also be paid to the nature of the corporation's business and any evidence of legitimate calls on its corporate income for the purposes of that business. Money needed to maintain the value of the business as a viable going concern will not be available for support purposes and should not be included in determining a parent's annual income.

- Although an appellate court should not tinker with a trial judge's exercise of discretion, it may reduce the amount of corporate income attributed to a parent where the trial judge has paid insufficient regard to the evidence of legitimate business needs in determining what portion of pretax corporate income to include in the parent's annual income.

The second important appellate judgment interpreting section 18 of the *Federal Child Support Guidelines*, and its provincial counterpart under the *Manitoba Child Support Guidelines* whereunder subtle differences exist, is *Nesbitt v. Nesbitt*,[354] wherein the Manitoba Court of Appeal formulated the following conclusions: Some cases assert that section 18 of the *Federal Child Support Guidelines* and their provincial counterparts should only be applied where a parent deliberately seeks to avoid child support obligations by, for example, artificially reducing income by leaving funds in his or her private company, or charging personal or living expenses to the company. Other cases interpret section 18 of the Guidelines more broadly to encompass situations where the parent's income, as determined under section 16 of the Guidelines, is perceived as not "fairly" reflecting all the income available to the parent for the purpose of determining child support. A parent in control of a corporation who chooses to build up retained corporate earnings, rather than take the money out as personal income, has the onus of proving that there are legitimate business reasons for leaving the earnings in the corporation. If this onus is not discharged, a court may impute all the retained corporate earnings for the most recent taxation year to the parent for the purpose of applying the Guidelines. Pursuant to section 17 of the Guidelines, a court may average corporate income over the last three years to determine the annual income "that is fair and reasonable" to impute to the parent for the purpose of determining support under the Guidelines. Although section 18 of the Guidelines allows the court to attribute corporate income to a parent only for the immediately preceding year, it may be possible to

---

354　[2001] M.J. No. 291 (C.A.); see also *Gossen v. Gossen*, [2003] N.S.J. No. 113 (S.C.).

apply section 19(1)(e)[355] of the Guidelines as an additional potential source to impute retained corporate earnings to a parent.

In determining the annual income of a spouse or former spouse, section 19 of the *Federal Child Support Guidelines* entitles the court to impute such income to the spouse or former spouse as it considers appropriate in specified circumstances. The listed circumstances include the following:

a) the spouse or former spouse is intentionally under-employed or unemployed, other than where the under-employment or unemployment is required by the needs of a child of the marriage or any child under the age of majority or by reasonable educational or health needs of the spouse or former spouse;

b) the spouse or former spouse is exempt from paying federal or provincial income tax;

c) the spouse or former spouse lives in a country that has effective rates of income tax that are significantly lower than those in Canada;

d) it appears that income has been diverted that would affect the level of child support to be determined under the Guidelines;

e) the property of the spouse or former spouse is not reasonably utilized to generate income;

f) the spouse or former spouse has failed to provide income information when under a legal obligation to do so;[356]

g) the spouse or former spouse unreasonably deducts expenses from income;

h) the spouse or former spouse derives a significant portion of income from dividends,[357] capital gains, or other sources that are taxed at a lower rate than employment or business income; and

i) the spouse or former spouse is a beneficiary under a trust and has been or may be in receipt of income or other benefits from the trust.

The list of circumstances under section 19 of the Guidelines that entitles a court to impute income to a spouse is not comprehensive and does not purport to limit the power of a court to impute income in other

---

355 Section 19 of the *Federal Child Support Guidelines* empowers a court to impute income to a parent whose "property is not reasonably utilized to generate income."

356 *Snyder v. Pictou*, [2008] N.S.J. No. 77 (C.A.).

357 *Austin v. Austin*, [2007] O.J. No. 4283 (Sup. Ct.).

circumstances.[358] However, a court should decline to attribute income to an obligor on the basis of his or her lifestyle, insofar as that lifestyle is enhanced by the independent income of the obligor's new spouse.[359] Income may, nevertheless, be imputed to an obligor who diverts income to his or her spouse or common-law spouse by means of a corporate entity that engages in non-arm's-length transactions.[360] Although income has been attributed to an obligor whose household expenses are shared by a new wife or an unmarried cohabitant,[361] widespread adoption of this practice would undermine the predictability and certainty sought to be achieved by the provincial and territorial tables under the *Federal Child Support Guidelines.* Different considerations apply, however, in those situations where the Guidelines expressly confer a judicial discretion, in the exercise of which the court is required to take account of the means or ability to pay of the parties.

Section 19(1)(a) of the *Federal Child Support Guidelines* empowers a court to impute such income as it deems appropriate to a spouse who "is intentionally under-employed or unemployed, other than where the under-employment or unemployment is required by the needs of a child of the marriage or any child under the age of majority or by reasonable educational or health needs of the spouse." Appellate courts in British Columbia,[362] Manitoba,[363] Nova Scotia,[364] and Ontario[365] have concluded that section 19(1)(a) of the Guidelines is not confined to circumstances where a parent deliberately seeks to evade his or her child support obligations or recklessly disregards his or her children's financial needs while pursuing his or her personal choice of employment or lifestyle. Although such deliberate or reckless conduct, where it exists, weighs heavily in the

---

358 *Charles v. Charles,* [1997] B.C.J. No. 1981 (S.C.); *D.L.M. v. J.A.M.,* 2008 NBCA 2, [2008] N.B.J. No. 9; *Bak v. Dobell,* 2007 ONCA 304, [2007] O.J. No. 1489.

359 *Risen v. Risen,* [1998] O.J. No. 3184 (Gen. Div.). As to parental gifts, see *Bak v. Dobell,* 2007 ONCA 304, [2007] O.J. No. 1489.

360 *Kowalewich v. Kowalewich,* [2001] B.C.J. No. 1406 (S.C.).

361 See, for example, *Courchesne v. Charlebois,* [1998] O.J. No. 2625 (Prov. Ct.); *Chace v. Chace,* [1998] P.E.I.J. No. 64 (S.C.T.D.).

362 *Van Gool v. Van Gool,* [1998] B.C.J. No. 2513 (C.A.); *Watts v. Willie,* [2004] B.C.J. No. 2482 (C.A.); *Barker v. Barker,* [2005] B.C.J. No. 687 (C.A.).

363 *Donovan v. Donovan,* [2000] M.J. No. 407 (C.A.); *Schindle v. Schindle,* [2001] M.J. No. 564 (C.A.); *Steele v. Koppanyi,* [2002] M.J. No. 201 (C.A.).

364 *Montgomery v. Montgomery,* [2000] N.S.J. No. 1 (C.A.).

365 *A.M.D. v. A.J.P.,* [2002] O.J. No. 3731, *(sub nom. Drygala v. Pauli)* (2002), 29 R.F.L. (5th) 293 (C.A.); *Kaye v. Kaye,* [2002] O.J. No. 3747 (Div. Ct.); *Riel v. Holland,* [2003] O.J. No. 3901 (C.A.); *Lawson v. Lawson,* [2006] O.J. No. 3179 (C.A.).

exercise of the court's discretion to impute income to a parent, the proper test for the judicial imputation of income to a parent pursuant to section 19(1)(a) of the Guidelines is perceived in the aforementioned appellate judgments as being a test of reasonableness. According to this criterion, the court must have regard to the parent's capacity to earn in light of such factors as employment history, age, education, skills, health, available employment opportunities, and the standard of living enjoyed during the marriage. This criterion was accepted in the dissenting opinion of Picard J.A., of the Alberta Court of Appeal, in *Hunt v. Smolis-Hunt*.[366] A contrary opinion was voiced, however, by Berger J.A., with whom Wittmann J.A. concurred.[367] Their majority judgment spoke of two irreconcilable lines of authority interpreting section 19(1)(a) of the Guidelines. The one line of authority would allow a court to impute income to parents only when they have engaged in a deliberate course of conduct for the purpose of undermining or avoiding their child support obligations. The second line is reflected in the test of reasonableness previously outlined. The majority judgment's endorsement of a test based on the deliberate evasion of child support obligations is difficult to reconcile with the overall content of section 19(1)(a) of the *Federal Child Support Guidelines*. As Veit J., of the Alberta Court of Queen's Bench, has observed, section 19(1)(a) of the Guidelines, when read in its entirety, appears to negate any requirement that a parent intend to evade his or her child support obligations. If such an intention were required, it would not have been necessary to create an express exemption in section 19(1)(a) of the Guidelines for a parent who is underemployed or unemployed because of the needs of a child or because of the reasonable educational or health needs of the parent.[368]

In *Donovan v. Donovan*,[369] Steele J.A., of the Manitoba Court of Appeal, endorsed the following six principles as relevant when determining whether income should be imputed to a parent pursuant to section 19(1)(a) of the *Federal Child Support Guidelines*:

---

366 [2001] A.J. No. 1170 (C.A.).

367 See also *P.E.K. v. B.W.K.*, [2003] A.J. No. 1706 (C.A.); *Demers v. Moar*, [2004] A.J. No. 1331 (C.A.); *Normandin v. Kovalench*, [2007] N.W.T.J. No. 105 (S.C.).

368 *Phipps v. Phipps*, [2001] A.J. No. 1206 (Q.B.). See also *Barker v. Barker*, [2005] B.C.J. No. 687 (C.A.).

369 (2000), 150 Man. R. (2d) 116 (C.A.). See also *Watts v. Willie*, [2004] B.C.J. No. 2482 (C.A.); *M.E.E.T. v. C.M.W.*, [2007] B.C.J. No. 1647 (S.C.); *D.L.M. v. J.A.M.*, 2008 NBCA 2, [2008] N.B.J. No. 9; *Beisel v. Henderson*, [2006] 2 W.W.R. 502 (Sask. Q.B.); *Moore v. Tymiak*, [2006] S.J. No. 326 (Q.B.). For a more detailed summary of the principles applicable under s. 19(1)(a) of the *Federal Child Support Guidelines*, see *Algner v. Algner*, [2008] S.J. No. 182 (Q.B.), Ryan-Froslie J.

1. There is a duty to seek employment in a case where a parent is healthy and there is no reason why the parent cannot work. It is "no answer for a person liable to support a child to say he is unemployed and does not intend to seek work or that his potential to earn income is an irrelevant factor" (*Van Gool v. Van Gool* (1998), 113 B.C.A.C. 200; 184 W.A.C. 200; 166 D.L.R. (4th) 528 (C.A.)).

2. When imputing income on the basis of intentional under-employment, a court must consider what is reasonable under the circumstances. The age, education, experience, skills and health of the parent are factors to be considered in addition to such matters as availability of work, freedom to relocate and other obligations.

3. A parent's limited work experience and job skills do not justify a failure to pursue employment that does not require significant skills, or employment in which the necessary skills can be learned on the job. While this may mean that job availability will be at the lower end of the wage scale, courts have never sanctioned the refusal of a parent to take reasonable steps to support his or her children simply because the parent cannot obtain interesting or highly paid employment.

4. Persistence in unremunerative employment may entitle the court to impute income.

5. A parent cannot be excused from his or her child support obligations in furtherance of unrealistic or unproductive career aspirations.

6. As a general rule, a parent cannot avoid child support obligations by a self-induced reduction of income.

A father, who is currently earning far less than the annual income previously earned, must provide a satisfactory explanation for the change or run the risk that income will be imputed to him on the basis of his previously demonstrated earning capacity.[370]

Courts have frequently declined to impute income to mothers who have temporarily withdrawn from the work force so as to provide stay-at-home care for their child of a second family. In *Burke v. Burke*,[371] the father sought to reduce the amount of child support payable under a separation agreement in consequence of his subsequent retirement from the military at the age of forty-two. At the time of the application, which was joined with a divorce proceeding, the father was living with his common-law

---

370 *Steele v. Koppanyi*, [2002] M.J. No. 201 (C.A.).
371 [2005] N.S.J. No. 74 (S.C.).

spouse and their infant son. His common-law spouse's earning capacity exceeded that of the father when he was in the military and they decided that he would be a "stay-at-home dad" for their child. In addressing his application to reduce the agreed amount of child support to reflect his current retirement income, Coady J. found that the father's decision to retire after twenty-two years in the military was reasonable, as was his decision to personally provide primary daily care for his infant son. Consequently, Coady J. refused to impute income to the father under section 19(1)(a) of the Guidelines, being of the opinion that to do so would constitute a gender-based double standard. In the result, child support was fixed on the basis of the retirement income being received by the father.

A judge cannot act on personal or privately acquired information. Furthermore, a judge cannot take judicial notice of a fact, unless (i) the matter is so notorious as to be indisputable by reasonable people; or (ii) the matter is capable of immediate accurate demonstration by resort to readily reliable sources of indisputable accuracy. A judge should proceed with the utmost caution, if he or she is tempted to take judicial notice of a fact that is vital to the resolution of the case, especially where counsel has not been afforded an opportunity to speak to the matter. Where a self-employed parent has provided unchallenged evidence of his annual earnings and business expenses and there is no evidence that the parent is intentionally underemployed, or that his property is underutilized, or that he has unreasonably deducted business expenses, a court is not entitled to impute additional income to that parent by relying on information that the judge possesses with respect to the income earned and the cost of services rendered by people in similar occupations to the parent. Should a judge pursue such a course of action, it constitutes a palpable and overriding error that warrants reversal on appeal.[372]

An appellate court should not interfere with a trial judge's conclusion that a parent acted reasonably in seeking lesser paid employment in order to spend more time with his children, where the trial judge chose to accept the husband's explanation for the change of employment. The fact that the appellate court is troubled by the finding of the trial judge is an insufficient basis for overturning it. An appellate court may intervene only where there is a material error, a serious misapprehension of the evidence, or an error in law. An appellate court cannot overturn a support order simply because it would have made a different decision or balanced the factors differently.[373]

---

372 *Dean v. Brown*, [2002] N.S.J. No. 439 (C.A.).
373 *Schindle v. Schindle*, [2001] M.J. No. 564 (C.A.).

The *Federal Child Support Guidelines* base support payments on the payor's gross taxable income. One of the objectives of the Guidelines is to ensure "consistent treatment" of those who are in "similar circumstances." Thus, there are provisions to impute income where a parent is exempt from paying tax, lives in a lower taxed jurisdiction, or derives income from sources that are taxed at a lower rate. Where a parent arranges his or her affairs to pay substantially less tax on income, the income must be grossed up before the table is applied. This is the only way to ensure the consistency mandated by the legislation.[374] In addition to the express powers to impute income under section 19 of the *Federal Child Support Guidelines*, a failure to file income tax returns and other financial data, as required by section 21(1) of the *Federal Child Support Guidelines*, entitles the other spouse to have an application for child support set down for a hearing in accordance with section 22(1)(a) of the Guidelines and, at such a hearing, the court may, pursuant to section 23 of the Guidelines, impute income to the offending spouse in such amount as is considered appropriate.[375] The inadequacy of the income information provided by the obligor may entitle the court to impute an income based on all of the evidence presented. The court may take cognizance that the lifestyle of the obligor indicates a higher income than that indicated.[376] Income may be imputed to a parent whose banking records are indicative of a higher income than that asserted.[377]

Section 19(1)(g) of the *Federal Child Support Guidelines* empowers a court to impute income to a parent who unreasonably deducts expenses from income. Section 19(2) of the Guidelines provides that the reasonableness of an expense deduction is not solely governed by whether the deduction is permissible under the *Income Tax Act*.[378] Although there may

---

374 *Orser v. Grant*, [2000] O.J. No. 1429 (Sup. Ct.); *Manis v. Manis*, [2000] O.J. No. 4539 (Sup. Ct.).

375 *Cole v. Cole*, [2000] N.S.J. No. 74 (S.C.); *Guillena v. Guillena*, [2003] N.S.J. No. 76 (S.C.); *Alexander v. Alexander*, [1999] O.J. No. 3694 (Sup. Ct.).

376 *Davari v. Namazi*, [1999] B.C.J. No. 116 (S.C.); *Motyka v. Motyka*, [2001] B.C.J. No. 52 (C.A.); *Manis v. Manis*, [2000] O.J. No. 4539 (Sup. Ct.); *Muir-Lang v. Lang*, [2002] O.J. No. 869 (Sup. Ct.); *Jonas v. Jonas*, [2002] O.J. No. 2117 (Sup. Ct.); *Scholes v. Scholes*, [2003] O.J. No. 3432 (Sup. Ct.); *Arlt v. Arlt*, [2003] S.J. No. 713 (Q.B.); *Kelly v. Lyle*, [2001] Y.J. No. 90 (S.C.).

377 *Schluessel v. Schluessel*, [1999] A.J. No. 1555 (Q.B.); *Van Deventer v. Van Deventer*, [2000] B.C.J. No. 37 (C.A.).

378 *Hall v. Hall*, [2006] A.J. No. 563 (Q.B.); *P.C.J.R. v. D.C.R.*, [2003] B.C.J. No. 792 (C.A.); *Cook v. McManus*, [2006] N.B.J. No. 334 (Q.B.); *Guderyan v. Meyers*, [2006] S.J. No. 797 (Q.B.).

be good reason to look behind the income tax return of a self-employed spouse to determine whether business expenses should be allowed in the context of the Guidelines, a court is fully entitled to find that the expenses are reasonable and should not be added back into the spouse's income for the purpose of determining the child support to be paid.[379] Various courts in Canada have addressed the question whether capital cost allowances for farming or business equipment should be allowed when determining a parent's income under the *Federal Child Support Guidelines* or their provincial counterparts. The leading case in this context is *Cornelius v. Andres*,[380] wherein the Manitoba Court of Appeal listed the following factors as relevant for consideration in deciding whether or not capital cost allowances should be imputed back into income.

1. Was the CCA deduction an actual expense in the year?
2. Was the CCA deduction greater than or less than the cost of acquisitions during the same time period?
3. Was the CCA deduction greater than or less than the repayments of principal with respect to chattels in question?
4. Was the CCA deduction the maximum allowable CCA deduction?
5. Was it necessary to take the CCA deduction in that year?
6. How much of a loss in a business year resulted in that year?
7. Are the chattels for which the CCA was claimed truly needed for business purposes?
8. [Have] the chattels for which the CCA was claimed truly depreciated?
9. Is it foreseeable that future chattel purchases will not be required?
10. Is there a pattern of spending which establishes a greater real income than income tax returns indicate?
11. If the children were living with the spouse, would they benefit from the actual income earned by the spouse?
12. Is there a dire need for child support?

After enumerating these factors, the Manitoba Court of Appeal affirmed that no general rule can be readily established as to when capital cost allowances should be imputed as income under section 19 of the Guidelines. Each case must be decided on its own merits, after scrutinizing the

---

379   *Gossen v. Gossen*, [2003] N.S.J. No. 113 (S.C.); *T.H. v. W.H.*, [2007] N.S.J. No. 27 (S.C.).
380   *Cornelius v. Andres* (1999), 45 R.F.L. (4th) 200, (*sub nom. Andres v. Andres*) [1999] M.J. No. 130 (C.A.).

business in respect of which the capital cost allowance is being claimed, the equipment on which the deduction is being claimed, and the capital cost allowances claimed in the past years, as well as the justification advanced by the party making the claim.[381] Where capital cost allowance deductions are made through a private corporation in which the parent is the sole shareholder, the court may pierce the corporate veil in the interests of achieving justice under the Guidelines and add back the deductions into the parent's personal income for the purpose of applying the Guidelines.[382] As was observed by the Prince Edward Island Court of Appeal in *Koren v. Blum*,[383] where the determination of a parent's income under the Guidelines involves capital cost adjustments or optional inventory adjustments, such as are available to farmers, the parent claiming the expenses must justify the deductions and this requires much more than merely providing copies of relevant income tax returns as required by section 21 of the Guidelines. However, a strong case can be made for the view that, where a parent has made full financial disclosure in accordance with the *Federal Child Support Guidelines* and relevant provincial Rules of Court, an onus falls on the parent asserting the "unreasonableness" of the expense to establish a *prima facie* case, in the absence of which the court should not disallow or adjust the expense in determining the parent's Guidelines income.[384]

While offsetting farm losses may lower the obligor's income tax payable on off-farm income, it does not follow that such losses will be allowed to reduce the obligor's income for the purposes of the *Federal Child Support Guidelines*. Some courts have allowed such losses, at least in part;[385] others have asserted that such losses should not normally be allowed.[386]

---

381 See also *Trueman v. Trueman*, [2000] A.J. No. 1301 (Q.B.); *Balaban v. Balaban*, [2001] A.J. No. 505 (Q.B.); *Egan v. Egan*, [2002] B.C.J. No. 896 (C.A.); *Blaine v. Sanders*, [2000] M.J. No. 149 (Q.B.); *Koren v. Blum*, [2000] P.E.I.J. No. 121 (S.C.A.D.); *Rush v. Rush*, [2002] P.E.I.J. No. 29 (S.C.T.D.); *Huber v. Yaroshko*, [2000] S.J. No. 201 (Q.B.); *Shillington v. Shillington*, [2007] S.J. No. 241 (Q.B.).

382 *Trueman v. Trueman*, [2000] A.J. No. 1301 (Q.B.); *Rudachyk v. Rudachyk*, [1999] S.J. No. 312 (C.A.).

383 [2000] P.E.I.J. No. 121 (S.C.A.D.).

384 *Rush v. Rush*, [2002] P.E.I.J. No. 29 (S.C.T.D.); see also *Egan v. Egan*, [2002] B.C.J. No. 896 (C.A.), concurring judgment of Newbury J.A.; *Monney v. Monney*, [1999] M.J. No. 17 (Q.B.).

385 *Cole v. McNeil*, [2001] N.B.J. No. 37 (Q.B.); *Dreger v. Dreger*, [2000] S.J. No. 11 (Q.B.).

386 *L.A.K. v. A.A.W.*, [2005] A.J. No. 1140 (Q.B.); *T.L.K. v. D.N.K.*, [1999] S.J. No. 401 (Q.B.); see also *Botha v. Botha*, [2000] A.J. No. 1533 (Q.B.); *Hollett v. Vessey*, [2005] N.S.J. No. 538 (S.C.).

In the final analysis, the issue would appear to be one of reasonableness. Consequently, in *Myketiak v. Myketiak*,[387] the Saskatchewan Court of Appeal concluded that a court may impute income under the Guidelines to a parent who sets off farm losses against his or her taxable income from other sources, where the losses are likely to continue unless the parent reorganizes his or her affairs, as for example, by renting the farm to third parties.

Where business expenses are added back into a parent's income under the *Federal Child Support Guidelines*, they should be grossed up to reflect their tax-free status to the parent.[388]

Section 20 of the *Federal Child Support Guidelines*, as amended by SOR/2005-400, provides as follows:

> 20.(1) Subject to subsection (2), where a spouse is a non-resident of Canada, the spouse's annual income is determined as though the spouse were a resident of Canada.
>
> (2) Where a spouse is a non-resident of Canada and resides in a country that has effective rates of income tax that are significantly higher than those applicable in the province in which the other spouse ordinarily resides, the spouse's annual income is the amount that the court determines to be appropriate taking those rates into consideration.

Section 20(1) serves no other purpose than to convert the spouse's foreign income into Canadian currency and to determine the spouse's annual income by using Schedule III of the Guidelines to allow for those deductions from the foreign tax return that are allowable expenses in Canada. A parent cannot invoke section 20(1) to reduce the annual income to be attributed to him in light of the currency exchange rate on his foreign income by asserting a high cost of living in the foreign country, although such an assertion might be examined in the context of section 19(1)(c) of the Guidelines, which empowers but does not compel a court to impute additional income to a spouse whose foreign income generates significantly lower income tax liabilities than those applicable in Canada. Absent undue hardship, the court cannot deviate from the ap-

---

387 [2001] S.J. No. 85 (C.A.).

388 *Cabernel v. Cabernel*, [1997] M.J. No. 375 (Q.B.); *Voth v. Voth*, [2004] M.J. No. 137 (Q.B.); *Riel v. Holland*, [2003] O.J. No. 3901 (C.A.); see also *Sarafinchin v. Sarafinchin*, [2000] O.J. No. 2855 (Sup. Ct.); *Iselmoe v. Iselmoe*, [2003] O.J. No. 4078 (Sup. Ct.); *Naidoo v. Naidoo*, [2004] O.J. No. 1458 (Sup. Ct.); compare *Johnson v. Johnson*, [2000] B.C.J. No. 2065 (S.C.).

plicable table amount of child support under the Guidelines on the basis of the high cost of living in the foreign country.[389] Section 20(2) now permits the court to adjust the income of a foreign resident to accommodate significantly higher income tax liabilities than would be imposed if that parent resided and paid taxes in Canada. It includes no provision for circumstances where the non-resident parent faces a significantly higher cost of living in the foreign jurisdiction that is unrelated to the operative income tax regime.[390]

A court may order financial disclosure in the face of a separation agreement that purports to specify that the agreed amount of child support shall be final and not subject to variation and that purports to waive any future right to financial disclosure. While it might be superficially persuasive that a parent should not be required to provide any financial information when he or she has conceded the ability to pay anything the court orders, such an approach is inconsistent with the legal framework of the *Federal Child Support Guidelines* and would not allow a court to make the appropriate analysis to determine whether to vary the support or to determine quantum. The Guidelines provide for mandatory disclosure regardless of any purported waiver by the parents. Where there is a legitimate concern that full financial disclosure would be costly and potentially prejudicial, the court may limit the amount of disclosure and seal sensitive information, provided that the financial disclosure ordered is sufficient to enable the court to determine the amount of support required to meet the children's reasonable needs. In *Quinn v. Keiper*,[391] the father, who conceded that his annual income exceeded $5 million, was ordered to provide the information required by sections 21(1)(a) and (b) of the Guidelines and complete a financial statement as required by Ontario Rule 13. In addition to his income tax returns for 2002, 2003, and 2004, he was ordered to disclose the amounts that he paid in meeting 100 percent of the children's special expenses that he undertook to pay under the terms of the 2001 separation agreement, which also provided for basic monthly support in the indexed amount of $5,000. Accepting that detailed additional financial disclosure in this case would have limited relevance and would be difficult, time-consuming, and expensive, the court was not satisfied that all the information in sections 21(1)(c)

---

389 *J.G.T. v. T.N.*, [2001] A.J. No. 1426 (Q.B.); *A.D.B. v. S.A.M.*, [2006] N.S.J. No. 252
(S.C.); *Connelly v. McGouran*, [2006] O.J. No. 993 (C.A.).

390 *Ibid.*

391 [2005] O.J. No. 5034 (Sup. Ct.).

to (g) of the Guidelines was necessary to determine the amount of child support to be ordered; consequently, it declined to order the father to provide additional back-up documentation with respect to partnerships or companies and with respect to values set out in his financial statement. The court reserved the right to order additional financial disclosure, if the need should become apparent in the future. Because public disclosure of the father's investment and trading strategies would be prejudicial to him and contrary to the best interests of the children in terms of his ongoing earning capacity, the court issued a sealing order with respect to the father's financial statement and income tax returns for a period of twelve months, with a reserved right for him to apply for an extension thereafter.

Sections 21 to 26 of the *Federal Child Support Guidelines* set out detailed provisions with respect to the acquisition and disclosure of information concerning spousal income and sanctions for non-disclosure. These provisions provide a new minimum standard of financial disclosure in child support proceedings. They are complemented by section 10(4) of the *Federal Child Support Guidelines*, which together with Schedule II of the Guidelines, requires additional financial disclosure to enable a court to undertake a comparison of the household living standards in cases where undue hardship exists.[392] The disclosure requirements of the *Federal Child Support Guidelines* may be supplemented by different, but not conflicting, provincial rules of practice and procedure.[393]

O. DISABILITY PAYMENTS AND CHILD SUPPORT

As illustrated in *Vickers v. Vickers*,[394] given that the table amount of child support is determined solely by reference to the obligor's income, federal or provincial monthly benefits paid to or for a child of a disabled parent are not deductible from the applicable table amount of child support that

---

392 *Buhr v. Buhr*, [1997] M.J. No. 565 (Q.B.).

393 *Le Bourdais v. Le Bourdais*, [1998] B.C.J. No. 2488 (S.C.).

394 [2001] N.S.J. No. 218 (C.A.). For decisions to similar effect, see *Trehearne v. Trehearne*, [2000] A.J. No. 1632 (Q.B.); *Wadden v. Wadden*, [2000] B.C.J. No. 1287 (S.C.); *Callaghan v. Brett*, [2000] N.J. No. 354 (S.C.); *Sayong v. Aindow*, [1999] N.W.T.J. No. 43 (S.C.); *St. Croix v. Maxwell*, [1999] O.J. No. 4824 (Sup. Ct.); *Sipos v. Sipos*, [2007] O.J. No. 711 (C.A.); *Rousseau v. Rousseau*, [1999] S.J. No. 76 (Q.B.); *Jones v. Jones*, [2005] S.J. No. 284 (Q.B.); *Peterson v. Horan*, [2006] S.J. No. 333 (C.A.); see *contra*: *Mullen v. Mullen*, [1998] N.B.J. No. 338 (Q.B.).

is payable under the *Federal Child Support Guidelines*. The income of the custodial parent or child is relevant only where there are special or extraordinary expenses within the meaning of section 7 of the Guidelines or where the court has a discretion,[395] such as under section 3(2) of the Guidelines if the child has attained the provincial age of majority,[396] or under section 5 of the Guidelines, which relates to the child support obligation of a spouse who stands in the place of a biological or adoptive parent,[397]or in shared-parenting arrangements under section 9 of the Guidelines,[398] or under section 10 of the Guidelines in circumstances of undue hardship.[399] On an application for special or extraordinary expenses under section 7 of the Guidelines, an obligor is not entitled to be credited dollar for dollar with respect to Canada Pension Plan payments made to children in consequence of the obligor's disability, but the amount received by the other parent will be included in that parent's income for the purpose of determining the proportionate parental contributions towards the expenses.[400] In Saskatchewan, the benefits payable under the Canada Pension Plan to the children of a disabled parent have been held not to constitute "special provisions" for the benefit of the children within the meaning of section 3(4)(a) of the *Family Maintenance Act*[401] and similar reasoning can be applied to sections 15.1(5) and 17(6.2) of the *Divorce Act*.

P. TYPES OF ORDERS

1) Interim Orders

Section 15.1(3) of the *Divorce Act* empowers a court to grant an interim order for child support. Interim and permanent orders fall subject to the same criteria under the *Divorce Act* and the *Federal Child Support Guidelines*. An interim order continues in force until a permanent order is

---

395 *Vickers v. Vickers*, [2001] N.S.J. No. 218 (C.A.); *Jones v. Jones*, [2005] S.J. No. 284 (Q.B.); *Peterson v. Horan*, [2006] S.J. No. 333 (C.A.).

396 *Burhoe v. Goff*, [1999] N.B.J. No. 296 (Q.B.); *Welsh v. Welsh*, [1998] O.J. No. 4550 (Gen. Div.).

397 *Fedoruk v. Jamieson*, [2002] B.C.J. No. 503 (S.C.).

398 *Jones v. Jones*, [2005] S.J. No. 284 (Q.B.).

399 *Alfaro v. Alfaro*, [1999] A.J. No. 1062 (Q.B.); *Dixon v. Fleming*, [2000] O.J. No. 1218 (Sup. Ct.).

400 *M.J.B. v. W.P.B.*, [1999] M.J. No. 314 (Q.B.).

401 *Peterson v. Horan*, [2006] S.J. No. 333 (C.A.).

granted and is not automatically terminated by divorce.[402] Although section 17 of the *Divorce Act* relates only to applications to vary permanent orders and section 15.1 of the *Divorce Act* includes no express provision for the variation of interim orders, a court has an inherent jurisdiction to vary an interim order.[403] In ordering permanent child support, a trial judge is not bound by a pre-existing order for interim child support. An amount payable under an interim order may be adjusted retroactively by a trial judge, if an erroneous assumption was made concerning the obligor's income.[404] However, a trial judge is not compelled to top up a pre-existing interim support order by a lump sum or supplementary periodic payments in light of a subsequent attribution of income.[405] Appellate courts have endorsed a general policy of not disturbing interim orders, unless there is a manifest error that requires immediate correction.[406]Interim variation orders, even though permissible under sections 15.1, 15.2, 16, and 17 of the *Divorce Act*, are not available as a matter of course. They should be regarded as exceptional. Courts generally frown upon multiplying interim proceedings and seek to encourage the parties to move without delay to a final resolution. If any inequities ensue, they can be addressed at trial.[407]

2) Periodic and Lump Sum Orders

Section 11 of the *Federal Child Support Guidelines* empowers a court to order payments under a child support order to be made by way of periodic sums, a lump sum, or a combination of both. Given that the provincial and territorial tables under the Guidelines fix a monthly sum for child support based on the obligor's annual income and the number of children, there appear to be significant limitations of the right of a court to order lump sum child support, although no corresponding limitations apply to orders for spousal support.[408] In the rare case where a lump sum order for

---

402 *Boznick v. Boznick* (1993), 45 R.F.L. (3d) 354 (B.C.S.C.).

403 See *Lipson v. Lipson* (1972), 7 R.F.L. 186 (Ont. C.A.); *Carvell v. Carvell*, [1969] 2 O.R. 513 (C.A.).

404 *Lewkoski v. Lewkoski*, [1998] O.J. No. 1736 (Gen. Div.).

405 *L'Heureux v. L'Heureux*, [1999] S.J. No. 437 (Q.B.).

406 *Phillips v. Phillips* (1985), 43 R.F.L. (2d) 462 (B.C.C.A.); *Chevalier v. Chevalier*, 2007 MBCA 131, [2007] M.J. No. 392.

407 *Hayden v. Stockwood*, [2006] N.J. No. 97 (U.F.C.); *Connell v. Connell*, [2006] P.E.I.J. No. 12 (S.C.T.D.). Compare *Werden v. Werden*, [2005] O.J. No. 5257 (Sup. Ct.).

408 *Finlay v. Finlay*, [2004] N.B.J. No. 448 (Q.B.); *Scorgie v. Scorgie*, [2006] O.J. No. 225 (Sup. Ct.), Timms J.; and *Chamanlall v. Chamanlall*, [2006] O.J. No. 251 (Sup. Ct.), Timms J. For a more detailed analysis of lump sum child support orders, see Julien

basic child support is granted, the court should capitalize the periodic payments that would otherwise have been ordered.[409] Such capitalization may warrant actuarial evidence being adduced.[410] Capitalization of child support payments is exceptional, but may be found appropriate where a parent has previously failed to discharge support obligations or is likely to do so in the future[411] or where the parent has a history of irresponsible money management.[412] An order for retroactive lump sum child support may be appropriate, where a non-custodial parent has failed to assume his or her fair share of financial responsibility for a child following spousal separation, thereby shifting an undue burden of child support to the custodial parent.[413] A lump sum may also be appropriate when a parent is ordered to make a contribution to special or extraordinary expenses falling within the ambit of section 7 of the *Federal Child Support Guidelines*.[414] Unless there has been a failure to recognize an obvious obligation or an attempt to avoid it, a parent should not ordinarily be ordered to pay a lump sum amount for child support on an interim basis.[415]

Adult children who pursue post-secondary education may be entitled to lump sum support payable out of a deceased parent's modest estate. Such an order may be granted pursuant to the Ontario *Family Law Act*, even if a corollary relief claim is unavailable under the *Divorce Act* following the respondent's death. The jurisdiction of a court to order lump sum support in the above circumstances is exercisable pursuant to the conjoint operation of sections 3(2)(b) and 11 of the *Federal Child Support Guidelines*. In assessing the amount of lump sum child support to be paid, the child support obligation takes priority over the rights of ordinary creditors and the declared beneficiaries of the deceased's estate. Due account must be taken, however, of the federal Crown's superior right to enforce the deceased's tax liabilities.[416]

D. Payne & Marilyn A. Payne, *Child Support Guidelines in Canada, 2006* (Toronto: Irwin Law, 2006) at 383–89.

409 See, for example, *Megaval v. Megaval*, [1997] B.C.J. No. 2454 (S.C.).
410 *Assinck v. Assinck*, [1998] O.J. No. 875 (Gen. Div.).
411 *Megaval v. Megaval*, [1997] B.C.J. No. 2454 (S.C.); *Bartole v. Parker*, [2006] S.J. No. 349 (Q.B.).
412 *Lobo v. Lobo*, [1999] A.J. No. 113 (Q.B.).
413 *Lackie v. Lackie*, [1998] O.J. No. 888 (Gen. Div.); *Krawczyk v. Krawczyk*, [1998] O.J. No. 2526 (Gen. Div.).
414 *Harrison v. Harrison*, [1998] B.C.J. No. 3090 (S.C.).
415 *Letourneau v. Letourneau* (1998), 131 Man. R. (2d) 123 (C.A.); *Chevalier v. Chevalier*, 2007 MBCA 131, [2007] M.J. No. 392.
416 *Hillock v. Hillock*, [2001] O.J. No. 3837 (Sup. Ct.).

3) Orders to Pay and Secure Child Support

Section 12 of the *Federal Child Support Guidelines* expressly empowers a court to order that child support be paid or secured, or paid and secured, in the manner specified in the order. The mutual exclusivity of orders to pay child support and orders to secure the payments, which was endorsed by the Supreme Court of Canada in *Nash v. Nash*,[417] no longer prevails under section 12 of the Guidelines. A court may now grant an order for the payment of child support, combined with an order to secure those payments. When granting an order to secure child support, a court should make it abundantly clear that the order is an order "to pay and secure" the child support ordered. Orders for security may be made against personal or real or personal property but should only be granted when there is a risk of default. It is an open question whether an obligor can be ordered to acquire life insurance to secure child support payments, where no policy existed on the date when relief was sought.[418]

Q. RETROACTIVE CHILD SUPPORT ORDERS UNDER THE *DIVORCE ACT*

Prior to the judgments of the Supreme Court of Canada in *D.B.S. v. S.R.G.; L.J.W. v. T.A.R.; Henry v. Henry; Hiemstra v. Hiemstra*,[419] provincial appellate courts in Canada were divided on two fundamental issues relating to retroactive child support orders. The first issue related to whether Canadian courts could order retroactive child support to be paid for a period of time that preceded the commencement of divorce proceedings.[420] The second issue related to the criteria to be applied in determining whether retroactive child support should be ordered in the diverse situations where such jurisdiction is possessed by the court.[421] On the first issue,

---

417 [1975] 2 S.C.R. 507.

418 See *Laczko v. Laczko*, [1999] O.J. No. 2577 (Sup. Ct.); compare *Berki v. Berki*, [1999] O.J. No. 843 (Gen. Div.); see also *Muslake v. Muslake* (1987), 6 R.F.L. (3d) 280 (Ont. U.F.C.).

419 [2006] S.C.J. No. 37.

420 For a review of the conflicting provincial appellate rulings, see *Mellway v. Mellway*, [2004] M.J. No. 300 (C.A.).

421 See, for example, *L.S. v. E.P.*, [1999] B.C.J. No. 1451 (C.A.); *Cabot v. Mikkelson*, [2004] M.J. No. 240 (C.A.); *Lu v. Sun*, [2005] N.S.J. No. 314 (C.A.); *Marinangeli v. Marinangeli*, [2003] O.J. No. 2819 (C.A.); compare the Alberta Court of Appeal judgments in *D.B.S. v. S.R.G.*, [2005] A.J. No. 2 (C.A.); *L.J.W. v. T.A.R.*, [2005] A.J.

the Supreme Court of Canada has accepted the reasoning of the majority judgment of the Alberta Court of Appeal in *Hunt v. Smolis-Hunt*[422] that "[a]n order for retroactive child support pre-dating the issuance [of] a petition for divorce is … a necessary incident to the dissolution of a marriage" and falls within the legislative authority of the Parliament of Canada. On the second issue, the Supreme Court of Canada was divided four-to-three. Subject to a potential finding of "undue hardship" within the meaning of section 10 of the *Federal Child Support Guidelines*, the minority judgment was disposed to holding parents fully accountable for any failure to pay increased child support in accordance with the Guidelines as and when their incomes materially increased. The majority judgment adopted a somewhat more conservative approach in endorsing the following conclusions:

1. So-called retroactive orders for child support are not truly retroactive. They simply enforce the pre-existing legal obligation of parents to pay an amount of child support commensurate with their income.[423]

2. When an application for retroactive child support is brought, it is incumbent on the court to analyze the federal or provincial statutory scheme under which the application is brought. Different policy choices by the federal and provincial governments must be judicially respected.

3. The propriety of a retroactive award can only be evaluated after a detailed examination of the facts of the particular case.

4. Retroactive orders should not be regarded as exceptional orders to be granted only in exceptional circumstances. Although the propriety of a retroactive order should not be presumed, it is not confined to rare cases.[424]

5. Child support is a right of the child that cannot be bargained away by the parents. Sections 15.1(5) to (8) and 17(6.2) to (6.5) of the *Divorce Act* control the extent to which parents can consensually determine their child obligations and the criteria defined therein take account of the standards prescribed by the *Federal Child Support*

No. 3 (C.A.); *Henry v. Henry*, [2005] A.J. No. 4 (C.A.); *Hiemstra v. Hiemstra*, [2005] A.J. No. 27 (C.A.).

422 [2001] A.J. No. 1170 at para. 32 (C.A.). See also *S. v. S.*, [2007] N.B.J. No. 422 (Q.B.).

423 *Ferguson v. Thorne*, [2007] N.B.J. No. 45 (Q.B.).

424 *Morgan v. Morgan*, [2006] B.C.J. No. 1795 (S.C.); *Ferguson v. Thorne*, [2007] N.B.J. No. 45 (Q.B.).

Guidelines.[425] Corresponding legislation is to be found under provincial child support regimes. Courts may order retroactive child support where circumstances have changed or were not as they appeared when a prior parental agreement was reached or court order was made.[426]

6. The underlying premise of both federal and provincial child support guidelines is that the amount of child support should reflect the obligor's income.[427]

7. Quite independently of any court order or any steps taken by the prospective recipient, there is a free-standing obligation on parents to support their children commensurate with their income. A parent who fails to do so will have failed to fulfill his or her child support obligation. Consequently, a parent has an obligation to increase the child support payments when his or her income increases.

8. Although the Guidelines do not impose a direct obligation on an obligor to automatically disclose income increases and adjust child support payments accordingly, this does not mean that a parent will satisfy his or her child support obligation by doing nothing. If his or her income increases without an appropriate increase in the amount of child support paid, there exists an unfulfilled legal obligation that may subsequently merit enforcement by means of a retroactive child support award.

9. The obligor's interest in certainty must be balanced with the need for fairness and flexibility. Relevant factors for consideration in determining whether a retroactive child support award is justified include whether there is a reasonable excuse why support was not sought earlier by the obligee; the conduct, blameworthy or otherwise, of the obligor; the circumstances of the child; and hardship that would be occasioned by a retroactive award. None of these factors is, in itself, determinative; the court should take an holistic approach.[428]

---

425 See *J.M.B. v. A.C.B.*, [2006] A.J. No. 487 (C.A.).

426 *Ewing v. Ewing*, [2007] A.J. No. 217 (C.A.).

427 *Morgan v. Morgan*, [2006] B.C.J. No. 1795 (S.C.).

428 *Albo v. Albo*, [2006] A.J. No. 1330 (Q.B.); *Ewing v. Ewing*, [2007] A.J. No. 217 (C.A.); *Loughlin v. Loughlin*, [2007] A.J. No. 74 (Q.B.); *Repchuk v. Repchuk*, [2007] A.J. No. 1482 (Q.B.); *St. Onge v. Bozarth*, [2008] A.J. No. 204 (Q.B.); *Morgan v. Morgan*, [2006] B.C.J. No. 1795 (S.C.); *C.A.R. v. G.F.R.*, [2006] B.C.J. No. 2102 (S.C.); *Boniface v. Boniface*, [2007] B.C.J. No. 614 (S.C.); *S.L.C. v. R.M.C.*, [2007] B.C.J. No. 773

10. An unreasonable delay in seeking support militates against a retro-active child support award but the court must bear in mind that child support is the right of the child and cannot be waived by par-ental agreement. Courts should not hesitate to find a reasonable excuse for the delay where the applicant harbours fears about a vindictive response from the obligor or lacks the financial or emo-tional means to bring an application or was given inadequate legal advice. Conversely, a parent who discloses income increases in a timely manner and who does nothing to pressure or intimidate the applicant will have gone a long way towards ensuring that the delay is characterized as unreasonable. Such a characterization does not inevitably preclude a retroactive award. It is simply one factor to consider when the court seeks to balance the obligor's interest in certainty with fairness to the children.

11. Blameworthy conduct, though not a prerequisite to retroactivity,[429] is an important factor to consider in determining the propriety of a retroactive child support award. Blameworthy conduct is accorded an expansive definition and arises whenever a parent knowingly chooses to ignore or evade his or her child support obligations. An obligor who does not automatically increase his or her child sup-port payments to reflect his or her increased income is not neces-sarily engaging in blameworthy conduct but objective factors can be used to determine whether the obligor had a reasonable belief that he or she was meeting his or her child support obligations.

12. In assessing the obligor's conduct, the court is not confined to looking at blameworthy conduct. Sometimes, an obligor's positive

(S.C.); *McConnell v. McConnell*, [2007] B.C.J. No. 1151 (S.C.); *J.W. v. M.H.W.*, [2007] B.C.J. No. 1597 (S.C.); *Leachman v. Leachman*, [2007] B.C.J. No. 1712 (S.C.); *H.(U.V.) v. H.(M.W.)*, 2008 BCCA 177, [2008] B.C.J. No. 717; *K.A.M. v. P.K.M.*, [2008] B.C.J. No. 121 (S.C.); *S.M.H. v. R.P.*, [2008] B.C.J. No. 254 (S.C.); *Ferguson v. Thorne*, [2007] N.B.J. No. 45 (Q.B.); *Dickson v. Dickson*, [2007] N.B.J. No. 259 (Q.B.); *S. v. S.*, [2007] N.B.J. No. 422 (Q.B.); *Fisher v. Munroe*, [2006] N.S.J. No. 439 (S.C.); *Kelly v. Kelly*, [2006] N.S.J. No. 494 (S.C.); *Doherty v. Decoff*, [2007] N.S.J. No. 263 (S.C.); *A.W.H. v. C.G.S.*, [2007] N.S.J. No. 262 (S.C.); *Allen v. Esau*, [2007] N.W.T.J. No. 64 (S.C.); *Debora v. Debora*, [2006] O.J. No. 4826 (C.A.); *Shea v. Fraser*, [2007] O.J. No. 1142 (C.A.); *Walkiewicz v. Walkiewicz*, [2007] O.J. No. 2249 (Sup. Ct.): *Baldwin v. Funston*, 2007 ONCA 381, [2007] O.J. No. 1986; *Connelly v. McGouran*, 2007 ONCA 578, [2007] O.J. No. 3201; *Banning v. Bobrowski*, [2007] O.J. No. 3927 (Sup. Ct.); *Emery v. Emery*, [2008] O.J. No. 844 (Sup. Ct.); *Smith v. Goethals*, [2006] S.J. No. 763 (Q.B.); *S.K. v. T.Z.*, [2007] S.J. No. 351 (Q.B.); *Gaspers v. Gaspers*, [2007] S.J. No. 507 (Q.B.); *Jarvis v. Parker*, [2008] S.J. No. 47 (Q.B.); *Dansereau v. Dansereau*, [2008] S.J. No. 114 (Q.B.).

429 *Tedham v. Tedham* (2003), 20 B.C.L.R. (4th) 56 (C.A.).

conduct will militate against a retroactive child support award. For example, an obligor who contributes to specific child-related expenses over and above his or her statutory obligations may be deemed to have met any increased child support obligation, although it must be borne in mind that the obligor is not free to decide how his or her child support obligation shall be discharged.[430] A court may, nevertheless, conclude that such contributions negate any justification for a retroactive child support award.

13. In determining whether a retroactive child support award is justified, the court should have regard to the circumstances of the child as they exist at the time of the application, as well as the circumstances of the child as they existed at the time when the support should have been paid.[431] For example, a child who is currently enjoying a relatively high standard of living may benefit less from a retroactive award than a child who is currently in need. And a child who suffered hardship in the past may be compensated through a retroactive award, although trial judges should not delve into the past to remedy all old familial injustices, such as the sacrifices made by a custodial parent on behalf of the child.

14. Hardship to the obligor and his or her new family dependants is a relevant factor to be considered in determining whether a retroactive child support award is justified. The minority judgment clearly spells out that the hardship must be "undue hardship" that satisfies the requirements of section 10 of the *Child Support Guidelines*. While the majority judgment accepts the premise that the Guidelines govern both retroactive and prospective child support orders, Bastarache J.'s analysis with respect to the impact of hardship[432] is not so clearly defined as to expressly confine its application to circumstances in which the very stringent requirements of section 10 of the Guidelines are satisfied. He does volunteer the statement that "[w]hile hardship for the payor parent is much less of a concern where it is the product of his/her blameworthy conduct, it remains a strong one where this is not the case."[433] He also acknowledges that courts should craft their retroactive awards so as to minimize hardship, for example, by ordering periodic pay-

---

430 *Haisman v. Haisman* (1994), 22 Alta. L.R. (2d) 56 at paras. 79–80 (C.A.).
431 *Morgan v. Morgan*, [2006] B.C.J. No. 1795 (S.C.).
432 *D.B.S. v. S.R.G.; L.J.W. v. T.A.R.; Henry v. Henry; Hiemstra v. Hiemstra*, [2006] S.C.J. No. 37 at paras. 114–16.
433 *Ibid.* at para. 116; see *Dansereau v. Dansereau*, [2008] S.J. No. 114 (Q.B.).

ments over a period of time to discharge the overall amount due. The exercise of this jurisdiction is consistent with section 11 of the *Federal Child Support Guidelines*.[434] Furthermore, if a court wishes to defer the payment of retroactive support or order payment by instalments, it may do so pursuant to sections 15.1(4) (original child support orders), or 17(3) of the *Divorce Act* (variation orders) which empower the court to impose "terms, conditions or restrictions" on its orders.[435]

15. There are two aspects to the judicial determination of the amount of any retroactive child support award. First, the court must determine the date to which the award should be retroactive. Second, the court must determine the dollar value of its order.

(i) Date of Retroactivity

The majority judgment examines four options as to the appropriate date when retroactive child support becomes payable, namely (i) the date when the application was made to the court; (ii) the date when formal notice was given to the obligor; (iii) the date when effective notice was given to the obligor; and (iv) the date when the amount of child support should have increased. Given the desirability of parents resolving the issue of child support promptly and without recourse to costly and emotionally draining litigation, the majority judgment favoured the third option. This option does not require the applicant to take any legal action. All that is required is that the topic be broached.[436] After that, the obligor can no longer assume that the *status quo* is fair to the child, and his or her interest in certainty in the management of his or her financial affairs is less compelling. While the date of effective notice will usually signal the applicant's attempt to change the child support obligation, an unwarranted, prolonged period of inactivity should not be ignored. Consistent with this approach and with section 25(1)(a) of the *Federal Child Support Guidelines*, which limits an applicant's request for financial disclosure by the obligor to the preceding three years, the majority judgment states that "it will usually be inappropriate to make a support award retroactive to a date more than three

---

434 See also *Michaud v. Michaud*, [2005] A.J. No. 1095 (Q.B.).

435 See, for example, *J.C.R. v. J.J.R.*, [2006] B.C.J. No. 2150 (S.C.).

436 *Neill v. Boudreau*, [2007] O.J. No. 169 (C.A.); see also *Lust v. Lust*, 2007 ABCA 202, [2007] A.J. No. 654; *Normandin v. Kovalench*, [2007] N.W.T.J. No. 105 (S.C.).

years before formal notice was given to the obligor." However, the date when increased support should have been paid will sometimes be a more appropriate date from which the retroactive order should start. Such will be the case where the obligor engages in blameworthy conduct, such as intimidation or misrepresentation, and a failure to disclose a material income increase itself constitutes blameworthy conduct. Given such conduct, the presumptive date of retroactivity will move back to the time when the obligor's circumstances materially changed.[437]

(ii) Amount

The *Divorce Act* confers a discretion on the courts to determine whether a child support order should be granted but the amount of any order after 1 May 1997 must be "in accordance with the applicable guidelines."[438] However, blind adherence to the table amounts set out in the Guidelines is neither required nor recommended. The first method whereby the court may deviate from the table amount of child support arises where undue hardship is established within the meaning of section 10 of the Guidelines. In addition to cases of undue hardship, courts may exercise their discretion with respect to amount in the diverse circumstances prescribed by sections 3(2) (adult children), 4 (parental annual income in excess of $150,000), and 9 (shared custody) of the Guidelines. A second method of adjusting the amount of support payable is exercisable by altering the time period encompassed by the retroactive award.[439] For example, where a court finds that there has been an unreasonable delay after effective notice of the child support claim was first given, the period of excessive delay might be excluded in calculating the retroactive award. Unless the statutory provisions mandate a different outcome, a court should not order retroactive child support in an amount that it considers unfair in light of all the attendant circumstances of the case.

16. The use of the phrase "at the material time" in the definition of "child of the marriage" in section 2(1) of the *Divorce Act* refers to the time of the application. Consequently, a child who is over the

---

437   *Shea v. Fraser*, [2007] O.J. No. 1142 (C.A.).
438   See *Divorce Act*, R.S.C. 1985 (2d Supp.), c. 3, ss. 15.1(3) and 17(6.1); *C.A.R. v. G.F.R.*, [2006] B.C.J. No. 2102 (S.C.).
439   *C.A.R. v. G.F.R., ibid.*

provincial age of majority and no longer economically dependent on his or her parents at that time is ineligible for a retroactive child award.[440] However, the fact that an application for the enforcement of child support arrears is brought after the children have ceased to be eligible for support does not necessarily preclude the recovery of arrears that accrued prior thereto, although it may be a relevant consideration.[441]

17. The aforementioned principles are inapplicable to the issue of retroactivity in the context of the cancellation of child support arrears.[442] The *D.B.S.* judgment, nevertheless, reiterates some principles of child support that are generally applicable, namely, the cardinal principle that support is the right of the child and both parents are obligated to support their children and monitor child support payments.

One issue that was not specifically addressed by the Supreme Court of Canada relates to whether a retroactive adjustment of Guidelines support payments should take place after the filing of income tax returns indicating that the amount of child support previously ordered was either too low or too high. In *Lavergne v. Lavergne*,[443] the Alberta Court of Appeal favoured such retroactive adjustment, stating that "[t]he child is entitled to be supported according to the payor's current income, if ascertainable, and if not, by a reasonably accurate estimate of the payor's current income with an adjustment at year's end once the actual income is known."

As a preventative measure that could significantly reduce the number of future claims for retroactive child support, the Alberta Court of Appeal in *D.B.S. v. S.R.G.*[444] stated that court orders and negotiated agreements should expressly provide an appropriate mechanism for the future varia-

---

440 *R.D.W. v. T.L.W.*, [2007] A.J. No. 489 (Q.B.); *D.M.B. v. J.R.B.*, [2007] A.J. No. 712 (Q.B.); *Oyama v. Oyama*, [2007] B.C.J. No. 643 (S.C.); *Stemmler v. May*, [2007] O.J. No. 3773 (Sup. Ct.); *Johnston v. Johnston*, [2006] S.J. No. 653 (Q.B.). Compare *Doherty v. Decoff*, [2007] N.S.J. No. 263 (S.C.).

441 *Ross v. Vermette*, [2007] S.J. No. 483 (Q.B.). See, generally, Section M(4), above in this chapter.

442 *C.A.R. v. G.F.R.*, [2006] B.C.J. No. 2102 (S.C.); *Adamson v. Steed*, [2006] O.J. No. 5306 (Sup. Ct.); *Matthews v. Matthews*, [2007] Y.J. No. 12 (S.C.).

443 2007 ABCA 169, [2007] A.J. No. 580 at para. 22. For trial judgment, see *R.E.L. v. S.M.L.*, [2006] A.J. No. 154 (Q.B.); see also *E.S. v. J.S.S.*, [2007] A.J. No. 832 (Q.B.); compare *Chalifoux v. Chalifoux*, [2006] A.J. No. 883 at para. 72 (Q.B.); *R.L.W. v. R.G.W.*, [2006] A.J. No. 1316 (Q.B.) (spousal support); *Martin v. Schaeffer*, [2001] S.J. No. 210 (Q.B.).

444 [2005] A.J. No. 2 (C.A.).

tion of child support obligations to reflect changes in parental income. It is incumbent on courts to ensure the recalculation of child support on a regular basis. At a minimum, orders for child support should routinely include the following provisions unless the attendant circumstances render them inappropriate. First, the payor should be required to annually disclose the financial information, including income tax returns, outlined in section 25 of the *Federal Child Support Guidelines*. Second, the court order should specify that the amount is subject to annual recalculation based on the then current income or as agreed upon between the parents. Third, the court order should provide that, if the parents are unable to agree on the amount of child support payable or the date when the adjusted payments will commence, then either parent may apply to the court to resolve the issues and/or make use of available alternative dispute resolution services.

It is open to a court to back-date an order for child support to the date of the commencement of the proceedings wherein notice of the statutory-based claim is provided. Such back-dating should not be characterized as an order for retroactive support that requires judicial consideration of the criteria identified by the Supreme Court of Canada in *D.B.S. v. S.R.G.*; *L.J.W. v. T.A.R.*; *Henry v. Henry*; *Hiemstra v. Hiemstra*, above.[445] A court may direct that child support as ordered shall be recalculated and retroactively adjusted in light of the obligor's income as revealed by his income tax return filed in the following year. Such an order will also be enforced without regard to the aforementioned criteria.[446]

A child support order may provide for a retroactive contribution to allowable expenses under section 7 of the *Federal Child Support Guidelines*. Whether such provision should be ordered will depend on the circumstances of the case, including but not limited to voluntary arrangements between the parents, the extent to which the expenditures were known, the custodial arrangements for the children, and the date of the application.[447] Many of the policy issues and factors that are addressed in relation to retroactive basic child support are also applicable to claims for a contribution to section 7 expenses under the *Federal Child Support Guidelines*. However, there is one fundamental difference. Basic child

---

445   *Hawco v. Myers*, [2005] N.J. No. 378 (C.A.). See also *MacKinnon v. MacKinnon*, [2005] O.J. No. 1552 (C.A.) (spousal support). Compare *Dillon v. Dillon*, [2005] N.S.J. No. 548 (C.A.).

446   *Chertow v. Chertow*, [2005] O.J. No. 1662 (C.A.).

447   *P.C.J.R. v. D.C.R.*, [2003] B.C.J. No. 729 (C.A.); see also *Clegg v. Downing*, [2004] A.J. No. 1511 (Q.B.).

support reflects the right of the child to have his or her essential needs met. Extraordinary expenses for extracurricular activities are not a basic right of the child and there is no inherent obligation in the parents to pay for such activities. An order for a retroactive contribution to such expenses may be deemed unfair where the father had no knowledge of these expenses and no idea that he might ultimately be called upon to contribute towards them.[448]

Retroactive variation of a child support order may result in a reduction, rather than an increase, in the amount payable, where the obligor's annual income had decreased from that originally accepted in a prior order. Lack of knowledge of the relevant facts may entitle a payor to reimbursement of overpayments of child support by means of a retroactive variation order, but such relief should not be granted to a payor who knew the facts but failed to take timely action to remedy the situation.[449] The decision whether to make a retroactive variation is a matter of broad discretionary authority. An order for a retroactive decrease was refused in *Simmonds v. Turner*,[450] in which the overpayment was minimal, the father had suffered no financial hardship, and the mother was unaware of the father's financial circumstances until he filed and served his application to vary. In *Hendrickson v. Hendrickson*,[451] institutional delays had occurred over which the father had no control but the mother had been advised of the father's intention to seek a reduction in the amount of child support within one month of the trial judge's written reasons. Under these circumstances, a substantial retroactive reduction in the table amount of child support and in the father's contribution towards section 7 expenses was deemed appropriate from the month following that in which the mother was advised of the father's intention to seek a variation order. The mother was given seven months to repay the overpayments of child support, if necessary by refinancing one of her two residential properties.

A non-custodial parent's obligation to support a child that is imposed pursuant to the *Family Maintenance Act* (Saskatchewan) or the *Divorce Act* terminates after the adoption of the child by a third party.[452]

---

448 *Clegg v. Downing*, [2004] A.J. No. 1511 (Q.B.).

449 *Collison v. Collison*, [2001] B.C.J. No. 2080 (S.C.).

450 [2005] N.S.J. No. 460 (S.C.). See also *Vance v. Kovacs*, [2005] N.B.J. No. 540 (Q.B.). Compare *Lawrence v. Gold*, [2007] A.J. No. 1199 (Q.B.).

451 [2005] N.S.J. No. 395 (S.C.).

452 *Reiss v. Reiss*, [2001] S.J. No. 37 (Q.B.). For differing judicial opinions on the retroactive impact of adoption on the enforcement of previously accrued support arrears, see *Musolino-Pearson v. Musolino* (1991), 35 R.F.L. (3d) 312 (N.S. Fam. Ct.),

R. PRIORITY OF CHILD SUPPORT OVER SPOUSAL SUPPORT; EFFECT OF CHILD SUPPORT ORDER ON ASSESSMENT OF SPOUSAL SUPPORT[453]

1) Relevant Statutory Provisions

Section 15.3 of the *Divorce Act* provides as follows:

Priority to child support

15.3(1) Where a court is considering an application for a child support order and an application for a spousal support order, the court shall give priority to child support in determining the applications.

Reasons

15.3(2) Where, as a result of giving priority to child support, the court is unable to make a spousal support order or the court makes a spousal support order in an amount that is less than it otherwise would have been, the court shall record its reasons for having done so.[454]

Consequences of reduction or termination of child support order

15.3(3) Where, as a result of giving priority to child support, a spousal support order was not made, or the amount of a spousal support order is less than it otherwise would have been, any subsequent reduction or termination of that child support constitutes a change of circumstances for the purposes of applying for a spousal support order, or a variation order in respect of the spousal support order, as the case may be.

2) Commentary

Section 15.3 of the *Divorce Act* addresses the situation where the application for child support and the application for spousal support involve members of the same family.[455] It does not establish priorities as between sequential families. For example, a former divorced wife's order for

---

Williams Fam. Ct. J., as he then was; *Smith v. Smith*, [2001] N.S.J. No. 87 (S.C.), Kennedy J.; compare *British Columbia (Maintenance Enforcement Director) v. Lagore*, [1993] B.C.J. No. 899 (Prov. Ct.), Rae Prov. Ct. J.

453 See D.A. Rollie Thompson, "The Chemistry of Support: The Interaction of Child and Spousal Support" (2006) 25 Can. Fam. L.Q. 251.

454 See *Pitt v. Pitt*, [1997] B.C.J. No. 1949 (S.C.), wherein the judgment was amended to reflect s. 15.3(2) of the *Divorce Act*.

455 *Hilborn v. Hilborn*, [2007] O.J. No. 3068 (Sup. Ct.).

spousal support will not be subject to a statutory priority in favour of the obligor's children from a second subsequently dissolved marriage. The difficulties that have plagued the courts respecting the competing claims of sequential families remain unresolved.

In consequence of the priority accorded to child support by section 15.3 of the *Divorce Act*, a court may be unable to grant a spousal support order because the obligor has no ability to pay any amount to satisfy the demonstrated need of the other spouse.[456] In granting an order for periodic spousal support, a court may acknowledge the amount to be less than would have been ordered but for the priority to be accorded to the needs of the children under section 15.3 of the *Divorce Act*.[457] A similar acknowledgment of the priority accorded to child support may be made where an order for lump sum spousal support is granted,[458] or where an order for spousal support is denied.[459]

Although periodic spousal support may be reduced or denied where child support obligations impair the obligor's ability to pay,[460] a lump sum spousal support payment may be practical.[461] In granting a lump sum order for spousal support, the court may expressly acknowledge a potential future right to periodic spousal support under section 15.3(3) of the *Divorce Act*.[462] Where the amount of spousal support has been reduced to accommodate child support payments, spousal support may be increased when these obligations cease.[463] A court may direct that an order for periodic spousal support shall be increased by the amount by which child support

456 *Bell v. Bell*, [1997] B.C.J. No. 2826 (S.C.); *Falbo v. Falbo*, [1998] B.C.J. No. 1497 (S.C.) (application for interim spousal support adjourned indefinitely); *Miao v. Chen*, [1998] B.C.J. No. 1926 (Prov. Ct.); *Cooper v. Cooper*, [2002] S.J. No. 226 (Q.B.).

457 *Langois v. Langois*, [1999] B.C.J. No. 1199 (S.C.); *Gray v. Gray*, [1998] O.J. No. 2291 (Gen. Div.); *Beatty v. Beatty*, [2000] O.J. No. 1755 (Sup. Ct.); *Whalen v. Whalen*, [2000] O.J. No. 2658 (Sup. Ct.).

458 *Lepage v. Lepage* (1999), 179 Sask. R. 34 (Q.B.).

459 *Falbo v. Falbo*, [1998] B.C.J. No. 1497 (S.C.).

460 *D'Entremont v. D'Entremont*, [2001] N.S.J. No. 586 (S.C.); *Norlander v. Norlander* (1989), 21 R.F.L. (3d) 317 (Sask. Q.B.); see also *Hunt v. Smolis-Hunt*, [2001] A.J. No. 1170 (C.A.) (spousal support to be revisited by trial court in light of appellate court's disposition of appeal respecting child support); *Kenning v. Kenning* (1995), 11 R.F.L. (4th) 216 (B.C.S.C.).

461 *Amaral v. Amaral* (1993), 50 R.F.L. (3d) 364 (Ont. Gen. Div.); *Kapogianes v. Kapogianes*, [2000] O.J. No. 2572 (Sup. Ct.); *Lepage v. Lepage*, [1999] S.J. No. 174 (Q.B.); compare *Whalen v. Whalen*, [2000] O.J. No. 2658 (Sup. Ct.).

462 *Lepage v. Lepage*, [1999] S.J. No. 174 (Q.B.).

463 *Sneddon v. Sneddon* (1993), 46 R.F.L. (3d) 373 (Alta. Q.B.); *Peters v. Peters*, [2002] N.S.J. No. 413 (S.C.); *MacArthur v. MacArthur*, [2004] N.S.J. No. 209 (S.C.).

is reduced when each of the children ceases to be entitled to support.[464] Before making any order, it is important to keep in mind that periodic payments for child support that are ordered after 1 May 1997 are tax-free, whereas periodic spousal support payments are deductible from the payor's taxable income and are taxable in the hands of the recipient spouse.[465] Courts must not overlook this difference when ordering what is, in effect, the conversion of child support payments into spousal support payments at some future date. An order whereby spousal support will be increased to a designated monthly amount on termination of the obligor's duty to pay court-ordered child support may be expressly declared to be subject to further variation by reason of a material change of circumstances,[466] although such a declaration is presumably unnecessary.

Although section 15.3(1) of the *Divorce Act* requires the court to give priority to child support over spousal support, this does not signify that special or exceptional expenses should be ordered under section 7 of the *Federal Child Support Guidelines* to supplement the basic amount of child support payable under the applicable provincial or territorial table, where such a supplementary allocation would render the custodial spouse destitute.[467] The priority of child support, including section 7 expenses,[468] over spousal support that is mandated by section 15.3 (1) of the *Divorce Act* does not preclude the court from giving consideration to spousal support and looking at the overall picture in determining the appropriate contribution, if any, to be made to special or extraordinary child-related expenses.[469]

A non-custodial parent who is ordered to pay periodic child support is not thereby disqualified from obtaining an order for periodic spousal support. Child support and spousal support, though necessarily intertwined, are separate concepts. The fact that the receipt of one may offset

---

464   *McLean v. McLean*, [1997] O.J. No. 5315 (Gen. Div.); see also *Smith v. Smith* (1998), 36 R.F.L. (4th) 419 at 425 (Ont. Ct. Gen. Div.); *Gritti v. Gritti*, [2001] O.J. No. 1363 (Sup. Ct.); *Cusack v. Cusack*, [1999] P.E.I.J. No. 90 (S.C.T.D.).

465   See *Rondeau v. Kirby*, [2003] N.S.J. No. 436 (S.C.).

466   *Lackie v. Lackie*, [1998] O.J. No. 888 (Gen. Div.).

467   *Lyttle v. Bourget*, [1999] N.S.J. No. 298 (S.C.); *Kaderly v. Kaderly*, [1997] P.E.I.J. No. 74 (S.C.T.D.); see also *Cameron-Masson v. Masson*, [1997] N.S.J. No. 207 (Fam. Ct.).

468   *Andrews v. Andrews*, [1999] O.J. No. 3578 (C.A.) (priority over spousal support given to extraordinary expenses for children's schooling pursuant to s. 38.1(i) of Ontario *Family Law Act*).

469   *Nataros v. Nataros*, [1998] B.C.J. No. 1417 (S.C.).

the payment of the other does not preclude an order for both kinds of relief in appropriate circumstances.[470]

Section 15.3 of the *Divorce Act* applies to both custodial and non-custodial parents.[471] Consequently, a custodial parent's obligation to provide financially for a child of the marriage takes priority over the obligation to pay spousal support to the non-custodial parent and may result in a reduction of the amount of spousal support that would otherwise be ordered.[472] A custodial parent cannot avoid the obligation to pay a reasonable amount of spousal support on the dissolution of a long marriage by calling upon the non-custodial parent to live at below the poverty level in order for the custodial parent to provide a child of the marriage with luxuries.[473]

Where a child has special needs due to a chronic illness, this may be taken into account in determining the ability to pay spousal support when the obligor is already committing significant resources to the child.[474]

Judicial opinions vary on the question whether it is appropriate or desirable to grant a nominal order for spousal support in circumstances where a substantial order is precluded by the priority accorded to a child support order. Some courts have ordered the nominal sum of $1 per year as spousal support because of the priority placed on child support obligations.[475] It has, nevertheless, been concluded that, where a parent with custody is unable to afford spousal support and the non-custodial parent is unable to pay child support, a court should decline to make any support order because "in case" nominal orders serve no useful purpose in that the parties are free to re-apply in the event of a change of circumstances.[476]

---

470 *Richter v. Vahamaki* (2000), 8 R.F.L. (5th) 194 (Ont. Sup. Ct.) (mother with annual income of $42,000; father with annual income of $104,000 and perhaps much more; father ordered to pay $1,000 per month as interim periodic spousal support; mother ordered to pay $605 per month for interim support of two children living with their father; child-care expenses to be totally assumed by father); see also *Varcoe v. Varcoe*, [2000] O.J. No. 229 (Sup. Ct.) (interim orders).

471 *Lockyer v. Lockyer*, [2000] O.J. No. 2939 at para. 52 (Sup. Ct.).

472 *Schick v. Schick*, [1997] S.J. No. 447 (Q.B.).

473 *Reyher v. Reyher* (1993), 48 R.F.L. (3d) 111 (Man. Q.B.).

474 *Broder v. Broder* (1994), 93 Man. R. (2d) 259 (Q.B.).

475 *Comeau v. Comeau*, [1997] N.S.J. No. 409 (T.D.); *Young v. Young*, [1999] N.S.J. No. 63 (S.C.).

476 *Frydrysek v. Frydrysek*, [1998] B.C.J. No. 394 (S.C.). See also *Gill-Sager v. Sager* (2003), 36 R.F.L. (5th) 369 (B.C.C.A.) and *Tierney-Hynes v. Hynes*, [2005] O.J. No. 2661 (C.A.), Chapter 8, Sections C(2) and R(4).

Where the spousal incomes are approximately equal after the payment of child support, a court may refuse to order spousal support until the child support obligation is eliminated.[477]

The cessation of child support payments does not inevitably justify an increase in the amount of spousal support payments.[478]

Where the combined income of the two spousal households has been substantially diminished in consequence of the application of the *Federal Child Support Guidelines* and accompanying amendments of the *Income Tax Act*, which took effect on 1 May 1997, a court may conclude that this constitutes a change of circumstances that warrants a reduction of the amount of spousal support under a pre-existing order so that the overall reduction in total income may be shared on some equitable basis by the former spouses.[479] On an application to vary the spousal support order on this basis, the court must be provided with accurate information concerning the after-tax income of the spouses before and after 1 May 1997.[480] In the absence of such information, an appellate court may conclude that a trial judge's order for a substantial reduction in the amount of court-ordered spousal support cannot be sustained, having regard to the financial disparity and apparent inconsistency between the old and new orders for spousal and child support, and may direct a new hearing on the issue of the amount of spousal support.[481]

Section 15.3(2) of the *Divorce Act* provides that, where a court is unable to make a spousal support order or makes an order in a reduced amount because of the priority accorded to child support, the court "shall record its reasons for having done so." Thomas Bastedo, a senior family law practitioner from Toronto, has concluded that "it is difficult to accept that the court will insist on section 15.3(2) as a precondition for its exercise of jurisdiction under subsection (3)."[482] But, as B. Lynn Reierson, a Halifax family law practitioner, has shrewdly observed,

> Although s. 15.3(3) of the *Divorce Act* establishes an automatic variation threshold, where the child support order relates to young children the

---

477 *Rupert v. Rupert*, [1999] N.B.J. No. 5 (Q.B.).

478 *Davis v. Davis*, [2000] N.S.J. No. 86 (S.C.).

479 *Desjardins v. Desjardins*, [1999] M.J. No. 70 (C.A.) (minority opinion of Huband J. The majority opinion of Scott C.J.M., with Monnin J.A. concurring, expressly declined to speculate on this issue.

480 *Ibid.*

481 *S.A.J.M. v. D.D.M.*, [1999] M.J. No. 118 (C.A.).

482 Thomas Bastedo, "Impact of *Child Support Guidelines* on Spousal Support" (November 1999) 11:3 *Matrimonial Affairs, CBAO Family Law Section Newsletter* 1 at 27.

opportunity to apply s. 15.3(3) to a spousal support variation application may not arise for many years. Entitlement on a compensatory basis, where need is not acute, may be very difficult to revisit at that future time.[483]

In the final analysis, there appear to be few, if any, distinct criteria to assist Canadian courts in balancing competing demands for child support and spousal support. Although the applicable table amount of periodic child support will normally be accorded priority over compensatory or even non-compensatory periodic spousal support, and the same priority may be accorded to necessary "special" expenses falling within section 7 of the *Federal Child Support Guidelines*, courts appear to be much less likely to accord priority to "extraordinary" expenses falling within the ambit of section 7 of the Guidelines, where there are insufficient funds to meet those expenses and also provide a basic level of necessary spousal support.

The impact of the *Federal Child Support Guidelines* on spousal support is not confined, however, to their substantive significance in light of section 15.3 of the *Divorce Act*. The effect of specific disclosure requirements under sections 21 to 26 of the *Federal Child Support Guidelines* has spread over into the context of spousal support.[484]

---

483 B. Lynn Reierson, "The Impact of *Child Support Guidelines* on Spousal Support Law and Practice" (Paper presented to Federation of Law Societies and Canadian Bar Association, The 2000 National Family Law Program, St. John's, Newfoundland 10–13 July 2000) c. 23-1 at 1.

484 *Ibid.* at 10–11.

CHAPTER 10

PARENTING ARRANGEMENTS AFTER DIVORCE[1]

A. INTRODUCTION

Since 1968, more than 1 million Canadian children have been affected by the divorce of their parents. More than 100,000 of these children have witnessed the breakdown of a second long-term relationship of their custodial parent.

Divorced mothers and their children have a high risk of living in poverty. Children who are raised in poverty by a single parent often encounter nutritional, health, and educational problems that significantly affect their adult lives.

Less than 4 percent of all divorce proceedings result in full-blown contested trials and, of these, very few involve disputes concerning the children. Less than 1 percent of contested divorce cases are confined to custody and access disputes.

More often than not, contested custody litigation is a reflection of continued and unresolved personal hostility between the spouses. Custody litigation may also disguise the real issue — which sometimes relates to money and property, rather than the children. A custodial parent may,

---

1   For sweeping proposals to change the law, see Canada, Parliament, Report of the Special Joint Committee on Child Custody and Access, *For the Sake of the Children* (Ottawa: Senate and House of Commons, December 1998) Summary of Recommendations 1–48 at xvii to xxiii.

for example, obtain an order for exclusive possession of the matrimonial home or an order for spousal support that would be unavailable if custody were denied to that parent.

A custodial parent has the authority to make decisions that affect the growth and development of a child, but is expected to exercise that authority in the best interests of the child. Where the parents disagree, either of them may institute legal proceedings to have the dispute resolved by a court.

B. PRESERVATION OF FAMILY BONDS; JOINT CUSTODY; MAXIMUM CONTACT PRINCIPLE

The history of custody during the last century has witnessed a radical judicial shift from a strong paternal preference, through a strong maternal preference, to the present-day philosophy that both parents are forever and marriage breakdown and divorce should not preclude continuing meaningful relationships between the child and both parents. Increased legal recognition of the importance of preserving the child-parent bond that evolved during the marriage is manifested by changes in orders for joint custody and access that have evolved over several decades. Before the first dominion-wide *Divorce Act* came into force in 1968, orders for joint custody were statistically insignificant. In recent years, courts have moved away from their former practice of granting sole responsibility for the children of separated or divorced parents to one of the parents and granting only access rights to the non-custodial parent. Today, some form of joint custody disposition is found in more than 40 percent of divorce cases. Thirty years ago, access orders entitled the non-custodial parent to spend a few hours with the child at the weekend and a few days with the child during school holidays. Today, a non-custodial parent is likely to be granted access privileges on one evening every week and overnight access from Friday to Sunday on alternate weekends. During the summer vacation, the non-custodial parent is frequently granted access for four to six weeks. Other vacations and statutory holidays will often be equally shared between the parents on a rotational basis.

Subsections 16(4), (5), and (10) of the *Divorce Act* go some way towards recognizing that divorce should not undermine the family bonds that a child develops during the marriage of his or her parents.

Subsection 16(4) of the *Divorce Act* empowers the court to make orders "granting custody of, or access to, any or all children of the marriage to any one or more persons." This subsection is of fundamental importance in that it recognizes a place for joint custody arrangements; it also entitles third parties, such as grandparents or other relatives, to enjoy access to the children of divorcing or divorced parents. Third-party applications for custody and access can only be brought by leave of court. Courts will only allow third-party applications to be brought by persons who have been previously involved in the child's life. Third-party custody orders are rare. Applications for access privileges by third parties, especially grandparents, are far more likely to be favourably received by the courts especially when such access will provide a measure of ongoing stability for the child. Grandparents have no presumptive right of access to their grandchildren and must discharge the onus of proving that they should have a continuing relationship with the child, notwithstanding the opposition of the custodial parent to access.[2]

Subsection 16(5) of the *Divorce Act* entitles a spouse who is granted access to make inquiries and to be given information concerning the health, education, and welfare of the children. Although subsection 16(5) falls short of giving equal participatory rights in the upbringing of the child to the non-custodial and the custodial parent, it provides the foundation for an exchange of opinions that may facilitate the non-custodial parent's meaningful involvement in decision making. While section 16(5) of the *Divorce Act* does not confer decision-making authority on the non-custodial parent, an equal right to participate in major decisions respecting a child's health, education, or welfare may be conferred by a joint custody order, notwithstanding that one of the parents is contemporaneously granted primary day-to-day care and control of the child. The mere fact that one parent is opposed to sharing major decision-making authority over the children does not preclude an order for joint custody. If the court is satisfied that the parents are capable of communicating and that the child would not be adversely affected, an order aimed at enhancing parental involvement in the child's life would generally seem consistent with the best interests of the child.[3]

Ongoing parental conflict is not an automatic bar to some form of joint custody or shared-parenting order but the degree of conflict may be sufficiently high to preclude any such order.[4] However, one parent can-

---

2   *C.M.L. v. R.S.T.*, [2000] S.J. No. 362 (Q.B.).

3   *V.L. v. D.L.*, [2001] A.J. No. 1259 (C.A.). In Ontario, guardianship of the person of a child is subsumed under "custody" of that child. "Guardianship" is a term that is confined to the guardianship of the property of a child: see *Children's Law Reform Act* (Ont.), R.S.O. 1990, c. C.12, Part III, especially ss. 20, 47–58, and 61.

4   *C.E.C. v. M.P.C.*, [2006] A.J. No. 383 (C.A.) (interim proceeding), citing *Richter v. Richter*, [2005] A.J. No. 616 at para. 11 (C.A.); see, generally, *Robinson v. Filyk*, [1996]

not create problems with the other parent and claim sole custody on the basis of a lack of co-operation.[5] In *Ladisa v. Ladisa*,[6] the Ontario Court of Appeal upheld the trial judge's order for joint custody, which provided for the two younger siblings, age thirteen and nine at the time of the appeal, to spend alternate weeks in each parental home. In dismissing the appeal in the absence of any demonstrated palpable and overriding error, the Ontario Court of Appeal observed that the trial judge's exercise of discretion properly took account of the history of co-parenting during the marriage, the wishes of the thirteen-year-old child, the absence of any compelling reason to separate the siblings, expert evidence presented by the Children's Lawyer who recommended joint custody, the evidence of third parties respecting the parent's interaction with the children, and the ability of the parents to communicate effectively and put their children's interests ahead of their own, notwithstanding ongoing parental strife. The provisions of the trial judge's order with respect to an older child, who was almost seventeen years of age at the time of the appeal, were vacated by the Ontario Court of Appeal on the basis that this child was now old enough to determine with whom she would live.

The judgment in *Ladisa v. Ladisa* may be compared with that of the same panel of judges of the Ontario Court of Appeal in *Kaplanis v. Kaplanis*.[7] In the latter case, the trial judge was found in error in granting an order for joint legal custody of a two-and-a-half-year-old child in the face of ongoing spousal conflict but in the hope parental co-operation would improve in the future after the parents received counselling. The trial judge was also found in error in ordering mandatory counselling for the parents with the unnamed counsellor being empowered to make decisions respecting the child's schools, activities, and hobbies, if the parents were unable to agree. While acknowledging that it might be desirable for parents to have recourse to a counsellor or parenting coach to resolve their disputes, the Ontario Court of Appeal stated that the

---

B.C.J. No. 2519, 84 B.C.A.C. 290; *Javid v. Kurytnik*, [2006] B.C.J. No. 3195 (C.A.); *D.C.R. v. T.M.R.*, [2007] B.C.J. No. 1684 (S.C.); *D.J.L. v. C.M.*, [2008] N.B.J. No. 7 (Q.B.); *Dubey v. Dubey*, [2008] B.C.J. No. 605 (S.C.) (joint custody inappropriate but joint guardianship ordered); *Newfoundland and Labrador (Director of Child, Youth and Family Services, Eastern Regional Integrated Health Authority) v. R.L.*, [2007] N.J. No. 420 (U.F.C.); *Radons v. Radons*, [2008] S.J. No. 116 (Q.B.); *E.J.M. v. D.D.I.*, [2008] Y.J. No. 18 (S.C.) (interim order).

5   *Lawson v. Lawson*, [2006] O.J. No. 3179 (C.A.).

6   [2005] O.J. No. 276 (C.A.). See also *Ursic v. Ursic*, [2006] O.J. No. 2178 (C.A.); *Cook v. Sacco*, [2006] O.J. No. 4379 (C.A.).

7   [2005] O.J. No. 275 (C.A.). See also *Roy v. Roy*, [2006] O.J. No. 1872 (C.A.).

counselling provisions of the order of the trial judge were problematic. In particular, the Ontario Court of Appeal observed that the legislation does not specifically authorize the court to order counselling, although some trial judges have held that such orders may be granted in the exercise of the court's inherent jurisdiction. In the present case, however, there was no evidence that the parties would be able to agree upon a counsellor and no agreed procedure was established for appointing a counsellor if the parents could not agree; nor was there any evidence that the parents were willing to have their disputes resolved by a counsellor outside the court process envisaged by the *Divorce Act* and without recourse to it. In addressing the broader issue of joint custody, the Ontario Court of Appeal expressed the opinion that the ongoing needs of the child require some evidence to be presented to the court that the parents, despite their differences, can effectively communicate with each other. Where such evidence is lacking or the evidence points to a parental inability to communicate, the hope that communication will improve once the litigation is over is an inadequate basis for making a joint custody order. Given its finding that this is what occurred in *Kaplanis v. Kaplanis*, the Ontario Court of Appeal substituted its own order for sole custody in favour of the mother and directed a rehearing of the issue of access, with the hope that the Children's Lawyer would become involved.

Where a court is concerned about the disruption caused by the children's frequent moves between the two parental households, the court may grant a "bird's nest" order whereby the children will reside in the home of one of the parents and each of the parents will be allotted specific blocks of time to spend with the children in that home. Although the benefits of a "bird's nest" order under which the parents visit the children rather than *vice versa* are best achieved where the children are able to stay in the matrimonial home, particularly if it is the only residence that they have known, all benefits are not lost merely because the matrimonial home has been sold and the parents have acquired separate residences.[8] As an alternative to an order whereby the children continue to reside in the matrimonial home and each parent lives in the home with the children at different periods of time, a court may grant exclusive possession of the home to one spouse but provide for specified access periods within the home by the non-custodial parent, during which time the custodial

---

8   *Hatton v. Hatton*, [1993] O.J. No. 2621 (Gen. Div.); *Greenough v. Greenough*, [2003] O.J. No. 4415 (Sup. Ct.).

parent must vacate the premises.[9] Given privacy concerns and the financial costs involved, "bird's nest" orders are exceptional even on a temporary basis, save in circumstances where the parents are agreeable to that form of order. Such orders, nevertheless, constitute one of the options available to promote shared parenting responsibilities.

Faced with a pattern of previous parental conflict, expert opinions may differ on the question whether the best interests of a child of separated or divorced parents will be served by a shared parenting regime. Judges in Quebec are inclined to grant orders for shared parenting only when the following conditions co-exist: (i) adequate parenting capacity; (ii) some minimal functional ability in the parents to communicate and co-operate; and (iii) geographic proximity of the two households. In a high-conflict situation where the expert evidence of a psychologist supports a finding that the parents are incapable of reaching a viable parenting plan that will meet the developmental needs of their child, the trial judge's refusal to grant an order for shared parenting should be upheld on appeal.[10]

Joint custody is a term that generates confusion. It may signify that separated or divorced parents will continue to share in making all major decisions concerning their child's health, education, and upbringing. In this context, it is sometimes called "joint legal custody" to differentiate it from "joint physical custody," which signifies that the child will reside with each parent for substantial periods. Joint physical custody may, but does not automatically, involve equal time sharing, such as three and one-half days a week with each parent, or alternating weeks or months with each parent. "Joint legal custody" usually exists when the parents have joint physical custody but "joint legal custody" can also exist independently of "joint physical custody."[11] Negotiated settlements and court orders should spell out parenting arrangements in unambiguous words that everyone can understand. This eliminates the risk that legal jargon such as "joint custody" will be misunderstood.[12] Although many Canad-

---

9   *Stefanyk v. Stefanyk* (1994), 1 R.F.L. (4th) 432 (N.S.S.C.).

10   *T.P.G. c. D.M.*, [2004] J.Q. no 5040 (C.A.).

11   *G.S. v. F.C.*, [2006] N.B.J. No. 477 (Q.B.); *L.B. v. B.B.*, [2007] N.B.J. No. 300 (Q.B.). Compare *T.(T.E.) v. L.(J.D.)* (2003), 16 R.F.L. (6th) 383 (Sask. Q.B.) and *Buxton v. Buxton*, [2006] S.J. No. 793 (Q.B.). For the most comprehensive judicial analysis in Canada of expert evidence relating to joint custody, see *G.V.C. v. G.E.*, [1992] Q.J. No. 337 (Sup. Ct.).

12   As to the inherent vagueness of the term "joint custody," see *Lennox v. Frender* (1990), 27 R.F.L. (3d) 181 at 185 (B.C.C.A.). See also *Gardiner v. Gardiner*, [2007] N.S.J. No. 367 (S.C.).

ian courts have been traditionally averse to granting any form of joint custody order where the parents have a history of ongoing substantial conflict after their separation, some courts have endorsed the concept of "parallel parenting" in cases where the parents are openly hostile and unco-operative.[13] Indeed, the conventional wisdom that joint custody and joint guardianship orders should only be granted when the parents can co-operate and communicate relatively well is being challenged in more and more cases, especially in Alberta,[14] British Columbia,[15] and Ontario.[16] The following characteristics of parallel parenting orders have been identified:

(i)   A parent assumes responsibility for the children during the time they are with that parent.

(ii)   A parent has no say or influence over the actions of the other parent while the children are in the other parent's care.

(iii) There is no expectation of flexibility or negotiation.

(iv)   A parent does not plan activities for the children during the other parent's time.

(v)   Contact between the parents is minimized.

(vi)   Children are not asked to deliver verbal messages.

(vii) Information about health, school, and vacations is shared in writing usually in the form of an access book.[17]

---

13 For a summary of the evolution of case law on joint custody in Alberta and Ontario, see *V.L. v. D.L.*, [2001] A.J. No. 1259 (C.A.); *Dagg v. Pereira* (2000), 12 R.F.L. (5th) 325 (Ont. Sup. Ct.). And see *Frame v. Frame*, [2007] M.J. No. 344 (C.A.); *Howard v. Howard*, [2007] S.J. No. 489 (C.A.). Compare the use of the "Joyce" style of joint guardianship order (elsewhere known as "joint legal custody"), which is frequently used in British Columbia, with or without a substantial child-parent time-sharing regime ("joint physical custody"): see for example, *S.D.N. v. M.D.N.*, [1997] B.C.J. No. 3027 (S.C.); *D.C.R. v. T.M.R.*, [2007] B.C.J. No. 1684 (S.C.).

14 *McCurry v. Hawkins*, [2004] A.J. No. 1290 (Q.B.); *Roberts v. Salvador*, [2006] A.J. No. 715 (Q.B.).

15 *Carr v. Carr*, [2001] B.C.J. No. 1219 (C.A.); *J.R. v. S.H.C.*, [2004] B.C.J. No. 2444 (Prov. Ct.); compare *Javid v. Kurytnyk*, [2006] B.C.J. No. 3195 (C.A.).

16 *T.J.M. v. P.G.M.*, [2002] O.J. No. 398 (Sup. Ct.); *Cox v. Down*, [2002] O.J. No. 2762 (Sup. Ct.), aff'd (*sub nom. Cox v. Stephen*), [2003] O.J. No. 4371 (C.A.); compare *Hildinger v. Carroll*, [2004] O.J. No. 291 (C.A.), leave to appeal to S.C.C. refused, [2004] S.C.C.A. 254. See also *Ursic v. Ursic*, [2006] O.J. No. 2178 (C.A.); *D.T.V. v. G.G.*, [2007] O.J. No. 3924 (Sup. Ct.); *J.T. v. S.C.-T.*, [2008] O.J. No. 426 (Sup. Ct.).

17 *Broder v. Broder*, [1998] A.J. No. 104 (Q.B.); *McCurry v. Hawkins*, [2004] A.J. No. 1290 (Q.B.). See also *Hensell v. Hensell*, [2007] O.J. No. 4189 (Sup. Ct.).

In *V.L. v. D.L.*,[18] the Alberta Court of Appeal summarized various judicial and legislative efforts to ensure that the children of separated or divorced parents continue to benefit from the input of both parents on the breakdown of the family unit. The task of the court is to find a parenting arrangement that optimizes the children's best interests. In some, but not all, cases in which the parents can no longer co-operate, an order for parallel parenting may constitute a viable option. Such an order has three advantages. First, it allows the court to make decisions on disputed evidence because an order for parallel parenting typically requires the parents to maintain a communications record, thereby enabling the court to decide which of the parents is unreasonable, controlling, or obstructive. Second, and more important, it gives primacy to the children's best interests rather than to the dispute between the parents. A parallel parenting regime avoids a destructive result in that it enables both parents to have continuing input into their children's lives, rather than have one of them reduced to the role of a passive observer or babysitter as a result of ongoing hostility and lack of co-operation between the parents. Because custody and access orders are never final, a parallel parenting order can always be revisited if it fails to accommodate the best interests of the children. In granting its initial order, therefore, a court does not have to make a permanently binding choice between optimism and prudence. It is well placed to monitor the effects of a parallel parenting regime and, if it becomes satisfied that an ongoing poor relationship between the parents is having a detrimental effect on the children, the parenting regime can be changed. The third advantage of parallel parenting is that it nurtures the objective of ensuring, insofar as is practicable, maximum contact between the children and their two parents, a legislative objective that has been endorsed by the Parliament of Canada in the *Divorce Act* and by provincial legislation that deals with both married and unmarried parents.

Subsections 16(10) and 17(9) of the *Divorce Act* extol the virtues of preserving the parent-child bond after divorce. They expressly require the court, in making an order for custody or access, or a variation order relating thereto, to give effect to the principle that a child of the marriage should have as much contact with each spouse or former spouse as is consistent with the best interests of the child and, for that purpose, shall

---

18   [2001] A.J. No. 1259 (C.A.). For a useful and succinct review of the increasing use of "parallel parenting" orders in high-conflict custody disputes, see *J.R. v. S.H.C.*, [2004] B.C.J. No. 2444 (Prov. Ct.), Tweedale Prov. Ct. J.

take into consideration the willingness of the person for whom custody is sought to facilitate such contact."[19] The maximum contact principle does not necessarily call for alternating weekly parenting arrangements or other equal time-sharing arrangements,[20] although such an order may be deemed appropriate in light of the attendant circumstances. [21]

An order for joint guardianship and custody confers equal decision-making authority on each parent with respect to major developments in their children's lives. Each of the joint guardians has what amounts to a veto concerning major decisions affecting the children. When one party exercises a veto, the only recourse for the other party is to apply to the court for a determination that the veto is not in the best interests of the children. When the parents disagree concerning a dangerous activity, the court may be required to determine whether the potential danger is outweighed by the potential benefit to the children. In *Chammout v. Chammout*,[22] Veit J., of the Alberta Court of Queen's Bench, observed that the court could take judicial notice of the political turmoil currently being experienced in Lebanon, which had been acknowledged in a travel advisory issued by the Canadian government. Pending stabilization of its political situation, Veit J. concluded that the potential dangers of the children travelling to Lebanon outweighed the importance of the children maintaining family ties with their paternal grandparents in Lebanon and the father was consequently precluded from taking or sending the children to Lebanon without the consent of the mother or a further order of the court. As to the future, Veit J. suggested that the parents might consider whether visits to Lebanon might be possible on stipulated conditions similar to those imposed by the Ontario Court of Appeal in *Kazdan v. Kazdan*.[23]

Where a joint custody order is inappropriate, section 16(10) of the *Divorce Act* endorses the principle that a child of divorcing or divorced parents has the right to a meaningful post-divorce relationship with both parents and the child's best interests are presumptively served, therefore, by an access order. Such an order enables the child and parent to develop or maintain a positive relationship and facilitates the parent's on-

19   See *Young v. Young*, [1993] 4 S.C.R. 3, 49 R.F.L. (3d) 117 at 150 at para. 17; *Lust v. Lust*, [2007] A.J. No. 654 (C.A.); *Wilkinson-Hughes v. Hughes*, [2008] O.J. No. 736 (Sup. Ct.); *Magnus v. Magnus*, [2006] S.J. No. 510 (C.A.).

20   *Dempsey v. Dempsey*, [2004] B.C.J. No. 2400 (S.C.).

21   *Moreau v. Moreau*, [2004] A.J. No. 1296 (Q.B.).

22   [2005] A.J. No. 219 (Q.B.).

23   [2002] O.J. No. 2478 (C.A.).

going contribution to the child's development during his or her formative years.[24]

Orders whereby infants and toddlers enjoy overnight access to their non-custodial parent should no longer be regarded as exceptional. The view formerly held by social scientists that overnight access for infants is undesirable, reflects an outdated perception of parent-child relationships and is inconsistent with current research on child development. Infants readily adapt to the different household environments provided that feeding and sleeping routines are similar in each household to ensure stability.[25] Consistent with this approach and with a recommendation that the father accept the primary-caregiving mother's advice respecting the child's routines and schedules, Wilson J. in *Lygouriatis v. Gohm*[26] granted the father interim access to a three-month-old child that included specified overnight access on alternate weekends. Different considerations may apply where a substantial block of summer access is sought. In *Ursic v. Ursic*,[27] Laskin J.A., of the Ontario Court of Appeal, accepted the opinion of an expert witness that the father's access to a three-year-old child for a full, uninterrupted month during the summer would be inappropriate, having regard to the child's age and state of development, and would likely be harmful to the child's sense of security and primary attachments.

C. TERMS AND CONDITIONS

1) General

Subsection 16(6) of the *Divorce Act* confers a broad discretion on the court to grant custody or access for a definite or indefinite period and subject to any such terms, conditions, or restrictions as the court thinks fit.[28] Where a divorce judgment incorporates the terms of a separation agreement that provides for a review of the residential care of the children

---

24 *M.E.E. v. T.R.E.*, [2002] N.S.J. No. 425 (S.C.); compare *K.R.C. v. C.A.C.*, [2007] N.S.J. No. 314 (S.C.).

25 *Cooper v. Cooper*, [2002] S.J. No. 226 (Q.B.), citing Joan B. Kelly & Michael E. Lamb, "Using Child Development Research to Make Appropriate Custody and Access Decisions for Young Children" (July 2000) 38:3 Family and Conciliation Courts Review 297 at 308–9. See also *Marsden v. Murphy*, [2007] A.J. No. 830 (Q.B.).

26 [2006] S.J. No. 609 (Q.B.).

27 [2006] O.J. No. 2178 (C.A.).

28 *Lust v. Lust*, [2007] A.J. No. 654 (C.A.) (interim custody order coupled with judicial directions for counselling).

after a designated period of time, such a review does not require proof of a material change of circumstances since the granting of the divorce.[29] Courts are generally reluctant to impose restrictions that limit the powers of the custodial parent, although they may be restrained from removing the children from the province where they ordinarily resided before the divorce. Some courts have issued an injunction to prohibit a custodial parent from leaving the province with the children when this would undermine the bond that the children have with the non-custodial parent. Although these decisions reflect the court's determination of what is in the child's best interests, no court has ever prohibited a non-custodial parent from leaving a province on the basis that the planned departure would undermine access to the children and be detrimental to their best interests. Whether prohibitions or restrictions on the right to remove children from the province may contravene the "mobility" right guaranteed by section 6 of the *Canadian Charter of Rights and Freedoms*, remains to be determined.

In the absence of spousal hostility, courts will often order "reasonable," "liberal," or "generous" access and leave it to the parents to work out the details. This provides flexibility that can accommodate the interests and needs of each parent and also those of the child. When spouses are still at war and cannot work out an access schedule, the court will step in to fill the vacuum by stipulating the time and place for access.

Where appropriate, a court may order supervised access, which signifies that a third party will be present when access privileges are being exercised. Supervised access may be ordered when some risk to the child is envisaged. Supervised access creates an artificial environment that inhibits the development of a natural, healthy parent-child relationship. Consequently, it should only be imposed by a court in unusual circumstances.[30] Supervised access may be found appropriate where there is reason to question a non-custodial parent's fitness to parent, or ability to protect the child, if domestic violence, child abuse, or parental alienation has occurred, or if there has been no contact between the parent and child for an appreciable length of time. Supervised access is used as a last resort and should not become a permanent feature of a child's life. It is intended to provide a temporary and time-limited means of resolving a parental impasse over access and should not be used as a long-term

---

29   *Sather v. McCallum*, [2006] A.J. No. 1241 (C.A.).

30   *C.(R.M.) v. C.(J.R.)* (1995), 12 R.F.L. (4th) 440 (B.C.S.C.); *Mitchell v. Mitchell* (1988), 16 R.F.L. (3d) 462 (Sask. Q.B.).

solution.[31] In *Markand v. Markand*,[32] the Ontario Court of Appeal dismissed the appellant's submission that the trial judge had erred in law by ordering supervised access to the children for an indefinite term, being of the opinion that the trial judge was aware that her order was exceptional in that it included no provision for a transition to unsupervised access nor any prescribed review date. While acknowledging that such an order should only be made in rare circumstances, the Ontario Court of Appeal found that the record fully supported the trial judge's decision to order the continuation of supervised access because of the appellant's attempts to manipulate the children and pressure them into living with him. In rejecting the appellant's submission that the order of the trial judge rendered it practically impossible for the appellant to obtain a future order for unsupervised access, the Ontario Court of Appeal pointed out that the trial judge's order in no way precluded a future application to vary the terms of access upon proof of a material change of circumstances.

2) Intended Change of Residence; Mobility Rights

Pursuant to subsection 16(7) of the *Divorce Act*, any person granted custody of a child may be required to give notice of any change of residence to any other person who has been granted access privileges. In the absence of any specified period to the contrary, such notice must be given thirty days in advance of the change of residence. Given such notice, the person with access privileges may apply to the court to challenge the intended change of residence of the child or seek variation of the custody or access arrangements in order to preserve meaningful contact with the child.

The issue of mobility rights was addressed by the Supreme Court of Canada in *Gordon v. Goertz*[33] wherein the custodial parent, the mother, intended to move to Australia and wished to take her daughter with her.

---

31   *M.(B.P.) v. M.(B.L.D.E.)* (1992), 42 R.F.L. (3d) 349 (Ont. C.A.), citing Judge Norris Weisman, "On Access after Parental Separation" (1992), 36 R.F.L. (3d) 35 at 74, leave to appeal to S.C.C. refused (1993), 48 R.F.L. (3d) 232 (S.C.C.). Compare *V.S.G. v. L.J.G.*, [2004] O.J. No. 2238 (Sup. Ct.), Blishen J. See also *C.T. v. J.T.*, [2007] B.C.J. No. 937 (Prov. Ct.).

32   [2006] O.J. No. 528 (C.A.).

33   [1996] 2 S.C.R. 27, 19 R.F.L. (4th) 177 at paras. 49–50. And see *C.L.R. v. R.A.R.*, [2006] B.C.J. No. 945 (C.A.); *Orring v. Orring*, [2006] B.C.J. No. 2996 (C.A.); *Harris v. Mouland*, [2006] N.S.J. No. 404 (C.A.); *Cameron v. Cameron*, [2006] N.S.J. No. 247 (C.A.); *K.C. c. N.P.*, [2006] Q.J. No. 8697 (C.A.). See also Nicholas Bala & Joanna Harris, "Parental Relocation: Applying the Best Interests of the Child Test in Ontario" (2006) 22 Can. J. Fam. L. 127.

Upon learning this, the non-custodial parent, the father, applied for custody of the child or, alternatively, an order restraining the mother from removing the child. The mother cross-applied to vary access so as to permit her to change the child's residence to Australia. In the majority judgment of McLachlin J., as she then was, which represented the opinion of seven of the nine judges, the law was summarized as follows:

1. The parent applying for a change in the custody or access order must meet the threshold requirement of demonstrating a material change in the circumstances affecting the child.

2. If the threshold is met, the judge on the application must embark on a fresh inquiry into what is in the best interests of the child, having regard to all the relevant circumstances relating to the child's needs and the ability of the respective parents to satisfy them.

3. This inquiry is based on the findings of the judge who made the previous order and evidence of the new circumstances.

4. The inquiry does not begin with a legal presumption in favour of the custodial parent, although the custodial parent's views are entitled to great respect.

5. Each case turns on its own unique circumstances. The only issue is the best interests of the child in the particular circumstances of the case.

6. The focus is on the best interests of the child, not the interests and rights of the parents.

7. More particularly the judge should consider, *inter alia*:

    (a) the existing custody arrangement and relationship between the child and the custodial parent;

    (b) the existing access arrangement and the relationship between the child and the access parent;

    (c) the desirability of maximizing contact between the child and both parents;

    (d) the views of the child;

    (e) the custodial parent's reason for moving, only in the exceptional case where it is relevant to that parent's ability to meet the needs of the child;[34]

    (f) disruption to the child of a change in custody;

    (g) disruption to the child consequent on removal from family, schools, and the community he or she has come to know.

---

34 See *MacPhail v. Karasek*, [2006] A.J. No. 982 (C.A.).

In the end, the importance of the child remaining with the parent to whose custody it has become accustomed in the new location must be weighed against the continuance of full contact with the child's access parent, its extended family and its community. The ultimate question in every case is this: what is in the best interests of the child in all the circumstances, old as well as new?

In applying the above criteria to the facts of the case, the Supreme Court of Canada, in both its majority and dissenting judgments, concluded that the mother's custody of the child should be continued, notwithstanding her intended move to Australia. However, the access arrangements were varied to provide for access to be exercisable in Canada so that the father's limited time with the child would be more natural and the child could maintain contact with friends and the extended family.

In determining whether a custodial parent should be entitled to relocate with the children, Burnyeat J., of the British Columbia Supreme Court, has identified the following twelve factors as relevant together with pertinent jurisprudence dealing with each of them:

(i)   the parenting capabilities of and the children's relationship with their parents and new partners;
(ii)   the employment security and the prospects of each parent and, where appropriate, their partner;
(iii)   access to and support of extended family members;
(iv)   any difficulty in exercising the proposed access and the quality of the proposed access if the move is allowed;
(v)   the effect upon the children's academic situation;
(vi)   the psychological/emotional well-being of the children;
(vii)   disruption of the children's existing social and community support and routines;
(viii) the desirability of the proposed new family unit for the children;
(ix)   the relative parenting capabilities of each parent and their respective ability to discharge parenting responsibilities;
(x)   the child's relationship with both parents;
(xi)   any separation of siblings; and
(xii)   retraining/educational opportunities for the moving parent.[35]

Gordon v. Goertz,[36] sets out the legal framework for analyzing cases involving a provincial change of residence by a custodial parent. The pri-

---

35   *One v. One*, [2000] B.C.J. No. 2178 (S.C.).
36   [1996] 2 S.C.R. 27, 19 R.F.L. (4th) 177.

mary issue is not the appropriateness of the move, unless there is evidence of the underlying purpose being to interfere with access by the non-custodial parent. Rather, where the move constitutes a material change of circumstances, the issue becomes a reconsideration of which parent is better qualified to have custody of the child under the present circumstances. *Gordon v. Goertz* acknowledges that a trial judge is entitled to give some weight to the existing custody order in determining whether the best interests of the child will be served by allowing the custodial parent to relocate with the child. Where the moving parent, after a reconsideration of all relevant factors, is still found to be the appropriate custodial parent, variation of the terms of access may be justified so as to reflect the new realities. If access problems have been encountered in the past, it may be necessary to spell out where access shall be exercised and at whose expense so that the maximum contact principle under section 17(9) of the *Divorce Act* can be accommodated.[37] In determining whether a custodial parent should be entitled to relocate with the child to another country, the custodial parent's perceptions of his or her personal academic and professional interests should not be confused with a detached appreciation of the child's best interests.[38]

In *Spencer v. Spencer,*[39] the Alberta Court of Appeal held that the chambers judge erred in finding that the mother's proposed relocation with the two children from Calgary, Alberta to Victoria, British Columbia constituted a material change of circumstances, given the father's extremely infrequent access to the children over the preceding five years and his exercise of regular access only after learning of the mother's intention to relocate to Victoria with her current spouse and the children. The Alberta Court of Appeal also concluded that, even if a material change were assumed, the chambers judge erred by overemphasizing the desirability of maximizing the children's contact with their father and by failing to give appropriate weight to the mother's wishes and the impact on the children if they were left in the custody of their father in Calgary. The Alberta Court of Appeal expressed concern about the "double bind" faced by custodial parents who acknowledge (as the mother did in this case) that they would abandon their relocation plans if the children were unable to accompany them. If a custodial mother, in response to an in-

---

37   *Brink v. Brink,* [2002] P.E.I.J. No. 7 (C.A.).
38   *K.C. c. N.P.,* [2006] Q.J. No. 8697 (C.A.). Compare *MacPhail v. Karasek,* [2006] A.J. No. 982 (C.A.). See also *H.S. v. C.S.,* [2006] S.J. No. 247 (C.A.).
39   [2005] A.J. No. 934 (C.A.).

quiry, states that she is unwilling to remain behind with the children, her answer raises the prospect of her being regarded as selfish in placing her own interests ahead of the best interests of the children. If, on the other hand, she is willing to forgo the relocation, her willingness to stay behind "for the sake of the children" renders the *status quo* an attractive option for the presiding judge to favour because it avoids the difficult decision that the application otherwise presents. In *Spencer v. Spencer,* the chambers judge was found to have erred in failing to address the effect on the children if they were left in Calgary without their mother, their stepfather, and their soon-to-be-born sibling, and the effect on them if they were left in the care of their father, who the chambers judge found was unable to assume primary care or even significant responsibility for the children. The mother's appeal was allowed and the order prohibiting her from taking the children to Victoria was set aside. Failing parental agreement on access, this issue was ordered to be returned to the Alberta Court of Queen's Bench for determination.

The criteria in *Gordon v. Goertz* apply whether mobility rights arise on an original application for custody or on an application to vary an existing custody order.[40] They also apply not only to proceedings under the *Divorce Act* but also to proceedings under provincial legislation. Geographically distant interprovincial relocations as well as extraprovincial relocations fall subject to the same criteria. The principles defined in *Gordon v. Goertz* do not provide a precise formula; each case must ultimately be determined on its own facts.[41] Where relocation issues arise on an interim motion, the following considerations have been regarded as important:

(i)   A court is more reluctant to disturb the *status quo* by permitting the move on an interim basis, where there is a genuine issue for trial.

(ii) There can be compelling circumstances that warrant relocation where, for example, financial benefits would be lost if relocation awaited a trial or the best interests of the children dictate that they commence school at a new location.

(iii) Although there may be a genuine issue for trial, the relocation may be authorized on an interim basis, if there is a strong probability that the custodial parent's position will prevail at trial.

---

40   *Nunweiler v. Nunweiler* (2000), 5 R.F.L. (5th) 442 (B.C.C.A.).

41   *Sulatyski-Waldack v. Waldack,* [2000] M.J. No. 412 (Q.B.).

Although relocation issues typically turn upon the facts of the particular case and previous case law is only of limited assistance, it is generally acknowledged that there should be a pressing reason for an immediate move before a court permits the relocation of children on a motion for interim relief.[42]

A court is not bound by the terms of a prior separation agreement in determining whether to permit the primary residential parent to relocate with the children, nor is an unforeseen material change of circumstances since the execution of the agreement a prerequisite to a court order that varies the terms of the agreement.[43]

With the increasing mobility of Canadian families, non-removal clauses have become fashionable in separation agreements and court orders regulating the custody of and access to children on the breakdown of spousal relationships. These clauses have been used to flag the notion that extraprovincial removal of the children must not occur without parental consent or a court order. The practical significance of such an express clause is that the task falls on the custodial parent to initiate an application to the court, if relocation is sought without the consent of the non-custodial parent. If a separation agreement or court order is silent with respect to removal, the non-custodial parent has the responsibility of bringing the matter to court to prevent the custodial parent's proposed removal of the children. In either situation, the court has the clear jurisdiction to determine whether the children can leave the province. When the agreement or court order is silent and the custodial parent chooses not to notify the non-custodial parent until after the relocation has occurred, the custodial parent runs a significant risk of incurring substantial expenses and losses in consequence of a subsequent court order requiring the children to reside in the province from which they have been unilaterally removed. Custodial parents who are not legally represented might not understand that they have a moral obligation to notify the non-custodial parent of any proposed relocation of the children but

---

42   The aforementioned three factors were identified by Marshman J. in *Plumley v. Plumley*, [1999] O.J. No. 3234 (Sup. Ct.) and have been endorsed in later cases: see *MacDonald v. MacDonald*, [2002] O.J. No. 2317 (Sup. Ct.); *Terris v. Terris*, [2002] O.J. No. 3018 (Sup. Ct.); *Vanderhyden v. Vanderhyden*, [2002] O.J. No. 3769 (Sup. Ct.); *Tiffin v. Verrette*, [2006] O.J. No. 4979 (Sup. Ct.); *Datars v. Graham*, [2007] O.J. No. 3179 (Sup. Ct.); *D.P. v. R.B.*, [2007] P.E.I.J. No. 53 (S.C.A.D.); *Ivens v. Ivens*, [2008] N.W.T.J. No. 11 (S.C.); compare *Comeau v. Dennison*, [2006] O.J. No. 5088 (Ct. Just.); *D.M. v. M.B.*, [2002] S.J. No. 621 (Q.B.).

43   *C.R.H. v. B.A.H.*, [2005] B.C.J. No. 1121 (C.A.).

common sense dictates that they should do so no matter how inconvenient it might be for the custodial parent to remain in the province and seek the necessary court approval. The *Divorce Act* does not expressly authorize a court to order the return of children or to order a divorced parent to live in a particular location. However, these consequences may ensue pursuant to section 17(3) of the *Divorce Act*, which incorporates by reference the provisions of section 16(6) of the *Divorce Act*, and thereby empowers the court on an application to vary a custody order to impose such "terms, conditions or restrictions in connection therewith as it thinks fit and just."

In custody cases involving mobility, the task of balancing the various factors that would affect the children's best interests in reaching a decision whether or not to permit the relocation of the children is an almost impossible one. The one tool available to the court in finding a balance is the ability to order block access. A relocation, no matter how valid the reasons, should not result in a termination of the relationship between the children and their non-custodial parent. Regular and frequent access is usually not possible when divorced parents live in different provinces or countries. Block access is often the only solution under these circumstances. A custodial parent may be required to accept a considerable amount of inconvenience and expense to facilitate block access, if the custodial parent seeks judicial approval of an extraprovincial relocation of the children. Having regard to the superior financial means of the custodial parent and the obligation of the non-custodial parent to pay the applicable table amount of child support, the court may order the custodial parent to cover all the transportation costs associated with the blocks of access ordered by the court.[44]

In the opinion of Professor D.A. Rollie Thompson, who has reviewed hundreds of judicial decisions on mobility since *Gordon v. Goertz*, "over time, the case law has become less predictable, not more so."[45]

Parliament and the provincial legislatures have devised a comprehensive scheme for dealing with child custody disputes and there is no ancillary right at common law for seeking damages in tort for a denial of access[46] or a parent's alleged wrongful relocation of a child.[47]

---

44   *R.B.N. v. M.J.N.*, [2002] N.S.J. No. 529 (S.C.), supplementary reasons [2002] N.S.J. No. 530 (S.C.), aff'd [2003] N.S.J. No. 192 (C.A.).

45   "Movin' On: Mobility and Bill C-22" (12th Annual Institute of Family Law, 2003, County of Carleton Law Association, Ottawa, 6 June 2003).

46   *Frame v. Smith*, [1987] 2 S.C.R. 99.

47   *Curle v. Lowe*, [2004] O.J. No. 3789 (Sup. Ct.).

D. BEST INTERESTS OF CHILD

Where custody and access issues arise on or after divorce, whether by way of an original application or an application to vary an existing order, the court must determine the application by reference only to the best interests of the child.[48]

The "best interests of a child" criterion does not constitute a denial of a parent's freedom of association under section 2(d) of the *Canadian Charter of Rights and Freedoms* nor does it contravene equality rights under section 15 of the *Charter*.[49]

The "best interests of the child" is an all-embracing concept that encompasses the physical, emotional, intellectual, and moral well-being of the child. The court must look not only at the day-to-day needs of the child but also to the longer-term growth and development of the child.[50]

Although many factors have been identified as appropriate for consideration in custody and access disputes, few attempts have been made to measure the relative significance of individual factors. The outcome of any trial may be largely influenced, therefore, by the attitudes and background of the presiding judge. Three factors have surfaced as of special importance where, as in most cases, either parent would be capable of raising the child. One important factor has been preservation of the *status quo* when the children are living in a stable home environment. Courts have frequently stated that preservation of the *status quo* is a compelling circumstance as a temporary measure in proceedings for interim custody but that it is of far less significance after a trial of the issues in open court. In reality, courts are reluctant to disturb the *status quo* whenever custody is in dispute.[51] A second important factor in custody disputes is the strong inclination of courts to grant day-to-day custody to the mother in circumstances where she was the primary caregiver during the marriage.

---

48   *Divorce Act*, R.S.C. 1985 (2d Supp.), c. 3, s. 16(8) (original application), s. 17(5) (variation proceeding).

49   *Green v. Millar*, [2004] B.C.J. No. 2422 (C.A.).

50   *Roberts v. Roberts*, [2000] N.S.J. No. 218 (Fam. Ct.); *D.P.O. v. P.E.O.*, [2006] N.S.J. No. 205 (S.C.); *K.R.C. v. C.A.C.*, [2007] N.S.J. No. 314 (S.C.).

51   *Kastner v. Kastner* (1990), 109 A.R. 241 (C.A.); *Richter v. Richter*, [2005] A.J. No. 616 (C.A.); *G.H. v. J.L.* (1996), 177 N.B.R. (2d) 184 (C.A.); *Whey v. Brenton* (1984), 49 Nfld. & P.E.I.R. 19 (Nfld. C.A.); *Stuyt v. Stuyt*, [2006] O.J. No. 4890 (Sup. Ct.); *Norland v. Norland*, [2006] O.J. No. 5126 (Sup. Ct.); *Haider v. Malach* (1999), 177 Sask. R. 285 (C.A.); *G.M.P. v. T.K.*, [2005] S.J. No. 218. (Q.B.). See Shelagh MacDonald & John Goodwin, "The Collision of Status Quo Principle with Children's Needs" Family Mediation Canada, *Resolve* (Fall 2004) at 2–7.

A third important factor is the disinclination of the courts to split the siblings between the parents.[52] In the final analysis, these three factors will be taken into account only insofar as they reflect the best interests of the children in the overall context of the facts of the particular case. Custody and access cases require an integrated assessment of all relevant factors and circumstances in order to determine the best interests of the child.[53]

With the passage of time, the relevance or significance of any particular factor may change as new attitudes and standards emerge. For example, the views and preferences of children are now an important consideration whereas religion plays a far less important role than it did many years ago. Although isolated cases may still centre upon the religious upbringing of a child,[54] most custody and access disputes pay little or no attention to religious matters, although ethnic and cultural diversity have emerged as a contemporary issue.[55] However, a child's racial and cultural heritage that is attributable to one but not both parents, is only one factor, albeit an important factor, to consider in determining the best interests of a child for the purpose of granting a custody/access order.[56] Where no evidence is adduced at the trial to indicate that race is an important consideration, a court, and especially an appellate court, is not entitled to treat the child's race as of paramount importance in determining which parent shall have custody of the child.[57]

Given the inherent vagueness of the concept of the "best interests of a child" in custody disputes, some courts have formulated lists of relevant considerations to complement those found in provincial or federal legislation. The following factors have been judicially identified in Alberta as relevant to determining the best interests of a child but they do not purport to constitute a comprehensive list:

(i)   the provision of the necessaries of life, including physical and health care and love;

---

52   *Consiglio v. Consiglio*, [2004] B.C.J. No. 2485 (S.C.) (splitting of siblings deemed appropriate).

53   *Gordon v. Goertz*, [1996] 2 S.C.R. 27, 19 R.F.L. (4th) 177 at 197; *Rail v. Rail* (1999), 180 D.L.R. (4th) 490 (B.C.C.A.), citing *Poole v. Poole* (1999), 173 D.L.R. (4th) 299 (B.C.C.A.); *Magnus v. Magnus*, [2006] S.J. No. 510 (C.A.).

54   See, for example, *Young v. Young*, [1993] 4 S.C.R. 3; *Hockey v. Hockey* (1989), 21 R.F.L. (3d) 105 (Ont. Div. Ct.).

55   See, generally, John T. Syrtash, *Religion and Culture in Canadian Family Law* (Markham, ON: Butterworths, 1992).

56   *Van de Perre v. Edwards*, [2001] 2 S.C.R. 1014; *O'Connor v. Kenney*, [2000] O.J. No. 3303 (Sup. Ct.); *Sawatzky v. Campbell*, [2001] S.J. No. 317 (Q.B.).

57   *Van de Perre v. Edwards*, [2001] 2 S.C.R. 1014.

(ii)   stability and consistency and an environment that fosters good mental and emotional health;

(iii)   the opportunity to learn good cultural, moral, and spiritual values;

(iv)   the necessity of setting realistic boundaries on conduct and fair and consistent discipline in teaching appropriate behaviour and conduct;

(v)   the opportunity to relate to and love and be loved by immediate and extended family and the opportunity to form relationships;

(vi)   the opportunity to grow and fulfill his or her potential with responsible guidance;

(vii)   to have optimal access to the non-custodial parent in order to encourage and foster a good relationship;

(viii)   to be with the parent best able to fulfill the child's needs; and

(ix)   the provision of an environment that is safe, secure, free of strife and conflict, and positively guides the child in development.[58]

In New Brunswick, the following factors have been identified as relevant to the determination of a child's best interests in the context of the *Family Services Act*:

1.   Which parent offers the most stability as a family unit;

2.   Which parent appears most prepared to communicate in a mature and responsible manner with the other parent;

3.   Which parent is more able to set aside personal animosity and be generous with access arrangements;

4.   Which parent shows promise of being an appropriate role model for the children, and exhibits a sense of values and directions;

5.   Which parent is more prepared to broaden the scope of the child's life with learning, associations, and challenges;

6.   Are the extended families on either side polarized or are they generous of attitude with the opposite parent;

7.   Which parent provides the best cushion for the child against the stresses of marriage breakdown;

8.   Does the child have physical or mental problems that require special attention and care e.g. attention deficit disorder or asthma;

9.   Does one parent play mind games with the child and carelessly expose the child to domestic turmoil;

---

58   *Calahoo v. Calahoo*, [2000] A.J. No. 815 (Q.B.), citing *Starko v. Starko* (1990), 74 Alta. L.R. (2d) 168 (Q.B.). See also *Lambe v. Coish*, [2006] N.J. No. 377 (U.F.C.). For additional factors, see *D.L.S. v. D.E.S.*, [2001] A.J. No. 883 (Q.B.).

10. Where will the overall long-term intellectual and security interests of the child best be served;

11. Will there be material provisions that meet at least minimal standards;

12. Which parent appears most prepared to give priority to the child's best interest over and above his own;

13. Which parent exhibits the most maturity and ability to accept and deal with responsibility;

14. Does either parent appear more prone to litigate than communicate or negotiate;

15. Is there a positive or negative effect with respect to the involvement of third parties with either parent on the welfare of the child and is such effect financial or emotional;

16. Does the evidence disclose a more substantial bonding between the child and one parent or the other;

17. In consideration of the potential for joint custody, does the evidence reveal a couple with the maturity, self-control, ability, will, and communication skills to make proper joint decisions about their children.[59]

In *Foley v. Foley*,[60] Goodfellow J. of the Nova Scotia Supreme Court formulated the following list of seventeen factors to consider in determining the best interests of a child, namely,

(i)   statutory direction;

(ii)   physical environment;

(iii)   discipline;

(iv)   role model;

(v)   wishes of the children;

(vi)   religious and spiritual guidance;

(vii)   assistance of experts, such as social workers, psychologists, and psychiatrists;

(viii) time availability of parent for a child;

(ix)   the cultural development of a child;

(x)   the physical and character development of the child by such things as participation in sports;

(xi)   the emotional support to assist in a child developing self-esteem and confidence;

---

59   *Shaw v. Shaw*, [1997] N.B.J. No. 211 (Q.B.); *C.R. v. T.R.*, [2007] N.B.J. No. 460 (Q.B.); *L.L. v. S.B.*, [2007] N.B.J. No. 502 (Q.B.); *D.J.L. v. C.M.*, [2008] N.B.J. No. 7 (Q.B.).

60   [1993] N.S.J. No. 347 (S.C.).

(xii) the financial contribution to the welfare of a child;

(xiii) the support of an extended family, including uncles, aunts, and grandparents;

(xiv) the willingness of a parent to facilitate contact with the other parent;

(xv) the interim and long-range plan for the welfare of the children;

(xvi) the financial consequences of custody; and

(xvii) any other relevant factors.

The listed factors in *Foley v. Foley* merely serve as indicia of the best interests of the child. By their very nature, custody and access applications are fact-specific. The listed factors may, therefore, expand, contract, or vary, depending upon the circumstances of the particular case as manifested by the totality of the evidence. Courts must approach each decision with great care and caution. They must be mindful that there is no such thing as a "perfect parent" and should not be quick to judge litigants for common parenting mistakes.[61]

In *Westhaver v. Howard*,[62] Williams J. endorsed the following principles as applicable when a court is reviewing the issue of access:

1) While contact with each parent will usually promote the balanced development of the child, it is a consideration that must be subordinate to the determination of the best interests of the child.

2) While the burden of proving that access to a parent should be denied rests with the parent who asserts that position, it is not necessary to prove that access by a parent would be harmful to the children. The extent of the burden is to prove that the best interests of the children would be met by making such an order.

3) It is appropriate for a trial judge to consider the possible adverse effect on the mother of the father's behaviour, if the father were to be granted access.

4) The court must be slow to deny or extinguish access unless the evidence dictates that it is in the best interests of the child to do so.[63]

---

61   *M.E.E. v. T.R.E.*, [2002] N.S.J. No. 425 (S.C.).

62   [2007] N.S.J. No. 499 (S.C.).

63   *Ibid.* at para. 5.

E. CONDUCT

1) General

Subsections 16(9) and 17(6) of the *Divorce Act* stipulate that the court, in making or varying an order for custody or access, shall not take into consideration the past conduct of a person, unless the conduct is relevant to the ability of that person to act as a parent.[64]

Perceptions of morality have changed. In past generations, a parent living in an adulterous relationship would be automatically denied custody. Today, spousal conduct, which does not overtly reflect on parenting ability, is generally disregarded. A court may be concerned with the viability of a parent's non-marital cohabitational relationship but is unconcerned with historical perceptions of the morality of the relationship. Contemporary issues of misconduct are more likely to focus on domestic violence or parental alienation.

On an application to change the custody and guardianship of a ten-year-old child on the basis of the custodial mother's intransigent conduct in alienating the child from the non-custodial father, the immediate detrimental impact on the child of a court-ordered change of custody may be outweighed by the long-term detrimental impact that will be suffered by the child if the parental alienation continues unabated.[65]

Subsections 16(9) and 17(6) of the *Divorce Act* will not eliminate acrimonious custody or access litigation, unless lawyers and parents jointly pursue other avenues for resolving parenting disputes on or after divorce. The strategic use of mediation and court-ordered independent custody assessments can reduce the potential for protracted no-holds-barred litigation.[66]

---

64 *D.P.O. v. P.E.O.*, [2006] N.S.J. No. 205 (S.C.) (joint custody negated by spousal abuse); *Somerville v. Somerville*, 2007 ONCA 210, [2007] O.J. No. 1079 (husband's deceit at time of marriage breakdown not reflective of his parenting capacity). See also *Mertz v. Symchyck*, 2007 SKCA 121, [2007] S.J. No. 586 (application under the *Children's Law Act, 1997*).

65 *A.A. v. S.N.A.*, [2007] B.C.J. No. 1474 (C.A.); see also *A.A. v. S.N.A.*, [2007] B.C.J. No. 1475 (C.A.); *D.J.L. v. C.M.*, [2008] N.B.J. No. 7 (Q.B.).

66 For a succinct but penetrating analysis of the judicial management of highly conflictual parenting disputes, see Justice Marguerite Trussler, "High Conflict Family Law Cases" (2003), 32 R.F.L. (5th) 237–43.

2) Child Sexual Abuse Allegations

In contested custody or access proceedings, a parent who alleges that the other parent has sexually abused their child has the burden of proving the allegation on the balance of probabilities. If the evidence clearly establishes sexual abuse, such conduct will usually be determinative of future parenting arrangements. If the evidence leaves it uncertain whether sexual abuse occurred in the past, the court must still go on to assess the risk of future abuse. As was stated by Green J. in *C.C. v. L.B.*[67] "the issue in a custody and access case where sexual abuse is alleged is not whether abuse did occur in the past but whether there is a real risk to the child in the future and, if so, whether that factor, when weighed against all the other factors bearing upon the best interests of the children, mandates a particular result." Hearsay evidence respecting statements made by young children may be admitted where sexual abuse is alleged in a custody or access dispute, provided that such evidence satisfies the criteria of necessity and reliability set out in *R. v. Khan.*[68] The receipt of hearsay evidence is also subject to judicial evaluation as to the weight to be accorded to it. In *J.A.G. v. R.J.R.,*[69] Robertson J. formulated the following list of factors to consider in weighing the evidence to determine whether a young child was sexually abused by a parent:

1) What were the circumstances of disclosure — to whom, and where?

2) Did the disclosure of evidence of alleged abuse come from any disinterested witnesses?

3) Were the statements made by the child spontaneous?

4) Did the questions asked of the child suggest an answer?

5) Did the child's statement provide context such as a time frame or positioning of the parties?

6) Was there progression in the story about events?

7) How did the child behave before and after disclosure?

8) Is there physical evidence that would be available by medical examination? If so, and no medical report has been filed, is there a sufficient explanation for its lack?

9) Was there opportunity?

---

67   (1995), 136 Nfld. & P.E.I.R. 296 (Nfld. U.F.C.).
68   [1990] 2 S.C.R. 531.
69   [1998] O.J. No. 1415 (Gen. Div.).

10) What investigative or court action was taken by the parent alleging abuse?

11) Who provided background information to the experts and investigators, and is it accurate, complete, and consistent with both parties' recollections?

12) Was there other evidence supporting the allegations of sexual abuse?

13) Was the custodial parent co-operative regarding access, or was access resisted on other grounds prior to the allegations and after disclosure?

14) Was there harmony between the evidence of one witness and another, and between the evidence of the experts?

15) Was there consistency over time of the child's disclosure?

16) Did the child use wording in statements which appeared to be prompted, rehearsed, or memorized?

17) Was the language used by the child consistent and commensurate with the child's language skills?

18) Was the information given by the child beyond age-appropriate knowledge?

19) What was the comfort level of the child to deal with the subject matter, in particular with respect to the offering of detail?

20) Did the child exhibit sexualized behaviour?

21) Was there evidence of pre-existing inappropriate sexual behaviour by the alleged perpetrator?

22) Was a treatment plan put forth by either parent?

23) Was the child coached or prompted?

24) Did the evidence of the expert witnesses, as accepted by a trial Judge, support the allegations of sexual abuse?

Lists such as this may be helpful, but only when they are tailored to the facts of the particular case. There is no single list that can be used for all cases involving alleged sexual abuse. Nicholas Bala and John Schuman, in their commentary entitled "Allegations of Sexual Abuse When Parents Have Separated,"[70] observe that, given the distinction between the rules of evidence and the standard of proof in criminal and civil proceedings, "it seems inappropriate for a family law judge to place much weight on the decision of police not to charge or on a criminal court acquittal" of a parent against whom allegations of child sexual abuse have been made.

---

70   (1999) 17 C.F.L.Q. 191.

Bala and Schuman further observe that abused children often feel an attachment to the abusing parent, notwithstanding the abuse. Consequently, a "family law court" may allow access by the former abusing parent, if it is satisfied that such access is in the best interests of the child. The judge must be satisfied, however, that the child is not at risk, and this may require supervised access in a neutral setting, before access in the home of the non-custodial parent is allowed.

A five-year-old child is not a competent witness where sexual abuse of the child is alleged in contested custody or access proceedings and the reception of hearsay evidence as to statements made by the child may, therefore, be "reasonably necessary" to make a proper determination. The reliability of the child's statements is to be evaluated and weighed along with the evidence provided by other witnesses. Where "prompting" has definitely occurred and "coaching" may have occurred, this will adversely affect the reliability to be accorded to the child's disclosures and demonstrations. Circumstantial physical evidence that is relied upon to support the allegation of sexual abuse may be discounted where there is a reasonable and plausible explanation provided for the physical condition. Past incidents in which the child "made up stories" are also relevant to the issue of reliability of the hearsay evidence. Where a review of all the relevant and admissible evidence leads the court to conclude not only that the burden of proving sexual abuse has not been satisfied but also that the facts do not support a finding that there is a substantial possibility of future sexual abuse, the "maximum contact" principle should be applied and an order for joint custody with shared decision-making authority and for unsupervised access on alternate weekends is appropriate.[71]

In proceedings for interim custody and access wherein the custodial parent alleges that the non-custodial parent has sexually abused the children, the adage about erring on the side of caution has its place, but it does not merit absolute application. Allegations of sexual abuse are always troubling, but the court should not abdicate its responsibility by postponing a determination until trial and granting the non-custodial parent supervised access to the children in the meantime. Supervised access creates an artificial and stilted environment for the children and the parent and may undermine the preservation of a close bond such as the child enjoys with the custodial parent. Supervised access may be better than no access but it is not much better. Consequently, it should only be ordered when there is no reasonable alternative. Given that the *Divorce Act* endorses the principle

---

71   *B.S. v. R.T.*, [2002] N.J. No. 101 (S.C.), Cook J.

that it is in the best interests of children to enjoy a relationship with both parents to the extent reasonably possible, access to a non-custodial parent should not be denied or restricted in the absence of a compelling reason. Instead of deferring the issue until trial, the court, on an interim application, should examine the sexual abuse allegations with care and objectivity. Where the descriptions of the alleged abuse are vague, they were elicited by the custodial parent as opposed to being volunteered, the children made no incriminating disclosures to third-party professionals, including a social services agency and the police who looked into the custodial parent's allegations, and an examination of the children by a licensed physician finds no evidence of sexual abuse and provides a clinical explanation of their physical condition, an order for unsupervised access to the children by the non-custodial parent may be granted. When the custodial parent has been the children's primary caregiver, a more fundamental change in the parental roles may be inappropriate having regard to the best interests of the children, notwithstanding that the custodial parent has relocated with the children in contravention of a court order that is currently under appeal. Although such relocation might justify a change of custody in other circumstances, Gerein C.J. concluded that it would constitute an improper punitive sanction in this case and it would be contrary to the best interests of the children. However, for the purposes of achieving continued meaningful involvement of the non-custodial parent in the children's lives, Gerein C.J., while conceding that such a disposition was unusual, granted the non-custodial parent access to the children for the entire and every weekend.[72]

Determination of the credibility of witnesses is a function of the trier of fact, not an expert witness. The majority judgment of the Supreme Court of Canada in *R. v. Béland*[73] renders polygraph evidence inadmissible in a criminal proceeding because it contravenes certain basic rules of evidence, namely (i) the rule against oath-helping; (ii) the rule against the admission of past out-of-court consistent statements by a witness; (iii) the rule relating to character evidence; and (iv) the expert evidence rule. These rules of evidence, which were relied upon in *R. v. Béland* to exclude the admission of polygraph evidence that was sought to be used to determine the credibility of the accused, are equally applicable to a contested guardianship, or custody and access proceeding wherein a parent seeks to negate allegations of child sexual abuse by introducing polygraph evidence.[74]

---

72   *T.G.F. v. D.S.V.*, [2005] S.J. No. 582 (Q.B.).
73   [1987] 2 S.C.R. 398.
74   *E.W. v. D.W.*, [2005] B.C.J. No. 1345 (S.C.).

F. EFFECT OF AGREEMENT

An agreement between parents or between parents and third parties respecting a child's upbringing cannot oust the statutory obligation of a court to grant a custody order that reflects a full and balanced consideration of all factors relevant to a determination of the child's best interests. A prior parenting agreement between the disputants is only one factor to be considered, albeit an important factor.[75]

Although a separation agreement may include provisions whereby its terms shall only be varied in the event of a material change of circumstances, such provisions cannot oust the jurisdiction of a court to grant orders for custody and child support in subsequent divorce proceedings. In allowing an appeal in *Jay v. Jay*[76] because the chambers judge had erred by concluding that his jurisdiction under the *Divorce Act* was limited by the provisions of the separation agreement, the Appeal Division of the Prince Edward Island Supreme Court expressed the following opinion:

> Irrespective of the terms of any agreement between the parties, the court has the jurisdiction in a motion for corollary relief in connection with divorce proceedings to hear and deal with all issues of custody and child support. An agreement between the parties is only one factor to be taken into consideration when deciding upon the best interests of the child. While such an agreement provides strong evidence of what the parties accepted at the time as meeting the best interests of the child, it does not relieve the court of its responsibility under s. 16 of the *Divorce Act* to make an independent assessment of the best interests of the child. (See: *Willick v. Willick*, [1994] 3 S.C.R. 670.)[77]

In the context of custody and access orders, the above observations are clearly consistent with established case law and with the express provisions of section 16(8) of the *Divorce Act* whereby "[i]n making an order under this section, the court shall take into consideration only the best interests of the child of the marriage as determined by reference to the condition, means, needs and other circumstances of the child."

---

75   *A.L. v. D.K.*, [2000] B.C.J. No. 1763 (C.A.). See also *M.E.O. v. S.R.M.*, [2004] A.J. No. 202 (C.A.) and *Hearn v. Hearn*, [2004] A.J. No. 105 (Q.B.), applying *Miglin v. Miglin*, [2003] 1 S.C.R. 303.

76   [2003] P.E.I.J. No. 68 (C.A.).

77   *Ibid.* at para. 4.

G. VARIATION AND RESCISSION OF CUSTODY AND ACCESS ORDERS

It is rare for a motions judge to vary an interim order granted pursuant to the *Divorce Act*, but a judge always has the jurisdiction to decide the custody of a child as it relates to the best interests of that child, particularly where it can be demonstrated that there has been a change of circumstances raising concerns about the child's welfare. However, there must be compelling reasons that militate in favour of immediate action rather than waiting for a hearing on the matter and a final order. There is no section in the *Divorce Act* that expressly prohibits the court from varying an interim order. If it was the intention of Parliament to prohibit such variation orders, it surely would have included a provision to indicate its clear intention. Where there is a gap in the legislation that the court is required to apply, the *parens patriae* jurisdiction of the court may be exercisable. The court may draw upon its inherent jurisdiction whenever it is just or equitable to do so and the exercise of the court's inherent jurisdiction to vary an interim order does not contravene any provision of the *Divorce Act*.[78]

Although interim custody orders ordinarily preserve the *status quo* and any subsequent variation is unusual, special circumstances may warrant such variation. In *Lewis v. Lewis*,[79] the mother was granted sole custody of the children and the father supervised access pursuant to an interim consent order triggered by the mother's allegations of abuse. Subsequently, the court rejected these allegations and the mother's contention that she was a pawn who was being controlled by the father. For example, the court found that the parents' involvement in "phone sex" and watching pornographic movies was a joint and consensual adult activity that did not affect their parenting abilities or the best interests of the children and was therefore irrelevant to the issues of custody and access. Finding that an order for joint custody would be unworkable because of the parents' inability to communicate, the mother was granted sole custody of the children and the father was granted unsupervised access on specified terms.

Section 17 of the *Divorce Act* regulates the jurisdiction of the court to vary, rescind, or suspend a permanent custody order or any provision thereof. It involves a two-stage analysis. Before entering on the merits

---

78   *D.G. v. H.F.*, [2006] N.B.J. No. 158 (C.A.).
79   [2005] N.S.J. No. 368 (S.C.).

or an application to vary a custody order, the judge must be satisfied of a change in the condition, means, needs, or circumstances of the child, and/or the ability of the former spouses to meet the parenting needs of the child — this change materially affects the child and was either not foreseen or could not have been reasonably contemplated by the judge who made the order that is sought to be varied.[80] If the threshold condition of a material change is established, the court should reassess the parenting arrangements in light of all the circumstances existing at the time of the variation proceeding. The court should consider the matter afresh without defaulting to the existing arrangements and must make its determination having regard only to the best interests of the child.[81]

Section 17(1)(b) of the *Divorce Act* empowers a court to grant an interim order varying or suspending the provisions of an existing permanent custody/access order. A distinction is to be drawn between the existence of such jurisdiction and the exercise of such jurisdiction. Before granting an interim variation order, the court must be satisfied (i) that a *prima facie* case has been made out pointing to a change of circumstances of sufficient import as might well result in variation of the custody/access order at the final hearing; and (ii) that the best interests of the child lie in making an interim order of the nature of that being contemplated. The court should also have regard to the principle that a child should have as much contact with each parent as is consistent with the child's best interests. The court should exercise its jurisdiction to grant an interim variation order sparingly and solely in the best interests of the child, bearing in mind that a final order will be forthcoming and even a temporary change can be unsettling. Applying these principles to the facts in *Dorval v. Dorval*,[82] wherein the interim variation order prohibited the mother

---

80   *Gordon v. Goertz*, [1996] 2 S.C.R. 27; *Ryan v. Ryan*, [2008] A.J. No. 128 (C.A.); *Hornan v. Hornan*, [2007] M.J. No. 385 (Q.B.); *Peters v. Neville*, [2004] N.J. No. 157 (U.F.C.); *V.S.G. v. L.J.G.*, [2004] O.J. No. 2238 (Sup. Ct.); *Talbot v. Henry* (1990), 25 R.F.L. (3d) 415 (Sask. C.A.); *Carriere v. Carriere*, [2006] S.J. No. 371 (Q.B.); *Willford v. Schaffer*, [2007] S.J. No. 12 (C.A.); *Scott v. Higgs*, [2007] S.J. No. 457 (Q.B.); *Gray (formerly Wiegers) v. Wiegers*, 2008 SKCA 7, [2008] S.J. No. 12.

81   *Ibid*. See also *Kubel v. Kubel* (1995), 15 R.F.L. (4th) 356 (Alta. C.A.); *Baynes v. Baynes* (1987), 8 R.F.L. (3d) 139 (B.C.C.A.); *West v. West* (1994), 92 Man. R. (2d) 164 (C.A.); *Talbot v. Henry* (1990), 25 R.F.L. (3d) 415 (Sask. C.A.); *Wilson v. Grassick* (1994), 2 R.F.L. (4th) 291 (Sask. C.A.), leave to appeal to S.C.C. refused (1994), 7 R.F.L. (4th) 254 (S.C.C.); compare *Magnus v. Magnus*, [2006] S.J. No. 510 (C.A.) (variation of shared parenting regime should not be disproportionate to the proven change).

82   [2006] S.J. No. 94 (C.A.). See also *Carey v. Hanlon*, 2007 ABCA 391, [2007] A.J. No. 1325; *Patterson v. Publicover*, [2005] N.S.J. No. 243 (S.C.); *Rode v. Moyer*, [2007] S.J.

from relocating the child, the Saskatchewan Court of Appeal found no tenable reason for interfering with the order. Addressing the incidental question of appeals challenging interim orders of limited duration, the Saskatchewan Court of Appeal stated that, while a right of appeal exists, the appellate court will exercise its powers sparingly and only in extraordinary circumstances. The reasons for this are obvious. Such appeals generate additional costs and delay, even when they are heard on an expedited basis, whereas it is in everybody's best interests that the matter proceed to a final determination as soon as is practicable. The judgment in *Dorval v. Dorval* does not purport to resolve the "controversy" relating to the interim variation of spousal support orders. It rests content with the statement that "even in those cases in which it has been held that the courts are not empowered to make interim orders on applications under section 17 or its equivalent, allowance is consistently made for the *parens patriae* jurisdiction of the courts when it comes to children and their interests."[83]

On an application to vary a custody order pursuant to section 17(5) of the *Divorce Act*, the applicant must prove a material or pivotal change in the child's circumstances that requires variation of the order, having regard to the best interests of the child. Although common sense dictates that a child's parenting needs will change over the years from infancy to adulthood, the increased maturity of the child arising from the passage of time does not, in and of itself, constitute a material change as required by section 17(5) of the *Divorce Act*; nor is it sufficient that the non-custodial parent wishes to assume a more substantial role in the child's life. Common sense assumptions about the changing needs of children as they mature do not discharge the court's duty to consider whether the existing order should be varied because it no longer satisfies the child's parenting needs. In *Gray (Formerly Wiegers) v. Wiegers*,[84] the Saskatchewan Court of Appeal held that the chambers judge had erred by ordering a substantial change in the parenting regime in the absence of evidence that the existing regime no longer served the child's best interests. The Saskatchewan Court of Appeal distinguished *Elliott v. Loewen*,[85] wherein the Manitoba Court of Appeal held that the motions judge was entitled to take judicial notice of the fact that the needs of a three-year-old child in relation to

---

No. 397 (Q.B.).

83   [2006] S.J. No. 94 at para. 21 (C.A.).

84   2008 SKCA 7, [2008] S.J. No. 12; see also *M.R. v. G.V.G.V.*, [2008] S.J. No. 27 (Q.B.); *Fennig-Doll v. Doll*, [2008] S.J. No. 177 (Q.B.).

85   (1993), 44 R.F.L. (3d) 445 (Man. C.A.).

his father are different from the needs of an eighteen-month-old child. The Saskatchewan Court of Appeal observed that, in *Elliott*, limitations imposed on the father's access were specifically related to the child's very tender years when the order was made, which limitations were no longer appropriate and in the child's best interests as he emerged from infancy into early childhood. In contrast with *Elliott*, the child in *Wiegers* was just under four years of age when the parenting regime was established, and nine and one-half years old when the father brought his application for increased parenting time. The original order provided for joint custody, with the mother to have primary care of the child, and the father to have access midweek and on alternate weekends, in addition to equal time-sharing during school vacations and three weeks during the summer. These provisions, coupled with the fact that the parents had separated before the child was born and the mother had always been the primary caregiver, led the Saskatchewan Court of Appeal to conclude that there was no reason to assume that the order was contingent upon the child's tender years. Accordingly, the variation order of the chambers judge was set aside and the original order was reinstated, subject to a prior modification of midweek access to include overnight visits, which the parents had agreed to when the child was seven years old.

Ongoing or escalating conflict may constitute a change of circumstances that justifies variation of an existing custody order.[86]

A custodial parent's persistent attempts to alienate the children from the non-custodial parent may justify an order changing the custody of the children. In granting such an order, it may be wise to structure the change in the children's primary residence in such a way as to promote a gradual transition and as little disruption as possible for the children. In *Rogerson v. Tessaro*,[87] the Ontario Court of Appeal found the trial judge's remedy of granting custody to the father to be "dramatic" but justified by the mother's persistent, ingrained, and deep-rooted inability to support the children's relationship with their father. Since the appeal was primarily fact-driven and there was no manifest error of law, the mother's appeal was dismissed. Compare *Coyle v. Danylkiw*,[88] wherein a father's appeal

---

86   *D.L.W. v. J.J.M.V.* (2005), 234 N.S.R. (2d) 366 (C.A.); *Zinck v. Fraser* (2006), 240 N.S.R. (2d) 335 (S.C.); *MacKay v. Murray*, [2006] N.S.J. No. 270 (C.A.).

87   [2006] O.J. No. 1825 (C.A.). See also *C.M.B.E. v. D.J.E.*, [2006] N.B.J. No. 364 (C.A.); *C.L.J. v. J.M.J.*, [2006] N.S.J. No. 171 (S.C.). Compare *R.P.B. v. K.D.P.*, [2006] A.J. No. 1192 (Q.B.) (parental expert intervention ordered pursuant to *Family Law Practice Note No. 7*).

88   [2006] O.J. No. 2061 (C.A.).

from a judgment awarding the mother sole custody of the child and permitting her to move with the child out of Ontario was allowed in part. The relocation provision was vacated by reason of the mother's return with the child to Ontario. The Court of Appeal dismissed the father's request for sole or joint custody based on his submissions that the trial judge had erred in failing to give adequate consideration to the maximum contact principle in section 16(10) of the *Divorce Act* by making an unreasonable finding that the mother would facilitate access, and in failing to accept the findings of a custody assessor. The Ontario Court of Appeal concluded that the trial judge's decisions on both these issues turned primarily on her findings of fact and her appraisal of the evidence, which should not be interfered with in the absence of a palpable and overriding error.

Less compelling evidence is required to vary access arrangements under a subsisting order, although the best interests of the child again constitute the determinative consideration.[89] The test to alter an order for access is that a material change in circumstance must have occurred that affects the best interests of the child.[90] However, this statutory requirement of a material change does not signify that an order, once made, calcifies and defies re-examination in the face of a child's changed needs. The cumulative effect of unrelenting stress on a child may constitute a material change that justifies termination of access.[91] As Helper J.A., of the Manitoba Court of Appeal, has observed,

> The needs of a child in relation to each of his parents change frequently over the years from infancy to adulthood. No court order can be crafted to address those ever-changing needs and the concerns of separated parents as they relate to their child; thus, the need for variation.[92]

For the purposes of section 17(5) of the *Divorce Act*, a former spouse's terminal illness or critical condition shall be considered a change of circumstances of the child of the marriage and the court shall make a variation order in respect of access that is in the best interests of the child.[93]

---

89 *Hamilton v. Hamilton* (1992), 43 R.F.L. (3d) 13 (Alta. Q.B.); *Magee v. Magee* (1993), 111 Sask. R. 211 (Q.B.).

90 *Cairns v. Cairns* (1995), 10 R.F.L. (4th) 234 (N.B.C.A.).

91 *M.(B.P.) v. M.(B.L.D.E.)* (1992), 42 R.F.L. (3d) 349 at 360 (Ont. C.A.), Abella J.A., with Tarnopolsky J.A. concurring; Finlayson J.A. dissenting (application under *Children's Law Reform Act*, R.S.O. 1990, c. C.12); leave to appeal to S.C.C. refused (1993), 48 R.F.L. (3d) 232 (S.C.C.).

92 *Elliott v. Loewen* (1993), 44 R.F.L. (3d) 445 at 447 (Man. C.A.).

93 Bill C-252, *An Act to Amend the Divorce Act*, 1st Sess., 39th Parl., 2006, s. 1 (Royal Assent 31 May 2007).

The wishes of the child may be taken into consideration when those wishes are free from interference or manipulation by either parent.[94] Discontinuance of access will only be ordered in exceptional circumstances. It may be reinstated where the custodial parent's objection to access is based on the child's fear of the non-custodial parent, which fear is attributable to the custodial parent's own improper influence,[95] although counselling may be necessary to avoid any threat to the child's emotional or psychological well-being. A *bona fide* change of residence by the custodial parent does not, of itself, warrant a change of custody, but may justify variation of the access arrangements so as to ensure that the child has as much contact with both parents as is consistent with the best interests of the child.[96]

Where an abusive relationship has left the custodial parent fearful of his or her former spouse and unwilling to continue to provide access, the trial judge may consider the possible adverse effects on the parent in continuing even limited access.[97] Allegations of sexual abuse that have surfaced since the making of the original order may require the variation of access arrangements.[98]

Access arrangements may be varied because of a child entering full-time attendance at school. The arrangements for a younger sibling may be varied to match these new arrangements, since it is appropriate that child-care arrangements should involve both children for the same periods of time.[99]

A judge may set out conditions in an original order, which, if followed by the access parent, may lead to a variation allowing increased access.[100]

Although the "best interests of the child" is the governing criterion in determining whether an access order should be varied pursuant to section 17(5) of the *Divorce Act*, this criterion is imprecise, vague, and dif-

---

94   *Keyes v. Gordon* (1989), 93 N.S.R. (2d) 383 (Fam. Ct.).

95   *Clothier v. Ettinger* (1989), 91 N.S.R. (2d) 428 (Fam. Ct.) (Compare *M.(B.P.) v. M.(B. L.D.E.)* (1992), 42 R.F.L. (3d) 349 (Ont. C.A.)); *Powley v. Wagner* (1987), 11 R.F.L. (3d) 136 (Sask. Q.B.).

96   *Matthews v. Matthews* (1988), 72 Nfld. & P.E.I.R. 217 (Nfld. U.F.C.); *Wainwright v. Wainwright* (1987), 10 R.F.L. (3d) 387 (N.S.T.D.), aff'd (1988), 15 R.F.L. (3d) 174 (N.S.C.A.), leave to appeal to S.C.C. refused (1989), 27 R.F.L (3d) xxxiii (note); *Sweeney v. Hartnell* (1987), 81 N.S.R. (2d) 203 (T.D.).

97   *Abdo v. Abdo* (1993), 50 R.F.L. (3d) 17 (N.S.C.A.) (application to terminate access under *Family Maintenance Act*, R.S.N.S. 1989, c. 160).

98   *McIsaac v. Stewart* (1993), 119 N.S.R. (2d) 102 (Fam. Ct.).

99   *Peters v. Karr* (1994), 93 Man. R. (2d) 222 (Q.B.).

100 *Sparks v. Sparks* (1994), 159 A.R. 187 (Q.B.).

ficult to define. While a wide variety of relevant factors should be taken into account, section 17(9) of the *Divorce Act* specifically endorses the guiding principle that a child should have maximum contact with his or her divorced parents to the extent that this is compatible with the child's best interests. The risk of harm to the child, while not the ultimate legal test, is also a factor to be considered.[101] There is a presumption that regular access to the non-custodial parent is in the best interests of a child. The right of the child to have contact with and maintain an attachment to the non-custodial parent is a fundamental right that should only be judicially withheld in the most extreme and unusual circumstances. Relevant case law provides no standard criteria for terminating access orders, but in *V.S.G. v. L.J.G.*,[102] Blishen J. of the Ontario Superior Court of Justice has identified the following factors as those most frequently relied upon when courts terminate an access order:

1. Long-term harassment or harmful conduct towards the custodial parent that creates fear or stress for the child.

2. A history of violence; unpredictable, uncontrollable behaviour; alcohol or drug abuse that is witnessed by the child or presents a risk to the child's safety or well-being.

3. Extreme parental alienation.

4. Persistent denigration of the other parent.

5. The absence of any relationship or attachment between the child and the non-custodial parent.

6. Neglect or abuse of the child during access visits.

7. The wishes or preference of an older child to terminate access.

Most of these factors would also be relevant in reviewing the alternative of supervised access. The judicial termination of access is a remedy of last resort that should be ordered only in the most exceptional circumstances. A court must carefully consider the option of supervision prior to termination. A supervision order has the potential to protect a child from the risk of harm, to foster the parent-child relationship, to ensure counselling or treatment that will improve parenting ability, to create a bridge between no relationship and a normal parenting relationship, and to avoid or reduce parental conflict and its detrimental effect on the child. Supervised access orders are normally granted for a limited time; they are seldom regarded as providing a long-term solution. There may, neverthe-

---

101   *Young v. Young*, [1993] 4 S.C.R. 3 at para. 210.
102   [2004] O.J. No. 2238 (Sup. Ct.).

less, be situations in which medium- or longer-term supervised access is in the child's best interests. In Blishen J.'s opinion, supervised access, whether of short, medium, or long duration, should always be examined as an alternative to a complete termination of the parent-child relationship, unless the viability of supervised access has been negated by past experience or by the unwillingness of the non-custodial parent to abide by court-imposed conditions relating to treatment or counselling.

H. PARENTAL CONFLICT RESOLUTION

Custody litigation is relatively rare; access litigation is more common.[103] It is generally acknowledged that litigation should be the last resort for resolving parenting disputes. It is costly, not only in terms of money, but also in terms of emotional wear-and-tear. Litigation is not a therapeutic catharsis for the resolution of custody and access disputes. Children pay a heavy price when their parents engage in embittered custody and access disputes that lead to warfare in the courts. If litigation can be avoided without damage to the psychological, physical, or moral well-being of the children, it should be avoided. There will be exceptional cases where allegations of psychological, physical, or sexual abuse necessitate judicial intervention. In the vast majority of cases, however, both parents are fit to continue to discharge their responsibilities to the children after marriage breakdown or divorce.

Roadblocks to shared parental responsibilities after separation or divorce are often attributable to a lack of knowledge and to the inability of parents to communicate and segregate their interpersonal hostility from their role as parents. It is for these reasons that the Law Reform Commission of Canada recommended that a mandatory family conference be held in cases involving dependent children. In its *Report on Family Law*, the Law Reform Commission of Canada recommended as follows:

3.   Whenever children over whom the court has jurisdiction in dissolution proceedings are involved, the law should require that there be an immediate informal meeting of the parties — an "assessment conference" — before the court, a court officer, a support staff per-

---

103 See Department of Justice, Canada, *Evaluation of the* Divorce Act, *Phase II: Monitoring and Evaluation* (May 1990) at 61 and 110–15. See also Bruce Ziff, "Recent Developments in Canadian Law: Marriage and Divorce" (1990) 22 Ottawa L. Rev. 139 at 211–13.

son or a community-based service or facility designated by the court, for the following purposes:

(a) to ascertain whether the spouses have made appropriate arrangements respecting the care, custody and upbringing of the children during the dissolution process, and if not, to ascertain whether such arrangements can be agreed to by the spouses;

(b) to ascertain whether the appointment of legal representation for children is indicated;

(c) to ascertain whether a formal investigative report by a public authority (e.g. an Official Guardian or Superintendent of Child Welfare) is indicated;

(d) to ascertain whether a mandatory psychiatric or psychological assessment of the situation is indicated;

(e) to acquaint the husband and wife with the availability of persons, services and facilities in the court or the community to assist them in negotiating temporary arrangements respecting children during the dissolution process as well as permanent arrangements applicable on dissolution;

(f) to enable the court to ascertain the need for, and where necessary to order the further appearance of the husband and wife before the court or a person, service or facility designated by the court to engage in one or more sessions of mandatory negotiation respecting the children; and

(g) generally to help the husband and wife, where possible, to avoid contested temporary or permanent custody proceedings through negotiation and agreement, and otherwise to avoid bringing matters involving the children before the court for adjudication.[104]

Although these proposals are confined to divorce, they are equally adaptable to proceedings for custody and access under provincial and territorial legislation. If we accept that children are entitled to enjoy the benefits and contributions of both of their parents, notwithstanding separation or divorce, the accessibility of relevant information would appear to be a vital first step on the road towards the sharing of continued parental privileges and responsibilities after separation.

---

104 Law Reform Commission of Canada, *Report on Family Law* (Ottawa: Information Canada, 1976) at 64–65.

I. VOICE OF THE CHILD

Statutes in several provinces stipulate that the wishes of a child are a relevant factor to be considered in determining the best interests of a child in contested custody or access proceedings. Although there is no explicit provision to this effect in the *Divorce Act*, judicial practice has long acknowledged the relevance of an older child's wishes in custody and access proceedings arising under that Act. The best interests of a child are not to be confused with the wishes of the child, but a child's views and preferences fall within the parameters of a child's best interests. When children are under nine years of age, courts do not usually place much, if any, reliance on their expressed preference. The wishes of children aged ten to thirteen are commonly treated as an important but not a decisive factor. The wishes of the children increase in significance as they grow older and courts have openly recognized the futility of ignoring the wishes of children over the age of fourteen years. It is also unusual for a court to grant any order for custody after a child reaches the age of sixteen years.[105] However, in accordance with the definition of "child of the marriage" in section 2(1) of the *Divorce Act*, a court has jurisdiction under section 16 of the *Divorce Act* to grant an order for custody of or access to an adult child who is mentally and physically disabled. Where the central factual issue to be determined in the contested custody and access proceeding is whether it is the adult child himself or his mother who is effectively preventing the father from visiting the child, the court may order a medical examination of the child under Rule 30 of the *British Columbia Rules of Court* or appoint an independent expert under Rule 32A to inquire into and report on the facts.[106]

Although the child is the focal point of all disputed custody and access proceedings, the question arises as to who speaks for the child.[107] Even though judges apply the "best interests of the child" as the determinative criterion of custody and access disputes, the role of independent arbiter precludes a trial judge from acting as an advocate for the child. How then, can the child's interests be protected? In some provinces, courts have

---

105   *L.B. v. B.B*, [2007] N.B.J. No. 300 (Q.B.); *B.W. v. B.W.*, [2007] N.B.J. No. 420 (Q.B.); *Kemp v. Kemp*, [2007] O.J. No. 1131 (Sup. Ct.); *Paul v. Misselbrook*, [2006] O.J. No. 1659 (Sup. Ct.); *Shillington v. Shillington*, [2007] S.J. No. 241 (Q.B.); *Feist v. Feist*, [2007] S.J. No. 722 (Q.B.).

106   *Ross v. Ross*, [2004] B.C.J. No. 446 (C.A.).

107   See Christine Davies, "Access to Justice for Children: The Voice of the Child in Custody and Access Disputes" (2004) 22 Can. Fam. L.Q. 153.

exercised a discretionary jurisdiction to appoint an independent lawyer to represent the child in contested custody proceedings.[108] However, such appointments are exceptional and children are rarely represented by independent lawyers in settlement negotiations and their voices may go unheard if mediation[109] is used as a means of resolving parenting disputes. In contested proceedings, some judges will interview the children privately to ascertain their wishes; other judges are averse to this practice.[110]

J. PARENTING PLANS

When economic disputes arise on separation or divorce, lawyers and courts insist on full financial disclosure as a condition precedent to resolving issues relating to property division and spousal or child support. The need for access to all relevant and available information is no less compelling when custody and access disputes arise. All too easily, however, the interests of children can be overlooked in custody and access litigation as parents engage in forensic combat for the purpose of ventilating their personal hostilities. Although it is generally acknowledged that separation and divorce sever the marital bond but should not sever parent-child bonds, adversarial conflict on marriage breakdown can present major obstacles to a meaningful relationship being preserved between children and a non-custodial parent.

The difficulty faced by a court when embittered spouses engage in custody litigation was exposed in the dissenting judgment of Bayda J.A., of the Saskatchewan Court of Appeal, in *Wakaluk v. Wakaluk*.[111] He stated:

> From the standpoint of custody the hearing of the petition was, in my respectful view, quite unsatisfactory. Virtually no evidence was dir-

---

108 For examples of provincial legislation that expressly provide for independent representation of children, see *Family Relations Act*, R.S.B.C. 1979, c. 121, s. 2 (family advocate may act as counsel for the interests and welfare of the child); Quebec *Code of Civil Procedure*, R.S.Q. c. C-25, as amended, art. 816 (appointment of attorney to represent child); *Children's Act*, R.S.Y. 1986, c. 22, s. 167 (Official Guardian has exclusive right to determine whether any child requires independent representation); see also *Kalaserk v. Nelson*, [2005] N.W.T.J. No. 3 (S.C.); and see, generally, *Payne's Divorce and Family Law Digest* (Don Mills, ON: R. De Boo, 1982–93) tabs 22.39 "Legal Representation of Child; *Amicus Curiae.*"

109 See Bob Simpson, "The *Children Act* (England) 1989 and the Voice of the Child in Family Conciliation" (1991) 29 Family and Conciliation Courts Review 385.

110 See Chapter 11, Section E.

111 (1977), 25 R.F.L. 292 (Sask. C.A.).

ected to this issue. The parties primarily concerned themselves with adducing evidence to show whether, on the basis of the many marital battles engaged in by them, one or the other of them should be favoured by the trial judge in his determination of the issue of cruelty.

No one bothered to bring forward much information in respect of the two individuals who of all the persons likely to be affected by these proceedings least deserve to be ignored — the children. We know their names, sex and ages, but little else. Of what intelligence are they? What are their likes? Dislikes? Do they have any special inclinations (for the arts, sports or the like) that should be nurtured? Any handicaps? Do they show signs of anxiety? What are their personalities? Characters? What is the health of each? (This list of questions is not intended as exhaustive or as one that is applicable to all contested cases but only as illustrative of those questions which may be relevant.) In short, no evidence was led to establish the intellectual, moral, emotional and physical needs of each child. Apart from the speculation that these children are "ordinary" (whatever that means) there is nothing on which to base a reasoned objective conclusion as to what must be done for this child and that child, as individuals and not as mere members of general class, in order that the welfare and happiness of each may be assured and enhanced.

Nor was any direct evidence led to show which of the parents, by reason of training, disposition, character, personality, experience, identification with a child's pursuits, ability to cope with any special requirements of a child's health, religious observance and such other pertinent factors (again the list is intended as only illustrative of matters which may be relevant), is best equipped to meet the needs of each individual child. The evidence presented on behalf of each side was principally, if not exclusively, geared to do one thing: show how badly one spouse treated the other. Such evidence is hardly a proper basis upon which to make a determination — a crucial one indeed from the standpoint of the children — as to which parent is best suited to meet the needs of the children and upon which to found an order for custody. How inconsiderate one spouse is of the other, or how one spouse reacts towards the other in a marital battle and the ability of a spouse to come out of a marital battle a winner, either actual or moral, are not high-ranking factors, if factors they be at all, in determining where a child's happiness and welfare lie, particularly whether such happiness and welfare are better assured by placement with one parent or the other.

...

The welfare of the children dictates that a new trial be held, restricted to the issue of custody, and I would direct an order accordingly.[112]

Although spousal misconduct may sometimes provide insight into parenting capacity, it is more often than not put forward for ulterior motives that have nothing to do with the welfare of the child. The threat of mudslinging litigation can usually be avoided, however, unless both counsel pursue such a course of action. An astute counsel for either spouse may avoid allegations of blame and fault by focusing pleadings, evidence, and submissions on the past parent-child relationship and on future plans for the care and upbringing of the child. In the words of Boisvert J., of the New Brunswick Queen's Bench,

> Spousal censure, or condemnation, has no place in custody disputes, unless it is directly and unmistakably linked with the disablement of one parent to answer to the children's best interests. A cogent and positive proposal aimed at sound child management, will, in most instances, lay by the heels arguments founded mainly on blame and accusations.[113]

It is ironic that judicial proceedings between spouses, which involve matrimonial property, and spousal and child support, require sworn financial statements to be filed, yet no requirement is imposed in custody proceedings for the disputants to file detailed information concerning the children whose future is at risk. We hardly serve our children well when we insist on mandatory, financial statements in spousal economic disputes but, in custody disputes, require no specific information respecting the personality, character, and attributes of the child and the ability of the disputants to contribute to the child's growth and development.

What is needed on separation or divorce is a perspective based on past family history and prospective parenting plans that can accommodate the different contributions that each parent can make towards the upbringing of the child.[114] There is no reason why separated and divorced

---

112   *Ibid.* at 299–300 and 306.

113   *Pare v. Pare* (1987), 78 N.B.R. (2d) 10 (Q.B.).

114   See Julien D. Payne & Kenneth L. Kallish, "The Welfare or Best Interests of the Child: Substantive Criteria to Be Applied in Custody Dispositions Made Pursuant to the *Divorce Act*, R.S.C. 1970, c. D-8" in *Payne's Divorce and Family Law Digest* (Don Mills, ON: R. De Boo, 1982–93) 1983 tab, at 83-1201/1253, especially 83-1239/1243, and Essays tab, E-177 at 184–85. See also Julien D. Payne, "The Dichotomy between Family Law and Family Crises on Marriage Breakdown" (1989) 20 R.G.D. 109 at 121. For details concerning the use of parenting plans in the state of Washington, see Department of Justice, Canada, *Parents Forever: Making the Con-*

parents should not be required to submit a detailed plan concerning their past and future parenting privileges and responsibilities. Such parenting plans should also take account of the contribution to the child's growth and development that has been and may continue to be made by members of the extended families, and especially the maternal and paternal grandparents.

Parenting plans will not eliminate hostile negotiations and protracted litigation by parents who are intent on battling through lawyers and the courts. What they can do, however, is shift the focus of attention to the child. Although parenting plans are not required to be filed in custody litigation, there is nothing to prevent parents from formulating such plans regardless of whether or not litigation is contemplated. Parenting plans can serve a useful purpose in assisting both parents to make appropriate arrangements for the upbringing of their children. Such plans can specifically define the contributions to be made by each parent and by third parties in the day-to-day and long-term upbringing of the children.

In a study undertaken for the Department of Justice, Canada, in 1989, Judith P. Ryan, a practising mediator and lawyer in Toronto, recommended radical changes in the terminology of parenting disputes and innovative procedures for resolving such disputes.[115] In December 1998, a Special Joint Committee of the Senate and House of Commons published its report entitled "For the Sake of the Children," which proposed abandonment of the terminology of custody and access in favour of the concept of "shared parenting." This recommendation constitutes one of forty-eight specific proposals for changes in the law and in the processes for resolving parenting disputes. These proposals are currently being studied by the Department of Justice, Canada. Although a few Canadian courts have endorsed the abandonment of legal jargon,[116] most lawyers and judges still speak in terms of "custody" and "access" rather than in the everyday language of "shared parenting." It is interesting to observe, however, that legislative changes in England[117] have abandoned the ter-

---

cept a Reality for Divorcing Parents and Their Children by Judith P. Ryan (31 March 1989) at 44–95.

115   Ryan, *ibid.*

116   See *Abbott v. Taylor* (1986), 2 R.F.L. (3d) 163 (Man. C.A.); *Lennox v. Frender* (1990), 27 R.F.L. (3d) 181 at 185–87 (B.C.C.A.); *Harsant v. Portnoi* (1990), 27 R.F.L. (3d) 216 (Ont. H.C.J.).

117   *Children Act 1989* (U.K.), 1989, c. 41.

minology of "custody" and "access" and substituted the notion of "shared parental responsibilities" as well as minimal judicial intervention.[118]

K. THIRD PARTIES

In divorce proceedings between the parents of a child, leave to apply for custody under section 16(3) of the *Divorce Act* may be granted to non-parents whose claim is not frivolous or vexatious. The onus of proving that the claim is frivolous or vexatious falls on the party opposing the application. Maternal grandparents with whom the child had been living may be added as third parties to a divorce proceeding between the child's parents, both of whom were opposed to the leave application.[119]

L. PROCESS

The *Divorce Act* is primarily concerned with the substantive rights and obligations of divorcing and divorced spouses and parents. Matters relating to evidence and procedure are primarily regulated by provincial and territorial legislation and rules of court. Only a few aspects of the divorce process are regulated by the *Divorce Act*. They include the statutory duties of lawyers and the courts respecting reconciliation and the duties of lawyers to promote the use of negotiation and mediation in resolving custody and access disputes.[120]

The definition of "court" in subsection 2(1) of the *Divorce Act* signifies that divorce is a matter that must be adjudicated by courts presided over by federally appointed judges. Provincially appointed judges have no jurisdiction to deal with divorce, although they have power to enforce orders for support or custody that have been granted in divorce proceedings.

The *Divorce Act* does not require that a divorce petition be tried in open court. Many provinces and territories have introduced so-called "desktop" uncontested divorces where the spouses do not personally ap-

---

118   See Janet Walker, "From Rights to Responsibilities for Parents: Old Dilemmas, New Solutions" (1991) 29 Family and Conciliation Courts Review 361. See also Andrew Bainham, "The *Children Act, 1989*: Welfare and Non-Interventionism" [1990] Fam. Law 143.

119   *Boychuk v. Boychuk*, [2001] A.J. No. 1578 (Q.B.). See Chapter 11, Section E(6).

120   See Chapter 6, Section D.

pear in court. Instead, the relevant evidence is presented by way of affidavits.

The current *Divorce Act* introduced the innovative procedure of joint petitions for divorce and joint applications for support, custody, and access.[121] Joint petitions are only appropriate when the spouses are in agreement and there are no hotly contested issues. As stated previously, third parties, such as grandparents or other relatives, may be permitted to intervene in divorce proceedings for the purpose of pursuing claims for custody or access to the children of the marriage.

---

121 *Divorce Act*, R.S.C. 1985 (2d Supp.), c. 3, s. 8(1) (divorce), ss. 15.1(1) and 15.2(1) (support), 16(2) (custody and access), and s. 17(1) (variation proceedings).

CHAPTER 11

REMEDIES AVAILABLE UNDER PROVINCIAL AND TERRITORIAL LEGISLATION

A. SPOUSAL SUPPORT

1) Diversity under Provincial and Territorial Statutes

Separated spouses may opt to seek spousal support under provincial or territorial legislation or by way of corollary relief in divorce proceedings. Unmarried cohabitants of the opposite sex or of the same sex may also be entitled to seek "spousal" support under provincial or territorial legislation. Provincial spousal support legislation that discriminates against couples living in a "common-law relationship"[1] or in a same-sex relationship[2] has been struck down as contravening equality rights under section 15 of the *Canadian Charter of Rights and Freedoms*.

In most provinces and territories, both federally and provincially appointed judges may adjudicate spousal and child support claims that arise independently of divorce.

Provincial and territorial statutes differ widely from each other in their specific provisions respecting spousal support. They also differ substantially from the language of the federal *Divorce Act*, which regulates spousal support on or after divorce.

---

1   *Taylor v. Rossu* (1998), 39 R.F.L. (4th) 242 (Alta. C.A.).
2   *M. v. H.*, [1999] 2 S.C.R. 3.

British Columbia[3] provides very general statutory criteria for spousal support orders. Several provinces, including New Brunswick,[4] Newfoundland and Labrador,[5] Nova Scotia,[6] Ontario,[7] Prince Edward Island,[8] and the Northwest Territories[9] provide a detailed statutory list of factors that the courts should take into account in determining the right to, duration, and amount of spousal support. The shortcomings of an unrefined list of designated factors, which lead to unbridled judicial discretion, have been tempered in Newfoundland and Labrador,[10] the Northwest Territories,[11] Ontario,[12] and Saskatchewan[13] by the articulation of specific objectives for support orders. These objectives are similar but not identical to those defined in the current *Divorce Act*.[14] Accordingly, they promote consistency between provincial and federal statutory criteria but fall short of providing a blueprint for uniformity.

Provincial statutory spousal support rights and obligations are no longer conditioned on proof of a matrimonial offence. Alberta,[15] British Columbia,[16] Manitoba,[17] New Brunswick,[18] Newfoundland and Labrador,[19] the Northwest Territories,[20] Ontario,[21] Prince Edward Island,[22] Quebec,[23] Saskatchewan,[24] and the Yukon Territory[25] have all abandoned the trad-

---

3   *Family Relations Act*, R.S.B.C. 1996, c. 128, s. 89.
4   *Family Services Act*, S.N.B. 1980, c. F-2.2, s. 115(6).
5   *Family Law Act*, R.S.N.L. 1990, c. F-2, s. 39(9).
6   *Maintenance and Custody Act*, R.S.N.S. 1989, c. 160, s. 4.
7   *Family Law Act*, R.S.O. 1990, c. F.3, s. 33(9).
8   *Family Law Act*, S.P.E.I. 1995, c. 12, s. 33(9).
9   *Family Law Act*, S.N.W.T. 1997, c. 18, s. 16.
10   *Family Law Act*, R.S.N.L. 1990, c. F-2, s. 39(8).
11   *Family Law Act*, S.N.W.T. 1997, c. 18, ss. 16(4), (5), (6), (7), (8), & (9).
12   *Family Law Act*, R.S.O. 1990, c. F-3, s. 33(8).
13   *Family Maintenance Act*, S.S. 1997, c. F-6.2, s. 5.
14   R.S.C. 1985 (2d Supp.), c. 3, ss. 15.2(6) and 17(7); see Chapter 8, Section G.
15   *Family Law Act*, S.A. 2003, c. F-4.5, ss. 58–60.
16   *Family Relations Act*, R.S.B.C. 1996, c. 128, s. 89.
17   *Family Maintenance Act*, C.C.S.M. c. F20, ss. 4 and 7.
18   *Family Services Act*, S.N.B. 1980, c. F-2.2, ss. 112 and 115(6).
19   *Family Law Act*, R.S.N.L. 1990, c. F-2, ss. 36 and 39(9).
20   *Family Law Act*, S.N.W.T. 1997, c. 18, ss. 15 and 16(5), (6), (7), (8), & (9).
21   *Family Law Act*, R.S.O. 1990, c. F-3, ss. 31 and 33(9).
22   *Family Law Act*, S.P.E.I. 1995, c. 12, ss. 30, 33(6), and (9).
23   *Civil Code of Québec*, S.Q. 1991, c. 64, art. 493, 511, and 585–96 [*C.c.Q.*].
24   *Family Maintenance Act*, S.S. 1997, c. F-6.2, ss. 5 and 7.
25   *Family Property and Support Act*, R.S.Y. 2002, c. 83, ss. 32 and 34(5).

itional offence concept in favour of economic criteria that largely focus on needs and ability to pay. In Newfoundland and Labrador,[26] the Northwest Territories,[27] and Ontario,[28] the spousal support obligation "exists without regard to the conduct of either spouse, but the court may in determining the amount of support have regard to a course of conduct that is not unconscionable as to constitute an obvious and gross repudiation of the [spousal] relationship."[29] Although there has been some inconsistency in the application of these statutory provisions, there has been strong judicial resistance to spouses engaging in mutual recriminations.[30] Manitoba, which originally applied a similar criterion of unconscionability, abandoned conduct as a relevant consideration altogether by amending legislation in 1983.[31] In Alberta, the courts may take misconduct into account only where it arbitrarily or unreasonably (i) precipitates, prolongs, or aggravates the need for support, or (ii) affects the ability of the obligor to provide support.[32] In New Brunswick[33] and Nova Scotia,[34] the relevant legislation expressly stipulates that courts may take conduct into account if it unreasonably prolongs the need for support. These statutory provisions are consistent with the statutory obligation on each spouse to strive for financial self-sufficiency. In the Yukon Territory,[35] a court is specifically empowered to deny support to a spouse who has remarried or is cohabiting with a third party in a relationship of some permanence.

2) Differences between Federal *Divorce Act* and Provincial and Territorial Legislation

Differences in provincial and territorial legislation and in the federal divorce legislation are primarily differences of form rather than of sub-

---

26 *Family Law Act*, R.S.N.L. 1990, c. F-2, s. 39(9).

27 *Family Law Act*, S.N.W.T. 1997, c. 18, s. 16(10).

28 *Family Law Act*, R.S.O. 1990, c. F-3, s. 33(10).

29 Compare *Maintenance and Custody Act*, R.S.N.S. 1989, c. 160, s. 6(2).

30 See Julien D. Payne, "The Relevance of Conduct to the Assessment of Spousal Maintenance under the *Reform Act*, S.O. 1978, c. 2" (1980) 3 Fam. L. Rev. 103, reprinted in *Payne's Digest on Divorce in Canada, 1968–1980* (Don Mills, ON: R. De Boo, 1982) at 419.

31 *Family Maintenance Act*, S.M. 1983, c. 54, s. 4, now C.C.S.M. c. F20, s. 4(2).

32 *Family Law Act*, S.A. 2003, c. F-4.5, s. 59.

33 *Family Services Act*, S.N.B. 1980, c. F-2.2, s. 115(6)(t).

34 *Maintenance and Custody Act*, R.S.N.S. 1989, c. 160, s. 6(1).

35 *Family Property and Support Act*, R.S.Y. 2002, c. 83, s. 34(5).

stance,[36] whether the courts are dealing with conduct or any other matter. If Mrs. Jones is separated from her husband, a judge is unlikely to allow the right to, duration, and amount of support to depend on whether she has invoked the provisions of the applicable provincial or territorial statute or the relevant provisions of the *Divorce Act*.

Certain important differences remain between the provincial and territorial support regimes and the federal divorce regime. In particular, provincial and territorial legislation confers broader powers on the courts with respect to the types of order that can be granted in proceedings for spousal support. The federal *Divorce Act*[37] empowers a court to grant orders to pay and secure a lump sum or periodic sums for spousal support. It does not empower a court to order a transfer of property in lieu of support payments. Most provincial and territorial support statutes[38] expressly confer wide powers on the courts with respect to such relief as lump sum payments, periodic payments, transfers or settlements of property, exclusive possession of the matrimonial home, security for support payments, and designation of a spouse as a beneficiary under a life insurance policy or pension plan. For constitutional reasons, orders respecting property rights can only be made by courts presided over by federally appointed judges.

B. CHILD SUPPORT UNDER PROVINCIAL AND TERRITORIAL LEGISLATION

Provincial and territorial statutory support regimes in Canada generally

---

36   *Snyder v. Pictou*, 2008 NSCA 19, [2008] N.S.J. No. 77.

37   R.S.C. 1985 (2d Supp.), c. 3, s. 15(2).

38   See *Family Law Act*, S.A. 2003, c. F-4.5, s. 49; *Family Relations Act*, R.S.B.C. 1996, c. 128, s. 93(5); *Family Maintenance Act*, C.C.S.M. c. F20, s. 10(1); *Family Services Act*, S.N.B. 1980, c. F-2.2, s. 116; *Family Law Act*, R.S.N.L. 1990, c. F-2, s. 40; *Maintenance and Custody Act*, R.S.N.S. 1989, c. 160, ss. 7, 33, and 36; *Family Law Act*, S.N.W.T. 1997, c. 18, s. 21; *Family Law Act*, R.S.O. 1990, c. F.3, s. 34; *Family Law Act*, S.P.E.I. 1995, c. 12, s. 34; *Family Maintenance Act*, S.S. 1997, c. F-6.2, s. 9; *Family Property and Support Act*, R.S.Y. 2002, c. 83, s. 38.

stipulate that parents owe an obligation to support their children.[39] For example, section 31 of the Ontario *Family Law Act*[40] provides as follows:

Obligation of parent to support child

31.(1) Every parent has an obligation to provide support, in accordance with need, for his or her unmarried child who is a minor or is enrolled in a full-time program of education, to the extent that the parent is capable of doing so.

Idem

(2) The obligation under subsection (1) does not extend to a child who is sixteen years of age or older and has withdrawn from parental control.

Provincial and territorial statutory support regimes usually provide broad definitions of "parent" or "child" for the purpose of defining the ambit of child support rights and obligations. Although these definitions take a variety of forms, it is common for child support obligations to be statutorily imposed on persons other than the natural parents where they stand in the place of parents to the children.[41] In Manitoba, the legal obligations of natural parents and of persons standing in the place of parents are regulated by statute so as to place the primary responsibility on the natural parents.[42]

---

39 *Family Relations Act*, R.S.B.C. 1996, c. 128, s. 88; *Family Maintenance Act*, C.C.S.M. c. F20, s. 36; *Family Services Act*, S.N.B. 1980, c. F-2.2, s. 113; *Family Law Act*, R.S.N.L. 1990, c. F-2, s. 37; *Maintenance and Custody Act*, R.S.N.S. 1989, c. 160, s. 8; *Children's Law Act*, S.N.W.T. 1997, c. 14, s. 58; *Family Law Act*, R.S.O. 1990, c. F.3, s. 31; *Family Law Act*, S.P.E.I. 1995, c. 12, s. 31; *Civil Code of Québec, C.c.Q.*, s. 585; *Family Maintenance Act*, S.S. 1997, c. F-6.2, s. 3; *Family Property and Support Act*, R.S.Y 2002, c. 83, s. 32.

40 R.S.O. 1990, c. F.3.

41 *Family Law Act*, S.A. 2003, c. F-4.5, ss. 47–49; *Family Relations Act*, R.S.B.C. 1996, c. 128, ss. 1, 87, and 88; *Family Maintenance Act*, C.C.S.M. c. F20, s. 1; *Family Services Act*, S.N.B. 1980, c. F-2.2, s. 1; *Family Law Act*, R.S.N.L. 1990, c. F-2, s. 2; *Children's Law Act*, S.N.W.T. 1997, c. 14, s. 57; *Family Law Act*, R.S.O. 1990, c. F.3, s. 1; *Family Law Act*, S.P.E.I. 1995, c. 12, s. 1; *Family Maintenance Act*, S.S. 1997, c. F-6.2, s. 2; *Family Property and Support Act*, R.S.Y 2002, c. 83, s.1. See, generally, Nicholas Bala, "Who Is a 'Parent'? 'Standing in the Place of a Parent' and Section 5 of the *Child Support Guidelines*" in The Law Society of Upper Canada, *Special Lectures 2006: Family Law* (Toronto: Irwin Law, 2007) at 71–118.

42 See *Family Maintenance Act*, C.C.S.M. c. F20, s. 36.

Provincial and territorial statutes empower their courts to order support for children over the age of majority in circumstances involving illness, disability, or post-secondary education.[43]

Most jurisdictions in Canada have adopted provincial or territorial *Child Support Guidelines* that mirror the *Federal Child Support Guidelines*. Little or no attention was paid to the possibility of a child instituting proceedings for support against both parents. Such a claim cannot be maintained under the *Divorce Act* and the *Federal Child Support Guidelines* because a child of the marriage has no standing to bring such an application under the *Divorce Act*.[44] A similar bar to relief does not necessarily exist, however, under provincial and territorial legislation. In *J.D.F. v. H.M.F.*,[45] Levy J., of the Nova Scotia Family Court, concluded that a child has standing to apply for support against both parents under the *Maintenance and Custody Act*. In such proceedings, the *Nova Scotia Child Maintenance Guidelines* apply. Furthermore, there is nothing inherently inappropriate with a child recovering the full table amount of child support from each parent. Indeed, such concurrent orders may be required in circumstances where the child is under the provincial age of majority. If the child had attained the age of majority, however, the court may apply section 3(2) of the *Child Maintenance Guidelines* and order each parent to pay such an amount as the court deems appropriate having regard to the condition, means, needs, and other circumstances of the child and the financial ability of each parent to contribute to the child's maintenance.

Effective 1 October 2005, Alberta has implemented provincial *Child Support Guidelines* to be applied where child support is sought pursuant to provincial statute. Prior to that date, Alberta courts applied the *Federal Child Support Guidelines* as a yardstick for determining the amount of child support to be paid and no distinction was drawn between the children of

---

43   *Family Law Act*, S.A. 2003, c. F-4.5, s. 46; *Family Relations Act*, R.S.B.C. 1996, c. 128, s. 87; *Family Maintenance Act*, C.C.S.M. c. F20, s. 35.1; *Family Law Act*, R.S.N.L. 1990, c. F-2, s. 37(7); *Family Services Act*, S.N.B. 1980, c. F-2.2, s. 115(6), as amended; *Maintenance and Custody Act*, R.S.N.S. 1989, c. 160, s. 2; *Children's Law Act*, S.N.W.T. 1997, c. 14, s. 57; *Family Law Act*, R.S.O. 1990, c. F.3, s. 31(1) (full-time education); *Family Law Act*, S.P.E.I. 1995, c. 12, s. 31; *Family Maintenance Act*, S.S. 1997, c. F-6.2, s. 4.

44   *Levesque v. Levesque* (1994), 4 R.F.L. (4th) 375 (Alta. C.A.); *Tapson v. Tapson* (1970), 2 R.F.L. 305 (Ont. C.A.).

45   [2001] N.S.J. No. 456 (Fam. Ct.).

non-cohabiting unmarried parents and the children of divorcing or divorced parents.[46] In *W.R.A. (Next friend of) and G.F.A.*,[47] Kenny J., of the Alberta Court of Queen's Bench, calculated the amount of child support arrears payable under a court order to the legal guardian of a child by retroactively applying the *Federal Child Support Guidelines*. In so doing, Kenny J. resolved an issue that was previously unclear under Alberta law. She concluded that a person who voluntarily consents to and is appointed as the private guardian of a child under the *Child Welfare Act* (Alberta) has a legal obligation to financially contribute towards the needs of the child. Consequently, the legal guardian cannot look to the non-custodial father of the child to exclusively assume the burden of child support after the mother's death.

C. NEED FOR RATIONALIZATION OF INCOME SUPPORT SYSTEMS

Sooner or later, the state must take steps to rationalize the diverse systems of income security in Canada. If every dollar in spousal and child support is set off against public assistance benefits or earned income, custodial parents and their children are no further ahead. What is needed is a rationalization of the laws governing the relationship between diverse sources of income, be it earned income, support payments, state subsidies, or any combination of these.

Although today's family law problem may be one of spousal and child support, tomorrow's will be the problem of elderly and infirm family members. People are living longer. Canada's population is growing older. Today's children will have to carry the tax burden for tomorrow's elderly. One in six children in Canada is now living in poverty. How can these children be realistically expected to contribute towards the future costs generated by an ageing population? The state must invest in these children today in order for dividends to be reaped tomorrow.

---

46 *Cavanaugh v. Ziegler*, [1998] A.J. No. 1423 (C.A.); *D.B.S. v. S.R.G.*, [2005] A.J. No. 2 (C.A.).
47 [2001] A.J. No. 1472 (Q.B.).

D. ENFORCEMENT OF SUPPORT

One of the problems that has plagued Canadian law over many years is the degree to which court orders for spousal and child support have fallen into default. The enforcement of support orders, even those granted in divorce, is regulated primarily by provincial and territorial legislation. Provincial and territorial automatic enforcement processes have been established whereby the enforcement of orders is no longer left to the spouses or parents to whom the money is payable. Orders for support are now registered with provincial or territorial agencies that monitor the payments and take any necessary steps to enforce orders that have fallen into default. Ontario and several other provinces have a system for automatic deduction of spousal and child support payments from an employee's pay cheque. Employers must make the necessary deduction and forward it to the appropriate regional enforcement office.[48]

E. CUSTODY OF AND ACCESS TO CHILDREN UNDER PROVINCIAL AND TERRITORIAL LEGISLATION

1) Welfare or Best Interests of Child

Custody or access disputes involving unmarried parents, third parties, or married parents who have separated without instituting divorce proceedings are regulated by provincial and territorial statutes. Provincial and territorial legislation also regulates wardship proceedings where child protection agencies seek to intervene in dysfunctional family situations that threaten the physical, emotional, or economic well-being of any child.

The "welfare" or "best interests" of the child has long been considered the paramount consideration in custody and access disputes between parents or between parents and third parties. Approximately seventy years ago, a judge of the Alberta Court of Appeal defined the criteria to be applied in contested custody proceedings in the following words:

---

48   See Statistics Canada, "Maintenance Enforcement Survey: Child and Spousal Support" *The Daily* (3 March 2008); Statistics Canada, Canadian Centre for Judicial Statistics, *Child and Spousal Support: Maintenance Enforcement Survey Statistics, 2006/2007* (Ottawa: Statistics Canada, 2008).

The paramount consideration is the welfare of the children; subsidiary to this and as a means of arriving at the best answer to that question are the conduct of the respective parents, the wishes of the mother as well as of the father, the ages and sexes of the children, the proposals of each parent for the maintenance and education of the children; their station and aptitudes and prospects in life; the pecuniary circumstance of the father and the mother — not for the purpose of giving the custody to the parent in the better financial position to maintain and educate the children, but for the purpose of fixing the amount to be paid by one or both parents for the maintenance of the children. The religion in which the children are to be brought up is always a matter for consideration, even, I think, in a case like the present where both parties are of the same religion, for the probabilities as to the one or the other of the parents fulfilling their obligations in this respect ought to be taken into account. Then an order for the custody of some or all of the children having been given to one parent, the question of access by the other must be dealt with.[49]

Provincial and territorial statutes across Canada have endorsed "the welfare of the child" or more commonly "the best interests of the child" as the determinative criterion in custody and access disputes.[50] In Alberta,

---

49 *O'Leary v. O'Leary* (1923), 19 Alta. L.R. 224 at 253 (C.A.), Beck J.A. See also *Leboeuf v. Leboeuf* (1928), 23 Alta. L.R. 328 (C.A.), Beck J.A.

50 *Family Law Act*, S.A. 2003, c. F-4.5, s. 18 (best interests of child is determinative with respect to "parenting" and "contact" orders; relevant factors listed); *R.L. v. M.P.*, [2008] A.J. No. 182 (Q.B.); *T.S. v. A.V.T.*, [2008] A.J. No. 293 (Q.B.); *Family Relations Act*, R.S.B.C. 1996, c. 128, s. 24 (best interests of child are paramount; specific factors designated as indicative of child's best interests; conduct only relevant to parenting capacity and impact on child); *Family Maintenance Act*, C.C.S.M. c. F20, s. 2 (best interests of child are paramount; child's views to be considered), s. 39(3) (conduct only relevant to parenting ability); *Family Services Act*, S.N.B. 1980, c. F-2.2, s. 1 (definition of "best interests of the child" by reference to specific factors), s. 129(2) (custody orders to be based on best interests of child); s. 129(3) (access to be determined on basis of best interests of child); *Children's Law Act*, R.S.N.L. 1990, c. C-13, s. 31 (custody and access to be determined on basis of best interests of child; specific factors designated as indicative of child's best interests; domestic violence to be taken into account but past conduct otherwise considered only when relevant to parenting ability), s. 71 (child entitled to be heard); *Maintenance and Custody Act*, R.S.N.S. 1989, c. 160, s. 18(5) (welfare of child is paramount); *Children's Law Act*, S.N.W.T. 1997, c. 14, s. 17 (custody and access to be determined on basis of best interests of child; specific factors designated; domestic violence to be considered but past conduct otherwise considered only when relevant to parenting ability; economic circumstances are not relevant to parenting ability); *Children's Law*

the terms custody and access orders have been displaced by new terminology, namely, "parenting" and "contact" orders.[51] Several provinces and territories, including Alberta, British Columbia, New Brunswick, Newfoundland and Labrador, Ontario, Saskatchewan, and the Yukon Territory, have statutorily designated particular factors that the courts must take into account in determining the best interests of a child.[52] Most of the provincial and territorial statutes, like the *Divorce Act*, expressly stipulate that the conduct of the parties is only relevant insofar as it affects parenting ability.[53]

To exemplify the type of statutory provisions found in most provinces and territories, it is appropriate to set out section 31 of the Newfoundland and Labrador *Children's Law Act*,[54] which provides as follows:

Merits of application for custody or access

31.(1) The merits of an application under this Part in respect of custody of or access to a child shall be determined on the basis of the best interests of the child.

Best interests of child

(2) In determining the best interests of a child for the purpose of an application under this Part in respect of custody of or access to a child, a court shall consider all the needs and circumstances of the child including,

    (a)   the love, affection and emotional ties between the child and,

        (i)   each person entitled to or claiming custody of or access to the child,

---

Reform Act, R.S.O. 1990, c. C.12, s. 24 (custody and access to be determined having regard to best interests of child in light of designated factors; past conduct only relevant to parenting ability); *Custody Jurisdiction and Enforcement Act*, R.S.P.E.I. 1988, c. C-33, s. 15 (custody and access to be determined on basis of best interests of child); *Children's Law Act*, S.S. 1997, c. C-8.2, ss. 8 & 9 (custody and access to be determined having regard only to best interests of child; specific factors identified as relevant); *Children's Act*, R.S.Y. 2002, c. 31, s. 1 (best interests of child are paramount and prevail over wishes of parent), s. 30 (specific factors designated as indicative of child's best interests; past conduct not considered, unless relevant to parenting ability; no presumption based on age or sex of child; rebuttable presumption in favour of sole physical custody but joint legal custody).

51   *Family Law Act*, S.A. 2003, c. F-4.5, ss. 32 and 35.

52   *Ibid.*

53   *Ibid.*

54   R.S.N.L. 1990, c. C-13.

      (ii) other members of the child's family who reside with the child, and

      (iii) persons involved in the care and upbringing of the child;

  (b) the views and preferences of the child, when the views and preferences can reasonably be ascertained;

  (c) the length of time the child has lived in a stable home environment;

  (d) the ability and willingness of each person applying for custody of the child to provide the child with guidance and education, the necessaries of life and the special needs of the child;

  (e) the ability of each parent seeking the custody or access to act as a parent;

  (f) plans proposed for the care and upbringing of the child;

  (g) the permanence and stability of the family unit with which it is proposed that the child will live; and

  (h) the relationship by blood or through an adoption order between the child and each person who is a party to the application.

Domestic violence and other past conduct

(3) In assessing a person's ability to act as a parent, the court shall consider whether the person has ever acted in a violent manner towards

  (a) his or her spouse or child;

  (b) his or her child's parent; or

  (c) another member of the household,

otherwise a person's past conduct shall only be considered if the court thinks it is relevant to the person's ability to act as a parent.

In New Brunswick, where the "best interests of the child" criterion applies equally to custody and access proceedings and to child protection proceedings, "the child's cultural and religious heritage" is included in the list of factors to be considered.[55]

---

55 *Family Services Act*, S.N.B. 1980, c. F-2.2, s. 1.

2) Types of Order

Provincial and territorial legislation,[56] like the federal *Divorce Act*,[57] confers wide powers on the courts in the exercise of their discretionary jurisdiction over custody and access. For example, courts may grant:

---

56   *Family Relations Act*, R.S.B.C. 1996, c. 128, s. 9 (interim orders), s. 10 (consent orders), s. 11 (incorporation of agreement in court orders), s. 35 (joint custody, access), s. 36 (apprehension of child by peace officer and return of child to custodial parent), s. 37 (non-molestation orders); *Family Maintenance Act*, C.C.S.M. c. F20, s. 11 (tracing whereabouts of parent), s. 13 (occupation of family residence), s. 48 (consent orders), s. 49 (disclosure of address), s. 50 (penalties); *Family Services Act*, S.N.B. 1980, c. F-2.2, s. 128 (non-molestation orders), s. 129 (custody and access), s. 132 (restraining orders), s. 132.1 (apprehension of child; role of police), s. 132.2 (prevention of removal of child; passports); *Children's Law Act*, R.S.N.L. 1990, c. C-13, s. 33 (custody, incidents of custody, access), s. 40 (supervision orders), s. 41 (enforcement of access, compensatory access, expenses, mediation), s. 42 (non-molestation), s. 43 (unlawful withholding of child), s. 44 (prohibiting removal of child), s. 45 (contempt powers of provincial courts), s. 46 (information as to address), s. 75 (consent orders), s. 79 (interim orders); *Children's Law Act*, S.N.W.T. 1997, c. 14, s. 20 (custody, incidents of custody, access), s. 23 (supervision orders), s. 28 (interim orders), s. 30 (enforcement of access, compensatory access, reimbursement of expenses, mediation), s. 31 (unlawful withholding of child), s. 32 (prohibiting removal of child), s. 33 (order for disclosure of information); *Children's Law Reform Act*, R.S.O. 1990, c. C.12, s. 28 (custody incidents of custody, access), s. 35 (supervision orders), s. 36 (non-molestation), s. 37 (unlawful withholding of child), s. 38 (prohibiting removal of child), s. 39 (contempt powers of provincial courts), s. 40 (information as to address), s. 75 (interim orders); *Custody Jurisdiction and Enforcement Act*, R.S.P.E.I. 1988, c. C-33, s. 5 (custody, incidents of custody, access), s. 10 (consent orders, incorporation of contract), s. 20 (non-molestation), s. 21 (order where child unlawfully withheld), s. 22 (prohibiting removal of child), s. 25 (information as to address of persons); *Children's Law Act*, S.S. 1997, c. C-8.2, s. 6 (custody, incidents of custody, access, any additional order, authorization of parent to appoint guardian, interim orders, notice of change of residence, sharing parental responsibilities), s. 7 (ex *parte* interim orders), s. 18 (powers to enforce custody and access orders), s. 23 (non-molestation), s. 24 (unlawful withholding of child), s. 26 (enforcement of access, compensatory access, security, mediation), s. 27 (payment of expenses), s. 28 (information as to address), s. 29 (contempt of court); *Children's Act*, R.S.Y. 2002, c. 31, s. 33 (joint custody; incidents of custody; additional orders), s. 35 (supervision orders), s. 36 (restraining orders), s. 42 (mediation), s. 43 (investigation orders), ss. 44 & 45 (extraprovincial evidence orders), s. 46 (apprehension orders), s. 47 (prohibiting removal of child), s. 48 (information about respondent's whereabouts).

57   R.S.C. 1985, (2d Supp.), c. 3, s. 6 (jurisdiction; transfer of proceedings), s. 16 (custody and access orders, interim orders, joint custody, and access, terms, and conditions, notice of change of residence), s. 17 (variation, terms, and conditions), ss. 18 & 19 (provisional orders for variation), s. 20 (enforcement throughout Canada). And see Chapter 10.

- interim or temporary orders,
- review orders, consent orders,
- joint guardianship and custody orders,
- third-party custody and access orders,
- orders dividing the incidents of custody,
- non-molestation or restraining orders,
- supervision orders,
- conditional orders restricting mobility or providing for notice of any intended change of residence,
- orders for the tracing of missing children,
- orders for the apprehension of children to prevent parental abduction,
- orders for the return of a child from outside the province or territory,
- orders for the enforcement of custody and access arrangements, and
- orders for the variation and termination of custody and access.

Absent some compelling reason, courts are hesitant to vary interim custody orders, which constitute temporary measures that are put in place until the parenting dispute can be resolved by agreement or a trial judgment.[58]

Review orders are unusual in custody and access cases because some degree of finality is usually desirable to promote stability in the lives of the children. However, a trial judge may find it appropriate to order an automatic review and to remain seized with jurisdiction, where he or she perceives a real prospect that his or her original order may not prove to be in the best interests of the children having regard to foreseeable future problems. The doctrines of *res judicata* and *functus officio* constitute no bar to the trial judge remaining seized with custody and access issues for the purpose of the review. Section 17(5) of the *Divorce Act* does not exclude the possibility of providing a fast-track review procedure under section 16(6) of the *Divorce Act*, which co-exists with the right of either parent to seek a variation order upon proof of a material change of circumstances. The triggering factor under section 16(6) may be the passage of time, the occurrence of some event, or the existence of some condition. In upholding the review provision in the current appeal, the Newfound-

---

58 *Koeckeritz v. Secord*, [2008] S.J. No. 129 (Q.B.).

land and Labrador Court of Appeal in *J.M.M. v. K.A.M.*[59] observed that the availability of the fast-track review procedure enabled the trial judge to grant an order for increased access to the children by the father on a five-day rotational basis, secure in the knowledge that this order could be expeditiously revisited if the father's previous conduct in seeking to alienate the children from their mother were resumed in the future.

3) Wishes of Child; Judicial Interviews; Legal Representation

With respect to custody and access proceedings, statutes in several provinces expressly acknowledge that the wishes of the child are a relevant factor to be considered in determining the "best interests of the child."[60] The significance of a child's wishes will depend on a number of factors including the child's age and maturity.[61]

Courts can take various steps to prevent either parent from embroiling their children in a contested custody/access proceeding. The presiding judge may exclude the children from the court, notwithstanding a parent's wish to have them present. Furthermore, although the children may be competent to give evidence, either sworn or unsworn, the judge may refuse to admit such evidence in the exercise of his or her inherent *parens patriae* jurisdiction, given that other avenues, such as assessments and home studies, are available to obtain the views and preferences of the children. A trial judge has the discretion to interview the children in chambers but this should not be undertaken lightly and a record must be kept of the interview. A judicial interview should not go beyond ascertaining

---

59   [2005] N.J. No. 325 (C.A.). For additional insights on review orders in custody/access proceedings, see *Sappier v. Francis* (2004), 276 N.B.R. (2d) 183 (C.A.) and see the annotation in (2004), 8 R.F.L. (6th) 218, which is cited in *J.M.M. v. K.A.M., ibid.* at para. 26.

60   *Family Law Act*, S.A. 2003, c. F-4.5, s. 18(2)(iv); *Family Relations Act*, R.S.B.C. 1996, c. 128, s. 24(1); *Family Maintenance Act*, C.C.S.M. c. F20, s. 2; *Family Services Act*, S.N.B. 1980, c. F-2.2, s. 1; *Children's Law Act*, R.S.N.L. 1990, c. C-13, s. 31(2)(b); *Children's Law Act*, S.N.W.T. 1997, c. 14, s. 17(2)(b); *Children's Law Reform Act*, R.S.O. 1990, c. C.12, s. 24(2)(b); *Custody Jurisdiction and Enforcement Act*, R.S.P.E.I. 1988, c. C-33, s. 8; *Civil Code of Québec*, C.c.Q., s. 34; *Children's Law Act*, S.S. 1997, c. C-8.2, s. 8(a)(vii) (custody) and s. 9(1)(iv) (access); *Children's Act*, R.S.Y 1986, c. 22, s. 131(h).

61   *L.E.G. v. A.G.*, [2002] B.C.J. No. 2319 (S.C.); *Poole v. Poole*, [2005] N.S.J. No. 68 (Q.B.); *Kittelson-Schurr v. Schurr*, [2005] S.J. No. 111 (Q.B.).

the wishes of the children; otherwise they become private witnesses and there is no basis in law for a court to admit such testimony.[62]

The three most common methods of ascertaining the views and preferences of a child are (i) judicial interview; (ii) the appointment of an independent expert able to ascertain the child's views; and (iii) the appointment of independent legal counsel for the child.[63] Most judges discourage parents and their lawyers from calling the children as witnesses in contested custody or access litigation.[64] Some judges will, however, interview the children privately in chambers, in the absence of the parents, but with counsel and/or a court reporter present.[65] Several provincial statutes specifically empower a judge to privately interview a child without imposing any requirement of parental consent. Judicial interviews of children without parental consent have also been endorsed by appellate courts in Manitoba and Saskatchewan.[66] In *A.(L.J.) v. A.(L.)*,[67] the British Columbia Court of Appeal expressed concern about the danger of a trial judge deciding a case on evidence of which the parents had no knowledge and no opportunity for cross-examination. Faced with significant cutbacks to legal aid services and in the use of third-party neutrals to ascertain a child's wishes, parents and their children may be denied justice if the voice of the child is not heard. In addressing these and other concerns, Martinson J., of the Supreme Court of British Columbia has formulated the following conclusions:

1.   A judge, at a trial, has the jurisdiction to interview a child in private, even in the absence of the consent of one or both parents. The

---

62   *M.E.S. v. D.A.S.*, [2001] A.J. No. 1521 (Q.B.); *Chovin v. Dancer-Chovin*, [2003] S.J. No. 598 (Q.B.).

63   *Kalaserk v. Nelson*, [2005] 8 W.W.R. 638 (N.W.T.S.C.), Vertes J., citing Christine Davies, "Access to Justice for Children: The Voice of the Child in Custody and Access Disputes" (2004) 22 Can. Fam. L.Q. 153; *Puszczak v. Puszczak*, [2005] A.J. No. 1715 (C.A.).

64   *Stefureak v. Chambers*, [2004] O.J. No. 4253 (Sup. Ct.).

65   Express statutory authority for judicial interviews, including the conditions applicable thereto, is found in several provinces: *Children's Law Act*, R.S.N.L. 1990, c. C-13, s. 70; *Children's Law Act*, S.N.W.T. 1997, c. 14, s. 83; *Children's Law Reform Act*, R.S.O. 1990, c. C.12, s. 65; *Custody Jurisdiction and Enforcement Act*, R.S.P.E.I. 1988, c. C-33, s. 8. See also David M. Siegel & Suzanne Hurley, "The Role of the Child's Preference in Custody Proceedings" (1977) 11 Fam. L. Q. 1.

66   See *Jandrisch v. Jandrisch* (1980), 16 R.F.L. (2d) 239 (Man. C.A.) and *Hamilton v. Hamilton* (1989), 20 R.F.L. (3d) 152 (Sask. C.A.). See also *R.A.L. v. R.D.R.*, [2006] A.J. No. 1474 (Q.B.).

67   (2002), 25 R.F.L. (5th) 8 (B.C.C.A.).

judge must, on a case by case basis, decide whether such an interview is in the best interests of the child in question.

2. In exercising this discretion, the judge can consider the general purposes of such an interview, and the general benefits of and concerns relating to the judge interview process. In addition, the judge can consider case specific factors by looking at:

    a. the relevance of the information that would be obtained to the issues that have to be decided,

    b. the reliability of the information that might be obtained, and

    c. the necessity of conducting the interview rather than obtaining the information in another way. Other options might include evidence presented:

        i.   by the parties in the form of expert evidence or no expert evidence

        ii. by a neutral third party expert

        iii. by a lawyer, acting as a lawyer for the child, an *amicus curiae*, (friend of the court), or a family advocate.

3. While a parent cannot simply veto an interview, a parent's specific reasons for withholding consent may be important to a determination of relevance, reliability, and necessity.[68]

In *Stefureak v. Chambers*,[69] where it was concluded that the wishes of a seven-year-old child may be relevant, but are not decisive, on a mother's application to vary an order for shared parenting, Quinn J. of the Ontario Superior Court of Justice reviewed the following five methods whereby a court may ascertain the views and preferences of a child:

a) Hearsay Evidence

Since the judgments of the Supreme Court of Canada in *R. v. Khan*,[70] and *R. v. Smith*,[71] hearsay evidence of out-of-court statements of a child are admissible for their truth, if they meet the tests of necessity and reliability. The nature and extent of the inquiry on the issue of necessity will depend on the facts of the particular case. Relevant factors for consideration would include counsel's consent to the admission of the evidence, and the child's age, emotional fragility, and level of understanding. The out-of-court statements of a child will satisfy the "necessity" test where

---

68   *L.E.G. v. A.G.*, [2002] B.C.J. No. 2319 (S.C.).
69   [2004] O.J. No. 4253 (Sup. Ct.).
70   [1990] 2 S.C.R. 531.
71   [1992] 2 S.C.R. 915.

the direct evidence of the child would be inadmissible. The reliability test will vary with the particular child and the attendant circumstances. There are many relevant considerations, such as timing, demeanour, the personality of the child, the intelligence and understanding of the child, and the absence of any reason to expect fabrication in the statement. The reliability test is satisfied where there are sufficient guarantees that the statements made are trustworthy. There may be some merit in a submission that the requirements of necessity and threshold reliability should be relaxed in custody cases, as compared to child protection proceedings and criminal prosecutions, if the custody case does not involve allegations of abuse, but this should not be regarded as a rigid rule; the degree of relaxation will depend on all the circumstances. Threshold reliability may be established if the out-of-court statements under consideration are made to more than one person but their ultimate reliability will only be determined after all the evidence in the case is known.

With respect to out-of-court statements that had already been included in the mother's testimony without objection from the father's counsel, Quinn J. concluded that it was impractical and inappropriate to revisit that evidence for the purpose of conducting after-the-fact *voir dires*. Insofar as future testimony was concerned, he made a blanket ruling that the necessity criterion had been met because it would be inappropriate for the child to be called as a witness. On the reliability issue, he concluded that the best approach would be to conduct a *voir dire* for each statement with the onus falling on the proponent of the hearsay evidence to establish threshold reliability.

b) In-Court Testimony of Young Children

There are no age-based statutory limitations on the competence of a child to testify. Testimony has been received by Canadian courts from children as young as four and, by the age of seven, "most children who are proposed as witnesses are ruled competent."[72] In the same article, the authors state that it is rare for children to suffer any long-term emotional disturbance from testifying in court. Indeed, giving such testimony may be cathartic. In the absence of some reasonably perceived psychological trauma to the child, there are two major obstacles to allowing a young child to testify in contested custody and access cases, namely,

---

72   See John Philippe Schuman, Professor Nicholas Bala, & Professor Kang Lee, "Developmentally Appropriate Questions for Child Witnesses" (1999) 25 Queen's Law J. 251.

(i)   the typical absence of a developmentally appropriate explanation to the child regarding the need for his or her testimony; and

(ii) the lack of training of the Bench and Bar in asking developmentally appropriate questions.

While conceding that it might not be too late to remove the first obstacle, Quinn J. found it to be too late for the second obstacle to be removed.

c)   Interviewing Child in Chambers

In responding to counsel's request for a judicial interview of the seven-year-old child in chambers, Quinn J. referred to section 64 of the Ontario *Children's Law Reform Act*, which expressly permits such interviews in custody and access proceedings instituted pursuant to that Act. Section 64 does not impose any duty on the judge to conduct an interview nor does it provide any criteria that must be met before an interview can take place. It is a matter of judicial discretion. The only requirement is that the interview be recorded. Customarily, the parents are not present but counsel may be present at the discretion of the judge. Case law and academic opinion suggest that a judge should only interview a child in chambers when other methods of ascertaining the child's views and preferences are unavailable. This suggestion is premised on the assumption that judges are not trained to interview children and the formality of a judicial interview in chambers is an intimidating environment in which it is difficult for the child to speak freely. Ultimately, however, the discretion whether to interview the child in chambers rests with the judge and it may be exercised over the objections of either or both of the parents and their counsel.

If a judge decides to interview the child in chambers, case law clarifies the use that may be made of the interview. The primary concern is to ensure that the views and preferences of the child are not confused with the child's best interests, which must be determined in light of the evidence as a whole. Judges must, nevertheless, face practical realities. For example, the wishes of a teenage child may be compelling because of the futility of ignoring those wishes. On the other hand, the wishes of a very young child, even if ascertainable, may carry little weight in the judicial determination of the child's best interests. In the final analysis, the weight to be given to any child's wishes will depend on the facts, including the child's age, intelligence, degree of maturity, and his or her ability to articulate an opinion. While some judges seek to obtain the views and preferences of the child, other judges may conduct an interview in chambers for the purpose of better understanding the child for the purpose of determining his or her best interests. Save in the most exceptional circumstances, it is wrong for a judge to obtain the confidence of a child by promising not to disclose any information provided. The judge has a discretion to decide whether anything should be disclosed about the results of the interview. In exercising this discretion, the judge must consider the ability of counsel to present argument at trial or on appeal, fairness to the parties, and potential embarrassment to the child. When a trial is already in progress, a properly conducted interview of the child in chambers may be the quickest and most efficient way to ascertain the views and preferences of a child, rather than ordering a lengthy adjournment for an assessment under section 30 of the Ontario *Children's Law Reform Act* or an investigation pursuant to section 112 of the Ontario *Courts of Justice Act*. Many judges are disinclined to interview a child in chambers, however, because of their lack of training in conducting such an interview. In *Stefureak v. Chambers*, Quinn J. found that a chambers interview was not feasible because he had no training or known skill in interviewing children.

d) Investigation by the Children's Lawyer

Section 112 of the *Courts of Justice Act* empowers the Children's Lawyer of Ontario to investigate, report, and make recommendations to the court on all matters concerning the custody of or access to a child that arise in proceedings under the *Divorce Act* or the Ontario *Children's Law Reform Act*. In *Novoa v. Molero*,[73] the Ontario Court of Appeal held that the use of the word "may" in sections 89(3.1) and 112 of the *Courts of Justice Act* clearly confers a discretion on the Children's Lawyer of Ontario to decide whether to act as the legal representative of a minor (section 89(3.1)) or to undertake an investigation and make a report and recommendations to the court on matters concerning the custody of and access to a child (section 112). Furthermore, there is no statutory or common-law obligation on the Children's Lawyer to give reasons for its decisions. *In Re K.*,[74] the Full Court of the Family Court of Australia set out the following non-exhaustive list of criteria for the appointment of a child representative:

(a)   Cases involving allegations of child abuse, whether physical, sexual, or psychological.

---

73   2007 ONCA 800, [2007] O.J. No. 4591.
74   (1994), 17 Fam. L.R. 537 at paras. 93–107 (Aust. Fam. Ct.).

(b) Cases where there is an apparently intractable conflict between the parents.

(c) Cases where the child is apparently alienated from one or both parents.

(d) Where there are real issues of cultural or religious difference affecting the child.

(e) Where the sexual preferences of either or both of the parents or some other person having significant contact with the child are likely to impinge upon the child's welfare.

(f) Where the conduct of either or both of the parents or some other person having significant contact with the child is alleged to be anti- social to the extent that it seriously impinges on the child's welfare.

(g) Where there are issues of significant medical, psychiatric, or psychological illness or personality disorder in relation to either party or a child or other persons having significant contact with the children.

(h) Any case in which, on the material filed by the parents, neither parent seems a suitable custodian.

(i) Any case in which a child of mature years is expressing strong views, the giving of effect to which would involve changing a long-standing custodial arrangement or a complete denial of access to one parent.

(j) Where one of the parties proposes that the child will either be permanently removed from the jurisdiction or permanently removed to such a place within the jurisdiction as to greatly restrict or for all practical purposes exclude the other party from the possibility of access to the child.

(k) Cases where it is proposed to separate siblings.

(l) Custody cases where none of the parties is legally represented.

(m) Applications in the court's welfare jurisdiction relating in particular to the medical treatment of children where the child's interests are not adequately represented by one of the parties.

In *Stefureak v. Chambers*, Quinn J. stated that paragraphs (a)–(c) and (f)–(h) might arguably apply to the case before him. While acknowledging that section 112 could be invoked mid-trial or even mid-appeal, Quinn J. held that section 112 should only be resorted to when there is a clearly-defined need that merits an investigation. Such a need did not exist in the present case because the views and preferences of the seven-year-old child were unlikely to have a significant role in the final decision. Given the father's belated mid-trial request for an investigation under section 112 of the *Courts of Justice Act*, Quinn J. harboured a strong suspicion that the father might be seeking to prop up a weak case by requesting the intervention of the Children's Lawyer.

In *Puszczak v. Puszczak*,[75] the Alberta Court of Appeal also cited the aforementioned thirteen factors in *Re K*.[76] and further stated that the Full Court of the Family Court of Australia has observed in the later case of *B. and R. and the Special Representative*[77] that cases may fall within those guidelines that do not require the appointment of a separate legal representative for the child. Furthermore, before appointing counsel for the child, the court must be satisfied that the child has the capacity to instruct counsel and that an appointee is independent and not aligned with or partial to either parent.

e) Court-Ordered Independent Assessment

Section 30(1) of the Ontario *Children's Law Reform Act* empowers a court to order an independent expert assessment of a child's needs and the ability and willingness of the parents to satisfy those needs. While conceding that section 30(1) might be invoked mid-trial to ascertain the views and preferences of a child, Quinn J. observed that the subsection is permissive in nature and case law indicates that assessments should only be ordered when there are clinical issues to be determined. In the circumstances before him in *Stefureak v. Chambers*, Quinn J. concluded that a court-ordered independent assessment was inappropriate for the same reasons as those indicated in the context of section 112 of the *Courts of Justice Act*.

Where an independent lawyer is appointed to act on behalf of a child in high-conflict custody or access proceedings, the role of the lawyer is to act as an advocate for the child and to ensure that the child's voice is heard in the dispute. If the child is sufficiently mature to express a preference on the vital issue of parental custody or access, the child has the right to have his or her wishes put in evidence before the court. Counsel representing the child has a professional right and duty to advise the child as to the possible consequences of the child's preferences. Counsel may also advise the child of counsel's perception of the child's best interests. In the final analysis, however, a mature child with powers of discernment

---

75 [2005] A.J. No. 1715 (C.A.).
76 (1994), 17 Fam. L.R. 537 (Aust. Fam. Ct.).
77 (1995), FLC 92-636 (Aust. Fam. Ct.).

has the right to have his or her personal wishes heard and advanced by counsel in court. The role of counsel is to serve as an advocate for the child and to put forward the evidence and submissions required to support the wishes of the child so that the child's voice can be heard. Counsel for the child is not a witness and is not entitled to press his or her opinions on the court as to what he or she perceives as being in the child's best interests. Counsel appointed to represent a child in a custody or access dispute is not there to determine what is in the child's best interests. That is the function of the trial judge, who will determine the best interests of the child after hearing all the evidence, including the evidence as to the child's wishes and his or her relationship with each parent. If there has been any improper manipulation or alienation of the child, the judge will weigh the wishes of the child in light of any evidence of that manipulation. Counsel for a mature child has no right to make recommendations to the court that are contrary to the child's own wishes. If counsel finds himself or herself unable to advocate for the child's wishes, then a new appointment of counsel for the child may be necessary.[78]

Although a thirteen-year-old child may be competent to give evidence in a highly conflictual parenting dispute, the court has discretion to refuse to permit the child to testify. Relevant factors to be considered in the exercise of the judicial discretion include the child's age; the child's aversion to or fear of testifying; the trauma that the child would suffer from testifying, even if those trauma do not involve long-term damage; the significance and probable weight of the child's evidence; whether the evidence could be obtained from another source; and the overall best interests of the child. In *S.E.C. v. G.P.*,[79] the father sought to call his thirteen-year-old daughter to testify on his behalf in response to the mother's allegations that the father had engaged in violent and abusive conduct during their cohabitation. The father also sought to have his daughter testify as to her wishes respecting future contact with her father. On the mother's application, Perkins J. set aside the father's summons of his daughter as a witness because her emotional well-being would not be served by

---

78   *M.F. c. J.*, [2002] J.Q. no 480 (C.A.), leave to appeal to S.C.C. refused, [2002] C.S.C.R. no 218. In this case, the appellant mother of the child sought the removal and replacement of counsel representing the child on the ground that counsel intended to rely on the expert opinion of a psychologist and seek increased contact between the child and his father as being in the best interests of the child, notwithstanding that the child was averse to this. The appeal was successful and an order was made for the replacement of the child's current lawyer.

79   [2003] O.J. No. 2744 (Sup. Ct.).

requiring her to testify, her evidence would not carry great weight having regard to the already available evidence addressing the general climate in the home over the years, and the reliability of any evidence presented would be suspect because the child was attached to her father and did not want to displease him.

A parental-capacity assessment sought pursuant to section 32F(1) of the *Judicature Act* (Nova Scotia) is appropriate where relevant clinical information would not otherwise be available to the court. Assessments are intrusive and involve additional costs and delay in the adjudicative process. They should not be ordered as a matter of course, nor should they be used as a fishing expedition. In *Lewis v. Lewis*,[80] an interim application for a parental-capacity assessment was denied because the applicant failed to show that it was necessary and in the best interests of the children, and the court had grave concerns that the proposed assessment would be used as an attempt to put forward highly prejudicial sexual abuse allegations that would not otherwise be admissible as evidence.

Professionals with expertise in various social sciences may provide insights into a child's particular circumstances and the capacity of one or both of the parties to parent the child. Two distinctions between an expert retained by one of the parents and an expert appointed by the court pursuant to section 97 of the *Queen's Bench Act* (Saskatchewan) are found in subsections 97(2) and (3) of the Act, namely, (i) when a report is ordered for the assistance of the court, the expert may be called as a witness by the court and is subject to cross-examination by any party; and (ii) a court-appointed expert is statutorily immune from civil liability for anything done or omitted to be done in good faith. Section 97 of the *Queen's Bench Act* (Saskatchewan) does not preclude a parent from calling as his or her own witness an expert who is qualified to make observations and proffer opinions on the custody, access, and welfare of children. The admissibility of expert-opinion evidence in this area is subject to the same set of criteria that govern opinion evidence in other areas of expertise. The evidence must be necessary, relevant, and provide information likely to be outside the experience of the trier of fact. The evidence must not offend any other exclusionary rule, and the person offering the evidence must be suitably qualified. In *Johnston v. Kurz*,[81] a section 97 assessment was not ordered but the parents agreed that the father would retain and pay for his own assessor and the mother would co-operate in the assessment.

---

80   [2005] N.S.J. No. 368 (S.C.).
81   [2005] S.J. No. 558 (Q.B.).

The evidence of the assessor was deemed admissible. After reviewing the best interests of the children in light of all the evidence, and the criteria defined in sections 6(1), (5), (7), and (8) of the *Children's Law Act* (Saskatchewan), and in *Gordon v. Goertz*,[82] M-E. Wright J. concluded that the mother, who had been the child's primary caregiver, should be granted permission to relocate with the child from Saskatchewan to New Brunswick to marry her fiancé and pursue available career opportunities there. The mother's wish to relocate under these circumstances was found to outweigh the consequential disruption of the child's close relationship with the father and paternal grandparents, which could be ameliorated to some degree by arrangements for frequent visits and contact by means of letters, telephone calls, e-mails, and webcam.

Where an assessment report is ordered pursuant to section 97 of the *Queen's Bench Act* (Saskatchewan), there can be no doubt that the report is for the assistance of the court and both parents are afforded the liberty of full cross-examination. As *Larre v. Cross*[83] demonstrates, where parents have jointly retained an assessor without recourse to section 97, one parent or the other is required to take "ownership" of the witness based on the assessor's subjective assessment of which of them came off better in the assessment. Because assessments are frequently critical of both parents and they may recommend joint custody for parents who are each seeking sole custody, *Larre v. Cross* may result in the unintended consequence that neither parent calls the assessor, thus denying valuable evidence to the court. Such a result is contrary to the long-standing principle, which is acknowledged in *Redshaw v. Redshaw*,[84] that all evidence that bears on the seminal question of a child's best interests should be made available to the court. In *Cozart v. Cozart*,[85] the parents had agreed to a joint custody and access assessment at a pre-trial conference. Before the assessment was undertaken, the mother launched a "mobility" application seeking to relocate the children from Central Butte to Saskatoon. The father contended that a custody and access assessment was essential to determine that issue and, since the parents had previously agreed to the completion of an assessment by a designated expert, the mother's application was adjourned on condition that it not be returned prior to the receipt of the assessor's report and resumption of the pre-trial

---

82   [1996] 2 S.C.R. 27.
83   [1998] S.J. No. 851 (Q.B.).
84   (1985), 47 R.F.L. (2d) 104 (Sask. C.A.).
85   [2005] S.J. No. 555 (Q.B.).

conference. Although there was no specific reference made to section 97 of the *Queen's Bench Act* (Saskatchewan), there was no doubt that the assessor's report was required for the court's assistance rather than for the edification of the parents or as a vehicle to promote settlement. In the result, Wilkinson J. granted an order pursuant to section 97 of the *Queen's Bench Act* (Saskatchewan) in terms of the draft order filed by the father, thus rendering the assessor subject to cross-examination by either parent.

4) Mediation and Reconciliation Attempts; Confidentiality of Process

In several provinces and territories, including British Columbia,[86] Manitoba,[87] Newfoundland and Labrador,[88] the Northwest Territories,[89] Ontario,[90] Quebec,[91] Saskatchewan,[92] and the Yukon,[93] enactments regulate the confidentiality of reconciliation counselling and of the mediation process in economic and parenting disputes on marriage breakdown. Provincial and territorial statutes regulating reconciliation and mediation or conciliation processes differ substantially in content. They do, however, have one feature in common. With the exception of Saskatchewan,[94] the provincial and territorial legislation presupposes judicial control or intervention and, unlike section 9 of the federal *Divorce Act*,[95] does not impose specific duties on lawyers who represent clients in family disputes. In other particulars, there are wide variations. Some statutory provisions are confined to reconciliation;[96] others are confined to

---

86 *Family Relations Act*, R.S.B.C. 1996, c. 128, s. 3 (family court counsellor).

87 Compare *Family Maintenance Act*, C.C.S.M. c. F20, ss. 12 and 47 (reconciliation).

88 *Family Law Act*, R.S.N.L. 1990, c. F-2, s. 4 (mediation); *Children's Law Act*, R.S.N.L. 1990, c. C-13, ss. 37 (mediation) and 41 (access enforcement).

89 *Family Law Act*, S.N.W.T. 1997, c. 18, s. 58 (mediation); *Children's Law Act*, S.N.W.T. 1997, c. 14, s. 71 (mediation).

90 *Family Law Act*, R.S.O. 1990, c. F.3, s. 3 (mediation); *Children's Law Reform Act*, R.S.O. 1990, c. C.12, s. 31 (mediation).

91 Quebec *Code of Civil Procedure*, R.S.Q. c. C-25, ss. 815.2 to 815.3 (reconciliation and mediation).

92 *Children's Law Act*, S.S. 1997, c. C-8.2, ss. 10 & 11 (mediation) and 26 (access enforcement); *Family Maintenance Act*, S.S. 1997, c. F-6.2, ss. 15 & 16 (mediation).

93 *Children's Act*, R.S.Y. 2002, c. 31, s. 42.

94 *Children's Law Act*, S.S. 1997, c. C-8.2, s. 11.

95 See Chapter 6, Section D(1).

96 *Family Maintenance Act*, C.C.S.M. c. F20, s. 12 (duty of court to promote reconciliation).

mediation;[97] still others apply to both reconciliation and mediation.[98] In addition, some statutes render evidence of statements made to a counsellor or mediator inadmissible except on consent of the parties,[99] while others specifically distinguish "open" or "closed" mediation.[100] This latter statutory approach originated in Ontario with the enactment of section 31 of the *Children's Law Reform Act*,[101] which regulates the potential confidentiality of the mediation process with respect to parenting disputes. Court-ordered mediation on consent of the parties under section 31 requires the parties to decide whether the mediator will file a full report of the mediation or a report that simply stipulates the outcome of the mediation process. If parties elect the latter, evidence of any admission or communication made in the course of the mediation is inadmissible in any legal proceeding except on consent of all parties to the proceeding.[102] Even in the absence of statutory provisions, however, judge-made law has accorded a common-law privilege to communications made in an attempt to settle disputes.[103]

5) Court-Ordered Investigations, Assessments, and Reports

Several provinces and territories have enacted statutory provisions whereby their courts may order investigations, assessments, and reports to be undertaken by independent experts in custody and access proceed-

---

97 *Family Services Act*, S.N.B. 1980, c. F-2.2, s. 131 (court-ordered conciliation); *Family Law Act*, R.S.N.L. 1990, c. C-13, s. 4; *Children's Law Act*, R.S.N.L. 1990, c. C-13, s. 37; *Children's Law Act*, S.N.W.T. 1997, c. 14, s. 71; *Family Law Act*, S.N.W.T. 1997, c. 18, s. 58; *Children's Law Reform Act*, R.S.O. 1990, c. C.12, s. 31; *Family Law Act*, R.S.O. 1990, c. F.3, s. 3; *Children's Law Act*, S.S. 1997, c. C-8.2, ss. 10 & 11; *Family Maintenance Act*, S.S. 1997, c. F-6.2, ss. 15 & 16; *Children's Act*, R.S.Y. 2002, c. 31, s. 42.

98 Quebec *Code of Civil Procedure*, R.S.Q. c. C-25.

99 *Family Relations Act*, R.S.B.C. 1996, c. 128, s. 3; Quebec *Code of Civil Procedure*, R.S.Q. c. C-25, s. 815.3; *Children's Law Act*, S.S. 1997, c. C-8.2, s. 10; *Family Maintenance Act*, S.S. 1997, c. F-6.2, s. 15.

100 See Section E(4), above in this chapter. See also *Children's Law Act*, R.S.N.L. 1990, c. C-13, s. 37; *Family Law Act*, R.S.N.L. 1990, c. C-13, s. 4; *Children's Law Act*, S.N.W.T. 1997, c. 14, s. 71; *Family Law Act*, S.N.W.T. 1997, c. 18, s. 58; *Children's Law Reform Act*, R.S.O. 1990, c. C-12, s. 31; *Family Law Act*, R.S.O. 1990, c. F-3, s. 3; *Children's Act*, R.S.Y. 2002, c. 31, s. 42.

101 R.S.O. 1990, c. C.12.

102 *Ibid.*, s. 31(7).

103 *Sinclair v. Roy* (1985), 47 R.F.L. (2d) 15 (B.C.S.C.); *Porter v. Porter* (1983), 32 R.F.L. (2d) 413 (Ont. U.F.C.).

ings.[104] Some statutes confer this discretionary authority on the courts in very general terms; others provide more detailed statutory provisions to regulate the judicial discretion. By way of example, Ontario falls into the latter category. In that province, the power of the court to order an "assessment" of the child's needs and the ability of the parties to meet those needs is defined in section 30 of the Ontario *Children's Law Reform Act*.[105] This power is exercisable as soon as an application for custody or access is brought. An assessment may be ordered before or during the hearing of the application.[106] The court may order an assessment on the request of any party to the application or on its own initiative. Where possible, the court will appoint an assessor chosen by the parties, but their failure to agree does not preclude the court from appointing an assessor who is willing to undertake the assessment and report to the court within the period of time designated by the court. The court may direct the parties to the application, the child, and other persons (for example, a "common-law spouse") to submit to an assessment, and any refusal to do so entitles the court to draw adverse inferences against a non-consenting adult respecting his or her ability or willingness to meet the needs of the child.

The report of the assessor is filed with the court and copies are provided to the parties and to counsel, if any, for the child. The assessor may be required to attend as a witness at any subsequent hearing of the application for custody or access. The costs of the assessment are to be borne by the parties in such proportions as the court directs, but the court may relieve a party from all or any of his or her financial responsibilities where serious pecuniary hardship would otherwise ensue. A court-ordered assessment does not preclude the parties or counsel representing the child from submitting other expert evidence respecting the needs of the child and the ability or willingness of the parties or any of them to satisfy those needs.

The role of an independent assessor, who is usually a psychiatrist, psychologist, or social worker, is to assist the court in its search for a custody or access disposition that reflects the best interests of the child.

---

104 *Family Relations Act*, R.S.B.C. 1996, c. 128, s. 15; *Family Maintenance Act*, C.C.S.M. c. F20, s. 3; *Children's Law Act*, R.S.N.L. 1990, c. C-13, s. 36; *Children's Law Act*, S.N.W.T. 1997, c. 14, s. 29; *Maintenance and Custody Act*, R.S.N.S. 1989, c. 160, s. 19; *Children's Law Reform Act*, R.S.O. 1990, c. C.12, s. 30; *Queen's Bench Act*, R.S.S. 1978, c. Q-1, s. 23.5 as amended by S.S. 1994, c. 27, s. 6; *Children's Act*, R.S.Y. 2002, c. 31, s. 43.

105 R.S.O. 1990, c. C.12.

106 *Stefureak v. Chambers*, [2004] O.J. No. 4253 (Sup. Ct.).

Although the assessor is entitled but not compelled to recommend a specific disposition or course of action, the decision-making authority remains vested in the trial judge. Assessment is not an exact science and the assessor's report and recommendation must be reviewed by the trial judge in light of all the evidence that has been adduced.

In custody and access proceedings, section 30 of the Ontario *Children's Law Reform Act* empowers the court to order an independent expert to assess and report to the court on the needs of the child and the willingness and ability of the parties to satisfy those needs. The party seeking a custody assessment must satisfy the court that it will likely provide evidence relating to the best interests of the child that would be otherwise unavailable. Court-ordered custody assessments are intrusive, costly, and may cause unwarranted delay. They should not be routinely ordered as a vehicle to promote settlement and should be limited to cases in which there are clinical issues to be determined.[107] In *Sheikh v. Sheikh*,[108] Flynn J., of the Ontario Superior Court of Justice, rejected the father's contention that "clinical issues" arose that called for an independent expert assessment in the context of the mother's proposal to relocate with the child to England, her premarital country of residence, because geographic and cultural alienation of the child from the father would be injurious to the child's emotional and psychological well-being. Flynn J. also concluded that there was a reasonable apprehension of bias on the part of the father's chosen expert who had already spoken to the father and manifested a predisposition against the move contemplated by the mother. Flynn J. further concluded that the father's belated motion for an independent assessment was indicative of a delaying tactic that should be addressed not only by dismissing the application for an independent assessment but also by issuing specific directions for an early trial, such as is mandated by section 26 of the Ontario *Children's Law Reform Act*. The mother was awarded costs of the motion on a partial indemnity basis, with the amount to be fixed after written submissions were made in accordance with judicial directions. In *Ursic v. Ursic*,[109] the Ontario Court of Appeal stated that, where there is a high degree of parental conflict and the child is only a toddler, the situation cries out for an expert assessment and the benefits such information can give a trial judge.

---

107   *Linton v. Clarke* (1994), 10 R.F.L. (4th) 92 (Ont. Div. Ct.).
108   [2004] O.J. No. 4384 (Sup. Ct.).
109   [2006] O.J. No. 2178 (C.A.). See also *R.P.B. v. K.D.P.*, [2006] A.J. No. 1192 (Q.B.).

Regarding the weight to be given to custody and access assessments, in *V.S.G. v. L.J.G.*[110] Blishen J. of the Superior Court of Justice observed that the court must consider the following:

1. the expertise of the assessors,
2. the methodology used,
3. the reliability of the factual underpinnings for opinions provided,
4. bias, and
5. whether the opinion evidence is based on solidly grounded scientific knowledge.

Blishen J. further observed that she was unaware of any standardized protocol for conducting assessments, although good assessments use a variety of methods to ensure the reliability of information obtained respecting a child and parents, including the following:

1. interviews with each parent and anyone living with the person seeking custody or access (e.g. new partners);
2. interviews with the child and observation of interaction between parents and children;
3. contact with others who have had significant involvement such as teachers or family doctors, as well as relatives who have a significant role in the lives of the children, such as grandparents;
4. a review of significant records or reports about the children or their parents; and,
5. psychological tests on parents and perhaps children, if a registered psychologist is involved.

The use and abuse of expert opinion evidence in guardianship, custody, and access disputes has attracted critical attention.[111] It is gener-

---

110 [2004] O.J. No. 2238 (Sup. Ct.).

111 Saul V. Levine, "The Role of the Mental Health Expert Witness in Family Law Disputes" in Rosalie S. Abella & Claire L'Heureux-Dubé, eds., *Family Law: Dimensions of Justice* (Markham, ON: Butterworths, 1983) at 129; R. Parry, *Custody Disputes: Evaluation and Intervention* (Toronto: Lexington Books, 1986); Gwynn Davis, *Partisans and Mediators: The Resolution of Divorce Disputes* (New York: Oxford University Press, 1988); Richard A. Gardner, "My Involvement in Custody Litigation: Past, Present and Future" (1989) 27 Family and Conciliation Courts Review 1; Faith K. Kaplan, Barbara L. Landau, & Robert L. McWhinney, "Custody/Access Assessment Guidelines: Report of the Interdisciplinary Committee for Custody/Access Assessments" (1989) 27 Family and Conciliation Courts Review 61; Paula J. Caplan & Jeffery Wilson, "Assessing the Child Custody Assessors" (1990) 27 R.F.L. (3d) 121.

ally conceded, however, that independent investigations, assessments, and reports can be of substantial assistance to courts and often produce parental settlements without recourse to protracted litigation. "Open assessments" and "closed mediation" as means of resolving guardianship, custody, and access disputes were the subject of a pilot project in Edmonton, Alberta, between 1 January 1985 and 31 December 1987. The success of this project[112] led to the implementation of a more broadly-based program in the Northern and Southern Regions of Alberta on 1 January 1991. *Family Law Practice Note 7* currently confers jurisdiction on the Alberta Court of Queen's Bench to authorize two kinds of procedure, namely, interventions and assessments. An intervention signifies a short-or long-term therapeutic involvement by a parenting expert that is resolution-oriented to assist families to overcome conflict. The intervention is intended to support the family in a collaborative, child-centred manner. The types of intervention may include counselling/therapy; educational sessions; assisting parents to develop and implement a parenting plan or parallel parenting plans; evaluation; remedial facilitated access; and formulating recommendations to the court for longer-term counselling, mediation, arbitration, or other forms of intervention. An assessment is an objective, neutral evaluation carried out by a parenting expert as an aid to litigation. An assessment may address only one home or parent or child. Assessments may include psychological testing. An assessment may also explore individual issues such as the educational needs of a child, the mental health of an individual, and anything else that the litigants identify and the court orders. Assessments include bilateral custody assessments. The parenting expert submits an assessment report to the court with copies to the parties or their counsel. A parenting expert may be required to give *viva voce* evidence and is subject to cross-examination by the parties in any proceedings wherein the best interests of the child are in issue.[113]

The court may authorize the court-appointed assessor to seek information from a psychologist who is counselling the children. Such authorization may be circumscribed by strict conditions that are designed to protect the privacy of the children and their non-involvement in the parental litigation as well as the confidentiality of their files.[114]

---

112   See R. Neil Dunne (Attorney General's Department) & Vincent Dwyer (Department of Social Services), *Edmonton Custody Mediation Project: Final Report* (Edmonton: Edmonton Custody Mediation Project, 1987) at 7–8.

113   See *R.P.B. v. K.D.P.*, [2006] A.J. No. 1192 (Q.B.).

114   *L.M.B. v. I.J.B.*, [2003] A.J. No. 1643 (Q.B.).

The admissibility of a report ordered pursuant to section 15 of the *Family Relations Act* (British Columbia) is not governed by the same evidentiary rules that apply when an expert's report is commissioned by one of the parties. A section 15 report may be admitted despite its inclusion of hearsay evidence and its reference to documents that will not be in evidence at the trial. The weight to be given to the opinions and recommendations of the assessor are to be determined in light of the evidence given at the trial relating to the facts and assumptions underlying the assessor's opinions.[115]

The preparation and reception of a court-ordered report under section 15 of the *Family Relations Act* (British Columbia) has built-in safeguards that are an inherent part of a process designed to place important and sensitive information before the court. Jurisdiction is vested in the court to approve the person to be appointed to carry out the investigation and the person so appointed reports to the court. Copies of the investigator's report are provided to the parties before it is placed before the court and any party is at liberty to compel the author's attendance for cross-examination and may lead evidence as to factual matters contained in the report. Given these various safeguards, the proper approach is to consider the factual aspects of the report to be *prima facie* evidence as to the truth of those facts. Where neither party challenges the report or requires the attendance of its author, the report should be considered a part of the evidence as a whole placed before the court. Faced with inaccurate and unreliable evidence on the part of both parents in *P.A.B. v. T.K.B*,[116] Parrett J. placed substantial weight on the report of the court-appointed expert in concluding that a joint custody regime was precluded by acrimony and bitterness that prevented the parents from maintaining the level of communication necessary to make such a regime workable. Consequently, sole custody was granted to the mother, with the father being entitled to reasonable and generous access to the children.

The opinions and recommendations of a court-appointed psychologist may be judicially discounted where the evidence as a whole leads the judge to assess the situation differently and parts of the report stray beyond the kind of investigation contemplated by section 15 of the *Family Relations Act* (British Columbia). In *Leontowicz v. Jacobsen*, the "recommendations" addressed a number of matters that the court was better qualified to evaluate, such as the significance of adherence to court or-

---

115   *Wu v. Sun*, 2006 BCSC 1891, [2006] B.C.J. No. 3276.
116   *P.A.B. v. T.K.B.*, [2004] B.C.J. No. 86 (S.C.).

ders, and some went directly to ultimate issues by applying the assessor's perception of the applicable legal criteria.[117]

A trial judge is not bound by the opinions and recommendations of an expert witness chosen by both parents to address issues of custody and mobility rights. The expert's opinion may be judicially dismissed where the evidence as a whole does not support significant factual assumptions made by the expert with respect to the parenting capabilities of the parties.[118]

An independent custody assessment report ordered pursuant to section 30 of the Ontario *Children's Law Reform Act* is admissible as expert evidence. Consequently, when asked to order an assessment, the court should consider the legal requirements relating to the admissibility of expert evidence. In *R. v. Mohan*,[119] the Supreme Court of Canada states that the admission of expert evidence depends on the application of the following criteria:

- relevance;
- necessity in assisting the trier of fact;
- the absence of any exclusionary rule; and
- a properly qualified expert.

The fact that expert evidence might be helpful is insufficient to satisfy the second requirement. Although necessity is not to be determined by too strict a standard, the expert's opinion must be necessary in the sense that it will provide information that is likely to be outside the experience and knowledge of the court. In *Linton v. Clarke*,[120] the Ontario Divisional Court ruled that assessments should not be routinely ordered in custody and access disputes but should be limited to cases in which clinical issues must be determined. Although the necessity requirement may well be met in some cases by the presence of clinical issues, there are also cases in which clinical issues exist but the court considers that an independent assessment under section 30 of the Ontario *Children's Law Reform Act* is unnecessary.

Where the children in a contested custody/access proceeding have independent legal counsel and an experienced social worker assigned by the Office of the Children's Lawyer, reports are available from a psych-

---

117   *Leontowicz v. Jacobsen*, [2003] B.C.J. No. 2723 (S.C.).
118   *Cade v. Rotstein*, [2004] O.J. No. 286 (C.A.).
119   [1994] 2 S.C.R. 9 at paras. 17 and 22.
120   (1994), 21 O.R. (3d) 568 (Div. Ct.).

ologist and from the children's family doctor, and direct evidence will also be provided by two Children's Aid Societies, the court may dismiss a parent's application for a court-ordered assessment under section 30 of the Ontario *Children's Law Reform Act* because the trial judge will be able to determine the issues raised in the case without the need for such an assessment. Any deficiencies identified by the applicant parent with respect to the work of the social worker appointed to assist the children's legal counsel may be dealt with by cross-examination and by direct evidence and they do not, in themselves, justify a court-ordered section 30 assessment. The fact that both parents had previously agreed to such an assessment does not circumscribe the court's discretion under section 30 of the Ontario *Children's Law Reform Act* and the agreement will carry little weight when it preceded the appointment of the lawyer and social worker by the Office of the Children's Lawyer.[121]

Expert critiques of independent custody assessments have frequently been introduced without any consideration of the question of their admissibility. The rule for admissibility of expert evidence in family law cases is the same as that applicable in other cases: the four-part test as originally set out in *R. v. Moran*, above, and refined in subsequent cases is applicable. In many cases relating to the evidence of a proposed expert, the critical question relates to necessity. Expert evidence will be necessary when it can provide a ready-made inference, which the judge, due to the technical nature of the facts, is unable to formulate; expert evidence is not necessary to address matters that fall within the scope of common sense. In most cases, it is neither necessary nor appropriate to introduce the evidence of a collateral critique of an independent custody assessment. Such a critique may be undertaken to assist counsel in formulating questions for cross-examination of the assessor or to assist counsel in developing an argument concerning the weight to be assigned to an assessment report, but it will not ordinarily be "necessary" to introduce the critique as original evidence or to call the expert who undertook the critique to give testimony.[122]

If the Children's Lawyer of Ontario becomes involved in a case pursuant to section 112 of the *Courts of Justice Act*, a judge may request, but cannot require, the Children's Lawyer to have a report prepared by someone other than the worker who prepared an earlier report in the case. Where such a course of action is favoured by the judge, the Children's

---

121 *J.J.B. v. G.G.B.*, [2003] O.J. No. 4073 (Sup. Ct.).
122 *Mayfield v. Mayfield*, [2001] O.J. No. 2212 (Sup. Ct.).

Lawyer should be given the opportunity to hear the judge's concerns and offer a response. Ultimately, it is up to the Children's Lawyer to decide how to proceed.[123]

In *Genovesi v. Genovesi*,[124] Granger J., of the Ontario General Division, held that an independent custody assessment is usually ordered for use at a trial and it is only in rare cases that the information obtained by the assessor might require immediate scrutiny on an interim application to determine whether there should be some variation of the existing parenting arrangement.

In Saskatchewan, custody/access assessments take a variety of forms, including full custody/access assessments, access assessments only, focused assessments that concentrate on a specific aspect of the parenting arrangement and/or the welfare of the child(ren), and "voices of the children" reports, which set out the wishes and/or concerns of the children. This list is not exhaustive. Such reports may be ordered by a judge at any stage of a proceeding and the reasons for ordering such reports differ widely. Given the wide variety of assessments in Saskatchewan, when they may be ordered, and the different purposes for which they are ordered, it is not prudent to endorse hard and fast rules with respect to their use.

There are a number of factors a court should consider in determining whether or not it is proper to consider an assessor's report. These circumstances include but are not limited to the following:

(i)   the nature of the application (i.e., whether it is an interim application or an application for variation);

(ii)   the nature of the relief sought (i.e., custody, access, a change from supervised to unsupervised visitations, etc.);

(iii)   the purpose of the assessment (i.e., whether it is for use by the chambers judge and/or at trial);

(iv)   the scope of the assessment (i.e., whether it is a full custody/access assessment, a focused assessment, a voices of the children report, etc.);

(v)   whether the assessment raises some immediate concern relating to the health and/or safety of the children;

(vi)   whether the parties agree to the use of the assessment;

(vii)   whether an evidentiary basis has been established for the opinions expressed in the assessment; and

---

123 *Dabirian v. Dabirian*, [2004] O.J. No. 846 (C.A.).

124 (1992), 41 R.F.L. (3d) 27 (Ont. Gen. Div.). See also *Stuyt v. Stuyt*, [2006] O.J. No. 4890 (Sup. Ct.).

(viii) whether the assessor can be subjected to cross-examination before the report is used.

In *Burka v. Burka*,[125] applying these criteria to a full custody/access assessment that had been ordered at a pre-trial conference and was obviously intended for use by the trial judge, Ryan-Froslie J., of the Saskatchewan Court of Queen's Bench, endorsed Granger J.'s approach in *Genovesi v. Genovesi* and refused to consider the assessment report on cross-applications by the parents to vary an interim order for joint custody by changing the child's primary residence so as to facilitate her attendance at a single kindergarten. Ryan-Froslie J., nevertheless, concluded that the existing interim order should be varied so that the child would ordinarily reside with the mother during the school week because it was not in the child's best interests to attend two different kindergartens in the separate communities in which the two parents lived.

While expert opinions are most helpful, and may be determinative in interim proceedings where there is no opportunity for the court to undertake a comprehensive inquiry into the family's circumstances, they cannot bind the court's hands at trial.[126]

In *Young v. Young*,[127] the Supreme Court of Canada confirmed that, although expert evidence may be helpful in some cases, it is not routinely required to establish the best interests of a child. That determination is normally possible from the evidence of the parties themselves and, in some cases, the testimony of the children involved. Under ordinary circumstances, a more limited role is appropriate for expert evidence, given the expense of such evidence, the time consumed in its preparation and presentation, and the often inconclusive results it generates. As L'Heureux-Dubé J. observed,

> I agree with my colleague [Madam Justice McLachlin] that expert evidence should not routinely be required to establish the best interests of the child. In my view, it is a modern-day myth that experts are always better placed than parents to assess the needs of the child. Common sense requires us to acknowledge that the person involved in day-to-day care may observe changes in the behaviour, mood, attitude, and development of a child that could go unnoticed by anyone else. The cus-

---

125 [2003] S.J. No. 609 (Q.B.). See also *Koeckeritz v. Secord*, [2008] S.J. No. 129 (Q.B.), Ryan-Froslie J.

126 *Tyabji v. Sandana* (1994), 2 R.F.L. (4th) 265 at 269–70 (B.C.S.C.).

127 [1993] 4 S.C.R. 3, 49 R.F.L (3d) 117 at 222.

todial parent normally has the best vantage point from which to assess the interests of the child, and thus will often provide the most reliable and complete source of information to the judge on the needs and interests of that child.

Furthermore, it is important to emphasize the importance of the evidence of children in custody and access disputes, and I would not wish to suggest that their testimony alone might not be a sufficient evidentiary basis upon which to restrict access. Courts have increasingly come to accept and understand in the criminal context that children themselves can be a reliable source of evidence to the judge (*R. v. Khan*, [1990] 2 S.C.R. 531). To disregard their evidence when their own interests are directly at issue would, in my opinion, be at odds with this clear evolutionary trend in the law.[128]

A court cannot delegate its authority under the *Divorce Act* to make an appropriate order. Accordingly, a direction by a trial judge that access privileges shall be determined by an appropriate professional will be deemed to have been made in excess of jurisdiction, and constitutes a reversible error on appeal.[129] Where parties choose not to seek alternative methods but instead rely on the adversarial process, the court has an obligation to render a judgment and not simply provide advice or instruct the parties as to how they may resolve their difficulties.[130]

6) Grandparents and Other Third Parties; Multiple Parents

Parents and grandparents are not on an equal footing in a contested custody proceeding. Unless there are grave reasons for concern about a child's well-being, a child should be placed in the custody of his or her parent.[131]

A parent who has been granted a consent order for sole custody does not enjoy an unfettered discretion to delegate his or her full-time par-

---

128 *Ibid.* at 212–13 [R.F.L.].

129 *Stewart v. Stewart* (1990), 30 R.F.L. (3d) 67 (Alta. C.A.); *Lake v. Lake* (1988), 11 R.F.L. (3d) 234 (N.S.C.A.); *Strobridge v. Strobridge* (1994), 4 R.F.L. (4th) 169 (Ont. C.A.); *C.A.M. v. D.M.*, [2003] O.J. No. 3707 (C.A.); *Azimi v. Mirzaei*, [2008] O.J. No. 1208 (Sup. Ct.). And see Chapter 6, Section J.

130 *Jarrett v. Jarrett* (1994), 10 R.F.L. (4th) 24 (Ont. Gen. Div.).

131 *J.B.E. v. F.S.L.*, [2004] B.C.J. No. 2438 (S.C.). Compare *S.F.R. v. J.V.H.*, [2006] N.J. No. 202 (U.F.C.), citing *Bailey v. Flood*, [1988] N.J. No. 36 (T.D.); *Penney v. Penney*, [2006] S.J. No. 175 (Q.B.). Compare *Hendricks v. Swan*, [2007] S.J. No. 30 (Q.B.).

enting responsibilities to a third party, such as the child's grandparent. Should this occur without the knowledge and approval of the non-custodial parent who has been exercising access to the child, the non-custodial parent may bring an application to vary the existing custody order.[132]

Orders for grandparental access may be granted but the right of separated parents to raise their children should not be lightly interfered with by an order for grandparental access that conflicts with the wishes of the parents and children. In the words of Abella J.A., of the Ontario Court of Appeal, as she then was, in *Chapman v. Chapman*, "in the absence of any evidence that the parents are behaving in a way which demonstrates an inability to act in accordance with the best interests of their children, their right to make decisions and judgments on the children's behalf should be respected, including decisions about whom they see, how often and under what circumstances they see them."[133] As Abella J.A. further observes, however, each case turns on its own facts and must be determined in light of the children's best interests.[134] A grandparent has the onus of proving on a balance of probabilities that proposed access to a grandchild is in the best interests of that child.[135] A court will decline to grant access when it would undermine the role of the custodial parent.[136] The following expansive list of relevant considerations is set out by Master Nitikman, of the British Columbia Supreme Court, in *Parmar v. Parmar*:

---

132   *O'Brien v. MacLearn*, [2004] N.S.J. No. 63 (C.A.).

133   [2001] O.J. No. 705 at para. 21 (C.A.).

134   *Chapman v. Chapman, ibid.*; see also *C.B. v. M.R.*, [2007] N.J. No. 378 (U.F.C.), citing Martha Shaffer, "To Grandmother's House We Go? An Examination of Grandparental Access" (2003–2004) 21 C.F.L.Q. 437, wherein two approaches, namely, the "parental autonomy" and the "pro-contact" approaches were compared; *Campbell v. Ramsden*, [2007] O.J. No. 1789 (Sup. Ct.); *Sochackey v. Sochackey; Boyle v. Gale*, [2007] O.J. No. 1873 (Sup. Ct.); *Ekvall v. Cooper*, [2007] S.J. No. 640 (Q.B.); compare *G.M.K. v. C.L.H.*, [2006] S.J. No. 399 (Q.B.), considering Dan L. Goldberg, "Background Paper, Grandparent-Grandchild Access: A Legal Analysis," online: www. justice.gc.ca/en/ps/pad/reports/2003-fcy-15.html. And see *Scott v. Walter*, [2006] M.J. No. 447 (Q.B.) (access denied to former wife of biological father).

135   *F.(N.) v. S.(H.L.)* (1999), 127 B.C.A.C. 66, [1999] B.C.J. No. 1438; *C.T. v. J.T.*, [2007] B.C.J. No. 937 (Prov. Ct.); *Chapman v. Chapman*, [1993] B.C.J. No. 316 (S.C.); *Sochackey v. Sochackey*, [2007] O.J. No. 1857 (Sup. Ct.); *Boyle v. Gale*, [2007] O.J. No. 1873 (Sup. Ct.).

136   *Chapman v. Chapman*, [2001] O.J. No. 705 at para. 21 (C.A.); *L.M. v. K.F.*, [2000] N.B.J. No. 512 (Q.B.); compare the *Civil Code of Québec, C.c.Q.*, art. 611 and see *D.C. v. B.R.*, [2000] Q.J. No. 6989 (Sup. Ct.); *Droit de la famille — 08544*, [2008] Q.J. No. 1886 (Sup. Ct.).

1. Grandparents may be granted legal standing to apply for custody of or access to their grandchildren, but they have no legal right to custody or access corresponding to that of the parents.

2. If grandparents make a successful application for access, their entitlement is different from that of a non-custodial parent.

3. The best interests of the child are the paramount concern.

4. The love, affection, and ties between the child and the grandparents are factors expressly recognized as relevant to a determination of the child's best interests under section 24(1) of the *Family Relations Act* (British Columbia).

5. In normal circumstances, the best interests of children are served by contact with their grandparents and other members of the extended family.

6. Considerable weight should be given to the wishes of the custodial parent and care should be taken to ensure that the court does not interfere unduly with the inherent right of the parent to determine the child's upbringing.

7. Grandparents are ordinarily expected to accommodate themselves to the parent's decision regarding the amount and type of access.

8. The child's wishes should be noted and accorded appropriate weight based on the child's age.

9. When the court finds grandparental access appropriate, the amount of time allotted is quite limited.[137]

In Alberta, an adoption order granted to the child's mother and her new partner severs the ties that the child previously had with the biological father and he loses his rights of access to the child, as do also those claiming through him. A paternal grandmother's application for continued access to the child following the adoption will accordingly be denied.[138]

Access orders under the *Children's Law Act, 1997* (Saskatchewan) are not confined to genetic parents or blood relatives. In *G.E.S. v. D.L.C.*,[139] the appellant mother had given birth to twins by means of *in vitro* fertilization. The respondent had declined the mother's request that he be the sperm donor but had been supportive both financially and otherwise of the mother's recourse to bio-technological child birth, having attended

---

137 [1997] B.C.J. No. 2094 (S.C.); see also *Lukyn v. Baynes*, [2008] B.C.J. No. 3 (S.C.).

138 *C.R. v. B.L.B.*, [2005] A.J. No. 726 (Q.B.). Compare *C.B. v. M.R.*, [2007] N.J. No. 378 (U.F.C.).

139 [2006] S.J. No. 419 (C.A.).

prenatal classes with the mother, being present at the birth of the twins, and having provided daily care for the twins after their birth. The mother's relationship with the respondent subsequently deteriorated and she no longer wished him to have any relationship with the twins. The trial judge found that the respondent had standing to apply for access to the twins as a person having a "sufficient interest" within the meaning of section 6(1) of the *Children's Law Act, 1997* (Saskatchewan), notwithstanding that he fell outside the traditional categories of third parties who seek access orders, namely, grandparents, other family relatives, and step-parents. In reaching this conclusion, the trial judge observed that the "primary focus must surely be on an assessment of what is in the true best interests of the child." While sharing the trial judge's finding that the respondent had a "sufficient interest" to bring an application for access to the twins, the Saskatchewan Court of Appeal concluded that the trial judge had erred in applying the best interests of the child in the context of section 6(1) of the *Children's Law Act, 1997*. The Saskatchewan Court of Appeal observed that the Act contemplates two separate stages of analysis where a non-parent seeks an access order under that Act. First, the court must apply section 6(1), which imposes the threshold requirement that the applicant be either a "parent" or "other person having, in the opinion of the court, a sufficient interest." Second, only if this threshold requirement is satisfied will the court proceed to apply section 9 of the Act, which provides that the substantive merits of an application for an access order are to be considered by reference to the best interests of the child. In the opinion of the Saskatchewan Court of Appeal, the trial judge blurred these two separate steps by focusing on the best interests of the child when considering the threshold requirement of sufficient interest. With respect to the first step, the Saskatchewan Court of Appeal formulated the following guidelines to the application of section 6(1) of *the Children's Law Act, 1997*:

> [para. 47] The proper focus of an inquiry in relation to the "sufficient interest" question, in my view, is the nature of the relationship between the applicant and the child. The question of the child's best interests does not enter the analysis at that point. In determining whether a non-family applicant is a person with a sufficient interest, the court should consider a variety of factors including, but not necessarily limited to: (a) the extent or degree of the applicant's involvement in the child's life, (b) the duration of that involvement, (c) the level of intimacy and the quality of the relationship between the applicant and the child, (d) how the relationship between the applicant and the child was represented

to the world, and (e) whether the applicant provided financially for the child. Further, at least in relation to situations such as the one at issue in the appeal where there is no traditional family or blood relationship between the applicant and the child, it is necessary to consider whether the applicant can show a settled commitment to the child and an intention to be a continuing and meaningful presence in the life of the child. Overall, in the kinds of circumstances involved here, s. 6 generally should be applied to screen out applicants who do not have both a significant relationship with the child and a demonstrated and settled ongoing commitment to the child.

Although the record was characterized by conflicting evidence, the Saskatchewan Court of Appeal found it capable of sustaining the trial judge's conclusion that the unique relationship between the parties, as reflected in the respondent's involvement in the pregnancy, birth, and care of the children, gave him a sufficient interest to bring the access application. In addressing the trial judge's further conclusion that access was in the best interests of the children, the Saskatchewan Court of Appeal stated that the trial judge appeared to have proceeded on the basis that, because the respondent had a "sufficient interest" and a positive relationship with the twins, access would be in their best interests. However, his approach and conclusion was held to be inconsistent with the overall trend of the law in cases involving an applicant who is not a parent, step-parent, or blood relative. In such cases, current case law in Saskatchewan and elsewhere confirms that the existence of an emotional bond between the applicant and the children is insufficient to justify an access order.[140] Thus, the court should not proceed on the assumption that ongoing contact is warranted, as would be the case in a dispute between parents in respect of whom the "maximum contact" principle applies. Where the application for access is brought by a person other than a parent, blood relative, or step-parent, it falls on the applicant to clearly and convincingly demonstrate that access is in the best interests of the child(ren). While case law does not always set out the rationale for this approach, it clearly stems from a deep social and legal norm that presumes fit parents generally act in their children's best interests. Consequently, a fit parent's assessment of a child's best interests should not be lightly interfered with. This does not signify that the court

---

140 See *Lindstrom v. Pearce*, 1999 SKQB 165; *Adams v. Martin*, 1992 CarswellOnt 1679 (Prov. Ct.); *Re Lapp and Dupuis* (1985), 17 D.L.R. (4th) 347 (Man. C.A.); *Cyrenne v. Moar* (1986), 41 Man. R. (2d) 108 (C.A.); *Elliott v. Mumford* (2004), 1 R.F.L. (6th) 193 (N.S.C.A.). Compare *Ekvall v. Cooper*, [2007] S.J. No. 640 (Q.B.).

must completely defer to the parent's opinion that access is inappropriate; it means only that the views of the custodial parent should be given very substantial weight in determining the best interests of the children. In *G.E.S. v. D.L.C.*, the evidence established that the mother was an excellent parent, the twins were happy, well-adjusted, and well cared for, and there was no suggestion that they would lack anything in their lives or suffer in any way in the absence of access to the respondent. Given the mother's opposition to such access based on the respondent's past conduct and her legitimate concerns about his ongoing preparedness to make the sacrifices necessary to sustain an enduring relationship with the twins, the Saskatchewan Court of Appeal concluded that the respondent had failed to demonstrate in a clear and convincing way that access would be in the best interests of the children and the trial judge had erred by failing to place any weight on the mother's objections to access and the reasons for her objections. The mother's appeal was accordingly allowed on the basis that the trial judge had committed material errors in the course of granting the respondent access to the twins.

It is interesting to compare the judgment of the Saskatchewan Court of Appeal in *G.E.S. v. D.L.C.*, above, with the judgment of the Alberta Court of Appeal in *D.W.H. v. D.J.R.*[141] This latter appeal raised the question whether the chambers judge erred in failing to determine that the appellant stood in the place of a parent to a three-and-a-half-year-old child and in concluding that he should be denied a contact order by virtue of section 35(5) of the *Family Law Act* (Alberta). The appellant lived with the male respondent in a same-sex relationship for approximately six and one-half years. They became friends of a female couple living in a same-sex relationship and it was decided that the female respondent would attempt to birth children, one for each couple, using assisted conception with the male respondent donating the sperm in each case. The parties agreed that the first child born would be raised in the home of the appellant and the male respondent. The female respondent would remain involved in the child's life and would reside with the appellant and the male respondent for the first two-and-a-half months of the child's life. These plans became a reality and the child lived with the appellant and the male respondent from May 2003 until their separation in June 2006. The female respondent played an active role in the child's life and enjoyed frequent contact. After the separation, the male and female respondents refused to allow the appellant to have contact with the child. The ap-

---

141 2007 ABCA 57, [2007] A.J. No. 187.

pellant sought a contact order under section 35 of the *Family Law Act* (Alberta). It was denied by the chambers judge who determined that the male and female respondents' wishes as guardians were entitled to considerable weight and the appellant had not shown how contact with the child would contribute to her best interests when her biological parents had decided otherwise. On appeal to the Alberta Court of Appeal, it was held that the chambers judge made a reversible error by failing to consider whether the appellant stood in the place of a parent to the child and in failing to assess the desirability of contact between the appellant and the child with that relationship in mind. Section 35(5) of the *Family Law Act* (Alberta) expressly provides that "[b]efore a court makes a contact order, the court shall satisfy itself that (a) contact between the child and the applicant is in the best interests of the child, (b) the child's physical, psychological or emotional health may be jeopardized if contact between the child and the applicant is denied, and (c) the guardians' denial of contact between the child and the applicant is unreasonable." While acknowledging that section 35(5) does not draw any distinction between parents or persons standing in the place of parents and other persons seeking a contact order, the Alberta Court of Appeal concluded that a *de facto* parent-child relationship remains an important consideration. Indeed, there is a presumption in favour of postseparation contact that is rooted in a recognition that the unique relationship between such persons ought not to be easily or readily abandoned or displaced. The fact that section 35(2) of the *Family Law Act* (Alberta) makes it clear that a person standing in the place of a parent is not required to seek leave to bring a contact application underlines that the legal nature of the relationship is an important consideration in determining whether contact is in the best interests of the child and in considering whether the requirements of section 35(5) have been met. Given the uncontested evidence that the appellant stood in the place of a parent to the child for most of the child's life, being known to the child as Papa, the Alberta Court of Appeal rejected the reasons offered by the respondents for the denial of contact. Their assertions that the appellant was HIV positive, had made poor choices in his love life, and was irrational for a short time following the separation were deemed an inadequate foundation for refusing a contact order in the circumstances of this case. Furthermore, their assertion that the child would suffer confusion and instability as a result of a contact order was not made out on the record. Indeed, their reasons failed to take into account the benefit that the child would derive from the affection of the appellant who had been directly involved in her parenting; they also ignored the potential for emotional harm occasioned by the sudden withdrawal of the appellant from the child's life. Accordingly, the Alberta Court of Appeal found that the respondents failed to provide any compelling reason to displace the presumption in favour of ongoing contact between the child and the appellant. The appeal was, therefore, allowed and the appellant was granted reasonable access as requested. It is noteworthy that, for the purpose of this interim application, the Alberta Court of Appeal found it unnecessary to determine whether it is possible to have more than one father or mother under the *Family Law Act* (Alberta) or whether the respondents satisfied the definitions of parent or guardian under the Act and what might flow as a result.

In a landmark decision in *A.A. v. B.B.*,[142] the Ontario Court of Appeal held that a five-year-old child had three parents, namely, his biological father and mother and the long-time lesbian partner of the biological mother. On this partner's uncontested application for a declaration of parentage, the trial judge, Aston J., held that section 4 of the *Children's Law Reform Act* (Ontario) "contemplates a single mother and a single father" and "does not afford authority for the court to grant this application."[143] Addressing the applicant's alternative submission that the court could grant the application by exercising its *parens patriae* jurisdiction to fill a legislative gap, Aston J. observed that, while a court may exercise such jurisdiction, it should not ignore the possibility that the gap may have been deliberate, in which case it is not a function of the court to exercise its *parens patriae* jurisdiction to rewrite legislation and social policy. While acknowledging that the granting of the application would serve the best interests of this particular child, whose primary care was being jointly provided by the biological mother and her lesbian partner and who had a meaningful relationship with the father through frequent visits, Aston J. held that this was insufficient reason to resort to the exercise of the court's *parens patriae* jurisdiction. He observed that the court must also have regard to the best interests of other children and the granting of the application in the present case would open the door to step-parents, extended family members, and others claiming parental status in less harmonious circumstances, and had the potential to generate or exacerbate custody or access litigation. The appellant's attempt to introduce a *Charter* challenge at the appellate level was rejected by the Ontario Court of Appeal on the basis that the appellant had not advanced

---

142 [2007] O.J. No. 2 (C.A.).
143 *A.A. v. B.B.*, [2003] O.J. No. 1215 (Sup. Ct.).

any satisfactory explanation for not raising the *Charter* issues at first instance and had failed to discharge the onus of proving the absence of tactical reasons for deferring the *Charter* challenge.[144] The Ontario Court of Appeal found no fault with Aston J.'s conclusion that the language of the *Children's Law Reform Act*, and especially section 4, contemplates a single mother and father. It rejected the conclusion of Aston J., however, respecting the exercise of the *parens patriae* jurisdiction. In the opinion of the Ontario Court of Appeal, the radical changes that have occurred in legal and social responses to same-sex relationships and the advent of reproductive technology were outside the contemplation of the Ontario legislature when it enacted the *Children's Law Reform Act* in 1978. Accordingly, the present case manifested a legislative gap that was not deliberate and the exercise of the *parens patriae* jurisdiction would conform to the purpose of the *Children's Law Reform Act*, which is to promote the equality of children born inside and outside of marriage. By way of clarifying the importance of the declaration of parentage that was designed to give the lesbian partner of the biological mother all the legal rights of a custodial parent, which include guardianship rights over the child under the *Children's Law Reform Act* (Ontario), Rosenberg J.A. listed the following results:

- the declaration of parentage is a lifelong immutable declaration of status;
- it allows the parent to fully participate in the child's life;
- the declared parent has to consent to any future adoption;
- the declaration determines lineage;
- the declaration ensures that the child will inherit on intestacy;
- the declared parent may obtain an OHIP card, a social insurance number, airline tickets, and passports for the child;
- the child of a Canadian citizen is a Canadian citizen, even if born outside of Canada (*Citizenship Act*, R.S.C. 1985, c. C-29, s. 3(1)(b));
- the declared parent may register the child in school; and
- the declared parent may assert her rights under various laws such as the *Health Care Consent Act, 1996*, S.O. 1996, c. 2, Sched. A., s. 20(1)5.[145]

It is noteworthy that in 1999 the Ontario legislature enacted the *Amendments Because of the Supreme Court of Canada Decision in* M. v. H. *Act*,

---

144   See *R. v. Brown* (1993), 83 C.C.C. (3d) 129 (S.C.C.).
145   [2007] O.J. No. 2 at para. 14 (C.A.).

which amended numerous Ontario statutes, including the *Children's Law Reform Act* (see S.O. 1999, c. 6, s. 7 (amending sections 24 and 78(2) of the *Children's Law Reform Act*) but saw no reason to amend section 4 of that Act to accommodate same-sex relationships and the science of reproductive technology. Consequently, it is open to question whether the Ontario Court of Appeal was correct in concluding that a legislative gap justified the exercise of the *parens patriae* jurisdiction in *A.A. v. B.B.*

7) Provincial Parenting Programs

Provincial legislation may require divorcing or divorced parents to attend parenting education programs before seeking substantive relief under the *Divorce Act*. Such provincial legislation is procedural rather than substantive in nature, and therefore falls within the constitutional authority of the provincial legislature in the absence of any functional conflict with the *Divorce Act*.[146]

Conflict may be inevitable if a grandparental access order is granted over the custodial parent's objections. However, the question to be resolved under section 32.1 of the *Provincial Court Act* (Alberta), which specifically empowers a court to grant grandparental access rights, is whether the conflict outweighs any long-term benefit of the child's growth and development that would result from an access order.[147]

---

146 *Flockhart v. Flockhart*, [2002] S.J. No. 94 (Q.B.).
147 *M.W. v. D.W.*, [2000] A.J. No. 1082 (Prov. Ct.).

CHAPTER 12

MATRIMONIAL PROPERTY RIGHTS

A. PROVINCIAL AND TERRITORIAL LEGISLATIVE DIVERSITY

Over thirty years ago, the Supreme Court of Canada in *Murdoch v. Murdoch*[1] concluded that a wife who had worked alongside her husband in the fields was not entitled to any interest in the ranch that had been originally purchased with his money. Her homemaking role and hard physical labour on the farm counted for nothing. Several years later, the Supreme Court of Canada saw the error of its ways and invoked the doctrine of unjust enrichment to enable wives[2] and unmarried cohabitants[3] to share in property acquired or preserved by their partners during cohabitation. In the meantime, provincial legislatures introduced statutory reforms to ameliorate the harshness of the *Murdoch* decision so far as married couples are concerned.

Every province and territory in Canada has enacted legislation to establish property-sharing rights between spouses on marriage breakdown or divorce and, in some provinces, on death.[4]

---

1   (1973), 13 R.F.L. 185 (S.C.C.).
2   *Rathwell v. Rathwell* (1978), 1 R.F.L. (2d) 1 (S.C.C.).
3   *Pettkus v. Becker* (1980), 19 R.F.L. (2d) 165 (S.C.C.); *Sorochan v. Sorochan* (1986), 2 R.F.L. (3d) 225 (S.C.C.). And see Chapter 3, Section E.
4   See *Matrimonial Property Act*, R.S.A. 2000, c. M-8; *Family Relations Act*, R.S.B.C., 1996, c. 128, Part 5; *Marital Property Act*, C.C.S.M. c. M45; *Marital Property Act*,

Three fundamental questions require consideration in any attempt to divide property between spouses on the termination of their relationship. They are as follows:

(i) what kind of property falls subject to division?
(ii) how is the property to be valued? and
(iii) how will the sharing of property be achieved?

In some provinces and territories, a wide judicial discretion exists and distinctions are drawn between "family assets" that both spouses use and "business" or "commercial" assets that are associated with only one of the spouses. In others, no such distinctions exist. In most provinces and territories, the courts are empowered to divide specific assets. In Ontario, it is the value of property, as distinct from the property itself, that is shared; all assets must be valued and each spouse is presumptively entitled to an equal share in the value of the assets acquired by either or both of them.

Provincial and territorial matrimonial property statutes usually exclude premarital assets from division and also certain postmarital assets, such as third-party gifts or inheritances and damages or monetary compensation received by a spouse from a third party as a result of personal injuries.

Statutory property-sharing regimes are not dependent on which spouse owned or acquired the assets. Prior to marriage breakdown, however, the control and management of an asset is legally vested in the owner. Provincial and territorial statutes, nevertheless, prohibit a title-holding spouse from disposing of or encumbering the matrimonial home without the consent of his or her spouse.

Many issues respecting property sharing between spouses remain unresolved by existing legislation. For example, complicated valuation and distribution problems can arise with respect to the sharing of em-

---

S.N.B. 1980, c. M-1.1; *Family Law Act*, R.S.N.L. 1990, c. F-2, Part I (Matrimonial Home), Part II (Matrimonial Assets), Part IV (Domestic Contracts); *Matrimonial Property Act*, R.S.N.S. 1989, c. 275; *Family Law Act*, S.N.W.T. 1997, c. 18, Part I (Domestic Contracts), Part III (Family Property), Part IV (Family Home); *Family Law Act*, R.S.O. 1990, c. F.3, Part I (Family Property), Part II (Matrimonial Home), Part IV (Domestic Contracts); *Family Law Act*, S.P.E.I. 1995, c. 12, Part I (Family Property), Part II (Family Home), Part IV (Domestic Contracts), *Civil Code of Québec*, S.Q. 1991, c. 64, Book 2; *Matrimonial Property Act, 1997*, S.S. 1997, c. M-6.11; *Family Property and Support Act*, R.S.Y. 1986, c. 63, Part I (Family Assets), Part 2 (Family Home), Part 4, ss. 1 and 58–65 (Domestic Contracts). Many of the aforementioned statutes have been amended from time to time.

ployment pensions, other than the Canada Pension Plan, which is subject to a splitting of credits on marriage breakdown. Canadian courts are also still grappling with the practical problems of property sharing when one of the spouses is in business and the dissolution of that business would reduce or eliminate that spouse's income-earning potential and consequential ability to provide spousal or child support on the breakdown of the marriage. For the most part, however, courts are coping well with these and other problems in their attempt to give effect to equality between spouses in the division of property or its value on marriage breakdown.

Because the relevant provincial and territorial statutes differ markedly in content and approach, it is impossible to provide a comprehensive analysis of the diverse provincial matrimonial property regimes in the following pages. The authors will consequently focus on the Ontario statute, which represents the most comprehensive provincial legislation on matrimonial property rights in Canada.

1) Introduction

In 1978, the province of Ontario enacted the *Family Law Reform Act*[5] to ameliorate the hardship and injustice arising under the doctrine of separation of property, whereby each spouse retained his or her own property on the breakdown or dissolution of marriage. Section 4 of the *Family Law Reform Act, 1978* empowered a court to order a division of "family assets" and, in exceptional circumstances, a division of non-family assets on marriage breakdown, regardless of which spouse was the owner of the assets. Generally speaking, a non-owning spouse would be granted an equal share of the family assets, which included the matrimonial home and other assets ordinarily used or enjoyed by the family, but no interest in business assets would be granted to the non-owning spouse.

As of 1 March 1986, Part I of the *Family Law Act*[6] eliminated the former distinction between "family assets" and "non-family assets" by providing for an equalization of the *value* of all assets accumulated by either spouse during the marriage in the event of marriage breakdown or death.

---

5   S.O. 1978, c. 2.
6   R.S.O. 1990, c. F.3. For proposed changes, see Ontario Law Reform Commission, *Report on Family Property Law* (including Executive Summary) (Toronto: Ontario Law Reform Commission, 1993); see also Ontario Law Reform Commission, *The Rights and Responsibilities of Cohabitants under the* Family Law Act (including Executive Summary) (Toronto: Ontario Law Reform Commission, 1993).

2) Objectives of *Family Law Act*

In general terms, the fundamental objective of Part I of the *Family Law Act* is to ensure that on marriage breakdown or death each spouse will receive a fair share, which will usually be an equal share, of the value of assets accumulated during the course of matrimonial cohabitation. Thus, subsection 5(7) of the *Family Law Act* provides as follows:

> *Purpose*
>
> 5.-(7) The purpose of this section is to recognize that child care, household management and financial provision are the joint responsibilities of the spouses and that inherent in the marital relationship there is equal contribution, whether financial or otherwise, by the spouses to the assumption of these responsibilities, entitling each spouse to the equalization of the net family properties, subject only to the equitable considerations set out in subsection (6).

This provision does not empower a court to deviate from the norm of equal division in the absence of circumstances that justify a finding of unconscionability within the meaning of subsection 5(6) of the *Family Law Act*.[7]

3) Definition of "Spouse"

For the purpose of Part I of the *Family Law Act*, subsection 1(1) specifically defines "spouse" as meaning a man and woman who are married to each other or who have entered into a void or voidable marriage, provided that in either of the latter circumstances, the person asserting a right under the Act acted in good faith. "Good faith" within the meaning of section 1(1) of the *Family Law Act* signifies an intention to comply with the *Marriage Act*.[8] Same-sex relationships and "common-law relationships" fall outside the ambit of Part I of the *Family Law Act*.

Pursuant to section 7(1) of the Ontario *Family Law Act*, a former spouse may seek equalization of the spousal net family properties under section 5 of the Act. After a valid foreign divorce has been granted, the Ontario Superior Court of Justice has no jurisdiction to hear and determine an application for spousal support under the *Divorce Act* or under the *Family Law Act* but the foreign divorce does not preclude the Ontario

---

7   *Brett v. Brett* (1999), 46 R.F.L. (4th) 433 (Ont. C.A.). See, generally, Section A(10), below in this chapter.

8   *Debora v. Debora*, [1999] O.J. No. 2 (C.A.).

Superior Court of Justice from adjudicating an application for the equalization of the spousal net family properties under the *Family Law Act*.[9]

4) Indian Lands; Foreign Immovable Property

The *Family Law Act* confers no jurisdiction on a court to interfere with interests in land on an Indian reserve, but the court is not precluded from making a monetary judgment for the purpose of equalizing the spousal net family properties.[10]

Canadian courts lack jurisdiction to order the sale of foreign immovable property, although the value of such property may be taken into account in ordering an equalization of the net spousal properties under Part I of the Ontario *Family Law Act*.[11]

5) Domestic Contracts

Subsection 2(10) of the *Family Law Act* provides that "[a] domestic contract dealing with a matter that is also dealt with in this Act prevails unless this Act provides otherwise."[12] A high threshold must be met before an Ontario court will find that an out-of-jurisdiction domestic contract prevails over the equalization provisions of the *Family Law Act*.[13]

6) Applications Respecting Ownership and Possession of Property

a) General

Section 10 of the *Family Law Act* empowers a spouse or former spouse to apply to the court for the determination of any question relating to the possession or ownership of property. It offers no direct guidelines to the court concerning the principles to be applied in determining questions of ownership and possession. The parties to such an application are entitled

---

9   *Okmyansky v. Okmyansky*, 2007 ONCA 427, [2007] O.J. No. 2298.

10   *Sandy v. Sandy* (1980), 13 R.F.L. (2d) 81 (Ont. C.A.).

11   *Bennett v. Bennett*, [2001] O.J. No. 224 (Sup. Ct.); *Aning v. Aning*, [2002] O.J. No. 2469 (Sup. Ct.); see also *Duke v. Andler*, [1932] S.C.R. 734; *Teczan v. Teczan* (1987), 11 R.F.L. (3d) 113 (B.C.C.A.); *Catania v. Giannattasio*, [1999] O.J. No. 1197 (C.A.); see, generally, James G. McLeod, *The Conflict of Laws* (Calgary: Carswell, 1983).

12   As to the validity and efficacy of a waiver of spousal property and equalization rights under a contract that predates the *Family Law Act*, see *Lay v. Lay* (2000), 4 R.F.L. (5th) 264 (Ont. C.A.), distinguishing *Bosch v. Bosch* (1991), 6 O.R. (3d) 168 (C.A.) and applying s. 70(3) of the *Family Law Act*.

13   *Webster v. Webster Estate*, [2006] O.J. No. 2749 (Sup. Ct.).

to invoke established principles of the common law and equity, including the doctrines of resulting and constructive trust. The right to assert the existence of a resulting or constructive trust in an application under section 10 of the *Family Law Act* is not precluded by an equalization of the net family properties under section 5 of the Act and may, indeed, be a prerequisite to calculating the net family property of each spouse for the purposes of any equalization claim.[14] A spouse may assert a beneficial ownership interest in property held in the other spouse's name where the value of that property has significantly increased between the date of the spousal separation and the date of trial.[15]

Section 10 of the *Family Law Act* cannot be invoked by third parties.[16] Where an application is brought by a spouse or former spouse, however, a third party may be added in accordance with the Ontario *Rules of Civil Procedure*.[17]

The assertion of ownership rights under subsection 10(1) of the *Family Law Act* is not conditioned on marriage breakdown. Such an application may be pursued even though the spouses are still cohabiting in a viable marriage. An application under subsection 10(1) may also be made or continued against the estate of a deceased spouse.[18]

b) Presumptions

At common law, when a husband purchased property in the name of his wife or transferred property to her, a presumption of advancement applied whereby he was presumed to have made a gift of the property to her. Where, however, the wife purchased property in her husband's name or transferred property to him, he would be presumed to hold the property on a resulting trust for his wife as the beneficial owner. The abolition of the presumption of advancement as between spouses, which was effectuated by paragraph 1(3)(d) of the *Family Law Reform Act, 1975* and continued under section 14 of the *Family Law Act*, establishes equality between the sexes in that, where either spouse purchases property in the name of the

---

14   *Rawluk v. Rawluk*, [1990] 1 S.C.R. 70, 23 R.F.L. (3d) 337; see also *Rarie v. Rarie* (1997), 32 R.F.L. (4th) 232 (Ont. C.A.) and Professor James G. McLeod's extremely lucid and informative Annotation at 233–37.

15   *Rawluk v. Rawluk*, [1990] 1 S.C.R. 70, 23 R.F.L. (3d) 337.

16   See *Chalmers v. Copfer* (1978), 7 R.F.L. (2d) 393 (Ont. Co. Ct.).

17   See *Bray v. Bray* (1979), 9 C.P.C. 241 (Ont. H.C.J.).

18   *Family Law Act*, R.S.O. 1990, c. F.3, s. 10(2); compare s. 5(2) of the Act, whereby an application for an equalization of net family properties can only be brought by a surviving spouse whose net family property is less than that of the deceased spouse.

other spouse or transfers property to the other spouse, the purchase or transfer gives rise to a presumption of resulting trust, whereby the transferee holds the property for the benefit of the transferor. The presumption of advancement arising from a parent's gratuitous transfer of assets to his or her child under the age of majority, and the presumption of resulting trust that arises when the child is an adult, are unaffected by the statutory abrogation of the presumption of advancement as between spouses.[19] However, a spouse cannot claim that property was received from a parent as a gift so as to be excluded from equalization of the spousal net family properties on marriage breakdown or death while asserting that the transfer was not a gift for tax purposes.[20]

Section 14 of the *Family Law Act* is confined in its application to questions of ownership or possession. It has no direct application to claims for an equalization of net family properties under section 5 of the Act.

The presumption arising under section 14 is a provisional presumption and not a conclusive presumption. It may be rebutted by cogent evidence that a gift was intended.[21]

The presumption of resulting trust has no application where property is held in the name of the spouses as joint tenants, and money on deposit in the name of both spouses is deemed to be held under joint tenancy. In either of these two circumstances, the beneficial interests of the spouses are governed by established principles of property law and they will be presumed to share equal beneficial interests.[22] The presumption may be rebutted by evidence that a gift was intended.[23]

A discussion of the significance of ownership to the resolution of an equalization claim under the *Family Law Act* appears later in this chapter.[24]

---

19   See *Pecore v. Pecore*, [2007] S.C.J. No. 17; *Madsen Estate v. Saylor*, [2007] S.C.J. No. 18.

20   *Karakatsanis v. Georgiou* (1991), 33 R.F.L. (3d) 263 (Ont. Gen. Div.). And see Section A(9)(n), below in this chapter.

21   See *Meszaros v. Meszaros* (1978), 22 O.R. (2d) 695 (Sup. Ct.); *DeBora v. DeBora*, [2004] O.J. No. 4826 (Sup. Ct.).

22   See *Ling v. Ling* (1980), 17 R.F.L. (2d) 62 at 66–67 (Ont. C.A.); *Berdette v. Berdette* (1991), 33 R.F.L. (3d) 113 (Ont. C.A.).

23   *DeBora v. DeBora*, [2004] O.J. No. 4826 (Sup. Ct.). And see Julie K. Hannaford, "Remedial Tool or Instrument of Reform: Resulting Trusts, the *Family Law Act*, and the *Launchbury* Decision" in The Law Society of Upper Canada, *Special Lectures 2006: Family Law* (Toronto: Irwin Law, 2007) 47–70.

24   See Section A(9)(b), below in this chapter. As to the effect of bankruptcy on equalization claims, see Robert A. Klotz, "Bankruptcy Problems in Family Law" in The

7) Triggering Events for Equalization of Net Family Properties

The *Family Law Act* preserves the doctrine of separation of property during matrimonial cohabitation. Subject to the provisions of section 21 of the Act, which ordinarily require spousal consent before the matrimonial home is disposed of or encumbered, each spouse has the freedom to acquire or dispose of property during matrimonial cohabitation.

The doctrine of separation of property may cease to apply, however, in the event of marriage breakdown or death. Pursuant to subsections 5(1), (2), and (3) of the *Family Law Act*, a system of deferred property sharing is activated by the occurrence of any of the following triggering events: (i) when a divorce is granted; (ii) when a marriage is declared a nullity; (iii) when the spouses are separated without any reasonable prospect of resuming cohabitation; (iv) when a spouse dies, if the net family property of the deceased spouse exceeds that of the surviving spouse; or (v) when, during cohabitation, there is a serious danger that one spouse may improvidently deplete his or her net family property.

a) Separation As a Triggering Event

Where spousal separation is relied upon as the triggering event under subsection 5(1) of the *Family Law Act*, the court must be satisfied that there is no reasonable prospect that they will resume cohabitation. The court must find that there is no reasonable prospect that the spouses will resume cohabitation where either spouse is adamantly opposed to reconciliation.[25] Spouses may be "separated" within the meaning of subsection 5(1), notwithstanding that they remain under the same roof, provided that they are living independent lives while sharing common accommodation.[26]

Law Society of Upper Canada, *Special Lectures, 1993: Family Law: Roles, Fairness and Equality* (Scarborough, ON: Carswell, 1994).

25 See *Challoner v. Challoner* (1973), 12 R.F.L. 311 (N.S.C.A.); compare *Sheriff v. Sheriff* (1982), 31 R.F.L. (2d) 434 at 436 (Ont. C.A.).

26 *Oswell v. Oswell* (1990), 28 R.F.L. (3d) 10 (Ont. H.C.J.), aff'd (1992), 43 R.F.L. (3d) 180 (Ont. C.A.); *De Mornay v. De Mornay* (1991), 34 R.F.L. (3d) 101 (Ont. Gen. Div.); *De Acetis v. De Acetis* (1991), 33 R.F.L. (3d) 372 (Ont. Gen. Div.), aff'd (1992), 39 R.F.L. (3d) 327 (Ont. C.A.).

b) Death As a Triggering Event[27]
The death of a spouse constitutes a triggering event for an equalization of net family properties but only where the net family property of the deceased spouse exceeds the net family property of the surviving spouse.[28]

The death of a spouse did not constitute a triggering event for the purpose of a court-ordered property division under section 4 of the *Family Law Reform Act, 1978*.[29] Consequently, widows or widowers sometimes found themselves in a substantially inferior position to that enjoyed by separated spouses. This injustice has been eliminated by subsection 5(2) of the *Family Law Act*.

c) Improvident Depletion of Net Family Property
Pursuant to subsection 5(3) of the *Family Law Act*, if there is a serious danger that one spouse may improvidently deplete his or her net family property, the other spouse, though still cohabiting, may apply to have the net family properties divided as though the spouses were separated and had no reasonable prospect of resuming cohabitation.

If an order for division is made by reason of the triggering event of an apprehended improvident depletion of net family property, neither spouse can thereafter pursue any further application based on some other triggering event. This is so even if the spouses continue to cohabit after the court-ordered division, unless a domestic contract provides otherwise.[30]

A serious danger that a spouse may improvidently deplete his or her net family property could be attributable to factors beyond the control of the spouse responsible for its management. Physical or mental disability may render a spouse incompetent to manage the property and thus give rise to a reasonable apprehension of improvident depletion. Alternatively, an improvident depletion may be apprehended in consequence of prospective intentional or negligent misconduct on the part of the title-holding spouse. In circumstances involving a disability, the threatened spouse may be wiser to apply for a guardianship order respecting the estate of the disabled spouse, because a successful application made pursuant to subsection 5(3) of the *Family Law Act* bars any subsequent application by reason of the express provisions of subsection 5(4) of the Act.

---

27   See Section A(11), below in this chapter.
28   *Family Law Act*, R.S.O. 1990, c. F.3, ss. 5(2) and 5(6).
29   S.O. 1978, c. 2; see *Palachik v. Kiss* (1983), 33 R.F.L. (2d) 225 (S.C.C.).
30   *Family Law Act*, R.S.O. 1990, c. F.3, ss. 5(4) & 5(5).

d) Alternative Triggering Events

Notwithstanding the special provisions of subsection 5(4) of the *Family Law Act*,[31] it is submitted that any successful application for division by reason of one of the several alternative triggering events under subsection 5(1) or (2) will bar a subsequent application based on some other triggering event, assuming that the parties do not remarry each other.[32]

8) Limitation Periods

Subsection 7(3) of the *Family Law Act*[33] provides that an application for equalization of spousal net family properties on marriage breakdown or death shall not be brought after the earliest of (a) two years after the day the marriage is terminated by divorce or judgment of nullity; (b) six years after the day the spouses separate and there is no reasonable prospect that they will resume cohabitation; or (c) six months after the first spouse's death.

The court may extend a limitation period arising under subsection 7(3) of the *Family Law Act* pursuant to the provisions of subsection 2(8) of the Act. Subsection 2(8) provides that the court may, on motion, extend a time prescribed by this Act if it is satisfied that (a) there are *prima facie* grounds for relief; (b) relief is unavailable because of delay that has been incurred in good faith; and (c) no person will suffer substantial prejudice by reason of the delay.[34]

9) Equalization of Net Family Properties

a) General Observations

Pursuant to section 15 of the *Family Law Act*, the property rights of spouses arising out of the marital relationship are governed by the internal law of the place where both spouses had their last common habitual residence or, if there is no place where they had a common habitual residence, by the law of Ontario. The last common habitual residence of the

---

31   *Ibid.*

32   Compare *Blomberg v. Blomberg*, 367 N.W.2d 643 (Minn. Ct. App. 1985) (pension benefits earned during first marriage excluded from division on dissolution of remarriage).

33   R.S.O. 1990, c. F.3.

34   *Shafer v. Shafer* (1998), 37 R.F.L. (4th) 104 (Ont. C.A.) (wife not precluded from pursuing equalization claim by s. 7(3) of *Family Law Act* where spouses had been engaged in ongoing negotiations); *Scherer v. Scherer*, [2002] O.J. No. 1661 (C.A.); *Webster v. Webster Estate*, [2006] O.J. No. 2749 (Sup. Ct.); *Poirier v. Alie*, [2007] O.J. No. 3798 (Sup. Ct.); *Katz v. Nimelman*, [2007] O.J. No. 4634 (Sup. Ct.).

spouses is the place where they last lived together as husband and wife and participated in everyday family life.[35]

Upon the occurrence of one of the triggering events specified in subsections 5(1), (2), and (3) of the *Family Law Act*, a spouse whose net family property is the lesser of the two net family properties is entitled to one-half of the difference between them, subject to the court's discretionary power to reapportion the sharing if an equalization of the net family properties would be unconscionable having regard to the specific factors enumerated in paragraphs (a) to (h) of subsection 5(6) of the Act.[36]

The concept of "net family property" is specifically defined in subsection 4(1) of the Act, which provides as follows:

net family property

"net family property" means the value of all the property, except property described in subsection (2), that a spouse owns on the valuation date, after deducting,

    (a) the spouse's debts and other liabilities, and

    (b) the value of property, other than a matrimonial home, that the spouse owned on the date of the marriage, after deducting the spouse's debts and other liabilities, calculated as of the date of the marriage.

The terms "property" and "valuation date" are also specifically defined in subsection 4(1) of the *Family Law Act*.[37] The current definitions read as follows:

property

"property" means any interest, present or future, vested or contingent, in real or personal property and includes:

    (a) property over which a spouse has, alone or in conjunction with another person, a power of appointment exercisable in favour of himself or herself,

    (b) property disposed of by a spouse but over which the spouse has, alone or in conjunction with another person, a power to

---

35   See, generally, *Pershadsingh v. Pershadsingh* (1987), 9 R.F.L. (3d) 359 (Ont. H.C.J.); *Vien v. Vien Estate* (1988), 12 R.F.L. 94 (Ont. C.A.); *Nicholas v. Nicholas* (1996), 24 R.F.L. (4th) 358 (Ont. C.A.); *Adam v. Adam* (1994), 7 R.F.L. (4th) 63 (Ont. Gen. Div.), aff'd (1996), 25 R.F.L. (4th) 50 (Ont. C.A.).

36   See Section A(10), below in this chapter.

37   S.O. 1986, c. 4, as amended by S.O. 1986, c. 35, now R.S.O. 1990, c. F.3.

revoke the disposition or a power to consume or dispose of the property, and

(c) in the case of a spouse's rights under a pension plan that have vested, the spouse's interest in the plan including contributions made by other persons.

valuation date

"valuation date" means the earliest of the following dates:

1. The date the spouses separate and there is no reasonable prospect that they will resume cohabitation.

2. The date a divorce is granted.

3. The date the marriage is declared a nullity.

4. The date one of the spouses commences an application based on subsection 5(3) (improvement depletion) that is subsequently granted.

5. The date before the date on which one of the spouses dies leaving the other spouse surviving.

A spouse owes no duty to disclose extramarital affairs to his or her marital partner and non-disclosure does not entitle a court to deviate from the statutorily defined "valuation date" in determining an application for equalization of spousal net family properties under Part I of the Ontario *Family Law Act*.[38]

In calculating a value as of a given date, the calculation shall be made as of the close of business on that date.[39]

Pursuant to the amended subsection 4(2) of the *Family Law Act*, the value of the following property that either spouse owns on the valuation date is excluded from the net family property:

- Property, other than a matrimonial home, that was acquired by gift or inheritance from a third person after the date of the marriage.
- Income from property referred to in paragraph 1, if the donor or testator has expressly stated that it is to be excluded from the spouse's net family property.
- Damages or a right to damages for personal injuries; nervous shock; mental distress; loss of guidance, care, and companionship; or the part of a settlement that represents those damages.

---

38 *Fleming v. Fleming*, [2001] O.J. No. 1052 (Sup. Ct.).
39 R.S.O. 1990, c. F.3, s. 4(4).

- Proceeds or a right to proceeds of a life insurance policy, as defined in the *Insurance Act*,[40] that are payable on the death of the life insured.
- Property, other than a matrimonial home, into which property referred to in paragraphs 1 to 4 can be traced.
- Property that the spouses have agreed by a domestic contract is not to be included in the spouse's net family property.

The onus of proving a "deduction" under the definition of "net family property" in subsection 4(1) of the Act and of proving an "exclusion" under subsection 4(2) of the *Family Law Act* falls on the person claiming the deduction or exclusion.[41] Spouses should, therefore, prepare an inventory of their assets at the date of their marriage and maintain ongoing records respecting these assets and any other assets that fall within the ambit of subsection 4(2) of the *Family Law Act*.

The *Family Law Act* provides for the equalization of net family properties but does not necessarily involve the equalization of spousal debts or liabilities, although this may occur in certain circumstances.[42] There is no authority under the *Family Law Act* to indemnify a spouse for a debt when there is no net family property.[43] Subsection 4(5) of the Act provides that the net family property of a spouse cannot be less than zero. If a spouse's net family property is less than zero, it is deemed to be equal to zero.

The overall significance of the aforementioned statutory provisions may be summarized in the following five steps:

(i)   Each spouse shall value his or her property, other than property excluded under subsection 4(2) of the Act, as of the date of the triggering event.

(ii) Each spouse shall calculate his or her debts and liabilities, apparently as of the date of the triggering event.

(iii) Each spouse shall calculate the value of property, other than a matrimonial home owned by that spouse on the date of the marriage,[44] and

---

40   R.S.O. 1990, c. I.8.
41   *Family Law Act*, R.S.O. 1990, c. F.3, s. 4(3).
42   *Hutton v. Hutton* (1985), 48 R.F.L. (2d) 451 (Ont. Co. Ct.).
43   *Leppek v. Leppek* (1991), 33 R.F.L. (3d) 66 (Ont. Gen. Div.); see also *Powers v. Naston-Powers* (1990), 28 R.F.L. (3d) 69 (Ont. S.C.).
44   See *Nahatchewitz v. Nahatchewitz* (1999), 1 R.F.L. (5th) 395 (Ont. C.A.); *Yeates v. Yeates*, [2007] O.J. No. 1376 (Sup. Ct.); compare *Kukolj v. Kukolj* (1986), 3 R.F.L. (3d) 359 (Ont. U.F.C.); *Michalofsky v. Michalofsky* (1989), 25 R.F.L. (3d) 316 (Ont. Div.

deduct from this value all debts and liabilities existing at the date of the marriage. The status of a matrimonial home is not immutable and a residence that was formerly occupied by the spouses, but is no longer so occupied prior to the cessation of matrimonial cohabitation, may entitle the owner spouse to a deduction of its premarital value under subsection 4(1) of the *Family Law Act*.[45]

(iv) The net family property of each spouse is then determined by subtracting the amounts calculated under paragraphs 2 and 3, above, from the amount calculated under paragraph 1, above. A spouse's net family property will be treated as having a zero value if the above calculations result in a deficit.

(v) When the net family property of each spouse has been calculated, the spouse whose net family property is the lesser of the two is *prima facie* entitled to one-half of the difference between them.

In *Oliva v. Oliva*,[46] the trial judge, McDermid L.J.S.C., identified the following ten steps to be followed for the purpose of determining an equalization claim under Part I of the *Family Law Act*:

1.   List and determine the value of all of the property owned by each spouse on the valuation date in this case the date of separation.

2.   List and determine the amount of each spouse's debts and other liabilities as of the valuation date.

3.   Deduct the total obtained in para. 2 from the total obtained in para. 1 for each spouse.

4.   List and determine the value of all the property, other than an interest in a matrimonial home, owned by each spouse on the date of the marriage.

5.   List and determine the amount of each spouse's debts and other liabilities calculated as of the date of the marriage.

6.   Deduct the total obtained in para. 5 from the total obtained in para. 4 for each spouse.

7.   Deduct the total obtained in para. 6 from the total obtained in para. 3 for each spouse.

Ct.), aff'd (1992), 39 R.F.L. (3d) 356 (Ont. C.A.); *Bosch v. Bosch* (1991), 38 R.F.L. (3d) 302 at 324 (Ont. C.A.), Arbour J.A.

45   *Folga v. Folga* (1986), 2 R.F.L. (3d) 358 (Ont. H.C.J.); *Zabiegalowski v. Zabiegalowski* (1992), 40 R.F.L. (3d) 321 (Ont. U.F.C.).

46   (1986), 2 R.F.L. (3d) 188 at 190–91 (Ont. S.C.), var'd (1988), 12 R.F.L. (3d) 334 (Ont. C.A.).

8. From the total obtained in para. 7 deduct the value of the exclusions, if any, to which each spouse is entitled under s. 4(2) of the Act.

9. Determine the amount which is 50 percent of the difference between the higher and lower values obtained for each spouse in para. 8.

10. Having regard to the factors contained in s. 5(6), decide whether the amount of the equalization payment is "unconscionable" and, if so, determine the proper amount which should be paid.

b) Significance of Ownership to Equalization Scheme

Sections 4 and 5 of the *Family Law Act* presuppose that the net family property of each spouse is distinct and separate. A determination of the net family property of each spouse may raise preliminary questions as to the ownership of particular assets. For example, where property, such as a bank account, is held in the joint names of the spouses, the beneficial interest(s) in the property may or may not be reflected by the legal title. The presumption of joint beneficial interests arising under section 14 of the *Family Law Act* is provisional and not conclusive. It may be rebutted by cogent evidence pointing to a contrary intention. Even where property is held in the name of only one spouse, the doctrines of resulting and constructive trusts may have an impact on the beneficial ownership of such property. A determination of the beneficial ownership rights of each spouse is a condition precedent to any equalization of the net family properties of the spouses.[47] The need for such a determination becomes more apparent if one spouse has debts exceeding his or her assets at the valuation date.

Consider, for example, the following circumstances. A husband and wife have a joint bank account at the time of separation with a value of $100,000. The spouses have no other assets and the husband owes his creditors $100,000. If the joint bank account were purely one of convenience and all deposits had been made by the husband, his net family property would be valued at zero and there would be nothing to divide between the spouses. If, however, the circumstances revealed that the wife owned the account of convenience, she being the sole depositor, her net family property would be valued at $100,000 and her husband's at zero. The husband would accordingly be entitled to a presumptive equalization right of

---

47   *Rawluk v. Rawluk*, [1990] 1 S.C.R. 70, 23 R.F.L. (3d) 337.

$50,000. If the joint bank account were beneficially owned in equal shares by both spouses, the husband's net family property would be zero and the wife's $50,000. The husband would accordingly be entitled to pursue an equalization claim in the amount of $25,000.

A monetary judgment based on the doctrine of unjust enrichment is unavailable as a remedy with respect to a premarital financial contribution towards the renovation of the matrimonial home where the contribution is adequately reflected in the subsequent transfer of title to the home into the names of both spouses as joint tenants.[48]

c) Definition of "Property"

The definition of "property" in subsection 4(1) of the *Family Law Act* is extremely broad. It includes the following:

- leasehold interests,
- life tenancies,[49]
- beneficial interests under wills or trusts,[50]
- pensions,[51]
- the cash surrender value of life insurance policies,[52]
- severance pay entitlements,[53]
- accumulated vacation pay,[54]
- accumulated sick leave,[55]

---

48 *Roseneck v. Gowling*, [2002] O.J. No. 4939 (C.A.).

49 See *Martin v. Martin* (1986), 2 R.F.L. (3d) 14 (Ont. Dist. Ct.); *Crutchfield v. Crutchfield* (1987), 10 R.F.L. (3d) 247 (Ont. H.C.J.); *Knapp v. Knapp* (1992), 40 R.F.L. (3d) 262 (Ont. Gen. Div.).

50 See *Brinkos v. Brinkos* (1989), 20 R.F.L. (3d) 445 (Ont. C.A.); *Black v. Black* (1989), 18 R.F.L. (3d) 303 (Ont. H.C.J.); compare *Dunning v. Dunning* (1987), 8 R.F.L. (3d) 289 (Ont. H.C.J.).

51 See Section A(9)(d), below in this chapter. Re unvested pensions, compare *Nix v. Nix* (1987), 11 R.F.L. (3d) 9 (Ont. H.C.J.) with *Ward v. Ward* (1988), 13 R.F.L. (3d) 259 (Ont. H.C.J.) and *Flynn v. Flynn* (1989), 68 O.R. (2d) 129 (Dist. Ct.).

52 *Blais v. Blais* (1992), 38 R.F.L. (3d) 256 (Gen. Div.).

53 *Marsham v. Marsham* (1987), 7 R.F.L. (3d) 1 (Ont. H.C.J.); *Miller v. Miller* (1987), 8 R.F.L. (3d) 113 (Ont. Dist. Ct.); *Emond v. Emond* (1987), 10 R.F.L. (3d) 107 (Ont. C.A.); *Klein v. Klein* (1987), 59 O.R. (2d) 781 (Dist. Ct.); *Butt v. Butt* (1989), 22 R.F.L. (3d) 415 (Ont. H.C.J.); *Melanson v. Melanson* (1991), 34 R.F.L. (3d) 323 (Ont. Gen. Div.); compare *Leckie v. Leckie*, [2004] O.J. No. 1550 (C.A.) (postseparation severance package excluded from equalization).

54 *Hodgins v. Hodgins* (1989), 23 R.F.L. (3d) 302 (Ont. H.C.J.).

55 *Hilderley v. Hilderley* (1989), 21 R.F.L. (3d) 383 (Ont. H.C.J.); *Alger v. Alger* (1989), 21 R.F.L. (3d) 211 (Ont. H.C.J.); *Cliche v. Cliche* (1991), 36 R.F.L. (3d) 297 (Ont. C.A.); compare *Rickett v. Rickett* (1989), 25 R.F.L. (3d) 188 (Ont. H.C.J.).

- worker's compensation benefits,[56]
- option rights,[57] partnership interests, business or professional goodwill,[58] and accounts receivable.[59]

In determining the wife's entitlement to an equalization of the spousal net family properties under Part I of the Ontario *Family Law Act* in *Ross v. Ross,*[60] a majority of the Ontario Court of Appeal (Rouleau J.A., with O'Connor A.C.J.O. concurring, Borins J.A. dissenting) upheld the trial judge's ruling that employee stock options "earned" by the husband prior to the spousal separation but received three-and-one-half months thereafter constituted property owned by him on the valuation date (i.e., the date of the spousal separation) and, therefore, had to be included in the calculation of his net family property. All three judges agreed, however, that the trial judge had erred by using an "if-and-when" approach to divide the husband's stock options instead of valuing them in accordance with the Black-Scholes method, which is an accepted model for valuing stock options where the underlying security is publicly traded. Application of this model resulted in a huge reduction of the wife's equalization entitlement. Unlike the situation in other provinces, Ontario courts have no jurisdiction to bypass the valuation of property by ordering a division *in specie.* And, as noted by Aitken J. in *Buttrum v. Buttrum,*[61] the "if-and-when" approach "is not a valuation technique but a method of dividing property."[62]

University degrees and professional licences, and future income resulting therefrom, are not "property" for the purposes of subsection 4(1) of the *Family Law Act.*[63]

---

56   *Kelly v. Kelly* (1987), 8 R.F.L. (3d) 212 (Ont. S.C.); *Buske v. Buske* (1988), 12 R.F.L. (3d) 388 (Ont. Dist. Ct.).

57   *Ross v. Ross,* [2006] O.J. No. 4916 (C.A.).

58   *Corless v. Corless* (1987), 5 R.F.L. (3d) 256 (Ont. U.F.C.); *Crutchfield v. Crutchfield* (1987), 10 R.F.L. (3d) 247 (Ont. H.C.J.); *Christian v. Christian* (1991), 37 R.F.L. (3d) 26 (Ont. Gen. Div.).

59   *Corless v. Corless* (1987), 5 R.F.L. (3d) 256 (Ont. U.F.C.); compare *Armstrong v. Armstrong* (1986), 39 A.C.W.S. (2d) 162 (Ont. Dist. Ct.).

60   [2006] O.J. No. 4916 (C.A.).

61   (2001), 15 R.F.L. (5th) 250 (Ont. Sup. Ct.).

62   See *Ross v. Ross,* [2006] O.J. No. 4916 at paras. 35–37 (C.A.), overruling *Reid v. Reid* (2003), 50 R.F.L. (5th) 170 (Ont. Sup. Ct.).

63   *Caratun v. Caratun* (1992), 42 R.F.L. (3d) 113 (Ont. C.A.), leave to appeal to S.C.C. refused (1993), 46 R.F.L. (3d) 314 (S.C.C.). And see Section A(9)(e), below in this chapter.

The definition of "property" under section 4(1) of the *Family Law Act* includes a future income stream payable pursuant to a non-competition agreement executed on the sale of an interest in a private company. Rights under such a contract fall within the definition of "property" under section 4(1) of the Act, where the right to the future income stream is not dependent on personal service. The non-taxability of such an income stream does not affect its characterization as "property" under section 4(1) of the *Family Law Act* but does preclude any discounting of its value in light of notional future tax liabilities. An inability to transfer the contractual right to a future income stream does not affect its characterization as "property" under the *Family Law Act*.[64] A spouse's right to future income from a trust established during the marriage has been held to fall within the definition of "property" in subsection 4(1) of the *Family Law Act*.[65] In *Da Costa v. Da Costa*,[66] a spouse's future interest in the capital of a deceased's estate, dependent as it was upon the spouse surviving the deceased's grandchildren, was characterized as a contingent interest and thus property within the meaning of section 4(1), but it was discounted in value to reflect the possibility that he might predecease the grandchildren. But a mere expectation of inheritance under a third-party will does not confer a vested or contingent interest until the death of the testator and does not, therefore, constitute "property" within the meaning of section 4(1) of the *Family Law Act*.[67]

d) Pensions

Paragraph (c) of the definition of "property" in subsection 4(1) of the *Family Law Act*[68] provides that "property" includes the following:

> in the case of a spouse's rights under a pension plan that have vested, the spouse's interest in the plan including contributions made by other persons.

Paragraph (c) does not imply that the valuation of a vested pension plan is always to be determined by reference to the contributions of the employee and employer, plus investment yield. Although this method of valuation may be appropriate for a defined contributions pension plan, its

---

64   *Clegg v. Clegg*, [2000] O.J. No. 2479 (Sup. Ct.).

65   *Brinkos v. Brinkos*, (1989), 20 R.F.L. (3d) 445 (Ont. C.A.); compare *Jordan v. Jordan* (1988), 13 R.F.L. (3d) 402 (Ont. C.A.).

66   *Da Costa v. Da Costa* (1992), 40 R.F.L. (3d) 216 (Ont. C.A.).

67   *Dunning v. Dunning* (1987), 8 R.F.L. (3d) 289 (Ont. H.C.J.).

68   S.O. 1986, c. 4, as amended by S.O. 1986, c. 35, now R.S.O. 1990, c. F.3.

validity is questionable when applied to a defined benefits pension plan. It is generally conceded that expert actuarial evidence is required in order to attribute a capitalized value to a defined benefits plan.[69] Many, but not all, of the difficulties arising in the context of actuarial valuation of defined benefits pension plans are canvassed by the Supreme Court of Canada in *Best v. Best*[70] but these complexities fall beyond the scope of this introductory text.[71] Actuarial capitalization of the value of a defined benefits plan may be avoided by the use of a so-called "if-and-when" order in most Canadian provinces. This form of order was endorsed by the British Columbia Court of Appeal in *Rutherford v. Rutherford*,[72] by the Manitoba Court of Appeal in *George v. George*,[73] and by the Alberta Court of Appeal in *Wilson v. Wilson*.[74] In the *Rutherford* and *George* cases, the courts endorsed the following formula to be applied where an "if-and-when" order is deemed appropriate to the division of pension benefits:

$$\frac{1}{2} \times \frac{\text{total number of months or years of matrimonial cohabitation in which pension contributions made}}{\text{total number of months or years during which pension contributions made}} \times \text{actual pension received}$$

In Alberta, a variation of this formula has been applied whereby the court looks to the total number of months or years during which the parties were married rather than to the period of matrimonial cohabitation.[75]

---

69   *Davies v. Davies* (1988), 13 R.F.L. (3d) 103 (Ont. H.C.J.); compare *Marsham v. Marsham* (1987), 7 R.F.L. (3d) 1 (Ont. H.C.J.). See, generally, Ontario Law Reform Commission, *Report on Pensions As Family Property: Valuation and Division* (including Executive Summary) (Toronto: Ontario Law Reform Commission, 1995). See also Canadian Institute of Actuaries, *Standard of Practice for the Computation of the Capitalized Value of Pension Entitlements on Marriage Breakdown for Purposes of Lump Sum Equalization Payments* (Ottawa: Canadian Institute of Actuaries, 1993).

70   [1999] 2 S.C.R. 868.

71   For an excellent overview of the complexities, see Professor James G. McLeod, Annotation, *Best v. Best* (1999), 31 R.F.L. (4th) 1 at 4–9.

72   [1980] 2 W.W.R. 330 (B.C.S.C.), aff'd in part (1981), 23 R.F.L. (2d) 337 (B.C.C.A.).

73   (1983), 35 R.F.L. (2d) 225 (Man. C.A.).

74   (1986), 2 R.F.L. (3d) 86 (Alta. C.A.).

75   *Ibid.*

The *Rutherford* and *George* formula has been applied in several Ontario judgments.[76] In *Nelson v. Nelson*,[77] Doyle L.J.S.C. diverged from the *Rutherford* and *George* formula by determining the value of the husband's defined benefits plan on the basis of his average annual salary for the best six years prior to the separation, because that date constituted the "valuation date" under the *Family Law Act*, and the wife was not entitled to benefit from her husband's contributions and increased pension benefits arising after separation.

In theory, it remains open to question whether an "if-and-when" order for the sharing of pension benefits upon maturity is consistent with a strict interpretation of the express provisions of the *Family Law Act*.[78] However, necessity is the mother of invention and an "if-and-when" approach may be essential in order to facilitate equitable and practicable discharge of an equalization entitlement.[79] In any event, the definition of "net family property" in subsection 4(1) of the *Family Law Act* specifically requires a valuation of all includable property as of the date of the triggering event.[80] An "if-and-when" approach to pensions in Ontario does not, therefore, avoid valuation of the pension for the purpose of determining the equalization entitlement and a lump sum payment based on the pension's capitalized value may be preferable to an "if-and-when" disposition.[81] Indeed, where practicable, "if-and-when" orders should be avoided by an immediate payment based on the capitalized value of the pension.[82] An "if-and-when" order is especially inappropriate where retirement is many years away and there is considerable bitterness between the part-

---

76 See, for example, *Porter v. Porter* (1986), 1 R.F.L. (3d) 12 (Ont. Dist. Ct.); *Harris v. Harris* (1986), 39 A.C.W.S. (2d) 68 (Ont. Dist. Ct.); *Klein v. Klein* (1987), 59 O.R. (2d) 781 (Dist. Ct.); *Rosenberg v. Rosenberg* (1987), 11 R.F.L. (3d) 126 at 131 (Ont. H.C.J.); *Wettlaufer v. Wettlaufer* (1988), 12 R.F.L. (3d) 379 (Ont. Dist. Ct.); *Storms v. Storms* (1988), 14 R.F.L. (3d) 317 (Ont. Dist. Ct.); *Rauf v. Rauf* (1992), 39 R.F.L. (3d) 63 (Ont. Div. Ct.).

77 [1986] O.J. No. 1483 (S.C.); see also *Thompson v. Thompson* (1987), 62 O.R. (2d) 425 (H.C.J.); compare *Weise v. Weise* (1992), 44 R.F.L. (3d) 22 (Ont. Gen. Div.).

78 See *Best v. Best*, [1999] 2 S.C.R. 868.

79 See *Marsham v. Marsham* (1987), 7 R.F.L. (3d) 1 (Ont. H.C.J.); *Hilderley v. Hilderley* (1989), 21 R.F.L. (3d) 383 at 394 (Ont. H.C.J.); *Lind v. Lind* (1992), 39 R.F.L. (3d) 227 (Ont. Gen. Div.).

80 *Marsham v. Marsham* (1987), 7 R.F.L. (3d) 1 (Ont. H.C.J.); *Miller v. Miller* (1987), 8 R.F.L. (3d) 113 (Ont. Dist. Ct.); *Woeller v. Woeller* (1988), 15 R.F.L. (3d) 120 (Ont. Dist. Ct.).

81 *Alger v. Alger* (1989), 21 R.F.L. (3d) 211 at 218–19 (Ont. H.C.J.); *Marsham v. Marsham* (1987), 7 R.F.L. (3d) 1 (Ont. H.C.J.).

82 *Fitzpatrick v. Fitzpatrick* (1989), 17 R.F.L. (3d) 278 at 279–80 (Ont. Dist. Ct.).

ners.[83] In deciding whether a lump sum or an "if-and-when" approach should be applied to the portion of the equalization payment representing the value of the pension, Weiler J.A. of the Ontario Court of Appeal[84] has suggested that a "critical factor" is the respective ages of the parties and the date when the pension is to begin. Where the spouses are close to retirement, a sharing of the pension benefit can be delayed because the waiting period is short, although the terms of postponement should contain protection for the payee spouse. If retirement is many years away, a lump sum pay-out is more appropriate. The court should balance any hardship to the payor spouse in making the payment against the hardship of the payee spouse in not receiving immediate payment. An income tax deduction should be allowed in attributing a lump sum value to the pension, but the court does not require expert evidence and may simply accept a reasonable estimate based upon the individual's tax situation. Paragraph 9(1)(c) of the *Family Law Act* precludes the deferral of an equalization payment beyond a maximum period of ten years and may thereby reduce the potential for an "if-and-when" order.[85] However, in *Marsham v. Marsham*,[86] Walsh J. circumvented the application of paragraph 9(1)(c) by invoking a trust pursuant to paragraph 9(1)(d) of the *Family Law Act*.[87]

A surviving spouse's benefits under a pension plan should not be included in the net family property of the spouse with the pension plan because that spouse has personally no interest therein.[88] Whether or not an actuarial valuation of such benefits will be attributed in determining the net family property of the surviving spouse will depend upon the probability of the spouses still being married to each other at the time of the pensioner's death. If the court finds it highly probable that the spouses

---

83   *Davies v. Davies* (1988), 13 R.F.L. (3d) 103 (Ont. H.C.J.).

84   *Best v. Best* (1992), 41 R.F.L. (3d) 383 (Ont. C.A.). And see Section A(13)(d), below in this chapter. For a classification of Ontario cases into the categories of lump sum payment, instalment payments, deferral of lump sum payment, and if-and-when orders, see Catherine D. Aitken, "Pensions under Part I of the *Family Law Act* of Ontario" in *Contemporary Issues in Family Law* (paper presented to Second Annual Institute of Family Law (1993), jointly sponsored by the Family Law Section of the County of Carleton Law Association and the Faculty of Law, University of Ottawa, 28 May 1993) tab 5.

85   See Sections A(13)(d) and A(13)(e), below in this chapter.

86   (1987), 7 R.F.L. (3d) 1 (Ont. H.C.J.).

87   See also *Hilderley v. Hilderley* (1989), 21 R.F.L. (3d) 383 (Ont. H.C.J.); *Rauf v. Rauf* (1992), 39 R.F.L. (3d) 63 (Ont. Div. Ct.).

88   *Marsham v. Marsham* (1987), 7 R.F.L. (3d) 1 (Ont. H.C.J.); *Miller v. Miller* (1987), 8 R.F.L. (3d) 113 (Ont. Dist. Ct.); *Davies v. Davies* (1988), 13 R.F.L. (3d) 103 (Ont. H.C.J.); *Hilderley v. Hilderley* (1989), 21 R.F.L. (3d) 383 (Ont. H.C.J.).

will be divorced before the pensioner's death, no amount will be attributed to the surviving spouse's net family property.[89]

Periodic pension benefits already being received are included in the calculation of the pensioned spouse's net family property.[90] Indeed, pension benefits already being received constitute both property and income. Consequently, the fact that a pension has been subject to spousal property division does not preclude the pension income from being considered in determining the pensioner's ability to pay court-ordered spousal support.[91]

Where a spouse's pension is vested and the proceeds can be rolled over into an RRSP without tax implications, the court should not allow a deduction to take account of notional income tax liabilities.[92]

Statutory development under federal pension legislation and Ontario pension legislation currently provide additional settlement options whereby a spouse's equalization entitlement under the *Family Law Act* may be satisfied by a division of pension benefits. For example, the *Pension Benefits Division Act*[93] provides a means whereby pension credits may be divided at source between spouses upon marriage breakdown. However, this statute does not displace Part I of the *Family Law Act*, which governs the equalization of spousal net family principles on marriage breakdown. The *Pension Benefits Division Act* simply provides a tool to transfer pension credits after they are valued and divided in accordance with provincial law. Indeed, the valuation of a pension in accordance with the criteria applicable under the *Pension Benefits Division Act* is quite different from the valuation of a pension pursuant to the *Family Law Act*. The purposes underlying the two statutes are fundamentally different. After determining the payment that must be made to achieve an equalization of the spousal net family properties under Part I of the *Family Law Act*, the transfer mechanism under the *Pension Benefit Division Act*

---

89 *Humphreys v. Humphreys* (1987), 7 R.F.L. (3d) 113 (Ont. H.C.J.). See also *Birce v. Birce*, [2001] O.J. No. 3910 (C.A.) (wife's survivorship benefit under husband's pension excluded where wife likely to predecease him).

90 *Abate v. Abate* (1988), 17 R.F.L. (3d) 251 (Ont. H.C.J.), aff'd (1989), 23 R.F.L. (3d) xli (note) (Ont. C.A.); see also *Clarke v. Clarke* (1990), 28 R.F.L. (3d) 113 (S.C.C.).

91 *Linton v. Linton* (1990), 30 R.F.L. (3d) 1 (Ont. C.A.); *Flett v. Flett* (1992), 43 R.F.L. (3d) 24 (Ont. U.F.C.); *Grainger v. Grainger* (1992), 39 R.F.L. (3d) 101 (Sask. C.A.); see also *Strang v. Strang* (1992), 39 R.F.L. (3d) 233 (S.C.C.); compare *Veres v. Veres* (1987), 9 R.F.L. (3d) 447 (Ont. H.C.J.); *Butt v. Butt* (1989), 22 R.F.L. (3d) 415 (Ont. H.C.J.).

92 *Forster v. Forster* (1987), 11 R.F.L. (3d) 121 (Ont. H.C.J.); see also *Aylsworth v. Aylsworth* (1987), 9 R.F.L. (3d) 105 (Ont. H.C.J.).

93 S.C. 1992, c. 46.

may be invoked, but to the extent that any portion of the equalization entitlement is not thereby realizable, the balance remains due pursuant to the *Family Law Act*.[94]

A wife's equalization claim may be barred by the husband's bankruptcy. A constructive trust claim may be sustainable against the husband's pension after his discharge from bankruptcy, but only where the three requirements of such a claim are established, namely, (i) the unjust enrichment of the husband; (ii) a corresponding deprivation of the wife; and (iii) the absence of any juristic reason for the enrichment.[95]

e) University Degrees; Professional Licences; Goodwill

The definition of "property" in subsection 4(1) of the *Family Law Act* is sufficiently broad to include an interest in a business or professional partnership. In valuing a professional practice, "goodwill" is a factor to be considered.[96] It has been held inappropriate to value the goodwill of a professional practice by capitalizing excess earnings, where the spouse is a sole practitioner and there is no continuum of returning patients[97] or where the practice has no value on the open market.[98] It has also been held that an anaesthetist employed by a hospital has no "practice" that constitutes divisible property and that his future income should not be regarded as a divisible asset.[99] Similarly, a spouse's professional degree or licence, with its consequential enhanced earning capacity, has been excluded from division. In *Brinkos v. Brinkos*,[100] Carthy J.A., of the Ontario Court of Appeal, presented the following opinion by way of *obiter dicta*:

> I cannot accept that the entitlement to earn income as a judge, or under a licence, is a contingent interest in the pool of money which may be earned in the future. There is no identifiable property, except perhaps the licence itself. If it is property, and if it has a value (and no opinion is here expressed), that value cannot be a capitalization of the future income stream. The licence will earn nothing without the services of the licensee and the earnings are based upon the value of the services provided, not upon the mere existence of a licence to perform. ...

94 *Lockyer v. Lockyer*, [2000] O.J. No. 2939 (Sup. Ct.), citing *Shafer v. Shafer* (1996), 25 R.F.L. (4th) 410 (Ont. Gen. Div.).
95 *Janakowski v. Janakowski*, [2000] O.J. No. 2650 (Sup. Ct.).
96 *Criton v. Criton* (1986), 50 R.F.L. (2d) 44 (Sask. C.A.).
97 *Nassar v. Nassar*, [1984] 6 W.W.R. 634 (Man. Q.B.).
98 *Smith v. Mackie* (1986), 48 R.F.L. (2d) 232 (B.C.S.C.).
99 *Barley v. Barley* (1984), 43 R.F.L. (2d) 100 (B.C.S.C.).
100 (1989), 20 R.F.L. (3d) 445 at 450 (Ont. C.A.).

In the case of a professional practising under a licence, it cannot be said
that there is a contingent entitlement to income in the future within the
legal meaning of those words where personal service and effort, rather
than an external event, are required to produce that income.

In *Caratun v. Caratun*,[101] the Ontario Court of Appeal specifically resolved the question whether a professional licence constitutes "property"
under subsection 4(1) of the *Family Law Act*. In view of the fact that a professional licence is non-transferable and its value depends on the future
labours of the licensee, the court concluded that a professional licence
is not "property" within the meaning of subsection 4 of the *Family Law
Act*, nor can it be subject to any proprietary interest in the form of a constructive trust. It was, nevertheless, concluded that the wife was entitled
to compensatory spousal support under subsection 11(1) of the *Divorce
Act*, 1968[102] in the amount of $30,000 for the sacrifice of her personal ca-
reer advancement and for her substantial contribution to her husband's
career aspirations.

f) Value

Although the notion of "value" is central to the application of Part I of
the *Family Law Act*, there is no definition of "value" in the Act. Where
practicable, the courts will apply the concept of fair market value, which
signifies "the highest price available in an open and unrestricted market
between informed and prudent parties acting at arms length and under
no compulsion to transact."[103]

Where the determination of a fair market value is impractical, as in
the case of pension benefits, the objectives of the *Family Law Act* necessitate that the court determine a "fair value" in light of the attendant
circumstances.[104]

g) Valuation of Business; Private Companies

In the words of Cameron J. in *Hart v. Hart (No. 3)*,

Generally there are four basic approaches to valuation of a business:

---

101 (1992), 42 R.F.L. (3d) 113 (Ont. C.A.).

102 S.C. 1967–68, c. 24.

103 *Christian v. Christian* (1991), 37 R.F.L. (3d) 26 (Ont. Gen. Div.); see also *Montague
v. Montague* (1996), 23 R.F.L. (4th) 62 (Ont. C.A.) (costs of pollution clean-up taken
into account in determining fair market value of husband's business).

104 *Marsham v. Marsham* (1987), 7 R.F.L. (3d) 1 (Ont. H.C.J.); *Menage v. Hedges* (1987), 8
R.F.L. (3d) 225 (Ont. U.F.C.).

1.   Market price (in the case of public company);
2.   Assets approach;
3.   Earnings or investment value approach; and
4.   A combination of the above. ...

The assets approach is generally used where the hypothetical purchaser is really looking to the company's underlying assets and not to the shares *per se*. This method may also be appropriate where the business being valued is a going concern, but not earning an adequate return on its invested capital. A determination of a liquidation value is an asset approach.

...

The earnings or investment value approach is appropriate when the business is earning a reasonable return on its capital. In this approach the hypothetical purchaser wishes to acquire the future earnings of the business.

...

In the combined approach, as the name implies, the appraiser uses the different approaches referred to above and weights the resulting values in light of particular factors to determine a final valuation.[105]

Factors to be considered in valuing the shares of a private company include the following:

(i)   the nature and history of the enterprise;
(ii)   the economic outlook;
(iii)   the book value and financial condition;
(iv)   the earning capacity;
(v)   the dividend-paying capacity;
(vi)   the goodwill or other intangible values;
(vii)   the size of the block to be valued; and
(viii) the market price of stock of similar corporations.

The valuation of the stock of a private company presents a unique factual situation that is not within the ambit of any exact science and the reasonableness of any valuation thus depends upon the judgment and experience of the appraiser and the completeness of the information relied

---

105   (1986), 60 Nfld. & P.E.I.R. 287 (Nfld. U.F.C.); see also *Kuderewko v. Kuderewko*, [2006] S.J. No. 726 (Q.B.).

upon to support the opinions presented.[106] The evidence of experts may yield to experience in light of a prior recorded sale of shares.[107] In determining the value of a business, the evidence of a person engaged in the "real world" of marketing such businesses may be preferred to that of a chartered accountant.[108]

Valuation is an art, not a science. In *Black v. Black*,[109] three expert opinions were submitted on the value of the husband's shares in privately held companies. The lowest estimate, submitted by one of two experts on behalf of the husband, produced a figure of $8,950,310. The husband's second expert suggested a figure of $14,707,000, which was subsequently revised to $13,261,000. The wife's expert valued the shares at $34,801,000. The lowest and highest estimates were consequently in excess of $25 million apart. The trial judge accepted the value of $14,707,000. The experience in *Black v. Black* suggests that there may be some advantage in spouses entering into a marriage contract to determine in advance the value of designated assets or, at least, a precise method for calculating value.

h) Valuation Date

The definitions of "net family property" and "valuation date" in subsection 4(1) of the *Family Law Act* imply that the court is unconcerned with changes in the value of property that occur between the valuation date and the date of the adjudication of an equalization claim.[110] In the absence of a resulting trust or constructive trust, any appreciation or depreciation in the value of property after the valuation date is irrelevant to a determination of the value of the net family property of each spouse, regardless of whether the change in value is attributable to extrinsic economic forces or to the conduct of a spouse.[111] The provisions of subsection 5(6) of the *Family Law Act* and particularly paragraphs (b), (d), (f), and (h)

---

106 *Indig v. Indig* (15 August 1986), Doc. Windsor 14,252/84 (Ont. S.C.), Carter L.J.S.C.; *Kuderewko v. Kuderewko*, [2006] S.J. No. 726 (Q.B.).

107 *Sheehan v. Sheehan* (31 March 1986) (Ont. S.C.), citing *Remus v. Remus* (1987), 5 R.F.L. (3d) 304 (Ont. H.C.J.). See also *Duff v. Duff* (1988), 12 R.F.L. (3d) 435 (Ont. S.C.).

108 *Sheehan v. Sheehan, ibid.*; compare *Duff v. Duff, ibid.*

109 (1989), 18 R.F.L. (3d) 303 (Ont. H.C.J.).

110 But see *Rawluk v. Rawluk*, [1990] 1 S.C.R. 70, 23 R.F.L. (3d) 337, and Sections A(6) and A(9)(b), above in this chapter.

111 *Kelly v. Kelly* (1986), 50 R.F.L. (2d) 360 (Ont. H.C.J.); *Arndt v. Arndt* (1991), 37 R.F.L. (3d) 423 (Ont. Gen. Div.), aff'd (1993), 48 R.F.L. 353 (Ont. C.A.), leave to appeal to S.C.C. refused (1994), 1 R.F.L. (4th) 63 (S.C.C.).

may enable the court to achieve equity between the spouses in the afore-mentioned circumstances by invoking its discretion to reapportion the entitlements of each spouse on the basis that an equalization of the net family properties as of the date of the triggering event would be uncon-scionable. The dissenting judgment of McLachlin J. in the Supreme Court of Canada decision of *Rawluk v. Rawluk*[112] concludes that subsection 5(6) of the Act may be used to address any unconscionability that might arise as a result of equalization of the parties' net family properties when the property has significantly appreciated in value by the date of trial.[113] Al-ternatively, a "reverse constructive trust" could perhaps be invoked by a title-holding spouse when property has depreciated in value between the valuation date and the date of trial.[114]

i)   Income Tax and Other Prospective Liabilities

In calculating the "net family property" of either spouse for the purposes of an equalization claim under section 5 of the *Family Law Act*, tax impli-cations may be taken into consideration.[115] In *Best v. Best*,[116] the Ontario Court of Appeal held that a 30 percent income tax deduction for pensions was appropriate because pensions are treated as income for tax purposes and therefore will inevitably attract income tax. The claimed deduction of 30 percent was deemed reasonable and consistent with the percentage allowed at trial in numerous instances.[117] Consideration should also be given to real estate and legal fees likely to be incurred in consequence of

---

112   *Rawluk v. Rawluk*, [1990] 1 S.C.R. 70, 23 R.F.L. (3d) 337.

113   See, generally, Section A(10)(a), below in this chapter.

114   See *McDonald v. McDonald* (1988), 11 R.F.L. (3d) 321 (Ont. S.C.), Forestell L.J.S.C. and James G. McLeod, "Annotation" at 322–23; see also *Arndt v. Arndt* (1991), 37 R.F.L. (3d) 423 (Ont. Gen. Div.), aff'd (1993), 48 R.F.L. 353 (Ont. C.A.), leave to appeal to S.C.C. refused (1994), 1 R.F.L. (4th) 63 (S.C.C.); *Socan v. Socan*, [2005] O.J. No. 3992 (Sup. Ct.).

115   As to the allocation of notional tax costs respecting an RRSP, which might be the subject of a tax-free rollover, see *Appleyard v. Appleyard* (1998), 41 R.F.L. (4th) 199 (Ont. C.A.) and see James G. McLeod, "Annotation" at 199–201.

116   (1992), 41 R.F.L. (3d) 383 (Ont. C.A.).

117   And see ranges from 10 to 40 percent in case listed by Catherine D. Aitken, "Pen-sions under Part I of the *Family Law Act* of Ontario" (paper presented to *Contem-porary Issues in Family Law*, Second Annual Institute of Family Law (1993), jointly sponsored by the Family Law Section of the County of Carleton Law Association and the Faculty of Law, University of Ottawa, 28 May 1993) tab 5.

any court-ordered equalization entitlement.[118] In the words of Finlayson J.A., of the Ontario Court of Appeal, in *McPherson v. McPherson,*

> An allowance should be made in the case where there is evidence that the disposition will involve a sale or transfer of property that attract tax consequences, and it should not be made in the case where it is not clear when, if ever, a sale or transfer of property will be made and thus the tax consequences of such an occurrence are so speculative that they can safely be ignored.[119]

Although this opinion was cited in the context of the *Family Law Reform Act, 1978*, it is equally applicable to its successor, the *Family Law Act*.[120] In the later appellate decision in *Sengmueller v. Sengmueller*, McKinlay J.A., delivering the opinion of the Ontario Court of Appeal, stated:

> From the *McPherson* case I glean three rules to apply in all cases:
> (1) Apply the overriding principle of fairness, *i.e.*, that costs of disposition as well as benefits should be shared equally;
> (2) Deal with each case on its own facts, considering the nature of the assets involved, evidence as to the probable timing of their disposition, and the probable tax and other costs of disposition at that time, discounted as of valuation day; and
> (3) Deduct disposition costs before arriving at the equalization payment, except in the situation where "it is not clear when, if ever" there will be a realization of the property.
>
> Under the *Family Law Act* it does not matter whether the third rule is applied as part of the valuation of the asset involved, or whether the deduction is made as an inevitable liability which exists on valuation day, although it is not payable until some time in the future.[121]

The Court of Appeal also rejected the submission of counsel for the appellant that disposition costs should only be allowed if it were necessary to dispose of the asset in order to satisfy the equalization entitlement.

---

118 *Kelly v. Kelly* (1986), 2 R.F.L. (3d) 1 (Ont. H.C.J.); *Sullivan v. Sullivan* (1986), 5 R.F.L. (3d) 28 at 35 (Ont. U.F.C.); but see *contra, Folga v. Folga* (1986), 2 R.F.L. (3d) 358 at 363 (Ont. S.C.).

119 (1988), 13 R.F.L. (3d) 1 at 9 (Ont. C.A.). See also *Livermore v. Livermore* (1992), 43 R.F.L. (3d) 163 (Ont. Gen. Div.).

120 *Starkman v. Starkman* (1990), 28 R.F.L. (3d) 208 (Ont. C.A.).

121 (1994), 2 R.F.L. (4th) 232 at 241 (Ont. C.A.).

j)   Expert Evidence: "Splitting the Difference"

Valuation is not an exact science and expert opinions may differ on the value of specific assets and even on the appropriate method for effectuating a valuation. For example, the valuation of a spouse's shares in an active company could be based on a future earnings approach or on a liquidation approach and the formula selected may radically affect the determination of their value.[122]

Where a court is faced with conflicting expert evidence respecting the value of specific assets, the court may find it appropriate to split the difference by averaging the appraisals submitted on behalf of the respective spouses. This practice cannot be universally applied, however, because it may lead to unjust and absurd results and would constitute an abrogation of the court's responsibility.[123]

In determining fair market value as of the "valuation date," which is usually the date on which the spouses separated, the court cannot invoke the benefit of hindsight.[124] While hindsight information cannot be used as part of the process of establishing the value of a private company on the valuation date, hindsight information relating to the actual results achieved after the valuation date may be compared against the projected or forecasted corporate results reached by the valuator and used to test the reasonableness of his or her assumptions.[125]

An order directing the transfer of property is unavailable under the *Family Law Act*[126] as a means of avoiding difficulties in valuation. Dispositive orders under section 9 of the *Family Law Act* presuppose that the equalization entitlement has already been established in light of the value of all relevant assets.[127]

---

122   See *Nurnberger v. Nurnberger* (1983), 25 Sask. R. 241 at 246–47 (Q.B.).

123   *Duff v. Duff* (1983), 43 Nfld. & P.E.I.R. 151 (Nfld. C.A.).

124   *Best v. Best*, [1999] 2 S.C.R. 868 (pension); *Harry v. Harry* (1987), 9 R.F.L. (3d) 121 (Ont. Dist. Ct.); *Woeller v. Woeller* (1988), 15 R.F.L. (3d) 120 (Ont. Dist. Ct.); *Martin v. Martin* (1989), 17 R.F.L. (3d) 78 (Ont. S.C.); *Ruster v. Ruster*, [2003] O.J. No. 3710 (C.A.) (premarital deduction).

125   *Debora v. Debora*, [2006] O.J. No. 4826 (C.A.).

126   R.S.O. 1990, c. F.3.

127   See *Marsham v. Marsham* (1987), 7 R.F.L. (3d) 1 (Ont. H.C.J.), Section A(9)(d), above in this chapter; *Henry v. Cymbalisty* (1986), 55 O.R. (2d) 51 at 54–55 (U.F.C.); *Humphreys v. Humphreys* (1987), 7 R.F.L. (3d) 113 (Ont. H.C.J.); *Cotter v. Cotter* (1988), 12 R.F.L. (3d) 209 (Ont. H.C.J.).

k) Deduction of Debts and Liabilities

In undertaking the statutory calculations for the purpose of determining the "net family property" of each spouse, subsection 4(1) provides for the deduction of "the spouse's debts and other liabilities."[128] Deductions are also to be made of the net value of premarital property, other than a matrimonial home.[129] For the purposes of subsection 4(1) of the *Family Law Act*, the value of debt-encumbered property is the equity in the property.[130] It appears that paragraph (a) of the definition of "net family property" in subsection 4(1) of the *Family Law Act* envisages the deduction of debts and other liabilities existing as of the "valuation date." It is immaterial whether the debts or liabilities were incurred for the benefit of the family as a whole or for the personal benefit of the spouse who incurred them. In calculating the equalization payment under Part I of the Ontario *Family Law Act*, the value of loans from the husband's parents may be substantially discounted where the debts are old and no demand was made for any repayment until after the spouses separated. In upholding the trial judge's finding in *Cade v. Rotstein*[131] that the debts should be discounted to 5 percent of their face value, the Court of Appeal observed that the husband's father had testified that he would not have looked for the money or taken any action against his son to collect the debts. The Court of Appeal concluded that the trial judge had properly followed the approach in *Poole v. Poole*[132] and *Salamon v. Salamon*,[133] and expressly agreed with the following statement of Heeney J. in *Poole v. Poole*:

> Even though debt may have a specified face value, if the evidence indicates that it is unlikely that the promissor will ever be called upon to pay the debt, the value of the debt should be discounted to reflect that reality.

---

128 See *Remus v. Remus* (1987), 5 R.F.L. (3d) 304 (Ont. H.C.J.); Section A(9)(i), above in this chapter.

129 See *Kivisto v. Kivisto* (1989), 17 R.F.L. (3d) 75 (Ont. Dist. Ct.); *Mittler v. Mittler* (1989), 17 R.F.L. (3d) 113 (Ont. H.C.J.); *Yee v. Yee* (1990), 26 R.F.L. (3d) 366 (Ont. C.A.); *Black v. Black* (1989), 18 R.F.L. (3d) 303 (Ont. H.C.J.); *Michalofsky v. Michalofsky* (1992), 32 R.F.L. (3d) 356 (Ont. C.A.).

130 *Reeson v. Kowalik* (1991), 36 R.F.L. (3d) 396 at 406–7 (Ont. Gen. Div.).

131 [2004] O.J. No 286 (C.A.). See also *Traversy v. Glover*, [2006] O.J. No. 2908 (Sup. Ct.).

132 [2001] O.J. No 2154 (Sup. Ct.).

133 [1997] O.J. No. 852 (Gen. Div.).

l)   Valuation of Premarital Property

In calculating the value of property, the definition of "net family property" in subsection 4(1) of the *Family Law Act* requires the deduction of "(b) the value of property, other than a matrimonial home, that the spouse owned on the date of the marriage, after deducting the spouse's debts and other liabilities, calculated as of the date of the marriage."[134]

If a spouse's premarital debts and liabilities exceed the value of his or her premarital assets, the deficit amount should be added to the net value of that spouse's assets at the valuation date for the purpose of determining the appropriate equalization payment to be ordered. Although judicial opinions have differed on this issue, the preponderance of authority asserts that debts that one spouse brings into a marriage and which are discharged during the marriage should be taken into account in calculating the appropriate equalization entitlement. This interpretation is endorsed in the reasons for judgment in *Jackson v. Jackson*[135] and in *McDonald v. McDonald*[136] and is exemplified by the calculation of the equalization payment in *Nahatchewitz v. Nahachewitz*.[137] These judgments reflect the objective of the *Family Law Act*, which is to equalize the value of property or wealth accumulated during the marriage, and this includes the reduction or elimination of a spouse's premarital debts.[138]

A spouse seeking to claim a deduction for a premarital asset bears the onus of proving its existence as of the date of marriage; the testimony of the spouse seeking the deduction may be insufficient without corroborating documentation.[139]

In determining the value of premarital property, paragraph (b) requires that the value be calculated as of the date of the marriage.[140] The value of this exemption cannot be indexed to any depreciation in the purchasing power of the dollar between the date of marriage and the "valuation date" as defined in subsection 4(1) of the Act.[141] Notional disposition

---

134   See *Collier v. Torbar*, [2002] O.J. No. 2879 (C.A.) (effect of unsecured premarital housing loan).

135   (1995), 5 R.F.L. (3d) 8 at 12 (Ont. H.C.J.), Kent J. See also *Menage v. Hedges* (1987), 8 R.F.L. (3d) 225 (Ont. U.F.C.).

136   (1995), 17 R.F.L. (4th) 258 at 260 (Ont. Gen. Div.), Rutherford J.

137   (1999), 178 D.L.R. (4th) 496 (Ont. C.A.).

138   See *McAndrew v. Rooney-McAndrew*, [2003] P.E.I.J. No. 95 (C.A.).

139   *Wasylyshyn v. Wasylyshyn* (1987), 8 R.F.L. (3d) 337 (Ont. Dist. Ct.); *Francis v. Francis* (1987), 8 R.F.L. (3d) 460 (Ont. S.C.); *Birce v. Birce*, [2001] O.J. No. 3910 (C.A.).

140   See *Oliva v. Oliva* (1986), 2 R.F.L. (3d) 188 (Ont. S.C.), var'd (1988), 12 R.F.L. (3d) 334 (Ont. C.A.).

141   See *Burgmaier v. Burgmaier* (1985), 47 R.F.L. (2d) 251 (Sask. Q.B.).

costs are also ignored in valuing the premarital property deduction for the purpose of determining an equalization entitlement under Part I of the Ontario *Family Law Act.*[142]

Any appreciation in the value of premarital property will be shared equally by the spouses on the valuation date, unless the court finds that this would be unconscionable having regard to subsection 5(6) of the Act, and particularly paragraph (h) thereof. Where the appreciation in value during matrimonial cohabitation is attributable to extrinsic considerations, such as inflation or market conditions, subsection 5(6) of the Act presumably has no application because an equal sharing of the increased value between the spouses would not appear to be unconscionable. In the converse situation, where premarital property has depreciated in value between the date of the marriage and the valuation date by reason of extrinsic economic conditions, the title-holding spouse is presumably entitled to a full deduction of the premarital value under paragraph (b) of the definition of "net family property" in subsection 4(1) of the Act, although paragraph 5(6)(h) of the Act might be deemed applicable in these circumstances.[143]

Pursuant to the provisions of paragraph (b), above, and paragraphs 4(2)(1) and 4(2)(5) of the *Family Law Act*, the value of a matrimonial home is included in the determination of the "net family property" of each spouse.[144] It is immaterial under paragraph (b) that the home was owned by a spouse prior to the marriage, provided that the residence was ordinarily occupied by the spouses as a family residence on the date of their separation.[145]

Similarly, it is immaterial under paragraphs 4(2)1 and 4(2)5 of the Act[146] that the matrimonial home was acquired by one of the spouses as a gift or inheritance from a third party after the date of the marriage or with the proceeds of such a gift or inheritance.[147]

---

142 *Pocs v. Pocs*, [2001] O.J. No. 2808 (Sup. Ct.).

143 See Section A(10)(i), below in this chapter.

144 *Shaver v. Shaver* (1991), 37 R.F.L. (3d) 117 (Ont. U.F.C.); see also Section A(9)(a), above in this chapter.

145 *Folga v. Folga* (1986), 2 R.F.L. (3d) 358 (Ont. S.C.); see also *Michalofsky v. Michalofsky* (1989), 25 R.F.L. (3d) 316 (Ont. Div. Ct.), aff'd (1992), 39 R.F.L. (3d) 356 (Ont. C.A.); *Bosch v. Bosch* (1991), 36 R.F.L. (3d) 302 (Ont. C.A.); *Nahatchewitz v. Nahatchewitz* (1999), 1 R.F.L. (5th) 395 (Ont. C.A.).

146 See Sections A(9)(m) and A(9)(r), below in this chapter.

147 *Harris v. Harris* (1986), 39 A.C.W.S. (2d) 68 (Ont. Dist. Ct.).

In *DeBora v. DeBora*,[148] a cottage had been purchased before the husband's marriage as an investment by a numbered company in which the husband was the sole shareholder. During the marriage, the cottage was ordinarily occupied by the spouses as an all-season recreational residence. The trial judge held that the cottage constituted a "matrimonial home" within the meaning of section 18(1) of the Ontario *Family Law Act*, which provides that "[e]very property in which a person has an interest and that is (or, if the spouses have separated, was) at the time of separation ordinarily occupied by the person and his or her spouse as their family residence, is their matrimonial home." Consequently, the husband could claim no deduction with respect to the premarital value of the cottage in light of the definition of "net family property" in section 4(1) of the Ontario *Family Law Act*. On appeal, the husband contended that he had no "interest" in the cottage within the meaning of section 18(1) of the Act because a shareholder does not own the assets of a corporation. Accordingly, he sought to deduct the value of his shares at the date of the marriage from their increased value on the date of the spousal separation as reflected in the market value of the cottage at these two dates. In addressing his contention, the Ontario Court of Appeal was called upon to examine section 18(2) of the Ontario *Family Law Act*, which provides that "[t]he ownership of a share or shares, or an interest in a share or shares, of a corporation entitling the owner to occupy a housing unit owned by a corporation shall be deemed to be an interest in the unit for the purposes of subsection (1)." In dismissing the husband's submission that section 18(2) primarily applies to a situation where a matrimonial home is a condominium or co-operative apartment or where the purpose of putting the home in the name of the corporation is to defeat the Ontario *Family Law Act*, the Ontario Court of Appeal stated:

> I disagree with this interpretation. The plain wording of the subsection does not limit a spouse's interest to a condominium or co-operative apartment and I can think of no reason to so limit it in this manner. The simple device of holding a house in the name of a personally owned corporation prior to the date of marriage would deprive the other spouse of the rights associated with the matrimonial home: an equal right to possession; the requirement that the consent of the other spouse to alienate or encumber the home be obtained; and the full value of the home

---

148   [2006] O.J. No. 4826 (C.A.). For further judicial insight on piercing the corporate veil, see *Wildman v. Wildman*, [2006] O.J. No. 3966 (C.A.) and *Lynch v. Segal*, [2006] O.J. No. 5014 (C.A.).

being included in the calculation of a spouse's net family property on separation. Such an interpretation would defeat the desired effect of the *FLA*, which regards the matrimonial home as a unique asset and gives it special treatment.[149]

While acknowledging that there is no single all-encompassing rule as to when a court will pierce the corporate veil and that a contextual approach is required that respects the interests of innocent third parties, the Ontario Court of Appeal concluded that the circumstances in *Debora* warranted a finding that the corporation was the *alter ego* of the husband that was being used by him to defeat his wife's legitimate claim and he ought not to be allowed to hide behind the corporate veil.

If property that includes a matrimonial home is normally used for a purpose other than residential, the matrimonial home is only the part of the property that may reasonably be regarded as necessary to the use and enjoyment of the residence.[150]

Where the matrimonial home represents only part of a multiple dwelling brought into the marriage, it will be necessary for the court to segregate the premarital value of the matrimonial home from the overall premarital value of the remainder of the property in order to determine the owner spouse's net family property.[151]

m) Excluded Property

Subsections 4(2) and 4(3) of the *Family Law Act*[152] provide as follows:

Excluded property

4.-(2) The value of the following property that a spouse owns on the valuation date does not form part of the spouse's net family property:

1. Property, other than a matrimonial home, that was acquired by gift or inheritance from a third person after the date of the marriage.

2. Income from property referred to in paragraph 1, if the donor or testator has expressly stated that it is to be excluded from the spouse's net family property.

---

149 [2006] O.J. No. 4826 at para. 18 (C.A.).
150 *Family Law Act*, R.S.O. 1990, c. F.3, s. 18(3); *Williams v. Williams*, [2006] O.J. No. 4986 (Sup. Ct.).
151 *Kraft v. Kraft*, [1999] O.J. No. 1995 (C.A.).
152 S.O. 1986, c. 4, as amended by S.O. 1986, c. 35, now R.S.O. 1990, c. F.3.

3. Damages or a right to damages for personal injuries, nervous shock, mental distress or loss of guidance, care and companionship, or the part of a settlement that represents those damages.

4. Proceeds or a right to proceeds of a policy of life insurance, as defined in the *Insurance Act*, [R.S.O. 1980, c. 218], that are payable on the death of the life insured.

5. Property, other than a matrimonial home, into which property referred to in paragraphs 1 to 4 can be traced.

6. Property that the spouses have agreed by a domestic contract is not to be included in the spouse's net family property.

(3) The onus of proving a deduction under the definition of "net family property" or an exclusion under subsection (2) is on the person claiming it.

There are no exclusions other than those listed in subsection 4(2). There is no deduction or exclusion from the net family property of a spouse for such things as children's furniture in the possession of that spouse.[153]

For the purposes of subsection 4(2) of the *Family Law Act*, the value of debt-encumbered property is the equity in the property.[154]

n) Property Acquired by Gift or Inheritance

The value of property that is acquired by one of the spouses by way of a gift or inheritance from a third party after the marriage is excluded from the determination of that spouse's net family property, except insofar as any portion thereof has been invested in the matrimonial home.[155] The value of such property is to be determined as of the valuation date rather than the date of acquisition. This means that the whole value, including any non-income based appreciation after the date of gift or inheritance, is excluded.[156]

Third-party gifts or inheritances that are no longer owned or traceable by the recipient on the "valuation date" do not fall within the category of excluded property under paragraph 4(2)1 of the *Family Law Act*.[157] The

---

153   *Davies v. Davies* (1988), 13 R.F.L. (3d) 103 (Ont. H.C.J.).

154   *Reeson v. Kowalik* (1991), 36 R.F.L. (3d) 396 (Ont. Gen. Div.).

155   *Family Law Act*, R.S.O. 1990, c. F.3, s. 4(2)1; see *Theberge v. Theberge* (1995), 17 R.F.L. (4th) 196 (Ont. C.A.).

156   See *Oliva v. Oliva* (1988), 12 R.F.L. (3d) 334 (Ont. C.A.).

157   *Vogel v. Vogel* (1989), 18 R.F.L. (3d) 445 (Ont. H.C.J.); *Sanders v. Sanders* (1992), 42 R.F.L. (3d) 198 (Ont. Gen. Div.).

provisions of paragraph 4(1)1 of the Act do not encompass interspousal gifts.[158]

Paragraph 4(2)5 of the *Family Law Act* makes it abundantly clear that the exclusion under paragraph 4(2)1 has no application to third-party postmarital gifts or inheritances to the extent that they have been invested in a matrimonial home.[159]

If an inheritance received during the marriage is placed by the recipient in a joint spousal bank account, a rebuttable presumption arises pursuant to section 14 of the *Family Law Act* that the spouses own the account as joint tenants and accordingly they share a joint beneficial interest in the account. If this presumption is not rebutted by evidence of a contrary intention, it is open to question whether the entire inheritance will be included in the calculation of the spousal net family properties for the purposes of the equalization process or whether the retained interest of the donor spouse remains exempt.[160]

o) Income from Third-Party Postmarital Gift or Inheritance

Subject to the express contrary intention of the donor or testator, the income generated by third-party postmarital gifts or inheritances is subject to inclusion in the determination of the net family property of the recipient spouse, provided that such income has not been spent on untraceable assets.[161] If the gift or inheritance is retained *in specie* and it is not a matrimonial home, its value will not form part of the spouse's net family property and a similar exclusion presumably applies under paragraph 4(2)5 to any substituted property, other than a matrimonial home, that is traceable to the gift or inheritance.

Although the word "income" in paragraph 4(2)2 does not apparently include any appreciation in the capital value of the property received by gift or inheritance from the date of acquisition to the valuation date, any

---

158 Compare *Family Law Act*, R.S.O. 1990, c. F.3, s. 5(6)(c), Section A(10)(d), below in this chapter.

159 *Lefevre v. Lefevre* (1992), 40 R.F.L. (3d) 372 (Ont. Gen. Div.). For the statutory definition of "matrimonial home," see s. 18 of the *Family Law Act*, R.S.O. 1990, c. F.3.

160 See *Cartier v. Cartier*, [2007] O.J. No. 4732 (Sup. Ct.). See also *Weeks v. Weeks*, [2005] P.E.I.J. No. 10 (C.A.) (no exclusion under *Family Law Act* (P.E.I.)); see *contra: Harrower v. Harrower*, [1989] A.J. No. 629 (C.A.), wherein Stevenson J.A. observed that "a gift to a spouse of a joint interest removes that joint interest from the category of exempt property [but the] interest held by the donor spouse remains exempt in accordance with and to the extent recognized by the [*Matrimonial Property*] *Act* [Alberta]."

161 *Family Law Act*, R.S.O. 1990, c. F.3, ss. 4(2)2 and 4(2)5.

income from the property that is used to pay or reduce the interest or principal of a mortgage or is used in any other way to increase the equity or value of the property is included.[162]

The right of the donor or testator to expressly stipulate that income from the gift or inheritance shall be excluded from the recipient's net family property is specifically recognized by paragraph 4(2)2 of the Act and will have a significant impact on the drafting of relevant documents or wills.

p) Damages

Paragraph 4(2)3 of the Act could be construed to exclude from a spouse's net family property any damages awarded for injury to the person, including that portion of the damages that represents compensation for a future loss of income." In *de Champlain v. de Champlain*,[163] Montgomery J. stated:

> This act is remedial in nature. It should therefore be broadly interpreted. In my opinion, "damages" in s. 4(2)(3) includes both special and general damages; it includes past and future loss of income, future care cost, general damages for pain, suffering and loss of amenities of life. It encompasses all heads of damages that might be awarded by a court and those heads of damages for which settlement is negotiated in personal injury cases.[164]

In *Shaver v. Shaver*,[165] however, a narrower interpretation of the meaning of section 4(2)3 was adopted by Mendes da Costa U.F.C.J., who concluded that "damages for lost wages and disability benefits do not satisfy the statutory test, and the value that qualified for exclusion was the general damage award of $25,000, which I understand, was compensation for pain and suffering." The latter exclusion was lost, however, pursuant to paragraph 4(2)5 of the *Family Law Act* because it formed part of the payment of an outstanding mortgage debt on the matrimonial home.[166] However,

---

162   *Oliva v. Oliva* (1988), 12 R.F.L. (3d) 334 (Ont. C.A.), var'g (1986), 2 R.F.L. (3d) 188 (Ont. S.C.).

163   (1986), 2 R.F.L. (3d) 22 at 23 (Ont. H.C.J.).

164   For a valuable commentary on divergent judicial opinions in the United States, see Kathy P. Holder, "In Sickness and in Health? Disability Benefits As Marital Property" (1985–86) 24 J. Fam. L. 657.

165   (1991), 37 R.F.L. (3d) 117 at 131 (Ont. U.F.C.).

166   *Ibid.* at 131–32.

the judgment of the Ontario Court of Appeal in *Lowe v. Lowe*[167] suggests a contrary conclusion. *Lowe v. Lowe* proceeded by way of an application under Rule 21.01(a) of the Ontario *Rules of Civil Procedure* to determine, as a point of law, whether the disabled husband's entitlement to a future income stream derived from Workplace Safety and Insurance Board benefits must be capitalized and included in his net family property for the purpose of determining spousal equalization rights and obligations under the Ontario *Family Law Act*. After pointing to a lack of consistency in previous trial judgments dealing with this subject, the Ontario Court of Appeal applied the modern purposive and contextual approach to statutory interpretation in concluding that, while the definition of "property" in section 4(1) of the Ontario *Family Law Act* is extremely broad, it does not include any and every interest, even those bearing no relationship to the marriage partnership, merely because the interest is not specifically excluded. The Ontario Court of Appeal accepted Aitken J.'s analysis in *Hamilton v. Hamilton*,[168] wherein she concluded that CPP and private insurance disability pensions should not be considered family property for equalization purposes. The Ontario Court of Appeal agreed with Aitken J.'s statement[169] that "the purpose of the disability payments is to replace in whole or in part the income that the person would have earned had he or she been able to work in the normal course." Thus, disability payments are "more comparable to a future income stream based on personal service" than to a retirement pension plan or a future stream of income from a trust,[170] both of which constitute "property" that falls subject to the equalization process. While conceding that disability benefits might be properly categorized as property when they are "part and parcel of an overall employee pension plan totally funded by the company,"[171] the Ontario Court of Appeal concluded that, ordinarily, disability payments replace income during the working life of the employee and, therefore, are appropriately treated as income, not property, in the context of property equalization and spousal support claims. The Ontario Court of Appeal acknowledged that it might be argued that the husband's permanent disability pension, which was payable for life, should be included as property because it was a fixed entitlement. However, it rejected that argument, being of the opinion that it is preferable, from the perspective of clarity

---

167 [2006] O.J. No. 132 (C.A.).
168 [2005] O.J. No. 3050 (Sup. Ct.).
169 *Ibid.* at para. 113.
170 See *Brinkos v. Brinkos* (1989), 69 O.R. (2d) 225 (C.A.).
171 See *McTaggart v. McTaggart* (1993), 50 R.F.L. (3d) 110 at para. 19 (Ont. Gen. Div.).

and predictability, to treat all disability benefits in the same way, whether they are calculated to reflect lost income or as compensation for impairment of earning capacity. Consequently, the Ontario Court of Appeal set aside the decision of the application judge and amended her order to provide that the respondent husband's WSIB pensions are not included property under Part I of the Ontario *Family Law Act*.

In *Maphangoh v. Maphangoh*,[172] the Ontario Court of Appeal found it necessary to distinguish between a retirement pension and disability benefits because a retirement pension constitutes "property," whereas disability payments do not constitute "property," for the purposes of an equalization of the spousal net family properties under Part I of the *Family Law Act*. In *Maphangoh*, the husband had worked for the federal government prior to his resignation in 1991. Six years later, at the age of fifty-six, he became disabled. Pursuant to his federal government pension plan, he became immediately entitled to a disability pension. This pension was characterized by the Ontario Court of Appeal as, in essence, an entitlement to take early retirement without penalty. But for his disability, the husband would have had to attain the age of sixty before being entitled to an unreduced pension. For the purpose of determining the wife's entitlement to an equalization of the spousal net family properties under Part I of the *Family Law Act*, the trial judge excluded the value of the disability benefits to which the husband was entitled until age sixty but included the value of the pension thereafter. The Ontario Court of Appeal held that the trial judge had adopted the correct approach on the record before him, which included information describing how the *Pension Benefits Division Act*, S.C. 1992, c. 46, Sch. II provided for the division of the husband's pension without regard to the disability benefits received prior to his attainment of the age of sixty.

Damages for breach of contract clearly fall outside section 4(2)3 of the *Family Law Act*.[173]

q) Life Insurance Policies

The provisions of paragraph 4(2)4 of the *Family Law Act* should be examined in the context of section 6, and particularly, subsections 6(4), 6(6), and 6(6a) of the Act.[174] Subsection 4(2)4, unlike subsection 6(6), of the

---

172   2007 ONCA 449, [2007] O.J. No. 2409.

173   *Docherty v. Docherty* (1994), 8 R.F.L. (4th) 155 (Ont. C.A.), aff'g (1992), 42 R.F.L. (3d) 87 (Ont. Gen. Div.).

174   See Section A(11)(b), below in this chapter.

Act is of general application in that it is not confined to a life insurance policy "taken out on the life of the deceased spouse" and "owned by the deceased spouse."

Although the proceeds or a right to the proceeds of a life insurance policy are excluded from the net family property of either spouse, the court has the authority under paragraph 34(1)(i) of the *Family Law Act*, in support proceedings, to make an *inter vivos* interim or final order requiring a spouse with a life insurance policy to designate the other spouse or a child as the irrevocable beneficiary under that policy.

r) Traceable Property

Where the value of property is excluded from the determination of a spouse's net family property under paragraphs 4(2)1 to 4 of the Act, a similar exclusion applies under paragraph 4(2)5 to any traceable substituted property. Paragraph 4(2)5 operates in relation to property "other than the matrimonial home" into which the "property referred to in paragraphs 1 to 4 can be traced." Consequently, an exclusion will be lost where the excluded property is traceable to the matrimonial home.[175]

The technical rules of tracing, which evolved to protect beneficiaries of trust funds that are improperly commingled with other assets by the trustees, ought not to be applied in the context of section 4(2)5 of the Ontario *Family Law Act* where equity demands that a portion of the exclusion claimed should be allowed.[176]

s) Property Excluded by Domestic Contract

Pursuant to paragraph 4(2)6 of the *Family Law Act, 1986*, spouses may exclude any property from their "net family property" by the terms of a domestic contract, as defined in section 51 of the Act. Paragraph 4(2)6 coexists with subsection 2(10) of the Act, which provides that "[a] domestic contract dealing with a matter that is also dealt with in this Act prevails unless this Act provides otherwise."[177]

Not all spousal agreements constitute "domestic contracts" as defined and regulated by Part IV of the *Family Law Act*.[178]

---

175 *Shaver v. Shaver* (1991), 37 R.F.L. (3d) 117 (Ont. U.F.C.), discussed in Section A(9)(p), above in this chapter. For general analysis of the doctrine of tracing, see D.W.M. Waters, *The Law of Trusts in Canada*, 2d ed. (Toronto: Carswell, 1984).

176 *McIsaac v. McIsaac*, [2004] O.J. No. 6 (Sup. Ct.).

177 *Armstrong v. Armstrong*, [2006] O.J. No. 3823 (C.A.).

178 See, for example, *Miller v. Miller* (1984), 41 R.F.L. (2d) 273 (S.C.C.), aff'g (1983), 29 R.F.L. (2d) 395 (Ont. C.A.).

Where a domestic contract takes the form of a separation agreement, spousal reconciliation terminates the agreement unless it is clear from the circumstances that the parties intended the separation agreement, or specific terms thereof, to survive the resumption of cohabitation.[179] A specific release of all rights to a particular property can be viewed as evidence that the parties considered the disposition of that property final and binding, notwithstanding the subsequent spousal reconciliation.[180]

t) Domestic Contracts: Canada Pension Plan

Although Canada Pension Plan benefits fall within the definition of "property" in subsection 4(1) of the *Family Law Act*, they should not be included in the calculation of the spousal net family properties because the federal legislation regulating such benefits itself provides for the splitting of credits between former spouses.[181] It is no longer possible in Ontario to contract out of the splitting of credits under the Canada Pension Plan.[182]

10) Unequal Division of Net Family Properties

a) Judicial Discretion Based on Unconscionability

Section 5(6) of the *Family Law Act* provides as follows:

Variation of share

5.-(6) The court may award a spouse an amount that is more or less than half the difference between the net family properties if the court is of the opinion that equalizing the net family properties would be unconscionable, having regard to,

---

179   *Bebenek v. Bebenek* (1979), 11 R.F.L. (2d) 137 (Ont. C.A.); *Bailey v. Bailey* (1982), 26 R.F.L. (2d) 209 (Ont. C.A.); *Livermore v. Livermore* (1992), 43 R.F.L. (3d) 163 (Ont. Gen. Div.); compare *Avery v. Avery* (1991), 33 R.F.L. (3d) 288 (Ont. Gen. Div.).

180   *Sydor v. Sydor* (2003), 44 R.F.L. (5th) 445 (Ont. C.A.); *Emery v. Emery*, [2008] O.J. No. 844 (Sup. Ct.).

181   *Payne v. Payne* (1988), 16 R.F.L. (3d) 8 (Ont. S.C.); see also *MacDonnell v. MacDonnell* (1991), 33 R.F.L. (3d) 52 (N.S.S.C.); *Czemeres v. Czemeres* (1991), 32 R.F.L. (3d) 243 (Sask. Q.B.).

182   *Albrecht v. Albrecht* (1989), 23 R.F.L. (3d) 8 (Ont. Dist. Ct.), rev'd (1991), 31 R.F.L. (3d) 325 (Ont. C.A.). And see *An Act to Amend the Canada Pension Plan and the Federal Court Act*, R.S.C. 1985 (2d Supp.), c. 30. For statutory amendments protecting the interests of divorced spouses who had waived their C.P.P. entitlements by way of a general release in an agreement executed before 4 June 1986, see *An Act to Amend the Canada Pension Plan (Spousal Agreement)*, S.C. 1991, c. 14, which received Royal Assent on 1 February 1991.

(a)   a spouse's failure to disclose to the other spouse debts or other liabilities existing at the date of the marriage;

(b)   the fact that debts or other liabilities claimed in reduction of a spouse's net family property were incurred recklessly or in bad faith;

(c)   the part of a spouse's net family property that consists of gifts made by the other spouse;

(d)   a spouse's intentional or reckless depletion of his or her net family property;

(e)   the fact that the amount a spouse would otherwise receive under subsection (1), (2) or (3) is disproportionately large in relation to a period of cohabitation that is less than five years;

(f)   the fact that one spouse has incurred a disproportionately larger amount of debts or other liabilities than the other spouse for the support of the family;

(g)   a written agreement between the spouses that is not a domestic contract; or

(h)   any other circumstances relating to the acquisition, disposition, preservation, maintenance or improvement of property.

Subsection 5(6) of the *Family Law Act* allows the court to award a spouse more or less than half the difference between the net family properties. A court is permitted to award an amount up to the whole of an offending spouse's net family property to compensate for unconscionable conduct.[183]

The court is empowered to deviate from the norm of equalization of the net family properties of the spouses only where equalization would be unconscionable and such unconscionability arises by reason of one or more of the factors specifically identified in paragraphs (a) to (h) of subsection 5(6) of the *Family Law Act*.[184]

The onus of proving unconscionability within the meaning of subsection 5(6) of the *Family Law Act* falls on the party asserting it and the term "unconscionable" will be given a strict, not a liberal, interpretation.[185] The

---

183   *Von Czieslik v. Ayuso*, [2007] O.J. No. 1513 (C.A.).

184   *Magee v. Magee* (1987), 6 R.F.L. (3d) 453 (Ont. U.F.C.); *Reeson v. Kowalik* (1991), 36 R.F.L. (3d) 396 (Ont. Gen. Div.); *Zabiegalowski v. Zabiegalowski* (1992), 40 R.F.L. (3d) 321 at 339 (Ont. U.F.C.); *Docherty v. Docherty* (1992), 42 R.F.L. (3d) 87 (Ont. Gen. Div.).

185   *Crane v. Crane* (1986), 3 R.F.L. (3d) 428 (Ont. S.C.), Mossop L.J.S.C.; *Balloch v. Balloch* (1991), 35 R.F.L. (3d) 325 (Ont. Gen. Div.); *Shaver v. Shaver* (1991), 37 R.F.L. (3d) 117 (Ont. U.F.C.); *Roseneck v. Gowling* (2002), 35 R.F.L. (5th) 177 (Ont. C.A.);

use of the word "unconscionable" should not be diluted so as to substitute the word "inequitable."[186] The term "unconscionable" signifies a threshold that precludes resort to subsection 5(6), unless the imbalance to be addressed is "harsh and shocking to the conscience," "patently unfair," or "inordinately inequitable," and "one that simply cannot be left as it is."[187]

An equalization of the differential in value of the spousal net family properties may be deemed "unconscionable" by reason of a spouse's neglect of his or her responsibilities for the economic and social welfare of the family or the wholly disproportionate contribution of one spouse to child care, household management, and financial provision as compared to that of the other spouse.[188] However, the failure of one spouse to contribute equally to child care, household management, and financial provision does not entitle the other spouse to invoke subsection 5(7) of the *Family Law Act* as an independent basis for judicial deviation from the norm of equalization.[189]

A spouse who has been denied specific deductions or exclusions based on the proper application of the statutory scheme cannot argue that such a result is "unconscionable" within the meaning of paragraph 5(6) of the *Family Law Act*.[190] In the words of Mendes da Costa U.F.C.J., "the equalization regime cannot be challenged where the circumstances relied upon as unconscionable have arisen merely from the application of

---

Parmigiani v. Parmigiani, [2006] O.J. No. 1268 (Sup. Ct.); *Haynes v. Haynes*, [2006] O.J. No. 4560 (Sup. Ct.); *Le Van v. Le Van*, [2006] O.J. No. 3584 (Sup. Ct.).

186   *Peake v. Peake* (1989), 21 R.F.L. (3d) 364 (Ont. H.C.J.); *Reeson v. Kowalik* (1991), 36 R.F.L. (3d) 396 (Ont. Gen. Div.); *Shaver v. Shaver* (1991), 37 R.F.L. (3d) 117 (Ont. U.F.C.); *Arndt v. Arndt* (1991), 37 R.F.L. (3d) 423 (Ont. Gen. Div.), aff'd (1993), 48 R.F.L. (3d) 353 (Ont. C.A.), leave to appeal to S.C.C. refused (1994), 1 R.F.L. (4th) 63 (S.C.C.); *Weddel v. Weddel*, [2006] O.J. No. 2574 (Sup. Ct.).

187   *MacDonald v. MacDonald* (1997), 33 R.F.L. (4th) 75 (Ont. C.A.); *Sullivan v. Sullivan* (1986), 5 R.F.L. (3d) 28 (Ont. U.F.C.); *Magee v. Magee* (1987), 6 R.F.L. (3d) 453 (Ont. U.F.C.); *Braaksma v. Braaksma (Public Trustee of)* (1992), 41 R.F.L. (3d) 304 (Ont. U.F.C.), aff'd (1996), 25 R.F.L. (4th) 307 (Ont. C.A.); *Balloch v. Balloch* (1991), 35 R.F.L. (3d) 325 (Ont. Gen. Div.); *Shaver v. Shaver* (1991), 37 R.F.L. (3d) 117 (Ont. U.F.C.); *Zabiegalowski v. Zabiegalowski* (1992), 40 R.F.L. (3d) 321 (Ont. U.F.C.); *Roseneck v. Gowling*, [2002] O.J. No. 4939 (C.A.); *Azimi v. Mirzaei*, [2007] O.J. No. 1824 (Sup. Ct.).

188   *McCutcheon v. McCutcheon* (1986), 2 R.F.L. (3d) 327 (Ont. Dist. Ct.); *Sullivan v. Sullivan* (1986), 5 R.F.L. (3d) 28 (Ont. U.F.C.); *Klein v. Klein* (1987), 59 O.R. (2d) 781 (Dist. Ct.); compare *Crane v. Crane* (1986), 3 R.F.L. (3d) 428 (Ont. S.C.); *Fenn v. Fenn* (1987), 10 R.F.L. (3d) 408 (Ont. H.C.J.).

189   *Brett v. Brett* (1999), 46 R.F.L. (4th) 433 (Ont. C.A.).

190   *Shaver v. Shaver* (1991), 37 R.F.L. (3d) 117 (Ont. U.F.C.).

the statutory scheme.[191] Nor can it be argued that an unequal division is warranted based on alleged unconscionability that arises from property having been excluded by a valid domestic contract.[192]

The language of subsection 5(6) of the *Family Law Act* appears to be sufficiently broad to permit the court to award a spouse all or any part of the other spouse's net family property. It has not yet been finally resolved whether subsection 5(6) of the *Family Law Act* is broad enough to address inequities that arise when assets increase or diminish in value between the valuation date and the date of trial.[193]

b) Undisclosed Premarital Debts or Liabilities

Pursuant to the definition of "net family property" in paragraph 4(1)(b) of the *Family Law Act,* premarital debts or other liabilities that are still outstanding on the "valuation date" are deducted from the value of the divisible property of the obligated spouse.[194] Where such debts or other liabilities were not disclosed to the other spouse prior to their marriage, injustice could obviously result from an equalization of their net family properties. Paragraph 5(6)(a) of the *Family Law Act* provides a means whereby such injustice may be averted by a court order for an unequal apportionment of the difference between the net family property of each spouse.[195] Such unequal apportionment must satisfy the general criterion of unconscionability set out in subsection 5(6).

c) Debts or Other Liabilities Incurred Recklessly or in Bad Faith

The right to deduct spousal debts and other liabilities from the value of the property owned on the valuation date is expressly recognized by the definition of "net family property" in subsection 4(1) of the *Family Law Act.* To offset the unconscionability that could result from an equalization of the net family property of each spouse, where debts or other liabilities were incurred recklessly or in bad faith, paragraph 5(6)(b) empowers the court to order an unequal apportionment between the spouses of their respective net family properties. Paragraph 5(6)(b) can only be invoked where the debts or other liabilities of the obligated spouse were incurred

---

191 *Ibid.*

192 *Avery v. Avery* (1991), 33 R.F.L. (3d) 288 (Ont. Gen. Div.).

193 See Section A(10)(i), below in this chapter.

194 See Section A(9)(l), above in this chapter.

195 See, for example, *Duff v. Duff* (1988), 12 R.F.L. (3d) 435 (Ont. S.C.).

either recklessly or in bad faith. Financial mismanagement, even if negligent, falls outside the ambit of paragraph 5(6)(b).[196]

d) Interspousal Gifts

Interspousal gifts form part of a spouse's net family property. Only gifts from third parties are excluded from a spouse's net family property under paragraph 4(2)1 of the *Family Law Act*.[197] Pursuant to paragraph 5(6)(c) of the Act, the court may order an unequal apportionment of the difference between the net family property of each spouse, if unconscionable results would ensue from an equalization of their net family properties, having regard to the nature or value of any interspousal gifts. In *Duff v. Duff*,[198] Hoilett L.J.S.C. ordered an unequal division of the net family properties because the wife had received jewellery and a car as gifts from the husband during their relatively short marriage. In *Braaksma v. Braaksma*,[199] an unequal division was ordered because the mentally-ill husband, in a period of lucidity one year prior to separation, had transferred the ownership of their only asset, the matrimonial home, into the wife's name and any court-ordered equalization of the spousal net family properties would undermine the wife's ability to take care of two disabled children of the marriage.

e) Depletion of Net Family Property

Pursuant to paragraph 5(6)(d) of the *Family Law Act*, the court may deviate from the norm of equalization of the net family properties of each spouse, where this would produce unconscionable results by reason of a spouse's intentional or reckless depletion of his or her net family property.

f) Duration of Cohabitation

Pursuant to paragraph 5(6)(e) of the *Family Law Act*, the court may order an unequal apportionment of the difference between the net family property of each spouse, where equalization would produce unconscionable results by yielding a disproportionately large allocation to a spouse having regard to the circumstance that cohabitation continued for less than

---

196   See *Moore v. Moore* (1987), 7 R.F.L. (3d) 390 (Ont. H.C.J.); *Cowan v. Cowan* (1987), 9 R.F.L. (3d) 401 (Ont. H.C.J.); see also *Crawford v. Crawford* (1997), 33 R.F.L. (4th) 381 (Ont. C.A.).

197   See Section A(9)(m), above in this chapter.

198   (1988), 12 R.F.L. (3d) 435 (Ont. S.C.).

199   (1992), 41 R.F.L. (3d) 304 (Ont. U.F.C.), aff'd (1996), 25 R.F.L. (4th) 307 (Ont. C.A.).

five years. The misconduct of a spouse in bringing the marriage to an end is irrelevant in determining whether an unequal division is justified by reason of the relatively short period of matrimonial cohabitation.[200]

> "Cohabitation" within the meaning of paragraph 5(6)(e) refers not only to matrimonial cohabitation but also to any period of premarital cohabitation.[201] Where the marriage has lasted close to five years, courts have tended either to not vary the share or to award a proportionate share based on the period of cohabitation.[202]

g) Debts and Other Liabilities Incurred for Support of Family

An unequal judicial apportionment of the difference between the value of the spousal net family properties may be ordered pursuant to paragraph 5(6)(f) of the *Family Law Act*, if equalization would be unconscionable having regard to the fact that one spouse has incurred a disproportionately larger amount of debts or other liabilities than the other spouse for the support of the family. Paragraph 5(6)(f) is presumably confined to debts or other liabilities that are still outstanding but is not restricted to third-party debts or liabilities.[203] The language of paragraph 5(6)(f) is, therefore, sufficiently broad to take account of existing consensual or court-ordered family support rights and obligations. An order for unequal apportionment might seem appropriate where family dependants have a continuing need for periodic support, and an equalization of the difference between the net family property of each spouse would be insufficient to accommodate that need and would in addition undermine the future ability of a spouse to pay support to his or her dependants. But in *Kelly v. Kelly*,[204] Potts J. was of the opinion that "debts or other liabilities" under paragraph 5(6)(f) and "other circumstances" under paragraph 5(6)(h) of the *Family Law Act* refer to debts or other liabilities and other circumstances in existence prior to, or as of, the date of separation. Even

---

200 *Futia v. Futia* (1990), 27 R.F.L. (3d) 81 at 83–85 (Ont. S.C.), West L.J.S.C.; *Reeson v. Kowalik* (1991), 36 R.F.L. (3d) 396 at 410 (Ont. Gen. Div.); *Pope v. Pope* (1999), 42 O.R. (3d) 514 (C.A.); *Mancuso v. Mancuso*, [2004] O.J. No. 4824 (C.A.); *Williams v. Williams*, [2006] O.J. No. 4986 (Sup. Ct.).

201 *MacNeill v. Pope* (1998), 43 R.F.L. (4th) 209 (Ont. C.A.); *Williams v. Williams*, [2006] O.J. No. 4986 (Sup. Ct.); *Linov v. Williams*, [2007] O.J. No. 907 (Sup. Ct.).

202 *Linov v. Williams*, [2007] O.J. No. 907 (Sup. Ct.).

203 Compare *Hammermeister v. Hammermeister* (1980), 19 R.F.L. (2d) 301 (Sask. Q.B.).

204 (1986), 50 R.F.L. (2d) 360 at 366 (Ont. H.C.J.).

if one prefers the opinion of Professor James G. McLeod[205] that such a restrictive interpretation of paragraphs 5(6)(f) and (h) is not "required in light of the language of the Act" and that the court may take account of circumstances arising between the date of separation and the date of adjudication, the words "has incurred" in paragraph 5(6)(f) may imply that court-ordered future support payments are to be ignored in determining whether an equalization of the net family property of each spouse would be unconscionable.[206] Perhaps the balancing of property and support entitlements in these circumstances could be achieved by an order deferring the property entitlement under the authority conferred on the court by paragraph 9(1)(c) of the *Family Law Act*. Any equalization or balancing payment must, however, be wholly discharged within the designated statutory period of ten years.

h) Written Agreement

Pursuant to paragraph 5(6)(g) of the *Family Law Act*, an unequal judicial apportionment of the difference between the net family property of each spouse may be ordered, where equalization would be unconscionable in light of a written agreement between the spouses that does not constitute a domestic contract.[207] An improperly constituted "domestic contract" that fails to comply with the formal requirements of section 55 of the *Family Law Act* may satisfy the requirements of paragraph 5(6)(g) of the Act.[208] Indeed, the words "written agreement" are sufficiently broad to encompass any mutual arrangements that have been reduced to writing by the spouses, regardless of whether these arrangements constitute a legally binding contract under established principles of the law of contracts.

i) Any Other Circumstance Relating to the Acquisition, Disposition, or Management of Property

An unequal judicial apportionment of the difference between the net family property of each spouse may be ordered under paragraph 5(6)(h) of

---

205 Annotation to *Kelly v. Kelly* (1986), 50 R.F.L. (2d) 360 at 361 (Ont. H.C.J.); see also dissenting opinion in *Rawluk v. Rawluk*, [1990] 1 S.C.R. 70, 23 R.F.L. (3d) 337; and see Section A(10)(i), below in this chapter.

206 See Section A(9)(k), above in this chapter.

207 *Braaksma v. Braaksma* (1992), 41 R.F.L. (3d) 304 (Ont. U.F.C.), aff'd (1996), 25 R.F.L. (4th) 307 (Ont. C.A.) (transfer of matrimonial home by deed); see also *Crawford v. Crawford* (1997), 33 R.F.L. (4th) 381 (Ont. C.A.).

208 Compare *Burton v. Burton* (1981), 24 R.F.L. (2d) 238 (Ont. C.A.).

the *Family Law Act* where equalization would be unconscionable having regard to "any other circumstance relating to the acquisition, disposition, preservation, maintenance or improvement of property."[209] Paragraph 5(6)(h) may be read in light of subsection 5(7) of the Act, which provides as follows:

Purpose

5.-(7) The purpose of this section is to recognize that child care, household management and financial provision are the joint responsibilities of the spouses and that inherent in the marital relationship there is equal contribution, whether financial or otherwise, by the spouses to the assumption of these responsibilities, entitling each spouse to the equalization of the net family properties, subject only to the equitable considerations set out in subsection (6).

Paragraph 5(6)(h) of the *Family Law Act* cannot be invoked to justify an unequal apportionment of the difference between the net family property of each spouse merely by reason of a traditional division of functions between spouses whereby one spouse discharges the responsibilities of a homemaker and the other spouse those of a breadwinner. If both spouses have pulled their weight in the marriage according to their respective abilities, talents, and mutual or agreed perceptions of their roles within the marriage, equalization is a fair result.[210] An unequal apportionment of the difference between the net family property of each spouse may be justified, however, where a spouse, without just cause, fails to discharge his or her marital responsibilities as defined in subsection 5(7) of the *Family Law Act*.[211]

---

209 See *Jordan v. Jordan* (1988), 13 R.F.L. (3d) 402 (Ont. C.A.); *De Mornay v. De Mornay* (1991), 34 R.F.L. (3d) 101 (Ont. Gen. Div.); *Braaksma v. Braaksma* (1992), 41 R.F.L. (3d) 304 (Ont. U.F.C.).

210 *Reeson v. Kowalik* (1991), 36 R.F.L. (3d) 396 at 409 (Ont. Gen. Div.).

211 *Klein v. Klein* (1987), 59 O.R. (2d) 781 (Ont. Dist. Ct.); *Henderson v. Henderson* (1987), 10 R.F.L. (3d) 150 (Ont. Dist. Ct.); compare *Robinson v. Robinson* (1982), 28 R.F.L. (2d) 342 at 346–47 (Sask. Q.B.); *Bray v. Bray* (1979), 16 R.F.L. (2d) 78 (Ont. Co. Ct.); *Grime v. Grime* (1980), 16 R.F.L. (2d) 365 (Ont. H.C.J.); *Fenn v. Fenn* (1987), 10 R.F.L. (3d) 408 (Ont. H.C.J.); and see *McCutcheon v. McCutcheon, Sullivan v. Sullivan, Moniz v. Moniz*, [1986] O.J. No. 1183 (H.C.J.), *Klein v. Klein*, and *Wasylyshyn v. Wasylyshyn*, discussed above in this chapter.

Postseparation events may be taken into account in determining that an equal division of the spousal net family properties is unconscionable within the meaning of section 5(6) of the Ontario *Family Law Act*.[212]

11) Entitlement on Death

a) Death As a Triggering Event

The death of a spouse constitutes a triggering event for an equalization of the net family property of each spouse, but only where the net family property of the deceased spouse exceeds that of the surviving spouse.[213] The right to an equalization of the net family property of each spouse on death is expressly confined to the surviving spouse and cannot be sought by the personal representative of a deceased spouse.

Public policy precludes a surviving spouse from pursuing an equalization claim where the survivor murdered the deceased spouse.[214]

b) Election by Surviving Spouse

The right of a surviving spouse to pursue an equalization claim under section 5 of the *Family Law Act* is subject to the exercise of an election under section 6 of the Act. A surviving spouse must make an election to assert his or her testate or intestate succession rights *or* to pursue an equalization claim under section 5 of the Act. The right of election is a personal right exercisable by the surviving spouse. Where no election has been exercised prior to the death of the surviving spouse, his or her personal representative is not entitled to file an election.[215]

Subsection 6(9) requires the election to be filed in an office of the Surrogate Clerk for Ontario within six months of the death.[216] This is subject to any extension of time permitted by the court under subsection 2(8) of the *Family Law Act*. Where no election has been filed within the

---

212 *Merklinger v. Merklinger* (1996), 26 R.F.L. (4th) 7 (Ont. C.A.); *Scherer v. Scherer*, [2002] O.J. No. 1661 (C.A.); *Weddel v. Weddel*, [2006] O.J. No. 2574 (Sup. Ct.); *LeVan v. LeVan*, [2006] O.J. No. 3584 (Sup. Ct.). See also dissenting judgment of McLachlin J., as she then was, in *Rawluk v. Rawluk* (1990), 23 R.F.L. (3d) 337 (S.C.C.).

213 *Family Law Act*, R.S.O. 1990, c. F.3, s. 5(2).

214 *Maljkovich v. Maljkovich Estate* (1995), 20 R.F.L. (4th) 222 (Ont. Gen. Div.), aff'd (1997), 33 R.F.L. (4th) 24 (Ont. C.A.).

215 *Rondberg Estate v. Rondberg Estate* (1989), 22 R.F.L. (3d) 27 (Ont. C.A.); compare *Anderson v. Anderson Estate* (1990), 74 O.R. (2d) 58 at 63–64 (H.C.J.).

216 See *Varga Estate v. Varga* (1987), 26 E.T.R. 172 (Ont. H.C.J.).

prescribed time limit, the surviving spouse is deemed to have elected to take under the will or intestacy, unless a court orders otherwise.[217]

Subsection 6(4) of the Act provides that a surviving spouse who elects to take under the will or intestacy "shall also receive the other property to which he or she is entitled because of the first spouse's death." Such "other property" might include benefits under any life insurance policy taken out on the life of the deceased spouse or under a pension plan that provides death benefits to the surviving spouse, or damages awarded in a wrongful death action under Part V of the *Family Law Act*. Subsection 6(4) of the Act may be contrasted with subsections 6(6) and 6(6a),[218] which apply to a spouse who elects to pursue an equalization claim. Such a spouse may assert rights as a beneficiary under a life insurance policy taken out on the life of the deceased spouse and owned by the deceased spouse, or under a pension or similar plan that provides for death benefits to the surviving spouse. However, any payment under the policy or plan must be credited against the surviving spouse's entitlement under section 5, unless a written designation by the deceased spouse provides that the surviving spouse shall receive such payment in addition to the entitlement under section 5.

Pursuant to subsection 6(5) of the *Family Law Act*, a testator may expressly provide in his or her will that testamentary gifts shall be in addition to the surviving spouse's equalization entitlement under section 5. In the absence of any such express provision, testamentary gifts to a surviving spouse who elects to receive his or her entitlement under section 5 are revoked and the will is to be interpreted as though the surviving spouse had predeceased the testator.[219]

A spouse who elects to receive the entitlement under section 5 is deemed to have disclaimed any intestate succession rights that would otherwise arise under Part II of the *Succession Law Reform Act*, R.S.O. 1990, c. S.26.[220] There are conflicting authorities as to whether an election under section 6(1) of the *Family Law Act* is irrevocable or the court has a residual discretion to set aside the election to avoid an injustice.[221] Section 6 of the *Family Law Act* does not address "multiple" wills and

---

217 Subsection 6(10); see *Webster v. Webster Estate*, [2006] O.J. No. 2749 (Sup. Ct.).

218 Enacted by *Family Law Amendment Act*, S.O. 1986, c. 35, s. 2(1), now R.S.O. 1990, c. F.3.

219 *Ibid.*, s. 6(7); *Cimetta v. Topler* (1989), 20 R.F.L. (3d) 102 (Ont. H.C.J.).

220 *Family Law Act*, R.S.O. 1990, c. F.3, s. 6(8).

221 *Re Bolfan Estate* (1992), 38 R.F.L. (3d) 250 (Ont. Gen. Div.); compare *Iasenza v. Iasenza Estate*, [2007] O.J. No. 2475 (Sup. Ct.).

only applies where there is a single will that is uncontested. Accordingly, a husband who would have received substantial benefits under his wife's former will, but who is excluded under her later will, may file an election under subsection 6(9) of the *Family Law Act* to preserve his rights under section 5, in the event that the later will is upheld. Under these circumstances, the election applies only with respect to the second will. Should the husband's challenge of that will prove successful, his election does not prevent or restrict his entitlement under the first will. Form 1 in Ontario Regulation 605/86 under the *Family Law Act*, which is technically deficient in that it is mandatory and does not permit a conditional election, should not be permitted to defeat the remedial nature of the *Act*, which was designed to enlarge rather than restrict the rights of spouses. In *Re Van der Wyngaard Estate*, the judge further observed that "an alternative suggestion, for future reference, might be to apply for an extension of time within which to file an election pursuant to (subsection 6(10) of the [*Family Law*] *Act*) until the issue as to the validity of the second will has been disposed of."[222]

Pursuant to paragraph 6(11)(a) and subsection 6(12) of the Act, a spouse's equalization entitlement under section 5 has priority over third-party testamentary gifts, excepting those made pursuant to a contract entered into by the deceased in good faith and for valuable consideration and insofar as the value of the gift does not exceed the consideration. The spousal entitlement under section 5 also takes priority over a third person's right of intestate succession and any order made against the deceased spouse's estate for the support of family dependants under Part V of the *Succession Law Reform Act*, except an order in favour of a "child" of the deceased spouse as defined under paragraph 57(a) of the *Succession Law Reform Act*.[223]

The personal representative of the deceased spouse is prohibited from distributing all or any of the deceased spouse's estate within six months of the death or after receiving notice of an application by the surviving spouse under section 5 of the Act, unless the surviving spouse gives written consent to the distribution or the court authorizes the distribution.[224] Contravention of these prohibitions renders the personal representative of the deceased spouse accountable for any improper distribution to the

---

222 *Re Van der Wyngaard Estate* (1987), 7 R.F.L. (3d) 81 (Ont. Surr. Ct.), McDermid Dist. Ct. J.

223 *Family Law Act*, R.S.O. 1990, c. F.3, s. 6(11)(c).

224 *Ibid.*, ss. 6(13) & 6(14).

extent that it undermines or injuriously affects the surviving spouse's entitlement under section 5.[225]

Pursuant to subsection 16(19) of the Act, a surviving spouse may bring a motion for an order to suspend the administration of the deceased spouse's estate for such time and to such extent as the court may determine.

Before exercising the statutory election or giving a written consent to the distribution of all or any of the deceased spouse's estate, the surviving spouse is presumably entitled to information respecting the extent and value of the deceased spouse's estate. Section 8 of the Act clearly requires disclosure of the party's property, debts, and other liabilities with respect to a section 7 application, but there is no corresponding requirement where an election is made pursuant to section 6. It would seem patently unfair to leave the surviving spouse to his or her own devices to ascertain the extent of the deceased's assets and liabilities given the limited time in which to do so before having to elect to take under the will or to pursue an equalization claim under the *Family Law Act*. It is uncertain, however, whether the personal representative of the deceased spouse must volunteer this information or await a demand for disclosure by the surviving spouse.

A determination of the value of the deceased spouse's estate may present significant difficulties by reason of the absence of any statutory definition of value and, more particularly, by reason of the definition of "valuation date" in subsection 4(1) of the *Family Law Act*. Pursuant to this subsection, the "valuation date" for the purposes of an equalization claim under section 5 where death is the triggering event is "[t]he date before the date on which one of the spouses dies leaving the other spouse surviving." This appears to indicate that any impact of the spouse's death on the value of his or her assets or even on their extent, as, for example, where property is held under joint tenancy with the surviving spouse, is to be ignored in determining the deceased spouse's net family property for the purposes of an equalization claim under section 5. As one commentator has observed, the results of this interpretation may be patently absurd.[226] Property such as pension and life insurance benefits, jointly owned real estate, businesses, or property subject to taxation might have

---

225 *Ibid.*, s. 6(18); but see also s. 6(15).

226 See Maurice C. Cullity, "The *Family Law Act, 1986*: Estates and Estate Planning" in The Law Society of Upper Canada Continuing Education Program, *The New* Family Law Act: *For Solicitors* (4 March 1986) at 25.29.

a substantial value to a spouse prior to death, but be worth little or nothing on death. Consequently, when the valuation date for equalization of net family property is the day prior to death, the deceased's estate will be credited with a fictitious amount resulting in the surviving spouse receiving an artificially high payment at the expense of other beneficiaries. A personal representative of the deceased spouse would be acting at risk, however, in ignoring the implications of the statutory valuation date by giving a realistic appraisal of the net worth of the deceased spouse following his or her death.

12) Property and Financial Statements

Section 8 of the *Family Law Act* provides as follows:

> *Statement of property*
>
> 8.   In an application under section 7, each party shall serve on the other and file with the court, in the manner and form prescribed by the rules of the court, a statement verified by oath or statutory declaration disclosing particulars of,
>
>   (a)   the party's property and debts and other liabilities,
>   (i)   as of the date of the marriage,
>   (ii)   as of the valuation date, and
>   (iii)   as of the date of the statement;
>   (b)   the deductions that the party claims under the definition of "net family property";
>   (c)   the exclusions that the party claims under subsection 4(2); and
>   (d)   all property that the party disposed of during the two years immediately preceding the making of the statement, or during the marriage, whichever period is shorter.

For the purpose of filing a financial statement, the ownership of property will be determined by reference to the title in which the property is registered.[227] Where property is jointly owned by the spouses, half of the value should be reported in the respective financial statements of each spouse.[228]

The objective of property and financial statements is to provide complete, up-to-date, and meaningful information to the parties and the

---

227   *Schaefer v. Schaefer* (1986), 38 A.C.W.S. (2d) 142 (Ont. C.A.).
228   *Ibid.* See also *Skrlj v. Skrlj* (1986), 2 R.F.L. (3d) 305 at 310 (Ont. H.C.J.).

court. The valuation of property by reference to its book value or depreciated cost value does not satisfy the requirements of section 8 of the *Family Law Act*. What is required is the estimated market value or actual worth of the property at the relevant time.[229] Where a party has filed a statement that is less than frank and complete, the court may draw unfavourable inferences against the party.[230] The court may also order costs against a party whose failure to comply with the letter and spirit of section 8 has resulted in unnecessary prolonging of the proceedings.[231] In addition, Ontario Rule 70.14(4) specifically provides that "[w]here a financial statement is required to be filed or delivered with a petition or counterpetition, or an answer to it, the registrar shall not accept the petition, counterpetition or answer for issuing of filing without the financial statement."

13) Powers of Court

a) General Observations

Section 9 of the *Family Law Act* provides as follows:

> *Powers of court*
>
> 9.-(1) In an application under section 7, the court may order,
>
> (a)   that one spouse pay to the other spouse the amount to which the court finds that spouse to be entitled under this Part;
>
> (b)   that security, including a charge on property, be given for the performance of an obligation imposed by the order;
>
> (c)   that, if necessary to avoid hardship, an amount referred to in paragraph (a) be paid in instalments during a period not exceeding ten years or that payment of all or part of the amount be delayed for a period not exceeding ten years; and
>
> (d)   that, if appropriate to satisfy an obligation imposed by the order,
>
>> (i)   property be transferred to or in trust for or vested in a spouse, whether absolutely, for life or for a term of years, or
>>
>> (ii)   any property be partitioned or sold.

---

229   *Silverstein v. Silverstein* (1978), 1 R.F.L. (2d) 239 at 241–42 (Ont. H.C.J.), Galligan J.; see Section A(9)(f), above in this chapter.

230   *Ibid.* See also *Stoikiewicz v. Filas* (1978), 7 R.F.L. (2d) 366 at 371 (Ont. U.F.C.) (child support).

231   *Silverstein v. Silverstein* (1978), 1 R.F.L. (2d) 239 (Ont. H.C.J.); *Payne v. Payne* (1983), 31 R.F.L. (2d) 211 at 217 (Ont. U.F.C.); *Skrlj v. Skrlj* (1986), 2 R.F.L. (3d) 305 (Ont. S.C.).

Financial information, inspections

(2) The court may, at the time of making an order for instalment or delayed payments or on motion at a later time, order that the spouse who has the obligation to make payments shall,

  (a) furnish the other spouse with specified financial information, which may include periodic financial statements; and

  (b) permit inspections of specified property of the spouse by or on behalf of the other spouse, as the court directs.

Variation

(3) If the court is satisfied that there has been a material change in the circumstances of the spouse who has the obligation to make instalment or delayed payments, the court may, on motion, vary the order, but shall not vary the amount to which the court found the spouse to be entitled under this Part.

Ten year period

(4) Subsections (3) and 2(8) (extension of times) do not permit the postponement of payment beyond the ten year period mentioned in paragraph (1)(c).

Section 5 of the *Family Law Act,* which constitutes the basis of the statutory property-sharing regime on marriage breakdown or death, is premised on a sharing of the value of property, and not on a division of property *in specie*.[232] It endorses an accounting procedure that will ordinarily result in a money judgment that leaves the title to property undisturbed. Section 9 of the *Family Law Act,* nevertheless, provides a variety of means whereby a successful equalization claim may be satisfied. The court may select a combination of the various remedies provided by section 9 so that a fair and reasonable solution may be attained.[233]

Section 9 of the Act is expressly confined to equalization claims. It does not extend to applications under section 10 of the Act, which involve questions of ownership. Although section 10 confers certain powers on the court similar to those defined in section 9, they are by no means iden-

---

232 *Henry v. Cymbalisty* (1986), 55 O.R. (2d) 51 at 55 (U.F.C.); *Skrlj v. Skrlj* (1986), 2 R.F.L. (3d) 305 at 309 (Ont. H.C.J.).

233 *Kukolj v. Kukolj* (1986), 3 R.F.L. (3d) 359 (Ont. U.F.C.); see also *Marsham v. Marsham* (1987), 7 R.F.L. (3d) 1 (Ont. H.C.J.).

tical; see, however, section 11, which applies to orders made under both sections 9 and 10.[234]

b) Order for Payment

Paragraph 9(1)(a) of the *Family Law Act* empowers the court to order one spouse to pay to the other spouse a lump sum in satisfaction of the equalization entitlement under section 5 of the Act.[235]

The Ontario Superior Court of Justice has inherent jurisdiction to grant an interim order for an advance payment to be made against the recipient's entitlement to equalization of the spousal net family properties under Part I of the Ontario *Family Law Act*.[236]

c) Order for Security

Paragraph 9(1)(b) of the *Family Law Act* empowers the court to order that security be given for the performance of any obligation imposed by any order of the court made pursuant to subsection 9(1). The security may include a charge on property or on the proceeds of sale of designated property[237] and such a charge may presumably be made on "excluded property" within the meaning of subsection 4(2) of the *Family Law Act*. An order for security lies in the discretion of the court and is not available as of right. The court may impose such an order where the conduct of one spouse indicates that there may be difficulty collecting a lump sum equalization payment.[238] Where payment of the amount due is deferred or involves instalments pursuant to an order under paragraph 9(1)(c) of the Act, an order for security is appropriate,[239] particularly where assets are located in a foreign jurisdiction.[240] An order for security may be varied or discharged pursuant to section 13 of the Act.[241]

---

234 See Section A(13)(h), below in this chapter.
235 See *Leslie v. Leslie* (1987), 9 R.F.L. (3d) 82 (Ont. H.C.J.); *Forster v. Forster* (1987), 11 R.F.L. (3d) 121 (Ont. H.C.J.).
236 *Zagdanski v. Zagdanski*, [2001] O.J. No. 2886 (Sup. Ct.).
237 *Jackson v. Jackson* (1987), 5 R.F.L. (3d) 8 (Ont. S.C.); *Duff v. Duff* (1988), 12 R.F.L. (3d) 435 (Ont. S.C.).
238 *Verboom v. Verboom* (1991), 34 R.F.L. (3d) 312 (Ont. Gen. Div.).
239 *Best v. Best* (1992), 41 R.F.L. (3d) 383 (Ont. C.A.); *Kukolj v. Kukolj* and *Benke v. Benke* at Section A(13)(d), below in this chapter, [1986] O.J. No. 2073 (Dist. Ct.).
240 *Da Costa v. Da Costa* (1992), 40 R.F.L. (3d) 216 (Ont. C.A.).
241 See Section A(15), below in this chapter.

d) Deferred or Instalment Payments

Where there is evidence that an order for immediate payment would create hardship, the court has a discretionary jurisdiction under paragraph 9(1)(c) of the Act to order that the due amount be paid in instalments over a maximum period of ten years or that all or any part of the due amount be deferred for a period not exceeding ten years.[242] The terms of any such order may be subsequently varied under section 9(3) of the Act, but the court is expressly precluded from varying the amount or from extending the ten-year period for payment by the express provisions of subsections 9(3) and 9(4) of the Act.

If an Ontario court favours an "if-and-when" order with respect to a spousal pension, paragraph 9(1)(c) presents obstacles where the pension benefits will not mature or be fully realized within the ten-year period. The provisions of paragraph 9(1)(c) of the Act will only be met where the amount due is fully paid within the stipulated time period. It is not sufficient that such payments commence within that period, but are not fully extinguished on the expiration thereof.[243] The ten-year maximum payout period has no application where the court orders that property be transferred to or in trust for a spouse pursuant to paragraph 9(1)(d) of the Act.[244]

e) Transfers of Property; Partition and Sale

Paragraph 9(1)(d) of the *Family Law Act* empowers the court to order that a spousal equalization entitlement shall be satisfied by property being transferred to, or in trust for, or vested in a spouse, whether absolutely, for life, or for a term of years.[245] The court may alternatively order the partition and sale of *any* property.[246]

242　*Oliva v. Oliva* (1986), 2 R.F.L. (3d) 188 (Ont. S.C.), var'd (1988), 12 R.F.L. (3d) 334 (Ont. C.A.); *Messier v. Messier* (1986), 5 R.F.L. (3d) 251 (Ont. Dist. Ct.); *Marsham v. Marsham* (1987), 7 R.F.L. (3d) 1 (Ont. H.C.J.); *Leslie v. Leslie* (1987), 9 R.F.L. (3d) 82 (Ont. H.C.J.); *Randolf v. Randolf* (1991), 34 R.F.L. (3d) 444 (Ont. Gen. Div.); *Roach v. Roach* (1997), 33 R.F.L. (4th) 157 (Ont. C.A.); *Arndt v. Arndt* (1991), 37 R.F.L. (3d) 423 (Ont. Gen. Div.), aff'd (1993), 48 R.F.L. (3d) 353 (Ont. C.A.), leave to appeal to S.C.C. refused (1994), 1 R.F.L. (4th) 63 (S.C.C.).

243　Compare *Porter v. Porter* (1986), 1 R.F.L. (3d) 12 (Ont. Dist. Ct.); *Kroone v. Kroone* (1992), 41 R.F.L. (3d) 111 (Ont. Gen. Div.); see also *Kukolj v. Kukolj* (1986), 3 R.F.L. (3d) 359 (Ont. U.F.C.); *Klein v. Klein* (1987), 59 O.R. (2d) 781 (Dist. Ct.).

244　See *Marsham v. Marsham* (1987), 7 R.F.L. (3d) 1 (Ont. H.C.J.); see also *Best v. Best* (1992), 41 R.F.L. (3d) 383 at 388 (Ont. C.A.).

245　See *Oliva v. Oliva* (1986), 2 R.F.L. (3d) 188 (Ont. S.C.), var'd (1988), 12 R.F.L. (3d) 334 (Ont. C.A.); *Da Costa v. Da Costa* (1992), 40 R.F.L. (3d) 216 (Ont. C.A.).

246　See *Leslie v. Leslie* (1987), 9 R.F.L. (3d) 82 (Ont. H.C.J.).

Paragraph 9(1)(d) does not empower the court to order a division of specific property in lieu of undertaking the calculations necessary to determine a spouse's equalization entitlement, although such a division could be achieved by a valid domestic contract.[247] In *Humphreys v. Humphreys*,[248] Galligan J. categorically stated that the court has no power "to rearrange assets between the parties and compensate for any difference in value by way of an equalizing payment."

f) Financial Information and Inspections

The power of the court to order financial disclosure or inspections of property pursuant to subsection 9(2) of the Act is confined to circumstances where the court makes an order for instalments or deferred payments under paragraph 9(1)(c) or on a motion to vary such an order brought pursuant to subsection 9(3) of the Act.

g) Variation of Order for Instalment or Deferred Payments

Subsection 9(3) of the *Family Law Act* empowers the court to vary an order made pursuant to paragraph 9(1)(c) for instalment or deferred payments in the event of a material change in the circumstances of the spouse obligated by such order. No corresponding statutory jurisdiction is vested in the court to accommodate material changes in the circumstances of the entitled spouse; for example, the death of this spouse. The powers of variation are expressly restricted under subsection 9(3) in that the court cannot vary the amount to which a spouse is entitled. Furthermore, subsection 9(4) of the Act precludes the court from postponing any payment beyond the ten-year period specified in paragraph 9(1)(c) of the Act.

h) Operating Business or Farm

In both interspousal ownership and equalization disputes, court orders must avoid the sale of an operating business or farm or the serious impairment of its operation, unless there is no reasonable alternative method of satisfying the claim.[249] An order requiring the disposition or impairment of an operating business or farm may be made where there are no practicable means of otherwise satisfying the award.[250]

---

247 See *Wilson v. Wilson* (1988), 14 R.F.L. (3d) 98 (Ont. H.C.J.).
248 (1987), 7 R.F.L. (3d) 113 (Ont. H.C.J.); see also *Cotter v. Cotter* (1988), 12 R.F.L. (3d) 209 (Ont. H.C.J.).
249 *Family Law Act*, R.S.O. 1990, c. F.3, s. 11.
250 *Postma v. Postma* (1987), 6 R.F.L. (3d) 50 (Ont. S.C.); *Leslie v. Leslie* (1987), 9 R.F.L. (3d) 82 (Ont. H.C.J.); see also *Godinek v. Godinek* (1992), 40 R.F.L. (3d) 78 (Ont. Gen.

i) Interest

As a general principle, prejudgment interest is payable on an equalization payment. Exceptions have been admitted where the payor spouse cannot realize on the asset giving rise to the equalization payment until after the trial, does not have the use of it prior to trial, the asset generates no income, and the payor spouse has not delayed the case being brought to trial. Many of the exceptional cases involve the matrimonial home or a pension.[251] While prejudgment interest may be denied on an equalization payment because it is based largely on the payor's pension, postjudgment interest may be ordered.[252] Postjudgment interest is payable on an equalization payment, unless the court makes an order disallowing postjudgment interest.[253]

Trial judges have a wide discretion under section 130 of the Ontario *Courts of Justice Act* to allow prejudgment or postjudgment interest at a higher or lower rate than that prescribed. In *Debora v. Debora*,[254] the wife's appeal respecting the amount of prejudgment interest was dismissed. The trial judge had taken account of fluctuations in the applicable rates of interest during the lengthy litigation and the rate selected was rationally connected to the interest rates that prevailed over the relevant period.

14) Restraining Orders and Preservation Orders

Section 12 of the *Family Law Act* empowers the court to make an interim or final order to restrain the depletion of a spouse's property, and for the possession, delivering up, safekeeping, and preservation of the property. The purpose of such an order is to ensure that there are sufficient assets available to satisfy any subsequent order for equalization of the spousal net family properties.[255] A court should decline to tie up all assets where this is unnecessary in light of the *prima facie* equalization entitlement of

---

Div.).

251 *McQuay v. McQuay* (1992), 39 R.F.L. (3d) 184 (Ont. Div. Ct.); *Bigelow v. Bigelow* (1995), 15 R.F.L. (4th) 12 (Ont. Div. Ct.); *Burgess v. Burgess* (1995), 16 R.F.L. (4th) 388 (Ont. C.A.); *Purcell v. Purcell* (1996), 26 R.F.L. (4th) 267 (Ont. C.A.); *Calvert v. Calvert* (1997), 32 O.R. (3d) 281 (Gen. Div.); *DeBora v. DeBora*, [2004] O.J. No. 4826 (Sup. Ct.).

252 *Kennedy v. Kennedy* (1995), 19 R.F.L. (4th) 454 (Ont. C.A.).

253 *Bigelow v. Bigelow* (1995), 15 R.F.L. (4th) 12 (Ont. Div. Ct.).

254 [2006] O.J. No. 4826 (C.A.).

255 *Lasch v. Lasch* (1988), 13 R.F.L. (3d) 434 (Ont. H.C.J. (Master)); *Both v. Both*, [2008] O.J. No. 1358 (Sup. Ct.).

the party seeking a restraining order under section 12 of the *Family Law Act*.[256]

Interim preservation orders under section 12 of the Ontario *Family Law Act* are designed to prevent the dissipation of assets pending determination of an application for equalization of the spousal net family properties under Part I of the Act. In exercising its discretionary jurisdiction, the court should consider (i) the relative strength of the equalization claim; (ii) the balance of convenience; and (iii) the prospect of irreparable harm.[257]

An order granted pursuant to section 12 of the *Family Law Act* does not confer any property right on the successful applicant nor priority over third-party creditors of the spouse against whom the order is obtained.[258]

Section 12 of the *Family Law Act* is preventive rather than curative in nature. It cannot be invoked to set aside transactions that have already been completed. Relief, if any, in these circumstances, must be found elsewhere — as, for example, under the provisions of the *Fraudulent Conveyances Act*, which has been successfully invoked to prevent a husband from frustrating his wife's right to seek an equalization of their net family properties by disposing of property to his adult children by *inter vivos* gifts.[259]

15) Variation and Realization of Security

An order for security or for the charging of property granted pursuant to paragraphs 9(1)(c) or 10(1)(d) of the *Family Law Act* may be varied or discharged under section 13 of the Act. In the alternative, the court may direct a sale of the property for the purpose of realizing the security, provided that notice of the motion to vary is given to all persons with an interest in the property.

16) Retrospective Operation

Part I of the *Family Law Act* applies to property owned by spouses whether they were married before or after the date when the Act came into force,

---

256 *Ibid.*

257 *Bronfman v. Bronfman*, [2000] O.J. No. 4591 (Sup. Ct.); *Both v. Both*, [2008] O.J. No. 1358 (Sup. Ct.).

258 *Nevarc Holdings Ltd. v. Orchid Communications Inc.* (1990), 28 R.F.L. (3d) 330 (Ont. Gen. Div.); *Gaudet (Litigation Guardian of) v. Young Estate* (1995), 11 R.F.L. (4th) 284 (Ont. Gen. Div.).

259 *Stone v. Stone*, [2001] O.J. No. 3282 (C.A.).

namely, 1 March 1986.[260] Part I of the *Family Law Act* also applies regardless of whether the property was acquired before or after the commencement of the Act.

17) Occupation Rent and Accountancy Claims

A spouse who remains in exclusive possession of the jointly owned matrimonial home after spousal separation may seek an accounting and contribution from the non-occupying spouse with respect to mortgage instalments, repairs, maintenance, or property taxes that have been paid by the occupying spouse. Where such an accounting is sought, the occupying spouse is subject to a counterclaim for occupation rent. In assessing an application for occupation rent, the court must exercise a certain amount of discretion in balancing the relevant factors in order to determine whether occupation rent is appropriate in the overall circumstances of the case. The following factors may be relevant in determining whether an order for occupation rent is appropriate:

(i)   the conduct of the non-occupying spouse, including the failure to pay support;

(ii)   the conduct of the occupying spouse, including the failure to pay support;

(iii)   delay in making the claim;

(iv)   the extent to which the non-occupying spouse has been prevented from having access to his or her equity in the home;

(v)   whether the non-occupying spouse moved for the sale of the home and, if not, why not;

(vi)   whether the occupying spouse paid the mortgage and other carrying charges of the home;

(vii)   whether the children resided with the occupying spouse and, if so, whether the non-occupying spouse paid, or was able to pay, child support; and

(viii) whether the occupying spouse has increased the selling value of the property.

Ouster is not required, as once was thought in some early decisions.[261] The following factors have been identified by the Ontario Court of Appeal as consistently taken into account where occupation rent is sought:

---

260 See *Vivier v. Vivier* (1987), 5 R.F.L. (3d) 450 (Ont. Dist. Ct.).

261 *Higgins v. Higgins*, [2001] O.J. No. 3011 (Sup. Ct.); *Guziolek v. Guziolek*, [2006] O.J. No. 1361 (Sup. Ct.); *Haynes v. Haynes*, [2006] O.J. No. 4560 (Sup. Ct.); *Rezel v. Rezel*,

- the timing of the claim for occupation rent;
- the duration of the occupancy;
- the inability of the non-occupying spouse to realize on his or her equity in the property;
- any reasonable credits to be set off against occupation rent; and
- any other competing claims in the litigation.[262]

18) Disposition and Possession of the Matrimonial Home

a) General Observations
Part II of the *Family Law Act* of Ontario includes special provisions concerning the disposition and possession of the matrimonial home.[263]

b) Definition and Designation of "Matrimonial Home"
Section 18 of the *Family Law Act* defines the "matrimonial home" as every property in which either spouse has an interest that the spouses ordinarily occupy as their family residence or did so at the time of their separation. Where the matrimonial home is on land that is normally used for a non-residential purpose, the matrimonial home only extends to that part of the property that is reasonably necessary for the use and enjoyment of the residence.[264]

Section 18 of the *Family Law Act* clearly envisages that spouses may have more than one matrimonial home; as, for example, where they enjoy an urban residence as well as cottage property.[265] However, section 20 of the *Family Law Act* permits the spouses to jointly designate and register one specific property as the matrimonial home, in which event any other non-designated property that would otherwise constitute a matrimonial home within the meaning of section 18 of the *Family Law Act* ceases to be a matrimonial home. A designation may be subsequently cancelled by the spouses, in which event other residences regain their status as matrimonial homes under section 18 of the Act.

[2007] O.J. No. 1460 (Sup. Ct.).

262   *Griffiths v. Zambosco* (2001), 54 O.R. (3d) 397 (C.A.).

263   As to the special status accorded to the matrimonial home in the context of equalization claims under Part I of the *Family Law Act*, see Sections A(9)(l), A(9)(m), and A(9)(r), above in this chapter.

264   *Williams v. Williams*, [2006] O.J. No. 4986 (Sup. Ct.).

265   *Reeson v. Kowalik* (1991), 36 R.F.L. (3d) 396 (Ont. Gen. Div.); *DeBora v. DeBora*, [2004] O.J. No. 4826 (Sup. Ct.).

c) Disposition of Matrimonial Home

Section 21 of the *Family Law Act* imposes a general prohibition against a spouse unilaterally disposing of or encumbering an interest in the matrimonial home. The need for spousal consent may be waived by the terms of a separation agreement. A court may also dispense with spousal consent to the disposition or encumbrance of the matrimonial home under section 23 of the *Family Law Act*. If a spouse unlawfully disposes of or encumbers an interest in the matrimonial home, the transaction may be set aside under section 23 of the *Family Law Act*, but the court's jurisdiction to set aside the transaction cannot be invoked against a *bona fide* purchaser for value without notice that the property was a matrimonial home.[266]

d) Possessory Rights in Matrimonial Home

Pursuant to subsection 19(1) of the *Family Law Act*, both spouses have an equal right to possession of the matrimonial home, regardless of whether title is vested in one or both spouses. The statutory right conferred by subsection 19(1) applies without regard to the conduct of the spouses or the state of their marital relationship. Pursuant to subsection 19(2) of the *Family Law Act*, this equal right of possession is a personal right as between the spouses[267] and expires when they cease to be spouses, unless a separation agreement or court order provides otherwise.[268] Section 19 of the *Family Law Act* has no application to spouses who co-own the matrimonial home because conjoint possessory rights in such a case derive from their ownership. During the existence of the marriage, either spouse may apply to a court for an exclusive possession order with respect to the matrimonial home, and such an application may be pursued regardless of the ownership or of the right of possession conferred by section 19 of the *Family Law Act*. However, section 24 of the Act is only available to a spouse as defined in section 1(1) of the *Family Law Act*; it cannot be invoked by a former spouse. If a divorced co-owning spouse wishes to pursue a possessory remedy, he or she must bring an application under section 2 of the *Partition Act*,[269] although Ontario courts have consistently acknowledged that where spouses co-own the matrimonial home

---

266 *McCaskie v. McCaskie* (2002), 26 R.F.L. (5th) 401 (Ont. Sup. Ct.).
267 *Royal Bank v. King* (1994), 35 R.F.L. (3d) 325 (Ont. Gen. Div.); *Manufacturers Life Insurance Company v. Riviera* (1998), 29 R.F.L. (4th) 1 (Ont. C.A.).
268 *Miller v. Miller* (1996), 20 R.F.L. (4th) 191 (Ont. C.A.).
269 *Ibid.*

under joint tenancy, there is a *prima facie* right to partition and sale that should not lightly be interfered with.[270]

Subsection 24(3) of the *Family Law Act* identifies the following six factors that must be considered on an application to the court for exclusive possession of the matrimonial home:

(i) the best interests of the children affected;
(ii) any existing orders under Part I of the *Family Law Act* and any existing support orders;
(iii) the financial position of both spouses;
(iv) any written agreement between the parties;
(v) the availability of other suitable and affordable accommodation; and
(vi) any violence committed by a spouse against the other spouse or children.

For the purposes of paragraph 24(3)(b) of the Act, subsection 24(4) requires the court to determine the best interests of a child having regard to

(a) the possible disruptive effects on the child of a move to other accommodation; and
(b) the child's views and preferences, if they can reasonably be ascertained.

The factors listed in subsection 24(4) of the *Family Law Act* are not necessarily exhaustive and do not exclude the court from considering other factors, such as the psychological stress to a child arising from persistent friction between the parents[271] or which party has the greater emotional attachment to the home.[272]

In *Caines v. Caines*,[273] Fleury Co. Ct. J. listed the following relevant considerations:

(a) Any agreement, formal or informal, between the parties as to the future use of the home.
(b) The date when the property was acquired.
(c) The historical ties of any parties to the property in question.

270　See *Arlow v. Arlow* (1990), 27 R.F.L. (3d) 348 (Ont. Div. Ct.), aff'd (1991), 33 R.F.L. (3d) 44 (Ont. C.A.).
271　See *Pifer v. Pifer* (1986), 3 R.F.L. (3d) 167 (Ont. Dist. Ct.).
272　*Hill v. Hill* (1987), 10 R.F.L. (3d) 225 (Ont. Dist. Ct.).
273　(1985), 42 R.F.L. (2d) 1 (Ont. Co. Ct.).

(d) The extent to which the property may have been acquired by one of the spouses by gift or by special efforts.

(e) The number of children who would continue to reside in the home.

(f) The financial ability of the parties to continue to maintain the property as well as to continue to dwell under separate roofs.

(g) The special character of the neighbourhood including such considerations as the presence of friends, relatives, members of a specific ethnic community.

(h) The need of the respondent for immediate funds.

(i) The impact of a move on the children's ability to attend school or university or to continue extracurricular activities.

(j) The health of the children.

(k) The reaction of the children to the marriage breakdown and their need for continued stability.

An order for exclusive possession of the matrimonial home is a drastic order in that it is likely to cause hardship to the dispossessed spouse, but this is to be balanced against the hardship that would be sustained by an unsuccessful applicant.[274] Inconvenience is not enough to justify an exclusive possession order.[275] Where the children are healthy and well-adjusted and there is no difficulty in the custodial parent obtaining suitable accommodation in the same area, an application for an exclusive possession order should be dismissed.[276]

Orders for exclusive possession of the matrimonial home are difficult to obtain if there are no children. Even when there are children, long-term exclusive possession orders are relatively rare. It is not unusual, however, for courts to grant exclusive possession of the matrimonial home to a sole custodial parent and the children until the end of the children's school year. This avoids the upheaval of a change in schools at a time when the children are already encountering stress as a result of the breakdown of their parents' relationship.

The onus of proving that an order for exclusive possession of the matrimonial home is justified falls on the person seeking exclusive pos-

---

274 *Bassett v. Bassett*, [1975] 1 All E.R. 513 at 517 (Eng. C.A.), Ormrod L.J.; see also *Re Ali* (1987), 5 R.F.L. (3d) 228 (Ont. H.C.J.).

275 *Bassett v. Bassett*, [1975] 1 All E.R. 513 at 521 (Eng. C.A.), Cummings-Bruce J.

276 See *Allen v. Allen* (1982), 24 R.F.L. (2d) 152 (Ont. Co. Ct.); see also *Koziarz v. Koziarz* (1984), 39 R.F.L. (2d) 417 (Ont. H.C.J.); compare *Jaremkow v. Jaremkow* (1985), 48 R.F.L. (2d) 206 (Ont. Dist. Ct.).

session.[277] In determining whether there is other suitable and affordable accommodation within the meaning of paragraph 24(3)(e) of the *Family Law Act*, the following criteria apply:

(i)   it need not match the present accommodation, but must be reasonably suitable for the needs required and relate to the standard of living previously enjoyed;

(ii) if it provides reasonable amenities, the court will ignore the niceties of its physical layout; and

(iii) the financial ability to secure and maintain such alternative accommodation should be considered.

In determining the best interests of the children with respect to alternative accommodation, the critical factors are the quality of the respective homes, their proximity to schools and other facilities, traffic hazards, and the effect of a change of environment on the children. Where the custodial parent's financial circumstances make the purchase or rental of alternative accommodation impossible and there is no pressing need for the non-custodial parent to realize the equity in the matrimonial home, an order for exclusive possession in favour of the custodial parent is justified.[278] In *Rosenthal v. Rosenthal*,[279] McMahon L.J.S.C. concluded that the requirements of subsection 24(3) of the *Family Law Act* had not been satisfied where two of the three children were emancipated and the husband was contributing towards the college education of the third child. McMahon L.J.S.C. further concluded that an exclusive possession order was not justified by reason only of the emotional stress of the applicant resulting from the marriage breakdown and that an order should be denied where it is apparent that there are insufficient funds available to permit the continued occupation of the home by one of the spouses.

The provisions of a separation agreement take precedence over the statutory rights conferred by section 24 of the *Family Law Act*.[280] A provision in a marriage contract that purports to limit possession rights in the matrimonial home is unenforceable pursuant to subsection 52(2) of the

---

277 See *Rondeau v. Rondeau* (1979), 12 R.F.L. (2d) 45 (Ont. Co. Ct.) and *Gies v. Gies* (1983), 30 R.F.L. (2d) 122 (Ont. Co. Ct.).

278 *Gies v. Gies* (1983), 30 R.F.L. (2d) 122 (Ont. Co. Ct.); *Francis v. Francis* (1987), 8 R.F.L. (3d) 460 (Ont. S.C.); *Tward v. Tward* (1982), 31 R.F.L. (2d) 251 (Ont. H.C.J.); *Jaremkow v. Jaremkow* (1985), 48 R.F.L. (2d) 206 (Ont. Dist. Ct.).

279 (1986), 3 R.F.L. (3d) 126 at 136–38 (Ont. H.C.J.).

280 *Family Law Act*, R.S.O. 1990, c. F.3, ss. 2(10) and 54.

Family Law Act. It does not follow that such a provision is to be ignored. A written agreement that does not satisfy the statutory definition of "domestic contract" may be relevant under paragraph 24(3)(d) of the *Family Law Act.*

Proof of any violence committed by one spouse against the other spouse or the children is expressly recognized by paragraph 24(3)(f) of the *Family Law Act, 1986* as of vital importance in determining whether an order for exclusive possession should be granted. In *Hill v. Hill,*[281] Fitzgerald D.C.J. concluded that "violence" under subsection 24(f) includes "psychological assault upon the sensibilities of the other spouse to a degree that renders continued sharing of the matrimonial dwelling impractical."

e) Penalties for Contravention of Exclusive Possession Order

Subsection 24(5) of the *Family Law Act*[282] introduces significant penal sanctions that may be imposed for contravention of an order for exclusive possession. A person who is convicted of contravening an order for exclusive possession is liable in the case of a first offence to a fine not exceeding $5,000 and/or to imprisonment for a term not exceeding three months. In the event of a second or subsequent offence, the maximum penalty increases to $10,000 and/or imprisonment for two years.

Pursuant to subsection 24(6) of the Act, a police officer is expressly empowered to arrest without warrant a person the police officer believes on reasonable and probable grounds to have contravened an order for exclusive possession.

f) Variation of Possessory Orders

Orders respecting the exclusive possession of the matrimonial home are subject to judicial discharge, variation, or suspension in the event of a material change in the circumstances. An application for this purpose may be brought by a person named in the order or by his or her personal representative.[283]

---

281 (1987), 10 R.F.L. (3d) 225 (Ont. Dist. Ct.); see also *Kutlesa v. Kutlesa,* [2008] O.J. No. 1157 (Sup. Ct.); compare *Gainer v. Gainer,* [2006] O.J. No. 1631 (Sup. Ct.).

282 S.O. 1986, c. 4, as amended by S.O. 1989, c. 72, s. 18, now R.S.O. 1990, c. F.3, s. 24(5).

283 *Family Law Act,* R.S.O. 1990, c. F.3, s. 25.

g) Severance of Third-Party Joint Tenancy in Matrimonial Home

Pursuant to subsection 26(1) of the *Family Law Act*, if a spouse dies owning an interest in the matrimonial home as a joint tenant with a person other than his or her spouse, the joint tenancy is deemed to be severed with a consequential loss of the right of survivorship immediately before the time of death. Subsection 26(1) is applicable regardless of whether a surviving spouse elects to take under the *Family Law Act* or the *Succession Law Reform Act*.[284] Consequently, the value of the deceased's interest as a tenant in common is included in the calculation of his or her net family property for the purposes of an equalization claim brought against the deceased's estate pursuant to subsection 5(2) of the Act. Subsection 26(1) of the *Family Law Act* has no application to a joint tenant who died prior to the commencement of the Act; namely, 1 March 1986.[285]

Pursuant to subsection 26(2) of the Act, a spouse who is occupying the matrimonial home without any proprietary interest therein at the time of the other spouse's death, is entitled to retain possession on a rent-free basis against the deceased spouse's estate for sixty days after the death. This right is exercisable notwithstanding the provisions of paragraphs 19(2)(a) and (b) of the Act and regardless whether or not the possession right arose pursuant to an order for exclusive possession. The provisions of subsection 26(2) presumably override any order made pursuant to paragraph 24(1)(d) of the Act that required the spouse with exclusive possession to make periodic payments as occupation rent to the dispossessed spouse.

19) Registration of Orders against Land

Orders granted pursuant to Part II of the *Family Law Act* are registerable against land under the *Registry Act*[286] and the *Land Titles Act*.[287]

20) *Situs* of Matrimonial Home; Retrospective Operation of Part II of *Family Law Act*

The application of Part II of the *Family Law Act* is expressly confined to matrimonial homes that are situated in Ontario.[288] Pursuant to subsec-

---

284 *Fulton v. Fulton* (1994), 17 O.R. (3d) 641 (C.A.).

285 *Re Vaillancourt* (1986), 4 R.F.L. (3d) 263 (Ont. H.C.J.).

286 R.S.O. 1990, c. R.20.

287 R.S.O. 1990, c. L.5.

288 *Family Law Act*, R.S.O. 1990, c. F.3, s. 28(1).

tion 28(2) of the Act, Part II applies whether the spouses were married before or after 1 March 1986, and whether the matrimonial home was acquired before or after that date.

DIVORCE ACT

R.S.C. 1985, c. 3 (2nd Supp.)

Current to May 5, 2008

An Act respecting divorce and corollary relief

SHORT TITLE

Short title
   1. This Act may be cited as the *Divorce Act*.

R.S.C. 1985, c. 3 (2nd Supp.), s. 1.

INTERPRETATION

Definitions
   2. (1) In this Act,

"age of majority"
"age of majority", in respect of a child, means the age of majority as deter-
      mined by the laws of the province where the child ordinarily resides,
      or, if the child ordinarily resides outside of Canada, eighteen years of
      age;

"appellate court"
"appellate court", in respect of an appeal from a court, means the court
      exercising appellate jurisdiction with respect to that appeal;

"applicable guidelines"

"applicable guidelines" means

  (a) where both spouses or former spouses are ordinarily resident in the same province at the time an application for a child support order or a variation order in respect of a child support order is made, or the amount of a child support order is to be recalculated pursuant to section 25.1, and that province has been designated by an order made under subsection (5), the laws of the province specified in the order, and

  (b) in any other case, the Federal Child Support Guidelines;

"child of the marriage"

"child of the marriage" means a child of two spouses or former spouses who, at the material time,

  (a) is under the age of majority and who has not withdrawn from their charge, or

  (b) is the age of majority or over and under their charge but unable, by reason of illness, disability or other cause, to withdraw from their charge or to obtain the necessaries of life;

"child support order"

"child support order" means an order made under subsection 15.1(1);

"corollary relief proceeding"

"corollary relief proceeding" means a proceeding in a court in which either or both former spouses seek a child support order, a spousal support order or a custody order;

"court"

"court", in respect of a province, means

  (a)   for the Province of Ontario, the Superior Court of Justice,

  (a.1) for the Province of Prince Edward Island or Newfoundland, the trial division of the Supreme Court of the Province,

  (b)   for the Province of Quebec, the Superior Court,

  (c)   for the Provinces of Nova Scotia and British Columbia, the Supreme Court of the Province,

  (d)   for the Province of New Brunswick, Manitoba, Saskatchewan or Alberta, the Court of Queen's Bench for the Province, and

  (e)   for Yukon or the Northwest Territories, the Supreme Court, and in Nunavut, the Nunavut Court of Justice, and includes such other court in the province the judges of which are appointed by the Governor General as is designated by the Lieutenant Governor in Council of the province as a court for the purposes of this Act;

"custody"
"custody" includes care, upbringing and any other incident of custody;

"custody order"
"custody order" means an order made under subsection 16(1);

"divorce proceeding"
"divorce proceeding" means a proceeding in a court in which either or both spouses seek a divorce alone or together with a child support order, a spousal support order or a custody order;

"Federal Child Support Guidelines"
"Federal Child Support Guidelines" means the guidelines made under section 26.1;

"provincial child support service"
"provincial child support service" means any service, agency or body designated in an agreement with a province under subsection 25.1(1);

"spousal support order"
"spousal support order" means an order made under subsection 15.2(1);

"spouse"
"spouse" means either of two persons who are married to each other;

"support order"
"support order" means a child support order or a spousal support order;

"variation order"
"variation order" means an order made under subsection 17(1);

"variation proceeding"
"variation proceeding" means a proceeding in a court in which either or both former spouses seek a variation order.

Child of the marriage

(2) For the purposes of the definition "child of the marriage" in sub-section (1), a child of two spouses or former spouses includes

(a) any child for whom they both stand in the place of parents; and

(b) any child of whom one is the parent and for whom the other stands in the place of a parent.

Term not restrictive

(3) The use of the term "application" to describe a proceeding under this Act in a court shall not be construed as limiting the name under which and the form and manner in which that proceeding may be taken in that court, and the name, manner and form of the proceeding in that court shall be such as is provided for by the rules regulating the practice and procedure in that court.

Idem

(4) The use in section 21.1 of the terms "affidavit" and "pleadings" to describe documents shall not be construed as limiting the name that may be used to refer to those documents in a court and the form of those documents, and the name and form of the documents shall be such as is provided for by the rules regulating the practice and procedure in that court.

Provincial child support guidelines

(5) The Governor in Council may, by order, designate a province for the purposes of the definition "applicable guidelines" in subsection (1) if the laws of the province establish comprehensive guidelines for the determination of child support that deal with the matters referred to in section 26.1. The order shall specify the laws of the province that constitute the guidelines of the province.

Amendments included

(6) The guidelines of a province referred to in subsection (5) include any amendments made to them from time to time.

R.S.C. 1985, c. 3 (2nd Supp.), s. 2; c. 27 (2nd Supp.), s. 10; S.C. 1990, c. 18, s. 1; S.C. 1992, c. 51, s. 46; S.C. 1997, c. 1, s. 1; S.C. 1999, c. 3, s. 61; S.C. 1998, c. 30, ss. 13 (F), 15 (E); S.C. 2002, c. 7, s. 158 (E); S.C. 2005, c. 33, s. 8(1) and (2) (F).

JURISDICTION

Jurisdiction in divorce proceedings

3. (1) A court in a province has jurisdiction to hear and determine a divorce proceeding if either spouse has been ordinarily resident in the province for at least one year immediately preceding the commencement of the proceeding.

Jurisdiction where two proceedings commenced on different days

(2) Where divorce proceedings between the same spouses are pending in two courts that would otherwise have jurisdiction under subsection (1) and were commenced on different days and the proceeding that was commenced first is not discontinued within thirty days after it was commenced, the court in which a divorce proceeding was commenced first has exclusive jurisdiction to hear and determine any divorce proceeding then pending between the spouses and the second divorce proceeding shall be deemed to be discontinued.

Jurisdiction where two proceedings commenced on same day

(3) Where divorce proceedings between the same spouses are pending in two courts that would otherwise have jurisdiction under subsection (1) and were commenced on the same day and neither proceeding is discontinued within thirty days after it was commenced, the Federal Court has exclusive jurisdiction to hear and determine any divorce proceeding then pending between the spouses and the divorce proceedings in those courts shall be transferred to the Federal Court on the direction of that Court.

R.S.C. 1985, c. 3 (2nd Supp.), s. 3; S.C. 2002, c. 8, s. 183.

Jurisdiction in corollary relief proceedings

4. (1) A court in a province has jurisdiction to hear and determine a corollary relief proceeding if

(a) either former spouse is ordinarily resident in the province at the commencement of the proceeding; or

(b) both former spouses accept the jurisdiction of the court.

Jurisdiction where two proceedings commenced on different days

(2) Where corollary relief proceedings between the same former spouses and in respect of the same matter are pending in two courts that would otherwise have jurisdiction under subsection (1) and were com-

menced on different days and the proceeding that was commenced first is not discontinued within thirty days after it was commenced, the court in which a corollary relief proceeding was commenced first has exclusive jurisdiction to hear and determine any corollary relief proceeding then pending between the former spouses in respect of that matter and the second corollary relief proceeding shall be deemed to be discontinued.

Jurisdiction where two proceedings commenced on same day
(3) Where proceedings between the same former spouses and in respect of the same matter are pending in two courts that would otherwise have jurisdiction under subsection (1) and were commenced on the same day and neither proceeding is discontinued within thirty days after it was commenced, the Federal Court has exclusive jurisdiction to hear and determine any corollary relief proceeding then pending between the former spouses in respect of that matter and the corollary relief proceedings in those courts shall be transferred to the Federal Court on the direction of that Court.

R.S.C. 1985, c. 3 (2nd Supp.), s. 4; S.C. 1993, c. 8, s. 1; S.C. 2002, c. 8, s. 183.

Jurisdiction in variation proceedings
5. (1) A court in a province has jurisdiction to hear and determine a variation proceeding if
   (a) either former spouse is ordinarily resident in the province at the commencement of the proceeding; or
   (b) both former spouses accept the jurisdiction of the court.

Jurisdiction where two proceedings commenced on different days
(2) Where variation proceedings between the same former spouses and in respect of the same matter are pending in two courts that would otherwise have jurisdiction under subsection (1) and were commenced on different days and the proceeding that was commenced first is not discontinued within thirty days after it was commenced, the court in which a variation proceeding was commenced first has exclusive jurisdiction to hear and determine any variation proceeding then pending between the former spouses in respect of that matter and the second variation proceeding shall be deemed to be discontinued.

Jurisdiction where two proceedings commenced on same day
(3) Where variation proceedings between the same former spouses and in respect of the same matter are pending in two courts that would

otherwise have jurisdiction under subsection (1) and were commenced on the same day and neither proceeding is discontinued within thirty days after it was commenced, the Federal Court has exclusive jurisdiction to hear and determine any variation proceeding then pending between the former spouses in respect of that matter and the variation proceedings in those courts shall be transferred to the Federal Court on the direction of that Court.

R.S.C. 1985, c. 3 (2nd Supp.), s. 5; S.C. 2002, c. 8, s. 183.

Transfer of divorce proceeding where custody application

6. (1) Where an application for an order under section 16 is made in a divorce proceeding to a court in a province and is opposed and the child of the marriage in respect of whom the order is sought is most substantially connected with another province, the court may, on application by a spouse or on its own motion, transfer the divorce proceeding to a court in that other province.

Transfer of corollary relief proceeding where custody application

(2) Where an application for an order under section 16 is made in a corollary relief proceeding to a court in a province and is opposed and the child of the marriage in respect of whom the order is sought is most substantially connected with another province, the court may, on application by a former spouse or on its own motion, transfer the corollary relief proceeding to a court in that other province.

Transfer of variation proceeding where custody application

(3) Where an application for a variation order in respect of a custody order is made in a variation proceeding to a court in a province and is opposed and the child of the marriage in respect of whom the variation order is sought is most substantially connected with another province, the court may, on application by a former spouse or on its own motion, transfer the variation proceeding to a court in that other province.

Exclusive jurisdiction

(4) Notwithstanding sections 3 to 5, a court in a province to which a proceeding is transferred under this section has exclusive jurisdiction to hear and determine the proceeding.

R.S.C. 1985, c. 3 (2nd Supp.), s. 6.

Exercise of jurisdiction by judge

7. The jurisdiction conferred on a court by this Act to grant a divorce shall be exercised only by a judge of the court without a jury.

R.S.C. 1985, c. 3 (2nd Supp.), s. 7.

DIVORCE

Divorce

8. (1) A court of competent jurisdiction may, on application by either or both spouses, grant a divorce to the spouse or spouses on the ground that there has been a breakdown of their marriage.

Breakdown of marriage

(2) Breakdown of a marriage is established only if

(a) the spouses have lived separate and apart for at least one year immediately preceding the determination of the divorce proceeding and were living separate and apart at the commencement of the proceeding; or

(b) the spouse against whom the divorce proceeding is brought has, since celebration of the marriage,

(i) committed adultery, or

(ii) treated the other spouse with physical or mental cruelty of such a kind as to render intolerable the continued cohabitation of the spouses.

Calculation of period of separation

(3) For the purposes of paragraph (2)(a),

(a) spouses shall be deemed to have lived separate and apart for any period during which they lived apart and either of them had the intention to live separate and apart from the other; and

(b) a period during which spouses have lived separate and apart shall not be considered to have been interrupted or terminated

(i) by reason only that either spouse has become incapable of forming or having an intention to continue to live separate and apart or of continuing to live separate and apart of the spouse's own volition, if it appears to the court that the separation would probably have continued if the spouse had not become so incapable, or

(ii) by reason only that the spouses have resumed cohabitation during a period of, or periods totalling, not more than ninety days with reconciliation as its primary purpose.

R.S.C. 1985, c. 3 (2nd Supp.), s. 8.

Duty of legal adviser

9. (1) It is the duty of every barrister, solicitor, lawyer or advocate who undertakes to act on behalf of a spouse in a divorce proceeding

(a) to draw to the attention of the spouse the provisions of this Act that have as their object the reconciliation of spouses, and

(b) to discuss with the spouse the possibility of the reconciliation of the spouses and to inform the spouse of the marriage counselling or guidance facilities known to him or her that might be able to assist the spouses to achieve a reconciliation,

unless the circumstances of the case are of such a nature that it would clearly not be appropriate to do so.

Idem

(2) It is the duty of every barrister, solicitor, lawyer or advocate who undertakes to act on behalf of a spouse in a divorce proceeding to discuss with the spouse the advisability of negotiating the matters that may be the subject of a support order or a custody order and to inform the spouse of the mediation facilities known to him or her that might be able to assist the spouses in negotiating those matters.

Certification

(3) Every document presented to a court by a barrister, solicitor, lawyer or advocate that formally commences a divorce proceeding shall contain a statement by him or her certifying that he or she has complied with this section.

R.S.C. 1985, c. 3 (2nd Supp.), s. 9.

Duty of court — reconciliation

10. (1) In a divorce proceeding, it is the duty of the court, before considering the evidence, to satisfy itself that there is no possibility of the reconciliation of the spouses, unless the circumstances of the case are of such a nature that it would clearly not be appropriate to do so.

Adjournment

(2) Where at any stage in a divorce proceeding it appears to the court from the nature of the case, the evidence or the attitude of either or both spouses that there is a possibility of the reconciliation of the spouses, the court shall

    (a) adjourn the proceeding to afford the spouses an opportunity to achieve a reconciliation; and

    (b) with the consent of the spouses or in the discretion of the court, nominate

       (i) a person with experience or training in marriage counselling or guidance, or

       (ii) in special circumstances, some other suitable person,

       to assist the spouses to achieve a reconciliation.

Resumption

(3) Where fourteen days have elapsed from the date of any adjournment under subsection (2), the court shall resume the proceeding on the application of either or both spouses.

Nominee not competent or compellable

(4) No person nominated by a court under this section to assist spouses to achieve a reconciliation is competent or compellable in any legal proceedings to disclose any admission or communication made to that person in his or her capacity as a nominee of the court for that purpose.

Evidence not admissible

(5) Evidence of anything said or of any admission or communication made in the course of assisting spouses to achieve a reconciliation is not admissible in any legal proceedings.

R.S.C. 1985, c. 3 (2nd Supp.), s. 10.

Duty of court — bars

    11. (1) In a divorce proceeding, it is the duty of the court

    (a) to satisfy itself that there has been no collusion in relation to the application for a divorce and to dismiss the application if it finds that there was collusion in presenting it;

    (b) to satisfy itself that reasonable arrangements have been made for the support of any children of the marriage, having regard to the applicable guidelines, and, if such arrangements have not been made, to stay the granting of the divorce until such arrangments are made; and

(c) where a divorce is sought in circumstances described in paragraph 8(2)(b), to satisfy itself that there has been no condonation or connivance on the part of the spouse bringing the proceeding, and to dismiss the application for a divorce if that spouse has condoned or connived at the act or conduct complained of unless, in the opinion of the court, the public interest would be better served by granting the divorce.

Revival

(2) Any act or conduct that has been condoned is not capable of being revived so as to constitute a circumstance described in paragraph 8(2)(b).

Condonation

(3) For the purposes of this section, a continuation or resumption of cohabitation during a period of, or periods totalling, not more than ninety days with reconciliation as its primary purpose shall not be considered to constitute condonation.

Definition of "collusion"

(4) In this section, "collusion" means an agreement or conspiracy to which an applicant for a divorce is either directly or indirectly a party for the purpose of subverting the administration of justice, and includes any agreement, understanding or arrangement to fabricate or suppress evidence or to deceive the court, but does not include an agreement to the extent that it provides for separation between the parties, financial support, division of property or the custody of any child of the marriage.

R.S.C. 1985, c. 3 (2nd Supp.), s. 11; S.C. 1997, c. 1, s. 1.1.

Effective date generally

12. (1) Subject to this section, a divorce takes effect on the thirty-first day after the day on which the judgment granting the divorce is rendered.

Special circumstances

(2) Where, on or after rendering a judgment granting a divorce,

(a) the court is of the opinion that by reason of special circumstances the divorce should take effect earlier than the thirty-first day after the day on which the judgment is rendered, and

(b) the spouses agree and undertake that no appeal from the judgment will be taken, or any appeal from the judgment that was taken has been abandoned,

the court may order that the divorce takes effect at such earlier time as it considers appropriate.

Effective date where appeal

(3) A divorce in respect of which an appeal is pending at the end of the period referred to in subsection (1), unless voided on appeal, takes effect on the expiration of the time fixed by law for instituting an appeal from the decision on that appeal or any subsequent appeal, if no appeal has been instituted within that time.

Certain extensions to be counted

(4) For the purposes of subsection (3), the time fixed by law for instituting an appeal from a decision on an appeal includes any extension thereof fixed pursuant to law before the expiration of that time or fixed thereafter on an application instituted before the expiration of that time.

No late extensions of time for appeal

(5) Notwithstanding any other law, the time fixed by law for instituting an appeal from a decision referred to in subsection (3) may not be extended after the expiration of that time, except on an application instituted before the expiration of that time.

Effective date where decision of Supreme Court of Canada

(6) A divorce in respect of which an appeal has been taken to the Supreme Court of Canada, unless voided on the appeal, takes effect on the day on which the judgment on the appeal is rendered.

Certificate of divorce

(7) Where a divorce takes effect in accordance with this section, a judge or officer of the court that rendered the judgment granting the divorce or, where that judgment has been appealed, of the appellate court that rendered the judgment on the final appeal, shall, on request, issue to any person a certificate that a divorce granted under this Act dissolved the marriage of the specified persons effective as of a specified date.

Conclusive proof

(8) A certificate referred to in subsection (7), or a certified copy thereof, is conclusive proof of the facts so certified without proof of the signature or authority of the person appearing to have signed the certificate.

R.S.C. 1985, c. 3 (2nd Supp.), s. 12.

Legal effect throughout Canada

13. On taking effect, a divorce granted under this Act has legal effect throughout Canada.

R.S.C. 1985, c. 3 (2nd Supp.), s. 13.

Marriage dissolved

14. On taking effect, a divorce granted under this Act dissolves the marriage of the spouses.

R.S.C. 1985, c. 3 (2nd Supp.), s. 14.

COROLLARY RELIEF

Interpretation

Definition of "spouse"

15. In sections 15.1 to 16, "spouse" has the meaning assigned by subsection 2(1), and includes a former spouse.

R.S.C. 1985, c. 3 (2nd Supp.), s. 15; S.C. 1997, c. 1, s. 2.

Child Support Orders

Child support order

15.1 (1) A court of competent jurisdiction may, on application by either or both spouses, make an order requiring a spouse to pay for the support of any or all children of the marriage.

Interim order

(2) Where an application is made under subsection (1), the court may, on application by either or both spouses, make an interim order requiring a spouse to pay for the support of any or all children of the marriage, pending the determination of the application under subsection (1).

Guidelines apply

(3) A court making an order under subsection (1) or an interim order under subsection (2) shall do so in accordance with the applicable guidelines.

Terms and conditions

(4) The court may make an order under subsection (1) or an interim order under subsection (2) for a definite or indefinite period or until a specified event occurs, and may impose terms, conditions or restrictions in connection with the order or interim order as it thinks fit and just.

Court may take agreement, etc., into account

(5) Notwithstanding subsection (3), a court may award an amount that is different from the amount that would be determined in accordance with the applicable guidelines if the court is satisfied

(a) that special provisions in an order, a judgment or a written agreement respecting the financial obligations of the spouses, or the division or transfer of their property, directly or indirectly benefit a child, or that special provisions have otherwise been made for the benefit of a child; and

(b) that the application of the applicable guidelines would result in an amount of child support that is inequitable given those special provisions.

Reasons

(6) Where the court awards, pursuant to subsection (5), an amount that is different from the amount that would be determined in accordance with the applicable guidelines, the court shall record its reasons for having done so.

Consent orders

(7) Notwithstanding subsection (3), a court may award an amount that is different from the amount that would be determined in accordance with the applicable guidelines on the consent of both spouses if it is satisfied that reasonable arrangements have been made for the support of the child to whom the order relates.

Reasonable arrangements

(8) For the purposes of subsection (7), in determining whether reasonable arrangements have been made for the support of a child, the court

shall have regard to the applicable guidelines. However, the court shall not consider the arrangements to be unreasonable solely because the amount of support agreed to is not the same as the amount that would otherwise have been determined in accordance with the applicable guidelines.

S.C. 1997, c. 1, s. 2.

Spousal Support Orders

Spousal support order

15.2 (1) A court of competent jurisdiction may, on application by either or both spouses, make an order requiring a spouse to secure or pay, or to secure and pay, such lump sum or periodic sums, or such lump sum and periodic sums, as the court thinks reasonable for the support of the other spouse.

Interim order

(2) Where an application is made under subsection (1), the court may, on application by either or both spouses, make an interim order requiring a spouse to secure or pay, or to secure and pay, such lump sum or periodic sums, or such lump sum and periodic sums, as the court thinks reasonable for the support of the other spouse, pending the determination of the application under subsection (1).

Terms and conditions

(3) The court may make an order under subsection (1) or an interim order under subsection (2) for a definite or indefinite period or until a specified event occurs, and may impose terms, conditions or restrictions in connection with the order as it thinks fit and just.

Factors

(4) In making an order under subsection (1) or an interim order under subsection (2), the court shall take into consideration the condition, means, needs and other circumstances of each spouse, including

(a) the length of time the spouses cohabited;

(b) the functions performed by each spouse during cohabitation; and

(c) any order, agreement or arrangement relating to support of either spouse.

Spousal misconduct

(5) In making an order under subsection (1) or an interim order under subsection (2), the court shall not take into consideration any misconduct of a spouse in relation to the marriage.

Objectives of spousal support order

(6) An order made under subsection (1) or an interim order under subsection (2) that provides for the support of a spouse should

(a) recognize any economic advantages or disadvantages to the spouses arising from the marriage or its breakdown;

(b) apportion between the spouses any financial consequences arising from the care of any child of the marriage over and above any obligation for the support of any child of the marriage;

(c) relieve any economic hardship of the spouses arising from the breakdown of the marriage; and

(d) in so far as practicable, promote the economic self-sufficiency of each spouse within a reasonable period of time.

S.C. 1997, c. 1, s. 2.

Priority

Priority to child support

15.3 (1) Where a court is considering an application for a child support order and an application for a spousal support order, the court shall give priority to child support in determining the applications.

Reasons

(2) Where, as a result of giving priority to child support, the court is unable to make a spousal support order or the court makes a spousal support order in an amount that is less than it otherwise would have been, the court shall record its reasons for having done so.

Consequences of reduction or termination of child support order

(3) Where, as a result of giving priority to child support, a spousal support order was not made, or the amount of a spousal support order is less than it otherwise would have been, any subsequent reduction or termination of that child support constitutes a change of circumstances for the purposes of applying for a spousal support order, or a variation order in respect of the spousal support order, as the case may be.

S.C. 1997, c. 1, s. 2.

Custody Orders

Order for custody

16. (1) A court of competent jurisdiction may, on application by either or both spouses or by any other person, make an order respecting the custody of or the access to, or the custody of and access to, any or all children of the marriage.

Interim order for custody

(2) Where an application is made under subsection (1), the court may, on application by either or both spouses or by any other person, make an interim order respecting the custody of or the access to, or the custody of and access to, any or all children of the marriage pending determination of the application under subsection (1).

Application by other person

(3) A person, other than a spouse, may not make an application under subsection (1) or (2) without leave of the court.

Joint custody or access

(4) The court may make an order under this section granting custody of, or access to, any or all children of the marriage to any one or more persons.

Access

(5) Unless the court orders otherwise, a spouse who is granted access to a child of the marriage has the right to make inquiries, and to be given information, as to the health, education and welfare of the child.

Terms and conditions

(6) The court may make an order under this section for a definite or indefinite period or until the happening of a specified event and may impose such other terms, conditions or restrictions in connection therewith as it thinks fit and just.

Order respecting change of residence

(7) Without limiting the generality of subsection (6), the court may include in an order under this section a term requiring any person who has custody of a child of the marriage and who intends to change the place of residence of that child to notify, at least thirty days before the

change or within such other period before the change as the court may specify, any person who is granted access to that child of the change, the time at which the change will be made and the new place of residence of the child.

Factors

(8) In making an order under this section, the court shall take into consideration only the best interests of the child of the marriage as determined by reference to the condition, means, needs and other circumstances of the child.

Past conduct

(9) In making an order under this section, the court shall not take into consideration the past conduct of any person unless the conduct is relevant to the ability of that person to act as a parent of a child.

Maximum contact

(10) In making an order under this section, the court shall give effect to the principle that a child of the marriage should have as much contact with each spouse as is consistent with the best interests of the child and, for that purpose, shall take into consideration the willingness of the person for whom custody is sought to facilitate such contact.

R.S.C. 1985, c. 3 (2nd Supp.), s. 16.

Variation, Recission or Suspension of Orders

Order for variation, rescission or suspension

17. (1) A court of competent jurisdiction may make an order varying, rescinding or suspending, prospectively or retroactively,

- (a) a support order or any provision thereof on application by either or both former spouses; or
- (b) a custody order or any provision thereof on application by either or both former spouses or by any other person.

Application by other person

(2) A person, other than a former spouse, may not make an application under paragraph (1)(b) without leave of the court.

Terms and conditions

(3) The court may include in a variation order any provision that under this Act could have been included in the order in respect of which the variation order is sought.

Factors for child support order

(4) Before the court makes a variation order in respect of a child support order, the court shall satisfy itself that a change of circumstances as provided for in the applicable guidelines has occurred since the making of the child support order or the last variation order made in respect of that order.

Factors for spousal support order

(4.1) Before the court makes a variation order in respect of a spousal support order, the court shall satisfy itself that a change in the condition, means, needs or other circumstances of either former spouse has occurred since the making of the spousal support order or the last variation order made in respect of that order, and, in making the variation order, the court shall take that change into consideration.

Factors for custody order

(5) Before the court makes a variation order in respect of a custody order, the court shall satisfy itself that there has been a change in the condition, means, needs or other circumstances of the child of the marriage occurring since the making of the custody order or the last variation order made in respect of that order, as the case may be, and, in making the variation order, the court shall take into consideration only the best interests of the child as determined by reference to that change.

Variation order

(5.1) For the purposes of subsection (5), a former spouse's terminal illness or critical condition shall be considered a change of circumstances of the child of the marriage, and the court shall make a variation order in respect of access that is in the best interests of the child.

Conduct

(6) In making a variation order, the court shall not take into consideration any conduct that under this Act could not have been considered in making the order in respect of which the variation order is sought.

Guidelines apply

(6.1) A court making a variation order in respect of a child support order shall do so in accordance with the applicable guidelines.

Court may take agreement, etc., into account

(6.2) Notwithstanding subsection (6.1), in making a variation order in respect of a child support order, a court may award an amount that is different from the amount that would be determined in accordance with the applicable guidelines if the court is satisfied

    (a) that special provisions in an order, a judgment or a written agreement respecting the financial obligations of the spouses, or the division or transfer of their property, directly or indirectly benefit a child, or that special provisions have otherwise been made for the benefit of a child; and

    (b) that the application of the applicable guidelines would result in an amount of child support that is inequitable given those special provisions.

Reasons

(6.3) Where the court awards, pursuant to subsection (6.2), an amount that is different from the amount that would be determined in accordance with the applicable guidelines, the court shall record its reasons for having done so.

Consent orders

(6.4) Notwithstanding subsection (6.1), a court may award an amount that is different from the amount that would be determined in accordance with the applicable guidelines on the consent of both spouses if it is satisfied that reasonable arrangements have been made for the support of the child to whom the order relates.

Reasonable arrangements

(6.5) For the purposes of subsection (6.4), in determining whether reasonable arrangements have been made for the support of a child, the court shall have regard to the applicable guidelines. However, the court shall not consider the arrangements to be unreasonable solely because the amount of support agreed to is not the same as the amount that would otherwise have been determined in accordance with the applicable guidelines.

Objectives of variation order varying spousal support order

(7) A variation order varying a spousal support order should

(a) recognize any economic advantages or disadvantages to the former spouses arising from the marriage or its breakdown;

(b) apportion between the former spouses any financial consequences arising from the care of any child of the marriage over and above any obligation for the support of any child of the marriage;

(c) relieve any economic hardship of the former spouses arising from the breakdown of the marriage; and

(d) in so far as practicable, promote the economic self-sufficiency of each former spouse within a reasonable period of time.

(8) REPEALED: S.C. 1997, c. 1, s. 5(5), effective May 1, 1997 (SI/97-43).

Maximum contact

(9) In making a variation order varying a custody order, the court shall give effect to the principle that a child of the marriage should have as much contact with each former spouse as is consistent with the best interests of the child and, for that purpose, where the variation order would grant custody of the child to a person who does not currently have custody, the court shall take into consideration the willingness of that person to facilitate such contact.

Limitation

(10) Notwithstanding subsection (1), where a spousal support order provides for support for a definite period or until a specified event occurs, a court may not, on an application instituted after the expiration of that period or the occurrence of the event, make a variation order for the purpose of resuming that support unless the court is satisfied that

(a) a variation order is necessary to relieve economic hardship arising from a change described in subsection (4.1) that is related to the marriage; and

(b) the changed circumstances, had they existed at the time of the making of the spousal support order or the last variation order made in respect of that order, as the case may be, would likely have resulted in a different order.

Copy of order

(11) Where a court makes a variation order in respect of a support order or a custody order made by another court, it shall send a copy of the variation order, certified by a judge or officer of the court, to that other court.

R.S.C. 1985, c. 3 (2nd Supp.), s. 17; S.C. 1997, c. 1, s. 5; S.C. 2007, c. 14, s. 1.

Variation order by affidavit, etc.

17.1 Where both former spouses are ordinarily resident in different provinces, a court of competent jurisdiction may, in accordance with any applicable rules of the court, make a variation order pursuant to subsection 17(1) on the basis of the submissions of the former spouses, whether presented orally before the court or by means of affidavits or any means of telecommunication, if both former spouses consent thereto.

S.C. 1993, c. 8, s. 2.

Provisional Orders

Definitions

18. (1) In this section and section 19,

"Attorney General"

"Attorney General", in respect of a province, means

    (a)   for Yukon, the member of the Executive Council of Yukon designated by the Commissioner of Yukon,

    (b)   for the Northwest Territories, the member of the Council of the Northwest Territories designated by the Commissioner of the Northwest Territories,

    (b.1) for Nunavut, the member of the Executive Council of Nunavut designated by the Commissioner of Nunavut, and

    (c)   for the other provinces, the Attorney General of the province, and includes any person authorized in writing by the member or Attorney General to act for the member or Attorney General in the performance of a function under this section or section 19;

"provisional order"

"provisional order" means an order made pursuant to subsection (2).

Provisional order

(2) Notwithstanding paragraph 5(1)(a) and subsection 17(1), where an application is made to a court in a province for a variation order in respect of a support order and

  (a) the respondent in the application is ordinarily resident in another province and has not accepted the jurisdiction of the court, or both former spouses have not consented to the application of section 17.1 in respect of the matter, and

  (b) in the circumstances of the case, the court is satisfied that the issues can be adequately determined by proceeding under this section and section 19,

the court shall make a variation order with or without notice to and in the absence of the respondent, but such order is provisional only and has no legal effect until it is confirmed in a proceeding under section 19 and, where so confirmed, it has legal effect in accordance with the terms of the order confirming it.

Transmission

(3) Where a court in a province makes a provisional order, it shall send to the Attorney General for the province

  (a) three copies of the provisional order certified by a judge or officer of the court;

  (b) a certified or sworn document setting out or summarizing the evidence given to the court; and

  (c) a statement giving any available information respecting the identification, location, income and assets of the respondent.

Idem

(4) On receipt of the documents referred to in subsection (3), the Attorney General shall send the documents to the Attorney General for the province in which the respondent is ordinarily resident.

Further evidence

(5) Where, during a proceeding under section 19, a court in a province remits the matter back for further evidence to the court that made the provisional order, the court that made the order shall, after giving notice to the applicant, receive further evidence.

Transmission

(6) Where evidence is received under subsection (5), the court that received the evidence shall forward to the court that remitted the matter back a certified or sworn document setting out or summarizing the evidence, together with such recommendations as the court that received the evidence considers appropriate.

R.S.C. 1985, c. 3 (2nd Supp.), s. 18; S.C. 1993, c. 8, s. 3; S.C. 1993, c. 28, s. 78 (Sch. III, s. 43); S.C. 2002, c. 7, s. 159.

Transmission

19. (1) On receipt of any documents sent pursuant to subsection 18(4), the Attorney General for the province in which the respondent is ordinarily resident shall send the documents to a court in the province.

Procedure

(2) Subject to subsection (3), where documents have been sent to a court pursuant to subsection (1), the court shall serve on the respondent a copy of the documents and a notice of a hearing respecting confirmation of the provisional order and shall proceed with the hearing, in the absence of the applicant, taking into consideration the certified or sworn document setting out or summarizing the evidence given to the court that made the provisional order.

Return to Attorney General

(3) Where documents have been sent to a court pursuant to subsection (1) and the respondent apparently is outside the province and is not likely to return, the court shall send the documents to the Attorney General for that province, together with any available information respecting the location and circumstances of the respondent.

Idem

(4) On receipt of any documents and information sent pursuant to subsection (3), the Attorney General shall send the documents and information to the Attorney General for the province of the court that made the provisional order.

Right of respondent

(5) In a proceeding under this section, the respondent may raise any matter that might have been raised before the court that made the provisional order.

Further evidence

(6) Where, in a proceeding under this section, the respondent satisfies the court that for the purpose of taking further evidence or for any other purpose it is necessary to remit the matter back to the court that made the provisional order, the court may so remit the matter and adjourn the proceeding for that purpose.

Order of confirmation or refusal

(7) Subject to subsection (7.1), at the conclusion of a proceeding under this section, the court shall make an order

    (a) confirming the provisional order without variation;

    (b) confirming the provisional order with variation; or

    (c) refusing confirmation of the provisional order.

Guidelines apply

(7.1) A court making an order under subsection (7) in respect of a child support order shall do so in accordance with the applicable guidelines.

Further evidence

(8) The court, before making an order confirming the provisional order with variation or an order refusing confirmation of the provisional order, shall decide whether to remit the matter back for further evidence to the court that made the provisional order.

Interim order for support of children

(9) Where a court remits a matter pursuant to this section in relation to a child support order, the court may, pending the making of an order under subsection (7), make an interim order in accordance with the applicable guidelines requiring a spouse to pay for the support of any or all children of the marriage.

Interim order for support of spouse

(9.1) Where a court remits a matter pursuant to this section in relation to a spousal support order, the court may make an interim order requiring a spouse to secure or pay, or to secure and pay, such lump sum or periodic sums, or such lump sum and periodic sums, as the court thinks reasonable for the support of the other spouse, pending the making of an order under subsection (7).

Terms and conditions

(10) The court may make an order under subsection (9) or (9.1) for a definite or indefinite period or until a specified event occurs, and may impose terms, conditions or restrictions in connection with the order as it thinks fit and just.

Provisions applicable

(11) Subsections 17(4), (4.1) and (6) to (7) apply, with such modifications as the circumstances require, in respect of an order made under subsection (9) or (9.1) as if it were a variation order referred to in those subsections.

Report and filing

(12) On making an order under subsection (7), the court in a province shall

(a) send a copy of the order, certified by a judge or officer of the court, to the Attorney General for that province, to the court that made the provisional order and, where that court is not the court that made the support order in respect of which the provisional order was made, to the court that made the support order;

(b) where an order is made confirming the provisional order with or without variation, file the order in the court; and

(c) where an order is made confirming the provisional order with variation or refusing confirmation of the provisional order, give written reasons to the Attorney General for that province and to the court that made the provisional order.

R.S.C. 1985, c. 3 (2nd Supp.), s. 19; S.C. 1993, c. 8, s. 4; S.C. 1997, c. 1, s. 7.

Definition of "court"

20. (1) In this section, "court", in respect of a province, has the meaning assigned by subsection 2(1) and includes such other court having jurisdiction in the province as is designated by the Lieutenant Governor in Council of the province as a court for the purposes of this section.

Legal effect throughout Canada

(2) Subject to subsection 18(2), an order made under any of sections 15.1 to 17 or subsection 19(7), (9) or (9.1) has legal effect throughout Canada.

Enforcement

(3) An order that has legal effect throughout Canada pursuant to subsection (2) may be

(a) registered in any court in a province and enforced in like manner as an order of that court; or

(b) enforced in a province in any other manner provided for by the laws of that province, including its laws respecting reciprocal enforcement between the province and a jurisdiction outside Canada.

Variation of orders

(4) Notwithstanding subsection (3), a court may only vary an order that has legal effect throughout Canada pursuant to subsection (2) in accordance with this Act.

R.S.C. 1985, c. 3 (2nd Supp.), s. 20; S.C. 1997, c. 1, s. 8.

Assignment of order

20.1 (1) A support order may be assigned to

(a) any minister of the Crown for Canada designated by the Governor in Council;

(b) any minister of the Crown for a province, or any agency in a province, designated by the Lieutenant Governor in Council of the province;

(c) any member of the Legislative Assembly of Yukon, or any agency in Yukon, designated by the Commissioner of Yukon;

(d) any member of the Council of the Northwest Territories, or any agency in the Northwest Territories, designated by the Commissioner of the Northwest Territories; or

(e) any member of the Legislative Assembly of Nunavut, or any agency in Nunavut, designated by the Commissioner of Nunavut.

Rights

(2) A minister, member or agency referred to in subsection (1) to whom an order is assigned is entitled to the payments due under the order, and has the same right to be notified of, and to participate in, proceedings under this Act to vary, rescind, suspend or enforce the order as the person who would otherwise be entitled to the payments.

S.C. 1997, c. 1, s. 9; S.C. 1993, c. 28, s. 78 (Sch. III, s. 43.1) as amended by S.C. 1998, c. 15, s. 23; S.C. 2002, c. 7, s. 160.

APPEALS

Appeal to appellate court

21. (1) Subject to subsections (2) and (3), an appeal lies to the appellate court from any judgment or order, whether final or interim, rendered or made by a court under this Act.

Restriction on divorce appeals

(2) No appeal lies from a judgment granting a divorce on or after the day on which the divorce takes effect.

Restriction on order appeals

(3) No appeal lies from an order made under this Act more than thirty days after the day on which the order was made.

Extension

(4) An appellate court or a judge thereof may, on special grounds, either before or after the expiration of the time fixed by subsection (3) for instituting an appeal, by order extend that time.

Powers of appellate court

(5) The appellate court may
 (a) dismiss the appeal; or
 (b) allow the appeal and
   (i) render the judgment or make the order that ought to have been rendered or made, including such order or such further or other order as it deems just, or
   (ii) order a new hearing where it deems it necessary to do so to correct a substantial wrong or miscarriage of justice.

Procedure on appeals

(6) Except as otherwise provided by this Act or the rules or regulations, an appeal under this section shall be asserted, heard and decided according to the ordinary procedure governing appeals to the appellate court from the court rendering the judgment or making the order being appealed.

R.S.C. 1985, c. 3 (2nd Supp.), s. 21.

GENERAL

Definition of "spouse"
  21.1 (1) In this section, "spouse" has the meaning assigned by subsection 2(1) and includes a former spouse.

Affidavit re removal of barriers to religious remarriage
  (2) In any proceedings under this Act, a spouse (in this section referred to as the "deponent") may serve on the other spouse and file with the court an affidavit indicating
  (a) that the other spouse is the spouse of the deponent;
  (b) the date and place of the marriage, and the official character of the person who solemnized the marriage;
  (c) the nature of any barriers to the remarriage of the deponent within the deponent's religion the removal of which is within the other spouse's control;
  (d) where there are any barriers to the remarriage of the other spouse within the other spouse's religion the removal of which is within the deponent's control, that the deponent
     (i) has removed those barriers, and the date and circumstances of that removal, or
     (ii) has signified a willingness to remove those barriers, and the date and circumstances of that signification;
  (e) that the deponent has, in writing, requested the other spouse to remove all of the barriers to the remarriage of the deponent within the deponent's religion the removal of which is within the other spouse's control;
  (f) the date of the request described in paragraph (e); and
  (g) that the other spouse, despite the request described in paragraph (e), has failed to remove all of the barriers referred to in that paragraph.

Powers of court where barriers not removed
  (3) Where a spouse who has been served with an affidavit under subsection (2) does not
  (a) within fifteen days after that affidavit is filed with the court or within such longer period as the court allows, serve on the deponent and file with the court an affidavit indicating that all of the barriers referred to in paragraph (2)(e) have been removed, and

(b) satisfy the court, in any additional manner that the court may require, that all of the barriers referred to in paragraph (2)(e) have been removed,

the court may, subject to any terms that the court considers appropriate,

(c) dismiss any application filed by that spouse under this Act, and

(d) strike out any other pleadings and affidavits filed by that spouse under this Act.

Special case

(4) Without limiting the generality of the court's discretion under subsection (3), the court may refuse to exercise its powers under paragraphs (3)(c) and (d) where a spouse who has been served with an affidavit under subsection (2)

(a) within fifteen days after that affidavit is filed with the court or within such longer period as the court allows, serves on the deponent and files with the court an affidavit indicating genuine grounds of a religious or conscientious nature for refusing to remove the barriers referred to in paragraph (2)(e); and

(b) satisfies the court, in any additional manner that the court may require, that the spouse has genuine grounds of a religious or conscientious nature for refusing to remove the barriers referred to in paragraph (2)(e).

Affidavits

(5) For the purposes of this section, an affidavit filed with the court by a spouse must, in order to be valid, indicate the date on which it was served on the other spouse.

Where section does not apply

(6) This section does not apply where the power to remove the barrier to religious remarriage lies with a religious body or official.

S.C. 1990, c. 18, s. 2.

Recognition of foreign divorce

22. (1) A divorce granted, on or after the coming into force of this Act, pursuant to a law of a country or subdivision of a country other than Canada by a tribunal or other authority having jurisdiction to do so shall be recognized for all purposes of determining the marital status in Canada of any person, if either former spouse was ordinarily resident in that country or subdivision for at least one year immediately preceding the commencement of proceedings for the divorce.

Idem

(2) A divorce granted, after July 1, 1968, pursuant to a law of a country or subdivision of a country other than Canada by a tribunal or other authority having jurisdiction to do so, on the basis of the domicile of the wife in that country or subdivision determined as if she were unmarried and, if she was a minor, as if she had attained the age of majority, shall be recognized for all purposes of determining the marital status in Canada of any person.

Other recognition rules preserved

(3) Nothing in this section abrogates or derogates from any other rule of law respecting the recognition of divorces granted otherwise than under this Act.

R.S.C. 1985, c. 3 (2nd Supp.), s. 22.

Provincial laws of evidence

23. (1) Subject to this or any other Act of Parliament, the laws of evidence of the province in which any proceedings under this Act are taken, including the laws of proof of service of any document, apply to such proceedings.

Presumption

(2) For the purposes of this section, where any proceedings are transferred to the Federal Court under subsection 3(3) or 5(3), the proceedings shall be deemed to have been taken in the province specified in the direction of the Court to be the province with which both spouses or former spouses, as the case may be, are or have been most substantially connected.

R.S.C. 1985, c. 3 (2nd Supp.), s. 23; S.C. 2002, c. 8, s. 183.

Proof of signature or office

24. A document offered in a proceeding under this Act that purports to be certified or sworn by a judge or an officer of a court shall, unless the contrary is proved, be proof of the appointment, signature or authority of the judge or officer and, in the case of a document purporting to be sworn, of the appointment, signature or authority of the person before whom the document purports to be sworn.

R.S.C. 1985, c. 3 (2nd Supp.), s. 24.

Definition of "competent authority"

25. (1) In this section, "competent authority", in respect of a court, or appellate court, in a province means the body, person or group of persons ordinarily competent under the laws of that province to make rules regulating the practice and procedure in that court.

Rules

(2) Subject to subsection (3), the competent authority may make rules applicable to any proceedings under this Act in a court, or appellate court, in a province, including, without limiting the generality of the foregoing, rules

(a) regulating the practice and procedure in the court, including the addition of persons as parties to the proceedings;

(b) respecting the conduct and disposition of any proceedings under this Act without an oral hearing;

(b.1) respecting the application of section 17.1 in respect of proceedings for a variation order;

(c) regulating the sittings of the court;

(d) respecting the fixing and awarding of costs;

(e) prescribing and regulating the duties of officers of the court;

(f) respecting the transfer of proceedings under this Act to or from the court; and

(g) prescribing and regulating any other matter considered expedient to attain the ends of justice and carry into effect the purposes and provisions of this Act.

Exercise of power

(3) The power to make rules for a court or appellate court conferred by subsection (2) on a competent authority shall be exercised in the like manner and subject to the like terms and conditions, if any, as the power to make rules for that court conferred on that authority by the laws of the province.

Not statutory instruments

(4) Rules made pursuant to this section by a competent authority that is not a judicial or quasi-judicial body shall be deemed not to be statutory

instruments within the meaning and for the purposes of the *Statutory Instruments Act.*

R.S.C. 1985, c. 3 (2nd Supp.), s. 25; S.C. 1993, c. 8, s. 5.

Agreements with provinces

25.1 (1) With the approval of the Governor in Council, the Minister of Justice may, on behalf of the Government of Canada, enter into an agreement with a province authorizing a provincial child support service designated in the agreement to

(a) assist courts in the province in the determination of the amount of child support; and

(b) recalculate, at regular intervals, in accordance with the applicable guidelines, the amount of child support orders on the basis of updated income information.

Effect of recalculation

(2) Subject to subsection (5), the amount of a child support order as recalculated pursuant to this section shall for all purposes be deemed to be the amount payable under the child support order.

Liability

(3) The former spouse against whom a child support order was made becomes liable to pay the amount as recalculated pursuant to this section thirty-one days after both former spouses to whom the order relates are notified of the recalculation in the manner provided for in the agreement authorizing the recalculation.

Right to vary

(4) Where either or both former spouses to whom a child support order relates do not agree with the amount of the order as recalculated pursuant to this section, either former spouse may, within thirty days after both former spouses are notified of the recalculation in the manner provided for in the agreement authorizing the recalculation, apply to a court of competent jurisdiction for an order under subsection 17(1).

Effect of application

(5) Where an application is made under subsection (4), the operation of subsection (3) is suspended pending the determination of the application, and the child support order continues in effect.

Withdrawal of application

(6) Where an application made under subsection (4) is withdrawn before the determination of the application, the former spouse against whom the order was made becomes liable to pay the amount as recalculated pursuant to this section on the day on which the former spouse would have become liable had the application not been made.

S.C. 1997, c. 1, s. 10; S.C. 1999, c. 31, s. 74 (F).

Regulations

26. (1) The Governor in Council may make regulations for carrying the purposes and provisions of this Act into effect and, without limiting the generality of the foregoing, may make regulations

(a) respecting the establishment and operation of a central registry of divorce proceedings in Canada; and

(b) providing for uniformity in the rules made pursuant to section 25.

Regulations prevail

(2) Any regulations made pursuant to subsection (1) to provide for uniformity in the rules prevail over those rules.

R.S.C. 1985, c. 3 (2nd Supp.), s. 26.

Guidelines

26.1 (1) The Governor in Council may establish guidelines respecting the making of orders for child support, including, but without limiting the generality of the foregoing, guidelines

(a) respecting the way in which the amount of an order for child support is to be determined;

(b) respecting the circumstances in which discretion may be exercised in the making of an order for child support;

(c) authorizing a court to require that the amount payable under an order for child support be paid in periodic payments, in a lump sum or in a lump sum and periodic payments;

(d) authorizing a court to require that the amount payable under an order for child support be paid or secured, or paid and secured, in the manner specified in the order;

(e) respecting the circumstances that give rise to the making of a variation order in respect of a child support order;

(f) respecting the determination of income for the purposes of the application of the guidelines;

(g) authorizing a court to impute income for the purposes of the application of the guidelines; and

(h) respecting the production of income information and providing for sanctions when that information is not provided.

Principle

(2) The guidelines shall be based on the principle that spouses have a joint financial obligation to maintain the children of the marriage in accordance with their relative abilities to contribute to the performance of that obligation.

Definition of "order for child support"

(3) In subsection (1), "order for child support" means

(a) an order or interim order made under section 15.1;

(b) a variation order in respect of a child support order; or

(c) an order or an interim order made under section 19.

S.C. 1997, c. 1, s. 11.

Fees

27. (1) The Governor in Council may, by order, authorize the Minister of Justice to prescribe a fee to be paid by any person to whom a service is provided under this Act or the regulations.

Agreements

(2) The Minister of Justice may, with the approval of the Governor in Council, enter into an agreement with the government of any province respecting the collection and remittance of any fees prescribed pursuant to subsection (1).

R.S.C. 1985, c. 3 (2nd Supp.), s. 27.

Review and report

28. The Minister of Justice shall undertake a comprehensive review of the provisions and operation of the Federal Child Support Guidelines and the determination of child support under this Act and shall cause a report on the review to be laid before each House of Parliament within five years after the coming into force of this section.

R.S.C. 1985, c. 3 (2nd Supp.), s. 28; S.C. 1997, c. 1, s. 12.

REPEALED
   29. REPEALED: S.C. 1997, c. 1, s. 12, effective May 1, 1997 (SI/97-43)

R.S.C. 1985, c. 3 (2nd Supp.), s. 29; S.C. 1997, c. 1, s. 12.

REPEALED
   30. REPEALED: S.C. 1997, c. 1, s. 12, effective May 1, 1997 (SI/97-43)

R.S.C. 1985, c. 3 (2nd Supp.), s. 30; S.C. 1997, c. 1, s. 12.

REPEALED
   31. REPEALED: S.C. 1997, c. 1, s. 12, effective May 1, 1997 (SI/97-43)

R.S.C. 1985, c. 3 (2nd Supp.), s. 31; S.C. 1997, c. 1, s. 12.

TRANSITIONAL PROVISIONS

Proceedings based on facts arising before commencement of Act
   32. Proceedings may be commenced under this Act notwithstanding that the material facts or circumstances giving rise to the proceedings or to jurisdiction over the proceedings occurred wholly or partly before the day on which this Act comes into force.

R.S.C. 1985, c. 3 (2nd Supp.), s. 32.

Divorce Act, R.S. 1970, c. D-8

Proceedings commenced before commencement of Act
   33. Proceedings commenced under the *Divorce Act*, chapter D-8 of the Revised Statutes of Canada, 1970, before the day on which this Act comes into force and not finally disposed of before that day shall be dealt with and disposed of in accordance with that Act as it read immediately before that day, as though it had not been repealed.

R.S.C. 1985, c. 3 (2nd Supp.), s. 33.

Variation and enforcement of orders previously made
   34. (1) Subject to subsection (1.1), any order made under subsection 11(1) of the *Divorce Act*, chapter D-8 of the Revised Statutes of Canada, 1970, including any order made pursuant to section 33 of this Act, and any order to the like effect made corollary to a decree of divorce granted in Canada before July 2, 1968 or granted on or after that day pursuant to subsection 22(2) of that Act may be varied, rescinded, suspended or en-

forced in accordance with sections 17 to 20, other than subsection 17(10), of this Act as if

> (a) the order were a support order or custody order, as the case may be; and
>
> (b) in subsections 17(4), (4.1) and (5), the words "or the last order made under subsection 11(2) of the *Divorce Act*, chapter D-8 of the Revised Statutes of Canada, 1970, varying that order" were added immediately before the words "or the last variation order made in respect of that order".

Combined orders

(1.1) Where an application is made under subsection 17(1) to vary an order referred to in subsection (1) that provides a single amount of money for the combined support of one or more children and a former spouse, the court shall rescind the order and treat the application as an application for a child support order and an application for a spousal support order.

Enforcement of interim orders

(2) Any order made under section 10 of the *Divorce Act*, chapter D-8 of the Revised Statutes of Canada, 1970, including any order made pursuant to section 33 of this Act, may be enforced in accordance with section 20 of this Act as if it were an order made under subsection 15.1(1) or 15.2(1) or section 16 of this Act, as the case may be.

Assignment of orders previously made

(3) Any order for the maintenance of a spouse or child of the marriage made under section 10 or 11 of the *Divorce Act*, chapter D-8 of the Revised Statutes of Canada, 1970, including any order made pursuant to section 33 of this Act, and any order to the like effect made corollary to a decree of divorce granted in Canada before July 2, 1968 or granted on or after that day pursuant to subsection 22(2) of that Act may be assigned to any minister, member or agency designated pursuant to section 20.1.

R.S.C. 1985, c. 3 (2nd Supp.), s. 34; S.C. 1997, c. 1, s. 14.

Procedural laws continued

35. The rules and regulations made under the *Divorce Act*, chapter D-8 of the Revised Statutes of Canada, 1970, and the provisions of any other law or of any rule, regulation or other instrument made thereunder respecting any matter in relation to which rules may be made under sub-section 25(2) that were in force in Canada or any province immediately before the day on which this Act comes into force and that are not incon-sistent with this Act continue in force as though made or enacted by or under this Act until they are repealed or altered by rules or regulations made under this Act or are, by virtue of the making of rules or regulations under this Act, rendered inconsistent with those rules or regulations.

R.S.C. 1985, c. 3 (2nd Supp.), s. 35.

Divorce Act, R.S. 1985, c. 3 (2nd Supp.)

Variation and enforcement of support orders previously made
    35.1 (1) Subject to subsection (2), any support order made under this Act before the coming into force of this section may be varied, rescinded, suspended or enforced in accordance with sections 17 to 20 as if the sup-port order were a child support order or a spousal support order, as the case may be.

Combined orders
    (2) Where an application is made under subsection 17(1) to vary a sup-port order made under this Act before the coming into force of this sec-tion that provides for the combined support of one or more children and a former spouse, the court shall rescind the order and treat the application as an application for a child support order and an application for a spousal support order.

Assignment of orders previously made
    (3) Any support order made under this Act before the coming into force of this section may be assigned to any minister, member or agency designated pursuant to section 20.1.

S.C. 1997, c. 1, s. 15.

COMMENCEMENT

Commencement
    36. This Act shall come into force on a day to be fixed by proclama-tion.

FEDERAL CHILD SUPPORT GUIDELINES

SOR/97-175

Current to Canada Gazette Part II
dated April 30, 2008

[Note: These Guidelines were amended by SOR/97-563 effective December 9, 1997, by SOR/99-136 effective April 1, 1999, by SOR/2000-337 effective November 1, 2000, by SOR/2001-292 effective August 1, 2001, by SOR/2005-400, effective May 1, 2006, and by SOR/2007-59, effective April 1, 2007. The amendments have been incorporated into the text of the Guidelines. The French version of the Guidelines was amended by SOR/2000-390 effective November 1, 2000, in order to correct an inconsistency between the English and French versions. For the text of that amendment see the Canada Gazette Part II, Vol. 134, No. 23, p. 2371.]

His Excellency the Governor General in Council, on the recommendation of the Minister of Justice, pursuant to section 26.1 (S.C. 1997, c. 1, s. 11) of the *Divorce Act* (R.S.C. 1985, c. 3 (2nd Supp.)), hereby establishes the annexed Federal Child Support Guidelines.

TABLE OF PROVISIONS
FEDERAL CHILD SUPPORT GUIDELINES
(This table is not part of the Guidelines.)

OBJECTIVES

1. Objectives

INTERPRETATION

2. Definitions

AMOUNT OF CHILD SUPPORT

3. Presumptive rule
4. Incomes over $150,000
5. Spouse in place of a parent
6. Medical and dental insurance
7. Special or extraordinary expenses
8. Split custody
9. Shared custody
10. Undue hardship

ELEMENTS OF A CHILD SUPPORT ORDER

11. Form of payments
12. Security
13. Information to be specified in order

VARIATION OF CHILD SUPPORT ORDERS

14. Circumstances for variation

INCOME

15. Determination of annual income
16. Calculation of annual income
17. Pattern of income
18. Shareholder, director or officer
19. Imputing income
20. Non-resident

INCOME INFORMATION

21. Obligation of applicant
22. Failure to comply

23. Adverse inference

24. Failure to comply with court order

25. Continuing obligation to provide income information

26. Provincial child support services

COMING INTO FORCE

27. Coming into force

Schedule I   — Notes to Federal Child Support Tables

Schedule II   — Comparison of Household Standards of Living Test

Schedule III — Adjustments to Income

OBJECTIVES

Objectives

1. The objectives of these Guidelines are

(a) to establish a fair standard of support for children that ensures that they continue to benefit from the financial means of both spouses after separation;

(b) to reduce conflict and tension between spouses by making the calculation of child support orders more objective;

(c) to improve the efficiency of the legal process by giving courts and spouses guidance in setting the levels of child support orders and encouraging settlement; and

(d) to ensure consistent treatment of spouses and children who are in similar circumstances.

INTERPRETATION

Definitions

2. (1) The definitions in this subsection apply in these Guidelines.

"Act"

"Act" means the *Divorce Act*.

"child"

"child" means a child of the marriage.

"income"

"income" means the annual income determined under sections 15 to 20.

"order assignee"
"order assignee" means a minister, member or agency referred to in sub-section 20.1(1) of the Act to whom a child support order is assigned in accordance with that subsection.

"spouse"
"spouse" has the meaning assigned by subsection 2(1) of the Act, and includes a former spouse.

"table"
"table" means a federal child support table set out in Schedule I.

universal child care benefit"
"universal child care benefit" means a benefit provided under section 4 of the *Universal Child Care Benefit Act.*

Income Tax Act
(2) Words and expressions that are used in sections 15 to 21 and that are not defined in this section have the meanings assigned to them under the *Income Tax Act.*

Most current information
(3) Where, for the purposes of these Guidelines, any amount is determined on the basis of specified information, the most current information must be used.

Application of Guidelines
(4) In addition to child support orders, these Guidelines apply, with such modifications as the circumstances require, to
 (a) interim orders under subsections 15.1(2) and 19(9) of the Act;
 (b) orders varying a child support order;
 (c) orders referred to in subsection 19(7) of the Act; and
 (d) recalculations under paragraph 25.1(1)(b) of the Act.

Recalculations
(5) For greater certainty, the provisions of these Guidelines that confer a discretionary power on a court do not apply to recalculations under paragraph 25.1(1)(b) of the Act by a provincial child support service.

SOR/2007-59, s. 1.

AMOUNT OF CHILD SUPPORT

Presumptive rule

   3. (1) Unless otherwise provided under these Guidelines, the amount of a child support order for children under the age of majority is

   (a)   the amount set out in the applicable table, according to the number of children under the age of majority to whom the order relates and the income of the spouse against whom the order is sought; and

   (b)   the amount, if any, determined under section 7.

Child the age of majority or over

   (2) Unless otherwise provided under these Guidelines, where a child to whom a child support order relates is the age of majority or over, the amount of the child support order is

   (a)   the amount determined by applying these Guidelines as if the child were under the age of majority; or

   (b)   if the court considers that approach to be inappropriate, the amount that it considers appropriate, having regard to the condition, means, needs and other circumstances of the child and the financial ability of each spouse to contribute to the support of the child.

Applicable table

   (3) The applicable table is

   (a)   if the spouse against whom an order is sought resides in Canada,

      (i)   the table for the province in which that spouse ordinarily resides at the time the application for the child support order, or for a variation order in respect of a child support order, is made or the amount is to be recalculated under section 25.1 of the Act,

      (ii) where the court is satisfied that the province in which that spouse ordinarily resides has changed since the time described in subparagraph (i), the table for the province in which the spouse ordinarily resides at the time of determining the amount of support, or

      (iii) where the court is satisfied that, in the near future after determination of the amount of support, that spouse will ordinarily reside in a given province other than the province in which the spouse ordinarily resides at the time of that determination, the table for the given province; and

(b) if the spouse against whom an order is sought resides outside of Canada, or if the residence of that spouse is unknown, the table for the province where the other spouse ordinarily resides at the time the application for the child support order or for a variation order in respect of a child support order is made or the amount is to be recalculated under section 25.1 of the Act.

SOR/97-563, s. 1.

Incomes over $150,000

4. Where the income of the spouse against whom a child support order is sought is over $150,000, the amount of a child support order is

(a) the amount determined under section 3; or

(b) if the court considers that amount to be inappropriate,

    (i) in respect of the first $150,000 of the spouse's income, the amount set out in the applicable table for the number of children under the age of majority to whom the order relates;

    (ii) in respect of the balance of the spouse's income, the amount that the court considers appropriate, having regard to the condition, means, needs and other circumstances of the children who are entitled to support and the financial ability of each spouse to contribute to the support of the children; and

    (iii) the amount, if any, determined under section 7.

Spouse in place of a parent

5. Where the spouse against whom a child support order is sought stands in the place of a parent for a child, the amount of a child support order is, in respect of that spouse, such amount as the court considers appropriate, having regard to these Guidelines and any other parent's legal duty to support the child.

Medical and dental insurance

6. In making a child support order, where medical or dental insurance coverage for the child is available to either spouse through his or her employer or otherwise at a reasonable rate, the court may order that coverage be acquired or continued.

Special or extraordinary expenses

7. (1) In a child support order the court may, on either spouse's request, provide for an amount to cover all or any portion of the following expenses, which expenses may be estimated, taking into account the necessity of the expense in relation to the child's best interests and the reasonableness of the expense in relation to the means of the spouses and those of the child and to the family's spending pattern prior to the separation:

(a) child care expenses incurred as a result of the custodial parent's employment, illness, disability or education or training for employment;

(b) that portion of the medical and dental insurance premiums attributable to the child;

(c) health-related expenses that exceed insurance reimbursement by at least $100 annually, including orthodontic treatment, professional counselling provided by a psychologist, social worker, psychiatrist or any other person, physiotherapy, occupational therapy, speech therapy and prescription drugs, hearing aids, glasses and contact lenses;

(d) extraordinary expenses for primary or secondary school education or for any other educational programs that meet the child's particular needs;

(e) expenses for post-secondary education; and

(f) extraordinary expenses for extracurricular activities.

SOR/2000-337, s. 1(1), (2), (3).

Definition of "extraordinary expenses"

(1.1) For the purposes of paragraphs (1)(d) and (f), the term "extraordinary expenses" means

(a) expenses that exceed those that the spouse requesting an amount for the extraordinary expenses can reasonably cover, taking into account that spouse's income and the amount that the spouse would receive under the applicable table or, where the court has determined that the table amount is inappropriate, the amount that the court has otherwise determined is appropriate; or

(b) where paragraph (a) is not applicable, expenses that the court considers are extraordinary taking into account

(i)   the amount of the expense in relation to the income of the spouse requesting the amount, including the amount that the spouse would receive under the applicable table or, where the court has determined that the table amount is inappropriate, the amount that the court has otherwise determined is appropriate,

(ii) the nature and number of the educational programs and extracurricular activities,

(iii) any special needs and talents of the child or children,

(iv) the overall cost of the programs and activities, and

(v)   any other similar factor that the court considers relevant.

SOR/2005/400, s. 1.

Sharing of expense

(2) The guiding principle in determining the amount of an expense referred to in subsection (1) is that the expense is shared by the spouses in proportion to their respective incomes after deducting from the expense, the contribution, if any, from the child.

Subsidies, tax deductions, etc.

(3) Subject to subsection (4), in determining the amount of an expense referred to in subsection (1), the court must take into account any subsidies, benefits or income tax deductions or credits relating to the expense, and any eligibility to claim a subsidy, benefit or income tax deduction or credit relating to the expense.

Universal child care benefit

(4) In determining the amount of an expense referred to in subsection (1), the court shall not take into account any universal child care benefit or any eligibility to claim that benefit.

SOR/2000-337, s. 1; SOR/2000-390, s. 1(F); SOR/2005-400, s. 1; SOR/2007-59, s. 2.

Split custody

8. Where each spouse has custody of one or more children, the amount of a child support order is the difference between the amount that each spouse would otherwise pay if a child support order were sought against each of the spouses.

Shared custody

9. Where a spouse exercises a right of access to, or has physical custody of, a child for not less than 40 per cent of the time over the course of a year, the amount of the child support order must be determined by taking into account

(a)   the amounts set out in the applicable tables for each of the spouses;

(b)   the increased costs of shared custody arrangements; and

(c)   the conditions, means, needs and other circumstances of each spouse and of any child for whom support is sought.

Undue hardship

10. (1) On either spouse's application, a court may award an amount of child support that is different from the amount determined under any of sections 3 to 5, 8 or 9 if the court finds that the spouse making the request, or a child in respect of whom the request is made, would otherwise suffer undue hardship.

Circumstances that may cause undue hardship

(2) Circumstances that may cause a spouse or child to suffer undue hardship include the following:

(a)   the spouse has responsibility for an unusually high level of debts reasonably incurred to support the spouses and their children prior to the separation or to earn a living;

(b)   the spouse has unusually high expenses in relation to exercising access to a child;

(c)   the spouse has a legal duty under a judgment, order or written separation agreement to support any person;

(d)   the spouse has a legal duty to support a child, other than a child of the marriage, who is

(i)   under the age of majority, or

(ii)   the age of majority or over but is unable, by reason of illness, disability or other cause, to obtain the necessaries of life; and

(e)   the spouse has a legal duty to support any person who is unable to obtain the necessaries of life due to an illness or disability.

Standards of living must be considered

(3) Despite a determination of undue hardship under subsection (1), an application under that subsection must be denied by the court if it is

of the opinion that the household of the spouse who claims undue hardship would, after determining the amount of child support under any of sections 3 to 5, 8 or 9, have a higher standard of living than the household of the other spouse.

Standards of living test

(4) In comparing standards of living for the purpose of subsection (3), the court may use the comparison of household standards of living test set out in Schedule II.

Reasonable time

(5) Where the court awards a different amount of child support under subsection (1), it may specify, in the child support order, a reasonable time for the satisfaction of any obligation arising from circumstances that cause undue hardship and the amount payable at the end of that time.

Reasons

(6) Where the court makes a child support order in a different amount under this section, it must record its reasons for doing so.

ELEMENTS OF A CHILD SUPPORT ORDER

Form of payments

11. The court may require in a child support order that the amount payable under the order be paid in periodic payments, in a lump sum or in a lump sum and periodic payments.

Security

12. The court may require in the child support order that the amount payable under the order be paid or secured, or paid and secured, in the manner specified in the order.

Information to be specified in order

13. A child support order must include the following information:
  (a) the name and birth date of each child to whom the order relates;
  (b) the income of any spouse whose income is used to determine the amount of the child support order;
  (c) the amount determined under paragraph 3(1)(a) for the number of children to whom the order relates;

(d) the amount determined under paragraph 3(2)(b) for a child the age of majority or over;

(e) the particulars of any expense described in subsection 7(1), the child to whom the expense relates, and the amount of the expense or, where that amount cannot be determined, the proportion to be paid in relation to the expense; and

(f) the date on which the lump sum or first payment is payable and the day of the month or other time period on which all subsequent payments are to be made.

VARIATION OF CHILD SUPPORT ORDERS

Circumstances for variation

14. For the purposes of subsection 17(4) of the Act, any one of the following constitutes a change of circumstances that gives rise to the making of a variation order in respect of a child support order:

(a) in the case where the amount of child support includes a determination made in accordance with the applicable table, any change in circumstances that would result in a different child support order or any provision thereof;

(b) in the case where the amount of child support does not include a determination made in accordance with a table, any change in the condition, means, needs or other circumstances of either spouse or of any child who is entitled to support; and

(c) in the case of an order made before May 1, 1997, the coming into force of section 15.1 of the Act, enacted by section 2 of chapter 1 of the Statutes of Canada, (1997).

SOR/97-563, s. 2; SOR/2000-337, s. 2.

INCOME

Determination of annual income

15. (1) Subject to subsection (2), a spouse's annual income is determined by the court in accordance with sections 16 to 20.

Agreement

(2) Where both spouses agree in writing on the annual income of a spouse, the court may consider that amount to be the spouse's income for the purposes of these Guidelines if the court thinks that the amount

is reasonable having regard to the income information provided under section 21.

Calculation of annual income

16. Subject to sections 17 to 20, a spouse's annual income is determined using the sources of income set out under the heading "Total income" in the T1 General form issued by the Canada Revenue Agency and is adjusted in accordance with Schedule III.

SOR/2000-337, s. 3.

Pattern of income

17. (1) If the court is of the opinion that the determination of a spouse's annual income under section 16 would not be the fairest determination of that income, the court may have regard to the spouse's income over the last three years and determine an amount that is fair and reasonable in light of any pattern of income, fluctuation in income or receipt of a non-recurring amount during those years.

Non-recurring losses

(2) Where a spouse has incurred a non-recurring capital or business investment loss, the court may, if it is of the opinion that the determination of the spouse's annual income under section 16 would not provide the fairest determination of the annual income, choose not to apply sections 6 and 7 of Schedule III, and adjust the amount of the loss, including related expenses and carrying charges and interest expenses, to arrive at such amount as the court considers appropriate.

SOR/2000-337, s. 4.

Shareholder, director or officer

18. (1) Where a spouse is a shareholder, director or officer of a corporation and the court is of the opinion that the amount of the spouse's annual income as determined under section 16 does not fairly reflect all the money available to the spouse for the payment of child support, the court may consider the situations described in section 17 and determine the spouse's annual income to include

    (a)   all or part of the pre-tax income of the corporation, and of any corporation that is related to that corporation, for the most recent taxation year; or

(b) an amount commensurate with the services that the spouse provides to the corporation, provided that the amount does not exceed the corporation's pre-tax income.

Adjustment to corporation's pre-tax income

(2) In determining the pre-tax income of a corporation for the purposes of subsection (1), all amounts paid by the corporation as salaries, wages or management fees, or other payments or benefits, to or on behalf of persons with whom the corporation does not deal at arm's length must be added to the pre-tax income, unless the spouse establishes that the payments were reasonable in the circumstances.

Imputing income

19. (1) The court may impute such amount of income to a spouse as it considers appropriate in the circumstances, which circumstances include the following:

(a) the spouse is intentionally under-employed or unemployed, other than where the under-employment or unemployment is required by the needs of a child of the marriage or any child under the age of majority or by the reasonable educational or health needs of the spouse;

(b) the spouse is exempt from paying federal or provincial income tax;

(c) the spouse lives in a country that has effective rates of income tax that are significantly lower than those in Canada;

(d) it appears that income has been diverted which would affect the level of child support to be determined under these Guidelines;

(e) the spouse's property is not reasonably utilized to generate income;

(f) the spouse has failed to provide income information when under a legal obligation to do so;

(g) the spouse unreasonably deducts expenses from income;

(h) the spouse derives a significant portion of income from dividends, capital gains or other sources that are taxed at a lower rate than employment or business income or that are exempt from tax; and

(i) the spouse is a beneficiary under a trust and is or will be in receipt of income or other benefits from the trust.

Reasonableness of expenses

(2) For the purpose of paragraph (1)(g), the reasonableness of an expense deduction is not solely governed by whether the deduction is permitted under the *Income Tax Act*.

SOR/2000-337, s. 5.

Non-resident

20. (1) Subject to subsection (2), where a spouse is a non-resident of Canada, the spouse's annual income is determined as though the spouse were a resident of Canada.

Non-resident taxed at higher rates

(2) Where a spouse is a non-resident of Canada and resides in a country that has effective rates of income tax that are significantly higher than those applicable in the province in which the other spouse ordinarily resides, the spouse's annual income is the amount that the court determines to be appropriate taking those rates into consideration.

SOR/2006-400, s. 2.

INCOME INFORMATION

Obligation of applicant

21. (1) A spouse who is applying for a child support order and whose income information is necessary to determine the amount of the order must include the following with the application:

(a) a copy of every personal income tax return filed by the spouse for each of the three most recent taxation years;

(b) a copy of every notice of assessment and reassessment issued to the spouse for each of the three most recent taxation years;

(c) where the spouse is an employee, the most recent statement of earnings indicating the total earnings paid in the year to date, including overtime or, where such a statement is not provided by the employer, a letter from the spouse's employer setting out that information including the spouse's rate of annual salary or remuneration;

(d) where the spouse is self-employed, for the three most recent taxation years

   (i) the financial statements of the spouse's business or professional practice, other than a partnership, and

     (ii) a statement showing a breakdown of all salaries, wages, management fees or other payments or benefits paid to, or on behalf of, persons or corporations with whom the spouse does not deal at arm's length;

(e) where the spouse is a partner in a partnership, confirmation of the spouse's income and draw from, and capital in, the partnership for its three most recent taxation years;

(f) where the spouse controls a corporation, for its three most recent taxation years

     (i) the financial statements of the corporation and its subsidiaries, and

     (ii) a statement showing a breakdown of all salaries, wages, management fees or other payments or benefits paid to, or on behalf of, persons or corporations with whom the corporation, and every related corporation, does not deal at arm's length;

(g) where the spouse is a beneficiary under a trust, a copy of the trust settlement agreement and copies of the trust's three most recent financial statements; and

(h) in addition to any income information that must be included under paragraphs (c) to (g), where the spouse receives income from employment insurance, social assistance, a pension, workers compensation, disability payments or any other source, the most recent statement of income indicating the total amount of income from the applicable source during the current year, or if such a statement is not provided, a letter from the appropriate authority stating the required information.

Obligation of respondent

    (2) A spouse who is served with an application for a child support order and whose income information is necessary to determine the amount of the order, must, within 30 days after the application is served if the spouse resides in Canada or the United States or within 60 days if the spouse resides elsewhere, or such other time limit as the court specifies, provide the court, as well as the other spouse or the order assignee, as the case may be, with the documents referred to in subsection (1).

Special expenses or undue hardship

    (3) Where, in the course of proceedings in respect of an application for a child support order, a spouse requests an amount to cover expenses

referred to in subsection 7(1) or pleads undue hardship, the spouse who would be receiving the amount of child support must, within 30 days after the amount is sought or undue hardship is pleaded if the spouse resides in Canada or the United States or within 60 days if the spouse resides elsewhere, or such other time limit as the court specifies, provide the court and the other spouse with the documents referred to in subsection (1).

Income over $150,000

(4) Where, in the course of proceedings in respect of an application for a child support order, it is established that the income of the spouse who would be paying the amount of child support is greater than $150,000, the other spouse must, within 30 days after the income is established to be greater than $150,000 if the other spouse resides in Canada or the United States or within 60 days if the other spouse resides elsewhere, or such other time limit as the court specifies, provide the court and the spouse with the documents referred to in subsection (1).

Making of rules not precluded

(5) Nothing in this section precludes the making of rules by a competent authority, within the meaning of section 25 of the Act, respecting the disclosure of income information that is considered necessary for the purposes of the determination of an amount of a child support order.

SOR/2000-337, s. 6.

Failure to comply

22. (1) Where a spouse fails to comply with section 21, the other spouse may apply

(a) to have the application for a child support order set down for a hearing, or move for judgment; or

(b) for an order requiring the spouse who failed to comply to provide the court, as well as the other spouse or order assignee, as the case may be, with the required documents.

Costs of the proceedings

(2) Where a court makes an order under paragraph (1)(a) or (b), the court may award costs in favour of the other spouse up to an amount that fully compensates the other spouse for all costs incurred in the proceedings.

Adverse inference

23. Where the court proceeds to a hearing on the basis of an application under paragraph 22(1)(a), the court may draw an adverse inference against the spouse who failed to comply and impute income to that spouse in such amount as it considers appropriate.

Failure to comply with court order

24. Where a spouse fails to comply with an order issued on the basis of an application under paragraph 22(1)(b), the court may

(a) strike out any of the spouse's pleadings;

(b) make a contempt order against the spouse;

(c) proceed to a hearing, in the course of which it may draw an adverse inference against the spouse and impute income to that spouse in such amount as it considers appropriate; and

(d) award costs in favour of the other spouse up to an amount that fully compensates the other spouse for all costs incurred in the proceedings.

Continuing obligation to provide income information

25. (1) Every spouse against whom a child support order has been made must, on the written request of the other spouse or the order assignee, not more than once a year after the making of the order and as long as the child is a child within the meaning of these Guidelines, provide that other spouse or the order assignee with

(a) the documents referred to in subsection 21(1) for any of the three most recent taxation years for which the spouse has not previously provided the documents;

(b) as applicable, any current information, in writing, about the status of any expenses included in the order pursuant to subsection 7(1); and

(c) as applicable, any current information, in writing, about the circumstances relied on by the court in a determination of undue hardship.

Below minimum income

(2) Where a court has determined that the spouse against whom a child support order is sought does not have to pay child support because his or her income level is below the minimum amount required for application of the tables, that spouse must, on the written request of the other spouse, not more than once a year after the determination and as long as

the child is a child within the meaning of these Guidelines, provide the other spouse with the documents referred to in subsection 21(1) for any of the three most recent taxation years for which the spouse has not previously provided the documents.

Obligation of receiving spouse
(3) Where the income information of the spouse in favour of whom a child support order is made is used to determine the amount of the order, the spouse must, not more than once a year after the making of the order and as long as the child is a child within the meaning of these Guidelines, on the written request of the other spouse, provide the other spouse with the documents and information referred to in subsection (1).

Information requests
(4) Where a spouse or an order assignee requests information from the other spouse under any of subsections (1) to (3) and the income information of the requesting spouse is used to determine the amount of the child support order, the requesting spouse or order assignee must include the documents and information referred to in subsection (1) with the request.

Time limit
(5) A spouse who receives a request made under any of subsections (1) to (3) must provide the required documents within 30 days after the request's receipt if the spouse resides in Canada or the United States and within 60 days after the request's receipt if the spouse resides elsewhere.

Deemed receipt
(6) A request made under any of subsections (1) to (3) is deemed to have been received 10 days after it is sent.

Failure to comply
(7) A court may, on application by either spouse or an order assignee, where the other spouse has failed to comply with any of subsections (1) to (3)

    (a) consider the other spouse to be in contempt of court and award costs in favour of the applicant up to an amount that fully compensates the applicant for all costs incurred in the proceedings; or

(b) make an order requiring the other spouse to provide the required documents to the court, as well as to the spouse or order assignee, as the case may be.

Unenforceable provision
(8) A provision in a judgment, order or agreement purporting to limit a spouse's obligation to provide documents under this section is unenforceable.

SOR/97-563, s. 3.

Provincial child support services
26. A spouse or an order assignee may appoint a provincial child support service to act on their behalf for the purposes of requesting and receiving income information under any of subsections 25(1) to (3), as well as for the purposes of an application under subsection 25(7).

COMING INTO FORCE

Coming into force
27. These Guidelines come into force on May 1, 1997.

SCHEDULE I
(Subsection 2(1))

FEDERAL CHILD SUPPORT TABLES

Notes:
1. The federal child support tables set out the amount of monthly child support payments for each province on the basis of the annual income of the spouse ordered to pay child support (the "support payer") and the number of children for whom a table amount is payable. Refer to these Guidelines to determine whether special measures apply.
2. There is a threshold level of income below which no amount of child support is payable. Child support amounts are specified for incomes up to $150,000 per year. Refer to section 4 of these Guidelines to determine the amount of child support payments for support payers with annual incomes over $150,000.
3. Income is set out in the tables in intervals of $1,000. Monthly amounts are determined by adding the applicable basic amount and the amount calculated by multiplying the applicable percentage by

the portion of the income that exceeds the lower amount within that interval of income.

Example:

Province: British Columbia
Number of children: 2
Annual income of support payer: $33,760
Basic amount: $515
Percentage: 1.39%
Lower amount of the income interval: $33,000
The amount of monthly child support is calculated as follows:
$515 + [1.39% × ($33,760-$33,000)]
$515 + [1.39/100 × $760]
$515 + [0.0139 × $760]
$515 + $10.56 = $525.56

4. There are separate tables for each province. The amounts vary from one province to another because of differences in provincial income tax rates. The tables are in the following order:

> (a) Ontario; (b) Quebec; (c) Nova Scotia; (d) New Brunswick; (e) Manitoba; (f) British Columbia; (g) Prince Edward Island; (h) Saskatchewan; (i) Alberta; (j) Newfoundland and Labrador; (k) Yukon; (l) Northwest Territories; and (m) Nunavut.

5. The amounts in the tables are based on economic studies of average spending on children in families at different income levels in Canada. They are calculated on the basis that child support payments are no longer taxable in the hands of the receiving parent and no longer deductible by the paying parent. They are calculated using a mathematical formula and generated by a computer program.

6. The formula referred to in note 5 sets support amounts to reflect average expenditures on children by a spouse with a particular number of children and level of income. The calculation is based on the support payer's income. The formula uses the basic personal amount for non-refundable tax credits to recognize personal expenses, and takes other federal and provincial income taxes and credits into account. Federal Child Tax benefits and Goods and Services Tax credits for children are excluded from the calculation. At lower income levels, the formula sets the amounts to take into account the combined im-

pact of taxes and child support payments on the support payer's limited disposable income.

SOR/97-563, ss. 4 to 9; SOR/99-136, ss. 1, 2; SOR/2005-400, ss. 3 to 5.

SCHEDULE II
(Subsection 10(4))

COMPARISON OF HOUSEHOLD STANDARDS OF LIVING TEST

Definitions
1. The definitions in this section apply in this Schedule.

"average tax rate"
"average tax rate" Repealed SOR/2000-337, s. 7(1).

"child"
"child" means a child of the marriage or a child who
   (a) is under the age of majority; or
   (b) is the age of majority or over but is unable, by reason of illness, disability or other cause to obtain the necessaries of life.

"household"
"household" means a spouse and any of the following persons residing with the spouse
   (a) any person who has a legal duty to support the spouse or whom the spouse has a legal duty to support,
   (b) any person who shares living expenses with the spouse or from whom the spouse otherwise receives an economic benefit as a result of living with that person, if the court considers it reasonable for that person to be considered part of the household; and
   (c) any child whom the spouse or the person described in paragraph (a) or (b) has a legal duty to support.

"taxable income"
"taxable income" means the annual taxable income determined using the calculations required to determine "Taxable Income" in the T1 General form issued by the Canada Revenue Agency.

Test

2. The comparison of household standards of living test is as follows:

STEP 1

Establish the annual income of each person in each household by applying the formula

$$A - B - C$$

where

A   is the person's income determined in accordance with sections 15 to 20 of these Guidelines,

B   is the federal and provincial taxes payable on the person's taxable income, and

C   is the person's source deductions for premiums paid under the *Employment Insurance Act* and contributions made to the *Canada Pension Plan* and the *Quebec Pension Plan*.

Where the information on which to base the income determination is not provided, the court may impute income in the amount it considers appropriate.

STEP 2

Adjust the annual income of each person in each household by

(a)   deducting the following amounts, calculated on an annual basis:

(i)   any amount relied on by the court as a factor that resulted in a determination of undue hardship, except any amount attributable to the support of a member of the household that is not incurred due to a disability or serious illness of that member,

(ii)   the amount that would otherwise be payable by that person in respect of a child to whom the order relates, if the pleading of undue hardship was not made,

(A)   under the applicable table, or

(B)   as is considered by the court to be appropriate, where the court considers the table amount to be inappropriate,

(iii)   any amount of support that is paid by the person under a judgment, order or written separation agreement, except

(A) an amount already deducted under subparagraph (i), and

(B) an amount paid by the person in respect of a child to whom the order referred to in subparagraph (ii) relates; and

(b) adding the following amounts, calculated on an annual basis:

(i) any amount that would otherwise be receivable by the person in respect of a child to whom the order relates, if the pleading of undue hardship was not made,

(A) under the applicable table, or

(B) as is considered by the court to be appropriate, where the court considers the table amount to be inappropriate,

(ii) any amount of child support that the person has received for any child under a judgment, order or written separation agreement.

STEP 3

Add the amounts of adjusted annual income for all the persons in each household to determine the total household income for each household.

STEP 4

Determine the applicable low-income measures amount for each household based on the following:

Low-income Measures

Household Size	Low-income Measures Amount
One person	
1 adult	$10,382

Two persons	
2 adults	$14,535
1 adult and 1 child	$14,535
Three persons	
3 adults	$18,688
2 adults and 1 child	$17,649
1 adult and 2 children	$17,649

Household Size	Low-income Measures Amount
Four persons	
4 adults	$22,840
3 adults and 1 child	$21,802
2 adults and 2 children	$20,764
1 adult and 3 children	$20,764

Household Size	Low-income Measures Amount
Five persons	
5 adults	$26,993
4 adults and 1 child	$25,955
3 adults and 2 children	$24,917
2 adults and 3 children	$23,879
1 adult and 4 children	$23,879

Household Size	Low-income Measures Amount
Six persons	
6 adults	$31,145
5 adults and 1 child	$30,108
4 adults and 2 children	$29,070
3 adults and 3 children	$28,031
2 adults and 4 children	$26,993
1 adult and 5 children	$26,993

Household Size	Low-income Measures Amount
Seven persons	
7 adults	$34,261
6 adults and 1 child	$33,222
5 adults and 2 children	$32,184
4 adults and 3 children	$31,146
3 adults and 4 children	$30,108
2 adults and 5 children	$29,070
1 adult and 6 children	$29,070

Household Size	Low-income Measures Amount
Eight persons	
8 adults	$38,413
7 adults and 1 child	$37,375

Household Size	Low-income Measures Amount
6 adults and 2 children	$36,337
5 adults and 3 children	$35,299
4 adults and 4 children	$34,261
3 adults and 5 children	$33,222
2 adults and 6 children	$32,184
1 adult and 7 children	$32,184

STEP 5

Divide the household income amount (Step 3) by the low-income measures amount (Step 4) to get a household income ratio for each household.

STEP 6

Compare the household income ratios. The household that has the higher ratio has the higher standard of living.

SOR/97-563, ss. 10, 11; SOR/2000-337, s. 7; SOR/2005-400, s. 6; SOR/2007-59, s. 4.

SCHEDULE III
(Section 16)

ADJUSTMENTS TO INCOME

Employment expenses

1. Where the spouse is an employee, the spouse's applicable employment expenses described in the following provisions of the *Income Tax Act* are deducted:

(a) Repealed SOR/2000-337, s. 8(1);

(b) paragraph 8(1)(*d*) concerning expenses of teacher's exchange fund contribution;

(c) paragraph 8(1)(*e*) concerning expenses of railway employees;

(d) paragraph 8(1)(*f*) concerning sales expenses;

(e) paragraph 8(1)(*g*) concerning transport employee's expenses;

(f) paragraph 8(1)(*h*) concerning travel expenses;

(f.1) paragraph 8(1)(*h.1*) concerning motor vehicle travel expenses;

(g) paragraph 8(1)(*i*) concerning dues and other expenses of performing duties;

(h) paragraph 8(1)(*j*) concerning motor vehicle and aircraft costs;

(i)   paragraph 8(1)(*l.1*) concerning *Canada Pension Plan* contributions and *Employment Insurance Act* premiums paid in respect of another employee who acts as an assistant or substitute for the spouse;

(j)   paragraph 8(1)(*n*) concerning salary reimbursement;

(k)   paragraph 8(1)(*o*) concerning forfeited amounts;

(l)   paragraph 8(1)(*p*) concerning musical instrument costs; and

(m) paragraph 8(1)(*q*) concerning artists' employment expenses.

Child support

2. Deduct any child support received that is included to determine total income in the T1 General form issued by the Canada Revenue Agency.

Spousal support and universal child care benefit

3. To calculate income for the purpose of determining an amount under an applicable table, deduct

(a)   the spousal support received from the other spouse; and

(b)   any universal child care benefit that is included to determine the spouse's total income in the T1 General form issued by the Canada Revenue Agency.

Special or extraordinary expenses

3.1 To calculate income for the purpose of determining an amount under section 7 of these Guidelines, deduct the spousal support paid to the other spouse and, as applicable, make the following adjustment in respect of universal child care benefits:

(a)   deduct benefits that are included to determine the spouse's total income in the T1 General form issued by the Canada Revenue Agency and that are for a child for whom special or extraordinary expenses are not being requested; or

(b)   include benefits that are not included to determine the spouse's total income in the T1 General form issued by the Canada Revenue Agency and that are received by the spouse for a child for whom special or extraordinary expenses are being requested.

Social assistance

4. Deduct any amount of social assistance income that is not attributable to the spouse.

Dividends from taxable Canadian corporations

5. Replace the taxable amount of dividends from taxable Canadian corporations received by the spouse by the actual amount of those dividends received by the spouse.

Capital gains and capital losses

6. Replace the taxable capital gains realized in a year by the spouse by the actual amount of capital gains realized by the spouse in excess of the spouse's actual capital losses in that year.

Business investment losses

7. Deduct the actual amount of business investment losses suffered by the spouse during the year.

Carrying charges

8. Deduct the spouse's carrying charges and interest expenses that are paid by the spouse and that would be deductible under the *Income Tax Act*.

Net self-employment income

9. Where the spouse's net self-employment income is determined by deducting an amount for salaries, benefits, wages or management fees, or other payments, paid to or on behalf of persons with whom the spouse does not deal at arm's length, include that amount, unless the spouse establishes that the payments were necessary to earn the self-employment income and were reasonable in the circumstances.

Additional amount

10. Where the spouse reports income from self-employment that, in accordance with sections 34.1 and 34.2 of the *Income Tax Act*, includes an additional amount earned in a prior period, deduct the amount earned in the prior period, net of reserves.

Capital cost allowance for property

11. Include the spouse's deduction for an allowable capital cost allowance with respect to real property.

Partnership income

12. Where the spouse earns income through a partnership or sole proprietorship, deduct any amount included in income that is properly required by the partnership or sole proprietorship for purposes of capitalization.

Employee stock options

13. (1) Where the spouse has received, as an employee benefit, options to purchase shares of a Canadian-controlled private corporation, or a publicly traded corporation that is subject to the same tax treatment with reference to stock options as a Canadian-controlled private corporation, and has exercised those options during the year, add the difference between the value of the shares at the time the options are exercised and the amount paid by the spouse for the shares, and any amount paid by the spouse to acquire the options to purchase the shares, to the income for the year in which the options are exercised.

Disposal of shares

(2) If the spouse has disposed of the shares during a year, deduct from the income for that year the difference determined under subsection (1).

SOR/97-563, ss. 12 to 14; SOR/2000-337, ss. 8 to 11, 12(E); SOR/2001-292, s. 1; SOR/2007-59, ss. 3, 4.

FAMILY LAW ACT

R.S.O. 1990, Chapter F.3

Current to May 1, 2008

CONTENTS

Preamble

1. Definitions
2. Procedural and other miscellaneous matters
3. Mediation

PART I
FAMILY PROPERTY

4. Definitions
5. Equalization of net family properties
6. Election
7. Application to court
8. Statement of property
9. Powers of court
10. Determination of questions of title between spouses
11. Operating business or farm
12. Orders for preservation
13. Variation and realization of security
14. Presumptions
15. Conflict of laws
16. Application of Part

PART II
MATRIMONIAL HOME

17. Definitions
18. Matrimonial home
19. Possession of matrimonial home
20. Designation of matrimonial home
21. Alienation of matrimonial home
22. Right of redemption and to notice
23. Powers of court respecting alienation
24. Order for possession of matrimonial home
25. Variation
26. Spouse without interest in matrimonial home
27. Registration of order
28. Application of Part

PART III
SUPPORT OBLIGATIONS

29. Definitions
30. Obligation of spouses for support
31. Obligation of parent to support child
32. Obligation of child to support parent
33. Order for support
34. Powers of court
35. Domestic contract, etc., may be filed with court
36. Effect of divorce proceeding
37. Application for variation
38. Indexing existing orders
38.1 Priority to child support
39. Existing orders
40. Restraining orders
41. Financial statement
42. Obtaining information
43. Arrest of absconding debtor
44. Provisional orders
45. Necessities of life
46. Order restraining harassment
47. Application for custody
48. Appeal from Ontario Court of Justice
49. Contempt of orders of Ontario Court of Justice

PART IV
DOMESTIC CONTRACTS

51.   Definitions
52.   Marriage contracts
53.   Cohabitation agreements
54.   Separation agreements
55.   Form and capacity
56.   Provisions that may be set aside or disregarded
57.   Rights of donors of gifts
58.   Contracts made outside Ontario
59.   Paternity agreements
59.1 Family arbitrations, agreements and awards
59.2 Other third-party decision-making processes in family matters
59.3 Contracting out
59.4 No agreement in advance of dispute
59.5 Status of awards
59.6 Conditions for enforceability
59.7 Secondary arbitration
59.8 Enforcement
60.   Application of Act to existing contracts

PART V
DEPENDANTS' CLAIM FOR DAMAGES

61.   Right of dependants to sue in tort
62.   Offer to settle for global sum
63.   Assessment of damages, insurance

PART VI
AMENDMENTS TO THE COMMON LAW

64.   Unity of legal personality abolished
65.   Actions between parent and child
66.   Recovery for prenatal injuries
67.   Domicile of minor

GENERAL

69.   Regulations
70.   Transition

Preamble

Whereas it is desirable to encourage and strengthen the role of the family; and whereas for that purpose it is necessary to recognize the equal position of spouses as individuals within marriage and to recognize marriage as a form of partnership; and whereas in support of such recognition it is necessary to provide in law for the orderly and equitable settlement of the affairs of the spouses upon the breakdown of the partnership, and to provide for other mutual obligations in family relationships, including the equitable sharing by parents of responsibility for their children;

Therefore, Her Majesty, by and with the advice and consent of the Legislative Assembly of the Province of Ontario, enacts as follows:

Definitions
   1. (1) In this Act,

"child" includes a person whom a parent has demonstrated a settled intention to treat as a child of his or her family, except under an arrangement where the child is placed for valuable consideration in a foster home by a person having lawful custody; ("enfant")

"child support guidelines" means the guidelines established by the regulations made under subsections 69 (2) and (3); ("lignes directrices sur les aliments pour les enfants")

"cohabit" means to live together in a conjugal relationship, whether within or outside marriage; ("cohabiter")

"court" means the Ontario Court of Justice, the Family Court of the Superior Court of Justice or the Superior Court of Justice; ("tribunal")

"domestic contract" means a domestic contract as defined in Part IV (Domestic Contracts); ("contrat familial")

"parent" includes a person who has demonstrated a settled intention to treat a child as a child of his or her family, except under an arrangement where the child is placed for valuable consideration in a foster home by a person having lawful custody; ("père ou mère")

"paternity agreement" means a paternity agreement as defined in Part IV (Domestic Contracts); ("accord de paternité")

"spouse" means either of two persons who,
      (a) are married to each other, or

(b) have together entered into a marriage that is voidable or void, in good faith on the part of a person relying on this clause to assert any right. ("conjoint") R.S.O. 1990, c. F.3, s. 1 (1); 1997, c. 20, s. 1; 1999, c. 6, s. 25 (1); 2005, c. 5, s. 27 (1, 2); 2006, c. 19, Sched. C, s. 1 (1, 2, 4).

Polygamous marriages

(2) In the definition of "spouse", a reference to marriage includes a marriage that is actually or potentially polygamous, if it was celebrated in a jurisdiction whose system of law recognizes it as valid. R.S.O. 1990, c. F.3, s. 1 (2).

Procedural and Other Miscellaneous Matters

Staying application

2. (1) If, in an application under this Act, it appears to the court that for the appropriate determination of the spouses' affairs it is necessary or desirable to have other matters determined first or simultaneously, the court may stay the application until another proceeding is brought or determined as the court considers appropriate. R.S.O. 1990, c. F.3, s. 2 (1).

All proceedings in one court

(2) Except as this Act provides otherwise, no person who is a party to an application under this Act shall make another application under this Act to another court, but the court may order that the proceeding be transferred to a court having other jurisdiction where, in the first court's opinion, the other court is more appropriate to determine the matters in issue that should be determined at the same time. R.S.O. 1990, c. F.3, s. 2 (2).

Applications in Superior Court of Justice

(3) In the Superior Court of Justice, an application under this Act may be made by action or application. R.S.O. 1990, c. F.3, s. 2 (3); 2006, c. 19, Sched. C, s. 1 (1).

Statement re removal of barriers to remarriage

(4) A party to an application under section 7 (net family property), 10 (questions of title between spouses), 33 (support), 34 (powers of court) or 37 (variation) may serve on the other party and file with the court a statement, verified by oath or statutory declaration, indicating that,

(a) the author of the statement has removed all barriers that are within his or her control and that would prevent the other spouse's remarriage within that spouse's faith; and

(b) the other party has not done so, despite a request. R.S.O. 1990, c. F.3, s. 2 (4).

Idem

(5) Within ten days after service of the statement, or within such longer period as the court allows, the party served with a statement under subsection (4) shall serve on the other party and file with the court a statement, verified by oath or statutory declaration, indicating that the author of the statement has removed all barriers that are within his or her control and that would prevent the other spouse's remarriage within that spouse's faith. R.S.O. 1990, c. F.3, s. 2 (5).

Dismissal, etc.

(6) When a party fails to comply with subsection (5),
(a) if the party is an applicant, the proceeding may be dismissed;
(b) if the party is a respondent, the defence may be struck out. R.S.O. 1990, c. F.3, s. 2 (6).

Exception

(7) Subsections (5) and (6) do not apply to a party who does not claim costs or other relief in the proceeding. R.S.O. 1990, c. F.3, s. 2 (7).

Extension of times

(8) The court may, on motion, extend a time prescribed by this Act if it is satisfied that,
(a) there are apparent grounds for relief;
(b) relief is unavailable because of delay that has been incurred in good faith; and
(c) no person will suffer substantial prejudice by reason of the delay. R.S.O. 1990, c. F.3, s. 2 (8).

Incorporation of contract in order

(9) A provision of a domestic contract in respect of a matter that is dealt with in this Act may be incorporated in an order made under this Act. R.S.O. 1990, c. F.3, s. 2 (9).

Act subject to contracts

(10) A domestic contract dealing with a matter that is also dealt with in this Act prevails unless this Act provides otherwise. R.S.O. 1990, c. F.3, s. 2 (10).

Registration of orders

(11) An order made under this Act that affects real property does not affect the acquisition of an interest in the real property by a person acting in good faith without notice of the order, unless the order is registered in the proper land registry office. R.S.O. 1990, c. F.3, s. 2 (11).

Mediation

3. (1) In an application under this Act, the court may, on motion, appoint a person whom the parties have selected to mediate any matter that the court specifies. R.S.O. 1990, c. F.3, s. 3 (1).

Consent to act

(2) The court shall appoint only a person who,

   (a) has consented to act as mediator; and

   (b) has agreed to file a report with the court within the period of time specified by the court. R.S.O. 1990, c. F.3, s. 3 (2).

Duty of mediator

(3) The mediator shall confer with the parties, and with the children if the mediator considers it appropriate to do so, and shall endeavour to obtain an agreement between the parties. R.S.O. 1990, c. F.3, s. 3 (3).

Full or limited report

(4) Before entering into mediation, the parties shall decide whether,

   (a) the mediator is to file a full report on the mediation, including anything that he or she considers relevant; or

   (b) the mediator is to file a limited report that sets out only the agreement reached by the parties or states only that the parties did not reach agreement. R.S.O. 1990, c. F.3, s. 3 (4).

Filing and copies of report

(5) The mediator shall file with the clerk or registrar of the court a full or limited report, as the parties have decided, and shall give a copy to each of the parties. R.S.O. 1990, c. F.3, s. 3 (5).

Admissions, etc., in the course of mediation

(6) If the parties have decided that the mediator is to file a limited report, no evidence of anything said or of any admission or communication made in the course of the mediation is admissible in any proceeding, except with the consent of all parties to the proceeding in which the mediator was appointed. R.S.O. 1990, c. F.3, s. 3 (6).

Fees and expenses

(7) The court shall require the parties to pay the mediator's fees and expenses and shall specify in the order the proportions or amounts of the fees and expenses that each party is required to pay. R.S.O. 1990, c. F.3, s. 3 (7).

Idem, serious financial hardship

(8) The court may require one party to pay all the mediator's fees and expenses if the court is satisfied that payment would cause the other party or parties serious financial hardship. R.S.O. 1990, c. F.3, s. 3 (8).

PART I
FAMILY PROPERTY

Definitions

4. (1) In this Part,

"court" means a court as defined in subsection 1 (1), but does not include the Ontario Court of Justice; ("tribunal")

"matrimonial home" means a matrimonial home under section 18 and includes property that is a matrimonial home under that section at the valuation date; ("foyer conjugal")

"net family property" means the value of all the property, except property described in subsection (2), that a spouse owns on the valuation date, after deducting,
- (a) the spouse's debts and other liabilities, and
- (b) the value of property, other than a matrimonial home, that the spouse owned on the date of the marriage, after deducting the spouse's debts and other liabilities, calculated as of the date of the marriage; ("biens familiaux nets")

"property" means any interest, present or future, vested or contingent, in real or personal property and includes,

(a) property over which a spouse has, alone or in conjunction with another person, a power of appointment exercisable in favour of himself or herself,

(b) property disposed of by a spouse but over which the spouse has, alone or in conjunction with another person, a power to revoke the disposition or a power to consume or dispose of the property, and

(c) in the case of a spouse's rights under a pension plan that have vested, the spouse's interest in the plan including contributions made by other persons; ("bien")

"valuation date" means the earliest of the following dates:

1. The date the spouses separate and there is no reasonable prospect that they will resume cohabitation.

2. The date a divorce is granted.

3. The date the marriage is declared a nullity.

4. The date one of the spouses commences an application based on subsection 5 (3) (improvident depletion) that is subsequently granted.

5. The date before the date on which one of the spouses dies leaving the other spouse surviving. ("date d'évaluation") R.S.O. 1990, c. F.3, s. 4 (1); 2006, c. 19, Sched. C, s. 1 (2).

Excluded property

(2) The value of the following property that a spouse owns on the valuation date does not form part of the spouse's net family property:

1. Property, other than a matrimonial home, that was acquired by gift or inheritance from a third person after the date of the marriage.

2. Income from property referred to in paragraph 1, if the donor or testator has expressly stated that it is to be excluded from the spouse's net family property.

3. Damages or a right to damages for personal injuries, nervous shock, mental distress or loss of guidance, care and companionship, or the part of a settlement that represents those damages.

4. Proceeds or a right to proceeds of a policy of life insurance, as defined under the *Insurance Act*, that are payable on the death of the life insured.

5. Property, other than a matrimonial home, into which property referred to in paragraphs 1 to 4 can be traced.

6. Property that the spouses have agreed by a domestic contract is not to be included in the spouse's net family property. R.S.O. 1990, c. F.3, s. 4 (2); 2004, c. 31, Sched. 38, s. 2 (1).

Onus of proof re deductions and exclusions
(3) The onus of proving a deduction under the definition of "net family property" or an exclusion under subsection (2) is on the person claiming it. R.S.O. 1990, c. F.3, s. 4 (3).

Close of business
(4) When this section requires that a value be calculated as of a given date, it shall be calculated as of close of business on that date. R.S.O. 1990, c. F.3, s. 4 (4).

Net family property not to be less than zero
(5) If a spouse's net family property as calculated under subsections (1), (2) and (4) is less than zero, it shall be deemed to be equal to zero. R.S.O. 1990, c. F.3, s. 4 (5).

Equalization of Net Family Properties

Divorce, etc.
5. (1) When a divorce is granted or a marriage is declared a nullity, or when the spouses are separated and there is no reasonable prospect that they will resume cohabitation, the spouse whose net family property is the lesser of the two net family properties is entitled to one-half the difference between them. R.S.O. 1990, c. F.3, s. 5 (1).

Death of spouse
(2) When a spouse dies, if the net family property of the deceased spouse exceeds the net family property of the surviving spouse, the surviving spouse is entitled to one-half the difference between them. R.S.O. 1990, c. F.3, s. 5 (2).

Improvident depletion of spouse's net family property
(3) When spouses are cohabiting, if there is a serious danger that one spouse may improvidently deplete his or her net family property, the other spouse may on an application under section 7 have the difference between the net family properties divided as if the spouses were separated and there were no reasonable prospect that they would resume cohabitation. R.S.O. 1990, c. F.3, s. 5 (3).

No further division

(4) After the court has made an order for division based on subsection (3), neither spouse may make a further application under section 7 in respect of their marriage. R.S.O. 1990, c. F.3, s. 5 (4).

Idem

(5) Subsection (4) applies even though the spouses continue to cohabit, unless a domestic contract between the spouses provides otherwise. R.S.O. 1990, c. F.3, s. 5 (5).

Variation of share

(6) The court may award a spouse an amount that is more or less than half the difference between the net family properties if the court is of the opinion that equalizing the net family properties would be unconscionable, having regard to,

(a) a spouse's failure to disclose to the other spouse debts or other liabilities existing at the date of the marriage;

(b) the fact that debts or other liabilities claimed in reduction of a spouse's net family property were incurred recklessly or in bad faith;

(c) the part of a spouse's net family property that consists of gifts made by the other spouse;

(d) a spouse's intentional or reckless depletion of his or her net family property;

(e) the fact that the amount a spouse would otherwise receive under subsection (1), (2) or (3) is disproportionately large in relation to a period of cohabitation that is less than five years;

(f) the fact that one spouse has incurred a disproportionately larger amount of debts or other liabilities than the other spouse for the support of the family;

(g) a written agreement between the spouses that is not a domestic contract; or

(h) any other circumstance relating to the acquisition, disposition, preservation, maintenance or improvement of property. R.S.O. 1990, c. F.3, s. 5 (6).

Purpose

(7) The purpose of this section is to recognize that child care, household management and financial provision are the joint responsibilities of the spouses and that inherent in the marital relationship there is equal con-

tribution, whether financial or otherwise, by the spouses to the assumption of these responsibilities, entitling each spouse to the equalization of the net family properties, subject only to the equitable considerations set out in subsection (6). R.S.O. 1990, c. F.3, s. 5 (7).

Election

Spouse's will

6. (1) When a spouse dies leaving a will, the surviving spouse shall elect to take under the will or to receive the entitlement under section 5. R.S.O. 1990, c. F.3, s. 6 (1).

Spouse's intestacy

(2) When a spouse dies intestate, the surviving spouse shall elect to receive the entitlement under Part II of the *Succession Law Reform Act* or to receive the entitlement under section 5. R.S.O. 1990, c. F.3, s. 6 (2).

Spouse's partial intestacy

(3) When a spouse dies testate as to some property and intestate as to other property, the surviving spouse shall elect to take under the will and to receive the entitlement under Part II of the *Succession Law Reform Act*, or to receive the entitlement under section 5. R.S.O. 1990, c. F.3, s. 6 (3).

Property outside estate

(4) A surviving spouse who elects to take under the will or to receive the entitlement under Part II of the *Succession Law Reform Act*, or both in the case of a partial intestacy, shall also receive the other property to which he or she is entitled because of the first spouse's death. R.S.O. 1990, c. F.3, s. 6 (4).

Gifts by will

(5) The surviving spouse shall receive the gifts made to him or her in the deceased spouse's will in addition to the entitlement under section 5 if the will expressly provides for that result. R.S.O. 1990, c. F.3, s. 6 (5).

Insurance, etc.

(6) Where a surviving spouse,

    (a) is the beneficiary,

        (i) of a policy of life insurance, as defined under the *Insurance Act*, that was taken out on the life of the deceased spouse and owned by the deceased spouse or was taken out on the lives of a group of which he or she was a member, or

(ii) of a lump sum payment provided under a pension or similar plan on the death of the deceased spouse; and

(b) elects or has elected to receive the entitlement under section 5, the payment under the policy or plan shall be credited against the surviving spouse's entitlement under section 5, unless a written designation by the deceased spouse provides that the surviving spouse shall receive payment under the policy or plan in addition to the entitlement under section 5. R.S.O. 1990, c. F.3, s. 6 (6); 2004, c. 31, Sched. 38, s. 2 (2).

Idem

(7) If a surviving spouse,

(a) elects or has elected to receive the entitlement under section 5; and

(b) receives payment under a life insurance policy or a lump sum payment provided under a pension or similar plan that is in excess of the entitlement under section 5,

and there is no written designation by the deceased spouse described in subsection (6), the deceased spouse's personal representative may recover the excess amount from the surviving spouse. R.S.O. 1990, c. F.3, s. 6 (7).

Effect of election to receive entitlement under s. 5

(8) When a surviving spouse elects to receive the entitlement under section 5, the gifts made to him or her in the deceased spouse's will are revoked and the will shall be interpreted as if the surviving spouse had died before the other, unless the will expressly provides that the gifts are in addition to the entitlement under section 5. R.S.O. 1990, c. F.3, s. 6 (8).

Idem

(9) When a surviving spouse elects to receive the entitlement under section 5, the spouse shall be deemed to have disclaimed the entitlement under Part II of the *Succession Law Reform Act.* R.S.O. 1990, c. F.3, s. 6 (9).

Manner of making election

(10) The surviving spouse's election shall be in the form prescribed by the regulations made under this Act and shall be filed in the office of the Estate Registrar for Ontario within six months after the first spouse's death. R.S.O. 1990, c. F.3, s. 6 (10).

Deemed election

(11) If the surviving spouse does not file the election within that time, he or she shall be deemed to have elected to take under the will or to receive the entitlement under the *Succession Law Reform Act*, or both, as the case may be, unless the court, on application, orders otherwise. R.S.O. 1990, c. F.3, s. 6 (11).

Priority of spouse's entitlement

(12) The spouse's entitlement under section 5 has priority over,

(a) the gifts made in the deceased spouse's will, if any, subject to subsection (13);

(b) a person's right to a share of the estate under Part II (Intestate Succession) of the *Succession Law Reform Act*;

(c) an order made against the estate under Part V (Support of Dependants) of the *Succession Law Reform Act*, except an order in favour of a child of the deceased spouse. R.S.O. 1990, c. F.3, s. 6 (12).

Exception

(13) The spouse's entitlement under section 5 does not have priority over a gift by will made in accordance with a contract that the deceased spouse entered into in good faith and for valuable consideration, except to the extent that the value of the gift, in the court's opinion, exceeds the consideration. R.S.O. 1990, c. F.3, s. 6 (13).

Distribution within six months of death restricted

(14) No distribution shall be made in the administration of a deceased spouse's estate within six months of the spouse's death, unless,

(a) the surviving spouse gives written consent to the distribution; or

(b) the court authorizes the distribution. R.S.O. 1990, c. F.3, s. 6 (14).

Idem, notice of application

(15) No distribution shall be made in the administration of a deceased spouse's death after the personal representative has received notice of an application under this Part, unless,

(a) the applicant gives written consent to the distribution; or

(b) the court authorizes the distribution. R.S.O. 1990, c. F.3, s. 6 (15).

Extension of limitation period

(16) If the court extends the time for a spouse's application based on subsection 5 (2), any property of the deceased spouse that is distributed before the date of the order and without notice of the application shall not be brought into the calculation of the deceased spouse's net family property. R.S.O. 1990, c. F.3, s. 6 (16).

Exception

(17) Subsections (14) and (15) do not prohibit reasonable advances to dependants of the deceased spouse for their support. R.S.O. 1990, c. F.3, s. 6 (17).

Definition

(18) In subsection (17),
"dependant" has the same meaning as in Part V of the *Succession Law Reform Act.* R.S.O. 1990, c. F.3, s. 6 (18).

Liability of personal representative

(19) If the personal representative makes a distribution that contravenes subsection (14) or (15), the court makes an order against the estate under this Part and the undistributed portion of the estate is not sufficient to satisfy the order, the personal representative is personally liable to the applicant for the amount that was distributed or the amount that is required to satisfy the order, whichever is less. R.S.O. 1990, c. F.3, s. 6 (19).

Order suspending administration

(20) On motion by the surviving spouse, the court may make an order suspending the administration of the deceased spouse's estate for the time and to the extent that the court decides. R.S.O. 1990, c. F.3, s. 6 (20).

Application to court

7. (1) The court may, on the application of a spouse, former spouse or deceased spouse's personal representative, determine any matter respecting the spouses' entitlement under section 5. R.S.O. 1990, c. F.3, s. 7 (1).

Personal action; estates

(2) Entitlement under subsections 5 (1), (2) and (3) is personal as between the spouses but,

(a) an application based on subsection 5 (1) or (3) and commenced before a spouse's death may be continued by or against the deceased spouse's estate; and

(b) an application based on subsection 5 (2) may be made by or against a deceased spouse's estate. R.S.O. 1990, c. F.3, s. 7 (2).

Limitation

(3) An application based on subsection 5 (1) or (2) shall not be brought after the earliest of,

(a) two years after the day the marriage is terminated by divorce or judgment of nullity;

(b) six years after the day the spouses separate and there is no reasonable prospect that they will resume cohabitation;

(c) six months after the first spouse's death. R.S.O. 1990, c. F.3, s. 7 (3).

Statement of property

8. In an application under section 7, each party shall serve on the other and file with the court, in the manner and form prescribed by the rules of the court, a statement verified by oath or statutory declaration disclosing particulars of,

(a) the party's property and debts and other liabilities,

   (i)   as of the date of the marriage,

   (ii) as of the valuation date, and

   (iii) as of the date of the statement;

(b) the deductions that the party claims under the definition of "net family property";

(c) the exclusions that the party claims under subsection 4 (2); and

(d) all property that the party disposed of during the two years immediately preceding the making of the statement, or during the marriage, whichever period is shorter. R.S.O. 1990, c. F.3, s. 8.

Powers of court

9. (1) In an application under section 7, the court may order,

(a) that one spouse pay to the other spouse the amount to which the court finds that spouse to be entitled under this Part;

(b) that security, including a charge on property, be given for the performance of an obligation imposed by the order;

(c) that, if necessary to avoid hardship, an amount referred to in clause (a) be paid in instalments during a period not exceeding ten years or that payment of all or part of the amount be delayed for a period not exceeding ten years; and

(d) that, if appropriate to satisfy an obligation imposed by the order,

    (i) property be transferred to or in trust for or vested in a spouse, whether absolutely, for life or for a term of years, or

    (ii) any property be partitioned or sold. R.S.O. 1990, c. F.3, s. 9 (1).

Financial information, inspections

(2) The court may, at the time of making an order for instalment or delayed payments or on motion at a later time, order that the spouse who has the obligation to make payments shall,

(a) furnish the other spouse with specified financial information, which may include periodic financial statements; and

(b) permit inspections of specified property of the spouse by or on behalf of the other spouse, as the court directs. R.S.O. 1990, c. F.3, s. 9 (2).

Variation

(3) If the court is satisfied that there has been a material change in the circumstances of the spouse who has the obligation to make instalment or delayed payments, the court may, on motion, vary the order, but shall not vary the amount to which the court found the spouse to be entitled under this Part. R.S.O. 1990, c. F.3, s. 9 (3).

Ten-year period

(4) Subsections (3) and 2 (8) (extension of times) do not permit the postponement of payment beyond the ten-year period mentioned in clause (1) (c). R.S.O. 1990, c. F.3, s. 9 (4).

Determination of questions of title between spouses

10. (1) A person may apply to the court for the determination of a question between that person and his or her spouse or former spouse as to the ownership or right to possession of particular property, other than a question arising out of an equalization of net family properties under section 5, and the court may,

   (a) declare the ownership or right to possession;

   (b) if the property has been disposed of, order payment in compensation for the interest of either party;

   (c) order that the property be partitioned or sold for the purpose of realizing the interests in it; and

   (d) order that either or both spouses give security, including a charge on property, for the performance of an obligation imposed by the order,

and may make ancillary orders or give ancillary directions. R.S.O. 1990, c. F.3, s. 10 (1).

Estates

   (2) An application based on subsection (1) may be made by or continued against the estate of a deceased spouse. R.S.O. 1990, c. F.3, s. 10 (2).

Operating business or farm

   11. (1) An order made under section 9 or 10 shall not be made so as to require or result in the sale of an operating business or farm or so as to seriously impair its operation, unless there is no reasonable alternative method of satisfying the award. R.S.O. 1990, c. F.3, s. 11 (1).

Idem

   (2) To comply with subsection (1), the court may,

   (a) order that one spouse pay to the other a share of the profits from the business or farm; and

   (b) if the business or farm is incorporated, order that one spouse transfer or have the corporation issue to the other shares in the corporation. R.S.O. 1990, c. F.3, s. 11 (2).

Orders for preservation

   12. In an application under section 7 or 10, if the court considers it necessary for the protection of the other spouse's interests under this Part, the court may make an interim or final order,

   (a) restraining the depletion of a spouse's property; and

   (b) for the possession, delivering up, safekeeping and preservation of the property. R.S.O. 1990, c. F.3, s. 12.

Variation and realization of security

13. If the court has ordered security or charged a property with security for the performance of an obligation under this Part, the court may, on motion,

(a) vary or discharge the order; or

(b) on notice to all persons having an interest in the property, direct its sale for the purpose of realizing the security or charge. R.S.O. 1990, c. F.3, s. 13.

Presumptions

14. The rule of law applying a presumption of a resulting trust shall be applied in questions of the ownership of property between spouses, as if they were not married, except that,

(a) the fact that property is held in the name of spouses as joint tenants is proof, in the absence of evidence to the contrary, that the spouses are intended to own the property as joint tenants; and

(b) money on deposit in the name of both spouses shall be deemed to be in the name of the spouses as joint tenants for the purposes of clause (a). R.S.O. 1990, c. F.3, s. 14; 2005, c. 5, s. 27 (3).

Conflict of laws

15. The property rights of spouses arising out of the marital relationship are governed by the internal law of the place where both spouses had their last common habitual residence or, if there is no place where the spouses had a common habitual residence, by the law of Ontario. R.S.O. 1990, c. F.3, s. 15.

Application of Part

16. (1) This Part applies to property owned by spouses,

(a) whether they were married before or after the 1st day of March, 1986; and

(b) whether the property was acquired before or after that day. R.S.O. 1990, c. F.3, s. 16 (1).

Application of s. 14

(2) Section 14 applies whether the event giving rise to the presumption occurred before or after the 1st day of March, 1986. R.S.O. 1990, c. F.3, s. 16 (2).

PART II
MATRIMONIAL HOME

Definitions

17. In this Part,

"court" means a court as defined in subsection 1 (1) but does not include the Ontario Court of Justice; ("tribunal")

"property" means real or personal property. ("bien") R.S.O. 1990, c. F.3, s. 17; 2006, c. 19, Sched. C, s. 1 (2).

Matrimonial home

18. (1) Every property in which a person has an interest and that is or, if the spouses have separated, was at the time of separation ordinarily occupied by the person and his or her spouse as their family residence is their matrimonial home. R.S.O. 1990, c. F.3, s. 18 (1).

Ownership of shares

(2) The ownership of a share or shares, or of an interest in a share or shares, of a corporation entitling the owner to occupy a housing unit owned by the corporation shall be deemed to be an interest in the unit for the purposes of subsection (1). R.S.O. 1990, c. F.3, s. 18 (2).

Residence on farmland, etc.

(3) If property that includes a matrimonial home is normally used for a purpose other than residential, the matrimonial home is only the part of the property that may reasonably be regarded as necessary to the use and enjoyment of the residence. R.S.O. 1990, c. F.3, s. 18 (3).

Possession of matrimonial home

19. (1) Both spouses have an equal right to possession of a matrimonial home. R.S.O. 1990, c. F.3, s. 19 (1).

Idem

(2) When only one of the spouses has an interest in a matrimonial home, the other spouse's right of possession,

    (a) is personal as against the first spouse; and

    (b) ends when they cease to be spouses, unless a separation agreement or court order provides otherwise. R.S.O. 1990, c. F.3, s. 19 (2).

Designation of matrimonial home

20. (1) One or both spouses may designate property owned by one or both of them as a matrimonial home, in the form prescribed by the regulations made under this Act. R.S.O. 1990, c. F.3, s. 20 (1).

Contiguous property

(2) The designation may include property that is described in the designation and is contiguous to the matrimonial home. R.S.O. 1990, c. F.3, s. 20 (2).

Registration

(3) The designation may be registered in the proper land registry office. R.S.O. 1990, c. F.3, s. 20 (3).

Effect of designation by both spouses

(4) On the registration of a designation made by both spouses, any other property that is a matrimonial home under section 18 but is not designated by both spouses ceases to be a matrimonial home. R.S.O. 1990, c. F.3, s. 20 (4).

Effect of designation by one spouse

(5) On the registration of a designation made by one spouse only, any other property that is a matrimonial home under section 18 remains a matrimonial home. R.S.O. 1990, c. F.3, s. 20 (5).

Cancellation of designation

(6) The designation of a matrimonial home is cancelled, and the property ceases to be a matrimonial home, on the registration or deposit of,

(a) a cancellation, executed by the person or persons who made the original designation, in the form prescribed by the regulations made under this Act;

(b) a decree absolute of divorce or judgment of nullity;

(c) an order under clause 23 (e) cancelling the designation; or

(d) proof of death of one of the spouses. R.S.O. 1990, c. F.3, s. 20 (6).

Revival of other matrimonial homes

(7) When a designation of a matrimonial home made by both spouses is cancelled, section 18 applies again in respect of other property that is a matrimonial home. R.S.O. 1990, c. F.3, s. 20 (7).

Alienation of matrimonial home

21. (1) No spouse shall dispose of or encumber an interest in a matrimonial home unless,

(a) the other spouse joins in the instrument or consents to the transaction;

(b) the other spouse has released all rights under this Part by a separation agreement;

(c) a court order has authorized the transaction or has released the property from the application of this Part; or

(d) the property is not designated by both spouses as a matrimonial home and a designation of another property as a matrimonial home, made by both spouses, is registered and not cancelled. R.S.O. 1990, c. F.3, s. 21 (1).

Setting aside transaction

(2) If a spouse disposes of or encumbers an interest in a matrimonial home in contravention of subsection (1), the transaction may be set aside on an application under section 23, unless the person holding the interest or encumbrance at the time of the application acquired it for value, in good faith and without notice, at the time of acquiring it or making an agreement to acquire it, that the property was a matrimonial home. R.S.O. 1990, c. F.3, s. 21 (2).

Proof that property not a matrimonial home

(3) For the purpose of subsection (2), a statement by the person making the disposition or encumbrance,

(a) verifying that he or she is not, or was not, a spouse at the time of the disposition or encumbrance;

(b) verifying that the person is a spouse who is not separated from his or her spouse and that the property is not ordinarily occupied by the spouses as their family residence;

(c) verifying that the person is a spouse who is separated from his or her spouse and that the property was not ordinarily occupied by the spouses, at the time of their separation, as their family residence;

(d) where the property is not designated by both spouses as a matrimonial home, verifying that a designation of another property as a matrimonial home, made by both spouses, is registered and not cancelled; or

(e) verifying that the other spouse has released all rights under this Part by a separation agreement,

shall, unless the person to whom the disposition or encumbrance is made had notice to the contrary, be deemed to be sufficient proof that the property is not a matrimonial home. R.S.O. 1990, c. F.3, s. 21 (3).

Idem, attorney's personal knowledge

(4) The statement shall be deemed to be sufficient proof that the property is not a matrimonial home if it is made by the attorney of the person making the disposition or encumbrance, on the basis of the attorney's personal knowledge. R.S.O. 1990, c. F.3, s. 21 (4).

Liens arising by operation of law

(5) This section does not apply to the acquisition of an interest in property by operation of law or to the acquisition of a lien under section 48 of the *Legal Aid Services Act, 1998.* R.S.O. 1990, c. F.3, s. 21 (5); 1998, c. 26, s. 102.

Right of redemption and to notice

22. (1) When a person proceeds to realize upon a lien, encumbrance or execution or exercises a forfeiture against property that is a matrimonial home, the spouse who has a right of possession under section 19 has the same right of redemption or relief against forfeiture as the other spouse and is entitled to the same notice respecting the claim and its enforcement or realization. R.S.O. 1990, c. F.3, s. 22 (1).

Service of notice

(2) A notice to which a spouse is entitled under subsection (1) shall be deemed to be sufficiently given if served or given personally or by registered mail addressed to the spouse at his or her usual or last known address or, if none, the address of the matrimonial home, and, if notice is served or given by mail, the service shall be deemed to have been made on the fifth day after the day of mailing. R.S.O. 1990, c. F.3, s. 22 (2).

Idem: power of sale

(3) When a person exercises a power of sale against property that is a matrimonial home, sections 33 and 34 of the *Mortgages Act* apply and subsection (2) does not apply. R.S.O. 1990, c. F.3, s. 22 (3); 1993, c. 27, Sched.

Payments by spouse

(4) If a spouse makes a payment in exercise of the right conferred by subsection (1), the payment shall be applied in satisfaction of the claim giving rise to the lien, encumbrance, execution or forfeiture. R.S.O. 1990, c. F.3, s. 22 (4).

Realization may continue in spouse's absence

(5) Despite any other Act, when a person who proceeds to realize upon a lien, encumbrance or execution or exercises a forfeiture does not have sufficient particulars of a spouse for the purpose and there is no response to a notice given under subsection (2) or under section 33 of the *Mortgages Act*, the realization or exercise of forfeiture may continue in the absence and without regard to the interest of the spouse and the spouse's rights under this section end on the completion of the realization or forfeiture. R.S.O. 1990, c. F.3, s. 22 (5); 1993, c. 27, Sched.

Powers of court respecting alienation

23. The court may, on the application of a spouse or person having an interest in property, by order,

- (a) determine whether or not the property is a matrimonial home and, if so, its extent;
- (b) authorize the disposition or encumbrance of the matrimonial home if the court finds that the spouse whose consent is required,
  - (i) cannot be found or is not available,
  - (ii) is not capable of giving or withholding consent, or
  - (iii) is unreasonably withholding consent,

  subject to any conditions, including provision of other comparable accommodation or payment in place of it, that the court considers appropriate;
- (c) dispense with a notice required to be given under section 22;
- (d) direct the setting aside of a transaction disposing of or encumbering an interest in the matrimonial home contrary to subsection 21 (1) and the revesting of the interest or any part of it on the conditions that the court considers appropriate; and
- (e) cancel a designation made under section 20 if the property is not a matrimonial home. R.S.O. 1990, c. F.3, s. 23.

Order for possession of matrimonial home

24. (1) Regardless of the ownership of a matrimonial home and its contents, and despite section 19 (spouse's right of possession), the court may on application, by order,

    (a) provide for the delivering up, safekeeping and preservation of the matrimonial home and its contents;

    (b) direct that one spouse be given exclusive possession of the matrimonial home or part of it for the period that the court directs and release other property that is a matrimonial home from the application of this Part;

    (c) direct a spouse to whom exclusive possession of the matrimonial home is given to make periodic payments to the other spouse;

    (d) direct that the contents of the matrimonial home, or any part of them,

        (i) remain in the home for the use of the spouse given possession, or

        (ii) be removed from the home for the use of a spouse or child;

    (e) order a spouse to pay for all or part of the repair and maintenance of the matrimonial home and of other liabilities arising in respect of it, or to make periodic payments to the other spouse for those purposes;

    (f) authorize the disposition or encumbrance of a spouse's interest in the matrimonial home, subject to the other spouse's right of exclusive possession as ordered; and

    (g) where a false statement is made under subsection 21 (3), direct,

        (i) the person who made the false statement, or

        (ii) a person who knew at the time he or she acquired an interest in the property that the statement was false and afterwards conveyed the interest,

    to substitute other real property for the matrimonial home, or direct the person to set aside money or security to stand in place of it, subject to any conditions that the court considers appropriate. R.S.O. 1990, c. F.3, s. 24 (1).

Temporary or interim order

(2) The court may, on motion, make a temporary or interim order under clause (1) (a), (b), (c), (d) or (e). R.S.O. 1990, c. F.3, s. 24 (2).

Order for exclusive possession: criteria

(3) In determining whether to make an order for exclusive possession, the court shall consider,

    (a) the best interests of the children affected;

    (b) any existing orders under Part I (Family Property) and any existing support orders;

    (c) the financial position of both spouses;

    (d) any written agreement between the parties;

    (e) the availability of other suitable and affordable accommodation; and

    (f) any violence committed by a spouse against the other spouse or the children. R.S.O. 1990, c. F.3, s. 24 (3).

Best interests of child

(4) In determining the best interests of a child, the court shall consider,

    (a) the possible disruptive effects on the child of a move to other accommodation; and

    (b) the child's views and preferences, if they can reasonably be ascertained. R.S.O. 1990, c. F.3, s. 24 (4).

Offence

(5) A person who contravenes an order for exclusive possession is guilty of an offence and upon conviction is liable,

    (a) in the case of a first offence, to a fine of not more than $5,000 or to imprisonment for a term of not more than three months, or to both; and

    (b) in the case of a second or subsequent offence, to a fine of not more than $10,000 or to imprisonment for a term of not more than two years, or to both. R.S.O. 1990, c. F.3, s. 24 (5).

Arrest without warrant

(6) A police officer may arrest without warrant a person the police officer believes on reasonable and probable grounds to have contravened an order for exclusive possession. R.S.O. 1990, c. F.3, s. 24 (6).

Existing orders

(7) Subsections (5) and (6) also apply in respect of contraventions, committed on or after the 1st day of March, 1986, of orders for exclusive possession made under Part III of the *Family Law Reform Act*, being

chapter 152 of the Revised Statutes of Ontario, 1980. R.S.O. 1990, c. F.3, s. 24 (7).

Variation

Possessory order

25. (1) On the application of a person named in an order made under clause 24 (1) (a), (b), (c), (d) or (e) or his or her personal representative, if the court is satisfied that there has been a material change in circumstances, the court may discharge, vary or suspend the order. R.S.O. 1990, c. F.3, s. 25 (1).

Conditions

(2) On the motion of a person who is subject to conditions imposed in an order made under clause 23 (b) or (d) or 24 (1) (g), or his or her personal representative, if the court is satisfied that the conditions are no longer appropriate, the court may discharge, vary or suspend them. R.S.O. 1990, c. F.3, s. 25 (2).

Existing orders

(3) Subsections (1) and (2) also apply to orders made under the corresponding provisions of Part III of the *Family Law Reform Act*, being chapter 152 of the Revised Statutes of Ontario, 1980. R.S.O. 1990, c. F.3, s. 25 (3).

Spouse Without Interest in Matrimonial Home

Joint tenancy with third person

26. (1) If a spouse dies owning an interest in a matrimonial home as a joint tenant with a third person and not with the other spouse, the joint tenancy shall be deemed to have been severed immediately before the time of death. R.S.O. 1990, c. F.3, s. 26 (1).

Sixty-day period after spouse's death

(2) Despite clauses 19 (2) (a) and (b) (termination of spouse's right of possession), a spouse who has no interest in a matrimonial home but is occupying it at the time of the other spouse's death, whether under an order for exclusive possession or otherwise, is entitled to retain possession against the spouse's estate, rent free, for sixty days after the spouse's death. R.S.O. 1990, c. F.3, s. 26 (2).

Registration of order

27. Orders made under this Part or under Part III of the *Family Law Reform Act*, being chapter 152 of the Revised Statutes of Ontario, 1980 are registrable against land under the *Registry Act* and the *Land Titles Act*. R.S.O. 1990, c. F.3, s. 27.

Application of Part

28. (1) This Part applies to matrimonial homes that are situated in Ontario. R.S.O. 1990, c. F.3, s. 28 (1).

Idem

(2) This Part applies,

(a) whether the spouses were married before or after the 1st day of March, 1986; and

(b) whether the matrimonial home was acquired before or after that day. R.S.O. 1990, c. F.3, s. 28 (2).

PART III
SUPPORT OBLIGATIONS

Definitions

29. In this Part,

"dependant" means a person to whom another has an obligation to provide support under this Part; ("personne à charge")

"spouse" means a spouse as defined in subsection 1 (1), and in addition includes either of two persons who are not married to each other and have cohabited,

(a) continuously for a period of not less than three years, or

(b) in a relationship of some permanence, if they are the natural or adoptive parents of a child. ("conjoint") R.S.O. 1990, c. F.3, s. 29; 1999, c. 6, s. 25 (2); 2005, c. 5, s. 27 (4–6).

Obligation of spouses for support

30. Every spouse has an obligation to provide support for himself or herself and for the other spouse, in accordance with need, to the extent that he or she is capable of doing so. R.S.O. 1990, c. F.3, s. 30; 1999, c. 6, s. 25 (3); 2005, c. 5, s. 27 (7).

Obligation of parent to support child

31. (1) Every parent has an obligation to provide support for his or her unmarried child who is a minor or is enrolled in a full time program of education, to the extent that the parent is capable of doing so. R.S.O. 1990, c. F.3, s. 31 (1); 1997, c. 20, s. 2.

Idem

(2) The obligation under subsection (1) does not extend to a child who is sixteen years of age or older and has withdrawn from parental control. R.S.O. 1990, c. F.3, s. 31 (2).

Obligation of child to support parent

32. Every child who is not a minor has an obligation to provide support, in accordance with need, for his or her parent who has cared for or provided support for the child, to the extent that the child is capable of doing so. R.S.O. 1990, c. F.3, s. 32.

Order for support

33. (1) A court may, on application, order a person to provide support for his or her dependants and determine the amount of support. R.S.O. 1990, c. F.3, s. 33 (1).

Applicants

(2) An application for an order for the support of a dependant may be made by the dependant or the dependant's parent. R.S.O. 1990, c. F.3, s. 33 (2).

Same

(2.1) The *Limitations Act, 2002* applies to an application made by the dependant's parent or by an agency referred to in subsection (3) as if it were made by the dependant himself or herself. 2002, c. 24, Sched. B, s. 37.

Same

(3) An application for an order for the support of a dependant who is the respondent's spouse or child may also be made by one of the following agencies,

(a) the Ministry of Community and Social Services in the name of the Minister;

(b) a municipality, excluding a lower-tier municipality in a regional municipality;

(c) a district social services administration board under the *District Social Services Administration Boards Act*;

(d) REPEALED: 2006, c. 19, Sched. B, s. 9.

(e) a delivery agent under the *Ontario Works Act, 1997,*

if the agency is providing or has provided a benefit under the *Family Benefits Act*, assistance under the *General Welfare Assistance Act* or the *Ontario Works Act, 1997* or income support under the *Ontario Disability Support Program Act, 1997* in respect of the dependant's support, or if an application for such a benefit or assistance has been made to the agency by or on behalf of the dependant. 1997, c. 25, Sched. E, s. 1; 1999, c. 6, s. 25 (4); 2002, c. 17, Sched. F, Table; 2005, c. 5, s. 27 (8); 2006, c. 19, Sched. B, s. 9.

Setting aside domestic contract

(4) The court may set aside a provision for support or a waiver of the right to support in a domestic contract and may determine and order support in an application under subsection (1) although the contract contains an express provision excluding the application of this section,

(a) if the provision for support or the waiver of the right to support results in unconscionable circumstances;

(b) if the provision for support is in favour of or the waiver is by or on behalf of a dependant who qualifies for an allowance for support out of public money; or

(c) if there is default in the payment of support under the contract at the time the application is made. R.S.O. 1990, c. F.3, s. 33 (4); 2006, c. 1, s. 5 (1).

Adding party

(5) In an application the court may, on a respondent's motion, add as a party another person who may have an obligation to provide support to the same dependant. R.S.O. 1990, c. F.3, s. 33 (5).

Idem

(6) In an action in the Superior Court of Justice, the defendant may add as a third party another person who may have an obligation to provide support to the same dependant. R.S.O. 1990, c. F.3, s. 33 (6); 2006, c. 19, Sched. C, s. 1 (1).

Purposes of order for support of child

(7) An order for the support of a child should,

(a) recognize that each parent has an obligation to provide support for the child;

(b) apportion the obligation according to the child support guidelines. R.S.O. 1990, c. F.3, s. 33 (7); 1997, c. 20, s. 3 (1).

Purposes of order for support of spouse

(8) An order for the support of a spouse should,

(a) recognize the spouse's contribution to the relationship and the economic consequences of the relationship for the spouse;

(b) share the economic burden of child support equitably;

(c) make fair provision to assist the spouse to become able to contribute to his or her own support; and

(d) relieve financial hardship, if this has not been done by orders under Parts I (Family Property) and II (Matrimonial Home). R.S.O. 1990, c. F.3, s. 33 (8); 1999, c. 6, s. 25 (5); 2005, c. 5, s. 27 (9).

Determination of amount for support of spouses, parents

(9) In determining the amount and duration, if any, of support for a spouse or parent in relation to need, the court shall consider all the circumstances of the parties, including,

(a) the dependant's and respondent's current assets and means;

(b) the assets and means that the dependant and respondent are likely to have in the future;

(c) the dependant's capacity to contribute to his or her own support;

(d) the respondent's capacity to provide support;

(e) the dependant's and respondent's age and physical and mental health;

(f) the dependant's needs, in determining which the court shall have regard to the accustomed standard of living while the parties resided together;

(g) the measures available for the dependant to become able to provide for his or her own support and the length of time and cost involved to enable the dependant to take those measures;

(h) any legal obligation of the respondent or dependant to provide support for another person;

(i)   the desirability of the dependant or respondent remaining at home to care for a child;

(j)   a contribution by the dependant to the realization of the respondent's career potential;

(k)   REPEALED: 1997, c. 20, s. 3 (3).

(l)   if the dependant is a spouse,

    (i)   the length of time the dependant and respondent cohabited,

    (ii)   the effect on the spouse's earning capacity of the responsibilities assumed during cohabitation,

    (iii) whether the spouse has undertaken the care of a child who is of the age of eighteen years or over and unable by reason of illness, disability or other cause to withdraw from the charge of his or her parents,

    (iv)   whether the spouse has undertaken to assist in the continuation of a program of education for a child eighteen years of age or over who is unable for that reason to withdraw from the charge of his or her parents,

    (v)   any housekeeping, child care or other domestic service performed by the spouse for the family, as if the spouse were devoting the time spent in performing that service in remunerative employment and were contributing the earnings to the family's support,

    (v.1) REPEALED: 2005, c. 5, s. 27 (12).

    (vi)   the effect on the spouse's earnings and career development of the responsibility of caring for a child; and

(m)   any other legal right of the dependant to support, other than out of public money. R.S.O. 1990, c. F.3, s. 33 (9); 1997, c. 20, s. 3 (2, 3); 1999, c. 6, s. 25 (6–9); 2005, c. 5, s. 27 (10–13).

Conduct

(10) The obligation to provide support for a spouse exists without regard to the conduct of either spouse, but the court may in determining the amount of support have regard to a course of conduct that is so unconscionable as to constitute an obvious and gross repudiation of the relationship. R.S.O. 1990, c. F.3, s. 33 (10); 1999, c. 6, s. 25 (10); 2005, c. 5, s. 27 (14).

Application of child support guidelines

(11) A court making an order for the support of a child shall do so in accordance with the child support guidelines. 1997, c. 20, s. 3 (4).

Exception: special provisions

(12) Despite subsection (11), a court may award an amount that is different from the amount that would be determined in accordance with the child support guidelines if the court is satisfied,

    (a) that special provisions in an order or a written agreement respecting the financial obligations of the parents, or the division or transfer of their property, directly or indirectly benefit a child, or that special provisions have otherwise been made for the benefit of a child; and

    (b) that the application of the child support guidelines would result in an amount of child support that is inequitable given those special provisions. 1997, c. 20, s. 3 (4).

Reasons

(13) Where the court awards, under subsection (12), an amount that is different from the amount that would be determined in accordance with the child support guidelines, the court shall record its reasons for doing so. 1997, c. 20, s. 3 (4).

Exception: consent orders

(14) Despite subsection (11), a court may award an amount that is different from the amount that would be determined in accordance with the child support guidelines on the consent of both parents if the court is satisfied that,

    (a) reasonable arrangements have been made for the support of the child to whom the order relates; and

    (b) where support for the child is payable out of public money, the arrangements do not provide for an amount less than the amount that would be determined in accordance with the child support guidelines. 1997, c. 20, s. 3 (4).

Reasonable arrangements

(15) For the purposes of clause (14) (a), in determining whether reasonable arrangements have been made for the support of a child,

    (a) the court shall have regard to the child support guidelines; and

(b) the court shall not consider the arrangements to be unreasonable solely because the amount of support agreed to is not the
same as the amount that would otherwise have been determined in accordance with the child support guidelines. 1997, c.
20, s. 3 (4).

Powers of court

34. (1) In an application under section 33, the court may make an
interim or final order,

(a) requiring that an amount be paid periodically, whether annually or otherwise and whether for an indefinite or limited period, or until the happening of a specified event;

(b) requiring that a lump sum be paid or held in trust;

(c) requiring that property be transferred to or in trust for or vested
in the dependant, whether absolutely, for life or for a term of
years;

(d) respecting any matter authorized to be ordered under clause 24
(1) (a), (b), (c), (d) or (e) (matrimonial home);

(e) requiring that some or all of the money payable under the order
be paid into court or to another appropriate person or agency
for the dependant's benefit;

(f) requiring that support be paid in respect of any period before
the date of the order;

(g) requiring payment to an agency referred to in subsection 33 (3)
of an amount in reimbursement for a benefit or assistance referred to in that subsection, including a benefit or assistance
provided before the date of the order;

(h) requiring payment of expenses in respect of a child's prenatal
care and birth;

(i) requiring that a spouse who has a policy of life insurance as
defined under the *Insurance Act* designate the other spouse or a
child as the beneficiary irrevocably;

(j) requiring that a spouse who has an interest in a pension plan or
other benefit plan designate the other spouse or a child as beneficiary under the plan and not change that designation; and

(k) requiring the securing of payment under the order, by a charge
on property or otherwise. R.S.O. 1990, c. F.3, s. 34 (1); 1999, c. 6,
s. 25 (11); 2004, c. 31, Sched. 38, s. 2 (3); 2005, c. 5, s. 27 (15).

Limitation on jurisdiction of Ontario Court of Justice

(2) The Ontario Court of Justice shall not make an order under clause (1) (b), (c), (i), (j) or (k) except for the provision of necessities or to prevent the dependant from becoming or continuing to be a public charge, and shall not make an order under clause (d). R.S.O. 1990, c. F.3, s. 34 (2); 2006, c. 19, Sched. C, s. 1 (2).

Assignment of support

(3) An order for support may be assigned to an agency referred to in subsection 33 (3). R.S.O. 1990, c. F.3, s. 34 (3).

Same

(3.1) An agency referred to in subsection 33 (3) to whom an order for support is assigned is entitled to the payments due under the order and has the same right to be notified of and to participate in proceedings under this Act to vary, rescind, suspend or enforce the order as the person who would otherwise be entitled to the payments. 1997, c. 20, s. 4 (1).

Support order binds estate

(4) An order for support binds the estate of the person having the support obligation unless the order provides otherwise. R.S.O. 1990, c. F.3, s. 34 (4).

Indexing of support payments

(5) In an order made under clause (1) (a), other than an order for the support of a child, the court may provide that the amount payable shall be increased annually on the order's anniversary date by the indexing factor, as defined in subsection (6), for November of the previous year. R.S.O. 1990, c. F.3, s. 34 (5); 1997, c. 20, s. 4 (2).

Definition

(6) The indexing factor for a given month is the percentage change in the Consumer Price Index for Canada for prices of all items since the same month of the previous year, as published by Statistics Canada. R.S.O. 1990, c. F.3, s. 34 (6).

Domestic contract, etc., may be filed with court

35. (1) A person who is a party to a domestic contract may file the contract with the clerk of the Ontario Court of Justice or of the Family Court of the Superior Court of Justice together with the person's affidavit stating that the contract is in effect and has not been set aside or varied by a court or agreement. R.S.O. 1990, c. F.3, s. 35 (1); 2006, c. 1, s. 5 (2); 2006, c. 19, Sched. C, s. 1 (2, 4).

Effect of filing

(2) A provision for support or maintenance contained in a contract that is filed in this manner,

    (a) may be enforced;

    (b) may be varied under section 37; and

    (c) except in the case of a provision for the support of a child, may be increased under section 38,

as if it were an order of the court where it is filed. 1997, c. 20, s. 5; 2006, c. 1, s. 5 (3).

Setting aside available

(3) Subsection 33 (4) (setting aside in unconscionable circumstances, etc.) applies to a contract that is filed in this manner. R.S.O. 1990, c. F.3, s. 35 (3); 2006, c. 1, s. 5 (4).

Enforcement available despite waiver

(4) Subsection (1) and clause (2) (a) apply despite an agreement to the contrary. R.S.O. 1990, c. F.3, s. 35 (4).

Existing contracts, etc.

(5) Subsections (1) and (2) also apply to contracts made before the 1st day of March, 1986. R.S.O. 1990, c. F.3, s. 35 (5); 2006, c. 1, s. 5 (5).

Existing arrears

(6) Clause (2) (a) also applies to arrears accrued before the 1st day of March, 1986. R.S.O. 1990, c. F.3, s. 35 (6).

Effect of divorce proceeding

36. (1) When a divorce proceeding is commenced under the *Divorce Act* (Canada), an application for support under this Part that has not been adjudicated is stayed, unless the court orders otherwise. R.S.O. 1990, c. F.3, s. 36 (1).

Arrears may be included in order

(2) The court that deals with a divorce proceeding under the *Divorce Act* (Canada) may determine the amount of arrears owing under an or-

der for support made under this Part and make an order respecting that amount at the same time as it makes an order under the *Divorce Act* (Canada). R.S.O. 1990, c. F.3, s. 36 (2).

Idem

(3) If a marriage is terminated by divorce or judgment of nullity and the question of support is not adjudicated in the divorce or nullity proceedings, an order for support made under this Part continues in force according to its terms. R.S.O. 1990, c. F.3, s. 36 (3).

Application for variation

37. (1) An application to the court for variation of an order made or confirmed under this Part may be made by,

  (a) a dependant or respondent named in the order;
  (b) a parent of a dependant referred to in clause (a);
  (c) the personal representative of a respondent referred to in clause (a); or
  (d) an agency referred to in subsection 33 (3). 1997, c. 20, s. 6.

Powers of court: spouse and parent support

(2) In the case of an order for support of a spouse or parent, if the court is satisfied that there has been a material change in the dependant's or respondent's circumstances or that evidence not available on the previous hearing has become available, the court may,

  (a) discharge, vary or suspend a term of the order, prospectively or retroactively;
  (b) relieve the respondent from the payment of part or all of the arrears or any interest due on them; and
  (c) make any other order under section 34 that the court considers appropriate in the circumstances referred to in section 33. 1997, c. 20, s. 6; 1999, c. 6, s. 25 (12); 2005, c. 5, s. 27 (16).

Powers of court: child support

(2.1) In the case of an order for support of a child, if the court is satisfied that there has been a change in circumstances within the meaning of the child support guidelines or that evidence not available on the previous hearing has become available, the court may,

  (a) discharge, vary or suspend a term of the order, prospectively or retroactively;

(b) relieve the respondent from the payment of part or all of the arrears or any interest due on them; and

(c) make any other order for the support of a child that the court could make on an application under section 33. 1997, c. 20, s. 6.

Application of child support guidelines

(2.2) A court making an order under subsection (2.1) shall do so in accordance with the child support guidelines. 1997, c. 20, s. 6.

Exception: special provisions

(2.3) Despite subsection (2.2), a court may award an amount that is different from the amount that would be determined in accordance with the child support guidelines if the court is satisfied,

(a) that special provisions in an order or a written agreement respecting the financial obligations of the parents, or the division or transfer of their property, directly or indirectly benefit a child, or that special provisions have otherwise been made for the benefit of a child; and

(b) that the application of the child support guidelines would result in an amount of child support that is inequitable given those special provisions. 1997, c. 20, s. 6.

Reasons

(2.4) Where the court awards, under subsection (2.3), an amount that is different from the amount that would be determined in accordance with the child support guidelines, the court shall record its reasons for doing so. 1997, c. 20, s. 6.

Exception: consent orders

(2.5) Despite subsection (2.2), a court may award an amount that is different from the amount that would be determined in accordance with the child support guidelines on the consent of both parents if the court is satisfied that,

(a) reasonable arrangements have been made for the support of the child to whom the order relates; and

(b) where support for the child is payable out of public money, the arrangements do not provide for an amount less than the amount that would be determined in accordance with the child support guidelines. 1997, c. 20, s. 6.

Reasonable arrangements

(2.6) For the purposes of clause (2.5) (a), in determining whether reasonable arrangements have been made for the support of a child,

(a) the court shall have regard to the child support guidelines; and

(b) the court shall not consider the arrangements to be unreasonable solely because the amount of support agreed to is not the same as the amount that would otherwise have been determined in accordance with the child support guidelines. 1997, c. 20, s. 6.

Limitation on applications for variation

(3) No application for variation shall be made within six months after the making of the order for support or the disposition of another application for variation in respect of the same order, except by leave of the court. R.S.O. 1990, c. F.3, s. 37 (3).

Indexing Existing Orders

Non-application to orders for child support

38. (1) This section does not apply to an order for the support of a child. 1997, c. 20, s. 7.

Application to have existing order indexed

(2) If an order made or confirmed under this Part is not indexed under subsection 34 (5), the dependant, or an agency referred to in subsection 33 (3), may apply to the court to have the order indexed in accordance with subsection 34 (5). R.S.O. 1990, c. F.3, s. 38 (1); 1997, c. 20, s. 7.

Power of court

(3) The court shall, unless the respondent shows that his or her income, assets and means have not increased sufficiently to permit the increase, order that the amount payable be increased by the indexing factor, as defined in subsection 34 (6), for November of the year before the year in which the application is made and be increased in the same way annually thereafter on the anniversary date of the order under this section. R.S.O. 1990, c. F.3, s. 38 (2); 1997, c. 20, s. 7.

Priority to child support

38.1 (1) Where a court is considering an application for the support of a child and an application for the support of a spouse, the court shall give priority to the support of the child in determining the applications. 1997, c. 20, s. 8; 1999, c. 6, s. 25 (13); 2005, c. 5, s. 27 (17).

Reasons

(2) Where as a result of giving priority to the support of a child, the court is unable to make an order for the support of a spouse or the court makes an order for the support of a spouse in an amount less than it otherwise would have, the court shall record its reasons for doing so. 1997, c. 20, s. 8; 1999, c. 6, s. 25 (14); 2005, c. 5, s. 27 (18).

Consequences of reduction or termination of child support

(3) Where as a result of giving priority to the support of a child, an order for the support of a spouse is not made or the amount of the order for the support of a spouse is less than it otherwise would have been, any material reduction or termination of the support for the child constitutes a material change of circumstances for the purposes of an application for the support of the spouse or for variation of an order for the support of the spouse. 1997, c. 20, s. 8; 1999, c. 6, s. 25 (15); 2005, c. 5, s. 27 (19).

(4) REPEALED: 2002, c. 24, Sched. B, s. 25.

Existing orders

39. (1) Sections 36 to 38 also apply to orders for maintenance or alimony made before the 31st day of March, 1978 or in proceedings commenced before the 31st day of March, 1978 and to orders for support made under Part II of the *Family Law Reform Act*, being chapter 152 of the Revised Statutes of Ontario, 1980. R.S.O. 1990, c. F.3, s. 39.

Combined support orders

(2) Where an application is made under section 37 to vary an order that provides a single amount of money for the combined support of one or more children and a spouse, the court shall rescind the order and treat the application as an application for an order for the support of a child and an application for an order for the support of a spouse. 1997, c. 20, s. 9; 1999, c. 6, s. 25 (17); 2005, c. 5, s. 27 (20).

Existing proceedings

(3) Where an application for the support of a child, including an application under section 37 to vary an order for the support of a child, is made before the day the *Uniform Federal and Provincial Child Support Guidelines Act, 1997* comes into force and the court has not considered

any evidence in the application, other than in respect of an interim order, before that day, the proceeding shall be deemed to be an application under the *Family Law Act* as amended by the *Uniform Federal and Provincial Child Support Guidelines Act, 1997*, subject to such directions as the court considers appropriate. 1997, c. 20, s. 9.

Restraining orders

40. The court may, on application, make an interim or final order restraining the depletion of a spouse's property that would impair or defeat a claim under this Part. R.S.O. 1990, c. F.3, s. 40; 1999, c. 6, s. 25 (18); 2005, c. 5, s. 27 (21).

Financial statement

41. In an application under section 33 or 37, each party shall serve on the other and file with the court a financial statement verified by oath or statutory declaration in the manner and form prescribed by the rules of the court. R.S.O. 1990, c. F.3, s. 41.

Obtaining Information

Order for return by employer

42. (1) In an application under section 33 or 37, the court may order the employer of a party to the application to make a written return to the court showing the party's wages or other remuneration during the preceding twelve months. R.S.O. 1990, c. F.3, s. 42 (1).

Return as evidence

(2) A return purporting to be signed by the employer may be received in evidence as proof, in the absence of evidence to the contrary, of its contents. R.S.O. 1990, c. F.3, s. 42 (2).

Order for access to information

(3) The court may, on motion, make an order under subsection (4) if it appears to the court that, in order to make an application under section 33 or 37, the moving party needs to learn or confirm the proposed respondent's whereabouts. R.S.O. 1990, c. F.3, s. 42 (3).

Idem

(4) The order shall require the person or public body to whom it is directed to provide the court or the moving party with any information that is shown on a record in the person's or public body's possession or

control and that indicates the proposed respondent's place of employment, address or location. R.S.O. 1990, c. F.3, s. 42 (4).

Crown bound

(5) This section binds the Crown in right of Ontario. R.S.O. 1990, c. F.3, s. 42 (5).

Arrest of absconding debtor

43. (1) If an application is made under section 33 or 37 and the court is satisfied that the respondent is about to leave Ontario and that there are reasonable grounds for believing that the respondent intends to evade his or her responsibilities under this Act, the court may issue a warrant for the respondent's arrest for the purpose of bringing him or her before the court. R.S.O. 1990, c. F.3, s. 43 (1).

Bail

(2) Section 150 (interim release by justice of the peace) of the *Provincial Offences Act* applies with necessary modifications to an arrest under the warrant. R.S.O. 1990, c. F.3, s. 43 (2).

Provisional orders

44. (1) In an application under section 33 or 37 in the Ontario Court (Provincial Division) or the Unified Family Court, the court shall proceed under this section, whether or not the respondent in the application files a financial statement, if,

    (a) the respondent fails to appear;

    (b) it appears to the court that the respondent resides in a locality in Ontario that is more than 150 kilometres away from the place where the court sits; and

    (c) the court is of the opinion, in the circumstances of the case, that the issues can be adequately determined by proceeding under this section. R.S.O. 1990, c. F.3, s. 44 (1).

Idem

(2) If the court determines that it would be proper to make a final order, were it not for the respondent's failure to appear, the court shall make an order for support that is provisional only and has no effect until it is confirmed by the Ontario Court (Provincial Division) or the Unified Family Court sitting nearest the place where the respondent resides. R.S.O. 1990, c. F.3, s. 44 (2).

Transmission for hearing

(3) The court that makes a provisional order shall send to the court in the locality in which the respondent resides copies of such documents and records, certified in such manner, as are prescribed by the rules of the court. R.S.O. 1990, c. F.3, s. 44 (3).

Show cause

(4) The court to which the documents and records are sent shall cause them to be served upon the respondent, together with a notice to file with the court the financial statement required by section 41, and to appear and show cause why the provisional order should not be confirmed. R.S.O. 1990, c. F.3, s. 44 (4).

Confirmation of order

(5) At the hearing, the respondent may raise any defence that might have been raised in the original proceeding, but if the respondent fails to satisfy the court that the order ought not to be confirmed, the court may confirm the order without variation or with the variation that the court considers proper having regard to all the evidence. R.S.O. 1990, c. F.3, s. 44 (5).

Adjournment for further evidence

(6) If the respondent appears before the court and satisfies the court that for the purpose of a defence or for the taking of further evidence or otherwise it is necessary to remit the case to the court where the applicant resides, the court may remit the case and adjourn the proceeding for that purpose. R.S.O. 1990, c. F.3, s. 44 (6).

Where order not confirmed

(7) If the respondent appears before the court and the court, having regard to all the evidence, is of the opinion that the order ought not to be confirmed, the court shall remit the case to the court sitting where the order was made with a statement of the reasons for doing so, and the court sitting where the order was made shall dispose of the application in accordance with the statement. R.S.O. 1990, c. F.3, s. 44 (7).

Certificates as evidence

(8) A certificate certifying copies of documents or records for the purpose of this section and purporting to be signed by the clerk of the court is, without proof of the clerk's office or signature, admissible in evi-

dence in a court to which it is transmitted under this section as proof, in the absence of evidence to the contrary, of the copy's authenticity. R.S.O. 1990, c. F.3, s. 44 (8).

Right of appeal

(9) No appeal lies from a provisional order made under this section, but a person bound by an order confirmed under this section has the same right of appeal as he or she would have had if the order had been made under section 34. R.S.O. 1990, c. F.3, s. 44 (9).

Necessities of Life

Pledging credit of spouse

45. (1) During cohabitation, a spouse has authority to render himself or herself and his or her spouse jointly and severally liable to a third party for necessities of life, unless the spouse has notified the third party that he or she has withdrawn the authority. R.S.O. 1990, c. F.3, s. 45 (1); 1999, c. 6, s. 25 (19); 2005, c. 5, s. 27 (22).

Liability for necessities of minor

(2) If a person is entitled to recover against a minor in respect of the provision of necessities for the minor, every parent who has an obligation to support the minor is liable for them jointly and severally with the minor. R.S.O. 1990, c. F.3, s. 45 (2).

Recovery between persons jointly liable

(3) If persons are jointly and severally liable under this section, their liability to each other shall be determined in accordance with their obligation to provide support. R.S.O. 1990, c. F.3, s. 45 (3).

Common law supplanted

(4) This section applies in place of the rules of common law by which a wife may pledge her husband's credit. R.S.O. 1990, c. F.3, s. 45 (4).

Order restraining harassment

46. (1) On application, a court may make an interim or final order restraining the applicant's spouse or former spouse from molesting, annoying or harassing the applicant or children in the applicant's lawful custody, or from communicating with the applicant or children, except as the order provides, and may require the applicant's spouse or former spouse to enter into the recognizance that the court considers appropriate. R.S.O. 1990, c. F.3, s. 46 (1); 1999, c. 6, s. 25 (20); 2005, c. 5, s. 27 (23).

Offence

(2) A person who contravenes a restraining order is guilty of an offence and upon conviction is liable,

    (a) in the case of a first offence, to a fine of not more than $5,000 or to imprisonment for a term of not more than three months, or to both; and

    (b) in the case of a second or subsequent offence, to a fine of not more than $10,000 or to imprisonment for a term of not more than two years, or to both. R.S.O. 1990, c. F.3, s. 46 (2).

Note: On a day to be named by proclamation of the Lieutenant Governor, subsection (2) is repealed by the Statutes of Ontario, 2000, chapter 33, subsection 22 (1). See: 2000, c. 33, ss. 22 (1), 23.

Note: Despite the repeal of subsection (2), any prosecution begun under that subsection before its repeal shall continue as if it were still in force. See: 2000, c. 33, s. 22 (3).

Arrest without warrant

(3) A police officer may arrest without warrant a person the police officer believes on reasonable and probable grounds to have contravened a restraining order. R.S.O. 1990, c. F.3, s. 46 (3).

Existing orders

(4) Subsections (2) and (3) also apply in respect of contraventions, committed on or after the 1st day of March, 1986, of restraining orders made under Part II of the *Family Law Reform Act*, being chapter 152 of the Revised Statutes of Ontario, 1980. R.S.O. 1990, c. F.3, s. 46 (4).

Note: On a day to be named by proclamation of the Lieutenant Governor, section 46 is repealed by the Statutes of Ontario, 2000, chapter 33, subsection 22 (2). See: 2000, c. 33, ss. 22 (2), 23.

Note: Despite the repeal of section 46, any proceeding begun under that section before its repeal shall continue as if section 46 were still in force, and any order made under section 46, after its repeal, remains in force until it terminates by its own terms or is rescinded or terminated by a court. See: 2000, c. 33, s. 22 (4).

Application for custody

47. The court may direct that an application for support stand over until an application for custody under the *Children's Law Reform Act* has been determined. R.S.O. 1990, c. F.3, s. 47.

Appeal from Ontario Court of Justice

48. An appeal lies from an order of the Ontario Court of Justice under this Part to the Superior Court of Justice. R.S.O. 1990, c. F.3, s. 48; 2006, c. 19, Sched. C, s. 1 (1, 2).

Contempt of orders of Ontario Court of Justice

49. (1) In addition to its powers in respect of contempt, the Ontario Court of Justice may punish by fine or imprisonment, or by both, any wilful contempt of or resistance to its process, rules or orders under this Act, but the fine shall not exceed $5,000 nor shall the imprisonment exceed ninety days. R.S.O. 1990, c. F.3, s. 49 (1); 2006, c. 19, Sched. C, s. 1 (2).

Conditions of imprisonment

(2) An order for imprisonment under subsection (1) may be conditional upon default in the performance of a condition set out in the order and may provide for the imprisonment to be served intermittently. R.S.O. 1990, c. F.3, s. 49 (2).

50. REPEALED: 2002, c. 24, Sched. B, s. 25.

PART IV
DOMESTIC CONTRACTS

Definitions

51. In this Part,

"cohabitation agreement" means an agreement entered into under section 53; ("accord de cohabitation")

"domestic contract" means a marriage contract, separation agreement, cohabitation agreement, paternity agreement or family arbitration agreement; ("contrat familial")

"family arbitration" means an arbitration that,

    (a) deals with matters that could be dealt with in a marriage contract, separation agreement, cohabitation agreement or paternity agreement under this Part, and

(b) is conducted exclusively in accordance with the law of Ontario or of another Canadian jurisdiction; ("arbitrage familial")

"family arbitration agreement" and "family arbitration award" have meanings that correspond to the meaning of "family arbitration"; ("convention d'arbitrage familial", "sentence d'arbitrage familial")

"marriage contract" means an agreement entered into under section 52; ("contrat de mariage")

"paternity agreement" means an agreement entered into under section 59; ("accord de paternité")

"separation agreement" means an agreement entered into under section 54. ("accord de séparation") R.S.O. 1990, c. F.3, s. 51; 2006, c. 1, s. 5 (6, 7).

Marriage contracts

52. (1) Two persons who are married to each other or intend to marry may enter into an agreement in which they agree on their respective rights and obligations under the marriage or on separation, on the annulment or dissolution of the marriage or on death, including,

(a) ownership in or division of property;

(b) support obligations;

(c) the right to direct the education and moral training of their children, but not the right to custody of or access to their children; and

(d) any other matter in the settlement of their affairs. R.S.O. 1990, c. F.3, s. 52 (1); 2005, c. 5, s. 27 (25).

Rights re matrimonial home excepted

(2) A provision in a marriage contract purporting to limit a spouse's rights under Part II (Matrimonial Home) is unenforceable. R.S.O. 1990, c. F.3, s. 52 (2).

Cohabitation agreements

53. (1) Two persons who are cohabiting or intend to cohabit and who are not married to each other may enter into an agreement in which they agree on their respective rights and obligations during cohabitation, or on ceasing to cohabit or on death, including,

(a) ownership in or division of property;

(b) support obligations;

(c) the right to direct the education and moral training of their children, but not the right to custody of or access to their children; and

(d) any other matter in the settlement of their affairs. R.S.O. 1990, c. F.3, s. 53 (1); 1999, c. 6, s. 25 (23); 2005, c. 5, s. 27 (26).

Effect of marriage on agreement

(2) If the parties to a cohabitation agreement marry each other, the agreement shall be deemed to be a marriage contract. R.S.O. 1990, c. F.3, s. 53 (2).

Separation agreements

54. Two persons who cohabited and are living separate and apart may enter into an agreement in which they agree on their respective rights and obligations, including,

(a) ownership in or division of property;

(b) support obligations;

(c) the right to direct the education and moral training of their children;

(d) the right to custody of and access to their children; and

(e) any other matter in the settlement of their affairs. R.S.O. 1990, c. F.3, s. 54; 1999, c. 6, s. 25 (24); 2005, c. 5, s. 27 (27).

Form and Capacity

Form of contract

55. (1) A domestic contract and an agreement to amend or rescind a domestic contract are unenforceable unless made in writing, signed by the parties and witnessed. R.S.O. 1990, c. F.3, s. 55 (1).

Capacity of minor

(2) A minor has capacity to enter into a domestic contract, subject to the approval of the court, which may be given before or after the minor enters into the contract. R.S.O. 1990, c. F.3, s. 55 (2).

Guardian of property

(3) If a mentally incapable person has a guardian of property other than his or her own spouse, the guardian may enter into a domestic contract or give any waiver or consent under this Act on the person's behalf, subject to the approval of the court, given in advance. 1992, c. 32, s. 12.

P.G.T.

(4) In all other cases of mental incapacity, the Public Guardian and Trustee has power to act on the person's behalf in accordance with subsection (3). 1992, c. 32, s. 12.

Provisions that May Be Set Aside or Disregarded

Contracts subject to best interests of child

56. (1) In the determination of a matter respecting the education, moral training or custody of or access to a child, the court may disregard any provision of a domestic contract pertaining to the matter where, in the opinion of the court, to do so is in the best interests of the child. R.S.O. 1990, c. F.3, s. 56 (1); 1997, c. 20, s. 10 (1).

Contracts subject to child support guidelines

(1.1) In the determination of a matter respecting the support of a child, the court may disregard any provision of a domestic contract pertaining to the matter where the provision is unreasonable having regard to the child support guidelines, as well as to any other provision relating to support of the child in the contract. 1997, c. 20, s. 10 (2); 2006, c. 1, s. 5 (8).

Clauses requiring chastity

(2) A provision in a domestic contract to take effect on separation whereby any right of a party is dependent upon remaining chaste is unenforceable, but this subsection shall not be construed to affect a contingency upon marriage or cohabitation with another. R.S.O. 1990, c. F.3, s. 56 (2).

Idem

(3) A provision in a domestic contract made before the 1st day of March, 1986 whereby any right of a party is dependent upon remaining chaste shall be given effect as a contingency upon marriage or cohabitation with another. R.S.O. 1990, c. F.3, s. 56 (3).

Setting aside domestic contract

(4) A court may, on application, set aside a domestic contract or a provision in it,

    (a) if a party failed to disclose to the other significant assets, or significant debts or other liabilities, existing when the domestic contract was made;

    (b) if a party did not understand the nature or consequences of the domestic contract; or

    (c) otherwise in accordance with the law of contract. R.S.O. 1990, c. F.3, s. 56 (4).

Barriers to remarriage

(5) The court may, on application, set aside all or part of a separation agreement or settlement, if the court is satisfied that the removal by one spouse of barriers that would prevent the other spouse's remarriage within that spouse's faith was a consideration in the making of the agreement or settlement. R.S.O. 1990, c. F.3, s. 56 (5).

Idem

(6) Subsection (5) also applies to consent orders, releases, notices of discontinuance and abandonment and other written or oral arrangements. R.S.O. 1990, c. F.3, s. 56 (6).

Application of subss. (4, 5, 6)

(7) Subsections (4), (5) and (6) apply despite any agreement to the contrary. R.S.O. 1990, c. F.3, s. 56 (7).

Rights of donors of gifts

57. If a domestic contract provides that specific gifts made to one or both parties may not be disposed of or encumbered without the consent of the donor, the donor shall be deemed to be a party to the contract for the purpose of enforcement or amendment of the provision. R.S.O. 1990, c. F.3, s. 57.

Contracts made outside Ontario

58. The manner and formalities of making a domestic contract and its essential validity and effect are governed by the proper law of the contract, except that,

    (a) a contract of which the proper law is that of a jurisdiction other than Ontario is also valid and enforceable in Ontario if entered into in accordance with Ontario's internal law;

    (b) subsection 33 (4) (setting aside provision for support or waiver) and section 56 apply in Ontario to contracts for which the proper law is that of a jurisdiction other than Ontario; and

(c)   a provision in a marriage contract or cohabitation agreement respecting the right to custody of or access to children is not enforceable in Ontario. R.S.O. 1990, c. F.3, s. 58.

Paternity agreements

59. (1) If a man and a woman who are not spouses enter into an agreement for,

(a)   the payment of the expenses of a child's prenatal care and birth;

(b)   support of a child; or

(c)   funeral expenses of the child or mother,

on the application of a party, or a children's aid society, to the Ontario Court of Justice or the Family Court of the Superior Court of Justice, the court may incorporate the agreement in an order, and Part III (Support Obligations) applies to the order in the same manner as if it were an order made under that Part. R.S.O. 1990, c. F.3, s. 59 (1); 2006, c. 19, Sched. C, s. 1 (2, 4).

Child support guidelines

(1.1) A court shall not incorporate an agreement for the support of a child in an order under subsection (1) unless the court is satisfied that the agreement is reasonable having regard to the child support guidelines, as well as to any other provision relating to support of the child in the agreement. 1997, c. 20, s. 11.

Absconding respondent

(2) If an application is made under subsection (1) and a judge of the court is satisfied that the respondent is about to leave Ontario and that there are reasonable grounds to believe that the respondent intends to evade his or her responsibilities under the agreement, the judge may issue a warrant in the form prescribed by the rules of the court for the respondent's arrest. R.S.O. 1990, c. F.3, s. 59 (2).

Bail

(3) Section 150 (interim release by justice of the peace) of the *Provincial Offences Act* applies with necessary modifications to an arrest under the warrant. R.S.O. 1990, c. F.3, s. 59 (3).

Capacity of minor

(4) A minor has capacity to enter into an agreement under subsection (1) that is approved by the court, whether the approval is given before or after the minor enters into the agreement. R.S.O. 1990, c. F.3, s. 59 (4).

Application to existing agreements

(5) This section applies to paternity agreements that were made before the 1st day of March, 1986. R.S.O. 1990, c. F.3, s. 59 (5).

Transitional provision

(6) A paternity agreement that is made before the day section 4 of the *Family Statute Law Amendment Act, 2006* comes into force is not invalid for the reason only that it does not comply with subsection 55 (1). 2006, c. 1, s. 5 (9).

Family arbitrations, agreements and awards

59.1 (1) Family arbitrations, family arbitration agreements and family arbitration awards are governed by this Act and by the *Arbitration Act, 1991.* 2006, c. 1, s. 5 (10).

Conflict

(2) In the event of conflict between this Act and the *Arbitration Act, 1991,* this Act prevails. 2006, c. 1, s. 5 (10).

Other third-party decision-making processes in family matters

59.2 (1) When a decision about a matter described in clause (a) of the definition of "family arbitration" in section 51 is made by a third person in a process that is not conducted exclusively in accordance with the law of Ontario or of another Canadian jurisdiction,

    (a) the process is not a family arbitration; and

    (b) the decision is not a family arbitration award and has no legal effect. 2006, c. 1, s. 5 (10).

Advice

(2) Nothing in this section restricts a person's right to obtain advice from another person. 2006, c. 1, s. 5 (10).

Contracting out

59.3 Any express or implied agreement by the parties to a family arbitration agreement to vary or exclude any of sections 59.1 to 59.7 is without effect. 2006, c. 1, s. 5 (10).

No agreement in advance of dispute

59.4 A family arbitration agreement and an award made under it are unenforceable unless the family arbitration agreement is entered into after the dispute to be arbitrated has arisen. 2006, c. 1, s. 5 (10).

Status of awards

59.5 A family arbitration award may be enforced or set aside in the same way as a domestic contract. 2006, c. 1, s. 5 (10).

Conditions for enforceability

59.6 (1) A family arbitration award is enforceable only if,

(a) the family arbitration agreement under which the award is made is made in writing and complies with any regulations made under the *Arbitration Act, 1991*;

(b) each of the parties to the agreement receives independent legal advice before making the agreement;

(c) the requirements of section 38 of the *Arbitration Act, 1991* are met (formal requirements, writing, reasons, delivery to parties); and

(d) the arbitrator complies with any regulations made under the *Arbitration Act, 1991.* 2006, c. 1, s. 5 (10).

Certificate of independent legal advice

(2) When a person receives independent legal advice as described in clause (1) (b), the lawyer who provides the advice shall complete a certificate of independent legal advice, which may be in a form approved by the Attorney General. 2006, c. 1, s. 5 (10).

Secondary arbitration

59.7 (1) The following special rules apply to a secondary arbitration and to an award made as the result of a secondary arbitration:

1. Despite section 59.4, the award is not unenforceable for the sole reason that the separation agreement was entered into or the court order or earlier award was made before the dispute to be arbitrated in the secondary arbitration had arisen.

2.   Despite clause 59.6 (1) (b), it is not necessary for the parties to receive independent legal advice before participating in the secondary arbitration.

3.   Despite clause 59.6 (1) (c), the requirements of section 38 of the *Arbitration Act, 1991* need not be met. 2006, c. 1, s. 5 (10).

Definition

(2) In this section,

"secondary arbitration" means a family arbitration that is conducted in accordance with a separation agreement, a court order or a family arbitration award that provides for the arbitration of possible future disputes relating to the ongoing management or implementation of the agreement, order or award. 2006, c. 1, s. 5 (10).

Enforcement

59.8 (1) A party who is entitled to the enforcement of a family arbitration award may make an application to the Superior Court of Justice or the Family Court to that effect. 2006, c. 1, s. 5 (10).

Application or motion

(2) If there is already a proceeding between the parties to the family arbitration agreement, the party entitled to enforcement shall make a motion in that proceeding rather than an application. 2006, c. 1, s. 5 (10).

Notice, supporting documents

(3) The application or motion shall be made on notice to the person against whom enforcement is sought and shall be supported by,

    (a)   the original award or a certified copy;

    (b)   a copy of the family arbitration agreement; and

    (c)   copies of the certificates of independent legal advice. 2006, c. 1, s. 5 (10).

Order

(4) If the family arbitration award satisfies the conditions set out in subsection 59.6 (1), the court shall make an order in the same terms as the award, unless,

    (a)   the period for commencing an appeal or an application to set the award aside has not yet elapsed;

    (b)   there is a pending appeal, application to set the award aside or application for a declaration of invalidity; or

(c) the award has been set aside or the arbitration is the subject of a declaration of invalidity. 2006, c. 1, s. 5 (10).

Pending proceeding

(5) If clause (4) (a) or (b) applies, the court may,

(a) make an order in the same terms as the award; or

(b) order, on such conditions as are just, that enforcement of the award is stayed until the period has elapsed without an appeal or application being commenced or until the pending proceeding is finally disposed of. 2006, c. 1, s. 5 (10).

Unusual remedies

(6) If the family arbitration award gives a remedy that the court does not have jurisdiction to grant or would not grant in a proceeding based on similar circumstances, the court may,

(a) make an order granting a different remedy, if the applicant requests it; or

(b) remit the award to the arbitrator with the court's opinion, in which case the arbitrator may award a different remedy. 2006, c. 1, s. 5 (10).

Application of Act to existing contracts

60. (1) A domestic contract validly made before the 1st day of March, 1986 shall be deemed to be a domestic contract for the purposes of this Act. R.S.O. 1990, c. F.3, s. 60 (1).

Contracts entered into before the 1st day of March, 1986

(2) If a domestic contract was entered into before the 1st day of March, 1986 and the contract or any part would have been valid if entered into on or after that day, the contract or part is not invalid for the reason only that it was entered into before that day. R.S.O. 1990, c. F.3, s. 60 (2).

Idem

(3) If property is transferred, under an agreement or understanding reached before the 31st day of March, 1978, between spouses who are living separate and apart, the transfer is effective as if made under a domestic contract. R.S.O. 1990, c. F.3, s. 60 (3).

PART V
DEPENDANTS' CLAIM FOR DAMAGES

Right of dependants to sue in tort

61. (1) If a person is injured or killed by the fault or neglect of another under circumstances where the person is entitled to recover damages, or would have been entitled if not killed, the spouse, as defined in Part III (Support Obligations), children, grandchildren, parents, grandparents, brothers and sisters of the person are entitled to recover their pecuniary loss resulting from the injury or death from the person from whom the person injured or killed is entitled to recover or would have been entitled if not killed, and to maintain an action for the purpose in a court of competent jurisdiction. R.S.O. 1990, c. F.3, s. 61 (1); 1999, c. 6, s. 25 (25); 2005, c. 5, s. 27 (28).

Damages in case of injury

(2) The damages recoverable in a claim under subsection (1) may include,

(a) actual expenses reasonably incurred for the benefit of the person injured or killed;

(b) actual funeral expenses reasonably incurred;

(c) a reasonable allowance for travel expenses actually incurred in visiting the person during his or her treatment or recovery;

(d) where, as a result of the injury, the claimant provides nursing, housekeeping or other services for the person, a reasonable allowance for loss of income or the value of the services; and

(e) an amount to compensate for the loss of guidance, care and companionship that the claimant might reasonably have expected to receive from the person if the injury or death had not occurred. R.S.O. 1990, c. F.3, s. 61 (2).

Contributory negligence

(3) In an action under subsection (1), the right to damages is subject to any apportionment of damages due to contributory fault or neglect of the person who was injured or killed. R.S.O. 1990, c. F.3, s. 61 (3).

(4) REPEALED: 2002, c. 24, Sched. B, s. 25.

Offer to settle for global sum

62. (1) The defendant may make an offer to settle for one sum of money as compensation for his or her fault or neglect to all plaintiffs, without specifying the shares into which it is to be divided. R.S.O. 1990, c. F.3, s. 62 (1).

Apportionment

(2) If the offer is accepted and the compensation has not been otherwise apportioned, the court may, on motion, apportion it among the plaintiffs. R.S.O. 1990, c. F.3, s. 62 (2).

Payment before apportionment

(3) The court may direct payment from the fund before apportionment. R.S.O. 1990, c. F.3, s. 62 (3).

Payment may be postponed

(4) The court may postpone the distribution of money to which minors are entitled. R.S.O. 1990, c. F.3, s. 62 (4).

Assessment of damages, insurance

63. In assessing damages in an action brought under this Part, the court shall not take into account any sum paid or payable as a result of the death or injury under a contract of insurance. R.S.O. 1990, c. F.3, s. 63.

PART VI
AMENDMENTS TO THE COMMON LAW

Unity of legal personality abolished

64. (1) For all purposes of the law of Ontario, a married person has a legal personality that is independent, separate and distinct from that of his or her spouse. R.S.O. 1990, c. F.3, s. 64 (1).

Capacity of married person

(2) A married person has and shall be accorded legal capacity for all purposes and in all respects as if he or she were an unmarried person and, in particular, has the same right of action in tort against his or her spouse as if they were not married. R.S.O. 1990, c. F.3, s. 64 (2).

Purpose of subss. (1, 2)

(3) The purpose of subsections (1) and (2) is to make the same law apply, and apply equally, to married men and married women and to remove any difference in it resulting from any common law rule or doctrine. R.S.O. 1990, c. F.3, s. 64 (3).

Actions between parent and child

65. No person is disentitled from bringing an action or other proceeding against another for the reason only that they are parent and child. R.S.O. 1990, c. F.3, s. 65.

Recovery for prenatal injuries

66. No person is disentitled from recovering damages in respect of injuries for the reason only that the injuries were incurred before his or her birth. R.S.O. 1990, c. F.3, s. 66.

Domicile of minor

67. The domicile of a person who is a minor is,

(a) if the minor habitually resides with both parents and the parents have a common domicile, that domicile;

(b) if the minor habitually resides with one parent only, that parent's domicile;

(c) if the minor resides with another person who has lawful custody of him or her, that person's domicile; or

(d) if the minor's domicile cannot be determined under clause (a), (b) or (c), the jurisdiction with which the minor has the closest connection. R.S.O. 1990, c. F.3, s. 67.

68. REPEALED: 2000, C. 4, S. 12.

GENERAL

Regulations

69. (1) The Lieutenant Governor in Council may make regulations respecting any matter referred to as prescribed by the regulations. R.S.O. 1990, c. F.3, s. 69.

Same

(2) The Lieutenant Governor in Council may make regulations establishing,

(a) guidelines respecting the making of orders for child support under this Act; and

(b) guidelines that may be designated under subsection 2 (5) of the *Divorce Act* (Canada). 1997, c. 20, s. 12.

Same

(3) Without limiting the generality of subsection (2), guidelines may be established under subsection (2),

(a) respecting the way in which the amount of an order for child support is to be determined;

(b) respecting the circumstances in which discretion may be exercised in the making of an order for child support;

(c) respecting the circumstances that give rise to the making of a variation order in respect of an order for the support of a child;

(d) respecting the determination of income for the purposes of the application of the guidelines;

(e) authorizing a court to impute income for the purposes of the application of the guidelines;

(f) respecting the production of income information and providing for sanctions when that information is not provided. 1997, c. 20, s. 12.

Transition

Application of ss. 5–8

70. (1) Sections 5 to 8 apply unless,

(a) an application under section 4 of the *Family Law Reform Act,* being chapter 152 of the Revised Statutes of Ontario, 1980 was adjudicated or settled before the 4th day of June, 1985; or

(b) the first spouse's death occurred before the 1st day of March, 1986. R.S.O. 1990, c. F.3, s. 70 (1).

Application of Part II

(2) Part II (Matrimonial Home) applies unless a proceeding under Part III of the *Family Law Reform Act,* being chapter 152 of the Revised Statutes of Ontario, 1980 to determine the rights between spouses in respect of the property concerned was adjudicated or settled before the 4th day of June, 1985. R.S.O. 1990, c. F.3, s. 70 (2).

Interpretation of existing contracts

(3) A separation agreement or marriage contract that was validly made before the 1st day of March, 1986 and that excludes a spouse's property from the application of sections 4 and 8 of the *Family Law Reform Act,* being chapter 152 of the Revised Statutes of Ontario, 1980,

(a) shall be deemed to exclude that property from the application of section 5 of this Act; and

(b) shall be read with necessary modifications. R.S.O. 1990, c. F.3, s. 70 (3).

CHILDREN'S LAW REFORM ACT

R.S.O. 1990, Chapter C.12

Current to May 1, 2008

CONTENTS

PART I
EQUAL STATUS OF CHILDREN

1. Rule of parentage
2. Rule of construction

PART II
ESTABLISHMENT OF PARENTAGE

3. Court under ss. 4 to 7
4. Paternity and maternity declarations
5. Application for declaration of paternity where no presumption
6. Reopening on new evidence
7. Appeal
8. Presumption of paternity
9. Admissibility in evidence of acknowledgment against interest
10. Leave for blood tests and DNA tests
12. Statutory declaration of parentage
13. Copies of statutory declarations under *Vital Statistics Act*
14. Filing of court decisions respecting parentage
15. Certified copies as evidence
16. Duties of Registrar General

17. Regulations for forms

PART III
CUSTODY, ACCESS AND GUARDIANSHIP

INTERPRETATION
18. Definitions, Part III
19. Purposes, Part III

CUSTODY AND ACCESS
20. Father and mother entitled to custody
21. Application for custody or access
22. Jurisdiction
23. Serious harm to child
24. Merits of application for custody or access
25. Declining jurisdiction
26. Delay
27. Effect of divorce proceedings

CUSTODY AND ACCESS — ORDERS
28. Powers of court
28a. Application to fix times or days of access
29. Order varying an order

CUSTODY AND ACCESS — ASSISTANCE TO COURT
30. Assessment of needs of child
31. Mediation
32. Further evidence from outside Ontario
33. Request from outside Ontario for further evidence

CUSTODY AND ACCESS — ENFORCEMENT
34. Supervision of custody or access
34a. Motions re right of access
35. Order restraining harassment
36. Order where child unlawfully withheld
37. Court orders, removal and return of children
38. Contempt of orders of Ontario Court of Justice
39. Information as to address

CUSTODY AND ACCESS — EXTRA-PROVINCIAL MATTERS
40. Interim powers of court
41. Enforcement of extra-provincial orders
42. Superseding order, material change in circumstances
43. Superseding order, serious harm

44. True copy of extra-provincial order

45. Court may take notice of foreign law

46. Convention on Civil Aspects of International Child Abduction

CONVENTION ON THE CIVIL ASPECTS OF INTERNATIONAL CHILD
ABDUCTION

CHAPTER I — SCOPE OF THE CONVENTION

CHAPTER II — CENTRAL AUTHORITIES

CHAPTER III — RETURN OF CHILDREN

CHAPTER IV — RIGHTS OF ACCESS

CHAPTER V — GENERAL PROVISIONS

CHAPTER VI — FINAL CLAUSES

GUARDIANSHIP

47. Appointment of guardian

48. Parents and joint guardians

49. Criteria

50. Effect of appointment

51. Payment of debt due to child if no guardian

52. Accounts

53. Transfer of property to child

54. Management fees and expenses

55. Bond by guardian

56. Where child has support obligation

57. Removal and resignation of guardian

58. Notice to Estate Registrar for Ontario

DISPOSITION OF PROPERTY

59. Court order re property of child

60. Order for maintenance where power of appointment in favour of
children

TESTAMENTARY CUSTODY AND GUARDIANSHIP

61. Appointments by will

PROCEDURE

62. Procedure, general

63. Application or response by minor

64. Child entitled to be heard

65. Where child is sixteen or more years old
66. All proceedings in one court
67. Consent and domestic contracts
68. Part subject to contracts
69. Jurisdiction of Superior Court of Justice
71. Where to apply for interim orders and variations
72. Interim order
73. Appeal from Ontario Court of Justice
74. Order effective pending appeal
75. Rule of construction, guardianship of person and property

PART I
EQUAL STATUS OF CHILDREN

Rule of parentage

1. (1) Subject to subsection (2), for all purposes of the law of Ontario a person is the child of his or her natural parents and his or her status as their child is independent of whether the child is born within or outside marriage. R.S.O. 1990, c. C.12, s. 1(1).

Exception for adopted children

(2) Where an adoption order has been made, section 158 or 159 of the *Child and Family Services Act* applies and the child is the child of the adopting parents as if they were the natural parents. R.S.O. 1990, c. C.12, s. 1(2).

Kindred relationships

(3) The parent and child relationships as determined under subsections (1) and (2) shall be followed in the determination of other kindred relationships flowing therefrom. R.S.O. 1990, c. C.12, s. 1(3).

Common law distinction of legitimacy abolished

(4) Any distinction at common law between the status of children born in wedlock and born out of wedlock is abolished and the relationship of parent and child and kindred relationships flowing therefrom shall be determined for the purposes of the common law in accordance with this section. R.S.O. 1990, c. C.12, s. 1(4).

Rule of construction

2. (1) For the purposes of construing any instrument, Act or regulation, unless the contrary intention appears, a reference to a person or group or class of persons described in terms of relationship by blood or marriage to another person shall be construed to refer to or include a person who comes within the description by reason of the relationship of parent and child as determined under section 1. R.S.O. 1990, c. C.12, s. 2(1).

Application

(2) Subsection (1) applies to,

    (a) any Act of the Legislature or any regulation, order or by-law made under an Act of the Legislature enacted or made before, on or after the 31st day of March, 1978; and

    (b) any instrument made on or after the 31st day of March, 1978. R.S.O. 1990, c. C.12, s. 2(2).

PART II
ESTABLISHMENT OF PARENTAGE

Court under ss. 4 to 7

3. The court having jurisdiction for the purposes of sections 4 to 7 is,

    (a) the Family Court, in the areas where it has jurisdiction under subsection 21.1(4) of the *Courts of Justice Act*;

    (b) the Superior Court of Justice, in the rest of Ontario. 1996, c. 25, s. 3(1); 2001, c. 9, Sched. B, s. 4(7).

Paternity and maternity declarations

4. (1) Any person having an interest may apply to a court for a declaration that a male person is recognized in law to be the father of a child or that a female person is the mother of a child. R.S.O. 1990, c. C.12, s. 4(1).

Declaration of paternity recognized at law

(2) Where the court finds that a presumption of paternity exists under section 8 and unless it is established, on the balance of probabilities, that the presumed father is not the father of the child, the court shall make a declaratory order confirming that the paternity is recognized in law. R.S.O. 1990, c. C.12, s. 4(2).

Declaration of maternity

(3) Where the court finds on the balance of probabilities that the relationship of mother and child has been established, the court may make a declaratory order to that effect. R.S.O. 1990, c. C.12, s. 4(3).

Idem

(4) Subject to sections 6 and 7, an order made under this section shall be recognized for all purposes. R.S.O. 1990, c. C.12, s. 4(4).

Application for declaration of paternity where no presumption

5. (1) Where there is no person recognized in law under section 8 to be the father of a child, any person may apply to the court for a declaration that a male person is his or her father, or any male person may apply to the court for a declaration that a person is his child. R.S.O. 1990, c. C.12, s. 5(1).

Limitation

(2) An application shall not be made under subsection (1) unless both the persons whose relationship is sought to be established are living. R.S.O. 1990, c. C.12, s. 5(2).

Declaratory order

(3) Where the court finds on the balance of probabilities that the relationship of father and child has been established, the court may make a declaratory order to that effect and, subject to sections 6 and 7, the order shall be recognized for all purposes. R.S.O. 1990, c. C.12, s. 5(3).

Reopening on new evidence

6. Where a declaration has been made under section 4 or 5 and evidence becomes available that was not available at the previous hearing, the court may, upon application, discharge or vary the order and make such other orders or directions as are ancillary thereto. R.S.O. 1990, c. C.12, s. 6.

Appeal

7. An appeal lies from an order under section 4 or 5 or a decision under section 6 in accordance with the rules of the court. R.S.O. 1990, c. C.12, s. 7.

Presumption of paternity

8. (1) Unless the contrary is proven on a balance of probabilities, there is a presumption that a male person is, and he shall be recognized in law to be, the father of a child in any one of the following circumstances:

1. The person is married to the mother of the child at the time of the birth of the child.

2. The person was married to the mother of the child by a marriage that was terminated by death or judgment of nullity within 300 days before the birth of the child or by divorce where the decree *nisi* was granted within 300 days before the birth of the child.

3. The person marries the mother of the child after the birth of the child and acknowledges that he is the natural father.

4. The person was cohabiting with the mother of the child in a relationship of some permanence at the time of the birth of the child or the child is born within 300 days after they ceased to cohabit.

5. The person has certified the child's birth, as the child's father, under the *Vital Statistics Act* or a similar Act in another jurisdiction in Canada.

6. The person has been found or recognized in his lifetime by a court of competent jurisdiction in Canada to be the father of the child. R.S.O. 1990, c. C.12, s. 8(1).

Where marriage void

(2) For the purpose of subsection (1), where a man and woman go through a form of marriage with each other, in good faith, that is void and cohabit, they shall be deemed to be married during the time they cohabit and the marriage shall be deemed to be terminated when they cease to cohabit. R.S.O. 1990, c. C.12, s. 8(2).

Conflicting presumptions

(3) Where circumstances exist that give rise to a presumption or presumptions of paternity by more than one father under subsection (1), no presumption shall be made as to paternity and no person is recognized in law to be the father. R.S.O. 1990, c. C.12, s. 8(3).

Admissibility in evidence of acknowledgment against interest

9. A written acknowledgment of parentage that is admitted in evidence in any civil proceeding against the interest of the person making the acknowledgment is proof, in the absence of evidence to the contrary, of the fact. R.S.O. 1990, c. C.12, s. 9.

Leave for blood tests and DNA tests

10. (1) On the application of a party in a civil proceeding in which the court is called on to determine a child's parentage, the court may give the party leave to obtain blood tests or DNA tests of the persons who are named in the order granting leave and to submit the results in evidence. 2006, c. 19, Sched. B, s. 4.

Conditions

(2) The court may impose conditions, as it thinks proper, on an order under subsection (1). 2006, c. 19, Sched. B, s. 4.

Consent to procedure

(3) The *Health Care Consent Act, 1996* applies to the blood test or DNA test as if it were treatment under that Act. 2006, c. 19, Sched. B, s. 4.

Inference from refusal

(4) If a person named in an order under subsection (1) refuses to submit to the blood test or DNA test, the court may draw such inferences as it thinks appropriate. 2006, c. 19, Sched. B, s. 4.

Exception

(5) Subsection (4) does not apply if the refusal is the decision of a substitute decision-maker as defined in section 9 of the *Health Care Consent Act, 1996*. 2006, c. 19, Sched. B, s. 4.

11. REPEALED: 2006, c. 19, Sched. B, s. 4.

Statutory declaration of parentage

12. (1) A person may file in the office of the Registrar General a statutory declaration, in the form prescribed by the regulations, affirming that he or she is the father or mother, as the case may be, of a child. R.S.O. 1990, c. C.12, s. 12(1).

Idem

(2) Two persons may file in the office of the Registrar General a statutory declaration, in the form prescribed by the regulations, jointly affirm-

ing that they are the father and mother of a child. R.S.O. 1990, c. C.12, s. 12(2).

Copies of statutory declarations under Vital Statistics Act

13. Upon application and upon payment of the fee prescribed under the *Vital Statistics Act*, any person who has an interest, furnishes substantially accurate particulars and satisfies the Registrar General as to the reason for requiring it may obtain from the Registrar General a certified copy of a statutory declaration filed under section 12. R.S.O. 1990, c. C.12, s. 13.

Filing of court decisions respecting parentage

14. (1) Every registrar or clerk of a court in Ontario shall furnish the Registrar General with a statement in the form prescribed by the regulations respecting each order or judgment of the court that confirms or makes a finding of parentage. R.S.O. 1990, c. C.12, s. 14(1); 1993, c. 27, Sched.

Inspection by public

(2) Upon application and upon payment of the fee prescribed under the *Vital Statistics Act*, any person may inspect a statement respecting an order or judgment filed under subsection (1) and obtain a certified copy thereof from the Registrar General. R.S.O. 1990, c. C.12, s. 14(2).

Certified copies as evidence

15. A certificate certifying a copy of a document to be a true copy, obtained under section 12, 13 or 14, purporting to be signed by the Registrar General or Deputy Registrar General or on which the signature of either is lithographed, printed or stamped is, without proof of the office or signature of the Registrar General or Deputy Registrar General, receivable in evidence as proof, in the absence of evidence to the contrary, of the filing and contents of the document for all purposes in any action or proceeding. R.S.O. 1990, c. C.12, s. 15.

Duties of Registrar General

16. Nothing in this Act shall be construed to require the Registrar General to amend a registration showing parentage other than in recognition of an order made under section 4, 5 or 6. R.S.O. 1990, c. C.12, s. 16.

Regulations for forms

17. The Lieutenant Governor in Council may make regulations prescribing forms for the purposes of this Part. R.S.O. 1990, c. C.12, s. 17.

PART III
CUSTODY, ACCESS AND GUARDIANSHIP

Interpretation

Definitions, Part III

18. (1) In this Part,

"court" means the Ontario Court of Justice, the Family Court or the Superior Court of Justice; ("tribunal")

"extra-provincial order" means an order, or that part of an order, of an extra-provincial tribunal that grants to a person custody of or access to a child; ("ordonnance extraprovinciale")

"extra-provincial tribunal" means a court or tribunal outside Ontario that has jurisdiction to grant to a person custody of or access to a child; ("tribunal extraprovincial")

"separation agreement" means an agreement that is a valid separation agreement under Part IV of the *Family Law Act.* ("accord de séparation") R.S.O. 1990, c. C.12, s. 18(1); 1996, c. 25, s. 3(2); 2001, c. 9, Sched. B, s. 4(7, 8).

Child

(2) A reference in this Part to a child is a reference to the child while a minor. R.S.O. 1990, c. C.12, s. 18(2).

Purposes, Part III

19. The purposes of this Part are,

(a) to ensure that applications to the courts in respect of custody of, incidents of custody of, access to and guardianship for children will be determined on the basis of the best interests of the children;

(b) to recognize that the concurrent exercise of jurisdiction by judicial tribunals of more than one province, territory or state in respect of the custody of the same child ought to be avoided, and to make provision so that the courts of Ontario will, unless there are exceptional circumstances, refrain from exercising or decline jurisdiction in cases where it is more appropriate for the matter to be determined by a tribunal having jurisdiction in another place with which the child has a closer connection;

(c) to discourage the abduction of children as an alternative to the determination of custody rights by due process; and

(d) to provide for the more effective enforcement of custody and access orders and for the recognition and enforcement of custody and access orders made outside Ontario. R.S.O. 1990, c. C.12, s. 19.

Custody and Access

Father and mother entitled to custody

20. (1) Except as otherwise provided in this Part, the father and the mother of a child are equally entitled to custody of the child. R.S.O. 1990, c. C.12, s. 20(1).

Rights and responsibilities

(2) A person entitled to custody of a child has the rights and responsibilities of a parent in respect of the person of the child and must exercise those rights and responsibilities in the best interests of the child. R.S.O. 1990, c. C.12, s. 20(2).

Authority to act

(3) Where more than one person is entitled to custody of a child, any one of them may exercise the rights and accept the responsibilities of a parent on behalf of them in respect of the child. R.S.O. 1990, c. C.12, s. 20(3).

Where parents separate

(4) Where the parents of a child live separate and apart and the child lives with one of them with the consent, implied consent or acquiescence of the other of them, the right of the other to exercise the entitlement of custody and the incidents of custody, but not the entitlement to access, is suspended until a separation agreement or order otherwise provides. R.S.O. 1990, c. C.12, s. 20(4).

Note: On a day to be named by proclamation of the Lieutenant Governor, section 20 is amended by section 77 by adding the following subsection:

Duty of separated parents

(4a) Where the parents of a child live separate and apart and the child is in the custody of one of them and the other is entitled to access under the terms of a separation agreement or order, each shall, in the best interests of the child, encourage and support the child's continuing parent-child relationship with the other. R.S.O. 1990, c. C.12, s. 77.

See: R.S.O. 1990, c. C.12, ss. 77, 85.

Access

(5) The entitlement to access to a child includes the right to visit with and be visited by the child and the same right as a parent to make inquiries and to be given information as to the health, education and welfare of the child. R.S.O. 1990, c. C.12, s. 20(5).

Marriage of child

(6) The entitlement to custody of or access to a child terminates on the marriage of the child. R.S.O. 1990, c. C.12, s. 20(6).

Entitlement subject to agreement or order

(7) Any entitlement to custody or access or incidents of custody under this section is subject to alteration by an order of the court or by separation agreement. R.S.O. 1990, c. C.12, s. 20(7).

Application for custody or access

21. A parent of a child or any other person may apply to a court for an order respecting custody of or access to the child or determining any aspect of the incidents of custody of the child. R.S.O. 1990, c. C.12, s. 21.

Jurisdiction

22. (1) A court shall only exercise its jurisdiction to make an order for custody of or access to a child where,

    (a) the child is habitually resident in Ontario at the commencement of the application for the order;

    (b) although the child is not habitually resident in Ontario, the court is satisfied,

        (i) that the child is physically present in Ontario at the commencement of the application for the order,

        (ii) that substantial evidence concerning the best interests of the child is available in Ontario,

(iii) that no application for custody of or access to the child is pending before an extra-provincial tribunal in another place where the child is habitually resident,

(iv) that no extra-provincial order in respect of custody of or access to the child has been recognized by a court in Ontario,

(v) that the child has a real and substantial connection with Ontario, and

(vi) that, on the balance of convenience, it is appropriate for jurisdiction to be exercised in Ontario. R.S.O. 1990, c. C.12, s. 22(1).

Habitual residence

(2) A child is habitually resident in the place where he or she resided,

(a) with both parents;

(b) where the parents are living separate and apart, with one parent under a separation agreement or with the consent, implied consent or acquiescence of the other or under a court order; or

(c) with a person other than a parent on a permanent basis for a significant period of time,

whichever last occurred. R.S.O. 1990, c. C.12, s. 22(2).

Abduction

(3) The removal or withholding of a child without the consent of the person having custody of the child does not alter the habitual residence of the child unless there has been acquiescence or undue delay in commencing due process by the person from whom the child is removed or withheld. R.S.O. 1990, c. C.12, s. 22(3).

Serious harm to child

23. Despite sections 22 and 41, a court may exercise its jurisdiction to make or to vary an order in respect of the custody of or access to a child where,

(a) the child is physically present in Ontario; and

(b) the court is satisfied that the child would, on the balance of probabilities, suffer serious harm if,

(i) the child remains in the custody of the person legally entitled to custody of the child,

(ii) the child is returned to the custody of the person legally entitled to custody of the child, or

(iii) the child is removed from Ontario. R.S.O. 1990, c. C.12, s. 23.

Merits of application for custody or access

24. (1) The merits of an application under this Part in respect of custody of or access to a child shall be determined on the basis of the best interests of the child, in accordance with subsections (2), (3) and (4). 2006, c. 1, s. 3(1).

Best interests of child

(2) The court shall consider all the child's needs and circumstances, including,

    (a) the love, affection and emotional ties between the child and,

        (i) each person entitled to or claiming custody of or access to the child,

        (ii) other members of the child's family who reside with the child, and

        (iii) persons involved in the child's care and upbringing;

    (b) the child's views and preferences, if they can reasonably be ascertained;

    (c) the length of time the child has lived in a stable home environment;

    (d) the ability and willingness of each person applying for custody of the child to provide the child with guidance and education, the necessaries of life and any special needs of the child;

    (e) any plans proposed for the child's care and upbringing;

    (f) the permanence and stability of the family unit with which it is proposed that the child will live;

    (g) the ability of each person applying for custody of or access to the child to act as a parent; and

    (h) the relationship by blood or through an adoption order between the child and each person who is a party to the application. 2006, c. 1, s. 3(1).

Past conduct

(3) A person's past conduct shall be considered only,

    (a) in accordance with subsection (4); or

    (b) if the court is satisfied that the conduct is otherwise relevant to the person's ability to act as a parent. 2006, c. 1, s. 3(1).

Violence and abuse

(4) In assessing a person's ability to act as a parent, the court shall consider whether the person has at any time committed violence or abuse against,

    (a) his or her spouse;

    (b) a parent of the child to whom the application relates;

    (c) a member of the person's household; or

    (d) any child. 2006, c. 1, s. 3(1).

Same

(5) For the purposes of subsection (4), anything done in self-defence or to protect another person shall not be considered violence or abuse. 2006, c. 1, s. 3(1).

Declining jurisdiction

25. A court having jurisdiction under this Part in respect of custody or access may decline to exercise its jurisdiction where it is of the opinion that it is more appropriate for jurisdiction to be exercised outside Ontario. R.S.O. 1990, c. C.12, s. 25.

Delay

26. (1) Where an application under this Part in respect of custody of or access to a child has not been heard within six months after the commencement of the proceedings, the clerk or local registrar of the court shall list the application for the court and give notice to the parties of the date and time when and the place where the court will fix a date for the hearing of the application. R.S.O. 1990, c. C.12, s. 26(1).

Exception

(1.1) Subsection (1) does not apply to an application under this Part that relates to the custody of or access to a child if the child is the subject of an application or order under Part III of the *Child and Family Services Act*, unless the application under this Part relates to,

    (a) an order in respect of the child that was made under subsection 57.1(1) of the *Child and Family Services Act*;

    (b) an order referred to in subsection 57.1(3) of the *Child and Family Services Act* that was made at the same time as an order under subsection 57.1(1) of that Act; or

    (c) an access order in respect of the child under section 58 of the *Child and Family Services Act* that was made at the same time as an order under subsection 57.1(1) of that Act. 2006, c. 5, s. 51(1).

Directions

(2) At a hearing of a matter listed by the clerk or local registrar in accordance with subsection (1), the court by order may fix a date for the hearing of the application and may give such directions in respect of the proceedings and make such order in respect of the costs of the proceedings as the court considers appropriate. R.S.O. 1990, c. C.12, s. 26(2).

Early date

(3) Where the court fixes a date under subsection (2), the court shall fix the earliest date that, in the opinion of the court, is compatible with a just disposition of the application. R.S.O. 1990, c. C.12, s. 26(3).

Effect of divorce proceedings

27. Where an action for divorce is commenced under the *Divorce Act* (Canada), any application under this Part in respect of custody of or access to a child that has not been determined is stayed except by leave of the court. R.S.O. 1990, c. C.12, s. 27.

Custody and Access — Orders

Powers of court

28. (1) The court to which an application is made under section 21,
  (a) by order may grant the custody of or access to the child to one or more persons;
  (b) by order may determine any aspect of the incidents of the right to custody or access; and
  (c) may make such additional order as the court considers necessary and proper in the circumstances. R.S.O. 1990, c. C.12, s. 28.

Exception

(2) If an application is made under section 21 with respect to a child who is the subject of an order made under section 57.1 of the *Child and Family Services Act*, the court shall treat the application as if it were an application to vary an order made under this section. 2006, c. 5, s. 51(2).

Same

(3) If an order for access to a child was made under Part III of the *Child and Family Services Act* at the same time as an order for custody of the child was made under section 57.1 of that Act, the court shall treat an application under section 21 relating to access to the child as if it were an application to vary an order made under this section. 2006, c. 5, s. 51(2).

Note: On a day to be named by proclamation of the Lieutenant Governor, the Act is amended by section 79 by adding the following section:

Application to fix times or days of access

28a. (1) If an order in respect of access to a child provides for a person's access to the child without specifying times or days, a party to the order may apply to the court that made it to vary it by specifying times or days. R.S.O. 1990, c. C.12, s. 79.

Order

(2) The court may vary the order by specifying the times or days agreed to by the parties, or the times or days the court considers appropriate if the parties do not agree. R.S.O. 1990, c. C.12, s. 79.

Separation agreements

(3) Subsection (1) also applies, with necessary modifications, in respect of a separation agreement under section 54 of the *Family Law Act* or a predecessor of that section that provides for a person's access to a child without specifying times or days. R.S.O. 1990, c. C.12, s. 79.

Exception

(4) Subsection (1) does not apply in respect of orders made under the *Divorce Act* (Canada) or a predecessor of that Act. R.S.O. 1990, c. C.12, s. 79.

See: R.S.O. 1990, c. C.12, ss. 79, 85.

Order varying an order

29. (1) A court shall not make an order under this Part that varies an order in respect of custody or access made by a court in Ontario unless there has been a material change in circumstances that affects or is likely to affect the best interests of the child. R.S.O. 1990, c. C.12, s. 29.

Note: On a day to be named by proclamation of the Lieutenant Governor, section 29 is amended by section 80 by adding the following subsection:

Exception

(2) Subsection (1) does not apply in respect of orders made under subsection 28a(2) (fixing times or days of access) or 34a(2) or (6) (access enforcement, etc.). R.S.O. 1990, c. C.12, s. 80.

See: R.S.O. 1990, c. C.12, ss. 80, 85.

Custody and Access — Assistance to Court

Assessment of needs of child

30. (1) The court before which an application is brought in respect of custody of or access to a child, by order, may appoint a person who has technical or professional skill to assess and report to the court on the needs of the child and the ability and willingness of the parties or any of them to satisfy the needs of the child. R.S.O. 1990, c. C.12, s. 30(1).

When order may be made

(2) An order may be made under subsection (1) on or before the hearing of the application in respect of custody of or access to the child and with or without a request by a party to the application. R.S.O. 1990, c. C.12, s. 30(2).

Agreement by parties

(3) The court shall, if possible, appoint a person agreed upon by the parties, but if the parties do not agree the court shall choose and appoint the person. R.S.O. 1990, c. C.12, s. 30(3).

Consent to act

(4) The court shall not appoint a person under subsection (1) unless the person has consented to make the assessment and to report to the court within the period of time specified by the court. R.S.O. 1990, c. C.12, s. 30(4).

Attendance for assessment

(5) In an order under subsection (1), the court may require the parties, the child and any other person who has been given notice of the proposed

order, or any of them, to attend for assessment by the person appointed by the order. R.S.O. 1990, c. C.12, s. 30(5).

Refusal to attend

(6) Where a person ordered under this section to attend for assessment refuses to attend or to undergo the assessment, the court may draw such inferences in respect of the ability and willingness of any person to satisfy the needs of the child as the court considers appropriate. R.S.O. 1990, c. C.12, s. 30(6).

Report

(7) The person appointed under subsection (1) shall file his or her report with the clerk or local registrar of the court. R.S.O. 1990, c. C.12, s. 30(7).

Copies of report

(8) The clerk or local registrar of the court shall give a copy of the report to each of the parties and to counsel, if any, representing the child. R.S.O. 1990, c. C.12, s. 30(8).

Admissibility of report

(9) The report mentioned in subsection (7) is admissible in evidence in the application. R.S.O. 1990, c. C.12, s. 30(9).

Assessor may be witness

(10) Any of the parties, and counsel, if any, representing the child, may require the person appointed under subsection (1) to attend as a witness at the hearing of the application. R.S.O. 1990, c. C.12, s. 30(10).

Directions

(11) Upon motion, the court by order may give such directions in respect of the assessment as the court considers appropriate. R.S.O. 1990, c. C.12, s. 30(11).

Fees and expenses

(12) The court shall require the parties to pay the fees and expenses of the person appointed under subsection (1). R.S.O. 1990, c. C.12, s. 30(12).

Idem, proportions or amounts

(13) The court shall specify in the order the proportions or amounts of the fees and expenses that the court requires each party to pay. R.S.O. 1990, c. C.12, s. 30(13).

Idem, serious financial hardship

(14) The court may relieve a party from responsibility for payment of any of the fees and expenses of the person appointed under subsection (1) where the court is satisfied that payment would cause serious financial hardship to the party. R.S.O. 1990, c. C.12, s. 30(14).

Note: On a day to be named by proclamation of the Lieutenant Governor, subsection (14) is repealed by section 81 and the following substituted:

Idem, serious financial hardship

(14) The court may require one party to pay all the fees and expenses of the person appointed under subsection (1) if the court is satisfied that payment would cause the other party or parties serious financial hardship. R.S.O. 1990, c. C.12, s. 81.

See: R.S.O. 1990, c. C.12, ss. 81, 85.

Other expert evidence

(15) The appointment of a person under subsection (1) does not prevent the parties or counsel representing the child from submitting other expert evidence as to the needs of the child and the ability and willingness of the parties or any of them to satisfy the needs of the child. R.S.O. 1990, c. C.12, s. 30(15).

Mediation

31. (1) Upon an application for custody of or access to a child, the court, at the request of the parties, by order may appoint a person selected by the parties to mediate any matter specified in the order. R.S.O. 1990, c. C.12, s. 31(1).

Consent to act

(2) The court shall not appoint a person under subsection (1) unless the person,

    (a) has consented to act as mediator; and

(b) has agreed to file a report with the court within the period of time specified by the court. R.S.O. 1990, c. C.12, s. 31(2).

Duty of mediator

(3) It is the duty of a mediator to confer with the parties and endeavour to obtain an agreement in respect of the matter. R.S.O. 1990, c. C.12, s. 31(3).

Form of report

(4) Before entering into mediation on the matter, the parties shall decide whether,

(a) the mediator is to file a full report on the mediation, including anything that the mediator considers relevant to the matter in mediation; or

(b) the mediator is to file a report that either sets out the agreement reached by the parties or states only that the parties did not reach agreement on the matter. R.S.O. 1990, c. C.12, s. 31(4).

Filing of report

(5) The mediator shall file his or her report with the clerk or local registrar of the court in the form decided upon by the parties under subsection (4). R.S.O. 1990, c. C.12, s. 31(5).

Copies of report

(6) The clerk or local registrar of the court shall give a copy of the report to each of the parties and to counsel, if any, representing the child. R.S.O. 1990, c. C.12, s. 31(6).

Admissions made in the course of mediation

(7) Where the parties have decided that the mediator's report is to be in the form described in clause (4)(b), evidence of anything said or of any admission or communication made in the course of the mediation is not admissible in any proceeding except with the consent of all parties to the proceeding in which the order was made under subsection (1). R.S.O. 1990, c. C.12, s. 31(7).

Fees and expenses

(8) The court shall require the parties to pay the fees and expenses of the mediator. R.S.O. 1990, c. C.12, s. 31(8).

Idem, proportions or amounts

(9) The court shall specify in the order the proportions or amounts of the fees and expenses that the court requires each party to pay. R.S.O. 1990, c. C.12, s. 31(9).

Idem, serious financial hardship

(10) The court may relieve a party from responsibility for payment of any of the fees and expenses of the mediator where the court is satisfied that payment would cause serious financial hardship to the party. R.S.O. 1990, c. C.12, s. 31(10).

Note: On a day to be named by proclamation of the Lieutenant Governor, subsection (10) is repealed by section 82 and the following substituted:

Idem, serious financial hardship

(10) The court may require one party to pay all the mediator's fees and expenses if the court is satisfied that payment would cause the other party or parties serious financial hardship. R.S.O. 1990, c. C.12, s. 82.

See: R.S.O. 1990, c. C.12, ss. 82, 85.

Further evidence from outside Ontario

32. (1) Where a court is of the opinion that it is necessary to receive further evidence from a place outside Ontario before making a decision, the court may send to the Attorney General, Minister of Justice or similar officer of the place outside Ontario such supporting material as may be necessary together with a request,

(a) that the Attorney General, Minister of Justice or similar officer take such action as may be necessary in order to require a named person to attend before the proper tribunal in that place and produce or give evidence in respect of the subject-matter of the application; and

(b) that the Attorney General, Minister of Justice or similar officer or the tribunal send to the court a certified copy of the evidence produced or given before the tribunal. R.S.O. 1990, c. C.12, s. 32(1).

Cost of obtaining evidence

(2) A court that acts under subsection (1) may assess the cost of so acting against one or more of the parties to the application or may deal with such cost as costs in the cause. R.S.O. 1990, c. C.12, s. 32(2).

Request from outside Ontario for further evidence

33. (1) Where the Attorney General receives from an extra-provincial tribunal a request similar to that referred to in section 32 and such supporting material as may be necessary, it is the duty of the Attorney General to refer the request and the material to the proper court. R.S.O. 1990, c. C.12, s. 33(1).

Obtaining evidence

(2) A court to which a request is referred by the Attorney General under subsection (1) shall require the person named in the request to attend before the court and produce or give evidence in accordance with the request. R.S.O. 1990, c. C.12, s. 33(2).

Custody and Access — Enforcement

Supervision of custody or access

34. (1) Where an order is made for custody of or access to a child, a court may give such directions as it considers appropriate for the supervision of the custody or access by a person, a children's aid society or other body. R.S.O. 1990, c. C.12, s. 34(1).

Consent to act

(2) A court shall not direct a person, a children's aid society or other body to supervise custody or access as mentioned in subsection (1) unless the person, society or body has consented to act as supervisor. R.S.O. 1990, c. C.12, s. 34(2).

Note: On a day to be named by proclamation of the Lieutenant Governor, the Act is amended by section 83 by adding the following section:

Motions re right of access

Motion to enforce right of access

34a. (1) A person in whose favour an order has been made for access to a child at specific times or on specific days and who claims that a person in whose favour an order has been made for custody of the child has wrongfully denied him or her access to the child may make a motion for relief under subsection (2) to the court that made the access order. R.S.O. 1990, c. C.12, s. 83.

Order for relief

(2) If the court is satisfied that the responding party wrongfully denied the moving party access to the child, the court may, by order,

   (a) require the responding party to give the moving party compensatory access to the child for the period agreed to by the parties, or for the period the court considers appropriate if the parties do not agree;

   (b) require supervision as described in section 34;

   (c) require the responding party to reimburse the moving party for any reasonable expenses actually incurred as a result of the wrongful denial of access;

   (d) appoint a mediator in accordance with section 31 as if the motion were an application for access. R.S.O. 1990, c. C.12, s. 83.

Period of compensatory access

(3) A period of compensatory access shall not be longer than the period of access that was wrongfully denied. R.S.O. 1990, c. C.12, s. 83.

What constitutes wrongful denial of access

(4) A denial of access is wrongful unless it is justified by a legitimate reason such as one of the following:

1. The responding party believed on reasonable grounds that the child might suffer physical or emotional harm if the right of access were exercised.

2. The responding party believed on reasonable grounds that he or she might suffer physical harm if the right of access were exercised.

3. The responding party believed on reasonable grounds that the moving party was impaired by alcohol or a drug at the time of access.

4. The moving party failed to present himself or herself to exercise the right of access within one hour of the time specified in the order or the time otherwise agreed on by the parties.

5. The responding party believed on reasonable grounds that the child was suffering from an illness of such a nature that it was not appropriate in the circumstances that the right of access be exercised.

6. The moving party did not satisfy written conditions concerning access that were agreed to by the parties or that form part of the order for access.
7. On numerous occasions during the preceding year, the moving party had, without reasonable notice and excuse, failed to exercise the right of access.
8. The moving party had informed the responding party that he or she would not seek to exercise the right of access on the occasion in question. R.S.O. 1990, c. C.12, s. 83.

Motion re failure to exercise of right of access, etc.

(5) A person in whose favour an order has been made for custody of a child and who claims that a person in whose favour an order has been made for access to the child has, without reasonable notice and excuse, failed to exercise the right of access or to return the child as the order requires, may make a motion for relief under subsection (6) to the court that made the access order. R.S.O. 1990, c. C.12, s. 83.

Order for relief

(6) If the court is satisfied that the responding party, without reasonable notice and excuse, failed to exercise the right of access or to return the child as the order requires, the court may, by order,
  (a) require supervision as described in section 34;
  (b) require the responding party to reimburse the moving party for any reasonable expenses actually incurred as a result of the failure to exercise the right of access or to return the child as the order requires;
  (c) appoint a mediator in accordance with section 31 as if the motion were an application for access. R.S.O. 1990, c. C.12, s. 83.

Speedy hearing

(7) A motion under subsection (1) or (5) shall be heard within ten days after it has been served. R.S.O. 1990, c. C.12, s. 83.

Limitation

(8) A motion under subsection (1) or (5) shall not be made more than thirty days after the alleged wrongful denial or failure. R.S.O. 1990, c. C.12, s. 83.

Oral evidence only

(9) The motion shall be determined on the basis of oral evidence only, unless the court gives leave to file an affidavit. R.S.O. 1990, c. C.12, s. 83.

Scope of evidence at hearing limited

(10) At the hearing of the motion, unless the court orders otherwise, evidence shall be admitted only if it is directly related to,

(a) the alleged wrongful denial of access or failure to exercise the right of access or return the child as the order requires; or

(b) the responding party's reasons for the denial or failure. R.S.O. 1990, c. C.12, s. 83.

Separation agreement may be filed with court

(11) A person who is a party to a separation agreement made under section 54 of the *Family Law Act* or a predecessor of that section may file the agreement with the clerk of the Ontario Court (Provincial Division) or of the Unified Family Court, together with the person's affidavit stating that the agreement is in effect and has not been set aside or varied by a court or agreement. R.S.O. 1990, c. C.12, s. 83.

> **Note: Subsection (11) is amended by the Statutes of Ontario, 2001, chapter 9, Schedule B, subsection 4(8) by striking out "Ontario Court (Provincial Division)" and substituting "Ontario Court of Justice". See: 2001, c. 9, Sched. B, s. 4(8).**

> **Note: Subsection (11) is amended by the Statutes of Ontario, 2001, chapter 9, Schedule B, subsection 4(9) by striking out "Unified Family Court" and substituting "Family Court". See: 2001, c. 9, Sched. B, s. 4(9).**

Effect of filing

(12) When a separation agreement providing for access to a child at specific times or on specific days is filed in this manner, subsections (1) and (5) apply as if the agreement were an order of the court where it is filed. R.S.O. 1990, c. C.12, s. 83.

Motions made in bad faith

(13) If the court is satisfied that a person has made a motion under subsection (1) or (5) in bad faith, the court may prohibit him or her from making further motions without leave of the court. R.S.O. 1990, c. C.12, s. 83.

Idem

(14) Subsections (1) and (5) do not apply in respect of orders made under the *Divorce Act* (Canada) or a predecessor of that Act. R.S.O. 1990, c. C.12, s. 83.

Application

(15) Subsections (1) and (5) do not apply in respect of a denial of access or a failure to exercise a right of access or to return a child as the order or agreement requires that takes place before the day this section comes into force. R.S.O. 1990, c. C.12, s. 83.

See: R.S.O. 1990, c. C.12, ss. 83, 85.

Order restraining harassment

35. (1) On application, a court may make an interim or final order restraining a person from molesting, annoying or harassing the applicant or children in the applicant's lawful custody and may require the person to enter into the recognizance or post the bond that the court considers appropriate. R.S.O. 1990, c. C.12, s. 35(1).

Note: On a day to be named by proclamation of the Lieutenant Governor, subsection (1) is repealed by section 84 and the following substituted:

Order restraining harassment

(1) On application, a court may make an interim or final order restraining a person from molesting, annoying or harassing the applicant or children in the applicant's lawful custody, or from communicating with the applicant or children, except as the order provides, and may require the person to enter into the recognizance that the court considers appropriate. R.S.O. 1990, c. C.12, s. 84.

See: R.S.O. 1990, c. C.12, ss. 84, 85.

Offence

(2) A person who contravenes a restraining order is guilty of an offence and on conviction is liable to either or both a fine of $5,000 and imprisonment for a term of not more than three months for a first offence and not more than two years for a subsequent offence. R.S.O. 1990, c. C.12, s. 35(2).

Note: On a day to be named by proclamation of the Lieutenant Governor, subsection (2) is repealed by the Statutes of Ontario, 2000, chapter 33, subsection 21(1). See: 2000, c. 33, ss. 21(1), 23.

Note: Despite the repeal of subsection (2), any prosecution begun under that subsection before its repeal shall continue as if it were still in force. See: 2000, c. 33, s. 21(3).

Arrest without warrant

(3) A police officer may arrest without warrant a person the police officer believes on reasonable and probable grounds to have contravened a restraining order. R.S.O. 1990, c. C.12, s. 35(3).

Existing orders

(4) Subsections (2) and (3) also apply in respect of contraventions, committed after those subsections come into force, of restraining orders made under a predecessor of this section. R.S.O. 1990, c. C.12, s. 35(4).

Note: On a day to be named by proclamation of the Lieutenant Governor, section 35 is repealed by the Statutes of Ontario, 2000, chapter 33, subsection 21(2). See: 2000, c. 33, ss. 21(2), 23.

Note: Despite the repeal of section 35, any proceeding begun under that section before its repeal shall continue as if section 35 were still in force, and any order made under section 35, after its repeal, remains in force until it terminates by its own terms or is rescinded or terminated by a court. See: 2000, c. 33, s. 21(4).

Order where child unlawfully withheld

36. (1) Where a court is satisfied upon application by a person in whose favour an order has been made for custody of or access to a child that there are reasonable and probable grounds for believing that any person is unlawfully withholding the child from the applicant, the court by order may authorize the applicant or someone on his or her behalf to apprehend the child for the purpose of giving effect to the rights of the applicant to custody or access, as the case may be. R.S.O. 1990, c. C.12, s. 36(1).

Order to locate and take child

(2) Where a court is satisfied upon application that there are reasonable and probable grounds for believing,

(a)   that any person is unlawfully withholding a child from a person entitled to custody of or access to the child;

(b)   that a person who is prohibited by court order or separation agreement from removing a child from Ontario proposes to remove the child or have the child removed from Ontario; or

(c)   that a person who is entitled to access to a child proposes to remove the child or to have the child removed from Ontario and that the child is not likely to return,

the court by order may direct a police force, having jurisdiction in any area where it appears to the court that the child may be, to locate, apprehend and deliver the child to the person named in the order. R.S.O. 1990, c. C.12, s. 36(2).

Application without notice

(3) An order may be made under subsection (2) upon an application without notice where the court is satisfied that it is necessary that action be taken without delay. R.S.O. 1990, c. C.12, s. 36(3).

Duty to act

(4) The police force directed to act by an order under subsection (2) shall do all things reasonably able to be done to locate, apprehend and deliver the child in accordance with the order. R.S.O. 1990, c. C.12, s. 36(4).

Entry and search

(5) For the purpose of locating and apprehending a child in accordance with an order under subsection (2), a member of a police force may enter and search any place where he or she has reasonable and probable grounds for believing that the child may be with such assistance and such force as are reasonable in the circumstances. R.S.O. 1990, c. C.12, s. 36(5).

Time

(6) An entry or a search referred to in subsection (5) shall be made only between 6 a.m. and 9 p.m. standard time unless the court, in the order, authorizes entry and search at another time. R.S.O. 1990, c. C.12, s. 36(6).

Expiration of order

(7) An order made under subsection (2) shall name a date on which it expires, which shall be a date not later than six months after it is made

unless the court is satisfied that a longer period of time is necessary in the circumstances. R.S.O. 1990, c. C.12, s. 36(7).

When application may be made

(8) An application under subsection (1) or (2) may be made in an application for custody or access or at any other time. R.S.O. 1990, c. C.12, s. 36(8).

Court orders, removal and return of children

To prevent unlawful removal of child

37. (1) Where a court, upon application, is satisfied upon reasonable and probable grounds that a person prohibited by court order or separation agreement from removing a child from Ontario proposes to remove the child from Ontario, the court in order to prevent the removal of the child from Ontario may make an order under subsection (3). R.S.O. 1990, c. C.12, s. 37(1).

To ensure return of child

(2) Where a court, upon application, is satisfied upon reasonable and probable grounds that a person entitled to access to a child proposes to remove the child from Ontario and is not likely to return the child to Ontario, the court in order to secure the prompt, safe return of the child to Ontario may make an order under subsection (3). R.S.O. 1990, c. C.12, s. 37(2).

Order by court

(3) An order mentioned in subsection (1) or (2) may require a person to do any one or more of the following:

1. Transfer specific property to a named trustee to be held subject to the terms and conditions specified in the order.
2. Where payments have been ordered for the support of the child, make the payments to a specified trustee subject to the terms and conditions specified in the order.
3. Post a bond, with or without sureties, payable to the applicant in such amount as the court considers appropriate.
4. Deliver the person's passport, the child's passport and any other travel documents of either of them that the court may specify to the court or to an individual or body specified by the court. R.S.O. 1990, c. C.12, s. 37(3).

Idem, Ontario Court of Justice

(4) The Ontario Court of Justice shall not make an order under paragraph 1 of subsection (3). R.S.O. 1990, c. C.12, s. 37(4); 2001, c. 9, Sched. B, s. 4(8).

Terms and conditions

(5) In an order under paragraph 1 of subsection (3), the court may specify terms and conditions for the return or the disposition of the property as the court considers appropriate. R.S.O. 1990, c. C.12, s. 37(5).

Safekeeping

(6) A court or an individual or body specified by the court in an order under paragraph 4 of subsection (3) shall hold a passport or travel document delivered in accordance with the order in safekeeping in accordance with any directions set out in the order. R.S.O. 1990, c. C.12, s. 37(6).

Directions

(7) In an order under subsection (3), a court may give such directions in respect of the safekeeping of the property, payments, passports or travel documents as the court considers appropriate. R.S.O. 1990, c. C.12, s. 37(7).

Contempt of orders of Ontario Court of Justice

38. (1) In addition to its powers in respect of contempt, the Ontario Court of Justice may punish by fine or imprisonment, or both, any wilful contempt of or resistance to its process or orders in respect of custody of or access to a child, but the fine shall not in any case exceed $5,000 nor shall the imprisonment exceed ninety days. R.S.O. 1990, c. C.12, s. 38(1); 2001, c. 9, Sched. B, s. 4(8).

Conditions of imprisonment

(2) An order for imprisonment under subsection (1) may be made conditional upon default in the performance of a condition set out in the order and may provide for the imprisonment to be served intermittently. R.S.O. 1990, c. C.12, s. 38(2).

Information as to address

39. (1) Where, upon application to a court, it appears to the court that,

(a) for the purpose of bringing an application in respect of custody or access under this Part; or

(b) for the purpose of the enforcement of an order for custody or access,

the proposed applicant or person in whose favour the order is made has need to learn or confirm the whereabouts of the proposed respondent or person against whom the order referred to in clause (b) is made, the court may order any person or public body to provide the court with such particulars of the address of the proposed respondent or person against whom the order referred to in clause (b) is made as are contained in the records in the custody of the person or body, and the person or body shall give the court such particulars as are contained in the records and the court may then give the particulars to such person or persons as the court considers appropriate. R.S.O. 1990, c. C.12, s. 39(1).

Exception

(2) A court shall not make an order on an application under subsection (1) where it appears to the court that the purpose of the application is to enable the applicant to identify or to obtain particulars as to the identity of a person who has custody of a child, rather than to learn or confirm the whereabouts of the proposed respondent or the enforcement of an order for custody or access. R.S.O. 1990, c. C.12, s. 39(2).

Compliance with order

(3) The giving of information in accordance with an order under subsection (1) shall be deemed for all purposes not to be a contravention of any Act or regulation or any common law rule of confidentiality. R.S.O. 1990, c. C.12, s. 39(3).

Section binds Crown

(4) This section binds the Crown in right of Ontario. R.S.O. 1990, c. C.12, s. 39(4).

Custody and Access — Extra-Provincial Matters

Interim powers of court

40. Upon application, a court,

(a) that is satisfied that a child has been wrongfully removed to or is being wrongfully retained in Ontario; or

(b) that may not exercise jurisdiction under section 22 or that has declined jurisdiction under section 25 or 42,

may do any one or more of the following:

1. Make such interim order in respect of the custody or access as the court considers is in the best interests of the child.
2. Stay the application subject to,
    i. the condition that a party to the application promptly commence a similar proceeding before an extra-provincial tribunal, or
    ii. such other conditions as the court considers appropriate.
3. Order a party to return the child to such place as the court considers appropriate and, in the discretion of the court, order payment of the cost of the reasonable travel and other expenses of the child and any parties to or witnesses at the hearing of the application. R.S.O. 1990, c. C.12, s. 40.

Enforcement of extra-provincial orders

41. (1) Upon application by any person in whose favour an order for the custody of or access to a child has been made by an extra-provincial tribunal, a court shall recognize the order unless the court is satisfied,

(a) that the respondent was not given reasonable notice of the commencement of the proceeding in which the order was made;
(b) that the respondent was not given an opportunity to be heard by the extra-provincial tribunal before the order was made;
(c) that the law of the place in which the order was made did not require the extra-provincial tribunal to have regard for the best interests of the child;
(d) that the order of the extra-provincial tribunal is contrary to public policy in Ontario; or
(e) that, in accordance with section 22, the extra-provincial tribunal would not have jurisdiction if it were a court in Ontario. R.S.O. 1990, c. C.12, s. 41(1).

Effect of recognition of order

(2) An order made by an extra-provincial tribunal that is recognized by a court shall be deemed to be an order of the court and enforceable as such. R.S.O. 1990, c. C.12, s. 41(2).

Conflicting orders

(3) A court presented with conflicting orders made by extra-provincial tribunals for the custody of or access to a child that, but for the conflict, would be recognized and enforced by the court under subsection (1) shall recognize and enforce the order that appears to the court to be most in accord with the best interests of the child. R.S.O. 1990, c. C.12, s. 41(3).

Further orders

(4) A court that has recognized an extra-provincial order may make such further orders under this Part as the court considers necessary to give effect to the order. R.S.O. 1990, c. C.12, s. 41(4).

Superseding order, material change in circumstances

42. (1) Upon application, a court by order may supersede an extra-provincial order in respect of custody of or access to a child where the court is satisfied that there has been a material change in circumstances that affects or is likely to affect the best interests of the child and,

(a) the child is habitually resident in Ontario at the commencement of the application for the order; or

(b) although the child is not habitually resident in Ontario, the court is satisfied,

(i) that the child is physically present in Ontario at the commencement of the application for the order,

(ii) that the child no longer has a real and substantial connection with the place where the extra-provincial order was made,

(iii) that substantial evidence concerning the best interests of the child is available in Ontario,

(iv) that the child has a real and substantial connection with Ontario, and

(v) that, on the balance of convenience, it is appropriate for jurisdiction to be exercised in Ontario. R.S.O. 1990, c. C.12, s. 42(1).

Declining jurisdiction

(2) A court may decline to exercise its jurisdiction under this section where it is of the opinion that it is more appropriate for jurisdiction to be exercised outside Ontario. R.S.O. 1990, c. C.12, s. 42(2).

Superseding order, serious harm

43. Upon application, a court by order may supersede an extra-provincial order in respect of custody of or access to a child if the court is satisfied that the child would, on the balance of probability, suffer serious harm if,

(a)   the child remains in the custody of the person legally entitled to custody of the child;

(b)   the child is returned to the custody of the person entitled to custody of the child; or

(c)   the child is removed from Ontario. R.S.O. 1990, c. C.12, s. 43.

True copy of extra-provincial order

44. A copy of an extra-provincial order certified as a true copy by a judge, other presiding officer or registrar of the tribunal that made the order or by a person charged with keeping the orders of the tribunal is proof, in the absence of evidence to the contrary, of the making of the order, the content of the order and the appointment and signature of the judge, presiding officer, registrar or other person. R.S.O. 1990, c. C.12, s. 44.

Court may take notice of foreign law

45. For the purposes of an application under this Part, a court may take notice, without requiring formal proof, of the law of a jurisdiction outside Ontario and of a decision of an extra-provincial tribunal. R.S.O. 1990, c. C.12, s. 45.

Convention on Civil Aspects of International Child Abduction

Definition

46. (1) In this section,

"convention" means the Convention on the Civil Aspects of International Child Abduction, set out in the Schedule to this section. R.S.O. 1990, c. C.12, s. 46(1).

Convention in force

(2) On, from and after the 1st day of December, 1983, except as provided in subsection (3), the convention is in force in Ontario and the provisions thereof are law in Ontario. R.S.O. 1990, c. C.12, s. 46(2).

Crown, legal costs under convention

(3) The Crown is not bound to assume any costs resulting under the convention from the participation of legal counsel or advisers or from court proceedings except in accordance with the *Legal Aid Services Act, 1998.* R.S.O. 1990, c. C.12, s. 46(3); 1998, c. 26, s. 101.

Central Authority

(4) The Ministry of the Attorney General shall be the Central Authority for Ontario for the purpose of the convention. R.S.O. 1990, c. C.12, s. 46(4).

Application to court

(5) An application may be made to a court in pursuance of a right or an obligation under the convention. R.S.O. 1990, c. C.12, s. 46(5).

Request to ratify convention

(6) The Attorney General shall request the Government of Canada to submit a declaration to the Ministry of Foreign Affairs of the Kingdom of the Netherlands, declaring that the convention extends to Ontario. R.S.O. 1990, c. C.12, s. 46(6).

Regulations

(7) The Lieutenant Governor in Council may make such regulations as the Lieutenant Governor in Council considers necessary to carry out the intent and purpose of this section. R.S.O. 1990, c. C.12, s. 46(7).

Conflict

(8) Where there is a conflict between this section and any other enactment, this section prevails.

SCHEDULE

Convention on the Civil Aspects of International Child Abduction

The States signatory to the present Convention,

Firmly convinced that the interests of children are of paramount importance in matters relating to their custody,

Desiring to protect children internationally from the harmful effects of their wrongful removal or retention and to establish procedures to ensure their prompt return to the State of their habitual residence, as well as to secure protection for rights of access,

Have resolved to conclude a Convention to this effect and have agreed upon the following provisions:

Chapter I — Scope of the Convention

Article 1

The objects of the present Convention are:
  (a) to secure the prompt return of children wrongfully removed to or retained in any Contracting State; and
  (b) to ensure that rights of custody and of access under the law of one Contracting State are effectively respected in the other Contracting States.

Article 2

Contracting States shall take all appropriate measures to secure within their territories the implementation of the objects of the Convention. For this purpose they shall use the most expeditious procedures available.

Article 3

The removal or the retention of a child is to be considered wrongful where:
  (a) it is in breach of rights of custody attributed to a person, an institution or any other body, either jointly or alone, under the law of the State in which the child was habitually resident immediately before the removal or retention; and
  (b) at the time of removal or retention those rights were actually exercised, either jointly or alone, or would have been so exercised but for the removal or retention.

The rights of custody mentioned in sub-paragraph (a) above, may arise in particular by operation of law or by reason of a judicial or administrative decision, or by reason of an agreement having legal effect under the law of that State.

Article 4

The Convention shall apply to any child who was habitually resident in a Contracting State immediately before any breach of custody or access rights. The Convention shall cease to apply when the child attains the age of 16 years.

Article 5
For the purposes of this Convention:
  (a) "rights of custody" shall include rights relating to the care of the person of the child and, in particular, the right to determine the child's place of residence;
  (b) "rights of access" shall include the right to take a child for a limited period of time to a place other than the child's habitual residence.

Chapter II — Central Authorities

Article 6

A Contracting State shall designate a Central Authority to discharge the duties which are imposed by the Convention upon such authorities.

Federal States, States with more than one system of law or States having autonomous territorial organizations shall be free to appoint more than one Central Authority and to specify the territorial extent of their powers. Where a State has appointed more than one Central Authority, it shall designate the Central Authority to which applications may be addressed for transmission to the appropriate Central Authority within that State.

Article 7

Central Authorities shall co-operate with each other and promote co-operation amongst the competent authorities in their respective States to secure the prompt return of children and to achieve the other objects of this Convention.

In particular, either directly or through any intermediary, they shall take all appropriate measures:
  (a) to discover the whereabouts of a child who has been wrongfully removed or retained;
  (b) to prevent further harm to the child or prejudice to interested parties by taking or causing to be taken provisional measures;
  (c) to secure the voluntary return of the child or to bring about an amicable resolution of the issues;
  (d) to exchange, where desirable, information relating to the social background of the child;

(e) to provide information of a general character as to the law of their State in connection with the application of the Convention;

(f) to initiate or facilitate the institution of judicial or administrative proceedings with a view to obtaining the return of the child and, in a proper case, to make arrangements for organizing or securing the effective exercise of rights of access;

(g) where the circumstances so require, to provide or facilitate the provision of legal aid and advice, including the participation of legal counsel and advisers;

(h) to provide such administrative arrangements as may be necessary and appropriate to secure the safe return of the child;

(i) to keep each other informed with respect to the operation of this Convention and, as far as possible, to eliminate any obstacles to its application.

Chapter III — Return of Children

Article 8

Any person, institution or other body claiming that a child has been removed or retained in breach of custody rights may apply either to the Central Authority of the child's habitual residence or to the Central Authority of any other Contracting State for assistance in securing the return of the child.

The application shall contain:

(a) information concerning the identity of the applicant, of the child and of the person alleged to have removed or retained the child;

(b) where available, the date of birth of the child;

(c) the grounds on which the applicant's claim for return of the child is based;

(d) all available information relating to the whereabouts of the child and the identity of the person with whom the child is presumed to be.

The application may be accompanied or supplemented by:

(e) an authenticated copy of any relevant decision or agreement;

(f) a certificate or an affidavit emanating from a Central Authority, or other competent authority of the State of the child's habitual residence, or from a qualified person, concerning the relevant law of that State;

(g) any other relevant document.

Article 9

If the Central Authority which receives an application referred to in Article 8 has reason to believe that the child is in another Contracting State, it shall directly and without delay transmit the application to the Central Authority of that Contracting State and inform the requesting Central Authority, or the applicant, as the case may be.

Article 10

The Central Authority of the State where the child is shall take or cause to be taken all appropriate measures in order to obtain the voluntary return of the child.

Article 11

The judicial or administrative authorities of Contracting States shall act expeditiously in proceedings for the return of children.

If the judicial or administrative authority concerned has not reached a decision within six weeks from the date of commencement of the proceedings, the applicant or the Central Authority of the requested State, on its own initiative or if asked by the Central Authority of the requesting State, shall have the right to request a statement of the reasons for the delay. If a reply is received by the Central Authority of the requested State, that Authority shall transmit the reply to the Central Authority of the requesting State, or to the applicant, as the case may be.

Article 12

Where a child has been wrongfully removed or retained in terms of Article 3 and, at the date of commencement of the proceedings before the judicial or administrative authority of the Contracting State where the child is, a period of less than one year has elapsed from the date of the wrongful removal or retention, the authority concerned shall order the return of the child forthwith.

The judicial or administrative authority, even where the proceedings have been commenced after the expiration of the period of one year referred to in the preceding paragraph, shall also order the return of the child, unless it is demonstrated that the child is now settled in its new environment.

Where the judicial or administrative authority in the requested State has reason to believe that the child has been taken to another State, it may stay the proceedings or dismiss the application for the return of the child.

Article 13

Despite the provisions of the preceding Article, the judicial or administrative authority of the requested State is not bound to order the return of the child if the person, institution or other body which opposes its return establishes that:

(a) the person, institution or other body having the care of the person of the child was not actually exercising the custody rights at the time of removal or retention, or had consented to or subsequently acquiesced in the removal or retention; or

(b) there is a grave risk that his or her return would expose the child to physical or psychological harm or otherwise place the child in an intolerable situation.

The judicial or administrative authority may also refuse to order the return of the child if it finds that the child objects to being returned and has attained an age and degree of maturity at which it is appropriate to take account of its views.

In considering the circumstances referred to in this Article, the judicial and administrative authorities shall take into account the information relating to the social background of the child provided by the Central Authority or other competent authority of the child's habitual residence.

Article 14

In ascertaining whether there has been a wrongful removal or retention within the meaning of Article 3, the judicial or administrative authorities of the requested State may take notice directly of the law of, and of judicial or administrative decisions, formally recognized or not in the State of the habitual residence of the child, without recourse to the specific procedures for the proof of that law or for the recognition of foreign decisions which would otherwise be applicable.

Article 15

The judicial or administrative authorities of a Contracting State may, prior to the making of an order for the return of the child, request that the applicant obtain from the authorities of the State of the habitual residence of the child a decision or other determination that the removal or retention was wrongful within the meaning of Article 3 of the Convention, where such a decision or determination may be obtained in that State. The Central Authorities of the Contracting States shall so far as practicable assist applicants to obtain such a decision or determination.

Article 16

After receiving notice of a wrongful removal or retention of a child in the sense of Article 3, the judicial or administrative authorities of the Contracting State to which the child has been removed or in which it has been retained shall not decide on the merits of rights of custody until it has been determined that the child is not to be returned under this Convention or unless an application under this Convention is not lodged within a reasonable time following receipt of the notice.

Article 17

The sole fact that a decision relating to custody has been given in or is entitled to recognition in the requested State shall not be a ground for refusing to return a child under this Convention, but the judicial or administrative authorities of the requested State may take account of the reasons for that decision in applying this Convention.

Article 18

The provisions of this Chapter do not limit the power of a judicial or administrative authority to order the return of the child at any time.

Article 19

A decision under this Convention concerning the return of the child shall not be taken to be a determination on the merits of any custody issue.

Article 20

The return of the child under the provisions of Article 12 may be refused if this would not be permitted by the fundamental principles of the requested State relating to the protection of human rights and fundamental freedoms.

Chapter IV — Rights of Access

Article 21

An application to make arrangements for organizing or securing the effective exercise of rights of access may be presented to the Central Authorities of the Contracting States in the same way as an application for the return of a child.

The Central Authorities are bound by the obligations of co-operation which are set forth in Article 7 to promote the peaceful enjoyment of access rights and the fulfilment of any conditions to which the exercise of those rights may be subject. The Central Authorities shall take steps to remove, as far as possible, all obstacles to the exercise of such rights.

The Central Authorities, either directly or through intermediaries, may initiate or assist in the institution of proceedings with a view to organizing or protecting these rights and securing respect for the conditions to which the exercise of these rights may be subject.

Chapter V — General Provisions

Article 22

No security, bond or deposit, however described, shall be required to guarantee the payment of costs and expenses in the judicial or administrative proceedings falling within the scope of this Convention.

Article 23

No legalization or similar formality may be required in the context of this Convention.

Article 24

Any application, communication or other document sent to the Central Authority of the requested State shall be in the original language, and shall be accompanied by a translation into the official language or one of the official languages of the requested State or, where that is not feasible, a translation into French or English.

However, a Contracting State may, by making a reservation in accordance with Article 42, object to the use of either French or English, but not both, in any application, communication or other document sent to its Central Authority.

Article 25

Nationals of the Contracting States and persons who are habitually resident within those States shall be entitled in matters concerned with the application of this Convention to legal aid and advice in any other Contracting State on the same conditions as if they themselves were nationals of and habitually resident in that State.

Article 26

Each Central Authority shall bear its own costs in applying this Convention.

Central Authorities and other public services of Contracting States shall not impose any charges in relation to applications submitted under this Convention. In particular, they may not require any payment from the applicant towards the costs and expenses of the proceedings or, where applicable, those arising from the participation of legal counsel or advisers. However, they may require the payment of the expenses incurred or to be incurred in implementing the return of the child.

However, a Contracting State may, by making a reservation in accordance with Article 42, declare that it shall not be bound to assume any costs referred to in the preceding paragraph resulting from the participation of legal counsel or advisers or from court proceedings, except insofar as those costs may be covered by its system of legal aid and advice.

Upon ordering the return of a child or issuing an order concerning rights of access under this Convention, the judicial or administrative authorities may, where appropriate, direct the person who removed or retained the child, or who prevented the exercise of rights of access, to pay necessary expenses incurred by or on behalf of the applicant, including travel expenses, any costs incurred or payments made for locating the child, the costs of legal representation of the applicant, and those of returning the child.

Article 27

When it is manifest that the requirements of this Convention are not fulfilled or that the application is otherwise not well founded, a Central Authority is not bound to accept the application. In that case, the Central Authority shall forthwith inform the applicant or the Central Authority through which the application was submitted, as the case may be, of its reasons.

Article 28

A Central Authority may require that the application be accompanied by a written authorization empowering it to act on behalf of the applicant, or to designate a representative so to act.

Article 29

This Convention shall not preclude any person, institution or body who claims that there has been a breach of custody or access rights within the meaning of Article 3 or 21 from applying directly to the judicial or administrative authorities of a Contracting State, whether or not under the provisions of this Convention.

Article 30

Any application submitted to the Central Authorities or directly to the judicial or administrative authorities of a Contracting State in accordance with the terms of this Convention, together with documents and any other information appended thereto or provided by a Central Authority, shall be admissible in the courts or administrative authorities of the Contracting States.

Article 31

In relation to a State which in matters of custody of children has two or more systems of law applicable in different territorial units:
    (a) any reference to habitual residence in that State shall be construed as referring to habitual residence in a territorial unit of that State;
    (b) any reference to the law of the State of habitual residence shall be construed as referring to the law of the territorial unit in that State where the child habitually resides.

Article 32

In relation to a State which in matters of custody of children has two or more systems of law applicable to different categories of persons, any reference to the law of that State shall be construed as referring to the legal system specified by the law of that State.

Article 33

A State within which different territorial units have their own rules of law in respect of custody of children shall not be bound to apply this Convention where a State with a unified system of law would not be bound to do so.

Article 34

This Convention shall take priority in matters within its scope over the *Convention of 5 October 1961 concerning the powers of authorities and the law applicable in respect of the protection of minors*, as between Parties to both Conventions. Otherwise the present Convention shall not restrict the application of an international instrument in force between the State of origin and the State addressed or other law of the State addressed for the purposes of obtaining the return of a child who has been wrongfully removed or retained or of organizing access rights.

Article 35

This Convention shall apply as between Contracting States only to wrongful removals or retentions occurring after its entry into force in those States.

Where a declaration has been made under Article 39 or 40, the reference in the preceding paragraph to a Contracting State shall be taken to refer to the territorial unit or units in relation to which this Convention applies.

Article 36

Nothing in this Convention shall prevent two or more Contracting States, in order to limit the restrictions to which the return of the child may be subject, from agreeing among themselves to derogate from any provisions of this Convention which may imply such a restriction.

Chapter VI — Final Clauses

Article 37

The Convention shall be open for signature by the States which were Members of the Hague Conference on Private International Law at the time of its Fourteenth Session.

It shall be ratified, accepted or approved and the instruments of ratification, acceptance or approval shall be deposited with the Ministry of Foreign Affairs of the Kingdom of the Netherlands.

Article 38

Any other State may accede to the Convention.

The instrument of accession shall be deposited with the Ministry of Foreign Affairs of the Kingdom of the Netherlands.

The Convention shall enter into force for a State acceding to it on the first day of the third calendar month after the deposit of its instrument of accession.

The accession will have effect only as regards the relations between the acceding State and such Contracting States as will have declared their acceptance of the accession. Such a declaration will also have to be made by any Member State ratifying, accepting or approving the Convention after an accession. Such declaration shall be deposited at the Ministry of Foreign Affairs of the Kingdom of the Netherlands; this Ministry shall forward, through diplomatic channels, a certified copy to each of the Contracting States.

The Convention will enter into force as between the acceding State and the State that has declared its acceptance of the accession on the first day of the third calendar month after the deposit of the declaration of acceptance.

Article 39

Any State may, at the time of signature, ratification, acceptance, approval or accession, declare that the Convention shall extend to all the territories for the international relations of which it is responsible, or to one or more of them. Such a declaration shall take effect at the time the Convention enters into force for that State.

Such declaration, as well as any subsequent extension, shall be notified to the Ministry of Foreign Affairs of the Kingdom of the Netherlands.

Article 40

If a Contracting State has two or more territorial units in which different systems of law are applicable in relation to matters dealt with in this Convention, it may at the time of signature, ratification, acceptance, approval or accession declare that this Convention shall extend to all its territorial units or only to one or more of them and may modify this declaration by submitting another declaration at any time.

Any such declaration shall be notified to the Ministry of Foreign Affairs of the Kingdom of the Netherlands and shall state expressly the territorial units to which the Convention applies.

Article 41

Where a Contracting State has a system of government under which executive, judicial and legislative powers are distributed between central and other authorities within that State, its signature or ratification, acceptance or approval of, or accession to this Convention, or its making of any declaration in terms of Article 40 shall carry no implication as to the internal distribution of powers within that State.

Article 42

Any State may, not later than the time of ratification, acceptance, approval or accession, or at the time of making a declaration in terms of Article 39 or 40, make one or both of the reservations provided for in Article 24 and Article 26, third paragraph. No other reservation shall be permitted.

Any State may at any time withdraw a reservation it has made. The withdrawal shall be notified to the Ministry of Foreign Affairs of the Kingdom of the Netherlands.

The reservation shall cease to have effect on the first day of the third calendar month after the notification referred to in the preceding paragraph.

Article 43

The Convention shall enter into force on the first day of the third calendar month after the deposit of the third instrument of ratification, acceptance, approval or accession referred to in Articles 37 and 38.

Thereafter the Convention shall enter into force:

1. for each State ratifying, accepting, approving or acceding to it subsequently, on the first day of the third calendar month after the deposit of its instrument of ratification, acceptance, approval or accession;
2. for any territory or territorial unit to which the Convention has been extended in conformity with Article 39 or 40, on the first day of the third calendar month after the notification referred to in that Article.

Article 44

The Convention shall remain in force for five years from the date of its entry into force in accordance with the first paragraph of Article 43 even for States which subsequently have ratified, accepted, approved it or acceded to it. If there has been no denunciation, it shall be renewed tacitly every five years.

Any denunciation shall be notified to the Ministry of Foreign Affairs of the Kingdom of the Netherlands at least six months before the expiry of the five year period. It may be limited to certain of the territories or territorial units to which the Convention applies.

The denunciation shall have effect only as regards the State which has notified it. The Convention shall remain in force for the other Contracting States.

Article 45

The Ministry of Foreign Affairs of the Kingdom of the Netherlands shall notify the States Members of the Conference, and the States which have acceded in accordance with Article 38, of the following:

1. the signatures and ratifications, acceptances and approvals referred to in Article 37;
2. the accessions referred to in Article 38;
3. the date on which the Convention enters into force in accordance with Article 43;

4. the extensions referred to in Article 39;
5. the declarations referred to in Articles 38 and 40;
6. the reservations referred to in Article 24 and Article 26, third paragraph, and the withdrawals referred to in Article 42;
7. the denunciations referred to in Article 44.

Done at The Hague, on the 25th day of October, 1980.

R.S.O. 1990, c. C.12, s. 46(8).

Guardianship

Appointment of guardian

47. (1) Upon application by a child's parent or by any other person, on notice to the Children's Lawyer, a court may appoint a guardian of the child's property. 2001, c. 9, Sched. B, s. 4(1).

Responsibility of guardian

(2) A guardian of the property of a child has charge of and is responsible for the care and management of the property of the child. R.S.O. 1990, c. C.12, s. 47(2).

Parents and joint guardians

Parents as guardians

48. (1) As between themselves and subject to any court order or any agreement between them, the parents of a child are equally entitled to be appointed by a court as guardians of the property of the child. R.S.O. 1990, c. C.12, s. 48(1).

Parent and other person

(2) As between a parent of a child and a person who is not a parent of the child, the parent has a preferential entitlement to be appointed by a court as a guardian of the property of the child. R.S.O. 1990, c. C.12, s. 48(2).

More than one guardian

(3) A court may appoint more than one guardian of the property of a child. R.S.O. 1990, c. C.12, s. 48(3).

Guardians jointly responsible

(4) Where more than one guardian is appointed of the property of a child, the guardians are jointly responsible for the care and management of the property of the child. R.S.O. 1990, c. C.12, s. 48(4).

Criteria

49. In deciding an application for the appointment of a guardian of the property of a child, the court shall consider all the circumstances, including,

    (a)   the ability of the applicant to manage the property of the child;

    (b)   the merits of the plan proposed by the applicant for the care and management of the property of the child; and

    (c)   the views and preferences of the child, where such views and preferences can reasonably be ascertained. R.S.O. 1990, c. C.12, s. 49; 2001, c. 9, Sched. B, s. 4(2).

Effect of appointment

50. The appointment of a guardian by a court under this Part has effect in all parts of Ontario. R.S.O. 1990, c. C.12, s. 50.

Payment of debt due to child if no guardian

51. (1) If no guardian of a child's property has been appointed, a person who is under a duty to pay money or deliver personal property to the child discharges that duty, to the extent of the amount paid or the value of the personal property delivered, subject to subsection (1.1), by paying money or delivering personal property to,

    (a)   the child, if the child has a legal obligation to support another person;

    (b)   a parent with whom the child resides; or

    (c)   a person who has lawful custody of the child. 2001, c. 9, Sched. B, s. 4(3).

Same

(1.1) The total of the amount of money paid and the value of personal property delivered under subsection (1) shall not exceed the prescribed amount or, if no amount is prescribed, $10,000. 2001, c. 9, Sched. B, s. 4(3).

Money payable under judgment

(2) Subsection (1) does not apply in respect of money payable under a judgment or order of a court. R.S.O. 1990, c. C.12, s. 51(2).

Receipt for payment

(3) A receipt or discharge for money or personal property not in excess of the amount or value set out in subsection (1) received for a child by a parent with whom the child resides or a person who has lawful custody of the child has the same validity as if a court had appointed the parent or the person as a guardian of the property of the child. R.S.O. 1990, c. C.12, s. 51(3).

Responsibility for money or property

(4) A parent with whom a child resides or a person who has lawful custody of a child who receives and holds money or personal property referred to in subsection (1) has the responsibility of a guardian for the care and management of the money or personal property. R.S.O. 1990, c. C.12, s. 51(4).

Regulations

(5) The Lieutenant Governor in Council may, by regulation, prescribe an amount for the purpose of subsection (1.1). 2001, c. 9, Sched. B, s. 4(4).

Accounts

52. A guardian of the property of a child may be required to account or may voluntarily pass the accounts in respect of the care and management of the property of the child in the same manner as a trustee under a will may be required to account or may pass the accounts in respect of the trusteeship. R.S.O. 1990, c. C.12, s. 52.

Transfer of property to child

53. A guardian of the property of a child shall transfer to the child all property of the child in the care of the guardian when the child attains the age of eighteen years. R.S.O. 1990, c. C.12, s. 53.

Management fees and expenses

54. A guardian of the property of a child is entitled to payment of a reasonable amount for fees for and expenses of management of the property of the child. R.S.O. 1990, c. C.12, s. 54.

Bond by guardian

55. (1) A court that appoints a guardian of the property of a child shall require the guardian to post a bond, with or without sureties, payable to the child in such amount as the court considers appropriate in respect of the care and management of the property of the child. R.S.O. 1990, c. C.12, s. 55(1).

Where parent appointed guardian

(2) Subsection (1) does not apply where the court appoints a parent of a child as guardian of the property of the child and the court is of the opinion that it is appropriate not to require the parent to post a bond. R.S.O. 1990, c. C.12, s. 55(2).

Where child has support obligation

56. Upon application by a child who has a legal obligation to support another person, the court that appointed a guardian of the property of the child or a co-ordinate court by order shall end the guardianship for the child. R.S.O. 1990, c. C.12, s. 56.

Removal and resignation of guardian

Removal

57. (1) A guardian of the property of a child may be removed by a court for the same reasons for which a trustee may be removed. R.S.O. 1990, c. C.12, s. 57(1).

Resignation

(2) A guardian of the property of a child, with the permission of a court, may resign as guardian upon such conditions as the court considers appropriate. R.S.O. 1990, c. C.12, s. 57(2).

Notice to Estate Registrar for Ontario

58. A notice of every application to a court for appointment of a guardian of the property of a child shall be transmitted by the clerk or local registrar of the court to the Estate Registrar for Ontario. R.S.O. 1990, c. C.12, s. 58; 1993, c. 27, Sched.

Disposition of Property

Court order re property of child

59. (1) Upon application by a child's parent or by any other person, on notice to the Children's Lawyer, the Superior Court of Justice by order may require or approve, or both,

(a) the disposition or encumbrance of all or part of the interest of the child in land;

(b) the sale of the interest of the child in personal property; or

(c) the payment of all or part of any money belonging to the child or of the income from any property belonging to the child, or both. R.S.O. 1990, c. C.12, s. 59(1); 2001, c. 9, Sched. B, s. 4(5).

Criteria

(2) An order shall be made under subsection (1) only where the Court is of the opinion that the disposition, encumbrance, sale or payment is necessary or proper for the support or education of the child or will substantially benefit the child. R.S.O. 1990, c. C.12, s. 59(2).

Conditions

(3) An order under subsection (1) may be made subject to such conditions as the Court considers appropriate. R.S.O. 1990, c. C.12, s. 59(3).

Limitation

(4) The Court shall not require or approve a disposition or encumbrance of the interest of a child in land contrary to a term of the instrument by which the child acquired the interest. R.S.O. 1990, c. C.12, s. 59(4).

Execution of documents

(5) The Court, where it makes an order under subsection (1), may order that the child or another person named in the order execute any documents necessary to carry out the disposition, encumbrance, sale or payment. R.S.O. 1990, c. C.12, s. 59(5).

Directions

(6) The Court by order may give such directions as it considers necessary for the carrying out of an order made under subsection (1). R.S.O. 1990, c. C.12, s. 59(6).

Validity of documents

(7) Every document executed in accordance with an order under this section is as effectual as if the child by whom it was executed was eighteen years of age or, if executed by another person in accordance with the order, as if the child had executed it and had been eighteen years of age at the time. R.S.O. 1990, c. C.12, s. 59(7).

Liability

(8) No person incurs or shall be deemed to incur liability by making a payment in accordance with an order under clause (1) (c). R.S.O. 1990, c. C.12, s. 59(8).

Order for maintenance where power of appointment in favour of children

60. (1) Upon application by or with the consent of a person who has an estate for life in property with power to devise or appoint the property to one or more of his or her children, the Superior Court of Justice may order that such part of the proceeds of the property as the Court considers proper be used for the support, education or benefit of one or more of the children. R.S.O. 1990, c. C.12, s. 60(1); 2001, c. 9, Sched. B, s. 4(7).

Idem

(2) An order may be made under subsection (1) whether or not,
  (a) there is a gift over in the event that there are no children to take under the power; or
  (b) any person could dispose of the property in the event that there are no children to take under the power. R.S.O. 1990, c. C.12, s. 60(2).

Testamentary Custody and Guardianship

Appointments by will

Custody

61. (1) A person entitled to custody of a child may appoint by will one or more persons to have custody of the child after the death of the appointor. R.S.O. 1990, c. C.12, s. 61(1).

Guardianship

(2) A guardian of the property of a child may appoint by will one or more persons to be guardians of the property of the child after the death of the appointor. R.S.O. 1990, c. C.12, s. 61(2).

Appointment by minor

(3) An unmarried parent who is a minor may make an appointment mentioned in subsection (1) or (2) by a written appointment signed by the parent. R.S.O. 1990, c. C.12, s. 61(3).

Limitation

(4) An appointment under subsection (1), (2) or (3) is effective only,

(a) if the appointor is the only person entitled to custody of the child or who is the guardian of the property of the child, as the case requires, on the day immediately before the appointment is to take effect; or

(b) if the appointor and any other person entitled to custody of the child or who is the guardian of the property of the child, as the case requires, die at the same time or in circumstances that render it uncertain which survived the other. R.S.O. 1990, c. C.12, s. 61(4).

Where more than one appointment

(5) Where two or more persons are appointed to have custody of or to be guardians of the property of a child by appointors who die as mentioned in clause (4) (b), only the appointments of the persons appointed by both or all of the appointors are effective. R.S.O. 1990, c. C.12, s. 61(5).

Consent of appointee

(6) No appointment under subsection (1), (2) or (3) is effective without the consent of the person appointed. R.S.O. 1990, c. C.12, s. 61(6).

Expiration of appointment

(7) An appointment under subsection (1), (2) or (3) for custody of a child or guardianship of the property of a child expires ninety days after the appointment becomes effective or, where the appointee applies under this Part for custody of the child or guardianship of the property of the child within the ninety-day period, when the application is disposed of. R.S.O. 1990, c. C.12, s. 61(7).

Application or order under ss. 21, 47

(8) An appointment under this section does not apply to prevent an application for or the making of an order under section 21 or 47. R.S.O. 1990, c. C.12, s. 61(8).

Application

(9) This section applies in respect of,

(a)   any will made on or after the 1st day of October, 1982; and

(b)   any will made before the 1st day of October, 1982, if the testator is living on that day. R.S.O. 1990, c. C.12, s. 61(9).

Procedure

Procedure, general

Joinder of proceedings

62. (1) An application under this Part may be made in the same proceeding and in the same manner as an application under the *Family Law Act,* or in another proceeding. R.S.O. 1990, c. C.12, s. 62(1).

Nature of order

(2) An application under this Part may be an original application or for the variance of an order previously given or to supersede an order of an extra-provincial tribunal. R.S.O. 1990, c. C.12, s. 62(2).

Parties

(3) The parties to an application under this Part in respect of a child shall include,

(a)   the mother and the father of the child;

(b)   a person who has demonstrated a settled intention to treat the child as a child of his or her family;

(c)   a person who had the actual care and upbringing of the child immediately before the application; and

(d)   any other person whose presence as a party is necessary to determine the matters in issue. R.S.O. 1990, c. C.12, s. 62(3).

Combining of applications

(4) Where, in an application under this Part, it appears to the court that it is necessary or desirable in the best interests of the child to have other matters first or simultaneously determined, the court may direct

that the application stand over until such other proceedings are brought or determined as the court considers appropriate, subject to section 26. R.S.O. 1990, c. C.12, s. 62(4).

Where identity of father not known

(5) Where there is no presumption of paternity and the identity of the father is not known or is not reasonably capable of being ascertained, the court may order substituted service or may dispense with service of documents upon the father in the proceeding. R.S.O. 1990, c. C.12, s. 62(5).

Application or response by minor

63. (1) A minor who is a parent may make an application under this Part without a next friend and may respond without a litigation guardian. R.S.O. 1990, c. C.12, s. 63(1).

Consent by minor

(2) A consent in respect of a matter provided for by this Part is not invalid by reason only that the person giving the consent is a minor. R.S.O. 1990, c. C.12, s. 63(2).

Child entitled to be heard

64. (1) In considering an application under this Part, a court where possible shall take into consideration the views and preferences of the child to the extent that the child is able to express them. R.S.O. 1990, c. C.12, s. 64(1).

Interview by court

(2) The court may interview the child to determine the views and preferences of the child. R.S.O. 1990, c. C.12, s. 64(2).

Recording

(3) The interview shall be recorded. R.S.O. 1990, c. C.12, s. 64(3).

Counsel

(4) The child is entitled to be advised by and to have his or her counsel, if any, present during the interview. R.S.O. 1990, c. C.12, s. 64(4).

Where child is sixteen or more years old

65. Nothing in this Part abrogates the right of a child of sixteen or more years of age to withdraw from parental control. R.S.O. 1990, c. C.12, s. 65.

All proceedings in one court

66. Except as otherwise provided, where an application is made to a court under this Part, no person who is a party to the proceeding shall make an application under this Part to any other court in respect of a matter in issue in the proceeding, but the court may order that the proceeding be transferred to a court having other jurisdiction where, in the opinion of the court, the court having other jurisdiction is more appropriate to determine the matters in issue that should be determined at the same time. R.S.O. 1990, c. C.12, s. 66.

Consent and domestic contracts

Consent orders

67. (1) Upon the consent of the parties in an application under this Part, the court may make any order that the court is otherwise empowered to make by this Part, subject to the duty of the court to have regard to the best interests of the child. R.S.O. 1990, c. C.12, s. 67(1).

Incorporation of contract in order

(2) Any matter provided for in this Part and in a domestic contract as defined in the *Family Law Act* may be incorporated in an order made under this Part. R.S.O. 1990, c. C.12, s. 67(2).

Part subject to contracts

68. Where a domestic contract as defined in the *Family Law Act* makes provision in respect of a matter that is provided for in this Part, the contract prevails except as otherwise provided in Part IV of the *Family Law Act*. R.S.O. 1990, c. C.12, s. 68.

Jurisdiction of Superior Court of Justice

69. This Part does not deprive the Superior Court of Justice of its *parens patriae* jurisdiction. R.S.O. 1990, c. C.12, s. 69; 2001, c. 9, Sched. B, s. 4(7).

70. REPEALED: 2001, c. 9, Sched. B, s. 4(6).

Where to apply for interim orders and variations

Place of application for interim order
71. (1) An application for an interim order shall be made to the court in which the original proceeding was taken. R.S.O. 1990, c. C.12, s. 71(1).

Place of application to vary order
(2) An application under this Part to vary an order may be made to the court in which the original proceeding was taken or to a co-ordinate court in another part of Ontario. R.S.O. 1990, c. C.12, s. 71(2).

Interim order
72. In a proceeding under this Part, the court may make such interim order as the court considers appropriate. R.S.O. 1990, c. C.12, s. 72.

Appeal from Ontario Court of Justice
73. An appeal from an order of the Ontario Court of Justice under this Part lies to the Superior Court of Justice. R.S.O. 1990, c. C.12, s. 73; 2001, c. 9, Sched. B, s. 4(7, 8).

Order effective pending appeal
74. An order under this Part is effective even if an appeal is taken from the order, unless the court that made the order or the court to which the appeal is taken orders otherwise. R.S.O. 1990, c. C.12, s. 74.

Rule of construction, guardianship of person and property
75. (1) For the purposes of construing any instrument, Act or regulation, unless the contrary intention appears, a reference to a guardian with respect to the person of a child shall be construed to refer to custody of the child and a reference to a guardian with respect to property of a child shall be construed to refer to guardianship of the property of the child. R.S.O. 1990, c. C.12, s. 75(1).

Application
(2) Subsection (1) applies to any instrument, any Act of the Legislature or any regulation, order or by-law made under an Act of the Legislature enacted or made before, on or after the 1st day of October, 1982. R.S.O. 1990, c. C.12, s. 75(2).

76. REPEALED: 2001, c. 9, Sched. B, s. 4(6).

77. OMITTED (PROVIDES FOR AMENDMENTS TO THIS ACT). R.S.O. 1990, c. C.12, s. 77.

78. REPEALED: 2006, c. 1, s. 3(2).

79.–84. OMITTED (PROVIDES FOR AMENDMENTS TO THIS ACT). R.S.O. 1990, c. C.12, ss. 79–84.

85. OMITTED (PROVIDES FOR COMING INTO FORCE OF PROVISIONS OF THIS ACT). R.S.O. 1990, c. C.12, s. 85.

TABLE OF CASES

A. v. B.   31
A.(C.) v. F.(W.)   308
A.(D.R.) v. M.(R.M.)   357, 359
A.(L.J.) v. A.(L.)   533
A.A. v. B.B. (2003 Ont.)   561
A.A. v. B.B. (2007 Ont.)   561, 563
A.A. v. S.N.A.   497
A.C. c. O.F.   241
A.C. v. R.R.   427
A.D.B. v. S.A.M.   425, 427, 453
A.E. v. M.G.   430
A.H. v. J.T.H.   145
A.L. v. D.K.   502
A.L.Y. v. L.M.Y.   419
A.M.D. v. A.J.P. (sub nom. Drygala v.
   Pauli)   445
A.S. v. A.S.   33
A.W.H. v. C.G.S.   461
Abate v. Abate   585
Abbott v. Taylor (1986 Man. C.A.)   516
Abbott v. Taylor (1988 Man. C.A.)   237
Abdo v. Abdo   508
Acchione v. Acchione   141, 219
Achari v. Sami   290

Ackland v. Brooks   423
Acorn v. DeRoche   417
Adam v. Adam   574
Adams v. Adams (1997 Man. Q.B.)   390
Adams v. Adams (2003 N.B.C.A.)   261
Adams v. Loov   404
Adams v. Martin   140
Adamson v. Steed (2006 Ont. Sup. Ct.)   432,
   465
Adamson v. Steed (2007 Ont. Sup. Ct.)   431
Adler v. Jonas (1998 B.C.S.C.)   364
Adler v. Jonas (1999 B.C.S.C.)   364
Ahn v. Ahn   317
Aisaican v. Khanapace   43
Aker v. Howard   406
Aksugyuk v. Aksugyuk   356
Albert v. Albert   312, 377–78
Albo v. Albo   377–78, 460
Albrecht v. Albrecht   604
Alexander v. Alexander   449
Alfaro v. Alfaro   455
Alger v. Alger   579, 583
Algner v. Algner   446
Ali v. Ahmed   29, 37

Ali v. Ali   27–28

Ali v. Canada (Minister of Citizenship and Immigration)   29

Ali, Re   628

Allaire v. Allaire   253, 264

Allaire v. Greyeyes   431

Allen v. Allen   628

Allen v. Esau   461

Almeida v. Almeida   219

Alspector v. Alspector   30

Amaral v. Amaral   231, 469

Ambler v. Ambler   285

Anderson v. Anderson (1972 Alta. C.A.)   206, 211

Anderson v. Anderson (1990 Man. Q.B.)   109

Anderson v. Anderson (2002 Man. C.A.)   267

Anderson v. Anderson Estate   612

Anderson v. Lambert   357, 359

Anderson v. Luoma   50–51, 65

Andrews v. Andrews (1992 N.S.T.D.)   282

Andrews v. Andrews (1992 Sask. C.A.)   357

Andrews v. Andrews (1995 B.C.S.C.)   230

Andrews v. Andrews (1999 Ont. C.A.)   239, 420, 470

Andrews v. Ross   32

Andries v. Andries   437

Anema v. Anema   189–90

Aning v. Aning   568

Appleyard v. Appleyard   590

Arlow v. Arlow   627

Arlt v. Arlt   449

Armitage v. Attorney General   194

Armstrong v. Armstrong (1986 Ont. Dist. Ct.)   580

Armstrong v. Armstrong (2006 Ont. C.A.)   289, 603

Arndt v. Arndt   589–90, 606, 620

Arsenault v. Arsenault   184–85

Aschenbrenner v. Aschenbrenner   225

Ashworth v. Ashworth   200

Asselin v. Canada   293

Assinck v. Assinck   457

Astle v. Walton   182–83

Attwood v. Attwood   260

Au v. Au   294

Aucoin v. Aucoin   107, 206, 216

Aujla v. Aujla   290

Austin v. Austin (2007 Ont. Sup. Ct.)   239

Austin v. Austin (2008 Ont. Sup. Ct.)   436, 444

Austin v. Goerz   53

Avery v. Avery   604, 607

Aylsworth v. Aylsworth   585

Azimi v. Mirzaei (2007 Ont. Sup. Ct.)   606

Azimi v. Mirzaei (2008 Ont. Sup. Ct.)   554

Aziz v. Aziz   428

B. v. B. (1935 S.C.C.)   43

B. v. B. (1970 Que. S.C.)   208

B. v. R.   209

B.(G.) v. G.(L.)   285, 295, 298

B.(K.L.) v. B.(K.E.)   128

B.(P.) v. B.(W.)   128

B.A.C. v. D.L.C.   420

B.D. v. S.D.   349

B.G.D. v. R.W.D.   224, 269, 284, 308–9

B.K.K. v. H.D.   211

B.L. v. S.S.   432

B.S. v. R.T.   500

B.W. v. B.W.   512

Babowech v. Von Como   230

Bachorick v. Verdejo   391

Baia v. Baia   191–92

Bailey v. Bailey   604

Bailey v. Flood   554

Bainbridge v. Bainbridge   385

Bak v. Dobell   445

Baker v. Baker (1970 B.C.S.C.)   207

Baker v. Baker (1994 Alta. Q.B.)   376

Baker v. Baker (1997 Ont. Ct. Gen. Div.)   373

Baker v. Baker (2003 Alta. Q.B.)   230–32

Baker, Re   90

Bakes v. Bakes   54, 279

Balaban v. Balaban   451

Balcombe v. Balcombe   89

Baldwin v. Funston   461

Balloch v. Balloch 605–6

Balogh v. Balogh 229

Bance v. Bance 200–1

Banning v. Bobrowski 461

Baram v. Bakshy 418

Barbeau v. Barbeau 389

Baril v. Obelnicki 106

Barker v. Barker (1993 Alta. Q.B.) 230

Barker v. Barker (2000 B.C.S.C.) 420

Barker v. Barker (2005 B.C.C.A.) 445–46

Barley v. Barley 586

Barnard v. Barnard 307

Barrett Estate v. Dexter 32

Barter v. Barter 350

Bartlett v. Bartlett 304, 427

Bartole v. Parker 245, 457

Basi v. Basi 427

Bassett v. Bassett 628

Bast v. Bast 191–92

Battagin v. Battagin 191

Battaglini v. Battaglini 230

Baum v. Baum 411

Baxter v. Baxter 40

Baynes v. Baynes 504

Beaton v. Beaton 291

Beaton, Re 189

Beatty v. Beatty (1997 B.C.C.A.) 364

Beatty v. Beatty (2000 Ont. Sup. Ct.) 469

Beaudoin v. Beaudoin 432

Beaulac v. Beaulac 263

Beaumont v. Beaumont 305

Bebenek v. Bebenek 604

Beeching v. Beeching 441

Beisel v. Henderson 446

Belcourt v. Belcourt 431

Belcourt v. Chartrand 225

Bell v. Bell 469

Bell v. Griffin 418–19

Bell-Angus v. Angus 421

Bell-Ginsburg v. Ginsburg 112

Bellman v. Bellman 419

Bemrose v. Fetter (2005 Ont. Sup. Ct.) 239

Bemrose v. Fetter (2007 Ont. C.A.) 239, 298

Beninger v. Beninger 315, 332, 336

Bennett v. Bennett (2001 Ont. Sup. Ct.) 568

Bennett v. Bennett (2003 Ont. Sup. Ct.) 291

Bennett v. Bennett (2005 Alta. Q.B.) 243, 246

Benson v. Benson 298, 344

Bentley v. Bentley 313

Berdette v. Berdette 81, 570

Berger v. Berger 215

Bergeron v. Bergeron 236–37, 239

Bergman-Illnik v. Illnik 393

Berki v. Berki 458

Berman v. Berman 90

Bernard v. Bernard 430, 432

Berthiaume v. Dastou 29

Best v. Best (1992 Ont. C.A.) 584, 590, 619–20

Best v. Best (1999 S.C.C.) 582–83, 592

Betts v. Betts 209

Bhatti v. Bhatti 230

Bhopal v. Bhopal 440

Bigelow v. Bigelow 62, 622

Biggar v. Biggar 409

Birce v. Birce 585, 594

Birks v. Birks 426–27

Birss v. Birss 405

Bitard v. Ritztallah 193

Black v. Black (1989 Ont. S.C.) 579, 589, 593

Black v. Black (1995 B.C.C.A.) 288

Blaine v. Sanders 451

Blair v. Chung 189

Blais v. Blais (1992 Ont. Ct. Gen. Div.) 579

Blais v. Blais (2001 Sask. Q.B.) 425

Blake v. Blake 377

Bland v. Bland 413, 424

Blomberg v. Blomberg 573

Blyth v. Brooks 430

Boehmer v. Boehmer 431

Boland v. Boland 229–30, 293

Bolentiru v. Radulescu 38

Bolfan Estate, Re 613

Boniface v. Boniface 435, 460

Borger v. Jan 225

Borrett v. Borrett 272, 275

Bosch v. Bosch 73, 568, 577, 595

Bosley v. Bosley   90

Boston v. Boston   291–92, 328

Botchett v. Botchett   247

Both v. Both   622–23

Botha v. Botha   451

Botros v. Botros   139

Boudreau v. Brun   246, 260, 352

Boulos v. Boulos   200

Bourget v. Bourget   348

Bourque v. Bourque   286

Bourque v. Phillips   406

Boutilier v. Nova Scotia (Attorney
General)   24

Boychuk v. Boychuk   517

Boyd v. Boyd   247

Boyle v. Gale   555

Boznick v. Boznick   456

Braaksma v. Braaksma   606, 608, 610–11

Bracewell v. Bracewell   306

Bracklow v. Bracklow   56, 243–44, 252–55,
258, 261–62, 265–67, 270, 300, 309, 327,
332, 349

Bradley v. Bradley   297

Bradley v. Zaba   378, 380

Bramley v. Bramley   210

Brandner v. Brandner   378

Bray v. Bray   569, 611

Bray-Long v. Long   240

Bremer v. Bremer   312

Brett v. Brett   567, 606

Brewer v. Brewer   108, 210

Brink v. Brink   488

Brinkos v. Brinkos   579, 581, 586, 601

British Columbia (Maintenance Enforcement
Director) v. Lagore   468

Brockie v. Brockie   248, 255, 267, 302

Broder v. Broder (1994 Man. Q.B.)   471

Broder v. Broder (1998 Alta. Q.B.)   480

Brodytsch v. Brodytsch   230

Bronfman v. Bronfman   623

Brook v. Brook   29

Brooks v. Alker   81

Brophy v. Brophy   268

Brosseau v. Belland   32

Brown v. Brown (1907 B.C. Co. Ct.)   31

Brown v. Brown (1980 P.E.I.T.D.)   191–92

Brown v. Brown (1993 B.C.S.C.)   380

Brown v. Brown (2007 Ont. Sup. Ct.)   237

Brown v. Brown (2007 N.B.Q.B.)   316

Brown v. Rae   264

Brown, Re   123

Brownie v. Hoganson   62

Bruehler v. Bruehler   376

Bruker v. Marcovitz   220

Bruno v. Bruno   423

Bryant v. Gordon   315

Buckland v. Buckland   33

Budden v. Combden   419

Budyk v. Sol   380

Buhr v. Buhr   454

Bumbacco v. Bumbacco   356

Burgess v. Burgess   622

Burgmaier v. Burgmaier   594

Burgoyne v. Burgoyne   200

Burhoe v. Goff   455

Burka v. Burka   553

Burke v. Burke   447

Burns v. Burns   400–1

Burt v. Burt (1974 N.S.T.D.)   201

Burt v. Burt (1990 Nfld. T.D.)   304

Burton v. Burton (1981 Ont. C.A.)   610

Burton v. Burton (1982 B.C.C.A.)   296

Burton v. Burton (1994 Ont. Ct. Gen.
Div.)   304

Burton v. Burton (1997 N.S.T.D.)   421

Bush v. Bush   305

Bushell v. Bushell   427

Buske v. Buske   580

Butt v. Butt   579, 585

Buttrum v. Buttrum   580

Buxton v. Buxton   479

Byerley v. Byerley   225

Byrn v. Mackin   189

Byzruki v. Byzruki   201

Bzowy v. Grover   54

C. v. C. (1921 U.K.) 41

C. v. C. (1942 N.Z.) 34

C. v. C. (1949 Man. Q.B.) 41

C.(R.M.) v. C.(J.R.) 484

C.A.M. v. D.M. 177, 554

C.A.R. v. G.F.R. 460, 464–65

C.B. v. M.R. 555–56

C.C. v. L.B. 498

C.E.C. v. M.P.C. 476

C.G.E. (No. 1), Re 64

C.L.B. v. B.T.C. 376

C.L.J. v. J.M.J. 506

C.L.R. v. R.A.R. 485

C.M.B.E. v. D.J.E. 506

C.N.G. v. S.M.R. 287

C.R. v. B.L.B. 556

C.R. v. T.R. 495

C.R.H. v. B.A.H. 490

C.T. v. J.T. 485, 555

C.W. v. L.G.M. 131

Cabernel v. Cabernel 452

Cable v. Cable 189

Cabot v. Mikkelson 458

Cade v. Rotstein 550, 593

Cadot v. Cadot 189

Caines v. Caines 627

Cairns v. Cairns 507

Calahoo v. Calahoo 494

Callaghan v. Brett 420, 454

Callaghan v. Callaghan 383

Calvert v. Calvert 622

Cameron v. Cameron 485

Cameron-Masson v. Masson 470

Camilleri v. Camilleri 290

Campbell v. Campbell (1976 Sask. Q.B.) 87, 274

Campbell v. Campbell (1986 Ont. H.C.J.) 77

Campbell v. Campbell (1991 Ont. Ct. Gen. Div.) 77

Campbell v. Campbell (1998 Sask. Q.B.) 357

Campbell v. Campbell (2008 B.C.S.C.) 315

Campbell v. Martijn 424

Campbell v. Ramsden 555

Campbell v. Rooney 305

Campese v. Campese 246

Campolin v. Campolin 395

Canadian Foundation for Children Youth and the Law v. Canada (Attorney General) 120

Cane v. Newman 423

Caratun v. Caratun 254, 580, 587

Carey v. Hanlon 504

Carlsen v. Carlsen 280

Carmichael v. Carmichael (1976 B.C.C.A.) 230

Carmichael v. Carmichael (2007 Alta. C.A.) 261

Carnall v. Carnall 387

Caro v. Cebryk 35

Caron v. Caron 305, 307, 309

Carr v. Carr 480

Carrier v. Carrier 341

Carriere v. Carriere 504

Carson v. Carson 205

Carter v. Carter (1978 Nfld. S.C.) 229

Carter v. Carter (1991 B.C.C.A.) 303

Cartier v. Cartier 599

Carvell v. Carvell 225, 456

Carwick v. Carwick 89

Casals v. Casals 420

Cass v. Cass 305

Cassar-Fleming v. Fleming 357, 359

Caston v. Caston 293

Catania v. Giannattasio 568

Cavalier v. Cavalier 210

Cavanaugh v. Ziegler 525

Cawker v. Cawker 287

Ceulemans v. Ceulemans 304

Chadder v. Chadder 234

Chadderton v. Chadderton 191

Chaitos v. Christopoulos 281

Chalifoux v. Chalifoux 243, 246, 253–54, 465

Challoner v. Challoner 141, 571

Chalmers v. Copfer 569

Chamanlall v. Chamanlall 456

Chambers v. Chambers   415, 422

Chammout v. Chammout   482

Champion v. Champion   287

Chapman v. Chapman (1993 B.C.S.C.)   555

Chapman v. Chapman (2001 Ont. C.A.)   555

Chapple v. Campbell   373

Chaput v. Chaput   416

Charles v. Charles (1991 B.C.S.C.)   282

Charles v. Charles (1997 B.C.S.C.)   445

Chartier v. Chartier   356–57, 359–61, 363, 368

Chaudhry v. Chaudhry   213

Cheni (otherwise Rodriguez) v. Cheni   27

Chenkie v. Chenkie   183

Chertkow v. Feinstein   33

Chertow v. Chertow   466

Chetti v. Chetti   27

Chevalier v. Chevalier   456–57

Children's Aid Society of Brant v. R.(E.)   121

Childs v. Childs Estate   173

Choquette v. Choquette   239

Chorney v. Chorney   209

Chouinard v. Chouinard   206

Chovin v. Dancer-Chovin   533

Chrispen v. Topham   50, 52, 62, 65

Christian v. Christian   580, 587

Christofferson v. Christofferson   90

Ciardullo v. Ciardullo   380

Cimetta v. Topler   613

Cipens v. Cipens   76, 86–88

Ciresi (Ahmad) v. Ahmad   37

Clark v. Clark   389

Clarke v. Clarke (1974 Alta. C.A.)   230

Clarke v. Clarke (1990 S.C.C.)   585

Clarke v. Clarke (1998 B.C.S.C.)   369

Clause v. Clause   30

Claxton v. Jones   395

Clegg v. Clegg   581

Clegg v. Downing   466–67

Cliche v. Cliche   579

Clifford v. Clifford   43

Clothier v. Ettinger   508

Coates v. Coates   205

Cochrane v. Cochrane   208

Cofell v. Moyer   406

Coghill v. Coghill   435

Cohen v. Cohen   229

Cohen v. Sellar   22

Cole v. Cole (1995 N.S. Fam. Ct.)   378

Cole v. Cole (2000 N.S.S.C.)   449

Cole v. McNeil   451

Collier v. Torbar   594

Collins v. Collins (1978 Alta. S.C.T.D.)   308

Collins v. Collins (2003 Nfld. S.C.)   427

Collison v. Collison   467

Colp (Silmarie) v. Colp   265

Comeau v. Comeau   471

Comeau v. Dennison   490

Connell v. Connell   456

Connelly v. Connelly   248

Connelly v. McGouran (2006 Ont. C.A.)   453

Connelly v. McGouran (2007 Ont. C.A.)   461

Connor v. Rakievich   262

Consiglio v. Consiglio   493

Contino v. Leonelli-Contino   396, 400, 402–3

Cook v. Kilduff   369

Cook v. McManus   427, 437, 441, 449

Cook v. Sacco   477

Cooper v. Cooper (1969 N.S.S.C.)   192

Cooper v. Cooper (1972 Ont. H.C.J.)   75, 200

Cooper v. Cooper (1983 Ont. Prov. Ct.)   308

Cooper v. Cooper (1998 Nfld. U.F.C.)   54

Cooper v. Cooper (2002 Sask. Q.B.)   469, 483

Corbeil v. Corbeil   246, 263, 312

Corkum v. Clarke   418

Corless v. Corless   580

Cormier v. Cormier   183

Cornelius v. Andres (sub nom. Andres v. Andres)   435, 450

Correia v. Correia   413, 415, 422

Correia v. Danyluk   140

Cosper v. Cosper   140

Costa v. Costa   173

Costa v. Petipas   398–400

Cotter v. Cotter (1986 Ont. C.A.)   309

Cotter v. Cotter (1988 Ont. H.C.J.)   592, 621

Cottreau v. Pothier   299

Courchesne v. Charlebois   445

Court v. McQuaid   403

Cowan v. Cowan (1987 Ont. Sup. Ct.)   608

Cowan v. Cowan (2001 Alta. Q.B.)   420

Coward v. Coward   293

Cowell v. Prince   31

Cox v. Cox   361

Cox v. Down (sub nom. Cox v. Stephen)   480

Coyle v. Danylkiw   506–7

Cozart v. Cozart   542

Cram v. Cram   394

Crane v. Crane   605–6

Crawford v. Crawford (1973 B.C.S.C.)   173

Crawford v. Crawford (1987 Ont. H.C.J.)   229

Crawford v. Crawford (1997 Ont. C.A.)   608, 610

Crawley v. Tobin   417

Creelman v. Creelman   269

Creighton v. Klyne   431

Criddle v. Mohl   431

Cridge v. Cridge   201

Criton v. Criton   586

Crofton v. Sturko   420

Cronkwright v. Cronkwright   142

Cross v. Cross   395

Crutchfield v. Crutchfield   579–80

Culen v. Culen   282–83

Cullen v. Cullen   191

Cunningham v. Cunningham   229

Curle v. Lowe   491

Curniski v. Aubert   406

Curran v. Curran   209

Currie v. Currie (1987 Man. Q.B.)   184

Currie v. Currie (1991 P.E.I.S.C.A.D.)   243

Cusack v. Cusack   470

Cushman v. Cushman   85

Cusick v. Squire   395

Cymbalisty v. Cymbalisty (2002 Man. Q.B.)   262

Cymbalisty v. Cymbalisty (2003 Man. C.A.)   292

Cyrenne v. Moar   558

Czemeres v. Czemeres   604

Czora v. Lonergan   110

D. v. A.   40

D.(T.W.) v. D.(Y.M.)   183

D.A.W. v. W.M.Z.   288

D.B. (Litigation guardian of) v. Children's Aid Society of Durham Region   131

D.B.S. v. S.R.G.   458, 465, 525

D.B.S. v. S.R.G.; L.J.W. v. T.A.R.; Henry v. Henry; Hiemstra v. Hiemstra   458, 462, 466

D.C. v. B.R.   555

D.C.R. v. T.M.R.   476–77, 480

D.G. v. H.F.   503

D.J.F. v. E.K.   379

D.J.L. v. C.M.   477, 495, 497

D.K.N. v. M.J.O.   271

D.L.M. v. J.A.M.   341, 445–46

D.L.S. v. D.E.S.   494

D.L.W. v. J.J.M.V.   506

D.M. v. M.B.   490

D.M.B. v. J.R.B.   465

D.P. v. R.B.   490

D.P.C. v. T.N.C.   186

D.P.O. v. P.E.O.   255, 492, 497

D.R.D. v. S.E.G.   356

D.R.M. v. R.B.M.   315, 317

D.S. v. D.A.M.   128

D.S. v. M.S.   348

D.T.V. v. G.G.   480

D.W.H. v. D.J.R.   559

d'Entremont v. d'Entremont (1992 N.S.C.A.)   205

D'Entremont v. D'Entremont (2001 N.S.S.C.)   469

D'Urzo v. D'Urzo   395

D'Vaz v. D'Vaz   225

Da Costa v. Da Costa   581, 619–20

Dabirian v. Dabirian   552

Dagg v. Pereira   480

Daher v. Daher   297

Daku v. Daku   427

Dalep v. Dalep   362

Danchuk v. Danchuk   409

Dansereau v. Dansereau   461–62

Darlington v. Darlington   362, 378

Darvill v. Chorney   428

Datars v. Graham   490

Davari v. Namazi   449

Davidson v. Davidson (1987 Ont. S.C.)   88

Davidson v. Davidson (1998 Alta. Q.B.)   412

Davies v. Davies (1980 N.B.Q.B.)   201

Davies v. Davies (1988 Ont. S.C.)   582, 584, 598

Davis v. Davis (1999 B.C.S.C.)   394

Davis v. Davis (2000 N.S.S.C.)   472

Davison v. Sweeney   29, 31–33, 40

De Acetis v. De Acetis   571

de Araujo v. de Araujo   142

de Champlain v. de Champlain   600

De Mornay v. De Mornay   571, 611

De Reneville v. De Reneville   29, 31

Deal v. Deal   33

Dean v. Brown   448

Dean v. Friesen   404

Deane v. Pawluk   174

Dearing v. Dearing   80

Debacker v. Debacker   277

Debora v. Debora (1999 Ont. C.A.)   567

Debora v. Debora (2004 Ont. Sup. Ct.)   570, 622, 626

Debora v. Debora (2006 Ont. C.A.)   392, 461, 592, 596, 622

Degagne v. Sargeant   384

Dejardin v. Dejardin   44

Delaney v. Delaney   211

Delorme v. Woodham   432

Demchuk v. Demchuk   79

Demeria v. Demeria   427

Demers v. Moar   446

Dempsey v. Dempsey (1997 N.S.T.D.)   418

Dempsey v. Dempsey (2004 B.C.S.C.)   482

Dennis v. Dennis   203

Denton v. Denton   350

Deo v. Kumar   41

Desimone v. Desimone   280

Desjardins v. Desjardins   472

Deslippe v. Deslippe   75, 201

Desramaux v. Desramaux   86

Desrochers v. Desrochers   232

Devani v. Devani   199

Deveau v. Groskopf   404

Dick v. Dick   201

Dickinson v. Dickinson   418

Dickson v. Dickson   460–61

Diebel v. Diebel   430

Diebert v. Calder   56

DiFrancesco v. Couto   430–31

Dillon v. Dillon   399, 466

DiPasquale v. DiPasquale   423–25

Dippel v. Dippel   192

Dipper v. Dipper   308

Ditullio v. Ditullio   88

Dixon v. Dixon   187, 297

Dixon v. Fleming   455

Do Carmo v. Etzkorn   357

Dobson v. Dobson   236

Docherty v. Docherty (1992 Ont. Gen. Div.)   605

Docherty v. Docherty (1994 Ont. C.A.)   602

Doe v. Alberta   52, 359

Doherty v. Decoff   461, 465

Doherty v. Doherty   234, 239, 423

Doiron v. Doiron   231

Domanski v. Domanski   432

Donovan v. Donovan   428, 445–46

Doole v. Doole   304, 432

Dorchester v. Dorchester   200

Dormer v. McJannet   173

Dorval v. Dorval   504–5

Douglas v. Campbell   377, 380

Douglas v. Ward   405

Douglas/Kwantlen Faculty Association v. Douglas College   94

Dowell v. Dowell   209

Downton v. Royal Trust Co.   42, 196

Doyle v. Doyle   400–1

Dreger v. Dreger   451

Dreichel v. Dreichel   262

Drewery v. Drewery   276

Droit de la Famille – 08316   244

Droit de la famille – 08544   555

Droit de la famille – 1006   190

Droit de la famille – 1115   232

Droit de la famille – 1184   230

Droit de la famille – 1221   194

Droit de la famille – 1404   305

Droit de la famille – 221   228

Droit de la famille – 304   199

Droit de la famille – 3148 (sub nom. O.M. v. A.K.)   185

Droit de la famille – 333   307

Droit de la famille – 360   190

Droit de la famille – 382   308–9

Droit de la famille – 471   199

Droit de la famille – 541   187

Droit de la famille – 683   234

Dubey v. Dubey   315, 350, 477

Duder v. Rowe   225, 315, 360

Dudka v. Dudka   393–94

Dudla v. Lemay   232

Duff v. Duff (1983 Nfld. C.A.)   592

Duff v. Duff (1988 Ont. S.C.)   589, 607–8, 619

Duguay v. Thompson-Duguay   176

Duits v. Duits   144

Duke v. Andler   568

Dumas v. Dumas   219, 413

Dumont v. Dumont   225

Dunbar v. Yukon   24

Dunnigan v. Park   333

Dunning v. Dunning   579, 581

Dupere v. Dupere   75, 200

Durant v. Durant   210

Durham v. Durham   33

Dusseault v. Dolfo   364

Dutrisac v. Ulm (1999 B.C.S.C.)   361

Dutrisac v. Ulm (2000 B.C.C.A.)   363, 368

Dyal v. Dyal   254

E.C.H. v. W.E.H.   416

E.J.M. v. D.D.I.   477

E.M.V. v. T.D.H.V.   430

E.S. v. J.S.S.   312, 465

E.W. v. D.W.   501

Earle v. Earle   428, 430

Earles v. Earles   400

Eastwood v. Eastwood   315, 350

Ebenal v. Ebenal   205–6

Ebrahim v. Ebrahim   420

Eddy v. Eddy   218

Edward v. Edward Estate   195

Edwards v. Edwards (1973 B.C.C.A.)   206

Edwards v. Edwards (1994 N.S.C.A.)   304

Egale Canada Inc. v. Canada (Attorney General)   24

Egan v. Egan   451

Eilers v. Eilers   410, 412

Ekvall v. Cooper   555, 558

Elias v. Elias   260

Ellet v. Ellet   188

Elligott v. Elligott   205

Elliot v. Elliot   229, 247, 254, 260, 312

Elliott v. Loewen   505, 507

Elliott v. Mumford   558

Ells v. Ells   209

Emery v. Emery (2007 B.C.S.C.)   315

Emery v. Emery (2008 Ont. Sup. Ct.)   312, 461, 604

Emond v. Emond   579

English v. English   379

Enman v. Enman   416

Epp v. Robertson   410

Epstein v. Epstein   234

Erhardt v. Erhardt   188

Erickson v. Erickson (2001 B.C.S.C.)   416

Erickson v. Erickson (2007 N.S.S.C.)   379

Estey v. Estey   394

Evans v. Evans (1987 B.C.S.C.)   184

Evans v. Evans (1988 Ont. H.C.J.)   231

Evans v. Evans (1998 Sask. Q.B.)   381, 389–90

Evely v. Evely   54, 278

Ewart v. Ewart   307

Ewasiuk v. Ewasiuk   205

Ewing v. Ewing (1990 B.C.S.C.)   304

Ewing v. Ewing (2007 Alta. S.C.)   460

F.(N.) v. S.(H.L.)   555

F.(R.D.) v. F.(S.L.)   218–19

F.(R.L.) v. F.(S.)   359

F.C.W. v. B.E.W.   352

Fair v. Jones   357

Falbo v. Falbo   469

Farden v. Farden   362, 378, 380

Faremouth v. Watson   31

Farkasch v. Farkasch   211

Farquar v. Farquar   79

Faulkner v. Faulkner (1986 B.C.S.C.)   259

Faulkner v. Faulkner (1997 Alta. Q.B.)   418

Fedoruk v. Jamieson   455

Fehr v. Fehr   295–96, 298

Feist v. Feist   512

Feldman v. Feldman   207

Fell v. Fell   323

Feng v. Sung Estate   32

Fenn v. Fenn   606, 611

Fennig-Doll v. Doll   505

Fenton v. Livingstone   31

Ferguson v. Thorne   387, 459, 461

Fernandez (Alarcio) v. Fernandez   36–37

Fernandez v. Fernandez   213

Fernquist v. Garland   362

Ferster v. Ferster   400

Filipich v. Filipich   430–31

Finlay v. Finlay   456

Finn v. Levine   435

Finney v. Finney   409

Finnie and Rae, Re   284

Firth v. Firth   304

Fisher v. Fisher (1978 Alta. T.D.)   209

Fisher v. Fisher (2001 N.S.C.A.)   249

Fisher v. Fisher (2008 Ont. C.A.)   225, 236–38, 246, 253, 260, 315, 317, 344–46, 349–50

Fisher v. Giles   260

Fisher v. Heron   410

Fisher v. Munroe   461

Fisher v. Pade   420

Fitzell v. Weisbrood   432

Fitzpatrick v. Fitzpatrick (1989 Ont. Dist. Ct.)   583

Fitzpatrick v. Fitzpatrick (2000 Nfld. U.F.C.)   393

Fleet v. Fleet   215

Fleming v. Fleming (1934 Ont. C.A.)   31

Fleming v. Fleming (2001 Ont. Div. Ct.)   248

Fleming v. Fleming (2001 Ont. Sup. Ct.)   575

Fleming v. Fleming (2005 Sask. Q.B.)   350–51

Flett v. Flett   585

Flockhart v. Flockhart   563

Flynn v. Flynn   579

Foley v. Foley   495–96

Folga v. Folga   577, 591, 595

Follwell v. Holmes   182, 184

Fong v. Charbonneau   415, 422

Fonseca v. Fonseca   411

Foran v. Foran   235, 240

Ford v. Stier   34

Forrester v. Forrester   416

Forster v. Forster   485, 619

Foster v. Foster   230, 236, 332

Fournier v. Fournier (1990 N.B.Q.B.)   304

Fournier v. Fournier (1997 B.C.S.C.)   357

Fowler v. Szabo-Fowler   219

Frame v. Frame   480

Frame v. Smith   491

Francis v. Baker   391–93

Francis v. Francis   594, 629

Fransoo v. Fransoo   395, 423–24

Fraser v. Capital Trust Corp.   90

Fraser v. Fraser (1994 N.B.C.A.)   229

Fraser v. Fraser (2001 Ont. Sup. Ct.)   395

Fraser v. Gallant   394

Fraser v. Jones   362, 380

Frazer v. van Rootselaar   284

Fredrickson v. Fredrickson   304

Frey v. Frey   296

Friedt v. Friedt Estate   293

Fritz v. Day   262

Fritz v. Tate   413

Frydrysek v. Frydrysek   471

Fulton v. Fulton   631

Furlong v. Furlong   204

Futia v. Futia   609

G. v. G. (1924 U.K.)   41

G. v. G. (1960 U.K.)   43

G. v. M.   43

G.E.S. v. D.L.C.   556, 559

G.H. v. J.L.   492

G.M. c. M.A.F.   185

G.M.K. v. C.L.H.   555

G.M.P. v. T.K.   492

G.S. v. F.C.   479

G.V. c. C.G.   348–49

G.V.C. v. G.E.   479

Gabel v. Gabel   225

Gaetz v. Gaetz   405

Gainer v. Gainer   245, 249, 630

Galbraith v. Galbraith   200, 206

Gale v. Gale (2002 Man. C.A.)   267

Gale v. Gale (2007 Man. C.A.)   225

Galeano v. Dubail   312

Galloway v. Galloway   435

Gammon v. Gammon   271

Gandy v. Gandy   403

Garad v. Garad   364

Garard v. Garard   411

Garchinski v. Garchinski   182–83

Gardiner v. Gardiner   395, 479

Garland v. Garland   350

Gartner v. Gartner   376

Garwood v. Garwood   304

Gaspers v. Gaspers   461

Gaudet (Litigation guardian of) v. Young
   Estate   623

Gauthier v. Gauthier   271

Gavigan v. Gavigan   360

Geci v. Gravel   191

Gehla v. Gehla   312

Genovesi v. Genovesi   552–53

Gentles v. Gentles   213

George v. George (1950 Ont. C.A.)   205

George v. George (1983 Man. C.A.)   582

Geransky v. Geransky   201

Gergely v. Gergely   85

Geropoulos v. Geropoulos   77

Ghisleri v. Ghisleri   428

Gidey v. Abay   290

Giebelhaus v. Bell   391

Gies v. Gies   629

Giesbrecht v. Giesbrecht   209

Giguere v. Giguere   254

Gilchrist v. Keith   431

Giles v. Villeneuve   415, 419

Gilham v. Steele   30

Gillett v. Gillett   213

Gillham v. Gillham   307

Gillis v. Gillis   302

Gill-Sager v. Sager   224, 284, 308–9, 471

Ginn v. Ginn   285

Ginter v. Ginter   200

Giorno v. Giorno   247

Girouard v. Girouard   330

Glazier v. Glazier   229

Glen v. Glen   382, 384, 387

Gobeil v. Gobeil   275, 286, 288, 407

Goddard v. Hambleton   61

Godinek v. Godinek   621

Goldberg v. Goldberg   440

Goldenberg v. Triffon   195

Goldstein v. Goldstein   207, 217

Gollins v. Gollins (No. 2)   207

Gollins v. Gollins (1963 U.K. H.L.)   108

Gollins v. Gollins (1964 U.K. H.L.)   206–7

Goodman v. Goodman   41

Gordon v. Goertz   485, 487–89, 491, 493,
   504, 542

Gordon v. Keyes (1985 N.S.C.A.)   141

Gordon v. Keyes (1986 N.S.T.D.)   193

Gordon v. Paquette   364

Gormley v. Gormley   417

Gossen v. Gossen   228, 231–32, 237, 239,
   259, 290, 443, 450

Gostlin v. Kergin   53

Goudie v. Buchanan   404
Goudie v. Goudie   206, 208
Goudy v. Malbeuf   301
Gould v. Sandau   61
Graham v. Graham   247
Grainger v. Grainger   304, 585
Grams v. Grams   259
Grandy v. Grandy   216
Grant v. Grant   217
Grant-Hose v. Grant-Hose   304–5
Graves v. Legg   89
Gray (formerly Wiegers) v. Wiegers   504
Gray v. Gray (1983 Ont. H.C.J.)   431
Gray v. Gray (1998 Ont. Ct. Gen. Div.)   469
Greco v. Levin   304–5
Green v. Green   378, 403, 405, 437
Green v. Millar   492
Greenall v. Greenall   232
Greenlees v. Greenlees   41
Greenough v. Greenough   478
Greenstreet v. Cumyns   41
Greenwood v. Greenwood (1988 Ont.
   H.C.J.)   80
Greenwood v. Greenwood (1998
   B.C.S.C.)   421
Greggain v. Hunter   107
Greither v. Greither   352
Grewal v. Sohal   31, 36, 41
Grierson v. Brunton   421
Griffith v. Griffith (1944 Ireland)   33
Griffith v. Griffith (2001 Sask. Q.B.)   89
Griffiths v. Griffiths   389
Griffiths v. Zambosco   625
Grime v. Grime   611
Grinyer v. Grinyer   344, 346
Gritti v. Gritti   470
Grohmann v. Grohmann   254
Grossmann v. Grossmann   81
Guderyan v. Meyers   449
Guerin v. R.   294
Guillena v. Guillena   449
Guillet v. Guillet   425
Guziolek v. Guziolek   624

H. v. H. (1953 U.K.)   33, 36
H. v. H. (1978 Ont. H.C.J.)   216
H.(U.V.) v. H.(M.W.)   361, 363–64, 368–69,
   461
H.L. v. M.H.L.   285
H.L.C. v. M.A.L.   40–41
H.R. v. R.P.   356
H.S. v. C.S.   488
Hagen v. Rankin   388
Haider v. Malach   492
Haimanot v. Haimanot   435, 436
Haisman v. Haisman   373, 430, 462
Hall v. Hall (1997 B.C.S.C.)   411
Hall v. Hall (2006 Alta. Q.B.)   449
Halley v. Halley   437
Halliday v. Halliday (1997 Ont. C.A.)   56
Halliday v. Halliday (1998 Sask. Q.B.)   357
Halpern v. Canada   24, 27, 197–98
Hama v. Werbes   225
Hamel v. Hamel   380
Hamilton v. Hamilton (1989 Sask. C.A.)   533
Hamilton v. Hamilton (1992 Alta. Q.B.)   507
Hamilton v. Hamilton (2005 Ont. Sup.
   Ct.)   601
Hamilton v. Hamilton (2006 B.C.S.C.)   295
Hamilton v. Pearce   433
Hammermeister v. Hammermeister   609
Hamonic v. Gronvold   394
Hancock v. Hancock   303
Handy v. Handy   394, 411
Hanmore v. Hanmore   403
Hannah v. Warner   441
Hanson v. Hanson   375
Hansvall v. Hansvall   414
Hardick v. Fox   41
Harding v. Harding (1985 Man. Q.B.)   191
Harding v. Harding (2006 Nfld. S.C.)   350
Harrington v. Harrington   374
Harris v. Harris (1978 B.C.S.C.)   296
Harris v. Harris (1986 Ont. Dist. Ct.)   583,
   595
Harris v. Harris (2005 Ont. Sup. Ct.)   250
Harris v. Harris (2006 Ont. C.A.)   375

Harris v. Mouland   485

Harris v. Murray   184

Harrison v. Canada (Attorney General)   24

Harrison v. Harrison (1917 Ont. C.A.)   172

Harrison v. Harrison (1975 N.S.T.D.)   204

Harrison v. Harrison (1998 B.C.S.C.)   457

Harrower v. Harrower   599

Harry v. Harry   592

Harsant v. Portnoi   173, 516

Hart v. Hart (No. 3)   587–88

Hart v. Neufeld   428

Harthan v. Harthan   32, 40, 43

Hartshorne v. Hartshorne   23, 66, 69, 70, 283

Harvey v. Harvey   304

Hassan and Hassan, Re   28

Hassan v. Hassan   29

Hatton v. Hatton   478

Hauff v. Hauff   229, 312

Havrot v. Moore   344, 347

Hawco v. Myers   466

Hawkins v. Hawkins   247

Hawko v. Knapp   431

Hayden v. Stockwood   456

Haynes v. Haynes   606, 624

Hayward v. Hayward (1961 U.K.)   44

Hayward v. Hayward (2006 N.B.Q.B.)   298, 301

Hearn v. Bacque   359

Hearn v. Hearn   502

Hébert v. Dame Houle   200

Hedley v. Hedley   259

Heiden v. British Columbia (Director of Maintenance Enforcement)   430

Heil v. Heil   40–41

Heimbecker v. Heimbecker   306

Hein v. Hein   225

Heinemann v. Heinemann   260

Hellinckx v. Large   375

Henderson v. Henderson (1944 U.K.)   216

Henderson v. Henderson (1987 Ont. Dist. Ct.)   312, 611

Henderson v. Henderson (1999 B.C.S.C.)   357

Henderson v. Sharma-Henderson   231

Hendricken v. Canada   53–54

Hendricks c. Québec (Procureur général)   24

Hendricks v. Swan   555

Hendrickson v. Hendrickson   467

Henry v. Cymbalisty   592, 618

Henry v. Henry   458–59

Hensell v. Hensell   480

Henteleff v. Henteleff   275

Hercus v. Hercus   175

Herman v. Herman   75, 207

Hersey v. Hersey   303

Hesketh v. Hesketh   349

Hickey v. Hickey (1999 S.C.C.)   299, 333, 351

Hickey v. Hickey (2002 S.C.C.)   431

Hiebert v. Hiebert (2005 B.C.S.C.)   182

Hiebert v. Hiebert (2007 Sask. Q.B.)   377–79, 384, 387

Hiemstra v. Hiemstra (2005 Alta. C.A.)   458

Higgins v. Higgins (2001 Ont. Sup. Ct.)   260, 624

Higgins v. Higgins (2006 Alta. Q.B.)   303

Hilborn v. Hilborn   468

Hilderley v. Hilderley   579, 583, 584

Hildinger v. Carroll   480

Hill v. Davis   375

Hill v. Hill (1959 U.K.)   43

Hill v. Hill (1987 Ont. Dist. Ct.)   110, 627, 630

Hill v. Hill (2003 N.S.C.A.)   237

Hill v. Hill (2008 Sask. Q.B.)   280

Hillhouse v. Hillhouse   243

Hillock v. Hillock   457

Hiltz v. Hiltz   206

Hinz v. Hinz   237, 238

Hiscock v. Dickie   285

Hiscocks v. Marshman   187

Hladun v. Hladun   394

Hock v. Hock (1970 B.C.S.C.)   211

Hock v. Hock (1971 B.C.C.A.)   211

Hockey v. Hockey   493

Hockey-Sweeney v. Sweeney   248

Hodgins v. Hodgins   579

Hofsteede v. Hofsteede   401–2

Hogan v. Johnston   420

Hogkinson v. Hodgkinson   393

Holeman v. Holeman   413, 415

Holizki v. Reeves   379, 387

Hollenbach v. Hollenbach   392

Hollett v. Vessey   451

Hollett-Collins v. Hollett   404

Holman v. Bignell   394

Holtby v. Holtby   435

Holtskog v. Holtskog   407

Holub v. Holub   195

Hoover v. Hoover   420

Hope v. Hope   225

Horlock v. Horlock   307

Horn v. Horn   277

Hornan v. Hornan   504

Horne v. Roberts   87, 284

Horner v. Horner (1973 N.S.C.A.)   206

Horner v. Horner (2004 Ont. C.A.)   312

Horvath v. Horvath   381

House v. House   296, 300

Howard v. Howard   480

Howe v. Kendall   411

Hrecka v. Andries   362

Hubbell v. Hubbell   280

Huber v. Yaroshko   437, 451

Hudson v. Hudson   234

Humeniuk v. Humeniuk   209

Humphreys v. Humphreys   585, 592, 621

Hunt v. Smolis-Hunt   446, 459, 469

Hunter v. Hunter   178

Hutton v. Hutton   576

Hyde v. Hyde and Woodmansee   24–25,
   28, 38

Hyldtoft v. Hyldtoft   77, 81

Iantsis (Papatheodorou) v.
   Papatheodorou   34, 36

Iasenza v. Iasenza Estate   613

Ickovich v. Tonken   235

Ierullo v. Ierullo   267

Ifield v. Ifield   207–8

Impey v. Impey   309

Indig v. Indig   589

Indyka v. Indyka   194

Inglis v. Inglis   216

Ingram v. Ingram   235

Iselmoe v. Iselmoe   452

Ivany v. Ivany (1971 B.C.S.C.)   209

Ivany v. Ivany (1996 Nfld. S.C.)   374, 378–79

J. v. J.   43

J.(L.A.) v. J.(H.)   131

J.A.G. v. R.J.R.   498

J.B.E. v. F.S.L.   554

J.C. v. A.M.M.   379, 384

J.C.R. v. J.J.R.   379, 463

J.D.F. v. H.M.F.   524

J.G.T. v. T.N.   453

J.G.W. v. A.C.S.   12

J.H.A. v. C.G.A.   255

J.J.B. v. G.G.B.   551

J.K. v. S.D.   362

J.M.B. v. A.C.B.   460

J.M.M. v. K.A.M. (2005 Nfld. S.C.)   177

J.M.M. v. K.A.M. (2005 Nfld. C.A.)   532

J.P. v. B.G.   393

J.R. v. S.H.C.   481

J.S. v. D.W.   356

J.T. v. S.C.-T.   480

J.W. v. M.H.W.   312, 461

Jablonowski v. Jablonowski   189

Jackson v. Holloway   418

Jackson v. Jackson (1987 Ont. S.C.)   619

Jackson v. Jackson (1993 Ont. Ct. Gen.
   Div.)   305

Jackson v. Jackson (1995 Ont. H.C.J.)   594

Jackson v. Punga   415

Jacobs v. Davies   22

Jahangiri-Mavaneh v. Taheri-Zengekan   185

James v. James   293

Jamieson v. Jamieson   379

Janakowski v. Janakowski   586

Jandrisch v. Jandrisch   533

Janes v. Janes   363, 369

Janes v. Pardo   194

Jansen v. Montgomery   53

Janz v. Harris   307

Jarbeau v. Pelletier   434

Jaremkow v. Jaremkow   628, 629

Jarocki v. Rice   395

Jarrett v. Jarrett   554

Jarvis v. Parker   461

Jarzebinski v. Jarzebinski   379, 391

Jasinski v. Jasinski   70

Javid v. Kurytnik   477

Jay v. Jay   287, 502

Jean v. Jean   234, 245, 377–78, 381

Jeffreys v. Luck   22

Jenkins v. Jenkins   304

Jensen v. Jensen   229, 231

Johnson v. Ahmad   37, 213

Johnson v. Checkowy   435, 439

Johnson v. Johnson (1998 B.C.S.C.)   389

Johnson v. Johnson (2000 B.C.S.C.)   452

Johnson v. Smith   36

Johnston v. Burns   287

Johnston v. Johnston (1997 B.C.C.A.)   430

Johnston v. Johnston (2004 Alta. Q.B.)   424

Johnston v. Johnston (2004 Ont. Sup. Ct.)   347

Johnston v. Johnston (2006 Sask. Q.B.)   430, 465

Johnston v. Kurz   541–42

Johnstone v. Wright   56–57

Jonas v. Jonas   420, 449

Jonasson v. Jonasson   380, 381

Jones v. Jones (1975 U.K. C.A.)   109

Jones v. Jones (2005 Sask. Q.B.)   454–55

Jordahl v. Jordahl   208

Jordan v. Jordan   581, 611

Juretic v. Ruiz   41

Juvatopolos v. Juvatopolos   307, 352

K.(L.A.) v. K.(G.N.)   218

K., Re (1995 Aust.)   537, 539

K., Re (1995 Ont. Prov. Div.)   64

K.A.M. v. P.K.M.   307, 315–16, 461

K.C. c. N.P.   485, 488

K.H.L. v. G.Q.L.   40–41

K.J.W. v. M.D.W.W.   35

K.K.C. v. A.P.C.   232

K.L.B. v. British Columbia   129–30

K.O. v. C.O.   394

K.R.C. v. C.A.C.   483, 492

Kaatz v. Kaatz   404

Kaderly v. Kaderly   470

Kahl v. Kahl   203

Kainz v. Potter   171

Kalaserk v. Nelson   513, 533

Kalyan v. Lal   37

Kaplanis v. Kaplanis   176, 477–78

Kapogianes v. Kapogianes   469

Karakatsanis v. Georgiou   570

Karol v. Karol   374

Kassim v. Kassim   35

Kastner v. Kastner   492

Kastrau v. Kastrau   210

Katapodis v. Katapodis   211

Katz v. Katz   275

Katz v. Nimelman   573

Kaur v. Brar   36, 37

Kaur v. Ginder   28

Kavanagh v. Kavanagh   394

Kawaluk v. Kawaluk   33

Kay v. Korakianitis   173

Kaye v. Kaye   445

Kazdan v. Kazdan   482

Keast v. Keast   254

Kehler v. Kehler   276, 286

Keizars v. Keizars   145

Keller v. Black   420

Kelly v. Kelly (1932 U.K.)   34

Kelly v. Kelly (1986 Ont. H.C.J.)   591

Kelly v. Kelly (1986 Ont. H.C.J.)   589, 609, 610

Kelly v. Kelly (1987 Ont. S.C.)   580

Kelly v. Kelly (1992 P.E.I.T.D.)   304

Kelly v. Kelly (2004 Ont. C.A.)   281

Kelly v. Kelly (2006 N.S.S.C.)   461

Kelly v. Lyle   449

Kemp v. Kemp   286, 378, 512

Kendry v. Cathcart   435

Kennedy v. Kennedy (1995 Ont. C.A.)   622

Kennedy v. Kennedy (1997 N.S. Fam. Ct.)   420

Kennedy-Dalton v. Dalton   418

Kenning v. Kenning   469

Kenward v. Kenward   35

Keogan v. Weekes   297

Kermeen v. Kermeen   188

Kern v. Kern   183

Kerr v. Kerr (2003 B.C.S.C.)   280

Kerr v. Kerr (2005 N.S.S.C.)   272, 275

Kerr v. Kerr (2005 Ont. Sup. Ct.) 351

Ketler v. Peacey   183

Keyes v. Gordon (1985 N.S.C.A.)   173

Keyes v. Gordon (1989 N.S. Fam. Ct.)   508

Khoee-Solomonescu v. Solomonescu (1997 Ont. Ct. Gen. Div.)   362, 394

Khoee-Solomonescu v. Solomonescu (2000 Ont. Div. Ct.)   425, 427

Kinasewich v. Kinasewich   423

King Estate v. King   284

King v. King   207

Kinghorn v. Kinghorn   304

Kingston v. Kelly   418

Kirby v. Kirby   285

Kirkpatrick v. Kirkpatrick   380

Kittelson-Schurr v. Schurr   532

Kivisto v. Kivisto   593

Klassen v. Klassen   432

Klein v. Klein   580, 583, 606, 611, 620

Knapp v. Knapp   579

Knoll v. Knoll   205–08

Kobayashi v. Kobayashi   201

Koch v. Koch (1978 Man. Co. Ct.)   210

Koch v. Koch (1985 Sask. Q.B.)   190

Koeckeritz v. Secord   531, 553

Kofoed v. Fichter   422

Kokkalas v. Kokkalas   34

Kolada v. Kolada   426

Koop v. Polson   304

Kopelow v. Warkentin   332–33, 348

Koren v. Blum   451

Kornberg v. Kornberg   184

Kovich v. Kreut   379

Kovitch v. Kovitch   225

Kowalewich v. Kowalewich   441, 445

Kowalski v. Grant   225

Koziarz v. Koziarz   628

Kozub v. Kozub   428

Kraft v. Kraft   597

Kramer v. Kramer (1983 B.C.S.C.)   287

Kramer v. Kramer (1999 Man. Q.B.)   417

Kranenburg v. Kranenburg   246

Krangle (Guardian ad litem of) v. Brisco   375

Krause v. Krause (1975 Alta. Q.B.)   206,

Krause v. Krause (1976 Alta. C.A.)   207, 211, 229–31, 293

Krawczyk v. Krawczyk   457

Kristoff v. Kristoff   76, 80, 81

Kroone v. Kroone   620

Krueger v. Tunison   384, 388

Kubel v. Kubel   504

Kuderewko v. Kuderewko   588, 589

Kudoba v. Kudoba   288, 407

Kukolj v. Kukolj   576, 618–20

Kulyk v. Kulyk   210

Kurcz v. Kurcz   249

Kutlesa v. Kutlesa   630

L. v. L.   209

L.(B.) v. B.(A.R.)   128

L.(G.M.) v. L.(V.A.)   304

L.A.K. v. A.A.W.   437, 452

L.B. v. B.B   479, 512

L.C. v. R.O.C.   395

L.E.G. v. A.G.   532, 534

L.J.W. v. T.A.R.   459

L.L. v. S.B.   495

L.L.M. v. W.L.K.   375

L.M. v. I.M.   284

L.M. v. K.F.   556

L.M.B. v. I.J.B. (2003 Alta. Q.B.)   549

L.M.B. v. I.J.B. (2005 Alta. Q.B.)   143

L.R.V. v. A.A.V.   185–86

L.S. v. E.P.   312, 459

L'Heureux v. L'Heureux   456

Labell v. Labell   430

Lachman v. Lachman   200

Lackie v. Lackie   457, 470

Lacroix c. Valois   231

Lacroix v. Lacroix   235

Laczko v. Laczko   458

Ladisa v. Ladisa   481

Lagacé v. Lagacé   306

Lake v. Lake (1983 B.C.S.C.)   208

Lake v. Lake (1988 N.S.C.A.)   177, 554

Lalonde v. Lalonde   173

Lamb v. Lamb   86

Lambe v. Coish   494

Landry v. Landry   140

Lang v. Lang   273, 277

Langdon v. Langdon   344

Langois v. Langois   469

Lapp and Dupuis, Re   559

Lapp v. Lapp   225, 332

Large v. Large   351

Larre v. Cross   542

Lasch v. Lasch   623

Laskosky v. Laskosky   415

Lauder v. Lauder   207

Laurie v. Laurie   415, 422

Lavergne v. Lavergne   434, 437, 465

Lavoie v. Canada   53

Lavoie v. Wills   420, 423

Lavoie v. Yawrenko   187

Law v. Canada (Minister of Employment and
    Immigration)   57–58

Law v. Law   329

Lawrence v. Gold   467

Lawson v. Lawson   445, 477

Lay v. Lay   568

Le Blanc v. Le Blanc   210

Le Bourdais v. Le Bourdais   454

Le Mesurier v. Le Mesurier   194

Le Van v. Le Van   606

Leachman v. Leachman   461

Leaderhouse v. Leaderhouse   75, 201,
    215–16

LeBlanc v. LeBlanc   40

Leboeuf v. Leboeuf   526

Leckie v. Leckie   579

Lee v. Lee   437

Lefevre v. Lefevre   599

Lehman v. Lehman   211

Leibel v. Davis   415

Lennox v. Frender   479, 516

Leonard v. Booker   185, 188

Leonard v. Leonard   381

Leonotion v. Leonotion   36

Leontowicz v. Jacobsen   550

Lepage v. Lepage   395, 469

Leppek v. Leppek   576

Leskun v. Leskun   237–39, 244–45, 248,
    300, 341

Leslie v. Leslie   619–21

Letourneau v. Letourneau   457

Levesque v. Levesque (1994 Alta. C.A.)   524

Levesque v. Levesque (1999 Ont. Sup.
    Ct.)   417

Levinson v. Levinson   296

Lewcock v. Natili-Lewcock   359

Lewi v. Lewi   387, 388, 389, 390

Lewis v. Lewis (1983 N.B.Q.B.)   211

Lewis v. Lewis (2005 N.S.S.C.)   503, 541

Lewkoski v. Lewkoski   456

Liang v. Liang   78

Lidstone v. Lidstone   239

Lietz v. Lietz   189

Lim v. Lim   28

Lind v. Lind   583

Lindstrom v. Pearce   559

Ling v. Ling   570

Linov v. Williams   609

Linton v. Clarke   546, 550

Linton v. Linton   253, 585

Lipson v. Lipson (1972 Ont. C.A.)   225, 456

Lipson v. Lipson (1986 Ont. Master)   86

Litton v. Litton   238, 293

Livermore v. Livermore   90, 591, 604

Lobo v. Lobo   457

Locke v. Ledrew   306

Lockyer v. Lockyer   242, 269, 306, 471, 586

Logan v. Logan   316

Long-Beck v. Beck   239

Longstaff v. Longstaff   430

Loos v. Schneider   377, 378

Loshney v. Hankins   431

Lotton v. Lotton   81

Lougheed v. Lougheed   375

Lowe v. Lowe   601

Loy v. Loy   79, 81–82, 86

Lu v. Sun   352, 373, 383, 384, 458

Luckett v. Luckett   437, 439

Lukyn v Baynes   556

Luney v. Luney   428

Lust v. Lust   331, 463, 482, 483

Lygouriatis v. Gohm   483

Lynch v. Lundrigan   432

Lynch v. Segal   596

Lyons v. Lyons   217

Lyttle v. Bourget   470

M. v. H.   10, 49–50, 52–53, 59, 74, 519

M. v. K.   145–46

M. v. M. (1971 Ont. C.A.)   108

M. v. M. (1974 Ont. H.C.J.)   210

M. v. M. (1975 N.B.C.A.)   108

M.(A.) v. Ryan   143–44

M.(B.J.) v. M.(J.H.)   218

M.(B.P.) v. M.(B.L.D.E.)   485, 507, 508

M.(C.F.) v. M.(M.F.)   360, 361

M.(K) v. M.(H.)   128

M.B. v. British Columbia   129

M.D.L. v. C.R.   418

M.E.E. v. T.R.E.   483, 496

M.E.E.T. v. C.M.W.   446

M.E.O. v. S.R.M.   502

M.E.S. v. D.A.S.   533

M.F. c. J.   540

M.J.B. v. W.P.B.   455

M.L. v. R.S.E   357

M.L.C. v. G.C.C.   430

M.M. v. J.H.   197–98, 222

M.R. v. G.V.G.V.   505

M.T.R. v. I.S.R.   362

M.V. v. D.V.   373, 381, 384

M.W. v. D.W.   563

Maber v. Maber   232, 237, 239–40

MacArthur v. Demers   364, 367

MacArthur v. MacArthur   469

MacCurdy v. MacCurdy   205

MacDonald v. MacDonald (1997 Ont.
    C.A.)   606

MacDonald v. MacDonald (2002
    B.C.C.A.)   392

MacDonald v. MacDonald (2002 Ont. Sup.
    Ct.)   490

MacDonald v. MacDonald (2004
    N.S.C.A.)   264

MacDonald v. Rasmussen   377, 378, 384, 389

MacDonnell v. MacDonnell   604

MacDougall v. MacDougall   216

MacDougall v. MacRae   305

MacFarlane v. MacFarlane   404

MacIntosh v. MacIntosh   422

MacKay v. Bucher   410

MacKay v. MacKay   207

MacKay v. Murray   506

MacKinnon v. MacKinnon (1986
    N.S.S.C.)   219

MacKinnon v. MacKinnon (2005 Ont.
    C.A.)   312, 413, 466

Mackrell v. Mackrell   215–16

MacLean v. MacLean (2003
    P.E.I.S.C.T.D.)   393

MacLean v. MacLean (2004 N.B.C.A.)   236,
    254, 256, 261, 263

MacLellan v. MacLellan   419

MacLennan v. MacLennan (1958 Scot-
    land)   203

MacLennan v. MacLennan (2003
    N.S.C.A.)   234, 378

MacLeod v. MacLeod   209

MacMillan-Dekker v. Dekker   53, 56

MacNaughton v. MacNaughton   231–32

MacNeil v. MacNeil (1976 N.S.C.A.) 211

MacNeil v. MacNeil (1994 N.S.C.A.) 229, 231, 232

MacNeill v. Pope 609

MacPhail v. Karasek 486, 488

MacPhail v. MacPhail 406

MacPhee v. Russel 62

MacPherson v. MacPherson (1976 Ont. C.A.) 189

MacPherson v. MacPherson (2007 N.B.Q.B.) 237

Macy v. Macy 280

Maddock v. Maddock 214–15

Madsen Estate v. Saylor 570

Magder v. Magder 305

Magee v. Magee (1987 Ont. U.F.C.) 254, 605, 606

Magee v. Magee (1993 Sask. Q.B.) 507

Magne v. Magne 230

Magnes v. Magnes 389

Magnus v. Magnus 482, 493, 504

Mahadervan v. Mahadervan 33

Maillet v. Maillet 230

Main v. Main 229

Maljkovich v. Maljkovich Estate 612

Maloney v. Maloney (1993 Ont. Ct. Gen. Div.) 62

Maloney v. Maloney (2004 Ont. Ct. Gen. Div.) 420

Mancuso v. Mancuso 609

Mancuso v. Weinrath 365–67

Manis v. Manis 449

Mannarino v. Mannarino 228–29

Manufacturers Life Insurance Company v. Riviera 622

Maphangoh v. Maphangoh 602

Marchese v. Marchese 172, 175

Marcon v. Cicchelli 22

Marcus v. Marcus 260

Maresich v. Penner 54

Magee v. Magee 435

Marinangeli v. Marinangeli 275–76, 312, 458

Mark v. Mark 205, 210

Markand v. Markand 485

Marks v. Tokarewicz 277

Marsden v. Murphy 483

Marsellus v. Marsellus 188

Marsh v. Marsh 374

Marshall v. Marshall (1923 Sask. C.A.) 89–90

Marshall v. Marshall (1998 N.S.S.C.) 373

Marshall v. Marshall (2002 Ont. Sup. Ct.) 268

Marsham v. Marsham 579, 582–86, 587, 592, 618, 620

Marsland v. Gibb 362

Martel v. Martel 417

Martell v. Height 374, 378–79

Martell v. Martell 435

Martin v. Blanchard 312

Martin v. Martin (1970 Aust.) 191

Martin v. Martin (1971 B.C.S.C.) 207

Martin v. Martin (1986 Ont. Dist. Ct.) 579

Martin v. Martin (1989 Ont. S.C.) 592

Martin v. Martin (1993 Sask. C.A.) 249

Martin v. Martin (2000 B.C.S.C.) 427

Martin v. Martin (2004 Ont. Sup. Ct.) 311

Martin v. Martin (2006 Ont. C.A.) 246

Martin v. Martin (2007 Man. Q.B.) 398

Martin v. Martin (2007 Ont. Sup. Ct.) 324

Martin v. Schaeffer 465

Marud v. Marud 357, 363

Mason v. Mason 253, 262

Masse v. Sykora 189

Massler v. Massler 418

Mather v. Mahoney 194

Matthews v. Matthews (1988 Nfld. U.F.C.) 508

Matthews v. Matthews (2007 Yukon S.C.) 465

Matwichuk v. Stephenson 378, 379, 389

Maxwell v. Maxwell 377, 378

May v. May 304–6

Mayberry v. Mayberry 200

Mayer v. Mayer 394

Mayfield v. Mayfield (1969 U.K.)   194

Mayfield v. Mayfield (2001 Ont. Sup.
Ct.)   551

McAdam v. McAdam   376

McAllister v. McAllister   216

McAndrew v. Rooney-McAndrew   594

McArthur v. McArthur   379

McArthur v. Zaduk   22

McBride v. McBride   370, 402

McCaskie v. McCaskie   626

McConnell v. McConnell (1975
N.B.C.A)   233

McConnell v. McConnell (1980 Ont.
H.C.J.)   90

McConnell v. McConnell (2007
B.C.S.C)   461

McCorriston v. McCorriston   350

McCowan v. McCowan   286, 309

McCoy v. Hucker   423

McCulloch v. Bawtinheimer   317, 330, 349

McCullough v. Ralph   38

McCurry v. Hawkins   480

McCutcheon v. McCutcheon   606, 611

McDermid v. McDermid   141

McDonald v. McDonald (1987 B.C.S.C.)   144

McDonald v. McDonald (1988 N.S.T.D.)   200

McDonald v. McDonald (1988 Ont.
S.C.)   590

McDonald v. McDonald (1995 Ont.
S.C.)   594

McDonald v. McDonald (1998 B.C.S.C.)   355

McDonald v. McDonald (2001
B.C.C.A.)   421

McEachern v. McEachern (1998 Sask.
Q.B.)   420, 423

McEachern v. McEachern (2006
B.C.C.A.)   276, 333, 335

McEvoy v. McEvoy   209

McEvoy v. New Brunswick (A.G.) (sub nom.
Re Court of Unified Criminal
Jurisdiction)   181

McGeachy v. McGeachy   201

McGee v. Ranson   54, 56

McGoey v. McGoey   398

McGrath v. McGrath (1977 N.B.Q.B.)   207,
211

McGrath v. McGrath (2006 Nfld.
U.F.C.)   395

McIllwraith v. McIllwraith   412

McIntosh v. McIntosh   428

McIsaac v. McIsaac   603

McIsaac v. Stewart   508

McKean v. McKean   243

McKenna v. McKenna   201

McKenzie v. McKenzie   213

McKenzie v. Singh   37

McKinney v. Polston   308

McKinney v. University of Guelph   94

McLaughlin v. Braun   431

McLean v. McLean   470

McLeod v. McLeod   87, 284

McMeekin v. McMeekin   86

McMullen v. McMullen   307

McMurchy v. McMurchy   398

McPherson v. McPherson   591

McQuay v. McQuay   622

McTaggart v. McTaggart   601

Medora v. Kohn   54, 56

Megaval v. Megaval   457

Megyesi v. Megyesi   328

Mehta v. Mehta   34

Meiklejohn v. Meiklejohn   291, 311

Meilen v. Anderson   32

Melanson v. Melanson (1990 N.B.Q.B.)   259

Melanson v. Melanson (1991 Ont. Ct. Gen.
Div.)   579

Mellway v. Mellway   462

Meltzer v. Meltzer (1989 Man. Q.B.)   231,
293

Meltzer v. Meltzer (1992 Man. C.A.)   293

Memisoglu v. Memiche   232

Menage v. Hedges   587, 594

Menzies v. Farnon   42

Merchant v. Dossani   36, 213

Merklinger v. Merklinger   612

Mero v. Mero   243

Merrell v. Merrell   172

Merritt v. Merritt   373, 388

Mertz v. Symchyck   497

Messier v. Baines   405

Messier v. Delage   259, 328

Messier v. Messier   620

Meszaros v. Meszaros   570

Metz v. Metz   233

Metz v. Weisgerber   12

Metzner v. Metzner   392

Meunier v. Meunier   31, 38

Meuser v. Meuser   427

Miao v. Chen   469

Michalofsky v. Michalofsky (1989 Ont. Div.
   Ct.)   577, 595

Michalofsky v. Michalofsky (1992 Ont.
   C.A.)   593

Michaud v. Michaud   463

Middleton v. MacPherson   403, 420

Mighton v. Mighton   381

Miglin v. Miglin   23, 68, 139, 269–280, 281,
   282, 283, 285–89, 309, 315, 502

Miles v. Chilton (falsely called Miles)   32

Miller v. Bozzi   77

Miller v. Joynt   378, 441

Miller v. Miller (1984 S.C.C.)   603

Miller v. Miller (1987 Ont. Dist. Ct.)   579,
   583–84

Miller v. Miller (1996 Ont. C.A.)   626

Mills v. Butt   189

Mills v. Mills   388

Milne v. Milne   213

Milot v. Canada   53

Milson v. Hough   32

Minaei v. Brae Centre Ltd.   234

Miron v. Trudel   48

Misener v. Muir   431

Mitchell v. Mitchell   484

Mittler v. Mittler   593

Modry v. Modry   326, 330, 350

Moge v. Moge   228, 234–35, 239, 243, 246,
   251–57, 259, 260, 261–63, 265, 266, 267,
   270, 272, 277, 288, 301–2, 309, 320, 327,
   332, 349–50

Mohrbutter v. Mohrbutter   183

Mollot v. Mollot   228

Molodowich v. Penttinen   53, 55, 279

Money v. Money   219

Mongillo v. Mongillo   86

Monks v. Monks   231

Monney v. Monney   451

Montague v. Montague   587

Montgomery v. Montgomery   445

Moore v. Moore   608

Moore v. Tymiak   446

Morash v. Morash   350

Moreau v. Moreau   482

Morgan v. Morgan (1959 U.K.)   43

Morgan v. Morgan (2001 B.C.S.C.)   233

Morgan v. Morgan (2006 B.C.S.C.)   373, 378,
   387, 428, 459–460, 462

Morgan v. Morgan (2006 Nfld. S.C.)   342–43

Moriarty v. Hood   431

Morice v. Morice   205

Morley v. Morley   440

Moro v. Miletich   434

Morrissette v. Ball   423

Morrone v. Morrone   406

Morrow v. Morrow   201

Mosher v. Mosher   228, 231–32

Moss v. Moss (1897 U.K.)   30, 34

Moss v. Moss (1997 Nfld. S.C.)   418

Motuzas v. Yarnell   357

Motyka v. Motyka   449

Mroz v. Mroz   232

Muchekeni v. Muchekeni   225

Muir-Lang v. Lang   449

Mullen v. Mullen   454

Mullin v. Mullin   253

Mundinger v. Mundinger   82

Mundle v. Jurgaitis   193

Mundle v. Mundle   415

Murdoch v. Murdoch   10, 560

Murdoch v. Ransom   90

Murphy v. Murphy (1989 Nfld. U.F.C.)   230

Murphy v. Murphy (1998 Nfld. S.C.)   415

Murphy v. Murphy (2000 B.C.S.C.)   433

Murphy v. Murphy (2002 N.S.S.C.)   298

Murphy v. Murphy (2007 B.C.C.A.)   306,
   425

Murphy v. Wulkowicz   188, 189

Murray v. Murray (1982 Sask. Q.B.)   376

Murray v. Murray (1991 Alta. Q.B.)   416

Muslake v. Muslake, Re   242, 458

Musolino-Pearson v. Musolino   468

Myers v. Myers   423

Myketiak v. Myketiak   452

N.B. v. K.J.B.   427

N.K. c. R.V.   188

N.M.M. v. N.S.M.   420

N.W. v. Canada (Attorney General)   24

Nachimson v. Nachimson   27

Nador v. Nador   88

Nagoda v. Nagoda   173

Nahatchewitz v. Nahatchewitz   577, 595

Naidoo v. Naidoo   452

Nane (Sykiotis) v. Sykiotis   34–35

Napper v. Napper   291

Narayan v. Narayan   334

Nasby v. Nasby   349

Nash v. Nash (1940 U.K.)   36

Nash v. Nash (1975 S.C.C.)   458

Nassar v. Nassar   586

Nathoo v. Nathoo   290

Navas v. Navas   190

Nay v. Nay   364

Naylen v. Naylen   188

Necemer v. Necemer   361, 362

Needham v. Needham   440

Negus v. Forster   90

Neill v. Boudreau   463

Nelson v. Nelson   583

Nesbitt v. Nesbitt   443

Neufeld v. Neufeld   307

Nevarc Holdings Ltd. v. Orchid
    Communications Inc.   623

Newfoundland and Labrador (Director of
    Child, Youth and Family Services, Eastern
    Regional Integrated Health Authority) v.
    R.L.   477

Newham v. Newham   173

Newman v. Newman (1971 Ont. C.A.)   201

Newman v. Newman (1979
    N.S.S.C.A.D.)   260

Newman v. Newman (1993 Man. Q.B.)   183

Newson v. Newson   229, 253

Newson v. Newson and Davidson   23

Newstone v. Newstone   228

Nicholas v. Nicholas   574

Nichols v. Nichols   106, 209

Nielsen v. Nielsen (1971 Ont. H.C.J.)   217

Nielsen v. Nielsen (2007 B.C.C.A)   428

Nitkin v. Nitkin   362, 378

Nix v. Nix   579

Noonan v. Noonan   225

Norland v. Norland   492

Norlander v. Norlander   469

Norman v. Norman (1973 N.S.C.A.)   200

Norman v. Norman (1979 Ont. U.F.C.)   43

Normandin v. Kovalench   446, 463

Nova Scotia (Attorney General) v. Walsh and
    Bona (sub nom. Walsh v. Bona)   57, 198

Nova Scotia Birth Registration No 1999-02-
    004200, Re   64

Novak v. Novak   207

Novoa v. Molero   537

Nowlan v. Nowlan   189

Nunan v. Nunan   189

Nunweiler v. Nunweiler   489

Nurmi v. Nurmi   73–74, 232

Nurnberger v. Nurnberger   592

O. v. C.   246

O'Brien v. MacLearn   555

O'Brien v. O'Brien   418

O'Connor v. Kenney   493

O'Leary v. O'Leary   527

O'Neill v. Wolfe   303

Oakley v. Oakley   286, 295

Odermatt v. Odermatt   388

Oeming v. Oeming   89

Okmyansky v. Okmyansky   185, 568

Oliva v. Oliva (1986 Ont. S.C.)   577, 594,
    600, 620

Oliva v. Oliva (1988 Ont. C.A.)   577, 594, 598, 600, 620

Ollinger v. Ollinger   361, 362

Olmstead v. Olmstead   173

Olsen v. Olsen   381

Olson v. Olson   377

Omah-Maharajh v. Howard   423, 424, 434

One v. One   487

Orabi v. El Qaoud   194, 195

Ordano v. Moore (sub nom. M.E.O. v. S.R.M.)   502

Orford v. Orford   203

Orring v. Orring   485

Orser v. Grant   449

Osborne v. Osborne   228, 293

Osmar v. Osmar   427

Osmond v. Osmond   142

Ostlund v. Ostlund   421

Oswell v. Oswell (1990 Ont. Sup. Ct.)   571

Oswell v. Oswell (1992 Ont. C.A.)   200

Othberg v. Othberg   209

Owen v. Sears   432

Owokalu v. Owokalu   225

Oxenham v. Oxenham   305

Oyama v. Oyama   465

P. v. P.   219

P.A. v. C.G.   39

P.A.B. v. T.K.B.   549

P.C.J.R. v. D.C.R.   449, 466

P.E.C. v. C.E.G.   145

P.E.K. v. B.W.K.   446

P.G.A. v. B.M.A.   331

P.H. v. P.H.   432

Paff v. Postnikoff   54

Pagani v. Pagani   427

Pagnotta v. Malozewski   344

Palachik v. Kiss   574

Palahnuk v. Palahnuk   185

Palmer v. Palmer   280–81

Pare v. Pare   515

Paredes v. Paredes   285

Parish v. Parish   230

Park v. Thompson   387, 413

Parker v. Vik   239

Parlee v. Lavallée   297

Parmar v. Parmar   555

Parmigiani v. Parmigiani   606

Parojcic v. Parojcic   33

Pascuzzi v. Pascuzzi   33

Pastoor v. Pastoor   77

Patan v. Patan   289

Patrick v. Patrick (1994 B.C.S.C.)   301

Patrick v. Patrick (1999 B.C.S.C.)   395

Patten v. Patten   231, 234

Patterson v. Publicover   504

Paul v. Misselbrook   512

Paulina v. Dudas   290

Pavlinek v. Pavlinek   209

Pawelko v. Pawelko   206

Payne v. Payne (1983 Ont. U.F.C.)   617

Payne v. Payne (1988 Ont. S.C.)   604

Peake v. Peake   606

Pearson v. Pearson (1992 Yukon S.C.)   144

Pearson v. Pearson (1995 Man. Q.B.)   231

Pecore v. Pecore   571

Pelech v. Pelech   309

Pellegrini v. Pellegrini   216

Pelletier v. Kakakaway   405

Penney v. Penney   554

Perchaluk v. Perchaluk   141

Perry v. Perry (1971 P.E.I.S.C.T.D.)   211

Perry v. Perry (2008 Ont. Sup. Ct.)   291

Pershadisingh v. Pershadisingh   574

Peskett v. Peskett   209

Peter v. Beblow   10, 61

Peters v. Graham   355

Peters v. Karr   508

Peters v. Murray   36, 38

Peters v. Neville   504

Peters v. Peters   469

Peterson v. Horan   454–54

Peterson v. Peterson   237

Petrowski v. Waskul   298

Pettigrew v. Pettigrew   228, 246, 254, 260, 312, 344, 352

Pettit v. Pettit   43
Pettkus v. Becker   10, 61, 564
Petz v. McNulty-Petz   246
Pevach v. Spalding   368
Phillipchuk v. Phillipchuk   388
Phillips v. Phillips   456
Phinney v. Phinney   254, 343
Phipps v. Phipps   446
Pickford v. Pickford   317
Pidgeon v. Hickman   432
Piercy v. Piercy   142, 143
Piette v. Therrien   211
Pifer v. Pifer   627
Pilon v. Pilon   304
Pires v. Pires   141
Pitcher v. Pitcher   423
Pitre v. Nguyen   195
Pitt v. Pitt   468
Plumley v. Plumley   490
Plummer, Re   196
Pocs v. Pocs   595
Poelen v. Poelen   290
Poirier v. Alie   573
Poisson v. Poisson   230–31
Poitras v. Poitras   275, 299
Pollock v. Rioux   385, 387, 388
Polsinelli v. Polsinelli   192
Pomroy v. Greene   423
Pongor v. Pongor   107, 206, 208
Poole v. Poole (1999 B.C.C.A.)   493
Poole v. Poole (2001 Ont. Sup. Ct.)   593
Poole v. Poole (2005 N.S.Q.B.)   532
Pope v. Pope   609
Porter v. Porter (1979 Ont. S.C.)   85
Porter v. Porter (1983 Ont. U.F.C.)   145, 544
Porter v. Porter (1986 Ont. Dist. Ct.)   583,
  620
Posener v. Posener   287
Postma v. Postma   621
Pottle v. Canada (Attorney General)   24
Poulter v. Poulter   295
Pousette v. Pousette   287
Powell v. Cockburn   195

Powell v. Powell   206
Power v. Hunt   387
Powers v. Naston-Powers   576
Powers v. Powers   229, 247
Powley v. Wagner   508
Poyntz Estate v. Poyntz   431
Prendergast v. Prendergast   291, 300
Price v. Price   312
Prieur v. Prieur   357
Propper v. Vanleeuwen   432
Puddifant v. Puddifant   324, 341
Pugh v. Pugh   32
Puopolo v. Puopolo   76
Purcell v. Purcell   622
Purdy v. Hazelden   296
Puszczak v. Puszczak   533, 539

Quigley v. Willmore   189
Quinn v. Keiper   453
Quinn v. Quinn   89

R. v. B.S.   120
R. v. Bear's Shin Bone   29
R. v. Béland   501
R. v. Bell (1857 U.C.Q.B.)   38
R. v. Bell (1992 Alta. C.A.)   103
R. v. Brown (1992 Alta. C.A.)   103
R. v. Brown (1993 S.C.C.)   562
R. v. Khan   498, 534, 554
R. v. L.(D.O.)   121
R. v. Lavallee   96, 105
R. v. Levogiannis   121
R. v. Mohan   550
R. v. Nan-E-Quis-A-Ka   29
R. v. R.   393
R. v. Salituro   203
R. v. Smith   534
R.A.L. v. R.D.R.   53
R.B. c. N.A   240
R.B. v. I.B.   229, 233, 249
R.B.N. v. M.J.N.   407, 491
R.D.W. v. T.L.W.   465
R.E.L. v. E.L.   40, 43– 44

R.E.L. v. S.M.L. 465

R.K. c. H.S. 298

R.L. v. M.P. 527

R.L.W. v. R.G.W. 465

R.M. v. M.M. 296, 298

R.P.B. v. K.D.P. 505, 546, 548

R.S. v. T.S. 438

R.S.M. v. M.S.M. 271

R.S.R. v. S.M.R. 306, 333

R.W.G. v. S.I.G. 375

Radons v. Radons 477

Raffin v. Raffin 229

Raftus v. Raftus 423

Rafuse v. Rafuse 229

Rail v. Rail 493

Ralph v. Ralph 304

Ramantanis v. Ramantanis 229

Ramboer v. Ramboer 73–74

Ramdatt v. Ramdatt 240

Randolf v. Randolf 620

Raney v. Raney 217

Range v. Range 305

Rankin v. Rankin 108, 207

Rarie v. Rarie 569

Rasmussen v. MacDonald 437

Ratcliffe v. Ratcliffe 107, 209

Rathwell v. Rathwell 10, 564

Rauch v. Rauch 210

Rauf v. Rauf 583, 584

Raven v. Raven 199

Rawluk v. Rawluk 569, 578, 589–90, 610, 612

Ray v. Ray 255

Rayvals v. Rayvals 234

Razavi-Brahimi v. Ershadi 390

Rea v. Rea 237

Rebenchuk v. Rebenchuk 362, 378–80, 384, 387–89

Rector v. Hamilton 432

Redl v. Redl 195

Redpath v. Redpath 332–33, 337–38

Redshaw v. Redshaw 542

Reeson v. Kowalik 593, 598, 605, 606, 609, 611, 625

Reference Re S. 6 of Family Relations Act 86

Reference Re Same-Sex Marriage 24

Reid v. Catalano 177

Reid v. Reid 580

Reiss v. Reiss 467

Rempel v. Reynolds 188

Remus v. Remus 589, 593

Renouf v. Bertol-Renouf 253

Repchuk v. Repchuk 460

Retail, Wholesale and Department Store Union, Local 558 v. Pepsi-Cola Canada Beverages 203, 204

Reyher v. Reyher 471

Reynolds v. Reynolds 32

Rezel v. Rezel 624

Riad v. Riad 235, 246

Richards v. Richards 90, 304

Richardson v. Richardson 65, 287, 309, 359

Richter v. Richter 476, 492

Richter v. Vahamaki 471

Rickett v. Rickett 579

Rideout v. Rideout 306

Riehl v. Key 185

Riel v. Holland 445, 452

Rimmer v. Adshead 291

Ripley v. Ripley 235

Risen v. Risen 445

Rivas v. Rivas 191, 220

Rivett v. Bylund 420

Roach v. Roach 620

Roadburg v. Braut 201

Roberts v. Beresford 299, 387

Roberts v. Clough 57, 61

Roberts v. Roberts 492

Roberts v. Salvador 283, 480

Robichaud v. Robichaud (1974 N.B.Q.B.) 190

Robichaud v. Robichaud (1988 B.C.C.A.) 243

Robichaud v. Robichaud (1992 N.B.Q.B.) 243

Robinson v. Cumming   22

Robinson v. Filyk   476

Robinson v. Robinson (1982 Sask. Q.B.)   611

Robinson v. Robinson (1993 Ont. C.A.)   253, 265

Robinson v. Robinson (2000 Ont. Sup. Ct.)   174

Robinson-Scott v. Robinson-Scott   194

Robski v. Robski   418

Robson v. Robson   142

Rode v. Moyer   504

Rodrigues v. Rodrigues   281

Rogers v. Rogers (1830 U.K.)   214

Rogers v. Rogers (1962 Aust.)   247

Rogers v. Rogers (1992 N.B.Q.B.)   307

Rogerson v. Rogerson   71, 271

Rogerson v. Tessaro   506

Romanoff v. Romanoff   259

Rondberg Estate v. Rondberg Estate   612

Rondeau v. Kirby (2003 N.S.S.C.)   470

Rondeau v. Kirby (2004 N.S.C.A.)   240

Rondeau v. Rondeau   630

Rosario v. Rosario   306

Roschuk v. Roschuk   216

Rose v. Ferguson   241

Rosen v. Rosen   82

Rosenberg v. Rosenberg (1987 Ont. H.C.J.)   583

Rosenberg v. Rosenberg (2003 Ont. Sup. Ct.)   390

Roseneck v. Gowling   579, 605, 616

Rosenthal v. Rosenthal   629

Ross v. Reaney   54

Ross v. Ross (1993 Ont. C.A.)   232, 235, 254

Ross v. Ross (1995 N.B.C.A.)   261, 265, 267

Ross v. Ross (1999 Ont. Sup. Ct.)   174

Ross v. Ross (2001 N.S.C.A.)   405

Ross v. Ross (2004 B.C.C.A.)   512

Ross v. Ross (2006 Ont. C.A.)   580

Ross v. Vermette   430, 431, 465

Rossi v. Rossi   350

Rossiter-Forrest v. Forrest   230

Rother v. Rother   140, 141

Rothgiesser v. Rothgiesser   184–86, 188

Rouleau v. Wells   211

Rousseau v. Rousseau   454

Routley v. Paget   275

Rowe v. Rowe   209

Roy v. Roy (2006 Ont. C.A.)   477

Roy v. Roy (2007 N.B.Q.B.)   287

Royal Bank v. King   627

Royko v. Royko   387

Rudachyk v. Rudachyk   452

Rudd v. Trossacs Investments Inc.   145

Rude v. Rude   183

Rudulier v. Rudulier   362, 385, 393–94, 418

Ruel v. Ruel   405

Rupert v. Rupert   472

Rush v. Rush   451

Rushton v. Rushton   200

Russell v. Russell   435

Rust v. Rust (1972 Alta. C.A.)   90

Rust v. Rust (1975 N.B.C.A.)   232

Ruster v. Ruster   592

Ruth v. Young   364

Rutherford v. Rutherford   582, 583

Ruyter v. Samson   183

Ryan v. Ryan (1985 N.S.S.C.)   41

Ryan v. Ryan (2008 Alta. S.C.)   504

S. v. S. (1956 U.K.)   41

S. v. S. (2007 N.B.Q.B.)   388, 459, 461

S.A.J.M. v. D.D.M.   472

S.C. v. J.C.   234, 331, 338–41

S.D.N. v. M.D.N.   480

S.D.P. v. P.W.   384

S.E. v. D.E.   356

S.E.C. v. G.P.   540

S.E.H. v. S.R.M.   393

S.E.J. v. G.P.J.   238

S.E.P. v. D.D.P.   197, 203, 204

S.F.R. v. J.V.H.   554

S.K. v. T.Z.   461

S.L.T. v. A.K.T.   177

S.M. c. S.K.   273

S.M. v. R.P.   363, 416

S.M.A. v. S.F.H. 327

S.M.H. v. R.P. 462

Saari v. Nykanen 44

Saby v. MacIntosh 426

Said v. Said 36

Salamon v. Salamon 593

Saleh v. Saleh 233

Sallam v. Sallam 40, 41

Salzmann v. Salzmann 281

Sampson v. Sampson (1994 N.B.Q.B.) 202–3

Sampson v. Sampson (1998 Alta. Q.B.) 432

Sanders v. Sanders 598

Sandy v. Sandy 568

Sangha v. Aujla 31, 41

Sangha v. Mander 29

Sappier v. Francis 532

Sapsford v. Sapsford 203

Sarafinchin v. Sarafinchin 452

Sarai v. Sarai 290

Sather v. McCallum 484

Sattar v. Sattar 213

Sawatzky v. Campbell 493

Sayong v. Aindow 396, 454

Schaefer v. Schaefer 616

Scheel v. Henkelman 86

Schenkeveld v. Schenkeveld 403–5

Scherer v. Scherer 573, 612

Schick v. Schick 434, 471

Schindle v. Schindle 444, 448

Schluessel v. Schluessel 449

Schmidt v. Schmidt 237

Schmuck v. Reynolds-Schmuck 240

Schnell v. Schnell 439, 440

Schnerch v. Schnerch 207

Scholes v. Scholes 449

Schultz v. Schultz 273

Schwebel v. Ungar 195

Scorgie v. Scorgie 456

Scott v. Higgs 504

Scott v. Scott (1959 U.K.) 43

Scott v. Scott (2007 B.C.S.C.) 245

Seeley v. McKay 359

Seeman v. Seeman 78

Segal v. Ou 290

Seguin v. Masterson 400

Seiler v. Funk 22

Seminuk v. Seminuk 201

Sengmueller v. Sengmueller 591

Sewell v. Grant 430

Shafer v. Shafer (1996 Ont. Ct. Gen. Div.) 586

Shafer v. Shafer (1998 Ont. C.A.) 573

Shakotko v. Shakotko 142

Shambrook v. Shambrook 424

Shankman v. Shankman 421

Sharf v. Sharf 414, 418, 419

Shaver v. Shaver 595, 600, 603, 605, 606

Shaw v. Shaw 435, 495

Shea v. Fraser 461, 464

Sheehan v. Sheehan 589

Sheikh v. Sheikh 546

Sheldon v. Sheldon 211

Shellito v. Bensimhon 332, 334

Shepherd v. Shepherd 33

Sheriff v. Sheriff (1982 Ont. C.A.) 571

Sheriff v. Sheriff (1983 Ont. S.C.) 141

Sherlock v. Sherlock 373

Sherlow v. Zubko 377, 387

Sherwood v. Ray 31

Shields v. Shields 183

Shillington v. Shillington 387, 451, 512

Shipka v. Shipka 416

Shokohyfard v. Sotoodeh 185

Shore-Kalo v. Kalo 218, 347

Shorten v. Shorten 199

Shumila v. Shumila 206

Sibbet v. Sibbet 249

Sikler v. Snow 426

Silver v. Silver (1955 U.K.) 36

Silver v. Silver (1985 Ont. C.A.) 352

Silverstein v. Silverstein 617

Simmonds v. Simmonds 350

Simmonds v. Turner 467

Simon v. Simon 391

Simpson v. Grignon 347

Simpson v. Simpson 218

Simpson v. Trowsdale 414

Sinclair v. Roy 145, 544

Singh v. Singh (1976 Ont. H.C.J.) 199

Singh v. Singh (1977 B.C.S.C.) 213

Singh v. Singh (1982 Man. Q.B.) 201

Singh v. Singh (1997 B.C.S.C.) 365, 366

Single v. Single 427

Sipos v. Sipos 454

Skelly v. Skelly 237

Skiba v. Skiba 415

Skolney v. Herman 373

Skrlj v. Skrlj 616–18

Slade v. Slade 399, 414

Sleigh v. Sleigh 78

Sloat v. Sloat 360

Smith v. Goethals 461

Smith v. Mackie 586

Smith v. Smith (1970 B.C.S.C.) 201

Smith v. Smith (1977 Ont. Co. Ct.) 81

Smith v. Smith (1980 P.E.I.T.D.) 201

Smith v. Smith (1985 Nfld. S.C.) 229

Smith v. Smith (1987 Man. Q.B.) 308

Smith v. Smith (1990 Man. C.A.) 379, 432

Smith v. Smith (1992 N.S. Fam. Ct.) 305

Smith v. Smith (1998 Ont. Ct. Gen.
    Div.) 470

Smith v. Smith (2001 Alta. C.A.) 420

Smith v. Smith (2001 N.S.S.C., Coughlan
    J.) 417

Smith v. Smith (2001 N.S.S.C., Kennedy
    C.J.S.C.) 468

Smith v. Smith (2006 B.C.S.C.) 328, 334

Smith v. Smith (2007 Man. Q.B.) 298, 306

Smyth v. Smyth 263

Sneddon v. Sneddon 469

Snodgrass v. Snodgrass 267

Snyder v. Pictou 316, 319, 444, 522

Sobush v. Sobush 34

Socan v. Socan 590

Sochackey v. Sochackey 555

Somers v. Somers 304

Somerville v. Somerville 497

Soper v. Soper (1985 N.S.C.A.) 53

Soper v. Soper (2006 Ont. Sup. Ct.) 312

Sorochan v. Sorochan 10, 61, 564

South v. South (1992 Man. C.A.) 248

South v. South (B.C.S.C.) 406

Sparks v. Sparks 508

Spek v. Lawson 188

Spencer v. Spencer (2002 B.C.C.A) 236

Spencer v. Spencer (2005 Alta. C.A.) 488,
    489

Spier v. Bergen 31

Spiers v. Spiers 243

Spinney v. Spinney 201

Spooner v. Spooner 87

Sprackin v. Kichton 54

Spring v. Spring 359

Springer v. Springer 183

Sproule v. Sproule 376

Squires v. Severs 363

Srini Vassan v. Srini Vassan 27

St. Amour v. St. Amour 388

St. Arnaud v. St. Arnaud 385

St. Croix v. Maxwell 454

St. Onge v. Bozarth 460

Stacey v. Hacking 432

Stacey v. Stacey 204

Standing v. Standing 184

Stapleton v. Stapleton 190

Staranowicz v. Staranowicz 188

Starkman v. Starkman 591

Starko v. Starko 494

Statia v. Statia 78

Steele v. Koppanyi 405, 421, 445, 447

Stefanyk v. Stefanyk 479

Stefureak v. Chambers 533, 534, 537–39,
    545

Stein v. Stein 237, 332, 333

Stelter v. Klingsphon 421

Stemmler v. May 465

Stening-Riding v. Riding 275

Stephen v. Stephen 435, 440

Stephens v. Falchi 196

Stevens v. Stevens 205, 206

Stevenson v. Stevenson 31, 38

Stewart v. Stewart (1990 Alta. C.A.)   178, 554

Stewart v. Stewart (2000 Sask. Q.B.)   432, 435

Stewart v. Stewart (2004 Alta. Q.B.)   423

Stewart v. Stewart (2007 Man. C.A.) 396, 397, 399

Stier v. Stier   266

Stocchero v. Stocchero   381

Stoffman v. Vancouver General Hospital   96

Stoikiewicz v. Filas   617

Stone v. Stone   623

Stones v. Stones   275

Storey v. Storey   206

Storms v. Storms   583

Strang v. Strang   244, 585

Stricker v. Stricker (1991 Alta. Q.B.)   229

Stricker v. Stricker (1994 Alta. C.A.)   230

Strickland v. Strickland   424

Strobridge v. Strobridge   177, 554

Stuyt v. Stuyt   492, 552

Sulatyski-Waldack v. Waldack   489

Sullivan v. Sullivan (sub nom. Sullivan v. Oldacre) (1818 U.K.)   32

Sullivan v. Sullivan (1986 Ont. U.F.C.)   591, 606, 611

Summerfelt v. Summerfelt   208

Sutcliffe v. Sutcliffe   394, 395

Swaine v. Swaine   362

Swallow v. De Lara   323

Sweeney v. Hartnell   508

Swift v. Kelly   34

Swindler v. Belanger   360, 361

Switzer v. Switzer   233

Sword v. Sword   231

Sydor v. Sydor   605

Sylvestre v. Sylvestre   257, 259

Synge v. Synge   42

Sypher v. Sypher   227

Szczur v. Szczur   290

T. v. T.   89

T.(T.E.) v. L.(J.D.)   479

T.A. v. R.C.A.   356

T.A.E. v. M.E.E.   229

T.G.F. v. D.S.V.   501

T.H. v. W.H.   237, 413, 450

T.J.M. v. P.G.M.   480

T.L.K. v. D.N.K.   451

T.L.R. v. R.W.R.   402

T.P.G. c. D.M.   479

T.S. v. A.V.T.   527

Takenaka v. Takenaka   206

Talbot v. Henry   504

Tallman v. Tomke   417

Tang v. Tang   417

Tanner v. Simpson   394

Tannis v. Tannis   213

Tanny v. Tanny   220

Tanouye v. Tanouye   55

Tapson v. Tapson   373, 524

Tauber v. Tauber (1999 Ont. Ct. Gen. Div.)   412

Tauber v. Tauber (2003 Ont. C.A.)   230

Taylor v. Rossu   519

Teczan v. Teczan   568

Tedham v. Tedham (2003 B.C.C.A.)   463

Tedham v. Tedham (2005 B.C.C.A.)   234, 237, 332, 334, 348

Tefera v. Yergu   37

Templeton v. Templeton   287

Terris v. Terris   490

The Queen v. McKimmon   293

Thebeau v. Thebeau   197

Theberge v. Theberge   598

Therrien-Cliché v. Cliché   303

Thomas v. Thomas and Abel v. Abel (2004 Alta. Q.B.) 243, 246–47, 256

Thomas v. Thomas and Abel v. Abel (2005 Alta. C.A.) 235, 241

Thompson v. Thompson (1939 U.K.)   203

Thompson v. Thompson (1971 Sask. Q.B.)   33

Thompson v. Thompson (1987 Ont. H.C.J.)   583

Thompson v. Thompson (1999 Sask. Q.B.) 377

Thorogood v. Thorogood 200, 202

Threlfall v. Threlfall 226

Thurber v. Thurber 182

Thynne v. Thynne 192

Tibbs v. Tibbs 183

Tierney-Hynes v. Hynes 224, 284, 309, 471

Tiffin v. Verrette 490

Tit v. Manitoba (Director of Vital Statistics) 190

Tomberg (Gilbert), Re 38

Tomberg v. Tomberg (Gilbert) 38

Tooth v. Knott 395

Torfehnejad v. Salimi 37

Torres v. Marin 225, 244, 317

Toth v. Kun 332, 335

Travers v. Holley 194

Travers v. Travers 253

Traversy v. Glover 224, 594

Trehearne v. Trehearne 454

Tremaine, Re 205

Tremblett v. Tremblett 228

Trinchan v. Trinchan 280

Trueman v. Trueman 423, 425, 451

Tschudi v. Tschudi 192

Tsurugida v. Romero 239

Tubbs v. Phillips 418, 420

Tully v. Tully 277

Turecki v. Turecki 431

Turk v. Turk 224

Turnbull v. Turnbull (1977 Man. Q.B.) 209

Turnbull v. Turnbull (1989 Sask. Q.B.) 188

Turnbull v. Turnbull (1998 Yukon S.C.) 432

Tutiah v. Tutiah 79

Tuxford v. Tuxford 80

Tward v. Tward 629

Tweel v. Tweel (1994 P.E.I.S.C.T.D.) 228, 231, 257, 265

Tweel v. Tweel (2000 P.E.I.S.C.T.D.) 400

Tyabji v. Sandana 553

Tynan v. Moses 435

U.S. v. Rubenstein 36

Underwood v. Underwood 308

Upadyhaha v. Sehgal 30

Upshall v. Janvier 304

Upshall v. Upshall 341

Ursic v. Ursic 477, 480, 483, 546

V.L. v. D.L. 477, 480, 481

V.S.G. v. L.J.G. 485, 504, 509, 547

Vaillancourt, Re 631

Valenti v. Valenti 131

Valier v. Valier 34

Vamvakidis v. Kirkoff 34

Van de Perre v. Edwards 493

Van der Wyngaard Estate, Re 614

Van Deventer v. Van Deventer 420, 449

Van Gool v. Van Gool 403, 405, 445, 447

Van Harten v. Van Harten 419

Van Stavern v. Van Stavern 232

Van Wynsberghe v. Van Wynsberghe 377

Vance v. Kovacs 467

Vanderhyden v. Vanderhyden 490

Vanderlinden v. Vanderlinden 315, 317, 343

Varcoe v. Varcoe 471

Varga Estate v. Varga 612

Vargo v. Saskatchewan (Family Justice Services Branch) 195

Vauclair v. Vauclair 225

Vazzaz v. Vazzaz 334

Verboom v. Verboom 619

Verdun v. Verdun 230

Veres v. Veres 260, 585

Vezina v. Vezina 427

Vickers v. Vickers 224, 454, 455

Vieira v. Vieira 232

Vien v. Vien Estate 83, 574

Virani v. Virani 185

Vivier v. Vivier 625

Voegelin v. Voegelin 78

Vogel v. The Attorney General of Canada, The Attorney General of Manitoba and Director of Vital Statistics Agency 24

Vogel v. Vogel 598

Von Czieslik v. Ayuso   605

Voth v. Voth   452

Vynnk v. Baisa   228, 230

W. v. W. (1952 U.K.)   43

W. v. W. (1973 U.K.)   355

W. v. W. (2005 B.C.S.C.)   332, 334, 348

W.C.P. v. C.P.   299

W.P.N. v. B.J.N.   379, 385, 387, 388

W.R.A. (Next friend of) v. G.F.A.   525

Wadden v. Wadden   454

Wagstaff v. Wagstaff   246

Wahl v. Wahl   362

Wainman v. Clairmont   404

Wainwright v. Wainwright   508

Wait v. Wait   417

Wakaluk v. Wakaluk   513

Wakefield v. Schrogl   207, 209

Walker v. Rutledge   395

Walker v. Tymofichuk 173, 284

Walker v. Walker   257

Walkiewicz v. Walkiewicz   461

Wallace v. Wallace   219

Wallin v. Wallin   219

Wallis v. Wallis   304

Walls v. Walls   373

Walsh v. Walsh (1988 N.B.C.A)   259

Walsh v. Walsh (2006 N.B.Q.B.)   235, 238, 341

Walsh v. Walsh (2006 Nfld. U.F.C.)   341

Walsh v. Walsh (2006 Ont. Sup. Ct)   300

Wang v. Wang   409, 410

Ward v. Ward (1985 N.B.Q.B.)   31, 32

Ward v. Ward (1988 Ont. H.C.J.)   579

Wasylyshyn v. Wasylyshyn   594, 611

Waterman v. Waterman   228

Watkins v. Watkins   216

Watson v. Watson (1991 B.C.S.C)   304

Watson v. Watson (1999 N.S.S.C)   393

Watt v. Thomas   208

Watt v. Watt   294

Watts v. Willie   444, 446

Webster v. Webster Estate   73, 568, 573, 613

Weddel v. Weddel   606, 612

Wedsworth v. Wedsworth 416

Weeks v. Weeks   599

Wegert v. Wegert   231

Weicholz v. Weicholz   360

Weir v. Weir   277

Weise v. Weise   583

Wellman v. Gilcash   227

Welsh v. Welsh   384, 455

Wentzell v. Schumacher   173

Werden v. Werden   456

Wesemann v. Wesemann   373, 385, 387

West v. West   504

Westcott v. Westcott 434

Westhaver v. Howard   496

Weston v. Weston   191

Wettlaufer v. Wettlaufer   583

Whalen v. Whalen   469

Whelan v. Whelan   227

Whey v. Brenton   492

White v. Gallant   430

White v. Rushton   364

White v. White   207

Whitley v. Whitley   385, 389

Widdis v. Widdis   359

Wiegers v. Wiegers   504, 505, 506

Wildman v. Wildman   596

Wilkinson v. Wilkinson 40

Wilkinson-Hughes v. Hughes   482

Willford v. Schaffer   504

Williams v. Smith   405

Williams v. Williams (1964 U.K.)   206, 207

Williams v. Williams (1971 N.S.S.C.)   218

Williams v. Williams (1991 N.W.T.S.C.)   200, 202

Williams v. Williams (1997 N.W.T.S.C.)   426

Williams v. Williams (2006 Ont. Sup Ct)   597, 609, 625

Williams v. Williams (2007 Nfld. U.F.C)   315

Willick v. Willick (1994 Alta. Q.B.)   173

Willick v. Willick (1994 S.C.C.)   262, 285, 287, 298, 302, 305, 427, 502

Williston v. Williston   333

Wills v. Wills   305

Wilm v. Wilm   331

Wilson v. Grassick   504

Wilson v. Wilson (1985 N.S.S.C.)   229

Wilson v. Wilson (1986 Alta. C.A.)   582

Wilson v. Wilson (1988 Ont. H.C.J.)   621

Wilson v. Wilson (1998 Sask. Q.B.)   435, 439

Wilson v. Wilson (2005 Ont. Sup. Ct.)   305, 307

Winmill v. Winmill   189

Winram v. Cassidy   187

Winsemann v. Donaldson   378, 385

Winsor v. Winsor   298

Wiome v. Wiome   430, 431

Wittstock v. Wittstock   206, 207

Wlodarczyk v. Spriggs 185

Woeller v. Woeller   583, 592

Woerz v. Woerz   216

Wolfe v. Wolfe   305

Wolinski v. Olynyk   54

Wood v. Wood (1944 Ont. H.C.J.)   216

Wood v. Wood (1987 P.E.I.S.C.T.D.)   189

Woode v. Woode   418

Woods v. Woods (1976 Ont. H.C.J.)   81, 88

Woods v. Woods (1998 Sask. Q.B.)   384

Woolgar v. Woolgar   201

Wouters v. Wouters   400–2

Wright v. Wright (1974 Ont. C.A.)   78

Wright v. Wright (2002 B.C.S.C.)   394

Wright v. Zaver   368, 409–11

Wrixon v. Wrixon   189

Wrobel v. Wrobel   305

Wu v. Sun   549

Wurmlinger v. Cyca   420, 431

Wuzinski v. Wuzinski   357

Wyatt v. Wyatt   308

Wylie v. Leclair   61

Wyman v. Wyman   208

Xu v. Leung   237

Yakiwchuk v. Oaks   54

Yashuk v. Logan   375

Yeates v. Yeates   576

Yee v. Yee   593

Yemchuk v. Yemchuk   330, 332, 332, 335, 336, 339, 345, 348

Yeo v. Yeo (1998 P.E.I.S.C.A.D.)   296, 297

Yeo v. Yeo (1998 P.E.I.S.C.T.D.)   424, 424

Yeoman v. Luhtala   139

Yew v. British Columbia (Attorney General)   28

Young v. Konkle   305, 432

Young v. Vincent   417

Young v. Young (1993 S.C.C.)   228, 482, 493, 509, 553

Young v. Young (1999 N.S.S.C.)   471

Zaba v. Bradley   389

Zabiegalowski v. Zabiegalowski   577, 606

Zagdanski v. Zagdanski   619

Zalesky v. Zalesky   205

Zawada v. Zawada   431

Zawatsky v. Zawatsky   205

Ziemann v. Ziemann   188

Zimmer v. Zimmer   259

Zimmerman v. Lazare   22

Zimmerman v. Shannon   287, 288

Zinck v. Fraser   506

Zinck v. Zinck   304

Ziniuk v. Ziniuk   280

Zoldester v. Zoldester   190

Zsiak v. Bell   416

Zunti v. Zunti   206

Zwicker v. Zwicker   208

INDEX

Aboriginal 2, 4, 7, 11, 14, 93, 116, 123, 133, 568

Abuse — *See* Child abuse, Elder abuse,
    Spousal abuse

Access — *See* Custody and access

Adoption 2, 37, 39, 49–50, 64, 125–26, 467,
    556, 562

Arbitration — *See* Dispute resolution

Best interests of child
    child protection proceedings 122–26
    custody and access 63–64, 492–96,
        503–10, 512–13, 526–29, 532
    domestic contracts 74, 80, 88

Change of name
    marriage 23
Child abuse
    "child in need of guidance," determination
        proceedings 122–23
    "child in need of protection," determina-
        tion proceedings 123–24
    custody proceedings 125–26
    "endangered child," determination
        proceedings 123–24
    family law proceedings 126–27
    nature 117–18
    sexual abuse 117–18

social and legal responses to 118–33
    abuse in institutions 132–33
    allegations by spouse 127
    child protection proceedings 122–26
    criminal sanctions 119–22
    damages 127–32

Child support — *See* Support

Children — *See also* Adoption, Child abuse,
    Custody and access, Domestic
    contracts
    cohabitants 63–64
    paternity agreements 83–84

Children's Law Reform Act (Ontario) 758–818

Cohabitational relationships 45–64
    agreements 50–53, 65–66, 74–75, 282–84
    child custody and access 63–64
    debts and liabilities 62–63
    legal status and consequences 48–50
    marriage, comparison with 48–50
    property rights 57–62
    reasons for 47–48
    succession 49
    support rights and obligations 53–57

Common-law relationships — *See* Cohabita-
    tional relationships

Custody and access — *See also* Best interests
    of child

agreement, effect of 502–3
child abuse allegations 126–27, 498–502,
    508, 510
child's voice 512–13
child's wishes 508, 509, 512–13, 532–40
cohabitational relationships 63–64
conduct of parent 63, 109, 356, 497–502
disclosure of information 513–17
domestic contracts 78
joint custody 7, 475–83, 503, 506–7,
    530–31, 542, 549, 553
litigation, effect of 510–12
objectives 475–83
parental conflict resolution 510–12
parenting agreements, prior 502–3
parenting plans 513–17
preservation of family bonds 475–83
process 21–22
provincial and territorial legislation
    519–63
    amicus curiae 513, 534
    assessments, court ordered 539–43,
        545–54
    child's wishes 532–43
    grandparents and third parties 517,
        555–63
    investigations, court–ordered 537–39,
        545–54
    judicial interviews 532–43
    legal representation 532–43
    mediation 543–44
    orders 530–32
    parenting programs 563
    reconciliation 543–44
rescission 503–10
residence, change of 485–91
spousal abuse, effect of 109–10
supervised access 110, 484–85, 500–1,
    503–4, 509–10
terms and conditions 483–91
variation 503–10

Death of partner — *See* Property division
Dispute resolution
    arbitration 169–76
        advantages 170–72

court-annexed 173
disadvantages 172–73
judicial and legislative responses
    173–76
mediation and 175–76
parenting co-ordination 176–77
religious laws and 174–75
counselling 138, 147–48
Divorce Act 138–45, 152, 167–68, 174
lawyers, duty to promote 139–41
mediation 138–39, 153–69, 543–44
    advantages 166
    approaches 153
    arbitration and 176
    children, involvement of 157
    confidentiality 145–46, 156–57,
        543–44
    court–connected 165–66
    disadvantages 166
    disclosure 156–57
    fair settlements 155
    future of 167–69
    goals 155–56
    impediments to 159–60
        emotional barriers 159
        power imbalance 160, 163
        stuck spots 159–62
        war games 160
    inappropriate circumstances 156
    issues 158–59
    lawyers, involvement of 157–58
    legal ethics 139–40
    mediator neutrality 159
    nature of 153
    Ontario *Family Law Act* 138–39, 167
    professional and community
        responses 167
    reasons for 154–55
    solutions 160–63
        anger and hostility management
            160–61
        power imbalance, redressing 163
        private caucusing 162
        stuck spots, circumventing 161–62
        trust and respect, restoring 162–63
    steps in 163–65
    third parties, and 157

negotiation 138–39, 148–52
    importance of 148
    privilege 143
    success of 150–52
    techniques 149–50
reconciliation 139–42
    confidentiality of 142–46, 543–44
    courts, duty of 141–42
    evidence, rules of 142–43
trends in 138–39
Divorce 179–221
    bars to 211–21
        arrangements for child support
            217–19
        collusion 213
        condonation 214–17
        connivance 214–17
        religious remarriage 220–21
    foreign 193–96
    ground for divorce 196–211
        marriage breakdown 196–99
            adultery, as evidence 202–5
            cruelty, as evidence 202, 205–11
            spousal separation, as evidence
                199–202
            no-fault divorce 211
    joint petitions 518
    judgments 191–93
        appeal 191–92
        effective date of 191–92
        expedition of 192–93
        national effect of 193
        rescission of 191–92
        right to remarry 193
    judicial separation 179–80
    jurisdiction 181–91
        corollary relief proceedings 184–87
        divorce proceedings 181–83
        ordinarily resident 188–91
        variation proceedings 187–88
    parenting arrangements after 474–518;
        See also Custody and access
    settlements 179–80
Divorce Act 633–70
Domestic contracts 65–90
    judicial separation 179–80
    Ontario *Family Law Act* and 71–90

access to children 74–76, 78, 83, 87
best interests of child 78, 86
capacity 77
child support 78, 85–86
children, provisions for 78
cohabitation agreements 50–53,
    65–66, 74–77, 282–84
custody 74–76, 78, 83, 87
dum casta clauses, 78–79, 277–78
extraprovincial contracts 83
formal requirements 76–77
general observations 71–72
gifts, rights of donor 82–83
marriage contracts 65–66, 67–70,
    72–74
matrimonial property 568
paternity agreements 83–84
pre-existing contracts, application to
    84–85
provisions regarding 85–89
    enforcement 88–89
    filing 88–89
    judgment, incorporation in 87
    order, incorporation in 86–87
    spousal and child support 85–86
    variation 88–89
remedies for breach 89–90
separation agreements 65–66, 75–76,
    179–80, 269–89
setting aside contracts 79–82, 85–86
    duress 79, 82
    lack of understanding 81
    non-disclosure 79–81
    undue influence 81
termination 90
types of 65–71

Elder abuse 92–94
Engagement 21
    termination and property disputes 21–22

Family
    definition of 1–8
    structures and Canadian family law 1–20
Family Law Act (Ontario) 699–757
Federal Child Support Guidelines 671–98

Gifts
   domestic contracts and rights of donors
      82–84

Judicial separation — *See* Divorce, Marriage
   breakdown and how to deal with
   crises
Jurisdiction
   divorce, over 181–90
   domestic contracts 78–79
   family law, over 16–20
   federal-provincial split 16–17

Marriage — *See also* Divorce, Marriage
   breakdown and how to deal with
   crises, Property division
   annulment
      bars to 41–44
      collusion 42
      estoppel 42
      insincerity 42–44
      religious annulments and divorce 44
   change of name 23
   consent 32–37
      alcohol 32–33
      convenience 35–37
      drugs 32–33
      duress 33
      fraud 34
      intention 35–37
      mistake 34–35
      motive 35–37
      unsoundness of mind 32–33
   consummation 39–41
   contracts 23, 66, 72–74, 75–76
   counselling 146–48
   defined 24–29
   engagements 21–22
   formalities 29–30
   jurisdiction 30–31
   legal capacity 37–39
      age 37–38
      prior marriage 38
      prohibited degrees of relatedness 39
      sex of parties 37
   monogamy 27–28

polygamy 27–29
   same–sex marriages 6, 24–27, 37, 39, 45,
      197–98, 222
   validity 29–30
   void and voidable marriages 31–32
Marriage breakdown and how to deal with
      crises 134–78 — *See also* Dispute
      resolution, Divorce
   crises of 134–35
   emotional aspects 135–38
Marriage (Prohibited Degrees) Act, 1990 39
Matrimonial home
   Act, retrospective application of 631–32
   definition of 625
   disposition 625–26
   exclusive possession, order for 106,
      110–11, 114, 180, 626–30
   joint tenancy severance with third party
      631
   "net family property" defined 574–75
   partition and sale 620–21
   possession of 625–31
   possessory rights 626–30
   spousal abuse, effect on possession
      110–11
   variation 630–31
Matrimonial property — *See* Matrimonial
      home, Property division
Maximum contact principle — *See* Divorce
Mediation — *See* Dispute resolution
Monogamy 27–28

Negotiation — *See* Dispute resolution
Non-molestation orders
   custody and access 530–31
   spousal abuse 111

Paternity
   agreements 83–84
Polygamy 27–29
Property division
   determination of ownership, Ontario
      568–72, 572
      presumptions applicable 569–70
   domestic contracts, Ontario 568
   family property rights, Ontario 566–632

Indian lands 568
legislation 564–66
  objectives 567
  overview 564–66
net family property, Ontario
  business, valuation 588–89
  Canada Pension Plan 604
  damages 600–2
  death
    election by spouse 612–16
    triggering division 572, 612
  debt 593
  definition of 574
  equalization of 571, 573–604, 616
  excluded property 575–76, 597–98,
    603–4
  gifts 598–600
  goodwill 586–87
  improvident depletion 572
  income tax 590–92
  inheritance 575, 581, 596, 597,
    598–600
  liabilities 590–93
  licences 581, 586–87
  life insurance policies 576, 579, 598,
    602–3
  limitation periods 573
  orders 617–22
  ownership, significance of 578–79
  pensions 581–86
  preservation order 622–23
  private companies 588–89
  professional licences 581, 586–87
  property, defined 574–75, 579–81
  restraining order 622–23
  security 619, 623–24
  separation 571
  traceable property 603
  triggering events 571–73
  trusts 579
  unequal division, Ontario 604–12
    agreements, written 610
    debts or liabilities 607, 609–10
    depletion of net family property
      608
    depreciation of assets 589, 594,
      610–12

  duration of cohabitation 608–9
    interspousal gifts 608
    judicial discretion 604–7
    marital responsibilities 611
    postseparation events 612
    unconscionability 604–7
    university degrees 581, 586–87
    valuation 587–90, 594–97
Ontario *Family Law Act* 566–87, 589–632
orders, Ontario
  registration of order against land 631
  security 233–34, 619, 623–24
  support 234–41
  variation 301–2
powers of court 617–22
  deferred payment 620–21
  family farm, regarding 621–22
  financial information 621
  inspections 621
  instalment payment 620–21
  interest 622
  occupation rent 624–25
  partition and sale 620–21
  payment 619
  preservation 622–23
  restraining 622–23
  retrospective 624
  security 619, 623–24
  transfer of property 620–21
property and financial statements 616–17
property ownership and possession
  568–70
provincial and territorial legislation
  564–66
spouse, defined 567–68
valuation, Ontario
  business 588–89
  expert evidence 592
  premarital property 594–97
  private company 588–89
  valuation date 575, 589–90
  value, defined 587
variation, Ontario
  instalment 620–21
  order for possession of matrimonial
    home 630
  security 623–24

Reconciliation — *See* Dispute resolution
Restraining orders
  depletion of spousal property 622–23
  spousal abuse 111

Separation — *See* Divorce, Marriage break-
    down and how to deal with crises
Separation agreements — *See* Domestic
    contracts
Spousal abuse
  defined 94–96
  *Domestic Violence and Stalking
      Prevention, Protection and
      Compensation Act* 106
  nature of 94–96
  reform proposals 115–17
  social and legal responses to 97–113
    actions for damages 112–13
    counselling services 98
    Criminal Code offences 100–5
    custody and access, effect on 109–10
    Divorce Act 107–8
    legal system 99–100
    matrimonial home, exclusive
        possession 110–11
    matrimonial proceedings 107–11
    non–molestation order 111
    provincial legislation 107–8
    restraining order 111
    shelters 97–98
    specialized courts 105
    support, child and spousal 108–9
    transition houses 97
    Victims of Domestic Violence Act 106
  victim's response to 113–14
Spousal separation — *See* Divorce, Marriage
    breakdown and how to deal with
    crises
Spousal Support Advisory Guidelines 14,
    312–51
Succession
  unmarried cohabitants — *See* Cohabita-
      tional relationships
Support
  child 353–474
    adult children 371–91

arrears remission 429–33
cost-of-living indexation 311
custody and access 526–63
de facto parent 355–70
disability payments 454–55
Divorce Act 355–56, 358, 361–63,
    371, 373–77, 380–81, 385, 392,
    395, 406–12, 419, 424–26, 441,
    454–60, 463–65, 468–73
domestic contracts 78, 85–86
enforcement 526
expenses
  section 7 of *Federal Child Support
      Guidelines* 354–55
  special and extraordinary 412–24
Federal Child Support Guidelines
    353–54, 356, 359–60, 362–72,
    376, 381–429, 432–37, 439–67,
    470, 472–73, 522–23
income, determination and disclosure
    433–55
income support systems, and 524–25
income tax 353–54
incomes over $150,000 391–93
judicial discretion 185, 364, 366–70,
    415, 444–45, 459–65, 466, 422
obligors
  income of 353–54, 364, 387,
      391–93, 425–27, 432–54,
      455–56, 460
  residence of 426
orders
  effects of 407–12
  types 455–58, 530–32
presumptive rule 354–55
  exceptions to 355
provincial guidelines 353
provincial legislation 522–24
retroactive orders 458–68
shared custody, and 324, 394–402
social assistance, and 435
split custody, and 324, 394–95
spousal abuse, where 108–9
spousal support, priority over 468–69
table amount 354–55
territorial legislation 522–24
undue hardship 402–6

variation 424–32
cohabitants 53–57
spousal 223–352
  appeals 351–52
  arrears, remission of 428–32
  child care 267
  common-law relationship and 307–8
  condition of spouse 243–44
  conduct, effect of 248–50
  cost-of-living indexation 311
  defined 222, 567–68
  domestic contracts 85–86, 269–89
  double dipping 290–93
  enforcement 525
  equality in obligations and rights 223
  equitable sharing principle 263–64
  factors affecting 242–48
  finality of orders 308–11
  fixed term 234–41, 302–3
  guidelines 313–52
  income support systems, and 525
  income tax, effect of 293–95
  interim support 224–28
  judicial discretion 261–63
  lump sum support 228–32
  means 244–46
  needs and capacity to pay 246–47,
    265–67
  no pat formula 268–69
  nominal support 224
  objectives of 250–61, 263–64, 265–67
  orders, types 223–41
  periodic support 228, 230, 232
  poverty, feminization of 268
  provincial legislation 407–10
  remarriage and 304–7
  remedies available under legislation
    519–63
  retroactive 293–95, 311–12
  security 233
  separation agreement and later
    support 269–79
  social assistance, and 230
  sponsorship agreement 290
  spousal abuse, where 108
  termination 295–311
  terms, conditions, and restrictions 242

territorial legislation 407–10
  variation orders 284–87, 295–311

Violence 91–133; *See also* Child abuse, Elder
  abuse, Spousal abuse
Void and voidable marriages 29–35, 37–40,
  42–44, 72, 192–93, 567

ABOUT THE AUTHORS

Julien D. Payne, C.M., Q.C., LL.D., L.S.M., F.R.S.C., one of Canada's foremost family law specialists, has been called the architect of the United Family Courts and No-Fault Divorce. He has taught family law at the Universities of Ottawa and Saskatchewan, and written extensively about divorce and family law. He was awarded the Law Society Medal by the Law Society of Upper Canada in 2002 and was made a member of the Order of Canada in 2004.

Julien D. Payne is the co-author of *Child Support Guidelines in Canada, 2006*, published by Irwin Law.

Marilyn A. Payne is an experienced author and the founding editor of *Payne's Divorce and Family Law Digest*. She is the co-author of *Child Support Guidelines in Canada, 2006*, published by Irwin Law.